Perspectives from the Past

PRIMARY SOURCES IN WESTERN CIVILIZATIONS

VOLUME 2

From the Early Modern Era through
Contemporary Times

JAMES M. BROPHY • STEVEN EPSTEIN • CAT NILAN

JOHN ROBERTSON • THOMAS MAX SAFLEY

W · W · NORTON & COMPANY   NEW YORK · LONDON

Copyright © 2002, 1998 by W. W. Norton & Company, Inc.

Library of Congress Cataloging-in-Publication Data
Perspectives from the past : primary sources in Western civilizations /
James M. Brophy . . . [et al.]—2nd ed.
    p.   cm.
    Contents: v. 1. From the ancient Near East through the age of absolutism
—v. 2. From early modern era through contemporary times.
    ISBN 0-393-97821-4 (v. 1: pbk.) — ISBN 0-393-97822-2 (v. 2: pbk.)
    1. Civilization, Western—History—Sources. I. Brophy, James M.
CB245 .P45   2002
909'.09812—dc21

                                                                2001055859

ISBN 0-393-97822-2 (pbk.)

W. W. Norton & Company, Inc., 500 Fifth Avenue, New York, NY 10110
www.wwnorton.com

W. W. Norton & Company Ltd., Castle House, 75/76 Wells Street, London W1T 3QT

1 2 3 4 5 6 7 8 9 0

ABOUT THE AUTHORS

JAMES M. BROPHY is associate professor of modern European history at the University of Delaware. He received his B.A. from Vassar College and did his graduate training at the Universität Tübingen and Indiana University, where he specialized in the social and political history of nineteenth-century Europe. He is the author of *Capitalism, Politics, and Railroads in Prussia, 1830–1870* (1998) and has published numerous articles on nineteenth-century German history. He regularly teaches the Western civilization survey as well as specialized courses and seminars on historiography, modern European history, modern German history, and European nationalisms.

STEVEN EPSTEIN teaches history at the University of Colorado-Boulder. He was educated at Swarthmore College, St John's College Cambridge, and Harvard, where he developed his interests in medieval social and economic history. He is the author of *Speaking of Slavery: Color, Ethnicity, and Human Bondage in Italy* (2001), *Genoa and the Genoese 958–1528* (1996), *Wage Labor and Guilds in Medieval Europe* (1991), and other works on medieval history. He has taught the first half of the Western civilizations survey for over seventeen years.

CAT NILAN earned her undergraduate degree in French studies and Ph.D. in western European history at Yale University and holds an M.A. in women's history from Sarah Lawrence College. She has taught a wide range of survey courses in European and world history, as well as seminars on the history of women, the family, the working classes, and crime and the prison system. Her research and writing focuses on the social and cultural history of childhood in Romantic-era France, with an emphasis on the problems of juvenile delinquency and child abuse.

JOHN ROBERTSON received both his M.A. (1976) and his Ph.D. (1981) in ancient history from the University of Pennsylvania. A specialist in the social and economic history of the ancient Near East, Professor Robertson has published several articles in major scholarly journals and contributed articles to such major reference works as the *Anchor Bible Dictionary* and the recently published *Civilizations of the Ancient Near East.* He has also participated in archaeological excavations in Syria and Greece as well as the American Southwest. Since 1982, Professor Robertson has been a member of the faculty of the department of history at Central Michigan University, where he has taught the history of Western civilization for both the department of history and the university honors program, as well as more specialized courses in the history of the ancient Near East and the Islamic and modern Middle East.

THOMAS MAX SAFLEY teaches the history of early modern Europe at the University of Pennsylvania. A specialist in economic and social history, his particular research interests include the history of marriage and the family, of poverty and charity, and of labor and business. In addition to numerous articles and reviews, Professor Safley is the author of *Let No Man Put Asunder: The Control of Marriage in the German Southwest, 1550–1620* (1984), *Charity and Economy in the Orphanages of Early Modern Augsburg* (1996), and *Matheus Miller's Memoir: A Merchant's Life in the Seventeenth Century* (2000). He is also co-editor of *The Workplace before the Factory: Artisans and Proletarians, 1500–1800* (1993) and serves on the editorial board of the *Sixteenth Century Journal*. At the University of Pennsylvania, Professor Safley regularly teaches the introductory survey of European history and advanced lecture courses on the early modern period. He also offers a broad array of undergraduate and graduate seminars.

CONTENTS

CHAPTER 13 ∿ THE CIVILIZATION OF THE RENAISSANCE, c. 1350–1550   46

CHAPTER 14 ∿ THE PROTESTANT REFORMATION   86

CHAPTER 15 ❧ RELIGIOUS WARS AND STATE BUILDING, 1540–1660   127

CHAPTER 16 ❧ THE ECONOMY AND SOCIETY OF EARLY MODERN EUROPE   179

CHAPTER 17 ✑ THE AGE OF ABSOLUTISM, 1660–1789   234

CHAPTER 18 ✑ THE SCIENTIFIC REVOLUTION   271

CHAPTER **19** ☙ THE ENLIGHTENMENT   311

CHAPTER 22 ⌘ CONSEQUENCES OF INDUSTRIALIZATION: URBANIZATION AND CLASS CONSCIOUSNESS, 1800–1850   454

CHAPTER 23 ⌘ REVOLUTION AND LIBERAL REFORM, 1815–1870   494

CHAPTER 24 ✐ REVOLUTION, NATIONALISM, AND NATION BUILDING, 1815–1870   531

CHAPTER 25 ❧ IMPERIALISM AND COLONIALISM, 1870–1914   565

CHAPTER 26 ❧ THE CHALLENGE OF THE MODERN WEST   602

CHAPTER 27 ❧ THE FIRST WORLD WAR   649

CHAPTER 28 ❧ TURMOIL BETWEEN THE WARS   684

CHAPTER 29 ∽ THE SECOND WORLD WAR   719

CHAPTER 30 ∽ COLD WAR POLITICS, ECONOMIC BOOM, AND CULTURAL CHANGE   759

CHAPTER 31 ∽ PROBLEMS OF WORLD CIVILIZATION   796

PREFACE FOR INSTRUCTORS

The authors of this text are very pleased to have been afforded the opportunity to design and compile this reader, which is the outgrowth of approximately seventy-five years of combined experience teaching the history of Western civilization. In the course of acquiring that experience, the authors were frustrated by what we perceived as serious shortcomings in most of the available supplementary readers. Among the more notable deficiencies are a frequent overemphasis on political and intellectual history at the expense of social and economic history and on elite culture at the expense of sources relating to the experiences of people of lesser socioeconomic station and, especially, of women. There is also an underinclusion of sources representative of the experiences and perspectives of European societies east of what is today Germany and a focus on Western civilization that often has neglected to address the West's important interactions with, and development of attitudes toward, non-Western peoples and civilizations. Some texts, in a laudable attempt to be more inclusive, incorporate more selections to serve up a veritable smorgasbord of thematically unlinked snippets, many of them so abbreviated or cited so disjointedly that the student can hardly gain a proper appreciation of their context or of the nature and structure of the documents from which they are derived. For ancient and medieval sources, this problem is all too often compounded by the use of translations that are either obsolete (from the standpoint of recent advances in philology) or rendered in an antiquated idiom that is hardly conducive to engaging students' interest. Finally, many readers are compiled by only one editor, who, whatever his or her experience and scholarly credentials, may understandably be hard pressed to command adequately the range and variety of primary sources available for examining the diverse aspects of Western civilization.

We by no means have the hubris to believe that what we have assembled will satisfy all the desiderata of every instructor. Nonetheless, to address the concerns noted above, and others, we have endeavored to produce a text that incorporates, as much as possible, the following features:

- Selections that consist of complete texts or lengthy excerpts of primary-source documents, ranging from one to eight pages in length and rendered in authoritative and eloquent, yet idiomatic, translations.

- Recognition that visual artifacts are also meaningful primary sources. Each chapter of this edition contains two visual features (photographs, paintings, posters, cartoons, sculptures, etc.), intended to help students learn how to analyze and interpret visual sources.

- An appropriate balance of primary sources from the Western canon, works that are illustrative of the origins and development of Western political institutions, intellectual life, and high culture or that illustrate aspects of social and economic history as well as more mundane aspects of life in Western societies. In other words, we have strived to provide selections pertinent to the lives, roles, achievements, and contributions of elite and commoner, ruler and ruled, master and servant, man and woman.

- Selections that reflect the experiences and perspectives of women and the dynamics of gender relations, including family and household structure.

- Selections that attempt to place a focus on the western European experience within a broader, even global perspective, by including selections relating to eastern Europe, the ancient and Islamic Middle East, Africa, Asia, and the Western Hemisphere. Thus, interspersed among the works of Western authors are excerpts from ancient Egyptian and Babylonian literature and private letters, the Quran, and works of such figures as Ibn Khaldun, Ibn Battuta, Bernal Diaz de Castillo, Edward Morel, Mohandas Ghandi, Frantz Fanon, Chai Ling, and the Ayatollah Ruhollah Khomeini. Readings such as these are intended to help students trace the evolution of the concept of the West and its relations with the non-West—matters of immense significance as an increasingly global society stands at the beginning of the twenty-first century.

- The incorporation of several unifying questions and issues to link documents both within and among chapters in a coherent, pedagogically useful internal framework. The documents in this reader have been chosen with an overarching purpose of interweaving a number of thematic threads that compose vital elements in the colorful fabrics of Western civilization: What are the status, responsibilities, and rights of the individual within the local community and broader society, and how have they changed over time? How have people defined their own communities, and how have they viewed outsiders? Who should have power within and over the community and society, and why? How have people responded to changes in the material world around them? Who or what controls the cosmos, and how have humankind's perceptions of its appropriate role and function within the cosmos changed?

The pedagogical and critical apparatus provided in this reader has been designed to guide the student to an appreciation of the sources but without imparting too much in the way of historical interpretation. For each chapter we have supplied an introduction that provides an historical context for the readings and alerts the student to the thematic threads that link them. Each reading in turn has an introduction that supplies an even more specific context and alerts the student to issues of interpretation or biased perspective. Finally, each selection is accompanied by several questions intended to stimulate analysis and discussion. The placement of these questions after each selection is quite intentional, as it is our hope that students will engage each document without a preconceived or predetermined sense of why it may be important and will instead learn to trust their own critical capacities and discern the significance of a reading on their own.

Obviously, to organize a project as complex as a reader of this kind and to bring it to a successful and timely fruition require the skills, support, inspiration, and dedication of many people other than the authors. We wish to express our admiration and profound gratitude to the editorial and marketing staff of W. W. Norton, especially to Kate Nash, Sarah Caldwell, Susan Upson, Jane Carter, Aaron Javsicas, and, most especially, to Jon Durbin, who assembled the team, helped us to define and refine our work, organized the project, offered useful insight and judicious criticism, and kept all of us on task and on time. The credit for this reader is surely as much his, and theirs, as ours.

PREFACE FOR STUDENTS

The purpose of this collection of illustrations and documents is to provide the student with the raw materials of history, the sources, in the form of the objects and written words that survive from the past. Your textbook relies on such documents, known as primary sources, as well as on the works of many past and present historians who have analyzed and interpreted these sources—the secondary literature. In some cases the historians were themselves sources, eyewitnesses to the events they recorded. Authors of textbooks select which facts and interpretations you should know, and so the textbook filters what you think about the human past by limiting the information available to you. Textbooks are useful because they provide a coherent historical narrative for students of history, but it is important to remember that they are only an introduction to the rich complexity of human experience over time.

A collection of historical documents and artifacts provides a vital supplement to the textbook, but it also has problems. First, the sources, mostly not intended for us to read and study, exist for the reasons that prompted some people to create them and others to preserve them. These reasons may include a measure of lies, self-deception, or ignorance about what was really happening and being recorded. So we must ask the following questions about any document or object—a treaty, contract, painting, photograph, poem, newspaper article, or sculpture: Why does it exist? What specific purpose did it serve when it was done? Who is its author? What motives prompted the creator to produce this material in this form?

The second major problem is that we, the editors of this collection, have selected, from millions of possible choices, these particular documents and objects, and not others. Even in this process, because of the limitations of space and our own personal experiences, we present a necessarily partial and highly selective view of Western civilization (also because of space limitations, it has been necessary to delete portions from some of the longer sections*). Our purpose is not to repeat what you can find in the textbook but to give you the opportunity to see and discuss how historians, now including you, make history out of documents and objects, and their understanding of why people behave the way they do.

The illustrations in this collection provide a glimpse at the millions of material objects that survive from the past. These churches, buildings, paintings, mosaics, sculptures, photographs, and other items make up an important set of sources for the historian to consider about the past. It is certainly difficult to appreciate an immense building or a small manuscript painting from a photograph. Nevertheless, the editors of this collection added illustrations to the Second Edition in order to make clear the full range of sources historians utilize. Also, the illustrations in many cases complement the written documents and in every case provide opportunities for a broader discussion of historical questions and the variety of sources that can help answer them.

Before exploring in more detail what documents are, we should be clear about what history is. Simply put, history is what we can say about the human past, in this case about the vast area of Western civilization from its origins to the most recent past. We can say, or write, things about the past because people left us their words, in the form of documents, and we can, like detectives, question these sources and then try to understand what happened. Before the written word, there is no history in the strictest sense; instead there are preliterate societies and the tens of thousands of years for which we know only what the anthropologists and archeologists can tell us from the physical remains of bodies and objects made by human hands. And yet during this time profoundly important human institutions like language, the family, and religion first appeared. History begins with writing because that is when the documentation starts.

Although history cannot exist without written documents, we must remember that this evidence is complex and ambiguous. In the first place, it first appears in ancient languages, and the majority of documents in this book were not originally in English. The act of translating the documents into modern English raises another barrier or filter, and we must use our imaginations to recreate the past worlds in which modern words like *liberty, race,* or *sin* had different meanings. One job of the historian is to understand the language of the documents in their widest possible contexts. All the authors intended their

---

* We indicate omissions, no matter how brief, with three spaced asterisks (* * *), running them in when the opening, middle, or closing of a paragraph has been deleted and centering them between lines when a full paragraph is dropped. Why asterisks, when ellipsis dots are the standard? Because authors use ellipsis dots, and we want to distinguish our deletions from theirs.

documents to communicate something, but as time passes, languages and contexts change, and so it becomes more difficult for us to figure out what a document meant then and may mean now. Language is an imperfect way to communicate, but we must make the best of what we have. If we recollect how difficult it is sometimes to understand the events we see and experience, then we can perhaps understand how careful we must be when we interpret someone else's report about an event in the past, especially when that past is far removed in space and time from our experience.

The documents give us the language, or testimony, of witnesses, observers, or people with some point to make. This evidence, like any other, must be examined for flaws, contradictions, lies, and what it tells us that the writer did not necessarily intend to reveal. Like a patient detective, we must question our witnesses with a full awareness of their limited and often-biased perception, piecing together our knowledge of their history with the aid of multiple testimonies and a broad context. Consider the document, whatever it is, as testimony and a piece of a bigger puzzle, many of the remaining pieces of which are missing or broken. It is useful at the beginning to be clear about the simple issues—What type of document is this evidence? Who wrote it? Where and when was it written? Why does it exist? Try to understand the context of the document by relating it to the wider world—how do words by Plato or about the Nazi Party fit with what you already know about ancient Greece or twentieth-century Germany?

When the document, or witness, has been correctly identified and placed in some context, we may then interrogate it further by asking questions about the words before us. Not all documents suggest the same questions, but there are some general questions that apply to nearly every document. One place to begin is to ask, Who or what is left out? Once you see the main point, it is interesting to ask what the documents tell us about people and subjects often left out of the records—women, children, or religious or ethnic minorities, for example. Or, if the document is about a religious minority, we can ask what it tells us about the majority. Take the document and try to turn it inside out by determining the basic assumptions or biases of its author, and then explore what has been intentionally or unintentionally left out. Another way to ask a fresh question of an old witness is to look beneath the surface and see what else is there. For example, if the document in question seems mainly to offer evidence on religion, ask what it tells us about the economy or contemporary eating habits or whatever else might occur to you. Documents frequently reveal excellent information on topics far from their ostensible subjects, if we remember to ask.

Every document in this collection is some kind of story, either long or short. The stories are almost all nonfiction, at least in theory, but they all have characters; a plot, or story line; and above all a point to the story, the meaning.

We have suggested some possible meanings in the sample questions at the end of each document, but these questions are just there to help your thinking or get a discussion going, about the many possible meanings of the documents. You can ask what the meaning was in the document's own time, as well as what we might now see as a meaning that makes sense to us of some pieces of the past. The point of the story in a document may often concern a central issue in history, the process of change. If history is what we can say about the human past, then the most important words describe how change occurs, for example, rapidly, as in revolutions and wars, or more slowly, as in marriage or family life. Every document casts some light on human change, and the meaning of the story often relates to why something changed.

History is often at its dullest when a document simply describes a static situation, for example, a law or farming. However, even a good description reveals choices and emphasis. If you ask, Why this law now? Why farm in this way? How did these activities influence human behavior? you can see that the real subject of nearly all documents is human change, on some level. You will find that people can and will strongly disagree about the meaning of a story: they can and will use the same evidence from a document to draw radically different meanings. This is one of the challenges of history and what makes it fun, for some explanations and meanings make more sense than others in the broader context of what you know about an episode or period of history. Argue about meaning, and you will learn something about not only your own biases and values but also the process of sifting facts for good arguments and answers. These skills have a value well beyond the study of history.

The documents and objects in this collection, even the most general works of philosophy or social analysis, reveal the particular and contingent aspects of history. Even the most abstract of these documents and objects comes from a specific time, place, and person and sheds some light on a unique set of circumstances. When history is like the other social sciences (economics, sociology, political science, and others), it tries to deal with typical or average people, societies, or behavior. When history is like the other humanities (literature, religion, art, and others), it stresses individual people, their quirks and uniqueness. The documents and objects also illustrate the contingent aspect of history, which unlike the social or natural sciences but like the humanities, appears to lack rules or laws. History depends on what people did, subject to the restrictions of their natures, resources, climate, and other natural factors—people with histories of their own! Rerunning this history is not like a movie, and it would never turn out the same way twice, for it is specific and contingent to the way it turned out this time. The documents and objects do not tell a story of an orderly progression from simple to complex societies or from bad to good ones. Instead, history continues, and people cope, or not, with the issues of religious faith, family life, making a living, and creating artifacts and documents. These documents and objects collectively provide perspectives on how experiments in living succeeded or failed. We invite you to use them to learn more about the people of the past than the textbooks can say and to use your imaginations to get these witnesses to answer your questions about the process and meaning of human change.

WHERE TO BEGIN?

This checklist is a series of questions that can be used to analyze most of the documents and objects in this reader.

✔ What type of document or object is this evidence?

✔ Why does the document or object exist? What motives prompted the author to create the material in this form?

✔ Who created this work?

✔ Who or what is left out—women, children, minorities, members of the majority?

✔ In addition to the main subject, what other kinds of information can be obtained?

✔ How do the subjects of the document or object relate to what we know about broader society?

✔ What was the meaning of the document or object in its own time? What is its meaning for the audience?

✔ What does the document or object tell us about change in society?

12 ∾ COMMERCE, CONQUEST, AND COLONIZATION, 1300–1600

The commercial revolution of the Middle Ages built on and fostered a desire by Europeans to extend trading networks beyond their homelands. Trade was not the only motive for travel. Religious pilgrimages and missions, Crusades, and a desire to pillage their neighbors still motivated some people to venture beyond the frontiers of Western Christendom—their Europe. Successful trade depended on reliable knowledge about the world. Better maps and accounts of travels made it possible for people to find their way over the vast stretches of Asia to China or across the Atlantic to Vinland. The most adventurous travel was by sea, and better ships, sails, ropes, compasses, and astrolabes made it easier to sail long distances out of the sight of land. Traveling by galleys in the Mediterranean was a little easier than sailing in the Atlantic. The great inland sea, the Mediterranean, whose waters touched Africa, Asia, and Europe, witnessed the first advances in sailing techniques, and also the first experiments in European colonization on islands like Crete and Cyprus.

After 1250 Europeans increasingly visited, traded with, and eventually colonized the various "new worlds" that lay in all directions. These places were, of course, not new to their indigenous inhabitants. Northern travel was the least promising because of the difficult Arctic climate, yet the Scandinavians had established around 1000 a precarious settlement on Greenland that lasted until about 1450. Plague, climatic changes, and the hardships of making a living in the Arctic may explain the eventual retreat of the Vikings from parts of the north. Yet memories persisted about the mysterious Vinland. Modern excavations have proved that Vikings visited and for a time lived on North American soil. English and French fishing ships continued to visit the Grand Banks for its wonderful supplies of cod. In the 1490s both states resumed efforts to explore the North Atlantic. English kings supported the voyages of John and Sebastian Cabot out of Bristol to find a northern passage to China and the fabled riches of the East.

1

Beginning in the mid–thirteenth century, missionaries like William of Ru-bruck and intrepid merchants like the Polos of Venice followed the Silk Road across central Asia to China, "the east beyond the east." A small trade contin-ued along this route to Europe until the mid–fourteenth century, when plague and changes in the Mongol Empire made travel across Asia more difficult. Ac-counts of the East and its immense riches in spices, precious gems and gold, and silk continued to intrigue Europeans. Muslim travelers like Ibn Battuta displayed a similar curiosity about Muslim states across Asia. In the fifteenth century, Chinese explorers made it all the way to Madagascar off the coast of southern Africa. The impulse to explore so far from home waned when the emperors stopped supporting these trading voyages. If Europeans wanted regular trade with China, they needed to find new, safe routes not controlled by the emerging Islamic Ottoman and Mamluk Empires in the East. The Ottoman conquest of Constantinople in 1453 choked off trade routes to the East and encouraged west-ern Europeans like Columbus to look for new ways of reaching Asia. When the Turks absorbed the Mamluk state in 1517, they became an important presence in the Indian Ocean and found the Portuguese already there.

The Portuguese, facing the Atlantic, the Ocean Sea, began to explore the west coast of Africa in search of gold. In the fourteenth century, Portuguese and Italian sailors found the islands—the Azores and Madeira, both uninhabited, and the Canaries, peopled by the Canarians. Spanish and French traders and explorers also took an interest in the opportunities for trade and settlement, but only the Portuguese continued to sail south beyond the Saharan coast. Mer-chants and sailors from Lisbon hoped to confirm ancient speculations that it was possible to circumnavigate Africa and find a way to the Indian Ocean. Explora-tions of the West African coast opened up a lucrative trade in gold and slaves that made tiny Portugal a world power. The patronage of the infante Henry the Navigator (1394–1460) established a seafaring tradition that enabled Bartolo-meu Dias to round the Cape of Good Hope in 1488. Vasco de Gama in 1497 sailed for India and eventually rewarded his investors with fabulous profits in spices. The opening up of sub-Saharan Africa to trade was not yet followed by significant colonization, as Europeans did not thrive in the tropics.

Only after reaching the "new worlds" of Asia and Africa did Europeans again "discover" the last new world, the Americas. It is important to recognize that Europeans had some previous experiences with colonies and new peoples be-fore Columbus. The Italian-born Christopher Columbus (c. 1450–1506) con-vinced Isabella of Castile and Ferdinando of Aragon to gamble on a sea route across the perilous Atlantic to the East. Until his dying day Columbus remained convinced that the people he called Indians lived off the coast of Asia, though he must have been puzzled by his repeated failures to reach the Chinese and Japa-nese. Still, Columbus's accomplishments as a sailor were striking. His search for

*wealth and trade was frustrated, however, and he laid the foundations for trad-
ing in slaves and exploiting the Indians and their lands in the search for gold
that reached its bloody conclusion with Hernando Cortéz in Mexico in 1519 and
and the Pizarros in Peru in 1533. In the sixteenth century the Spanish, and
soon the Portuguese in Brazil, began to establish permanent colonies in their
new territories. Soon other European powers, notably the Dutch, English, and
French, would follow in their wake, first as explorers, traders, pirates, and slave
traders.*

 *At the same time a demographic catastrophe occurred in the Americas as
the new diseases like smallpox which the Europeans brought with them wiped
out a high percentage, in some places perhaps as much as 90 percent, of the
Indians. As the Indians completely disappeared in some places and were greatly
reduced in numbers in others, colonists planning to make money in the mines or
the newly established sugar plantations increasingly relied on African slaves for
labor. Supplying slaves to the last new world became an increasingly lucrative
trade for the Portuguese, and soon enough for the Dutch and English as well.
This first global economy, involving trade networks that stretched from Lisbon to
Nanking, from the Senegal River in Africa to Vera Cruz in Mexico, enriched
some Europeans and laid the foundations for colonial empires on which the sun
never set.*

WILLIAM OF RUBRUCK

FROM *On the Mongols*

*William of Rubruck, a Franciscan monk from Flanders, was sent in 1253 to the
Mongols by Louis IX of France, then on crusade in the East. The Mongol Empire,
established by Chingis, or Genghis, Chan (1167–1227) and extended by successors
like Mangu (1251–1259), had sent scouting parties as far west as Poland and Hungary. In the first section of this account, William describes Mongol culture to the
French king. In the second section he is at the Mongol capital of Caracorum in
Mongolia, seeking another audience with Mangu.*

From *Mission to Asia*, edited by Christopher Dawson (Cambridge, Mass.: Medieval Academy
of America, 1980), pp. 95–98, 100–6, 194–97.

*   *   *

Commerce and Conquest

The married women make for themselves really beautiful carts which I would not know how to describe for you except by a picture; in fact I would have done you paintings of everything if I only knew how to paint. A wealthy Mongol or Tartar may well have a hundred or two hundred such carts with chests. Baatu has twenty-six wives and each of these has a large house, not counting the other small ones which are placed behind the large one and which are, as it were, chambers in which their attendants live; belonging to each of these houses are a good two hundred carts. When they pitch their houses the chief wife places her dwelling at the extreme west end and after her the others according to their rank, so that the last wife will be at the far east end, and there will be the space of a stone's throw between the establishment of one wife and that of another. And so the orda of a rich Mongol will look like a large town and yet there will be very few men in it.

One woman will drive twenty or thirty carts, for the country is flat. They tie together the carts, which are drawn by oxen or camels, one after the other, and the woman will sit on the front one driving the ox while all the others follow in step. If they happen to come on a bad bit of track they loose them and lead them across it one by one. They go at a very slow pace, as a sheep or an ox might walk.

When they have pitched their houses with the door facing south, they arrange the master's couch at the northern end. The women's place is always on the east side, that is, on the left of the master of the house when he is sitting on his couch looking towards the south; the men's place is on the west side, that is, to his right.

On entering a house the men would by no means hang up their quiver in the women's section. Over the head of the master there is always an idol like a doll or little image of felt which they call the master's brother, and a similar one over the head of the mistress, and this they call the mistress's brother; they are fastened on to the wall. Higher up between these two is a thin little one which is, as it were, the guardian of the whole house. The mistress of the house places on her right side, at the foot of the couch, in a prominent position, a goat-skin stuffed with wool or other material, and next to it a tiny image turned towards her attendants and the women. By the entrance on the women's side is still another idol with a cow's udder for the women who milk the cows, for this is the women's job. On the other side of the door towards the men is another image with a mare's udder for the men who milk the mares.

When they have foregathered for a drink they first sprinkle with the drink the idol over the master's head, then all the other idols in turn; after this an attendant goes out of the house with a cup and some drinks; he sprinkles thrice towards the south, genuflecting each time; this is in honour of fire; next towards the east in honour of the air, and after that to the west in honour of water; they cast it to the north for the dead. When the master is holding his cup in his hand and is about to drink, before he does so he first pours some out on the earth as its share. If he drinks while seated on a horse, before he drinks he pours some over the neck or mane of the horse. And so when the attendant has sprinkled towards the four quarters of the earth he returns into the house; two servants with two cups and as many plates are ready to carry the drink to the master and the wife sitting beside him upon his couch. If he has several wives, she with whom he sleeps at night sits next to him during the day, and on that day all the others have to come to her dwelling to drink, and the court is held there, and the gifts which are presented to the master are placed in the treasury of that wife. Standing in the entrance is a bench with a skin of milk or some other drink and some cups.

In the winter they make an excellent drink from rice, millet, wheat and honey, which is clear like wine. Wine, too, is conveyed to them from distant regions. In the summer they do not bother about anything except cosmos. Cosmos is always to be found inside the house before the entrance door, and near it stands a musician with his instrument. Our lutes and viols I did not see there but many other instruments such as are not known among us. When the master begins to drink, then one of the attendants cries out in a loud voice "Ha!" and the musician strikes his instrument. And when it is a big feast they are holding, they all clap their hands and also dance to the sound of the instrument, the men before the master and the women before the mistress. After the master has drunk, then the attendant cries out as before and the instrument-player breaks off. Then they drink all round, the men and the women, and sometimes vie with each other in drinking in a really disgusting and gluttonous manner.

When they want to incite anyone to drink they seize him by the ears and pull them vigorously to make his gullet open, and they clap and dance in front of him. Likewise when they want to make a great feast and entertainment for anyone, one man takes a full cup and two others stand, one on his right and one on his left, and in this manner the three, singing and dancing, advance right up to him to whom they are to offer the cup, and they sing and dance before him; when he stretches out his hand to take the cup they suddenly leap back, and then they advance again as before; and in this way they make fun of him, drawing back the cup three or four times until he is in a really lively mood and wants it: then they give him the cup and sing and clap their hands and stamp with their feet while he drinks.

The Food of the Tartars

As for their food and victuals I must tell you they eat all dead animals indiscriminately and with so many flocks and herds you can be sure a great many animals do die. However, in the summer as long as they have any cosmos, that is mare's milk, they do not care about any other food. If during that time an ox or a horse happens to die, they dry the flesh by cutting it into thin strips and hanging it in the sun and the wind, and it dries immediately without salt and without any unpleasant smell. Out of the intestines of horses they make sausages which are better than pork sausages and they eat these fresh; the rest of the meat they keep for the winter. From the hide of oxen they make large jars which they dry in a wonderful way in the smoke. From the hind part of horses' hide they make very nice shoes.

They feed fifty or a hundred men with the flesh of a single sheep, for they cut it up in little bits in a dish with salt and water, making no other sauce; then with the point of a knife or a fork especially made for this purpose—like those with which we are accustomed to eat pears and apples cooked in wine—they offer to each of those standing round one or two mouthfuls, according to the number of guests. Before the flesh of the sheep is served, the master first takes what pleases him; and also if he gives anyone a special portion then the one receiving it has to eat it himself and may give it to no one else. But if he cannot eat it all he may take it away with him or give it to his servant, if he is there, to keep for him; otherwise he may put it away in his *captargac*, that is, a square bag which they carry to put all such things in: in this they also keep bones when they have not the time to give them a good gnaw, so that later they may gnaw them and no food be wasted.

*   *   *

The Animals They Eat, Their Clothes and Their Hunting

The great lords have villages in the south from which millet and flour are brought to them for the winter; the poor provide for themselves by trading sheep and skins; and the slaves fill their bellies with dirty water and are content with this. They also catch mice, of which many kinds abound there; mice with long tails they do not eat but give to their birds; they eat dormice and all kinds of mice with short tails. There are also many marmots there which they call *sogur* and these congregate in one burrow in the winter, twenty or thirty of them together, and they sleep for six months; these they catch in great quantities.

Also to be found there are conies with a long tail like a cat and having at the tip of the tail black and white hairs. They have many other little animals as well which are good to eat, and they are very clever at knowing the difference. I saw no deer there, I saw few hares, many gazelles; wild asses I saw in great quantities and these are like mules. I also saw another kind of animal which is called *arcali* and which has a body just like a ram's and horns twisted like a ram's but of such a size that I could scarce lift the two horns with one hand; and they make large cups out of these horns.

They have hawks, gerfalcons and peregrine falcons in great numbers and these they carry on their right hand, and they always put a little thong round the hawk's neck. This thong hangs down the middle of its breast and by it they pull down with the left hand the head and breast of the hawk when they cast it at its prey, so that it is not beaten back by the wind or carried upwards. They procure a large part of their food by the chase.

When they want to hunt wild animals they gather together in a great crowd and surround the district in which they know the animals to be, and gradually they close in until between them they shut in the animals in a circle and then they shoot at them with their arrows.

I will tell you about their garments and their clothing. From Cathay and other countries to the east, and also from Persia and other districts of the south, come cloths of silk and gold and cotton materials which they wear in the summer. From Russia, Moxel, Great Bulgaria and Pascatu, which is Greater Hungary, and Kerkis, which are all districts towards the north, and full of forests, and from many other regions in the north which are subject to them, valuable furs of many kinds are brought for them, such as I have never seen in our part of the world; and these they wear in winter. In the winter they always make at least two fur garments, one with the fur against the body, the other with the fur outside to the wind and snow, and these are usually of the skins of wolves or foxes or monkeys, and when they are sitting in their dwelling they have another softer one. The poor make their outer ones of dog and goat.

They also make trousers out of skins. Moreover, the rich line their garments with silk stuffing which is extraordinarily soft and light and warm. The poor line their clothes with cotton material and with the softer wool which they are able to pick out from the coarser. With the coarse they make felt to cover their dwellings and coffers and also for making bedding. Also with wool mixed with a third part horse-hair they make their ropes. From felt they make saddle pads, saddle cloths and rain cloaks, which means they use a great deal of wool. You have seen the men's costume.

How the Men Shave and the Women Adorn Themselves

The men shave a square on the top of their heads and from the front corners of this they continue the shaving in strips along the sides of the head as far as the temples. They also shave their temples and neck to the top of the cervical cavity and their forehead in front to the top of the frontal bone, where they leave a tuft of hair which hangs down as far as the eyebrows. At the sides and the back of the head they leave the hair, which they make into plaits, and these they braid round the head to the ears.

The costume of the girls is no different from that of the men except that it is somewhat longer. But on the day after she is married a woman shaves from the middle of her head to her forehead, and she has a tunic as wide as a nun's cowl, and in every respect wider and longer, and open in front, and this they tie on the right side. Now in this matter the Tartars differ from the Turks, for the Turks tie their tunics on the left, but the Tartars always on the right.

They also have a head-dress which they call *bocca,* which is made out of the bark of a tree or of any other fairly light material which they can find; it is large and circular and as big as two hands can span around, a cubit and more high and square at the top like the capital of a column. This *bocca* they cover with costly silk material, and it is hollow inside, and on the capital in the middle or on the side they put a rod of quills or slender canes, likewise a cubit and more in length; and they decorate this rod at the top with peacock feathers and throughout its length all round with little feathers from the mallard's tail and also with precious stones. The wealthy ladies wear such an ornament on the top of their head and fasten it down firmly with a hood which has a hole in the top for this purpose, and in it they stuff their hair, gathering it up from the back on to the top of the head in a kind of knot and putting over it the *bocca* which they then tie firmly under the chin. So when several ladies ride together and are seen from a distance, they give the appearance of soldiers with helmets on their heads and raised lances; for the *bocca* looks like a helmet and the rod on top like a lance.

All the women sit on their horses like men, astride, and they tie their cowls with a piece of sky-blue silk round the waist, and with another strip they bind their breasts, and they fasten a piece of white stuff below their eyes which hangs down to the breast.

The women are wondrous fat and the less nose they have the more beautiful they are considered. They disfigure themselves hideously by painting their faces. They never lie down on a bed to give birth to their children.

The Duties of the Women and Their Work

It is the duty of the women to drive the carts, to load the houses on to them and to unload them, to milk the cows, to make the butter and *grut,* to dress the skins and to sew them, which they do with thread made out of tendons. They split the tendons into very thin threads and then twist these into one long thread. They also sew shoes and

socks and other garments. They never wash their clothes, for they say that that makes God angry and that it would thunder if they hung them out to dry; they even beat those who do wash them and take them away from them. They are extraordinarily afraid of thunder. At such a time they turn all strangers out of their dwellings and wrap themselves in black felt in which they hide until it has passed over. They never wash their dishes, but when the meat is cooked, they wash out the bowl in which they are going to put it with some boiling broth from the cauldron which they afterwards pour back. The women also make the felt and cover the houses.

The men make bows and arrows, manufacture stirrups and bits and make saddles; they build the houses and carts, they look after the horses and milk the mares, churn the cosmos, that is the mares' milk, and make the skins in which it is kept, and they also look after the camels and load them. Both sexes look after the sheep and goats, and sometimes the men, sometimes the women, milk them. They dress skins with the sour milk of ewes, thickened and salted.

When they want to wash their hands or their head, they fill their mouth with water and, pouring this little by little from their mouth into their hands, with it they wet their hair and wash their head.

As for their marriages, you must know that no one there has a wife unless he buys her, which means that sometimes girls are quite grown up before they marry, for their parents always keep them until they sell them. They observe the first and second degrees of consanguinity, but observe no degrees of affinity; they have two sisters at the same time or one after the other. No widow among them marries, the reason being that they believe that all those who serve them in this life will serve them in the next, and so of a widow they believe that she will always return after death to her first husband. This gives rise to a shameful custom among them whereby a son sometimes takes to wife all his father's wives, except his own mother; for the orda of a father and mother always falls to the youngest son and so he himself has to provide for all his father's wives who come to him with his father's effects; and then, if he so wishes, he uses them as wives, for he does not consider an injury has been done to him if they return to his father after death.

And so when anyone has made an agreement with another to take his daughter, the father of the girl arranges a feast and she takes flight to relations where she lies hid. Then the father declares: "Now my daughter is yours; take her wherever you find her." Then he searches for her with his friends until he finds her; then he has to take her by force and bring her, as though by violence, to his house.

Of Their Justice and Judgments, Death and Burial

Concerning their penal laws I can tell you that when two men fight no one dares to interfere, even a father dare not help his son, but he who comes off the worse may appeal to the court of the lord and if the other touches him after the appeal, he is put to death. But he must go immediately without any delay and the one who has suffered the injury leads the other like a captive.

They inflict capital punishment on no one unless he has been caught in the act or confesses; but when a man is accused by a number of people, they torture him well, so that he confesses. Murder they punish by the death sentence, and also cohabiting with a woman not one's own. By one's own I mean wife or servant, for it is lawful for a man to use his slave as he will. Robbery on a grand scale they likewise punish by death. For a petty theft, such as one sheep, so long as a man has not been caught doing it often, they beat him cruelly, and if they deal him a hundred strokes, then they have to have a hundred rods. I am speaking of those who are beaten as a result of the court's sentence. Similarly they put to death false ambassadors, that is to say men who pretend they are ambassadors but are not; also sorceresses, of whom however I will tell you more later, for they consider them to be witches.

When anyone dies they mourn, wailing in a loud voice, and then they are free from paying taxes until the year is up. And if anyone is present at the death of an adult, he does not enter the dwelling of Mangu Chan for a year; if it is a child who dies he does not enter it for a month.

Near the grave of a dead man they always leave a dwelling, if he is of the nobility, that is of the family of Chingis, who was their first father and lord. The burial place of him who dies is not known; and always around those places where they bury their nobles there is a camp of men who guard the tombs. It has not come to my knowledge that they bury treasure with the dead. The Comans make a great mound over the dead man and set up a statue to him, facing the east and holding a cup in its hand in front of its navel. They also make pyramids for the rich, that is, little pointed houses; and in some places I saw large towers of baked tiles, and in others stone houses, although stones are not to be found there. I saw a man recently dead for whom they had hung up, between tall poles, the skins of sixteen horses, four facing each quarter of the earth, and they had put cosmos there for him to drink and meat for him to eat, and in spite of this they said of him that he had been baptised. Further east I saw other tombs, namely large areas strewn with stones, some round, some square and then four tall stones upright round the plot facing the four quarters of the earth.

When anyone is ill he takes to his bed and places a sign above his dwelling that there is a sick person there and that no one may enter. And so nobody visits the invalid except the one who looks after him. When anyone from one of the great ordas is sick, they place guards at a distance round the orda and they do not allow anyone to cross these bounds, for they are afraid an evil spirit or wind may come in with those entering. They summon their soothsayers as if they were their priests.

*　　*　　*

Friar William's Last Audience with Mangu

On the day of Pentecost Mangu Chan summoned me and the *tuin* with whom I had debated to his presence; before I went in the interpreter, Master William's son, told me we would have to return to our own country and that I was not to offer any objection for he had learned this was settled. When I came before the Chan I had to kneel down with the *tuin* beside me together with his interpreter. Then the Chan said to me: "Tell me if it is true that the other day when I sent my scribes to you, you said I was a *tuin*." I replied: "My lord, I did not say that, but, if you allow me, I will tell you the words I used." I then repeated to him what I had said and he answered: "I well thought you had not said it, for that was not the sort of thing you ought to say, but your interpreter translated badly." And he stretched out towards me the staff on which he was leaning, saying "Fear not." I smiled and said quietly: "If I were afraid I would not have come here." He enquired of the interpreter what I had said and he repeated it to him.

He then began to make a profession of his faith to me. "We Mongols," said he, "believe that there is but one God, by Whom we live and by Whom we die and towards Him we have an upright heart." I said, "God Himself will grant this for it cannot come about but by His gift." He asked what I had said and the interpreter told him. Afterwards the Chan continued: "But just as God gave different fingers to the hand so has He given different ways to men. To you God has given the Scriptures and you Christians do not observe them. You do not find in the Scriptures that a man ought to disparage another, now do you?" he said. "No," I replied, "but from the beginning I made it clear to you that I had no wish to wrangle with anyone." "My words do not apply to you," said he. "Similarly you do not find that a man ought to turn aside from justice for the sake of money." "No, my Lord," I said, "and for a truth I have not come to these parts in order to gain money, rather have I refused that which was offered to me." There was a scribe present, who bore witness to the fact that I had refused a *iascot* and some pieces of silk. "My words do not apply to you," he said. "As I was saying, God has given you the Scriptures and you do not keep them; to us, on the other hand, He has given soothsayers, and we do what they tell us, and live in peace." He drank four times, I believe, before he finished saying these things.

And while I was listening closely to hear if there was still more he wished to declare concerning his faith, he began to speak of my return saying: "You have stayed here a long time, it is my wish that you go back. You have said that you dare not take my envoys with you; are you willing to take a message and letter from me?"

From then onwards I had neither the opportunity nor the time to put the Catholic Faith before him, for a man may not say more in his presence than he desires, unless he be an envoy; an envoy can say whatever he will, and they always enquire whether he wishes to say still more. I, however, was not allowed to continue speaking, but had to listen to him and reply to the questions he put.

I then answered him that if he would have his message explained to me and put down in writing, I would gladly take it to the best of my ability. He next asked if I desired gold or silver or costly garments. I said: "Such things we do not accept, but we have no provisions and without your aid cannot leave your country." He answered: "I will arrange for you to have all that you need as far as my territory stretches, do you wish for more?" I replied, "That is sufficient for me." He then enquired: "How far do you wish to be conducted?" I said: "We can manage for ourselves when we reach the land of the King of Armenia. If I were given a guide as far as that I would be satisfied." He answered: "I will have you accompanied thus far, after that you can fend for yourselves." And he added, "There are two eyes in a head, yet although they are two, nevertheless they have but one sight, and whither the vision of one is directed so is that of the other; you came from Baatu, it therefore behoves you to return by way of him."

When he had said this I asked his leave to say

a few words. "You may speak," he answered. Then I said: "My Lord, we are not warlike men, we would like to see those holding dominion over the world who would govern it most justly according to the will of God. Our duty is to teach men to live according to the will of God; for this reason did we come to these parts and we would gladly have remained here if you had allowed it. Since it is your good pleasure that we return, it must needs be; I will go back and carry your letter to the best of my ability in accordance with your commands. I would like to ask of your Eminence that, when I have taken your letter, I may be granted your permission to return to you, especially as you have some poor serfs at Bolac who speak our language and need a priest to teach them and their children their faith, and I would gladly abide with them." He replied: "Provided your masters send you back to me." I then said: "My Lord, I do not know what my masters have in mind, but I have permission from them to go wherever I will, where there is need to preach the word of God; and it seems to me that it is most necessary in these parts, therefore whether he send back an envoy to you or not, given your permission I would return."

He kept silent and sat for a long time as if turning things over in his mind, and the interpreter told me not to speak any more. However, I anxiously awaited his reply. At last he spoke: "You have a long journey ahead of you, fortify yourself with food so that you may be strong enough to reach your own country." And he had me given something to drink. I then left his presence, and never afterwards returned. If I had had the power of working miracles like Moses, he might have humbled himself.

*   *   *

REVIEW QUESTIONS

1. If William were a spy or an anthropologist, what valuable insights would he offer about Mongol culture?
2. In particular, according to William, how does the role of women in Mongol society compare with that of European women?
3. What ideas about religion determine the ways Mangu and William think about it?

IBN BATTUTA

FROM *The Travels*

Ibn Battuta (1304–c. 1377), from Tangier in Morocco, was an extraordinary traveler whose journeys took him as far as China and India. He wrote extensive accounts of his travels; here he describes Muslim Cairo in its prime before the plague.

From *The Travels of Ibn Battuta*, edited by H. A. R. Gibb (Cambridge, Mass.: Harvard University Press, 1958), pp. 41–53.

*   *   *

Commerce

I arrived at length at the city of Miṣr, mother of cities and seat of Pharaoh the tyrant, mistress of broad provinces and fruitful lands, boundless in multitude of buildings, peerless in beauty and splendour, the meeting-place of comer and goer, the stopping-place of feeble and strong. Therein is what you will of learned and simple, grave and gay, prudent and foolish, base and noble, of high estate and low estate, unknown and famous; she surges as the waves of the sea with her throngs of folk and can scarce contain them for all the capacity of her situation and sustaining power. Her youth is ever new in spite of length of days, and the star of her horoscope does not move from the mansion of fortune; her conquering capital (*al-Qāhira*) has subdued the nations, and her kings have grasped the forelocks of both Arab and non-Arab. She has as her peculiar possession the majestic Nile, which dispenses her district from the need of entreating the distillation [of the rain]; her territory is a month's journey for a hastening traveller, of generous soil, and extending a friendly welcome to strangers.

Ibn Juzayy remarks: Of Cairo the poet says—

No common town is Cairo, by thy life! Nay, she
Is heaven on earth for those with eyes to see;
Her youth those boys and maids with lustrous
    eyes,
Kawthar her Nile, her Rawḍa Paradise.

*   *   *

It is said that in Cairo there are twelve thousand water-carriers who transport water on camels, and thirty thousand hirers of mules and donkeys, and that on its Nile there are thirty-six thousand vessels belonging to the Sultan and his subjects, which sail upstream to Upper Egypt and downstream to Alexandria and Damietta, laden with goods and commodities of all kinds. On the bank of the Nile opposite Cairo is the place known as al-Rawḍa ['the Garden'], which is a pleasure park and promenade, containing many beautiful gardens. The people of Cairo are fond of pleasure and amusement. I once witnessed a fête there which was held for al-Malik al-Nāṣir's recovery from a fracture which he had suffered in his hand. All the merchants decorated their bazaars and had rich stuffs, ornaments, and silken fabrics hung up in their shops for several days.

The Mosque of 'Amr b. al-'Āṣ, and the Colleges, Hospital, and Convents

The Mosque of 'Amr b. al-'Āṣ is a noble mosque, highly venerated and widely celebrated. The Friday service is held in it, and the road runs right through it from east to west. To the west of it is the cell where the Imām Abū 'Abdallāh al-Shāfi'ī used to teach. As for the madrasas in Cairo, they are too many for anyone to count; and as for the Māristān, which is "between the two castles" near the mausoleum of al-Malik al-Manṣūr Qalā'ūn, no description is adequate to its beauties. It is equipped with innumerable conveniences and medicaments, and its revenue is reported to be a thousand dinars a day. The convents too are numerous. The people there call them *khawāniq*, the singular being *khānqa*, and the amīrs in Cairo vie with one another in building them.

Each convent in Cairo is affected to the use of a separate congregation of poor brethren, most of whom are Persians, men of good education and adepts in the 'way' of Sufism. Each has a shaikh and a warden, and the organization of their affairs is admirable. It is one of their customs in the matter of their food that the steward of the house comes in the morning to the faqīrs, each of whom then specifies what food he desires. When they assemble for meals, each person is given his bread and soup in a separate dish, none sharing with another. They eat twice a day. They receive winter clothing and summer clothing and a monthly allowance varying from twenty to thirty dirhams each. Every Thursday night they are given sugar cakes, soap to wash their clothes, the price of admission to the bath-house, and oil to feed their lamps. These men are celibate; the married men have separate convents. Amongst the stipulations required of them are attendance at the five daily prayers, spending the night in the convent, and assembly in mass in a chapel within the convent. Another of their customs is that each one of them sits upon a prayer-carpet reserved for his exclusive use. When they pray the dawn prayer they recite the chapters of *Victory*, of *the Kingdom*, and of *'Amma*. After this copies of the Holy Qur'ān are brought, divided into sections, and each faqīr takes a section. After 'sealing' the Qur'ān and reciting a *dhikr*, the Qur'ān-readers give a recital according to the custom of the Easterners. They hold a similar service following the mid-afternoon prayer.

They have a regular ritual for the admission of newcomers. The applicant comes to the gate of the convent and takes up his stand there, with his waist girt, a prayer mat on his shoulder, the staff in his right hand and the jug in his left. The gate-keeper informs the steward of the convent that he is there. The steward then comes out to him and asks him from what country he has come, what convents he has stayed in on his way, and who was his spiritual director (*shaikh*). When he has ascertained the truth of his answers, he admits him into the convent, spreads his prayer-mat for him in a place befitting his station, and shows him the lavatory. The newcomer renews his ablutions and, returning to his mat, ungirds his waist, and prays two prostrations, then he clasps the hand of the shaikh and those of the others present, and takes his seat amongst them. Another custom of theirs is that on Fridays the servant collects all their prayer-mats and takes them to the mosque, where he spreads them in readiness for their coming. The faqīrs come out in a body, accompanied by their shaikh, proceed to the mosque, and pray each on his own mat. When they have finished the prayer they recite the Qur'ān according to their custom, and thereafter return in a body to the convent, accompanied by their shaikh.

The Qarāfa of Cairo and Its Sanctuaries

At [Old] Cairo too is [the cemetery called] al-Qarāfa, a place of vast repute for blessed power, whose special virtue is affirmed in a tradition related by al-Qurṭubī amongst others, for it is a part of the amount al-Muqaṭṭam, of which God has promised that it shall be one of the gardens of Paradise. These people build in the Qarāfa beautiful domed chapels and surround them by walls, so that they look like houses, and they construct chambers in them and hire the services of Qur'ān-readers, who recite night and day in beautiful voices. There are some of them who build a religious house or a madrasa by the side of the mausoleum. They go out every Thursday evening to spend the night there with their children and womenfolk and make a circuit of the famous sanctuaries. They go out also to spend the night there on the night of mid-Sha'bān, and the market-people take out all kinds of eatables.

Among the celebrated sanctuaries is the imposing holy shrine where rests the head of al-Ḥusain b. 'Alī * * *. Beside it is a vast convent, of wonderful workmanship, on the doors of which there are silver rings, and plates also on them of the same metal. This shrine is paid its full meed of respect and veneration.

Amongst the monuments is the tomb of the Lady (*Sayyida*) Nafisa, daughter of Zaid b. 'Alī b. al-Ḥusain b. 'Alī (upon them peace). She was a woman answered in prayer and zealous in her devotions. This mausoleum is of elegant construction and resplendent brightness, and beside it is a convent which is visited by a great concourse during the days of the feast dedicated to her. Another is the tomb of the Imām Abū 'Abdallāh Muḥammad b. Idrīs al-Shāfi'ī, close by which is a large convent. The mausoleum enjoys an immense revenue and is surmounted by the famous dome, of admirable workmanship and marvellous construction, an exceedingly fine piece of architecture and exceptionally lofty, the diameter of which exceeds thirty cubits. The Qarāfa of Cairo contains also an incalculable number of graves of men eminent for learning and religion, and in it lie a goodly number of the Companions and of the leading figures of both earlier and later generations (God be pleased with them). ⋆ ⋆ ⋆

⋆   ⋆   ⋆

The Egyptian Nile

The Egyptian Nile surpasses all rivers of the earth in sweetness of taste, breadth of channel and magnitude of utility. Cities and villages succeed one another along its banks without interruption and have no equal in the inhabited world, nor is any river known whose basin is so intensively cultivated as that of the Nile. There is no river on earth but it which is called a sea; God Most High has said "If thou fearest for him, cast him into the *yamm*," thus calling it *yamm*, which means "sea" (*bahr*). It is related in an unimpeachable Tradition that the Prophet of God (God's blessing and peace upon him) reached on the night of his Ascension the Lote-Tree of the Extremity, and lo, at its base were four streams, two outer streams and two inner streams. He asked Gabriel (peace be upon him) what streams these were, and he replied 'The two inner streams flow through Paradise, and as for the two outer streams they are the Nile and Euphrates'. It is also related in the Traditions of the Prophet that the Nile, Euphrates, Saihān and Jaihān are, each one, rivers of Paradise. The course of the Nile is from south to north, contrary to all the great rivers. One extraordinary thing about it is that it begins to rise in the extreme hot weather, at the time when rivers generally diminish and dry up, and begins to subside at the time when rivers increase in volume and overflow. The river of Sind [Indus] resembles it in this respect, and will be mentioned later. The first beginning of the Nile flood is in Ḥazīrān, that is June; and when its rise amounts to sixteen cubits, the land-tax due to the Sultan is payable in full. If it rises another cubit, there is plenty in that year, and complete well-being. But if it reaches eighteen cubits it does damage to the cultivated lands and causes an outbreak of plague. If it falls short of sixteen by a cubit, the Sultan's land-tax is diminished, and if it is two cubits short the people make solemn prayers for rain and there is the greatest misery.

The Nile is one of the five great rivers of the world, which are the Nile, Euphrates, Tigris, Saiḥūn [Syr Darya] and Jaiḥūn [Amu Darya]; five other rivers rival these, the river of Sind, which is called Panj Ab [i.e. Five Rivers], the river of Hindustān which is called the Kank [or Gang, i.e. Ganges]—to it the Hindus go on pilgrimage, and when they burn their dead they throw the ashes of them into it, and they say that it comes from Paradise—the river Jūn, also in Hindustān, the river Itil [Volga] in the Qifjaq [Kipchak] steppe, on the shore of which is the city of al-Sarā, and the river Sarū in the land of al-Khiṭā [Cathay], on the banks of which is the city of Khān-Bāliq [Peking], whence it descends to the city of al-Khansā [Hang-chow] and from there to the city of al-Zaitūn [Zayton] in the land of China. We shall speak of all these in their proper places, if God will. Some distance below Cairo the Nile divides into three sections, and none of these streams can be crossed except by boat, winter or summer. The inhabitants of every township have canals led off the Nile; when it is in flood it fills these and they inundate the cultivated fields.

The Pyramids and Berbās

These are among the marvels which have been celebrated through the course of ages, and there is much talk and theorizing amongst men about them, their significance and the origin of their construction. They aver that all branches of knowledge which came into existence before the Deluge were derived from Hermes the Ancient, who lived in the remotest part of the Saʿīd [Upper Egypt]; he is also called by the name of Khanūkh [Enoch] that is Idrīs (on him be peace). It is said that he was the first to speculate on the movements of the spheres and the celestial bodies, and the first to construct temples and glorify God in them; and that he warned men of the coming of the Deluge, and fearing for the disappearance of knowledge and destruction of the practical arts built the pyramids and berbas, in which he depicted all the practical arts and their tools, and made diagrams of the sciences, in order that they might remain immortalized. It is said also that the seat of learning and kingship in Egypt was the city of Manūf [Memphis], which is one *barīd* from al-Fusṭāṭ. When Alexandria was built, the people removed to it, and it became the seat of learning and kingship until the coming of Islām, when 'Amr b. al-'Āṣ (God be pleased with him) laid out the city of al-Fusṭāṭ, which remains the capital of Egypt to this day.

The pyramids is an edifice of solid hewn stone, of immense height and circular plan, broad at the base and narrow at the top, like the figure of a cone. They have no doorways and the manner of their erection is unknown. One of the tales related about them is that a certain king of Egypt before the Flood dreamed a dream which filled him with terror and determined him to build these pyramids on the western side of the Nile, as a depository for the sciences and for the bodies of the kings. He asked the astrologers whether they would be opened in the future at any spot, and they told him that an opening would be made on the north side, and informed him of the exact spot where the opening would begin, and of the sum of money which would be expended in making the opening. He then ordered to be deposited in that place the sum of money which they had told him would be spent in breaching it. By pressing forward its construction, he completed it in sixty years, and wrote this inscription upon them: "We erected these pyramids in the space of sixty years; let him who will, pull them down in the space of six hundred years; yet to pull down is easier than to build." Now when the Caliphate devolved upon the Commander of the Faithful al-Ma'mūn, he proposed to pull them down, and although one of the Egyptian shaikhs advised him not to do so he persisted in his design and ordered that they should be breached from the north side. So they set about lighting fires up against them and then sprinkling them with vinegar and battering them with a mangonel, until the breach which is still to be seen in them was opened up. There they found, facing the hole, a sum of money which the Commander of the Faithful ordered to be weighted. He then calculated what had been spent on making the breach, and finding the two sums equal, was greatly astonished. At the same time they found the breadth of the wall to be twenty cubits.

The Sultan of Egypt

The Sultan of Egypt at the time of my entry was al-Malik al-Nāṣir Abu'l-Fatḥ Muḥammad, son of al-Malik al-Manṣūr Saif al-Dīn Qalā'ūn al-Ṣāliḥī. Qalā'ūn was known as al-Alfī ['the Thousandman'] because al-Malik al-Ṣāliḥ bought him for a thousand dinars of gold. He came originally from Qifjaq [Kipchak]. Al-Malik al-Nāṣir (God's mercy upon him was a man of generous character and great virtues, and sufficient proof of his nobility is furnished by his devotion to the service of the two holy sanctuaries of Mecca and Madīna and the works of beneficence which he does every year to assist the pilgrims, in furnishing camels loaded with provisions and water for those without means and the helpless, and for carrying those who cannot keep up with the caravan or are too weak to walk on foot, both on the Egyptian pilgrim-road and on that from Damascus. He also built a great convent at Siryāqus, in the outskirts of Cairo. But the convent built by our lord the Commander of the Faithful and Defender of the Faith, the refuge of the poor and needy, Caliph of God upon earth, whose zeal in the Holy War transcends its obligations, Abū 'Inān (God be his strength and aid, and grant him the signal victory, and prosper him), in the outskirts of his sublime residence, the luminous city (God guard it), has no equal to it in the inhabited world for perfection of architecture, beauty of construction, and plaster carving such as none of the Easterners can accomplish. We shall speak in due course of the schools, hospitals, and convents which he (God be his strength) has founded in his land (God guard it and preserve it by the prolongation of his reign).

*   *   *

REVIEW QUESTIONS

1. How does old Cairo compare to a contemporary European city?

2. What did Ibn Battuta think was important about a city?

3. What did he actually know about the pyramids and the Nile?

DOUKAS

FROM *Decline and Fall of Byzantium to the Ottoman Turks*

Doukas (also appears as Ducas), a fifteenth-century Byzantine historian, descended from a noble Greek family. For a time he worked for the Genoese colonial administration at New Phocaea in Asia Minor. Doukas wrote his history to illustrate what he hoped were temporary Ottoman triumphs over the Greek world. The historian was present at the Ottoman siege of Lesbos in 1462, during which he disappeared from the historical record, probably through death or enslavement. This section of Doukas's history concerns the conquest of Constantinople in 1453.

From *Decline and Fall of Byzantium to the Ottoman Turks,* by Doukas, translated by Harry J. Magoulias (Detroit, Mich.: Wayne State University Press, 1975), pp. 220–27, 240–41.

*   *   *

When all preparations had been completed according to plan, Mehmed sent an envoy to the emperor inside the City with the following message, "The preparations for the assault have been concluded. It is now time to consummate what we planned long ago. Let us leave the outcome of this undertaking to God. What say you? Do you wish to quit the City and go wherever you like together with your officials and their possessions, leaving behind the populace unharmed by us and by you? Or do you choose to resist and to lose your life and belongings, and to have the Turks take the populace captive and scatter them throughout the earth?" The emperor and the senate answered, "If you so wish, as your fathers did before you, you too, by the grace of God, can live peacefully with us. They regarded my parents as their fathers, and as such honored them, and they looked upon this City as their fatherland. In time of difficulty, they entered within her walls and were saved. No one who resisted her lived long. Keep the fortresses and the lands which have been unjustly seized from us as justly yours. Extract as much tribute annually as we are able to pay you, and depart in peace. Can you be certain that victory instead of defeat awaits you? The right to surrender the City to you belongs neither to me nor to anyone who dwells therein. Rather than to have our lives spared, it is our common resolve willingly to die."

When the tyrant heard this reply, he despaired of a peaceful surrender of the City. He therefore instructed the heralds to announce to the entire army the day on which the assault would be launched. He also affirmed on oath that he desired for himself no gain other than the buildings and walls of the City. As for the treasures and captives to be taken, he declared, "Let those be your reward." The troops shouted their approval.

As night fell, he sent heralds around the camp with instructions that large torches and fires should be lighted at every tent. And once the torches were burning, they were all to chant and shout in their foul and impious tongue. This strange spectacle was indeed incredible. As the torches poured their light over land and sea, brighter than the sun, they illuminated the entire City, Galata, all the islands, ships and boats as far as Skutari. The entire surface of the water flashed so brightly that it was like lightning. Would that it had been lightning, the lightning which not only produces light but also burns and utterly consumes everything! The Romans thought that fire had fallen on the camp and ran up to the breach in the wall. When they saw the Turks dancing and heard their joyous shouts, they foresaw the future. With a contrite heart they prayed to God, "Spare us, O Lord, from Thy just wrath and deliver us from the hands of the enemy." The spectacle and din affected the citizens so much that they appeared to be half-dead, unable to breathe either in or out.

Giovanni labored throughout the night. He ordered all the brushwood in the City gathered and placed at the breach. He also constructed a second fosse within for protection where the walls had been destroyed. The Romans realized that their movements were conspicuous and that they could not pass through the gate to oppose the Turks at the outer fortifications because the fallen walls exposed them. There were, however, some old men who knew of an underground sallyport located at the lower end of the palace that, many years before, had been sealed shut. When the emperor was informed of its existence, he commanded that it be opened. The soldiers could now sally through because it was screened by solid walls, and they gave battle to the Turks in the enclosure. The name of this hidden door was Kerkoporta.

On Sunday, the tyrant began to engage in full scale warfare. Right into the evening and through the night he gave no rest to the Romans. That Sunday was the Feast of All Saints, the twenty-seventh day of May.

From daybreak he engaged in light skirmishes until the ninth hour [3 p.m.], and after the ninth hour he arrayed the army from the palace to the Golden Gate. He also deployed the eighty ships from the Xyloporta Gate to the Plataea Gate. The remaining ships, which were stationed at the Double Columns, began an encircling maneuver, starting from the Horaia Gate and continuing past the Acropolis of Demetrios the Great and the small postern located at the Hodegetria monastery. Sailing past the Great Palace and crossing the harbor, they completed the encirclement as far as Vlangas. In addition to all kinds of equipment, each vessel carried a scaling ladder equal to the height of the walls.

Just as the sun set, the call to battle rang out. The battle array was most formidable indeed! The tyrant himself was on horseback on Monday evening. Exactly opposite the fallen walls he gave battle with his faithful slaves, young and all-powerful, fighting like lions, more than ten thousand of them. To the rear and on both flanks there were more than one hundred thousand fighting cavalrymen. To the south of these and as far as the harbor of the Golden Gate there were another hundred thousand troops and more. From the spot where the ruler was standing to the extremities of the palace there were another fifty thousand soldiers. The troops on the ships and at the bridge were beyond number.

The City's defenders were deployed in the following manner: The emperor and Giovanni Giustiniani were stationed at the fallen walls, outside the stockade in the enclosure, with about three thousand Latins and Romans. The grand duke was posted at the Imperial Gate with about five hundred troops. At the sea walls and along the battlements from the Xyloporta Gate to the Horaia Gate, more than five hundred crossbowmen and archers were arrayed. Making the complete circuit from the Horaia Gate to the Golden Gate there was stationed in each bastion a single archer, crossbowman, or gunner. They spent the entire night on watch with no sleep at all.

The Turks with Mehmed rushed to the walls, carrying a great number of scaling ladders which had been constructed beforehand. Behind the lines, the tyrant, brandishing an iron mace, forced his archers to the walls by using both flattery and threats. The City's defenders fought back bravely with all the strength they could muster. Giovanni and his men, supported by the emperor in arms, together with all his troops, fought back courageously.

But just as Fortune's feats of arms were about to snatch victory from Turkish hands, from the very middle of the embattled Roman troops, God removed their general, a mighty warrior of gigantic stature. He was wounded just before dawn by lead shot which went through the back of his arm, penetrating his iron breastplate which had been forged in the manner of Achilles' weapons. Unable to relieve the pain of the wound, he cried out to the emperor, "Stand your ground bravely, and I will retire to the ship to attend to my wound. Then I will quickly return." It was in that hour that the words spoken by Jeremias to the Jews were fulfilled, "Thus shall ye say to Sedekias: Thus saith the Lord God of Israel. Behold, I will turn back the weapons of war *which are in your hands,* wherewith ye fight against the king of Babylon and the Chaldeans that have besieged you from outside the wall; and I will gather them into the midst of this city. And I will fight against you with an outstretched hand *or* with an *uplifted* arm with wrath and anger and *great irritation.* And I will smite the dwellers in this city, both men and cattle with grievous death, and they shall die. I will not spare them, and I will not have compassion upon them!"[1] When the emperor beheld Giovanni in retreat, he lost heart and so did his companions. Yet they continued the fight with all their strength.

The Turks gradually made their way to the walls, and, using their shields for cover, threw up their scaling ladders. Thwarted, however, by

stone-throwers from above, they achieved nothing. Their assault, therefore, was repulsed. All the Romans with the emperor held their ground against the enemy, and all their strength and purpose were exerted to prevent the Turks from entering through the fallen walls. Unbeknown to them, however, God willed that the Turks would be brought in by another way. When they saw the sallyport, to which we referred above, open, some fifty of the tyrant's renowned slaves leaped inside. They climbed to the top of the walls and zealously slew anyone they met and struck down the sentinels who discharged missiles from above. It was a sight filled with horror! Some of the Romans and Latins who were preventing the Turks from attaching scaling ladders to the walls were cut to pieces, while others, closing their eyes, jumped from the wall and ended their lives horribly by smashing their bodies. Unimpeded, the Turks threw up the scaling ladders and ascended like soaring eagles.

The Romans and the emperor did not know what had happened because the entry of the Turks took place at a distance; indeed, their paramount concern was the enemy before them. The fierce Turkish warriors outnumbered the Romans twenty to one. The Romans, moreover, were not as experienced in warfare as the ordinary Turks. Their attention and concern, therefore, were focused on the Turkish ground attack. Then suddenly arrows fell from above, slaughtering many Romans. When they looked up and saw the Turks, they fled behind the walls. Unable to enter through the Gate of Charisios because of the press of the multitude, only those got through who were stronger and able to trample down the weaker. When the tyrant's troops witnessed the rout of the Romans, they shouted with one voice and pursued them inside, trampling upon the wretches and slaughtering them. When they reached the gate, they were unable to get through because it was blocked by the bodies of the dead and the dying. The majority entered through the breaches in the walls and they cut down all those they met.

The emperor, despairing and hopeless, stood with sword and shield in hand and poignantly

---

[1]Jeremiah 21: 3–6. Doukas's additions are in italics.

cried out, "Is there no one among the Christians who will take my head from me?" He was abandoned and alone. Then one of the Turks wounded him by striking him flush, and he, in turn, gave the Turk a blow. A second Turk delivered a mortal blow from behind and the emperor fell to the earth. They slew him as a common soldier and left him, because they did not know he was the emperor.

Only three Turks perished and all the rest made their way inside. It was the first hour of the day [6 a.m.], and the sun had not yet risen. As they entered the City and spread out from the Gate of Charisios to the palace, they slew those who resisted and those who fled. Some two thousand fighting men were slaughtered. The Turks were apprehensive because they had estimated that within the City there must be at least fifty thousand soldiers. Consequently, they slew the two thousand. Had they known that the total number of armed troops did not exceed eight thousand men, they would not have killed any of them. This nation is a lover of money and if a patricide fell into their hands, they would release him for gold. How much truer this would be for him who had done no wrong but had instead been wronged by them. After the conflict I met many Turks who related the following to me, "Fearful of those ahead of us, we slew as many as we met. Had we known that there was such a dearth of men in the City, we would have sold them all like sheep."

Some of the Azabs, that is, the tyrant's retinue who are also called Janissaries, overran the palace. Others swarmed over the Monastery of the Great Forerunner called Petra and the Monastery of Chora in which was found the icon of my Immaculate Mother of God. O tongue and lips, how can I relate what happened there to the icon because of your sins? While the apostates were anxious to go elsewhere for more plunder, one of the infidels, extending his befouled hands, hacked the icon into four pieces with an axe. Casting lots, each received his equal share and its accompanying ornament. After they seized the monastery's precious vessels, they rode off.

Breaking into the protostrator's home, they broke open the coffers full of treasures amassed long ago. In so doing, they aroused the noblewomen from their sleep. It was the twenty-ninth day of May, and the morning sleep of the youths and maidens was sweet indeed; they slept unafraid and carefree as they had done yesterday and the day before.

Then a great horde of mounted infidels charged down the street leading to the Great Church. The actions of both Turks and Romans made quite a spectacle! In the early dawn, as the Turks poured into the City and the citizens took flight, some of the fleeing Romans managed to reach their homes and rescue their children and wives. As they moved, bloodstained, across the Forum of the Bull and passed the Column of the Cross [Forum of Constantine], their wives asked, "What is to become of us?" When they heard the fearful cry, "The Turks are slaughtering Romans within the City's walls," they did not believe it at first. They cursed and reviled the ill-omened messenger instead. But behind him came a second, and then a third, and all were covered with blood, and they knew that the cup of the Lord's wrath had touched their lips. Monks and nuns, therefore, and men and women, carrying their infants in their arms and abandoning their homes to anyone who wished to break in, ran to the Great Church. The thoroughfare, overflowing with people, was a sight to behold!

Why were they all seeking refuge in the Great Church? Many years before they had heard from some false prophets that the City was fated to be surrendered to the Turks who would enter with great force, and that the Romans would be cut down by them as far as the Column of Constantine the Great. Afterwards, however, an angel, descending and holding a sword, would deliver the empire and the sword to an unknown man, extremely plain and poor, standing at the Column. "Take this sword," the angel would say, "and avenge the people of the Lord." Then the Turks would take flight and the Romans would follow hard upon them, cutting them down. They would drive them from the City and from the West, and from the East as far as the borders of Persia, to a place called Monodendrion. Because they fully expected these prophecies to be realized, some ran and advised others to run also. This was the conviction of the Romans who long ago had contemplated what their present action would be, contending, "If we leave the Column of the Cross behind us, we will avoid future wrath." This was the cause then of the flight into the Great Church. In one hour's time that enormous temple was filled with men and women. There was a throng too many to count, above and below, in the courtyards and everywhere. They bolted the doors and waited, hoping to be rescued by the anonymous savior.

O miserable Romans! O wretches! The temple which only yesterday you called a cave and altar of heretics, and not one of you would enter so as not to be defiled because the liturgy was offered by clerics who had embraced Church Union, and now, because of the impending wrath you push your way inside, seeking to be saved. But not even the impending just wrath could move your hearts to peace. And even if, in such a calamity, an angel were to descend from heaven and say to you, "If you will accept the Union and a state of peace in the Church, I will expel the enemy from the City," even then you would not assent. And if you did assent, it would only be a lie! They who but a few days before had said, "It would be better to fall into the hands of the Turks than into the clutches of the Franks," knew this was true.

Pillaging, slaughtering, and taking captives on the way, the Turks reached the temple before the termination of the first hour. The gates were barred, but they broke them with axes. They entered with swords flashing and, beholding the myriad populace, each Turk caught and bound his own captive. There was no one who resisted or who did not surrender himself like a sheep. Who can recount the calamity of that time and place? Who can describe the wailing and the cries of the babes, the mothers' tearful screams and the fathers' lamentations? The commonest Turk sought the most tender maiden. The lovely nun, who heretofore belonged only to the one God, was now seized and bound by another master. The rapine caused the tugging and pulling of braids of hair, the exposure of bosoms and breasts, and outstretched arms. The female slave was bound with her mistress, the master with his slave, the archimandrite with the doorkeeper, tender youths with virgins, who had never been exposed to the sun and hardly ever seen by their own fathers, were dragged about, forcibly pushed together and flogged. The despoiler led them to a certain spot, and placing them in safekeeping, returned to take a second and even a third prize. The abductors, the avengers of God, were in a great hurry. Within one hour they had bound everyone, the male captives with cords and the women with their own veils. The infinite chains of captives who like herds of kine and flocks of sheep poured out of the temple and the temple sanctuary made an extraordinary spectacle! They wept and wailed and there was none to show them mercy.

What became of the temple treasures? What shall I say and how shall I say it? My tongue is stuck fast in my larynx. I am unable to draw breath through my sealed mouth. In that same hour the dogs hacked the holy icons to pieces, removing the ornaments. As for the chains, candelabra, holy altar coverings, and lamps, some they destroyed and the rest they seized. All the precious and sacred vessels of the holy sacristy, fashioned from gold and silver and other valuable materials, they collected in an instant, leaving the temple desolate and naked; absolutely nothing was left behind.

*   *   *

Three days after the Fall, Mehmed released the ships so that they might sail to their own province and city. They carried so much cargo that they almost sank from the weight. What cargo did they carry? Costly apparel, silver, gold, copper and tin vessels, and books beyond number. They were filled to capacity with captives—priests and laymen, nuns and monks. The tents at the fosse were also teeming with captives and with the multifarious articles enumerated above. It was indeed spectacular to see a barbarian wearing an episcopal *sakkos*,[2] and another girded about with a golden stole and leading around dogs that were arrayed in fabrics embroidered with golden lambs instead of in coarse blankets. Others were sitting and feasting, eating a variety of fruits from the sacred patens in front of them, and drinking unwatered wine from the sacred chalices. Innumerable books were loaded onto the wagons and hauled in all directions; they were dispersed throughout East and West. For a single gold coin, ten books were sold—the works of Aristotle and Plato, books of theological content and on every subject. Gold and silver were pulled from the Evangelistaries which were adorned with many different jewels; some were sold and the rest were thrown away. All the icons were thrown to the flames and the meats they ate were roasted by the fire that was kindled.

On the fifth day Mehmed visited Galata. Ordering a census taken of all the inhabitants, he found that many of the homes had been bolted because the Latins had fled in the ships. He ordered the homes opened and an inventory taken of their belongings. He stipulated that should the owners return within a period of three months, they would be allowed to repossess their possessions, but if they failed to return, all would then be confiscated by the ruler. Afterwards, he commanded the entire army with the assistance of the outlying villages to demolish and raze the walls of Galata. Once this was accomplished they would be dismissed. His orders were executed. The land walls were overthrown but the walls along the harbor were allowed to stand.

In order to prepare enough lime to rebuild the fallen walls of the City, Mehmed ordered the lime-slakers to work the whole month of August. After five thousand families were registered from both the eastern and western provinces, Mehmed instructed them and their entire households to take up residence in the City by September on penalty of death. He next appointed his slave Sulayman *eparch*. He converted the Great Church into an altar for his God and Muhammad, but left the other churches desolate. He returned triumphant to Adrianople with innumerable captives and booty.

He departed from the City on the eighteenth day of June, taking with him in wagons and on horseback all the noblewomen and their daughters. The wife of the grand duke died en route near the village of Mesene and she was buried there. She was renowned for her charity and compassion for the indigent and for being a prudent woman who exercised restraint over the many passions of the spirit.

Mehmed's majestic triumphal entry into Adrianople was followed—and what a spectacle it was—by all the noble-women and Christian governors and rulers streaming in and greeting him with "Hail!" With what heart and intent did their lips and mouths say this? Afraid that they might suffer the same fate as the City, they involuntarily made their submission with gifts. The tyrant was sitting on his throne, haughty and proud, boasting about the fall of the City. The Christian rulers stood there trembling and wondering what the future held in store for them.

First, he demanded of the Serb ambassador the annual payment of twelve thousand gold coins to the Turkish throne. The despots of the Peloponnesos were instructed to appear in person annually with gifts to make their obeisance and to submit the payment of ten thousand gold coins. The lord of Chios was to make an annual payment of six thousand gold coins and the lord of Mitylene three thousand gold coins annually. The emperor of Trebizond and all those who resided along the Black Sea were to come annually with gifts to make obeisance and to pay the tribute.

*   *   *

---

[2] An episcopal garment.

REVIEW QUESTIONS

1. How does Doukas explain the reason for the fall of Constantinople?
2. What difference did the end of the Byzantine state make to the history of the eastern Mediterranean? Why did the Byzantines receive so little help from the West?
3. What signs of bias appear in Doukas's account of the Turks and Sultan Mehmed?

AŞIKPAŞAZADE

FROM *History of the House of Osman*

Aşikpaşazade (also appears as Ashiq Pasha-Zade) (1400–after 1484), the grandson of a famous Turkish poet of the fourteenth century, descended from a dervish family. In his youth he participated in Ottoman campaigns in the Balkans. He wrote in the 1480s his history of the Ottoman sultans beginning with the founder of the family line Osman. This excerpt from his chronicle describes the fall of Constantinople and the end of the vizier Halil Pasha from a Turkish perspective.

From *Islam: From the Prophet Muhammad to the Capture of Constantinople*, vol. 1, edited and translated by Bernard Lewis (New York: Oxford University Press, 1987), pp. 144–48.

*　　*　　*

The Capture of Constantinople

WHAT SULTAN MEḤMED KHAN GĀZI DID WHEN HE HAD RETURNED FROM KARAMAN, AND WHAT BUILDINGS HE RAISED

He wanted to cross to Rumeli at Gallipoli, but they said to him, "O mighty Sultan! Infidel ships have come and have closed the straits at Gallipoli."

So they took the Sultan and led him to Kojaeli. They made camp at Akčahisar, on the shore of the Bosphorus above Istanbul.

There, where his father had crossed, he crossed to Rumeli and made camp opposite Akčahisar.

He said to Halīl Pasha, "Lala, here I need a fortress!" In short, he gave orders at once and had the fortress built, and it was completed.

Then he despatched Akčayluoglu Meḥmed Bey, saying, "Make haste and besiege Istanbul."

Meḥmed Bey came, cleared the people from the city gates, and drove away the sheep and goats from the adjoining villages. The Emperor was told, "The Turk has struck us to the heart and pulled our house down on our heads."

The Emperor said, "Neighborliness between them and us is like the neighborliness of the falcon and the crow."

Then he said, "If there is any way of saving ourselves from this Turk, we must appeal again to our friend Halīl Pasha. Now we must send Halīl Pasha some little fish."

He filled the bellies of these fish with florins and sent them to Halīl Pasha. The Emperor had a vizier whose name was Master Luke.[1] He said, "Ha! Halīl Pasha will swallow the fish and it won't do you any good. He is no longer concerned about helping you. Look to your own resources."

They brought Halīl the fish. He ate the fish and put the contents in his money chest. Then he acted for the infidels. He went to the Sultan and spoke many words to him about the infidels. The Sultan said, "Ha Lala, let the summer come and then we shall see. What God commands, that we shall do."

They had been busy for some time with preparations for the conquest of the city. When all was ready and summer came, Sultan Mehmed said, "We shall spend this summer in Istanbul."

They came and made camp around the walls of Istanbul. From the land side and with ships on the sea they enclosed the city all around. There were 400 ships on the sea, and 70 ships sailed over Galata across the dry land. The warriors stood ready and unfurled their flags. At the foot of the walls they went into the sea and made a bridge over the water. They attacked.

The fighting went on, day and night, for fifty days. On the fifty-first day the Sultan ordered free plunder. They attacked. On the fifty-first day, a Tuesday, the citadel was captured. There was good booty and plunder. Gold and silver and jewels and fine stuffs were brought and stacked in the camp market. They began to sell them. They made the people of the city slaves and killed their Emperor, and the *gāzīs* embraced their pretty girls. On Wednesday they arrested Halīl Pasha and his sons and his officers and put them in prison. Theirs is a long story, but I have cut it short, because all this is well known, concerning what they did to Halīl Pasha.

In short, on the first Friday after the conquest, they recited the communal prayer in Santa Sofia, and the Islamic invocation was read in the name of Sultan Mehmed Khan Gāzī, the son of Sultan Murād Khan Gāzī, the son of Sultan Mehmed Khan Gāzī, the son of Sultan Bāyezīd Khan, the son of Murād Hünkâr Gāzī, the son of Orkhan

Gāzī Khan, the son of Osmān Gāzī Khan, the son of Ertugrul Gāzī Khan, the son of Sultan Süleymānshāh Gāzī Khan of the house of Gökalp, the son of Oguz Khan. I have set forth their family tree in the first chapter.

This victory was achieved by Sultan Mehmed Khan in the year 857 of the Hijra [1453].

HOW ISTANBUL WAS DESTROYED WHEN IT WAS CAPTURED AND HOW IT AGAIN BECAME A FLOURISHING CITY

When Sultan Mehmed Khan Gāzī had captured Istanbul, he made his servant Süleymān Bey city commandant. Then he sent messengers to all his lands saying, "Whoever wishes, let him come, and let him become owner of houses, vineyards, and gardens in Istanbul." And they gave them to all who came.

This was, however, not enough to repopulate the city. This time, therefore, the Sultan gave orders to dispatch families, both rich and poor, from every province. The Sultan's servants were sent with orders to the qādīs and the military commandants of every province and, in accordance with these orders, conscripted and brought very many families. These newcomers were also given houses, and this time the city began to flourish.

On the houses which were given to these newcomers a rental [*muqāṭaʿa*] was imposed, which bore heavily upon them. They said, "Did you remove us from our own property and bring us here just to pay rent for these infidel houses?" And some abandoned their wives and children and ran away.

Sultan Mehmed had a servant called Kula Shahin who had served his father and grandfather and had been a vizier. Kula Shahin said to the Pādishāh, "O mighty Sultan! Your father and your grandfather conquered so many lands but in none did they impose a rental. It would be more fitting for my Sultan not to do this."

The Pādishāh accepted what he said and forewent the rental. He issued orders, "Every house which you assign, assign as freehold [*mülk*]." Henceforth, with every house which was assigned,

---

[1] The Byzantine *Megadux* Lucas Notaras.

they gave a letter that it was to be their freehold. In this way the city again began to flourish. They began to build mosques. Some of them built dervish convents, some of them private houses, and the city returned to its previous state.

Then a new vizier, who was the son of an infidel, came to the Pādishāh and became the Pādishāh's close confidant. The father and friends of this vizier were infidels, old residents of Istanbul. They came to him and said, "Hey, what are you doing? The Turks have repopulated this city. Have you no loyalty? They have taken your father's home and our home and make free with it before our eyes. But you are the confidant of the Pādishāh; therefore, do all you can so that these people should give up the rebuilding of this city, and then it will remain in our hands as before."

The vizier said, "We shall reimpose that rental which they had imposed at the time. Then these people will stop building private houses, and in this way the city will again fall in ruins and finally be left in the hands of our community."

One day this vizier found an occasion to persuade the Pādishāh, and he reintroduced the rental. . . . Whatever this scheming infidel said, he did, and they wrote it down.

Question: Who then was this vizier?

Answer: It was the Greek Meḥmed Pasha, whom he later had strangled like a dog.

Question: What buildings did Sultan Meḥmed Khan Gāzī build in Istanbul?

He built eight *medreses,* with a great cathedral mosque in their midst, and facing the mosque a fine hospice and a hospital, and at the side of the eight *medreses* he built eight more small *medreses,* to house the students. Apart from this, he had a fine mausoleum built over the grave of the holy Eyyūb-ī Ensārī, with a hospice, a *medrese,* and a mosque nearby.

*   *   *

Because of this rental people began to flee the rebuilding of Istanbul. . . . The imposing of this rental, which still stands, was the fault of this Greek Mehmed.

*   *   *

REVIEW QUESTIONS

1. How does this account of the conquest of Constantinople compare with the one by Doukas?
2. Why is it easier to criticize the vizier than the sultan? What is the role of the vizier in the Ottoman Empire?

"The Tale of the White Cowl": A Russian Tale

The Russian story "The Tale of the White Cowl" was written down in this form in Novogorod by church officials sometime in the late fifteenth century. The white cowl, a simple woolen hood, passed from the classical first Rome, briefly to the Byzantine state, and finally to the Russian people, after 1453 the only remaining defenders of eastern Orthodoxy. Russia became the easternmost state that traced some of its culture back to the Mediterranean world.

From *Medieval Russia's Epics, Chronicles and Tales,* edited by Serge A. Zenkovsky (New York: Dutton, 1963).

At that time the Patriarch of Constantinople was Philotheus, who was distinguished by his strict fasting and his virtuous ways. Once, he had a vision in the night of a youth from whom emanated light and who told him:

"Blessed teacher, in the olden times the Roman Emperor, Constantine, who, through the vision of the Holy Apostles Peter and Paul, was enlightened by God, decided to give Blessed Pope Sylvester the White Cowl to glorify the Holy Apostolic Church. Later, the unfaithful popes of the Latin heresies wanted to profane and destroy this cowl, but I appeared to the evil pope, and now this pope has sent this cowl to you. When the messengers arrive with it, you must accept it with all honors. Then send the White Cowl to the Russian land, to the city of Novgorod the Great with your written blessing. And there this cowl will be worn on the head of Vasily, Archbishop of Novgorod so that he may glorify the Holy Apostolic Cathedral of Holy Sophia and laud the Orthodox. There, in that land, the faith of Christ is verily glorified. And the popes, because of their shamelessness, will receive the vengeance of God." And having spoken these words, the youth became invisible.

The patriarch awoke filled with awe and joy, and was unable to sleep throughout the remainder of the night. And he contemplated this vision. In the morning he ordered that the bells should sound the Matins, and when day came he summoned the Church council and revealed his vision. And all praised God, perceiving that a holy angel had appeared to the patriarch. Yet they did not fully understand the meaning of the message. When they were still in council and were filled with awe due to their great joy, there arrived a servant of the patriarch, and he announced to them that messengers had arrived from the Pope of Rome. The patriarch ordered that they be brought before him. The messengers came, bowed lowly to the patriarch, and gave him the message. The patriarch read the message and pondered it, praising God. He announced its contents to Emperor John who was reigning at that time and whose name was Kantakuzen. And then he went

with the entire council to meet the bringers of the divine treasure which lay in an ark. He accepted it with all honors, broke the seal, and took from the ark the Holy White Cowl. He kissed it with reverence, and looked upon it with wonderment both for its creation and for the wonderful fragrance that emanated from it.

At that time the patriarch had diseased eyes and constant headaches, but when he placed the White Cowl upon his head, these afflictions immediately ceased to be. And he rejoiced with great joy and rendered glory to Christ, our Lord, to Constantine's blessed memory for his creating this wonderful cowl for Blessed Pope Sylvester. And he put the Holy Cowl on the golden salver that was also sent by the pope. He placed them in the great church in an honorable place until he could make a decision with the emperor's counseling.

After the White Cowl was sent from Rome, the evil pope, who was counseled by heretics, became angered against the Christian faith and was driven to a frenzy, extremely regretting his allowing the White Cowl to be sent to Constantinople. And he wrote an evil letter to the patriarch, in which he demanded the return of the White Cowl on the golden salver. The patriarch read this letter and, understanding the pope's evil and cunning design, sent him a letter in return that was based on Holy Scripture, and in it he called the pope both evil and godless, the apostate and precursor of the Antichrist. And the patriarch cursed the pope in the name of our Lord, Jesus Christ, the Holy Apostles, and the Church Fathers. And this letter came to the pope.

When the pope had read the letter and learned that the patriarch intended to send the White Cowl with great honor to the Russian land, to the city of Novgorod the Great, he uttered a roar. And his face changed and he fell ill, for he, the infidel, disliked the Russian land and could not even bear to hear of this land where the Christian faith was professed.

Patriarch Philotheus, having seen that the White Cowl was illumined with grace, began to ponder how he might keep it in Constantinople and wear it on his own head. He consulted with the emperor about the matter several times, and wanted to write to the other patriarchs and metropolitans to summon them to a council. After Matins one Sunday, the patriarch returned to his chambers and, after the usual prayers, lay down to rest. But he slept but lightly, and in this sleep he saw that two men, who were unknown to him, came through the door. And from them there emanated light. One of them was armed as a warrior and had an imperial crown upon his head. The other wore a bishop's vestments and was distinguished by his venerable white hair.

The latter spoke to the patriarch, saying: "Patriarch! Stop pondering your wearing of the White Cowl on your own head. If this were to be, our Lord, Jesus Christ, would have so predestined it from the founding of this city. And for a long time did divine enlightenment come from heaven, and then God's voice came to me and I learned that Rome had to betray God and embrace their Latin heresies. That is the reason I did not wish to wear this cowl upon my head, and thus I instructed other popes not to do so. And this imperial city of Constantinople will be taken by the sons of Hagar because of its sins, and all holy shrines will be defiled and destroyed. Thus has it been predestined since the founding of this city.

"The ancient city of Rome will break away from the glory and faith of Christ because of its pride and ambition. In the new Rome, which will be the City of Constantinople, the Christian faith will also perish through the violence of the sons of Hagar. In the third Rome, which will be the land of Russia, the Grace of the Holy Spirit will be revealed. Know then, Philotheus, that all Christians will finally unite into one Russian nation because of its orthodoxy. Since ancient times and by the will of Constantine, Emperor of the Earth, the imperial crown of the imperial city is predestined to be given to the Russian tsar. But the White Cowl, by the will of the King of Heaven, Jesus Christ, will be given to the archbishop of Novgorod the Great. And this White Cowl is more honorable than the crown of the tsar, for it is an imperial crown of the archangelic spiritual order.

Thus, you must send this Holy White Cowl to the Russian land, to the city of Novgorod the Great, as you were told to do in the vision of the angel. You should believe and trust in what I say. And when you send it to the Russian land, the Orthodox Faith will be glorified and the cowl will be safe from seizure by the infidel sons of Hagar and from the intended profanation by the Latin pope. And the grace, glory, and honor which were taken from Rome, as well as the Grace of the Holy Spirit, will be removed from the imperial city of Constantinople after its capture by the sons of Hagar. And all holy relics will be given to the Russian land in the predestined moment. And the Russian tsar will be elevated by God above other nations, and under his sway will be many heathen kings. And the power of the patriarch of this imperial ruling city will pass to the Russian land in the predestined hour. And that land will be called Radiant Russia, which, by the Grace of God, will be glorified with blessings. And its majesty will be strengthened by its orthodoxy, and it will become more honorable than the two Romes which preceded it."

And saying this, the man of the vision who was dressed in a bishop's vestment wished to leave, but the patriarch, seized by great awe, fell before the bishop and said: "Who are you, my lord? Your vision has seized me with great awe; my heart has been frightened by your words, and I tremble to my very bones."

The man in the bishop's vestments answered: "Don't you know who I am? I am Pope Sylvester, and I came to you because I was ordered by God to reveal to you the great mystery which will come to pass in the predestined time." Then, pointing to the other man in the vision, he added: "This is blessed Emperor Constantine of Rome to whom I gave rebirth in the holy font and whom I won over to the faith of our Lord, Jesus Christ. He was the first Christian emperor, my child in Christ, who created and gave me the White Cowl in place of the imperial crown." And saying this, he blessed the patriarch, and became invisible.

Waking up, the patriarch was seized with awe, remembering the words about the White Cowl and the conquest of Constantinople by the pagan sons of Hagar. And he wept for a long time. When the hour of the divine Mass arrived, the patriarch went to the church, fell before the icon of the Holy Mother of God, and remained lying there for some time. Then he arose, took the White Cowl with great reverence, kissed it piously, placed it upon his head, and then put it to his eyes and his heart. And his adoration for this cowl increased even more. And doing this, he wept. His clerics, who were around him and saw that he wept inconsolably, did not dare to inquire as to why he was weeping. Finally the patriarch ceased crying and told his clerics in detail of the vision of Pope Sylvester and Emperor Constantine. Having heard these words, the clerics wept sorrowfully, and exclaimed, "Thy will be done!"

The patriarch, mourning the forthcoming misfortunes of the city of Constantinople and fearing to trespass the divine will, told them that he must fulfill the will of the Lord and do with the White Cowl as he was commanded to do. After having deliberated with blessed Emperor John, he took the White Cowl and the golden salver, put them in the aforementioned ark, sealed it with his seal, and, as he was commanded by the holy angel and Blessed Pope Sylvester, put in his epistle with his blessings, and in it he commanded Archbishop Vasily and all other bishops who would follow Vasily to wear the White Cowl upon their heads. He added many other honorable and marvelous gifts from his clergy for the bishopric of Novgorod the Great. And he also sent vestments with their embroidered crosses for the glorification of the Holy Apostolic Church. And all this was placed in another ark. And he gave these arks to a bishop named Eumeny, and sent him forth with both joy and sorrow.

In the bishopric of the city of Novgorod the Great was Archbishop Vasily who distinguished himself by his fasting and virtuous ways. Once, in the night, he prayed to God and then lay down to rest, but he slept but lightly, and had a dream in which he saw the angel of God. This angel of God, who had a handsome appearance and radiant face, appeared before him in the garb of a monk and

with the White Cowl upon his head. With his finger he pointed to his head and in a low voice announced: "Vasily! This White Cowl which you see on my head is from Rome. In olden times the Christian Emperor Constantine created it in honor of Sylvester, Pope of Rome. He gave it to this pope to wear upon his head. But God Almighty did not permit the White Cowl to remain there because of their Latin heresies. Tomorrow morning you must go from the city with your clergymen and meet the bishop and messengers sent by the patriarch. And they will bring an ark, and in this ark you will find the White Cowl upon a golden salver. Accept it with all honors, for this White Cowl symbolizes the radiant Resurrection which came to pass on the third day. And from now, you and all other archbishops of this city will wear it on your heads. And I have come to you to assure you before hand that all is as God wills it and to assuage any doubts you may have." And saying this, the angel became invisible.

Waking up, Archbishop Vasily was seized with awe and joy, pondering the meaning of the vision. The next morning he sent his clerics outside the city, to the crossroads, to see whether the messengers really would appear. In the vicinity of the city the servant of Archbishop Vasily met a Greek bishop who was unknown to him and who traveled to the city of Novgorod. They made a low obeisance and returned to the archbishop and told them all they had seen. The bishop then sent his messenger into the city to summon the clerics and the entire population. And he ordered the tolling of the bells, and both he and his clerics donned their vestments.

The procession had not gone far from the Cathedral of Holy Sophia when they met the aforementioned bishop, sent by the patriarch and bearing the ark that had been sealed by the patriarch, and which contained the venerable gifts, came to Archbishop Vasily, made a low obeisance before him, and gave him the epistles of the patriarch. They blessed and greeted each other in Christ's name. Archbishop Vasily accepted the epistles of the patriarch and the arks bearing the venerable gifts. And he went with them to the Cathedral of Holy Sophia, the Wisdom of God. There he put them in the middle of the church in an honorable place, and ordered that the patriarchal epistles be read aloud. When the Orthodox people, who were in the cathedral, heard these writings read aloud, they rendered glory to God and rejoiced with great joy. Archbishop Vasily opened one of the arks and removed the cover. And a wonderful fragrance and miraculous radiance spread through the church. Archbishop Vasily and all present were in wonderment, witnessing these happenings. And Bishop Eumeny, who was sent by the patriarch, wondered about these blessed deeds of God that he had witnessed. And they all rendered glory to God, and celebrated the service of thanksgiving.

Archbishop Vasily took the White Cowl from the ark and saw that it appeared exactly like the one he had seen on the angel's head in his vision. And he kissed it with reverence. At that same moment there came a sonorous voice from the icon of the Lord, which was in the cupola of the church, saying, "Holy, holy." And after a moment of silence there came the same voice, which thrice announced, "Ispola eti despota." And when the archbishop and all those present heard these voices, they were seized with awe and joy. And they said, "The Lord have mercy upon us!" And the archbishop then ordered that all present in the church be silent, and he revealed to them his vision of the angel and his words concerning the White Cowl. And he told of his vision as it had happened and in detail, even as it was told to him by the angel in the night.

Giving thanks to God for sending this cowl, the archbishop went forth from the church, preceded by the deacons in holy vestments carrying tapers and singing hymns. And they proceeded with serenity and piety. And the people crowded round, jostling each other and jumping so that they might see the White Cowl on the arch-bishop's head. And all were in wonderment. Thus, in this way, thanks to the Grace of our Lord, Jesus Christ, and to the blessing of his Holiness Philotheus, Patriarch of of Constantinople, the White Cowl became a symbol upon the heads of the archbishops of Novgorod. And Archbishop Vasily was overcome with great joy, and for seven days he feasted all priests, deacons, and clerics of the city of Novgorod the Great. And he also offered food and drink to the poor, to monks, and to prisoners. And he asked that the prisoners be released. During the divine service he placed the holy and venerable gifts of the patriarch in the Cathedral of Holy Sophia and with the blessings of all clerics. And the golden salver, on which the White Cowl was placed, was also deposited in the Cathedral of Holy Sophia during the Mass.

The messengers of the patriarch who brought the Holy White Cowl were also shown great honor and they received many gifts. The archbishop sent gifts to the Emperor and Patriarch of Constantinople and sent the messengers forth with great honors. Thereafter, multitudes arrived from many cities and kingdoms to look upon, as if it were a miracle, the archbishop in the White Cowl. And they were in wonderment about it, and told of it in many lands. This Holy White Cowl was created by the first pious Christian Emperor, Constantine, for Blessed Pope Sylvester in the year 297. And this is the history of the Holy White Cowl up to this day.

REVIEW QUESTIONS

1. What were the Russian attitudes toward the Roman Catholic Church, the Muslims, and the Eastern Orthodox Church?
2. Given these attitudes, why is anyone in Russia interested in portraying it as a third Rome?

ALVISE DA MOSTO

Voyage to Africa

Alvise da Mosto (died 1483), also known as Cadamosto, was a member of a prominent family in the Venetian nobility. Alvise passed his early years as a merchant, visiting Flanders and Portugal. In 1454 he accompanied a Portuguese expedition engaged in trade and exploration south of the Sahara. The account of this voyage and another one the following year constitutes one of the earliest European descriptions of black Africa. This excerpt contains Alvise's first impressions of the empire of Mali (here called Melli) in central Africa, inhabited by the people he called the Azanegi (Tuaregs) and the Wolof people, a large tribe south of the Senegal River.

From *The Voyages of Cadamosto,* translated and edited by G. R. Crone (London: Hakluyt Society, 1937), pp. 20–33.

*   *   *

You should know that these people have no knowledge of any Christians except the Portuguese, against whom they have waged war for [thirteen or] fourteen years, many of them having been taken prisoners, as I have already said, and sold into slavery. It is asserted that when for the first time they saw sails, that is, ships, on the sea (which neither they nor their forefathers had ever seen before), they believed that they were great sea-birds with white wings, which were flying, and had come from some strange place: when the sails were lowered for the landing, some of them, watching from far off, thought that the ships were fishes. Others again said that they were phantoms that went by night, at which they were greatly terrified. The reason for this belief was because these caravels within a short space of time appeared at many places, where attacks were delivered, especially at night, by their crews. Thus one such assault might be separated from the next by a hundred or more miles, according to the plans of the sailors, or as the winds, blowing hither and thither, served them. Perceiving this, they said amongst themselves, "If these be human creatures,

how can they travel so great a distance in one night, a distance which we could not go in three days?" Thus, as they did not understand the art of navigation, they all thought that the ships were phantoms. This I know is testified to by many Portuguese who at that time were trading in caravels on this coast, and also by those who were captured on these raids. And from this it may be judged how strange many of our ways appeared to them, if such an opinion could prevail.

Beyond the said mart of Edon [Oden], six days journey further inland, there is a place called Tagaza, that is to say in our tongue "cargador," where a very great quantity of rock-salt is mined. Every year large caravans of camels belonging to the above mentioned Arabs and Azanaghi, leaving in many parties, carry it to Tanbutu [Timbuktu]; thence they go to Melli, the empire of the Blacks, where, so rapidly is it sold, within eight days of its arrival all is disposed of at a price of two to three hundred *mitigalli* a load, according to the quantity [a *mitigallo* is worth about a ducat]: then with the gold they return to their homes.

In this empire of Melli it is very hot, and the pasturage is very unsuitable for fourfooted animals: so that of the majority which come with the caravans no more than twenty-five out of a hundred return. There are no quadrupeds in this country, because they all die, and many also of the Arabs and Azanaghi sicken in this place and die, on account of the great heat. It is said that on horseback it is about forty days from Tagaza to Tanbutu, and thirty from Tanbutu to Melli.

I enquired of them what the merchants of Melli did with this salt, and was told that a small quantity is consumed in their country. Since it is below the meridional and on the equinoctial, where the day is constantly about as long as the night, it is extremely hot at certain seasons of the year: this causes the blood to putrefy, so that were it not for this salt, they would die. The remedy they employ is as follows: they take a small piece of the salt, mix it in a jar with a little water, and drink it every day. They say that this saves them. The remainder of this salt they carry away on a long journey in pieces as large as a man can, with a certain knack, bear on his head.

You must know that when this salt is carried to Melli by camel it goes in large pieces [as it is dug out from the mines], of a size most easily carried on camels, two pieces on each animal. Then at Melli, these blacks break it in smaller pieces, in order to carry it on their heads, so that each man carries one piece, and thus they form a great army of men on foot, who transport it a great distance. Those who carry it have two forked sticks, one in each hand: when they are tired, they plant them in the ground, and rest their load upon them. In this way they carry it until they reach certain waters: I could not learn from them whether it is fresh or sea water, so that I do not know if it is a river or the sea, though they consider it to be the sea. [I think however it must be a river, for if it were the sea, in such a hot country there would be no lack of salt.] These Blacks are obliged to carry it in this way, because they have no camels or other beasts of burden, as these cannot live in the great heat. It may be imagined how many men are required to carry it on foot, and how many are those who consume it every year. Having reached these waters with the salt, they proceed in this fashion: all those who have the salt

pile it in rows, each marking his own. Having made these piles, the whole caravan retires half a day's journey. Then there come another race of blacks who do not wish to be seen or to speak. They arrive in large boats, from which it appears that they come from islands, and disembark. Seeing the salt, they place a quantity of gold opposite each pile, and then turn back, leaving salt and gold. When they have gone, the negroes who own the salt return: if they are satisfied with the quantity of gold, they leave the salt and retire with the gold. Then the blacks of the gold return, and remove those piles which are without gold. By the other piles of salt they place more gold, if it pleases them, or else they leave the salt. In this way, by long and ancient custom, they carry on their trade without seeing or speaking to each other. Although it is difficult to believe this, I can testify that I have had this information from many merchants, Arab as well as Azanaghi, and also from persons in whom faith can be placed.

How the Emperor Sought to Take One of These Traders Prisoner

Reflecting upon this, I asked the merchants how it came to be that the Emperor of Melli, who, they said, was so great a lord, had not wished so to proceed as to find out by love or by other means what people these were who did not wish to speak or to be seen. They replied that, not many years previously, an Emperor of Melli determined at all costs to get one of them in his power, and having taken counsel about it, ordered some of his men to leave a few days before the salt caravan, and proceed to the place where it was customary to pile the salt, to dig trenches near by, in which to conceal themselves. When the Blacks returned to set the gold by the salt, they were to attack them and to take two or three, whom they were to convey under close guard to Melli. To be brief, this was done. They seized four, the others taking to flight: of the four they released three, surmising that one would satisfy the desires of the lord, and not wishing to anger these Blacks more. They spoke to this man in several Negro languages, but he would not reply, or speak at all, neither would he eat. He lived four days and then died. For this reason these blacks of Melli are of the opinion, after the experience they had with him who would not speak, that they are dumb. Others think that they behave thus from disdain [of doing what their ancestors had never done]. This death vexed all the blacks of Melli, for on account of it their lord could not achieve his intention. On returning to him they related the incident in due order.

Then the lord was very displeased with them, and asked what the blacks looked like. They replied they were very black in colour, with well-formed bodies, a span higher than they themselves. The lower lip, more than a span in width, hung down, huge and red, over the breast, displaying the inner part glistening like blood.[1] The upper lip was as small as their own. This form of the lips displayed the gums and teeth, the latter, they said, being bigger than their own: they had two large teeth on each side, and large black eyes. Their appearance is terrifying, and the gums exude blood, as do the lips.

Because of this incident, none of the emperor's men have since been willing to embroil themselves in similar affairs, since, as a result of the capture and death of this one Negro, it was three years before the others would resume the customary exchange of gold for salt. It was thought that their lips became putrid, being in a warmer country than ours: so that these blacks, having borne much sickness and death [for this space of time], and having no other way of obtaining the salt to cure themselves, resumed the accustomed trade. On this account, it is our opinion, being unable to live without salt, they set off their plight against our action, just as the Emperor did not care whether these blacks spoke or not, so long as he had the profit of the gold. This is what I understood from this incident, and since it is related by so many we can accept it. Because I have seen and understood such things in the world, I am one of those who

are willing to believe this and other matters to be possible.

The gold thus brought to Melli is divided in three parts: one portion goes with the caravan which takes the road from Melli to a place that is called Cochia. This is the route which runs towards Soria [and il Cairo]: the second and third portions go with a caravan from Melli to Tanbutu. There they are separated: one portion goes to Atoet, whence it is carried to Tunis in Barbary through all the coast beyond: the other part goes to the above mentioned Hoden, whence it spreads towards Orā and Hona, towns in Barbary within the Strecto de Zibelterra, Afezes, Amarochos, Arzib, Azafi, and Amessa, towns in Barbary beyond the Straits. In these places it is bought by us Italians and other Christians from the Moors with the various merchandize we give them.

To return to my first subject, this is the best thing that is brought from the said land and country of the Azanaghi, that is, the brown men. Of that portion of the gold which is brought every year to Hoden, as described already, some quantity is carried to the sea coast, and sold to the Spaniards who are continuously stationed on the said island of Argin for the trade of merchandize, in exchange for other things.

In this land of the brown men, no money is coined, and they have never used it. Nor, formerly, was money to be found in any of their towns. Their sole method is to barter article for article, or two articles for one, and by such means they live. It is true that I understand that inland these Azanaghi, and also the Arabs in some of their districts, are wont to employ white cowries, of those small kinds which are brought to Venice from the Levant. They give certain numbers of these according to the things they have to buy. I should explain that the gold they sell they give by the weight of a *mitigallo;* according to the practice in Barbary, this *mitigallo* is of the value of a ducat, more or less.

* * *

---

[1]This suggests the use of the labret, which is still worn by the Lobi women.

The Rio de Senega, Which Divides the Desert from the Fertile Land

When we had passed in sight of this Cauo Bianco, we sailed on our journey to the river called the Rio de Senega, the first river of the Land of the Blacks, which debouches on this coast. This river separates the Blacks from the brown people called Azanaghi, and also the dry and arid land, that is, the above mentioned desert, from the fertile country of the Blacks. The river is large; its mouth being over a mile wide, and quite deep. There is another mouth a little distance beyond, with an island between. Thus it enters the sea by two mouths, and before each of them about a mile out to sea are shoals and broad sand-banks. In this place the water increases and decreases every six hours, that is, with the rise and fall of the tide. The tide ascends the river more than sixty miles, according to the information I have had from Portuguese who have been [many miles] up it [in caravels]. He who wishes to enter this river must go in with the tide, on account of the shoals and banks at the mouth. From Cauo Bianco it is 380 miles to the river: all the coast is sandy to within about twenty miles of the mouth. It is called Costa de Antte rotte, and is of the Azanaghi, or brown men.

It appears to me a very marvellous thing that beyond the river all men are very black, tall and big, their bodies well formed; and the whole country green, full of trees, and fertile: while on this side, the men are brownish, small, lean, ill-nourished, and small in stature: the country sterile and arid. This river is said to be a branch of the river Nile, of the four royal rivers: it flows through all Ethiopia, watering the country as in Egypt: passing through "lo caiero," it waters all the land of Egypt. This river has many other very large branches, in addition to that of Senega, and they are great rivers on this coast of Ethiopia, of which more will be related later.

The Lords Who Rule on the Coast of Capo Verde

The country of these first blacks of the Kingdom of Senega is at the beginning of the first Kingdom of Ethiopia. It is all low-lying country, and many people live on the banks of this river. They are called Zilofi. For a great distance beyond, it is low country, and beyond the river likewise, except for Cauo Verde, which is the highest land on all this coast, for 400 miles beyond this Cauo Verde, and for 900 miles on this side of the said cape, the whole coast is flat. [And the people who dwell along its banks are called Gilofi. And all this coast and the known country behind is all lowland as far as the river, and also beyond this river to Capo Verde. This Cape is the highest land on the whole coast, that is for four hundred miles beyond the said Cape.]

The King of Senega in my time was called Zuchalin [Zucolin—a youth of twenty-two years. This Kingdom does not descend by inheritance] but in this land there are divers lesser lords, who [three or four of whom] through jealousy, at times agree among themselves, and set up a King of their own, if he is in truth of noble parentage. This King rules as long as is pleasing to the said lords [that is, according to the treatment they receive from him]. Frequently [they banish him by force: and as frequently] the King makes himself so powerful that he can defend himself against them. Thus his position is not stable and firm, as is that of the Soldan of Babilonia: but he is always in dread of deposition [death or exile].

You must know that this King is lord of a very poor people, and has no city in his country, but villages with huts of straw only. [They do not know how to build houses with walls:] they have no lime with which to build walls, and there is great lack of stones. This Kingdom, also, is very small; it extends no more than two hundred miles along the coast, and, from the information I had, about the same distance inland or a little more. The king lives thus: he has no fixed income [from taxes]: save that each year the lords of the country, in order to stand well with him, present him with horses, which are much esteemed owing to their scarcity, forage, beasts such as cows and goats, vegetables, millet, and the like. The King supports himself by raids, which result in many slaves from his own as well as neighbouring countries. He employs these slaves [in many ways, mainly] in cultivating the land allotted to him: but he also sells many to the Azanaghi [and Arab] merchants in return for horses and other goods, and also to Christians, since they have begun to trade with these blacks.

The King is permitted to have as many wives as he wishes, as also are all the chiefs and men of this country, that is, as many as they can support. Thus this King has always thirty of them, though he favours one more than another, according to those from whom they are descended. This is his manner of living with his wives: he has certain villages and places, in some of which he keeps eight or ten of them. Each has a house of her own, with young servants to attend her, and slaves to cultivate the possessions and lands assigned by the lord, [with the fruits of which they are able to support themselves]. They have also a certain number of beasts, such as cows and goats, for their use; in this way his wives have the land sown and the beasts tended, and so gain a living. When the King arrives at one of these villages, he goes to the house of one of his wives, for they are obliged to provide, out of this produce, for him and those accompanying him. Every morning, at sunrise, each prepares three or four dishes of various foods, either meat, fish, or other Moorish foods according to their practice. These are sent by their slaves to be put at the disposal of their lord, so that within an hour forty or fifty dishes are assembled; when the time at which the lord wishes to eat has arrived, he picks out whatever tempts him, and gives the remainder to those in his train. But he never gives his people abundance to eat, so that they are always hungry. In this fashion he journeys from place to place without giving any thought to his victuals, and lodges sometimes with one wife, sometimes with another, so that he begets numerous sons, for when one is pregnant he leaves her alone. All the other chiefs of this country live in this same fashion.

The Customs of the Blacks, and Their Beliefs

The faith of these first Blacks is Muhammadanism: they are not however, as are the white Moors, very resolute in this faith, especially the common people. The chiefs adhere to the tenets of the Muhammadans because they have around them priests of the Azanaghi or Arabs, [who have reached this country]. These give them some instruction in the laws of Muhammad, enlarging upon the great disgrace of being rulers and yet living without any divine law, and behaving as do their people and lowly men, who live without laws; and since they have converse with none but these Azanaghi and Arab priests, they are converted to the law of Muhammad. But since they have had converse with Christians, they believe less in it, for our customs please them, and they also realise our wealth and ingenuity in everything as compared with theirs. They say that the God, who has bestowed so many benefits, has shown his great love for us, which could only be if his law were good—but that, none the less, theirs is still the law of God, through which they will find salvation, as we through ours.

These people dress thus: almost all constantly go naked, except for a goatskin fashioned in the form of drawers, with which they hide their shame. But the chiefs and those of standing wear a cotton garment—for cotton grows in these lands. Their women spin it into cloth of a span in width. They are unable to make wider cloth because they do not understand how to card it for weaving. When they wish to make a larger piece, they sew four or five of these strips together. These garments are made to reach half way down the thigh, with wide sleeves to the elbow. They also wear breeches of this cotton, which are tied across, and reach to the ankles, and are otherwise so large as to be from thirty to thirty-five, or even forty *palmi* round the top; when they are girded round the waist, they are much crumpled and form a sack in front, and the hinder part reaches to the ground, and waggles like a tail—the most comical thing to be seen in the world. They would come in these wide petticoats with these tails and ask us if we had ever seen a more beautiful dress or fashion: for they hold it for certain that they are the most beautiful garments in the world. Their women, both married and single, all go covered with girdles, below which they wear a sheet of these cotton strips bound across, half way down their legs. Men and women always go barefoot. They wear nothing on their heads: the hair of both sexes is fashioned into neat tresses arranged in various styles, though their hair by nature is no longer than a span. You must know also that the men of these lands perform many women's tasks, such as spinning, washing clothes and such things. It is always very hot there, and the further one goes inland, the greater the heat: by comparison, it is no colder in these parts in January than it is in April in our country of Italy.

Men Clean in Their Persons and Filthy in Eating

The men and women are clean in their persons, since they wash themselves all over four or five times a day: but in eating they are filthy, and ill-mannered. In matters of which they have no experience they are credulous and awkward, but in those to which they are accustomed they are the equal of our skilled men. They are talkative, and never at a loss for something to say: in general they are great liars and cheats: but on the other hand, charitable, receiving strangers willingly, and providing a night's lodging and one or two meals without any charge.

*   *   *

REVIEW QUESTIONS

1. What does da Mosto's account reveal about the earliest phases of the African slave trade?
2. His description of the silent trade is the first extended account we have of this remarkable type of barter. How plausible is this account, and what might it teach the economic historian about markets?
3. Alvise da Mosto was also the first European ethnographer of the Wolof. What types of bias and questions did he bring to his view of the Wolof? What contrasts are there in the way he described them to the way William of Rubruck described the Mongols?

CHRISTOPHER COLUMBUS

Letter on His First Voyage

Christopher Columbus (c. 1450–1506) was born somewhere around Genoa and from an early age made his living as a sailor. Columbus saw much of the Mediter-ranean and Atlantic world and acquired real skill as a mapmaker and navigator. Self-taught in geography, Columbus developed a theory of the globe's size that made sailing across the Atlantic to China and Japan a daring but plausible adventure. After spending years looking for a patron among the rulers of Europe, at last in

SAPI-PORTUGUESE SALT CELLAR, IVORY (C. 1500)

Portuguese traders in West Africa commissioned art works from the indigenous Sapi people. Merchants then sold these imaginative ivory carvings across Europe; this salt cellar ended up in Italy. Why would a European collector have purchased this object? How does the style of Sapi art differ from contemporary works of art created by Europeans?

1492 Isabella of Castile took the lead along with her husband Ferdinando of Aragon in sponsoring Columbus's first voyage. This letter is one of his earliest accounts of this trip—but we do not know to whom the letter was sent.

From *Selected Documents Illustrating the Four Voyages of Christopher Columbus,* translated and edited by Cecil Jane (London: Hakluyt Society, 1930), pp. 3–18.

Sir, As I know that you will be pleased at the great victory with which Our Lord has crowned my voyage, I write this to you, from which you will learn how in thirty-three days, I passed from the Canary Islands to the Indies with the fleet which the most illustrious king and queen, our sovereigns, gave to me. And there I found very many islands filled with people innumerable, and of them all I have taken possession for their highnesses, by proclamation made and with the royal standard unfurled, and no opposition was offered to me. To the first island which I found, I gave the name *San Salvador,* in remembrance of the Divine Majesty, Who has marvellously bestowed all this; the Indians call it "Guanahani." To the second, I gave the name *Isla de Santa María de Concepción;* to the third, *Fernandina;* to the fourth, *Isabella;* to the fifth, *Isla Juana,* and so to each one I gave a new name.

When I reached Juana, I followed its coast to the westward, and I found it to be so extensive that I thought that it must be the mainland, the province of Catayo. And since there were neither towns nor villages on the seashore, but only small hamlets, with the people of which I could not have speech, because they all fled immediately, I went forward on the same course, thinking that I should not fail to find great cities and towns. And, at the end of many leagues, seeing that there was no change and that the coast was bearing me northwards, which I wished to avoid, since winter was already beginning and I proposed to make from it to the south, and as moreover the wind was carrying me forward, I determined not to wait for a change in the weather and retraced my path as far as a certain harbour known to me. And from that point, I sent two men inland to learn if there were a king or great cities. They travelled three days' journey and found an infinity of small hamlets and people without number, but nothing of importance. For this reason, they returned.

I understood sufficiently from other Indians, whom I had already taken, that this land was nothing but an island. And therefore I followed its coast eastwards for one hundred and seven leagues to the point where it ended. And from that cape, I saw another island, distant eighteen leagues from the former, to the east, to which I at once gave the name "Española." And I went there and followed its northern coast, as I had in the case of Juana, to the eastward for one hundred and eighty-eight great leagues in a straight line. This island and all the others are very fertile to a limitless degree, and this island is extremely so. In it there are many harbours on the coast of the sea, beyond comparison with others which I know in Christendom, and many rivers, good and large, which is marvellous. Its lands are high, and there are in it very many sierras and very lofty mountains, beyond comparison with the island of Teneriffe. All are most beautiful, of a thousand shapes, and all are accessible and filled with trees of a thousand kinds and tall, and they seem to touch the sky. And I am told that they never lose their foliage, as I can understand, for I saw them as green and as lovely as they are in Spain in May, and some of them were flowering, some bearing fruit, and some in another stage, according to their nature. And the nightingale was singing and other birds of a thousand kinds in the month of November there where I went. There are six or eight kinds of palm, which are a wonder to behold on account of their beautiful variety, but so are the other trees and fruits and plants. In it are marvellous pine groves, and there are very large tracts of cultivatable lands, and there is honey, and there are birds of many kinds and fruits in great diversity. In the interior are mines of metals, and the population is without number. Española is a marvel.

The sierras and mountains, the plains and arable lands and pastures, are so lovely and rich for planting and sowing, for breeding cattle of every kind, for building towns and villages. The harbours of the sea here are such as cannot be believed to exist unless they have been seen, and so with the rivers, many and great, and good waters, the majority of which contain gold. In the trees and fruits and plants, there is a great difference from those of Juana. In this island, there are many spices and great mines of gold and of other metals.

The people of this island, and of all the other islands which I have found and of which I have information, all go naked, men and women, as their mothers bore them, although some women cover a single place with the leaf of a plant or with a net of cotton which they make for the purpose. They have no iron or steel or weapons, nor are they fitted to use them, not because they are not well built men and of handsome stature, but because they are very marvellously timorous. They have no other arms than weapons made of canes, cut in seeding time, to the ends of which they fix a small sharpened stick. And they do not dare to make use of these, for many times it has happened that I have sent ashore two or three men to some town to have speech, and countless people have come out to them, and as soon as they have seen my men approaching they have fled, even a father not waiting for his son. And this, not because ill has been done to anyone; on the contrary, at every point where I have been and have been able to have speech, I have given to them of all that I had, such as cloth and many other things, without receiving anything for it; but so they are, incurably timid. It is true that, after they have been reassured and have lost their fear, they are so guileless and so generous with all they possess, that no one would believe it who has not seen it. They never refuse anything which they possess, if it be asked of them; on the contrary, they invite anyone to share it, and display as much love as if they would

give their hearts, and whether the thing be of value or whether it be of small price, at once with whatever trifle of whatever kind it may be that is given to them, with that they are content. I forbade that they should be given things so worthless as fragments of broken crockery and scraps of broken glass, and ends of straps, although when they were able to get them, they fancied that they possessed the best jewel in the world. So it was found that a sailor for a strap received gold to the weight of two and a half *castellanos,* and others much more for other things which were worth much less. As for new *blancas,* for them they would give everything which they had, although it might be two or three *castellanos'* weight of gold or an *arroba* or two of spun cotton. . . . They took even the pieces of the broken hoops of the wine barrels and, like savages, gave what they had, so that it seemed to me to be wrong and I forbade it. And I gave a thousand handsome good things, which I had brought, in order that they might conceive affection, and more than that, might become Christians and be inclined to the love and service of their highnesses and of the whole Castilian nation, and strive to aid us and to give us of the things which they have in abundance and which are necessary to us. And they do not know any creed and are not idolaters; only they all believe that power and good are in the heavens, and they are very firmly convinced that I, with these ships and men, came from the heavens, and in this belief they everywhere received me, after they had overcome their fear. And this does not come because they are ignorant; on the contrary, they are of a very acute intelligence and are men who navigate all those seas, so that it is amazing how good an account they give of everything, but it is because they have never seen people clothed or ships of such a kind.

And as soon as I arrived in the Indies, in the first island which I found, I took by force some of them, in order that they might learn and give me information of that which there is in those parts, and so it was that they soon understood us, and we them, either by speech or signs, and they have been very serviceable. I still take them with me, and they are always assured that I come from Heaven, for all the intercourse which they have had with me; and they were the first to announce this wherever I went, and the others went running from house to house and to the neighbouring towns, with loud cries of, 'Come! Come to see the people from Heaven!' So all, men and women alike, when their minds were set at rest concerning us, came, so that not one, great or small, remained behind, and all brought something to eat and drink, which they gave with extraordinary affection. In all the island, they have very many canoes, like rowing *fustas,* some larger, some smaller, and some are larger than a *fusta* of eighteen benches. They are not so broad, because they are made of a single log of wood, but a *fusta* would not keep up with them in rowing, since their speed is a thing incredible. And in these they navigate among all those islands, which are innumerable, and carry their goods. One of these canoes I have seen with seventy and eighty men in her, and each one with his oar.

In all these islands, I saw no great diversity in the appearance of the people or in their manners and language. On the contrary, they all understand one another, which is a very curious thing, on account of which I hope that their highnesses will determine upon their conversion to our holy faith, towards which they are very inclined.

I have already said how I have gone one hundred and seven leagues in a straight line from west to east along the seashore of the island Juana, and as a result of that voyage, I can say that this island is larger than England and Scotland together, for, beyond these one hundred and seven leagues, there remain to the westward two provinces to which I have not gone. One of these provinces they call "Avan," and there the people are born with tails; and these provinces cannot have a length of less than fifty or sixty leagues, as I could understand from those Indians whom I have and who know all the islands.

The other, Española, has a circumference greater than all Spain, from Colibre, by the sea-coast, to Fuenterabia in Vizcaya, since I voyaged along one side one hundred and eighty-eight great leagues in a straight line from west to east. It is a land to be desired and, seen, it is never to be left. And in it, although of all I have taken possession for their highnesses and all are more richly endowed than I know how, or am able, to say, and I hold them all for their highnesses, so that they may dispose of them as, and as absolutely as, of the kingdoms of Castile, in this Española, in the situation most convenient and in the best position for the mines of gold and for all intercourse as well with the mainland here as with that there, belonging to the Grand Khan, where will be great trade and gain, I have taken possession of a large town, to which I gave the name *Villa de Navidad,* and in it I have made fortifications and a fort, which now will by this time be entirely finished, and I have left in it sufficient men for such a purpose with arms and artillery and provisions for more than a year, and a *fusta,* and one, a master of all sea-craft, to build others, and great friendship with the king of that land, so much so, that he was proud to call me, and to treat me as, a brother. And even if he were to change his attitude to one of hostility towards these men, he and his do not know what arms are and they go naked, as I have already said, and are the most timorous people that there are in the world, so that the men whom I have left there alone would suffice to destroy all that land, and the island is without danger for their persons, if they know how to govern themselves.

In all these islands, it seems to me that all men are content with one woman, and to their chief or king they give as many as twenty. It appears to me that the women work more than the men. And I have not been able to learn if they hold private property; what seemed to me to appear was that, in that which one had, all took a share, especially of eatable things.

In these islands I have so far found no human monstrosities, as many expected, but on the contrary the whole population is very well-formed, nor are they Negroes as in Guinea, but their hair is flowing, and they are not born where there is intense force in the rays of the sun; it is true that the sun has there great power, although it is distant from the equinoctial line twenty-six degrees. In these islands, where there are high mountains, the cold was severe this winter, but they endure it, being used to it and with the help of meats which they eat with many and extremely hot spices. As I have found no monsters, so I have had no report of any, except in an island "Quaris," the second at the coming into the Indies, which is inhabited by a people who are regarded in all the islands as very fierce and who eat human flesh. They have many canoes with which they range through all the islands of India and pillage and take as much as they can. They are no more malformed than the others, except that they have the custom of wearing their hair long like women, and they use bows and arrows of the same cane stems, with a small piece of wood at the end, owing to lack of iron which they do not possess. They are ferocious among these other people who are cowardly to an excessive degree, but I make no more account of them than of the rest. These are those who have intercourse with the women of "Matinino," which is the first island met on the way from Spain to the Indies, in which there is not a man. These women engage in no feminine occupation, but use bows and arrows of cane, like those already mentioned, and they arm and protect themselves with plates of copper, of which they have much.

In another island, which they assure me is larger than Española, the people have no hair. In it, there is gold incalculable, and from it and from the other islands, I bring with me Indians as evidence.

In conclusion, to speak only of that which has been accomplished on this voyage, which was so hasty, their highnesses can see that I will give them as much gold as they may need, if their highnesses will render me very slight assistance; moreover, spice and cotton, as much as their highnesses shall command; and mastic, as much as they shall order to be shipped and which, up to now, has been found only in Greece, in the island of Chios, and the Seignory sells it for what it pleases; and aloe wood, as much as they shall order to be shipped, and slaves, as many as they shall order to be shipped and who will be from the idolaters. And I believe that I have found rhubarb and cinamon, and I shall find a thousand other things of value, which the people whom I have left there will have discovered, for I have not delayed at any point, so far as the wind allowed me to sail, except in the town of Navidad, in order to leave it secured and well established, and in truth, I should have done much more, if the ships had served me, as reason demanded.

This is enough . . . and the eternal God, our Lord, Who gives to all those who walk in His way triumph over things which appear to be impossible, and this was notably one; for, although men have talked or have written of these lands, all was conjectural, without suggestion of ocular evidence, but amounted only to this, that those who heard for the most part listened and judged it to be rather a fable than as having any vestige of truth. So that, since Our Redeemer has given this victory to our most illustrious king and queen, and to their renowned kingdoms, in so great a matter, for this all Christendom ought to feel delight and make great feasts and give solemn thanks to the Holy Trinity with many solemn prayers for the great exaltation which they shall have, in the turning of so many peoples to our holy faith, and afterwards for temporal benefits, for not only Spain but all Christians will have hence refreshment and gain.

This, in accordance with that which has been accomplished, thus briefly.

Done in the caravel, off the Canary Islands, on the fifteenth of February, in the year one thousand four hundred and ninety-three.

At your orders.   El Almirante.

After having written this, and being in the sea of Castile, there came on me so great a south-south-west wind, that I was obliged to lighten ship. But I ran here to-day into this port of Lisbon, which was the greatest marvel in the world, whence I decided to write to their highnesses. In all the Indies, I have always found weather like May; where I went in thirty-three days and I had returned in twenty-eight, save for these storms which have detained me for fourteen days, beating about in this sea. Here all the sailors say that never has there been so bad a winter nor so many ships lost.

Done on the fourth day of March.

REVIEW QUESTIONS

1. What can we learn about Columbus's personality and motives from this letter?
2. Columbus also provided here the first Western account of the people he called Indians. What do we learn about his interests and abilities as an ethnographer?

MANUEL I

"The Letter Which the King, Our Lord, Wrote to the King and Queen of Castile, His Kin, Concerning the News of India"

In 1501 King Manuel I of Portugal wrote this letter to his relatives Isabella of Castile and Ferdinando of Aragon. The king was clearly proud of the journey Pedro Alvarez Cabral made to India the previous year. As this letter explains, Cabral's fleet also "discovered" Brazil (here called Santa Cruz) during this voyage. The letter describes Cabral's visit to Kilwa (here Quilon) in East Africa as well. But most of the letter concerns Cabral's long stay in Calicut in India.

From *The Voyage of Pedro Álvares Cabral to Brazil and India,* translated by William Brooks Greenlee (London: Hakluyt Society, 1937), pp. 43–52.

Most high and most excellent and most powerful Sovereigns, Father and Mother:

During these past days, after the first news arrived from India, I did not write at once to Your Majesties concerning the matters there because Pedro Alvarez Cabral, my chief captain of the fleet, which I had sent there, had not yet returned. And after his arrival I also delayed in doing so because two ships of his company had not yet come. One of these he had sent to Çofalla, a gold-mine which was discovered recently, not to establish trade, but only to have true information of what was there; because of the two ships which went there for this purpose, one was lost at sea, and the other was separated from the fleet in stormy weather and did not go there. And after the aforesaid ships had arrived, and I was on the point of notifying Your Majesties, Pero Lopes de Padilha told me that you would be glad to have news of what had happened there. The following is briefly everything which took place. My aforesaid captain with thirteen ships departed from Lisboa the 9th of March of last year, and during the octave of Easter he reached a land which he newly

CONQUEST OF MEXICO, FLORENTINE CODEX (C. 1555)

The Franciscan friar Bernardino de Sahagún (d. 1590) directed a team of Nahua aides who produced the Florentine Codex. This book is an account of the Cortéz's expedition of 1519, which resulted in the destruction of the Aztec Empire. The book is in Nahuatl and is accompanied by over 100 illustrations. Scholars have debated the extent to which the text and pictures allowed the Nahua to express their own views on these events. Sahagún began collecting information in the 1540s, and this chapter may have been composed around 1555. The illustrations accompanying the text may also have been sketched by Nahua people. These six pictures show characteristic battle scenes; in the last one the Mexica have captured a Spanish cannon. Guns and steel certainly played a role in the Spanish conquest of Mexico. What evidence do these pictures provide of this? Perhaps even more striking were the roles of horses and large dogs (not pictured here). What advantages did these animals provide the Spaniards?

discovered, to which he gave the name of Santa Cruz. In it he found the people nude as in the first innocence, gentle, and peaceable. It seemed that Our Lord miraculously wished it to be found, because it is very convenient and necessary for the voyage to India, because he repaired his ships and took water there. And on account of the long voyage which he had to make, he did not stop to obtain information about the said land; he only sent me a ship from there to notify me how he found it; and he pursued his route by way of the Cape of Good Hope. In that gulf, before arriving at it, he encountered great storms, in which, during one single day, four ships foundered together before his eyes, of which not a single person escaped. At this time, also, another of his ships disappeared, of which no news has been received up to this time. And that in which he went, with the others which remained, passed through great danger. And thus he went his way to make port at the kingdom of Quiloa, which belongs to the Moors, under whose sovereignty is the said mine of Çofalla, because he carried my letters and messages for its king, to establish peace with him, and a treaty concerning purchases and trade at the said mine. And before reaching the aforesaid kingdom, he found two ships with a great quantity of gold, which he took possession of, and because they belonged to the said King of Quiloa, after doing them much honour, he let them go. He was very well received by that king, who came in person to converse with my said captain on the sea, and entered with him in his boat, and he sent him presents; and after receiving my letters and messages, he agreed to the treaty. And since the ships which were destined for that mine were among those which were lost, no trade was begun there at that time, because the merchandise which the other ships carried was not suitable for what was needed for that land. And he departed from there and went to another kingdom, Melinde, for which he also was carrying my letters and messages, because its king, who likewise is a Moor, had done good deeds to Dom Vasco, who first went there to discover it. This king likewise visited him on the sea and also sent him presents, and confirmed and

established peace and friendship with him, and gave him the pilots whom he needed for his voyage. These kingdoms extend from the Red Sea in this direction, and in the interior they border on Gentiles, and these Gentiles border on the land of Prester John, whom they call the *abechy*. In their language this means "branded with iron," because, as a matter of fact, they do this, and they are branded with iron as a sign that they are baptized in water. From there he departed for Calecut, which is seven hundred leagues beyond. This city, as I believe you must already know, is of the Gentiles who worship many things and believe that there is only one God. And it is very populous, and there are in it many Moors who, until now, always traded there in spices, because it is thus like Bruges in Flanders, the principal trading place for the things of India, which come to it from outside; and in it there are only cassiafistula and ginger. He arrived at this city five months after having departed from Lisbon. And he was very honourably received by the king, who came to a house beside the sea to speak to him, with all his lords and many other people. And there he gave him my messages and established with him my peace and concord. Concerning this agreement the aforesaid king ordered a letter written on a sheet of silver with his seal inlaid in gold, for this is the custom in his land in matters of great importance, and other letters written on leaves of trees which resemble palms, on which they ordinarily write. And from these trees and their fruit are made the following things: sugar, honey, oil, wine, water, vinegar, charcoal, and cordage for ships, and for everything else, and matting of which they make some sails for ships, and it serves them for everything which they need. And the aforesaid fruit, in addition to what is thus made of it, is their chief food, particularly at sea. After the agreement had thus been made with the said king, my factor sent on shore the entire establishment which I had ordered for the above-mentioned factory, and at once he began to trade with his merchandise and to load the ships with spices. In the meantime, the King of Calecut sent word to my captain that a very large and well-armed ship which had annoyed him on previous occasions, belonging to another king, his enemy, had sent word to him that it was passing before his port, without any fear of him, and he begged him to order it to be captured, enlarging on the matter, as it greatly concerned his estate and honour.

And the said captain, in view of the good treatment which he and also my factor were beginning to receive, and in order to confirm further peace and friendship, agreed to do it. And in order to show him the strength of our people in ships and artillery, he sent against it only the smallest ship which he had, with a large bombard. And it overtook them within the harbour of another king, his neighbour, and before his eyes and those of all his people he captured it, and brought it to Calecut with 400 bowmen and some artillery and with seven elephants, trained in warfare, on board (there these would be worth thirty thousand cruzados, for they gave five thousand for only one of them), and with other merchandise of spices. This ship my captain ordered to be presented to him, and he gave it to him with everything which came in it, and he came to the shore with all his state and pomp to see it, since it was to them a very great surprise that so small a ship with so few men should take so large a ship with so many people, and to receive the message which the said captain was sending him concerning it. And the Moors, especially those of Mecca, who were there, seeing that they were in this concord and friendship, and that two ships were already loaded with spices, and seeing also the great loss which they were suffering, sought all the means that they could to put discord between my factor and the king. And they stirred up a tumult on land to hinder them; and because all the merchandise was in the hands of the Moors they hid it, and secretly sent it elsewhere. When he learned this, the aforesaid captain sent word to the King of Calecut, complaining to him and asking him to fulfil what he had agreed, which was that in twenty days he would give him merchandise with which to load the said ships, and that until they were loaded, he would not give authority to load to any others. And the king answered him that he would at once order all the

merchandise which there was in the land to be given to him, and that if any ship should be loaded in his harbour without the knowledge of his officials, he gave him the authority and power to detain it until he sent his said officials, so that they might arrange to turn it over to him. As soon as the Moors learned of this, they agreed to load a ship publicly with great diligence, using still greater care in hiding the merchandise than they had previously done, and this, in order to give an excuse for an outbreak to begin, for they are powerful. And the city is of many nationalities and of extensive population, in which the king can, with difficulty, attend to the tumults of the populace. And when my factor saw that the ship was being loaded, he asked the said captain to detain it, as the king had agreed. And the said captain, fearing an outbreak, hesitated to do it; and the said factor again asked him to detain it, telling him that the chief Moors and also some Gentiles told him that if the said ship were not held they could in no way load their ships. According to what followed it appears that they were doing it in order to give rise to the said outbreak. And my captain, after hesitating many times, fearing what followed, ordered the people of that ship to be told that, because of the authority which he had for this, it should not leave; but they were not willing to agree to this. And then it was necessary to order it to be held. And he commanded his boats to bring it inside the harbour, where it surely could not leave without his permission. And as soon as the Moors saw this, since it was the end which they desired, at that very moment they came quickly with all the rest of the population, whom they had already stirred up, to attack the said factor and his house, and fought with him. And he with those few whom he had with him, defended themselves for some time, and leaving the house, rallied at the sea. And my captain, who was then ill, as soon as he was told of the uprising on land, ordered all his boats to aid him, and although the sea was very rough he nevertheless gathered up some of the people. They killed the factor and with him fifty people were lost, either dead or captives. After this was done, when my captain saw that the king had not come to help and that he sent no message and was providing himself with some equipment implying war, and also had taken possession of my property which had remained on shore, he waited one day to see if he would make amends for the said matter. When he saw that he was sending him no message, fearing that he was arming himself effectively, as he afterwards did, to prevent him from taking the vengeance he could take at that time, he decided to act at once, and he took ten large ships which were in the harbour, and ordered all the people who were on them to be put to the sword, with the exception of a few who, concealing themselves, escaped death, and whom afterwards he did not wish to kill, but brought captive to me. And he ordered the said ships to be burned in front of the port, which caused great horror to the king and to the people of the land. On the ships there were three elephants which died there. In this manner he spent the entire day; and as soon as it was night, he went with all the ships, and placed himself as near land as he could in front of the city; and as soon as it was dawn, he began to fire with artillery, and bombarded it until night, especially the houses of the king. In this he did much damage, and killed many of his people, as he learned afterwards, and he killed one of the chief men who was near the king. On account of this, the king immediately departed from the city, for it seemed to him that he was not safe anywhere. And he sailed from there to another port of his, which was called Fandarene [Pandarani], which he also damaged with artillery, and killed people. And from there he sailed to the kingdom of Cochim, which is the region from which spices come, 30 leagues beyond Calecut, and on the way, he found two other ships of Calecut, which he also captured and ordered to be burned. And when he reached Cochim, after having informed the king of what had happened in Calecut, he was very well received by him, and made an agreement with him in the same manner which he had done in Calecut. Then he immediately sent my factor and certain men with him on shore, for whom they gave him honourable men as hostages, whom he brought to me; and they

loaded his ships in 16 days; and the merchandise they brought to him in their boats was brought with so much greater friendliness and security that it appeared that Our Lord permitted the outbreak at Calecut in order that this other agreement might take place, which is of greater profit and security, because the harbour is much better and of much more extensive trade, since, of almost all the merchandise which goes to Calecut, most of it is to be found in that land, and because others go there first without going to Calecut. In this city of Cochim there are many ships, and he learned that two merchants alone had as many as 50 ships. In that kingdom there are many true Christians of the conversion of Saint Thomas, and their priests follow the manner of life of the apostles with much strictness, having nothing of their own except what is given them as alms. And they practise celibacy, and have churches in which they say mass, and they consecrate unleavened bread, and wine which they make from dried fruit with water, for they cannot make other. In their churches they have no images save the cross, and all the Christians wear the apostolic garments, and never cut their beards and hair. And there he found definite information concerning where the body of Saint Thomas lies, which is 150 leagues from there, on the sea coast, in a city which is called Maliapor [Mailapur], of a small population; and he brought me earth from his tomb. And all the Christians and also the Moors and Gentiles, on account of the great miracles which are performed, go to his house on pilgrimage. He also brought us two Christians who came of their own accord and with the permission of their prelate, so that we might send them to Rome and to Jerusalem, to see the things of the Church there, and to be informed about them, for they consider that they are better ruled by being ordained by Saint Peter, who, they believe, was the chief of the apostles. And he also learned certain news of great Christian nations which are on the other side of that kingdom, who come on pilgrimage to the aforesaid house of Saint Thomas, and have very great kings who obey One only. They are white men of fair hair, and are considered strong. The land is called Malchima, and from it come porcelain, and musk and amber, and aloe-wood, which they bring from the river Ganges, which is on this side of them. And there are such fine vases of porcelain there, that a single one of them is worth a hundred cruzados. And while he was in the kingdom of Cochim, when the treaty had been agreed to and the ships loaded, there came to him messages from the King of Cananor, and from the King of Colum [Quilon] who are near by, requesting him to come to them because they would make more profitable trade with him, but, because he had already made the treaty, he declined to go. At this time, as he was about to depart from Cochim, the same king sent word to him that a large fleet from Calecut was coming against him, and that as many as 15,000 men were in it. It did not seem well to my captain to fight with it, because he had his ships loaded, and had few men, and it did not seem to him that there was time or necessity for taking the risk, since he feared that they might kill or disable some of them, and on account of the length of the journey which he had to go, which was 4,000 leagues from here. But he set sail, with them following him, and as they did not dare to go far out to sea, they turned back, because they feared to go against him. From there he went his way, which was to the kingdom of Cananor, [ruled by] one of those kings who invited him. And as he was passing, as soon as those on land caught sight of him, they sent him another message, asking him to stop there, because the king wanted to send a messenger to me by him, whom he brought me. And in the single day that he was there, he ordered so much spicery to be brought to the ships that he might have entirely filled them, had they been empty; and they gave what they might carry free, as a present to win my friendship. And all his chief men came also to my captain, telling him on behalf of the king that they would see to it that he was treated there in a different manner than in Calecut, assuring him that if he wanted to make war on Calecut they would help him, and that he in person would go on land, and all his fleet on the sea. And after thanking him greatly in my name, he took leave of him, saying to him that in

the other fleet which I was to send soon, I would send him my answer regarding everything. He went his way, and in the middle of that crossing he took a very large ship loaded with merchandise. It appeared to him that it was a ship of Mecca which was just coming from Calecut. And finding that the aforesaid ship belonged to the King of Cambaia [Cambay], he abandoned it, sending word by it to the said king that he had released it because he did not intend to make war with any one; he had made it only on those who had broken the word which they had given to him in my name. Continuing farther on his way, he lost one of the ships which was laden, for it ran aground during the night. Its people were saved, and he ordered the ship to be burned because it could not be dislodged safely. From this place he sent a ship to obtain news of the mine of Çofalla which I have mentioned before. This has just arrived, and brought me definite information of it and also concerning the trade and the merchandise of the country and of the great quantity of gold which is there; and there he found news, that among the men who carry gold from there to the coasts, they saw many who have four eyes, namely, two in front and two behind. The men are small of body and strong, and it is said that they are cruel, and that they eat the men with whom they have war, and that the cows of the king wear collars of heavy gold around their necks. Near this mine there are two islands on which they gather much pearl and amber. My aforesaid captain departed from there, and reached Lisboa 16 months from the day he had left it, and, blessed be Our Lord, in all this voyage he lost only three men from sickness, and all the others are healthy and of good spirits.[1] And now a certain message comes to me saying that one of the ships that was going to Çoffala which he believed lost, is coming, and will be here shortly. They say that it entered the Red Sea, and that it is bringing from there some silver and also some information concerning matters there, although I am already informed in detail concerning

---

[1]This is a mistake, since many had died of scurvy.

the said Red Sea, having been informed thereof by my above-mentioned captain, who had information concerning it in many ways. I leave the other details of this matter to Pero Lopes, who was present at everything. Very exalted and very excellent and very puissant Sovereigns, Father and Mother, may Our Lord have your life and royal estate in His holy care.

Written in Santarem the 29th of July, 1501.

El Rey.

REVIEW QUESTIONS

1. One theme here concerns Portuguese rivalry with the Moors—Muslims in East Africa and India. What were these relationships like?
2. What types of trade did the Portuguese hope to conduct in India?
3. Even though the information in the letter is at second hand, we still have an extensive view of the people of Calicut. What image of India has Manuel constructed for his readers?

13 – THE CIVILIZATION OF THE RENAISSANCE, C. 1350–1550

The Renaissance began as an Italian phenomenon, occurring between c. 1300 and 1520, that spread to the rest of Europe over the course of the 1500s and early 1600s. Its principal manifestations were the revival of classicism and naturalism in arts and literature, the rise of the modern dynastic state as the dominant political structure, and an economic crisis fueled by industrial change and economic contraction.

Until recently, scholars have traditionally viewed the Renaissance as a period of great change. Contemporaries used the term rinascita *to express their sense of a rebirth, a perfection in the arts. Many modern scholars view the period as one of fundamental change, an abrupt departure from the past, and have identified the following several characteristics that set the Renaissance apart as a discrete period of history. Scholars and artists revived classical antiquity as a subject of study and emulation. The state emerged as a work of art, that is, as a calculated design by persons in pursuit of power. The universal man, well rounded in physical and intellectual endeavors, became the political and pedagogical ideal of the age. The social mobility born of a rapidly changing economy led to an aristocracy of merit, a fusion of nobility and bourgeoisie in which achievement mattered more than lineage.*

All of these characteristics have been criticized and reviewed by latter-day historians of the Renaissance, most of whom would emphasize its continuity with the Middle Ages. Few, however, would disagree that the age was unusually self-conscious—aware of its achievements, intrigued by its potential, and impatient of its limits. The following selections capture something of this mentality.

LEON BATTISTA ALBERTI

FROM *I Libri della Famiglia*

Leon Battista Alberti (1404–1474) embodied the Renaissance universal man. Born the illegitimate son of a Florentine merchant, he was an athlete, polymath, and artist. He earned a degree in canon law at the University of Bologna in 1428, and migrated to Rome and entered papal service. It was there, in 1438, that he began to write On the Family. *Written in the form of a dialogue among the members of the Alberti family, gathered at the deathbed of Leon Battista's father in 1421, it examines the ideal family as a unit for the begetting and rearing of children, for the amassing and maintaining of fortunes, and for the accumulation and exercise of power. It was also a sly exercise in satire, insofar as it indirectly criticizes his brothers and uncles for violating his father's dying wish that Leon Battista be treated as a legitimate member of the family.*

From *I Libri della Famiglia,* translated by Renee New Watkins (Columbia: University of South Carolina Press, 1969).

*   *   *

XIII

Lionardo: If I had children, you may be sure I should think about them, but my thoughts would be untroubled. My first consideration would only be to make my children grow up with good character and virtue. Whatever activities suited their taste would suit me. Any activity which is not dishonest is not displeasing to an honorable mind. The activities which lead to honor and praise belong to honorable and wellborn men. Certainly I will admit that every son cannot achieve all that his father might wish. If he does something he is able to do, however, I like that better than to have him strike out in a direction where he cannot follow through. I also think it is more praiseworthy for a man, even if he does not altogether succeed, to do his best in some field rather than sit inactive, inert, and idle. There is an old saying which our ancestors often repeated: "Idleness is the mother of vice." It is an ugly and hateful thing to see a

man keep himself forever useless, like that idle fellow who when they asked him why he spent all day as if condemned to sit or lie on public benches, answered "I am waiting to get fat." The man who heard him was disgusted, and asked him rather to try to fatten up a pig, since at least something useful might come of it. Thus quite correctly he showed him what an idle fellow amounts to, which is less than a pig.

I'll go further, Adovardo. However rich and noble a father may be, he should try to have his son learn, besides the noble skills, some occupation which is not degrading. By means of this occupation in case of misfortune he can live honestly by his own labor and the work of his hands. Are the vicissitudes of this world so little or so infrequent that we can ignore the possibility of adverse circumstances? Was not the son of Perseus, king of Macedonia, seen sweating and soiled in a Roman factory, employed in making his living with heavy and painful labor? If the instability of things could thus transport the son of a famous and powerful king to such depths of poverty and need, it is right for us private citizens as well as for men of higher station to provide against every misfortune. If none in our house ever had to devote himself to such laboring occupations, thank fortune for it, and let us make sure that none will have to in the future. A wise and foresightful pilot, to be able to survive in adverse storms, carries more rope, anchors, and sheets than he needs for good weather. So let the father see that his sons enjoy some praiseworthy and useful activity. In this matter let him consider first of all the honesty of the work, and then adapt his course to what he knows his son can actually accomplish, and finally try to choose a field in which, by applying himself, the young man can hope to earn a reputation.

*   *   *

Battista: Whatever you think. The only question we have is what are the things that make a family fortunate. Go on with what you have to say and we shall listen.

*   *   *

Lionardo: In our discussion we may establish four general precepts as sound and firm foundation for all the other points to be developed or added. I shall name them. In the family the number of men must not diminish but augment; possessions must not grow less, but more; all forms of disgrace are to be shunned—a good name and fine reputation is precious and worth pursuing; hatreds, enmities, rancor must be carefully avoided, while good will, numerous acquaintances, and friendships are something to look for, augment, and cultivate.

*   *   *

If a family is not to fall for these reasons into what we have described as the most unfortunate condition of decline, but is to grow, instead, in fame and in the prosperous multitude of its youth, we must persuade our young men to take wives. We must use every argument for this purpose, offer incentive, promise reward, employ all our wit, persistence, and cunning. A most appropriate reason for taking a wife may be found in what we

were saying before, about the evil of sensual indulgence, for the condemnation of such things may lead young men to desire honorable satisfactions. As other incentives, we may also speak to them of the delights of this primary and natural companionship of marriage. Children act as pledges and securities of marital love and kindness. At the same time they offer a focus for all a man's hopes and desires. Sad, indeed, is the man who has labored to get wealth and power and lands, and then has no true heir and perpetuator of his memory. No one can be more suited than a man's true and legitimate sons to gain advantages by virtue of his character, position, and authority, and to enjoy the fruits and rewards of his labor. If a man leaves such heirs, furthermore, he need not consider himself wholly dead and gone. His children keep his own position and his true image in the family. Dido, the Phoenician, when Aeneas left her, his mistress, cried out with tears, among her great sorrows no desire above this one: "Ah, had I but a small Aeneas now, to play beside me." As you were first poisoned, wretched and abandoned woman, by that man whose fatal and consuming love you did embrace, so another little Aeneas might by his similar face and gestures have offered you some consolation in your grief and anguish.

*   *   *

When, by the urging and counsel of their elders and of the whole family, young men have arrived at the point of marriage, their mothers and other female relatives and friends, who have known the virgins of the neighborhood from earliest childhood and know the way their upbringing has formed them, should select all the well-born and well-brought-up girls and present that list to the new groom-to-be. He can then choose the one who suits him best. The elders of the house and all of the family shall reject no daughter-in-law unless she is tainted with the breath of scandal or bad reputation. Aside from that, let the man who will have to satisfy her satisfy himself. He should act as do wise heads of families before they acquire some property—they like to look it over several times before they actually sign a contract. It is good in the case of any purchase and contract to inform oneself fully and to take counsel. One should consult a good number of persons and be very careful in order to avoid belated regrets. The man who has decided to marry must be still more cautious. I recommend that he examine and anticipate in every way, and consider for many days, what sort of person it is he is to live with for all his years as husband and companion. Let him be minded to marry for two purposes: first to perpetuate himself in his children, and second to have a steady and constant companion all his life. A woman is needed, therefore, who is likely to bear children and who is desirable as a perpetual mate.

*   *   *

To sum up this whole subject in a few words, for I want above all to be brief on this point, let a man get himself new kinsmen of better than plebeian blood, of a fortune more than diminutive, of a decent occupation, and of modest and respectable habits. Let them not be too far above himself, lest their greatness overshadow his own honor and position. Too high a family may disturb his own and his family's peace and tranquillity, and also, if one of them falls, you cannot help to support him without collapsing or wearing yourself out as you stagger under a weight too great for your arms and your strength. I also do not want the new relatives to rank too low, for while the first error puts you in a position of servitude, the second causes expense. Let them be equals, then, and, to repeat, modest and respectable people.

*   *   *

We have, as I said, made the house numerous and full of young people. It is essential to give them something to do now, and not let them grow lazy. Idleness is not only useless and generally despised in young men, but a positive burden and danger to the family. I do not need to teach you to shun idleness, when I know you are hard workers and active. I do encourage you to continue as

you are doing in every sort of activity and hard discipline that you may attain excellence and deserve fame. Only think this matter over and consider whether any man, even if he is not necessarily ambitious of gaining glory but merely a little shy of falling into disgrace, can ever be, in actuality or even if we merely try to imagine him, a man not heartily opposed to idleness and to mere sitting. Who has ever dreamed he might reach any grace or dignity without hard work in the noblest arts, without assiduous efforts, without plenty of sweat poured out in manly and strenuous exertions? Certainly a man who would wish for the favor of praise and fame must avoid and resist idleness and inertia just as he would do major and hateful enemies. There is nothing that leads more quickly to dishonor and disgrace than idleness. The lap of the idler has always been the nest and lair of vice. Nothing is so harmful and pestilent in public and private life as the lazy and passive citizen. From idleness springs lasciviousness; from lasciviousness comes a contempt for the law; from disobedience to law comes ruin and the destruction of the country itself. To the extent that men tolerate the first resistance of men's will to the customs and ways of the country, their spirits soon turn to arrogance, pride, and the harmful power of avarice and greed. Thieves, murderers, adulterers, and all sorts of criminals and evil men run wild.

*   *   *

To this I might add that man ought to give some reward to God, to satisfy him with good works in return for the wonderful gifts which He gave to the spirit of man exalting and magnifying it beyond that of all other earthly beings. Nature, that is, God, made man a composite of two parts, one celestial and divine, the other most beautiful and noble among mortal things. He provided him with a form and a body suited to every sort of movement, so as to enable him to perceive and to flee from that which threatened to harm and oppose him. He gave him speech and judgment so that he would be able to seek after and to find what he needed and could use. He gave him movement and sentiment, desire and the power of excitement, so that he might clearly appreciate and pursue useful things and shun those harmful and dangerous to him. He gave him intelligence, teachability, memory and reason, qualities divine in themselves and which enable man to investigate, to distinguish, to know what to avoid and what to desire in order best to preserve himself. To these great gifts, admirable beyond measure, God added still another power of the spirit and mind of man, namely moderation. As a curb on greed and on excessive lusts, he gave him modesty and the desire for honor. Further, God established in the human mind a strong tie to bind together human beings in society, namely justice, equity, liberality, and love. These are the means by which a man can gain the favor and praise of other men, as well as the mercy and grace of the creator. Beyond this, God filled the manly breast with powers that make man able to bear fatigue, adversity, and the hard blows of fortune. He is able to undertake what is difficult, to overcome sorrow, not even to fear death—such are his qualities of strength, of endurance and fortitude, such can be his contempt for transitory things. These are qualities which enable us to honor and serve God as fully as we should, with piety, with moderation, and with every other perfect and honorable deed. Let us agree, then, that man was not born to languish in idleness but to labor and create magnificent and great works, first for the pleasure and glory of God, and second for his own enjoyment of that life of perfect virtue and its fruit, which is happiness.

*   *   *

Let men seek their own happiness first, and they will obtain the happiness of their family also. As I have said, happiness cannot be gained without good works and just and righteous deeds. Works are just and good which not only do no harm to anyone, but which benefit many. Works are righteous if they are without a trace of the dishonorable or any element of dishonesty. The best works are those which benefit many people. Those are most virtuous, perhaps, which cannot

be pursued without strength and nobility. We must give ourselves to manly effort, then, and follow the noblest pursuits.

It seems to me, before we dedicate ourselves to any particular activity, it would be wise to think over and examine the question of what is our easiest way to reach or come near to happiness. Not every man easily attains happiness. Nature did not make all men of the same humor, or of the same intelligence or will, or equally endowed with skill and power. Rather nature planned that where I might be weak, you would make good the deficiency, and in some other way you would lack the virtue found in another. Why this? So that I should have need of you, and you of him, he of another, and some other of me. In this way one man's need for another serves as the cause and means to keep us all united in general friendship and alliance. This may, indeed, have been the source and beginning of republics. Laws may have begun thus rather than as I was saying before; fire and water alone may not have been the cause of so great a union among men as society gives them. Society is a union sustained by laws, by reason, and by custom.

Let us not digress. To decide which is the most suitable career for himself, a man must take two things into account: the first is his own intelligence, his mind and his body, everything about himself; and the second, the question requiring close consideration, is that of outside supports, the help and resources which are necessary or useful and to which he must have early access, welcome, and free right of use if he is to enter the field for which he seems more suited than for any other. Take an example: if a man wished to perform great feats of arms while he knew he was himself but a weak fellow, not very robust, incapable of bearing up through dust and storm and sun, this would not be the right profession for him to pursue. If I, being poor, longed to devote my life to letters, though I had not the money to pay the considerable expenses attached to such a career, again this would be a poor choice of career. If you are equipped with numerous relatives, plenty of friends, abundant wealth, and if you possess within yourself intelligence, eloquence, and such tact as to keep you out of any rough or awkward situations, and you decide to dedicate yourself to civic affairs, you might do extremely well.

*   *   *

We should also consider at this point how much reward and profit, how much honor and fame, you can gain from any work or achievement you undertake to perform. The only condition is that you surpass everyone else in the field. In every craft the most skilled master, as you know, gains most riches and has the best position and the greatest stature among his companions. Think how even in so humble a profession as shoemaking men search out the best among the cobblers. If it is true of the humblest occupations that the most skilled practitioners are ever most in demand and so become most famous, consider whether in the highest professions the opposite suddenly holds true. In fact you will find it still more to the point to be the best in these, or at least one of the best. If you succeed in these fields, you know that you have been given a greater portion of happiness than other men. If you are learned, you realize the misfortune of the ignorant. You know, in addition, that the unhappiest lot falls to those who, being ignorant, desire still to appear learned.

*   *   *

Consider in your own mind what a boon to know more than others and to put the knowledge to good use at the right time and place. If you think it over, I am sure you will realize that in every field a man who would appear to be valuable must be valuable in fact. Now we have stated this much: that youth should not be wasted but should be directed to some honorable kind of work, that a man should do his utmost in that work, and that he should choose the field which will be most helpful to his family and bring him most fame. A career should suit our own nature and the state of our fortunes, and should be pursued in such a way that we may never, by our own fault at least, fall short of the first rank.

Riches, however, are for nearly everyone the primary reason for working at all. They are also most useful in making it possible to persevere in our undertakings until we win approval and attain public favor, position, and fame. This is the time, therefore, to explain how wealth is acquired and how it is kept. It was also one of the four things which we said were necessary to bring about and to preserve contentment in a family. Now, then, let us begin to accumulate wealth. Perhaps the present moment, as the evening grows dark, is just right for this subject, for no occupation seems less attractive to a man of large and liberal spirit than the kind of labor by which wealth is in fact gathered. If you will count over in your imagination the actual careers that bring great profits, you will see that all basically concern themselves with buying and selling or with lending and collecting the returns. Having neither petty nor vulgar minds, I imagine you probably find these activities, which are solely directed to making a profit, somewhat below you. They seem entirely to lack honor and distinction.

*   *   *

Those who thus dismiss all mercenary activities are wrong, I believe. If the pursuit of wealth is not as glorious as are other great pursuits, yet a man is not contemptible if, being unsuited by nature to achieve anything much in other finer fields of work, he devotes himself to this kind of activity. Here, it may be, he knows he is not inadequately equipped to do well. Here everyone admits he is very useful to the republic and still more to his own family. Wealth, if it is used to help the needy, can gain a man esteem and praise. With wealth, if it is used to do great and noble things and to show a fine magnanimity and splendor, fame and dignity can be attained. In emergencies and times of need we see every day how useful is the wealth of private citizens to the country itself. From public funds alone it is not always possible to pay the wages of those whose arms and blood defend the country's liberty and dignity. Nor can republics increase their glory and their might without enormous expenditure.

* * *

Why have I gone on at length on these topics? Only to show you that, among occupations, there are quite a few, both honorable and highly esteemed, by means of which wealth in no small measure may be gained. One of these occupations, as you know, is that of merchant. You can easily call to mind other similar careers which are both honorable and highly profitable. You want to know, then, what they are. Let us run through them. We shall spread out all the occupations before us and choose the best among them, then we shall try to define how they make us wealthy and prosperous. Occupations that do not bring profit and gain will never make you rich. Those that bring frequent and large profits are the ones that make you rich. The only system for becoming rich, by our own industry and by the means that luck, friends, or anyone's favor can give us, is to make profits. And how do men grow poor? Ill fortune certainly plays a part, this I admit, but excluding fortune, let us speak here of industry. If riches come through profits, and these through labor, diligence, and hard work, then poverty, which is the reverse of profit, will follow from the reverse of these virtues, namely from neglect, laziness, and sloth. These are the fault neither of fortune nor of others, but of oneself. One grows poor, also, by spending too much. Prodigality dissipates wealth and throws it away. The opposite of prodigality, the opposite of neglect, are carefulness and conscientiousness, in short, good management. Good management is the means to preserve wealth. Thus we have found out that to become rich one must make profits, keep what one has gained, and exercise rational good management.

* * *

REVIEW QUESTIONS

1. What, according to Alberti, is the role and nature of a father?
2. How is his authority different from other kinds of authority?
3. What is the role of education in the formation of human nature?
4. How does this view differ from that of other authors?
5. What is honor?
6. What is its relationship to the family and why is it so important to Alberti?
7. How might Alberti define the family?

BENVENUTO CELLINI

FROM *The Autobiography*

Benvenuto Cellini (1500–1571) was a native of Florence. Apprenticed as a young man to a goldsmith, he eventually wandered to Rome, where he established himself as an independent craftsman and artist. Supported by the patronage of merchants, aristocrats, and prelates, his success knew no bounds, at least in his own telling. Indeed, Cellini's individualism, self-confidence, and talent, expressed in both art and violence, are recorded in his autobiography. It is both a fascinating portrait of the Renaissance artist and a valuable window on the era.

From *The Autobiography of Benvenuto Cellini,* translated by John Addington Symonds (New York: Modern Library, 1995).

*   *   *

All the while I was at Florence, I studied the noble manner of Michel Agnolo, and from this I have never deviated. About that time I contracted a close and familiar friendship with an amiable lad of my own age, who was also in the goldsmith's trade. He was called Francesco, son of Filippo, and grandson of Fra Lippo Lippi, that most excellent painter. Through intercourse together, such love grew up between us that, day or night, we never stayed apart. The house where he lived was still full of the fine studies which his father had made, bound up in several books of drawings by his hand, and taken from the best antiquities of Rome. The sight of these things filled me with passionate enthusiasm; and for two years or thereabouts we lived in intimacy. At that time I fashioned a silver bas-relief of the size of a little child's hand. It was intended for the clasp to a man's belt; for they were then worn as large as that. I carved on it a knot of leaves in the antique style, with figures of children and other masks of great beauty. This piece I made in the workshop of one Francesco Salimbene; and on its being exhibited to the trade, the goldsmiths praised me as the best young craftsman of their art.

There was one Giovan Battista, surnamed Il Tasso, a wood-carver, precisely of my own age, who one day said to me that if I was willing to go to Rome, he should be glad to join me. Now we had this conversation together immediately after dinner; and I being angry with my father for the same old reason of the music, said to Tasso: "You are a fellow of words, not deeds." He answered: "I too have come to anger with my mother; and if I had cash enough to take me to Rome, I would not turn back to lock the door of that wretched little workshop I call mine." To these words I re-

plied that if that was all that kept him in Florence I had money enough in my pockets to bring us both to Rome. Talking thus and walking onwards, we found ourselves at the gate San Piero Gattolini without noticing that we had got there; whereupon I said: "Friend Tasso, this is God's doing that we have reached this gate without either you or me noticing that we were there; and now that I am here, it seems to me that I have finished half the journey." And so, being of one accord, we pursued our way together, saying, "Oh, what will our old folks say this evening?" We then made an agreement not to think more about them till we reached Rome. So we tied our aprons behind our backs, and trudged almost in silence to Siena. When we arrived at Siena, Tasso said (for he had hurt his feet) that he would not go farther, and asked me to lend him money to get back. I made answer: "I should not have enough left to go forward; you ought indeed to have thought of this on leaving Florence; and if it is because of your feet that you shirk the journey, we will find a return horse for Rome, which will deprive you of the excuse." Accordingly I hired a horse; and seeing that he did not answer, I took my way toward the gate of Rome. When he knew that I was firmly resolved to go, muttering between his teeth, and limping as well as he could, he came on behind me very slowly and at a great distance. On reaching the gate, I felt pity for my comrade, and waited for him, and took him on the crupper, saying: "What would our friends speak of us to-morrow, if, having left for Rome, we had not pluck to get beyond Siena?" Then the good Tasso said I spoke the truth; and as he was a pleasant fellow, he began to laugh and sing; and in this way, always singing and laughing, we travelled the whole way to Rome. I had just nineteen years then, and so had the century.

When we reached Rome, I put myself under a master who was known as Il Firenzuola. His name was Giovanni, and he came from Firenzuola in Lombardy, a most able craftsman in large vases and big plate of that kind. I showed him part of the model for the clasp which I had made in Florence at Salimbene's. It pleased him exceedingly; and turning to one of his journeymen, a Florentine called Giannotto Giannotti, who had been several years with him, he spoke as follows: "This fellow is one of the Florentines who knows something, and you are one of those who know nothing." Then I recognised the man, and turned to speak with him; for before he went to Rome, we often went to draw together, and had been very intimate comrades. He was so put out by the words his master flung at him, that he said he did not recognise me or know who I was; whereupon I got angry, and cried out: "O Giannotto, you who were once my friend—for have we not been together in such and such places, and drawn, and ate, and drunk, and slept in company at your house in the country? I don't want you to bear witness on my behalf to this worthy man, your master, because I hope my hands are such that without aid from you they will declare what sort of a fellow I am."

XIV

When I had thus spoken, Firenzuola, who was a man of hot spirit and brave, turned to Giannotto, and said to him: "You vile rascal, aren't you ashamed to treat a man who has been so intimate a comrade with you in this way?" And with the same movement of quick feeling, he faced round and said to me: "Welcome to my workshop; and do as you have promised; let your hands declare what man you are."

He gave me a very fine piece of silver plate to work on for a cardinal. It was a little oblong box, copied from the porphyry sarcophagus before the door of the Rotonda. Beside what I copied, I enriched it with so many elegant masks of my invention, that my master went about showing it through the art, and boasting that so

good a piece of work had been turned out from his shop. It was about half a cubit in size, and was so constructed as to serve for a salt-cellar at table. This was the first earning that I touched at Rome, and part of it I sent to assist my good father; the rest I kept for my own use, living upon it while I went about studying the antiquities of Rome, until my money failed, and I had to return to the shop for work. Battista del Tasso, my comrade, did not stay long in Rome, but went back to Florence.

After undertaking some new commissions, I took it into my head, as soon as I had finished them, to change my master; I had indeed been worried into doing so by a certain Milanese, called Pagolo Arsago. My first master, Firenzuola, had a great quarrel about this with Arsago, and abused him in my presence; whereupon I took up speech in defence of my new master. I said that I was born free, and free I meant to live, and that there was no reason to complain of him, far less of me, since some few crowns of wages were still due to me; also that I chose to go, like a free journeyman, where it pleased me, knowing I did wrong to no man. My new master then put in with his excuses, saying that he had not asked me to come, and that I should gratify him by returning with Firenzuola. To this I replied that I was not aware of wronging the latter in any way, and as I had completed his commissions, I chose to be my own master and not the man of others, and that he who wanted me must beg me of myself. Firenzuola cried: "I don't intend to beg you of yourself; I have done with you; don't show yourself again upon my premises." I reminded him of the money he owed me. He laughed me in the face; on which I said that if I knew how to use my tools in handicraft as well as he had seen, I could be quite as clever with my sword in claiming the just payment of my labour. While we were exchanging these words, an old man happened to come up, called Maestro Antonio, of San Marino. He was the chief among the Roman goldsmiths, and had been Firenzuola's master. Hearing what I had to say, which I took good care that he should understand, he immediately espoused my cause, and bade Firenzuola pay me. The dispute waxed warm, because Firenzuola was an admirable swordsman, far better than he was a goldsmith. Yet reason made itself heard; and I backed my cause with the same spirit, till I got myself paid. In course of time Firenzuola and I became friends, and at his request I stood godfather to one of his children.

*   *   *

REVIEW QUESTIONS

1. What distinguishes the artist according to Cellini?
2. How is genius dependent on wealth?
3. What does Cellini tell us about patronage and its effects on art?
4. In what ways is the artist like a courtier?

GIORGIO VASSARI

FROM *The Lives of the Artists*

Giorgio Vassari (1511–1574) was one of the most fashionable and prolific painters of his age. He spent most of his life traveling about Italy on various commissions. During these travels, he gathered specific information about artists and their works that he later incorporated into The Lives of the Artists *(1500). Its biographical sketches reveal not only fascinating insights into the practice of art in the Renaissance but also the taste and perspective of an accomplished artist. As a young man, Vassari studied painting under Michelangelo Buonarotti (1475–1564) and remained a lifelong disciple and admirer. Michelangelo began his career in 1492 under the patronage of Lorenzo de Medici. In 1505 he moved to Rome to design the tomb of Pope Julius II (1502–1513). Among his more famous commissions are the ceiling of the Sistine Chapel and the Basilica of St. Peter's. His career stretched to the middle of the sixteenth century, "bringing to perfection" (in Vassari's words) the three branches of the fine arts.*

From *The Lives of the Artists,* by Giorgio Vassari, translated by George Bull (New York: Penguin Books, 1965), pp. 325–26, 349–54.

*   *   *

Enlightened by what had been achieved by the renowned Giotto and his school, all artists of energy and distinction were striving to give the world proof of the talents with which fortune and their own happy temperaments had endowed them. They were all anxious (though their efforts were in vain) to reflect in their work the glories of nature and to attain, as far as possible, perfect artistic discernment or understanding. Meanwhile, the benign ruler of heaven graciously looked down to earth, saw the worthlessness of what was being done, the intense but utterly fruitless studies, and the presumption of men who were farther from true art than night is from day, and resolved to save us from our errors. So he decided to send into the world an artist who would be skilled in each and every craft, whose work alone would teach us how to attain perfection in design (by correct drawing and by the use of contour and light and shadows, so as to obtain relief in painting) and how to use right judgment in sculpture and, in architecture, create buildings which would be comfortable and secure, healthy, pleasant to look at, well-proportioned and richly ornamented. Moreover, he determined to give this artist the knowledge of true moral philosophy and the gift of poetic expression, so that everyone might admire and follow him as their perfect exemplar in life, work, and behaviour and in every endeavour, and he would be acclaimed as divine. He also saw that in the practice of these exalted disciplines and arts, namely, painting, sculpture, and architecture, the Tuscan genius has always been preeminent, for the Tuscans have devoted to all the various branches of art more labour and study than all the other Italian peoples. And therefore he chose to have Michelangelo born a Florentine, so that one of her own citizens might bring to absolute perfection the achievements for which Florence was already justly renowned.

So in the year 1474 in the Casentino, under a fateful and lucky star, the virtuous and noble wife of Lodovico di Leonardo Buonarroti gave birth to a baby son. That year Lodovico (who was said to be related to the most noble and ancient family of the counts of Canossa) was visiting magistrate at the township of Chiusi and Caprese near the Sasso della Vernia (where St. Francis received the stigmata) in the diocese of Arezzo. The boy was born on Sunday, 6 March, about the eighth hour of the night; and without further thought his father decided to call him Michelangelo, being inspired by heaven and convinced that he saw in him something supernatural and beyond human experience. This was evident in the child's horoscope which showed Mercury and Venus in the house of Jupiter, peaceably disposed; in other words, his mind

and hands were destined to fashion sublime and magnificent works of art.

*   *   *

Meanwhile, the Pope had returned to Rome while Michelangelo remained in Bologna to finish the statue. In his absence Bramante was constantly plotting with Raphael of Urbino to remove from the Pope's mind the idea of having Michelangelo finish the tomb on his return. Bramante did this (being a friend and relation of Raphael and therefore no friend of Michelangelo's) when he saw the way his holiness kept praising and glorifying Michelangelo's work as a sculptor. He and Raphael suggested to Pope Julius that if the tomb were finished it would bring nearer the day of his death, and they said that it was bad luck to have one's tomb built while one was still alive. Eventually they persuaded his holiness to get Michelangelo on his return to paint, as a memorial for his uncle, Pope Sixtus IV, the ceiling of the chapel that he had built in the Vatican. In this way Bramante and Michelangelo's other rivals thought they would divert his energies from sculpture, in which they realized he was supreme. This, they argued, would make things hopeless for him, since as he had no experience of colouring in fresco he would certainly, they believed, do less creditable work as a painter. Without doubt, they thought, he would be compared unfavourably with Raphael, and even if the work were a success, being forced to do it would make him angry with the Pope; and thus one way or another they would succeed in their purpose of getting rid of him. So when Michelangelo returned to Rome he found the Pope resolved to leave the tomb as it was for the time being, and he was told to paint the ceiling of the chapel. Michelangelo, being anxious to finish the tomb, and considering the magnitude and difficulty of the task of painting the chapel, and his lack of experience, tried in every possible way to shake the burden off his shoulders. But the more he refused, the more determined he made the Pope, who was a wilful man by nature and who in any case was again being prompted by Michelangelo's rivals, and especially Bramante. And finally, being the hot-tempered man he was, his holiness was all ready to fly into a rage.

However, seeing that his holiness was persevering, Michelangelo resigned himself to doing what he was asked. Then the Pope ordered Bramante to make the ceiling ready for painting, and he did so by piercing the surface and supporting the scaffolding by ropes. When Michelangelo saw this he asked Bramante what he should do, when the painting was finished, to fill up the holes. Bramante said: "We'll think of it when it's time." And he added that there was no other way. Michelangelo realized that Bramante either knew nothing about the matter or else was no friend of his, and he went to the Pope and told him that the scaffolding was unsatisfactory and that Bramante had not known how to make it; and the Pope replied, in the presence of Bramante, that Michelangelo should do it himself in his own way. So he arranged to have the scaffolding erected on props which kept clear of the wall, a method for use with vaults (by which many fine works have been executed) which he subsequently taught to various people, including Bramante. In this instance he enabled a poor carpenter, who rebuilt the scaffolding, to dispense with so many of the ropes that when Michelangelo gave him what was over he sold them and made enough for a dowry for his daughter.

Michelangelo then started making the cartoons for the vaulting; and the Pope also decided that the walls that had been painted by previous artists in the time of Sixtus should be scraped clean and that Michelangelo should have fifteen thousand ducats for the cost of the work, the price being decided through Giuliano da Sangallo. Then being forced reluctantly, by the magnitude of the task, to take on some assistants, Michelangelo sent for help to Florence. He was anxious to show that his paintings would surpass the work done there earlier, and he was determined to show modern artists how to draw and paint. Indeed, the circumstances of this undertaking encouraged Michelangelo to aim very high, for the sake both of his own reputation and the art of painting; and in this mood he started and finished the cartoons. He was then ready to begin the frescoes, but he lacked the necessary experience. Meanwhile, some of his friends, who were painters, came to Rome from Florence in order to assist him and let him see their technique. Several of them were skilled painters in fresco, and they included Granaccio, Giuliano Bugiardini, Jacopo di Sandro, the elder Indaco, Angelo di Donnino, and Aristotile. Having started the work, Michelangelo asked them to produce some examples of what they could do. But when he saw that these were nothing like what he wanted he grew dissatisfied, and then one morning he made up his mind to scrap everything they had done. He shut himself up in the chapel, refused to let them in again, and would never let them see him even when he was at home. So, when they thought the joke was wearing thin, they accepted their dismissal and went back ashamed to Florence.

Thereupon, having arranged to do all the work by himself, Michelangelo carried it well on the way to completion; working with the utmost solicitude, labour, and study he refused to let anyone see him in case he would have to show what he was painting. As a result every day the people became more impatient.

Pope Julius himself was always keen to see whatever Michelangelo was doing, and so naturally he was more anxious than ever to see what was being hidden from him. So one day he resolved to go and see the work, but he was not allowed in, as Michelangelo would never have consented. (This was the cause of the quarrel described earlier, when Michelangelo had to leave Rome as he would not let the Pope see what he was painting.) Now when a third of the work was completed (as I found out from Michelangelo himself, to clear up any uncertainty) during the winter when the north wind was blowing several spots of mould started to appear on the surface. The reason for this was that the Roman lime, which is white in colour and made of travertine, does not dry very quickly, and when mixed with pozzolana, which is a brownish colour, forms a dark mixture which is very watery before it sets; then after the wall has been thoroughly soaked, it often effloresces when it is drying. Thus this salt efflorescence appeared in many places, although in time the air dried it up. When Michelangelo saw what was happening he despaired of the whole undertaking and was reluctant to go on. However, his holiness sent Giuliano da Sangallo to see him and explain the reason for the blemishes. Sangallo explained how to remove the moulds and encouraged him to continue. Then, when the work was half finished, the Pope who had subsequently gone to inspect it several times (being helped up the ladders by Michelangelo) wanted it to be thrown open to the public. Being hasty and impatient by nature, he simply could not bear to wait until it was perfect and had, so to say, received the final touch.

As soon as it was thrown open, the whole of Rome flocked to see it; and the Pope was the first, not having the patience to wait till the dust had settled after the dismantling of the scaffolds. Raphael da Urbino (who had great powers of imitation) changed his style as soon as he had seen Michelangelo's work and straight away, to show his skill, painted the prophets and sibyls of Santa Maria della Pace; and Bramante subsequently tried to persuade the Pope to let Raphael paint the other half of the chapel. When Michelangelo heard about this he complained of Bramante and revealed to the Pope, without reserve, many faults in his life and in his architectural works. (He himself, as it happened, was later to correct the mistakes made by Bramante in the fabric of St. Peter's.) However, the Pope recognized Michelangelo's genius more clearly every day and wanted him to carry on the work himself; and after he had seen it displayed he was of the opinion that Michelangelo would do the other half even better. And so in twenty months Michelangelo brought the project to perfect completion without the assistance even of someone to grind his colours. Michelangelo at times complained that because of the haste the Pope imposed on him he was unable to finish it in the way he would have liked; for his

holiness was always asking him importunately when it would be ready. On one of these occasions Michelangelo retorted that the ceiling would be finished "when it satisfies me as an artist."

And to this the Pope replied: "And we want you to satisfy us and finish it soon."

Finally, the Pope threatened that if Michelangelo did not finish the ceiling quickly he would have him thrown down from the scaffolding. Then Michelangelo, who had good reason to fear the Pope's anger, lost no time in doing all that was wanted; and after taking down the rest of the scaffolding he threw the ceiling open to the public on the morning of All Saints' Day, when the Pope went into the chapel to sing Mass, to the satisfaction of the entire city.

Michelangelo wanted to retouch some parts of the painting *a secco,* as the old masters had done on the scenes below, painting backgrounds, draperies, and skies in ultramarine, and in certain places adding ornamentation in gold, in order to enrich and heighten the visual impact. The Pope, learning that this ornamentation was lacking, and hearing the work praised so enthusiastically by all who saw it, wanted him to go ahead. However, he lacked the patience to rebuild the scaffolding, and so the ceiling stayed as it was. His holiness used to see Michelangelo often and he would ask him to have the chapel enriched with colours and gold, since it looked impoverished. And Michelangelo would answer familiarly:

"Holy Father, in those days men did not bedeck themselves in gold and those you see painted there were never very rich. They were holy men who despised riches."

For this work Michelangelo was paid by the Pope three thousand crowns in several instalments, of which he had to spend twenty-five on colours. He executed the frescoes in great discomfort, having to work with his face looking upwards, which impaired his sight so badly that he could not read or look at drawings save with his head turned backwards; and this lasted for several months afterwards. I can talk from personal experience about this, since when I painted five rooms in the great apartments of Duke Cosimo's palace if I had not made a chair where I could rest my head and relax from time to time I would never have finished; even so this work so ruined my sight and injured my head that I still feel the effects, and I am astonished that Michelangelo bore all that discomfort so well. In fact, every day the work moved him to greater enthusiasm, and he was so spurred on by his own progress and improvements that he felt no fatigue and ignored all the discomfort.

*   *   *

REVIEW QUESTIONS

1. What distinguishes the artist according to Vassari?
2. What is the source of artistic genius?
3. What does the experience of Michelangelo tell us about human art and human nature as viewed by Vassari?

LEONARDO DA VINCI

FROM *The Notebooks*

Leonardo da Vinci (1452–1519) was born in the countryside of Florence, the illegitimate son of a notary in the town of Vinci. He was self-taught and could read Latin poorly. He was left-handed, a condition viewed by contemporaries as a deformity. Sometime around 1481 he moved to Milan, where his patrons were the Dukes Gian Galeazzo (1476–94) and Ludovico Sforza (1494–1500). During the French invasion of 1499 Leonardo fled Milan and led a peripatetic existence until 1508, when he returned to the city. In 1513 he was taken to France, where he lived the remainder of his days. He is widely acclaimed as a genius, the designer of futuristic machines of many sorts. Among these was a device for grinding concave mirrors and lenses that made possible the invention of the telescope in 1509. He was a great artist in many media as well as a keen observer of nature. His interests ranged from aerodynamics to physics to biology to anatomy to optics. His writings on perspective are drawn from his notebooks, which he wrote backward, in a mirror hand, and in no particular order, and which were never published in his lifetime.

From *The Notebooks of Leonardo da Vinci*, translated by Edward MacCurdy (London: Cape, 1958).

*   *   *

Principle of Perspective

All things transmit their image to the eye by means of pyramids; the nearer to the eye these are intersected the smaller the image of their cause will appear.

If you should ask how you can demonstrate these points to me from experience, I should tell you, as regards the vanishing point which moves with you, to notice as you go along by lands ploughed in straight furrows, the ends of which start from the path where you are walking, you will see that continually each pair of furrows seem to approach each other and to join at their ends.

As regards the point that comes to the eye, it may be comprehended with greater ease; for if you look in the eye of anyone you will see your own image there; consequently if you suppose two lines to start from your ears and proceed to the ears of the image which you see of yourself in the eye of the other person, you will clearly recognise that these lines contract so much that when they have continued only a little way beyond your image as mirrored in the said eye they will touch one another in a point.

The thing that is nearer to the eye always appears larger than another of the same size which is more remote.

Perspective is of such a nature that it makes what is flat appear in relief, and what is in relief appear flat.

The perspective by means of which a thing is represented will be better understood when it is seen from the view-point at which it was drawn.

If you wish to represent a thing near, which should produce the effect of natural things, it is impossible for your perspective not to appear false, by reason of all the illusory appearances and errors in proportion of which the existence may be assumed in a mediocre work, unless whoever is looking at this perspective finds himself surveying it from the exact distance, elevation, angle of vision or point at which you were situated to make this perspective. Therefore it would be necessary to make a window of the size of your face or in truth a hole through which you would look at the said work. And if you should do this, then without any doubt your work will produce the effect of nature if the light and shade are correctly rendered, and you will hardly be able to convince yourself that these things are painted. Otherwise do not trouble yourself about representing anything, unless you take your view-point at a distance of at least twenty times the maximum width and height of the thing that you represent; and this will satisfy every beholder who places himself in front of the work at any angle whatever.

If you wish to see a proof of this quickly, take a piece of a staff like a small column eight times as high as its width without plinth or capital, then measure off on a flat wall forty equal spaces which are in conformity with the spaces; they will make between them forty columns similar to your small column. Then let there be set up in front of the middle of these spaces, at a distance of four braccia from the wall, a thin band of iron, in the centre of which there is a small round hole of the size of a large pearl; place a light beside this hole so as to touch it, then go and place your column above each mark of the wall and draw the outline of the shadow, then shade it and observe it through the hole in the iron.

In Vitolone there are eight hundred and five conclusions about perspective.

Perspective

No visible body can be comprehended and well judged by human eyes, except by the difference of the background where the extremities of this body terminate and are bounded, and so far as its contour lines are concerned no object will seem to be separated from this background. The moon, although far distant from the body of the sun, when by reason of eclipses it finds itself between our eyes and the sun, having the sun for its background will seem to human eyes to be joined and attached to it.

Perspective comes to aid us where judgment fails in things that diminish.

It is possible to bring about that the eye does not see distant objects as much diminished as they are in natural perspective, where they are diminished by reason of the convexity of the eye, which is obliged to intersect upon its surface the pyramids of every kind of image that approach the eye at a right angle. But the method that I show here in the margin cuts these pyramids at right angles near the surface of the pupil. But whereas the convex pupil of the eye can take in the whole of our hemisphere, this will show only a single star; but where many small stars transmit their images to the surface of the pupil these stars are very small; here only one will be visible but it will be large; and so the moon will be greater in size and its spots more distinct. You should place close to the eye a glass filled with the water mentioned in chapter four of book 113 'Concerning Natural Things', water which causes things congealed in balls of crystalline glass to appear as though they were without glass.

Of the eye. Of bodies less than the pupil of the eye that which is nearest to it will be least discerned by this pupil—and from this experience it follows that the power of sight is not reduced to a point.

But the images of objects which meet in the pupil of the eye are spread over this pupil in the same way as they are spread about in the air; and the proof of this is pointed out to us when we look at the starry heavens without fixing our gaze more upon one star than upon another, for then the sky shows itself to us strewn with stars, and they bear to the eye the same proportions as in the sky, and the spaces between them also are the same.

Natural perspective acts in the opposite way, for the greater the distance the smaller does the thing seen appear, and the less the distance the larger it appears. But this invention constrains the beholder to stand with his eye at a small hole, and then with this small hole it will be seen well. But since many eyes come together to see at the same time one and the same work produced by this art, only one of them will have a good view of the function of this perspective and all the others will only see it confusedly. It is well therefore to shun this compound perspective, and to keep to the simple which does not purport to view planes foreshortened but as far as possible in exact form.

And of this simple perspective in which the plane intersects the pyramid that conveys the images to the eye that are at an equal distance from the visual faculty, an example is afforded us by the curve of the pupil of the eye upon which these pyramids intersect at an equal distance from the visual faculty.

Of Equal Things the More Remote Appears Smaller

The practice of perspective is divided into two parts, of which the first treats of all the things seen by the eye at whatsoever distance, and this in itself shows all these things diminished as the eye beholds them, without the man being obliged to stand in one place rather than in another, provided that the wall does not foreshorten it a second time.

But the second practice is a combination of perspective made partly by art and partly by nature, and the work done according to its rules has no part that is not influenced by natural and accidental perspective. Natural perspective I understand has to do with the flat surface on which this perspective is represented; which surface, although it is parallel to it in length and height, is constrained to diminish the distant parts more than its near ones. And this is proved by the first of what has been said above, and its diminution is natural.

Accidental perspective, that is that which is created by art, acts in the contrary way; because it causes bodies equal in themselves to increase on the foreshortened plane, in proportion as the eye is more natural and nearer to the plane, and as the part of this plane where it is represented is more remote from the eye.

*   *   *

REVIEW QUESTIONS

1. According to da Vinci, what is the relationship between perspective in nature and perspective in the human eye?
2. What is the relationship between perspective and mathematical principles?
3. Is perspective a constant or contingent?
4. What implications does this have for painting?
5. How might it shape the enterprise of reading?

BALDESAR CASTIGLIONE

FROM *The Book of the Courtier*

Baldesar Castiglione (1478–1529) was born near Mantua and educated in Milan. He entered the service of the duke of Milan in 1496. After the duke was carried prisoner to France, Castiglione returned to Mantua. In 1504, he entered the court of Guidobaldo of Montefeltro, duke of Urbino, where he remained until 1524; this is the setting of The Book of the Courtier. *Although he wrote elegant verse in Latin and Italian, this reflection on courtly life was Castiglione's claim to fame. Fashioned as a discourse among courtiers and courtesans, it described the ideal courtier and presented the Renaissance man.*

From *The Book of the Courtier*, by Baldesar Castiglione, translated by Charles S. Singleton (New York: Bantam Doubleday Dell, 1959), pp. 29–30, 32–34, 70–72, 205–8, 289–90.

*   *   *

"Thus, I would have our Courtier born of a noble and genteel family; because it is far less becoming for one of low birth to fail to do virtuous things than for one of noble birth, who, should he stray from the path of his forebears, stains the family name, and not only fails to achieve anything but loses what has been achieved already. For noble birth is like a bright lamp that makes manifest and visible deeds both good and bad, kindling and spurring on to virtue as much for fear of dishonor as for hope of praise. And since this luster of nobility does not shine forth in the deeds of the lowly born, they lack that spur, as well as that fear of dishonor, nor do they think themselves obliged to go beyond what was done by their forebears; whereas to the wellborn it seems a reproach not to attain at least to the mark set them by their ancestors. Hence, it almost always happens that, in the profession of arms as well as in other worthy pursuits, those who are most distinguished are men of noble birth, because nature has implanted in everything that hid-

LAST SUPPER (1498)

LEONARDO DA VINCI

Perhaps da Vinci's greatest painting, the Last Supper *captures the drama of the moment in which Jesus reveals to his disciples that one of them will betray him. For all its moment, however, it remains compellingly intimate in the individuality of expressions and gestures and in the conversational groupings of three. What do you think makes the* Last Supper *representative of Renaissance art in general? How might the artistic device of perspective be said to be an extension of urban, mercantile culture, the very culture that gave rise to the Renaissance? What does the* Last Supper *reveal about religious faith during the Renaissance?*

den seed which gives a certain force and quality of its own essence to all that springs from it, making it like itself: as we can see not only in breeds of horses and other animals, but in trees as well, the shoots of which nearly always resemble the trunk; and if they sometimes degenerate, the fault lies with the husbandman. And so it happens with men, who, if they are tended in the right way, are almost always like those from whom they spring, and often are better; but if they lack someone to tend them properly, they grow wild and never attain their full growth.

*   *   *

"But, to return to our subject, I say that there is a mean to be found between such supreme grace on the one hand and such stupid ineptitude on the other, and that those who are not so perfectly endowed by nature can, with care and effort, polish and in great part correct their natural defects. Therefore, besides his noble birth, I would wish the Courtier favored in this other respect, and endowed by nature not only with talent and with beauty of countenance and person, but with that certain grace which we call an 'air,' which shall make him at first sight pleasing and lovable to all who see him; and let this be an adornment informing and attending all his actions, giving the promise outwardly that such a one is worthy of the company and the favor of every great lord."

*   *   *

"But to come to some particulars: I hold that the principal and true profession of the Courtier must be that of arms; which I wish him to exercise with vigor; and let him be known among the others as bold, energetic, and faithful to whomever he serves. And the repute of these good qualities will be earned by exercising them in every time and place, inasmuch as one may not ever fail therein without great blame. And, just as among women the name of purity, once stained, is never restored, so the reputation of a gentleman whose profession is arms, if ever in the least way he sullies himself through cowardice or other disgrace, always remains defiled before the world and covered with ignominy. Therefore, the more our Courtier excels in this art, the more will he merit praise; although I do not deem it necessary that he have the perfect knowledge of things and other qualities that befit a commander, for since this would launch us on too great a sea, we shall be satisfied, as we have said, if he have complete loyalty and an undaunted spirit, and be always seen to have them. For oftentimes men are known for their courage in small things rather than in great. And often in important perils and where there are many witnesses, some men are found who, although their hearts sink within them, still, spurred on by fear of shame or by the company of those present, press forward with eyes shut, as it were, and do their duty, God knows how; and in things of little importance and when they think they can avoid the risk of danger, they are glad to play safe. But those men who, even when they think they will not be observed or seen or recognized by anyone, show courage and are not careless of anything, however slight, for which they could be blamed, such have the quality of spirit we are seeking in our Courtier.

"However, we do not wish him to make a show of being so fierce that he is forever swaggering in his speech, declaring that he has wedded his cuirass, and glowering with such dour looks as we have often seen Berto do; for to such as these one may rightly say what in polite society a worthy lady jestingly said to a certain man (whom I do not now wish to name) whom she sought to honor by inviting him to dance, and who not only declined this but would not listen to music or take any part in the other entertainments offered him, but kept saying that such trifles were not his business. And when finally the lady said to him: 'What then is your business?' he answered with a scowl: 'Fighting.' Whereupon the lady replied at once: 'I should think it a good thing, now that you are not away at war or engaged in fighting, for you to have yourself greased all over and stowed away in a closet along with all your battle harness, so that you won't grow any rustier than you already are';

and so, amid much laughter from those present, she ridiculed him in his stupid presumption. Therefore, let the man we are seeking be exceedingly fierce, harsh, and always among the first, wherever the enemy is; and in every other place, humane, modest, reserved, avoiding ostentation above all things as well as that impudent praise of himself by which a man always arouses hatred and disgust in all who hear him."

*   *   *

"I would have him more than passably learned in letters, at least in those studies which we call the humanities. Let him be conversant not only with the Latin language, but with Greek as well, because of the abundance and variety of things that are so divinely written therein. Let him be versed in the poets, as well as in the orators and historians, and let him be practiced also in writing verse and prose, especially in our own vernacular; for, besides the personal satisfaction he will take in this, in this way he will never want for pleasant entertainment with the ladies, who are usually fond of such things. And if, because of other occupations or lack of study, he does not attain to such a perfection that his writings should merit great praise, let him take care to keep them under cover so that others will not laugh at him, and let him show them only to a friend who can be trusted; because at least they will be of profit to him in that, through such exercise, he will be capable of judging the writing of others. For it very rarely happens that a man who is unpracticed in writing, however learned he may be, can ever wholly understand the toils and industry of writers, or taste the sweetness and excellence of styles, and those intrinsic niceties that are often found in the ancients.

These studies, moreover, will make him fluent, and (as Aristippus said to the tyrant) bold and self-confident in speaking with everyone. However, I would have our Courtier keep one precept firmly in mind, namely, in this as in everything else, to be cautious and reserved rather than forward, and take care not to get the mistaken notion that he knows something he does not know.

*   *   *

"Let us leave these blind ones to their error, and let us have our Courtier be of such good judgment that he will not let himself be persuaded that black is white, or presume of himself more than he clearly knows to be true; and especially in those points which (if your memory serves you) messer Cesare said we had often used as the means of bringing to light the folly of many persons. Indeed, even if he knows that the praises bestowed upon him are true, let him avoid error by not assenting too openly to them, nor concede them without some protest; but let him rather disclaim them modestly, always showing and really esteeming arms as his chief profession, and the other good accomplishments as ornaments thereto; and do this especially when among soldiers, in order not to act like those who in studies wish to appear as soldiers, and, when in the company of warriors, wish to appear as men of letters. In this way, for the reasons we have stated, he will avoid affectation and even the ordinary things he does will appear to be very great things."

*   *   *

Then said the Duchess: "Do not exceed bounds, signor Magnifico, but hold to the order given, and describe the Court Lady so that such a noble lady may have someone capable of serving her worthily."

The Magnifico continued: "Then, Madam, in order to show that your commands can induce me to attempt what I do not even know how to do, I will speak of this excellent Lady as I would wish her to be; and when I have fashioned her to my taste, and since then I may not have another, like Pygmalion I will take her for my own. And, though signor Gasparo has said that the same rules which serve for the Courtier serve also for the Lady, I am of a different opinion; for although some qualities are common to both and are as necessary for a man as for a woman, there are yet others that befit a woman more than a man, and others that befit a man and to which a woman ought to be a complete stranger. I say this of bodily exercises; but above all I think that in her ways, manners, words, gestures, and bearing, a woman ought to be very unlike a man; for just as he must show a certain solid and sturdy manliness, so it is seemly for a woman to have a soft and delicate tenderness, with an air of womanly sweetness in her every movement, which, in her going and staying, and in whatever she says, shall always make her appear the woman without any resemblance to a man.

"Now, if this precept be added to the rules which these gentlemen have taught the Courtier, then I think she ought to be able to follow many such and adorn herself with the best accomplishments, as signor Gasparo says. For I hold that many virtues of the mind are as necessary to a woman as to a man; also, gentle birth; to avoid affectation, to be naturally graceful in all her actions, to be mannerly, clever, prudent, not arrogant, not envious, not slanderous, not vain, not contentious, not inept, to know how to gain and hold the favor of her mistress and of all others, to perform well and gracefully the exercises that are suitable for women. And I do think that beauty is more necessary to her than to the Courtier, for truly that woman lacks much who lacks beauty. Also she must be more circumspect, and more careful not to give occasion for evil being said of her, and conduct herself so that she may not only escape being sullied by guilt but even by the suspicion of it, for a woman has not so many ways of defending herself against false calumnies as a man has. But since Count Ludovico has set forth in great detail the chief profession of the Courtier, and has insisted that this be arms, I think it is also fitting to state what I judge that of the Court Lady to be, and when I have done this I shall think to have discharged the greater part of my assignment.

"Leaving aside, then, those virtues of the mind which she is to have in common with the Courtier (such as prudence, magnanimity, continence, and many others), as well as those qualities that befit all (such as kindness, discretion, ability to manage her husband's property and house and children, if she is married, and all qualities that are requisite in a good mother), I say that, in my opinion, in a Lady who lives at court a certain pleasing affability is becoming above all else, whereby she will be able to entertain graciously every kind of man with agreeable and comely conversation suited to the time and place and to the station of the person with whom she speaks, joining to serene and modest manners, and to that comeliness that ought to inform all her actions, a quick vivacity of spirit whereby she will show herself a stranger to all boorishness; but with such a kind manner as to cause her to be thought no less chaste, prudent, and gentle than she is agreeable, witty, and discreet: thus, she must observe a certain mean (difficult to achieve and, as it were, composed of contraries) and must strictly observe certain limits and not exceed them.

"Now, in her wish to be thought good and pure, this Lady must not be so coy, or appear so to abhor gay company or any talk that is a little loose, as to withdraw as soon as she finds herself involved, for it might easily be thought that she was pretending to be so austere in order to hide something about herself which she feared others might discover; for manners so unbending are always odious. Yet, on the other hand, for the sake of appearing free and amiable she must not utter unseemly words or enter into any immodest and unbridled familiarity or into ways such as might cause others to believe about her what is perhaps not true; but when she finds herself present at such talk, she ought to listen with a light blush of shame.

"Likewise, she must avoid an error into which I have seen many women fall, which is to gossip and eagerly listen to evil spoken of other women. For those women who, when they hear of the unchaste ways of other women, bristle and pretend that the thing is incredible and that a woman so immodest is a monster, in making so much of the fault give cause to think that they might be guilty of it themselves. And those others who continually go about prying into other women's love affairs, relating them in such detail and with such glee, appear envious and desirous that everyone should know of this case in order that the same thing may not through error be imputed to them; and thus they emit certain laughs and assume certain attitudes, making it evident that they relish it all. And the result of this is that men, although they appear to listen to them willingly, usually conceive a bad opinion of such women and have little respect for them, and take these ways of theirs to be an invitation to go further; and they often do go so far with them that it quite justly brings shame upon them, and in the end they esteem them so little as to care nothing for their company, and even come to despise them. On the other hand, there is no man so profligate and so forward as not to have reverence for those women who are esteemed to be good and virtuous, because a certain gravity, tempered with wisdom and goodness, is like a shield against the insolence and brutishness of presumptuous men; wherefore we see that a word, a laugh, or an act of kindness, however small, coming from a virtuous woman is more esteemed by everyone than all the blandishments and caresses of those who so openly show their want of shame—and if they are not unchaste, by their wanton laughter, loquacity, insolence, and scurrilous behavior of this sort, they appear to be so.

*   *   *

"Therefore, I think that the aim of the perfect Courtier, which we have not spoken of up to now, is so to win for himself, by means of the accomplishments ascribed to him by these gentlemen, the favor and mind of the prince whom he serves that he may be able to tell him, and always will tell him, the truth about everything he needs to know, without fear or risk of displeasing him; and that when he sees the mind of his prince inclined to a wrong action, he may dare to oppose him and in a gentle manner avail himself of the favor acquired by his good accomplishments, so as to dissuade him of every evil intent and bring him to the path of virtue. And thus, having in himself the goodness which these gentlemen attributed to

him, together with readiness of wit, charm, prudence, knowledge of letters and of many other things—the Courtier will in every instance be able adroitly to show the prince how much honor and profit will come to him and to his from justice, liberality, magnanimity, gentleness, and the other virtues that befit a good prince; and, on the other hand, how much infamy and harm result from the vices opposed to these virtues. Hence, I think that even as music, festivals, games, and the other pleasant accomplishments are, as it were, the flower; so to bring or help one's prince toward what is right and to frighten him away from what is wrong are the true fruit of Courtiership. And because the real merit of good deeds consists chiefly in two things, one of which is to choose a truly good end to aim at, and the other is to know how to find means timely and fitting to attain that good end—it is certain that a man aims at the best end when he sees to it that his prince is deceived by no one, listens to no flatterers or slanderers or liars, and distinguishes good from evil, loving the one and hating the other."

*   *   *

REVIEW QUESTIONS

1. What does Castiglione mean by grace? How is it created?
2. To what extent is it the product of birth or nature?
3. How is it gendered?
4. What does a courtier's conduct tell others about his status?
5. If status was once thought to reside in one's birth and lineage, how does the courtier alter that notion?
6. How does Castiglione's courtier differ from a medieval monk or knight?
7. Is his virtue the expression of his nature, cultivation, or education?

PORTRAIT OF POPE LEO X AND TWO CARDINALS (1518)   RAPHAEL

This intriguing portrait of Pope Leo X and two of his cardinals, relatives elevated through acts of nepotism, reveals the full sophistication of Raphael's artistry. He created an attractive painting of his patron in full papal regalia. At the same time he subtly included less attractive hints about the subject's office and character. What might this portrait tell us of Leo's character? What does the portrait tell us about Renaissance values? Is Raphael exercising a subtle criticism of the church through his portrait of its head, and, if so, what elements of his criticism are explicit in the painting?

68

GIOVANNI PICO DELLA MIRANDOLA

FROM "Oration on the Dignity of Man"

Giovanni Pico della Mirandola (1463–1494) is a singular figure in the history of Renaissance humanism. While the corpus of his published works remained small as a result of his early death, the breadth of his learning won him the admiration of scholars past and present. He received a thorough classical education in Greek and Latin, and studied the scholastic tradition of the Middle Ages as well as Jewish and Arabic philosophy. His conception of the dignity of man and harmony among philosophers found expression in his "Oration on the Dignity of Man." In 1486, Pico published his 900 theses, inviting all scholars to a public debate in January 1487. Before it could take place, however, Pope Innocent VIII appointed a commission to examine the theses, some of which were found to be heretical. An attempt to defend the incriminated points plunged Pico into a conflict with ecclesiastical authorities that lasted several years. The oration, never published in its author's lifetime, was written as an introductory speech for the disputation.

From *Renaissance Philosophy of Man,* edited by Ernest Cassirer (Chicago: University of Chicago Press, 1948).

I have read in the records of the Arabians, reverend Fathers, that Abdala the Saracen, when questioned as to what on this stage of the world, as it were, could be seen most worthy of wonder, replied: "There is nothing to be seen more wonderful than man." In agreement with this opinion is the saying of Hermes Trismegistus: "A great miracle, Asclepius, is man." But when I weighed the reason for these maxims, the many grounds for the excellence of human nature reported by many men failed to satisfy me—that man is the intermediary between creatures, the intimate of the gods, the king of the lower beings, by the acuteness of his senses, by the discernment of his reason, and by the light of his intelligence the interpreter of nature, the interval between fixed eternity and fleeting time, and (as the Persians say) the bond, nay, rather, the marriage song of the world, on David's testimony but little lower than the angels. Admittedly great though these reasons be, they are not the principal grounds, that is, those which may rightfully claim for themselves the privilege of the highest admiration. For why should we not admire more the angels themselves and the blessed choirs of heaven? At last it seems to me I have come to understand why man is the most fortunate of creatures and consequently worthy of all admiration and what precisely is that rank which is his lot in the universal chain of Being—a rank to be envied not only by brutes but even by the stars and by minds beyond this world. It is a matter past faith and a wondrous one. Why should it not be? For it is on this very account that man is rightly called and judged a great miracle and a wonderful creature indeed.

But hear, Fathers, exactly what this rank is and, as friendly auditors, conformably to your kindness, do me this favor. God the Father, the supreme Architect, had already built this cosmic home we behold, the most sacred temple of His godhead, by the laws of His mysterious wisdom. The region above the heavens He had adorned with Intelligences, the heavenly spheres He had quickened with eternal souls, and the excrementary and filthy parts of the lower world He had filled with a multitude of animals of every kind. But, when the work was finished, the Craftsman kept wishing that there were someone to ponder the plan of so great a work, to love its beauty, and to wonder at its vastness. Therefore, when everything was done (as Moses and Timaeus bear witness), He finally took thought concerning the creation of man. But there was not among His archetypes that from which He could fashion a new offspring, nor was there in His treasure-houses anything which He might bestow on His new son as an inheritance, nor was there in the seats of all the world a place where the latter might sit to contemplate the universe. All was now complete; all things had been assigned to the highest, the middle, and the lowest orders. But in its final creation it was not the part of the Father's power to fail as though exhausted. It was not the part of His wisdom to waver in a needful matter through poverty of counsel. It was not the part of His kindly love that he who was to praise God's divine generosity in regard to others should be compelled to condemn it in regard to himself.

At last the best of artisans ordained that that creature to whom He had been able to give nothing proper to himself should have joint possession of whatever had been peculiar to each of the different kinds of being. He therefore took man as a creature of indeterminate nature and, assigning him a place in the middle of the world, addressed him thus: "Neither a fixed abode nor a form that is thine alone nor any function peculiar to thyself have we given thee, Adam, to the end that according to thy longing and according to thy judgment thou mayest have and possess what abode, what form, and what functions thou thyself shalt desire. The nature of all other beings is limited and constrained within the bounds of laws prescribed by Us. Thou, constrained by no limits, in accordance with thine own free will, in whose hand We have placed thee, shalt ordain for thyself the limits of thy nature. We have set thee at the world's center that thou mayest from thence more easily observe whatever is in the world. We have made thee neither of heaven nor of earth, neither mortal nor immortal, so that with freedom of choice and with honor, as though the maker and molder of thyself, thou mayest fashion thyself in whatever shape thou shalt prefer. Thou shalt have the power to degenerate into the lower forms of life, which are brutish. Thou shalt have the power, out of thy soul's judgment, to be reborn into the higher forms, which are divine."

O supreme generosity of God the Father, O highest and most marvelous felicity of man! To him it is granted to have whatever he chooses, to be whatever he wills. Beasts as soon as they are born (so says Lucilius) bring with them from their mother's womb all they will ever possess. Spiritual beings, either from the beginning or soon thereafter, become what they are to be for ever and ever. On man when he came into life the Father conferred the seeds of all kinds and the germs of every way of life. Whatever seeds each man cultivates will grow to maturity and bear in him their own fruit. If they be vegetative, he will be like a plant. If sensitive, he will become brutish. If rational, he will grow into a heavenly being. If intellectual, he will be an angel and the son of God. And if, happy in the lot of no created thing, he withdraws into the center of his own unity, his spirit, made one with God, in the solitary darkness of God, who is set above all things, shall surpass them all. Who would not admire this our chameleon? Or who could more greatly admire aught else whatever? It is man who Asclepius of Athens, arguing from his mutability of character and from his self-transforming nature, on just grounds says was symbolized by Proteus in the mysteries. Hence those metamorphoses renowned among the Hebrews and the Pythagoreans.

*   *   *

REVIEW QUESTIONS

1. How is Pico reordering the hierarchy of creation?
2. What does he claim for human nature that sets it apart?
3. How does Pico conceive of human will?
4. What implications does that conception have?
5. What is Pico's understanding of the relationship of humankind to God?
6. What are its implications?

NICCOLO MACHIAVELLI

FROM *The Prince*

Niccolò Machiavelli (1469–1527) was the son of a Florentine lawyer. Little is known of him until 1498, when he entered the service of the Florentine Republic of Pier Soderini as secretary to the second chancery, a minor bureaucratic post he held for fourteen years. From this position, Machiavelli observed the political process of his day. A staunch republican, he lost his position in government in 1512, when Soderini's republic was toppled and the Medici of Florence restored to power by a papal army. He spent the rest of his days in retirement, possibly trying to restore himself to the graces of the Medici and the pope, but certainly engaged in the scholarly and literary pursuits that would establish his reputation as a political analyst. Among the fruits of these labors was The Prince, written in 1513. Of the many observations and ideas expressed in this short work, two at least became fundamental truths of modern politics. One was the necessity of national unity based on a common language, culture, and economy. The other was the preservation of national unity through the concentration and exercise of power by the state. As controversial as they were prescient in Machiavelli's day, these ideas encouraged later scholars to number him among the first modern students of politics.

From *The Prince*, by Niccolo Machiavelli, translated by Robert M. Adams, A Norton Critical Edition (2d ed.; New York: Norton, 1977), pp. 31–32, 44–50.

How to Measure the Strength of Any Prince's State

There is one other consideration to bear in mind regarding these civil principates; that is, whether a prince is strong enough to stand on his own feet in case of need, or whether he is in constant need of help from others. And to make the matter clearer, let me say that in my opinion princes control their own destiny when they command enough money or men to assemble an adequate army and make a stand against anyone who attacks them. I think princes who need outside protection are those who can't take the field against their foes, but have to hide behind their walls and defend themselves there. I've already mentioned the first class, and will save whatever else I have to say about them till later. As for the others, all I can say is that they should keep their cities well fortified and well supplied, and pay no heed to the surrounding countryside. Whenever a man has fortified his city strongly, and has dealt with his subjects as I described above and will describe further below, people will be slow to attack him; men are always wary of tasks that seem hard, and it can't seem easy to attack a prince whose city is in fine fettle, and whose people do not hate him.

*   *   *

Thus a prince who has a strong city and does not earn his people's hatred cannot be attacked, or if he were, that attacker would be driven off to his own disgrace; because the way things keep changing in this world, it's almost impossible for a prince with his armies to devote an entire year to a siege while doing nothing else. Maybe someone will object: when the people see their possessions outside the walls being burnt up, they will get impatient; a long siege and their own self-interest will make them forget the prince. But to this I answer that a brave, strong prince will overcome all these problems, giving his subjects hope at one minute that the storm will soon pass, stirring them up at another moment to fear the enemy's cruelty, and on still other occasions restraining those who seem too rash. Besides, the enemy will generally do his burning and ravishing of the countryside as soon as he begins the siege, when men's minds are still passionate and earnest for the defense; thus the prince has less reason to worry, because, after a few days, when tempers have cooled, the harm will already have been done, the losses inflicted, and there will clearly be no cure. At that point, the people will rally even more strongly behind their prince, because they will feel he owes them something, since their houses were burnt and their fields ravaged in defense of his cause. Indeed, men are so constructed that they feel themselves committed as much by the benefits they grant as by those they receive. Hence, all things considered, it should not be hard for a prudent prince to keep his subjects in good

spirits throughout a siege, as long as he does not run short of food or weapons.

*   *   *

On the Reasons Why Men Are Praised or Blamed—Especially Princes

It remains now to be seen what style and principles a prince ought to adopt in dealing with his subjects and friends. I know the subject has been treated frequently before, and I'm afraid people will think me rash for trying to do so again, especially since I intend to differ in this discussion from what others have said. But since I intend to write something useful to an understanding reader, it seemed better to go after the real truth of the matter than to repeat what people have imagined. A great many men have imagined states and princedoms such as nobody ever saw or knew in the real world, for there's such a difference between the way we really live and the way we ought to live that the man who neglects the real to study the ideal will learn how to accomplish his ruin, not his salvation. Any man who tries to be good all the time is bound to come to ruin among the great number who are not good. Hence a prince who wants to keep his post must learn how not to be good, and use that knowledge, or refrain from using it, as necessity requires.

Putting aside, then, all the imaginary things that are said about princes, and getting down to the truth, let me say that whenever men are discussed (and especially princes because they are prominent), there are certain qualities that bring them either praise or blame. Thus some are considered generous, others stingy (I use a Tuscan term, since "greedy" in our speech means a man who wants to take other people's goods; we call a man "stingy" who clings to his own); some are givers, others grabbers; some cruel, others merciful; one man is treacherous, another faithful; one is feeble and effeminate, another fierce and spirited; one humane, another proud; one lustful, another chaste; one straightforward, another sly; one harsh, another gentle; one serious, another playful; one religious, another skeptical, and so on. I know everyone will agree that among these many qualities a prince certainly ought to have all those that are considered good. But since it is impossible to have and exercise them all, because the conditions of human life simply do not allow it, a prince must be shrewd enough to avoid the public disgrace of those vices that would lose him his state. If he possibly can, he should also guard against vices that will not lose him his state; but if he cannot prevent them, he should not be too worried about indulging them. And furthermore, he should not be too worried about incurring blame for any vice without which he would find it hard to save his state. For if you look at matters carefully, you will see that something resembling virtue, if you follow it, may be your ruin, while something else resembling vice will lead, if you follow it, to your security and well-being.

On Liberality and Stinginess

Let me begin, then, with the first of the qualities mentioned above, by saying that a reputation for liberality is doubtless very fine; but the generosity that earns you that reputation can do you great harm. For if you exercise your generosity in a really virtuous way, as you should, nobody will know of it, and you cannot escape the odium of the opposite vice. Hence if you wish to be widely known as a generous man, you must seize every opportunity to make a big display of your giving. A prince of this character is bound to use up his entire revenue in works of ostentation. Thus, in the end, if he wants to keep a name for generosity, he will have to load his people with exorbitant taxes and squeeze money out of them in every way he can. This is the first step in making him odious to his subjects; for when he is poor, nobody will respect him. Then, when his generosity has angered many and brought rewards to a few, the slightest difficulty will trouble him, and at the first approach of danger, down he goes. If by chance he foresees this, and tries to change his ways, he will immediately be labelled a miser.

Since a prince cannot use this virtue [*virtù*] of liberality in such a way as to become known for it unless he harms his own security, he won't mind, if he judges prudently of things, being known as a miser. In due course he will be thought the more liberal man, when people see that his parsimony enables him to live on his income, to defend himself against his enemies, and to undertake major projects without burdening his people with taxes. Thus he will be acting liberally toward all those people from whom he takes nothing (and there are an immense number of them), and in a stingy way toward those people on whom he bestows nothing (and they are very few). In our times, we have seen great things being accomplished only by men who have had the name of misers; all the others have gone under. Pope Julius II, though he used his reputation as a generous man to gain the papacy, sacrificed it in order to be able to make war; the present king of France has waged many wars without levying a single extra tax on his people, simply because he could take care of the extra expenses out of the savings from his long parsimony. If the present king of Spain had a reputation for generosity, he would never have been able to undertake so many campaigns, or win so many of them.

*   *   *

On Cruelty and Clemency: Whether It Is Better to Be Loved or Feared

Continuing now with our list of qualities, let me say that every prince should prefer to be considered merciful rather than cruel, yet he should be careful not to mismanage this clemency of his. People thought Cesare Borgia was cruel, but that cruelty of his reorganized the Romagna, united it, and established it in peace and loyalty. Anyone who views the matter realistically will see that this prince was much more merciful than the people of Florence, who, to avoid the reputation of cruelty, allowed Pistoia to be destroyed. Thus, no prince should mind being called cruel for what he does to keep his subjects united and loyal; he may make examples of a very few, but he will be more merciful in reality than those who, in their tenderheartedness, allow disorders to occur, with their attendant murders and lootings. Such turbulence brings harm to an entire community, while the executions ordered by a prince affect only one individual at a time. A new prince, above all others, cannot possibly avoid a name for cruelty, since new states are always in danger. And Virgil, speaking through the mouth of Dido, says:

> Res dura et regni novitas me talia cogunt
> Moliri, et late fines custode tueri.[1]

Yet a prince should be slow to believe rumors and to commit himself to action on the basis of them. He should not be afraid of his own thoughts; he ought to proceed cautiously, moderating his conduct with prudence and humanity, allowing neither overconfidence to make him careless, nor overtimidity to make him intolerable.

Here the question arises: is it better to be loved than feared, or vice versa? I don't doubt that every prince would like to be both; but since it is hard to accommodate these qualities, if you have to make a choice, to be feared is much safer than to be loved. For it is a good general rule about men, that they are ungrateful, fickle, liars and deceivers, fearful of danger and greedy for gain. While you serve their welfare, they are all yours, offering their blood, their belongings, their lives, and their children's lives, as we noted above—so long as the danger is remote. But when the danger is close at hand, they turn against you. Then, any prince who has relied on their words and has made no other preparations will come to grief; because friendships that are bought at a price, and not with greatness and nobility of soul, may be paid for but they are not acquired, and they cannot be used in time of need. People are less concerned with offending a man who makes himself loved than one who makes himself feared: the reason is that love

is a link of obligation which men, because they are rotten, will break any time they think doing so serves their advantage; but fear involves dread of punishment, from which they can never escape.

Still, a prince should make himself feared in such a way that, even if he gets no love, he gets no hate either; because it is perfectly possible to be feared and not hated, and this will be the result if only the prince will keep his hands off the property of his subjects or citizens, and off their women. When he does have to shed blood, he should be sure to have a strong justification and manifest cause; but above all, he should not confiscate people's property, because men are quicker to forget the death of a father than the loss of a patrimony. Besides, pretexts for confiscation are always plentiful; it never fails that a prince who starts living by plunder can find reasons to rob someone else. Excuses for proceeding against someone's life are much rarer and more quickly exhausted.

*   *   *

Returning to the question of being feared or loved, I conclude that since men love at their own inclination but can be made to fear at the inclination of the prince, a shrewd prince will lay his foundations on what is under his own control, not on what is controlled by others. He should simply take pains not to be hated, as I said.

The Way Princes Should Keep Their Word

How praiseworthy it is for a prince to keep his word and live with integrity rather than by craftiness, everyone understands; yet we see from recent experience that those princes have accomplished most who paid little heed to keeping their promises, but who knew how craftily to manipulate the minds of men. In the end, they won out over those who tried to act honestly.

You should consider then, that there are two ways of fighting, one with laws and the other with

---

[1]"Severe pressures and the newness of the regime compel me to these measures. I must maintain the borders against foreign enemies."

force. The first is properly a human method, the second belongs to beasts. But as the first method does not always suffice, you sometimes have to turn to the second. Thus a prince must know how to make good use of both the beast and the man. Ancient writers made subtle note of this fact when they wrote that Achilles and many other princes of antiquity were sent to be reared by Chiron the centaur, who trained them in his discipline. Having a teacher who is half man and half beast can only mean that a prince must know how to use both these two natures, and that one without the other has no lasting effect.

Since a prince must know how to use the character of beasts, he should pick for imitation the fox and the lion. As the lion cannot protect himself from traps, and the fox cannot defend himself from wolves, you have to be a fox in order to be wary of traps, and a lion to overawe the wolves. Those who try to live by the lion alone are badly mistaken. Thus a prudent prince cannot and should not keep his word when to do so would go against his interest, or when the reasons that

made him pledge it no longer apply. Doubtless if all men were good, this rule would be bad; but since they are a sad lot, and keep no faith with you, you in your turn are under no obligation to keep it with them.

*　　*　　*

REVIEW QUESTIONS

1. What, according to Machiavelli, is the basis of political authority?
2. How does his theory differ from others of his day?
3. When he claims that a prince must assume many guises, what is Machiavelli saying about his understanding of human nature?
4. What is the role of artifice in political authority?
5. What might Machiavelli's prince have in common with Castiglione's courtier?

DESIDERIUS ERASMUS OF ROTTERDAM

FROM *Ten Colloquies*

Desiderius Erasmus of Rotterdam (1476–1536) was one of the greatest scholars, measured in terms of his writings and their influence, of his day. Educated at Deventer in the Netherlands and in Paris, he began his career as an editor, translator, and popularizer of classical texts. In the humanistic tradition, he used classical tropes as models for his own society, a practice that made him not only a great scholar but also a great satirist. His chief intellectual commitment, however, was the renewal of Christian piety through the study of Christian literature, the Bible and church fathers above all. In this context he is often viewed as the great exponent of Christian humanism, the northern European variant of classical Italian humanism. His translation of the Bible inspired the biblical scholarship of sixteenth-century reformers. His editions of patristic sources remain authoritative to this day. His Ten

Colloquies *were written as popular texts to inculcate elegant Latin and to inspire Christian conduct.*

From *Ten Colloquies,* by Desiderius Erasmus, translated by Craig R. Thompson (Upper Saddle River, N.J.: Prentice-Hall, 1986).

"Cyclops, or the Gospel Bearer"

CANNIUS. What's Polyphemus hunting here?

POLYPHEMUS. What could I be hunting without dogs or spear? Is that your question?

CANNIUS. Some wood nymph, perhaps.

POLYPHEMUS. A good guess. Look, here's my hunting net.

CANNIUS. What a sight! Bacchus in a lion's skin —Polyphemus with a book—a cat in a saffron gown!

POLYPHEMUS. I've painted this little book not only in saffron but bright red and blue, too.

CANNIUS. I'm not talking about saffron; I said something in Greek. Seems to be a soldierly book, for it's protected by bosses, plates, and brass clasps.

POLYPHEMUS. Take a good look at it.

CANNIUS. I'm looking. Very fine, but you haven't yet decorated it enough.

POLYPHEMUS. What's lacking?

CANNIUS. You should have added your coat of arms.

POLYPHEMUS. What coat of arms?

CANNIUS. The head of Silenus peering out of a wine jug. But what's the book about? The art of drinking?

POLYPHEMUS. Be careful you don't blurt out blasphemy.

CANNIUS. What, you don't mean it's something sacred?

POLYPHEMUS. The most sacred of all, the Gospels.

CANNIUS. By Hercules! What has Polyphemus to do with the Gospels?

POLYPHEMUS. You might as well ask what a Christian has to do with Christ.

CANNIUS. I'm not sure a halberd isn't more fitting for the likes of you. If I were at sea and met a stranger who looked like this, I'd take him for a pirate; if I met him in a wood, for a bandit.

POLYPHEMUS. Yet this very Gospel teaches us not to judge a man by appearances. Just as a haughty spirit often lurks under an ash-colored cowl, so a cropped head, curled beard, stern brow, wild eyes, plumed cap, military cloak, and slashed breeches sometimes cover a true Christian heart.

CANNIUS. Of course. Sometimes a sheep lurks in wolf's clothing, too. And if you trust fables, an ass in a lion's skin.

POLYPHEMUS. What's more, I know a man who has a sheep's head and a fox's heart. I could wish him friends as fair as his eyes are dark, and a character as shining as his complexion.

CANNIUS. If a man with a sheepskin cap has a sheep's head, what a load *you* carry, with both a sheep and an ostrich on your head. And isn't it rather ridiculous to have a bird on your head and an ass in your heart?

POLYPHEMUS. That hurt!

CANNIUS. But it would be well if, as you've decorated the Gospels with various ornaments, the Gospels in turn adorned you. You've decorated them with colors; I wish they might embellish you with good morals.

POLYPHEMUS. I'll take care of that.

CANNIUS. After your fashion, yes.

POLYPHEMUS. But insults aside, you don't condemn those who carry a volume of the Gospels about, do you?

CANNIUS. I'd be the last person in the world to do that.

POLYPHEMUS. What? I seem to you the least person in the world, when I'm taller than you by an ass's head?

CANNIUS. I don't believe you'd be that much taller even if the ass pricked up its ears.

POLYPHEMUS. Certainly by a buffalo's.

CANNIUS. I like the comparison. But I said "last"; I wasn't calling you "least."

POLYPHEMUS. What's the difference between an egg and an egg?

CANNIUS. What's the difference between middle finger and little finger?

POLYPHEMUS. The middle one's longer.

CANNIUS. Very good! What's the difference between ass ears and wolf ears?

POLYPHEMUS. Wolf ears are shorter.

CANNIUS. That's right.

POLYPHEMUS. But I'm in the habit of measuring long and short by span and ell, not by ears.

CANNIUS. Well, the man who carried Christ was called Christopher. You, who carry the Gospels, ought to be called Gospel-bearer instead of Polyphemus.

POLYPHEMUS. Don't you think it's holy to carry the Gospels?

CANNIUS. No—unless you'd agree that asses are mighty holy.

POLYPHEMUS. How so?

CANNIUS. Because one of them can carry three thousand books of this kind. I should think you'd be equal to that load if fitted with the right packsaddle.

POLYPHEMUS. There's nothing farfetched in thus crediting an ass with holiness because he carried Christ.

CANNIUS. I don't envy you that holiness. And if you like, I'll give you relics of the ass that carried Christ, so you can kiss them.

POLYPHEMUS. A gift I'll be glad to get. For by touching the body of Christ that ass was consecrated.

CANNIUS. Obviously those who smote Christ touched him too.

POLYPHEMUS. But tell me seriously, isn't carrying the Gospel about a reverent thing to do?

CANNIUS. Reverent if done sincerely, without hypocrisy.

POLYPHEMUS. Let monks have hypocrisy! What has a soldier to do with hypocrisy?

CANNIUS. But first tell me what hypocrisy is.

POLYPHEMUS. Professing something other than what you really mean.

CANNIUS. But what does carrying a copy of the Gospels profess? A gospel life, doesn't it?

POLYPHEMUS. I suppose so.

CANNIUS. Therefore, when the life doesn't correspond to the book, isn't that hypocrisy?

POLYPHEMUS. Apparently. But what is it truly to bear the Gospel?

CANNIUS. Some bear it in their hands, as the Franciscans do their Rule. Parisian porters, and asses and geldings, can do the same. There are those who bear it in their mouths, harping on nothing but Christ and the Gospel. That's pharisaical. Some bear it in their hearts. The true Gospel bearer, then, is one who carries it in hands and mouth *and* heart.

POLYPHEMUS. Where are these?

CANNIUS. In churches—the deacons, who bear the book, read it to the congregation, and have it by heart.

POLYPHEMUS. Though not all who bear the Gospel in their hearts are devout.

CANNIUS. Don't quibble. A man doesn't bear it in his heart unless he loves it through and through. Nobody loves it wholeheartedly unless he emulates the Gospel in his manner of living.

POLYPHEMUS. I don't follow these subtleties.

CANNIUS. But I'll tell you more bluntly. If you carry a jar of Beaune wine on your shoulder, it's just a burden, isn't it?

POLYPHEMUS. That's all.

CANNIUS. But if you hold the wine in your throat, and presently spit it out?

POLYPHEMUS. Useless—though, really, I'm not accustomed to doing that!

CANNIUS. But if—as you *are* accustomed—you take a long drink?

POLYPHEMUS. Nothing more heavenly.

CANNIUS. Your whole body glows; your face turns rosy; your expression grows merry.

POLYPHEMUS. Exactly.

CANNIUS. The Gospel has the same effect when it penetrates the heart. It makes a new man of you.

POLYPHEMUS. So I don't seem to you to live according to the Gospel?

CANNIUS. You can best decide that question yourself.

POLYPHEMUS. If it could be decided with a battle-ax—

CANNIUS. If someone called you a liar or a rake to your face, what would you do?

POLYPHEMUS. What would I do? He'd feel my fists.

CANNIUS. What if someone hit you hard?

POLYPHEMUS. I'd break his neck for that.

CANNIUS. But your book teaches you to repay insults with a soft answer; and "Whosoever shall smite thee on thy right cheek, turn to him the other also."

POLYPHEMUS. I've read that, but it slipped my mind.

CANNIUS. You pray frequently, I dare say.

POLYPHEMUS. That's pharisaical.

CANNIUS. Long-winded but ostentatious praying is pharisaical. But your book teaches us to pray without ceasing, yet sincerely.

POLYPHEMUS. Still, I do pray sometimes.

CANNIUS. When?

POLYPHEMUS. Whenever I think of it—once or twice a week.

CANNIUS. What do you pray?

POLYPHEMUS. The Lord's Prayer.

CANNIUS. How often?

POLYPHEMUS. Once. For the Gospel forbids vain repetitions as "much speaking."

CANNIUS. Can you concentrate on the Lord's Prayer while repeating it?

POLYPHEMUS. Never tried. Isn't it enough to say the words?

CANNIUS. I don't know, except that God hears only the utterance of the heart. Do you fast often?

POLYPHEMUS. Never.

CANNIUS. But your book recommends prayer and fasting.

POLYPHEMUS. I'd recommend them too, if my belly did not demand something else.

CANNIUS. But Paul says that those who serve their bellies aren't serving Jesus Christ. Do you eat meat on any day whatever?

POLYPHEMUS. Any day it's offered.

CANNIUS. Yet a man as tough as you are could live on hay or the bark of trees.

POLYPHEMUS. But Christ said that a man is not defiled by what he eats.

CANNIUS. True, if it's eaten in moderation, without giving offense. But Paul, the disciple of Christ, prefers starvation to offending a weak brother by his food; and he calls upon us to follow his example, in order that we may please all men in all things.

POLYPHEMUS. Paul's Paul, and I'm me.

CANNIUS. But Egon's job is to feed she-goats.

POLYPHEMUS. I'd rather eat one.

CANNIUS. A fine wish! You'll be a billygoat rather than a she-goat.

POLYPHEMUS. I said *eat* one, not *be* one.

CANNIUS. Very prettily said. Are you generous to the poor?

POLYPHEMUS. I've nothing to give.

CANNIUS. But you would have, if you lived soberly and worked hard.

POLYPHEMUS. I'm fond of loafing.

CANNIUS. Do you keep God's commandments?

POLYPHEMUS. That's tiresome.

CANNIUS. Do you do penance for your sins?

POLYPHEMUS. Christ has paid for us.

CANNIUS. Then why do you insist you love the Gospel?

POLYPHEMUS. I'll tell you. A certain Franciscan in our neighborhood kept babbling from the pulpit against Erasmus' New Testament. I met the man privately, grabbed him by the hair with my left hand, and punched him with my right. I gave him a hell of a beating; made his whole face swell. What do you say to that? Isn't that promoting the Gospel? Next I gave him absolution by banging him on the head three times with this very same book, raising three lumps, in the name of Father, Son, and Holy Ghost.

CANNIUS. The evangelical spirit, all right! This is certainly defending the Gospel with the Gospel.

POLYPHEMUS. I ran across another member of the same order who never stopped raving against Erasmus. Fired with evangelical zeal, I threatened the fellow so much he begged pardon on both knees and admitted the devil had put him up to saying what he said. If he hadn't done this, my halberd would have bounced against his head. I looked as fierce as Mars in battle. This took place before witnesses.

CANNIUS. I'm surprised the man didn't drop dead on the spot. But let's go on. Do you live chastely?

POLYPHEMUS. I may when I'm old. But shall I confess the truth to you, Cannius?

CANNIUS. I'm no priest. If you want to confess, find somebody else.

POLYPHEMUS. Usually I confess to God, but to you I admit I'm not yet a perfect follower of the Gospel; just an ordinary fellow. My kind have four Gospels. Four things above all we Gospelers seek: full bellies; plenty of work for the organs below the belly; a livelihood from somewhere or other; finally, freedom to do as we please. If we get these, we shout in our cups, "Io, triumph; Io, Paean! The Gospel flourishes! Christ reigns!"

CANNIUS. That's an Epicurean life, surely, not an evangelical one.

POLYPHEMUS. I don't deny it, but you know Christ is omnipotent and can turn us into other men in the twinkling of an eye.

CANNIUS. Into swine, too, which I think is more likely than into good men.

POLYPHEMUS. I wish there were no worse creatures in the world than swine, oxen, asses, and camels! You can meet many men who are fiercer than lions, greedier than wolves, more lecherous than sparrows, more snappish than dogs, more venomous than vipers.

CANNIUS. But now it's time for you to begin changing from brute to man.

POLYPHEMUS. You do well to warn me, for prophets these days declare the end of the world is at hand.

CANNIUS. All the more reason to hurry.

POLYPHEMUS. I await the hand of Christ.

CANNIUS. See that you are pliant material for his hand! But where do they get the notion that the end of the world is near?

POLYPHEMUS. They say it's because men are be-

having now just as they did before the Flood overwhelmed them. They feast, drink, stuff themselves, marry and are given in marriage, whore, buy, sell, pay and charge interest, build buildings. Kings make war, priests are zealous to increase their wealth, theologians invent syllogisms, monks roam through the world, the commons riot, Erasmus writes colloquies. In short, no calamity is lacking: hunger, thirst, robbery, war, plague, sedition, poverty. Doesn't this prove human affairs are at an end?

CANNIUS. In this mass of woes, what worries you most?

POLYPHEMUS. Guess.

CANNIUS. That your purse is full of cobwebs.

POLYPHEMUS. Damned if you haven't hit it!—Just now I'm on my way back from a drinking party. Some other time, when I'm more sober, I'll argue with you about the Gospel, if you like.

CANNIUS. When shall I see you sober?

POLYPHEMUS. When I'm sober.

CANNIUS. When will you be so?

POLYPHEMUS. When you see me so. Meantime, my dear Cannius, good luck.

CANNIUS. I hope you, in turn, become what you're called.

POLYPHEMUS. To prevent you from outdoing me in courtesy, I pray that Cannius, as the name implies, may never be lacking a can!

REVIEW QUESTIONS

1. Why does Erasmus use the dialogue form?
2. What might he be saying, not only about his readers but also about voice and perspective?
3. What is the older mode of Christianity that Erasmus parodies?
4. What is wrong with it?
5. What ideal of Christian behavior emerges in the colloquy?
6. How might it differ from the older form?
7. How might it be better suited to the instabilities of life in Renaissance Europe?

SIR THOMAS MORE

FROM *Utopia*

Sir Thomas More (1478–1535) was born on Milk Street, in London, the "brightest star that ever shined in the via lactea,*" according to Thomas Fuller. His father, John More, was a butler at Lincoln's Inn, later raised to the knighthood and made a judge first in the court of common pleas and later on the king's bench. The son was educated in the household of John Morton, archbishop of Canterbury, and at Christ Church, Oxford. Compelled by his father to study law, More entered New Inn in 1494 and Lincoln's Inn in 1496. He lived with the monks at the London Charterhouse and developed there the discipline and devotion that would serve him well in later troubles. Yet, he decided on married rather than monastic life. He wed Jane Colet in 1505 and they had four children. More was an early advocate of education for women; he insisted that his son and daughters be taught by the best tutors available. Despite his many interests—intellectual, religious, and domestic—the law remained his career. City, monarchy, and church called on his services.*

He was part of a London trade delegation to the cities of the Hanse in 1515. During this service he wrote Book II of Utopia, *describing a pagan, communist city-state in which all policies and institutions were governed by reason. Such a state contrasted notably with the polity of Christian Europe with its greed, self-interest, and violence, as More described it in Book I. The complete work, which drew heavily on descriptions of the new world as well as passages from classical literature, was published in 1516 in Louvain. It established More's international reputation as a man of letters. But public affairs constantly drew him out of his study. In 1523, he served as speaker of the House of Commons, and, in 1529, he succeeded Cardinal Wolsey as lord chancellor under Henry VIII. The king favored More, keeping him in attendance, visiting him at home, and enjoying his learned conversation. They fell out over Henry's growing dispute with the Catholic Church. More resigned office in 1532, the day after the clergy were deprived of the power to enact constitutions without royal consent. Refusal to swear the Oath of Supremacy in 1534, by which he would have recognized Henry as the supreme head of the church in England, made More guilty of treason. He was martyred in 1535, in his own words "the king's good servant but God's first."*

From *Utopia*, by Sir Thomas More, translated by Robert M. Adams, A Norton Critical Edition (2d ed.; New York: Norton, 1975), pp. 30–33, 40–42, 50–51, 64.

*   *   *

"But as a matter of fact, my dear More, to tell you what I really think, as long as you have private property, and as long as cash money is the measure of all things, it is really not possible for a nation to be governed justly or happily. For justice cannot exist where all the best things in life are held by the worst citizens; nor can anyone be happy where property is limited to a few, since those few are always uneasy and the many are utterly wretched.

"So I reflect on the wonderfully wise and sacred institutions of the Utopians who are so well governed with so few laws. Among them virtue has its reward, yet everything is shared equally, and all men live in plenty. I contrast them with the many other nations which are constantly passing new ordinances and yet can never order their affairs satisfactorily. In these other nations, whatever a man can get he calls his own private property; but all the mass of laws old and new don't enable him to secure his own, or defend it, or even distinguish it from someone else's property. Different men lay claim, successively or all at once, to the same property; and thus arise innumerable and interminable lawsuits—fresh ones every day. When I consider all these things, I become more sympathetic to Plato and do not wonder that he declined to make laws for any people who refused to share their goods equally. Wisest of men, he easily perceived that the one and only road to the welfare of all lies through the absolute equality of goods. I doubt whether such equality can ever be achieved where property belongs to individual men. However abundant goods may be, when every man tries to get as much as he can for his own exclusive use, a handful of men end up sharing the whole thing, and the rest are left in poverty. The result generally is two sorts of people whose fortunes ought to be interchanged: the rich are rapacious, wicked, and useless, while the poor are unassuming, modest men who work hard, more for the benefit of the public than of themselves.

"Thus I am wholly convinced that unless private property is entirely done away with, there can be no fair or just distribution of goods, nor can mankind be happily governed. As long as private property remains, by far the largest and the best part of mankind will be oppressed by a heavy and inescapable burden of cares and anxieties. This load, I admit, may be lightened a little bit under

the present system, but I maintain it cannot be entirely removed. Laws might be made that no one should own more than a certain amount of land or receive more than a certain income. Or laws might be passed to prevent the prince from becoming too powerful and the populace too unruly. It might be made unlawful for public offices to be solicited, or put up for sale, or made burdensome for the officeholder by great expense. Otherwise, officeholders are tempted to get their money back by fraud or extortion, and only rich men can afford to seek positions which ought to be held by wise men. Laws of this sort, I agree, may have as much effect as good and careful nursing has on men who are chronically or even terminally sick. The social evils I mentioned may be alleviated and their effects mitigated for a while, but so long as private property remains, there is no hope at all of effecting a cure and restoring society to good health. While you try to cure one part, you aggravate the disease in other parts. Suppressing one symptom causes another to break out, since you cannot give something to one man without taking it away from someone else."

"But I don't see it that way," I replied. "It seems to me that men cannot possibly live well where all things are in common. How can there be plenty of commodities where every man stops working? The hope of gain will not spur him on; he will rely on others, and become lazy. If a man is driven by want of something to produce it, and yet cannot legally protect what he has gained, what can follow but continual bloodshed and turmoil, especially when respect for magistrates and their authority has been lost? I for one cannot conceive of authority existing among men who are equal to one another in every respect."

*   *   *

"As for the relative ages of the governments," Raphael replied, "you might judge more accurately if you had read their histories. If we believe these records, they had cities before there were even human inhabitants here. What ingenuity has discovered or chance hit upon could have turned up just as well in one place as the other. As a matter of fact, I believe we surpass them in natural intelligence, but they leave us far behind in their diligence and zeal to learn.

"According to their chronicles, they had heard nothing of men-from-beyond-the-equator (that's their name for us) until we arrived, except that once, some twelve hundred years ago, a ship which a storm had blown toward Utopia was wrecked on their island. Some Romans and Egyptians were cast ashore, and never departed. Now note how the Utopians profited, through their diligence, from this one chance event. They learned every single useful art of the Roman civilization either directly from their guests, or indirectly from hints and surmises on which they based their own investigations. What benefits from the mere fact that on a single occasion some Europeans landed there! If a similar accident has hitherto brought any men here from their land, the incident has been completely forgotten, as it will be forgotten in time to come that I was ever in their country. From one such accident they made themselves masters of all our useful inventions, but I suspect it will be a long time before we accept any of their institutions which are better than ours. This willingness to learn, I think, is the really important reason for their being better governed and living more happily than we do, though we are not inferior to them in brains or resources."

*   *   *

Their Occupations

Agriculture is the one occupation at which everyone works, men and women alike, with no exceptions. They are trained in it from childhood, partly in the schools where they learn theory, and partly through field trips to nearby farms, which make something like a game of practical instruction. On these trips they not only watch the work being done, but frequently pitch in and get a workout by doing the jobs themselves.

Besides farm work (which, as I said, everybody performs), each person is taught a particular trade of his own, such as wool-working, linen-making, masonry, metal-work, or carpentry. There is no other craft that is practiced by any considerable number of them. Throughout the island people wear, and down through the centuries they have always worn, the same style of clothing, except for the distinction between the sexes, and between married and unmarried persons. Their clothing is attractive, does not hamper bodily movement, and serves for warm as well as cold weather; what is more, each household can make its own.

Every person (and this includes women as well as men) learns a second trade, besides agriculture. As the weaker sex, women practice the lighter crafts, such as working in wool or linen; the heavier crafts are assigned to the men. As a rule, the son is trained to his father's craft, for which most feel a natural inclination. But if anyone is attracted to another occupation, he is transferred by adoption into a family practicing the trade he prefers. When anyone makes such a change, both his father and the authorities make sure that he is assigned to a grave and responsible householder. After a man has learned one trade, if he wants to learn another, he gets the same permission. When he has learned both, he pursues whichever he likes better, unless the city needs one more than the other.

The chief and almost the only business of the syphogrants is to manage matters so that no one sits around in idleness, and assure that everyone works hard at his trade. But no one has to exhaust himself with endless toil from early morning to late at night, as if he were a beast of burden. Such wretchedness, really worse than slavery, is the common lot of workmen in all countries, except Utopia. Of the day's twenty-four hours, the Utopians devote only six to work. They work three hours before noon, when they go to dinner. After dinner they rest for a couple of hours, then go to work for another three hours. Then they have supper, and at eight o'clock (counting the first hour after noon as one), they go to bed and sleep eight hours.

The other hours of the day, when they are not working, eating, or sleeping, are left to each man's individual discretion, provided he does not waste them in roistering or sloth, but uses them busily in some occupation that pleases him. Generally these periods are devoted to intellectual activity. For they have an established custom of giving public lectures before daybreak; attendance at these lectures is required only of those who have been specially chosen to devote themselves to learning, but a great many other people, both men and women, choose voluntarily to attend. Depending on their interests, some go to one lecture, some to another. But if anyone would rather devote his spare time to his trade, as many do who don't care for the intellectual life, this is not discouraged; in fact, such persons are commended as especially useful to the commonwealth.

*   *   *

But in all this, you may get a wrong impression, if we don't go back and consider one point more carefully. Because they allot only six hours to work, you might think the necessities of life would be in scant supply. This is far from the case. Their working hours are ample to provide not only enough but more than enough of the necessities and even the conveniences of life. You will easily appreciate this if you consider how large a part of the population in other countries exists without doing any work at all. In the first place, hardly any of the women, who are a full half of the population, work; or, if they do, then as a rule their husbands lie snoring in the bed. Then there is a great lazy gang of priests and so-called religious men. Add to them all the rich, especially the landlords, who are commonly called gentlemen and nobility. Include with them their retainers, that mob of swaggering bullies. Finally, reckon in with these the sturdy and lusty beggars, who go about feigning some disease as an excuse for their idleness. You will certainly find that the things which satisfy our needs are produced by far fewer hands than you had supposed.

And now consider how few of those who do work are doing really essential things. For where money is the standard of everything, many superfluous trades are bound to be carried on simply to satisfy luxury and licentiousness. Suppose the multitude of those who now work were limited to a few trades, and set to producing more and more of those conveniences and commodities that nature really requires. They would be bound to produce so much that the prices would drop, and the workmen would be unable to gain a living. But suppose again that all the workers in useless trades were put to useful ones, and that all the idlers (who now guzzle twice as much as the workingmen who make what they consume) were assigned to productive tasks—well, you can easily see how little time each man would have to spend working, in order to produce all the goods that human needs and conveniences require—yes, and human pleasure too, as long as it's true and natural pleasure.

*   *   *

Their Gold and Silver

For these reasons, therefore, they have accumulated a vast treasure, but they do not keep it like a treasure. I'm really quite ashamed to tell you how they do keep it, because you probably won't believe me. I would not have believed it myself if someone had just told me about it; but I was there, and saw it with my own eyes. It is a general rule that the more different anything is from what people are used to, the harder it is to accept. But, considering that all their other customs are so unlike ours, a sensible man will not be surprised that they use gold and silver quite differently than we do. After all, they never do use money among themselves, but keep it only for a contingency which may or may not actually arise. So in the meanwhile they take care that no one shall overvalue gold and silver, of which money is made, beyond what the metals themselves deserve. Anyone can see, for example, that iron is far superior to either; men could not live without iron, by heaven, any more than without fire or water. But gold and silver have, by nature, no function that we cannot easily dispense with. Human folly has made them precious because they are rare. Like a most wise and generous mother, nature has placed the best things everywhere and in the open, like air, water, and the earth itself; but she has hidden away in remote places all vain and unprofitable things.

If in Utopia gold and silver were kept locked up in some tower, foolish heads among the common people might well concoct a story that the prince and the senate were out to cheat ordinary folk and get some advantage for themselves. They might indeed put the gold and silver into beautiful plate-ware and rich handiwork, but then in case of necessity the people would not want to give up such articles, on which they had begun to fix their hearts, only to melt them down for soldiers' pay. To avoid all these inconveniences, they thought of a plan which conforms with their institutions as clearly as it contrasts with our own. Unless we've actually seen it working, their plan may seem ridiculous to us, because we prize gold so highly and are so careful about protecting it. With them it's just the other way. While they eat from pottery dishes and drink from glass cups, well made but inexpensive, their chamber pots and stools—all their humblest vessels, for use in the common halls and private homes—are made of gold and silver. The chains and heavy fetters of slaves are also made of these metals. Finally, criminals who are to bear through life the mark of some disgraceful act are forced to wear golden rings on their ears, golden bands on their fingers, golden chains around their necks, and even golden crowns on their heads. Thus they hold gold and silver up to scorn in every conceivable way. As a result, when they have to part with these metals, which other nations give up with as much agony as if they were being disemboweled, the Utopians feel it no more than the loss of a penny.

*   *   *

Slaves

The Utopians enslave prisoners of war only if they are captured in wars fought by the Utopians themselves. The children of slaves are not automatically enslaved, nor are any men who were enslaved in a foreign country. Most of their slaves are either their own former citizens, enslaved for some heinous offense, or else men of other nations who were condemned to death in their own land. Most are of the latter sort. Sometimes the Utopians buy them at a very modest rate, more often they ask for them, get them for nothing, and bring them home in considerable numbers. These kinds of slaves are kept constantly at work, and are always fettered. The Utopians deal with their own people more harshly than with others, feeling that their crimes are worse and deserve stricter punishment because, as it is argued, they had an excellent education and the best of moral training, yet still couldn't be restrained from wrongdoing. A third class of slaves consists of hardworking penniless drudges from other nations who voluntarily choose to become slaves in Utopia. Such people are treated well, almost as well as citizens, except that they are given a little extra work, on the score that they're used to it. If one of them wants to leave, which seldom happens, no obstacles are put in his way, nor is he sent off empty-handed.

*   *   *

REVIEW QUESTIONS

1. Why did More choose to call the place *Utopia*, literally "Nowhere"?
2. What possibilities created by the discovery of a new world does More explore in *Utopia*?

3. How are More's Utopians different from what medieval Europeans would have considered Christian?

4. How does More's attitude toward the people of Utopia reflect attitudes of the Renaissance?

5. How might *Utopia* be critical of Renaissance society?

6. What do More's Utopians have in common with the kind of Christians Erasmus described in his colloquy "Cyclops, the Gospel-Bearer"?

14 ❦ THE PROTESTANT REFORMATION

The year 1492 marks both the end of the expansion of Christianity in Europe, with the final expulsion of the Jews and Muslims from the Iberian Peninsula, and the beginning of the expansion of European Christianity across the globe. So, too, it marks the nadir of papal ambition, venality, and corruption, and thereby the medieval Christian hierarchy. In that year the Borgia pope, Alexander VI, whom contemporaries such as Machiavelli knew to be rapacious, murderous, treacherous, and ambitious, was elected.

Within a generation of the Reconquista of Spain, the German lands of the grandson of Ferdinando and Isabella of Spain would be split between two very different understandings of Christianity: what it meant to be a Christian, what the Church was and how it was to be constituted, and what the nature of worship was. In part, the Reformation arose in response to perceptions of papal bellicosity and immorality; it belonged to an older tradition of reformatio. Equally, however, the Reformation was heir to the Renaissance: the philological skills and discoveries of fifteenth-century humanists enabled new approaches to the study of the Bible, and the humanist emphasis on historical accuracy led to a call for a return to apostolic Christianity. That return to the text of Scripture, along with a new sensitivity to historical periods, brought theologians such as Martin Luther to reconsider not only devotional practices but the very structure of authority of medieval Christendom—the papal hierarchy—and others, such as John Calvin, to return to the Acts of the Apostles for a vision of the true church.

Even as Christendom divided against itself in Europe, it expanded through the persons of conquistadores to create worlds unimagined in the European tradition. Reformation and expansion both came through bloodshed. In Germany, peasants and artisans fought lords and emperor to institute the godly law they *found in the Bible, only to be massacred. In France, the Low Countries, and England, as well as the Holy Roman Empire, Christians executed Christians over questions of the Eucharist, the place of images in worship, and the cult of the saints. Churches divided from one another, each defining itself against the others, even as all confronted worlds for which neither the Bible nor the classical tradition had prepared them.*

GIOVANNI MICHIEL

FROM A Venetian Ambassador's Report on the St. Bartholomew's Day Massacre

The struggle for supremacy in northern Italy, which marked the last half of the fifteenth century, gave rise to a new form of diplomacy, including structures and procedures that would be fundamental to relations among all modern states. Requiring continuous contact and communication, Renaissance states turned to permanent diplomacy, distinguished by the use of accredited resident ambassadors rather than ad hoc missions of medieval legates. The tasks of a permanent ambassador were to represent his government at state ceremonies, to gather information, and, occasionally, to enter into negotiations. Nowhere was this system more fully and expertly articulated than by the Republic of Venice in the late fifteenth and sixteenth centuries. Its ambassadors were chosen with unusual care from the most prominent families of the city. They were highly educated, and their duties were carefully defined. Among the latter were weekly dispatches reporting all matters of any interest to Venice. These reports were regularly read and debated in the senate, which replied with questions, instructions, and information of its own. As a result, Venetian ambassadors were among the most skilled and respected in early modern Europe. In this report, Giovanni Michiel interprets the events of St. Bartholomew's Day in 1572. The massacre of Huguenots, instigated by the Queen Mother, Catherine de Medici, outraged Protestant Europe and dashed all hopes for peace in France. Of particular interest is the ambassador's harshly realistic account of the political motives for so violent an act of statecraft.

From *Pursuit of Power: Venetian Ambassadors' Reports on Spain, Turkey and France in the Age of Phillip II, 1560–1600*, by James C. Davis (New York: HarperCollins, 1970), pp. 72–76, 78–79.

*   *   *

Turning to the queen, Admiral de Coligny said, "Madame, the king refuses to involve himself in one war. God grant that he may not be caught up in another which he cannot avoid."

By these words he meant, some say, that if they abandoned the prince of Orange things might go badly for him, and there would be a danger that if the prince failed to win or was actually driven out by the Spanish or for some other reason, then he might enter France with his French and German followers and it might be necessary to drive him out by force. However, everyone understood his words in a very different sense, namely that he was giving notice that he planned to stir up new storms and renew the rioting and civil war. When the queen carefully pondered this it became the chief reason, taken together with the other considerations, why she hurried to prepare that fate for him which he eventually met.

*   *   *

Then, at the dinner hour on Friday, while the admiral was returning on foot from the court to his lodgings and reading a letter, someone fired an arquebus at him. The shot came from a window which faced a bit obliquely on the street, near the royal palace called the Louvre. But it did not strike him in the chest as intended because it so happened that the admiral was wearing a pair of slippers which made walking difficult and, wanting to take them off and hand them to a page, he had just started to turn around. So the arquebus shot tore off a finger on his left hand and then hit his right arm near the wrist and passed through it to the other side near the elbow. If he had simply walked straight ahead it would have hit him in the chest and killed him.

As you can imagine, news of the event caused great excitement, especially at court. Everyone supposed it had been done by order of the duke of Guise to avenge his family, because the window from which the shot was fired belonged to his mother's house, which had purposely been left empty after she had gone to stay in another. When

the news was reported to the king, who happened to be playing tennis with the duke of Guise, they say he turned white and looked thunderstruck. Without saying a word he withdrew into his chambers and made it obvious that he was extremely angry.

*   *   *

On Saturday the admiral's dressings were changed and the word was given out—which may or may not have been true—that the wound was not a mortal one and that there was no danger even that he would lose the arm. The Huguenots only blustered all the more, and everyone waited to see what would happen next. The duke of Guise knew he might be attacked, so he armed himself and stuck close to his uncle, the duke of Aumale, and as many relatives, friends and servants as possible.

But before long the situation changed. Late Saturday night, just before the dawn of Saint Bartholomew's Day, the massacre or slaughter was carried out. The French say the king ordered it. How wild and terrifying it was in Paris (which has a larger population than any other city in Europe), no one can imagine. Nor can one imagine the rage and frenzy of those who slaughtered and sacked, as the king ordered the people to do. Nor what a marvel, not to say a miracle, it was that the common people did not take advantage of this freedom to loot and plunder from Catholics as well as Huguenots, and ravenously take whatever they could get their hands on, especially since the city is incredibly wealthy. No one would ever imagine that a people could be armed and egged on by their ruler, yet not get out of control once they were worked up. But it was not God's will that things should reach such a pass.

The slaughter went on past Sunday for two or three more days, despite the fact that edicts were issued against it and the duke of Nevers was sent riding through the city along with the king's natural brother to order them to stop the killing. The massacre showed how powerfully religion can affect men's minds. On every street one could see the barbarous sight of men cold-bloodedly outraging others of their own people, and not just men who had never done them any harm but in most cases people they knew to be their neighbors and even their relatives. They had no feeling, no mercy on anyone, even those who kneeled before them and humbly begged for their lives. If one man hated another because of some argument or lawsuit all he had to say was "This man is a Huguenot" and he was immediately killed. (That happened to many Catholics.) If their victims threw themselves in the river as a last resort and tried to swim to safety, as many did, they chased them in boats and then drowned them. There was a great deal of looting and pillaging and they say the goods taken amounted to two million because many Huguenots, including some of the richest of them, had come to live in Paris after the most recent edict of pacification. Some estimate the number who were killed as high as four thousand, while others put it as low as two thousand.

The killing spread to all the provinces and most of the major cities and was just as frenzied there, if not more so. They attacked anyone, even the gentry, and as a result all the leaders who did not escape have been killed or thrown in prison.

It is true that Montgomery and some others who were pursued by the duke of Guise escaped to England, but they are not major figures. And the king has terrified them enough so they won't make any trouble.

*   *   *

REVIEW QUESTIONS

1. According to the report, at what level of society did the St. Bartholomew's Day Massacre originate?
2. Who was said to have initiated it?
3. How was a person identified as Huguenot or Catholic?
4. What does that say about religious identity in early modern France?
5. Do we know from this report who ordered the assassination?
6. Who caused the massacre?
7. What do we learn about the relation of religion to politics and political action?

ST. IGNATIUS OF LOYOLA

FROM *The Spiritual Exercises*

St. Ignatius of Loyola (1491–1556), the great mystic and founder of the Society of Jesus, was born into a hidalgo family and spent his early manhood in military service to the king of Spain. Wounded in battle, he spent his convalescence reading the lives of saints, which awoke in him a sense of spiritual inadequacy not unlike those which fired the religious engagements of Martin Luther and John Calvin. His early attempts at reconciliation, in the form of physical austerities practiced on pilgrimage to Montserrat and in the hermitage at Manresa, failed to reassure him of his soul's salvation, just as they failed to ease the spiritual torments of the young Luther. The scholastically trained Luther sought solace in the systematic study of the Bible; the uneducated Loyola found it in visions of God. Loyola spent the next decade educating himself and seeking his mission. After a pilgrimage to the Holy Land in 1523,

Loyola began his formal education by studying elementary Latin with schoolboys in Barcelona. He attended the universities in Alcala and Salamanca, preached in the streets, and was arrested by the Inquisition on suspicion of heresy. He attended the University of Paris from 1528 to 1535 and began to gather around him the companions who would form the initial core of the Society of Jesus. In 1534, he and nine companions swore an oath of poverty and chastity and promised either to undertake a crusade to the Holy Land or, failing that, to offer absolute obedience to the pope. At the center of this group was not only the man Loyola but his series of devotions and meditations that would later be published as The Spiritual Exercises *(1548). These exercises offered a practical and ascetic meditation on the life and death of Christ that drew much from the systematic meditations of the* devotio moderna *("modern devotions"). It instructed those who made or directed a religious retreat in order to stimulate an imitation of Christ that would be expressed in apostolic action as well as religious devotion. In 1535, Loyola and his company left for Italy. He was ordained in Venice in 1537. Finding no passage to the Holy Land, they continued to Rome, where they preached in the streets and ministered to the poor. Introduced to Pope Paul III by Gasparo Contarini, a great advocate of monastic reform, the company received a charter of foundation as the Society of Jesus in 1540. Constituted an order of clerks regular, devoted to educating the young and propagating the faith, sworn to poverty and obedience, the Jesuits grew quickly to become one of the most influential Catholic orders of the early modern period, a model of piety, discipline, education, and service.*

From *The Spiritual Exercises of St. Ignatius,* translated by Anthony Molho (New York: Bantam Doubleday Dell, 1989), pp. 139–42.

Rules for Thinking with the Church

In order to have the proper attitude of mind in the Church Militant we should observe the following rules:

1. Putting aside all private judgment, we should keep our minds prepared and ready to obey promptly and in all things the true spouse of Christ our Lord, our Holy Mother, the hierarchical Church.

2. To praise sacramental confession and the reception of the Most Holy Sacrament once a year, and much better once a month, and better still every week, with the requisite and proper dispositions.

3. To praise the frequent hearing of Mass, singing of hymns and psalms, and the recitation of long prayers, both in and out of church; also the hours arranged for fixed times for the whole Divine Office, for prayers of all kinds and for the canonical hours.

4. To praise highly religious life, virginity, and continence; and also matrimony, but not as highly as any of the foregoing.

5. To praise the vows of religion, obedience, poverty, chastity, and other works of perfection and supererogation. It must be remembered that a vow is made in matters that lead to evangelical perfection. It is therefore improper to make a vow in matters that depart from this perfection; as, for example, to enter business, to get married, and so forth.

6. To praise the relics of the saints by venerating them and by praying to these saints. Also to praise the stations, pilgrimages, indulgences, jubilees, Crusade indulgences, and the lighting of candles in the churches.

7. To praise the precepts concerning fasts and

abstinences, such as those of Lent, Ember Days, Vigils, Fridays, and Saturdays; likewise to praise acts of penance, both interior and exterior.

8. To praise the adornments and buildings of churches as well as sacred images, and to venerate them according to what they represent.

9. Finally, to praise all the precepts of the Church, holding ourselves ready at all times to find reasons for their defense, and never offending against them.

10. We should be more inclined to approve and praise the directions and recommendations of our superiors as well as their personal behavior. Although sometimes these may not be or may not have been praiseworthy, to speak against them when preaching in public or in conversation with people would give rise to murmuring and scandal rather than to edification. As a result, the people would be angry with their superiors, whether temporal or spiritual. Still, while it does harm to our superiors in their absence to speak ill of them in the presence of the people, it might be useful to speak of their bad conduct to those who can apply a remedy.

11. To praise both positive and scholastic theology, for as it is more characteristic of the positive doctors, such as St. Augustine, St. Jerome, St. Gregory, and others, to encourage the affections to greater love and service of God our Lord in all things, so it also is more characteristic of the scholastic doctors, such as St. Thomas, St. Bonaventure, and the Master of the Sentences, etc., to define and explain for our times the things necessary for eternal salvation, and to refute and expose all errors and fallacies. Also, the scholastic doctors, being of more recent date, not only have a clearer understanding of the Holy Scripture and of the teachings of the positive and holy doctors, but also, being enlightened and inspired by the Divine Power, they are helped by the Councils, Canons, and Constitutions of our Holy Mother Church.

12. We must be on our guard against making comparisons between the living and those who have already gone to their reward, for it is no small error to say, for example: "This man knows more than St. Augustine"; "He is another St. Francis, or even greater"; "He is another St. Paul in goodness, holiness, etc."

13. If we wish to be sure that we are right in all things, we should always be ready to accept this principle: I will believe that the white that I see is black, if the hierarchical Church so defines it. For, I believe that between the Bridegroom, Christ our Lord, and the Bride, His Church, there is but one spirit, which governs and directs us for the salvation of our souls, for the same Spirit and Lord, who gave us the Ten Commandments, guides and governs our Holy Mother Church.

14. Although it be true that no one can be saved unless it be predestined and unless he have faith and grace, still we must be very careful of our manner of discussing and speaking of these matters.

15. We should not make predestination an habitual subject of conversation. If it is sometimes mentioned we must speak in such a way that no person will fall into error, as happens on occasion when one will say, "It has already been determined whether I will be saved or lost, and in spite of all the good or evil that I do, this will not be changed." As a result, they become apathetic and neglect the works that are conducive to their salvation and to the spiritual growth of their souls.

16. In like manner, we must be careful lest by speaking too much and with too great emphasis on faith, without any distinction or explanation, we give occasion to the people to become indolent and lazy in the performance of good works, whether it be before or after their faith is founded in charity.

17. Also in our discourse we ought not to emphasize the doctrine that would destroy free will. We may therefore speak of faith and grace to the extent that God enables us to do so, for the greater praise of His Divine Majesty. But, in these dangerous times of ours, it must not be done in such a way that good works or free will suffer any detriment or be considered worthless.

18. Although the generous service of God for motives of pure love should be most highly esteemed, we should praise highly the fear of His Divine

Majesty, for filial fear and even servile fear are pious and most holy things. When one cannot attain anything better or more useful, this fear is of great help in rising from mortal sin, and after this first step one easily advances to filial fear which is wholly acceptable and pleasing to God our Lord, since it is inseparable from Divine Love.

*   *   *

REVIEW QUESTIONS

1. What do you suppose Loyola means by the *church militant*?
2. How might the Jesuits have been soldiers of Christ?
3. Loyola asks the members of his order to "praise" in order to be "thinking with the Church." How does this serve the Church?
4. What specifically does Loyola ask the Jesuits to praise?
5. What do the "Rules for Thinking with the Church" tell us about the Church?

FROM *The Trial of Klaus Hottinger of Zurich:* Iconoclasm

Among the most dramatic manifestations of reformation in the sixteenth century were instances of iconoclasm. Traditionally understood as a direct response to reformed teaching against the veneration of saints and the reliance on images, occasionally leavened with social and economic antagonism, iconoclasm has more recently been interpreted as a popular form of reformation, a point at which the common folk put into action the religious ideals of an educated elite. The following is a transcription of one of the earliest trials of iconoclasts, which occurred in the Swiss city of Zurich in September 1523. Three men pulled down and broke up a large crucifix that stood at a crossing in the suburb of Stadelhofen, just outside the city walls of Zurich. Such crosses were often quite tall; this one is described variously as eight to ten feet tall. This account retains some of the legal distinctions that would have been important to the iconoclasts, not only the ownership of the crucifix but the nature of that ownership. It also gives evidence of the common interpretation of images, an issue at the heart of the Reformation.

From *The Trial of Klaus Hottinger of Zurich*, translated by L. P. Wandel (Zurich: Staatsarchiv).

*   *   *

Witnesses

1. Hans Ockenfuss stated: Klaus Hottinger came to him and asked a favor of him, to help Hottinger remove a crucifix at Stadelhofen. The miller had given it free and clear to Hottinger to do with as he pleased. Since one hears daily, that such crucifixes and all other images of God, our Savior, are forbidden, Ockenfuss was of the opinion, that he had not behaved inappropriately or done anything illegal.

2. Heini Hirt, the miller of Stadelhofen, stated: days past, this witness, with his brothers, had gone out from the lower grainary, planning to have a drink together, when Klaus Hottinger ran after him and spoke: Hey, Hirt, when are you going to put away your idols? Hirt answered him, they did not bother him; he simply must not pray to them. He wished to leave this issue to his Lords (the magistrate of Zurich), for he was not learned in scripture and had no understanding of the matter. To this, Hottinger replied, if he (Hirt) were a good Christian man, he would remove them, because he had been informed from God's Word, that such idols should not be. When Hirt heard this, as he did not want trouble, he said to Hottinger, in so far as Hirt had the power and right to put away such idols, he transferred them and his jurisdiction over them, such as he had, to Hottinger for his own. Hottinger then told Hirt he must also help him to do this. But Hirt wanted nothing more to do with it, to be nowhere near it. Hottinger said, he would certainly find others who would help him. Hirt did not note, that Hottinger was so agitated. Hottinger came to him again after had been to Ulrich Trinkler, a magistrate, and said, "I have removed the idols," and further, he had not done it without involving my honorable Lords. He had namely sought counsel from Claus Setzstab, a magistrate, telling him what he wished to do. Furthermore, as my Lords had acknowledged, when they arrested the said Hottinger and his associates, Hottinger had come to him and said, would he

do so well as to go to Mr. Setzstab, and ask him not to put the case behind him, that he had talked with him. Hirt did not go to Setzstab—he did not wish to bring the whole matter upon himself. Hottinger also said that he had sold the woodwork and given out the money that had been "released" from it to the poor.

3. Lorenz Hochruetiner stated: He had already been imprisoned, along with Wolf the cabinetmaker, on account of the oil lamps, which the two had broken two weeks earlier in Our Lady's Church in Zurich, and was therefore, entirely of the opinion that he should steer clear of this; my Lords would not wish him to take part in such a case anymore. Then Claus Hottinger came up to him and told him of the crucifix in Stadelhofen, how he and Hans Ockenfuss had removed it, and asked him that he would help them tomorrow, for Ockenfuss had something else to do and could not help him anymore. He also said to him, how the miller had transferred the crucifix to him freely, to have as his own, with my Lord Ulrich Trinkler as witness. Finally upon his word, and because other people carried images of saints and crucifixes out of the churches, and no one marked it, he opined that it was not illegal, and he did as Hottinger wished, and unearthed the said sul.

The Accused

Klaus Hottinger gave his answer concerning the crucifix: A few days ago he talked over a lot of things with Heini Hirt, the miller from Stadelhofen, namely about images and other things. And the same Hirt said, if it were not right, then he would suffer to have his crucifix in Stadelhofen removed. And the two talked so much with one another, that he (Hirt) gave him the crucifix as a gift, free and clear, with Mr. Ulrich Trinkler as witness. And along with Hans Ockenfuss, he then removed that crucifix and in the morning, Lorenz Hochruetiner helped him to unearth the sul. And it was their opinion and their agreement that the best course would be to sell the wood from it, and give the money from it to the poor. He had not done this without the knowledge and will of certain lords of the Great and Small Councils, Mr. Claus Setzstab, Mr. Thoma Spruengli, and Heinrich Trueben. They did not warn him away, but instead said that by their understanding, they held and acknowledged it to be a good work, that such images come away. And namely, Mr. Stezstab said he had been there when Hans Huobers of Augsburg gave it to him to remove as he pleased. And he thought, no one talked him out of it.

And, so that no one thought, he sought counsel only after he had done the deed, he went in that very hour, in which Hirt had given him the crucifix, to Mr. Ulrich Trinkler, and understood nothing else from him, than that he held it for a good work. And had the forementioned either all together or singly warned him away with a single word, he would not have taken this on and would have away quietly. The said Mr. Trinkler also showed him certain images, which stood under the stairs in his house, and said, though it had cost him a great deal, he had them carried out of the church, so that no one would pray to them.

Further finding of the court: It was put before him, that he had said, he would give as a gift either to my Lords or to the poor in the hospice a measure of wine. He answered, not to his knowledge and he could not make sense of it, that he would have said such a thing. In so far as they nonetheless found this true of him, he could say nothing contrary, he would lie to no one. On the contrary, if an honest man said it of him, he could well believe it and not oppose it. Further: he went to Heini Hirt afterwards, and informed him, he had to go to the tower, and told him, he lied and contradicted to my Lords how he had given the crucifix as a gift.

Upon this Hirt became outraged and said, he had given it to him to do with as he wished insofar as he had the power and right, but gave it to me free and clear, as my own to do with as I pleased. And he reminded the said Hirt so much that Hirt said, it had occurred as Hottinger said, and if it came to that, he would also tell my Lords that.

Judgment

1. Klaus Hottinger, by his sworn oath to God and the Saints, is banned for two years and all costs are bound over to him. To have the oath lifted, he must return to the authorities. 2. Lorenz Hochruetiner, the weaver, had to swear "an oath out of my Lords' city and country" and to assume the costs. 3. Hans Ockenfuss is allowed to leave prison on parole, but should keep cognizance of my Lords and assume the costs. The latter two men were penalized for being participants in Hottinger's transgression.

REVIEW QUESTIONS

1. Why does this trial indicate iconoclasts appear before the city council, a civil authority?
2. What does that tell you about the nature of the crime of iconoclasm?
3. What does Hottinger tell us about the crucifix?
4. Why does he tear it down?
5. What does he turn it into?
6. What do we learn about the meaning of images and the process of reformation for ordinary Christians?

ST. TERESA OF AVILA

FROM *The Life of Teresa of Jesus*

St. Teresa of Avila (1515–1582) was a Spanish mystic, spiritual author, and monastic reformer. Her worldly achievements were great, to which the Discalced Carmelites still bear witness; in addition, the beauty of her inner life, as revealed in her writings, earned her recognition as one of the world's great female religious authors. Teresa was born in central Spain, the daughter of a wealthy hidalgo. At age fourteen, she was sent to a boarding school, where she became ill and began to consider her life's vocation. Despite paternal opposition, Teresa became a novice in a Carmelite convent around 1535. Her health collapsed again, leaving her an invalid for three years. During her convalescence she began the series of meditations that would establish her reputation as a mystic. It took fifteen years to perfect the prayers and meditations that would lead to her ecstatic visions and conversations with God. Her most celebrated work, The Life, *written in obedience to her confessors and directors, captured this process as the history of a soul, much like Augustine's* Confessions. *They combine religious ardor with human candor, an insistence that her experiences were a gift of God with an unwillingness to claim any spiritual distinction.*

In 1558, Teresa began to consider the restoration of Carmelite life to its original observance of austerity. It required complete separation from the world to promote prayerful meditation, such as was enjoined in the Primitive Carmelite Rule of 1247. In 1562, with the authorization of Pope Pius IV, Teresa and four companions opened the first convent of the Carmelite reform. Despite intense opposition from secular and ecclesiastical officials, her efforts eventually won the approval of the Carmelite general as well as his mandate to extend her reform to men. In 1567, she met a young Carmelite priest, Juan de Yepes, later canonized as St. John of the Cross, a brilliant friar who helped her initiate the Carmelite reform for men. In her lifetime, she saw sixteen convents and twelve monasteries established. The last decades of her life were given to this work. Forty years after her death, she was canonized; in 1970 she was made a doctor of the Church.

From *The Life of Theresa of Jesus: The Autobiography of Teresa of Avila,* translated by E. Allison Peters (New York: Bantam Doubleday Dell, 1991), pp. 68–71.

*   *   *

I have strayed far from any intention, for I was trying to give the reasons why this kind of vision cannot be the work of the imagination. How could we picture Christ's Humanity by merely studying the subject or form any impression of His great beauty by means of the imagination? No little time would be necessary if such a reproduction was to be in the least like the original. One can indeed make such a picture with one's imagination, and spend time in regarding it, and considering the form and the brilliance of it; little by little one may even learn to perfect such an image and store it up in the memory. Who can prevent this? Such a picture can undoubtedly be fashioned with the understanding. But with regard to the vision which we are discussing there is no way of doing this: we have to look at it when the Lord is pleased to reveal it to us—to look as He wills and at whatever He wills. And there is no possibility of our subtracting from it or adding to it, or any way in which we can obtain it, whatever we may do, or look at it when we like or refrain from looking at it. If we try to look at any particular part of it, we at once lose Christ.

For two years and a half things went on like this and it was quite usual for God to grant me this favour. It must now be more than three years since He took it from me as a continually recurring favour, by giving me something else of a higher kind, which I shall describe later. Though I saw that He was speaking to me, and though I was looking upon that great beauty of His, and experiencing the sweetness with which He uttered those words—sometimes stern words—with that most lovely and Divine mouth, and though, too, I was extremely desirous of observing the colour of His eyes, or His height, so that I should be able to describe it, I have never been sufficiently worthy to see this, nor has it been of any use for me to attempt to do so; if I tried, I lost the vision altogether. Though I sometimes see Him looking at me compassionately, His gaze has such power that my soul cannot endure it and remains in so sublime a rapture that it loses this beauteous vision in order to have the greater fruition of it all. So there is no question here of our wanting or not wanting to see the vision. It is clear that the Lord wants of us only humility and shame, our acceptance of what is given us and our praise of its Giver.

This refers to all visions, none excepted. There is nothing that we can do about them; we cannot see more or less of them at will; and we can neither call them up nor banish them by our own efforts. The Lord's will is that we shall see quite clearly that they are produced, not by us but by His Majesty. Still less can we be proud of them: on the contrary, they make us humble and fearful, when we find that, just as the Lord takes from us the power of seeing what we desire, so He can also take from us these favours and His grace, with the result that we are completely lost. So while we live in this exile let us always walk with fear.

Almost invariably the Lord showed Himself to me in His resurrection body, and it was thus, too, that I saw Him in the Host. Only occasionally, to strengthen me when I was in tribulation, did He show me His wounds, and then He would appear sometimes as He was on the Cross and sometimes as in the Garden. On a few occasions I saw Him wearing the crown of thorns and sometimes He would also be carrying the Cross—because of my necessities, as I say, and those of others—but always in His glorified flesh. Many are the affronts and trials that I have suffered through telling this and many are the fears and persecutions that it has brought me. So sure were those whom I told of it that I had a devil that some of them wanted to exorcize me. This troubled me very little, but I was sorry when I found that my confessors were afraid to hear my confessions or when I heard that people were saying things to them against me. None the less, I could never regret having seen these heavenly visions and I would not exchange them for all the good things and delights of this world. I always considered them a great favour from the Lord, and I think they were the greatest of treasures; often the Lord Himself would reassure me about them. I found my love for Him growing exceedingly: I used to go to Him and tell Him about all these trials and I always came away from prayer comforted and with new strength. I did not dare to argue with my critics, because I saw that that made things worse, as they thought me lacking in humility. With my confessor, however, I did discuss these matters; and whenever he saw that I was troubled he would comfort me greatly.

As the visions became more numerous, one of those who had previously been in the habit of helping me and who used sometimes to hear my confessions when the minister was unable to do so, began to say that it was clear I was being deceived by the devil. So, as I was quite unable to resist it, they commanded me to make the sign of the Cross whenever I had a vision, and to snap my fingers at it so as to convince myself that it came from the devil, whereupon it would not come again: I was not to be afraid, they said, and God would protect me and take the vision away. This caused me great distress: as I could not help believing that my visions came from God, it was a terrible thing to have to do; and, as I have said, I could not possibly wish them to be taken from me. However, I did as they commanded me. I besought God often to set me free from deception; indeed, I was continually doing so and with many tears. I would also invoke Saint Peter and Saint Paul, for the Lord had told me (it was on their festival that He had first appeared to me) that they would prevent me from being deluded; and I used often to see them very clearly on my left hand, though not in an imaginary vision. These glorious Saints were in a very real sense my lords.

To be obliged to snap my fingers at a vision in which I saw the Lord caused me the sorest distress. For, when I saw Him before me, I could not have believed that the vision had come from the devil even if the alternative were my being cut to pieces. So this was a kind of penance to me, and a heavy one. In order not to have to be so continually crossing myself, I would carry a cross in my hand. This I did almost invariably; but I was not so particular about snapping my fingers at the vision, for it hurt me too much to do that. It reminded me of the way the Jews had insulted Him, and I would beseech Him to forgive me, since I did it out of obedience to him who was in His own place, and not to blame me, since he was one of the ministers whom He had placed in His Church. He told me not to worry about it and said I was quite right to obey, but He would see that my confessor learned the truth. When they made me stop my prayer He seemed to me to have become angry, and He told me to tell them that this was tyranny. He used to show me ways of knowing that the visions were not of the devil; some of these I shall describe later.

*   *   *

REVIEW QUESTIONS

1. What distinguishes Teresa's spirituality from that of Ignatius Loyola?
2. Might we call her spirituality feminine?
3. Is Teresa's piety private or public? In what ways?
4. Are visions portable?
5. Are they entirely private?
6. How does language fail Teresa?

SEBASTIAN LOTZER

The Twelve Articles of the Peasants of Swabia

The Twelve Articles of the Peasants of Swabia, adopted at the free imperial city of Memmingen in 1525, is one of the signal documents of the great agrarian revolt known as the Peasants' War of 1525. More than any other such document, it specifically linked the social and political grievances of the peasants with the evangelical principles of the Reformation. Ironically, the Twelve Articles of the Peasants of Swabia was not composed by a peasant but by a townsman, the journeyman furrier and lay preacher Sebastian Lotzer. To do so, he summarized and condensed the long

THE ECSTASY OF ST. TERESA (1652) GIAN LORENZO BERNINI

Bernini's masterful rendering of the spiritual transport of St. Teresa is considered one of the great works of the Catholic Reformation. It captures all the inarticulate emotional and mystical elements of worship that were thought to be a counterpoint to the Protestant emphasis on the spoken word. How might art of this sort be considered an effective response to the propagandistic content of broadsides such as The Godly Mill? *What does the rendering of the angel reveal about the artist's conception of God's love? What does the rendering of St. Teresa reveal about the artist's conception of religious truth?*

(several hundred articles) list of demands put forward by the peasants of Baltringen. The Memmingen preacher Christoph Schappeler added a preamble and supplied biblical references in the margins. The document acquired its importance because it was quickly printed and widely disseminated. In many areas of the revolt, it was adopted as the basis for lists of grievances and proposals for settlement.

From *The Revolution of 1525: The German Peasants from a New Perspective,* translated by Thomas A. Brady Jr. (Baltimore: Johns Hopkins University Press, 1981), pp. 195–201.

The Just and Fundamental Articles of All the Peasantry and Tenants of Spiritual and Temporal Powers by Whom They Think Themselves Oppressed

To the Christian reader, the peace and grace of God through Jesus Christ.

There are many antichrists who, now that the peasants are assembled together, seize the chance to mock the gospel, saying, "Is this the fruit of the new gospel: to band together in great numbers and plot conspiracies to reform and even topple the spiritual and temporal powers—yes, even to murder them?" The following articles answer all these godless, blasphemous critics. We want two things: first, to make them stop mocking the word of God; and second, to establish the Christian justice of the current disobedience and rebellion of all the peasants.

First of all, the gospel does not cause rebellions and uproars, because it tells of Christ, the promised Messiah, whose words and life teach nothing but love, peace, patience, and unity. And all who believe in this Christ become loving, peaceful, patient, and one in spirit. This is the basis of all the articles of the peasants (as we will clearly show): to hear the gospel and to live accordingly. How then can the antichrists call the gospel a cause of rebellion and of disobedience? It is not the gospel that drives some antichrists and foes of the gospel to resist and reject these demands and requirements, but the devil, the deadliest foe of the gospel, who arouses through unbelief such opposition

in his own followers. His aim is to suppress and abolish the word of God, which teaches love, peace, and unity.

Second, it surely follows that the peasants, whose articles demand this gospel as their doctrine and rule of life, cannot be called "disobedient" or "rebellious." For if God deigns to hear the peasants' earnest plea that they may be permitted to live according to his word, who will dare deny his will? Who indeed will dare question his judgment? Who will dare oppose his majesty? Did he not hear the children of Israel crying to him and deliver them out of Pharaoh's hand? And can he not save his own today as well? Yes, he will save them, and soon! Therefore, Christian reader, read these articles diligently, and then judge for yourself.

These are the Articles.

THE FIRST ARTICLE

First of all, we humbly ask and beg—and we all agree on this—that henceforth we ought to have the authority and power for the whole community to elect and appoint its own pastor. We also want authority to depose a pastor who behaves improperly. This elected pastor should preach to us the holy gospel purely and clearly, without human additions or human doctrines or precepts. For constant preaching of the true faith impels us to beg God for his grace, that he may instill in us and confirm in us that same true faith. Unless we have his grace in us, we remain mere, useless flesh and blood. For the Scripture clearly teaches that we may come to God only through true faith and can be saved only through His mercy. This is why we need such a guide and pastor; and thus our demand is grounded in Scripture.

THE SECOND ARTICLE

Second, although the obligation to pay a just tithe prescribed in the Old Testament is fulfilled in the New, yet we will gladly pay the large tithe on grain—but only in just measure. Since the tithe should be given to God and distributed among his servants, so the pastor who clearly preaches the word of God deserves to receive it. From now on we want to have our church wardens, appointed by the community, collect and receive this tithe and have our elected pastor draw from it, with the whole community's consent, a decent and adequate living for himself and his. The remainder should be distributed to the village's own poor, again with the community's consent and according to need. What then remains should be kept in case some need to be called up to defend the country; and then the costs can be met from this reserve, so that no general territorial tax will be laid upon the poor folk.

Wherever one or more villages have sold off the tithe to meet some emergency, those purchasers who can show that they bought the tithe with the consent of the whole village shall not be simply expropriated. Indeed we hope to reach fair compromises with such persons, according to the facts of the case, and to redeem the tithe in installments. But wherever the tithe holder—be he clergyman or layman—did not buy the tithe from the whole village but has it from ancestors who simply seized it from the village, we will not, ought not, and do not intend to pay it any longer, except (as we said above) to support our elected pastor. And we will reserve the rest or distribute it to the poor, as the Bible commands. As for the small tithe, we will not pay it at all, for the Lord God created cattle for man's free use; and it is an unjust tithe invented by men alone. Therefore, we won't pay it anymore.

THE THIRD ARTICLE

Third, it has until now been the custom for the lords to own us as their property. This is deplorable, for Christ redeemed and bought us all with his precious blood, the lowliest shepherd as well as the greatest lord, with no exceptions. Thus the Bible proves that we are free and want to be free. Not that we want to be utterly free and subject to no authority at all; God does not teach us that. We ought to live according to the commandments, not according to the lusts of the flesh. But we should love God, recognize him as our Lord in our neighbor, and willingly do all things God commanded us at his Last Supper. This means we should live according to his commandment, which does not teach us to obey only the rulers, but to humble ourselves before everyone. Thus we should willingly obey our elected and rightful ruler, set over us by God, in all proper and Christian matters. Nor do we doubt that you, as true and just Christians, will gladly release us from bondage or prove to us from the gospel that we must be your property.

THE FOURTH ARTICLE

Fourth, until now it has been the custom that no commoner might catch wild game, wildfowl, or fish in the running waters, which seems to us altogether improper, unbrotherly, selfish, and contrary to God's Word. In some places the rulers protect the game to our distress and great loss, for we must suffer silently while the dumb beasts gobble up the crops God gave for man's use, although this offends both God and neighbor. When the Lord God created man, he gave him dominion over all animals, over the birds of the air, and the fish in the waters. Thus we demand that if someone owns a stream, lake, or pond, he should have to produce documentary proof of ownership and show that it was sold to him with the consent of the whole village. In that case we do not want to seize it from him with force but only to review the matter in a Christian way for the sake of brotherly love. But whoever cannot produce adequate proof of ownership and sale should surrender the waters to the community, as is just.

THE FIFTH ARTICLE

Fifth, we have another grievance about woodcutting, for our lords have seized the woods for themselves alone; and when the poor commoner needs some wood, he has to pay twice the price for it. We think that those woods whose lords, be they clergymen or laymen, cannot prove ownership by purchase should revert to the whole community. And the community should be able to allow in an orderly way each man to gather firewood for his home and building timber free, though only with permission of the community's elected officials. If all the woods have been fairly purchased, then a neighborly and Christian agreement should be reached with their owners about their use. Where the woods were simply seized and then sold to a third party, however, a compromise should be reached according to the facts of the case and the norms of brotherly love and Holy Writ.

THE SIXTH ARTICLE

Sixth, there is our grievous burden of labor services, which the lords daily increase in number and kind. We demand that these obligations be properly investigated and lessened. And we should be allowed, graciously, to serve as our forefathers did, according to God's word alone.

THE SEVENTH ARTICLE

Seventh, in the future we will not allow the lords to oppress us any more. Rather, a man shall have his holding on the proper terms on which it has been leased, that is, by the agreement between lord and peasant. The lord should not force or press the tenant to perform labor or any other service without pay, so that the peasant may use and enjoy his land unburdened and in peace. When the lord needs labor services, however, the peasant should willingly serve his own lord before others; yet a peasant should serve only at a time when his own affairs do not suffer and only for a just wage.

THE EIGHTH ARTICLE

Eighth, we have a grievance that many of us hold lands that are overburdened with rents higher than the land's yield. Thus the peasants lose their property and are ruined. The lords should have honorable men inspect these farms and adjust the rents fairly, so that the peasant does not work for nothing. For every laborer is worthy of his hire.

THE NINTH ARTICLE

Ninth, we have a grievance against the way serious crimes are punished, for they are constantly making new laws. We are not punished according to the severity of the case but sometimes out of great ill will and sometimes out of favoritism. We think that punishments should be dealt out among us according to the ancient written law and the circumstances of the case, and not according to the judge's bias.

THE TENTH ARTICLE

Tenth, we have a grievance that some people have seized meadows and fields belonging to the community. We shall restore these to the community, unless a proper sale can be proved. If they were improperly bought, however, then a friendly and brotherly compromise should be reached, based on the facts.

THE ELEVENTH ARTICLE

Eleventh, we want the custom called death taxes totally abolished. We will not tolerate it or allow widows and orphans to be so shamefully robbed of their goods, as so often happens in various ways, against God and all that is honorable. The very ones who should be guarding and protecting our goods have skinned and trimmed us of them instead. Had they the slightest legal pretext, they would have grabbed everything. God will suffer this no longer but will wipe it all out. Henceforth no one shall have to pay death taxes, whether small or large.

CONCLUSION

Twelfth, we believe and have decided that if any one or more of these articles is not in agreement with God's Word (which we doubt), then this should be proved to us from Holy Writ. We will abandon it, when this is proved by the Bible. If some of our articles should be approved and later found to be unjust, they shall be dead, null, and void from that moment on. Likewise, if Scripture truly reveals further grievances as offensive to God and a burden to our neighbor, we will reserve a place for them and declare them included in our list. We, for our part, will live and exercise our- selves in all Christian teachings, for which we will

pray to the Lord God. For he alone, and no other, can give us the truth. The peace of Christ be with us all.

REVIEW QUESTIONS

1. What does the Twelve Articles tell you about relations between the common man and his lords?
2. What are the priorities of the Twelve Articles?
3. What is most important to the petitioners?
4. Why is a pastor so important?
5. What is second in importance?
6. What changes are the petitioners asking for the tithe?
7. What is Godly Law?
8. What might be its applications?
9. What are the implications of Godly Law for the lords?

FROM *Canons and Decrees of the Council of Trent*

The great centerpiece of Catholic reform and reaction was the ecumenical Council of Trent, held in several sessions between 1545 and 1563. From the beginning of the sixteenth century, Catholic clergy, secular leaders, and Protestant reformers had called for an ecumenical council to heal the inadequacies of the Catholic Church. Popes had resisted the tactic just as insistently for fear that such a council might be used to limit papal authority, as, indeed, had been the case in the fifteenth century. Pope Paul III, however, realized that a council might serve the cause of papal au- thority as well as that of church reform and accordingly called a council to meet in the city of Trent, located in imperial territory but still close to Rome. Agreements on procedures and the leadership of papal legates assured that the council remained firmly under papal direction and set a tone of doctrinal and disciplinary conserva- tism. Its deliberations and decisions divide themselves into three great periods. The first period, 1545–1547, was devoted to dogma. The council rejected the Protestant teaching on scripture as the sole source of religious truth and insisted that scripture and tradition were equally authoritative. It retained the traditional seven sacra-

ments. Most important, it rejected the Protestant doctrine of justification. During the second period, 1551–1552, the council reasserted the traditional Catholic teaching on the Eucharist, rejecting the interpretations of Luther, Zwingli, and Calvin. Long delayed by political events and papal indifference, the council reconvened for the third and last time in 1562. In its final year, the council defined the Mass, addressed various liturgical issues, and resolved disciplinary issues such as clerical residency and training. Viewed in its entirety, the Council of Trent strengthened the authority of the papacy in the Catholic Church. If its decrees and canons were largely conservative, they were also unmistakable in their clarity and uniformity. In its pronouncements on discipline, it laid the foundations for a better-educated, more conscientious clergy. The Council of Trent clearly defined Catholic Christianity in opposition to Protestantism.

From *Canons and Decrees of the Council of Trent,* translated by H. J. Schroeder (London: Herder, 1941).

*   *   *

Fourth Session
Celebrated on the Eighth Day
of April 1546

DECREE CONCERNING THE CANONICAL SCRIPTURES

The holy, ecumenical and general Council of Trent, lawfully assembled in the Holy Ghost, the same three legates of the Apostolic See presiding, keeps this constantly in view, namely, that the purity of the Gospel may be preserved in the Church after the errors have been removed. This, of old promised through the Prophets in the Holy Scriptures, our Lord Jesus Christ, the Son of God, promulgated first with His own mouth, and then commanded it to be preached by His Apostles to every creature as the source at once of all saving truth and rules of conduct. It also clearly perceives that these truths and rules are contained in the written books and in the unwritten traditions, which, received by the Apostles from the mouth of Christ Himself, or from the Apostles themselves, the Holy Ghost dictating, have come down to us, transmitted as it were from hand to hand. Following, then, the examples of the orthodox Fathers, it receives and venerates with a feeling of piety and reverence all the books both of the Old and New Testaments, since one God is the author of both; also the traditions, whether they relate to faith or to morals, as having been dictated either orally by Christ or by the Holy Ghost, and preserved in the Catholic Church in unbroken succession. It has thought it proper, moreover, to insert in this decree a list of the sacred books, lest a doubt might arise in the mind of someone as to which are the books received by this council. They are the following: of the Old Testament, the five books of Moses, namely, Genesis, Exodus, Leviticus, Numbers, Deuteronomy; Josue, Judges, Ruth, the four books of Kings, two of Paralipomenon, the first and second of Esdras, the latter of which is called Nehemias, Tobias, Judith, Esther, Job, the Davidic Psalter of 150 Psalms, Proverbs, Ecclesiastes, the Canticle of Canticles, Wisdom, Ecclesiasticus, Isaias, Jeremias, with Baruch, Ezechiel, Daniel, the twelve minor Prophets, namely, Osee, Joel, Amos, Abdias, Jonas, Micheas, Nahum, Habacuc, Sophonias, Aggeus, Zacharias, Malachias; two books of Machabees, the first and second. Of the New Testament, the four Gospels, according to Matthew, Mark, Luke and John; the Acts of the Apostles written by Luke the Evangelist; fourteen Epistles of Paul the Apostle, to the Romans, two to the Corinthians, to the Galatians, to the Ephesians, to the Philippians, to the Colossians, two to the Thessalonians, two to Timothy, to Titus, to Philemon, to the Hebrews; two of Peter the Apostle, three of John the Apostle, one of James the Apostle, one of Jude the Apostle, and the Apocalypse of John the Apostle. If anyone does not accept as sacred and canonical the aforesaid books in their entirety and with all their parts, as they have been accustomed to be read in the Catholic Church and as they are contained in the old Latin Vulgate Edition, and knowingly and deliberately rejects the aforesaid traditions, let him be anathema. Let all understand, therefore, in what order and manner the council, after having laid the foundation of the confession of faith, will proceed, and who are the chief witnesses and supports to whom it will appeal in confirming dogmas and in restoring morals in the Church.

DECREE CONCERNING THE EDITION AND USE OF THE SACRED BOOKS

Moreover, the same holy council considering that not a little advantage will accrue to the Church of God if it be made known which of all the Latin editions of the sacred books now in circulation is to be regarded as authentic, ordains and declares that the old Latin Vulgate Edition, which, in use for so many hundred years, has been approved by the Church, be in public lectures, disputations, sermons and expositions held as authentic, and that no one dare or presume under any pretext whatsoever to reject it.

Furthermore, to check unbridled spirits, it decrees that no one relying on his own judgment shall, in matters of faith and morals pertaining to the edification of Christian doctrine, distorting the Holy Scriptures in accordance with his own conceptions, presume to interpret them contrary to that sense which holy mother Church, to whom it belongs to judge of their true sense and interpretation, has held and holds, or even contrary to the unanimous teaching of the Fathers, even though such interpretations should never at any time be published. Those who act contrary to this shall be made known by the ordinaries and punished in accordance with the penalties prescribed by the law.

And wishing, as is proper, to impose a restraint in this matter on printers also, who, now without restraint, thinking what pleases them is permitted them, print without the permission of ecclesiastical superiors the books of the Holy Scriptures and the notes and commentaries thereon of all persons indiscriminately, often with the name of the press omitted, often also under a fictitious press-name, and what is worse, without the name of the author, and also indiscreetly have for sale such books printed elsewhere, this council decrees and ordains that in the future the Holy Scriptures, especially the old Vulgate Edition, be printed in the most correct manner possible, and that it shall not be lawful for anyone to print or to have printed any books whatsoever dealing with sacred doctrinal matters without the name of the author, or in the future to sell them, or even to have them in possession, unless they have first been examined and approved by the ordinary, under penalty of anathema and fine prescribed by the last Council of the Lateran. If they be regulars they must in addition to this examination and approval obtain permission also from their own superiors after these have examined the books in accordance with their own statutes. Those who lend or circulate them in manuscript before they have been examined and approved, shall be subject to the same penalties as the printers, and those who have them in their possession or read them, shall, unless they make known the authors, be themselves regarded as the authors. The approbation of such books, however, shall be given in writing and shall appear authentically at the beginning of the book, whether it be written or printed, and all this, that is, both the examination and approbation, shall be done gratuitously, so that what ought to be approved may be approved and what ought to be condemned may be condemned.

Furthermore, wishing to repress that boldness whereby the words and sentences of the Holy Scriptures are turned and twisted to all kinds of profane usages, namely, to things scurrilous, fabulous, vain, to flatteries, detractions, superstitions, godless and diabolical incantations, divinations, the casting of lots and defamatory libels, to put an end to such irreverence and contempt, and that no one may in the future dare use in any manner the words of Holy Scripture for these and similar purposes, it is commanded and enjoined that all people of this kind be restrained by the bishops as violators and profaners of the word of God, with the penalties of the law and other penalties that they may deem fit to impose.

*   *   *

Twenty-third Session Which Is the Seventh under the Supreme Pontiff, Pius IV, Celebrated on the Fifteenth Day of July 1563 The True and Catholic Doctrine Concerning the Sacrament of Order, Defined and Published by the Holy Council of Trent in the Seventh Session in Condemnation of Current Errors

FROM CHAPTER I
THE INSTITUTION OF THE PRIESTHOOD OF THE NEW LAW

Sacrifice and priesthood are by the ordinance of God so united that both have existed in every law. Since therefore in the New Testament the Catholic Church has received from the institution of Christ the holy, visible sacrifice of the Eucharist, it must also be confessed that there is in that Church a new, visible and external priesthood, into which the old has been translated. That this was instituted by the same Lord our Savior, and that to the Apostles and their successors in the priesthood was given the power of consecrating, offering and administering His body and blood, as also of forgiving and retaining sins, is shown by the Sacred Scriptures and has always been taught by the tradition of the Catholic Church.

CHAPTER II
THE SEVEN ORDERS

But since the ministry of so holy a priesthood is something divine, that it might be exercised in a more worthy manner and with greater veneration, it was consistent that in the most well-ordered arrangement of the Church there should be several distinct orders of ministers, who by virtue of their office should minister to the priesthood, so distributed that those already having the clerical tonsure should ascend through the minor to the major orders. For the Sacred Scriptures mention unmistakably not only the priests but also the deacons, and teach in the most definite words what is especially to be observed in their ordination; and from the very beginning of the Church the names of the following orders and the duties proper to each one are known to have been in use, namely, those of the subdeacon, acolyte, exorcist, lector and porter, though these were not of equal rank; for the subdiaconate is classed among the major orders by the Fathers and holy councils, in which we also read very often of other inferior orders.

CHAPTER III
THE ORDER OF THE PRIESTHOOD IS TRULY A SACRAMENT

Since from the testimony of Scripture, Apostolic tradition and the unanimous agreement of the Fathers it is clear that grace is conferred by sacred ordination, which is performed by words and outward signs, no one ought to doubt that order is truly and properly one of the seven sacraments of holy Church. For the Apostle says: *I admonish thee that thou stir up the grace of God which is in thee by the imposition of my hands. For God has not given us the spirit of fear, but of power and of love and of sobriety.*

CHAPTER IV
THE ECCLESIASTICAL HIERARCHY
AND ORDINATION

But since in the sacrament of order, as also in baptism and confirmation, a character is imprinted which can neither be effaced nor taken away, the holy council justly condemns the opinion of those who say that the priests of the New Testament have only a temporary power, and that those who have once been rightly ordained can again become laymen if they do not exercise the ministry of the word of God. And if anyone should assert that all Christians without distinction are priests of the New Testament, or that they are all *inter se* endowed with an equal spiritual power, he seems to do nothing else than derange the ecclesiastical hierarchy, which is *an army set in array*; as if, contrary to the teaching of St. Paul, all are apostles, all prophets, all evangelists, all pastors, all doctors. Wherefore, the holy council declares that, besides the other ecclesiastical grades, the bishops, who have succeeded the Apostles, principally belong to this hierarchical order, and have been placed, as the same Apostle says, by the Holy Ghost to rule the Church of God; that they are superior to priests, administer the sacrament of confirmation, ordain ministers of the Church, and can perform many other functions over which those of an inferior order have no power. The council teaches furthermore, that in the ordination of bishops, priests and the other orders, the consent, call or authority, whether of the people or of any civil power or magistrate is not required in such wise that without this the ordination is invalid; rather does it decree that all those who, called and instituted only by the people or by the civil power or magistrate, ascend to the exercise of these offices, and those who by their rashness assume them, are not ministers of the Church, but are to be regarded as thieves and robbers, who have not entered by the door. These are the things which in general it has seemed good to the holy council to teach to the faithful of Christ regarding the sacrament of order. The contrary, however, it has resolved to condemn in definite and appropriate canons in the following manner, in order that all, making use with the help of Christ of the rule of faith, may in the midst of the darkness of so many errors recognize more easily the Catholic truth and adhere to it.

CANONS ON THE SACRAMENT OF ORDER

Canon 1. If anyone says that there is not in the New Testament a visible and external priesthood, or that there is no power of consecrating and offering the true body and blood of the Lord and of forgiving and retaining sins, but only the office and bare ministry of preaching the Gospel; or that those who do not preach are not priests at all, let him be anathema.

Canon 2. If anyone says that besides the priesthood there are not in the Catholic Church other orders, both major and minor, by which, as by certain steps, advance is made to the priesthood, let him be anathema.

Canon 3. If anyone says that order or sacred ordination is not truly and properly a sacrament instituted by Christ the Lord, or that it is some human contrivance devised by men unskilled in ecclesiastical matters, or that it is only a certain rite for choosing ministers of the word of God and of the sacraments, let him be anathema.

Canon 4. If anyone says that by sacred ordination the Holy Ghost is not imparted and that therefore the bishops say in vain: *Receive ye the Holy Ghost,* or that by it a character is not imprinted, or that he who has once been a priest can again become a layman, let him be anathema.

Canon 5. If anyone says that the holy unction which the Church uses in ordination is not only not required but is detestable and pernicious, as also are the other ceremonies of order, let him be anathema.

Canon 6. If anyone says that in the Catholic Church there is not instituted a hierarchy by divine ordinance, which consists of bishops, priests and ministers, let him be anathema.

Canon 7. If anyone says that bishops are not superior to priests, or that they have not the power to confirm and ordain, or that the power which they have is common to them and to priests, or that orders conferred by them without the consent or call of the people or of the secular power are invalid, or that those who have been neither rightly ordained nor sent by ecclesiastical and canonical authority, but come from elsewhere, are lawful ministers of the word and of the sacraments, let him be anathema.

Canon 8. If anyone says that the bishops who are chosen by the authority of the Roman pontiff are not true and legitimate bishops, but merely human deception, let him be anathema.

*   *   *

Twenty-fifth Session Which Is the Ninth and Last under the Supreme Pontiff, Pius IV, Begun on the Third and Closed on the Fourth Day of December 1563

DECREE CONCERNING PURGATORY

Since the Catholic Church, instructed by the Holy Ghost, has, following the sacred writings and the ancient tradition of the Fathers, taught in sacred councils and very recently in this ecumenical council that there is a purgatory, and that the souls there detained are aided by the suffrages of the faithful and chiefly by the acceptable sacrifice of the altar, the holy council commands the bishops that they strive diligently to the end that the sound doctrine of purgatory, transmitted by the Fathers and sacred councils, be believed and maintained by the faithful of Christ, and be everywhere taught and preached. The more difficult and subtle questions, however, and those that do not make for edification and from which there is for the most part no increase in piety, are to be excluded from popular instructions to uneducated people. Likewise, things that are uncertain or that have the appearance of falsehood they shall not permit to be made known publicly and discussed. But those things that tend to a certain kind of curiosity or superstition, or that savor of filthy lu-

cre, they shall prohibit as scandals and stumbling blocks to the faithful. The bishops shall see to it that the suffrages of the living, that is, the sacrifice of the mass, prayers, alms and other works of piety which they have been accustomed to perform for the faithful departed, be piously and devoutly discharged in accordance with the laws of the Church, and that whatever is due on their behalf from testamentary bequests or other ways, be discharged by the priests and ministers of the Church and others who are bound to render this service not in a perfunctory manner, but diligently and accurately.

ON THE INVOCATION, VENERATION, AND RELICS OF SAINTS, AND ON SACRED IMAGES

The holy council commands all bishops and others who hold the office of teaching and have charge of the *cura animarum,* that in accordance with the usage of the Catholic and Apostolic Church, received from the primitive times of the Christian religion, and with the unanimous teaching of the holy Fathers and the decrees of sacred councils, they above all instruct the faithful diligently in matters relating to intercession and invocation of the saints, the veneration of relics, and the legitimate use of images, teaching them that the saints who reign together with Christ offer up their prayers to God for men, that it is good and beneficial suppliantly to invoke them and to have recourse to their prayers, assistance and support in order to obtain favors from God through His Son, Jesus Christ our Lord, who alone is our redeemer and savior; and that they think impiously who deny that the saints who enjoy eternal happiness in heaven are to be invoked, or who assert that they do not pray for men, or that our invocation of them to pray for each of us individually is idolatry, or that it is opposed to the word of God and inconsistent with the honor of the *one mediator of God and men, Jesus Christ,* or that it is foolish to pray vocally or mentally to those who reign in heaven. Also, that the holy bodies of the holy martyrs and of others living with Christ, which were the living members of Christ and the temple of the Holy Ghost, to be awakened by Him to eternal life and to be glorified, are to be venerated by the faithful, through which many benefits are bestowed by God on men, so that those who maintain that veneration and honor are not due to the relics of the saints, or that these and other memorials are honored by the faithful without profit, and that the places dedicated to the memory of the saints for the purpose of obtaining their aid are visited in vain, are to be utterly condemned, as the Church has already long since condemned and now again condemns them. Moreover, that the images of Christ, of the Virgin Mother of God, and of the other saints are to be placed and retained especially in the churches, and that due honor and veneration is to be given them; not, however, that any divinity or virtue is believed to be in them by reason of which they are to be venerated, or that something is to be asked of them, or that trust is to be placed in images, as was done of old by the Gentiles who placed their hope in idols; but because the honor which is shown them is referred to the prototypes which they represent, so that by means of the images which we kiss and before which we uncover the head and prostrate ourselves, we adore Christ and venerate the saints whose likeness they bear. That is what was defined by the decrees of the councils, especially of the Second Council of Nicaea, against the opponents of images.

Moreover, let the bishops diligently teach that by means of the stories of the mysteries of our redemption portrayed in paintings and other representations the people are instructed and confirmed in the articles of faith, which ought to be borne in mind and constantly reflected upon; also that great profit is derived from all holy images, not only because the people are thereby reminded of the benefits and gifts bestowed on them by Christ, but also because through the saints the miracles of God and salutary examples are set before the eyes of the faithful, so that they may give God thanks for those things, may fashion their own life and conduct in imitation of the saints and be moved to adore and love God and cultivate piety. But if anyone should teach or maintain any-

thing contrary to these decrees, let him be anathema. If any abuses shall have found their way into these holy and salutary observances, the holy council desires earnestly that they be completely removed, so that no representation of false doctrines and such as might be the occasion of grave error to the uneducated be exhibited. And if at times it happens, when this is beneficial to the illiterate, that the stories and narratives of the Holy Scriptures are portrayed and exhibited, the people should be instructed that not for that reason is the divinity represented in picture as if it can be seen with bodily eyes or expressed in colors or figures. Furthermore, in the invocation of the saints, the veneration of relics, and the sacred use of images, all superstition shall be removed, all filthy quest for gain eliminated, and all lasciviousness avoided, so that images shall not be painted and adorned with a seductive charm, or the celebration of saints and the visitation of relics be perverted by the people into boisterous festivities and drunkenness, as if the festivals in honor of the saints are to be celebrated with revelry and with no sense of decency. Finally, such zeal and care should be exhibited by the bishops with regard to these things that nothing may appear that is disorderly or unbecoming and confusedly arranged, nothing that is profane, nothing disrespectful, since holiness becometh the house of God. That these things may be the more faithfully observed, the holy council decrees that no one is permitted to erect or cause to be erected in any place or church, howsoever exempt, any unusual image unless it has been approved by the bishop; also that no new miracles be accepted and no relics recognized unless they have been investigated and approved by the same bishop, who, as soon as he has obtained any knowledge of such matters, shall, after consulting theologians and other pious men, act thereon as he shall judge consonant with truth and piety. But if any doubtful or grave abuse is to be eradicated, or if indeed any graver question concerning these matters should arise, the bishop, before he settles the controversy, shall await the decision of the metropolitan and of the bishops of the province in a provincial synod; so, however, that nothing new or anything that has not hitherto been in use in the Church, shall be decided upon without having first consulted the most holy Roman pontiff.

*   *   *

REVIEW QUESTIONS

1. How does the Council of Trent approach the question of the authority of Scripture?

2. Why did it set that discussion in terms of a list of books the council recognized as sacred?

3. On what basis might the council claim the authority to name the books of the Bible and determine the correct translation?

4. What are the seven orders? What is their place in Christianity and their function? What is the nature of their authority?

5. What do these decrees suggest about the practice of Catholicism in the years following the Reformation?

JOHN CALVIN

FROM Draft Ecclesiastical Ordinances, September and October 1541

John Calvin (1509–1564) was born of bourgeois parents in the city of Noyon in Picardy. Destined by his father for an ecclesiastical career, he received several benefices to finance his education as early as 1521. In 1523, he transferred to the University of Paris, where he imbibed the spirit of humanism from such teachers as Mathurin Cordier and Guillaume Bude. Calvin earned a master of arts degree at Paris and, without abandoning his study of classical languages and literature, turned to law at Orleans in 1528. By 1532, he had earned a doctorate of law. Sometime during his legal training or shortly thereafter, Calvin converted to Protestantism. The year 1534 was decisive for Calvin. Forced to flee Paris because of the proscription of Protestantism, he made his way to Basel, where he began work on his great systematic theology, Institutes of the Christian Religion *(1536). It was immediately recognized as a superb normative statement of reformed theology and established Calvin's stature as a leader among Protestants despite his youth. As the first edition went to press, Calvin made his way to Geneva, where Guillaume Farel enlisted his aid in the reform of the city. The early years of the Reformation in Geneva were stormy, and there was considerable opposition to the doctrines advocated by Calvin. In a dispute over church discipline, the city council banished the Protestant pastors. Calvin made his way to Strasbourg, where he remained as a colleague of Martin Bucer and minister to the French refugee church until 1541. Meanwhile, political and religious chaos in Geneva eventually forced the government to seek the return of Calvin. He reluctantly consented, but only with the assurance that his entire original scheme of church polity would be instituted. The ecclesiastical ordinance adopted in 1541 encapsulated that polity and became influential for reformed churches throughout Europe. Calvin remained in Geneva from 1541 until his death in 1564, by which time the city that had accepted reform so reluctantly had been transformed into the center of an international Reformation.*

From *Calvin: Theological Treatises,* translated by J. K. S. Reid (Louisville: Westminster John Knox Press, 1954).

There are four orders of office instituted by our Lord for the government of his Church. First, pastors; then doctors; next elders; and fourth deacons.

Hence if we will have a Church well ordered and maintained we ought to observe this form of government.

As to the pastors, whom Scripture also sometimes calls elders and ministers, their office is to proclaim the Word of God, to instruct, admonish, exhort and censure, both in public and private, to administer the sacraments and to enjoin brotherly corrections along with the elders and colleagues.

Now in order that nothing happen confusedly in the Church, no one is to enter upon this office without a calling. In this it is necessary to consider three things, namely: the principal thing is the examination; then what belongs to the institution of the ministers; third, what ceremony or method of procedure it is good to observe in introducing them to office.

The examination contains two parts, of which the first concerns doctrine—to ascertain whether the candidate for ordination has a good and holy knowledge of Scripture; and also whether he be a fit and proper person to communicate it edifyingly to the people.

Further to avoid all danger of the candidate holding some false opinion, it will be good that he profess his acceptance and maintenance of the doctrine approved by the Church.

To know whether he is fit to instruct, it would be necessary to proceed by interrogation and by hearing him discuss in private the doctrine of the Lord.

The second part concerns life, to ascertain whether he is of good habits and conducts himself always without reproach. The rule of procedure in this matter which it is needful to follow is very well indicated by Paul.

There Follows, to Whom It Belongs to Institute Pastors

It will be good in this connection to follow the order of the ancient Church, for it is the only practice which is shown us in Scripture. The order is that ministers first elect such as ought to hold office; afterwards that he be presented to the Council; and if he is found worthy the Council receive and accept him, giving him certification to produce finally to the people when he preaches, in order that he be received by the common consent of the company of the faithful. If he be found unworthy, and show this after due probation, it is necessary to proceed to a new election for the choosing of another.

As to the manner of introducing him, it is good to use the imposition of hands, which ceremony was observed by the apostles and then in the ancient Church, providing that it take place without superstition and without offence. But because there has been much superstition in the past and scandal might result, it is better to abstain from it because of the infirmity of the times.

When he is elected, he has to swear in front of the Seigneury. Of this oath there will be a prescribed form, suitable to what is required of a minister.

Now as it is necessary to examine the ministers well when they are to be elected, so also it is necessary to have good supervision to maintain them in their duty.

First it will be expedient that all the ministers, for conserving purity and concord of doctrine among themselves, meet together one certain day each week, for discussion of the Scriptures; and none are to be exempt from this without legitimate excuse. If anyone be negligent, let him be admonished.

As for those who preach in the villages, throughout the Seigneury, they are to be exhorted to come as often as they are able. For the rest, if they default an entire month, it is to be held to be very great negligence, unless it is a case of illness or other legitimate hindrance.

If there appear difference of doctrine, let the ministers come together to discuss the matter. Afterwards, if need be, let them call the elders to assist in composing the contention. Finally, if they are unable to come to friendly agreement because of the obstinacy of one of the parties, let the case be referred to the magistrate to be put in order.

To obviate all scandals of living, it will be proper that there be a form of correction to which all submit themselves. It will also be the means by which the ministry may retain respect, and the Word of God be neither dishonoured nor scorned because of the ill reputation of the ministers. For as one is to correct those who merit it, so it will be proper to reprove calumnies and false reports which are made unjustly against innocent people.

But first it should be noted that there are crimes which are quite intolerable in a minister, and there are faults which may on the other hand be endured while direct fraternal admonitions are offered.

Of the first sort are:

heresy, schism, rebellion against ecclesiastical order, blasphemy open and meriting civil punishment, simony and all corruption in presentations, intrigue to occupy another's place, leaving one's Church without lawful leave or just calling, duplicity, perjury, lewdness, larceny, drunkenness, assault meriting punishment by law, usury, games forbidden by the law and scandalous, dances and similar dissoluteness, crimes carrying with them loss of civil rights, crime giving rise to another separation from the Church.

Of the second sort are:

strange methods of treating Scripture which turn to scandal, curiosity in investigating idle questions, advancing some doctrine or kind of practice not received in the Church, negligence in studying and reading the Scriptures, negligence in rebuking vice amounting to flattery, negligence in doing everything required by his office, scurrility, lying, slander, dissolute words, injurious words, foolhardiness and evil devices, avarice and too great parsimony, undisciplined anger, quarrels and contentions, laxity either of manner or of gesture and like conduct improper to a minister.

In the case of the crimes which cannot at all be tolerated, if some accusation and complaint arise, let the assembly of ministers and elders investigate it, in order to proceed reasonably and according to whatever is discovered in judging the case, and then report judgment to the magistrate in order that if required the delinquent be deposed.

In the case of the lesser vices which may be corrected by simple admonition, one is to proceed according to the command of our Lord, so that as a last step it come for ecclesiastical judgment.

To keep this discipline in operation, let the ministers every three months take special notice whether there be anything to discuss among themselves, to remedy it as is reasonable.

Of the Number, Place and Time of Preachings

Each Sunday, there is to be sermon at St. Peter and St. Gervais at break of day, and at the usual hour at the said St. Peter and St. Gervais.

At midday, there is to be catechism, that is, instruction of little children in all the three churches, the Magdalene, St. Peter and St. Gervais.

At three o'clock second sermon in St. Peter and St. Gervais.

For bringing children to catechism, and for receiving the sacraments, the boundaries of the parishes should as far as possible be observed; that is, St. Gervais embracing what it had in the past, the Magdalene similarly, St. Peter what belonged formerly to St. Germain, St. Cross, Our Lady the New, and St. Legier.

Besides the two preachings which take place, on working days there will be a sermon at St. Peter three times a week, on Monday, Tuesday and Friday one hour before beginning is made at the other places.

To maintain these charges and others pertaining to the ministry, it will be necessary to have five ministers and three coadjutors who will also be ministers, to aid and assist as necessity requires.

Concerning the Second Order, Which We Have Called Doctors

The office proper to doctors is the instruction of the faithful in true doctrine, in order that the purity of the Gospel be not corrupted either by ignorance or by evil opinions. As things are disposed today, we always include under this title aids and instructions for maintaining the doctrine of God and defending the Church from injury by the fault of pastors and ministers. So to use a more intelligible word, we will call this the order of the schools.

The degree nearest to the minister and most closely joined to the government of the Church is the lecturer in theology, of which it will be good to have one in Old Testament and one in New Testament.

But because it is only possible to profit from such lectures if first one is instructed in the languages and humanities, and also because it is necessary to raise offspring for time to come, in order not to leave the Church deserted to our children, a college should be instituted for instructing children to prepare them for the ministry as well as for civil government.

For the first, a proper place ought to be assigned for both doing lessons and accommodating the children and others who would profit. There must be a man learned and expert in arranging both the house and the instruction, who is able also to lecture. He is to be chosen and remunerated on condition that he have under his charge lecturers both in languages and in dialectic, if it can be done. Likewise there should be some matriculated persons to teach the little children; and these we hope shortly to appoint to assist the master.

All who are there will be subject like ministers to ecclesiastical discipline.

There need be no other school in the city for the little children, but let the girls have their school apart, as has hitherto been the case.

Let no one be received if he is not approved by the ministers on their testimony, for fear of impropriety.

Concerning the Third Order Which Is That of Elders

Their office is to have oversight of the life of everyone, to admonish amicably those whom they see to be erring or to be living a disordered life, and, where it is required, to enjoin fraternal corrections themselves and along with others.

In the present condition of the Church, it would be good to elect two of the Little Council, four of the Council of Sixty, and six of the Council of Two Hundred, men of good and honest life, without reproach and beyond suspicion, and above all fearing God and possessing spiritual prudence. These should be so elected that there be some in every quarter of the city, to keep an eye on everybody.

The best way of electing them seems to be this, that the Little Council suggest the nomination of the best that can be found and the most suitable; and to do this, summon the ministers to confer with them; after this they should present those whom they would commend to the Council of Two Hundred, which will approve them. If it find them worthy, let them take the special oath, whose form will be readily drawn up. And at the end of the year, let them present themselves to the Seigneury for consideration whether they ought to be continued or changed. It is inexpedient that they be changed often without cause, so long as they discharge their duty faithfully.

The Fourth Order of Ecclesiastical Government, That Is, the Deacons

There were always two kinds in the ancient Church, the one deputed to receive, dispense and hold goods for the poor, not only daily alms, but also possessions, rents and pensions; the other to tend and care for the sick and administer allowances to the poor. This custom we follow again now for we have procurators and hospitallers.

The number of procurators appointed for this hospital seems to us to be proper; but we wish that there be also a separate reception office, so that not only provisions be in time made better, but that those who wish to do some charity may be more certain that the gift will not be employed otherwise than they intend. And if the revenue assigned by their Lordships be insufficient, or should extraordinary necessity arise, the Seigneury will advise about adjustment, according to the need they see.

The election of both procurators and hospitallers is to take place like that of the elders; and in electing them the rule proposed by Paul for deacons is to be followed.

With regard to the office of procurator, we think the rules which have already been imposed on them by us are good, by means of which, in urgent affairs, and where there is danger in deferment, and chiefly when there is no grave difficulty or question of great expense, they are not obliged always to be meeting, but one or two can do what is reasonable in the absence of the others.

It will be their duty to watch diligently that the public hospital is well maintained, and that this be so both for the sick and the old people unable to work, widowed women, orphaned children and

other poor creatures. The sick are always to be lodged in a set of rooms separate from the other people who are unable to work, old men, widowed women, orphaned children and the other poor.

Moreover, care for the poor dispersed through the city should be revived, as the procurators may arrange it.

Moreover, besides the hospital for those passing through which must be maintained, there should be some attention given to any recognized as worthy of special charity. For this purpose, a special room should be set aside to receive those who ought to be assisted by the procurators, which is to be reserved for this business.

It should above all be demanded that the families of the hospitallers be honourably ruled in accordance with the will of God, since they have to govern houses dedicated to God.

The ministers must on their side enquire whether there be any lack or want of anything, in order to ask and desire the Seigneury to put it in order. To do this, some of their company with the procurators should visit the hospital every three months, to ascertain if all is in order.

It would be good, not only for the poor of the hospital, but also for those of the city who cannot help themselves, that they have a doctor and a surgeon of their own who should still practise in the city, but meanwhile be required to have care of the hospital and to visit the other poor.

As for the hospital for plague, it should be wholly separate and apart, and especially if it happen that the city be visited by this scourge of God.

For the rest, to discourage mendicancy which is contrary to good order, it would be well, and we have so ordered it, that there be one of our officials at the entrance of the churches to remove from the place those who loiter; and if there be any who give offence or offer insolence to bring them to one of the Lords Syndic. Similarly for the rest of the time, let the Overseers of Tens take care that the total prohibition of begging be well observed.

*   *   *

REVIEW QUESTIONS

1. What is the church according to Calvin?
2. What is its structure?
3. What do the four offices tell us about the function of the church?
4. What is the purpose of the church?
5. What are its goals?
6. What are the practices of the church and the relation of those practices to the process of becoming a Christian?
7. What is the relation between the church and salvation?

MARTIN LUTHER

FROM "Appeal to the Christian Nobility of the German Nation"

Martin Luther (1483–1546), the founder of Protestantism, was born of peasant stock. His father had left his fields for the copper mines of Mansfeld in Saxony, where he flourished economically and rose to the status of town councillor. His son Martin received a primary education from the Brethren of the Common Life and enrolled at the University of Erfurt in 1501, where he earned his bachelor of arts in 1502 and his master of arts in 1505. His father hoped that his son would continue the family's rise to prominence by pursuing a legal career. These aspirations were shattered when Luther unexpectedly entered a monastery in 1505. As a member of the order of Augustinian Hermits, Luther began formal training in theology. Selected for advanced training in theology, he made his way to the University of Wittenberg, where he received his doctorate in 1512 and occupied the chair of biblical theology. Even as his academic career prospered, his inner life suffered. Luther was beset by doubts about his own salvation, the result of a consciousness both of his own weakness and of divine righteousness. Long study and meditation led him to a resolution that became the basis for his theology of justification. Salvation was the result of divine grace, freely given; the forgiven conscience could be at peace; the soul could serve God joyfully. Given this new conviction, it is not surprising that the extravagant claims surrounding the sale of indulgences in 1517 provoked Luther to public protest. His objection to the notion that the pope could remit the temporal punishment for sins led him deeper and deeper into controversy and ultimately to schism. By 1520, the rift between Luther and the Catholic Church had become irreparable and extended to far more issues than papal power. In that year, he published three manifestos of reform, the first of which, "Appeal to the Christian Nobility of the German Nation," is excerpted below. It addressed the princes and rulers of Germany, recited the many grievances against the Church, and urged them

*to call a council for the reform of religion. It found a deep response in the nation
and mobilized the forces of the Reformation.*

From *The American Edition of Luther's Works*, edited by Jaroslav Pelikan (Minneapolis,
Minn.: Augsburg Press, 1943), pp. 7–12, 18–24.

Jesus

To the Esteemed and Reverend Master, Nicholas
von Amsdorf, Licentiate of Holy Scripture, and
Canon of Wittenberg, my special and kind friend,
from Doctor Martin Luther.

The grace and peace of God be with you, esteemed, reverend, and dear sir and friend.

The time for silence is past, and the time to
speak has come, as Ecclesiastes says. I am carrying
out our intention to put together a few points on
the matter of the reform of the Christian estate,
to be laid before the Christian nobility of the
German nation, in the hope that God may help
his church through the laity, since the clergy, to
whom this task more properly belongs, have
grown quite indifferent. I am sending the whole
thing to you, reverend sir, that you may give an
opinion on it and, where necessary, improve it.

I know full well that I shall not escape the
charge of presumption because I, a despised, inferior person, venture to address such high and
great estates on such weighty matters, as if there
were nobody else in the world except Doctor Luther to take up the cause of the Christian estate
and give advice to such high-ranking people. I
make no apologies no matter who demands them.
Perhaps I owe my God and the world another
work of folly. I intend to pay my debt honestly.
And if I succeed, I shall for the time being become a court jester. And if I fail, I still have one
advantage—no one need buy me a cap or put scis-
sors to my head. It is a question of who will put
the bells on whom. I must fulfil the proverb,
"Whatever the world does, a monk must be in the
picture, even if he has to be painted in. More
than once a fool has spoken wisely, and wise men
have often been arrant fools. Paul says, "He who
wishes to be wise must become a fool." Moreover,

since I am not only a fool, but also a sworn doctor
of Holy Scripture, I am glad for the opportunity
to fulfil my doctor's oath, even in the guise of a
fool.

I beg you, give my apologies to those who are
moderately intelligent, for I do not know how to
earn the grace and favor of the superintelligent. I
have often sought to do so with the greatest pains,
but from now on I neither desire nor value their
favor. God help us to seek not our own glory but
his alone. Amen.

At Wittenberg, in the monastery of the Augus-
tinians, on the eve of St. John Baptist in the year
fifteen hundred and twenty.

To His Most Illustrious, Most Mighty, and
Imperial Majesty, and to the Christian Nobility of
the German Nation, from Doctor Martin Luther.

Grace and power from God, Most Illustrious
Majesty, and most gracious and dear lords.

It is not from sheer impertinence or rashness
that I, one poor man, have taken it upon myself
to address your worships. All the estates of Christendom, particularly in Germany, are now oppressed by distress and affliction, and this has
stirred not only me but everybody else to cry out
time and time again and to pray for help. It has
even compelled me now at this time to cry aloud
that God may inspire someone with his Spirit
to lend a helping hand to this distressed and
wretched nation. Often the councils have made
some pretense at reformation, but their attempts
have been cleverly frustrated by the guile of certain
men, and things have gone from bad to worse.
With God's help I intend to expose the wiles and
wickedness of these men, so that they are shown
up for what they are and may never again be so
obstructive and destructive. God has given us a
young man of noble birth as head of state, and in

him has awakened great hopes of good in many hearts. Presented with such an opportunity we ought to apply ourselves and use this time of grace profitably.

The first and most important thing to do in this matter is to prepare ourselves in all seriousness. We must not start something by trusting in great power or human reason, even if all the power in the world were ours. For God cannot and will not suffer that a good work begin by relying upon one's own power and reason. He dashes such works to the ground, they do no good at all. As it says in Psalm 33, "No king is saved by his great might and no lord is saved by the greatness of his strength." I fear that this is why the good emperors Frederick I and Frederick II and many other German emperors were in former times shamefully oppressed and trodden underfoot by the popes, although all the world feared the emperors. It may be that they relied on their own might more than on God, and therefore had to fall. What was it in our own times that raised the bloodthirsty Julius II to such heights? Nothing else, I fear, except that France, the Germans, and Venice relied upon themselves. The children of Benjamin slew forty-two thousand Israelites because the latter relied on their own strength, Judges 30.

That it may not so fare with us and our noble Charles, we must realize that in this matter we are not dealing with men, but with the princes of hell. These princes could fill the world with war and bloodshed, but war and bloodshed do not overcome them. We must tackle this job by renouncing trust in physical force and trusting humbly in God. We must seek God's help through earnest prayer and fix our minds on nothing else than the misery and distress of suffering Christendom without regard to what evil men deserve. Otherwise, we may start the game with great prospects of success, but when we get into it the evil spirits will stir up such confusion that the whole world will swim in blood, and then nothing will come of it all. Let us act wisely, therefore, and in the fear of God. The more force we use, the greater our disaster if we do not act humbly and in the

fear of God. If the popes and Romanists have hitherto been able to set kings against each other by the devil's help, they may well be able to do it again if we were to go ahead without the help of God on our own strength and by our own cunning.

The Romanists have very cleverly built three walls around themselves. Hitherto they have protected themselves by these walls in such a way that no one has been able to reform them. As a result, the whole of Christendom has fallen abominably.

In the first place, when pressed by the temporal power they have made decrees and declared that the temporal power had no jurisdiction over them, but that, on the contrary, the spiritual power is above the temporal. In the second place, when the attempt is made to reprove them with the Scriptures, they raise the objection that only the pope may interpret the Scriptures. In the third place, if threatened with a council, their story is that no one may summon a council but the pope.

In this way they have cunningly stolen our three rods from us, that they may go unpunished. They have ensconced themselves within the safe stronghold of these three walls so that they can practice all the knavery and wickedness which we see today. Even when they have been compelled to hold a council they have weakened its power in advance by putting the princes under oath to let them remain as they were. In addition, they have given the pope full authority over all decision of a council, so that it is all the same whether there are many councils or no councils. They only deceive us with puppet shows and sham fights. They fear terribly for their skin in a really free council! They have so intimidated kings and princes with this technique that they believe it would be an offense against God not to be obedient to the Romanists in all their knavish and ghoulish deceits.

May God help us, and give us just one of those trumpets with which the walls of Jericho were overthrown to blast down these walls of straw and paper in the same way and set free the Christian rods for the punishment of sin, and bring to light the craft and deceit of the devil, to the end that through punishment we may reform ourselves and once more attain God's favor.

Let us begin by attacking the first wall. It is pure invention that pope, bishop, priests, and monks are called the spiritual estate while princes, lords, artisans, and farmers are called the temporal estate. This is indeed a piece of deceit and hypocrisy. Yet no one need be intimidated by it, and for this reason: all Christians are truly of the spiritual estate, and there is no difference among them except that of office. Paul says in I Corinthians 12 that we are all one body, yet every member has its own work by which it serves the others. This is because we all have one baptism, one gospel, one faith, and are all Christians alike; for baptism, gospel, and faith alone make us spiritual and a Christian people.

*   *   *

The second wall is still more loosely built and less substantial. The Romanists want to be the only masters of Holy Scripture, although they never learn a thing from the Bible all their life long. They assume the sole authority for themselves, and, quite unashamed, they play about with words before our very eyes, trying to persuade us that the pope cannot err in matters of faith, regardless of whether he is righteous or wicked. Yet they cannot point to a single letter. This is why so many heretical and unChristian, even unnatural, ordinances stand in the canon law. But there is no need to talk about these ordinances at present. Since these Romanists think the Holy Spirit never leaves them, no matter how ignorant and wicked they are, they become bold and decree only what they want. And if what they claim were true, why have Holy Scripture at all? Of what use is Scripture? Let us burn the Scripture and be satisfied with the unlearned gentlemen at Rome who possess the Holy Spirit! And yet the Holy Spirit can be possessed only by pious hearts. If I had not read the words with my own eyes, I would not have believed it possible for the devil to have made such stupid claims at Rome, and to have won supporters for them.

But so as not to fight them with mere words,

we will quote the Scriptures. St. Paul says in I Corinthians 14, "If something better is revealed to anyone, though he is already sitting and listening to another in God's word, then the one who is speaking shall hold his peace and give place." What would be the point of this commandment if we were compelled to believe only the man who does the talking, or the man who is at the top? Even Christ said in John 6 that all Christians shall be taught by God. If it were to happen that the pope and his cohorts were wicked and not true Christians, were not taught by God and were without understanding, and at the same time some obscure person had a right understanding, why should the people not follow the obscure man? Has the pope not erred many times? Who would help Christendom when the pope erred if we did not have somebody we could trust more than him, somebody who had the Scriptures on his side?

Therefore, their claim that only the pope may interpret Scripture is an outrageous fancied fable. They cannot produce a single letter of Scripture to maintain that the interpretation of Scripture or the confirmation of its interpretation belongs to the pope alone. They themselves have usurped this power. And although they allege that this power was given to St. Peter when the keys were given him, it is clear enough that the keys were not given to Peter alone but to the whole community. Further, the keys were not ordained for doctrine or government, but only for the binding or loosing of sin. Whatever else or whatever more they arrogate to themselves on the basis of the keys is a mere fabrication. But Christ's words to Peter, "I have prayed for you that your faith fail not," cannot be applied to the pope, since the majority of the popes have been without faith, as they must themselves confess. Besides, it is not only for Peter that Christ prayed, but also for all apostles and Christians, as he says in John 17, "Father, I pray for those whom thou hast given me, and not for these only, but for all who believe on me through their word." Is that not clear enough?

Just think of it! The Romanists must admit that there are among us good Christians who have the true faith, spirit, understanding, word, and mind of Christ. Why, then, should we reject the word and understanding of good Christians and follow the pope, who has neither faith nor the Spirit? To follow the pope would be to deny the whole faith as well as the Christian church. Again, if the article, "I believe in one holy Christian church," is correct, then the pope cannot be the only one who is right. Otherwise, we would have to confess, "I believe in the pope at Rome." This would reduce the Christian church to one man, and be nothing else than a devilish and hellish error.

Besides, if we are all priests, as was said above, and all have one faith, one gospel, one sacrament, why should we not also have the power to test and judge what is right or wrong in matters of faith? What becomes of Paul's words in I Corinthians 2, "A spiritual man judges all things, yet he is judged by no one"? And II Corinthians 4, "We all have one spirit of faith"? Why, then, should not we perceive what is consistent with faith and what is not, just as well as an unbelieving pope does?

We ought to become bold and free on the authority of all these texts, and many others. We ought not to allow the Spirit of freedom (as Paul calls him) to be frightened off by the fabrications of the popes, but we ought to march boldly forward and test all that they do, or leave undone, by our believing understanding of the Scriptures. We must compel the Romanists to follow not their own interpretation but the better one. Long ago Abraham had to listen to Sarah, although she was in more complete subjection to him than we are to anyone on earth. And Balaam's ass was wiser than the prophet himself. If God spoke then through an ass against a prophet, why should he not be able even now to speak through a righteous man against the pope? Similarly, St. Paul rebukes St. Peter as a man in error in Galatians 2. Therefore, it is the duty of every Christian to espouse the cause of the faith, to understand and defend it, and to denounce every error.

The third wall falls of itself when the first two are down. When the pope acts contrary to the Scriptures, it is our duty to stand by the Scriptures, to reprove him and to constrain him, according to the word of Christ, Matthew 18, "If your brother sins against you, go and tell it to him, between you and him alone; if he does not listen to you, then take one or two others with you; if he does not listen to them, tell it to the church; if he does not listen to the church, consider him a heathen." Here every member is commanded to care for every other. How much more should we do this when the member that does evil is responsible for the government of the church, and by his evil-doing is the cause of much harm and offense to the rest! But if I am to accuse him before the church, I must naturally call the church together.

The Romanists have no basis in Scripture for their claim that the pope alone has the right to call or confirm a council. This is just their own ruling, and it is only valid as long as it is not harmful to Christendom or contrary to the laws of God. Now when the pope deserves punishment, this ruling no longer obtains, for not to punish him by authority of a council is harmful to Christendom.

Thus we read in Acts 15 that it was not St. Peter who called the Apostolic Council but the apostles and elders. If then that right had belonged to St. Peter alone, the council would not have been a Christian council, but a heretical *conciliabulum*. Even the Council of Nicaea, the most famous of all councils, was neither called nor confirmed by the bishop of Rome, but by the emperor Constantine. Many other emperors after him have done the same, and yet these councils were the most Christian of all. But if the pope alone has the right to convene councils, then these councils would all have been heretical. Further, when I examine the councils the pope did summon, I find that they did nothing of special importance.

Therefore, when necessity demands it, and the pope is an offense to Christendom, the first man who is able should, as a true member of the whole body, do what he can to bring about a truly free council. No one can do this so well as the temporal authorities, especially since they are also fellow-Christians, fellow-priests, fellow-members of the spiritual estate, fellow-lords over all things. Whenever it is necessary or profitable they ought to exercise the office and work which they have received from God over everyone. Would it not be unnatural if a fire broke out in a city and everybody were to stand by and let it burn on and on and consume everything that could burn because nobody had the authority of the mayor, or because, perhaps, the fire broke out in the mayor's house? In such a situation is it not the duty of every citizen to arouse and summon the rest? How much more should this be done in the spiritual city of Christ if a fire of offense breaks out, whether in the papal government, or anywhere else! The same argument holds if an enemy were to attack a city. The man who first roused the others deserves honor and gratitude. Why, then, should he not deserve honor who makes known the presence of the enemy from hell and rouses Christian people and calls them together?

*   *   *

REVIEW QUESTIONS

1. Why does Luther address the German nobility?
2. How is Luther redefining temporal and spiritual authorities?
3. What is their relation to one another?
4. Where does Luther locate true authority?

"Statement of Grievances," Diet of Worms, 1521

The Diet of Worms in 1521, the first meeting of Emperor Charles V with the representatives of the German Estates and the occasion of Martin Luther's appearance before the emperor, is a dramatic moment in the history of the Reformation. It provided the setting for Luther's declaration of faith in Scripture and freedom of conscience: "Here I stand." It also provided the opportunity for an official statement of grievances concerning the state of the church. Thus, even as it condemned Luther, the diet reminded Charles both of the reformer's extraordinary popular support and of the necessity of addressing the "burdens and abuses" placed on the empire by Rome. Charles asked the representatives to submit a catalogue of these abuses for consideration and action. A committee of electors and princes, both secular and spiritual, drew up the following list, probably using complaints submitted by individual representatives. Though no formal action was taken at Worms, the "Statement of Grievances" provided the basis of a document sent to Rome after the Diet of Nuremberg in 1523.

From *Manifestations of Discontent in Germany on the Eve of the Reformation*, edited by Gerald Strauss (Bloomington: Indiana University Press, 1971), pp. 52–63.

HIS ROMAN IMPERIAL MAJESTY desiring the electors, princes, and General Estates of the Empire to acquaint him with the burdens placed on the German nation by His Holiness the Pope and other ecclesiastics, and to make known to him our counsel and opinions as to how these burdens might be lifted from us, we have in all haste set down the following points, beginning with matters touching His Holiness the Pope.

   1. *Secular cases are transferred to Rome for trial*

THE GODLY MILL (1521)

Church reformers—both Protestant and Catholic—made full use of the new technology of printing to broadcast their ideological message to the common folk. Often, a printed image was worth a thousand words to a still largely illiterate population. The Godly Mill distills the early Lutheran message of reliance on Scripture as the sole source of religious truth: As the truth of the Gospel is disseminated, as in the workings of a mill, those institutions and traditions not explicitly established in it are banished. What is the significance of the grouping of the four figures: Christ, Erasmus, Luther, and Karsthans, the common man? Why would Lutherans choose a mill as their symbol for the dissemination of the Gospel? Given the year in which it was printed, 1521, how might this image be directly related to significant political events?

in the first instance. Our Most Holy Father the Pope, heeding the clamor of his priests, causes numerous persons to be summoned for trial in Rome in matters of inheritance, mortgage and similar worldly concerns, a practice conducive to the curtailment of the competence of secular authorities. We ask that Your Imperial Majesty undertake to ensure that no person, spiritual or worldly, be summoned to Rome for first trial in any matter, spiritual or worldly, but that he be allowed instead to appear in the first instance before the bishop or archdeacon of his province or, if he is a layman and the matter at issue is secular, before the prince, government, or ordinary judge with appropriate competence.

*   *   *

7. *Rome often grants benefices to unworthy persons.* Rome awards German benefices to unqualified, unlearned, and unfit persons such as gunners, falconers, bakers, donkey drivers, stable grooms, and so on, most of whom know not a word of German and never assume the duties connected with their benefices, shifting them instead to worthless vicars who are content with a pittance in pay. Thus the German laity receives neither spiritual care nor worldly counsel from the Church, while a hoard of money flows yearly to Italy with no return to us, least of all gratitude. We think that German benefices should be awarded to native Germans only and that beneficed persons ought to be required to reside in the place to which they are assigned.

*   *   *

9. *Concerning annates.* In former times emperors granted annates to Rome for a limited term of years only and for no purpose other than to enable the Church to hold back the Turk and support Christendom. In the course of time, however, the payment of annates grew into a regular custom, and, as is generally known, the German nation has been excessively burdened with them. . . .

10. *Annates are constantly increased in amount.* Not only are annates almost daily raised in amount, but they are also being extended from archbishoprics and bishoprics to abbeys, priories, parishes, and other ecclesiastical prebends. . . . Al-

though the old regulations placed a pallium fee of not more than ten thousand gulden upon the bishoprics of Mainz, Cologne, Salzburg, and others, the pallium cannot now be fetched home for less than twenty thousand to twenty-four thousand gulden.

11. *Concerning new devices employed by Rome.* The main reason for the constant rise in the cost of episcopal confirmations and pallium fees is the proliferation of offices in Rome, such as chamberlains, shield-bearers, and others, for whose emoluments our bishops' subjects must pay taxes and tributes. Furthermore, Rome obtains money by means of a number of cunning and novel devices, especially the following: a certain newly elected bishop has been given papal leave to pay his pallium fees not in cash but instead in the form of a pledge from certain sponsors to make payment at a given time. Suddenly, and for no reason, these sponsors are excommunicated and, almost at once, absolved again, for which absolution the bishop-elect must pay from three to five hundred ducats. It has been made known to us that His Holiness has this year created several new offices and is now personally served by more than 150 retainers who make their living off the proceeds of ecclesiastical benefices, for which the German nation furnishes the money.

*   *   *

19. *Concerning papal dispensation and absolution.* Popes and bishops reserve to themselves certain sins and offenses from which, they say, only they can absolve us. Whenever such a "case" occurs and a man wishes absolution, he discovers that only money can procure it for him. Nor does Rome give out a dispensation except on payment of gold. A poor man without money will not see his matter despatched. A rich man can, moreover, for a sum, obtain papal letters of indult, which entitle him to priestly absolution for any sin he might commit in the future, murder, for example, or perjury. All this shows how Roman greed and covetousness cause sins and vices to multiply in the world.

20. *Concerning the depredations of papal courtiers.* The German nation also suffers exceedingly from

the greed of papal and curial hangers-on who are bent on occupying ecclesiastical benefices in our land. These courtiers compel honorable old clerics, long established and blameless in their offices, to go to Rome, where they are subjected to humiliating chicaneries. There they must wait until Rome gets what it wants through reservations and pensions obtained by means of so-called Chancellery Rules, setting aside old agreements and replacing them with new ones. In this way, honorable old clerics who are not schooled in courtiers' tricks are defrauded of their benefices *lite pendente,* no matter what the outcome of their case will be.

* * *

22. *Concerning indulgences.* We also regard it in the highest degree objectionable that His Holiness should permit so many indulgences to be sold in Germany, a practice through which simple-minded folk are misled and cheated of their savings. When His Holiness sends nuncios or emissaries to a country, he empowers them to offer indulgences for sale and retain a portion of the income for their traveling expenses and salaries. . . . Bishops and local secular authorities also get their share for helping with the arrangements for the sale. All this money is obtained from poor and simple people who cannot see through the curia's cunning deceptions.

23. *Concerning mendicants, relic hawkers, and miracle healers.* These riffraff go back and forth through our land, begging, collecting, offering indulgences, and extracting large sums of money from our people. We think these hawkers ought to be kept out of our country. . . .

* * *

31. *How some clerics escape punishment for their misdeeds.* If an ordained cleric going about in the world on secular business and in secular clothes is brought before a secular court on some charge and is detained by it, he need only say "I am ordained" and demand to be transferred to an ecclesiastical court, and he will go free. His bishop will support him, notwithstanding the fact that the man was apprehended without tonsure and wearing worldly dress. And if the secular court does

not release him within twenty-four hours, its judges are excommunicated. Are not such practices bound to encourage clerics to wicked acts, the more since ecclesiastical courts let them go scot-free, no matter what their offense? . . .

32. *How secular property comes into ecclesiastical hands.* Seeing that the spiritual estate is under papal instructions never to sell or otherwise transfer the Church's real estate and immobilia to the laity, we think it advisable for His Roman Imperial Majesty to cause a corresponding law to be made for the secular estate, to wit, that no secular person be allowed to make over any part of his real property to any ecclesiastical person or institution, and that this proscription apply to inheritance as well. If such a law is not introduced without delay, it is possible that the secular estate will, in the course of time, be altogether bought out by the Church . . . and the secular estate of the Holy Roman Empire eventually be entirely beholden to the Church.

* * *

37. *Ecclesiastical courts give support to Jewish usury.* Everyone knows that the Jews' usury in Germany pauperizes and corrupts Christian society. But whenever a secular authority sets out to curb the Jews, the latter call upon an ecclesiastical court for help and cause the Christians to be excommunicated. For although the debtors swear that the money owed the Jews was not procured on terms of usury, the court knows that Jews do not lend except usuriously and that the poor, in their great need, perjure themselves. Canon and civil law forbids the rendering of judicial or other aid in matters of usury, but bishops and prelates permit it nonetheless.

* * *

39. *Sinners are given fines to pay rather than spiritual penance to do.* Although spiritual penance ought to be imposed upon sinners for one reason only, to gain salvation for their souls, ecclesiastical judges tend nowadays to make penalties so formidable that the sinner is obliged to buy his way out of them, through which practice untold amounts of money flow into the Church's treasury . . . .

*   *   *

43. *Excommunication is used indiscriminately, even in trivial matters.* Notwithstanding the original and true purpose of spiritual censure and excommunication, namely, to aid and direct Christian life and faith, this weapon is now flung at us for the most inconsequential debts—some of them amounting to no more than a few pennies—or for non-payment of court or administrative costs after the principal sum has already been returned. With such procedures the very life blood is sucked out of the poor, untutored laity, who are driven to distraction by the fear of the Church's ban. . . .

*   *   *

54. *There are too many vagrant mendicants in our land.* The poor in Germany are sorely oppressed by the extraordinary number of mendicant monks, especially by begging friars maintained by mendicant orders in violation of their own rules. Some villages and towns have two, three, or four of these begging brothers going about with hands outstretched, and the alms that should go to old and indigent householders who can no longer support themselves fill the monks' pouches instead. Bishops condone this practice in return for a portion of the collection.

*   *   *

56. *Too many priests are ordained, many of them unlearned and unfit.* Archbishops and bishops have been ordaining base and uneducated persons whose only claim to the priesthood is that they are needy. Such people, either because of their low estate or because of some native inclination to wickedness, lead reckless and dishonorable lives, bringing the whole spiritual estate into disrepute and setting the common folk a bad example. Before making ordination, the bishop is obliged to consult six witnesses on the candidate's fitness for the priestly office; but as things are now, the witnesses have, likely as not, never seen or heard of the candidate. Thus our Christian laws are nothing but pretense and sham to them.

*   *   *

58. *Bishops ought to hold frequent synods.* All the above shortcomings would doubtless be alleviated if bishops fulfilled their obligation to meet in synods with their prelates and ecclesiastical subjects in order to seek the aid and counsel of all the clergy present, as the law of the Church obliges them to do.

*   *   *

66. *Certain clerics behave like laymen and are even seen brawling in taverns.* The majority of parish priests and other secular clerics mingle with the common people at inns and taverns. They frequent public dances and walk about the streets in lay garments, brandishing long knives. They engage in quarrels and arguments, which usually lead to blows, whereupon they fall upon poor folk, wound or even kill them, and then excommunicate them unless the innocently injured parties agree to offer money for a settlement with the offending priest.

67. *Clerics set bad examples by cohabiting with their serving women.* Most parish priests and other clerics have established domestic relations with women of loose morals. They dwell openly with the women and with their children. It is a dishonest, detestable life for priests and a wretched example to set for their parishioners.

*   *   *

69. *Many clerics have turned to tavern keeping and gambling.* Clerics can frequently be seen setting themselves up as inn keepers. On holidays, in places where they have proprietary rights, priests put up tables for dice, bowls, or cards and invite people to play. Then they take the winnings, shamelessly claiming that these belong to them by rights of sovereignty. . . .

*   *   *

85. *They try to gain exclusive jurisdiction over legal matters, which should be heard in secular courts.* Much legal business that, according to law, may be settled in either ecclesiastical or secular courts, has in fact been usurped by the clergy. For when a secular judge claims a case, it often happens that a spiritual judge steps forward and threatens the other with excommunication unless he lets go of the case. Thus the clergy take over what they wish. According to our laws, offenses like perjury, adultery, and black magic may be handled by either

spiritual or lay courts, depending on who first claimed the case. But the clergy make bold to grasp all such cases, thus undercutting secular authority.

* * *

88. *How they take over secular jurisdiction by falsely pleading prescription.* Some experts hesitate to call attention to the Church's practice of acquiring rights by possession, that is, by pleading prescriptive rights to gain legal jurisdiction over lay matters, though His Imperial Majesty's and the empire's highest dignities and jurisdictions are thereby being steadily eroded. But we know it to be according to right and law that no one may prescribe, or claim to have acquired by possession, against the high sovereignty of pope and emperor, no matter how many years he has held on to something or used it without interference.

* * *

91. *Money can buy tolerance of concubinage and usury.* If a man and a woman cohabit without being married, they may pay an annual fee to the clergy and be left to live in shame and sin. The same is done with usurers. . . . A married person whose spouse has disappeared but might still be living is, without any further search for the missing partner, allowed to take up cohabitation with another. This they call "*toleramus*," and it serves to bring contempt upon the holy sacrament of marriage.

* * *

95. *Innocent people who happen to live near an excommunicated person are themselves excommunicated.* In some towns and villages ten or twelve neighbors of an excommunicate are placed under the ban along with him, although they have nothing to do with his offense. And this is done for no reason other than the clergy's eagerness to establish its authority and to have it obeyed. Because of this practice, poor and innocent people are forced to buy their way out of the ban, or else to remove their families and belongings from their

homes. No distinction is made in these indiscriminate excommunications. No one asks: Is the man poor or not? Did he associate voluntarily with the excommunicated sinner? And even though their own canon law forbids declarations of interdict for debts or other money matters, they impose the ban on whole towns and villages, alleging disobedience as the cause in order to mask their illegal and unjust action.

* * *

97. *They demand a weekly tribute from artisans.* In many places the clergy demand a weekly tax or tribute from millers, inn keepers, bakers, shoe makers, smiths, tailors, shepherds, cowherds, and other craftsmen. If this tribute is refused, they enforce their demand with the threat of excommunication.

* * *

101. *They withhold the sacraments for trivial offenses.* If a man owes a small debt to the priest or to the parish, and if he is too poor to repay it on time and asks for a short extension of the loan, the priest often withholds the sacraments from him and nags and intimidates him, although the matter ought by rights to be brought before a secular judge.

REVIEW QUESTIONS

1. What are the general categories into which the grievances may be organized?
2. How would you characterize the list as a whole?
3. On the basis of the statement, what was the nature of discontent with the Roman Church on the eve of the Reformation?
4. What kind of action or reforms did the representatives at Worms hope to prompt from the pope in Rome?
5. To what extent does the statement reflect the spiritual yearnings of Christians like Luther?

The Oath of Allegiance

The "Form or Example of the Profession and Oath Exhibited to Henry VIII, King of England, by the Bishops and Clergy Assembled in the Convocation in Parliament Held Anno Domini 1534," indicates clearly the state of the Reformation in England during that year. The doctrinal split with Rome had not reached a crucial stage, but the political schism was nearly complete. In March Pope Clement VII pronounced Henry's marriage to Catherine of Aragon to be valid and declared the king excommunicate if he did not accept the decision. Thus ended Henry's hope for an annulment and remarriage within the Church. Yet, his desire for an heir drove him to defiance. The Oath of Allegiance effectively severed all ecclesiastical ties to Rome and established the monarch as the head of the Anglican Church.

From *Selections from the Sources of English History*, edited by Charles W. Colby (New York: Longmans, Green, 1899), pp. 145–47.

To the most invincible and our most pious Lord in Christ, the Lord Henry the eighth, by the grace of God, king of England and France, defender of the faith, lord of Ireland, and on earth, under Christ, supreme head of the Church of England, your humble subjects and most obliged supplicants.

Reverence and obedience due to, and worthy of so excellent and mighty a prince, with all honour of subjection.

We, not constrained by force or fear, not hereunto induced or seduced by any deceit or other sinister machination, but out of our own certain knowledge, deliberate minds and mere and spontaneous wills, do, purely of our own accord, and absolutely in the word of our priesthood, profess, promise and swear, unto your most illustrious majesty, our singular and most high lord and patron, Henry the eighth, by the grace of God King of England and France, defender of the faith, lord of Ireland, and on earth of the English Church, immediately under Christ, supreme head: That from henceforth we will promise or give, or cause to be given, to no foreign emperor, king, prince, or prelate, nor to the bishop of Rome (whom they call Pope) fidelity or obedience in word or writing, simple or by oath; but at all times, in every case

and condition, we will follow and observe, and to our power defend the parts of your royal majesty, and of your successors, against every man whom we shall know or suspect to be an adversary to your majesty, or to your successors: and we will sincerely and heartily perform fidelity and obedience to your royal majesty alone, as to our supreme prince, and head of the English Church: we profess that the papacy of Rome is not ordained by God in holy writ, but that it is of human tradition; we constantly affirm, and openly do declare, and will declare, and will diligently take care that others shall so publish the same. Neither will we privately or publicly treat with any mortal man, or give our consent, that the bishop of Rome may here have, or exercise any longer, any authority or jurisdiction, or that he may hereafter be restored to any. And we do knowingly, publicly aver the modern bishop of Rome or his successor in that bishopric whosoever, not to be pope, nor high priest, nor universal bishop, nor the most high lord, but only bishop or prelate of Rome, as by our ancestors used: and the laws and statutes of this realm, at any time set forth and enacted, for the extirpation and taking away of popery, and of the authority and jurisdiction of the said bishop of Rome, we will, after our strength, knowledge and wit, firmly observe ourselves, and, as much as in us lies, will take care, and cause the same to be in like manner observed by others: neither will we henceforth appeal to the said bishop of Rome, or consent to any that shall appeal: neither will we act in his court for right or justice, nor will answer to any that there doth act, nor will there take upon us the person of a plaintiff or defendant: and if the said bishop, by message, or by his letters, shall signify anything unto us, whatsoever it be, we will, as soon as conveniently we may, signify or cause the same to be signified, either to your royal majesty, or to your privy council, or to your successors, or to their privy council; and we will neither send, or cause to be sent, any letters or message to the said bishop of Rome, or to his court, unless your majesty or your successor first know or consent that such letter or message shall be sent to him. We will not procure any bulls, briefs or rescripts whatsoever, for ourselves or others, from the bishop of Rome or his court, neither will we counsel any such to be procured by any other. And if any such shall be procured generally or specially for us without our knowledge, or any otherwise shall be granted, we will renounce the same, nor will we consent thereto, nor any way use the same, but will take care that the same be delivered to your majesty, or to your successors. And we do by this writing expressly renounce all exemption whereby, mediately or immediately, we are or have been subject to the bishop of Rome, highest prelate (as they call him), or to him by what name soever he is called, or to his church of Rome, and all his grants, privileges, gifts, whatsoever conferred; and we profess ourselves to be subjects and vassals to your majesty alone, and we do thereto submit ourselves, and promise only to be subject thereunto. Neither will we by ourselves, or by any other interposed person or persons, pay or cause to be paid, to the said bishop of Rome,

or to his messengers, orators, collectors, or legates, any procuration, pension, portion, taxes, or any other sum of moneys, by what name soever it be called. Moreover, to confirm this our covenant, we profess and undertake, and in the word of a priest, and under the fidelity due to your majesty and our own conscience before God, we promise, that, against this our aforesaid profession and undertaking, we will use no dispensation, no exception, no appellation or provocation, and no remedy of law or of fact; and if we have made any profession to the hindrance of this our profession and undertaking, we do revoke the same, for the time present, and for all time to come, and to renounce the same by these present letters; whereunto we have subscribed our names, either under our own hands, or the hands of our procurators at our request: and the same we have caused to be confirmed by the fixing of our common seal thereto, and by the mark and subscription of the public notary under written. Dated and acted in our Chapter-House.

REVIEW QUESTIONS

1. What are the implications of declaring Henry "on earth of the Church of England, immediately under Christ, supreme head"?

2. What did it mean to declare the papacy a "human tradition"?

3. How might the prohibition of appeals "to the said bishop of Rome" influence the lives of the common folk?

4. What economic motives might have inspired the Oath of Allegiance?

5. How does the Oath of Allegiance compare with the "Statement of Grievances" presented to the Diet of Worms in 1521?

15 ∽ RELIGIOUS WARS AND STATE BUILDING, 1540–1660

The challenge to the authority of classical culture that the new worlds posed, combined with the fragmentation of the medieval Christian Church, the "body of all believers," laid the foundation in the second half of the sixteenth century for profound crises of political and social order and of epistemology, the very foundation of human knowledge. In their efforts to describe what they saw in the Americas, European conquistadores and clergy were forced to adopt analogies: hundreds of species of plants and animals were not to be found in Pliny, the great and trusted botanist and zoologist of the ancient world, or in the Bible. The cultures of the Americas posed new models of social and political relations, opening new possibilities for the ordering of political relations and calling into question the very nature of political authority.

Within Europe, civil wars arose in the wake of the fragmentation of the Christian Church. The wars of religion in France, 1562–1598, led astute observers such as Montaigne to question the claim of each side to know the truth, and to question whether human reason was sufficient to discern the truth. In all the religious wars, beginning with the German Peasants' War of 1525 and culminating in the Thirty Years' War, 1618–1648, the social order was overthrown, as peasant killed lord, brother killed brother, son killed father, and neighbor killed neighbor. What was it to be human? To be savage? And where was God as Christian slaughtered Christian?

The crisis of the seventeenth century was not simply intellectual and spiritual but had real material aspects. The expansion of Europe into new worlds changed patterns of consumption and production, thus contributing to the overthrow of traditional work processes and lifestyles. It created a tremendous influx of wealth that aided the rise of new economic and political powers, both social *groups and nation-states, and that contributed to chronic inflation. Changes in society, economy, and politics created tensions that found expression in the violence of the period. Religious wars were seldom entirely religious in cause or in consequence. The almost constant march and countermarch of armies not only destroyed life and property but also disrupted agriculture and spread disease. The struggle for existence, difficult under the best of circumstances in the early modern period, became much more difficult in the age of crisis.*

By 1660, peasants had risen in unprecedented numbers against their lords; common Englishmen had executed their king; Europeans had witnessed multiple incidents of cannibalism in their own villages; and the medieval epistemology, that very base by which Europeans could be certain of the veracity of what they knew, had collapsed. New formulations were being tentatively put forward, but they did not yet replace the old certainties that had been irrecoverably lost.

JEAN BODIN

FROM *On Sovereignty*

Jean Bodin (1529–1596) was born a bourgeois in Angers. He entered a Carmelite monastery in 1545, apparently set on an ecclesiastical career, but obtained release from his vows around 1549. He pursued a course of study at the royal Collège de Quatre Langues in Paris. By 1550, he was well trained in humanist studies and went on to become one of the greatest scholars of his day. His continual search for religious truth placed him repeatedly under suspicion of heresy, but no clear evidence exists to support a conversion to Calvinism. Bodin continued his studies and attended the University of Toulouse, where he studied law during the 1550s. In 1561, he launched his public career by serving as an advocate before the parlement in Paris. Bodin soon rose to the attention of high officials and dignitaries and received special commissions from the king as early as 1570. In 1571, he entered the service of Francis, Duke of Alençon, a prince of the blood. During his service to Alençon, and in the aftermath of the St. Bartholomew's Day massacre, Bodin published his great work, Six livres de la république *(1576), a systematic exposition of public law. It included an absolutist theory of royal government, from which the following selection is drawn. Bodin's theory was based on the controversial notion, which proved highly influential in the development of royal absolutism, that sovereignty was indivisible and that high powers of government could not be shared by separate agents or agencies. His notion that all governmental powers were concentrated in the king of France, can be seen as a direct response to the anarchy of civil war that gripped the kingdom during the second half of the sixteenth century. In 1576, Bodin was chosen as a deputy for the Third Estate of the Estates-General of Blois. Though a royalist, Bodin opposed the civil wars that raged in France and became a leading spokesperson against royal requests for increased taxation and religious uniformity. It cost him royal favor and high office. With the death in 1584 of his patron, the duke of Alençon, Bodin's career in high politics ended. He retired to Laon, where he died.*

From *On Sovereignty,* by Jean Bodin, edited by Julian H. Franklin (Cambridge, Eng.: Cambridge University Press, 1992), pp. 46–50.

Book I

*   *   *

CHAPTER 8
ON SOVEREIGNTY

Sovereignty is the absolute and perpetual power of a commonwealth, which the Latins call *maiestas;* the Greeks *akra exousia, kurion arche,* and *kurion politeuma;* and the Italians *segnioria,* a word they use for private persons as well as for those who have full control of the state, while the Hebrews call it *tomech shévet*—that is, the highest power of command. We must now formulate a definition of sovereignty because no jurist or political philosopher has defined it, even though it is the chief point, and the one that needs most to be explained, in a treatise on the commonwealth. Inasmuch as we have said that a commonwealth is a just government, with sovereign power, of several households and of that which they have in common, we need to clarify the meaning of sovereign power.

*   *   *

We shall conclude, then, that the sovereignty of the monarch is in no way altered by the presence of the Estates. On the contrary, his majesty is all the greater and more illustrious when all his people publicly acknowledge him as sovereign, even though, in an assembly like this, princes, not wishing to rebuff their subjects, grant and pass many things that they would not consent to had

they not been overcome by the requests, petitions, and just complaints of a harassed and afflicted people which has most often been wronged without the knowledge of the prince, who sees and hears only through the eyes, ears, and reports of others.

We thus see that the main point of sovereign majesty and absolute power consists of giving the law to subjects in general without their consent. Not to go to other countries, we in this kingdom have often seen certain general customs repealed by edicts of our kings without hearing from the Estates when the injustice of the rules was obvious. Thus the custom concerning the inheritance by mothers of their children's goods, which was observed in this kingdom throughout the entire region governed by customary law, was changed without assembling either the general or local estates. Nor is this something new. In the time of King Philip the Fair, the general custom of the entire kingdom, by which the losing party in a case could not be required to pay expenses, was suppressed by an edict without assembling the Estates.

*   *   *

CHAPTER 10
ON THE TRUE MARKS OF SOVEREIGNTY

Since there is nothing greater on earth, after God, than sovereign princes, and since they have been established by Him as His lieutenants for commanding other men, we need to be precise about their status so that we may respect and revere their majesty in complete obedience, and do them honor in our thoughts and in our speech. Contempt for one's sovereign prince is contempt toward God, of whom he is the earthly image. That is why God, speaking to Samuel, from whom the people had demanded a different prince, said "It is me that they have wronged."

To be able to recognize such a person—that is, a sovereign—we have to know his attributes, which are properties not shared by subjects. For if they were shared, there would be no sovereign prince. Yet the best writers on this subject have not treated this point with the clarity it deserves, whether from flattery, fear, hatred, or forgetfulness.

We read that Samuel, after consecrating the king that God had designated, wrote a book about the rights of majesty. But the Hebrews have written that the kings suppressed his book so that they could tyrannize their subjects. Melanchthon thus went astray in thinking that the rights of majesty were the abuses and tyrannical practices that Samuel pointed out to the people in a speech. "Do you wish to know," said Samuel, "the ways of tyrants? It is to seize the goods of subjects to dispose of at his pleasure, and to seize their women and their children in order to abuse them and to make them slaves." The word *mishpotim* as it is used in this passage does not mean rights, but rather practices and ways of doing things. Otherwise this good prince, Samuel, would have contradicted himself. For when accounting to the people for the stewardship that God had given him, he said, "Is there anyone among you who can say that I ever took gold or silver from him, or any present whatsoever?" And thereupon the whole people loudly praised him for never having done a wrong or taken anything from anyone no matter who.

*　　*　　*

We may thus conclude that the first prerogative of a sovereign prince is to give law to all in general and each in particular. But this is not sufficient. We have to add "without the consent of any other, whether greater, equal, or below him." For if the prince is obligated to make no law without the consent of a superior, he is clearly a subject; if of an equal, he has an associate; if of subjects, such as the senate or the people, he is not sovereign. The names of grandees that one finds affixed to edicts are not put there to give the law its force, but to witness it and to add weight to it so that the enactment will be more acceptable. For there are very ancient edicts, extant at Saint Denys in France, issued by Philip I and Louis the Fat in 1060 and 1129 respectively, to which the seals of their queens Anne and Alix, and of Robert and Hugh, were affixed. For Louis the Fat, it was year twelve of his reign; for Adelaide, year six.

When I say that the first prerogative of sovereignty is to give law to all in general and to each in particular, the latter part refers to privileges, which are in the jurisdiction of sovereign princes to the exclusion of all others. I call it a privilege when a law is made for one or a few private individuals, no matter whether it is for the profit or the loss of the person with respect to whom it is decreed. Thus Cicero said, *Privilegium de meo capite latum est.* "They have passed," he said, "a capital privilege against me." He is referring to the authorization to put him on trial decreed against him by the commoners at the request of the tribune Clodius. He calls this the *lex Clodia* in many places, and he bitterly protests that privileges could be decreed only by the great Estates of the people as it was laid down by the laws of the Twelve Tables in the words: *Privilegia, nisi comitiis centuriatis irroganto, qui secus faxit capital esto.*[1] And all those who have written of regalian rights agree that only the sovereign can grant privileges, exemptions, and immunities, and grant dispensations from edicts and ordinances. In monarchies, however, privileges last only for the lifetime of the monarchs, as the emperor Tiberius, Suetonius reports, informed all those who had received privileges from Augustus.

*　　*　　*

---

[1] "Let no privileges be imposed except in the *comita centuriata;* let him who has done otherwise be put to death."

Book II

CHAPTER 5

WHETHER IT IS LAWFUL TO MAKE AN ATTEMPT
UPON THE TYRANT'S LIFE AND TO NULLIFY AND
REPEAL HIS ORDINANCES AFTER HE IS DEAD

Ignorance of the exact meaning of the term "tyrant" has led many people astray, and has been the cause of many inconveniences. We have said that a tyrant is someone who makes himself into a sovereign prince by his own authority—without election, or right of succession, or lot, or a just war, or a special calling from God. This is what is understood by tyrant in the writings of the ancients and in the laws that would have him put to death. Indeed, the ancients established great prizes and rewards for those who killed tyrants, offering titles of nobility, prowess, and chivalry to them along with statues and honorific titles, and even all the tyrant's goods, because they were taken as true liberators of the fatherland, or of the motherland, as the Cretans say. In this they did not distinguish, between a good and virtuous prince and a bad and wicked one, for no one has the right to seize the sovereignty and make himself the master of those who had been his companions, no matter what pretenses of justice and virtue he may offer. In strictest law, furthermore, use of the prerogatives reserved to sovereignty is punishable by death. Hence if a subject seeks, by whatever means, to invade the state and steal it from his king or, in a democracy or aristocracy, to turn himself from a fellow-citizen into lord and master, he deserves to be put to death. In this respect our question does not pose any difficulty.

*   *   *

At this point there are many questions one may ask, such as whether a tyrant, who I said may be justly killed without form or shape of trial, becomes legitimate if, after having encroached upon sovereignty by force or fraud, he has himself elected by the Estates. For it seems that the solemn act of election is an authentic ratification of the tyranny, an indication that the people have found it to their liking. But I say that it is nevertheless permissible to kill him, and to do so by force unless the tyrant, stripping off his authority, has given up his arms and put power back into the hands of the people in order to have its judgment. What tyrants force upon a people stripped of power cannot be called consent. Sulla, for example, had himself made dictator for eighty years by the Valerian law, which he got published with a powerful army camped inside the city of Rome. But Cicero said that this was not a law. Another example is Caesar, who had himself made permanent dictator by the Servian law; and yet another is Cosimo de Medici who, having an army inside Florence, had himself elected duke. When objections were raised, he set off a volley of gunfire in front of the palace, which induced the lords and magistrates to get on with it more quickly.

*   *   *

So much then for the tyrant, whether virtuous or wicked, who makes himself a sovereign lord on his own authority. But the chief difficulty arising from our question is whether a sovereign prince who has come into possession of the state by way of election, or lot, or right of succession, or just war, or by a special calling from God, can be killed if he is cruel, oppressive, or excessively wicked. For that is the meaning given to the word tyrant. Many doctors and theologians, who have touched upon this question, have resolved that it is permissible to kill a tyrant without distinction, and some, putting two words together that are incompatible, have spoken of a king-tyrant (*roi tyran*), which has caused the ruin of some very fine and flourishing monarchies.

But to decide this question properly we need to distinguish between a prince who is absolutely sovereign and one who is not, and between subjects and foreigners. It makes a great difference whether we say that a tyrant can be lawfully killed by a foreign prince or by a subject. For just as it is glorious and becoming, when the gates of justice have been shut, for someone, whoever he may be, to use force in defense of the goods, honor, and life of those who have been unjustly oppressed—as Moses did when he saw his brother being beaten and mistreated and had no way of getting justice—so is it a most beautiful and magnificent thing for a prince to take up arms in order to avenge an entire people unjustly oppressed by a tyrant's cruelty, as did Hercules, who traveled all over the world exterminating tyrant-monsters and was deified for his great feats. The same was done by Dion, Timoleon, Aratus, and other generous princes, who obtained the title of chastisers and correctors of tyrants. This, furthermore, was the sole cause for which Tamerlane, prince of the Tartars, declared war on Bajazet, who was then besieging Constantinople, Tamerlane saying that he had come to punish him for tyranny and to deliver the afflicted peoples. He defeated Bajazet in a battle fought on the plateau of Mount Stella, and after he had killed and routed three hundred thousand Turks, he had the tyrant chained inside a cage until he died. In this case it makes no difference whether this virtuous prince proceeds against a tyrant by force, deception, or judicial means. It is however true that if a virtuous prince has seized a tyrant, he will obtain more honor by putting him on trial and punishing him as a murderer, parricide, and thief, rather than acting against him by the common law of peoples (*droit des gens*).

But as for subjects, and what they may do, one has to know whether the prince is absolutely sovereign, or is properly speaking not a sovereign. For if he is not absolutely sovereign, it follows necessarily that sovereignty is in the people or the aristocracy. In this latter case there is no doubt that it is permissible to proceed against the tyrant either by way of law if one can prevail against him, or else by way of fact and open force, if one cannot otherwise have justice. Thus the Senate took the first way against Nero, the second against Maximinus inasmuch as the Roman emperors were no more than princes of the republic, in the sense of first persons and chief citizens, with sovereignty remaining in the people and the Senate.

*   *   *

But if the prince is sovereign absolutely, as are the genuine monarchs of France, Spain, England, Scotland, Ethiopia, Turkey, Persia, and Moscovy—whose power has never been called into question and whose sovereignty has never been shared with subjects—then it is not the part of any subject individually, or all of them in general, to make an attempt on the honor or the life of the monarch, either by way of force or by way of law, even if he has committed all the misdeeds, impieties, and cruelties that one could mention. As to the way of law, the subject has no right of jurisdiction over his prince, on whom all power and authority to command depends; he not only can revoke all the power of his magistrates, but in his presence, all the power and jurisdiction of all magistrates, guilds and corporations, Estates and communities, cease, as we have said and will say again even more elaborately in the proper place. And if it is not permissible for a subject to pass judgment on his prince, or a vassal on his lord, or a servant on his master—in short, if it is not permissible to proceed against one's king by way of law—how could it be licit to do so by way of force? For the question here is not to discover who is the strongest, but only whether it is permissible in law, and whether a subject has the power to condemn his sovereign prince.

A subject is guilty of treason in the first degree not only for having killed a sovereign prince, but also for attempting it, advising it, wishing it, or even thinking it. And the law finds this so monstrous [as to subject it to a special rule of sentencing]. Ordinarily, if someone who is accused, seized, and convicted dies before he has been sentenced, his personal status is not diminished, no matter what his crime, even if it was treason. But treason in the highest degree can never be purged by the death of the person accused of it, and even someone who was never accused is considered in law as having been already sentenced. And although evil thoughts are not subject to punishment, anyone who has thought of making an attempt on the life of his sovereign prince is held to be guilty of a capital crime, no matter whether he repented of it. In fact there was a gentleman from Normandy who confessed to a Franciscan friar that he had wanted to kill King Francis I but had repented of this evil wish. The Franciscan gave him absolution, but still told the king about it; he had the gentleman sent before the Parlement of Paris to stand trial, where he was condemned to death by its verdict and thereupon executed. And one cannot say that the court acted from fear, in view of the fact that it often refused to verify edicts and letters patent even when the king commanded it. And in Paris a man, named Caboche, who was completely mad and out of his senses, drew a sword against King Henry II without any effect or even attempt. He too was condemned to die without consideration of his insanity, which the law ordinarily excuses no matter what murder or crime the madman may have committed.

*   *   *

As for Calvin's remark that if there existed in these times magistrates especially constituted for the defense of the people and to restrain the licentiousness of kings, like the ephors in Sparta, the tribunes in Rome, and the demarchs in Athens, then those magistrates should resist, oppose, and prevent their licentiousness and cruelty—it clearly shows that it is never licit, in a proper monarchy, to attack a sovereign king, or defend one's self against him, or to make an attempt upon his life or honor, for he spoke only of democratic and aristocratic states. I have shown above that the kings of Sparta were but simple senators and captains. And when he speaks of the Estates, he says "possible," not daring to be definite. In any event there is an important difference between attacking the honor of one's prince and resisting his tyranny, between killing one's king and opposing his cruelty.

We thus read that the Protestant princes of Germany, before taking up arms against the emperor, asked Martin Luther if it were permissible. He frankly replied that it was not permissible no matter how great the charge of impiety or tyranny. But he was not heeded; and the outcome of the

affair was miserable, bringing with it the ruin of some great and illustrious houses of Germany. *Quia nulla iusta causa videri potest,* said Cicero, *adversus patriam arma capiendi.*[2] Admittedly, it is quite certain that the sovereignty of the German Empire does not lie in the person of the emperor, as we shall explain in due course. But since he is the chief, they could have taken up arms against him only with the consent of the Estates or its majority, which was not obtained. It would have been even less permissible against a sovereign prince.

I can give no better parallel than that of a son with respect to his father. The law of God says that he who speaks evil of his father or his mother shall be put to death. If the father be a murderer, a thief, a traitor to his country, a person who has committed incest or parricide, a blasphemer, an atheist, and anything else one wants to add, I confess that the entire gamut of penalties will not suffice for his punishment; but I say that it is not for his son to lay hands on him, *quia nulla tanta impietas, nullum tantum factum est quod sit parricidio vindicandum,*[3] as it was put by an orator of ancient times. And yet Cicero, taking up this question, says that love of country is even greater. Hence the prince of our country, being ordained and sent by God, is always more sacred and ought to be more inviolable than a father.

I conclude then that it is never permissible for a subject to attempt anything against a sovereign prince, no matter how wicked and cruel a tyrant he may be. It is certainly permissible not to obey him in anything that is against the law of God or nature—to flee, to hide, to evade his blows, to suffer death rather than make any attempt upon his life or honor. For oh, how many tyrants there would be if it were lawful to kill them! He who taxes too heavily would be a tyrant, as the vulgar understand it; he who gives commands that the

---

[2]"Because there can never be a just cause to take up arms against one's country."

[3]"Because there is no impiety so great, and no crime so great that it ought to be avenged by patricide."

people do not like would be a tyrant, as Aristotle defined a tyrant in the *Politics;* he who maintains guards for his security would be a tyrant; he who punishes conspirators against his rule would be a tyrant. How then should good princes be secure in their lives? I would not say that it is illicit for other princes to proceed against tyrants by force of arms, as I have stated, but it is not for subjects.

*   *   *

REVIEW QUESTIONS

1. What, according to Bodin, is the definition of sovereignty?
2. In describing its prerogatives, would Bodin have agreed with Machiavelli?
3. Can sovereignty be mixed? Why?
4. Is it permissible to resist a tyrant?
5. Can a sovereign ruler be a tyrant?
6. May one resist a sovereign?

FROM "Instructions of the Magistracy of Health in Florence for Justices in the Countryside * * * "

In 1348, an epidemic of bubonic plague erupted in the city of Genoa and swept across Europe. The effects were catastrophic. Population dropped sharply, especially in crowded cities. Without the advantages of medical science or even the rudiments of public hygiene, nothing could be done to control or resist the contagion. In Florence, the number of inhabitants dropped from about 100,000 in 1348 to less than 50,000 by 1351. Population loss translated into lost production and lost consumption. Markets shrank, industries declined, and firms went bankrupt. Serious social upheavals accompanied economic decline. Antagonism and violence followed disease and deprivation. France was shaken by the peasant revolt known as the Jacquerie (1358). Recovery proved slow and sporadic. Plague recurred intermittently and remained a threat, especially to cities, until the seventeenth century, and contributed notably to the general crisis of that period. In 1630, when plague raged in Florence and the surrounding countryside once again, the administration of the Grand Duchy of Tuscany released the following "Instructions of the Health Board of Florence for the Justices of the Countryside in Case of Infectious Sicknesses that Might be Discovered in the Areas under Their Jurisdiction." These were guidelines for fighting the disease. They reflect the seriousness with which the authorities viewed

THE SURRENDER OF BREDA (1635)

DIEGO VELÁZQUEZ

One of a series of marshal portraits by Velázquez, The Surrender of Breda *records the moment in which Dutch governor Justin de Nassau symbolically surrendered the keys of the Brabantine fortress town of Breda to Ambrosio de Spinola, commander of the besieging Spanish forces. The actual capitulation took place three days earlier. Spinola had offered honorable terms in order to end twelve months of determined resistance. The depiction of peaceful amity and order between bitter foes contrasted sharply with the harsh realities of warfare in early modern Europe. What might have been Velázquez's purpose, as a painter at the court of Spain, in capturing the surrender of Breda? What might be the symbolic intent of Spinola's (figure receiving key, right center) graceful smile and the peaceful attitudes of the* tercios *(soldiers with vertical lances, extreme right)? How and why does* The Surrender of Breda *describe and distort the realities of statecraft and warfare in the seventeenth century?*

epidemic disease, as a threat to the political, social, and economic order, and the
altogether insufficient measures they took against it.

From *Faith, Reason, and the Plague,* by Carlo Cipolla (Ithaca, N.Y.: Cornell University Press, 1981), pp. 87–92.

It being the task of all justices, criminal as well as civil, to watch over everything that concerns good government, they shall in particular, above all else, have an eye to good regulations regarding the interests of the Public Health, and for this purpose shall make shift to have notice of all cases of sickness believed to be infectious that should chance to occur in their jurisdictions and as soon as they come by news of any case whether of sickness or death, they shall observe the following and proceed to carry out the orders herein described against any persons whatsoever, even if they should be Florentine citizens or others in other ways privileged.

First, they shall give orders to whomever is concerned that those dead of suspected plague are not to be buried in the churches but in the countryside far from the high roads, and a hundred armslengths from the houses, and in a grave at least three armslengths deep with the benediction that will seem fit to the priests of the parish church where such deaths may be, and if there are no gravediggers, have the corpse put on a ladder and handling it as little as possible, carried to the grave, and, where possible, put on the said corpse lime and then earth.

As soon as the news arrives of the sickness being discovered in whatsoever house, the Justice shall give orders that the sick man be carried to the pesthouse, if it is near enough for him to be carried there.

Then he will have orders given to the occupants of the house where the sickness has been, if they are tenants, that they must not leave the house and the fields where they are, that they must not associate with anybody, and must not give away anything from their house or fields under pain, as transgressors, of their lives and confiscation of their goods.

If the sick of the said houses should be far from the pesthouses so that they could not with ease be carried thither, give in any case orders that none must leave home or fields, as above, being tenants.

If the said sick are subtenants or live in houses without land the order must be given to all the occupants, with the said penalty, not to leave the house.

As the said persons under orders need to be sustained with victuals, if they are tenants, give orders to the owners of the land that they supply the said victuals, giving them credit to repay at the harvests or in some other way.

If they are farmworkers, or occupants of houses without land, or poor, give order to the Chamberlain of the Council that he supply them with the necessary victuals from some innkeeper or shopkeeper nearby to the amount of eight *soldi* a day per head.

If the landlords of the said sick tenants should not live in the same jurisdiction so that the order cannot be given to them, then have the Chamberlain of the Council supply the said expenses for victuals for the said eight *soldi* a day for each one of those under orders as above.

And they shall give orders that the victuals be brought to those under orders, not in money, but in bread and eatables by the nearest innkeepers or shopkeepers or others they deem suitable, and such things should be delivered through the windows or in some other way such that whoever brings them does not approach and does not converse with the suspect cases and those under orders, and for this debt they must be reimbursed by the owners of the land who in turn shall reimburse themselves from the peasants on whom the money is being spent.

The said Justices will give order to the Health

Deputies nearest the dwelling of the suspects, or to other of their officials, who will from time to time go and inspect the affected areas and ensure that victuals are supplied them as above and that they do not leave the house and land respectively assigned to them as the place of disinfection, which they must do, proceeding against transgressors with every rigour, having them isolated and the doors of their houses nailed up; and then after the usual disinfection have them put into prison and advise the Magistrate of the Health Board of Florence and await orders from him, which will be given.

The quarantine and disinfection that are to be carried out in each house must be of twenty-two days at least from the day that the last person sick with the suspect sickness had died or recovered; after this period the said houses can be opened and freed.

It must be noted that before the houses closed or under orders are opened even where none of the occupants is left, it is very fitting and necessary that first the said houses be perfumed and purified in the following manner and with the diligence described, to wit:

First, whoever enters the house to perfume it should carry in his hand brushwood, or something like it, lighted and burning and should go upstairs with it and make fire with flames in the rooms. Then shut the windows tight and make smoke with sulphur all through the house.

Sweep the floors, benches, and walls well, and if possible, whitewash the house or, at least, wash the walls down with alkaline solution using a whitewashing brush. The woodwork should also be washed down with alkaline solution. Put the linen cloths to soak in water and wash the mattresses and put other cloths where they can get air, and keep them aired for many, many days before they are used again. And those that were used directly by the infected person are to be burnt if they be woollens or linen. The room where the dead or sick person had been must, for three days after it has come empty, be washed out with vinegar, and have it swept thoroughly every day, and the first time, scatter lime around the room and throw

vinegar over it until it has smoked and burnt itself out.

And since it often chances that the sick are peasants far away from lands and castles and from the advantage of being able to have physicians and medicines, make very sure that they know of some easy medicines proposed to the Magistrates of the Health Board as being easy by their physicians, with which the occupants of the said houses under orders and the sick themselves may make their own medicines.

And they shall do their utmost to save those, above all, who are healthy in the said closed houses; and for this purpose the latter, every morning, shall take some Venice treacle, oil themselves with oil against the poison, and other like preservatives, and if they have none of these, shall take nuts, and dried figs, and rue and, early in the morning, eat them or other things that are meant for the purpose.

Every morning the sick shall take a five-ounce glass of very hot chick-pea or goat's-rue juice, and shall cover themselves well so as to sweat; they must be informed that sweating is an excellent remedy for the infectious sickness that is latent. That they strive to bring out this sweat, however, with fire or with putting cloths on or as best they can.

Oil the swellings that appear with oil of white lilies or of camomile or flax seeds and place upon them a little wool soaked in one of these oils.

If these swellings do not come out, go about to make them do so with a cupping glass or by putting on them white onion roasted on the embers and mixed with Venice treacle.

If a blister or small carbuncle be found, put upon it devil's bit or scabious grass crushed between two stones, and, to remove the scab, put a little chicken fat on it and slit with a razor and then put a little Venice treacle on it. Around the small carbuncle put pomegranate juice together with the pomegranate seeds, well peeled and crushed together.

The sick must take good care of themselves, eating meat, eggs, and good things; they must abstain from wine, and drink boiled water with the soft part of a loaf and a few coriander seeds in it.

Note must be taken of these medicines for the use of those who cannot have, as above, the services of physicians or other medicines, those, that is, like the poor peasants who live in the countryside, etc.

REVIEW QUESTIONS

1. Why should those concerned with good government pay particular attention to public health?
2. What might be the relation of civic order to health?
3. What effect do you suppose quarantining had on civic order and public health?
4. What do you learn about the understanding of disease in early modern Europe?
5. How is illness a social issue?

GIANFRANCESCO MOROSINI

FROM A Venetian Ambassador's Report on Spain

The struggle for supremacy in northern Italy, which marked the last half of the fifteenth century, gave rise to a new form of diplomacy, structures and procedures that would be fundamental to relations among all modern states. Requiring continuous contact and communication, Renaissance states turned to permanent diplomacy, distinguished by the use of accredited resident ambassadors rather than ad hoc missions of medieval legates. The tasks of a permanent ambassador were to represent his government at state ceremonies, to gather information, and, occasionally, to enter into negotiations. Nowhere was this system more fully and expertly articulated than by the Republic of Venice in the late fifteenth and sixteenth centuries. Ambassadors were chosen with unusual care from the most prominent families of the city. They were highly educated, and their duties were carefully defined.

Among the ambassadors' duties were weekly dispatches reporting all matters of any interest to Venice. These reports were regularly read and debated in the senate, which replied with questions, instructions, and information of its own. As a result, Venetian ambassadors were among the most skilled and respected in early modern Europe. Their reports remain a singularly important source for the history of that period. Gianfrancesco Morosini is, perhaps, not typical among Venetian ambassadors. He had a particularly sharp eye for social structures and details. His reports to his principals, therefore, are unusually rich in observations on the states, in this case Spain, to which he was posted. He documented the distribution of wealth in Spain, the wealth and feebleness of its aristocrats, and the poverty and incompetence of its commoners. By so doing, he offers a firsthand account of the Spanish paradox, its power and its impotence.

From *Pursuit of Power: Venetian Ambassadors' Reports on Spain, Turkey and France in the Age of Phillip II, 1560–1600,* by James C. Davis (New York: HarperCollins, 1970), pp. 72–76, 78–79.

Most of the men in this country are small in stature and dark in complexion, haughty if they belong to the upper classes or prudently humble if they are common people, and unsuited for any kind of work. As farmers they are the most lackadaisical in the world, and as artisans they are so lazy and slow that work that would be done anywhere else in one month in Spain requires four. They are such stupid craftsmen that in all their provinces you can hardly find a building or anything else of interest except for antiquities done in Roman times or works built by the Moorish kings. Most of the Spanish live in houses so ineptly built of inferior materials that it is remarkable if one lasts as long as the man who built it. The cities are badly run and dirty; they throw all their refuse into the public streets instead of having the conveniences in their houses which are used in Italy and other parts of the world. They give no thought to food supplies; as a result the common people often have to fight each other to get bread, not so much because there is a shortage of grain as because there is no official whose job it is to make sure that there is bread. ＊ ＊ ＊

＊   ＊   ＊

Spain might be quick to rebel if there were a leader courageous enough to direct a revolt. All of the people are discontented with their king and his current ministers. The nobles are dissatisfied because they are virtually ignored, and everyone else because they pay such unbearably heavy taxes; no other people in the world carry such a tax burden as the Castilians. True, the Aragonese and Castilians have ended their quarrels and there have been no more of those rebellions of the cities against the kings which happened in the reign of the emperor Charles V, and earlier during the reign of King Ferdinand. But when the king dies —or if he should get into serious problems— these and even more unpleasant humors might recur in the body politic. There would be a special danger if the rebels used religion as a battle standard, since religious faith lends itself very well to subverting and destroying monarchies. Spain would be particularly susceptible because there are so many there who are Moors at heart, many others who secretly remain Jews, and even some heretics. They are all very cautious because they fear the Inquisition, a high tribunal so powerful and harsh that everyone is terrified of it. Without the Inquisition Spain would be more lost than Germany and England, even though the Spanish look at first glance like the most devout Catholics in the world.

Most Spaniards are either very rich or very poor, and there would seem to be a cause-and-effect relationship between the wealth of some and the poverty of the rest. It is as if four men had to divide this chamber among them. If one man took three-quarters there would be very little to divide among the other three. The Spanish clergy is very rich; the church in Toledo alone has revenues of 400,000 ducats a year, and all the other fifty-seven bishoprics are also very wealthy. The incomes of the churches have been estimated at four million in gold per year. Then there are twenty-two dukes, forty-seven counts, and thirty-six marquises in those lands, and their incomes total nearly three million in gold a year. The richest of all is said to be the duke of Medina Sidonia, the governor-elect of Milan, whose income exceeds 150,000 ducats a year.

*   *   *

Because the king does not use them in his service, very few of the grandees know anything about running a government, nor do they know anything else. They consider it beneath them to leave their estates unless to take major government positions; on the other hand, they are not suited for life on their own estates. They do not read; they do not discuss anything of value; they simply live in ignorance. The only noteworthy thing about them is a certain loftiness and dignity which in Italy we call "Spanish composure" and which makes all foreigners hate them. They let it be understood that not only is there no other people which bears comparison with them, but that everyone should be grateful to be ruled by them. And they do not forget to use this haughtiness even among themselves. Before addressing a person as "Señor," "Vuestra Merced," "you," . . . or "el," they give the matter a great deal of thought, because they believe that any distinction they confer on someone else reduces their own importance.

Because they remain on their own lands they have seen and they know nothing about the world. Their lack of schooling makes them ignorant and their lack of contacts with others makes them arrogant. This arrogance is very common among the young people, especially those who are surrounded by great wealth. Revered and deferred to by their own domestic servants, they soon come to believe that everyone should behave that way toward them, and that no one is so important as they. The result is that they look down on others —indeed, they often despise them—and only late or never do they realize their error, when they have been damaged and shamed.

The Spanish grandees consider attending to business matters just as ridiculous as book reading; both pursuits are detestable, or at least completely at odds with the life of a knight. And yet they do not take much pleasure in horsemanship. Instead they pass the time idly, even depravedly. The reasons for this are that they have been poorly brought up and they believe that exercise in Spain is "unhealthy," and also that the king lives in great seclusion and has no interest in watching tournaments.

*   *   *

The nobles and other aristocrats are all tax exempt; they pay the king no head or property tax at all. Their only obligation is to serve in his army at their own expense, and even then only when it is a question of defending Spain from attack. They are very firm and determined about guarding their tax immunity, just as the Aragonese defend all of their liberties. Once when the government tried to impose a very light tax on them they raised such an uproar that the matter was dropped.

The nobles and grandees of Castile have so little legal authority in their own jurisdictions that most of them have courts only of the first instance; and few of their courts may hear appeals. All appeals eventually go to the chancelleries and the royal council. Their own vassals can have them summoned to these higher courts on the slightest of grounds, and they are often treated worse there than the lowliest subjects. This happens both because such is the king's wish and because the judges usually come from the lower classes. The reason for this is that judges have to be university graduates; since the nobles consider it beneath them to study anything, the power of the courts goes by default into the hands of plebeians. Professional learning is the only route by which men from the lower classes can rise to important posts. This explains why not only the law courts but almost all of the bishoprics are also in the hands of commoners, who are enemies of the nobility. This in turn is another of the grudges the upper classes have against the present regime. At one time most of the bishoprics were given as a matter of course to younger sons of the grandees, as a way of compensating them for not being the heirs. Despite all I have said, however, the king still has ample means to gratify the nobles, since he has many knighthoods in the military orders to distribute, all of which may be conferred only on nobles.

Some of these have incomes of up to twelve thousand ducats.

*   *   *

REVIEW QUESTIONS

1. What were the sources of Spain's declining power according to Morosini?

2. How does Morosini depict the nobility?
3. What are their values?
4. What does Morosini suggest is significantly undervalued by the Spanish nobility? Why?
5. What do we learn about the distribution of authority in Spain?
6. How are political decisions made?

REGINALD SCOT

FROM *Discoverie of Witchcraft*

Reginald Scot (1538–1599) was a Kentish squire who witnessed a number of fraudulent accusations of witchcraft in the villages of his shire during the reign of Elizabeth I. In 1584 he wrote his Discoverie of Witchcraft, *which contains a remarkable exposition of magical elements in medieval Catholicism and a protest against the persecution of harmless old women. Scot doubted that God could ever have allowed witches to exercise supernatural powers, much less demand that they be persecuted for it. In this regard, he deserves to be ranked among the skeptics on the question of witchcraft, although he never denied the existence of witches. According to Scot, all "witches" fell into one of four categories. First were the innocent, those falsely accused. Second were the deluded, those convinced through their own misery that they were witches. Third were the malefactors, those who harmed people and damaged property, though not by supernatural means. Fourth were imposters, those who posed as witches and conjurers. Scot denied that any of these "witches" had access to supernatural powers. Malefactors and imposters were, in fact, the witches named in the Bible as not being suffered to live. They were the only witches Scot admitted. His work is said to have made a great impression in the magistracy and clergy of his day. Nonetheless, his remained a minority opinion. Most contemporaries understood as tantamount to atheism any denial of the reality of spirits or the possibility of the supernatural. The persecution of witches continued unabated into the eighteenth century; many thousands, mostly harmless old women, fell victim to the rage.*

From *Discoverie of Witchcraft, 1584,* edited by Hugh Ross Wilkinson (Carbondale: Southern Illinois Press, 1962).

*   *   *

The inconvenience growing by mens credulitie herein, with a reproofe of some churchmen, which are inclined to the common conceived opinion of witches omnipotencie, and a familiar example thereof. But the world is now so bewitched and over-run with this fond error, that even where a man shuld seeke comfort and counsell, there shall hee be sent (in case of necessitie) from God to the divell; and from the Physician, to the coosening witch, who will not sticke to take upon hir, by wordes to heale the lame (which was proper onelie to Christ: and to them whom he assisted with his divine power) yea, with hir familiar & charmes she will take upon hir to cure the blind: though in the tenth of S. *Johns* Gospell it be written, that the divell cannot open the eies of the blind. And they attaine such credit as I have heard (to my greefe) some of the ministerie affirme, that they have had in their parish at one instant, xvii. or xviii. witches: meaning such as could worke miracles superna-turallie. Whereby they manifested as well their infidelitie and ignorance, in conceiving Gods word; as their negligence and error in instructing their flocks. For they themselves might under-stand, and also teach their parishoners, that God onelie worketh great woonders; and that it is he which sendeth such punishments to the wicked, and such trials to the elect: according to the saieng of the Prophet *Haggai*, I smote you with blasting and mildeaw, and with haile, in all the labours of your hands; and yet you turned not unto me, saith the Lord. And therefore saith the same Prophet in another place; You have sowen much, and bring in little. And both in *Joel* and *Leviticus,* the like phrases and proofes are used and made. But more shalbe said of this hereafter.

*   *   *

At the assises holden at *Rochester,* Anno 1581, one *Margaret Simons,* the wife of *John Simons,* of *Brenchlie* in *Kent,* was araigned for witchcraft, at the instigation and complaint of divers fond and malicious persons; and speciallie by the meanes of one *John Ferrall* vicar of that parish: with whom I talked about that matter, and found him both fon-dlie assotted in the cause, and enviouslie bent to-wards hir: and (which is worse) as unable to make a good account of his faith, as shee whom he ac-cused. That which he, for his part, laid to the poore womans charge, was this.

His sonne (being an ungratious boie, and prentise to one *Robert Scotchford* clothier, dwelling in that parish of *Brenchlie*) passed on a daie by hir house; at whome by chance hir little dog barked. Which thing the boie taking in evill part, drewe his knife, & pursued him therewith even to hir doore: whom she rebuked with some such words as the boie disdained, & yet neverthelesse would not be persuaded to depart in a long time. At the last he returned to his maisters house, and within five or sixe daies fell sicke. Then was called to mind the fraie betwixt the dog and the boie: in-somuch as the vicar (who thought himselfe so privileged, as he little mistrusted that God would visit his children with sicknes) did so calculate; as he found, partlie through his owne judgement, and partlie (as he himselfe told me) by the relation of other witches, that his said sonne was by hir bewitched. Yea, he also told me, that this his sonne (being as it were past all cure) received perfect health at the hands of another witch.

He proceeded yet further against hir, affirm-ing, that alwaies in his parish church, when he desired to read most plainelie, his voice so failed him, as he could scant be heard at all. Which hee could impute, he said, to nothing else, but to hir inchantment. When I advertised the poore woman hereof, as being desirous to heare what she could saie for hir selfe; she told me, that in verie deed his voice did much faile him, speciallie when he strained himselfe to speake lowdest. How beit, she said that at all times his voice was hoarse and lowe: which thing I perceived to be true. But sir, said she, you shall understand, that this our vicar is diseased with such a kind of hoarsenesse, as di-vers of our neighbors in this parish, not long since, doubted that he had the French pox; & in that respect utterly refused to communicate with him: untill such time as (being therunto injoined by M. D. *Lewen* the Ordinarie) he had brought frō

London a certificat, under the hands of two physicians, that his hoarsenes proceeded from a disease in the lungs. Which certificat he published in the church, in the presence of the whole congregation: and by this meanes hee was cured, or rather excused of the shame of his disease. And this I knowe to be true by the relation of divers honest men of that parish. And truelie, if one of the Jurie had not beene wiser than the other, she had beene condemned thereupon, and upon other as ridiculous matters as this. For the name of a witch is so odious, and hir power so feared among the common people, that if the honestest bodie living chance to be arraigned thereupon, she shall hardlie escape condemnation.

A Confutation of the Common Conceived Opinion of Witches and Witchcraft, and How Detestable a Sinne It Is to Repaire to Them for Counsell or Helpe in Time of Affliction

But whatsoever is reported or conceived of such manner of witchcrafts, I dare avow to be false and fabulous (coosinage, dotage, and poisoning excepted:) neither is there any mention made of these kind of witches in the Bible. If Christ had knowne them, he would not have pretermitted to invaie against their presumption, in taking upon them his office: as, to heale and cure diseases; and to worke such miraculous and supernaturall things, as whereby he himselfe was speciallie knowne, beleeved, and published to be God; his actions and cures consisting (in order and effect) according to the power of our witchmoongers imputed to witches. Howbeit, if there be any in these daies afflicted in such strange sort, as Christs cures and patients are described in the new testament to have beene: we flie from trusting in God to trusting in witches, who doo not onelie in their coosening art take on them the office of Christ in this behalfe; but use his verie phrase of speech to such idolators, as com to seeke divine assistance at their hands, saieng; Go thy waies, thy sonne or thy daughter, &c. shall doo well, and be whole.

*   *   *

In like manner I say, he that attributeth to a witch, such divine power, as dulie and onelie apperteineth unto GOD (which all witchmongers doo) is in hart a blasphemer, an idolater, and full of grosse impietie, although he neither go nor send to hir for assistance.

A Further Confutation of Witches Miraculous and Omnipotent Power, by Invincible Reasons and Authorities, with Dissuasions from Such Fond Credulitie

If witches could doo anie such miraculous things, as these and other which are imputed to them, they might doo them againe and againe, at anie time or place, or at anie mans desire: for the divell is as strong at one time as at another, as busie by daie as by night, and readie enough to doo all mischeefe, and careth not whom he abuseth. And in so much as it is confessed, by the most part of witchmoongers themselves, that he knoweth not the cogitation of mans heart, he should (me thinks) sometimes appeere unto honest and credible persons, in such grosse and corporall forme, as it is said he dooth unto witches: which you shall never heare to be justified by one sufficient witnesse. For the divell indeed entreth into the mind, and that waie seeketh mans confusion.

The art alwaies presupposeth the power; so as, if they saie they can doo this or that, they must shew how and by what meanes they doo it; as neither the witches, nor the witchmoongers are able to doo. For to everie action is required the facultie and abilitie of the agent or dooer; the aptnes of the patient or subject; and a convenient and possible application. Now the witches are mortall, and their power dependeth upon the analogie and consonancie of their minds and bodies; but with their minds they can but will and understand; and with their bodies they can doo no more, but as the bounds and ends of terrene sense will suffer: and therefore their power extendeth not to doo such miracles, as surmounteth their owne sense, and the understanding of others which are wiser than they; so as here wanteth the vertue and power of the efficient. And in reason, there can be no more vertue in the thing caused, than in the cause, or that which proceedeth of or from the benefit of the cause. And we see, that ignorant and impotent women, or witches, are the causes of incantations and charmes; wherein we shall perceive there is none effect, if we will credit our owne experience and sense unabused, the rules of philosophie, or the word of God. For alas! What an unapt instrument is a toothles, old, impotent, and unweldie woman to flie in the aier? Truelie, the divell little needs such instruments to bring his purposes to passe.

It is strange, that we should suppose, that such persons can worke such feates: and it is more strange, that we will imagine that to be possible to be doone by a witch, which to nature and sense is impossible; speciallie when our neighbours life dependeth upon our credulitie therein; and when we may see the defect of abilitie, which alwaies is an impediment both to the act, and also to the presumption thereof. And bicause there is nothing possible in lawe, that in nature is impossible; therefore the judge dooth not attend or regard what the accused man saith; or yet would doo: but what is prooved to have beene committed, and naturallie falleth in mans power and will to doo. For the lawe saith, that To will a thing unpossible, is a signe of a mad man, or of a foole, upon whom no sentence or judgement taketh hold. Furthermore, what Jurie will condemne, or what Judge will give sentence or judgement against one for killing a man at *Berwicke;* when they themselves, and manie other sawe that man at *London,* that verie daie, wherein the murther was committed; yea though the partie confesse himself guiltie therein, and twentie witnesses depose the same? But in this case also I saie the judge is not to weigh their testimonie, which is weakened by lawe; and the judges authoritie is to supplie the imperfection of the case, and to mainteine the right and equitie of the same.

Seeing therefore that some other things might naturallie be the occasion and cause of such calamities as witches are supposed to bring; let not us that professe the Gospell and knowledge of Christ, be bewitched to beleeve that they doo such things, as are in nature impossible, and in sense and reason incredible. If they saie it is doone through the divels helpe, who can work miracles; whie doo not theeves bring their busines to passe miraculouslie, with whom the divell is as conversant as with the other? Such mischeefes as are imputed to witches, happen where no witches are; yea and continue when witches are hanged and burnt: whie then should we attribute such effect to that cause, which being taken awaie, happeneth neverthelesse?

*   *   *

What Testimonies and Witnesses Are Allowed to Give Evidence against Reputed Witches, by the Report and Allowance of the Inquisitors Themselves, and Such as Are Speciall Writers Heerein

Excommunicat persons, partakers of the falt, infants, wicked servants, and runnawaies are to be admitted to beare witnesse against their dames in this mater of witchcraft: bicause (saith *Bodin* the champion of witchmoongers) none that be honest are able to detect them. Heretikes also and witches shall be received to accuse, but not to excuse a witch. And finallie, the testimonie of all infamous persons in this case is good and allowed. Yea, one lewd person (saith *Bodin*) may be received to accuse and condemne a thousand suspected witches. And although by lawe, a capitall enimie may be challenged; yet *James Sprenger,* and *Henrie Institor,* (from whom *Bodin,* and all the writers that ever I have read, doo receive their light, authorities and arguments) saie (upon this point of lawe) that The poore frendlesse old woman must proove, that hir capitall enimie would have killed hir, and that hee hath both assalted & wounded hir; otherwise she pleadeth all in vaine. If the judge aske hir, whether she have anie capitall enimies; and she rehearse other, and forget hir accuser; or else answer that he was hir capital enimie, but now she hopeth he is not so: such a one is nevertheles admitted for a witnes. And though by lawe, single witnesses are not admittable; yet if one depose she hath bewitched hir cow; another, hir sow; and the third, hir butter: these saith (saith *M. Mal.* and *Bodin*) are no single witnesses; bicause they agree that she is a witch.

The Fifteene Crimes Laid to the Charge of Witches, by Witchmongers, Speciallie by Bodin, in Dæmonomania

They denie God, and all religion.

Answere. Then let them die therefore, or at the least be used like infidels, or apostataes.

They cursse, blaspheme, and provoke God with all despite.

Answere. Then let them have the law expressed in *Levit.* 24. and *Deut.* 13 & 17.

They give their faith to the divell, and they worship and offer sacrifice unto him.

Ans. Let such also be judged by the same lawe.

They doo solemnelie vow and promise all their progenie unto the divell.

Ans. This promise proceedeth from an unsound mind, and is not to be regarded; bicause they cannot performe it, neither will it be prooved true. Howbeit, if it be done by anie that is sound of mind, let the cursse of *Jeremie*, 32.36. light upon them, to wit, the sword, famine and pestilence.

They sacrifice their owne children to the divell before baptisme, holding them up in the aire unto him, and then thrust a needle into their braines.

Ans. If this be true, I maintaine them not herein: but there is a lawe to judge them by. Howbeit, it is so contrarie to sense and nature, that it were follie to beleeve it; either upon *Bodins* bare word, or else upon his presumptions; speciallie when so small commoditie and so great danger and inconvenience insueth to the witches thereby.

They burne their children when they have sacrificed them.

Ans. Then let them have such punishment, as they that offered their children unto *Moloch: Levit.* 20. But these be meere devises of witchmoongers and inquisitors, that with extreame tortures have wroong such confessions from them; or else with false reports have beelied them; or by flatterie & faire words and promises have woon it at their hands, at the length.

They sweare to the divell to bring as manie into that societie as they can.

Ans. This is false, and so prooved elsewhere.

They sweare by the name of the divell.

Ans. I never heard anie such oth, neither have we warrant to kill them that so doo sweare; though indeed it be verie lewd and impious.

They use incestuous adulterie with spirits.

Ans. This is a stale ridiculous lie, as is prooved apparentlie hereafter.

They boile infants (after they have murthered them unbaptised) untill their flesh be made potable.

Ans. This is untrue, incredible, and impossible.

They eate the flesh and drinke the bloud of men and children openlie.

Ans. Then are they kin to the *Anthropophagi* and *Canibals*. But I beleeve never an honest man in *England* nor in *France*, will affirme that he hath seene any of these persons, that are said to be witches, do so; if they shuld, I beleeve it would poison them.

They kill men with poison.

Ans. Let them be hanged for their labour.

They kill mens cattell.

Ans. Then let an action of trespasse be brought against them for so dooing.

They bewitch mens corne, and bring hunger and barrennes into the countrie; they ride and flie in the aire, bring stormes, make tempests, &c.

Ans. Then will I worship them as gods; for those be not the works of man nor yet of witch: as I have elsewhere prooved at large.

They use venerie with a divell called *Iucubus*, even when they lie in bed with their husbands, and have children by them, which become the best witches.

Ans. This is the last lie, verie ridiculous, and confuted by me elsewhere.

Of Foure Capitall Crimes Objected against Witches, All Fullie Answered and Confuted as Frivolous

First therefore they laie to their charge idolatrie. But alas without all reason: for such are properlie knowne to us to be idolaters, as doo externall worship to idols or strange gods. The furthest point that idolatrie can be stretched unto, is, that they, which are culpable therein, are such as hope for and seeke salvation at the hands of idols, or of anie other than God; or fixe their whole mind and love upon anie creature, so as the power of God be neglected and contemned thereby. But witches neither seeke nor beleeve to have salvation at the hands of divels, but by them they are onlie deceived; the instruments of their phantasie being corrupted, and so infatuated, that they suppose, confesse, and saie they can doo that, which is as farre beyond their power and nature to doo, as to kill a man at *Yorke* before noone, when they have beene seene at *London* in that morning, &c. But if these latter idolaters, whose idolatrie is spirituall, and committed onelie in mind, should be punished by death; then should everie covetous man, or other, that setteth his affection anie waie too much upon an earthlie creature, be executed, and yet perchance the witch might escape scotfree.

Secondlie, apostasie is laid to their charge, whereby it is inferred, that they are worthie to die. But apostasie is, where anie of sound judgement forsake the gospell, learned and well knowne unto them; and doo not onelie embrace impietie and infidelitie; but oppugne and resist the truth erstwhile by them professed. But alas these poore women go not about to defend anie impietie, but after good admonition repent.

Thirdlie, they would have them executed for seducing the people. But God knoweth they have small store of Rhetorike or art to seduce; except to tell a tale of Robin good-fellow be to deceive and seduce. Neither may their age or sex admit that opinion or accusation to be just: for they themselves are poore seduced soules. I for my part (as else-where I have said) have prooved this point to be false in most apparent sort.

Fourthlie, as touching the accusation, which all the writers use herein against them for their carnall copulation with *Incubus:* the follie of mens credulitie is as much to be woondered at and derided, as the others vaine and impossible confessions. For the divell is a spirit, and hath neither flesh nor bones, which were to be used in the performance of this action. And since he also lacketh all instruments, substance, and seed ingendred of bloud; it were follie to staie overlong in the confutation of that, which is not in the nature of things. And yet must I saie somewhat heerein, bicause the opinion hereof is so stronglie and universallie received, and the fables thereupon so innumerable; wherby *M. Mal. Bodin, Hemingius, Hyperius, Danaeus, Erastus,* and others that take upon them to write heerein, are so abused, or rather seeke to abuse others; as I woonder at their fond credulitie in this behalfe. For they affirme undoubtedlie, that the divell plaieth *Succubus* to the man, and carrieth from him the seed of generation, which he delivereth as *Incubus* to the woman, who manie times that waie is gotten with child; which will verie naturallie (they saie) become a witch, and such one they affirme *Merline* was.

*   *   *

By What Meanes the Common People Have Beene Made Beleeve in the Miraculous Works of Witches, a Definition of Witchcraft, and a Description Thereof

The common people have beene so assotted and bewitched, with whatsoever poets have feigned of witchcraft, either in earnest, in jest, or else in derision; and with whatsoever lowd liers and couseners for their pleasures heerein have invented, and with whatsoever tales they have heard from old doting women, or from their mothers maids, and with whatsoever the grandfoole their ghostlie father, or anie other morrow masse preest had informed them; and finallie with whatsoever they have swallowed up through tract of time, or through their owne timerous nature or ignorant conceipt, concerning these matters of hagges and witches: as they have so settled their opinion and credit thereupon, that they thinke it heresie to doubt in anie part of the matter; speciallie bicause they find this word witchcraft expressed in the scriptures; which is as to defend praieng to saincts, bicause *Sanctus, Sanctus, Sanctus* is written in *Te Deum.*

And now to come to the definition of witchcraft, which hitherto I did deferre and put off purposelie: that you might perceive the true nature thereof, by the circumstances, and therefore the rather to allow of the same, seeing the varietie of other writers. Witchcraft is in truth a cousening art, wherin the name of God is abused, prophaned and blasphemed, and his power attributed to a vile creature. In estimation of the vulgar people, it is a supernaturall worke, contrived betweene a corporall old woman, and a spirituall divell. The maner thereof is so secret, mysticall, and strange, that to this daie there hath never beene any credible witnes thereof. It is incomprehensible to the wise, learned or faithfull; a probable matter to children, fooles, melancholike persons and papists. The trade is thought to be impious. The effect and end thereof to be sometimes evill, as when thereby man or beast, grasse, trees, or corne, &c; is hurt: sometimes good, as whereby sicke folkes are healed, theeves bewraied, and true men come to their goods, &c. The matter and instruments, wherewith it is accomplished, are words, charmes, signes, images, characters, &c; the which words although any other creature do pronounce, in manner and forme as they doo, leaving out no circumstance requisite or usually for that action: yet none is said to have the grace or gift to perform the matter, except she

be a witch, and so taken either by hir owne consent, or by others imputation.

Reasons to Proove That Words and Characters Are But Bables, and That Witches Cannot Doo Such Things as the Multitude Supposeth They Can, Their Greatest Woonders Prooved Trifles, of a Yoong Gentleman Cousened

That words, characters, images, and such other trinkets, which are thought so necessarie instruments for witchcraft (as without the which no such thing can be accomplished) are but bables, devised by couseners, to abuse the people withall; I trust I have sufficientlie prooved. And the same maie be further and more plainelie perceived by these short and compendious reasons following.

First, in that *Turkes* and infidels, in their witchcraft, use both other words, and other characters than our witches doo and also such as are most contrarie. In so much as, if ours be bad, in reason theirs should be good. If their witches can doo anie thing, ours can doo nothing. For as our witches are said to renounce Christ, and despise his sacraments: so doo the other forsake *Mahomet,* and his lawes, which is one large step to christianitie.

It is also to be thought, that all witches are couseners; when mother *Bungie,* a principall witch, so reputed, tried, and condemned of all men, and continuing in that exercise and estimation manie yeares (having cousened & abused the whole realme, in so much as there came to hir, witchmongers from all the furthest parts of the land, she being in diverse bookes set out with authoritie, registred and chronicled by the name of the great witch of *Rochester,* and reputed among all men for the cheefe ringleader of all other witches) by good proofe is found to be a meere cousener; confessing in hir death bed freelie, without compulsion or inforcement, that hir cunning consisted onlie in deluding and deceiving the people: saying that she had (towards the maintenance of hir credit in that cousening trade) some sight in physicke and surgerie, and the assistance of a freend of hirs, called *Heron,* a professor thereof. And this I know, partlie of mine owne knowledge, and partlie by the testimonie of hir husband, and others of credit, to whome (I saie) in hir death bed, and at sundrie other times she protested these things; and also that she never had indeed anie materiall spirit or divell (as the voice went) nor yet knew how to worke anie supernaturall matter, as she in hir life time made men beleeve she had and could doo.

*   *   *

Againe, who will mainteine, that common witchcrafts are not cousenages, when the great and famous witchcrafts, which had stolne credit not onlie from all the common people, but from men of great wisdome and authoritie, are discovered to be beggerlie slights of cousening varlots? Which otherwise might and would have remained a perpetuall objection against me. Were there not three images of late yeeres found in a doonghill, to the terror & astonishment of manie thousands? In so much as great matters were thought to have beene pretended to be doone by witchcraft. But if the Lord preserve those persons (whose destruction was doubted to have beene intended thereby) from all other the lewd practises and attempts of their enimies; I feare not, but they shall easilie withstand these and such like devises, although

they should indeed be practised against them. But no doubt, if such bables could have brought those matters of mischeefe to passe, by the hands of traitors, witches, or papists; we should long since have beene deprived of the most excellent jewell and comfort that we enjoy in this world. Howbeit, I confesse, that the feare, conceipt, and doubt of such mischeefous pretenses may breed inconvenience to them that stand in awe of the same. And I wish, that even for such practises, though they never can or doo take effect, the practisers be punished with all extremitie: bicause therein is manifested a traiterous heart to the Queene, and a presumption against God.

*   *   *

REVIEW QUESTIONS

1. What is witchcraft?
2. How does Scot depict it?
3. According to Scot, what characterizes witches and witchcraft?
4. How does Scot confound the very notion of witchcraft?
5. Where does he locate the source of all power to override the laws of nature?
6. What sort of power is left to witches?
7. What, according to Scot, is the relation of witches to the natural world?

BLAISE PASCAL

FROM *Pensées*

Blaise Pascal (1623–1662) was born the son of a French official. During his life, he dabbled in many subjects, including science, religion, and literature. His conversion to Jansenism plunged him into controversy with the Jesuits, giving rise to his Lettres provinciales. *These, along with his* Pensées, *from which the current selection is drawn, established his literary fame. His thought contains a fascinating blend of confidence in human reason and consciousness of its limits. René Descartes viewed Pascal as the embodiment of a mentality of intellectual and spiritual crisis. Be that as it may, Pascal is also considered one of the great stylists of the French language.*

From *Pensées*, by Blaise Pascal, translated by A. J. Krailsheimer (New York: Penguin Books, 1995), pp. 58–64, 121–25.

The Wager

*   *   *

Infinity—nothing. Our soul is cast into the body where it finds number, time, dimensions; it reasons about these things and calls them natural, or necessary, and can believe nothing else.

Unity added to infinity does not increase it at all, any more than a foot added to an infinite measurement: the finite is annihilated in the presence of the infinite and becomes pure nothingness. So it is with our mind before God, with our justice before divine justice. There is not so great a disproportion between our justice and God's as between unity and infinity.

God's justice must be as vast as his mercy. Now his justice towards the damned is less vast and ought to be less startling to us than his mercy towards the elect.

We know that the infinite exists without knowing its nature, just as we know that it is untrue that numbers are finite. Thus it is true that there is an infinite number, but we do not know what it is. It is untrue that it is even, untrue that it is odd, for by adding a unit it does not change its nature. Yet it is a number, and every number is even or odd. (It is true that this applies to every finite number.)

Therefore we may well know that God exists without knowing what he is.

Is there no substantial truth, seeing that there are so many true things which are not truth itself?

Thus we know the existence and nature of the finite because we too are finite and extended in space.

We know the existence of the infinite without knowing its nature, because it too has extension but unlike us no limits.

But we do not know either the existence or the nature of God, because he has neither extension nor limits.

But by faith we know his existence, through glory we shall know his nature.

Now I have already proved that it is quite possible to know that something exists without knowing its nature.

Let us now speak according to our natural lights.

If there is a God, he is infinitely beyond our comprehension, since, being indivisible and without limits, he bears no relation to us. We are therefore incapable of knowing either what he is or whether he is. That being so, who would dare to attempt an answer to the question? Certainly not we, who bear no relation to him.

Who then will condemn Christians for being unable to give rational grounds for their belief, professing as they do a religion for which they cannot give rational grounds? They declare that it is a folly, *stultitiam,* in expounding it to the world, and then you complain that they do not prove it. If they did prove it they would not be keeping their word. It is by being without proof that they show they are not without sense. "Yes, but although that excuses those who offer their religion as such, and absolves them from the criticism of producing it without rational grounds, it does not absolve those who accept it." Let us then examine this point, and let us say: "Either God is or he is not." But to which view shall we be inclined? Reason cannot decide this question. Infinite chaos separates us. At the far end of this infinite distance a coin is being spun which will come down heads

...eason cannot make ... cannot prove either

...ot then condemn as wrong those who have made a choice, for you know nothing about it. "No, but I will condemn them not for having made this particular choice, but any choice, for, although the one who calls heads and the other one are equally at fault, the fact is that they are both at fault: the right thing is not to wager at all."

Yes, but you must wager. There is no choice, you are already committed. Which will you choose then? Let us see: since a choice must be made, let us see which offers you the least interest. You have two things to lose: the true and the good; and two things to stake: your reason and your will, your knowledge and your happiness; and your nature has two things to avoid: error and wretchedness. Since you must necessarily choose, your reason is no more affronted by choosing one rather than the other. That is one point cleared up. But your happiness? Let us weigh up the gain and the loss involved in calling heads that God exists. Let us assess the two cases: if you win you win everything, if you lose you lose nothing. Do not hesitate then; wager that he does exist. "That is wonderful. Yes, I must wager, but perhaps I am wagering too much." Let us see: since there is an equal chance of gain and loss, if you stood to win only two lives for one you could still wager, but supposing you stood to win three?

You would have to play (since you must necessarily play) and it would be unwise of you, once you are obliged to play, not to risk your life in order to win three lives at a game in which there is an equal chance of losing and winning. But there is an eternity of life and happiness. That being so, even though there were an infinite number of chances, of which only one were in your favour, you would still be right to wager one in order to win two; and you would be acting wrongly, being obliged to play, in refusing to stake one life against three in a game, where out of an infinite number of chances there is one in your favour, if there were an infinity of infinitely happy life to be won.

But here there is an infinity of infinitely happy life to be won, one chance of winning against a finite number of chances of losing, and what you are staking is finite. That leaves no choice; wherever there is infinity, and where there are not infinite chances of losing against that of winning, there is no room for hesitation, you must give everything. And thus, since you are obliged to play, you must be renouncing reason if you hoard your life rather than risk it for an infinite gain, just as likely to occur as a loss amounting to nothing.

For it is no good saying that it is uncertain whether you will win, that it is certain that you are taking a risk, and that the infinite distance between the certainty of what you are risking and the uncertainty of what you may gain makes the finite good you are certainly risking equal to the infinite good that you are not certain to gain. This is not the case. Every gambler takes a certain risk for an uncertain gain, and yet he is taking a certain finite risk for an uncertain finite gain without sinning against reason. Here there is no infinite distance between the certain risk and the uncertain gain: that is not true. There is, indeed, an infinite distance between the certainty of winning and the certainty of losing, but the proportion between the uncertainty of winning and the certainty of what is being risked is in proportion to the chances of winning or losing. And hence if there are as many chances on one side as on the other you are playing for even odds. And in that case the certainty of what you are risking is equal to the uncertainty of what you may win; it is by no means infinitely distant from it. Thus our argument carries infinite weight, when the stakes are finite in a game where there are even chances of winning and losing and an infinite prize to be won.

This is conclusive and if men are capable of any truth this is it.

"I confess, I admit it, but is there really no way of seeing what the cards are?"—"Yes. Scripture and the rest, etc."—"Yes, but my hands are tied and my lips are sealed; I am being forced to wager and I am not free; I am being held fast and I am so made that I cannot believe. What do you want me to do then?"—"That is true, but at least get it into your head that, if you are unable to believe, it is because of your passions, since reason impels you to believe and yet you cannot do so. Concentrate then not on convincing yourself by multiplying proofs of God's existence but by diminishing your passions. You want to find faith and you do not know the road. You want to be cured of unbelief and you ask for the remedy: learn from those who were once bound like you and who now wager all they have. These are people who know the road you wish to follow, who have been cured of the affliction of which you wish to be cured: follow the way by which they began. They behaved just as if they did believe, taking holy water, having masses said, and so on. That will make you believe quite naturally, and will make you more docile."—"But that is what I am afraid of."—"But why? What have you to lose? But to show you that this is the way, the fact is that this diminishes the passions which are your great obstacles. . . ."

End of this address.

"Now what harm will come to you from choosing this course? You will be faithful, honest, humble, grateful, full of good works, a sincere, true friend. . . . It is true you will not enjoy noxious pleasures, glory and good living, but will you not have others?

"I tell you that you will gain even in this life, and that at every step you take along this road you will see that your gain is so certain and your risk so negligible that in the end you will realize that

you have wagered on something certain and infinite for which you have paid nothing."

"How these words fill me with rapture and delight!—"

"If my words please you and seem cogent, you must know that they come from a man who went down upon his knees before and after to pray this infinite and indivisible being, to whom he submits his own, that he might bring your being also to submit to him for your own good and for his glory: and that strength might thus be reconciled with lowliness."

*   *   *

Review Questions

1. How does Pascal conceive of the human condition?
2. What does it mean for him to have a body?
3. How does he differ in this respect from Montaigne?
4. How does Pascal construct his proof for the existence of God?
5. Why does he begin with infinity, a mathematical concept?
6. What is he saying about the limits of human knowledge?
7. For whom might this essay have been written?
8. Why must we wager?

JOHN DONNE

FROM "The First Anniversarie"

John Donne (1572–1631) was esteemed by his contemporary Ben Jonson as "the first poet in the world in some things." He was born in London, the son of a prosperous merchant. His father died while Donne was still an infant, and he was raised by his mother, the daughter of the playwright John Heywood and grand-

daughter of Sir Thomas More's sister. His family was devoutly Roman Catholic. Donne matriculated at Hart Hall, Oxford, in 1584 but left without a degree because it was impossible for Catholics to take the oath of supremacy required at graduation. He entered Thavies Inn, London, as a law student in 1591 and transferred to Lincoln's Inn in 1592. At this point he began to write poetry. In 1596, he joined the earl of Essex's Cadiz expedition and on his return became secretary to Sir Thomas Egerton, the lord keeper of the Great Seal of England. Donne abjured his Catholic faith to join the Church of England and was about to embark on a diplomatic career when he secretly married Ann More, the niece of his employer's wife. He was imprisoned for marrying a minor without her guardian's consent, and the girl's father secured his dismissal from Egerton's service. On his release, Donne found himself without employment and his wife without a dowry. Years of poverty and dependence turned the poet toward religion and reflection, both of which found ready expression in his writing. His first published work, The Pseudo-Martyr *(1610), written to persuade Catholics to take the oath of allegiance, earned him an honorary master of arts degree from Oxford and the notice of the king. In 1614, he was elected to Parliament and, in 1615, became an Anglican priest. During these middle years, Donne wrote his "anniversaries," the first of which was published in 1611. The subject was Elizabeth Drury, who died in 1610 at the age of fourteen. The poem captures something of the weariness and insecurity that accompanied the crisis of the seventeenth century. His subsequent career was divided between the poet and the priest. When he died, as dean of St. Paul's, Donne had earned another reputation as the greatest preacher of his age.*

From *The Complete English Poems of John Donne,* edited by C. A. Patrides (New York: Everyman's Library, 1985).

An Anatomy of the World.
   Wherein, By occasion of the untimely
      death of Mistris
Elizabeth Drury the frailty and the decay of his
  whole
World is represented.

To The Praise of the Dead, and the Anatomy.
[by Joseph Hall?]

Wel dy'de the world, that we might live to see
This world of wit, in his Anatomee:
No evill wants his good: so wilder heyres
Bedew their fathers Toombs with forced teares,
Whose state requites their los: whils thus we
  gain
Well may wee walk in blacks, but not com-
  plaine.

          *   *   *

She, of whom th'Auncients seem'd to prophesie,
When they call'd vertues by the name of shee;
She in whom vertue was so much refin'd,
That for Allay unto so pure a minde
Shee tooke the weaker Sex, she that could drive
The poysonous tincture, and the stayne of *Eve,*
Out of her thoughts, and deeds; and purifie
All, by a true religious Alchimy;
Shee, shee is dead; shee's dead: when thou
  knowest this,
Thou knowest how poore a trifling thing man is.
And learn'st thus much by our Anatomee,
The heart being perish'd, no part can be free.
And that except thou feed (not banquet) on
The supernaturall food, Religion,
Thy better Grouth growes withered, and scant;

Be more then man, or thou'rt lesse then an Ant.
Then, as mankinde, so is the worlds whole frame
Quite out of joynt, almost created lame:
For, before God had made up all the rest,
Corruption entred, and deprav'd the best:
It seis'd the Angels, and then first of all
The world did in her Cradle take a fall,
And turn'd her braines, and tooke a generall
    maime
Wronging each joynt of th'universall frame.
The noblest part, man, felt it first; and than
Both beasts and plants, curst in the curse of
    man.
So did the world from the first houre decay,
The evening was beginning of the day,
And now the Springs and Sommers which we
    see,
Like sonnes of women after fifty bee.
And new Philosophy cals all in doubt,
The Element of fire is quite put out;
The Sun is lost, and th'earth, and no mans wit
Can well direct him, where to looke for it.
And freely men confesse, that this world's spent,
When in the Planets, and the Firmament
They seeke so many new; they see that this
Is crumbled out againe to his Atomis.
'Tis all in pieces, all cohærence gone;
All just supply, and all Relation:
Prince, Subject, Father, Sonne, are things forgot,
For every man alone thinkes he hath got
To be a Phœnix, and that there can bee
None of that kinde, of which he is, but hee.
This is the worlds condition now, and now
She that should all parts to reunion bow,
She that had all Magnetique force alone,
To draw, and fasten sundred parts in one;
She whom wise nature had invented then
When she observ'd that every sort of men
Did in their voyage in this worlds Sea stray,
And needed a new compasse for their way;
Shee that was best, and first originall
Of all faire copies; and the generall
Steward to Fate; shee whose rich eyes, and brest,
Guilt the West Indies, and perfum'd the East;
Whose having breath'd in this world, did bestow
Spice on those Isles, and bad them still smell so,

And that rich Indie which doth gold interre,
Is but as single money, coyn'd from her:
She to whom this world must it selfe refer,
As Suburbs, or the Microcosme of her,
Shee, shee is dead; shee's dead: when thou
    knowst this,
Thou knowst how lame a cripple this world is.
And learnst thus much by our Anatomy,
That this worlds generall sickenesse doth not lie
In any humour, or one certaine part;
But, as thou sawest it rotten at the hart,
Thou seest a Hectique fever hath got hold
Of the whole substance, not to be contrould,
And that thou hast but one way, not t'admit
The worlds infection, to be none of it.
For the worlds subtilst immateriall parts
Feele this consuming wound, and ages darts.
For the worlds beauty is decayd, or gone,
Beauty, that's colour, and proportion.
We thinke the heavens enjoy their Spherical
Their round proportion embracing all.
But yet their various and perplexed course,
Observ'd in divers ages doth enforce
Men to finde out so many Eccentrique parts,
Such divers downe-right lines, such overthwarts,
As disproportion that pure forme. It teares
The Firmament in eight and fortie sheeres,
And in those constellations there arise
New starres, and old do vanish from our eyes:
As though heav'n suffred earth-quakes, peace or
    war,
When new Townes rise, and olde demolish'd
    are.
They have empayld within a Zodiake
The free-borne Sunne, and keepe twelve signes
    awake
To watch his steps; the Goat and Crabbe
    controule,
And fright him backe, who els to eyther Pole,
(Did not these Tropiques fetter him) might
    runne:
For his course is not round; nor can the Sunne
Perfit a Circle, or maintaine his way
One inche direct; but where he rose to day
He comes no more, but with a cousening line,
Steales by that point, and so is Serpentine:

And seeming weary with his reeling thus,
He meanes to sleepe, being now falne nearer us.
So, of the stares which boast that they do runne
In Circle still, none ends where he begunne.
All their proportion's lame, it sinks, it swels.
For of Meridians, and Parallels,
Man hath weav'd out a net, and this net
    throwne
Upon the Heavens, and now they are his owne.
Loth to goe up the hill, or labor thus
To goe to heaven, we make heaven come to us.
We spur, we raine the stars, and in their race
They're diversly content t'obey our pace.
But keepes the earth her round proportion still?
Doth not a Tenarif, or higher Hill
Rise so high like a Rocke, that one might thinke
The floating Moone would shipwracke there, and
    sink?
Seas are so deepe, that Whales being strooke to
    day,
Perchance to morrow, scarse at middle way
Of their wish'd journeys end, the bottom, dye.
And men, to sound depths, so much line untie,
As one might justly thinke, that there would rise
At end thereof, one of th'Antipodies:
If under all, a Vault infernall be,

(Which sure is spacious, except that we
Invent another torment, that there must
Millions into a strait hote roome be thrust)
Then solidnes, and roundnes have no place.
Are these but warts, and pock-holes in the face
Of th'earth? Thinke so: But yet confesse, in this
The worlds proportion disfigured is,
That those two legges whereon it doth relie,
Reward and punishment are bent awrie.
And, Oh, it can no more be questioned,
That beauties best, proportion, is dead,
Since even griefe it selfe, which now alone
Is left us, is without proportion.

*   *   *

REVIEW QUESTIONS

1. Of the changes in the early modern period that
   Donne catalogues, which does he highlight?
2. Why do you suppose he chose these?
3. What has been lost according to Donne?
4. How might he understand Pascal's notion of
   infinity?

HANS JAKOB CHRISTOPH VON GRIMMELSHAUSEN

FROM *Simplicissimus*

Hans Jakob Christoph von Grimmelshausen (1621–1676), author of Simplicissimus,
*the greatest German novel of the seventeenth century and one of the great works of
all German literature, was born at Gelnhausen, near Hanau in Hesse Kassel. The
troubled times of the Thirty Years' War (1618–1648) that found eloquent consideration in his writing are reflected by his life. He lost his parents early, probably in the
1634 sack of Gelnhausen by troops under Ferdinand, general infanta of Spain, and
was himself kidnapped by marauding Hessian troops the following year. His experiences became the stuff of his novel. In 1636 he joined the Imperial army. In 1639
he became secretary to Reinhard von Schauenburg, the commandant at Offenburg,
on whose staff he served until 1647. At the end of the war, he was commandant on*

the Inn. Soon after the war he became steward of the Schauenburg estates, married, and converted to Catholicism. In 1667, Grimmelshausen was appointed magistrate and tax collector at Renchen, a town belonging to the Bishopric of Strasbourg. His duties evidently left him free to write; he published his masterpiece, Simplicissimus, *in 1669. Modeled on the Spanish picaresque romance,* Simplicissimus *sketched the development of a human soul measured against the background of a land riven by warfare. It gave free reign to its authors narrative gifts: his realist detail, coarse humor, and social criticism.* Simplicissimus *is widely considered a historical document for its vivid picture of seventeenth-century Germany. Grimmelshausen's life ended as it began, in the shadow of war. In 1674, Rechen was occupied by French troops and his household was broken up. He died in 1676, once more in military service.*

From *Simplicissimus,* by Hans Jakob Christoph von Grimmelshausen, translated by S. Goodrich (San Francisco: Daedalus Press, 1995).

Book I

CHAPTER I
TREATS OF SIMPLICISSIMUS'S RUSTIC DESCENT AND OF HIS UPBRINGING ANSWERING THERETO

There appeareth in these days of ours (of which many do believe that they be the last days) among the common folk, a certain disease which causeth those who do suffer from it (so soon as they have either scraped and higgled together so much that they can, besides a few pence in their pocket, wear a fool's coat of the new fashion with a thousand bits of silk ribbon upon it, or by some trick of fortune have become known as men of parts) forthwith to give themselves out gentlemen and nobles of ancient descent. Whereas it doth often happen that their ancestors were day-labourers, carters, and porters, their cousins donkey-drivers, their brothers turnkeys and catchpolls, their sisters harlots, their mothers bawds—yea, witches even: and in a word, their whole pedigree of thirty-two quarterings as full of dirt and stain as ever was the sugarbakers' guild of Prague. Yea, these new sprigs of nobility be often themselves as black as if they had been born and bred in Guinea.

With such foolish folk I desire not to even myself, though 'tis not untrue that I have often fancied I must have drawn my birth from some great lord or knight at least, as being by nature disposed to follow the nobleman's trade had I but the means and the tools for it. 'Tis true, moreover, without jesting, that my birth and upbringing can be well compared to that of a prince if we overlook the one great difference in degree. How! did not my dad (for so they call fathers in the Spessart) have his own palace like any other, so fine as no king could build with his own hands, but must let that alone for ever. 'Twas painted with lime, and in place of unfruitful tiles, cold lead and red copper, was roofed with that straw whereupon the noble corn doth grow, and that he, my dad, might make a proper show of nobility and riches, he had his wall round his castle built, not of stone, which men do find upon the road or dig out of the earth in barren places, much less of miserable baked bricks that in a brief space can be made and burned (as other great lords be wont to do), but he did use oak, which noble and profitable tree, being such that smoked sausage and fat ham doth grow upon it, taketh for its full growth no less than a hundred years; and where is the monarch that can imitate him therein? His halls, his rooms, and his chambers did he have thoroughly blackened with smoke, and for this reason only, that 'tis the most lasting colour in the world, and doth take longer to reach to real perfection than an artist will spend on his most excellent paintings. The tapestries were of the most delicate web in the world, wove for us by her that of old did challenge

Minerva to a spinning match. His windows were dedicated to St. Papyrius for no other reason than that that same paper doth take longer to come to perfection, reckoning from the sowing of the hemp or flax whereof 'tis made, than doth the finest and clearest glass of Murano: for his trade made him apt to believe that whatever was produced with much paint was also more valuable and more costly; and what was moss costly was best suited to nobility. Instead of pages, lackeys, and grooms, he had sheep, goats, and swine, which often waited upon me in the pastures till I drove them home. His armoury was well furnished with ploughs, mattocks, axes, hoes, shovels, pitchforks, and hayforks, with which weapons he daily exercised himself; for hoeing and digging he made his military discipline, as did the old Romans in time of peace. The yoking of oxen was his generalship, the piling of dung his fortification, tilling of the land his campaigning, and the cleaning out of stables his princely pastime and exercise. By this means did he conquer the whole round world so far as he could reach, and at every harvest did draw from it rich spoils. But all this I account nothing of, and am not puffed up thereby, lest any should have cause to jibe at me as at other newfangled nobility, for I esteem myself no higher than was my dad, which had his abode in a right merry land, to wit, in the Spessart, where the wolves do howl good-night to each other. But that I have as yet told you nought of my dad's family, race and name is for the sake of precious brevity, especially since there is here no question of a foundation for gentlefolks for me to swear myself into; 'tis enough if it be known that I was born in the Spessart.

Now as my dad's manner of living will be perceived to be truly noble, so any man of sense will easily understand that my upbringing was like and suitable thereto: and whoso thinks that is not deceived, for in my tenth year had I already learned the rudiments of my dad's princely exercises: yet as touching studies I might compare with the famous Amphistides, of whom Suidas reports that he could not count higher than five: for my dad

had perchance too high a spirit, and therefore followed the use of these days, wherein many persons of quality trouble themselves not, as they say with bookworms' follies, but have their hirelings to do their inkslinging for them. Yet was I a fine performer on the bagpipe, whereon I could produce most dolorous strains. But as to knowledge of things divine, none shall ever persuade me that any lad of my age in all Christendom could there beat me, for I knew nought of God or man, of Heaven or hell, of angel or devil, nor could discern between good and evil. So may it be easily understood that I, with such knowledge of theology, lived like our first parents in Paradise, which in their innocence knew nought of sickness or death or dying, and still less of the Resurrection. O noble life! (or, as one might better say, O noodle's life!) in which none troubles himself about medicine. And by this measure ye can estimate my proficiency in the study of jurisprudence and all other arts and sciences. Yea, I was so perfected in ignorance that I knew not that I knew nothing. So say I again, O noble life that once I led! But my dad would not suffer me long to enjoy such bliss, but deemed it right that as being nobly born, I should nobly act and nobly live: and therefore began to train me up for higher things and gave me harder lessons.

*   *   *

CHAPTER IV

HOW SIMPLICISSIMUS'S PALACE WAS STORMED, PLUNDERED, AND RUINATED, AND IN WHAT SORRY FASHION THE SOLDIERS KEPT HOUSE THERE

Although it was not my intention to take the peaceloving reader with these troopers to my dad's house and farm, seeing that matters will go ill therein, yet the course of my history demands that I should leave to kind posterity an account of what manner of cruelties were now and again practised in this our German war: yea, and moreover testify by my own example that such evils must often have been sent to us by the goodness of Almighty

God for our profit. For, gentle reader, who would ever have taught me that there was a God in Heaven if these soldiers had not destroyed my dad's house, and by such a deed driven me out among folk who gave me all fitting instruction thereupon? Only a little while before, I neither knew nor could fancy to myself that there were any people on earth save only my dad, my mother and me, and the rest of our household, nor did I know of any human habitation but that where I daily went out and in. But soon thereafter I understood the way of men's coming into this world, and how they must leave it again. I was only in shape a man and in name a Christian: for the rest I was but a beast. Yet the Almighty looked upon my innocence with a pitiful eye, and would bring me to a knowledge both of Himself and of myself. And although He had a thousand ways to lead me thereto, yet would He doubtless use that one only by which my dad and my mother should be punished: and that for an example to all others by reason of their heathenish upbringing of me.

The first thing these troopers did was, that they stabled their horses: thereafter each fell to his appointed task: which task was neither more nor less than ruin and destruction. For though some began to slaughter and to boil and to roast so that it looked as if there should be a merry banquet forward, yet others there were who did but storm through the house above and below stairs. Others stowed together great parcels of cloth and apparel and all manner of household stuff, as if they would set up a frippery market. All that they had no mind to take with them they cut in pieces. Some thrust their swords through the hay and straw as if they had not enough sheep and swine to slaughter: and some shook the feathers out of the beds and in their stead stuffed in bacon and other dried meat and provisions as if such were better and softer to sleep upon. Others broke the stove and the windows as if they had a never-ending summer to promise. Houseware of copper and tin they beat flat, and packed such vessels, all bent and spoiled, in with the rest. Bedsteads, tables, chairs, and benches they burned, though there lay many cords of dry wood in the yard. Pots and pipkins must all go to pieces, either because they would eat none but roast flesh, or because their purpose was to make there but a single meal.

Our maid was so handled in the stable that she could not come out; which is a shame to tell of. Our man they laid bound upon the ground, thrust a gag into his mouth, and poured a pailful of filthy water into his body: and by this, which they called a Swedish draught, they forced him to lead a party of them to a another place where they captured men and beasts, and brought them back to our farm, in which company were my dad, my mother, and our Ursula.

And now they began: first to take the flints out of their pistols and in place of them to jam the peasants' thumbs in and so to torture the poor rogues as if they had been about the burning of witches: for one of them they had taken they thrust into the baking oven and there lit a fire under him, although he had as yet confessed no crime: as for another, they put a cord round his head and so twisted it tight with a piece of wood that the blood gushed from his mouth and nose and ears. In a word each had his own device to torture the peasants, and each peasant his several torture. But as it seemed to me then, my dad was the luckiest, for he with a laughing face confessed what others must out with in the midst of pains and miserable lamentations: and such honour without doubt fell to him because he was the householder. For they set him before a fire and bound him fast so that he could neither stir hand nor foot, and smeared the soles of his feet with wet salt, and this they made our old goat lick off, and so tickle him that he well nigh burst his sides with laughing. And this seemed to me so merry a thing that I must needs laugh with him for the sake of fellowship, or because I knew no better. In the midst of such laughter he must needs confess all that they would have of him, and indeed revealed to them a secret treasure, which proved far richer in pearls, gold, and trinkets than any would have looked for among peasants. Of the women, girls, and maidservants whom they took, I have not much to say in particular, for the soldiers would not have me see how they dealt with them. Yet this I know, that one heard some of them scream most piteously in divers corners of the house; and well I can judge it fared no better with my mother and our Ursel than with the rest. Yet in the midst of all this miserable ruin I helped to turn the spit, and in the afternoon to give the horses drink, in which employ I encountered our maid in the stable, who seemed to me wondrously tumbled, so that I knew her not, but with a weak voice she called to me, "O lad, run away, or the troopers will have thee away with them. Look to it well that thou get hence: thou seest in what plight . . ." And more she could not say.

*　　*　　*

CHAPTER XV

HOW SIMPLICISSIMUS WAS PLUNDERED, AND HOW HE DREAMED OF THE PEASANTS AND HOW THEY FARED IN TIMES OF WAR

Now when I came home I found that my fireplace and all my poor furniture, together with my store of provisions, which I had grown during the summer in my garden and had kept for the coming winter, were all gone. "And whither now?" thought I. And then first did need teach me heartily to pray: and I must summon all my small wits together, to devise what I should do. But as my knowledge of the world was both small and evil, I could come to no proper conclusion, only that 'twas best to commend myself to God and to put my whole confidence in Him: for otherwise I must perish. And besides all this those things which I had heard and seen that day lay heavy on my mind: and I pondered not so much upon my food and my sustenance as upon the enmity which there is ever between soldiers and peasants. Yet could my foolish mind come to no other conclusion than this—that there must of a surety be two races of men in the world, and not one only, descended from Adam, but two, wild and tame, like other unreasoning beasts, and therefore pursuing one another so cruelly.

With such thoughts I fell asleep, for mere misery and cold, with a hungry stomach. Then it seemed to me, as if in a dream, that all the trees which stood round my dwelling suddenly changed and took on another appearance: for on every treetop sat a trooper, and the trunks were garnished, in place of leaves, with all manner of folk. Of these, some had long lances, others musquets, hangers, halberts, flags, and some drums and fifes. Now this was merry to see, for all was neatly distributed and each according to his rank. The roots, moreover, were made up of folk of little worth, as mechanics and labourers, mostly, however, peasants and the like; and these nevertheless gave its strength to the tree and renewed the same when it was lost: yea more, they repaired the loss of any fallen leaves from among themselves to their own great damage: and all the time they lamented over them that sat on the tree, and that with good reason, for the whole weight of the tree lay upon them and pressed them so that all the money was squeezed out of their pockets, yea, though it was behind seven locks and keys: but if the money would not out, then did the commissaries so handle them with rods (which thing they call military execution) that sighs came from their heart, tears from their eyes, blood from their nails, and the marrow from their bones. Yet among these were some whom men call light o' heart; and these made but little ado, took all with a shrug, and in the midst of their torment had, in place of comfort, mockery for every turn.

CHAPTER XVI

OF THE WAYS AND WORKS OF SOLDIERS NOWADAYS, AND HOW HARDLY A COMMON SOLDIER CAN GET PROMOTION

So must the roots of these trees suffer and endure toil and misery in the midst of trouble and complaint, and those upon the lower boughs in yet greater hardship: yet were these last mostly merrier than the first named, yea and moreover, insolent and swaggering, and for the most part godless folk, and for the roots a heavy unbearable burden at all times. And this was the rhyme upon them:

> Hunger and thirst, and cold and heat, and work and woe, and all we meet;
> And deeds of blood and deeds of shame, all may ye put to the landsknecht's name.

Which rhymes were the less like to be lyingly invented in that they answered to the facts. For gluttony and drunkenness, hunger and thirst, wenching and dicing and playing, riot and roaring, murdering and being murdered, slaying and being slain, torturing and being tortured, hunting and being hunted, harrying and being harried, robbing and being robbed, frighting and being frighted, causing trouble and suffering trouble, beating and being beaten: in a word, hurting and harming, and in turn being hurt and harmed—this was their whole life. And in this career they let nothing hinder them: neither winter nor summer, snow nor ice, heat nor cold, rain nor wind, hill nor dale, wet nor dry; ditches, mountain-passes, ramparts and walls, fire and water, were all the same to them. Father nor mother, sister nor brother, no, nor the danger to their own bodies, souls, and consciences, nor even loss of life and of heaven itself, or aught else that can be named, will ever stand in their way, for ever they toil and moil at their own strange work, till at last, little by little, in battles, sieges, attacks, campaigns, yea, and in their winter quarters too (which are the soldiers' earthly paradise, if they can but happen upon fat peasants) they perish, they die, they rot and consume away, save but a few, who in their old age, unless they have been right thrifty rievers and robbers, do furnish us with the best of all beggars and vagabonds.

Next above these hard-worked folk sat old henroost-robbers, who, after some years and much peril of their lives, had climbed up the lowest branches and clung to them, and so far had had the luck to escape death. Now these looked more serious, and somewhat more dignified than the lowest, in that they were a degree higher ascended: yet above them were some yet higher, who had yet loftier imaginings because they had to command the very lowest. And these people did

call coat-beaters, because they were wont to dust the jackets of the poor pikemen, and to give the musqueteers oil enough to grease their barrels with.

Just above these the trunk of the tree had an interval or stop, which was a smooth place without branches, greased with all manner of ointments and curious soap of disfavour, so that no man save of noble birth could scale it, in spite of courage and skill and knowledge, God knows how clever he might be. For 'twas polished as smooth as a marble pillar or a steel mirror. Just over that smooth spot sat they with the flags: and of these some were young, some pretty well in years: the young folk their kinsmen had raised so far: the older people had either mounted on a silver ladder which is called the Bribery Backstairs or else on a step which Fortune, for want of a better client, had left for them. A little further up sat higher folk, and these had also their toil and care and annoyance: yet had they this advantage, that they could fill their pokes with the fattest slices which they could cut out of the roots, and that with a knife which they called "War-contribution." And these were at their best and happiest when there came a commissary-bird flying overhead, and shook out a whole panfull of gold over the tree to cheer them: for of that they caught as much as they could, and let but little or nothing at all fall to the lowest branches: and so of these last more died of hunger than of the enemy's attacks, from which danger those placed above seemed to be free. Therefore was there a perpetual climbing and swarming going on on those trees; for each would needs sit in those highest and happiest places: yet were there some idle, worthless rascals, not worth their commissariat-bread, who troubled themselves little about higher places, and only did their duty. So the lowest, being ambitious, hoped for the fall of the highest, that they might sit in their place, and if it happened to one among ten thousand of them that he got so far, yet would such good luck come to him only in his miserable old age when he was more fit to sit in the chimney-corner and roast apples than to meet the foe in the field. And if any man dealt honestly and carried himself well, yet was he ever envied by others, and perchance by reason of some unlucky chance of war deprived both of office and of life. And nowhere was this more grievous than at the before-mentioned smooth place on the tree: for there an officer who had had a good sergeant or corporal under him must lose him, however unwillingly, because he was now made an ensign. And for that reason they would take, in place of old soldiers, ink-slingers, footmen, overgrown pages, poor noblemen, and at times poor relations, tramps and vagabonds. And these took the very bread out of the mouths of those that had deserved it, and forthwith were made Ensigns.

* * *

REVIEW QUESTIONS

1. Who is Simplicissimus?
2. What is his relation to nature?
3. What does he consider noble and base?
4. What does Grimmelshausen tell us about the conduct of the Thirty Years' War?
5. What happens to the character of Simplicissimus when he witnesses the violence of war?
6. What did the Thirty Years' War do to the land and its occupants?

THOMAS HOBBES

FROM *Leviathan*

Thomas Hobbes (1588–1679) was an English philosopher whose mechanistic and deterministic theories of political life were highly controversial in his own time. Born in Malmesbury, Hobbes attended Magdalen Hall, Oxford, and became tutor to William Cavendish, later earl of Devonshire, in 1608. With his student, he undertook several tours of the continent where he met and spoke with leading intellectual lights of the day, including Galileo and Descartes. Around 1637, he became interested in the constitutional struggle between parliament and Charles I and set to work writing a "little treatise in English" in defense of the royal prerogative. Before its publication in 1650, the book circulated privately in 1640 under the title Elements of Law, Natural and Politic. *Fearing arrest by parliament, Hobbes fled to Paris, where he remained for the next eleven years. While in exile, he served as math tutor to the Prince of Wales, Charles II, from 1646–1648. His great work,* Leviathan *(1651), was a forceful argument for political absolutism. Its title, taken from the horrifying sea monster of the Old Testament, suggested the power and authority Hobbes thought necessary to compel obedience and order in human society. Strongly influenced by mechanical philosophy, he treated human beings as matter in motion, subject to certain physical, rational laws. People feared one another and lived in a state of constant competition and conflict. For this reason, they must submit to the absolute, supreme authority of the state, a social contract among selfish individuals moved by fear and necessity. Once delegated, that authority was irrevocable and indivisible. Ironically, these theories found favor neither with royalists nor with anti-*

royalists. Charles II believed that it was written in justification of the Common-wealth. The French feared its attacks on the papacy. After the Restoration, Parliament added Leviathan *to a list of books to be investigated for atheistic tendencies. Despite frustrations over the reception of his political theories, Hobbes retained his intellectual vigor. At age eighty-four, he wrote an autobiography in Latin and translated the works of Homer into English. He died at age ninety-one.*

From *Leviathan,* by Thomas Hobbes, edited by E. Hershey Sneath (Needham: Ginn Press, 1898).

*   *   *

Of the Causes, Generation, and Definition of a Commonwealth

The final cause, end, or design of men, who naturally love liberty and dominion over others, in the introduction of that restraint upon themselves in which we see them live in commonwealths is the foresight of their own preservation, and of a more contented life thereby; that is to say, of getting themselves out from that miserable condition of war which is necessarily consequent . . . to the natural passions of men when there is no visible power to keep them in awe and tie them by fear of punishment to the performance of their covenants, and observation of the laws of nature. . . .

For the laws of nature, as "justice," "equity," "modesty," "mercy," and, in sum, "doing to others as we would be done to," of themselves, without the terror of some power to cause them to be observed, are contrary to our natural passions, that carry us to partiality, pride, revenge, and the like. And covenants without the sword are but words, and of no strength to secure a man at all. Therefore, notwithstanding the laws of nature, which every one has then kept when he has the will to keep them, when he can do it safely, if there be no power erected, or not great enough for our security; every man will, and may lawfully rely on his own strength and art, for protection against all other men. And in all places where men have lived by small families, to rob and spoil one another has been a trade, and so far from being reputed against the law of nature that the greater spoils they gained, the greater was their honor; and men observed no other laws therein but the laws of honor; that is, to abstain from cruelty, leaving to men their lives and instruments of livelihood. And as small families did then, so now do cities and kingdoms, which are but greater families, for their own security enlarge their dominions upon all pretenses of danger and fear of invasion or assistance that may be given to invaders, and endeavor as much as they can to subdue or weaken their neighbors by open force and secret arts, for lack of other protection, justly; and are remembered for it in later ages with honor.

Nor is it the joining together of a small number of men that gives them this security, because in small numbers small additions on the one side or the other make the advantage of strength so great as is sufficient to carry the victory; and therefore gives encouragement to an invasion. The multitude sufficient to confide in for our security is not determined by any certain number but by comparison with the enemy we fear; and is then sufficient when the advantage of the enemy is not so visible and conspicuous to determine the event of war as to move him to attempt it.

And should there not be so great a multitude, even if their actions be directed according to their particular judgments and particular appetites, they can expect thereby no defense nor protection, neither against a common enemy nor against the injuries of one another. For being distracted in opinions concerning the best use and application of their strength, they do not help but hinder one another, and reduce their strength by mutual opposition to nothing; whereby they are easily not only subdued by a very few that agree together, but also, when there is no common enemy, they make war upon each other for their particular interests. For if we could suppose a great multitude of men to consent in the observation of justice and other laws of nature without a common power to keep them all in awe, we might as well suppose all mankind to do the same; and then there neither would be, nor need to be, any civil government or commonwealth at all, because there would be peace without subjection.

Nor is it enough for the security which men desire should last all the time of their life that they be governed and directed by one judgment for a limited time, as in one battle or one war. For though they obtain a victory by their unanimous endeavor against a foreign enemy, yet afterwards, when either they have no common enemy or he that by one group is held for an enemy is by another group held for a friend, they must needs, by the difference of their interests, dissolve, and fall again into a war among themselves.

It is true that certain living creatures, as bees and ants, live sociably one with another, which are therefore by Aristotle numbered among political creatures, and yet have no other direction, than their particular judgments and appetites; nor speech whereby one of them can signify to another what he thinks expedient for the common benefit; and therefore some man may perhaps desire to know why mankind cannot do the same. To which I answer:

First, that men are continually in competition for honor and dignity, which these creatures are not; and consequently among men there arises on the ground envy and hatred and finally war, but among these not so.

Secondly, that among these creatures the common good differ not from the private; and being by nature inclined to their private, they procure thereby the common benefit. But man, whose joy consists in comparing himself with other men, can relish nothing but what is eminent.

Thirdly, that these creatures, having not, as man, the use of reason, do not see nor think they see any fault, in the administration of their common business; whereas among men, there are very many that think themselves wiser and abler to govern the public better than the rest; and these strive to reform and innovate, one this way, another that way, and thereby bring it into distraction and civil war.

Fourthly, that these creatures, though they have some use of voice in making known to one another their desires and other affections, yet lack that art of words by which some men can represent to others that which is good in the likeness of evil; and evil in the likeness of good; and augment or diminish the apparent greatness of good and evil, making men discontented and troubling their peace at their pleasure.

Fifthly, irrational creatures cannot distinguish between "injury" and "damage"; and, therefore, as long as they be at ease they are not offended with their fellows; whereas man is then most troublesome when he is most at ease; for then it is that he loves to show his wisdom and control the actions of them that govern the commonwealth.

Lastly, the agreement of these creatures is natural, that of men is by covenant only, which is artificial; and therefore, it is no wonder if there be somewhat else required besides covenant to make their agreement constant and lasting, which is a common power to keep them in awe and to direct their actions to the common benefit.

The only way to erect such a common power which may be able to defend them from the invasion of foreigners and the injuries of one another, and thereby to secure them in such sort so that by their own industry and by the fruits of the earth they may nourish themselves and live contentedly, is to confer all their power and strength upon one man, or upon one assembly of men that may reduce all their wills, by plurality of voices, unto one will; which is as much as to say, to appoint one man or assembly of men to bear their person; and every one to accept and acknowledge himself to be author of whatsoever he that so bears their person shall act or cause to be acted in those things which concern the common peace and safety, and therein to submit their wills every one to his will, and their judgments to his judgment. This is more than consent or concord; it is a real unity of them all in one and the same person, made by covenant of every man with every man, in such manner as if every man should say to every man, "I authorize and give up my right of governing myself to this man, or to this assembly of men, on this condition, that you give up your right to him and authorize all his actions in like manner." This done, the multitude so united in one person is called a "commonwealth," in Latin *civitas*. This is the generation of that great "leviathan," or rather, to speak more reverently, of that "mortal god," to which we owe, under the "immortal God," our peace and defense. For by this authority, given him by every particular man in the commonwealth, he has the use of so much power and strength conferred on him that, by terror thereof, he is enabled to form the wills of them all to peace at home and mutual aid against their enemies abroad. And in him consists the essence of the commonwealth, which, to define it, is "one person, of whose acts a great multitude, by mutual covenants one with another, have made themselves the author, to the end he may use the strength and means of them all as he shall think expedient for their peace and common defense."

And he that carries this person is called "sovereign" and said to have "sovereign power"; and every one besides, his "subject."

The attaining to this sovereign power is by two ways. One, by natural force, as when a man makes his children to submit themselves and their children to his government, as being able to destroy them if they refuse; or by war subdues his enemies to his will, giving them their lives on that condition. The other is when men agree among themselves to submit to some man or assembly of men voluntarily, on confidence that they will be protected by him against all others. This latter, may be called a political commonwealth, or commonwealth by "institution," and the former, a commonwealth by "acquisition." * * *

Of the Office of the Sovereign Representative

The office of the sovereign, be it a monarch or an assembly, consists in the end for which he was trusted with the sovereign power, namely, the securing of "the safety of the people"; to which he is obliged by the law of nature, and to render an account thereof to God, the author of that law, and to none but him. But by safety here is not meant a bare preservation but also all other contentments of life which every man by lawful industry, without danger or hurt to the commonwealth, shall acquire to himself.

And this is to be done, not by care applied to individuals further than their protection from injuries when they shall complain, but by a general provision contained in public instruction, both of doctrine and example, and in the making and executing of good laws to which individual persons may apply their own cases.

And because, if the essential rights of sovereignty . . . be taken away, the commonwealth is thereby dissolved and every man returns into the condition and calamity of a war with every other man, which is the greatest evil that can happen in this life; it is the office of the sovereign, to maintain those rights entire, and consequently against his duty, first, to transfer to another or to lay from himself any of them. For he that deserts the means deserts the ends; and he deserts the means when, being the sovereign, he acknowledges himself subject to the civil laws and renounces the power of supreme judicature, or of making war or peace by his own authority; or of judging of the necessities of the commonwealth; or of levying money and soldiers when and as much as in his own conscience he shall judge necessary; or of making officers and ministers both of war and peace; or of appointing teachers and examining what doctrines are conformable or contrary to the defense, peace, and good of the people. Secondly, it is against his duty to let the people be ignorant or misinformed of the grounds and reasons of those his essential rights, because thereby men are easy to be seduced and drawn to resist him when the commonwealth shall require their use and exercise.

And the grounds of these rights have the need to be diligently and truly taught, because they cannot be maintained by any civil law or terror of legal punishment. For a civil law that shall forbid rebellion (and such is all resistance to the essential rights of the sovereignty), is not, as a civil law, any obligation, but by virtue only of the law of nature that forbids the violation of faith; which natural obligation if men know not, they cannot know the right of any law the sovereign makes. And for the punishment, they take it but for an act of hostility which when they think they have strength enough, they will endeavor by acts of hostility, to avoid. * * *

To the care of the sovereign belongs the making of good laws. But what is a good law? By a good law I mean not a just law; for no law can be unjust. The law is made by the sovereign power, and all that is done by such power is warranted and owned by every one of the people; and that which every man will have so, no man can say is unjust. It is in the laws of a commonwealth as in the laws of gaming; whatsoever the gamesters all agree on is injustice to none of them. A good law is that which is "needed" for the "good of the people" and "perspicuous."

For the use of laws, which are but rules authorized, is not to bind the people from all voluntary actions but to direct and keep them in such a motion as not to hurt themselves by their own impetuous desires, rashness, or indiscretion; as hedges are set not to stop travellers, but to keep them in their way. And, therefore, a law that is not needed, having not the true end of a law, is not good. A law may be conceived to be good when it is for the benefit of the sovereign, though it be not necessary for the people, but it is not so. For the good of the sovereign and people cannot be separated. It is a weak sovereign, that has weak subjects, and a weak people, whose sovereign lacks power to rule them at his will. Unnecessary laws are not good laws but traps for money; which, where the right of sovereign power is acknowledged, are superfluous, and where it is

not acknowledged, insufficient to defend the people. * * *

It belongs also to the office of the sovereign to make a right application of punishments and rewards. And seeing the end of punishing is not revenge and discharge of anger, but correction, either of the offender, or of others by his example; the severest punishments are to be inflicted for those crimes that are of most danger to the public; such as are those which proceed from malice to the government established; those that spring from contempt of justice; those that provoke indignation in the multitude; and those which, unpunished, seem authorized, as when they are committed by sons, servants, or favorites of men in authority. For indignation carries men not only against the actors and authors of injustice, but against all power that is likely to protect them; as in the case of Tarquin, when for the insolent act of one of his sons he was driven out of Rome and the monarchy itself dissolved. But crimes of infirmity, such as are those which proceed from great provocation, from great fear, great need, or from ignorance, whether the fact be a great crime or not, there is place many times for leniency without prejudice to the commonwealth; and leniency, when there is such place for it, is required by the law of nature. The punishment of the leaders and teachers in a commotion, not the poor seduced people, when they are punished, can profit the commonwealth by their example. To be severe to the people is to punish that ignorance which may in great part be imputed to the sovereign, whose fault it was that they were no better instructed.

In like manner it belongs to the office and duty of the sovereign, to apply his rewards so that there may arise from them benefit to the commonwealth, wherein consists their use, and end; and is then done when they that have well served the commonwealth are, with as little expense of the common treasure as is possible, so well recompensed as others thereby may be encouraged both to serve the same as faithfully as they can and to study the arts by which they may be enabled to do it better. To buy with money or preferment from a popular ambitious subject to be quiet and desist from making ill impressions in the minds of the people has nothing of the nature of reward (which is ordained not for disservice, but for service past), nor a sign of gratitude, but of fear; nor does it tend to the benefit but to the damage of the public. It is a contention with ambition like that of Hercules with the monster Hydra which, having many heads, for every one that was vanquished there grew up three. For in like manner, when the stubbornness of one popular man is overcome with reward there arise many more, by the example, that do the same mischief in hope of like benefit; and as all sorts of manufacture, so also malice increases by being salable. And though sometimes a civil war may be deferred by such ways as that, yet the danger grows still the greater and the public ruin more assured. It is therefore against the duty of the sovereign, to whom the public safety is committed, to reward those that aspire to greatness by disturbing the peace of their country, and not rather to oppose the beginnings of such men with a little danger than after a longer time with greater. * * *

When the sovereign himself is popular, that is, revered and beloved of his people, there is no danger at all from the popularity of a subject. For soldiers are never so generally unjust as to side with their captain though they love him, against their sovereign, when they love not only his person but also his cause. And therefore those who by violence have at any time suppressed the power of their lawful sovereign, before they could settle themselves in his place have been always put to the trouble of contriving their titles to save the people from the shame of receiving them. To have a known right to sovereign power is so popular a quality as he that has it needs no more, for his own part, to turn the hearts of his subjects to him but that they see him able absolutely to govern his own family; nor, on the part of his enemies, but a disbanding of their armies. For the greatest and most active part of mankind has never hitherto been well contented with the present.

Concerning the offices of one sovereign to another, which are comprehended in that law which is commonly called the "law of nations," I need not say anything in this place because the law of nations and the law of nature is the same thing. And every sovereign has the same right, in securing the safety of his people that any particular man can have in securing the safety of his own body. And the same law that dictates to men that have no civil government what they ought to do and what to avoid in regard of one another dictates the same to commonwealths, that is, to the consciences of sovereign princes and sovereign assemblies, there being no court of natural justice but in the conscience only; where not man but God reigns whose laws, such of them as oblige all mankind, in respect of God as he is the author of nature are "natural," and in respect of the same God as he is King of kings are "laws."

* * *

REVIEW QUESTIONS

1. What is Hobbes's view of human nature?
2. What motivates human beings?
3. What, according to Hobbes, is the purpose of the state?
4. Why do human beings come together to form a political society?
5. What are the responsibilities of the sovereign?
6. What is the sovereign's highest obligation?
7. Does Hobbes hold out any hope that the state can improve human nature?

MICHEL EYQUEM DE MONTAIGNE

FROM "It Is Folly to Measure the True and False by Our Own Capacity"

Michel Eyquem de Montaigne (1533–1592) introduced the essay as a literary form. Born of a wealthy family in the Château de Montaigne, near Libourne, he was first educated by a tutor who spoke Latin but no French. Until he was six years old, Montaigne learned the classical language as his native tongue. He was further educated at the Collège du Guyenne, where his fluency intimidated some of the finest Latinists in France, and studied law at Toulouse. In 1554, his father purchased an office in the Cour des Aides of Périgeaux, a fiscal court later incorporated into the Parlement of Bordeaux, a position he soon resigned to his son. Montaigne spent thirteen years in office at work he found neither pleasant nor useful. In 1571, he retired to the family estate. Apart from brief visits to Paris and Rouen, periods of travel, and two terms as mayor of Bordeaux (1581–1585), Montaigne spent the rest of his life as a country gentleman. His life was not all leisure. He became gentleman-in-ordinary to the king's chamber and spent the period 1572–1576 trying to broker a peace between Catholics and Huguenots. His first two books of the Essais *appeared in 1580; the third and last volume appeared in 1588. These essays are known for their discursive, conversational style, in which Montaigne undertook explorations of custom, opinion, and institutions. They gave voice to his opposition to all forms of dogmatism that were without rational basis. He observed life with a degree of skepticism, emphasizing the limits of human knowledge and the contradictions in human behavior. Indeed, Montaigne's essays are often cited as examples of an epistemological crisis born of the new discoveries, theological debates, and social tensions that marked the early modern period.*

From *The Complete Essays of Montaigne*, translated by Donald M. Frame (Stanford, Calif.: Stanford University Press, 1958), pp. 132–35.

Perhaps it is not without reason that we attribute facility in belief and conviction to simplicity and ignorance; for it seems to me I once learned that belief was a sort of impression made on our mind, and that the softer and less resistant the mind, the easier it was to imprint something on it. *As the scale of the balance must necessarily sink under the weight placed upon it, so must the mind yield to evident things.* The more a mind is empty and without counterpoise, the more easily it gives beneath the weight of the first persuasive argument. That is why children, common people, women, and sick people are most subject to being led by the ears. But then, on the other hand, it is foolish presumption to go around disdaining and condemning as false whatever does not seem likely to us; which is an ordinary vice in those who think they have more than common ability. I used to do so once; and if

I heard of returning spirits, prognostications of future events, enchantments, sorcery, or some other story that I could not swallow,

> Dreams, witches, miracles, magic alarms,
> Nocturnal specters, and Thessalian charms,
>
> Horace

I felt compassion for the poor people who were taken in by these follies. And now I think that I was at least as much to be pitied myself. Not that experience has since shown me anything surpassing my first beliefs, and that through no fault of my curiosity; but reason has taught me that to condemn a thing thus, dogmatically, as false and impossible, is to assume the advantage of knowing the bounds and limits of God's will and of the power of our mother Nature; and that there is no more notable folly in the world than to reduce these things to the measure of our capacity and competence. If we call prodigies or miracles whatever our reason cannot reach, how many of these appear continually to our eyes! Let us consider through what clouds and how gropingly we are led to the knowledge of most of the things that are right in our hands; assuredly we shall find that it is rather familiarity than knowledge that takes away their strangeness,

> But no one now, so tired of seeing are our eyes,
> Deigns to look up at the bright temples of the
> skies,
>
> Lucretius

and that if those things were presented to us for the first time, we should find them as incredible as any others, or more so.

> If they were here for the first time for men to
> see,
> If they were set before us unexpectedly,
> Nothing more marvelous than these things
> could be told,
> Nothing more unbelievable for men of old.
>
> Lucretius

He who had never seen a river thought that the first one he came across was the ocean. And the things that are the greatest within our knowledge we judge to be the utmost that nature can do in that category.

> A fair-sized stream seems vast to one who until
> then
> Has never seen a greater; so with trees, with
> men.
> In every field each man regards as vast in size
> The greatest objects that have come before his
> eyes.
>
> Lucretius

The mind becomes accustomed to things by the habitual sight of them, and neither wonders nor inquires about the reasons for the things it sees all the time.

The novelty of things incites us more than their greatness to seek their causes.

We must judge with more reverence the infinite power of nature, and with more consciousness of our ignorance and weakness. How many things of slight probability there are, testified to by trustworthy people, which, if we cannot be convinced of them, we should at least leave in suspense! For to condemn them as impossible is to pretend, with rash presumption, to know the limits of possibility. If people rightly understood the difference between the impossible and the unusual, and between what is contrary to the orderly course of nature and what is contrary to the common opinion of men, neither believing rashly nor disbelieving easily, they would observe the rule of "nothing too much," enjoined by Chilo.

When we find in Froissart that the count of Foix, in Béarn, learned of the defeat of King John of Castile at Juberoth the day after it happened, and the way he says he learned it, we can laugh at it; and also at the story our annals tell, that Pope Honorius performed public funeral rites for King Philip Augustus and commanded them to be performed throughout Italy on the very day he died at Mantes. For the authority of these witnesses has perhaps not enough rank to keep us in check. But if Plutarch, besides several examples that he cites from antiquity, says that he knows with certain knowledge that in the time of Domitian, the news of the battle lost by Antonius in Germany was published in Rome, several days' journey from there, and dispersed throughout the whole world, on the same day it was lost; and if Caesar maintains that it has often happened that the report has preceded the event—shall we say that these simple men let themselves be hoaxed like the common herd, because they were not clear-sighted like ourselves? Is there anything more delicate, clearer, and more alert than Pliny's judgment, when he sees fit to bring it into play, or anything farther from inanity? Leaving aside the excellence of his knowledge, which I count for less, in which of these qualities do we surpass him? However, there is no schoolboy so young but he will convict him of falsehood, and want to give him a lesson on the progress of nature's works.

When we read in Bouchet about the miracles done by the relics of Saint Hilary, let it go: his credit is not great enough to take away our right to contradict him. But to condemn wholesale all similar stories seems to me a singular impudence. The great Saint Augustine testifies that he saw a blind child recover his sight upon the relics of Saint Gervase and Saint Protasius at Milan; a woman at Carthage cured of a cancer by the sign of the cross that a newly baptized woman made over her; Hesperius, a close friend of his, cast out the spirits that infested his house with a little earth from the sepulcher of our Lord, and a paralytic promptly cured by this earth, later, when it had been carried to church; a woman in a procession, having touched Saint Stephen's shrine with a bouquet, and rubbed her eyes with this bouquet, recover her long-lost sight; and he reports many other miracles at which he says he himself was present. Of what shall we accuse both him and two holy bishops, Aurelius and Maximinus, whom he calls upon as his witnesses? Shall it be of ignorance, simplicity, and credulity, or of knavery and imposture? Is there any man in our time so impudent that he thinks himself comparable to them, either in virtue and piety, or in learning, judgment, and ability? *Who, though they brought forth no proof, might crush me by their mere authority.*

It is a dangerous and fateful presumption, be-

sides the absurd temerity that it implies, to disdain what we do not comprehend. For after you have established, according to your fine understanding, the limits of truth and falsehood, and it turns out that you must necessarily believe things even stranger than those you deny, you are obliged from then on to abandon these limits. Now, what seems to me to bring as much disorder into our consciences as anything, in these religious troubles that we are in, is this partial surrender of their beliefs by Catholics. It seems to them that they are being very moderate and understanding when they yield to their opponents some of the articles in dispute. But, besides the fact that they do not see what an advantage it is to a man charging you for you to begin to give ground and withdraw, and how much that encourages him to pursue his point, those articles which they select as the most trivial are sometimes very important. We must either submit completely to the authority of our ecclesiastical government, or do without it completely. It is not for us to decide what portion of obedience we owe it.

Moreover, I can say this for having tried it. In other days I exercised this freedom of personal choice and selection, regarding with negligence certain points in the observance of our Church which seem more vain or strange than others; until, coming to discuss them with learned men, I found that these things have a massive and very solid foundation, and that it is only stupidity and ignorance that make us receive them with less reverence than the rest. Why do we not remember how much contradiction we sense even in our own judgment? How many things were articles of faith to us yesterday, which are fables to us today? Vainglory and curiosity are the two scourges of our soul. The latter leads us to thrust our noses into everything, and the former forbids us to leave anything unresolved and undecided.

REVIEW QUESTIONS

1. What are the limits of human knowledge?
2. What roles do authority and experience play in knowledge?
3. How does Montaigne's attitude toward prodigies or miracles compare with that of Reginald Scot?
4. How do their conceptions of nature differ?
5. How might Montaigne's reflection on knowledge indicate an intellectual crisis?

MICHEL EYQUEM DE MONTAIGNE

FROM "Of Cannibals"

From *The Complete Essays of Montaigne,* translated by Donald M. Frame (Stanford, Calif.: Stanford University Press, 1958).

When King Pyrrhus passed over into Italy, after he had reconnoitered the formation of the army that the Romans were sending to meet him, he said: "I do not know what barbarians these are" (for so the Greeks called all foreign nations), "but the formation of this army that I see is not at all barbarous." The Greeks said as much of the army that Flamininus brought into their country, and so did Philip, seeing from a knoll the order and distribution of the Roman camp, in his kingdom, under Publius Sulpicius Galba. Thus we should beware of clinging to vulgar opinions, and judge things by reason's way, not by popular say.

I had with me for a long time a man who had lived for ten or twelve years in that other world which has been discovered in our century, in the place where Villegaignon landed, and which he called Antarctic France. This discovery of a boundless country seems worthy of consideration. I don't know if I can guarantee that some other such discovery will not be made in the future, so many personages greater than ourselves having been mistaken about this one. I am afraid we have eyes bigger than our stomachs, and more curiosity than capacity. We embrace everything, but we clasp only wind.

*   *   *

This man I had was a simple, crude fellow—a character fit to bear true witness; for clever people observe more things and more curiously, but they interpret them; and to lend weight and conviction to their interpretation, they cannot help altering history a little. They never show you things as they are, but bend and disguise them according to the way they have seen them; and to give credence to their judgment and attract you to it, they are prone to add something to their matter, to stretch it out and amplify it. We need a man either very honest, or so simple that he has not the stuff to build up false inventions and give them plausibility; and wedded to no theory. Such was my man; and besides this, he at various times brought sailors and merchants, whom he had known on that trip, to see me. So I content myself with his information, without inquiring what the cosmographers say about it.

*   *   *

Now, to return to my subject, I think there is nothing barbarous and savage in that nation, from what I have been told, except that each man calls barbarism whatever is not his own practice; for indeed it seems we have no other test of truth and reason than the example and pattern of the opinions and customs of the country we live in. *There is always the perfect religion, the perfect government, the perfect and accomplished manners in all things.* Those people are wild, just as we call wild the fruits that Nature has produced by herself and in her normal course; whereas really it is those that we have changed artificially and led astray from the common order, that we should rather call wild. The former retain alive and vigorous their genuine, their most useful and natural, virtues and properties, which we have debased in the latter in adapting them to gratify our corrupted taste. And yet for all that, the savor and delicacy of some uncultivated fruits of those countries is quite as excellent, even to our taste, as that of our own. It is not reasonable that art should win the place of honor over our great and powerful mother Nature. We have so overloaded the beauty and richness of her works by our inventions that we have quite smothered her. Yet wherever her purity shines forth, she wonderfully puts to shame our vain and frivolous attempts:

Ivy comes readier without our care;
In lonely caves the arbutus grows more fair;
No art with artless bird song can compare.
> Propertius

All our efforts cannot even succeed in reproducing the nest of the tiniest little bird, its contexture, its beauty and convenience; or even the web of the puny spider. All things, says Plato, are produced by nature, by fortune, or by art; the greatest and most beautiful by one or the other of the first two, the least and most imperfect by the last.

These nations, then, seem to me barbarous in this sense, that they have been fashioned very little by the human mind, and are still very close to their original naturalness. The laws of nature still rule them, very little corrupted by ours; and they are in such a state of purity that I am sometimes vexed that they were unknown earlier, in the days when there were men able to judge them better than we. I am sorry that Lycurgus and Plato did not know of them; for it seems to me that what we actually see in these nations surpasses not only all the pictures in which poets have idealized the golden age and all their inventions in imagining a happy state of man, but also the conceptions and the very desire of philosophy. They could not imagine a naturalness so pure and simple as we see by experience; nor could they believe that our society could be maintained with so little artifice and human solder. This is a nation, I should say to Plato, in which there is no sort of traffic, no knowledge of letters, no science of numbers, no name for a magistrate or for political superiority, no custom of servitude, no riches or poverty, no contracts, no successions, no partitions, no occupations but leisure ones, no care for any but common kinship, no clothes, no agriculture, no metal, no use of wine or wheat. The very words that signify lying, treachery, dissimulation, avarice, envy, belittling, pardon—unheard of. How far from this perfection would he find the republic that he imagined: *Men fresh sprung from the gods.*

These manners nature first ordained.
> Virgil

For the rest, they live in a country with a very pleasant and temperate climate, so that according to my witnesses it is rare to see a sick man there; and they have assured me that they never saw one palsied, bleary-eyed, toothless, or bent with age. They are settled along the sea and shut in on the land side by great high mountains, with a stretch about a hundred leagues wide in between. They have a great abundance of fish and flesh which bear no resemblance to ours, and they eat them with no other artifice than cooking. The first man who rode a horse there, though he had had dealings with them on several other trips, so horrified them in this posture that they shot him dead with arrows before they could recognize him.

Their buildings are very long, with a capacity

of two or three hundred souls; they are covered with the bark of great trees, the strips reaching to the ground at one end and supporting and leaning on one another at the top, in the manner of some of our barns, whose covering hangs down to the ground and acts as a side. They have wood so hard that they cut with it and make of it their swords and grills to cook their food. Their beds are of a cotton weave, hung from the roof like those in our ships, each man having his own; for the wives sleep apart from their husbands.

They get up with the sun, and eat immediately upon rising, to last them through the day; for they take no other meal than that one. Like some other Eastern peoples, of whom Suidas tells us, who drank apart from meals, they do not drink then; but they drink several times a day, and to capacity. Their drink is made of some root, and is of the color of our claret wines. They drink it only luke-warm. This beverage keeps only two or three days; it has a slightly sharp taste, is not at all heady, is good for the stomach, and has a laxative effect upon those who are not used to it; it is a very pleasant drink for anyone who is accustomed to it. In place of bread they use a certain white substance like preserved coriander. I have tried it; it tastes sweet and a little flat.

The whole day is spent in dancing. The younger men go to hunt animals with bows. Some of the women busy themselves meanwhile with warming their drink, which is their chief duty. Some one of the old men, in the morning before they begin to eat, preaches to the whole barnful in common, walking from one end to the other, and repeating one single sentence several times until he has completed the circuit (for the buildings are fully a hundred paces long). He recommends to them only two things: valor against the enemy and love for their wives. And they never fail to point out this obligation, as their refrain, that it is their wives who keep their drink warm and seasoned.

There may be seen in several places, including my own house, specimens of their beds, of their ropes, of their wooden swords and the bracelets with which they cover their wrists in combats, and

of the big canes, open at one end, by whose sound they keep time in their dances. They are close shaven all over, and shave themselves much more cleanly than we, with nothing but a wooden or stone razor. They believe that souls are immortal, and that those who have deserved well of the gods are lodged in that part of heaven where the sun rises, and the damned in the west.

They have some sort of priests and prophets, but they rarely appear before the people, having their home in the mountains. On their arrival there is a great feast and solemn assembly of several villages—each barn, as I have described it, makes up a village, and they are about one French league from each other. The prophet speaks to them in public, exhorting them to virtue and their duty; but their whole ethical science contains only these two articles: resoluteness in war and affection for their wives. He prophesies to them things to come and the results they are to expect from their undertakings, and urges them to war or holds them back from it; but this is on the condition that when he fails to prophesy correctly, and if things turn out otherwise than he has predicted, he is cut into a thousand pieces if they catch him, and condemned as a false prophet. For this reason, the prophet who has once been mistaken is never seen again.

*   *   *

They have their wars with the nations beyond the mountains, further inland, to which they go quite naked, with no other arms than bows or wooden swords ending in a sharp point, in the manner of the tongues of our boar spears. It is astonishing what firmness they show in their combats, which never end but in slaughter and bloodshed; for as to routs and terror, they know nothing of either.

Each man brings back as his trophy the head of the enemy he has killed, and sets it up at the entrance to his dwelling. After they have treated their prisoners well for a long time with all the hospitality they can think of, each man who has a prisoner calls a great assembly of his acquaintances. He ties a rope to one of the prisoner's arms, by the end of which he holds him, a few steps away, for fear of being hurt, and gives his dearest friend the other arm to hold in the same way; and these two, in the presence of the whole assembly, kill him with their swords. This done, they roast him and eat him in common and send some pieces to their absent friends. This is not, as people think, for nourishment, as of old the Scythians used to do; it is to betoken an extreme revenge. And the proof of this came when they saw the Portuguese, who had joined forces with their adversaries, inflict a different kind of death on them when they took them prisoner, which was to bury them up to the waist, shoot the rest of their body full of arrows, and afterward hang them. They thought that these people from the other world, being men who had sown the knowledge of many vices among their neighbors and were much greater masters than themselves in every sort of wickedness, did not adopt this sort of vengeance without some reason, and that it must be more painful than their own; so they began to give up their old method and to follow this one.

I am not sorry that we notice the barbarous horror of such acts, but I am heartily sorry that, judging their faults rightly, we should be so blind to our own. I think there is more barbarity in eating a man alive than in eating him dead; and in tearing by tortures and the rack a body still full of feeling, in roasting a man bit by bit, in having him bitten and mangled by dogs and swine (as we have not only read but seen within fresh memory, not among ancient enemies, but among neighbors and fellow citizens, and what is worse, on the pretext of piety and religion), than in roasting and eating him after he is dead.

*   *   *

So we may well call these people barbarians, in respect to the rules of reason, but not in respect to ourselves, who surpass them in every kind of barbarity.

Their warfare is wholly noble and generous, and as excusable and beautiful as this human disease can be; its only basis among them is their rivalry in valor. They are not fighting for the conquest of new lands, for they still enjoy that natural abundance that provides them without toil and trouble with all necessary things in such profusion that they have no wish to enlarge their boundaries. They are still in that happy state of desiring only as much as their natural needs demand; anything beyond that is superfluous to them.

They generally call those of the same age, brothers; those who are younger, children; and the old men are fathers to all the others. These leave to their heirs in common the full possession of their property, without division or any other title at all than just the one that Nature gives to her creatures in bringing them into the world.

If their neighbors cross the mountains to attack them and win a victory, the gain of the victor is glory, and the advantage of having proved the master in valor and virtue; for apart from this they have no use for the goods of the vanquished, and they return to their own country, where they lack neither anything necessary nor that great thing, the knowledge of how to enjoy their condition happily and be content with it. These men of ours do the same in their turn. They demand of their prisoners no other ransom than that they confess and acknowledge their defeat. But there is not one in a whole century who does not choose to die rather than to relax a single bit, by word or look, from the grandeur of an invincible courage; not one who would not rather be killed and eaten than so much as ask not to be. They treat them very freely, so that life may be all the dearer to them, and usually entertain them with threats of their coming death, of the torments they will have to suffer, the preparations that are being made for that purpose, the cutting up of their limbs, and the feast that will be made at their expense. All this is done for the sole purpose of extorting from their lips some weak or base word, or making them want to flee, so as to gain the advantage of having terrified them and broken down their firmness. For indeed, if you take it the right way, it is in this point alone that true victory lies:

It is no victory
Unless the vanquished foe admits your mastery.
                                    Claudian

The Hungarians, very bellicose fighters, did not in olden times pursue their advantage beyond putting the enemy at their mercy. For having wrung a confession from him to this effect, they let him go unharmed and unransomed, except, at most, for exacting his promise never again to take up arms against them.

We win enough advantages over our enemies that are borrowed advantages, not really our own. It is the quality of a porter, not of valor, to have sturdier arms and legs; agility is a dead and corporeal quality; it is a stroke of luck to make our enemy stumble, or dazzle his eyes by the sunlight; it is a trick of art and technique, which may be found in a worthless coward, to be an able fencer. The worth and value of a man is in his heart and his will; there lies his real honor. Valor is the strength, not of legs and arms, but of heart and soul; it consists not in the worth of our horse or our weapons, but in our own. He who falls obstinate in his courage, *if he has fallen, he fights on his knees.* He who relaxes none of his assurance, no matter how great the danger of imminent death; who, giving up his soul, still looks firmly and scornfully at his enemy—he is beaten not by us, but by fortune; he is killed, not conquered.

*   *   *

To return to our story. These prisoners are so far from giving in, in spite of all that is done to them, that on the contrary, during the two or three months that they are kept, they wear a gay expression; they urge their captors to hurry and put them to the test; they defy them, insult them, reproach them with their cowardice and the number of battles they have lost to the prisoners' own people.

I have a song composed by a prisoner which contains this challenge, that they should all come boldly and gather to dine off him, for they will be eating at the same time their own fathers and grandfathers, who have served to feed and nourish his body. "These muscles," he says, "this flesh and these veins are your own, poor fools that you are. You do not recognize that the substance of your ancestors' limbs is still contained in them. Savor them well; you will find in them the taste of your own flesh." An idea that certainly does not smack of barbarity. Those that paint these people dying, and who show the execution, portray the prisoner spitting in the face of his slayers and scowling at them. Indeed, to the last gasp they never stop braving and defying their enemies by word and look. Truly here are real savages by our standards; for either they must be thoroughly so, or we must be; there is an amazing distance between their character and ours.

The men there have several wives, and the higher their reputation for valor the more wives they have. It is a remarkably beautiful thing about their marriages that the same jealousy our wives have to keep us from the affection and kindness of other women, theirs have to win this for them. Being more concerned for their husbands' honor than for anything else, they strive and scheme to have as many companions as they can, since that is a sign of their husbands' valor.

*   *   *

Three of these men, ignorant of the price they will pay some day, in loss of repose and happiness, for gaining knowledge of the corruptions of this side of the ocean; ignorant also of the fact that of this intercourse will come their ruin (which I suppose is already well advanced: poor wretches, to let themselves be tricked by the desire for new things, and to have left the serenity of their own sky to come and see ours!)—three of these men were at Rouen, at the time the late King Charles IX was there. The king talked to them for a long time; they were shown our ways, our splendor, the aspect of a fine city. After that, someone asked their opinion, and wanted to know what they had found most amazing. They mentioned three things, of which I have forgotten the third, and I am very sorry for it; but I still remember two of them. They said that in the first place they thought it very strange that so many grown men, bearded, strong, and armed, who were around the king (it is likely that they were talking about the Swiss of his guard) should submit to obey a child, and that one of them was not chosen to command instead. Second (they have a way in their language of speaking of men as halves of one another), they had noticed that there were among us men full and gorged with all sorts of good things, and that their other halves were beggars at their doors, emaciated with hunger and poverty; and they thought it strange that these needy halves could endure such an injustice, and did not take the others by the throat, or set fire to their houses.

I had a very long talk with one of them; but I had an interpreter who followed my meaning so badly, and who was so hindered by his stupidity in taking in my ideas, that I could get hardly any satisfaction from the man. When I asked him what profit he gained from his superior position among his people (for he was a captain, and our sailors called him king), he told me that it was to march foremost in war. How many men followed him? He pointed to a piece of ground, to signify as many as such a space could hold; it might have been four or five thousand men. Did all his authority expire with the war? He said that this much remained, that when he visited the villages dependent on him, they made paths for him through the underbrush by which he might pass quite comfortably.

All this is not too bad—but what's the use? They don't wear breeches.

*   *   *

REVIEW QUESTIONS

1. What lessons does Montaigne draw from accounts of the new world?
2. Why do you suppose Montaigne chose cannibalism, of all possible topics, to compare European and American cultures?
3. How does he reflect the crisis of the Iron Century?
4. Are there any human constants for Montaigne?
5. Does he believe in a single human nature, a single ideal of virtue?

HENRY BLOUNT

FROM *A Voyage into the Levant*

The Englishman Henry Blount was an adventurer and traveler. His acute, sympathetic observations of the Turkish Empire render vividly the great power of the Ottomans. In the 1630s, after more than a century of invasion and conquest, the Ottoman Turks were still considered a menace—aggressive, hostile, and heathen— to the Christian West. This particular passage, concerning the organization of the

*THE PLUNDERING AND BURNING OF A VILLAGE, A HANGING, AND
PEASANTS AVENGE THEMSELVES* (1633)   JACQUES CALLOT

These three prints, often referred to as The Horrors of War, *powerfully reveal commonplace events of the early seventeenth century: the ravages of war on a small village, the punishment of unruly troops, and the violence of the violated. They reveal the underbelly of early modern warfare in a way that contrasts starkly with the stately, heroic images of Velázquez and others. How do the troopers depicted by Callot differ from those depicted by Velázquez? How do their representations of warfare differ? How does Callot portray rural life? What general aspects of the Iron Century does Callot capture in his images?*

Turkish army, suggests that the perception was not misplaced. At the same time, however, the 1634 publication of his A Voyage into the Levant *signals Blount's growing fascination with a wider, non-European world.*

From *Documentary History of Eastern Europe,* edited by Alfred J. Bannan and Achilles Edelenyi (New York: Twayne, 1970), pp. 100–4.

*   *   *

Turkish Power in the 1630s

At length we reached Vallivoh, a pretty little town upon the confines of Hungary; where the camp staying some days, we left them behind, and being to pass a wood near the Christian country, doubting it to be (as confines are) full of thieves, we divided our caravan of six score horse in two parts; half with the persons, and goods of least esteem, we sent a day before the rest, that so the thieves, having a booty, might be gone before we came, which happened accordingly; they were robbed; one thief, and two of ours slain; some hundred dollars worth of goods lost. The next day we passed, and found sixteen thieves in a narrow passage, before whom we set a good guard of harquebuzes and pistols, till the weaker fort passed by; so in three days we came safe to Belgrada.

The city, anciently called Taurunum, or Alba Graeca, was the metropolis of Hungary, till won by sultan Soliman the second, in the year 1525. It is one of the most pleasant, stately, and commodious situations that I have seen; it stands most in a bottom, encompassed eastward by gentle and pleasant ascents, employed in orchards or vines; southward is an easy hill, part possessed with buildings, the rest a burying-place of well nigh three miles in compass, so full of graves as one can be by another; the west end yields a right magnificient aspect, by reason of an eminency of land jetting out further than the rest, and bearing a goodly strong castle, whose walls are two miles about, excellently fortified with a dry ditch and out works. This castle on the west side is washed by the great river Sava, which on the north of the city loses itself in the Danubius, of old called Ister,

now Duny, and is held the greatest river in the world, deep and dangerous for navigation, runs eastward into the Euxine or Black Sea, in its passage receiving fifty and odd rivers, most of them navigable. Two rarities, I was told of this river, and with my own experience found true; one was, that at mid-day and mid-night, the stream runs slower by much than at other times; this they find by the noise of those boat-mills, whereof there are about twenty, like those upon the Rhoane at Lions; their clackers beat much slower at those times than else, which argues like difference in the motion of the wheel, and by consequence of the stream; the cause is neither any reflux, nor stop of current by wind or otherwise, for there is no increase of water observed. The other wonder is, that where those two great currents meet, their waters mingle no more than water and oil; not that either floats above other, but join unmixed; so that near the middle of the river, I have gone in a boat, and tasted of the Danuby as clear and pure as a well; then putting my hand not an inch further, I have taken of the Sava as troubled as a street channel, tasting the gravel in my teeth; yet it did not tast unctious, as I expected, but hath some others secret ground of the antipathy, which though not easily found out, is very effectual; for they run thus threescore miles together, and for a day's journey I have been an eye witness thereof.

The castle is excellently furnished with artillery, and at the entrance there stands an arsenal with some forty or fifty fair brass pieces, most bearing the arms and inscription of Ferdinand the emperor. That which to me seemed strangest in this castle (for I had free liberty to pry up and down) was a round tower called the Zindana, a cruelty not by them devised, and seldom practiced; it is like old Rome's Gemoniae: the tower is large and round, but within severed into many squares of long beams, set on end about four feet asunder; each beam was stuck frequently with great flesh hooks; the person condemned was naked, let fall amongst those hooks, which gave him a quick or lasting misery, as he chanced to light; then at the bottom the river is let in by grates, whereby all the putrefaction was washed away. Within this great castle is another little one, with works of its own; I had like to have miscarried with approaching the entrance, but the rude noise, and worse looks of the guard, gave me a timely apprehension with sudden passage, and humiliation, to sweeten them, and get off; for, as I after learned, there is kept great part of the Grand Seignior's treasure, to be ready when he wars on that side the empire: it is death for any Turk or Christian to enter; and the captain is never to go forth without particular license from the emperor. Here the bashaw of Temesuar, joining the people of Buda, and his own with those of Belgrade and Bosnah, they were held encamped on the south side of the town, yet not so severely, but the Spahies, Janisaaries, and Venturiers, had leave to go before to the general rendezvous, as they pleased, though most of them staid to attend the bashaws; they there expected Murath bashaw; he, five days after our arrival, came in with a few foot, but four thousand horse, of the Spahy Timariot's; such brave horses, and men so dexterous in the use of the launce, I had not seen. Then was made public proclamation to hang all such Janissaries as should be found behind these forces. With them the next day we set forward for Sophia, which in twelve days we reached. The bashaws did not go all in company, but setting forth about an hour one after another, drew out their troops in length without confusion, not in much exact order of file and rank, as near no enemy. In this and our former march, I much admired that we had a caravan loaded with clothes, silks, tissues, and other rich commodities, were so safe, not only in the main army, but in straggling troops, amongst whom we often wandered, by reason of recovering the Jews sabbath; but I found the cause to be the cruelty of justice;

for thieves upon the way are empaled without delay; or mercy; and there was a Saniack, with two hundred horse, who did nothing but coast up and down the country, and every man who could not give a fair account of his being where he found him, was presently strangled, though not known to have offended; for their justice, although not so rash as we suppose, yet will rather cut off two innocent men, than let one offender escape; for in the execution of an innocent, they think if he be held guilty, the example works as well as if he were guilty indeed; and where a constant denial makes the fact doubted, in that execution, the resentment so violent terrifies the more: therefore to prevent disorders sometimes, in the beginnings of war, colourable punishments are used, where just ones are wanting. This speedy and remorseless severity makes that when then their great armies lie about any town or pass, no man is endamaged or troubles to secure his goods; in which respect it pretends more effect upon a bad age than our Christian compassion, which is so easily abused, as we cannot raise two or three companies of soldiers, but they pilfer and rifle wheresoever they pass; wherein the want of cruelty upon delinquents, causes much more oppression of the innocent, which is the greatest cruelty of all. Yet without their army there want not scandals, for in the way we passed by a Palanga, which is a village fortified with mud walls against thieves, where we found a small caravan to have been assaulted the day before, and divers remaining sore wounded; for through all Turkey, especially in desart places, there are many mountaineers, or outlaws, like the Wild Irish, who live upon spoil, and are not held members of the state, but enemies, and used accordingly. In all our march, though I could not perceive much discipline, as not near an adverse party, yet I wondered to see such a multitude so clear of confusion, violence, want, sickness, or any other disorder; and, though we were almost three score thousand, and sometimes found not a town in seven or eight days, yet was there such plenty of good bisket, rice, and mutton, as wheresoever I passed up and down to view the Spahies and others in their tents, they would often make me sit and eat with them very plentifully and well. . . .

*   *   *

REVIEW QUESTIONS

1. What does Blount's account reveal about the perils of travel within Europe during the seventeenth century?

2. Why do you suppose Blount reserved so much of his attention for the Turkish military force?

3. What does he most admire?

4. How does his account of Turkish soldiers contrast with that of Christian soldiers by Grimmelshausen?

5. Does the description of Turkish society and military organization serve as a deliberate contrast to and criticism of those organizations ravaging much of central Europe in the 1630s?

16 ❧ THE ECONOMY AND SOCIETY OF EARLY MODERN EUROPE

Transition best characterizes the economy and society of early modern Europe. While the forms of production and exchange remained corporatist and traditional, elements of individualism and capitalism exerted increasingly strong influence. Accordingly, a society that remained in large part hierarchical and patriarchal showed signs of an emergent class structure. Evidence of these changes remained largely regional, being more evident in certain places and times than in others. Nonetheless, the evidence of such a transition can be seen nearly everywhere in Europe, driven by forces that gripped the entire continent.

For much of the period, the population remained locked in a struggle to survive. Beset by periodic famine and disease, life seemed tenuous and expectancies were short. Given high and early mortality, marriages occurred relatively late in life and truncated families were commonplace. Beginning in the late seventeenth century, however, mortality began to decline. By the eighteenth century populations were expanding across Europe.

The principal cause of the change in demographic dynamics was an increase in food supply that may be attributed in turn to a gradual change in agricultural techniques. Throughout the early modern period, traditional agricultural practices gradually yielded to techniques known generally as scientific farming. Landowners who sought gain in the marketplaces of Europe needed more direct control over land use, an ability to respond flexibly to market conditions. As a result, they enclosed communal lands and turned to the kinds of husbandry that would increase harvests and profits. The result was an increased food supply the eventually freed Europe from its age-old cycle of feast and famine.

An increasing population put new pressures on industry by raising the demand for manufactured goods and supplying a ready labor force to produce them. Rural manufacturing in the form of extensive production networks, known as the putting-out system, increased industrial productivity and captured surplus population in industrial work processes. Those who could not find such employ-

ment fled to the cities, which also grew rapidly. It is interesting that urban manufacturing remained largely traditional, that is, highly regulated and guild based, throughout the early modern period.

The greatest single force for change between 1500 and 1800 was the expansion of long-distance commerce based on the development of overseas empires and the consolidation of central states. Capitalistic practices had existed since the late fourteenth century at least, but the possibility of large profits from direct trade with Asia and the Americas offered new scope for their application. The development of mercantilist theories that advocated the expansion of trade as a source of political power combined with capitalistic ambitions to facilitate global commerce. As a result, enterprises such as charter companies emerged on a larger scale. The supplies of goods traded and their profitability promoted the refinement of commercial facilities such as commodity exchanges, stock markets, and banking techniques. Moreover, the activities of these enterprises introduced new commodities in such volumes that new tastes emerged and old patterns of consumption were transformed.

Growing populations and expanding economies notwithstanding, the society of early modern Europe remained traditional. It was hierarchical in structure; each individual's place was fixed by birthright. Authority was patriarchal in nature, modeled on the supposedly absolute authority of the father within his family. Yet, change was also evident here. Economic change created mobility. New wealth encouraged social and political aspirations as bourgeois everywhere chaffed under the exclusivity of the aristocracy and sought admission to their ranks. New poverty created a class of have-nots that challenged the established order and threatened its security.

Observers and theorists viewed the transformation of Europe's economy and society with some trepidation. In most instances, their responses were reactionary. They returned to notions of fatherhood for a model of authority that could withstand the changing times. As the period progressed, however, more and more theorists turned to philosophical reason to find general laws of human interaction that might be applied to govern economic and social behavior.

LORENZO BERNARDO

FROM A Venetian Ambassador's Report on the Ottoman Empire

The struggle for supremacy in northern Italy, which marked the last half of the fifteenth century, gave rise to a new form of diplomacy, structures and procedures that would be fundamental to relations among all modern states. Requiring continuous contact and communication, Renaissance states turned to permanent diplomacy, distinguished by the use of accredited resident ambassadors rather than ad hoc missions of medieval legates. The tasks of a permanent ambassador were to represent his government at state ceremonies, to gather information, and, occasionally, to enter into negotiations. Nowhere was this system more fully and expertly articulated than by the Republic of Venice in the late fifteenth and sixteenth centuries. Ambassadors were chosen with unusual care from the most prominent families of the city. They were highly educated, and their duties were carefully defined.

Among the ambassadors' duties were weekly dispatches reporting all matters of any interest to Venice. These reports were regularly read and debated in the Senate, which replied with questions, instructions, and information of its own. As a result, Venetian ambassadors were among the most skilled and respected in early modern Europe. Their reports remain a singularly important source for the history of that period. Lorenzo Bernardo had the distinction of serving as the Venetian ambassador to a non-European state, Venice's chief rival in trade to the Middle East and the great power of the Moslem world, the Ottoman Empire. Though his assignment to Constantinople was brief (1591–1592), he offered the following analysis of the empire's strengths and weaknesses and of why Venice might expect its imminent decline. It offers insights into the political power in early modern Europe, as well as a Western perspective on non-Western states and civilizations.

From *Pursuit of Power: Venetian Ambassadors' Reports on Spain, Turkey and France in the Age of Phillip II, 1560–1600,* by James C. Davis (New York: HarperCollins, 1970), pp. 72–76, 78–79.

*   *   *

Three basic qualities have enabled the Turks to make such remarkable conquests, and rise to such importance in a brief period: religion, frugality, and obedience.

From the beginning it was religion that made them zealous, frugality that made them satisfied with little, and obedience that produced men ready for any dangerous campaign.

In an earlier report I discussed at length these three qualities, which were then and always had been typical of the Turks. Now I plan to follow the same order, but to discuss whether any changes have taken place subsequently that might lead us to hope that empire will eventually decline.

For nothing is more certain than that every living thing (including kingdoms and empires) has a beginning, a middle, and an end, or, you might say, a growth, maturity, and decline.

In former times, Serene Prince, all Turks held to a single religion, whose major belief is that it is "written" when and how a man will die, and that if he dies for his God and his faith he will go directly to Paradise. It is not surprising, then, that one reads in histories about Turks who vied for the chance to fill a ditch with their bodies, or made a human bridge for others to use crossing a river, going to their deaths without the slightest hesitation. But now the Turks have not a single religion, but three of them. The Persians are among the Turks like the heretics among us, because some of them hold the beliefs of Ali, and others those of Omar, both of whom were followers of Mohammed, but held different doctrines. Then there are the Arabs and Moors, who claim they alone preserve the true, uncorrupted religion and that the "Greek Turks" (as they call these in Constantinople) are bastard Turks with a corrupted religion, which they blame on their being mostly descended from Christian renegades who did not understand the Muslim religion. As a matter of fact, I have known many of these renegades who had no religious beliefs, and said religions were invented by men for political reasons. They hold that when the body dies the soul dies, just as it does with brute beasts, which they are.

The belief that one's death is "written" and that one has no free will to escape dangers is declining in Turkey with each passing day. Experience teaches them the opposite when they see that a man who avoids plague victims saves his life while one who has stayed with them catches plague and dies. During my time there as *bailo* I even saw their mufti flee Constantinople for fear of plague and go to the garden to live, and the Grand Signor himself took care to avoid all contacts with his generals. Having learned they can escape from plagues, they now apply the same lesson to wars. Everybody shirks war service as long as he can, and when he does go he hangs back from the front lines and concentrates on saving his own life. When the authorities announce a campaign in Persia there are outcries and revolts, and if the sultan wants to send janissaries there he creates new ones who are so glad to have the higher pay that they are willing to risk dangers which the regulars dread and flee. In short, nowadays they all look out for their own safety.

As for frugality, which I said was the second of the three sources of the Turks' great power, this used to be one of their marked characteristics. At one time the Turks had no interest in fine foods or, if they were rich, in splendid decorations in their houses. Each was happy with bread and rice, and a carpet and a cushion; he showed his importance only by having many slaves and horses with which he could better serve his ruler. No wonder then that they could put up with the terrible effort and physical discomfort involved in conquering and ruling. What a shameful lesson to our own state, where we equate military glory with sumptuous banquets and our men want to live in their camps and ships as if they were back home at weddings and feasts!

But now that the Turks have conquered vast, rich lands they too have fallen victims to the corruption of wealth. They are beginning to appreciate fine foods and game, and most of them drink wine. They furnish their houses beautifully and wear clothes of gold and silver with costly linings. Briefly, then, they become fonder every day of luxury, comfort, and display. They are happy to follow the example provided by the sultan, who cares nothing about winning glory on the battlefield and prefers to stay at home and enjoy the countless pleasures of the seraglio. Modeling themselves on him, all the splendid pashas, governors, and generals, and the ordinary soldiers too, want to stay in *their* homes and enjoy *their* pleasures and keep as far as possible from the dangers and discomforts of war. The pashas make use of their wives, who are related to the Grand Signor, to persuade him to keep their husbands at home. They do this not only to satisfy the men but also because they know that if they stay in Constantinople their husbands can win more favor by serving and fawning on the Grand Signor. If they go to war their rivals find it easier to slander them and they run a greater risk of losing the sultan's favor. And right behind the great men are all the lower ranks of soldiers, following in their footsteps, and trying to avoid being pulled away from the comforts of home.

Obedience was the third source of the great power of the Turkish empire. In the old days obedience made them united, union made them strong, and strength rendered their armies invincible. They are all slaves by nature, and the slaves of one single master; only from him can they hope to win power, honors, and wealth and only from him do they have to fear punishment and death. Why should it be surprising, then, that they used to compete with each other to perform stupendous feats in his presence? This is why it is said that the Turks' strict obedience to their master is the foundation of the empire's security and grandeur. But when the foundation weakens, when the brake is released, ruin could easily follow. The point is that with those other state-preserving qualities changing into state-corroding qualities, disobedience and disunion could be the agents which finally topple it.

This is all the more likely now that the chief officials have no other goal but to oppose each other bitterly. They have all the normal rivalries and ambitions of ministers of state, but they also have unusual opportunities for undercover competition with each other, because many of them have married daughters, sisters, and nieces of the Grand Signor. These women can speak with His Majesty whenever they want and they often sway him in favor of their husbands. This practice throws government affairs into confusion and is a real source of worry to the first vizier, who fears to take the smallest step without notifying the sultan. He knows that his rivals' wives might sometime find the Grand Signor in the right mood and bring about his ruin, something the *caiacadin* did to the first vizier Sinan when I was there.

*   *   *

REVIEW QUESTIONS

1. What were the causes of Ottoman success?
2. Why does Bernardo stress these particular strengths?
3. What caused the decline of the Ottoman Empire?
4. How does the ambassador define success and failure, rise and decline?

THOMAS MUN

FROM *Discourse on England's Treasure by Forraign Trade*

Thomas Mun (1571–1641) was the son of an English mercer and rose to become a noted writer on economics and the first to give a clear statement of the theory of balance of trade. He was a prominent figure in commercial circles as a member of the standing commission on trade and the committee of the East India Company. His most important publication, Discourse on England's Treasure by Forraign

Trade, published posthumously in 1664, developed his idea that the wealth of a nation could not decline significantly so long as the value of exports exceeded the value of imports. Both in its emphasis on trade, as opposed to agriculture or industry, as the source of wealth and in its vision of economic systems as incapable of expansion, this theory became a cornerstone of mercantilist thinking.

From *Early English Tracts on Commerce*, edited by J. R. McCulloch (Cambridge, Eng.: Cambridge University Press, 1954).

*   *   *

Chapter II
The Means to Enrich This Kingdom, and to Encrease Our Treasure

Although a Kingdom may be enriched by gifts received, or by purchase taken from some other Nations, yet these are things uncertain and of small consideration when they happen. The ordinary means therefore to increase our wealth and treasure is by *Forraign Trade*, wherein wee must ever observe this rule; to sell more to strangers yearly than wee consume of theirs in value. For suppose that when this Kingdom is plentifully served with the Cloth, Lead, Tinn, Iron, Fish and other native commodities, we doe yearly export the overplus to forraign Countreys to the value of twenty two hundred thousand pounds; by which means we are enabled beyond the Seas to buy and bring in forraign wares for our use and Consumptions, to the value of twenty hundred thousand pounds: By this order duly kept in our trading, we may rest assured that the Kingdom shall be enriched yearly two hundred thousand pounds, which must be brought to us in so much Treasure; because that part of our stock which is not returned to us in wares must necessarily be brought home in treasure.

For in this case it cometh to pass in the stock of a Kingdom, as in the estate of a private man; who is supposed to have one thousand pounds yearly revenue and two thousand pounds of ready money in his Chest: If such a man through excess shall spend one thousand five hundred pounds *per*

annum, all his ready mony will be gone in four years; and in the like time his said money will be doubled if he take a Frugal course to spend but five hundred pounds *per annum*, which rule never faileth likewise in the Commonwealth, but in some cases (of no great moment) which I will hereafter declare, when I shall shew by whom and in what manner this ballance of the Kingdoms account ought to be drawn up yearly, or so often as it shall please the State to discover how much we gain or lose by trade with forraign Nations. But first I will say something concerning those ways and means which will encrease our exportations and diminish our importations of wares; which being done, I will then set down some other arguments both affirmative and negative to strengthen that which is here declared, and thereby to show that all the other means which are commonly supposed to enrich the Kingdom with Treasure are altogether insufficient and meer fallacies.

Chapter III
The Particular Ways and Means to Encrease the Exportation of Our Commodities, and to Decrease Our Consumption of Forraign Wares

The revenue or stock of a Kingdom by which it is provided of forraign wares is either *Natural* or *Artificial*. The Natural wealth is so much only as can be spared from our own use and necessities to be exported unto strangers. The Artificial consists in our manufactures and industrious trading with forraign commodities, concerning which I will set down such particulars as may serve for the cause we have in hand.

1. First, although this Realm be already exceeding rich by nature, yet might it be much encreased by laying the waste grounds (which are infinite) into such employments as should no way hinder the present revenues of other manured lands, but hereby to supply our selves and prevent the importations of Hemp, Flax, Cordage, Tobacco, and divers other things which now we fetch from strangers to our great impoverishing.

2. We may likewise diminish our importations, if we would soberly refrain from excessive consumption of forraign wares in our diet and rayment, with such often change of fashions as is used, so much the more to encrease the waste and charge; which vices at this present are more notorious amongst us than in former ages. Yet might they easily be amended by enforcing the observation of such good laws as are strictly practised in other Countries against the said excesses; where likewise by commanding their own manufactures to be used, they prevent the coming in of others, without prohibition, or offence to strangers in their mutual commerce.

3. In our exportations we must not only regard our own superfluities, but also we must consider our neighbours necessities, that so upon the wares which they cannot want, nor yet be furnished thereof elsewhere, we may (besides the vent of the Materials) gain so much of the manufacture as we can, and also endeavour to sell them dear, so far forth as the high price cause not a less vent in the quantity. But the superfluity of our commodities which strangers use, and may also have the same from other Nations, or may abate their vent by the use of some such like wares from other places, and with little inconvenience; we must in this case strive to sell as cheap as possible we can, rather than to lose the utterance of such wares. For we have found of late years by good experience, that being able to sell our Cloth cheap in Turkey, we have greatly encreased the vent thereof, and the *Venetians* have lost as much in the utterance of theirs in those Countreys, because it is dearer. And on the other side a few years past, when by the

excessive price of Wools our Cloth was exceeding dear, we lost at the least half our clothing for forraign parts, which since is no otherwise (well neer) recovered again than by the great fall of price for Wools and Cloth. We find that twenty five in the hundred less in the price of these and some other Wares, to the loss of private mens revenues, may raise above fifty upon the hundred in the quantity vented to the benefit of the publique. For when Cloth is dear, other Nations doe presently practice clothing, and we know they want neither art nor materials to this performance. But when by cheapness we drive them from this employment, and so in time obtain our dear price again, then do they also use their former remedy. So that by these alterations we learn, that it is in vain to expect a greater revenue of our wares than their condition will afford, but rather it concerns us to apply our endeavours to the times with care and diligence to help our selves the best we may, by making our cloth and other manufactures without deceit, which will encrease their estimation and use.

4. The value of our exportations likewise may be much advanced when we perform it our selves in our own Ships, for then we get only not the price of our wares as they are worth here, but also the Merchants gains, the charges of ensurance, and fraight to carry them beyond the seas. As for example, if the *Italian* Merchants should come hither in their own shipping to fetch our Corn, our red Herrings or the like, in this case the Kingdom should have ordinarily but 25s. for a quarter of Wheat, and 20s. for a barrel of red herrings, whereas if we carry these wares our selves into *Italy* upon the said rates, it is likely that wee shall obtain fifty shillings for the first, and forty shillings for the last, which is a great difference in the utterance or vent of the Kingdoms stock. And although it is true that the commerce ought to be free to strangers to bring in and carry out at their pleasure, yet nevertheless in many places the exportation of victuals and munition are either prohibited, or at least limited to be done onely by the people and Shipping of those places where they abound.

5. The frugal expending likewise of our own nat-

ural wealth might advance much yearly to be exported unto strangers; and if in our rayment we will be prodigal, yet let this be done with our own materials and manufactures, as Cloth, Lace, Imbroderies, Cut-works and the like, where the excess of the rich may be the employment of the poor, whose labours notwithstanding of this kind, would be more profitable for the Commonwealth, if they were done to the use of strangers.

6. The Fishing in his Majesties seas of *England, Scotland,* and *Ireland* is our natural wealth, and would cost nothing but labour, which the *Dutch* bestow willingly, and thereby draw yearly a very great profit to themselves by serving many places of Christendom with our Fish, for which they return and supply their wants both of forraign Wares and Mony, besides the multitude of Mariners and Shipping, which hereby are maintain'd, whereof a long discourse might be made to show the particular manage of this important business. Our fishing plantation likewise in *New-England, Virginia, Groenland,* the *Summer Islands* and the *New-found-land,* are of the like nature, affording much wealth and employments to maintain a great number of poor, and to encrease our decaying trade.

7. A Staple or Magazin for forraign Corn, Indigo, Spices, Raw-silks, Cotton wool or any other commodity whatsoever, to be imported will encrease Shipping, Trade, Treasure, and the Kings customes, by exporting them again where need shall require, which course of Trading, hath been the chief means to raise *Venice, Genoa,* the *low-Countreys,* with some others; and for such a purpose *England* stands most commodiously, wanting nothing to this performance but our own diligence and endeavour.

8. Also wee ought to esteem and cherish those trades which we have in remote or far Countreys, for besides the encrease of Shipping and Mariners thereby, the wares also sent thither and receiv'd from thence are far more profitable unto the kingdom than by our trades neer at hand; As for example; suppose Pepper to be worth here two Shillings the pound constantly, if then it be brought from the *Dutch* at *Amsterdam,* the Merchant may give there twenty pence the pound, and gain well by the bargain; but if he fetch this Pepper from the *East-indies,* he must not give above three pence the pound at the most, which is a mighty advantage, not only in that part which serveth for our own use, but also for that great quantity which (from hence) we transport yearly unto divers other Nations to be sold at a higher price: whereby it is plain, that we make a far greater stock by gain upon these *Indian* Commodities, than those Nations doe where they grow, and to whom they properly appertain, being the natural wealth of their Countries. But for the better understanding of this particular, we must ever distinguish between the gain of the Kingdom, and the profit of the Merchant; for although the Kingdom payeth no more for this Pepper than is before supposed, nor for any other commodity bought in forraign parts more than the stranger receiveth from us for the same, yet the Merchant payeth not only that price, but also the fraight, ensurance, customes and other charges which are exceeding great in these long voyages; but yet all these in the Kingdoms accompt are but commutations among our selves, and no Privation of the Kingdoms stock, which being duly considered, together with the support also of our other trades in our best Shipping to *Italy, France, Turkey,* the *East Countreys* and other places, by transporting and venting the wares which we bring yearly from the *East Indies;* It may well stir up our utmost endeavours to maintain and enlarge this great and noble business, so much importing the Publique wealth, Strength, and Happiness. Neither is there less honour and judgment by growing rich (in this manner) upon the stock of other Nations, than by an industrious encrease of our own means, especially when this later is advanced by the benefit of the former, as we have found in the *East Indies* by sale of much of our Tin, Cloth, Lead and other Commodities, the vent whereof doth daily encrease in those Countreys which formerly had no use of our wares.

9. It would be very beneficial to export money as well as wares, being done in trade only, it would encrease our Treasure; but of this I write

more largely in the next Chapter to prove it plainly.

10. It were policie and profit for the State to suffer manufactures made of forraign Materials to be exported custome-free, as Velvets and all other wrought Silks, Fustians, thrown Silks and the like, it would employ very many poor people, and much encrease the value of our stock yearly issued into other Countreys, and it would (for this purpose) cause the more forraign Materials to be brought in, to the improvement of His Majesties Customes. I will here remember a notable increase in our manufacture of winding and twisting only of forraign raw Silk, which within 35. years to my knowledge did not employ more than 300. people in the City and suburbs of London, where at this present time it doth set on work above fourteen thousand souls, as upon diligent enquiry hath been credibly reported unto His Majesties Commissioners for Trade. And it is certain, that if the said forraign Commodities might be exported from hence, free of custome, this manufacture would yet encrease very much, and decrease as fast in *Italy* and in the *Netherlands*. But if any man allege the *Dutch* proverb, *Live and let others live;* I answer, that the Dutchmen notwithstanding their own Proverb, doe not onely in these Kingdoms, encroach upon our livings, but also in other forraign parts of our trade (where they have power) they do hinder and destroy us in our lawful course of living, hereby taking the bread out of our mouth, which we shall never prevent by plucking the pot from their nose, as of late years too many of us do practise to the great hurt and dishonour of this famous Nation; We ought rather to imitate former times in taking sober and worthy courses more pleasing to God and suitable to our ancient reputation.

11. It is needful also not to charge the native commodities with too great customes, lest by indearing them to the strangers use, it hinder their vent. And especially forraign wares brought in to be transported again should be favoured, for otherwise that manner of trading (so much importing the good of the Commonwealth) cannot prosper nor subsist. But the Consumption of such forraign wares in the Realm may be the more charged, which will turn to the profit of the kingdom in the *Ballance of the Trade,* and thereby also enable the King to lay up the more Treasure out of his yearly incomes, as of this particular I intend to write more fully in his proper place, where I shall shew how much money a Prince may conveniently lay up without the hurt of his subjects.

12. Lastly, in all things we must endeavour to make the most we can of our own, whether it be *Natural* or *Artificial;* And forasmuch as the people which live by the Arts are far more in number than they who are masters of the fruits, we ought the more carefully to maintain those endeavours of the multitude, in whom doth consist the greatest strength and riches both of King and Kingdom: for where the people are many, and the arts good, there the traffique must be great, and the Countrey rich. The *Italians* employ a greater number of people, and get more money by their industry and manufactures of the raw Silks of the Kingdom of *Cicilia,* than the King of *Spain* and his Subjects have by the revenue of this rich commodity. But what need we fetch the example so far, when we know that our own natural wares doe not yield us so much profit as our industry? For Iron oar in the Mines is of no great worth, when it is compared with the employment and advantage it yields being digged, tried, transported, bought, sold, cast into Ordnance, Muskets, and many other instruments of war for offence and defence, wrought into Anchors, bolts, spikes, nayles and the like, for the use of Ships, Houses, Carts, Coaches, Ploughs, and other instruments for Tillage. Compare our Fleece-wools with our Cloth, which requires shearing, washing, carding, spinning, Weaving, fulling, dying, dressing and other trimmings, and we shall find these Arts more profitable than the natural wealth, whereof I might instance other examples, but I will not be more tedious, for if I would amplify upon this and the other particulars before written, I might find matter sufficient to make a large volume, but my desire in all is only to prove what I propound with brevity and plainness.

THE SYNDICS OF THE DRAPERS' GUILD (1632)　　　　　　　　　　　　REMBRANDT VAN RIJN

One of Rembrandt's most recognizable works, The Syndics *captures all the sober solidity and confidence of Calvinist merchants in the young Dutch Republic. Convinced that worldly success indicated divine election, they look out on the world with purposeful determination to make of their lives a testimonial to God's grace. The work is a penetrating psychological study of these members of the urban elite. What elements of Rembrandt's painting might be characterized as bourgeois? Insofar as the syndics were leaders in Amsterdam society, what does their portrait reveal of that society? Reading into the expressions on the faces and the composition of the portrait, what was Rembrandt's relationship to the artisanal and mercantile world of Amsterdam?*

REVIEW QUESTIONS

1. What does Mun consider trade to be?
2. Of what does it consist?
3. What is his chief concern regarding trade?
4. What is the relation of trade to the nation?

5. What are the foundations of successful trade for Mun?
6. Why does he emphasize moral values in a treatise on economic policy?
7. What are the goods to be found in commerce?

JEAN BAPTISTE POQUELIN (MOLIÈRE)

FROM *The Citizen Who Apes the Nobleman*

Molière (1622–1673) was baptized Jean Baptiste Poquelin. His life might be considered unorthodox from a very early stage. Though educated at the Collège de Clermont, which would number among its alumni such illustrious literati as Voltaire, and clearly intended for a career in royal service, he broke with tradition and joined a traveling company of players in 1643. He adopted his stage name, Molière, the following year and devoted the rest of his life to the stage. His rise to prominence began in 1658, when, playing on an improvised stage in a guardroom of the Louvre, he performed Corneille's Nicomède *as well as a play of his own,* Le docteur amoureux, *before Louis XIV.* Le bourgeois gentilhomme *appeared at the royal palace at Chambord in 1670. It satirized the ambition of contemporary bourgeois to compete in magnificence with the aristocracy. Yet, it was a double-edged satire. Though the theme must have pleased Molière's noble audience, the figure of Jourdain is no unpleasant, boorish climber but rather a delightfully good-natured soul, foolish but naive, fatuous but genuine. An unwillingness to subordinate his art to his audience may help explain why Molière frequently struggled in his lifetime. His actors often abandoned his company. Pensions went unpaid. His best works were not always well received. His fame spread only slowly. Though considered one of the greatest French writers, Molière was no writer in the strict sense. Little of his work was published; his comedies were written to be performed. Publication occurred only after several texts were pirated by Jean Ribou, and several remained unpublished long after Molière's death. This occurred in 1672, when Molière was taken ill during a performance of* Le malade imaginaire. *He died that same night, without receiving the sacraments or renouncing his stage life, and was buried unceremoniously in a common grave.*

From *The Dramatic Words of Molière*, vol. 5 (Barrie, n.d.).

FROM **Act I**

The overture is played by a great many instruments; and in the middle of the stage, the pupil of the music-master is busy composing a serenade, ordered by M. Jourdain.

SCENE I. A MUSIC-MASTER, A DANCING-MASTER, THREE MUSICIANS, TWO VIOLIN PLAYERS, FOUR DANCERS

Mus.-Mas. (*To the musicians*) Come, retire into that room, and rest yourselves until he comes.

Dan.-Mas. (*To the dancers*) And you also, on that side.

Mus.-Mas. (*To his pupil*) Is it done?

Pup. Yes.

Mus.-Mas. Let me look. . . . That is right.

Dan.-Mas. It is something new?

Mus.-Mas. Yes, it is an air for a serenade, which I made him compose here, while waiting till our gentleman is awake.

Dan.-Mas. May one have a look at it?

Mus.-Mas. You shall hear it by-and-by with the dialogue, when he comes; he will not be long.

Dan.-Mas. Our occupations, yours and mine, are no small matter just at present.

Mus.-Mas. True: we have both of us found here the very man whom we want. It is a nice little income for us this Mr. Jourdain, with his notions of nobility and gallantry, which he has taken into his head; and your dancing and my music might wish that everyone were like him.

Dan.-Mas. Not quite; and I should like him to be more of a judge than he is, of the things we provide for him.

Mus.-Mas. It is true that he knows little about them, but he pays well; and that is what our arts require just now above aught else.

Dan.-Mas. As for myself, I confess, I hunger somewhat after glory. I am fond of applause, and I think that, in all the fine arts, it is an annoying torture to have to exhibit before fools, to have one's compositions subjected to the barbarism of a stupid man. Do not argue; there is a delight in having to work for people who are capable of appreciating the delicacy of an art, who know how to give a sweet reception to the beauties of a work, and who, by approbations which tickle one's fancy, reward one for his labour. Yes, the most pleasant recompense one can receive for the things which one does, is to find them understood, and made much of by applause which does one honour, There is nothing in my opinion, that pays us better for all our troubles; and enlightened praises are exquisitely sweet.

Mus.-Mas. I quite agree with you, and I enjoy them as much as you do. Assuredly, there is nothing that tickles our fancy more than the applause you speak of; but such incense does not give us our livelihood. Praise pure and simple does not provide for a rainy day: there must be something solid mixed withal; and the best way to praise is to put one's hand in one's pocket. M. Jourdain is a man, it is true, whose knowledge is very small, who discourses at random upon all things, and never applauds but at the wrong time; but his money makes up for his bad judgment; he has discernment in his purse; his praises are minted, and this ignorant citizen is of more value to us, as you see, than the great lord who introduced us here.

Dan.-Mas. There is some truth in what you say; but I think you make a little too much of money; and the interest in it is something so grovelling, that no gentleman ought ever to show any attachment to it.

Mus.-Mas. You are glad enough, however, to receive the money which our gentleman gives you.

Dan.-Mas. Assuredly; but I do not make it my whole happiness; and I could wish that with all his wealth he had also some good taste.

Mus.-Mas. I could wish the same; and that is what we are aiming at both of us. But, in any case, he gives us the means of becoming known in the world; and he shall pay for others, and others shall applaud for him.

Dan.-Mas. Here he comes.

* * *

SCENE III. MRS. JOURDAIN,
M. JOURDAIN, TWO LACQUEYS

Mrs. Jour. Ha! ha! this is something new again! What is the meaning of this curious get-up, husband? Are you setting the world at nought to deck yourself out in this fashion? and do you wish to become a laughing-stock everywhere?

M. Jour. None but he-fools and she-fools will make a laughing-stock of me, wife.

Mrs. Jour. In truth, they have not waited until now; and all the world has been laughing for a long while already at your vagaries.

M. Jour. Who is all this world, pray?

Mrs. Jour. All this world is a world which is right, and which has more sense than you have. As for myself, I am disgusted with the life which you lead. I do not know whether this is our own house or not. One would think it is Shrove Tuesday every day; and from early morn, for fear of being too late, one hears nothing but the noise of fiddles and singers disturbing the whole neighbourhood.

Nic. The mistress is right. I shall never see the ship-shape again with this heap of people that you bring to your house. They have feet that pick up the mud in every quarter of the town to bring it in here afterwards; and poor Françoise is almost worked off her legs, with rubbing the floors which your pretty tutors come to dirty again regularly every day.

M. Jour. Good gracious! Miss Nicole, your tongue is sharp enough for a country-lass!

Mrs. Jour. Nicole is right; and she has more sense than you have. I should much like to know what you want with a dancing-master, at your age.

Nic. And with a great hulking fencing-master, who shakes the whole house with his stamping, and uproots all the floor-tiles in our big room.

M. Jour. Hold your tongues, you girl and my wife.

Mrs. Jour. Do you wish to learn dancing against the time when you shall have no longer any legs?

Nic. Do you want to kill any one?

M. Jour. Hold your tongues, I tell you: you are ignorant women, both of you; and you do not know the benefits of all this.

Mrs. Jour. You ought rather to think of seeing your daughter married, who is of an age to be provided for.

M. Jour. I shall think of seeing my daughter married when a suitable party shall present himself for her; but I shall also think of acquiring some polite learning.

Nic. I have also heard, Mistress, that for fear of shortcoming, he has taken a philosophy-master to-day.

M. Jour. Very good. I wish to improve my mind, and to know how to argue about things amongst gentle-folks.

Mrs. Jour. Shall you not go, one of these days, to school, to get the birch, at your age?

M. Jour. Why not? Would to heaven I could have the birch at this hour before everybody, and that I could know all that they teach at school!

Nic. Yes, indeed! that would improve your legs.

M. Jour. No doubt it would.

Mrs. Jour. All this is highly necessary to manage your house!

M. Jour. Assuredly. You both talk like fools, and I am ashamed at your ignorance. (*To Mrs. Jourdain.*) For instance, do you know what you are saying at this moment?

Mrs. Jour. Yes. I know that what I say is very well said, and that you ought to think of leading a different life.

M. Jour. I am not speaking of that. I am asking you what these words are which you are speaking just now.

Mrs. Jour. They are very sensible words, and your conduct is scarcely so.

M. Jour. I am not speaking of that, I tell you. I ask you, what I am speaking with you, what I am saying to you at this moment, what that is?

MRS. JOUR. Nonsense.

M. JOUR. He, no, that is not it. What we are saying both of us, the language we are speaking at this moment?

MRS. JOUR. Well?

M. JOUR. What is it called?

MRS. JOUR. It is called whatever you like.

M. JOUR. It is prose, you stupid.

MRS. JOUR. Prose?

M. JOUR. Yes, prose. Whatever is prose is not verse, and whatever is not verse is prose. Eh? that comes from studying. (*To Nicole.*) And do you know what you are to do to say U?

NIC. How?

M. JOUR. Yes. What do you do when you say U?

NIC. What?

M. JOUR. Say U, just to see.

NIC. Well! U.

M. JOUR. What do you do?

NIC. I say U.

M. JOUR. Yes; but when you say U what do you do?

NIC. I do what you tell me to do.

M. JOUR. Oh! what a strange thing to have to do with fools? You pout the lips outwards, and bring the upper jaw near the lower one; U, do you see? I make a mouth, U.

NIC. Yes: that is fine.

MRS. JOUR. That is admirable!

M. JOUR. It is quite another thing, if you had seen O, and DA, DA, and FA, FA.

MRS. JOUR. But what is all this gibberish?

NIC. What are we the better for all this?

M. JOUR. It drives me mad when I see ignorant women.

MRS. JOUR. Go, you should send all these people about their business, with their silly stuff.

NIC. And above all, this great lout of a fencing-master, who fills the whole of my place with dust.

M. JOUR. Lord! this fencing-master sticks strangely in your gizzard! I will let you see your impertinence directly. (*After having had the foils brought, and giving one of them to Nicole.*) Stay,

reason demonstrative. The line of the body. When one thrusts in carte, one has but to do so, and when one thrusts in tierce, one has but to do so. This is the way never to be killed; and is it not very fine to be sure of one's game when one has to fight somebody? There, just thrust at me, to see.

(*Nicole thrusts several times at M. Jourdain.*)

NIC. Well, what!

M. JOUR. Gently! Hullo! ho! Softly! The devil take the hussy!

NIC. You tell me to thrust at you.

M. JOUR. Yes; but you thrust in tierce, before thrusting at me in carte, and you do not wait for me to parry.

MRS. JOUR. You are mad, husband, with all your fancies; and this has come to you only since you have taken it in your head to frequent the nobility.

M. JOUR. When I frequent the nobility, I show my judgment; and it is better than to frequent your citizens.

MRS. JOUR. Indeed! really there is much to gain by frequenting your nobles; and you have done a great deal of good with this beautiful count, with whom you are so smitten!

M. JOUR. Peace; take care what you say. Do you know, wife, that you do not know of whom you are speaking, when you speak of him? He is a personage of greater importance than you think, a nobleman who is held in great consideration at court, and who speaks to the King just as I speak to you. Is it not a great honour to me to see a person of such standing come so frequently to my house, who calls me his dear friend, and who treats me as if I were his equal? He has more kindness for me than one would ever imagine, and, before all the world, shows me such affection, that I am perfectly confused by it.

MRS. JOUR. Yes, he shows you kindness and affection; but he borrows your money.

M. JOUR. Well, is it not an honour to lend money to a man of that condition? and can I do less for a nobleman who calls me his dear friend?

MRS. JOUR. And this nobleman, what does he do for you?

M. JOUR. Things you would be astonished at, if you knew them.

MRS. JOUR. But what?

M. JOUR. That will do! I cannot explain myself. It is enough that if I have lent him money, he will return it to me, and before long.

MRS. JOUR. Yes, you had better wait for it.

M. JOUR. Assuredly. Has he not said so?

MRS. JOUR. Yes, yes, he will be sure not to fail in it.

M. JOUR. He has given me his word as a nobleman.

MRS. JOUR. Stuff!

M. JOUR. Good gracious, you are very obstinate, wife! I tell you that he will keep his word; I am sure of it.

MRS. JOUR. And I, I am sure that he will not, and that all the caresses he loads you with are only so much cajoling.

M. JOUR. Hold your tongue. Here he comes.

MRS. JOUR. It wanted nothing but this. He comes perhaps to ask you for another loan; and the very sight of him spoils my dinner.

M. JOUR. Hold your tongue, I tell you.

*   *   *

SCENE XII. CLÉONTE, M. JOURDAIN,
MRS. JOURDAIN, LUCILE, COVIELLE, NICOLE

CLE. Sir, I did not wish to depute any one else to prefer a request which I have long meditated. It concerns me sufficiently to undertake it in person; and without farther ado, I will tell you that the honour of being your son-in-law is a glorious favour which I beg of you to grant me.

M. JOUR. Before giving you your answer, Sir, I pray you to tell me whether you are a nobleman.

CLE. Sir, most people, on this question, do not hesitate much; the word is easily spoken. There is no scruple in assuming that name, and present custom seems to authorize the theft. As for me, I confess to you, my feelings on this point are rather more delicate. I think that all imposture is unworthy of an honest man, and that it is cowardice to disguise what Heaven has made us, to deck ourselves in the eyes of the world with a stolen title, and to wish to pass for what we are not. I am born of parents who, no doubt, have filled honourable offices; I have acquitted myself with honour in the army, where I served for six years; and I am sufficiently well to do to hold a middling rank in society; but with all this, I will not assume what others, in my position, might think they had the right to pretend to; and I will tell you frankly that I am not a nobleman.

M. JOUR. Your hand, Sir; my daughter is not for you.

CLE. How.

M. JOUR. You are not a nobleman: you shall not have my daughter.

MRS. JOUR. What is it you mean by your nobleman? Is it that we ourselves are descended from Saint Louis?

M. JOUR. Hold your tongue, wife; I see what you are driving at.

MRS. JOUR. Are we two descended from aught else than from plain citizens?

M. JOUR. If that is not a slander?

MRS. JOUR. And was your father not a tradesman as well as mine?

M. JOUR. Plague take the woman, she always harps upon that. If your father was a tradesman, so much the worse for him; but as for mine, they are impertinent fellows who say so. All that I have to say to you, is that I will have a nobleman for a son-in-law.

MRS. JOUR. Your daughter wants a husband who is suited to her; and it is much better for her that she should have a respectable man, rich and handsome, than a beggarly and deformed nobleman.

NIC. That is true; we have the son of our village squire, who is the greatest lout and the most stupid nincompoop that I have ever seen.

M. JOUR. (*To Nicole*). Hold your tongue, Miss Impertinence; you always thrust yourself into the conversation. I have sufficient wealth to give my daughter; I wish only for honours, and I will make her a marchioness.

Mrs. Jour. Marchioness?

M. Jour. Yes, marchioness.

Mrs. Jour. Alas! Heaven preserve me from it!

M. Jour. It is a thing I am determined on.

Mrs. Jour. It is a thing to which I shall never consent. Matches with people above one's own position are always subject to the most grievous inconvenience. I do not wish a son-in-law of mine to be able to reproach my daughter with her parents, or that she should have children who would be ashamed to call me their grand-mother. If she were to come and visit me with the equipage of a grand lady, and that, through inadvertency, she should miss curtseying to one of the neighbourhood, people would not fail to say a hundred silly things immediately. Do you see this lady marchioness, they would say, who is giving herself such airs? She is the daughter of M. Jourdain, who was only too glad, when she was a child, to play at ladyship with us. She has not always been so high up in the world, and her two grandfathers sold cloth near the St. Innocent gate. They amassed great wealth for their children, for which they are probably pay-ing very dearly in the other world; for people can scarcely become so rich by remaining hon-est folks. I will not have all this tittle-tattle, and in one word, I wish for a man who shall be grateful to me for my daughter, and to whom I shall be able to say: Sit down there, son-in-law, and dine with me.

M. Jour. These are the sentiments of a narrow mind, to wish to remain for ever in a mean condition. Do not answer me any more: my daughter shall be a marchioness in spite of all the world; and, if you put me in a passion, I shall make her a duchess.

*   *   *

REVIEW QUESTIONS

1. How are servants and masters, who operated in separate worlds, interdependent in Molière's comedy?
2. What is the relation between nobility and judgment?
3. Do women judge differently or according to different standards?

ROBERT FILMER

FROM *Patriarcha*

Robert Filmer (1588–1563), the English theorist of patriarchalism and absolutism, was born into the Kentish squirearchy. Filmer was educated at Trinity College, Cambridge, and at Lincoln's Inn and was knighted by Charles I. Though he never fought for the king, his house was sacked during the Civil War, and he was impris-oned in the royalist cause. He wrote many political tracts, but his most important work, Patriarcha *(1680), was not well received at the time. Common opinion seemed to follow that of John Locke, who wrote in his* Two Treatises of Govern-ment: *"There was never so much glib nonsense put together in well-sounding En-glish." Yet, Filmer remains interesting in his own right. He is the first English*

THE MEETING IN LYONS (1625)   PETER PAUL RUBENS

The Meeting in Lyons *is part of a cycle of twenty-one paintings, the largest commission in Rubens's career, for Marie de Medici, dowager queen of France. Intended to hang in her palace in Paris, they describe the important events of her life. It was not easy work; she was a difficult subject, neither beautiful nor interesting nor agreeable. She had quarreled with her late husband, Henri IV, and her son, Louis XIII, had banished her from Paris. Still, Rubens managed to complete the commission to his patroness's satisfaction and created images glorifying the French monarchy. What do the two allegorical figures—Hera, Goddess of Marriage, joining the King and his Queen, and Lyons, driving a chariot—mean in relationship to the royal pair? Why would Rubens choose to represent Henri and Marie as mythological, semidivine figures? Considering the dates of the paintings, after a prolonged civil war and before a great international conflict, what might the allegorical representations of monarch and aristocracy suggest about their strength or weakness?*

195

absolutist. Despite the publication date, Patriarcha was written before the Civil War and before publication of Leviathan, before the actions of Parliament prompted any defense of the monarchy and its prerogatives. Filmer believed that the state was a family, that the first king was a father, and that submission to patriarchal authority was the key to political obligation. Of particular interest is his interpretation of patriarchy, the social structure that characterized early modern Europe until the industrial revolution. Indeed, many scholars argue that Filmer's description of social relations is more realistic than the mechanical individualism put forward by Locke. His achievement notwithstanding, his historical significance rests solely on the fact that all of Locke's political thought was directed against him.

From *Patriarcha and Other Writings,* edited by Johann P. Sommerville (Cambridge, Eng.: Cambridge University Press, 1991), pp. 2–3, 5–12.

Since the time that school divinity began to flourish, there hath been a common opinion maintained as well by divines as by divers other learned men which affirms: "Mankind is naturally endowed and born with freedom from all subjection, and at liberty to choose what form of government it please, and that the power which any one man hath over others was at the first by human right bestowed according to the discretion of the multitude."

This tenet was first hatched in the schools, and hath been fostered by all succeeding papists for good divinity. The divines also of the reformed churches have entertained it, and the common people everywhere tenderly embrace it as being most plausible to flesh and blood, for that it prodigally distributes a portion of liberty to the meanest of the multitude, who magnify liberty as if the height of human felicity were only to be found in it—never remembering that the desire of liberty was the cause of the fall of Adam.

But howsoever this vulgar opinion hath of late obtained great reputation, yet it is not to be found in the ancient Fathers and doctors of the primitive church. It contradicts the doctrine and history of the Holy Scriptures, the constant practice of all ancient monarchies, and the very principles of the law of nature. It is hard to say whether it be more erroneous in divinity or dangerous in policy.

Yet upon the grounds of this doctrine both Jesuits and some over zealous favourers of the Ge-neva discipline have built a perilous conclusion, which is 'that the people or multitude have power to punish or deprive the prince if he transgress the laws of the kingdom'. Witness Parsons and Buchanan. The first, under the name of Doleman, in the third chapter of his first book labours to prove that kings have been lawfully chastised by their commonwealths. The latter in his book *De Jure Regni apud Scotos* maintains a liberty of the people to depose their prince. Cardinal Bellarmine and Mr Calvin both look asquint this way.

This desperate assertion, whereby kings are made subject to the censures and deprivations of their subjects, follows . . . as a necessary consequence of that former position of the supposed natural equality and freedom of mankind, and liberty to choose what form of government it please.

*   *   *

The rebellious consequence which follows this prime article of the natural freedom of mankind may be my sufficient warrant for a modest examination of the original truth of it. Much hath been said, and by many, for the affirmative. Equity requires that an ear be reserved a little for the negative.

*   *   *

To make evident the grounds of this question about the natural liberty of mankind, I will lay down some passages of Cardinal Bellarmine, that may best unfold the state of this controversy. "Secular or civil power," said he

> is instituted by men. It is in the people unless they bestow it on a prince. This power is immediately in the whole multitude, as in the subject of it. For this power is by the divine law, but the divine law hath given this power to no particular man. If the positive law be taken away, there is left no reason why amongst a multitude (who are equal) one rather than another should bear rule over the rest. Power is given by the multitude to one man, or to more by the same law of nature, for the commonwealth of itself cannot exercise this power, therefore it is bound to bestow it upon some one man, or some few. It depends upon the consent of the multitude to ordain over themselves a king, or consul, or other magistrate; and if there be a lawful cause, the multitude may change the kingdom into an aristocracy or democracy.

Thus far Bellarmine, in which passages are comprised the strength of all that ever I have read or heard produced for the natural liberty of the subject.

*　　*　　*

I come now to examine that argument which is used by Bellarmine, and is the one and only argument I can find produced by any author for the proof of the natural liberty of the people. It is thus framed: that God hath given or ordained power is evident by Scripture; but God hath given it to no particular man, because by nature all men are equal; therefore he hath given power to the people or multitude.

To answer this reason, drawn from the equality of mankind by nature, I will first use the help of Bellarmine himself, whose very words are these: 'if many men had been together created out of the earth, all they ought to have been princes over their posterity'. In these words we have an evident confession that creation made man prince of his posterity. And indeed not only Adam but the succeeding patriarchs had, by right of fatherhood, royal authority over their children. Nor dares Bellarmine deny this also. "That the patriarchs," saith he, "were endowed with kingly power, their deeds do testify." For as Adam was lord of his children, so his children under him had a command and power over their own children, but still with subordination to the first parent, who is lord paramount over his children's children to all generations, as being the grandfather of his people.

I see not then how the children of Adam, or of any man else, can be free from subjection to their parents. And this subjection of children is the only fountain of all regal authority, by the ordination of God himself. It follows that civil power not only in general is by divine institution, but even the assignment of it specifically to the eldest parent, which quite takes away that new and common distinction which refers only power universal as absolute to God, but power respective in regard of the special form of government to the choice of the people. Nor leaves it any place for such imaginary pactions between kings and their people as many dream of.

This lordship which Adam by creation had over the whole world, and by right descending from him the patriarchs did enjoy, was as large and ample as the absolutest dominion of any monarch which hath been since the creation. For power of life and death we find that Judah, the father, pronounced sentence of death against Thamar, his daughter-in-law, for playing the harlot. "Bring her forth," saith he, "that she may be burnt." Touching war, we see that Abraham commanded an army of 318 soldiers of his own family; and Esau met his brother Jacob with 400 men at arms. For matter of peace, Abraham made a league with Abimelech, and ratified the articles by an oath. These acts of judging in capital causes, of making war, and concluding peace, are the chiefest marks of sovereignty that are found in any monarch.

Not only until the Flood, but after it, this patriarchal power did continue—as the very name of patriarch doth in part prove. The three sons of Noah had the whole world divided amongst them by their father, for of them was the whole world overspread, according to the benediction given to him and his sons: "Be fruitful and multiply and replenish the earth." Most of the civillest nations in the world labour to fetch their original from some one of the sons or nephews of Noah, which were scattered abroad after the confusion of Babel. In this dispersion we must certainly find the establishment of regal power throughout the kingdoms of the world.

It is a common opinion that at the confusion of tongues there were seventy-two distinct nations erected. All which were not confused multitudes, without heads or governors, and at liberty to choose what governors or government they pleased, but they were distinct families, which had fathers for rulers over them. Whereby it appears that even in the confusion, God was careful to preserve the fatherly authority by distributing the diversity of languages according to the diversity of families.

* * *

In this division of the world, some are of opinion that Noah used lots for the distribution of it. Others affirm that he sailed about the Mediterranean sea in ten years and as he went about, pointed to each son his part, and so made the division of the then known world into Asia, Africa, and Europe, according to the number of his sons, the limits of which three parts are all found in that midland sea.

* * *

Some, perhaps, may think that these princes and dukes of families were but some pretty lords under some greater kings, because the number of them are so many that their particular territories could be but small, and not worthy the title of kingdoms. But they must consider that at first kings had no such large dominions as they have nowadays. We find in the time of Abraham, which was about 300 years after the Flood, that in a little corner of Asia nine kings at once met in battle, most of which were but kings of cities apiece, with the adjacent territories, as of Sodom, Gomorrha, Shinar, etc. In the same chapter is mention of Melchisedek, king of Salem, which was but the city

of Jerusalem. And in the catalogue of the kings of Edom, the name of each king's city is recorded as the only mark to distinguish their dominions. In the land of Canaan, which was but of a small circuit, Joshua destroyed thirty-one kings, and about the same time Adonibezek had seventy kings whose fingers and toes he had cut off, and made them feed under his table. A few ages after this, thirty-two kings came to Benhadad, king of Syria, and about seventy kings of Greece went to the wars of Troy. Caesar found more kings in France than there be now provinces there, and at his sailing over into this island he found four kings in our county of Kent. These heaps of kings in each nation are an argument that their territories were but small, and strongly confirm our assertion that erection of kingdoms came at first only by distinction of families.

By manifest footsteps we may trace this paternal government unto the Israelites coming into Egypt, where the exercise of supreme patriarchal jurisdiction was intermitted because they were in subjection to a stronger prince. After the return of these Israelites out of bondage, God, out of a special care of them, chose Moses and Joshua successively to govern as princes in the place and stead of the supreme fathers, and after them likewise for a time He raised up Judges to defend His people in times of peril. But when God gave the Israelites kings, He re-established the ancient and prime right of lineal succession to paternal government. And whensoever He made choice of any special person to be king, He intended that the issue also should have benefit thereof, as being comprehended sufficiently in the person of the father—although the father only were named in the grant.

It may seem absurd to maintain that kings now are the fathers of their people, since experience shows the contrary. It is true, all kings be not the natural parents of their subjects, yet they all either are, or are to be reputed as the next heirs to those progenitors who were at first the natural parents of the whole people, and in their right succeed to the exercise of supreme jurisdiction. And such heirs are not only lords of their own children, but also of their brethren, and all others that were subject to their fathers.

And therefore we find that God told Cain of his brother Abel: "His desires shall be subject unto thee, and thou shalt rule over him." Accordingly, when Jacob had bought his brother's birthright, Isaac blessed him thus: "Be lord over thy brethren, and let the sons of thy mother bow before thee." As long as the first fathers of families lived, the name of patriarchs did aptly belong unto them. But after a few descents, when the true fatherhood itself was extinct and only the right of the father descended to the true heir, then the title of prince or king was more significant to express the power of him who succeeds only to the right of that fatherhood which his ancestors did naturally enjoy. By this means it comes to pass that many a child, by succeeding a king, hath the right of a father over many a grey-headed multitude, and hath the title of *pater patriae*.

*   *   *

In all kingdoms or commonwealths in the world, whether the prince be the supreme father of the people or but the true heir of such a father, or whether he come to the crown by usurpation, or by election of the nobles or of the people, or by any other way whatsoever, or whether some few or a multitude govern the commonwealth, yet still the authority that is in any one, or in many, or in all of these, is the only right and natural authority of a supreme father. There is, and always shall be continued to the end of the world, a natural right of a supreme father over every multitude, although, by the secret will of God, many at first do most unjustly obtain the exercise of it.

To confirm this natural right of regal power, we find in the decalogue that the law which enjoins obedience to kings is delivered in the terms of "honour thy father" as if all power were originally in the father. If obedience to parents be im-

mediately due by a natural law, and subjection to princes but by the mediation of an human ordinance, what reason is there that the law of nature should give place to the laws of men, as we see the power of the father over his child gives place and is subordinate to the power of the magistrate?

If we compare the natural duties of a father with those of a king, we find them to be all one, without any difference at all but only in the latitude or extent of them. As the father over one family, so the king, as father over many families, extends his care to preserve, feed, clothe, instruct and defend the whole commonwealth. His wars, his peace, his courts of justice and all his acts of sovereignty tend only to preserve and distribute to every subordinate and inferior father, and to their children, their rights and privileges, so that all the duties of a king are summed up in an universal fatherly care of his people.

*   *   *

REVIEW QUESTIONS

1. According to Filmer, what is the relation between the authority of a father and the authority of a king?
2. Why does Filmer link political authority to domestic authority?
3. What is the relation between authority and nature for Filmer?
4. How does political authority come into being?
5. What are the implications of Filmer's rejection of the natural liberty of humankind?
6. What are its implications for his conception of human nature?
7. What are its implications for economic relations?
8. What are its implications for social status?

JEAN BAPTISTE COLBERT

A Memorandum, 1669, AND
A Memorandum, 1670

Jean-Baptiste Colbert (1619–1683), the son of a merchant of Reims, rose above his mercantile roots to become a statesman and minister of finance to Louis XIV. His chief concern was the economic reconstruction of France. He reorganized the fiscal administration of the state and made it more efficient. He also promoted commerce and industry in ways consistent with mercantilist theory. To improve exports, he promoted industries that produced high-quality goods, increased the merchant fleet, attracted foreign artisans, and limited foreign competition. Indeed, the system of state sponsorship and regulation that arose under Colbert and soon bore his name was widely resented by entrepreneurs anxious to innovate and expand. In his capacity as secretary of state for the king's household, from 1669, he was also concerned with the arts and education in France. He founded schools and learned societies to foster these endeavors, including the Academy of Science in 1666 to promote science. All these activities served to expand the power and magnificence of the French state, in the service of which he remained his entire life. That service proved profitable on a private level as well. He died a very wealthy man, whose estate had risen to that of an aristocrat by dint of loyal service. Yet, he was a disappointed man. Though the state had become stronger and more prosperous through his policies, he saw his ambition to reform and expand the French economy frustrated by wars that pursued the ends of the king he had served.

From *Colbert and a Century of French Mercantilism*, by Charles W. Cole (New York: Columbia University Press, 1939), p. 320.

A Memorandum, 1669

The commerce of all Europe is carried on by ships of every size to the number of 20,000, and it is perfectly clear that this number cannot be increased, since the number of people in all the states remains the same and consumption likewise remains the same. . . .

Commerce is a perpetual and peaceable war of wit and energy among all nations. Each nation works incessantly to have its legitimate share of commerce or to gain an advantage over another nation. The Dutch fight at present, in this war, with 15,000 to 16,000 ships, a government of merchants, all of whose maxims and power are directed solely toward the preservation and increase of their commerce, and much more care, energy, and thrift than any other nation.

The English with 3,000 to 4,000 ships, less energy and care, and more expenditures than the Dutch.

The French with 500 to 600.

Those two last cannot improve their commerce save by increasing the number of their vessels, and cannot increase this number save from the 20,000 which carry all the commerce and consequently by making inroads on the 15,000 to 16,000 of the Dutch.

A Memorandum, 1670

Formerly the Dutch, English, Hamburgers, and other nations bringing into the realm a much greater quantity of merchandise than that which they carried away, withdrew the surplus in circulating money, which produced both their abundance and the poverty of the realm, and indisputably resulted in their power and our weakness.

We must next examine the means which were employed to change this destiny.

Firstly, in 1662 Your Majesty maintained his right to 50 sols per ton of freight from foreign vessels, which produced such great results that we have seen the number of French vessels increase yearly; and in seven or eight years the Dutch have been practically excluded from port-to-port commerce, which is carried on by the French. The advantages received by the state through the increase in the number of sailors and seamen, through the money which has remained in the realm by this means and an infinity of others, would be too long to enumerate.

At the same time, Your Majesty ordered work done to abolish all the tolls which had long been established on all the rivers of the kingdom, and he began from then on to have an examination made of the rivers which could be rendered navigable in order to facilitate the descent of commodities and merchandise from inside the realm toward the sea to be transported into foreign lands. Although everything that invites the universal admiration of men was still in disorder in these first years and although the recovery work was a sort of abyss, Your Majesty did not delay in beginning the examination of the tariffs of the *cinq grosses fermes* and scrutinized the fact that the regulation and levying of these sorts of duties concerning commerce had always been done with a great deal of ignorance on the basis of memoranda by tax farmers, who, being solely concerned with their own interests and the increase in the profits

from their tax farms while they possessed them, had always overvalued the commodities, merchandise, and manufactured items of the realm which they saw leaving in abundance, and favored the entrance of foreign merchandise and manufactured items, in order to have a greater quantity of them enter, without being concerned about whether money was as a result leaving the realm, for they were indifferent to this as long as their tax farms produced gain for them during the period of their possession.

Finally, after having thoroughly studied this matter, Your Majesty ordered the tariff of 1664, in which the duties are regulated on a completely different principle, that is to say, that all merchandise and manufactured items of the realm were markedly favored and the foreign ones priced out of the market, though not completely; for having as yet no established manufacturers in the realm, this increase in duties, had it been excessive, would have been a great burden for the *peuple,* because of their need for the aforesaid foreign merchandise and manufactured items; but this change began to provide some means of establishing the same manufactures in the realm; and to this end:

The fabric manufacture of Sedan has been reestablished, and enlarged to 62 from the 12 looms there were then.

The new establishments of Abbeville, Dieppe, Fécamp, and Rouen have been built, in which there are presently more than 200 looms.

The factory for barracan was next established at La Ferré-sous-Jouarre, which is made up of 120 looms;

That of little damasks from Flanders, at Meaux, consisting of 80 looms;

That for carpeting, in the same city, made up of 20 looms . . .

That for tin, in Nivernois;

That for French lace, in 52 cities and towns, in which more than 20,000 workers toil;

The manufacture of brass, or yellow copper, set up in Champagne;

That for camlet of Brussels, in Paris, which will become large and extensive;

Brass wire, in Burgundy;

Gold thread of Milan, at Lyons . . .

And since Your Majesty has wanted to work diligently at reestablishing his naval forces, and since for that it has been necessary to make very great expenditures, since all merchandise, munitions and manufactured items formerly came from Holland and the countries of the North, it has been absolutely necessary to be especially concerned with finding within the realm, or with establishing in it, everything which might be necessary for this great plan.

To this end, the manufacture of tar was established in Médoc, Auvergne, Dauphiné, and Provence;

Iron cannons, in Burgundy, Nivernois, Saintonge, and Périgord;

Large anchors, in Dauphiné, Nivernois, Brittany, and Rochefort;

Sailcloth for the Levant, in Dauphiné;

Coarse muslin, in Auvergne;

All the implements for pilots and others, at Dieppe and La Rochelle;

The cutting of wood suitable for vessels, in Burgundy, Dauphiné, Brittany, Normandy, Poitou, Saintonge, Provence, Guyenne, and the Pyrenees;

Masts, of a sort once unknown in this realm, have been found in Provence, Languedoc, Auvergne, Dauphiné, and in the Pyrenees.

Iron, which was obtained from Sweden and Biscay, is currently manufactured in the realm.

Fine hemp for ropes, which came from Prussia and from Piedmont, is currently obtained in Burgundy, Mâconnais, Bresse, Dauphiné; and markets for it have since been established in Berry and in Auvergue, which always provides money in these provinces and keeps it within the realm.

In a word, everything serving for the construction of vessels is currently established in the realm, so that Your Majesty can get along without foreigners for the navy and will even, in a short time, be able to supply them and gain their money in this fashion. And it is with this same objective of having everything necessary to provide abundantly for his navy and that of his subjects that he is working at the general reform of all the forests in his realm, which, being as carefully preserved as they are at present, will abundantly produce all the wood necessary for this.

REVIEW QUESTIONS

1. How does Colbert speak of commerce?
2. What does it entail?
3. What causes its success?
4. Why is commerce a war?
5. What does Colbert see as the source of Dutch and English power?
6. What has strengthened French commerce?
7. What goods does Colbert describe?
8. Why do you suppose he pays particular attention to them?

ANNE ROBERT JACQUES TURGOT

FROM *Reflections on the Accumulation and Distribution of Wealth*

Anne Robert Jacques Turgot, Baron de l'Aulne (1727–1781), was born in Paris and educated at the Sorbonne. His entire career was spent in state service. After holding numerous posts, he was appointed intendant (chief administrative officer) of the district of Limoges in 1761. Influenced by physiocratic economic ideas that advocated the expansion of agriculture as the basis of all wealth, he instituted a number of fiscal reforms in his district, including the substitution of monetary payments for corvée (forced labor) service. While holding office in Limoges, Turgot published his economic treatise, Reflections on the Accumulation and Distribution of Wealth *(1766), which began with the physiocratic notions of land as the sole source of wealth and agriculture as the most important kind of production but developed in its course a surprisingly modern notion of capital. It provides an interesting perspective on rural labor, productivity, and wealth before industrialization. In 1774, Turgot was appointed comptroller-general of finance. In this capacity he undertook a series of reforms aimed at controlling expenditures and taxation. He delivered his* Six Edicts, *which urged the abolition of forced labor, the suppression of monopolies, and the taxation of the nobility, to the royal council in 1776. These sweeping reforms provoked such resistance from the nobility that Turgot was forced into permanent retirement.*

From *Turgot on Progress, Sociology and Economics,* edited by Ronald L. Meek (Cambridge, Eng.: Cambridge University Press, 1973), pp. 119–28.

I

Impossibility of Commerce on the assumption of an equal division of land, where each man would have only what was necessary for his own support.

If the land were distributed among all the inhabitants of a country in such a way that each of them had precisely the quantity necessary for his support, and nothing more, it is evident that, all being equal, no one would be willing to work for others. Also no one would have the means of paying for the labour of another; for each man, having only as much land as was necessary to produce his own subsistence, would consume all that he had gathered in, and would have nothing which he could exchange for the labour of others.

II

The above hypothesis has never existed, and could not have continued to exist. The diversity of soils and the multiplicity of needs lead to the exchange of the products of the land for other products.

This hypothesis could never have existed, because the lands were cultivated before being divided, cultivation itself having been the only motive for the division and for the law which secures to every man his property. The first men who engaged in cultivation probably cultivated as much land as their resources would permit, and consequently more than was necessary for their own support.

Even if this state of affairs could have existed, it could not have been a lasting one. If each man drew no more than his subsistence from his land, and did not have the means of paying for the labour of others, he would not be able to meet his other needs for housing, clothing, etc. except by means of his own labour, and this would be virtually impossible, since *all land falls far short of producing everything.*

The man whose land was suitable only for corn, and would produce neither cotton nor hemp, would lack cloth with which to clothe himself. Another man would have land suitable for cotton which would produce no corn. One would lack wood to keep himself warm, while another would lack corn to feed himself. Experience would soon teach each man the kind of product for which his land was most suitable; and he would confine himself to cultivating this, in order to procure for himself the things which he lacked by means of exchange with his neighbours, who, having in their turn reasoned in the same way, would have cultivated the produce best suited to their land and abandoned the cultivation of all others.

III

The products of the land require long and difficult preparations in order to render them suitable to meet men's needs.

The produce which the land yields in order to satisfy the different needs of men cannot for the most part serve to do this in the state in which nature affords it; it must be subjected to various changes and be prepared by means of art. Wheat must be converted into flour and then into bread; hides must be tanned or dressed; wool and cotton must be spun; silk must be drawn from the cocoons; hemp and flax must be soaked, peeled, and spun; then different fabrics must be woven from them; and then they must be cut and sewn in order to make them into clothing, footwear, etc. If the same man who caused these different things to be produced from his land, and who used them to meet his needs, were also obliged to subject them to all these intermediate preparations, it is certain that the result would turn out very badly. The greater part of these preparations demand an amount of care, attention, and long experience which is acquired only by working continuously and on a great quantity of materials. Take for example the preparation of hides. Where is the husbandman who could attend to all the details involved in this operation, which goes on for several months and sometimes for several years? If he could, would he be able to do it for a single hide? What a loss of time, space, and materials, which could have served at the same time, or successively, to tan a great number of hides! And even if he did succeed in tanning one single hide, he needs only one pair of shoes: what would he make out of the remainder? Shall he kill an ox in order to have this pair of shoes? Shall he cut down a tree to make himself a pair of clogs? The same may be said of all the other needs of each man, who, if he were reduced to his own land and his own labour, would involve himself in a great deal of time and trouble in order to be very badly equipped in every respect, and would cultivate his land very badly.

IV

The necessity for these preparations leads to the exchange of products for labour.

The same motive which brought about the exchange of one kind of produce for another as between the Cultivators of soils of different qualities was bound to lead also to the exchange of produce for labour as between the Cultivators and another part of society, which had come to prefer the occupation of preparing and working up the products of the land to that of growing them. Everyone gained as a result of this arrangement, for each man by devoting himself to a single kind of work succeeded much better in it. The Husbandman obtained from his land the greatest possible quantity of products, and by means of the exchange of his surplus procured for himself all the other things he needed much more easily than he would have done by means of his own labour. The Shoemaker, by making shoes for the Husbandman, appropriated to himself a portion of the latter's harvest. Each Workman worked to meet the needs of the Workmen of all the other kinds, who in their turn all worked for him.

V

Pre-eminence of the Husbandman who produces over the Artisan who prepares. The Husbandman is the prime mover in the circulation of men's labour; it is he who causes the land to produce the wages of all the Artisans.

It must however be noted that the Husbandman, who supplies everyone with the most important and considerable objects of their consumption (I mean their food and also the materials of almost all manufactures), has the advantage of a greater degree of independence. His labour, among the various kinds of labour which are shared out between the different members of society, retains the same primacy and the same pre-eminence that the labour which provided for his subsistence possessed among the different kinds of labour which he was obliged, when he was in a solitary state, to devote to his needs of all kinds. What we have here is a primacy arising not from honour or dignity, but from *physical necessity*. The Husbandman, generally speaking, can get on without the labour of the other Workmen, but no Workman can labour if the Husbandman does not support him. In this circulation, which by means of the reciprocal exchange of needs renders men necessary to one another and constitutes the bond of society, it is therefore the labour of the Husbandman which is the prime mover. Whatever his labour causes the land to produce over and above his personal needs is the unique fund from which are paid the wages which all the other members of society receive in exchange for their labour. The latter, in making use of the consideration which they receive in this exchange to purchase in their turn the produce of the Husbandman, do no more than return to him exactly what they have received from him. Here we have a very basic difference between these two kinds of labour, and before we deal with the innumerable consequences which spring from it we must dwell upon it in order that we may be fully aware of how self-evident it is.

VI

The wage of the Workman is limited to his subsistence as a result of competition between Workmen. He earns no more than a living.

The simple Workman, who possesses only his hands and his industry, has nothing except in so far as he succeeds in selling his toil to others. He sells it more or less dear; but this higher or lower price does not depend upon himself alone; it results from the agreement which he makes with the man who pays for his labour. The latter pays him as little as he is able; since he has a choice between a great number of Workmen he prefers the one who works most cheaply. Thus the Workmen are obliged to vie with one another and lower their price. In every kind of work it is bound to be the case, and in actual fact is the case, that the wage of the Workman is limited to what is necessary in order to enable him to procure his subsistence.

VII

The Husbandman is the only one whose labour produces anything over and above the wage of the labour. He is therefore the unique source of all wealth.

The position of the Husbandman is quite different. The land, independently of any other man and of any agreement, pays him directly the price of his labour. Nature never bargains with him in order to oblige him to content himself with what is absolutely necessary. What she grants is proportionate neither to his needs nor to a contractual evaluation of the price of his working day. It is the physical result of the fertility of the soil, and of the correctness, much more than of the difficulty, of the means he has employed to render it fruitful. As soon as the labour of the Husbandman produces something over and above his needs, he is able, with this surplus over and above the reward for his toil which nature affords him as a pure gift, to purchase the labour of other members of the society. The latter, when they sell to him, earn no more than their living; but the Husbandman obtains, besides his subsistence, an independent and disposable form of wealth, which he has never purchased but which he sells. He is therefore the unique source of all wealth, which, through its circulation, animates all the industry of society; because he is the only one whose labour produces anything over and above the wage of the labour.

VIII

Primary division of society into two classes: first, the *productive class,* or the Cultivators; and second, the *stipendiary class,* or the Artisans.

Here then we have the whole society divided, as the result of a necessity founded on the nature of things, into two classes, both of which are occupied in work. But one of these, through its labour, produces or rather extracts from the land wealth which is continually renascent, and which provides the whole of society with subsistence and the materials for all its needs. The other, engaged in preparing the produced materials and giving them forms which render them suitable for men's use, sells its labour to the first, and receives its subsistence from it in exchange. The first may be called the *productive class,* and the second the *stipendiary class.*

IX

In the earliest times the Proprietor could not have been distinguished from the Cultivator.

Up to now we have made no distinction at all between the Husbandman and the Proprietor of the land; and in the beginning they were not in fact distinguished at all. It was as a result of the labour of those who first worked the fields, and who enclosed them, in order to make certain of securing the harvest, that all the land ceased to be common to all and that landed property was established. Until societies were consolidated, and until public power, or the law, having come to predominate over individual power, was able to guarantee everyone the peaceful possession of his property against all invasion from without, one could maintain one's ownership of a piece of land only in the way that one had acquired it, and by continuing to cultivate it. It would not have been safe to have one's fields worked by another who, having undergone all the toil involved, would have had difficulty in understanding that the whole of the harvest did not belong to him. Moreover, in these early times every industrious man would be able to find as much land as he wanted, and could thus not be induced to till the soil for others. Every proprietor was obliged either to cultivate his fields or to abandon them completely.

X
Progress of society; all land comes to have an owner.

But the land became populated, and was brought into cultivation to a greater and greater extent. In the course of time all the best land came to be occupied. There remained for the last comers only the infertile soils which had been rejected by the first. But in the end all land found its owner; and those who could not possess properties had at first no course open to them other than to exchange the labour of their hands in the occupations of the *stipendiary* class for the surplus produce of the cultivating Proprietor.

XI
It begins to be possible for the Proprietors to shift the labour of cultivation on to paid Cultivators.

But since the land rendered the owner who cultivated it not only his subsistence, not only the means of procuring for himself by way of exchange the other things he needed, but also a large surplus, he was able with this surplus to pay men to cultivate his land. And for men who live on wages, it is just as good to earn them in this occupation as in any other. Thus ownership could be separated from the labour of cultivation, and soon it was.

XII
Inequality in the division of property: causes which make this inevitable.

The original Proprietors, as has already been said, at first occupied as much land as their resources allowed them and their families to cultivate. A man of greater strength, more industrious, and more anxious about the future took more land than a man with the opposite character. He whose family was larger, having more needs and more hands, extended his possessions further; here was already a first form of inequality. All land is not equally fertile: two men with the same area of land and the same labour may obtain very different products from it: a second source of inequality. Properties, in passing from fathers to children, are divided up into portions which are more or less small according to whether the families are more or less numerous. As one generation succeeds another, the inheritances at one time are further subdivided, and at another time are brought together again through the dying out of branches of the family: a third source of inequality. The contrast between the intelligence, the activity, and above all the thrift of some with the indolence, inactivity, and extravagance of others, constituted a fourth cause of inequality, and the most powerful one of all. The negligent and improvident Proprietor, who cultivates badly, and who in abundant years consumes the whole of his surplus in frivolities, on the occurrence of the slightest accident finds himself reduced to asking for help from his more prudent neighbour, and to living on loans. If, as the result of new accidents or the continuation of his negligence, he finds that he is not in a position to pay, and if he is obliged to have recourse to new loans, there will in the end be nothing left for him to do but abandon a part or even the whole of his estate to his creditor, who will take it as an equivalent; or to part with it to another in exchange for other assets with which he will discharge his obligation to his creditor.

XIII
Consequence of this inequality: the Cultivator distinguished from the Proprietor.

So here we have landed estates as objects of commerce, being bought and sold. The portion of the Proprietor who is extravagant or unfortunate serves to increase that of the Proprietor who is luckier or more prudent; and in the midst of this infinitely varied inequality of possessions it is impossible that a great number of Proprietors should not possess more than they are able to cultivate. Moreover it is natural enough that a wealthy man should wish to enjoy his wealth in peace, and that instead of employing all his time in arduous labour he should prefer to give a part of his surplus to people who will work for him.

XIV
Division of the product between the Cultivator and the Proprietor. *Net product* or revenue.

According to this new arrangement, the product of the land is divided into two parts. One comprises the subsistence and profits of the Husbandman, which are the reward for his labour and the condition upon which he undertakes to cultivate the Proprietor's fields. What remains is that independent and disposable part which the land gives as a pure gift to the one who cultivates it, over and above his advances and the wages of his toil; and this is the share of the Proprietor, or the *revenue*, with which the latter is able to live without working and which he takes wherever he wishes.

XV
New division of the Society into three classes, the Cultivators, the Artisans, and the Proprietors, or the *'productive' class*, the *'stipendiary' class*, and the *'disposable' class*.

So now we have the Society divided into three classes: the class of Husbandmen, for which we may keep the name *productive class*; the class of Artisans and other *stipendiaries* supported by the product of the land; and the class of *Proprietors*, the only one which, not being bound by the need for subsistence to one particular kind of work, may be employed to meet the general needs of the Society, for example in war and the administration of justice, whether through personal service, or through the payment of a part of its revenue with which the State or the Society may hire men to discharge these functions. The name which for this reason suits it best is the *disposable class*.

XVI
Resemblance between the two industrious or non-disposable classes.

The two classes of Cultivators and Artisans resemble one another in many respects, and above all in the fact that those of whom they are composed do not possess any revenue and live equally on the wages which are paid to them out of the product of the land. Both also have this in common, that they earn nothing but the price of their labour and of their advances, and this price is almost the same in the two classes. The Proprietor beats down those who cultivate his land in order to give up to them the smallest possible portion of the product, in the same way as he haggles with his Shoemaker in order to buy his shoes as cheaply as possible. In a word, neither the Cultivator nor the Artisan receive more than a recompense for their labour.

XVII
Essential difference between the two industrious classes.

But there is this difference between these two kinds of labour, that the Cultivator's labour produces his own wage, and in addition the revenue which serves to pay the whole class of Artisans and other stipendiaries, whereas the Artisans receive simply their wages, that is, their share of the product of the land, in exchange for their labour, and do not produce any revenue. The Proprietor enjoys nothing except through the labour of the Cultivator; he receives from him his subsistence and the means of paying for the work of the other stipendiaries. He has need of the Cultivator because of a necessity which arises from the physical order of things, by virtue of which the land produces nothing at all without labour; but the Cultivator has need of the Proprietor only by virtue of human conventions and the civil laws which guaranteed to the original Cultivators and their heirs the ownership of the land which they had occupied, even after they ceased to cultivate it. But these laws could guarantee to the man who took no part in the work himself only that part of the product which the land yields over and above the recompense due to the Cultivators. The Proprietor is forced to abandon the latter, on pain of losing the whole. The Cultivator, completely restricted though he is to the recompense for his labour, thus retains that natural and physical primacy which renders him the prime mover of the whole machine of Society, and which causes not only his own subsistence, but also the wealth of the Proprietor and the wages for all other kinds of work,

to depend upon his labour alone. The Artisan, on the other hand, receives his wages, either from the Proprietor or from the Cultivator, and gives them, by the exchange of his labour, only the equivalent of these wages and nothing over and above this.

Thus, although neither the Cultivator nor the Artisan earn more than a recompense for their labour, the Cultivator generates over and above this recompense the revenue of the Proprietor, and the Artisan does not generate any revenue, either for himself or for others.

XVIII
This difference justifies their being distinguished as the *productive class* and the *sterile class*.

Thus we may distinguish the two non-disposable classes as the *productive class,* which is that of the Cultivators, and the *sterile class,* which includes all the other stipendiary members of the Society.

REVIEW QUESTIONS

1. What is different about Turgot's economic thought?
2. Have we seen constant principles applied to land and its use?
3. What might be the principles Turgot applies?
4. Why is labor of central importance to Turgot?
5. How is labor measured?
6. By what criteria does Turgot evaluate labor?
7. What is the source of wealth, according to Turgot?
8. What constitutes progress?

WILLIAM GOUDGE

FROM *Of Domesticall Duties*

William Goudge was a Puritan clergyman best remembered for his tract on family life, a conduct book entitled Of Domesticall Duties *(1634). It captured the common attitude toward domestic governance in early modern Europe. All authority rested in the hands of a pater familias, the husband-father-master, who possessed absolute control over the family's property and labor and to whom all members of the household owed unflinching obedience and loyalty. Though observed most often in the breach, this pattern of discipline was universally prescribed in early modern Europe.*

From *Western Societies*, edited by Brian Tierney and Joan Scott (New York: Knopf, 1984).

*   *   *

But what if a man of lewd and beastly conditions, as a drunkard, a glutton, a profane swaggerer, an impious swearer and blasphemer, be married to a wise, sober, religious matron, must she account him her superior and worthy of an husband's honor?

Surely she must. For the evil quality and disposition of his heart and life doth not deprive a man of that civil honor which God hath given unto him. Though an husband in regard of evil qualities may carry the image of the devil, yet in regard of his place and office; he beareth the Image of God: so do Magistrates in the Commonwealth, Ministers in the Church, Parents and Masters in the Family. Note for our present purpose, the exhortation of St Peter to Christian wives which have infidel husbands, 'Be in subjection to them: let your conversation be in fear'. If Infidels carry not the devil's image and are not, so long as they are Infidels, vassals of Satan, who are? Yet wives must be subject to them.

*   *   *

REVIEW QUESTIONS

1. What is the conflict between order and nature Goudge depicts?
2. Why should a wife stay with a brutal husband?
3. What sort of order does Goudge invoke?

Marquis de Vauban AND Curé of Rumegies

Much of our knowledge about the economy and society of early modern Europe comes from contemporary accounts. For many reasons, individuals described the life and times of which they were part. Some, like Sébastien Le Prestre, Marquis de Vauban (1633–1707), labored in the service of the state. A French military engineer and genius in the construction of fortifications under Louis XIV, he studied the society and economy of the Kingdom of France to determine its military capacity, the human and material resources that could be mobilized for war in pursuit of royal policy. The result was a series of sober, accurate descriptions of the French population. Others, like Henri Platelle, an obscure parish priest in the village of Rumegies, chronicled their own experiences and observations. The chance survival of Platelle's 1693 journal provides us with a firsthand account of the starkness of daily life in early modern Europe and the struggles of poor peasants simply to survive.

From *Ancien Regime: French Society, 1600–1750,* by Pierre Goubert (New York: Harper-Collins, 1973), pp. 116–18.

Marquis de Vauban

FROM *Description Geographique de l'Election de Vezelay*

*   *   *

. . . All the so-called *bas peuple* live on nothing but bread of mixed barley and oats, from which they do not even remove the bran, which means that bread can sometimes be lifted by the straw sticking out of it. They also eat poor fruits, mainly wild, and a few vegetables from their gardens, boiled up with a little rape- or nut-oil sometimes, but more often not, or with a pinch of salt. Only the most prosperous eat bread made of rye mixed with barley and wheat.

. . . The general run of people seldom drink, eat meat not three times a year, and use little salt . . . So it is no cause for surprise if people who are so ill-nourished have so little energy. Add to this what they suffer from exposure: winter and summer, three fourths of them are dressed in nothing but half-rotting tattered linen, and are shod throughout the year with *sabots,* and no other covering for the foot. If one of them does have shoes he only wears them on saints' days and Sundays: the extreme poverty to which they are reduced, owning as they do not one inch of land, rebounds against the more prosperous town and country bourgeois, and against the nobility and the clergy. They lease their lands out to *métayage,* and the owner who wants a new *métayer* must begin by settling his obligations, paying his debts, stocking the holding with beasts and feeding him and his family for the coming year at his own expense . . .

The poor people are ground down in another manner by the loans of grain and money they take from the wealthy in emergencies, by means of which a high rate of usury is enforced, under the guise of presents which must be made after the debts fall due, so as to avoid imprisonment. After the term has been extended by only three or four months, either another present must be produced when the time is up, or they face the *sergent* who is sure to strip the house bare. Many others of these poor people's afflictions remain at my quill's tip, so as not to offend anybody.

Since hardship can hardly go much further, its normal effects are a matter of course: firstly, it makes people weak and unhealthy, especially the children, many of whom die for want of good food; secondly, the men become idle and apathetic, being persuaded that only the least and worst part of the fruit of their labours will turn to their own profit; thirdly, there are liars, robbers, men of bad faith, always willing to perjure themselves provided that it pays, and to get drunk as soon as they lay hands on the wherewithal . . .

. . . It only remains to take stock of two million men all of whom I suppose to be day-labourers or simple artisans scattered throughout the towns, *bourgs* and villages of the realm.

What I have to say about all these workers . . . deserves serious attention, for although this sector may consist of what are unfairly called the dregs of the people, they are nonetheless worthy of high consideration in view of the services which they render to the State. For it is they who undertake all the great tasks in town and country without which neither themselves nor others could live. It is they who provide all the soldiers and sailors and all the servants and serving women; in a word, without them the State could not survive. It is for this reason that they ought to be spared in the matter of taxes, in order not to burden them beyond their strength.

Let us begin with the town-dwellers. . . .

Among the smaller fry, particularly in the countryside, there are any number of people who, while they lay no claim to any special craft, are continually plying several which are most necessary and indispensable. Of such a kind are those whom we call *manoeuvriers*, who, owning for the most part nothing but their strong arms or very little more, do day- or piece-work for whoever wants to employ them. It is they who do all the major jobs such as mowing, harvesting, threshing, woodcutting, working the soil and the vineyards, clearing land, ditching, carrying soil to vineyards or elsewhere, labouring for builders and several other tasks which are all hard and laborious. These men may well find this kind of employment for part of the year, and it is true that they can usually earn a fair day's wage at haymaking, harvesting and grape-picking time, but the rest of the year is a different story . . .

It will not be inappropriate to give some particulars about what the country day-labourer can earn.

I shall assume that of the three hundred and sixty-five days in the year, he may be gainfully employed for one hundred and eighty, and earn nine *sols* a day. This is a high figure, and it is certain that except at harvest- and grape-picking time most earn not more than eight *sols* a day on average, but supposing we allow the nine *sols*, that would amount to eighty-five *livres* and ten *sols*, call

it ninety *livres*, from which we have to deduct his liabilities (taxes plus salt for a family of four say 14*l*. 16*s*) . . . leaving seventy-five *livres* four *sols*.

Since I am assuming that this family . . . consists of four people, it requires not less than ten *septiers* of grain, Paris measure, to feed them. This grain, half wheat, half rye . . . commonly selling at six *livres* per *septier* . . . will come to sixty *livres*, which leaves fifteen *livres* four *sols* out of the seventy-five *livres* four *sols*, out of which the labourer has to find the price of rent and upkeep for his house, a few chattels, if only some earthenware bowls, clothing and linen, and the needs of his entire family for one year.

But these fifteen *livres* four *sols* will not take him very far unless his industry or some particular business supervenes and his wife contributes to their income by means of her distaff, sewing, knitting hose or making small quantities of lace . . . also by keeping a small garden or rearing poultry and perhaps a calf, a pig or a goat for the better-off . . . ; by which means he might buy a piece of larding bacon and a little butter or oil for making soup. And if he does not additionally cultivate some small allotment, he will be hard pressed to subsist, or at least he will be reduced, together with his family, to the most wretched fare. And if instead of two children he has four, that will be worse still until they are old enough to earn their own living. Thus however we come at the matter, it is certain that he will always have the greatest difficulty in seeing the year out . . .

Curé of Rumegies

FROM *Journal*

. . . the final misfortune was the utter failure of the ensuing harvest, which caused grain to reach a tremendous price. And since the poor people were exhausted in like measure by the frequent demands of His Majesty and by these exorbitant taxes, they fell into such poverty as might just as well be called famine. Happy the man who could lay hands on a measure of rye to mix with oats, peas and beans and make bread to half fill his belly. I speak of two thirds of this village, if not more . . .

Throughout this time, the talk was all of thieves, murders and people dying of starvation. I do not know if it is to the credit of the *curé* of Rumegies to refer here to a death which occurred in his parish during that time: a man named Pierre du Gauquier, who lived by the statue of the Virgin, towards la Howardries. This poor fellow was a widower; people thought that he was not as poor as he was; he was burdened with three children. He fell ill, or rather he grew worn-out and feeble, but nobody informed the *curé,* until one Sunday, upon the final bell for mass, one of his sisters came and told the *curé* that her brother was dying of starvation, and that was all she said. The pastor gave her some bread to take to him forthwith, but perhaps the sister had need of it for herself, as seems likely to be the case. She did not take it to him, and at the second bell for vespers the poor man died of starvation. He was the only one to drop dead for want of bread, but several others died of that cause a little at a time, both here and in other villages, for that year saw a great mortality. In our parish alone, more people died than in several ordinary years . . . Truly men wearied of being of this world. Men of goodwill had their hearts wrung at the sight of the poor people's sufferings, poor people, without money while a measure of corn cost nine to ten *livres* at the end of the year, with peas and beans corresponding . . .

The ordinance made by His Majesty for the relief of his poor people cannot be forgotten here . . . Every community *had to* feed its poor. The pastors, mayors and men of law taxed the wealth-iest and the middling, each according to his capability, in order to succour the poor, whom it was also their duty to seek out. It was the right way to keep everybody provided . . . In this village, where there is no court and everybody is his own master, the *curé* read out and re-read that ordinance to no avail. The *mayeurs* and men of law, who were the richest and would therefore have to be taxed most, fought it with all their might. With much hardship, August was finally reached. A fortnight beforehand, people were harvesting the rye when it was still green, and putting it in ovens to dry it, and because this grain was unripe and unhealthy it caused several serious illnesses. May the Lord in his fatherly Providence vouchsafe us to be preserved henceforward from a like dearth . . .

REVIEW QUESTIONS

1. What does Vauban tell us about the lives of the great majority of French people?
2. How might they measure wealth?
3. How might they view taxes?
4. Would they be Turgot's workmen or husbandmen?
5. Who are the people Vauban describes?
6. What is their social place?
7. What is their economic function?
8. What services might they render to the state?
9. Who are the people Platelle describes as poor?
10. Do they cause their own poverty?
11. Does Platelle suggest any attributes that may have caused their poverty?
12. Whom do taxes serve in Platelle's parish?
13. What was the purpose of taxes?

ABBÉ GUILLAUME-THOMAS RAYNAL

FROM *A Philosophical and Political History of the Settlements and Trade of the Europeans in the East and West Indies*

The Abbé Guillaume-Thomas Raynal (1713–1796) was an author and propagandist, who helped set the intellectual climate for the French Revolution. Educated by the Jesuits, he initially joined the Society of Jesus but later left the religious life to concentrate on his writing. The author of several popular histories and the editor of the Mercure de France, *he established himself with the publication in 1770 of a six-volume history of the European colonies in the East Indies and North America, from which this passionate denunciation of slavery is drawn. The work's popularity can be measured by the fact that it went through thirty editions before the revolution. Elected to the Estates General in 1789, he refused to serve because of his opposition to violence. He later renounced radicalism in favor of a constitutional monarchy. His property was expropriated by the revolutionary regime he opposed, and Raynal died in poverty.*

From *A Philosophical and Political History of the Settlements and Trade of the Europeans in the East and West Indies,* by Abbé Raynal (Glasgow, Scot.: M'Kenzie, 1812), pp. 311–17.

*   *   *

Slavery is entirely contrary to humanity, reason, and justice.

We will not here so far demean ourselves, as to enlarge the ignominious list of those writers who devote their abilities to justify, by policy, what morality condemns. In an age where so many errors are boldly laid open, it would be unpardonable to conceal any truth that is interesting to humanity. If, whatever we have hitherto advanced, hath seemingly tended only to alleviate the burden of slavery, the reason is, that it was first necessary to give some comfort to those unhappy beings, whom we cannot set free; and convince their oppressors, that they are cruel, to the prejudice of real interests. But, in the meantime, until some great revolution makes the evidence of this great truth felt, it is proper to go on with the subject.

We shall then first prove, that there is no reason of state that can authorise slavery. We shall not be afraid to cite to the tribunal of reason and justice, those governments which tolerate this cruelty, or which even are not ashamed to make it the basis of their power.

Montesquieu could not resolve with himself to treat seriously the question concerning slavery. In reality it is degrading reason to employ it, I will not say in defending, but even in refuting an abuse so repugnant to it. Whoever justifies so odious a system, deserves the utmost contempt from a philosopher, and from the negro a stab with his dagger.

*   *   *

Will it be said, that he who wants to make me a slave does me no injury, but that he only makes use of his rights? Where are those rights? Who hath stamped upon them so sacred a character as to silence mine? From Nature I hold the right of self-defence; Nature, therefore, has not given to another the right of attacking me. If thou thinkest thyself authorised to oppress me, because thou art stronger and more ingenious than I am; do not complain if my vigorous arm shall plunge a dagger into thy breast; do not complain when in thy tortured entrails thou shalt feel the pangs of death conveyed by poison into thy food: I am stronger and more ingenious than thou; fall a victim, therefore, in thy, turn, and expiate the crime of having been an oppressor.

He who supports the system of slavery, is the enemy of the whole human race. He divides it into two societies of legal assassins; the oppressors, and the oppressed. It is the same thing as proclaiming to the world, if you would preserve your life, instantly take away mine, for I want to have yours.

But the right of slavery, you say, extends only to the right of labour and the privation of liberty, not of life. What! does not the master, who disposes of my strength at his pleasure, likewise dispose of my life, which depends on the voluntary and moderate use of my faculties. What is existence to him, who has not the disposal of it? I cannot kill my slave, but I can make him bleed under the whip of an excutioner; I can overwhelm him with sorrows, drudgery, and want; I can injure him every way, and secretly undermine the principles and springs of his life; I can smother, by slow punishments, the wretched infant, which a negro woman carries in her womb. Thus the laws protect the slave against violent death, only to leave to my cruelty the right of making him die by degrees.

Let us proceed a step farther: the right of slavery is that of perpetrating all sorts of crimes: those crimes which invade property; for slaves are not suffered to have any, even in their own persons: those crimes which destroy personal safety; for the slave may be sacrificed to the caprice of his master: those crimes, which make modesty shudder. My blood rises at these horrid images. I detest, I abhor the human species, made up only of victims and executioners; and, if it is never to become better, may it be anihilated!

*   *   *

But these negroes, say they, are a race of men born for slavery; their dispositions are narrow, treacherous, and wicked; they themselves allow the superiority of our understandings, and almost acknowledge the justice of our authority.

The minds of the negroes are contracted; because slavery spoils all the springs of the soul. They are wicked; but not half so wicked as you. They are treacherous, because they are under no obligation to speak truth to their tyrants. They acknowledge the superiority of our understandings, because we have abused their ignorance. They allow the justice of our authority, because we have abused their weakness. I might as well say, that the Indians are a species of men born to be crushed to death, because there are fanatics among them who throw themselves under the wheels of their idol's car, before the temple of Jaguernat.

But these negroes, it is farther urged, were born as slaves. Barbarians, will you persuade me, that a man can be the property of a sovereign, a son the property of a father, a wife the property of an husband, a domestic the property of a master, a negro the property of a planter?

But these slaves have sold themselves. Could ever a man, by compact, or by an oath, permit another to use and abuse him? If he assented to this compact, or confirmed it by an oath, it were a transport of ignorance or folly; and he is released from it, the moment that he either knows himself, or his reason returns.

But they had been taken in war. What have you to do with that? Suffer the conqueror to make what ill use he pleases of his own victory. Why do you make yourselves his accomplices?

But they were criminals, condemned in their own country to slavery. Who was it that condemned them? Do you not know, that in a despotic state there is no criminal but the despot?

The subject of a despotic prince is the same as the slave in a state repugnant to Nature. Every thing that contributes to keep a man in such a state, is an attempt against his person. Every power, which fixes him to the tyranny of one man, is the power of his enemies; and all those who are about him, are the authors or abettors of this violence. His mother, who taught him the first lessons of disobedience; his neighbour, who set him the example of it; his superiors, who compelled him into this state; and this equals, who led him into it by their opinion: All these are the ministers and instruments of tyranny. The tyrant can do nothing of himself; he is only the first mover of those efforts which all his subjects exert to their mutual oppression. He keeps them in a state of perpetual war, which renders robberies, treasons, and even assassinations, lawful. Thus, like the blood which flows in his veins, all crimes originate from his heart, and return thither, as to their primary source. Caligula used to say, that he wished the whole human race had but one head, that he might have the pleasure of cutting it off. Socrates would have said, that if all crimes were heaped upon one head, that should be the one which ought to be struck off.

Let us, therefore, endeavour to make the light of reason, and the sentiments of Nature, take place of the blind ferocity of our ancestors. Let us break the bonds of so many victims to our mercenary principles, should we even be obliged to discard a commerce which is founded only on injustice, and whose object is luxury.

But even this is not necessary. There is no occasion to give up those conveniences which custom hath so much endeared to us. We may draw them from our colonies, without peopling them with the slaves. These productions may be cultivated by the hands of free men, and then be reaped without remorse.

The islands are filled with blacks, whose fetters have been broken. They successfully clear the small plantations that have been given them, or which they have acquired by their industry. Such of these unhappy men, as should recover their independence, would live in quiet upon the same manual labours, that would then be free and advantageous to them. The vassals of Denmark, who have lately been made free, have not abandoned their ploughs.

Is it then apprehended, that the facility of acquiring subsistence without labour, on a soil naturally fertile, and of dispensing with the want of clothes under a burning sky, would plunge these men in idleness? Why then do not the inhabitants of Europe confine themselves to such labours as are of the first necessity? Why do they exhaust their powers in laborious employments, which tend only to the transient gratifications of a frivolous imagination? There are amongst us a thousand professions, some more laborious than others, which owe their origin to our institutions. Human laws have given rise to a variety of fictitious wants which otherwise would never have had an existence. By disposing of every species of property according to their capricious institutions, they have subjected an infinite number of people to the imperious will of their fellow-creatures, so far as even to make them sing and dance for a living. We have amongst us beings formed like ourselves, who have consented to inter themselves under mountains, to furnish us with metals and with copper, perhaps to poison us: Why do we imagine that the negroes are less dupes and less foolish than the Europeans?

At the time that we gradually confer liberty on these unhappy beings as a reward for their economy, their good behaviour, and their industry, we must be careful to subject them to our laws and manners, and to offer them our super fluities. We must give to them a country, give them interest to study, productions to cultivate, and an object adequate to their respective tastes, and our colonies will never want men, who, being eased of their chains, will be more active and robust.

To what tribunal shall we refer the cause of humanity, which so many men are in confederacy to betray, in order to over turn the whole system of slavery, which is supported by passions so universal, by laws so authentic, by the emulations of such powerful nations, and by prejudices still more powerful? Sovereigns of the earth, you alone can bring about this revolution. If you do not sport with the rest of mortals, if you do not regard the power of kings as the right of a successful plunder, and the obedience of subjects as artfully obtained from their ignorance, reflect on your own obligations. Refuse the sanction of your authority to the infamous and criminal traffic of men, turned into so many herds of cattle, and this trade will cease. For once unite, for the happiness of the world, those powers and designs which have been so often exerted for its ruin. If some one amongst you would venture to found the expectation of his opulence and grandeur on the generosity of all the rest, he instantly becomes an enemy of mankind, who ought to be destroyed. You may carry fire and sword into his territories. Your armies will soon be inspired with the sacred enthusiasm of humanity. You will then perceive what difference virtue makes between men who succour the oppressed, and mercenaries who serve tyrants.

But, what am I saying? Let the ineffectual calls of humanity be no longer pleaded with the people and their masters; perhaps they have never been consulted in any public transactions. If then, ye nations of Europe, interest alone can exert its influence over you, listen to me once more: Your slaves stand in no need either of your generosity or of your counsels, in order to break the sacrilegious yoke which oppresses them. Nature speaks a more powerful language than philosophy, or interest. Some white people, already massacred, have expiated a part of our crimes; already have two colonies of fugitive negroes been established, to whom treaties and power give a perfect security from your attempts. Poison hath at different times been the instrument of their vengeance. Several

have eluded your oppression by a voluntary death. These enterprizes are so many indications of the impending storm; and the negroes only want a chief, sufficiently courageous, to lead them on to vengeance and slaughter.

Where is this great man to be found, whom Nature, perhaps, owes to the honour of the human species? Where is this new Spartacus, who will not find a Crassus? Then will the *black code* be no more; and the *white code* will be dreadful, if the conqueror only regards the right of reprisals.

Till this revolution takes place, the negroes will groan under the yoke of oppression, the description of which cannot, but interest us more and more in their destiny.

*   *   *

REVIEW QUESTIONS

1. What is the philosophical basis of Raynal's condemnation of slavery?
2. According to Raynal, what abuses arise as a result of slavery?
3. What is the consequence of slavery for the enslaved?
4. What would be the consequence of emancipation for the colonial powers?

ADAM SMITH

FROM *The Wealth of Nations*

Though best remembered for his towering system of political economy, An Inquiry into the Nature and Causes of the Wealth of Nations *(1776), Adam Smith (1723–1790) was one of the towering social philosophers of the eighteenth century, whose economic writings constitute only a part of his larger view of social and political development. Born the son of a minor government official, he entered the University of Glasgow in 1737, already a center of what became known as the Scottish Enlightenment, where he was deeply influenced by another great moral and economic philosopher, Francis Hutcheson. After completing his education at Oxford, he returned to Scotland, where he embarked on a series of public lectures in Edinburgh. In 1752 he was appointed professor of logic at Glasgow, and in 1754 he assumed the chair in moral philosophy. He would look on his tenure as the happiest and most honorable of his life. It was certainly the most productive. There he made the acquaintance of some of the leading intellectual lights of his day: James Watt, of steam-engine fame; David Hume, the great philosopher; and Andrew Cochrane. The last was the founder of the Political Economy Club and the likely source of much of Smith's information on business and commerce. In 1759, Smith published his first important work,* The Theory of Moral Sentiments, *in which he attempted to describe universal principles of human nature. His answer to the question of moral judgment was the thesis of the "inner man," or "impartial spectator," which is the conscience in each human being and whose pronouncements cannot be ignored. Thus, human beings can be driven by passions and self-interests and simultaneously capable of ethics and generosity. This principle foreshadowed the "invisible hand" that would guide economic behavior in* The Wealth of Nations. *He began work on the classic text after resigning his post at Glasgow to serve as tutor to the young duke of Buccleuch. When it finally appeared, it continued the themes first addressed in* The Theory of Moral Sentiments, *the resolution of passion and reason in human behavior, and now, human history. Society evolves through four broad stages, each with appropriate institutions: simple hunters, nomadic herders, feudal farmers, and commercial workers. The guiding force in this development is human nature, motivated by self-interest but guided by disinterested reason. Most of the book is given over to a discussion of the function of the invisible hand in the final, current stage. Whereas conscience provided the necessary guidance in* The Theory of Moral Sentiments, *competition assumes that function in* The Wealth of Nations. *Competition rendered markets self-regulating and ensured that prices and wages never stray far from their "natural" levels. Much of the book, especially Book IV, where he places his discussion of colonies, is given over to a polemic against restriction, through both regulation and monopoly, in economic life.* The Wealth of Nations *appeared to great acclaim and earned its author fame and fortune. He published nothing more.*

From *An Inquiry into the Nature and Causes of the Wealth of Nations,* by Adam Smith (New York: Modern Library, 1950), pp. 599–609, 638–49.

*   *   *

Of the Motives for Establishing New Colonies

The interest which occasioned the first settlement of the different European colonies in America and the West Indies, was not altogether so plain and distinct as that which directed the establishment of those of ancient Greece and Rome.

GREEK COLONIES WERE SENT OUT WHEN THE POPULATION GREW TOO GREAT AT HOME.

All the different states of ancient Greece possessed, each of them, but a very small territory, and when the people in any one of them multiplied beyond what that territory could easily maintain, a part of them were sent in quest of a new habitation in some remote and distant part of the world; the warlike neighbours who surrounded them on all sides, rendering it difficult for any of them to enlarge very much its territory at home. * * *

THE MOTHER CITY CLAIMED NO AUTHORITY.

The mother city, though she considered the colony as a child, at all times entitled to great favour and assistance, and owing in return much gratitude and respect, yet considered it as an emancipated child, over whom she pretended to claim no direct authority or jurisdiction.

The colony settled its own form of government, enacted its own laws, elected its own magistrates, and made peace or war with its neighbours as an independent state, which had no occasion to wait for the approbation or consent of the mother city. Nothing can be more plain and distinct than the interest which directed every such establishment.

ROMAN COLONIES WERE SENT OUT TO SATISFY THE DEMAND FOR LANDS AND TO ESTABLISH GARRISONS IN CONQUERED TERRITORIES.

Rome, like most of the other ancient republics, was originally founded upon an Agrarian law, which divided the public territory in a certain proportion among the different citizens who composed the state. The course of human affairs, by marriage, by succession, and by alienation, necessarily deranged this original division, and frequently threw the lands, which had been allotted for the maintenance of many different families into the possession of a single person. To remedy this disorder, for such it was supposed to be, a law was made, restricting the quantity of land which any citizen could possess to five hundred jugera, about three hundred and fifty English acres. This law, however, though we read of its having been executed upon one or two occasions, was either neglected or evaded, and the inequality of fortunes went on continually increasing. The greater part of the citizens had no land, and without it the manners and customs of those times rendered it difficult for a freeman to maintain his independency. * * * The people became clamorous to get land, and the rich and the great, we may believe, were perfectly determined not to give them any part of theirs. To satisfy them in some measure, therefore, they frequently proposed to send out a new colony.

THEY WERE ENTIRELY SUBJECT TO THE MOTHER CITY.

But conquering Rome was, even upon such occasions, under no necessity of turning out her citizens to seek their fortune, if one may say so, through the wide world, without knowing where they were to settle. She assigned them lands generally in the conquered provinces of Italy, where, being within the dominions of the republic, they could never form any independent state; but were at best but a sort of corporation, which, though it had the power of enacting bye-laws for its own government, was at all times subject to the correction, jurisdiction, and legislative authority of the mother city. The sending out a colony of this kind, not only gave some satisfaction to the people, but often established a sort of garrison too in a newly conquered province, of which the obedience might otherwise have been doubtful. A Roman colony, therefore, whether we consider the nature of the establishment itself, or the motives for making it, was altogether different from a Greek one. The words accordingly, which in the original languages denote those different establishments, have very different meanings. The Latin word (*Colonia*) signifies simply a plantation. The Greek word (αποιηια), on the contrary, signifies a separation of dwelling, a departure from home, a going out of the house. But, though the Roman colonies were in many respects different from the Greek ones, the interest which prompted to establish them was equally plain and distinct. Both institutions derived their origin either from irresistible necessity, or from clear and evident utility.

THE UTILITY OF THE AMERICAN COLONIES IS NOT SO EVIDENT.

The establishment of the European colonies in America and the West Indies arose from no necessity: and though the utility which has resulted from them has been very great, it is not altogether so clear and evident. It was not understood at their first establishment, and was not the motive either of that establishment or of the discoveries which gave occasion to it; and the nature, extent, and limits of that utility are not, perhaps, well understood at this day.

THE VENETIANS HAD A PROFITABLE TRADE IN EAST INDIA GOODS.

The Venetians, during the fourteenth and fifteenth centuries, carried on a very advantageous commerce in spiceries, and other East India goods, which they distributed among the other nations of Europe. They purchased them chiefly in Egypt, at that time under the dominion of the Mammeluks, the enemies of the Turks, of whom the Venetians were the enemies; and this union of interest, assisted by the money of Venice, formed such a connection as gave the Venetians almost a monopoly of the trade.

THIS WAS ENVIED BY THE PORTUGUESE AND LED THEM TO DISCOVER THE CAPE OF GOOD HOPE PASSAGE.

The great profits of the Venetians tempted the avidity of the Portuguese. They had been endeavouring, during the course of the fifteenth century, to find out by sea a way to the countries from which the Moors brought them ivory and gold dust across the Desart. They discovered the Madeiras, the Canaries, the Azores, the Cape de Verd islands, the coast of Guinea, that of Loango, Congo, Angola, and Benguela, and finally, the Cape of Good Hope. They had long wished to share in the profitable traffic of the Venetians, and this last discovery opened to them a probable prospect of doing so. In 1497, Vasco de Gama sailed from the port of Lisbon with a fleet of four ships, and, after a navigation of eleven months, arrived upon the coast of Indostan, and thus completed a course of discoveries which had been pursued with great steadiness, and with very little interruption, for near a century together.

COLUMBUS ENDEAVOURED TO REACH THE EAST INDIES BY SAILING WESTWARDS.

Some years before this, while the expectations of Europe were in suspense about the projects of the Portuguese, of which the success appeared yet to be doubtful, a Genoese pilot formed the yet more daring project of sailing to the East Indies by the West. The situation of those countries was at that time very imperfectly known in Europe. The few European travellers who had been there had magnified the distance; perhaps through simplicity and ignorance, what was really very great, appearing almost infinite to those who could not measure it; or, perhaps, in order to increase somewhat more the marvellous of their own adventures in visiting regions so immensely remote from Europe. The longer the way was by the East, Columbus very justly concluded, the shorter it would be by the West. He proposed, therefore, to take that way, as both the shortest and the surest, and he had the good fortune to convince Isabella of Castile of the probability of his project. He sailed from the port of Palos in August 1492, near five years before the expedition of Vasco de Gama set out from Portugal, and, after a voyage of between two and three months, discovered first some of the small Bahama or Lucayan islands, and afterwards the great island of St. Domingo.

COLUMBUS MISTOOK THE COUNTRIES HE FOUND FOR THE INDIES.

But the countries which Columbus discovered, either in this or in any of his subsequent voyages, had no resemblance to those which he had gone in quest of. Instead of the wealth, cultivation and populousness of China and Indostan, he found, in St. Domingo, and in all the other parts of the new world which he ever visited, nothing but a country quite covered with wood, uncultivated, and inhabited only by some tribes of naked and miserable savages. He was not very willing, however, to believe that they were not the same with some of the countries described by Marco Polo, the first European who had visited, or at least had left behind him any description of China or the East Indies; and a very slight resemblance, such as that which he found between the name of Cibao, a mountain in St. Domingo, and that of Cipango, mentioned by Marco Polo, was frequently sufficient to make him return to this favourite prepossession, though contrary to the clearest evidence. In his letters to Ferdinand and Isabella he called the countries which he had discovered, the Indies. He entertained no doubt but that they were the extremity of those which had been described by Marco Polo, and that they were not very distant from the Ganges, or from the countries which had been conquered by Alexander. Even when at last convinced that they were different, he still flattered himself that those rich countries were at no great distance, and in a subsequent voyage, accordingly, went in quest of them along the coast of Terra Firma, and towards the isthmus of Darien.

HENCE THE NAMES EAST AND WEST INDIES.

In consequence of this mistake of Columbus, the name of the Indies has stuck to those unfortunate countries ever since; and when it was at last clearly discovered that the new were altogether different from the old Indies, the former were called the West, in contradistinction to the latter, which were called the East Indies.

THE COUNTRIES DISCOVERED WERE NOT RICH.

It was of importance to Columbus, however, that the countries which he had discovered, whatever they were, should be represented to the court of Spain as of very great consequence; and, in what

constitutes the real riches of every country, the animal and vegetable productions of the soil, there was at that time nothing which could well justify such a representation of them.

*   *   *

SO COLUMBUS RELIED ON THE MINERALS.

Finding nothing either in the animals or vegetables of the newly discovered countries, which could justify a very advantageous representation of them, Columbus turned his view towards their minerals; and in the richness of the productions of this third kingdom, he flattered himself, he had found a full compensation for the insignificancy of those of the other two. The little bits of gold with which the inhabitants ornamented their dress, and which, he was informed, they frequently found in the rivulets and torrents that fell from the mountains, were sufficient to satisfy him that those mountains abounded with the richest gold mines. St. Domingo, therefore, was represented as a country abounding with gold, and upon that account (according to the prejudices not only of the present times, but of those times), an inexhaustible source of real wealth to the crown and kingdom of Spain. * * *

THE COUNCIL OF CASTILE WAS ATTRACTED BY THE GOLD, COLUMBUS PROPOSING THAT THE GOVERNMENT SHOULD HAVE HALF THE GOLD AND SILVER DISCOVERED.

In consequence of the representations of Columbus, the council of Castile determined to take possession of countries of which the inhabitants were plainly incapable of defending themselves. The pious purpose of converting them to Christianity sanctified the injustice of the project. But the hope of finding treasures of gold there, was the sole motive which prompted to undertake it; and to give this motive the greater weight, it was proposed by Columbus that the half of all the gold and silver that should be found there should belong to the crown. This proposal was approved of by the council.

*   *   *

THE SUBSEQUENT SPANISH ENTERPRISES WERE ALL PROMPTED BY THE SAME MOTIVE.

All the other enterprises of the Spaniards in the new world, subsequent to those of Columbus, seem to have been prompted by the same motive. It was the sacred thirst of gold that carried Oieda, Nicuessa, and Vasco Nugnes de Balboa, to the isthmus of Darien, that carried Cortez to Mexico, and Almagro and Pizzarro to Chile and Peru. When those adventurers arrived upon any unknown coast, their first enquiry was always if there was any gold to be found there; and according to the information which they received concerning this particular, they determined either to quit the country or to settle in it.

*   *   *

IN THIS CASE EXPECTATIONS WERE TO SOME EXTENT REALISED, SO FAR AS THE SPANIARDS WERE CONCERNED.

In the countries first discovered by the Spaniards, no gold or silver mines are at present known which are supposed to be worth the working. The quantities of those metals which the first adventurers are said to have found there, had probably been very much magnified, as well as the fertility of the mines which were wrought immediately after the first discovery. What those adventurers were reported to have found, however, was sufficient to inflame the avidity of all their countrymen. Every Spaniard who sailed to America expected to find an Eldorado. Fortune too did upon this what she has done upon very few other occasions. She realized in some measure the extravagant hopes of her votaries, and in the discovery and conquest of Mexico and Peru (of which the one happened about thirty, the other about forty years after the first expedition of Columbus), she presented them with something not very unlike that profusion of the precious metals which they sought for.

A project of commerce to the East Indies, therefore, gave occasion to the first discovery of the West. A project of conquest gave occasion to all the establishments of the Spaniards in those newly discovered countries. The motive which excited them to this conquest was a project of gold and silver mines; and a course of accidents, which no human wisdom could foresee, rendered this project much more successful than the undertakers had any reasonable grounds for expecting.

BUT THE OTHER NATIONS WERE NOT SO SUCCESSFUL.

The first adventures of all the other nations of Europe, who attempted to make settlements in America, were animated by the like chimerical views; but they were not equally successful. It was more than a hundred years after the first settlement of the Brazils, before any silver, gold, or diamond mines were discovered there. In the English, French, Dutch, and Danish colonies, none have ever yet been discovered; at least none that are at present supposed to be worth the working. The first English settlers in North America, however, offered a fifth of all the gold and silver which should be found there to the king, as a motive for granting them their patents. In the patents to Sir Walter Raleigh, to the London and Plymouth companies, to the council of Plymouth, &c. this fifth was accordingly reserved to the crown. To the expectation of finding gold and silver mines, those first settlers too joined that of discovering a northwest passage to the East Indies. They have hitherto been disappointed in both.

Causes of the Prosperity of New Colonies

The colony of a civilized nation which takes possession either of a waste country, or of one so thinly inhabited, that the natives easily give place to the new settlers, advances more rapidly to wealth and greatness than any other human society.

COLONISTS TAKE OUT KNOWLEDGE AND REGULAR GOVERNMENT.

The colonists carry out with them a knowledge of agriculture and of other useful arts, superior to what can grow up of its own accord in the course of many centuries among savage and barbarous nations. They carry out with them too the habit of subordination, some notion of the regular government which takes place in their own country, of the system of laws which supports it, and of a regular administration of justice; and they naturally establish something of the same kind in the new settlement. But among savage and barbarous nations, the natural progress of law and government is still slower than the natural progress of arts, after law and government have been so far established, as is necessary for their protection.

LAND IS PLENTIFUL AND CHEAP.

Every colonist gets more land than he can possibly cultivate. He has no rent, and scarce any taxes to pay. No landlord shares with him in its produce, and the share of the sovereign is commonly but a trifle. He has every motive to render as great as possible a produce, which is thus to be almost entirely his own. But his land is commonly so extensive, that with all his own industry, and with all the industry of other people whom he can get to employ, he can seldom make it produce the tenth part of what it is capable of producing.

WAGES ARE HIGH.

He is eager, therefore, to collect labourers from all quarters, and to reward them with the most liberal wages. But those liberal wages, joined to the plenty and cheapness of land, soon make those labourers leave him, in order to become landlords themselves, and to reward, with equal liberality, other

labourers, who soon leave them for the same reason that they left their first master.

*   *   *

Of the Advantages Which Europe Has Derived from the Discovery of America, and from That of a Passage to the East Indies by the Cape of Good Hope

THE ADVANTAGES DERIVED BY EUROPE FROM AMERICA ARE (1) THE ADVANTAGES OF EUROPE IN GENERAL, AND (2) THE ADVANTAGES OF THE PARTICULAR COUNTRIES WHICH HAVE COLONIES.

Such are the advantages which the colonies of America have derived from the policy of Europe.

What are those which Europe has derived from the discovery and colonization of America?

Those advantages may be divided, first, into the general advantages which Europe, considered as one great country, has derived from those great events; and, secondly, into the particular advantages which each colonizing country has derived from the colonies which particularly belong to it, in consequence of the authority or dominion which it exercises over them.

(1) THE GENERAL ADVANTAGES TO EUROPE ARE (A) AN INCREASE OF ENJOYMENTS

The general advantages which Europe, considered as one great country, has derived from the discovery and colonization of America, consist, first, in the increase of its enjoyments; and secondly, in the augmentation of its industry.

The surplus produce of America, imported into Europe, furnishes the inhabitants of this great continent with a variety of commodities which they could not otherwise have possessed, some for conveniency and use, some for pleasure, and some for ornament, and thereby contributes to increase their enjoyments.

(B) AN AUGMENTATION OF INDUSTRY NOT ONLY IN THE COUNTRIES WHICH TRADE WITH AMERICA DIRECTLY, BUT ALSO IN OTHER COUNTRIES WHICH DO NOT SEND THEIR PRODUCE TO AMERICA OR EVEN RECEIVE ANY PRODUCE FROM AMERICA.

The discovery and colonization of America, it will readily be allowed, have contributed to augment the industry, first, of all the countries which trade to it directly; such as Spain, Portugal, France, and England; and, secondly, of all those which, without trading to it directly, send, through the medium of other countries, goods to it of their own produce; such as Austrian Flanders, and some provinces of Germany, which, through the medium of the countries before mentioned, send to it a considerable quantity of linen and other goods. All such countries have evidently gained a more extensive market for their surplus produce, and must consequently have been encouraged to increase its quantity.

*　　*　　*

Those great events may even have contributed to increase the enjoyments, and to augment the industry of countries which, not only never sent any commodities to America, but never received any from it. Even such countries may have received a greater abundance of other commodities from countries of which the surplus produce had been augmented by means of the American trade. This greater abundance, as it must necessarily have increased their enjoyments, so it must likewise have augmented their industry. A greater number of new equivalents of some kind or other must have been presented to them to be exchanged for the surplus produce of that industry. A more extensive market must have been created for that surplus produce, so as to raise its value, and thereby encourage its increase. The mass of commodities annually thrown into the great circle of European commerce, and by its various revolutions annually distributed among all the different nations comprehended within it, must have been augmented by the whole surplus produce of America. A greater share of this greater mass, therefore, is likely to have fallen to each of those nations, to

have increased their enjoyments, and augmented their industry.

*　　*　　*

(2) THE PARTICULAR ADVANTAGES OF THE COLONISING COUNTRIES ARE (A) THE COMMON ADVANTAGES DERIVED FROM PROVINCES, (B) THE PECULIAR ADVANTAGES DERIVED FROM PROVINCES IN AMERICA.

The particular advantages which each colonizing country derives from the colonies which particularly belong to it, are of two different kinds; first, those common advantages which every empire derives from the provinces subject to its dominion; and, secondly, those peculiar advantages which are supposed to result from provinces of so very peculiar a nature as the European colonies of America.

The common advantages which every empire derives from the provinces subject to its dominion, consist, first, in the military force which they furnish for its defence; and, secondly, in the revenue which they furnish for the support of its civil government. * * *

(A) THE COMMON ADVANTAGES ARE CONTRIBUTIONS OF MILITARY FORCES AND REVENUE, BUT NONE OF THE COLONIES HAVE EVER FURNISHED MILITARY FORCE.

The European colonies of America have never yet furnished any military force for the defence of the mother country. Their military force has never yet been sufficient for their own defence; and in the different wars in which the mother countries have been engaged, the defence of their colonies has generally occasioned a very considerable distraction of the military force of those countries. In this respect, therefore, all the European colonies have, without exception, been a cause rather of weakness than of strength to their respective mother countries.

AND THE COLONIES OF SPAIN AND PORTUGAL ALONE HAVE CONTRIBUTED REVENUE.

The colonies of Spain and Portugal only have contributed any revenue towards the defence of the mother country, or the support of her civil government. The taxes which have been levied upon those of other European nations, upon those of England in particular, have seldom been equal to the expence laid out upon them in time of peace, and never sufficient to defray that which they occasioned in time of war. Such colonies, therefore, have been a source of expence and not of revenue to their respective mother countries.

(B) THE EXCLUSIVE TRADE IS THE SOLE PECULIAR ADVANTAGE.

The advantages of such colonies to their respective mother countries, consist altogether in those peculiar advantages which are supposed to result from provinces of so very peculiar a nature as the European colonies of America; and the exclusive trade, it is acknowledged, is the sole source of all those peculiar advantages.

THE EXCLUSIVE TRADE OF EACH COUNTRY IS A DISADVANTAGE TO THE OTHER COUNTRIES.

In consequence of this exclusive trade, all that part of the surplus produce of the English colonies, for example, which consists in what are called enumerated commodities, can be sent to no other country but England. Other countries must afterwards buy it of her. It must be cheaper therefore in England than it can be in any other country, and must contribute more to increase the enjoyments of England than those of any other country. It must likewise contribute more to encourage her industry. For all those parts of her own surplus produce which England exchanges for those enumerated commodities, she must get a better price than any other countries can get for the like parts of theirs, when they exchange them for the same commodities. The manufactures of England, for example, will purchase a greater quantity of the sugar and tobacco of her own colonies, than the like manufactures of other countries can purchase of that sugar and tobacco. So far, therefore, as the manufactures of England and those of other countries are both to be exchanged for the sugar and tobacco of the English colonies, this superiority of price gives an encouragement to the former, beyond what the latter can in these circumstances enjoy. The exclusive trade of the colonies, therefore, as it diminishes, or, at least, keeps down below what they would otherwise rise to, both the enjoyments and the industry of the countries which do not possess it; so it gives an evident advantage to the countries which do possess it over those other countries.

*   *   *

REVIEW QUESTIONS

1. How, according to Smith, did the colonial empires of early modern Europe differ from those of the ancient world?
2. What was the motive force of empire?
3. How does Smith explain the eventual success of the colonies in America?
4. What benefits does he see derive from empire? What costs?
5. How does Smith's vision of labor in the colonies differ from Abbé Raynal's discussion of slavery? Why do they differ?
6. How do we explain Smith's apparent indifference to the exploitation of native or slave populations?

SAMUEL PEPYS

FROM *The Diary*

Samuel Pepys (1633–1703) was the son of a rural tailor. Despite this humble origin, he rose to become one of the great men of his day, England's first secretary of the Admiralty, a member of Parliament, president of the Royal Society, and a baron of the Cinque Ports. He was the confidant of kings, familiar with both Charles II and James II. Yet, he is best remembered as the author of his diary, which offers a lively and fascinating account of life in Restoration England from 1660 to 1669. Educated at Magdalene College, Cambridge, he entered the service of his cousin, Admiral Edward Montagu, a favorite of Lord Protector Cromwell. He sailed as his cousin's secretary with the fleet that brought Charles II home from exile, after which he was appointed a clerk in the Admiralty. He found his vocation attending to the business matters of the Royal Navy, studied shipbuilding, victualing, and accounting, and so began a distinguished career in the naval administration. He distinguished himself during the Second Dutch War (1665–1667), at which time plague and fire ravaged London. He eventually rose to a position that combined the authority of first lord and secretary for the Admiralty, a position he held until the end of James II's reign. He retired in 1689 and spent the remainder of his life amassing a library, corresponding with scholars, and preparing a history of the Royal Navy. Yet the work for which he is best remembered had been completed some twenty years prior. His diary is a singular combination of the small and large events that convey intimately and frankly the sense of a life and time.

From *The Diary of Samuel Pepys,* edited by Richard Le Gallienne (New York: Modern Library, 2001), pp. 142–68.

1665

*   *   *

JUNE 1ST. I took coach and to Westminster Hall, where I took the fairest flower, and by coach to Tothill Fields for the ayre till it was dark. I 'light, and in with the fairest flower to eat a cake, and there did do as much as was safe with my flower, and that was enough on my part. Broke up, and away without any notice, and, after delivering the rose where it should be, I to the Temple and 'light, and come to the middle door, and there took another coach, and so home to write letters, but very few, God knows, being by my pleasure made to forget everything that is. The coachman that carried [us] cannot know me again, nor the people at the house where we were. Home to bed, certain news being come that our fleete is in sight of the Dutch ships.

2ND. Up and to the Duke of Albemarle, but missed him. Thence to the Harp and Ball and to Westminster Hall, where I visited "the flowers" in each place, and so met with Mr. Creed, and he and I to Mrs. Croft's to drink and did, but saw not her daughter Borroughes.

3RD. All this day by all people upon the River, and almost every where else hereabout were heard the guns, our two fleets for certain being engaged; which was confirmed by letters from Harwich, but nothing particular: and all our hearts full of concernment for the Duke, and I particularly for my Lord Sandwich and Mr. Coventry after his Royall Highnesse.

4TH. (SUNDAY). Newes being come that our fleete is pursuing the Dutch, who, either by cunning, or by being worsted, do give ground, but nothing more for certain.

5TH. Thence home to dinner, after 'Change, where great talke of the Dutch being fled and we in pursuit of them, and that our ship Charity is lost upon our Captain's, Wilkinson, and Lieutenant's yielding, but of this there is no certainty.

7TH. This day, much against my will, I did in Drury Lane see two or three houses marked with a red cross upon the doors, and "Lord have mercy upon us" writ there; which was a sad sight to me, being the first of the kind that, to my remembrance, I ever saw. It put me into an ill conception of myself and my smell, so that I was forced to buy some roll-tobacco to smell to and chaw, which took away the apprehension.

8TH. Alone at home to dinner, my wife, mother, and Mercer dining at W. Joyce's; I giving her a caution to go round by the Half Moone to his house, because of the plague. I to my Lord Treasurer's by appointment of Sir Thomas Ingram's, to meet the Goldsmiths; where I met with the great news at last newly come, brought by Bab May from the Duke of Yorke, that we have totally routed the Dutch; that the Duke himself, the Prince, my Lord Sandwich and Mr. Coventry are all well which did put me into such joy, that I forgot almost all other thoughts. Admirall Opdam blown up, Trump killed, and said by Holmes; all the rest of their admiralls, as they say, but Everson are killed: we having taken and sunk, as is believed, about 24 of their best ships; killed and taken near 8 or 10,000 men, and lost, we think, not above 700. A great[er] victory never known in

the world. They are all fled, some 43 got into the Texell, and others elsewhere, and we in pursuit of the rest. Thence, when my heart full of joy, home, and to my office a little; then to my Lady Pen's, where they are all joyed and not a little puffed up at the good successe of their father; and good service indeed is said to have been done by him. Had a great bonfire at the gate; and I with my Lady Pen's people and others to Mrs. Turner's great room, and then down into the streete. I did give the boys 4s. among them, and mighty merry. So home to bed, with my heart at great rest and quiett, saving that the consideration of the victory is too great for me presently to comprehend.

9TH. Lay long in bed, my head akeing with too much thoughts I think last night.

10TH. In the evening home to supper; and there, to my great trouble, hear that the plague is come into the City (though it hath these three or four weeks since its beginning been wholly out of the City); but where should it begin but in my good friend and neighbour's, Dr. Burnett, in Fanchurch Street: which in both points troubles me mightily. To the office to finish my letters and then home to bed, being troubled at the sicknesse, and my head filled also with other business enough, and particularly how to put my things and estate in order, in case it should please God to call me away, which God dispose of to his glory.

11TH (LORD'S DAY). Up, and expected long a new suit; but, coming not, dressed myself in my late new black silke camelott suit; and, when fully ready, comes my new one of coloured ferrandin, which my wife puts me out of love with, which vexes me, but I think it is only my not being used to wear colours which makes it look a little unusual upon me. To my chamber and there spent the morning reading. I out of doors a little, to shew, forsooth, my new suit, and back again, and in going I saw poor Dr. Burnett's door shut; but he hath, I hear, gained great goodwill among his neighbours; for he discovered it himself first, and caused himself to be shut up of his own accord: which was very handsome.

15TH. The towne grows very sickly, and people to be afeard of it; there dying this last week of the plague 112, from 43 the week before, whereof but [one] in Fanchurch-streete, and one in Broad-streete, by the Treasurer's office.

16TH. I to White Hall, where the Court is full of the Duke and his courtiers returned from sea. All fat and lusty, and ruddy by being in the sun.

17TH. It struck me very deep this afternoon going with a hackney coach from my Lord Treasurer's down Holborne, the coachman I found to drive easily and easily, at last stood still, and come down hardly able to stand, and told me that he was suddenly struck very sicke, and almost blind, he could not see; so I 'light and went into another coach, with a sad heart for the poor man and trouble for myself, lest he should have been struck with the plague, being at the end of the towne that I took him up; but God have mercy upon us all!

20TH. This day I informed myself that there died four or five at Westminster of the plague in one alley in several houses upon Sunday last, Bell Alley, over against the Palace-gate; yet people do think that the number will be fewer in the towne than it was the last weeke.

21ST. So homewards and to the Cross Keys at Cripplegate, where I find all the towne almost going out of towne, the coaches and waggons being all full of people going into the country. Here I had some of the company of the tapster's wife a while, and so home to my office, and then home to supper and to bed.

23RD. So home by hackney coach, which is become a very dangerous passage now-a-days, the sickness increasing mightily, and to bed.

26TH. The plague encreases mightily, I this day seeing a house, at a bitt-maker's over against St.

Clement's Church, in the open street, shut up; which is a sad sight.

29TH. Up and by water to White Hall, where the Court full of waggons and people ready to go out of towne. To the Harp and Ball, and there drank and talked with Mary, she telling me in discourse that she lived lately at my neighbour's, Mr. Knightly, which made me forbear further discourse. This end of the towne every day grows very bad of the plague. The Mortality Bill is come to 267; which is about ninety more than the last: and of these but four in the City, which is a great blessing to us.

30TH. Thus this book of two years ends. Myself and family in good health, consisting of myself and wife, Mercer, her woman, Mary, Alice, and Susan our maids, and Tom my boy. In a sickly time of the plague growing on. Having upon my hands the troublesome care of the Treasury of Tangier, with great sums drawn upon me, and nothing to pay them with: also the business of the office great. Consideration of removing my wife to Woolwich; she lately busy in learning to paint, with great pleasure and successe. All other things well; especially a new interest I am making, by a match in hand between the eldest son of Sir G. Carteret, and my Lady Jemimah Montagu.

*   *   *

AUGUST 1ST. Slept, and lay long; then up and my Lord [Crew] and Sir G. Carteret being gone abroad, I first to see the bridegroom and bride, and found them both up, and he gone to dress himself. Both red in the face, and well enough pleased this morning with their night's lodging.

2ND. Up, it being a publique fast, as being the first Wednesday of the month, for the plague; I within doors all day, and upon my monthly accounts late, I did find myself really worth £1,900, for which the great God of Heaven and Earth be praised!

5TH. In the morning up, and my wife showed me several things of her doing, especially one fine woman's Persian head mighty finely done beyond what I could expect of her; and so away by water, having ordered in the yarde six or eight bargemen to be whipped, who had last night stolen some of the King's cordage from out of the yarde.

10TH. By and by to the office, where we sat all the morning; in great trouble to see the Bill this week rise so high, to above 4,000 in all, and of them above 3,000 of the plague. And an odd story of Alderman Bence's stumbling at night over a dead corps in the street, and going home and telling his wife, she at the fright, being with child, fell sicke and died of the plague. Thence to the office and, after writing letters, home, to draw over anew my will, which I had bound myself by oath to dispatch by to-morrow night; the town growing so unhealthy, that a man cannot depend upon living two days to an end.

11TH. Up, and all day long finishing and writing over my will twice, for my father and my wife, only in the morning a pleasant rencontre happened in having a young married woman brought me by her father, old Delkes, that carries pins always in his mouth, to get her husband off that he should not go to sea, *une contre pouvait avoir* done any *cose cum elle,* but I did nothing, *si ni baisser* her. After they were gone my mind run upon having them called back again, and I sent a messenger to Blackwall, but he failed. So I lost my expectation.

12TH. The people die so, that now it seems they are fain to carry the dead to be buried by day-light, the nights not sufficing to do it in. And my Lord Mayor commands people to be within at nine at night all, as they say, that the sick may have liberty to go abroad for ayre.

14TH. This night I did present my wife with the dyamond ring, awhile since given me by Mr. Dicke Vines's brother, for helping him to be a purser, valued at about £10, the first thing of that nature I did ever give her. Great fears we have that the plague will be a great Bill this weeke.

15TH. Up by 4 o'clock and walked to Greenwich, where called at Captain Cocke's and to his chamber, he being in bed, where something put my last night's dream into my head, which I think is the best that ever was dreamt, which was that I had my Lady Castlemayne in my armes and was admitted to use all the dalliance I desired with her, and then dreamt that this could not be awake, but that it was only a dream; but that since it was a dream, and that I took so much real pleasure in it, what a happy thing it would be if when we are in our graves (as Shakespeere resembles it) we could dream, and dream but such dreams as this, that then we should not need to be so fearful of death, as we are this plague time. It was dark before I could get home, and so land at Churchyard stairs, where, to my great trouble, I met a dead corps of the plague, in the narrow ally just bringing down a little pair of stairs. But I thank God I was not much disturbed at it. However, I shall beware of being late abroad again.

19TH. Our fleete is come home to our great grief with not above five weeks' dry, and six days' wet provisions: however, must out again. Having read all this news, and received commands of the Duke with great content, he giving me the words which to my great joy he hath several times said to me that his greatest reliance is upon me. And my Lord Craven also did come out to talk with me, and told me that I am in mighty esteem with the Duke, for which I bless God.

28TH. Up, and being ready I out to Mr. Colvill, the goldsmith's, having not for some days been in the streets; but now how few people I see, and those looking like people that had taken leave of the world.

30TH. Up betimes and to my business of settling my house and papers, and then abroad and met with Hadley, our clerke, who, upon my asking how the plague goes, he told me it increases much, and much in our parish; for, says he, there died nine this week, though I have returned but six: which is a very ill practice, and makes me think it is so in other places; and therefore the plague much greater than people take it to be. Thence, walked towards Moorefields to see (God forbid my presumption!) whether I could see any dead corps going to the grave; but, as God would have it, did not. But, Lord! how every body's looks, and discourse in the street is of death, and nothing else, and few people going up and down, that the towne is like a place distressed and forsaken.

31st. Up; and, after putting several things in order to my removal, to Woolwich; the plague having a great encrease this week, beyond all expectation of almost 2,000, making the general Bill 7,000, odd 100; and the plague above 6,000. Thus this month ends with great sadness upon the publick, through the greatness of the plague every where through the kingdom almost. Every day sadder and sadder news of its encrease. In the City died this week 7,496, and of them 6,102 of the plague. But it is feared that the true number of the dead this week is near 10,000; partly from the poor that cannot be taken notice of, through

the greatness of the number, and partly from the Quakers and others that will not have any bell ring for them. Our fleete gone out to find the Dutch, we having about 100 sail in our fleete, and in them the Soveraigne one; so that it is a better fleete than the former with the Duke was.

*   *   *

REVIEW QUESTIONS

1. How would you characterize life in Restoration England as it is portrayed in Pepys's diary?
2. Why is Pepys so little moved by the suffering of Londoners during the plague?
3. What image of domestic life do we derive from Pepys's accounts?
4. What is Pepys's relationship with Lady Castlemayne?
5. What sense does he offer of the relationship between aristocrats and commoners? How does it differ from accounts of France in the mid–seventeenth century? How might you explain the surprising degree of familiarity?

Coffee House Society

Coffee is an example of the impact of overseas trade and colonial empire on the consumption and lifestyle of ordinary Europeans. The beans' historical origins are shrouded in legend. What seems clear is that they were taken to Arabia from Africa during the fifteenth century and placed under cultivation. Introduced into Europe during the sixteenth and seventeenth centuries, they gained almost immediate popularity. Served at coffeehouses, the first of which was established in London around 1650, coffee's consumption became an occasion for transacting political, social, commercial, or literary business. So great was the demand for coffee that European mer-

chants took it from the Arabian Peninsula to Java, Indonesia, and the Americas. The following description gives some sense of the ways in which colonial products shaped European culture in the seventeenth century.

From *Selections from the Sources of English History*, edited by Charles W. Colby (New York: Longmans, Green, 1899), pp. 208–12.

*   *   *

1673

A coffee-house is a lay conventicle, good-fellowship turned puritan, ill-husbandry in masquerade, whither people come, after toping all day, to purchase, at the expense of their last penny, the repute of sober companions: A Rota [club] room, that, like Noah's ark, receives animals of every sort, from the precise diminutive band, to the hectoring cravat and cuffs in folio: a nursery for training up the smaller fry of virtuosi in confident tattling, or a cabal of kittling [carping] critics that have only learned to spit and mew; a mint of intelligence, that, to make each man his pennyworth, draws out into petty parcels, what the merchant receives in bullion: he, that comes often, saves twopence a week in Gazettes, and has his news and his coffee for the same charge, as at a threepenny ordinary they give in broth to your chop of mutton; it is an exchange, where haberdashers of political small-wares meet, and mutually abuse each other, and the public, with bottomless stories, and headless notions; the rendezvous of idle pamphlets, and persons more idly employed to read them; a high court of justice, where every little fellow in a camlet cloak takes upon him to transpose affairs both in church and state, to show reasons against acts of parliament, and condemn the decrees of general councils.

•   •   •

As you have a hodge-podge of drinks, such too is your company, for each man seems a leveller, and ranks and files himself as he lists, without regard to degrees or order; so that often you may see a silly fop and a worshipful justice, a griping rook and a grave citizen, a worthy lawyer and an errant pickpocket, a reverend nonconformist and a canting mountebank, all blended together to compose an oglio [medley] of impertinence.

If any pragmatic, to show himself witty or eloquent, begin to talk high, presently the further tables are abandoned, and all the rest flock round (like smaller birds, to admire the gravity of the madge-howlet [barn-owl]). They listen to him awhile with their mouths, and let their pipes go out, and coffee grow cold, for pure zeal of attention, but on the sudden fall all a yelping at once with more noise, but not half so much harmony, as a pack of beagles on the full cry. To still this bawling, up starts Capt. All-man-sir, the man of mouth, with a face as blustering as that of Æolus and his four sons, in painting, and a voice louder than the speaking trumpet, he begins you the story of a sea-fight; and though he never were further, by water, than the Bear-garden, . . . yet, having pirated the names of ships and captains, he persuades you himself was present, and performed miracles; that he waded knee-deep in blood on the upper-deck, and never thought to serenade his mistress so pleasant as the bullets whistling; how he stopped a vice-admiral of the enemy's under full sail; till she was boarded, with his single arm, instead of grappling-irons, and puffed out with his breath a fire-ship that fell foul on them. All this he relates, sitting in a cloud of smoke, and belching so many common oaths to vouch it, you can scarce guess whether the real engagement, or his romancing account of it, be the more dreadful: however, he concludes with railing at the conduct of some eminent officers (that, perhaps, he never saw), and protests, had they taken his advice at the council of war, not a sail had escaped us.

He is no sooner out of breath, but another begins a lecture on the Gazette, where, finding several prizes taken, he gravely observes, if this trade hold, we shall quickly rout the Dutch, horse and foot, by sea: he nicknames the Polish gentlemen wherever he meets them, and enquires whether Gayland and Taffaletta be Lutherans or Calvinists? *stilo novo* he interprets a vast new stile, or turnpike, erected by his electoral highness on the borders of Westphalia, to keep Monsieur Turenne's cavalry from falling on his retreating troops: he takes words by the sound, without examining their sense: Morea he believes to be the country of the Moors, and Hungary a place where famine always keeps her court, nor is there anything more certain, than that he made a whole room full of fops, as wise as himself, spend above two hours in searching the map for Aristocracy and Democracy, not doubting but to have found them there, as well as Dalmatia and Croatia.

1675

Though the happy Arabia, nature's spicery, prodigally furnishes the voluptuous world with all kinds of aromatics, and divers other rarities; yet I scarce know whether mankind be not still as much obliged to it for the excellent fruit of the humble coffee-shrub, as for any other of its more specious productions: for, since there is nothing we here enjoy, next to life, valuable beyond health, certainly those things that contribute to preserve us in good plight and eucrasy, and fortify our weak bodies against the continual assaults and batteries of disease, deserve our regards much more than those which only gratify a liquorish palate, or otherwise prove subservient to our delights. As for this salutiferous berry, of so general a use through all the regions of the east, it is sufficiently known, when prepared, to be moderately hot, and of a very drying attenuating and cleansing quality; whence reason infers, that its decoction must contain many good physical properties, and cannot but be an incomparable remedy to dissolve crudities, comfort the brain, and dry up ill humours in the stomach. In brief, to prevent or redress, in those that frequently drink it, all cold drowsy rheumatic distempers whatsoever, that proceed from excess of moisture, which are so numerous, that but to name them would tire the tongue of a mountebank.

• • •

Lastly, for diversion. It is older than Aristotle, and will be true, when Hobbes is forgot, that man is a sociable creature, and delights in company. Now, whither shall a person, wearied with hard study, or the laborious turmoils of a tedious day, repair to refresh himself? Or where can young gentlemen, or shop-keepers, more innocently and advantageously spend an hour or two in the evening, than at a coffee-house? Where they shall be sure to meet company, and, by the custom of the house, not such as at other places, stingy and reserved to themselves, but free and communicative; where every man may modestly begin his story, and propose to, or answer another, as he thinks fit. Discourse is *pabulum animi, cos ingenii;* the mind's best diet, and the great whetstone and incentive of ingenuity; by that we come to know men better than by their physiognomy. *Loquere, ut te videam,* speak, that I may see thee, was the philosopher's adage. To read men is acknowledged more useful than books; but where is there a better library for that study, generally, than here, amongst such a variety of humours, all expressing themselves on divers subjects, according to their respective abilities?

• • •

In brief, it is undeniable, that, as you have here the most civil, so it is, generally, the most intelligent society; the frequenting whose converse, and observing their discourses and department, cannot but civilise our manners, enlarge our understandings, refine our language, teach us a generous confidence and handsome mode of address, and brush off that *pudor rubrusticus* (as, I remember, Tully somewhere calls it), that clownish kind of modesty frequently incident to the best natures, which renders them sheepish and ridiculous in company.

So that, upon the whole matter, spite of the idle sarcasms and paltry reproaches thrown upon it, we may, with no less truth than plainness, give this brief character of a well-regulated coffee-house (for our pen disdains to be an advocate for any sordid holes, that assume that name to cloak the practice of debauchery), that it is the sanctuary of health, the nursery of temperance, the delight of frugality, an academy of civility, and free-school of ingenuity.

*   *   *

REVIEW QUESTIONS

1. How would you describe coffeehouse society in the late seventeenth century?
2. What is the attitude of each of our two anonymous authors? How and why do they differ?
3. What is the significance of reading the *Gazette*?
4. What are the virtues of coffee?
5. How can coffee drinking be a vice in early modern Europe?

17   THE AGE OF ABSOLUTISM, 1660–1789

Absolutism refers to a particular conception of political authority that emerged in the wake of the crises of the later sixteenth century. It asserted order, where Europeans felt order had been undermined in political and social relations, by positing a vision of a society which had its apex in the person of a single ruler. At the center of all conceptions of absolutism was the will of the ruler: for all theorists, that will was absolute, not merely sovereign but determinative of all political relations. The king stood at the peak of that pyramid, and the function of that pyramid was to realize his will. Theories of absolutism drew on an understanding of the will that had its origins in the writings of Italian humanists in the fifteenth century and its fullest expression in the writings of theologians such as John Calvin and Martin Luther. By the end of the period, there would be calls for enlightened absolutism, in which reason guided the will of the sovereign, but the will of the monarch was still the agent of political life.

Such an understanding of the nature and operation of political power required a number of developments, not the least of which was a military and a bureaucracy to carry out the king's will. In France and in Spain, over the course of some three centuries, elaborate machineries of rule had evolved: chanceries for the collection, supervision, management, and disbursement of various incomes; judiciaries to decide such diverse issues as disputes over property, relations between lords and servants, and, in some kingdoms, private relations among families; and the emergence of diplomatic professionals, as well as secretaries of various kinds for record-keeping, which increased exponentially in this period. Finally, certain theories that posited a hierarchy of human nature, from natural slavery to natural monarchy, supported an understanding of that pyramid as not only rational, but natural.

These developments did not go unopposed. Among theorists there arose several who countered the notion of absolute monarchy with that of sovereignty placed in the hands of property owners. Moreover, they argued persuasively that the exercise of sovereignty was limited in accordance with the principles of natu-ral law. In practice as in theory, social groups, especially the aristocracy, strug-gled to limit the expanding powers of the monarch, whom they viewed as one of their own, and to preserve their own political prerogatives.

No monarch in this period was truly absolute—such an effective expression of the will of the ruler requires greater technological and military support than any ruler prior to the nineteenth century could have. Many, however, were largely successful in representing themselves as the center of all political life in their states, nurturing courts and bureaucracies that reflected images of omnis-cient and powerful rulers. These same courts provided both a milieu and the financial support for philosophes such as Voltaire and scientists such as Galileo, even as those intellectuals were calling into question the ethics of and the social bases for absolutism.

LOUIS XIV AND THE DUC DE SAINT-SIMON

Revocation of the Edict of Nantes

The Edict of Nantes, signed by Henry IV in 1598, granted a measure of religious liberty to his Protestant subjects, the Huguenots. It granted them freedom of con-science and the right to hold public worship services anywhere they had done so in 1576, including two towns in every administrative unit of France, the houses of aristocrats, and within 5 kilometers of Paris. It also granted French Protestants full civil rights: to enter trade, inherit property, attend universities, and hold offices. The edict included one crucial political concession: the Huguenots were permitted to re-tain such fortified places as they held in 1597 as garrisoned strongholds at the ex-pense of the crown. The edict also restored Catholicism in all areas where it had been disrupted. Nonetheless, French Catholics resented it as being too tolerant of heresy. The monarchy soon came to view its political clause as a danger to the state. Cardinal Richilieu reduced the Protestant strongholds by force of arms, and the Edict of Alès rescinded the political agreement in 1629 Louis XIV revoked the edict in 1685 and deprived the Huguenots of all civil and religious liberties. Their clergy were forced into exile. Thousands of religious refugees fled France for the Protestant states of Europe and America, where their commercial and artisanal skills contrib-uted significantly to economic prosperity. The revocation provoked a storm of out-raged protest against an arbitrary act of state. The proclamation, extracted below, offers the monarch's justification, based on his absolute authority and its religious underpinnings. Entries from the Memoirs of the Duke of Saint-Simon, *an eyewit-*

ness at the royal court, The Declaration of the Gallican Church, *interested parties to the revocation, and from Louis's letter to his heir reflect on the political context and consequences of the deed.*

From *Readings in European History,* translated by J. H. Robinson (Oxford, Eng.: Ginn, 1906).

Louis XIV

FROM Revocation of the Edict of Nantes

1. Be it known that of our certain knowledge, full power, and royal authority, we have, by this present perpetual and irrevocable edict, suppressed and revoked, and do suppress and revoke, the edict of our said grandfather, given at Nantes in April 1598, in its whole extent. . . .

2. We forbid our subjects of the R.P.R. [Religion pretendue reformee, i.e., the so-called reformed religion] to meet any more for the exercise of the said religion in any place or private house, under any pretext whatever. . . .

3. We likewise forbid all noblemen, of what condition soever, to hold such religious exercises in their houses or fiefs, under penalty to be inflicted upon all our said subjects who shall engage in the said exercises, of imprisonment and confiscation.

4. We enjoin all ministers of the said R.P.R., who do not choose to become converts and to embrace the Catholic, apostolic, and Roman religion, to leave our kingdom and the territories subject to us within a fortnight of the publication of our present edict, without leave to reside therein beyond that period, or, during the said fortnight, to engage in any preaching, exhortation, or any other function, on pain of being sent to the galleys. . . .

*   *   *

7. We forbid private schools for the instruction of children of the said R.P.R., and in general all things whatever which can be regarded as a concession of any kind in favor of the said religion.

*   *   *

Duc de Saint-Simon

FROM *Memoirs*

*   *   *

The first-fruits of this dreadful plot were the wanton revocation of the Edict of Nantes, without a shadow of a pretext, and the proscriptions which followed it; its ultimate results were the depopulation of a fourth part of the kingdom and the ruin of our commerce. For a long time the country was given over to the authorised ravages of dragoons, which caused the deaths of, literally, thousands of innocent people of all ages and both sexes. Families were torn asunder; men of all classes, often old and infirm, highly respected for their piety and learning, were sent to toil in the galleys under the lash of the overseer; multitudes were driven penniless from their homes to seek refuge in foreign countries, to which they carried our arts and manufactures, enriching them and causing their cities to flourish at the expense of France.

*   *   *

I reminded the Regent of the disturbances and civil wars caused by the Huguenots from the reign of Henry II to that of Louis XIII; pointing out that even when they were comparatively quiet they had formed a body apart within the State, having their own chiefs, courts of justice specially appointed to deal with their affairs, even when they concerned Catholics, with strong places and garrisons at their disposal; corresponding with foreign Powers; always complaining and ready to take up arms: subjects, in short, merely in name, and yielding just as much or as little allegiance to their Sovereign as they thought fit. I recapitulated the heroic struggles by which his grandfather, Louis XIII, had at last beaten down this Hydra; thereby enabling his successor to get rid of it once for all by the mere expression of his will, without the slightest opposition.

I begged the Regent to reflect that he was now reaping the benefit of these struggles in a profound domestic tranquility; and to consider whether it was worth while, in time of peace when no foreign Power was thinking about the question, to make a concession which the late King had rejected with indignation when reduced to the utmost extremities by a long and disastrous war. I said, in conclusion, that if Louis XIV had made a mistake in revoking the Edict of Nantes it was not so much in the act itself as in the mode of carrying it out.

* * *

FROM Declaration of the Gallican Church

We, the archbishops and bishops assembled at Paris by order of the King, with other ecclesiastical deputies who represent the Gallican Church, have judged it necessary to make the regulations and the declaration which follows:

That St. Peter and his successors, Vicars of Jesus Christ, and the whole Church herself, have received power of God only in things spiritual, and pertaining to eternal salvation, not in things civil or temporal, the Lord Himself having said, "My kingdom is not of this world," and also "Render unto Caesar the things that be Caesar's, and unto God the things that are God's"; as also firmly declareth the Apostle, "Let every soul be subject unto the higher powers; for there is no power but of God; the powers that be are ordained of God; whosoever therefore resisteth the power, resisteth the ordinance of God."

Therefore kings and princes are in no wise subjected by God's appointment to any ecclesiastical power in temporal things; neither can the authority of the Keys of the Church directly or indirectly depose them, or their subjects be dis-

pensed from the obedience and fidelity of their oaths to the same; and this doctrine we affirm to be necessary for the maintenance of public peace, no less profitable to the Church than to the State, and to be everywhere and every way observed as agreeable to the Word of God, to the tradition of the Fathers and the example of the Saints. . . .

* * *

Louis XIV

FROM Letter to His Heir

* * *

I have never failed, when an occasion has presented itself, to impress upon you the great respect we should have for religion, and the deference we should show to its ministers in matters specially connected with their mission, that is to say, with the celebration of the Sacred Mysteries and the preaching of the doctrine of the Gospels. But because people connected with the Church are liable to presume a little too much on the advantages attaching to their profession, and are willing sometimes to make use of them in order to whittle down their most rightful duties, I feel obliged to explain to you certain points on this question which may be of importance.

The first is that Kings are absolute *seigneurs*, and from their nature have full and free disposal of all property both secular and ecclesiastical, to use it as wise dispensers, that is to say, in accordance with the requirements of their State.

The second is that those mysterious names, the Franchises and Liberties of the Church, with which perhaps people will endeavour to dazzle you, have equal reference to all the faithful whether they be laymen or tonsured, who are all equally sons of this common Mother; but that they exempt neither the one nor the other from subjection to Sovereigns, to whom the Gospel itself precisely enjoins that they should submit themselves.

*   *   *

REVIEW QUESTIONS

1. Why did Louis revoke the Edict of Nantes?
2. What does this tell us about his conception of royal authority?

3. Is there any aspect of life that is exempt from royal authority?
4. How does this contrast with the political theory of John Locke?
5. What, according the Duke of Saint-Simon, were the real consequences of the revocation?
6. How might Louis or his advisors have justified the act?
7. What, benefits might have been expected in the first place?

JOHN LOCKE

FROM *Two Treatises on Government*

John Locke (1632–1704) was an English philosopher whose thought contributed to the Enlightenment. He grew up in a liberal Puritan family, the son of an attorney who fought in the civil war against Charles I, and attended Christ's Church College, Oxford. He received his bachelor of arts in 1656, lectured in classical languages while earning his master of arts, and entered Oxford medical school to avoid being forced to join the clergy. In 1666, Locke attached himself to the household of the earl of Shaftesbury and his fortunes to the liberal Whig Party. Between 1675 and 1679, he lived in France, where he made contact with leading intellectuals of the late seventeenth century. On his return to England, he plunged into the controversy surrounding the succession of James II, an avowed Catholic with absolutist pretensions, to the throne of his brother, Charles II. Locke's patron, Shaftesbury, was imprisoned for his opposition, and Locke went into exile in 1683. Though he was involved to some extent in the Glorious Revolution of 1688, he returned to England in 1689, in the entourage of Mary, princess of Orange, who would assume the throne with her husband William. The Two Treatises on Government (1690) were published anonymously, although readers commonly assumed Locke's authorship. More interesting is the point at time in which they were written. Most scholars assume that they were written immediately before publication, as a justification of the revolution just completed. Many scholars believe, however, that the treatises were written from exile as a call to revolution, a much more inflammatory and risky project. The first treatise comprises a long attack on Robert Filmer's Patriarcha, *a denial of the patriarchal justification of the absolute monarch. The second treatise constructs in the place of patriarchy a theory of politics based on natural law, which provides the foundation of human freedom. The social contract creates a political structure by consent of the governed designed to preserve those freedoms established in natural law. Locke's treatises inspired the political theories of the Enlightenment.*

From *First Treatises* in *Two Treatises on Government*, edited by Ernst Rhys (New York: Dutton, 1993).

PALACE AND GARDENS OF VERSAILLES (1668)   PIERRE PATEL

Patel's famous print of the palace at Versailles captures the grand scale of monarchy in the seventeenth century. Note not only the size of the palace but also its location in the center of carefully planned gardens, boulevards, and buildings. Versailles was truly a theater for the display of political power. Why was such a theater of power necessary? What can be learned from the iconography of power that was built into Versailles, such as the function of gardens or the location of boulevards or alleys or broad open spaces? How might Versailles have functioned not only as a theater of power but also as a prison for the powerful?

239

* * *

Chapter VI
Of Paternal Power

It may perhaps be censured an impertinent criticism in a discourse of this nature to find fault with words and names that have obtained in the world. And yet possibly it may not be amiss to offer new ones when the old are apt to lead men into mistakes, as this of paternal power probably has done, which seems so to place the power of parents over their children wholly in the father, as if the mother had no share in it; whereas if we consult reason or revelation, we shall find she has an equal title, which may give one reason to ask whether this might not be more properly called parental power? For whatever obligation Nature and the right of generation lays on children, it must certainly bind them equal to both the concurrent causes of it. And accordingly we see the positive law of God everywhere joins them together without distinction, when it commands the obedience of children: "Honour thy father and thy mother"; "Whosoever curseth his father or his mother"; "Ye shall fear every man his mother and his father"; "Children, obey your parents" etc., is the style of the Old and New Testament.

* * *

Though I have said above "That all men by nature are equal," I cannot be supposed to understand all sorts of "equality." Age or virtue may give men a just precedency. Excellency of parts and merit may place others above the common level. Birth may subject some, and alliance or benefits others, to pay an observance to those to whom Nature, gratitude, or other respects, may have made it due; and yet all this consists with the equality which all men are in in respect of jurisdiction or dominion one over another, which was the equality I there spoke of as proper to the business in hand, being that equal right that every man hath to his natural freedom, without being subjected to the will or authority of any other man.

Children, I confess, are not born in this full state of equality, though they are born to it. Their parents have a sort of rule and jurisdiction over them when they come into the world, and for some time after, but it is but a temporary one. The bonds of this subjection are like the swaddling clothes they are wrapt up in and supported by in the weakness of their infancy. Age and reason as they grow up loosen them, till at length they drop quite off, and leave a man at his own free disposal.

Adam was created a perfect man, his body and mind in full possession of their strength and reason, and so was capable from the first instance of his being to provide for his own support and preservation, and govern his actions according to the dictates of the law of reason God had implanted in him. From him the world is peopled with his descendants, who are all born infants, weak and helpless, without knowledge or understanding. But to supply the defects of this imperfect state till the improvement of growth and age had removed them, Adam and Eve, and after them all parents were, by the law of Nature, under an obligation to preserve, nourish and educate the children they had begotten, not as their own workmanship, but the workmanship of their own Maker, the Almighty, to whom they were to be accountable for them.

The law that was to govern Adam was the same that was to govern all his posterity, the law of reason. But his offspring having another way of entrance into the world, different from him, by a natural birth, that produced them ignorant, and without the use of reason, they were not presently under that law. For nobody can be under a law that is not promulgated to him; and this law being promulgated or made known by reason only, he that is not come to the use of his reason cannot be said to be under this law; and Adam's children being not presently as soon as born under this law of reason, were not presently free. For law, in its true notion, is not so much the limitation as the direction of a free and intelligent agent to his proper interest, and prescribes no farther than is for the general good of those under that law. Could they be happier without it, the law, as a useless thing, would of itself vanish; and that ill deserves the name of confinement which hedges us in only from bogs and precipices. So that however it may be mistaken, the end of law is not to abolish or restrain, but to preserve and enlarge freedom. For in all the states of created beings, capable of laws, where there is no law there is no freedom. For liberty is to be free from restraint and violence from others, which cannot be where there is no law; and is not, as we are told, "a liberty for every man to do what he lists." For who could be free, when every other man's humour might domineer over him? But a liberty to dispose and order freely as he lists his person, actions, possessions, and his whole property within the allowance of those laws under which he is, and therein not to be subject to the arbitrary will of another, but freely follow his own.

The power, then, that parents have over their children arises from that duty which is incumbent on them, to take care of their offspring during the imperfect state of childhood. To inform the mind, and govern the actions of their yet ignorant nonage, till reason shall take its place and ease them of that trouble, is what the children want, and the parents are bound to. For God having given man an understanding to direct his actions, has allowed him a freedom of will and liberty of acting, as properly belonging thereunto within the bounds of that law he is under. But whilst he is in an estate wherein he has no understanding of his own to direct his will, he is not to have any will of his own to follow. He that understands for him must will for him too; he must prescribe to his will, and regulate his actions, but when he comes to the estate that made his father a free man, the son is a free man too.

This holds in all the laws a man is under, whether natural or civil. Is a man under the law of Nature? What made him free of that law? what gave him a free disposing of his property, according to his own will, within the compass of that law? I answer, an estate wherein he might be supposed capable to know that law, that so he might keep his actions within the bounds of it. When he has acquired that state, he is presumed to know how far that law is to be his guide, and how far he may make use of his freedom, and so comes

to have it; till then, somebody else must guide him, who is presumed to know how far the law allows a liberty. If such a state of reason, such an age of discretion made him free, the same shall make his son free too. Is a man under the law of England? what made him free of that law—that is, to have the liberty to dispose of his actions and possessions, according to his own will, within the permission of that law? a capacity of knowing that law. Which is supposed, by that law, at the age of twenty-one, and in some cases sooner. If this made the father free, it shall make the son free too. Till then, we see the law allows the son to have no will, but he is to be guided by the will of his father or guardian, who is to understand for him. And if the father die and fail to substitute a deputy in this trust, if he hath not provided a tutor to govern his son during his minority, during his want of understanding, the law takes care to do it: some other must govern him and be a will to him till he hath attained to a state of freedom, and his understanding be fit to take the government of his will. But after that the father and son are equally free, as much as tutor and pupil, after nonage, equally subjects of the same law together, without any dominion left in the father over the life, liberty, or estate of his son, whether they be only in the state and under the law of Nature, or under the positive laws of an established government.

*   *   *

The freedom then of man, and liberty of acting according to his own will, is grounded on his having reason, which is able to instruct him in that law he is to govern himself by, and make him know how far he is left to the freedom of his own will. To turn him loose to an unrestrained liberty, before he has reason to guide him, is not the allowing him the privilege of his nature to be free, but to thrust him out amongst brutes, and abandon him to a state as wretched and as much beneath that of a man as theirs. This is that which puts the authority into the parents' hands to govern the minority of their children. God hath made it their business to employ this care on their offspring, and hath placed in them suitable inclinations of tenderness and concern to temper this power, to apply it as His wisdom designed it, to the children's good as long as they should need to be under it.

But what reason can hence advance this care of the parents due to their offspring into an absolute, arbitrary dominion of the father, whose power reaches no farther than by such a discipline as he finds most effectual to give such strength and health to their bodies, such vigour and rectitude to their minds, as may best fit his children to be most useful to themselves and others, and, if it be necessary to his condition, to make them work when they are able for their own subsistence; but in this power the mother, too, has her share with the father.

Nay, this power so little belongs to the father by any peculiar right of Nature, but only as he is guardian of his children, that when he quits his care of them he loses his power over them, which goes along with their nourishment and education, to which it is inseparably annexed, and belongs as much to the foster-father of an exposed child as to the natural father of another. So little power does the bare act of begetting give a man over his issue, if all his care ends there, and this be all the title he hath to the name and authority of a father. And what will become of this paternal power in that part of the world where one woman hath more than one husband at a time? or in those parts of America where, when the husband and wife part, which happens frequently, the children are all left to the mother, follow her, and are wholly under her care and provision? And if the father die whilst the children are young, do they not naturally everywhere owe the same obedience to their mother, during their minority, as to their father, were he alive? And will any one say that the mother hath a legislative power over her children that she can make standing rules which shall be of perpetual obligation, by which they ought to regulate all the concerns of their property, and bound their liberty all the course of their lives, and enforce the observation of them with capital punishments? For this is the proper power of the magistrate, of which the father hath not so much as

the shadow. His command over his children is but temporary, and reaches not their life or property. It is but a help to the weakness and imperfection of their nonage, a discipline necessary to their education. And though a father may dispose of his own possessions as he pleases when his children are out of danger of perishing for want, yet his power extends not to the lives or goods which either their own industry, or another's bounty, has made theirs, nor to their liberty neither, when they are once arrived to the enfranchisement of the years of discretion. The father's empire then ceases, and he can from thenceforward no more dispose of the liberty of his son than that of any other man. And it must be far from an absolute or perpetual jurisdiction from which a man may withdraw himself, having licence from Divine authority to "leave father and mother and cleave to his wife."

*   *   *

Chapter VII
Of Political or Civil Society

God, having made man such a creature that, in His own judgment, it was not good for him to be alone, put him under strong obligations of necessity, convenience, and inclination, to drive him into society, as well as fitted him with understanding and language to continue and enjoy it. The first society was between man and wife, which gave beginning to that between parents and children, to which, in time, that between master and servant came to be added. And though all these might, and commonly did, meet together, and make up but one family, wherein the master or mistress of it had some sort of rule proper to a family, each of these, or all together, came short of "political society," as we shall see if we consider the different ends, ties, and bounds of each of these.

Conjugal society is made by a voluntary compact between man and woman, and though it consist chiefly in such a communion and right in one another's bodies as is necessary to its chief end, procreation, yet it draws with it mutual support and assistance, and a communion of interests too, as necessary not only to unite their care and affection, but also necessary to their common offspring, who have a right to be nourished and maintained by them till they are able to provide for themselves.

For the end of conjunction between male and female being not barely procreation, but the continuation of the species, this conjunction betwixt male and female ought to last, even after procreation, so long as is necessary to the nourishment and support of the young ones, who are to be sustained by those that got them till they are able to shift and provide for themselves. This rule, which the infinite wise Maker hath set to the works of His hands, we find the inferior creatures steadily obey. In those vivaporous animals which feed on grass the conjunction between male and female lasts no longer than the very act of copulation, because the teat of the dam being sufficient to nourish the young till it be able to feed on grass, the male only begets, but concerns not himself for the female or young, to whose sustenance he can contribute nothing. But in beasts of prey the conjunction lasts longer, because the dam, not being able well to subsist herself and nourish her numerous offspring by her own prey alone (a more laborious as well as more dangerous way of living than by feeding on grass), the assistance of the male is necessary to the maintenance of their common family, which cannot subsist till they are able to prey for themselves, but by the joint care of male and female. The same is observed in all birds (except some domestic ones, where plenty of food excuses the cock from feeding and taking care of the young brood), whose young, needing food in the nest, the cock and hen continue mates till the young are able to use their wings and provide for themselves.

And herein, I think, lies the chief, if not the only reason, why the male and female in mankind are tied to a longer conjunction than other creatures—viz., because the female is capable of conceiving, and, *de facto,* is commonly with child

again, and brings forth too a new birth, long before the former is out of a dependency for support on his parents' help and able to shift for himself, and has all the assistance due to him from his parents, whereby the father, who is bound to take care for those he hath begot, is under an obligation to continue in conjugal society with the same woman longer than other creatures, whose young, being able to subsist of themselves before the time of procreation returns again, the conjugal bond dissolves of itself, and they are at liberty till Hymen, at his usual anniversary season, summons them again to choose new mates. Wherein one cannot but admire the wisdom of the great Creator, who, having given to man an ability to lay up for the future as well as supply the present necessity, hath made it necessary that society of man and wife should be more lasting than of male and female amongst other creatures, that so their industry might be encouraged, and their interest better united, to make provision and lay up goods for their common issue, which uncertain mixture, or easy and frequent solutions of conjugal society, would mightily disturb.

But though these are ties upon mankind which make the conjugal bonds more firm and lasting in a man than the other species of animals, yet it would give one reason to inquire why this compact, where procreation and education are secured and inheritance taken care for, may not be made determinable, either by consent, or at a certain time, or upon certain conditions, as well as any other voluntary compacts, there being no necessity, in the nature of the thing, nor to the ends of it, that it should always be for life—I mean, to such as are under no restraint of any positive law which ordains all such contracts to be perpetual.

But the husband and wife, though they have but one common concern, yet having different understandings, will unavoidably sometimes have different wills too. It therefore being necessary that the last determination (i.e., the rule) should be placed somewhere, it naturally falls to the man's share as the abler and the stronger. But this, reaching but to the things of their common interest and property, leaves the wife in the full and true possession of what by contract is her peculiar right, and at least gives the husband no more power over her than she has over his life; the power of the husband being so far from that of an absolute monarch that the wife has, in many cases, a liberty to separate from him where natural right or their contract allows it, whether that contract be made by themselves in the state of Nature or by the customs or laws of the country they live in, and the children, upon such separation, fall to the father or mother's lot as such contract does determine.

For all the ends of marriage being to be obtained under politic government, as well as in the state of Nature, the civil magistrate doth not abridge the right or power of either, naturally necessary to those ends—viz., procreation and mutual support and assistance whilst they are together, but only decides any controversy that may arise between man and wife about them. If it were otherwise, and that absolute sovereignty and power of life and death naturally belonged to the husband, and were necessary to the society between man and wife, there could be no matrimony in any of these countries where the husband is allowed no such absolute authority. But the ends of matrimony requiring no such power in the husband, it was not at all necessary to it. The condition of conjugal society put it not in him; but whatsoever might consist with procreation and support of the children till they could shift for themselves—mutual assistance, comfort, and maintenance—might be varied and regulated by that contract which first united them in that society, nothing being necessary to any society that is not necessary to the ends for which it is made.

*   *   *

Let us therefore consider a master of a family with all these subordinate relations of wife, children, servants and slaves, united under the domestic rule of a family, with what resemblance soever it may have in its order, offices, and number too, with a little commonwealth, yet is very far from it both in its constitution, power, and end; or if it must be thought a monarchy, and the paterfamilias the absolute monarch in it, absolute monarchy will have but a very shattered and short power, when it is plain by what has been said before, that the master of the family has a very distinct and differently limited power both as to time and extent over those several persons that are in it; for excepting the slave (and the family is as much a family, and his power as paterfamilias as great, whether there be any slaves in his family or no) he has no legislative power of life and death over any of them, and none too but what a mistress of a family may have as well as he. And he certainly can have no absolute power over the whole family who has but a very limited one over every individual in it. But how a family, or any other society of men, differ from that which is properly political society, we shall best see by considering wherein political society itself consists.

Man being born, as has been proved, with a title to perfect freedom and an uncontrolled enjoyment of all the rights and privileges of the law of Nature, equally with any other man, or number of men in the world, hath by nature a power not only to preserve his property—that is, his life, liberty, and estate, against the injuries and attempts of other men, but to judge of and punish the breaches of that law in others, as he is persuaded the offence deserves, even with death itself, in crimes where the heinousness of the fact, in his opinion, requires it. But because no political society can be, nor subsist, without having in itself the power to preserve the property, and in order thereunto punish the offences of all those of that society, there, and there only, is political society where every one of the members hath quitted this natural power, resigned it up into the hands of the community in all cases that exclude him not from appealing for protection to the law established by it. And thus all private judgment of every particular member being excluded, the community comes to be umpire, and by understanding indifferent rules and men authorised by the community for their execution, decides all the differences that may happen between any members of that society concerning any matter of right, and punishes those offences which any member hath committed against the society with such penalties as the law has established; whereby it is easy to discern who are, and are not, in political society together. Those who are united into one body, and have a common established law and judicature to appeal to, with authority to decide controversies between them and punish offenders, are in civil society one with another; but those who have no such common appeal, I mean on earth, are still in the state of Nature, each being where there is no other, judge for himself and executioner; which is, as I have before showed it, the perfect state of Nature.

And thus the commonwealth comes by a power to set down what punishment shall belong to the several transgressions they think worthy of it, committed amongst the members of that society (which is the power of making laws), as well as it has the power to punish any injury done unto any of its members by any one that is not of it (which is the power of war and peace); and all this for the preservation of the property of all the members of that society, as far as is possible. But though every man entered into society has quitted his power to punish offences against the law of Nature in prosecution of his own private judgment, yet with the judgment of offences which he has given up to the legislative, in all cases where he can appeal to the magistrate, he has given up a right to the commonwealth to employ his force for the execution of the judgments of the commonwealth whenever he shall be called to it, which, indeed, are his own judgments, they being made by himself or his representative. And herein we have the original of the legislative and executive power of civil society, which is to judge by standing laws how far offences are to be punished when committed within the commonwealth; and also by occasional judgments founded on the present circumstances of the fact, how far injuries from without are to be vindicated, and in both these to employ all the force of all the members when there shall be need.

Wherever, therefore, any number of men so unite into one society as to quit every one his executive power of the law of Nature, and to resign it to the public, there and there only is a political or civil society. And this is done wherever any number of men, in the state of Nature, enter into society to make one people one body politic under one supreme government: or else when any one joins himself to, and incorporates with any government already made. For hereby he authorises the society, or which is all one, the legislative thereof, to make laws for him as the public good of the society shall require, to the execution whereof his own assistance (as to his own decrees) is due. And this puts men out of a state of Nature into that of a commonwealth, by setting up a judge on earth with authority to determine all the controversies and redress the injuries that may happen to any member of the commonwealth, which judge is the legislative or magistrates appointed by it. And wherever there are any number of men, however associated, that have no such decisive power to appeal to, there they are still in the state of Nature.

And hence it is evident that absolute monarchy, which by some men is counted for the only government in the world, is indeed inconsistent with civil society, and so can be no form of civil government at all. For the end of civil society being to avoid and remedy those inconveniencies of the state of Nature which necessarily follow from every man's being judge in his own case, by setting up a known authority to which every one of that society may appeal upon any injury received, or controversy that may arise, and which every one of the society ought to obey. Wherever any persons are who have not such an authority to appeal to, and decide any difference between them there, those persons are still in the state of Nature. And so is every absolute prince in respect of those who are under his dominion.

For he being supposed to have all, both legislative and executive, power in himself alone, there is no judge to be found, no appeal lies open to any one, who may fairly and indifferently, and with authority decide, and from whence relief and redress may be expected of any injury or inconveniency that may be suffered from him, or by his order. So that such a man, however entitled, Czar, or Grand Signior, or how you please, is as much

in the state of Nature, with all under his dominion, as he is with the rest of mankind. For wherever any two men are, who have no standing rule
and common judge to appeal to on earth, for the
determination of controversies of right betwixt
them, there they are still in the state of Nature,
and under all the inconveniencies of it, with only
this woeful difference to the subject, or rather
slave of an absolute prince. That whereas, in the
ordinary state of Nature, he has a liberty to judge
of his right, according to the best of his power to
maintain it; but whenever his property is invaded
by the will and order of his monarch, he has not
only no appeal, as those in society ought to have,
but, as if he were degraded from the common state
of rational creatures, is denied a liberty to judge
of, or defend his right, and so is exposed to all the
misery and inconveniencies that a man can fear
from one, who being in the unrestrained state of
Nature, is yet corrupted with flattery and armed
with power.

*   *   *

Chapter VIII
Of the Beginning of Political Societies

Men being, as has been said, by nature all free,
equal, and independent, no one can be put out of
this estate and subjected to the political power of
another without his own consent, which is done
by agreeing with other men, to join and unite into
a community for their comfortable, safe, and
peaceable living, one amongst another, in a secure
enjoyment of their properties, and a greater security against any that are not of it. This any number of men may do, because it injures not the
freedom of the rest; they are left, as they were, in
the liberty of the state of Nature. When any number of men have so consented to make one community or government, they are thereby presently
incorporated, and make one body politic, wherein
the majority have a right to act and conclude the
rest.

For, when any number of men have, by the
consent of every individual, made a community,
they have thereby made that community one
body, with a power to act as one body, which is
only by the will and determination of the majority.
For that which acts any community, being only
the consent of the individuals of it, and it being
one body, must move one way, it is necessary the
body should move that way whither the greater
force carries it, which is the consent of the majority, or else it is impossible it should act or
continue one body, one community, which the
consent of every individual that united into it
agreed that it should; and so every one is bound
by that consent to be concluded by the majority.
And therefore we see that in assemblies empow-
ered to act by positive laws where no number is
set by that positive law which empowers them, the
act of the majority passes for the act of the whole,
and of course determines as having, by the law of
Nature and reason, the power of the whole.

And thus every man, by consenting with others to make one body politic under one government, puts himself under an obligation to every
one of that society to submit to the determination
of the majority, and to be concluded by it; or else
this original compact, whereby he with others incorporates into one society, would signify nothing,
and be no compact if he be left free and under no
other ties than he was in before in the state of
Nature. For what appearance would there be of
any compact? What new engagement if he were
no farther tied by any decrees of the society than
he himself thought fit and did actually consent to?
This would be still as great a liberty as he himself
had before his compact, or any one else in the
state of Nature, who may submit himself and consent to any acts of it if he thinks fit.

*   *   *

Whosoever, therefore, out of a state of Nature
unite into a community, must be understood to
give up all the power necessary to the ends for
which they unite into society to the majority of
the community, unless they expressly agreed in

any number greater than the majority. And this is done by barely agreeing to unite into one political society, which is all the compact that is, or needs be, between the individuals that enter into or make up a commonwealth. And thus, that which begins and actually constitutes any political society is nothing but the consent of any number of freemen capable of majority, to unite and incorporate into such a society. And this is that, and that only, which did or could give beginning to any lawful government in the world.

*   *   *

Every man being, as has been showed, naturally free, and nothing being able to put him into subjection to any earthly power, but only his own consent, it is to be considered what shall be understood to be a sufficient declaration of a man's consent to make him subject to the laws of any government. There is a common distinction of an express and a tacit consent, which will concern our present case. Nobody doubts but an express consent of any man, entering into any society, makes him a perfect member of that society, a subject of that government. The difficulty is, what ought to be looked upon as a tacit consent, and how far it binds—*i.e.*, how far any one shall be looked on to have consented, and thereby submitted to any government, where he has made no expressions of it at all. And to this I say, that every man that hath any possession or enjoyment of any part of the dominions of any government doth hereby give his tacit consent, and is as far forth obliged to obedience to the laws of that government, during such enjoyment, as any one under it, whether this his possession be of land to him and his heirs for ever, or a lodging only for a week; or whether it be barely travelling freely on the highway; and, in effect, it reaches as far as the very being of any one within the territories of that government.

To understand this the better, it is fit to consider that every man when he at first incorporates himself into any commonwealth, he, by his uniting himself thereunto, annexes also, and submits to the community those possessions which he has,

or shall acquire, that do not already belong to any other government. For it would be a direct contradiction for any one to enter into society with others for the securing and regulating of property, and yet to suppose his land, whose property is to be regulated by the laws of the society, should be exempt from the jurisdiction of that government to which he himself, and the property of the land, is a subject. By the same act, therefore, whereby any one unites his person, which was before free, to any commonwealth, by the same he unites his possessions, which were before free, to it also; and they become, both of them, person and possession, subject to the government and dominion of that commonwealth as long as it hath a being. Whoever therefore, from thenceforth, by inheritance, purchases permission, or otherwise enjoys any part of the land so annexed to, and under the government of that commonweal, must take it with the condition it is under—that is, of submitting to the government of the commonwealth, under whose jurisdiction it is, as far forth as any subject of it.

But since the government has a direct jurisdiction only over the land and reaches the possessor of it (before he has actually incorporated himself in the society) only as he dwells upon and enjoys that, the obligation any one is under by virtue of such enjoyment to submit to the government begins and ends with the enjoyment; so that whenever the owner, who has given nothing but such a tacit consent to the government will, by donation, sale or otherwise, quit the said possession, he is at liberty to go and incorporate himself into any other commonwealth, or agree with others to begin a new one *in vacuis locis,* in any part of the world they can find free and unpossessed; whereas he that has once, by actual agreement and any express declaration, given his consent to be of any commonweal, is perpetually and indispensably obliged to be, and remain unalterably a subject to it, and can never be again in the liberty of the state of Nature, unless by any calamity the government he was under comes to be dissolved.

But submitting to the laws of any country, living quietly and enjoying privileges and protection under them, makes not a man a member of that society; it is only a local protection and homage due to and from all those who, not being in a state of war, come within the territories belonging to any government, to all parts whereof the force of its law extends. But this no more makes a man a member of that society, a perpetual subject of that commonwealth, than it would make a man a subject to another in whose family he found it convenient to abide for some time, though, whilst he continued in it, he were obliged to comply with the laws and submit to the government he found there. And thus we see that foreigners, by living all their lives under another government, and enjoying the privileges and protection of it, though they are bound, even in conscience, to submit to its administration as far forth as any denizen, yet do not thereby come to be subjects or members of that commonwealth. Nothing can make any man so but his actually entering into it by positive engagement and express promise and compact. This is that which, I think, concerning the beginning of political societies, and that consent which makes any one a member of any commonwealth.

Chapter IX
Of the Ends of Political Society and Government

If man in the state of Nature be so free as has been said, if he be absolute lord of his own person and possessions, equal to the greatest and subject to nobody, why will he part with his freedom, this empire, and subject himself to the dominion and control of any other power? To which it is obvious to answer, that though in the state of Nature he hath such a right, yet the enjoyment of it is very uncertain and constantly exposed to the invasion of others; for all being kings as much as he, every man his equal, and the greater part no strict observers of equity and justice, the enjoyment of the property he has in this state is very unsafe, very insecure. This makes him willing to quit this condition which, however free, is full of fears and continual dangers; and it is not without reason

that he seeks out and is willing to join in society with others who are already united, or have a mind to unite for the mutual preservation of their lives, liberties and estates, which I call by the general name—property.

The great and chief end, therefore, of men uniting into commonwealths, and putting themselves under government, is the preservation of their property; to which in the state of Nature there are many things wanting.

Firstly, there wants an established, settled, known law, received and allowed by common consent to be the standard of right and wrong, and the common measure to decide all controversies between them. For though the law of Nature be plain and intelligible to all rational creatures, yet men, being biased by their interest, as well as ignorant for want of study of it, are not apt to allow of it as a law binding to them in the application of it to their particular cases.

Secondly, in the state of Nature there wants a known and indifferent judge, with authority to determine all differences according to the established law. For every one in that state being both judge and executioner of the law of Nature, men being partial to themselves, passion and revenge is very apt to carry them too far, and with too much heat in their own cases, as well as negligence and unconcernedness, make them too remiss in other men's.

Thirdly, in the state of Nature there often wants power to back and support the sentence when right, and to give it due execution. They who by any injustice offended will seldom fail where they are able by force to make good their injustice. Such resistance many times makes the punishment dangerous, and frequently destructive to those who attempt it.

*   *   *

REVIEW QUESTIONS

1. According to Locke, what is the nature of political society?

2. How does political society come into being?

3. How does Locke's notion of a social contract compare with that of Hobbes?

4. What are the ends of political society?

5. What are the implications of Locke's reasoning for early modern economic thinking?

JACQUES-BENIGNE BOSSUET

FROM *Politics Drawn from the Very Words of Holy Scripture*

Jacques-Benigne Bossuet (1627–1704) was a French Roman Catholic clergyman and writer, considered by some to be the greatest French preacher in history. He was born in Dijon, and was educated at Jesuit schools and at the Collège de Navarre in Paris. Ordained a priest in 1652, he served at court as tutor to the dauphin, the son of Louis XIV, for whom he wrote his great Discourse on Universal History *(1681), in which he argued that all history is moved by providence. The same year he was elevated to bishop of Meaux, a dignity he possessed until his death. Though best remembered for his* Funeral Orations *(1689), panegyrics on important national figures, history records his theory of absolutism as well. Bossuet's* Politics Drawn from the Very Words of Holy Scripture *was published posthumously in 1708. It argued that because God created kingship, kings were answerable only to God. By so reasoning, Bossuet offered one of the most explicit and extreme arguments for the divine right of kings.*

From *Politics Drawn from the Very Words of Holy Scripture*, by Jacques Bossuet, translated by Patrick Riley (Cambridge, Eng.: Cambridge University Press, 1990), pp. 39–43, 46–69, 57–63, 81–83, 103–6.

* * *

Third Book
In Which One Begins to Explain the Nature and the Properties of Royal Authority

First Article
Taking Notice of the Essential Characteristics.

SOLE PROPOSITION
THERE ARE FOUR CHARACTERISTICS OR QUALITIES
ESSENTIAL TO ROYAL AUTHORITY.

First, royal authority is sacred;
Secondly, it is paternal;
Thirdly, it is absolute;
Fourthly, it is subject to reason.
All of this must be established, in order, in the following articles.

Article II
Royal Authority Is Sacred.

1ST PROPOSITION
GOD ESTABLISHES KINGS AS HIS MINISTERS, AND
REIGNS THROUGH THEM OVER THE PEOPLES.

We have already seen that all power comes from God.

"The prince, St. Paul adds, is God's minister to thee for good. But if thou do that which is evil, fear: for he beareth not the sword in vain. For he is God's minister: an avenger to execute wrath upon him that doth evil."

Thus princes act as ministers of God, and his lieutenants on earth. It is through them that he exercises his Empire. "And now say you that you are able to withstand the kingdom of the Lord, which he possesseth by the sons of David?"

It is in this way that we have seen that the royal throne is not the throne of a man, but the throne of God himself. "God hath chosen Solomon my son, to sit upon the throne of the kingdom of the Lord over Israel." And again: "Solomon sat on the throne of the Lord."

And in order that no one believe that it was peculiar to the Israelites to have kings established by God, here is what Ecclesiasticus says: "Over every nation he set a ruler. And Israel was made the manifest portion of God."

Thus he governs all peoples, and gives them, all of them, their kings; though he governs Israel in a more particular and announced fashion.

* * *

3RD PROPOSITION
ONE MUST OBEY THE PRINCE BY REASON
OF RELIGION AND CONSCIENCE.

St. Paul, after having said that the prince is the minister of God, concludes thus: "wherefore be subject of necessity, not only for wrath, but also for conscience' sake."

This is why "one must serve, not to the eye, as it were pleasing men, but, as the servants of Christ doing the will of God, from the heart."

And again: "Servants, obey in all things your temporal masters, not serving to the eye, as pleasing men, but in simplicity of heart, fearing God. Whatsoever you do, do it from the heart, as to the Lord, and not to men; knowing that you shall receive of the Lord the reward of inheritance. Serve ye the Lord Christ."

If the apostle speaks thus of slavery, a condition contrary to nature, what must we think of legitimate subjection to princes and to magistrates, the protectors of public liberty?

This is why St. Peter says: "Be ye subject therefore to every human creature for God's sake: whether it be to the king as excelling; Or to governors as sent by him for the punishment of evildoers, and for the praise of the good."

Even if rulers do not acquit themselves of this duty, one must respect in them their charge and their ministry. "Servants, be subject to your masters with all fear, not only to the good and gentle, but also to the angry and unjust."

There is thus something religious in the respect one gives to the prince. The service of God and respect for kings are inseparable things, and St. Peter places these two duties together: "Fear God, Honor the King."

God, moreover, has put something divine into kings. "I have said: You are Gods, and all of you the sons of the most High." It is God himself whom David makes speak in this way.

This accounts for the fact that the servants of God swear by the life and health of the king, as by a divine and sacred thing. Uriah spoke to David: "By thy welfare and by the welfare of thy soul I will not do this thing."

Even if the king should be an infidel, from the respect one should have for the ordination of God. "By the health of Pharaoh, you shall not depart hence."

Here one must listen to the first Christians, and to Tertullian, who speaks as follows in the name of all of them: "We shall swear, not by the genius of the Caesars, but by their life and by their health, which is the most august of all geniuses. Do you not know that geniuses are demons? But we, who see in the emperors the choice and judgment of God, who gave them the command over all peoples, respect in them what God has placed there, and we uphold that through a great oath."

He adds: "What more can I say about our religion and about our piety for the emperor, whom we must respect as he whom our God has chosen: such that I can say that Caesar is more to us than to you, because it is our God who has established him?"

Thus it is the spirit of Christianity to make kings respected in a kind of religious way—which Tertullian (again) calls very well "the religion of the second majesty."

This second majesty simply flows out of the first, that is to say the divine, which, for the good of human affairs, has lent some of its brilliance to kings.

*   *   *

Article III
Royal Authority Is Paternal, and Its Proper Character Is Goodness.

After the things which have been said, this truth has no further need of proofs.

We have seen that kings hold the place of God, who is the true Father of the human race.

We have also seen that the first idea of power that there was among men, is that of paternal power; and that kings were fashioned on the model of fathers.

Moreover, all the world agrees that obedience, which is due to public power, is only found (in the Decalogue) in the precept which obliges one to honor his parents.

From all of this it appears that the name "king" is a father's name, and that goodness is the most natural quality in kings.

Let us, nonetheless, reflect particularly on so important a truth.

1ST PROPOSITION
GOODNESS IS A ROYAL QUALITY, AND THE TRUE PREROGATIVE OF GREATNESS.

"The Lord your God is the God of gods, and the Lord of lords, a great and mighty and terrible, who accepteth no person nor taketh bribes. He doth judgment to the fatherless, and the widow, loveth the stranger, and giveth him food and raiment."

Because God is great and self-sufficient, he turns (as it were) entirely to do good to men, in conformity to this word: "For according to his greatness, also is his mercy with him."

He places an image of his greatness in kings, in order to oblige them to imitate his goodness.

He raises them to a condition in which they have nothing more to desire for themselves. We have heard David saying: "What can David add more, seeing thou hast thus glorified thy servant, and known him?"

And at the same time he declares to them that he gives them this greatness for love of the nations. "Because the Lord hath loved his people, therefore, he hath made thee king over them." And again: "God, whom thou hast pleased, . . . hath set thee upon the throne of Israel, because the Lord hath loved Israel for ever, and hath appointed thee king, to do judgment and justice."

That is why, in those passages where we read that the kingdom of David was raised over the people, the Hebrew and the Greek use *for* the people. This shows that greatness has for its object the good of subject peoples.

Indeed God, who has made all men from the same earth, bodily, and has placed equally in their souls his image and resemblance, has not established between them so many distinctions as to make on one side the proud and on the other slaves and wretches. He made the great only to protect the small; he gave his power to kings only to procure the public good, and for the support of the people.

*   *   *

Fourth Book
On the Characteristics of Royalty (continuation)

First Article
Royal Authority Is Absolute.

In order to make this term odious and insupportable, many pretend to confuse absolute government and arbitrary government. But nothing is more distinct, as we shall make clear when we speak of justice.

1ST PROPOSITION
THE PRINCE NEED ACCOUNT TO NO ONE FOR WHAT HE ORDAINS.

"Observe the mouth of the king, and the commandments of the oath of God. Be not hasty to depart from his face, and do not continue in an evil work: for he will do all that pleaseth him. And his word is full of power: neither can any man say to him: Why dost thou so? He that keepeth the commandment, shall find no evil."

Without this absolute authority, he can neither do good nor suppress evil: his power must be such that no one can hope to escape him; and, in fine, the sole defense of individuals against the public power, must be their innocence.

This doctrine is in conformity with the saying of St. Paul: "Wilt thou then not be afraid of the power? Do that which is good."

2ND PROPOSITION
WHEN THE PRINCE HAS DECIDED, THERE CAN BE NO OTHER DECISION.

The judgments of sovereigns are attributed to God himself. When Josaphat established judges to judge the people, he said: "It is not in the name of man that you judge, but in the name of God."

This is what Ecclesiasticus is made to say: "Judge not against a judge." For still stronger reasons against the sovereign judge who is the king. And the reason which is given is that, "he judgeth according to that which is just." It is not that he is always so judging, but that he is assumed to be so judging; and that no one has the right to judge or to review after him.

One must, then, obey princes as if they were justice itself, without which there is neither order nor justice in affairs.

They are gods, and share in some way in divine independence. "I have said: You are gods, and all of you the sons of the most High."

Only God can judge their judgments and their persons. "God hath stood in the congregation of gods, and being in the midst of them he judgeth gods."

It is for that reason that St. Gregory, Bishop of Tours, said to King Chilperic in a council: "We speak to you, but you listen to us only if you want to. If you do not want to, who will condemn you other than he who has said that he was justice itself?"

It follows from this that he who does not want

to obey the prince, is not sent to another tribunal; but he is condemned irremissibly to death as an enemy of public peace and of human society. "Whoever will be proud and will not obey the command of the pontiff and the ordinance of the judge will die, and you will thus eradicate the evil from among you." And again: "Whosoever shall refuse to obey all your orders, may he die." It is the people who speak thus to Joshua.

The prince can correct himself when he knows that he has done badly; but against his authority there can be no remedy except his authority.

This is why he must take care of what he orders. "Take heed what you do; and whatsoever you judge, it shall rebound to you. Let the fear of the Lord be with you, and do all things with great care."

It is thus that Joseph instructed the judges, to whom he was entrusting his authority: how much of this he recollected when he himself had to judge!

* * *

Fifth Book
Fourth and Final Characteristic of Royal Authority

First Article
Royal Authority Is Subject to Reason.

**1ST PROPOSITION
GOVERNMENT IS A WORK OF REASON AND INTELLIGENCE. "NOW, LISTEN, O KINGS, AND BE INSTRUCTED, JUDGES OF THE EARTH."**

All men are created capable of understanding. But principally you upon whom reposes an entire nation, you who should be the soul and intelligence of a state, in whom must be found the first reason for all its movements: the less it is necessary for you to justify yourself to others, the more you must have justification and intelligence within yourself.

The contrary of acting from reason is to act out of passion or anger. To act out of anger, as Saul acted against David, driven by his jealousy or possessed by his black melancholy, entails all kinds of irregularities, inconsistencies, inequalities, anomalies, injustice, and confusion in one's conduct.

Though one has only a horse to lead and a flock to guide, one cannot do it without reason. How much more is needed for the leadership of men and a rational flock!

"The Lord took David from the care of his sheep to have him conduct Jacob, his servant, and Israel, his inheritance. And he led them in the innocence of his heart with an able and intelligent hand."

Everything among men is accomplished through intelligence and through counsel. "Houses are built out of wisdom and become solid through prudence. Ability fills the granaries and amasses riches. The wise man is courageous. The able man is robust and strong because war is waged by strategy and by industry, and salvation is found where there is much counsel."

Wisdom herself says: "It is through me that kings rule and through me that legislators prescribe what is just."

She is so born to command that she gives the empire even to those born in servitude. "The wise servant will command the children of the house who lack wisdom, and he will apportion their lots." And furthermore: "Free people will subject themselves to a judicious servant."

God, upon installing Joshua, orders him to study the law of Moses, which was the law of the kingdom, "in order," he says, "that you should understand all that you do." And furthermore: "and then you will carry out your designs and you will understand what to do." David said as much to Solomon in the last instructions he gave to him upon dying. "Take care to observe the laws of God so that you may understand all that you do and to which side you are to turn.

"So that you may not be turned, turn yourself knowingly. Let reason direct all your movements. Know what you do and why you are doing it."

Solomon had learned from God himself how much wisdom is necessary to govern a great people. "God appeared to him in a dream during the night, and said to him: Ask what thou wilt that I should give thee. And Solomon said: Thou hast shown great mercy to thy servant David my father, even as he walked before thee in truth, and justice, and an upright heart with thee: and thou hast kept thy great mercy for him, and hast given him a son to sit on his throne, as it is this day. And now, O Lord God, thou hast made thy servant king instead of David my father: and I am but a child, and know not how to go out and come in (that is to say, I do not know how to conduct myself: where to begin or to end matters). And thy servant is in the midst of the people which thou hast chosen, an immense people, which cannot be numbered nor counted for multitude. Give therefore to thy servant an understanding heart, to judge thy people, and discern between good and evil. For who shall be able to judge this people, thy people which is so numerous? And the word was pleasing to the Lord that Solomon had asked such a thing. And the Lord said to Solomon: Because thou hast asked this thing, and hast not asked for thyself long life, or riches, nor the lives of thy enemies, but hast asked for thyself wisdom to discern judgment, Behold I have done for thee according to thy words, and have given thee a wise and understanding heart, insomuch that there hath been no one like thee before thee, nor shall arise after thee. Yea and the things also which thou didst not ask, I have given thee: to wit riches and glory, so that no one hath been like thee among the kings in all days heretofore."

This dream of Solomon's was an ecstasy in which the mind of this great king, separated from the senses and united to God, enjoyed true knowledge. He saw, while in this state, that wisdom is the sole grace that a prince should ask of God.

He saw the weightiness of the affairs and the immense multitude of the people whom he had to lead. So many temperaments, so many interests, so many artifices, so many passions, so many surprises to fear, so many things to consider, so many

people from every side to hear and know: what mind could be equal to it?

I am young, he said, and I still do not know how to conduct myself. He was not lacking in spirit, any more than in resolution. For he had already spoken in a masterly tone to his brother Adonias: and from the beginning of his reign he had done his part at a decisive juncture, with as much prudence as could be desired: and all the same he trembled still, when he saw this immense chain of cares and of matters that accompany royalty: and he saw well that he could only find his way out through consummate wisdom.

He asked it of God, and God gave it to him: but at the same time he gave him all the rest which he had not asked, that is to say riches and glory.

He teaches kings that they will lack nothing when they have wisdom, and that she alone draws all other goods to them.

We find a fine commentary on Solomon's prayer in the book of Wisdom, which makes this wise king speak as follows: "Wherefore I wished, and understanding was given me: and I called upon God, and the spirit of wisdom came upon me. And I preferred her before kingdoms and thrones, and esteemed riches nothing in comparison of her. Neither did I compare unto her any precious stone: for all gold in comparison of her, is as a little sand, and silver in respect to her shall be counted as clay. I loved her above health and beauty, and chose to have her instead of light: for her light cannot be put out. Now all good things came to me together with her, and innumerable riches through her hands."

*   *   *

LAS MENINAS (1656)

DIEGO VELÁZQUEZ

Velázquez's final masterpiece, a famous and curious reflection on court life, has long intrigued art historians. Why paint a picture of the infanta Margarita, followed by her entourage of ladies, dwarves, and pets? As legend has it, she burst into the artist's studio while he was painting a portrait of the king and queen, whose only representation remains a mirrored reflection in the background. He offers a strikingly realistic portrait of some of the members of the court of Philip IV of Spain and, at the same time, a subtle commentary on life in that court. How might Las Meninas *be considered a critique of the court? If the painting was intended as a criticism of royal manners and monarchical rule, what was the criticism? How might events in Spain and Europe at the middle of the seventeenth century have inspired the artist to risk such a statement?*

REVIEW QUESTIONS

1. Why does Bossuet begin his consideration of political authority with God?
2. What are the implications of this point of departure?
3. How is absolutism understood by Bossuet?
4. How does conscience relate to obedience according to Bossuet?
5. How does Bossuet's discussion of paternal authority compare with Filmer's?
6. Why is monarchy natural?
7. How is Bossuet construing nature?

DUC DE SAINT-SIMON

FROM *Historical Memoirs*

Louis de Rouvroy, duc de Saint-Simon (1675–1755), was a French soldier and diplomat, best remembered for his memoirs of court life during the reign of Louis XIV. Born the son of an aged nobleman, a parvenu raised to the aristocracy by Louis XIII, he was a remarkable figure. Physically unattractive, Saint-Simon possessed a violent and vindictive temper as well as great wit and intelligence. His career at court can best be described as disappointing. As his memoirs make clear, he never achieved the rank he sought because of his open and tactless opposition to Louis XIV on minor points of precedence and ceremony. Saint-Simon managed to attach himself to Philippe, duc de Orléans in 1712 and so persevered on the edge of affairs until his patron's death in 1723. From that point until his death in 1755, Saint-Simon remained in private life and devoted himself to writing his memoirs. A composite narrative, drawn from his own memory and papers as well as witness testimony and manuscript sources, it offers a wealth of information on life at the court and a close analysis of state affairs under an absolute monarch.

From *Historical Memoirs of the Duc de Saint-Simon*, vol. 1, translated by Lucy Norton (New York: McGraw-Hill, 1967).

*   *   *

After ten days at Givry the two armies separated and marched away, and two days later the siege of Namur was proclaimed, the King having covered that journey in a five-day march. Monseigneur, Monsieur, Monsieur le Prince, and the Maréchal d'Humières, in order of rank, led the army under the King's command. The Maréchal de Luxembourg, in sole command of his army, covered the siege and took observations. Meantime the ladies removed to Dinant. On the third day of the King's march Monsieur le Prince was sent on ahead to invest Namur town, for Vauban, the famous organizer of the King's sieges, had insisted on there being separate attacks for the town and the fortress. Nothing very eventful happened during the ten days of the siege; on the eleventh day of open trenches they sounded for a parley and a surrender was arranged on the defenders' terms. During all this time the King was living under canvas in very hot weather, for it had not rained since we left Paris. The army moved camp in order to besiege the fortress, and whilst that was taking place the King's own regiment of infantry found its new position held by a small detachment of the enemy digging trenches. There was a brisk engagement in which the royal troops greatly distinguished themselves, with very few losses, and the enemy were soon routed. The King was delighted by this, for he was particularly devoted to that regiment which he liked to think of as being his personal property.

The King's tents and those of his courtiers were pitched in a pleasant meadow five hundred paces from the monastery of Marlagne. By this time the weather had changed to abundant and continuous rain, such as no one in the army could remember and had thus greatly increased the reputation of St. Médard, whose feast-day is 8 June. It had poured on that day and, according to the saying, whatever the weather is then it will continue so for the next forty days, as it happened in that year. The soldiers were driven nearly to desperation by the floods, so that they cursed the saint heartily, breaking and burning his images wherever they could lay hands on them. The rain was indeed a perfect plague, and the King's tents could only be reached by laying down paths of brushwood which had daily to be renewed. The other tents were not more easily accessible and the trenches were soon full of muddy water. It sometimes took as much as three days to move a cannon from one battery to another. The waggons were unusable, and shells, cannon-balls, etc., had to be transported on mules and horses, which became the sole support of every service to the army and the Court. Without them nothing would have been possible. The flooding of the roads also prevented the army of M. de Luxembourg from using their waggons. They were near starvation for lack of fodder and would have died had not the King issued orders that detachments of his *maison* should ride each day carrying sacks of grain to a

certain village where M. de Luxembourg's officers would receive and count them.

Although the *maison* had had little rest on account of carrying brushwood, mounting the various guards, and their other daily duties, they were given this additional fatigue because the cavalry also had been continuously on duty and were down to leaves for forage. That consideration aroused no sympathy in the hearts of the pampered *maison*, who were accustomed to special privileges. They complained. The King was obdurate. The task remained theirs. On the very first day, however, the lifeguards and light cavalry were openly murmuring when they reached the depot in the early morning, and they so worked upon one another that the men actually threw the sacks down and refused to pick them up again. Cresnay, my brigadier, had most courteously asked me whether I was willing to take a sack, saying that otherwise he would find me some different duty; but I had consented, hoping thus to please the King, especially in view of all the grumbling. It so happened that I arrived on the scene with my troop of musketeers at the precise moment when the red-coats were about to mutiny, and I took up my sack before them all. Thereupon Marin, a cavalry-brigadier, who was supervising the loading by the King's orders and raging at the mutineers, called out my name, exclaiming that if I did not think myself too good for such work, lifeguardsmen and the light horse need not be ashamed to copy me. That argument and his stern eye had their effect; there was a rush to pick up the sacks, and never afterwards the smallest objection. Marin watched us go and then went to tell the King what had happened and the influence of my good example. That kind office resulted in the King saying some gracious things to me, and throughout the remainder of the siege he never saw me without saying something civil. I was all the more obliged to Marin because I had no acquaintance with him socially.

*   *   *

1700

The year began with an economy. The King announced that he would no longer pay for the changes made by courtiers in their lodgings, which had cost him more than sixty thousand livres since Fontainebleau. Mme de Mailly was thought to be the cause, for she had changed hers annually in the past three or four years. The new arrangement was better in that one could get alterations made as one wished without first obtaining the King's consent; on the other hand one had to pay for everything.

From Candlemas to Lent there was a continual succession of balls and entertainments at the Court. The King gave several at Versailles and Marly, with wonderfully ingenious masquerades and tableaux, a form of diversion that vastly pleased him under the guise of amusing Mme la Duchesse de Bourgogne. There were concerts and private theatricals at Mme de Maintenon's; Monseigneur gave balls, and the most distinguished persons took pride in offering entertainment to Mme la Duchesse de Bourgogne. Monsieur le Prince, though his rooms were few and small, contrived to astonish the Court with the most elegant party in the world, a full-evening-dress ball, masks, tableaux, booths with foreign merchandise, and a supper most exquisitely staged. No one at the Court was refused admittance to any part of it, and there was no crowding nor any other inconvenience.

One evening when there was no ball Mme de Pontchartrain gave one at the Chancellery, and it turned out to be the gayest of them all. The Chancellor received Monseigneur, the three princes, and Mme la Duchesse de Bourgogne at the front entrance at ten o'clock and then immediately went off to sleep at the Château. There were different rooms provided for a full-evening-dress ball, masks, a splendid supper, and booths for the merchants of various countries, China, Japan, etc., offering vast quantities of objects of beauty and virtue, all chosen with exquisite taste. No money was taken; all were presents offered to Mme la Duchesse de Bourgogne and the other ladies.

There was also a concert in her honour, a play, and tableaux. Never was anything better conceived, more sumptuous, nor more perfectly organized, and Mme de Pontchartrain in the midst of it all was as gay, civil, and unruffled as though she had no responsibilities.

Everyone enjoyed themselves immensely, and we did not reach home until eight in the morning. Mme de Saint-Simon, who was always in Mme la Duchesse de Bourgogne's retinue (a great favour), and I never saw the light of day in the last three weeks before Lent. Certain dancers were not allowed to leave the ball-room before the princess, and once at Marly when I tried to escape early she sent orders for me to be confined within its doors. The same thing occurred to others also. I was truly thankful when Ash Wednesday came, and for a couple of days after felt quite stunned. As for Mme de Saint-Simon, she was worn out by Shrove Tuesday and did not manage to stay the full course. The King amused himself also in Mme de Maintenon's room with some selected ladies, playing *brelan, petite prime,* and *reversis* on the days when he had no ministers or little work to do, and those diversions continued well into Lent.

*   *   *

1702

*   *   *

When the promotion of generals was finally put into execution it proved to be very sweeping, comprising seventeen lieutenants-general, fifty brigadiers, forty-one colonels of infantry, and thirty-eight of cavalry. But before recounting the action which that promotion led me to take, I must first describe how during that winter I was received into the Parlement.

In dealing with his bastards the King always gave immediate effect to the honours which he granted them, without waiting for the usual warrants, letters patent, notifications, or decrees to be published. Yet, for many years past, he had made it a rule that peers might not be received into the

Parlement without his consent. That he never refused, but he had lately begun to withhold permission if the peer were not yet twenty-five years old, thus gradually instituting a custom which might later become the general rule. I was aware of this and accordingly deferred my own reception until a year after my twenty-fifth birthday, on the plea of forgetfulness.

My first action was to call on President Harlay, who was overwhelmingly polite. I was then obliged to call on the princes of the blood and finally on the bastards. M. du Maine, when I visited him, asked me to repeat the date, then with a delight that appeared restrained only by modesty and good manners, he exclaimed, "I shall be most careful not to forget. Such an honour! So gratifying that you desire my presence! You may be sure of me," and so saying he escorted me as far as the gardens, for this was at a Marly, and I was of the house-party. The Comte de Toulouse and M. de Vendôme replied less effusively but no less pleasantly, and were as polite as M. du Maine. Cardinal de Noailles had never once attended at the Parlement since he received the Roman crimson because his hat did not entitle him to a seat higher than that of his rank as count and peer. I elected to visit him at one of his public audiences. "You are aware," said he, "that I no longer have a seat?" "On the contrary," I replied, "I know that you have a most splendid place, and I beg you to take it at my reception." He then smiled, and I smiled also, for we perfectly understood one another. Later he personally escorted me to the top of his staircase, both doors open wide, and we walked together side by side, I on his right hand. M. de Luxembourg was the only one not to hear from me on that occasion. I had never forgiven him those abominable warrants, but he was not my friend and I did him no wrong.

Dongeois was at that time acting as registrar of the Parlement. He was a man whose ability and constant attendance had made him very knowledgeable in the customs of that body. I knew him well, and therefore went to consult him about the correct procedure. Yet despite the honesty and kindness of his intentions the good man laid three

traps for me, but luckily I was on the watch and fell into none of them. He said that out of respect for the Parlement I should make my first appearance there in a plain black coat unadorned with gold lace; that out of respect for the princes of the blood, whose short mantles were worn longer than their coats, I should not allow mine to come below the level of my jacket, and that out of respect for the premier président I should call to thank him on the morning after my reception, still wearing parliamentary dress. He did not bluntly make these suggestions but tactfully hinted at them. I made no issue of it, but I did the exact opposite, and having been alerted I took care to warn all those who were received after me, and they defended themselves likewise. It is by such ruses that many humiliations have come upon the dukes, one after another, in a constant stream that almost passes belief.

The reforming of the army after the Peace of Ryswick was on a very large scale but very haphazard. The quality of the various regiments, especially of the cavalry, and the merits of their commanding officers were ignored by Barbezieux, who was young and impulsive, and to whom the King gave a free hand. I myself had no acquaintance with him; my regiment was re-formed, and as it was very good parts of it were allocated to the Royals and the rest incorporated in the Duras regiment. My company was added to that of Barbezieux's brother-in-law the Comte d'Uzès, of whom he took particular care. It was small consolation to hear that others were being treated in the same way, and I was deeply disappointed. The colonels of regiments re-formed like mine were placed at the bottom of the list in their new regiments, and I was ordered to serve under Saint-Mauris, a gentleman of Franche-Comté and a complete stranger to me, although his brother was a lieutenant-general and well regarded. Shortly after this, the petty discipline that runs alongside active service demanded two months' service from officers at the tail of new regiments. That seemed monstrous to me. I went, of course, but I had been indisposed for some time past, and having been recommended the waters of Plombières I asked for leave of absence and for the next three years spent there the two months when I should have been exiled to a strange regiment, with no troops to command and no work to do. The King did not seem to mind. I often went to Marly; he spoke to me sometimes, a very good sign that was much remarked upon; in a word he treated me kindly, indeed better than most of my age and rank.

From time to time officers junior to myself were promoted; but they were veterans who had earned regiments by long and distinguished service, and I could understand the reason. Talk of a general promotion did not excite me, for birth and rank counted for nothing. I was too junior to be made a brigadier; my entire ambition was to command a regiment and fight at its head in the coming war, thus avoiding the humiliation of having to serve as a supernumerary aide-de-camp to Saint-Mauris. The King had distinguished me after the Neerwinden campaign by giving me a regiment; and I had brought it up to strength, and, dare I say so, commanded it with care and honour in four successive campaigns until the war ended.

The promotion was announced; everyone was astonished at the numbers, for there had never been so large a list. I eagerly scanned the names of new cavalry brigadiers, hoping to find my own, and was mortified to see five junior to me mentioned. My pride was most deeply hurt but I kept silent for fear of saying something rash in my vexation. The Maréchal de Lorges was most indignant and his brother-in-law not less so, and they both insisted that I ought to quit the service. I myself felt so angry that I was much inclined to do so; but my youth, the war beginning, the thought of renouncing my ambitions in my chosen career, the boredom of being idle, the tedious summers when conversation would all turn on war and partings, the advancement that could be earned by distinguished conduct, were all powerful deterrents, and I spent two months in mental agony, resigning every morning and every night reversing my decision.

At last, driven to extremes and harried by the two marshals, I resolved to take advice from men on whom I could rely, and to choose them from different walks of life. I finally decided upon the Maréchal de Choiseul, M. de Beauvilliers, the Chancellor, and M. de La Rochefoucauld. They knew how I was placed and were indignant on my behalf, and, moreover, the three last were courtiers. This was most desirable, for what I wished to discover was what the best people would think, particularly the solid men about the King. Above all I sought for advice that would not leave me a prey to indecision, rash impulses, or afterthoughts. Their verdict, given unanimously and most firmly, was that I should leave the service. They all agreed that it would be both a shame and most unsuitable for a man of my rank who had served with honour at the head of a good regiment to return to fight without regiment, troops, or even a company to command. They added that no duke and peer, especially not one with an establishment, wife and children, should consent to be left a mere soldier of fortune, whilst others of lesser degree received employment and commands in a large-scale promotion.

I did not take them as my judges in order to ponder their advice. My course was clear; but though I knew they were right I still hesitated, and three months passed in a torment of doubt before I could bring myself to act. When I finally did so, I followed the advice of those same arbiters. I was very careful to display no hurt feelings, for I wished to leave public and especially military opinion to judge of my having been passed over. The King's anger was inevitable; my friends warned me of it, and I was fully prepared. Need I say how much I dreaded it? He invariably took offence when officers left the service, calling it desertion, especially where the nobility were concerned. What really nettled him, however, was that a man should leave him with a grudge, and anyone who did so felt his displeasure long afterwards, if not for ever. Yet my friends drew no comparison between the disadvantage of resigning, which, at my age, would soon cease to affect me, and the disgrace of continuing to serve under such humiliating conditions. At the same time they insisted on my taking all possible precautions.

I accordingly wrote a short letter to the King,

in which without complaining, or any sign of discontent, or mention of regiments or promotion, I stated my distress at being obliged to leave his service for reasons of health. I added that my consolation would be to attend on him assiduously, with the honour of seeing and paying my court to him all the time. My advisers approved my letter and on Tuesday in Holy Week I presented it myself, at the door of his study, as he returned from mass. I went thence to Chamillart, with whom I had little acquaintance at that time. He was leaving to go to the council, but I told him my story by word of mouth, showing no sign of discontent, and immediately set out for Paris. I had already put many of my friends, both men and women, on the alert, to report anything, no matter how trivial, that the King might say on the subject of my letter. I stayed away for a week; returning on Easter Tuesday, I learned that the Chancellor had found the King in the act of reading it, and that he had exclaimed angrily, 'Here is another deserter!' and had thereupon read my letter aloud word for word. On that same evening I attended on him for the first time since he had heard from me.

After that, for three consecutive years I received no sign of favour from him, and he never missed the smallest opportunity (for want of greater ones) to make me feel how deeply I had offended. He never spoke to or looked at me except by accident. He never mentioned my letter or the circumstances of my leaving his service. I was no longer invited to Marly, and after the first few visits I no longer gave him the satisfaction of refusing me. I must end this sorry tale. Fourteen or fifteen months later he paid a visit to Trianon and supped with the Princesses. The custom on those occasions was for him to make a list, a very short one, of the ladies whom he wished invited. This particular visit was from a Wednesday to a Saturday, and Mme de Saint-Simon and I were doing what we usually did when he went to Marly, that is to say, dining at L'Etang with the Chamillarts on our way to sleep in Paris. We were just sitting down to table when Mme de Saint-Simon received a message to say that she was on the King's supper-list for that evening. We were astounded and returned at once to Versailles. She then discovered that she was to be the only lady of her age at the King's table; the rest were Mme de Chevreuse, Mme de Beauvilliers, the Comtesse de Gramont, three or four chaperones, the palace ladies, and no others. She was invited again on the Friday, and thereafter the King always nominated her on his rare excursions to Trianon. I soon learned the reason for this favour and it struck me as absurd. He never invited her to Marly, because husbands had the right to go there with their wives. His intention was to show me that his disfavour was towards me alone and did not extend to my wife.

We none the less persevered in waiting on him as usual, but we never sought for invitations to Marly. We lived a pleasant enough life among our friends, and Mme de Saint-Simon continued to enjoy all the pleasures to which the King and Mme la Duchesse de Bourgogne summoned her, even although she could not share them with me. I have dealt with this matter at length because it throws light upon the King's nature.

*   *   *

REVIEW QUESTIONS

1. According to Saint-Simon, what is the relation between political power and military power?
2. What is the relation between nature and political power?
3. What does Saint-Simon tell us about the king's social and fiscal relations with his nobility?
4. What is part of the royal obligation?
5. What do balls and other festivities have to do with political power?
6. Why would legitimacy be both an issue and not an issue at the French court?
7. What are the relations of lineage to political power?

FREDERICK II, THE GREAT

FROM *Antimachiavell*

Frederick II, the Great (1712–1786), king of Prussia, was the third son of Frederick William II of Prussia and Sophia Dorothea of Hanover, sister of George II of England. As a boy, Frederick showed little interest in the military matters that fascinated his father and, led by his tutor, the French Calvinist refugee Jacob E. Duhan de Jandun, discovered a world of art and literature instead. He mastered the flute, for which he composed a number of pieces, and adopted a free-thinking philosophy. His father's efforts at discipline had little effect on the young Frederick, who tried to evade his duties by escaping to England in 1730. The plan was discovered, Frederick imprisoned, and his best friend executed. This brutal encounter had its desired effect: Frederick threw himself on his father's mercy and dedicated himself to the arts of kingship. After a period of military service, in 1735 Frederick withdrew to the castle of Rheinsberg, where he undertook a systematic program of reading. He corresponded with Voltaire and, through French literature, read widely in the philosophical works of the Enlightenment. His ideal of government became enlightened but absolute, serving the people but limited only by the ruler's sensibilities. In this period Frederick wrote a number of treatises on politics, among which was the Antimachiavell (1740), published by Voltaire at The Hague. In it, he developed his ideal of the enlightened, absolute monarch in contrast to those of the Florentine statesman. The work was widely read in France and praised as a formula for enlightened rule. In the same year, Frederick succeeded his father and began a long and illustrious reign as king of Prussia. He distinguished himself as the greatest military genius of his day. In peacetime, he transformed Prussia into the model of an enlightened despotism. His policies expanded education, promoted industry, and reformed justice, all in the interest of state power.

From *Frederick the Great on the Art of War*, edited and translated by Jay Luvaas (New York: Free Press, 1966).

The Duty of Sovereigns

Since Machiavelli wrote his political *Prince*, the face of Europe has changed so much that it can no longer be recognized. If some great general in the age of Louis XII were to come back into the world he would find himself much at a loss. He would see war now carried on by bodies of men so numerous that they can hardly be subsisted in the field, yet are kept up in peace as well as war, whereas in his age, to execute great enterprises and strike decisive blows a handful of men sufficed, and these were disbanded as soon as the war was over. Instead of coats of mail, lances, and harquebusses with matches, he would find the army furnished with uniforms, firelocks, and bayonets. He would see new methods of encamping, besieging, and giving battle, and find the art of subsisting the troops as necessary now as that of conquering was before.

But what would Machiavelli himself say upon seeing this new political face of Europe, and so many princes who were scarcely known in his day now being ranked with the greatest monarchs? What would he say upon seeing the power and authority of sovereigns firmly established, the present manner of negotiating, and that balance settled in Europe by the alliance of many princes and states against the over-powerful and ambitious, a balance solely designed for securing the peace and tranquility of mankind?

All of these things have produced such universal change that Machiavelli's maxims cannot be applied to modern politics. . . . He assumes that a prince who has a large territory, a numerous army, and a full treasury may defend himself against his enemies without foreign supplies. I venture to contradict. . . . Let a sovereign be ever so formidable, he cannot defend himself against powerful enemies without the assistance of allies. If the most formidable prince in Europe, Louis XIV, was reduced to the greatest distress and was nearly ruined by the war of the Spanish Succession, if for want of foreign assistance he was unable to defend himself against the alliance of so many kings and princes, how should a sovereign who is less powerful be able to resist the joint attacks of his neighbors, to which he may often be exposed, without allies?

It is often said—and often repeated without much reflection—that treaties are useless because they are never observed in all points, and that the present age is no more scrupulous in keeping faith than any other. I answer that although many examples may be produced, ancient, modern, and some very recent of princes who have not fulfilled all their engagements, yet it is always prudent and necessary to make alliances. For your allies otherwise will be so many enemies; and if they refuse to send you supplies when you need them, you may at least expect them to observe an exact neutrality.

It is a known truth in politics that the most natural and consequently the best allies are those who have common interests and who are not such close neighbors as to be involved in any dispute over frontiers. Sometimes it happens that strange accidents give birth to extraordinary alliances. In our own time we have seen nations that had always been rivals and even enemies united under the same banners. But these are events that rarely occur and that never can serve as examples, for such connections can only be momentary, whereas the other kind, which are contracted from a unity of interests, alone are capable of execution. In the present situation in Europe, when all her princes are armed and preponderating powers rise up capable of crushing the feeble, prudence requires that alliances should be formed with other powers, as much to secure aid in case of attack as to repress the dangerous plans of enemies, and to sustain all just pretensions by the help of such allies. . . .

Nor is this sufficient. We must have eyes and ears among our neighbors, especially among our enemies, which shall be open to receive and faithfully report what they have seen and heard. Men are wicked. Care must be taken especially not to suffer surprise, because surprises intimidate and terrify. This never happens when preparations are made, however vexatious the event anticipated. European politics are so fallacious that the wisest men may become dupes if they are not always alert and on their guard.

*   *   *

The military system ought . . . to rest on good principles that experience has shown to be valid. The genius of the nation ought to be understood —what it is capable of, and how far its safety may be risked by leading it against the enemy. . . .

There are states which, from their situation and constitution, must be maritime powers: such are England, Holland, France, Spain, and Denmark. They are surrounded by the sea, and their distant colonies force them to keep a navy and to maintain communication and trade between the mother country and these detached members. There are other states such as Austria, Poland, Prussia, and even Russia, some of which may well do without shipping and others that would commit an unpardonable error in politics if they were to . . . employ a part of their troops at sea when they stand indispensably in need of their services on land.

The number of troops maintained by a state ought to be in proportion to the troops maintained by its enemies. Their forces should be equal, or the weakest is in danger of being oppressed. Perhaps it may be argued that a king ought to depend on the aid of his allies. This reasoning would be good if allies were what they ought to be, but their zeal is only lukewarm, and he who shall depend upon another as upon himself will most certainly be deceived. If frontiers can be defended by fortresses, there must be no neglect in building nor any expense spared in bringing them to perfection. France has provided an example of this, and she has realized its advantages on different occasions.

But neither politics nor the army can prosper if the finances are not kept in the greatest order and if the prince himself be not a prudent economist. Money is like the magician's wand, for by its aid miracles are performed. Great political views, the maintenance of the military, and the best conceived plans for the well-being of the people will all remain lethargic if not animated by money. The economy of the sovereign is useful to the public good because, if he does not have sufficient funds in reserve either to supply the expenses of war without burdening his people with extraordinary taxes or to give relief to citizens in times of public calamity, all these burdens will fall on the subject, who will be without the means he needs most in such unhappy times.

*   *   *

All branches of the state administration are intimately tied together in one bundle: finances, politics, and military affairs are inseparable. Not one, but all of these departments must be uniformly well administered. They must be steered in a straight line, head to head, as the team of horses in the Olympic contest which, pulling with equal weight and speed, covered the course and brought victory to their driver. A prince who rules independently and has fashioned his political system himself will not find himself in difficulty when he must make a quick decision, for he directs everything toward his established goal.

Above all, he must have acquired the greatest knowledge conceivable in the details of military affairs. One produces poor campaign plans at the round table, and where do the best plans lead if they are wrecked through the ignorance of those entrusted with their execution? A King may be the most able man, the best economist, the most subtle statesman—he will still fail as commander in chief if he neither knows the needs of an army nor cares about the countless details of its maintenance, if he is unaware how an army is mobilized, remains ignorant of the rules of war, or understands nothing of training troops in the garrison and leading them in the field. . . .

*   *   *

So in Prussia the ruler must do that which is most useful for the good of the state and therefore he must place himself at the head of the army. In this way he gives esteem to the military profession and preserves our excellent discipline and the order introduced among the troops. . . . If he possesses no expert knowledge, how will the king judge order and discipline among the different regiments and units? How can he improve what he himself does not understand? How can he blame the colonels for their mistakes and indicate to them at once the way in which they have been wrong and instruct them how to put their regiments in good order? If the king himself understands nothing of regimental and company economy, of troop leading and the art of maneuver, will he be so imprudent as to interfere? In this event he would expose himself to ridicule just as much as he would through ordering false troop movements. All this knowledge demands constant exercise, which one can only acquire if he is a soldier and applies himself to military service with unbroken diligence.

Finally, I venture the assertion that only the ruler can introduce and maintain this admirable discipline in the army. For often he must summon his authority, strongly censure the individual without regard for person and rank, reward others generously, have the troops mustered whenever possible, and not overlook the slightest negligence. The king of Prussia therefore must of necessity be a soldier and commander in chief. This office, which is courted in all republics and monarchies with diligence and ambition, nevertheless is held in low regard by the kings of Europe, who believe that they lose some of their dignity if they lead their armies themselves. But the throne turns out to be a disgrace if effeminate and lazy princes abandon the leadership of their troops to generals, and thus implicitly avow their own cowardice or incapacity.

In Prussia it is certainly honorable to work with the flower of the nobility and the elite of the nation in strengthening discipline. For it is discipline that preserves the fame of the fatherland, gives it respect in peace, and produces victory in war. One would have to be a completely pitiful human being, bogged down in inertia and unnerved by high living, if he wished to shrink from the trouble and work that the maintenance of discipline in the army demands. But in exchange for his efforts, the king certainly would find his reward in victories and fame, which is even more valuable than the highest peak of grandeur or the pinnacle of power.

*   *   *

As for the manner in which a prince ought to make war, I agree entirely with Machiavelli. Indeed, a great king ought always to assume command of his troops and to regard the camp as his place of residence. This is what his interest, duty, and glory require. As he is the chief magistrate in distributing justice to his people in times of peace, so he ought to be their chief protector and defender in war. When a prince is his own general and present in the field, his orders are more easily suited to all sudden emergencies and are executed with greater dispatch. His presence prevents that misunderstanding among the generals which is so often prejudicial to the interests of the sovereign and fatal to the army. More care is taken of the magazines, ammunition, and provisions, without which Caesar himself at the head of 100,000 men would never be able to accomplish anything. As it is the prince himself who gives orders for the battle, it seems to be his province to direct the execution of these orders, and by his presence and example to inspire his troops with valor and confidence.

But it may be objected that every man is not born to be a soldier and that many princes have not the talents, experience, or courage necessary for commanding an army. This objection may be easily removed: a prince will always find generals skilful enough to advise him, and it is sufficient for him in this case to be directed by their advice. Besides, no war can be carried on with great success if the general is under the direction of a ministry which is not present in the camp and consequently is unable to judge of sudden occurrences and to give orders accordingly.

*   *   *

REVIEW QUESTIONS

1. According to Frederick, why does a state need allies?
2. What has the state become according to Frederick?
3. How does a ruler choose allies?
4. What is their relation to the state?
5. How do they reflect the state? Why does the state need a military?
6. What is the purpose of the military?
7. How is Frederick's idea different from Machiavelli's?

HUGO GROTIUS

FROM *On the Law of War and Peace*

Hugo Grotius (1583–1645) was a Dutch statesman, jurist, theologian, poet, philologist, and historian, a man of all-embracing knowledge, whose writings were of fundamental importance in the formulation of international law. He was born in Delft, the son of the burgomaster and curator at the University of Leiden. Grotius was precocious; he matriculated at the University of Leiden at age eleven. By age fifteen, he had edited the encyclopedia of Martianus Capella and accompanied a diplomatic mission to the king of France, who described Grotius as the "miracle of Holland." He earned his doctorate in law at the University of Orléans and became a distinguished jurist at The Hague. In 1601, he was appointed historiographer of the States of Holland.

He wrote a number of minor but memorable legal treatises before publishing his great work, On the Law of War and Peace, *in 1625. Grotius argued that the entire law of humankind was based on four fundamental precepts: neither state nor individual may attack another state or individual, neither state nor individual may appropriate what belongs to another state or individual, neither state nor individual may disregard treaties or contracts, and neither state nor individual may commit a crime. In the case of a violation of one of these precepts, compensation might be sought either by war or by individual action. These principles and the arguments that surrounded them significantly aided the development of a theory of state sovereignty and international relations in the early modern period. During the remainder of his life, Grotius remained involved in political as well as intellectual affairs of his day. Apart from the vast corpus of his written works, he participated in the government of the United Provinces of the Netherlands. He was eventually imprisoned for his support of Arminianism and managed to escape hidden in a trunk. He spent the rest of his life in exile, honored as one of the great intellectuals of the seventeenth century but unacknowledged by his own country.*

From *The Rights of War and Peace,* by M. Walter Dunn (1901).

*   *   *

VIII

And here is the proper place for refuting the opinion of those, who maintain that, every where and without exception, the sovereign power is vested in the people, so that they have a right to restrain and punish kings for an abuse of their power.

However there is no man of sober wisdom, who does not see the incalculable mischiefs, which such opinions have occasioned, and may still occasion; and upon the following grounds they may be refuted.

From the Jewish, as well as the Roman Law, it appears that any one might engage himself in private servitude to whom he pleased. Now if an individual may do so, why may not a whole people, for the benefit of better government and more certain protection, completely transfer their sovereign rights to one or more persons, without reserving any portion to themselves? Neither can it be alledged that such a thing is not to be presumed, for the question is not, what is to be presumed in a doubtful case, but what may lawfully be done. Nor is it any more to the purpose to object to the inconveniences, which may, and actually do arise from a people's thus surrendering their rights. For it is not in the power of man to devise any form of government free from imperfections and dangers. As a dramatic writer says, "you must either take these advantages with those imperfections, or resign your pretensions to both."

Now as there are different ways of living, some of a worse, and some of a better kind, left to the choice of every individual; so a nation, "under certain circumstances, WHEN for instance, the succession to the throne is extinct, or the throne has by any other means become vacant," may choose what form of government she pleases. Nor is this right to be measured by the excellence of this or that form of government, on which there may be varieties of opinion, but by the will of the people.

There may be many reasons indeed why a people may entirely relinquish their rights, and surrender them to another: for instance, they may have no other means of securing themselves from the danger of immediate destruction, or under the pressure of famine it may be the only way, through which they can procure support. For if the Campanians, formerly, when reduced by necessity surrendered themselves to the Roman people in the following terms:—"Senators of Rome, we consign to your dominion the people of Campania, and the city of Capua, our lands, our temples, and all things both divine and human," and if another people as Appian relates, offered to submit to the Romans, and were refused, what is there to prevent any nation from submitting in the same manner to one powerful sovereign? It may also happen that a master of a family, having large possessions, will suffer no one to reside upon them on any other terms, or an owner, having many

slaves, may give them their liberty upon condition of their doing certain services, and paying certain rents; of which examples may be produced. Thus Tacitus, speaking of the German slaves, says, "Each has his own separate habitation, and his own household to govern. The master considers him as a tenant, bound to pay a certain rent in corn, cattle, and wearing apparel. And this is the utmost extent of his servitude."

Aristotle, in describing the requisites, which fit men for servitude, says, that "those men, whose powers are chiefly confined to the body, and whose principal excellence consists in affording bodily service, are naturally slaves, because it is their interest to be so." In the same manner some nations are of such a disposition that they are more calculated to obey than to govern, which seems to have been the opinion which the Cappadocians held of themselves, who when the Romans offered them a popular government, refused to accept it, because the nation they said could not exist in safety without a king. Thus Philostratus in the life of Apollonius, says, that it was foolish to offer liberty to the Thracians, the Mysians, and the Getae, which they were not capable of enjoying. The example of nations, who have for many ages lived happily under a kingly government, has induced many to give the preference to that form. Livy says, that the cities under Eumenes would not have changed their condition for that of any free state whatsoever. And sometimes a state is so situated, that it seems impossible it can preserve its peace and existence, without submitting to the absolute government of a single person, which many wise men thought to be the case with the Roman Republic in the time of Augustus Cæsar. From these, and causes like these it not only may, but generally does happen, that men, as Cicero observes in the second book of his offices, willingly submit to the supreme authority of another.

Now as property may be acquired by what has been already styled just war, by the same means the rights of sovereignty may be acquired. Nor is the term sovereignty here meant to be applied to monarchy alone, but to government by nobles, from any share in which the people are excluded. For there never was any government so purely popular, as not to require the exclusion of the poor, of strangers, women, and minors from the public councils. Some states have other nations under them, no less dependent upon their will, than subjects upon that of their sovereign princes. From whence arose that question, Are the Collatine people in their own power? And the Campanians, when they submitted to the Romans, are said to have passed under a foreign dominion. In the same manner Acarnania and Amphilochia are said to have been under the dominion of the Aetolians; Peraea and Caunus under that of the Rhodians; and Pydna was ceded by Philip to the Olynthians. And those towns, that had been under the Spartans, when they were delivered from their dominion, received the name of the free Laconians. The city of Cotyora is said by Xenophon to have belonged to the people of Sinope. Nice in Italy, according to Strabo, was adjudged to the people of Marseilles; and the island of Pithecusa to the Neapolitans. We find in Frontinus, that the towns of Calati and Caudium with their territories were adjudged, the one to the colony of Capua, and the other to that of Beneventum. Otho, as Tacitus relates, gave the cities of the Moors to the Province of Baetia. None of these instances, any more than the cessions of other conquered countries could be admitted, if it were a received rule that the rights of sovereigns are under the controul and direction of subjects.

Now it is plain both from sacred and profane history, that there are kings, who are not subject to the controul of the people in their collective body; God addressing the people of Israel, says, if thou shalt say, "I will place a king over me"; and to Samuel "Shew them the manner of the king, who shall reign over them." Hence the King is said to be anointed over the people, over the inheritance of the Lord, over Israel. Solomon is styled King over all Israel. Thus David gives thanks to God, for subduing the people under him. And Christ says, "the Kings of the nations bear rule over them." There is a well known passage in Horace, "Powerful sovereigns reign over their own

subjects, and the supreme being over sovereigns themselves." Seneca thus describes the three forms of government, "Sometimes the supreme power is lodged in the people, sometimes in a senate composed of the leading men of the state, sometimes this power of the people, and dominion over the people themselves is vested in a single person." Of the last description are those, who, as Plutarch says, exercise authority not according to the laws, but over the laws. And in Herodutus, Otanes describes a monarch as one whose acts are not subject to controul. Dion Prusaeensis also and Pausanias define a monarchy in the same terms.

Aristotle says there are some kings, who have the same right, which the nation elsewhere possesses over persons and property. Thus when the Roman Princes began to exercise regal power, the people it was said had transferred all their own personal sovereignty to them, which gave rise to the saying of Marcus Antoninus the Philosopher, that no one but God alone can be judge of the Prince. Dion. L. liii. speaking of such a prince, says, "he is perfectly master of his own actions, to do whatever he pleases, and cannot be obliged to do any thing against his will." Such anciently was the power of the Inachidae established at Argos in Greece. For in the Greek Tragedy of the Suppliants, Aeschylus has introduced the people thus addressing the King: "You are the state, you the people; you the court from which there is no appeal, you preside over the altars, and regulate all affairs by your supreme will." King Theseus himself in Euripides speaks in very different terms of the Athenian Republic; "The city is not governed by one man, but in a popular form, by an annual succession of magistrates." For according to Plutarch's explanation, Theseus was the general in war, and the guardian of the laws; but in other respects nothing more than a citizen. So that they who are limited by popular controul are improperly called kings. Thus after the time of Lycurgus, and more particularly after the institution of the Ephori, the Kings of the Lacedaemonians are said by Polybius, Plutarch, and Cornelius Nepos, to have been Kings more in name than in reality. An example which was followed by the rest of Greece.

Thus Pausanias says of the Argives to the Corinthians, "The Argives from their love of equality have reduced their kingly power very low; so that they have left the posterity of Cisus nothing more than the shadow of Kings." Aristotle denies such to be proper forms of government, because they constitute only a part of an Aristocracy or Democracy.

Examples also may be found of nations, who have not been under a perpetual regal form, but only for a time under a government exempt from popular controul. Such was the power of the Amimonians among the Cnidians, and of the Dictators in the early periods of the Roman history, when there was no appeal to the people, from whence Livy says, the will of the Dictator was observed as a law. Indeed they found this submission the only remedy against imminent danger, and in the words of Cicero, the Dictatorship possessed all the strength of royal power.

It will not be difficult to refute the arguments brought in favour of the contrary opinion. For in the first place the assertion that the constituent always retains a controul over the sovereign power, which he has contributed to establish, is only true in those cases where the continuance and existence of that power depends upon the will and pleasure of the constituent: but not in cases where the power, though it might derive its origin from that constituent, becomes a necessary and fundamental part of the established law. Of this nature is that authority to which a woman submits when she gives herself to a husband. Valentinian the Emperor, when the soldiers who had raised him to the throne, made a demand of which he did not approve, replied; "Soldiers, your election of me for your emperor was your own voluntary choice; but since you have elected me, it depends upon my pleasure to grant your request. It becomes you to obey as subjects, and me to consider what is proper to be done."

Nor is the assumption true, that all kings are made by the people, as may be plainly seen from the instances adduced above, of an owner admitting strangers to reside upon his demesnes on condition of their obedience, and of nations submitting by right of conquest. Another argument is derived from a saying of the Philosophers, that all power is conferred for the benefit of the governed and not of the governing party. Hence from the nobleness of the end, it is supposed to follow, that subjects have a superiority over the sovereign. But it is not universally true, that all power is conferred for the benefit of the party governed. For some powers are conferred for the sake of the governor, as the right of a master over a slave, in which the advantage of the latter is only a contingent and adventitious circumstance. In the same manner the gain of a Physician is to reward him for his labour; and not merely to promote the good of his art. There are other kinds of authority established for the benefit of both parties, as for instance, the authority of a husband over his wife. Certain governments also, as those which are gained by right of conquest, may be established for the benefit of the sovereign; and yet convey no idea of tyranny, a word which in its original signification, implied nothing of arbitrary power or injustice, but only the government or authority of a Prince. Again, some governments may be formed for the advantage both of subjects and sovereign, as when a people, unable to defend themselves, put themselves under the protection and dominion of any powerful king. Yet it is not to be denied, but that in most governments the good of the subject is the chief object which is regarded: and that what Cicero has said after Herodotus, and Herodotus after Hesiod, is true, that Kings were appointed in order that men might enjoy complete justice.

Now this admission by no means goes to establish the inference that kings are amenable to the people. For though guardianships were invented for the benefit of wards, yet the guardian has a right to authority over the ward. Nor, though a guardian may for mismanagement be removed from his trust, does it follow that a king may for the same reason be deposed. The cases are quite different, the guardian has a superior to judge him; but in governments, as there must be some dernier resort, it must be vested either in an individual, or in some public body, whose misconduct, as there is no superior tribunal before which they can be called, God declares that he himself will judge. He either punishes their offences, should he deem it necessary; or permits them for the chastisement of his people.

This is well expressed by Tacitus: he says, "you should bear with the rapacity or luxury of rulers, as you would bear with drought, or excessive rains, or any other calamities of nature. For as long as men exist there will be faults and imperfections; but these are not of uninterrupted continuance, and they are often repaired by the succession of better times." And Marcus Aurelius speaking of subordinate magistrates, said, that they were under the controul of the sovereign: but that the sovereign was amenable to God. There is a remarkable passage in Gregory of Tours, where that Bishop thus addresses the King of France, "If any of us, Sir, should transgress the bounds of justice, he may be punished by you. But if you exceed them, who can call you to account? For when we address you, you may hear us if you please; but if you will not, who can judge you, except him, who has declared himself to be righteousness?" Among the maxims of the Essenes, Porphyry cites a passage, that "no one can reign without the special appointment of divine providence." Irenaeus has expressed this well, "Kings are appointed by him at whose command men are created; and their appointment is suited to the condition of those, whom they are called to govern." There is the same thought in the Constitutions of Clement, "You shall fear the King, for he is of the Lord's appointment."

Nor is it an objection to what has been said, that some nations have been punished for the offences of their kings, for this does not happen, because they forbear to restrain their kings, but because they seem to give, at least a tacit consent to their vices, or perhaps, without respect to this, God may use that sovereign power which he has over the life and death of every man to inflict a punishment upon the king by depriving him of his subjects.

*   *   *

REVIEW QUESTIONS

1. What is the relation between political power and will according to Grotius?
2. What is the state? The sovereign state?
3. Where does Grotius locate sovereignty?
4. Does sovereignty have a moral component?
5. What is its relation to property? To the good of the people?

18 ⌘ THE SCIENTIFIC REVOLUTION

The term scientific revolution *is commonly applied to the changes in scientific theory and practice that took root in the early seventeenth century and promoted the advance of science as we know it today. It grew initially out of changes in astronomy and physics, the creation of mechanical philosophy as a general theory of nature, and the adoption of mathematics as a basic language of science. Natural phenomena were conceived to be regular and rational. Given that nature was subject to reason, human beings could uncover its laws, which were assumed to be few in number and universal in application, by the right exercise of their own rational capacities. Among these laws were those of mechanics, which altered the scientific vision of the universe. They explained all physical phenomena in terms of matter and assumed that motion was the natural state of the world. Mechanical philosophy posited that all bodies were composed of a single, universal substance, matter. These natural phenomena, matter and motion, were so defined as to be measured and translated into numbers that could be manipulated in mathematical formulas. As a form of reason, therefore, mathematics could become the language of scientific inquiry. Reason and mathematics, it was believed, could teach reliable truths about nature. As such the scientific revolution created the basic intellectual milieu for enlightened thinking.*

FRANCIS BACON

FROM *The Great Instauration*

With Francis Bacon (1561–1626) we enter the so-called Age of Reason, the era of science and enlightenment. Son of Sir Nicholas Bacon, lord keeper of the Great Seal of England, he attended Trinity College, Cambridge, and entered the legal profession in 1582. His public life was not that of a natural philosopher but that of a states-man. Beginning his career under Elizabeth I, he rose to the position of lord chancel-lor and was created viscount St. Albans in 1621 under James I. His Great Instauration *(1620) was published in the eve of his advancement. After the collapse of his career in 1622, when he pleaded guilty to charges of bribery, Bacon withdrew into enforced retirement and, like Machiavelli, pursued his intellectual passion. In his writings, he envisioned the transformation of the human mind through the right use of reason. He called for the close observation of nature and scientific collabora-tion in the cause of human improvement. In this, Bacon was the prophet of the revolution in science.*

From *Works of Francis Bacon,* edited by Robert L. Ellis, James Spedding, and D. D. Heath (London: Longman, 1857–1874).

Preface

That the state of knowledge is not prosperous nor greatly advancing; and that a way must be opened for the human understanding entirely different from any hitherto known, and other helps provided, in order that the mind may exercise over the nature of things the authority which properly belongs to it.

It seems to me that men do not rightly understand either their store or their strength, but overrate the one and underrate the other. Hence it follows, that either from an extravagant estimate of the value of the arts which they possess, they seek no fur-ther; or else from too mean an estimate of their own powers, they spend their strength in small matters and never put it fairly to the trial in those which go to the main. These are as the pillars of fate set in the path of knowledge; for men have neither desire nor hope to encourage them to pen-etrate further. And since opinion of store is one of the chief causes of want, and satisfaction with the present induces neglect of provision for the future, it becomes a thing not only useful, but ab-solutely necessary, that the excess of honour and admiration with which our existing stock of in-ventions is regarded be in the very entrance and threshold of the work, and that frankly and with-out circumlocution, stripped off, and men be duly warned not to exaggerate or make too much of them. For let a man look carefully into all that variety of books with which the arts and sciences abound, he will find everywhere endless repeti-tions of the same thing, varying in the method of treatment, but not new in substance, insomuch that the whole stock, numerous as it appears at first view, proves on examination to be but scanty. And for its value and utility it must be plainly avowed that that wisdom which we have derived principally from the Greeks is but like the boy-hood of knowledge, and has the characteristic property of boys: it can talk, but it cannot gen-erate; for it is fruitful of controversies but barren of works. So that the state of learning as it now is appears to be represented to the life in the old fable of Scylla, who had the head and face of a virgin, but her womb was hung round with barking monsters, from which she could not be delivered. For in like manner the sciences to which we are accustomed have certain general positions which are specious and flattering; but as soon as they come to particulars, which are as the parts of generation, when they should produce fruit and works, then arise contentions and barking disputations, which are the end of the matter and all the issue they can yield. Observe also, that if sciences of this kind had any life in them, that could never have come to pass which has been the case now for many ages—that they stand almost at a stay, without receiving any augmentations worthy of the human race; insomuch that many times not only what was asserted once is asserted still, but what was a question once is a question still, and instead of being resolved by discussion is only fixed and fed; and all the tradition and succession of schools is still a succession of masters and scholars, not of inventors and those who bring to further perfection the things invented. In the mechanical arts we do not find it so; they, on the contrary, as having in them some breath of life, are continually growing and becoming more perfect. As originally invented they are commonly rude, clumsy, and shapeless; afterwards they acquire new powers and more commodious arrangements and constructions; in so far that men shall sooner leave the study and pursuit of them and turn to something else, than they arrive at the ultimate perfection of which they are capable. Philosophy and the intellectual sciences, on the contrary, stand like statues, worshipped and celebrated, but not moved or advanced. Nay, they sometimes flourish most in the hands of the first author, and afterwards degenerate. For when men have once made over their judgments to others' keeping, and (like those senators whom they called *Pedarii*) have agreed to support some one person's opinion, from that time they make no enlargement of the sciences themselves, but fall to the servile office of embellishing certain individual au-

thors and increasing their retinue. And let it not be said that the sciences have been growing gradually till they have at last reached their full stature, and so (their course being completed) have settled in the works of a few writers; and that there being now no room for the invention of better, all that remains is to embellish and cultivate those things which have been invented already. Would it were so! But the truth is that this appropriating of the sciences had its origin in nothing better than the confidence of a few persons and the sloth and indolence of the rest. For after the sciences had been in several parts perhaps cultivated and handled diligently, there has risen up some man of bold disposition, and famous for methods and short ways which people like, who has in appearance reduced them to an art, while he has in fact only spoiled all that the others had done. And yet this is what posterity like, because it makes the work short and easy, and saves further inquiry, of which they are weary and impatient. And if any one take this general acquiescence and consent for an argument of weight, as being the judgment of Time, let me tell him that the reasoning on which he relies is most fallacious and weak. For, first, we are far from knowing all that in the matter of sciences and arts has in various ages and places been brought to light and published; much less, all that has been by private persons secretly attempted and stirred; so neither the births nor the miscarriages of Time are entered in our records. Nor, secondly, is the consent itself and the time it has continued a consideration of much worth. For however various are the forms of civil polities, there is but one form of polity in the sciences; and that always has been and always will be popular. Now the doctrines which find most favour with the populace are those which are either contentious and pugnacious, or specious and empty; such, I say, as either entangle assent or tickle it. And therefore no doubt the greatest wits in each successive age have been forced out of their own course; men of capacity and intellect above the vulgar having been fain, for reputation's sake, to bow to the judgment of the time and the multitude; and thus if any contemplations of a higher order took light anywhere, they were presently blown out by the winds of vulgar opinions. So that Time is like a river, which has brought down to us things light and puffed up, while those which are weighty and solid have sunk. Nay, those very authors who have usurped a kind of dictatorship in the sciences and taken upon them to lay down the law with such confidence, yet when from time to time they come to themselves again, they fall to complaints of the subtlety of nature, the hiding-places of truth, the obscurity of things, the entanglement of causes, the weakness of the human mind; wherein nevertheless they show themselves never the more modest, seeing that they will rather lay the blame upon the common condition of men and nature than upon themselves. And then whatever any art fails to attain, they ever set it down upon the authority of that art itself as impossible of attainment; and how can art be found guilty when it is judge in its own cause? So it is but a device for exempting ignorance from ignominy. Now for those things which are delivered and received, this is their condition: barren of works, full of questions; in point of enlargement slow and languid; carrying a show of perfection in the whole, but in the parts ill filled up; in selection popular, and unsatisfactory even to those who propound them; and therefore fenced round and set forth with sundry artifices. And if there be any who have determined to make trial for themselves, and put their own strength to the work of advancing the boundaries of the sciences, yet have they not ventured to cast themselves completely loose from received opinions or to seek their knowledge at the fountain; but they think they have done some great thing if they do but add and introduce into the existing sum of science something of their own; prudently considering with themselves that by making the addition they can assert their liberty, while they retain the credit of modesty by assenting to the rest. But these mediocrities and middle ways so much praised, in deferring to opinions and customs, turn to the great detriment of the sciences. For it is hardly possible at once to admire an author and to go beyond him; knowledge being as water, which will not rise above the

level from which it fell. Men of this kind, therefore, amend some things, but advance little; and improve the condition of knowledge, but do not extend its range. Some, indeed, there have been who have gone more boldly to work, and taking it all for an open matter and giving their genius full play, have made a passage for themselves and their own opinions by pulling down and demolishing former ones; and yet all their stir has but little advanced the matter; since their aim has been not to extend philosophy and the arts in substance and value, but only to change doctrines and transfer the kingdom of opinions to themselves; whereby little has indeed been gained, for though the error be the opposite of the other, the causes of erring are the same in both. And if there have been any who, not binding themselves either to other men's opinions or to their own, but loving liberty, have desired to engage others along with themselves in search, these, though honest in intention, have been weak in endeavour. For they have been content to follow probable reasons, and are carried round in a whirl of arguments, and in the promiscuous liberty of search have relaxed the severity of inquiry. There is none who has dwelt upon experience and the facts of nature as long as is necessary. Some there are indeed who have committed themselves to the waves of experience, and almost turned mechanics; yet these again have in their very experiments pursued a kind of wandering inquiry, without any regular system of operations. And besides they have mostly proposed to themselves certain petty tasks, taking it for a great matter to work out some single discovery— a course of proceeding at once poor in aim and unskilful in design. For no man can rightly and successfully investigate the nature of anything in the thing itself; let him vary his experiments as laboriously as he will, he never comes to a resting-place, but still finds something to seek beyond. And there is another thing to be remembered; namely, that all industry in experimenting has begun with proposing to itself certain definite works to be accomplished, and has pursued them with premature and unseasonable eagerness; it has sought, I say, experiments of Fruit, not experiments of Light; not imitating the divine procedure, which in its first day's work created light only and assigned to it one entire day; on which day it produced no material work, but proceeded to that on the days following. As for those who have given the first place to Logic, supposing that the surest helps to the sciences were to be found in that, they have indeed most truly and excellently perceived that the human intellect left to its own course is not to be trusted; but then the remedy is altogether too weak for the disease; nor is it without evil in itself. For the Logic which is received, though it be very properly applied to civil business and to those arts which rest in discourse and opinion, is not nearly subtle enough to deal with nature; and in offering at what it cannot master, has done more to establish and perpetuate error than to open the way to truth.

Upon the whole therefore, it seems that men have not been happy hitherto either in the trust which they have placed in others or in their own industry with regard to the sciences; especially as neither the demonstrations nor the experiments as yet known are much to be relied upon. But the universe to the eye of the human understanding is framed like a labyrinth; presenting as it does on every side so many ambiguities of way, such deceitful resemblances of objects and signs, natures so irregular in their lines, and so knotted and entangled. And then the way is still to be made by the uncertain light of the sense, sometimes shining out, sometimes clouded over, through the woods of experience and particulars; while those who offer themselves for guides are (as was said) themselves also puzzled, and increase the number of errors and wanderers. In circumstances so difficult neither the natural force of man's judgment nor even any accidental felicity offers any chance of success. No excellence of wit, no repetition of chance experiments, can overcome such difficulties as these. Our steps must be guided by a clue, and the whole way from the very first perception of the senses must be laid out upon a sure plan. Not that I would be understood to mean that nothing whatever has been done in so many ages by so great labours. We have no reason to be ashamed of the discoveries which have been made, and no doubt the ancients proved themselves in everything that turns on wit and abstract meditation, wonderful men. But as in former ages when men sailed only by observation of the stars, they could indeed coast along the shores of the old continent or cross a few small and mediterranean seas; but before the ocean could be traversed and the new world discovered, the use of the mariner's needle, as a more faithful and certain guide, had to be found out; in like manner the discoveries which have been hitherto made in the arts and sciences are such as might be made by practice, meditation, observation, argumentation,—for they lay near to the senses, and immediately beneath common notions; but before we can reach the remoter and more hidden parts of nature, it is necessary that a more perfect use and application of the human mind and intellect be introduced.

For my own part at least, in obedience to the everlasting love of truth, I have committed myself to the uncertainties and difficulties and solitudes of the ways, and relying on the divine assistance have upheld my mind both against the shocks and embattled ranks of opinion, and against my own private and inward hesitations and scruples, and against the fogs and clouds of nature, and the phantoms flitting about on every side; in the hope of providing at last for the present and future generations guidance more faithful and secure. Wherein if I have made any progress, the way has been opened to me by no other means than the true and legitimate humiliation of the human spirit. For all those who before me have applied themselves to the invention of arts have but cast a glance or two upon facts and examples and experience, and straightway proceeded, as if invention were nothing more than an exercise of thought, to invoke their own spirits to give them oracles. I, on the contrary, dwelling purely and constantly among the facts of nature, withdraw my intellect from them no further than may suffice to let the images and rays of natural objects meet in a point, as they do in the sense of vision; whence it follows that the strength and excellency of the wit has but little to do in the matter. And the same humility which I use in inventing I employ likewise in teaching. For I do not endeavour either by triumphs of confutation, or pleadings of antiquity, or assumption of authority, or even by the veil of obscurity, to invest these inventions of mine with any majesty; which might easily be done by one who sought to give lustre to his own name rather than light to other men's minds. I have not sought (I say) nor do I seek either to force or ensnare men's judgments, but I lead them to things themselves and the concordances of things, that they may see for themselves what they have, what they can dispute, what they can add and contribute to the common stock. And for myself, if in anything I have been either too credulous or too little awake and attentive, or if I have fallen off by the way and left the inquiry incomplete, nevertheless I so present these things naked and open that my errors can be marked and set aside before the mass of knowledge be further infected by them: and it will be easy also for others to continue and carry on my labours. And by these means I suppose that I have established for ever a true and lawful marriage between the empirical and the rational faculty, the unkind and ill-starred divorce and separation of which has thrown into confusion all the affairs of the human family.

Wherefore, seeing that these things do not depend upon myself, at the outset of the work I most humbly and fervently pray to God the Father, God the Son, and God the Holy Ghost, that remembering the sorrows of mankind and the pilgrimage of this our life wherein we wear out days few and evil, they will vouchsafe through my hands to endow the human family with new mercies. This likewise I humbly pray, that things human may not interfere with things divine, and that from the opening of the ways of sense and the increase of natural light there may arise in our minds no incredulity or darkness with regard to the divine mysteries; but rather that the understanding being thereby purified and purged of fancies and vanity, and yet not the less subject and entirely submissive to the divine oracles, may give to faith that which is faith's. Lastly, that knowledge being now discharged of that venom which the serpent infused into it, and which makes the mind of man to swell, we may not be wise above measure and sobriety, but cultivate truth in charity.

And now having said my prayers I turn to men; to whom I have certain salutary admonitions to offer and certain fair requests to make. My first admonition (which was also my prayer) is that men confine the sense within the limits of duty in respect of things divine: for the sense is like the sun, which reveals the face of earth, but seals and shuts up the face of heaven. My next, that in flying from this evil they fall not into the opposite error, which they will surely do if they think that the inquisition of nature is in any part interdicted or forbidden. For it was not that pure and uncorrupted natural knowledge whereby Adam gave names to the creatures according to their propriety, which gave occasion to the fall. It was the ambitious and proud desire of moral knowledge to judge of good and evil, to the end that man may revolt from God and give laws to himself, which was the form and manner of the temptation. Whereas of the sciences which regard nature, the divine philosopher declares that "it is the glory of God to conceal a thing, but it is the glory of the King to find a thing out." Even as though the divine nature took pleasure in the innocent and kindly sport of children playing at hide and seek, and vouchsafed of his kindness and goodness to admit the human spirit for his playfellow at that game. Lastly, I would address one general admonition to all; that they consider what are the true ends of knowledge, and that they seek it not either for pleasure of the mind, or for contention, or for superiority to others, or for profit, or fame, or power, or any of these inferior things; but for the benefit and use of life; and that they perfect and govern it in charity. For it was from lust of power that the angels fell, from lust of knowledge that man fell; but of charity there can be no excess, neither did angel or man ever come in danger by it.

The requests I have to make are these. Of myself I say nothing; but in behalf of the business which is in hand I entreat men to believe that it is not an opinion to be held, but a work to be done; and to be well assured that I am labouring to lay the foundation, not of any sect or doctrine, but of human utility and power. Next, I ask them to deal fairly by their own interests, and laying aside all emulations and prejudices in favour of this or that opinion, to join in consultation for the common good; and being now freed and guarded by the securities and helps which I offer from the errors and impediments of the way, to come forward themselves and take part in that which remains to be done. Moreover, to be of good hope, nor to imagine that this Instauration of mine is a thing infinite and beyond the power of man, when it is in fact the true end and termination of infinite error; and seeing also that it is by no means forgetful of the conditions of mortality and humanity, (for it does not suppose that the work can be altogether completed within one generation, but provides for its being taken up by another); and finally that it seeks for the sciences not arrogantly in the little cells of human wit, but with reverence in the greater world. But it is the empty things that are vast: things solid are most contracted and lie in little room. And now I have only one favour more to ask (else injustice to me may perhaps imperil the business itself)—that men will consider well how far, upon that which I must needs assert (if I am to be consistent with myself), they are entitled to judge and decide upon these doctrines of mine; inasmuch as all that premature human reasoning which anticipates inquiry, and is abstracted from the facts rashly and sooner than is fit, is by me rejected (so far as the inquisition of nature is concerned), as a thing uncertain, confused, and ill built up; and I cannot be fairly asked to abide by the decision of a tribunal which is itself on its trial.

*　　*　　*

REVIEW QUESTIONS

1. What does Bacon believe to be the wrong relation to the past and to past authors?
2. Why does he think so?
3. What relation to the past and to past authors does he think a true scientist should hold?
4. Why does Bacon propose the necessity of a method, and what method he propose?
5. According to Bacon, what is invention, and what is its relation to experience and prior knowledge?

GALILEO GALILEI

FROM *The Starry Messenger* AND *The Assayer*

Galileo Galilei (1564–1642), an Italian astronomer, mathematician, and physicist, was a major contributor to the shift in scientific practice commonly called the Scientific Revolution. Born the son of a musician, Vincenzo Galilei, Galileo received his primary education from a tutor in Pisa and later from the monks of Santa Maria at Vallambrosa in Florence. From 1581 to 1585, he studied medicine at the University of Pisa and supplemented his education with private lessons in mathematics. Without formal instruction in that field, Galileo occupied the chair in mathematics at the University of Pisa from 1589 to 1591 and at the University of Padua from 1592 until 1610, when he was appointed court philosopher and mathematician to

THE HUMAN BODY (1543)   ANDREAS VESALIUS

Andreas Vesalius is considered one of the great pioneers of the scientific study of the human body as well as one of the great practitioners of empirical research. His masterwork, De Humani Corporis Fabrica, *was based on exact dissection and study and contained precise drawings that are valued as works of art as well as science. How is Vesalius's work representative of the scientific revolution? What does the work suggest about the connections among art, technique, and science in early modern Europe? Why is the drawing placed in a lifelike pose and natural setting?*

the grand duke of Tuscany. During his tenure at court, he published The Starry Messenger *(1610) and* The Assayer *(1619). The former gave evidence to confirm the heliocentric theory of the solar system. The latter offered a strong defense of the empirical basis of scientific reasoning. It was his advocacy of the Copernican theory that led him into conflict with the Roman Catholic Inquisition. Galileo was forced to abjure his scientific findings and was sentenced to perpetual house arrest. His books were burned. His trial, no less than his discoveries, secured his fame, and his books continued to circulate clandestinely throughout Europe.*

From *Discoveries and Opinions of Galileo,* translated by Stillman Drake (New York: Bantam Doubleday Dell, 1957), pp. 27–31, 237–38.

FROM The Starry Messenger

from ASTRONOMICAL MESSAGE
WHICH CONTAINS AND EXPLAINS RECENT OBSERVATIONS MADE WITH THE AID OF A NEW SPYGLASS CONCERNING THE SURFACE OF THE MOON, THE MILKY WAY, NEBULOUS STARS, AND INNUMERABLE FIXED STARS, AS WELL AS FOUR PLANETS NEVER BEFORE SEEN, AND NOW NAMED THE MEDICEAN STARS

Great indeed are the things which in this brief treatise I propose for observation and consideration by all students of nature. I say great, because of the excellence of the subject itself, the entirely unexpected and novel character of these things, and finally because of the instrument by means of which they have been revealed to our senses.

Surely it is a great thing to increase the numerous host of fixed stars previously visible to the unaided vision, adding countless more which have never before been seen, exposing these plainly to the eye in numbers ten times exceeding the old and familiar stars.

It is a very beautiful thing, and most gratifying to the sight, to behold the body of the moon, distant from us almost sixty earthly radii, as if it were no farther away than two such measures— so that its diameter appears almost thirty times larger, its surface nearly nine hundred times, and its volume twenty-seven thousand times as large

as when viewed with the naked eye. In this way one may learn with all the certainty of sense evidence that the moon is not robed in a smooth and polished surface but is in fact rough and uneven, covered everywhere, just like the earth's surface, with huge prominences, deep valleys, and chasms.

Again, it seems to me a matter of no small importance to have ended the dispute about the Milky Way by making its nature manifest to the very senses as well as to the intellect. Similarly it will be a pleasant and elegant thing to demonstrate that the nature of those stars which astronomers have previously called "nebulous" is far different from what has been believed hitherto. But what surpasses all wonders by far, and what particularly moves us to seek the attention of all astronomers and philosophers, is the discovery of four wandering stars not known or observed by any man before us. Like Venus and Mercury, which have their own periods about the sun, these have theirs about a certain star that is conspicuous among those already known, which they sometimes precede and sometimes follow, without ever departing from it beyond certain limits. All these facts were discovered and observed by me not many days ago with the aid of a spyglass which I devised, after first being illuminated by divine grace. Perhaps other things, still more remarkable, will in time be discovered by me or by other observers with the aid of such an instrument, the form and construction of which I shall first briefly explain, as well as the occasion of its having been devised. Afterwards I shall relate the story of the observations I have made.

About ten months ago a report reached my ears that a certain Fleming had constructed a spyglass by means of which visible objects, though very distant from the eye of the observer, were distinctly seen as if nearby. Of this truly remarkable effect several experiences were related, to which some persons gave credence while others denied them. A few days later the report was confirmed to me in a letter from a noble Frenchman at Paris, Jacques Badovere, which caused me to apply myself wholeheartedly to inquire into the means by which I might arrive at the invention of a similar instrument. This I did shortly afterwards, my basis being the theory of refraction. First I prepared a tube of lead, at the ends of which I fitted two glass lenses, both plane on one side while on the other side one was spherically convex and the other concave. Then placing my eye near the concave lens I perceived objects satisfactorily large and near, for they appeared three times closer and nine times larger than when seen with the naked eye alone. Next I constructed another one, more accurate, which represented objects as enlarged more than sixty times. Finally, sparing neither labor nor expense, I succeeded in constructing for myself so excellent an instrument that objects seen by means of it appeared nearly one thousand times larger and over thirty times closer than when regarded with our natural vision.

It would be superfluous to enumerate the number and importance of the advantages of such an instrument at sea as well as on land. But forsaking terrestrial observations, I turned to celestial ones, and first I saw the moon from as near at hand as if it were scarcely two terrestrial radii away. After that I observed often with wondering delight both the planets and the fixed stars, and since I saw these latter to be very crowded, I began to seek (and eventually found) a method by which I might measure their distances apart.

Here it is appropriate to convey certain cautions to all who intend to undertake observations of this sort, for in the first place it is necessary to prepare quite a perfect telescope, which will show all objects bright, distinct, and free from any haziness, while magnifying them at least four hundred times and thus showing them twenty times closer. Unless the instrument is of this kind it will be vain to attempt to observe all the things which I have seen in the heavens, and which will presently be set forth. Now in order to determine without much trouble the magnifying power of an instrument, trace on paper the contour of two circles or two squares of which one is four hundred times as large as the other, as it will be when the diameter of one is twenty times that of the other. Then, with both these figures attached to the same wall, observe them simultaneously from a distance, looking at the smaller one through the telescope and at the larger one with the other eye unaided. This may be done without inconvenience while holding both eyes open at the same time; the two figures will appear to be of the same size if the instrument magnifies objects in the desired proportion.

Such an instrument having been prepared, we seek a method of measuring distances apart. This we shall accomplish by the following contrivance.

Let ABCD be the tube and E be the eye of the observer. Then if there were no lenses in the tube, the rays would reach the object FG along the straight lines ECF and EDG. But when the lenses have been inserted, the rays go along the refracted lines ECH and EDI; thus they are brought closer together, and those which were previously directed freely to the object FG now include only the portion of it HI. The ratio of the distance EH to the line HI then being found, one may by means of a table of sines determine the size of the angle formed at the eye by the object HI, which we shall find to be but a few minutes of arc. Now, if to the lens CD we fit thin plates, some pierced with larger and some with smaller apertures, putting now one plate and now another over the lens as required, we may form at pleasure different angles subtending more or fewer minutes of arc, and by this means we may easily measure the intervals between stars which are but a few minutes apart, with no greater error than one or two minutes. And for the present let it suffice that we have touched lightly on these matters and scarcely more than mentioned them, as on some other occasion we shall explain the entire theory of this instrument.

*   *   *

Deserving of notice also is the difference between the appearances of the planets and of the fixed stars. The planets show their globes perfectly round and definitely bounded, looking like little moons, spherical and flooded all over with light; the fixed stars are never seen to be bounded by a circular periphery, but have rather the aspect of blazes whose rays vibrate about them and scintillate a great deal. Viewed with a telescope they appear of a shape similar to that which they present to the naked eye, but sufficiently enlarged so that a star of the fifth or sixth magnitude seems to equal the Dog Star, largest of all the fixed stars. Now, in addition to stars of the sixth magnitude, a host of other stars are perceived through the telescope which escape the naked eye; these are so numerous as almost to surpass belief. One may, in fact, see more of them than all the stars included among the first six magnitudes. The largest of these, which we may call stars of the seventh magnitude, or the first magnitude of invisible stars, appear through the telescope as larger and brighter than stars of the second magnitude when the latter are viewed with the naked eye. In order to give one or two proofs of their almost inconceivable number, I have adjoined pictures of two constellations. With these as samples, you may judge of all the others.

FROM *The Assayer*

*   *   *

In Sarsi I seem to discern the firm belief that in philosophizing one must support oneself upon the opinion of some celebrated author, as if our minds ought to remain completely sterile and barren unless wedded to the reasoning of some other person. Possibly he thinks that philosophy is a book of fiction by some writer, like the *Iliad* or *Orlando Furioso,* productions in which the least important thing is whether what is written there is true. Well, Sarsi, that is not how matters stand. Philosophy is written in this grand book, the universe, which stands continually open to our gaze. But the book cannot be understood unless one first learns to comprehend the language and read the letters in which it is composed. It is written in the language of mathematics, and its characters are triangles, circles, and other geometric figures without which it is humanly impossible to understand a single word of it; without these, one wanders about in a dark labyrinth.

Sarsi seems to think that our intellect should be enslaved to that of some other man. . . . But even on that assumption, I do not see why he selects Tycho. . . . Tycho could not extricate himself from his own explanation of diversity in the apparent motion of his comet; but now Sarsi expects my mind to be satisfied and set at rest by a little poetic flower that is not followed by any fruit at all. It is this that Guiducci rejected when he quite rightly said that nature takes no delight in poetry. That is a very true statement, even though Sarsi appears to disbelieve it and acts as if acquainted with neither nature nor poetry. He seems not to know that fables and fictions are in a way essential to poetry, which could not exist without them, while any sort of falsehood is so abhorrent to nature that it is as absent there as darkness is in light.

*   *   *

REVIEW QUESTIONS

1. How does a telescope work? What is its relation to human sight?
2. What does Galileo see? What does he discern?
3. What are the two books for Galileo?
4. What is the relation of one to the other?
5. What are the implications of Galileo's assertion that understanding depends on how one reads the book of the universe?

BLAISE PASCAL

FROM *Pensées*

*Blaise Pascal (1623–1662) was the son of a French official. During his life, he dab-
bled in many subjects, including science, religion, and literature. His conversion to
Jansenism plunged him into controversy with the Jesuits, giving rise to his* Lettres
provinciales. *These, along with his* Pensées *from which the following selection is
drawn, established his literary fame. His thought contained a fascinating blend of
confidence in human reason and consciousness of its limits. Descartes viewed Pascal
as the embodiment of a mentality of intellectual and spiritual crisis. Be that as it
may, Pascal raised profound questions about the purpose and potential of human
knowledge.*

From *Pensées* by Blaise Pascal, translated by A. J. Krailsheimer (New York: Penguin Books, 1995), pp. 58–64, 121–25.

*   *   *

XV. Transition from Knowledge of Man to Knowledge of God

DISPROPORTION OF MAN

*   *   *

This is where unaided knowledge brings us. If it
is not true, there is no truth in man, and if it is
true, he has good cause to feel humiliated; in either case he is obliged to humble himself.

And, since he cannot exist without believing
this knowledge, before going on to a wider inquiry
concerning nature, I want him to consider nature
just once, seriously and at leisure, and to look at
himself as well, and judge whether there is any
proportion between himself and nature by comparing the two.

Let man then contemplate the whole of nature
in her full and lofty majesty, let him turn his gaze
away from the lowly objects around him; let him
behold the dazzling light set like an eternal lamp
to light up the universe, let him see the earth as a
mere speck compared to the vast orbit described
by this star, and let him marvel at finding this vast
orbit itself to be no more than the tiniest point
compared to that described by the stars revolving
in the firmament. But if our eyes stop there, let
our imagination proceed further; it will grow
weary of conceiving things before nature tires of
producing them. The whole visible world is only
an imperceptible dot in nature's ample bosom. No
idea comes near it; it is no good inflating our conceptions beyond imaginable space, we only bring
forth atoms compared to the reality of things. Nature is an infinite sphere whose centre is everywhere and circumference nowhere. In short it is
the greatest perceptible mark of God's omnipo-
tence that our imagination should lose itself in
that thought.

Let man, returning to himself, consider what
he is in comparison with what exists; let him regard himself as lost, and from this little dungeon,
in which he finds himself lodged, I mean the universe, let him learn to take the earth, its realms,
its cities, its houses and himself at their proper
value.

What is a man in the infinite?

But, to offer him another prodigy equally astounding, let him look into the tiniest things he knows. Let a mite show him in its minute body incomparably more minute parts, legs with joints, veins in its legs, blood in the veins, humours in the blood, drops in the humours, vapours in the drops: let him divide these things still further until he has exhausted his powers of imagination, and let the last thing he comes down to now be the subject of our discourse. He will perhaps think that this is the ultimate of minuteness in nature.

I want to show him a new abyss. I want to depict to him not only the visible universe, but all the conceivable immensity of nature enclosed in this miniature atom. Let him see there an infinity of universes, each with its firmament, its planets, its earth, in the same proportions as in the visible world, and on that earth animals, and finally mites, in which he will find again the same results as in the first; and finding the same thing yet again in the others without end or respite, he will be lost in such wonders, as astounding in their minuteness as the others in their amplitude. For who will not marvel that our body, a moment ago imperceptible in a universe, itself imperceptible in the bosom of the whole, should now be a colossus, a world, or rather a whole, compared to the nothingness beyond our reach? Anyone who considers himself in this way will be terrified at himself, and, seeing his mass, as given him by nature, supporting him between these two abysses of infinity and nothingness, will tremble at these marvels. I believe that with his curiosity changing into wonder he will be more disposed to contemplate them in silence than investigate them with presumption.

For, after all, what is man in nature? A nothing compared to the infinite, a whole compared to the nothing, a middle point between all and nothing, infinitely remote from an understanding of the extremes; the end of things and their principles are unattainably hidden from him in impenetrable secrecy.

Equally incapable of seeing the nothingness from which he emerges and the infinity in which he is engulfed.

What else can he do, then, but perceive some semblance of the middle of things, eternally hopeless of knowing either their principles or their end? All things have come out of nothingness and are carried onwards to infinity. Who can follow these astonishing processes? The author of these wonders understands them: no one else can.

Because they failed to contemplate these infinities, men have rashly undertaken to probe into nature as if there were some proportion between themselves and her.

Strangely enough they wanted to know the principles of things and go on from there to know everything, inspired by a presumption as infinite as their object. For there can be no doubt that such a plan could not be conceived without infinite presumption or a capacity as infinite as that of nature.

When we know better, we understand that, since nature has engraved her own image and that of her author on all things, they almost all share her double infinity. Thus we see that all the sciences are infinite in the range of their researches, for who can doubt that mathematics, for instance, has an infinity of infinities of propositions to expound? They are infinite also in the multiplicity and subtlety of their principles, for anyone can see that those which are supposed to be ultimate do not stand by themselves, but depend on others, which depend on others again, and thus never allow of any finality.

But we treat as ultimate those which seem so to our reason, as in material things we call a point indivisible when our senses can perceive nothing beyond it, although by its nature it is infinitely divisible.

Of these two infinites of science, that of greatness is much more obvious, and that is why it has occurred to few people to claim that they know everything. 'I am going to speak about everything,' Democritus used to say.

But the infinitely small is much harder to see. The philosophers have much more readily claimed to have reached it, and that is where they have all tripped up. This is the origin of such familiar titles as *Of the principles of things, Of the principles of philosophy,* and the like, which are really as pretentious, though they do not look it, as this blatant one: *Of all that can be known.*

We naturally believe we are more capable of reaching the centre of things than of embracing their circumference, and the visible extent of the world is visibly greater than we. But since we in our turn are greater than small things, we think we are more capable of mastering them, and yet it takes no less capacity to reach nothingness than the whole. In either case it takes an infinite capacity, and it seems to me that anyone who had understood the ultimate principles of things might also succeed in knowing infinity. One depends on the other, and one leads to the other. These extremes touch and join by going in opposite directions, and they meet in God and God alone.

Let us then realize our limitations. We are something and we are not everything. Such being as we have conceals from us the knowledge of first principles, which arise from nothingness, and the smallness of our being hides infinity from our sight.

Our intelligence occupies the same rank in the order of intellect as our body in the whole range of nature.

Limited in every respect, we find this intermediate state between two extremes reflected in all our faculties. Our senses can perceive nothing extreme; too much noise deafens us, too much light dazzles; when we are too far or too close we cannot see properly; an argument is obscured by being too long or too short; too much truth bewilders us. I know people who cannot understand that 4 from 0 leaves 0. First principles are too obvious for us; too much pleasure causes discomfort; too much harmony in music is displeasing; too much kindness annoys us: we want to be able to pay back the debt with something over. *Kindness is welcome to the extent that it seems the debt can be paid back. When it goes too far gratitude turns into hatred.*

We feel neither extreme heat nor extreme cold. Qualities carried to excess are bad for us and cannot be perceived; we no longer feel them, we suffer them. Excessive youth and excessive age impair thought; so do too much and too little learning.

In a word, extremes are as if they did not exist for us nor we for them; they escape us or we escape them.

Such is our true state. That is what makes us incapable of certain knowledge or absolute ignorance. We are floating in a medium of vast extent, always drifting uncertainly, blown to and fro; whenever we think we have a fixed point to which we can cling and make fast, it shifts and leaves us behind; if we follow it, it eludes our grasp, slips away, and flees eternally before us. Nothing stands still for us. This is our natural state and yet the state most contrary to our inclinations. We burn with desire to find a firm footing, an ultimate, lasting base on which to build a tower rising up to infinity, but our whole foundation cracks and the earth opens up into the depth of the abyss.

Let us then seek neither assurance nor stability; our reason is always deceived by the inconsistency of appearances; nothing can fix the finite between the two infinites which enclose and evade it.

Once that is clearly understood, I think that each of us can stay quietly in the state in which nature has placed him. Since the middle station allotted to us is always far from the extremes, what does it matter if someone else has a slightly better understanding of things? If he has, and if he takes them a little further, is he not still infinitely remote from the goal? Is not our span of life equally infinitesimal in eternity, even if it is extended by ten years?

In the perspective of these infinites, all finites are equal and I see no reason to settle our imagination on one rather than another. Merely comparing ourselves with the finite is painful.

If man studied himself, he would see how incapable he is of going further. How could a part possibly know the whole? But perhaps he will aspire to know at least the parts to which he bears some proportion. But the parts of the world are all so related and linked together that I think it is impossible to know one without the other and without the whole.

There is, for example, a relationship between man and all he knows. He needs space to contain him, time to exist in, motion to be alive, elements to constitute him, warmth and food for nourishment, air to breathe. He sees light, he feels bodies, everything in short is related to him. To understand man therefore one must know why he needs air to live, and to understand air one must know how it comes to be thus related to the life of man, etc.

Flame cannot exist without air, so, to know one, one must know the other.

Thus, since all things are both caused or causing, assisted and assisting, mediate and immediate, providing mutual support in a chain linking together naturally and imperceptibly the most distant and different things, I consider it as impossible to know the parts without knowing the whole as to know the whole without knowing the individual parts.

The eternity of things in themselves or in God must still amaze our brief span of life.

The fixed and constant immobility of nature, compared to the continual changes going on in us, must produce the same effect.

And what makes our inability to know things absolute is that they are simple in themselves, while we are composed of two opposing natures of different kinds, soul and body. For it is impossible for the part of us which reasons to be anything but spiritual, and even if it were claimed that we are simply corporeal, that would still more preclude us from knowing things, since there is nothing so inconceivable as the idea that matter knows itself. We cannot possibly know how it could know itself.

Thus, if we are simply material, we can know nothing at all, and, if we are composed of mind and matter, we cannot have perfect knowledge of things which are simply spiritual or corporeal.

That is why nearly all philosophers confuse their ideas of things, and speak spiritually of corporeal things and corporeally of spiritual ones, for they boldly assert that bodies tend to fall, that they aspire towards their centre, that they flee from destruction, that they fear a void, that they have inclinations, sympathies, antipathies, all things pertaining only to things spiritual. And when they speak of minds, they consider them as being in a place, and attribute to them movement from one place to another, which are things pertaining only to bodies.

Instead of receiving ideas of these things in their purity, we colour them with our qualities and stamp our own composite being on all the simple things we contemplate.

Who would not think, to see us compounding everything of mind and matter, that such a mixture is perfectly intelligible to us? Yet this is the thing we understand least; man is to himself the greatest prodigy in nature, for he cannot conceive what body is, and still less what mind is, and least of all how a body can be joined to a mind. This is his supreme difficulty, and yet it is his very being. *The way in which minds are attached to bodies is beyond man's understanding, and yet this is what man is.*

*   *   *

REVIEW QUESTIONS

1. According to Pascal, what is the relation between universality and infinity?
2. Why does Pascal advocate the former?
3. Why can humans not know everything? What does Pascal's contention that nature is an infinite sphere teach us about human knowledge?
4. Why does nature hold forth abysses to human knowledge?
5. How has Pascal's concept of infinity, used earlier as a concept by which human beings might approach knowledge of God, changed in this passage?

RENÉ DESCARTES

FROM *Discourse on Method and Meditations on First Philosophy*

*René Descartes (1596–1650) was born of a family of the judicial nobility. He grad-
uated in 1612 from the Collège La Flèche and received a law degree in 1616 from
the University of Poitiers. From 1616 until 1624, he saw military service in the
Thirty Years' War. During the winter of 1620, while quartered near Ulm, Descartes
claimed to have achieved the philosophical insights that would form the basis of his
entire system of rational thought. In 1628 he left France, for reasons that are not
clear, and returned only for relatively brief periods of time. Until 1649, he lived in
the United Provinces of the Netherlands. There, with the publication of the Discourse on Method in 1637, he began to make public the ideas first glimpsed in
1620, the systematic philosophy that would make him famous. His was one of the
three great systems of rationalism of the seventeenth century, along with those created by Spinoza and Liebniz. Reacting to the skepticism of the early seventeenth
century, represented by the thought of philosophers like Pascal, Descartes decided to
subject every idea to critical scrutiny and retain as true only those ideas that were
"self-evident." The result was a geometric method of reasoning that consisted of four
simple rules: to start only with clear and distinct ideas, to simplify any difficulty in
thinking by dividing it into small parts, to think in an orderly process from simplest
to most complex, and to make thorough evaluations that overlook no part of the
problem. The Cartesian method gained enthusiastic popular support and served as
an important stimulus for the science of the Enlightenment.*

From *The European Philosophers from Descartes to Neitzsche,* edited by Monroe C. Beardsley
(New York: Modern Library, 1992), pp. 11–18.

*   *   *

Part 2

I was then in Germany, to which country I had
been attracted by the wars which are not yet at an
end. And as I was returning from the coronation
of the Emperor to join the army, the setting in of
winter detained me in a quarter where, since I
found no society to divert me, while fortunately I
had also no cares or passions to trouble me, I remained the whole day shut up alone in a stove-
heated room, where I had complete leisure to
occupy myself with my own thoughts. One of the
first of the considerations that occurred to me was
that there is very often less perfection in works
composed of several portions, and carried out by
the hands of various masters, than in those on
which one individual alone has worked. Thus we
see that buildings planned and carried out by one
architect alone are usually more beautiful and better proportioned than those which many have
tried to put in order and improve, making use
of old walls that were built with other ends in

view. * * * And similarly I thought that the sciences found in books—in those at least whose reasonings are only probable and which have no demonstrations, composed as they are of the gradually accumulated opinions of many different individuals—do not approach so near to the truth as the simple reasoning that a man of common sense can quite naturally carry out respecting the things which come immediately before him. Again I thought that since we have all been children before being men, and since it has for long fallen to us to be governed by our appetites and by our teachers (who often enough contradicted one another, and none of whom perhaps counselled us always for the best), it is almost impossible that our judgments should be so excellent or solid as they would have been had we had complete use of our Reason since our birth, and had we been guided by it alone.

It is true that we do not find that all the houses in a town are razed to the ground for the sole reason that the town is to be rebuilt in another fashion, with streets made more beautiful; but at the same time we see that many people cause their own houses to be knocked down in order to rebuild them, and that sometimes they are forced to do so where there is danger of the houses falling of themselves, and when the foundations are not secure. From such examples I argued to myself that there was no plausibility in the claim of any private individual to reform a state by altering everything, and by overturning it throughout, in order to set it right again. Nor is it likewise probable that the whole body of the Sciences, or the order of teaching established by the Schools, should be reformed. But as regards all the opinions which up to this time I had embraced, I thought I could not do better than endeavor once for all to sweep them completely away, so that they might later on be replaced, either by others that were better, or by the same, when I had made them conform to the uniformity of a rational scheme. And I firmly believed that by this means I should succeed in directing my life much better than if I had only built on old foundations, and relied on principles of which I allowed myself to be in youth persuaded without having inquired into their truth. For although in so doing I recognized various difficulties, these were at the same time not unsurmountable, nor comparable to those which are found in reformation of the most insignificant kind in matters which concern the public. * * *

* * * My design has never extended beyond trying to reform my own opinion and to build on a foundation that is entirely my own. If my work has given me a certain satisfaction, so that I here present to you a draft of it, I do not so do because I wish to advise anybody to imitate it. Those to whom God has been most beneficent in the bestowal of His grace will perhaps form designs that are more elevated; but I fear much that this particular one will seem too venturesome for many. The simple resolve to strip oneself of all opinions and beliefs formerly received is not to be regarded as an example that each man should follow, and the world may be said to be mainly composed of two classes of minds neither of which could prudently adopt it. There are those who, believing themselves to be cleverer than they are, cannot restrain themselves from being precipitate in judgment and have not sufficient patience to arrange their thoughts in proper order; hence, once a man of this description had taken the liberty of doubting the principles he formerly accepted, and had deviated from the beaten track, he would never be able to maintain the path which must be followed to reach the appointed end more quickly, and he would hence remain wandering astray all through his life. Secondly, there are those who having reason or modesty enough to judge that they are less capable of distinguishing truth from falsehood than some others from whom instruction might be obtained, are right in contenting themselves with following the opinions of these others rather than in searching better ones for themselves.

For myself I should doubtless have been of these last if I had never had more than a single master, or had I never known the diversities that have from all time existed between the opinions of men of the greatest learning. But I had been taught, even in my College days, that there is nothing imaginable so strange or so little credible that it has not been maintained by one philosopher or other, and I further recognized in the course of my travels that all those whose sentiments are very contrary to ours are yet not necessarily barbarians or savages, but may be possessed of Reason in as great or even a greater degree than ourselves. I also considered how very different the self-same man, identical in mind and spirit, may become, according as he is brought up from childhood amongst the French or Germans, or has passed his whole life amongst Chinese or cannibals. I likewise noticed how even in the fashions of one's clothing the same thing that pleased us ten years ago, and that will perhaps please us once again before ten years are passed, seems at the present time extravagant and ridiculous. I thus concluded that it is much more custom and example that persuade us than any certain knowledge, and yet in spite of this the voice of the majority is valueless as a proof of any truths that are a little difficult to discover, because such truths are much more likely to have been discovered by one man than by a nation. I could not, however, put my finger on a single person whose opinions seemed preferable to those of others, and I found that I was, so to speak, constrained myself to undertake the direction of my procedure.

But like one who walks alone and in the twilight I resolved to go so slowly, and to use so much circumspection in all things, that if my advance was but very small, at least I guarded myself well from falling. I did not wish to set about the final rejection of any single opinion which might formerly have crept into my beliefs without having been introduced there by means of Reason, until I had first of all employed sufficient time in planning out the task which I had undertaken, and in seeking the true Method of arriving at a knowledge of all the things of which my mind was capable.

Among the different branches of Philosophy, I had in my younger days to a certain extent studied Logic; and in those of Mathematics, Geometrical Analysis and Algebra—three arts or sciences which seemed as though they ought to contribute something to the design I had in view. But in examining them I observed in respect to Logic that the syllogisms and the greater part of the other teaching served better in explaining to others those things that one knows (or like the art of Lully, in enabling one to speak without judgment of those things of which one is ignorant) than in learning what is new. And although in reality Logic contains many precepts that are very true and very good, there are at the same time mingled with them so many others that are hurtful or superfluous, that it is almost as difficult to separate the two as to draw a Diana or a Minerva out of a block of marble that is not yet roughly hewn. And as to the Analysis of the ancients and the Algebra of the moderns, besides the fact that they embrace only matters the most abstract, such as appear to have no actual use, the former is always so restricted to the consideration of symbols that it cannot exercise the Understanding without greatly fatiguing the Imagination; and in the latter one is so subjected to certain rules and formulas that the result is the construction of an art that is confused and obscure, and that embarrasses the mind, instead of a science that contributes to its cultivation. This made me feel that some other Method must be found, which, comprising the advantages of the three, is yet exempt from their faults. And as a multiplicity of laws often furnishes excuses for evil-doing, and as a State is hence much better ruled when, having but very few laws, these are most strictly observed; so, instead of the great number of precepts of which Logic is composed, I believed that I should find the four which I shall state quite sufficient, provided that I adhered to a firm and constant resolve never on any single occasion to fail in their observance.

The first of these was to accept nothing as true which I did not clearly recognize to be so: that is to say, carefully to avoid precipitation and prejudice in judgments, and to accept in them nothing more than what was presented to my mind so clearly and distinctly that I could have no occasion to doubt it.

The second was to divide up each of the difficulties that I examined into as many parts as possible, and as seemed requisite in order that it might be resolved in the best manner possible.

The third was to carry on my reflections in due order, commencing with objects that were the most simple and easy to understand, in order to rise little by little, or by degrees, to knowledge of the most complex, assuming an order, even if a fictitious one, among those which do not follow a natural sequence relatively to one another.

The last was in all cases to make enumerations so complete and reviews so general that I should be certain of having omitted nothing.

Those long chains of reasoning, simple and easy as they are, of which geometricians make use in order to arrive at the most difficult demonstrations, had caused me to imagine that all those things which fall under the cognizance of man might very likely be mutually related in the same fashion; and that, provided only that we abstain from receiving anything as true that is not so, and always retain the order that is necessary in order to deduce the one conclusion from the other, there can be nothing so remote that we cannot reach to it, nor so recondite that we cannot discover it. And I had not much trouble in discovering which objects it was necessary to begin with, for I already knew that I must begin with the most simple and most easy to apprehend. Considering also that of all those who have hitherto sought for the truth in the Sciences, it has been the mathematicians alone who have been able to succeed in making any demonstrations, that is to say producing reasons that are evident and certain, I did not doubt that it had been by means of a similar kind that they carried on their investigations. I did not at the same time hope for any practical result in so doing, except that my mind would become accustomed to the nourishment of truth and would not content itself with false reasoning. But for all that I had no intention of trying to master all those particular sciences that receive in common the name of Mathematics; but observing that, although their objects are different, they do not fail to agree in this, that they take nothing under

consideration but the various relationships or proportions that are present in these objects, I thought it would be better if I only examined these proportions in their general aspect, and without viewing them otherwise than in the objects that would serve most to facilitate a knowledge of them. Not that I should in any way restrict them to these objects, for I might later on all the more easily apply them to all other objects to which they were applicable. Then, having carefully noted that in order to comprehend the proportions I should sometimes require to consider each one in particular, and sometimes merely keep them in mind, or take them in groups, I thought that, in order the better to consider them in detail, I should picture them in the form of lines, because I could find no method more simple nor more capable of being distinctly represented to my imagination and senses. I considered, however, that in order to keep them in my memory or to embrace several at once, it would be essential that I should explain them by means of certain formulas, the shorter the better. And for this purpose it was requisite that I should borrow all that is best in Geometrical Analysis and Algebra, and correct the errors of the one by the other.

*   *   *

But what pleased me most in this Method was that I was certain by its means of exercising my reason in all things, if not perfectly, at least as well as was in my power. And besides this, I felt in making use of it that my mind gradually accustomed itself to conceive of its objects more accurately and distinctly; and not having restricted this Method to any particular matter, I promised myself to apply it as usefully to the difficulties of other sciences as I had done to those of Algebra. Not that on this account I dared undertake to examine just at once all those which might present themselves; for that would itself have been contrary to the order that the Method prescribes. But having noticed that the knowledge of these difficulties must be dependent on principles derived from Philosophy in which I yet found nothing to be certain, I thought that it was requisite above all to try to establish certainty in it. I considered also that since this endeavor is the most important in all the world, and that in which precipitation and prejudice were most to be feared, I should not try to grapple with it till I had attained to a much riper age than that of three and twenty, which was the age I had reached. I thought, too, that I should first of all employ much time in preparing myself for the work by eradicating from my mind all the wrong opinions that I had up to this time accepted, and accumulating a variety of experiences fitted later on to afford matter for my reasonings, and by ever exercising myself in the Method I had prescribed, in order more and more to fortify myself in the power of using it.

*   *   *

REVIEW QUESTIONS

1. Why does Descartes reject the received knowledge of the past?
2. Why does Descartes not trust his own mind as a reasoning instrument?
3. What method does he propose, and what relationship does he see exists between experience and knowledge?
4. How does Descartes's epistemology compare with those of Montaigne and of Locke?

ISAAC NEWTON

FROM *Mathematical Principles of Natural Philosophy*

Isaac Newton (1642–1727) created the great reformulation of seventeenth-century mechanical philosophy. Born of yeoman stock, his intellectual gifts were recognized early by a teacher and an uncle, who urged that Newton be prepared for a university education. He entered Trinity College, Cambridge, in 1661 and received his Bachelor of Arts in 1665 and his Master of Arts in 1668. The next year, Newton was appointed Lucasian Professor, a position he held until 1701. As a natural philosopher, Newton agreed with Bacon that empiricism, that is, the gathering of experimental data, was the starting point for scientific inquiry. Yet he reserved a role for Cartesian rationalism by demonstrating the theoretical utility of mathematics in mechanical philosophy. In Mathematical Principles of Natural Philosophy *Newton laid out the quantitative framework of his mechanical philosophy and showed how it was possible, experimentally, to work with invisible bodies. In the following rules of reason, he offered a methodological guide to the study of reality.*

From *Mathematical Principles of Natural Philosophy,* vol. 2, by Isaac Newton, translated by Andrew Motte (London: Sherwood, Neely and Jones, 1919).

*   *   *

Book III

In the preceding books I have laid down the principles of philosophy; principles not philosophical, but mathematical; such, to wit, as we may build our reasonings upon in philosophical enquiries. These principles are the laws and conditions of certain motions, and powers or forces, which chiefly have respect to philosophy; but, lest they should have appeared of themselves dry and barren, I have illustrated them here and there with some philosophical scholiums, giving an account of such things as are of more general nature, and which philosophy seems chiefly to be founded on; such as the density and the resistance of bodies, spaces void of all bodies, and the motion of light and sounds. It remains that, from the same principles, I now demonstrate the frame of the System of the World. Upon this subject I had, indeed, composed the third book in a popular method, that it might be read by many; but afterwards, considering that such as had not sufficiently entered into the principles could not easily discern the strength of the consequences, nor lay aside the prejudices to which they had been many years accustomed, therefore, to prevent the disputes which might be raised upon such accounts, I chose to reduce the substance of this book into the form of propositions (in the mathematical way), which should be read by those only who had first made themselves masters of the principles established in the preceding books: not that I would advise any one to the previous study of every proposition of those books; for they abound with such as might cost too much time, even to readers of good mathematical learning. It is enough if one carefully reads the definitions, the laws of motions, and the first three sections of the first book. He may then pass on to this book, and consult such of the remaining propositions of the *first two books*, as the references in this, and his occasions, shall require.

Rules of Reasoning in Philosophy

RULE I
WE ARE TO ADMIT NO MORE CAUSES OF NATURAL THINGS THAN SUCH AS ARE BOTH TRUE AND SUFFICIENT TO EXPLAIN THEIR APPEARANCES.

To this purpose the philosophers say that Nature does nothing in vain, and more is in vain when less will serve; for Nature is pleased with simplicity, and affects not the pomp of superfluous causes.

RULE II
THEREFORE TO THE SAME NATURAL EFFECTS WE MUST, AS FAR AS POSSIBLE, ASSIGN THE SAME CAUSES.

As to respiration in a man and in a beast; the descent of stones in Europe and in America; the light of our culinary fire and of the sun; the reflection of light in the earth and in the planets.

RULE III
THE QUALITIES OF BODIES, WHICH ADMIT NEITHER INTENSION OR REMISSION OF DEGREES, AND WHICH ARE FOUND TO BELONG TO ALL BODIES WITHIN THE REACH OF OUR EXPERIMENTS, ARE TO BE ESTEEMED THE UNIVERSAL QUALITIES OF ALL BODIES WHATSOEVER.

For since the qualities of bodies are only known to us by experiments, we are to hold for universal all such as universally agree with experiments; and such as are not liable to diminution can never be quite taken away. We are certainly not to relinquish the evidence of experiments for the sake of dreams and vain fictions of our own devising; nor are we to recede from the analogy of Nature, which is wont to be simple, and always consonant to itself. We no other way know the extension of bodies than by our senses, nor do these reach it in all bodies; but because we perceive extension in all that are sensible, therefore we ascribe it universally to all others also. That abundance of bodies are hard, we learn by experience; and because the hardness of the whole arises from the hardness of the parts, we therefore justly infer the hardness of the undivided particles not only of the bodies we feel but of all others. That all bodies are impenetrable, we gather not from reason, but from sensation. The bodies which we handle we find impenetrable, and thence conclude impenetrability to be an universal property of all bodies whatsoever. That all bodies are moveable, and endowed with certain powers (which we call *vires inertiæ*) of persevering in their motion, or in their rest, we only infer from the like properties observed in the bodies which we have seen. The extension, hardness, impenetrability, mobility, and *vis inertiæ* of the whole, result from the extension, hardness, impenetrability, mobility, and *vires inertiæ* of the parts; and thence we conclude the least particles of all bodies to be also all extended, and hard, and impenetrable, and moveable, and endowed with their proper *vires inertiæ*. And this is the foundation of all philosophy. Moreover, that the divided but continuous particles of bodies may be separated from one another, is matter of observation; and, in the particles that remain undivided, our minds are able to distinguish yet lesser parts, as is mathematically demonstrated. But whether the parts so distinguished, and not yet divided, may, by the powers of Nature, be actually divided and separated from one another, we cannot certainly determine. Yet, had we the proof of but one experiment that any undivided particle, in breaking a hard and solid body, suffered a division, we might by virtue of this rule conclude that the undivided as well as the divided particles may be divided and actually separated to infinity.

Lastly, if it universally appears, by experiments and astronomical observations, that all bodies about the earth gravitate towards the earth, and that in proportion to the quantity of matter which they severally contain; that the moon likewise, according to the quantity of its matter, gravitates

towards the earth; that, on the other hand, our sea gravitates towards the moon; and all the planets mutually one towards another; and the comets in like manner towards the sun; we must, in consequence of this rule, universally allow that all bodies whatsoever are endowed with a principle of mutual gravitation. For the argument from the appearances concludes with more force for the universal gravitation of all bodies than for their impenetrability; of which, among those in the celestial regions, we have no experiments, nor any manner of observation. Not that I affirm gravity to be essential to bodies: by their *vis insita* I mean nothing but their *vis inertiæ*. This is immutable. Their gravity is diminished as they recede from the earth.

RULE IV

IN EXPERIMENTAL PHILOSOPHY WE ARE TO LOOK UPON PROPOSITIONS COLLECTED BY GENERAL INDUCTION FROM PHÆNOMENA AS ACCURATELY OR VERY NEARLY TRUE, NOTWITHSTANDING ANY CONTRARY HYPOTHESES THAT MAY BE IMAGINED, TILL SUCH TIME AS OTHER PHÆNOMENA OCCUR, BY WHICH THEY MAY EITHER BE MADE MORE ACCURATE, OR LIABLE TO EXCEPTIONS.

This rule we must follow, that the argument of induction may not be evaded by hypotheses.

*　　*　　*

REVIEW QUESTIONS

1. Why does Newton take mathematical principles as the principles of philosophy?
2. If nature, as Newton asserts, is "pleased with simplicity," what is the origin of "superfluous causes"?
3. What is the relation between cause and law?
4. How does Newton arrive at the universal?
5. How does his method differ from that of Pascal?

NICOLAUS COPERNICUS

FROM *Six Books Concerning the Revolutions of the Heavenly Orbs*

The Polish cleric and astronomer, Nicolaus Copernicus (1473–1543), is generally credited as the author of the heliocentric solar system. He proposed and demonstrated mathematically how the observed motions of stars and planets might be reconciled by assuming that the Sun was a fixed point and that the Earth rotated around the Sun while revolving on its own axis. His interest in the heavens probably began during a period of study at the University of Bologna, where he came into contact with Domenic Maria de Novara, the university's leading astronomer. While his principle interests were scientific, his career remained ecclesiastical. He served as a church canon, involved in administrative matters, and pursued astronomy in his spare time. Troubled by the discrepancies between theoretical descriptions and direct observations of planetary motion, he eventually postulated that, were the Sun assumed to be at rest and the Earth assumed to be in motion, the remaining planets would resolve themselves into an ordered progression according to their sidereal periods. While his findings solved the problem of ordering the planets, they created new ones by casting much of Aristotelian natural philosophy in doubt. Though he is thought to have developed his theory between 1508 and 1514, De revolutionibus orbium coelestium libri vi *("Six Books Concerning the Revolutions of the Heavenly Orbs") did not appear until the year of his death, 1543. Its full implications as a new theory concerning the fundamental structure of the universe would not be recognized until Kepler published his own theories a century later.*

From *On the Revolutions of the Heavenly Spheres*, by Nicolaus Copernicus, translated by Charles G. Walli (Amherst: Prometheus Books, 1996), pp. 4–7, 15–19.

*   *   *

Preface and Dedication to Pope Paul III

I can reckon easily enough, Most Holy Father, that as soon as certain people learn that in these books of mine which I have written about the revolutions of the spheres of the world I attribute certain motions to the terrestrial globe, they will immediately shout to have me and my opinion hooted off the stage. For my own works do not please me so much that I do not weigh what judgments others will pronounce concerning them. And although I realize that the conceptions of a philosopher are placed beyond the judgment of the crowd, because it is his loving duty to seek the truth in all things, in so far as God has granted that to human reason; nevertheless I think we should avoid opinions utterly foreign to rightness. And when I considered how absurd this "lecture" would be held by those who know that the opinion that the Earth rests immovable in the middle of the heavens as if their centre had been confirmed by the judgments of many ages—if I were to assert to the contrary that the Earth moves; for a long time I was in great difficulty as to whether I should bring to light my commentaries written to demonstrate the Earth's movement, or whether it would not be better to follow the example of the Pythagoreans and certain others who used to hand down the mysteries of their philosophy not in writing but by word of mouth and only to their relatives and friends—witness the letter of Lysis to Hipparchus. They however seem to me to have done that not, as some judge, out of a jealous unwillingness to communicate their doctrines but in order that things of very great beauty which have been investigated by the loving care of great men should not be scorned by those who find it a bother to expend any great energy on letters—except on the money-making variety—or who are provoked by the exhortations and examples of others to the liberal study of philosophy but on account of their natural stupidity hold the position among philosophers that drones hold among bees. Therefore, when I weighed these things in my mind, the scorn which I had to fear on account of the newness and absurdity of my opinion almost drove me to abandon a work already undertaken.

*   *   *

But perhaps Your Holiness will not be so much surprised at my giving the results of my nocturnal study to the light—after having taken such care in working them out that I did not hesitate to put in writing my conceptions as to the movement of the Earth—as you will be eager to hear from me what came into my mind that in opposition to the general opinion of mathematicians and almost in opposition to common sense I should dare to imagine some movement of the Earth. And so I am unwilling to hide from Your Holiness that nothing except my knowledge that mathematicians have not agreed with one another in their researches moved me to think out a different scheme of drawing up the movements of the spheres of the world. For in the first place mathematicians are so uncertain about the move-

ments of the sun and moon that they can neither demonstrate nor observe the unchanging magnitude of the revolving year. Then in setting u the solar and lunar movements and those of the other five wandering stars, they do not employ the same principles, assumptions, or demonstrations for the revolutions and apparent movements. * * * Moreover, they have not been able to discover or to infer the chief point of all, i.e., the form of the world and the certain commensurability of its parts. But they are in exactly the same fix as someone taking from different places hands, feet, head, and the other limbs—shaped very beautifully but not with reference to one body and without correspondence to one another—so that such parts made up a monster rather than a man. And so, in the process of demonstration which they call "method," they are found either to have omitted something necessary or to have admitted something foreign which by no means pertains to the matter; and they would by no means have been in this fix, if they had followed sure principles. For if the hypotheses they assumed were not false, everything which followed from the hypotheses would have been verified without fail; and though what I am saying may be obscure right now, nevertheless it will become clearer in the proper place.

Accordingly, when I had meditated upon this lack of certitude in the traditional mathematics concerning the composition of movements of the spheres of the world, I began to be annoyed that the philosophers, who in other respects had made a very careful scrutiny of the least details of the world, had discovered no sure scheme for the movements of the machinery of the world, which has been built for us by the Best and Most Orderly Workman of all. Wherefore, I took the trouble to reread all the books by philosophers which I could get hold of, to see if any of them even supposed that the movements of the spheres of the world were different from those laid down by those who taught mathematics in the schools. And as a matter of fact, I found first in Cicero that Nicetas thought that the Earth moved. And afterwards I found in Plutarch that there were some others of the same opinion: I shall copy out his words here, so that they may be known to all:

> Some think that the Earth is at rest; but Philolaus the Pythagorean says that it moves around the fire with an obliquely circular motion, like the sun and moon. Herakleides of Pontus and Ekphantus the Pythagorean do not give the Earth any movement of locomotion, but rather a limited movement of rising and setting around its centre, like a wheel.

Therefore I also, having found occasion, began to meditate upon the mobility of the Earth. And although the opinion seemed absurd, nevertheless because I knew that others before me had been granted the liberty of constructing whatever circles they pleased in order to demonstrate astral phenomena, I thought that I too, would be readily permitted to test whether or not, by the laying down that the Earth had some movement, demonstrations less shaky than those of my predecessors could be found for the revolutions of the celestial spheres.

And so, having laid down the movements which I attribute to the Earth farther on in the work, I finally discovered by the help of long and numerous observations that if the movements of the other wandering stars are correlated with the circular movement of the Earth, and if the movements are computed in accordance with the revolution of each planet, not only do all their phenomena follow from that but also this correlation binds together so closely the order and magnitudes of all the planets and of their spheres or orbital circles and the heavens themselves that nothing can be shifted around in any part of them without disrupting the remaining parts and the universe as a whole.

Accordingly, in composing my work I adopted the following order: in the first book I describe all the locations of the spheres or orbital circles together with the movements which I attribute to the earth, so that this book contains as it were the general set-up of the universe. But afterwards in the remaining books I correlate all the movements of the other planets and their spheres or orbital circles with the mobility of the Earth, so that it can be gathered from that how far the apparent movements of the remaining planets and their orbital circles can be saved by being correlated with the movements of the Earth. And I have no doubt that talented and learned mathematicians will agree with me, if—as philosophy demands in the first place—they are willing to give not superficial but profound thought and effort to what I bring forward in this work in demonstrating these things. And in order that the unlearned as well as the learned might see that I was not seeking to flee from the judgment of any man, I preferred to dedicate these results of my nocturnal study to Your Holiness rather than to anyone else; because, even in this remote corner of the earth where I live, you are held to be most eminent both in the dignity of your order and in your love of letters and even of mathematics; hence, by the authority of your judgment you can easily provide a guard against the bites of slanderers, despite the proverb that there is no medicine for the bite of a sycophant.

But if perchance there are certain "idle talkers" who take it upon themselves to pronounce judgment, although wholly ignorant of mathematics, and if by shamelessly distorting the sense of some passage in Holy Writ to suit their purpose, they dare to reprehend and to attack my work; they worry me so little that I shall even scorn their judgments as foolhardy. For it is not unknown that Lactantius, otherwise a distinguished writer but hardly a mathematician, speaks in an utterly childish fashion concerning the shape of the Earth, when he laughs at those who have affirmed that the Earth has the form of a globe. And so the studious need not be surprised if people like that laugh at us. Mathematics is written for mathematicians; and among them, if I am not mistaken, my labours will be seen to contribute something to the ecclesiastical commonwealth, the principate of which Your Holiness now holds. For not many years ago under Leo X when the Lateran Council was considering the question of reforming the Ecclesiastical Calendar, no decision was reached, for the sole reason that the magnitude of the year and the months and the movements of the sun and moon had not yet been measured with sufficient accuracy. From that time on I gave attention to making more exact observations of these things and was encouraged to do so by that most distinguished man, Paul, Bishop of Fossombrone, who had been present at those deliberations. But what have I accomplished in this matter I leave to the judgment of Your Holiness in particular and to that of all other learned mathematicians. And so as not to appear to Your Holiness to make more promises concerning the utility of this book than I can fulfill, I now pass on to the body of the work.

*   *   *

7. Why the Ancients Thought the Earth Was at Rest at the Middle of the World As Its Centre

Wherefore for other reasons the ancient philosophers have tried to affirm that the Earth is at rest at the middle of the world, and as principal cause they put forward heaviness and lightness. For Earth is the heaviest element; and all things of any weight are borne towards it and strive to move towards the very centre of it.

For since the Earth is a globe towards which from every direction heavy things by their own nature are borne at right angles to its surface, the heavy things would fall on one another at the centre if they were not held back at the surface; since a straight line making right angles with a plane surface where it touches a sphere leads to the centre. And those things which are borne toward the centre seem to follow along in order to be at rest at the centre. All the more then will the Earth be at rest at the centre; and, as being the receptacle for falling bodies, it will remain immovable because of its weight.

They strive similarly to prove this by reason of movement and its nature. For Aristotle says that the movement of a body which is one and simple is simple, and the simple movements are the rec-

tilinear and the circular. And of rectilinear movements, one is upward, and the other is downward. As a consequence, every simple movement is either toward the centre, i.e., downward, or away from the centre, i.e., upward, or around the centre, i.e., circular. Now it belongs to earth and water, which are considered heavy, to be borne downward, i.e., to seek the centre: for air and fire, which are endowed with lightness, move upward, i.e., away from the centre. It seems fitting to grant rectilinear movement to these four elements and to give the heavenly bodies a circular movement around the centre. So Aristotle. Therefore, said Ptolemy of Alexandria, if the Earth moved, even if only by its daily rotation, the contrary of what was said above would necessarily take place. For this movement which would traverse the total circuit of the Earth in twenty-four hours would necessarily be very headlong and of an unsurpassable velocity. Now things which are suddenly and violently whirled around are seen to be utterly unfitted for reuniting, and the more unified are seen to become dispersed, unless some constant force constrains them to stick together. And a long time ago, he says, the scattered Earth would have passed beyond the heavens, as is certainly ridiculous; and *a fortiori* so would all the living creatures and all the other separate masses which could by no means remain unshaken. Moreover, freely falling bodies would not arrive at the places appointed them, and certainly not along the perpendicular line which they assume so quickly. And we would see clouds and other things floating in the air always borne toward the west.

8. Answer to the Aforesaid Reasons and Their Inadequacy

For these and similar reasons they say that the Earth remains at rest at the middle of the world and that there is no doubt about this. But if someone opines that the Earth revolves, he will also say that the movement is natural and not violent. Now things which are according to nature produce effects contrary to those which are violent.

For things to which force or violence is applied get broken up and are unable to subsist for a long time. But things which are caused by nature are in a right condition and are kept in their best organization. Therefore Ptolemy had no reason to fear that the Earth and all things on the Earth would be scattered in a revolution caused by the efficacy of nature, which is greatly different from that of art or from that which can result from the genius of man. But why didn't he feel anxiety about the world instead, whose movement must necessarily be of greater velocity, the greater the heavens are than the Earth? Or have the heavens become so immense, because an unspeakably vehement motion has pulled them away from the centre, and because the heavens would fall if they came to rest anywhere else?

Surely if this reasoning were tenable, the magnitude of the heavens would extend infinitely. For the farther the movement is borne upward by the vehement force, the faster will the movement be, on account of the ever-increasing circumference which must be traversed every twenty-four hours: and conversely, the immensity of the sky would increase with the increase in movement. In this way, the velocity would make the magnitude increase infinitely, and the magnitude the velocity. And in accordance with the axiom of physics that *that which is infinite cannot be traversed or moved in any way*, then the heavens will necessarily come to rest.

But they say that beyond the heavens there isn't any body or place or void or anything at all; and accordingly it is not possible for the heavens to move outward: in that case it is rather surprising that something can be held together by nothing. But if the heavens were infinite and were finite only with respect to a hollow space inside, then it will be said with more truth that there is nothing outside the heavens, since anything which occupied any space would be in them; but the heavens will remain immobile. For movement is the most powerful reason wherewith they try to conclude that the universe is finite.

But let us leave to the philosophers of nature the dispute as to whether the world is finite or infinite, and let us hold as certain that the Earth is held together between its two poles and terminates in a spherical surface. Why therefore should we hesitate any longer to grant to it the movement which accords naturally with its form, rather than put the whole world in a commotion—the world whose limits we do not and cannot know? And why not admit that the appearance of daily revolution belongs to the heavens but the reality belongs to the Earth? And things are as when Aeneas said in Virgil: "We sail out of the harbor, and the land and the cities move away." As a matter of fact, when a ship floats on over a tranquil sea, all the things outside seem to the voyagers to be moving in a movement which is the image of their own, and they think on the contrary that they themselves and all the things with them are at rest. So it can easily happen in the case of the movement of the Earth that the whole world should be believed to be moving in a circle. Then what would we say about the clouds and the other things floating in the air or falling or rising up, except that not only the Earth and the watery element with which it is conjoined are moved in this way but also no small part of the air and whatever other things have a similar kinship with the Earth? whether because the neighbouring air, which is mixed with earthly and watery matter, obeys the same nature as the Earth or because the movement of the air is an acquired one, in which it participates without resistance on account of the contiguity and perpetual rotation of the Earth. Conversely, it is no less astonishing for them to say that the highest region of the air follows the celestial movement, as is shown by those stars which appear suddenly—I mean those called "comets" or "bearded stars" by the Greeks. For that place is assigned for their generation; and like all the other stars they rise and set. We can say that that part of the air is deprived of terrestrial motion on account of its great distance from the Earth. Hence the air which is nearest to the Earth and the things floating in it will appear tranquil, unless they are driven to and fro by the wind or some other force, as happens. For how is the wind in the air different from a current in the sea?

But we must confess that in comparison with the world the movement of falling and of rising bodies is twofold and is in general compounded of the rectilinear and the circular. As regards things which move downward on account of their weight because they have very much earth in them, doubtless their parts possess the same nature as the whole, and it is for the same reason that fiery bodies are drawn upward with force. For even this earthly fire feeds principally on earthly matter; and they define flame as glowing smoke. Now it is a property of fire to make that which it invades to expand; and it does this with such force that it can be stopped by no means or contrivance from breaking prison and completing its job. Now expanding movement moves away from the centre to the circumference; and so if some part of the Earth caught on fire, it would be borne away from the centre and upward. Accordingly, as they say, a simple body possesses a simple movement—this is first verified in the case of circular movement —as long as the simple body remain in its unity in its natural place. In this place, in fact, its movement is none other than the circular, which remains entirely in itself, as though at rest. Rectilinear movement, however, is added to those bodies which journey away from their natural place or are shoved out of it or are outside it somehow. But nothing is more repugnant to the order of the whole and to the form of the world than for anything to be outside of its place. Therefore rectilinear movement belongs only to bodies which are not in the right condition and are not perfectly conformed to their nature—when they are separated from their whole and abandon its unity. Furthermore, bodies which are moved upward or downward do not possess a simple, uniform, and regular movement—even without taking into account circular movement. For they cannot be in equilibrium with their lightness or their force of weight. And those which fall downward possess a slow movement at the beginning but increase their velocity as they fall. And conversely we note that this earthly fire—and we have experience of no other—when carried high up im-

mediately dies down, as if through the acknowledged agency of the violence of earthly matter.

Now circular movement always goes on regularly, for it has an unfailing cause; but [in rectilinear movement] the acceleration stops, because, when the bodies have reached their own place, they are no longer heavy or light, and so the movement ends. Therefore, since circular movement belongs to wholes and rectilinear to parts, we can say that the circular movement stands with the rectilinear, as does animal with sick. And the fact that Aristotle divided simple movement into three genera: away from the centre, toward the centre, and around the centre, will be considered merely as an act of reason, just as we distinguish between line, point, and surface, though none of them can subsist without the others or without body.

In addition, there is the fact that the state of immobility is regarded as more noble and godlike than that of change and instability, which for that reason should belong to the Earth rather than to the world. I add that it seems rather absurd to ascribe movement to the container or to that which provides the place and not rather to that which is contained and has a place, i.e., the Earth. And lastly, since it is clear that the wandering stars are sometimes nearer and sometimes farther away from the Earth, then the movement of one and the same body around the centre—and they mean the centre of the Earth—will be both away from the centre and toward the centre. Therefore it is necessary that movement around the centre should be taken more generally; and it should be enough if each movement is in accord with its own centre. You see therefore that for all these reasons it is more probably that the Earth moves than that it is at rest—especially in the case of the daily revolution, as it is the Earth's very own. And I think that is enough as regards the first part of the question.

9. Whether Many Movements Can Be Attributed to the Earth, and Concerning the Centre of the World

Therefore, since nothing hinders the mobility of the Earth, I think we should now see whether more than one movement belongs to it, so that it can be regarded as one of the wandering stars. For the apparent irregular movement of the planets and their variable distances from the Earth—which cannot be understood as occurring in circles homocentric with the Earth—make it clear that the Earth is not the centre of their circular movements. Therefore, since there are many centres, it is not foolhardy to doubt whether the centre of gravity of the Earth rather than some other is the centre of the world. I myself think that gravity or heaviness is nothing except a certain natural appetency implanted in the parts by the divine providence of the universal Artisan, in order that they should unite with one another in their oneness and wholeness and come together in the form of a globe. It is believable that this affect is present in the sun, moon, and the other bright planets and that through its efficacy they remain in the spherical figure in which they are visible, though they nevertheless accomplish their circular movements in many different ways. Therefore if the Earth too possesses movements different from the one around its centre, then they will necessarily be movements which similarly appear on the outside in the many bodies; and we find the yearly revo- lution among these movements. For if the annual revolution were changed from being solar to being terrestrial, and immobility were granted to the sun, the risings and settings of the signs and of the fixed stars—whereby they become morning or evening stars—will appear in the same way; and it will be seen that the stoppings, retrogressions, and progressions of the wandering stars are not their own, but are a movement of the Earth and that they borrow the appearances of this move- ment. Lastly, the sun will be regarded as occupying the centre of the world. And the ratio of order in which these bodies succeed one another and the harmony of the whole world teaches us their truth, if only—as they say—we would look at the thing with both eyes.

REVIEW QUESTIONS

1. Why did Copernicus dedicate his great work to Pope Paul III?
2. What assumptions about the nature of scien- tific knowledge caused Copernicus to revisit and revise the received natural philosophy?
3. How does Copernicus refute in this work the notion that the Earth is at rest in the universe?
4. What does this reveal about his scientific method?
5. What benefits would arise from the establish- ment of scientific truth?

FRIEDRICH WILHELM HEINRICH ALEXANDER VON HUMBOLDT

FROM *Personal Narrative*

The German naturalist and explorer, Friedrich Wilhelm Heinrich Alexander von Humboldt (1769–1859), was one of the leading figures in the classic period of geographic exploration and biological classification. Born on his family's estates near Berlin, he was educated at the universities of Frankfurt, Göttingen, and Hamburg, where his interests in the natural sciences took shape. After an initial period of scientific travel, the journals of which provided his first publications in natural philosophy, he accepted a position in the Prussian mining administration. His maternal inheritance provided him the means to pursue his interests in geography and biology. At his own expense, he undertook a five-year tour (1799–1804) of Spanish-American colonies, covering over 6,000 miles on foot, horseback, and canoe, penetrating deep into the unexplored interior, and observing not only the geology and biology but also the history, politics, societies, and cultures of the continent.

On his return, he settled in Paris, at that time one of the great scientific centers of Europe, and set about publishing his monumental Relation historique du voyage aux régions équinoxiales du nouveau continent, *which extended to thirty volumes by the time of its completion in 1834. His* Personal Narrative, *from which the current selection is taken, made up the last three volumes. The publication brought him fame, if not fortune, and resulted in his recall to Berlin to serve as chamberlain to Friedrich Wilhelm III and councillor of state to Friedrich Wilhelm IV of Prussia. It was an unhappy result for von Humboldt, who viewed Berlin as a backwater and longed for the cosmopolitanism of Paris. Still, his passion for science remained. Von Humboldt spent the last twenty-five years of his life writing* Kosmos, *a comprehensive account of the structure of the universe as understood in the early nineteenth century. The first four volumes appeared during his lifetime and were quickly translated into most European languages. The fifth volume appeared after the author's death at age ninety.*

From *Personal Narrative*, by Friedrich Wilhelm Heinrich Alexander von Humboldt, translated by Jason Wilson (New York: Penguin Books, 1996), pp. 15–23, 66–76.

Chapter 1
Preparations — Departure from Spain — Landing at the Canary Islands

From my earliest days I felt the urge to travel to distant lands seldom visited by Europeans. This urge characterizes a moment when our life seems to open before us like a limitless horizon in which nothing attracts us more than intense mental thrills and images of positive danger. I was brought up in a country that has no relations with either of the Indies, and I lived in mountains far from the sea and famous for their working mines, yet I felt an increasing passion for the sea and a yearning to travel far overseas. What we glean from travellers' vivid descriptions has a special charm; whatever is far off and suggestive excites our imagination; such pleasures tempt us far more than anything we may daily experience in the narrow circle of sedentary life. My taste for botanizing and the study of geology, with the chance of a trip to Holland, England and France accompanied by Georg Forster, who was lucky enough to travel with Captain Cook on his second world tour, helped determine the travel plans I had been hatching since I was eighteen years old. What attracted me about the torrid zone was no longer the promise of a wandering life full of adventures, but a desire to see with my own eyes a grand, wild nature rich in every conceivable natural product, and the prospect of collecting facts that might contribute to the progress of science. Personal circumstances prevented me from carrying out these absorbing plans, and for six years I had the leisure to prepare myself for the observations I would make in the New World by travelling through several European countries and exploring the Alps, whose structure I would later compare with the Andes between Quito and Peru.

During that time a voyage to explore the Pacific was being planned in France, under the direction of Captain Baudin. The early plan was daring and grand, and would have been better entrusted to a more enlightened man. The idea was to travel across the Spanish colonies in South America from the mouth of the River Plate to the kingdom of Quito and the Panama isthmus. The two corvettes would then proceed to New Holland through the Pacific archipelagoes, stopping at Madagascar and returning home round the Cape of Good Hope. I had arrived in Paris when the preparations for the voyage had just begun. I had little faith in Captain Baudin's character as he had given me cause to be suspicious in the Viennese Court when charged to accompany one of my friends to Brazil, but as I could never with my own resources have afforded such a far-reaching expedition, nor visited such a beautiful part of the earth, I decided to risk taking part in the expedition. I got permission to embark with my instruments on one of the corvettes destined for the Pacific, and I did this on the agreement that I could leave Captain Baudin whenever it suited me. Michaux, who had visited Persia and parts of North America, and Bonpland, who became and remained a close friend, were also to accompany this expedition as naturalists.

*   *   *

We resolved to spend the winter in Spain, hoping to embark from Cartagena or Cádiz in the spring, if the political situation in the east permitted this. We crossed the kingdoms of Catalonia and Valencia to reach Madrid. On the way we visited the ruins of Tarragona and ancient Saguntum. From Barcelona we made an excursion to Montserrat, whose elevated peaks are inhabited by hermits. The contrast between luxuriant vegetation and desolate, bare rocks forms a peculiar scenery.

Arriving at Madrid I soon congratulated myself on my decision to visit the peninsula. Baron de Forell, Saxon Ambassador to the Spanish Court, received me in a friendly way that greatly favoured my project. To his knowledge of mineralogy he added a great interest in the progress of science. He let me know that under the patronage of an enlightened minister, Don Mariano Luis de Urquijo, I might be permitted to make a journey to the interior of Spanish America, at my own expense. After all the set-backs I had suffered I did not hesitate to take up this suggestion.

In March 1799 I was presented at the Court of Aranjuez and the King received me graciously. I explained the motives that prompted me to undertake a journey to the New World and the Philippines, and presented a memoir of my plans to the Secretary of State. Señor de Urquijo supported my petition and overcame every obstacle in my path, proceeding with commendable generosity given I had no personal relationship with him. The zeal with which he helped me can be due only to his love for science.

I obtained two passports; one from the Secretary of State, the other from the Council of the Indies. Never before had such concessions been granted to a traveller, and never had the Spanish Government shown such confidence in a foreigner. To waylay all the possible reservations that the viceroys and captain-generals might raise concerning the nature and finality of my work, it said in my safe conduct from the First Secretary of State that "I was authorized to freely use my physical and geodesical instruments, that in all the Spanish possessions I could make astronomical observations, measure the height of mountains, collect whatever grew on the ground, and carry out any task that might advance the Sciences."

*   *   *

The moment of leaving Europe for the first time is impressive. We vainly recall the frequency of communications between the two worlds; we vainly reflect how, thanks to the improved state of navigation, we may now cross the Atlantic, which compared to the Pacific is but a shortish arm of the sea; yet what we feel when we begin our first long-distance voyage is none the less accompanied by a deep emotion, unlike any we may have felt in our youth. Separated from the objects of our dearest affections, and entering into a new life, we are forced to fall back on ourselves and we feel more isolated than we have ever felt before.

*   *   *

At sunset on the 8th of June the look-out sighted from his crow's-nest a British convoy sailing along the coast towards the south-east. To avoid it we altered our course during the night. We were also given orders not to put our lights on in the great cabin so that we would not be seen from afar. We constantly had to use dark-lanterns to make our observations of the sea's temperature, or read the markings on our astronomical instruments. In the torrid zone, where twilight lasts a few minutes, we were condemned to inaction, in similar circumstances, from six in the evening. For me this was particularly irritating as I have never suffered from seasickness and no sooner am I on board than I feel the urge to work more than ever.

From La Coruña to the 36th degree of latitude we had scarcely seen any living creature apart from sea swallows and a few dolphins. We searched in vain for seaweed and molluscs. On the 11th of June we were struck by a curious sight that later we would see often in the Pacific. We reached a zone where the sea seemed covered with an enormous amount of jellyfish. The boat could hardly move, though the jellyfish floated towards the south-east four times faster than the current. This procession lasted some forty-five minutes; then we saw a few scattered and exhausted ones struggling to follow the main bunch, as if tired of their journey.

Between Madeira and the African coast we were almost becalmed, which suited me perfectly as I could carry out my magnetic experiments. We never tired of admiring the magnificent nights; nothing approaches the clarity and serenity of the African sky. We were struck by the extraordinary number of shooting stars that crossed the night sky. The further south we advanced, the more we saw, especially near the Canary Islands. When we were about 40 leagues east of Madeira, a common swallow (*Hirundo rustica*) landed on the topmast. It was so exhausted we easily caught it. What drives a bird so far off its course at such a calm time of year?

*   *   *

The island of Lanzarote used to be called Titeroigotra. When the Spaniards arrived its inhabitants differed from those on the other islands by their superior culture. They built their houses with cut stones while the Guanches of Tenerife lived in caves like troglodytes. At that time a strange custom—repeated only in Tibet—prevailed. A woman had several husbands, who each took it in turn to exercise the rights of the head of the family. Each husband was known as such during a lunar month; then another took his place while he returned to being a servant in the house. In the fifteenth century the island of Lanzarote consisted of two states separated by a wall; a kind of monument, which outlives national enmities, found also in Scotland, Peru and China.

Guessing from some signs on an old Portuguese map, the captain of the *Pizarro* thought we were opposite a small fort built north of Teguise, the capital of Lanzarote. Mistaking some basaltic crags for a castle he saluted it properly by hoisting the Spanish flag and sending a boat with an officer to the supposed fort to find out if the English were lurking in these waters. We were not a little surprised to discover that the land we took for the coast of Lanzarote was the small island of Graciosa, and that for several leagues around there was not a sound of life.

We took the opportunity to use the boat to survey the land around the large bay. No words can evoke the feelings of a naturalist who first steps on soil outside Europe. So many objects call for his attention that it is hard to order his impression. At each step he thinks he is coming across something new, and in his excitement he does not recognize things that commonly feature in botanical gardens and natural history collections. Two hundred yards off the coast we saw a man fishing with a rod. We turned the boat towards him but he fled and hid behind a rock. It took our sailors some effort to capture him. The sight of the corvette, the thunder of our cannons in such a solitary place—possibly visited only by pirates—the launching of our boat, all this terrified the poor fisherman. He informed us that the island of Graciosa on which we had landed was separated from Lanzarote by a small channel called El Río. He offered to guide us to Los Colorados harbour to find out about the blockade at Tenerife but, when the man assured us that for weeks he had not seen any ships out at sea, the captain decided to set sail for Santa Cruz.

*   *   *

Chapter 5
The Araya peninsula — Salt marshes —
Ruins of the Santiago fort

We spent the first weeks of our stay in Cumaná testing our instruments, botanizing in the nearby countryside, and investigating the traces of the earthquake of the 14th of December 1797. Dazzled by the sheer amount of different objects we found

it awkward to stick to a systematic way of studying and observing. If everything that we saw around us excited us, our instruments in their turn awoke the curiosity of the local inhabitants. The numerous visitors disturbed us; in order not to disappoint all those who seemed so pleased to see the spots of the moon through Dollond's telescope,[31] the absorption of two gases in a eudiometrical tube, or the effects of galvanism on the motions of a frog, we had to answer many obscure questions and repeat the same experiments for hours.

This same situation repeated itself over the five years of our journey whenever we settled down in a place where people knew we had microscopes, telescopes and electrical apparatus. This was all the more tiresome as those who visited us held confused notions of astronomy or physics, two sciences that in the Spanish colonies are called by the bizarre name of new philosophy, *nueva filosofía*. The half-scientific looked at us scornfully when they heard we had not brought with us books like Abbé Pluche's *Spectacle de la nature* or Sigaud la Fond's *Cours de physique* or Valmont de Bomare's Dictionary. These, along with Baron Bielfeld's *Traité d'économie politique,* are the foreign works most admired in Spanish America. No one is deemed learned who cannot quote from them in translation. Only in the great capitals are the names of Haller, Cavendish and Lavoisier replacing those who have been famous for over fifty years.

Our house in Cumaná was magnificently situated for observing the sky and meteorological phenomena; on the other hand, during the day, we witnessed scenes that disgusted us. A part of the great plaza is surrounded with arcades above which runs a long wooden gallery, common to all hot countries. This is where the slaves brought from Africa were once sold. Of all European countries Denmark was the first and for ages the only government to abolish the slave-trade; yet the first slaves we saw here were transported by a Danish slave-ship. What silences the speculations of vile interest in its struggle with the duties of humanity, national honour and the laws of the fatherland?

The slaves put up for sale were young people

from fifteen to twenty years old. Every morning they were given coconut oil to rub into their bodies to make their skin black and shiny. All the time buyers would approach and, examining their teeth, would calculate their age and health; they forced open their mouths just as if dealing with horses at market. This debasing custom dates back to Africa as is faithfully shown in a play by Cervantes who, after a long captivity with the Moors, outlined the sale of Christian slaves in Algiers. It is distressing to think that still today in the Spanish West Indies slaves are branded with hot irons to identify them in case they escape. This is how one treats those "who save other men from the labour of sowing, working in the fields and harvesting."

The deep impression caused by our first sight of a slave sale in Cumaná was alleviated somewhat by the relief of finding ourselves with a people and on a continent where this spectacle is very rare, and the number of slaves, in general, insignificant. In 1800 there were not more than 600 slaves in the two provinces of Cumaná and New Barcelona, while the total population reached around 110,000. The trade in African slaves, never favoured by the Spanish Crown, has dwindled to almost nothing on these coasts where, in the sixteenth century, it reached a terrifying figure.

Our first excursion was to the Araya peninsula and those regions formerly so infamous for slave-trading and pearl fishing. On the 19th of August, at about two in the morning, we embarked on the Manzanares river, near the Indian settlement. Our main objectives on this short trip were to visit the ruins of the ancient Araya fort, the salt works and the mountains that form the narrow Maniquarez peninsula where we hoped to carry out some geological research. The night was deliciously cool, swarms of luminous insects (*Elater noctilucus*) shone in the air, on the ground covered with sesuvium, and in the mimosa (*Lampyris italica*) thickets bordering the river. We know how common glow-worms are in Italy and all southern Europe, yet the picturesque effect they produce cannot compare with these innumerable scattered and moving lights, which embellish the tropical

nights all over the plains, repeating the spectacle of the stars in the sky on the ground.

Descending the river we passed the plantations or *charas* where negroes had lit bonfires for their fiestas. A light billowing smoke rose above the palm-tree tops, giving a reddish colour to the moon's disk. It was a Sunday night and the slaves danced to the monotonous and noisy music of guitars. A fundamental feature of the black African races is their inexhaustible store of vitality and joy. After working painfully hard all week, they prefer to dance and sing on their fiesta days rather than sleep for a long time. We should be wary of criticizing this mixture of thoughtlessness and frivolity for it sweetens the evils of a life of deprivations and suffering!

The boat in which we crossed the Gulf of Cariaco was very spacious. They had spread large jaguar skins out so that we could rest at night. We had been scarcely two months in the torrid zone, and already our organs were so sensitive to the slightest temperature changes that cold stopped us sleeping. To our surprise we saw that the thermometer marked 21.8°C. This fact is familiar to those who have lived long in the Indies. During our stay at Guayaquil in January 1803, we watched the Indians cover themselves and complain of the cold when the temperature sank to 23.8°C, while they suffocated with heat at 30.5°C. A difference of 6°C or 7°C was sufficient to cause the opposite sensations of cold and heat. At Cumaná, during heavy showers, people in the streets are heard to complain "Qué hielo! Estoy emparamado," though the thermometer exposed to the rain sinks only to 21.5°C.

*   *   *

At dawn the next day we realized that the hut where we had spent the night formed part of a group of huts situated on the banks of a salt lake. They are the few remains left of a considerable village formed long ago around the fort. The ruins of the church were half buried in sand and covered with brushwood. When in 1762 the Araya fort was completely dismantled, to save the expense of maintaining a garrison, the Indians and other coloured residents who lived around about emigrated one by one to Maniquarez, Cariaco and the Guaiquerí suburb at Cumaná. Only a few remained in the wild and desolate village, deeply attached to their native land. These poor people live from fishing on the coast and in neighbouring shoals rich in fish. They seemed content with their fate and found it strange that I asked them why they had no gardens to cultivate nutritious plants. "Our gardens," they replied, "lie on the other side of the strait; we bring fish to Cumaná and they give us cassava, bananas and coconuts in return." This economic system, which flatters laziness, is followed at Maniquarez and throughout the Araya peninsula. The principal wealth of these inhabitants consists of large, beautiful goats. They move freely about like the goats on the Tenerife peak; they are completely wild, and are branded like the mules because it would be difficult to recognize them from their colour or spots. These fawn goats do not vary in colour like domestic ones. When a settler out hunting shoots a goat that is not his, he brings it to whichever neighbour it belongs to.

*   *   *

Benzoni relates the adventure of one Louis Lampagnano, to whom Charles V granted the privilege of proceeding with five caravels to the Cumaná coasts to fish for pearls. The settlers sent him back with the bold message that the Emperor, too liberal with what was not his own, had no right to dispose of the oysters living at the bottom of the sea.

The pearl fisheries diminished rapidly towards the end of the sixteenth century, and had long ceased by 1683. The industrious Venetians who imitated fine pearls perfectly, and the growing popularity of cut diamonds, made the Cubagua fisheries less lucrative. At the same time the oysters became scarcer, not because, according to popular legend, they were frightened by the sound of oars and moved away, but because the rash gathering of thousands at a time stopped them propagating themselves. To form an idea of the destruction of the shells caused by the divers, we must remember that a boat collects in two to three weeks more

than 35,000 oysters. The animal lives but nine to ten years, and only in its fourth year do pearls begin to show. In 10,000 shells there is often not a single pearl of value.

On the morning of the 20th the son of our host, a young, robust Indian, led us to the village of Maniquarez, passing through Barigon and Caney. It was a four-hour walk. Because of the reverberation of the sun's rays on the sand the thermometer remained at 31.3°C. The cylindrical cacti along the path made the landscape green, but without freshness or shade. We had walked barely a league when our guide decided, at every opportunity, to sit down and rest. When we got near to Casas de la Vela he even tried to lie down in the shade of a beautiful tamarind tree, to await nightfall. We observed this characteristic trait whenever we travelled with Indians; it has given rise to the most mistaken ideas about the physical constitutions of different races. The copper-coloured Indian, who is more used to the burning heat of these regions than a European, complains more because nothing stimulates his interest. Money is no bait, and if he is tempted by gain he repents of his decision as soon as he starts walking. This same Indian, who would complain when we loaded him with a box filled with plants while herborizing, would row his canoe against the strongest current for fourteen or fifteen hours in order to be back home.

We examined the remarkably solid ruins of Santiago. The 5-foot-thick walls of freestone have been toppled over by mines; but we still found huge sections with scarcely a crack in them. Our guide showed us a cistern (*el aljibe*), 30 feet deep, which though damaged furnishes water to the inhabitants of the Araya peninsula. This cistern was finished in 1681. As the basin is covered with an arched vault the excellent water remains very cool. Crossing the arid hills of Cape Cirial we detected a strong smell of petroleum. The wind blew from the place where the springs of petroleum, mentioned by the first chroniclers, are to be found.

The Maniquarez potteries, famous from time immemorial, are a specialized industry completely run by Indian women. They work with the same method that was used before the conquest. This reveals both the infancy of this craft and that immobility of manners so characteristic of American Indians. Three hundred years have not sufficed to introduce the potter's wheel to a coast not more than forty days' sailing from Spain. The Indians have a vague idea that something of the sort exists, and surely would adopt one should it be shown to them. The quarries where they extract their clay lie half a league to the east of Maniquarez. This clay is produced by the decomposition of a mica-slate stained red by iron oxide. The Indian women prefer the part most loaded with mica; and very skilfully shape vessels of 2 to 3 feet in diameter with regular curves. As they do not know how to use kilns they place scrub from desmanthus, cassia and arborescent capparis around the pots and bake them in the open air.

*   *   *

The inhabitants of Araya, whom we visited a second time when returning from the Orinoco, have not forgotten that their peninsula is one of the places most anciently populated by the Castilians. They like talking about the pearl fisheries, the ruins of the Santiago fort, which they hope will be rebuilt one day, and all that they call the ancient splendour of these countries. In China and Japan inventions are called recent if they are more than 2,000 years old: in the European colonies an event seems extremely ancient if it is three centuries old, dating back to the discovery.

This absence of memories, which characterizes these new people in the United States of America and in the Spanish and Portuguese possessions, is worthy of attention. It is not only distressing to the traveller, who becomes deprived of the pleasures of the imagination, it also influences the bonds that tie a settler to the land he inhabits, the form of the rocks around his hut, the trees shading his cradle.

Most of these modern colonies are founded in a zone where the climate, the produce, the sky and landscape, all differ completely from Europe. The settler vainly tries to name the mountains, rivers and valleys with names that recall his motherland; these names soon lose their charm, and mean nothing to later generations. Under the influence of an exotic nature new habits are born for new needs; national memories are slowly effaced, and those remembered, like ghosts of our imaginations, are not attached to any time or place. The glories of Don Pelayo or the Cid Campeador have penetrated the forests and mountains of America; people sometimes pronounce these famous names, but they seem to come from an ideal world, from vague, fabulous times.

Moreover, the American colonies are founded in countries where the dead leave barely any trace of their existence. To the north of Gila river, on the banks of the Missouri, and in the Andean plain, traditions date back only a century. In Peru, Guatemala and Mexico, ruins, historic paintings and sculptured monuments attest, it is true, to ancient Indian civilizations, but throughout an entire province only a few families have precise notions about Inca history or Mexican princesses. The Indian has kept his language, his customs and national character; but the loss of *quipus* and symbolic paintings, the introduction of Christianity, and other factors, have made the historic and religious traditions vanish. On the one hand the European settler scorns everything to do with the defeated Indians. Placed between memories of the metropolis and the actual country he was born in, he looks to both indifferently; in a climate where the equality of the seasons makes the succession of years almost indifferent he lives only for the pleasures of the moment and rarely looks to the past.

REVIEW QUESTIONS

1. Noting the style in which von Humboldt's narrative is written, what conclusions can be drawn about his intended audience and the function of science in the late eighteenth and early nineteenth centuries?
2. What methods does he employ and how do

these differ from those of Copernicus, Galileo, or Newton?

3. What is the nature and subject of science as practiced by von Humboldt?

4. Is there a purpose to his frequent observations of both the natural and the human world?

5. How does von Humboldt's discussion of slavery differ from those of Raynal and Smith?

JOHN WALLIS

FROM *A Defense of the Royal Society*

The Royal Society of London for the Promotion of Natural Knowledge was chartered in 1662, the first scientific society in Great Britain and one of the oldest in Europe. The account of its founding comes from the mathematician, Dr. John Wallis (1616–1703), one of its early members. He reveals its origins to have been small, informal discussion groups, which met in Oxford and London as early as 1645 to discuss matters of science, and a number of local academies, which promoted experimentation. A long tradition of independent discussion was little changed by royal patronage. The society attracted many of the great minds of early science, whose research and leadership made it internationally famous. Its publication, Philosophical Transactions, *was one of the first scientific publications in Europe and quickly became a leading clearinghouse for research. The society sponsored great voyages of exploration and observation, such as the expeditions of James Cook. Its maintains the role of fostering science in the broadest sense of the term to the present day.*

From *A Defence of the Royal Society,* by John Wallis (London, 1678), cited in *History of the Royal Society,* by C. R. Weld (London, 1848), pp. 35–36.

*   *   *

The Origin of the Royal Society (1645–1649)

*   *   *

(A) About the year 1645, while I lived in London (at a time when, by our civil wars, academical studies were much interrupted in both our Universities), beside the conversation of divers eminent divines, as to matters theological, I had the opportunity of being acquainted with divers worthy persons, inquisitive into natural philosophy, and other parts of human learning; and particularly of what hath been called the *New Philosophy,* or *Experimental Philosophy.* We did by agreements, divers of us, meet weekly in London on a certain day, to treat and discourse of such affairs; of which number were *Dr. John Wilkins* (afterward *Bishop of Chester*), *Dr Jonathan Goddard, Dr. George Ent, Dr. Glisson, Dr. Merret* (Drs. in Physic), *Mr. Samuel Foster,* then Professor of Astronomy at Gresham College, *Mr. Theodore Hank* (a German of the Palatinate, and then resident in London,

THE ANATOMY LESSON OF DR. TULP (1632)   Rembrandt Harmenszoon van Rijn

Rembrandt's painting, The Anatomy Lesson of Dr. Tulp, *established the artist's reputation as a painter of portraits. It is interesting for a number of reasons. First, the subject itself is unusual, not what one would necessarily expect of a renowned artist. Second, the subject is controversial in an age in which the dissection of the human body was neither widely accepted nor legal in all places. Thus, the painting captures not only the master's skill but also a moment in the growth of early modern science. What does Rembrandt seem to be saying about the scientist Niclaes Tulp and his science? What can we gather from the expressions and attitudes of the scientist's audience? What conclusions does the work permit concerning the study of anatomy and of science in general in early modern Europe?*

who, I think, gave the first occasion, and first suggested those meetings), and many others.

These meetings we held sometimes at *Dr. Goddard's* lodgings in *Wood Street* (or some convenient place near), on occasion of his keeping an operator in his house for grinding glasses for telescopes and microscopes; sometimes at a convenient place in *Cheapside,* and sometimes at *Gresham College,* or some place near adjoining.

Our business was (precluding matters of theology and state affairs) to discourse and consider of *Philosophical Enquiries,* and such as related thereunto; as *physic, anatomy, geometry, astronomy, navigation, statics, magnetics, chemics, mechanics,* and natural *experiments;* with the state of these studies, as then cultivated at home and abroad. We then discoursed of the *circulation of the blood, the valves in the veins, the venæ lactæ, the lymphatic vessels, the Copernican hypothesis, the nature of comets and new stars, the satellites of Jupiter, the oval shape* (as it then appeared) *of Saturn, the spots in the sun, and its turning on its own axis, the inequalities and selenography of the moon, the several phases of Venus and Mercury, the improvement of telescopes, and grinding of glasses for that purpose, the weight of air, the possibility, or impossibility of vacuities, and nature's abhorrence thereof, the Torricellian experiment in quicksilver, the descent of heavy bodies, and the degrees of acceleration therein;* and divers other things of like nature. Some of which were then but new discoveries, and others not so generally known and embraced, as now they are, with other things appertaining to what hath been called *The New Philosophy,* which from the times of *Galileo* at *Florence,* and *Sir Francis Bacon* (*Lord Verulam*) in England, hath been much cultivated in *Italy, France, Germany,* and other parts abroad, as well as with us in *England.*

About the year 1648, 1649, some of our company being removed to Oxford (first *Dr. Wilkins,* then I, and soon after *Dr. Goddard*), our company divided. Those in London continued to meet there as before (and we with them when we had occasion to be there), and those of us at Oxford; with *Dr. Ward* (since *Bishop of Salisbury*), *Dr. Ralph*

Bathurst (now *President of Trinity College in Oxford*), *Dr. Petty* (since *Sir William Petty*), *Dr. Willis* (then an eminent physician in *Oxford*), and divers others, continued such meetings in Oxford, and brought those studies into fashion there; meeting first at Dr. Petty's lodgings (in an apothecary's house), because of the convenience of inspecting drugs, and the like, as there was occasion; and after his remove to Ireland (though not so constantly), at the lodgings of Dr. Wilkin's, then Warden of Wadham College, and after his removal to Trinity College in Cambridge, at the lodgings of the Honourable Mr. Robert Boyle, then resident for divers years in Oxford.

(*B*) We would by no means be thought to slight or undervalue the philosophy of Aristotle, which hath for many ages obtained in the schools. But have (as we ought) a great esteem for him, and judge him to have been a very great man, and think those who do most slight him, to be such as are less acquainted with him. He was a great enquirer into the history of nature, but we do not think (nor did he think) that he had so exhausted the stock of knowledge of that kind as that there would be nothing left for the enquiry of after-times, as neither can we of this age hope to find out so much, but that there will be much left for those that come after us.

(*C*) I take its first ground and foundation to have been in London, about the year 1645, if not sooner, when Dr. Wilkins, (then chaplain to the Prince Elector Palatine, in London) and others, met weekly at a certain day and hour, under a certain penalty, and a weekly contribution for the charge of experiments, with certain rules agreed upon amongst us. When (to avoid diversion to other discourses, and for some other reasons) we barred all discourses of divinity, of state affairs, and of news, other than what concerned our business of Philosophy. These meetings we removed soon after to the Bull Head in Cheapside, and in term-time to Gresham College, where we met weekly at Mr. Foster's lecture (then Astronomy Professor there), and, after the lecture ended, repaired, sometimes to Mr. Foster's lodgings, sometimes to some other place not far distant, where we continued such enquiries, and our numbers increased.

About the years 1648–9 some of our company were removed to Oxford; first, Dr. Wilkins, then I, and soon after, Dr. Goddard, whereupon our company divided. Those at London (and we, when we had occasion to be there) met as before. Those of us at Oxford, with Dr. Ward, Dr. Petty, and many others of the most inquisitive persons in Oxford, met weekly (for some years) at Dr. Petty's lodgings, on the like account, to wit, so long as Dr. Petty continued in Oxford, and for some while after, because of the conveniences we had there (being the house of an apothecary) to view, and make use of, drugs and other like matters, as there was occasion.

Our meetings there were very numerous and very considerable. For, besides the diligence of persons studiously inquisitive, the novelty of the design made many to resort thither; who, when it ceased to be new, began to grow more remiss, or did pursue such inquiries at home. We did afterwards (Dr. Petty being gone for Ireland, and our numbers growing less) remove thence; and (some years before His Majesty's return) did meet at Dr. Wilkins's lodgings in Wadham College. In the meanwhile, our company at Gresham College being much again increased, by the accession of divers eminent and noble persons, upon His Majesty's return, we were (about the beginning of the year 1662) by His Majesty's grace and favour, incorporated by the name of the Royal Society.

*   *   *

REVIEW QUESTIONS

1. What does Wallis mean when he refers to the new philosophy?
2. What does his list of discussion topics tell us about early science?
3. What is the significance of the fact that the researches as well as the discussions of them were private, that is, not carried out under the state's sponsorship and guidance?
4. Why does Wallis refer to Aristotle?

19   THE ENLIGHTENMENT

The Enlightenment continued and extended the work begun by the revolution in science by spreading its new ideas to the general reading public and by extending them to new disciplines devoted to the study of human nature. As an intellectual and cultural movement of the eighteenth century, it was characterized by faith in the power of human reason to solve the basic problems of existence. Though centered in Paris, the Enlightenment was international in scope, manifesting itself throughout Europe and North America. Enlightened intellectuals turned critical reason on all received institutions and traditions with an eye to rebuilding human society according to the natural order of things. This natural order was born of three scientific cornerstones: mechanics, reason, and empiricism. Reason provided both an analogy for the universe and a tool for its analysis. Nature was assumed to be rational, to be ordered according to knowable, controllable relations—fundamental laws that could be discovered through observation and experimentation. Confidence in the existence of natural laws encouraged the search for similar laws governing human relations. Knowledge of these laws would serve humankind by making possible practical reforms at all levels of life.

By popularizing and extending the ideas of the scientific revolution, the Enlightenment encouraged a secular view of the world. In this way, it helped bring Europe into the modern era.

John Locke

FROM *An Essay Concerning Human Understanding*

John Locke (1632–1704) was an English philosopher whose thought contributed to the Enlightenment. He grew up in a liberal, Puritan family, the son of an attorney who fought in the Civil War against Charles I, and attended Christ's Church College, Oxford. He received his bachelor of arts in 1656, lectured in classical languages while earning his master of arts, and entered Oxford medical school to avoid being forced to join the clergy. In 1666, Lock attached himself to the household of the earl of Shaftesbury and his fortunes to the liberal Whig Party. Between 1675 and 1679, he lived in France, where he made contact with leading intellectuals of the late seventeenth century. On his return to England, he plunged into the controversy surrounding the succession of James II, an avowed Catholic with absolutist pretensions, to the throne of his brother, Charles II. Locke's patron, Shaftesbury, was imprisoned for his opposition, and Locke went into exile in 1683. Though he was involved to some extent in the Glorious Revolution of 1688, he returned to England in 1689, in the entourage of Mary, princess of Orange, who would assume the throne with her husband William. This was a period of intense political engagement for Locke, the fruits of which would be the publication of the Two Treatises on Government *(1690). Yet, he was also engaged in broader philosophical study. Locke's great work on epistemology,* An Essay Concerning Human Understanding, *appeared in the same year. It was a complete account of human knowledge, its source and its reliability. His argument was as simple as it was revolutionary. Rejecting all appeals to authority and theory, he showed that all knowledge derives from sensory perception and experience as considered and elaborated by reason. It was one of the most influential works in all of Western philosophy and had an immediate impact on enlightened thinkers. As Voltaire himself announced, "No Man ever had a more judicious or more methodical Genius . . . than Mr. Locke."*

From *An Essay Concerning Human Understanding*, by John Locke, edited by Roger Woolhouse (New York: Penguin Books, 1997), pp. 109–112.

*   *   *

Book II
Of Ideas

Chapter I
Of Ideas in General, and Their Original

IDEA IS THE OBJECT OF THINKING.

Every man being conscious to himself, that he thinks, and that which his mind is applied about, whilst thinking, being the ideas, that are there, 'tis past doubt, that men have in their minds several ideas, such as are those expressed by the words, *whiteness, hardness, sweetness, thinking, motion, man, elephant, army, drunkenness,* and others: it is in the first place then to be inquired, how he comes by them? I know it is a received doctrine, that men have native ideas, and original characters stamped upon their minds, in their very first being. This opinion I have at large examined already; and, I suppose, what I have said in the foregoing book, will be much more easily admitted, when I have shown, whence the understanding may get all the ideas it has, and by what ways and degrees they may come into the mind; for which I shall appeal to everyone's own observation and experience.

ALL IDEAS COME FROM SENSATION OR REFLECTION.

Let us then suppose the mind to be, as we say, white paper, void of all characters, without any ideas; how comes it to be furnished? Whence comes it by that vast store, which the busy and boundless fancy of man has painted on it, with an almost endless variety? Whence has it all the materials of reason and knowledge? To this I answer, in one world, from *experience* in that, all our knowledge is founded; and from that it ultimately derives itself. Our observation employed either about *external sensible objects; or about the internal operations of our minds, perceived and reflected on by ourselves, is that, which supplies our understandings with all the materials of thinking.* These two are the fountains of knowledge, from whence all the ideas we have, or can naturally have, do spring.

THE OBJECTS OF SENSATION ONE SOURCE OF IDEAS.

First, *our senses,* conversant about particular sensible objects, do *convey into the mind,* several distinct *perceptions* of things, according to those various ways, wherein those objects do affect them: and thus we come by those ideas, we have of *yellow, white, heat, cold, soft, hard, bitter, sweet,* and all those which we call sensible qualities, which when I say the senses convey into the mind, I mean, they from external objects convey into the mind what produces there those *perceptions.* This great source, of most of the ideas we have, depending wholly upon our senses, and derived by them to the understanding, I call *sensation.*

THE OPERATIONS OF OUR MINDS, THE OTHER SOURCE OF THEM.

Secondly, the other fountain, from which experience furnisheth the understanding with ideas, is the *perception of the operations of our own minds* within us, as it is employed about the ideas it has got; which operations, when the soul comes to reflect on, and consider, do furnish the understanding with another set of ideas, which could not be had from things without; and such are, *perception, thinking, doubting, believing, reasoning, knowing, willing,* and all the different actings of our own minds; which we being conscious of, and observing in ourselves, do from these receive into our understandings, as distinct ideas, as we do from bodies affecting our senses. This source of ideas, every man has wholly in himself: and though it be not sense, as having nothing to do with external objects; yet it is very like it, and might properly enough be called internal sense. But as I call the other *sensation,* so I call this *reflection,* the ideas it affords being such only, as the mind gets by reflecting on its own operations within itself. By *reflection* then, in the following part of this discourse, I would be understood to mean, that notice which the mind takes of its own operations, and the manner of them, by reason whereof, there come to be ideas of these operations in the understanding. These two, I say, *viz.* external, material things, as the objects of *sensation;* and the operations of our own minds within, as the objects of *reflection,* are, to me, the only originals, from whence all our ideas take their beginnings. The term *operations* here, I use in a large sense, as comprehending not barely the actions of the mind about its ideas, but some sort of passions arising sometimes from them, such as is the satisfaction or uneasiness arising from any thought.

ALL OUR IDEAS ARE OF THE ONE OR THE OTHER OF THESE.

The understanding seems to me, not to have the least glimmering of any ideas, which it doth not receive from one of these two. *External objects furnish the mind with the ideas of sensible qualities,* which are all those different perceptions they produce in us: and the *mind furnishes the understanding with ideas of its own operations.*

These, when we have taken a full survey of them, and their several modes, combinations, and relations, we shall find to contain all our whole stock of ideas; and that we have nothing in our minds, which did not come in, one of these two ways. Let anyone examine his own thoughts, and throughly search into his understanding, and then let him tell me, whether all the original ideas he has there, are any other than of the objects of his *senses;* or of the operations of his mind, considered as objects of his *reflection*: and how great a mass of knowledge soever he imagines to be lodged there, he will, upon taking a strict view, see, that he has *not any idea in his mind, but what one of these two have imprinted;* though, perhaps, with infinite variety compounded and enlarged by the understanding, as we shall see hereafter.

OBSERVABLE IN CHILDREN.

He that attentively considers the state of a *child,* at his first coming into the world, will have little reason to think him stored with plenty of ideas, that are to be the matter of his future knowledge. 'Tis by degrees he comes to be furnished with them: and though the ideas of obvious and familiar qualities, imprint themselves, before the memory begins to keep a register of time and order, yet 'tis often so late, before some unusual qualities come in the way, that there are few men that cannot recollect the beginning of their acquaintance with them: and if it were worthwhile, no doubt a child might be so ordered, as to have but a very few, even of the ordinary ideas, till he were grown up to a man. But all that are born into the world being surrounded with bodies, that perpetually and diversely affect them, variety of ideas, whether care be taken about it or no, are imprinted on the minds of children. *Light,* and *colours,* are busy at hand everywhere, when the eye is but open; *sounds,* and some *tangible qualities* fail not to solicit their proper senses, and force an entrance to the mind; but yet, I think, it will be granted easily, that if a child were kept in a place, where he never saw any other but black and white, till he were a man, he would have no more ideas of scarlet or green, than he that from his childhood never tasted an oyster, or a pineapple, has of those particular relishes.

MEN ARE DIFFERENTLY FURNISHED WITH THESE, ACCORDING TO THE DIFFERENT OBJECTS THEY CONVERSE WITH.

Men then come to be furnished with fewer or more simple ideas from without, according as the *objects,* they converse with, afford greater or less variety; and from the operation of their minds within, according as they more or less *reflect* on them. For, though he that contemplates the operations of his mind, cannot but have plain and clear *ideas* of them; yet unless he turn his thoughts that way, and considers them *attentively,* he will no more have clear and distinct ideas of all the *operations of his mind,* and all that may be observed therein, than he will have all the particular ideas of any landscape, or of the parts and motions of a clock, who will not turn his eyes to it, and with attention heed all the parts of it. The picture, or clock may be so placed, that they may come in his way every day; but yet he will have but a confused idea of all the parts they are made up of, till he *applies himself with attention,* to consider them each in particular.

IDEAS OF REFLECTION LATER, BECAUSE THEY NEED ATTENTION.

And hence we see the reason, why 'tis pretty late, before most children get ideas of the operations of their own minds; and some have not any very clear, or perfect ideas of the greatest part of them all their lives. Because, though they pass there continually; yet like floating visions, they make not deep impressions enough, to leave in the mind clear distinct lasting ideas, till the understanding turns inwards upon itself, *reflects* on its own *operations,* and makes them the object of its own contemplation. Children, when they come first into it, are surrounded with a world of new things, which, by a constant solicitation of their senses, draw the mind constantly to them, forward to take notice of new, and apt to be delighted with the variety of changing objects. Thus the first years are usually employed and diverted in looking abroad. Men's business in them is to acquaint themselves with what is to be found without; and so growing up in a constant attention to outward sensations, seldom make any considerable reflection on what passes within them, till they come to be of riper years; and some scarce ever at all.

THE SOUL BEGINS TO HAVE IDEAS, WHEN IT BEGINS TO PERCEIVE.

To ask, *at what time a man has first any ideas,* is to ask, when he begins to perceive; having ideas, and perception, being the same thing. I know it is an opinion, that the soul always thinks,[1] and that it has the actual perception of ideas in itself constantly, as long as it exists; and that actual thinking is as inseparable from the soul, as actual extension is from the body; which if true, to inquire after the beginning of a man's ideas, is the same, as to inquire after the beginning of his soul. For by this account, soul and its ideas, as body and its extension, will begin to exist both at the same time.

*　　*　　*

REVIEW QUESTIONS

1. What, according to Locke, is the source of human knowledge? How does this compare with the philosophy of Descartes?
2. How reliable is human knowledge as a source of truth?
3. What does Locke mean by *the soul?*
4. How does Locke arrive at his epistemology?

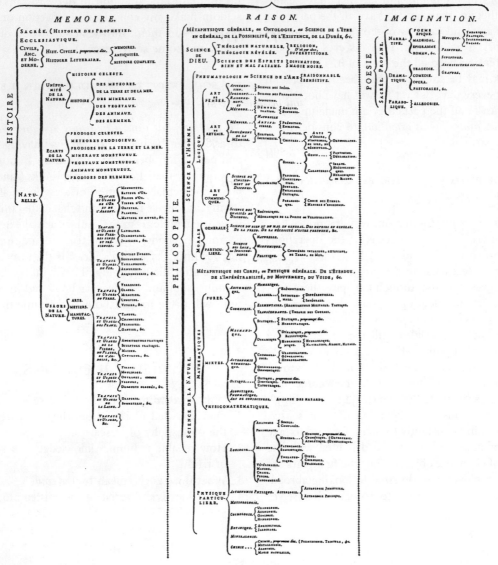

SYSTÉME FIGURÉ
DES CONNOISSANCES HUMAINES.

SYSTÊME FIGURÉ DES CONNOISSANCES HUMAINES (1751)

Denis Diderot

The Encyclopédie was perhaps the single most famous publication of the Enlightenment. Intended as a compendium of all useful knowledge, it became an exemplification of reason applied to human behavior. Representatives of all new schools of thought found a place in its pages. The encyclopedia soon became famous as well for its discussion of innovations in crafts and trades. Throughout, it served as a vehicle for skepticism toward and criticism of established institutions and practices and, so, established itself in the vanguard of progressive thought. What does the organization and content of the Système figuré reveal about Diderot's conception of human knowledge? Why does reason, so central to enlightened thought and reform, appear in the middle of the table rather than on the left, in the first position? What aspects of human thought and knowledge does the table exclude? Is the Système figuré a work of propaganda, and, if so, what is its ideological content?

VOLTAIRE

FROM *Letters Concerning the English Nation*

François-Marie Arouet (1694–1778) was the son of a Parisian notary and royal official at the Cour des Comptes and became one of the fathers of the Enlightenment in France. As a youngster, he attached himself to his godfather, the abbé de Chateauneuf, a freethinker who introduced him to progressive circles in the French capital. He attended the Jesuit Collège Louis-le-Grand, where he graduated in 1711 with a degree in philosophy. Though he enrolled in law school, he decided on a literary career and frequented the salons of Paris. His first success came in 1718 with the staging of Oedipus. *At this point, he adopted the pen name of Voltaire. Legal difficulties that followed a brawl with the servants of the chevalier de Rohan resulted in Voltaire's exile to England. From 1726 to 1729 he was brought into personal contact with English philosophy, science, politics, and culture. Voltaire considered English thought and institutions the best in human history and devoted himself to their introduction to France on his return. His* Letters Concerning the English Nation *(1734) brought fame and notoriety. A warrant for his arrest forced him to flee once again. In fact, his career was marked by a series of legal difficulties and exiles: to Circey in Champagne in 1734, to Berlin and the court of Frederick II in 1750, to Geneva in 1752, and to Ferney in 1757. His lifelong commitments to freedom, toleration, reform, and empiricism made Voltaire one of the great figures of the Enlightenment.*

From *Letters Concerning the English Nation,* by F. Arouet, edited by Nicholas Cronk (Oxford, Eng.: Oxford University Press, 1994), pp. 61–66.

*　　*　　*

Letter 13
On Mr. Locke

Perhaps no Man ever had a more judicious or more methodical Genius, or was a more acute Logician than Mr. *Locke,* and yet he was not deeply skill'd in the Mathematicks. This great Man could never subject himself to the tedious Fatigue of Calculations, nor to the dry Pursuit of Mathematical Truths, which do not at first present any sensible Objects to the Mind; and no one has given better Proofs than he, that 'tis possible for a Man to have a geometrical Head without the Assistance of Geometry. Before his Time, several great Philosophers had declar'd, in the most positive Terms, what the Soul of Man is; but as these absolutely knew nothing about it, they might very well be allow'd to differ entirely in opinion from one another.

In *Greece,* the infant Seat of Arts and of Errors, and where the Grandeur as well as Folly of the human Mind went such prodigious Lengths, the People us'd to reason about the Soul in the very same Manner as we do.

The divine *Anaxagoras,* in whose Honour an Altar was erected, for his having taught Mankind that the Sun was greater than *Peloponnesus,* that Snow was black, and that the Heavens were of

Stone; affirm'd that the Soul was an aerial Spirit, but at the same Time immortal. *Diogenes,* (not he who was a cynical Philosopher after having coyn'd base Money) declar'd that the Soul was a Portion of the Substance of God; an Idea which we must confess was very sublime. *Epicurus* maintain'd that it was compos'd of Parts in the same Manner as the Body.

Aristotle who has been explain'd a thousand Ways, because he is unintelligible, was of Opinion, according to some of his Disciples, that the Understanding in all Men is one and the same Substance.

The divine *Plato,* Master of the divine *Aristotle,* and the divine *Socrates* Master of the divine *Plato,* us'd-to say that the Soul was corporeal and eternal. No doubt but the Demon of *Socrates* had instructed him in the Nature of it. Some People, indeed, pretend, that a Man who boasted his being attended by a familiar Genius, must infallibly be either a Knave or a Madman, but this kind of People are seldom satisfied with any Thing but Reason.

With regard to the Fathers of the Church, several in the primitive Ages believ'd that the Soul was human, and the Angels and God corporeal. Men naturally improve upon every System. St. *Bernard,* as Father *Mabillon* confesses, taught that the Soul after Death does not see God in the celestial Regions, but converses with *Christ's* human Nature only. However, he was not believ'd this Time on his bare Word; the Adventure of the Crusade having a little sunk the Credit of his Oracles. Afterwards a thousand Schoolmen arose, such as the irrefragable Doctor, the subtil Doctor, the angelic Doctor, the seraphic Doctor, and the cherubic Doctor, who were all sure that they had a very clear and distinct Idea of the Soul, and yet wrote in such a Manner, that one would conclude they were resolv'd no one should understand a Word in their Writings. Our *Des Cartes,* born not to discover the Errors of Antiquity, but to substitute his own in the Room of them; and hurried away by that systematic Spirit which throws a Cloud over the Minds of the greatest Men, thought he had demonstrated that the Soul is the same Thing as

Thought, in the same Manner as Matter, in his Opinion, is the same as Extension. He asserted, that Man thinks eternally, and that the Soul, at its coming into the Body, is inform'd with the whole Series of metaphysical Notions; knowing God, infinite Space, possessing all abstract Ideas; in a Word, completely endued with the most sublime Lights, which it unhappily forgets at its issuing from the Womb.

Father *Malbranche,* in his sublime Illusions, not only admitted innate Ideas, but did not doubt of our living wholly in God, and that God is, as it were, our Soul.

Such a Multitude of Reasoners having written the Romance of the Soul, a Sage at last arose, who gave, with an Air of the greatest Modesty, the History of it. Mr. *Locke* has display'd the human Soul, in the same Manner as an excellent Anatomist explains the Springs of the human Body. He every where takes the Light of Physicks for his Guide. He sometimes presumes to speak affirmatively, but then he presumes also to doubt. Instead of concluding at once what we know not, he examines gradually what we wou'd know. He takes an Infant at the Instant of his Birth; he traces, Step by Step, the Progress of his Understanding; examines what Things he has in common with Beasts, and what he possesses above them. Above all he consults himself; the being conscious that he himself thinks.

I shall leave, says he, to those who know more of this Matter than my self, the examining whether the Soul exists before or after the Organization of our Bodies. But I confess that 'tis my Lot to be animated with one of those heavy Souls which do not think always; and I am even so unhappy as not to conceive, that 'tis more necessary the Soul should think perpetually, than that Bodies shou'd be for ever in Motion.

With regard to my self, I shall boast that I have the Honour to be as stupid in this Particular as Mr. *Locke.* No one shall ever make me believe, that I think always; and I am as little inclin'd as he cou'd be, to fancy that some Weeks after I was conceiv'd, I was a very learned Soul; knowing at that Time a thousand Things which I forgot at my

Birth; and possessing when in the Womb, (tho' to no Manner of Purpose,) Knowledge which I lost the Instant I had occasion for it; and which I have never since been able to recover perfectly.

Mr. *Locke* after having destroy'd innate Ideas; after having fully renounc'd the Vanity of believing that we think always; after having laid down, from the most solid Principles, that Ideas enter the Mind through the Senses; having examin'd our simple and complex Ideas; having trac'd the human Mind through its several Operations; having shew'd that all the Languages in the World are imperfect, and the great Abuse that is made of Words every Moment; he at last comes to consider the Extent or rather the narrow Limits of human Knowledge. 'Twas in this Chapter he presum'd to advance, but very modestly, the following Words, 'We shall, perhaps, never be capable of knowing, whether a Being, purely material, thinks or not.' This sage Assertion was, by more Divines than one, look'd upon as a scandalous Declaration that the Soul is material and mortal. Some *Englishmen,* devout after their Way, sounded an Alarm. The Superstitious are the same in Society as Cowards in an Army; they themselves are seiz'd with a panic Fear, and communicate it to others. 'Twas loudly exclaim'd, that Mr. *Locke* intended to destroy Religion; nevertheless, Religion had nothing to do in the Affair, it being a Question purely Philosophical, altogether independent on Faith and Revelation. Mr. *Locke*'s Opponents needed but to examine, calmly and impartially, whether the declaring that Matter can think, implies a Contradiction; and whether God is able to communicate Thought to Matter. But Divines are too apt to begin their Declarations with saying, that God is offended when People differ from them in Opinion; in which they too much resemble the bad Poets, who us'd to declare publickly that *Boileau* spake irreverently of *Lewis* the Fourteenth, because he ridicul'd their stupid Productions Bishop *Stillingfleet* got the Reputation of a calm and unprejudic'd Divine, because he did not expressly make use of injurious Terms in his Dispute with Mr. *Locke.* That Divine entred the Lists against him, but was defeated; for he argued as a Schoolman, and *Locke* as a Philosopher who was perfectly acquainted with the strong as well as the weak Side of the human Mind, and who fought with Weapons whose Temper he knew. If I might presume to give my Opinion on so delicate a Subject after Mr. *Locke,* I would say, that Men have long disputed on the Nature and the Immortality of the Soul. With regard to its Immortality 'tis impossible to give a Demonstration of it, since its Nature is still the Subject of Controversy; which however must be thoroughly understood, before a Person can be able to determine whether it be immortal or not. Human Reason is so little able, merely by its own Strength, to demonstrate the Immortality of the Soul, that 'twas absolutely necessary Religion should reveal it to us. 'Tis of Advantage to Society in general, that Mankind should believe the Soul to be immortal; Faith commands us to do this; nothing more is requir'd, and the Matter is clear'd up at once. But 'tis otherwise with respect to its Nature; 'tis of little Importance to Religion, which only requires the Soul to be virtuous, what Substance it may be made of. 'Tis a Clock which is given us to regulate, but the Artist has not told us of what Materials the Spring of this Clock is compos'd.

I am a Body and, I think, that's all I know of the Matter. Shall I ascribe to an unknown Cause, what I can so easily impute to the only second Cause I am acquainted with? Here all the School Philosophers interrupt me with their Arguments, and declare that there is only Extension and Solidity in Bodies, and that there they can have nothing but Motion and Figure. Now Motion, Figure, Extension and Solidity cannot form a Thought, and consequently the Soul cannot be Matter. All this, so often repeated, mighty Series of Reasoning, amounts to no more than this; I am absolutely ignorant what Matter is; I guess, but imperfectly, some Properties of it; now, I absolutely cannot tell whether these Properties may be joyn'd to Thought. As I therefore know nothing, I maintain positively that Matter cannot think. In this Manner do the Schools reason.

Mr. *Locke* address'd these Gentlemen in the candid, sincere Manner following. At least confess your selves to be as ignorant as I. Neither your Imaginations nor mine are able to comprehend in what manner a Body is susceptible of Ideas; and do you conceive better in what manner a Substance, of what kind soever, is susceptible of them? As you cannot comprehend either Matter or Spirit, why will you presume to assert any thing?

The superstitious Man comes afterwards, and declares, that all those must be burnt for the Good of their Souls, who so much as suspect that 'tis possible for the Body to think without any foreign Assistance. But what would these People say should they themselves be prov'd irreligious? And indeed, what Man can presume to assert, without being guilty at the same time of the greatest Impiety, that 'tis impossible for the Creator to form Matter with Thought and Sensation? Consider only, I beg you, what a Dilemma you bring yourselves into; you who confine in this Manner the Power of the Creator. Beasts have the same Organs, the same Sensations, the same Perceptions as we; they have Memory, and combine certain Ideas. In case it was not in the Power of God to animate Matter, and inform it with Sensation, the Consequence would be, either that Beasts are mere Machines, or that they have a spiritual Soul.

Methinks 'tis clearly evident that Beasts cannot be mere Machines, which I prove thus. God has given them the very same Organs of Sensation as to us: If therefore they have no Sensation, God has created a useless Thing; now according to your own Confession God does nothing in vain; he therefore did not create so many Organs of Sensation, merely for them to be uninform'd with this Faculty; consequently Beasts are not mere Machines. Beasts, according to your Assertion, cannot be animated with a spiritual Soul; you will therefore, in spight of your self, be reduc'd to this only Assertion, viz. that God has endued the Organs of Beasts, who are mere Matter, with the Faculties of Sensation and Perception, which you call Instinct in them. But why may not God if he pleases, communicate to our more delicate Organs, that Faculty of feeling, perceiving, and thinking, which we call human Reason? To whatever Side you turn, you are forc'd to acknowledge your own Ignorance, and the boundless Power of the Creator. Exclaim therefore no more against the sage, the modest Philosophy of Mr. *Locke,* which so far from interfering with Religion, would be of use to demonstrate the Truth of it, in case Religion wanted any such Support. For what Philosophy can be of a more religious Nature than that, which affirming nothing but what it conceives clearly; and conscious of its own Weakness, declares that we must always have recourse to God in our examining of the first Principles.

Besides, we must not be apprehensive, that any philosophical Opinion will ever prejudice the Religion of a Country. Tho' our Demonstrations clash directly with our Mysteries, that's nothing to the Purpose, for the latter are not less rever'd upon that Account by our Christian Philosophers, who know very well that the Objects of Reason and those of Faith are of a very different Nature. Philosophers will never form a religious Sect, the Reason of which is, their Writings are not calculated for the Vulgar, and they themselves are free from Enthusiasm. If we divide Mankind into twenty Parts, 'twill be found that nineteen of these consist of Persons employ'd in manual Labour, who will never know that such a Man as Mr. *Locke* existed. In the remaining twentieth Part how few are Readers? And among such as are so, twenty amuse themselves with Romances to one who studies Philosophy. The thinking Part of Mankind are confin'd to a very small Number, and these will never disturb the Peace and Tranquillity of the World.

Neither *Montagne, Locke, Bayle, Spinoza, Hobbes,* the Lord *Shaftsbury, Collins* nor *Toland* lighted up the Firebrand of Discord in their Countries; this has generally been the Work of Divines, who being at first puff'd up with the Ambition of becoming Chiefs of a Sect, soon grew very desirous of being at the Head of a Party. But what do I say? All the Works of the modern Philosophers put together will never make so much Noise as even the Dispute which arose among the *Franciscans,* merely about the Fashion of their Sleeves and of their Cowls.

Letter XIV.

On *Des Cartes* and Sir *Isaac Newton*.

A Frenchman who arrives in *London,* will find Philosophy, like every Thing else, very much chang'd there. He had left the World a *plenum,* and he now finds it a *vacuum.* At *Paris* the Universe is seen, compos'd of Vortices of subtile Matter; but nothing like it is seen in *London.* In *France,* 'tis the Pressure of the Moon that causes the Tides; but in *England* 'tis the Sea that gravitates towards the Moon; so that when you think that the Moon should make it Flood with us, those Gentlemen fancy it should be Ebb, which, very unluckily, cannot be prov'd. For to be able to do this, 'tis necessary the Moon and the Tides should have been enquir'd into, at the very instant of the Creation.

You'll observe farther, that the Sun, which in *France* is said to have nothing to do in the Affair, comes in here for very near a quarter of its Assistance. According to your *Cartesians,* every Thing is perform'd by an Impulsion, of which we have very little Notion; and according to Sir *Isaac Newton,* 'tis by an Attraction, the Cause of which is as much unknown to us. At *Paris* you imagine that the Earth is shap'd like a Melon, or of an oblique Figure; at *London* it has an oblate one. A *Cartesian* declares that Light exists in the Air; but a *Newtonian* asserts that it comes from the Sun in six Minutes and a half. The several Operations of your Chymistry are perform'd by Acids, Alkalies and subtile Matter; but Attraction prevails even in Chymistry among the *English.*

The very Essence of Things is totally chang'd. You neither are agreed upon the Definition of the Soul, nor on that of Matter. *Descartes,* as I observ'd in my last, maintains that the Soul is the same Thing with Thought, and Mr. *Locke* has given a pretty good Proof of the contrary.

Descartes asserts farther, that Extension alone constitutes Matter, but Sir *Isaac* adds Solidity to it.

How furiously contradictory are these Opinions! *Non nostrum inter vos tantas componere lites.*

VIRGIL, Eclogue III.

'Tis not for us to end such great Disputes.

This famous *Newton,* this Destroyer of the *Cartesian* System, died in *March Anno* 1727. His Countrymen honour'd him in his Life-Time, and interr'd him as tho' he had been a King who had made his People happy.

The *English* read with the highest Satisfaction, and translated into their Tongue, the Elogium of Sir *Isaac Newton,* which Mr. *de Fontenelle,* spoke in the Academy of Sciences. Mr. *de Fontenelle* presides as Judge over Philosophers; and the *English* expected his Decision, as a solemn Declaration of the Superiority of the *English* Philosophy over that of the *French.* But when 'twas found that this Gentleman had compar'd *Des Cartes* to Sir *Isaac,* the whole Royal Society in *London* rose up in Arms. So far from acquiescing with Mr. *Fontenelle's* Judgment, they criticis'd his Discourse. And even several (who however were not the ablest Philosophers in that Body) were offended at the Comparison; and for no other Reason but because *Des Cartes* was a Frenchman.

It must be confess'd that these two great Men differ'd very much in Conduct, in Fortune, and in Philosophy.

Nature had indulg'd *Des Cartes* a shining and strong Imagination, whence he became a very singular Person both in private Life, and in his Manner of Reasoning. This Imagination could not conceal itself even in his philosophical Works, which are every where adorn'd with very shining, ingenious Metaphors and Figures. Nature had almost made him a Poet; and indeed he wrote a Piece of Poetry for the Entertainment of *Christina* Queen of *Sweden,* which however was suppress'd in Honour to his Memory.

He embrac'd a Military Life for some Time, and afterwards becoming a complete Philosopher, he did not think the Passion of Love derogatory to his Character. He had by his Mistress a Daughter call'd *Froncine,* who died young, and was very much regretted by him. Thus he experienc'd every Passion incident to Mankind.

He was a long Time of Opinion, that it would be necessary for him to fly from the Society of his Fellow Creatures, and especially from his native Country, in order to enjoy the Happiness of cultivating his philosophical Studies in full Liberty.

Des Cartes was very right, for his Cotemporaries were not knowing enough to improve and enlighten his Understanding, and were capable of little else than of giving him Uneasiness.

He left *France* purely to go in search of Truth, which was then persecuted by the wretched Philosophy of the Schools. However, he found that Reason was as much disguis'd and deprav'd in the Universities of *Holland,* into which he withdrew, as in his own Country. For at the Time that the *French* condemn'd the only Propositions of his Philosophy which were true, he was persecuted by the pretended Philosophers of *Holland,* who understood him no better; and who, having a nearer View of his Glory, hated his Person the more, so that he was oblig'd to leave *Utrecht. Des Cartes* was injuriously accus'd of being an Atheist, the last Refuge of religious Scandal: And he who had employ'd all the Sagacity and Penetration of his Genius, in searching for new Proofs of the Existence of a God, was suspected to believe there was no such Being.

Such a Persecution from all Sides, must necessarily suppose a most exalted Merit as well as a very distinguish'd Reputation, and indeed he possess'd both. Reason at that Time darted a Ray upon the World thro' the Gloom of the Schools, and the Prejudices of popular Superstition. At last his Name spread so universally, that the *French* were desirous of bringing him back into his native Country by Rewards, and accordingly offer'd him an annual Pension of a thousand Crowns. Upon these Hopes *Des Cartes* return'd to *France;* paid the Fees of his Patent, which was sold at that Time, but no Pension was settled upon him. Thus disappointed, he return'd to his Solitude in *North-Holland,* where he again pursued the Study of Philosophy, whilst the great *Galileo,* at fourscore Years of Age, was groaning in the Prisons of the Inquisition, only for having demonstrated the Earth's Motion.

At last *Des Cartes* was snatch'd from the World in the Flower of his Age at *Stockholm.* His Death was owing to a bad Regimen, and he expir'd in the Midst of some *Literati* who were his Enemies, and under the Hands of a Physician to whom he was odious.

The Progress of Sir *Isaac Newton*'s Life was quite different. He liv'd happy, and very much honour'd in his native Country, to the Age of fourscore and five Years.

'Twas his peculiar Felicity, not only to be born in a Country of Liberty, but in an Age when all scholastic Impertinencies were banish'd from the World. Reason alone was cultivated, and Mankind cou'd only be his Pupil, not his Enemy.

One very singular Difference in the Lives of these two great Men is, that Sir *Isaac,* during the long Course of Years he enjoy'd was never sensible to any Passion, was not subject to the common Frailties of Mankind, nor ever had any Commerce with Women; a Circumstance which was assur'd me by the Physician and Surgeon who attended him in his last Moments.

We may admire Sir *Isaac Newton* on this Occasion, but then we must not censure *Des Cartes.*

The Opinion that generally prevails in *England* with regard to these two Philosophers is, that the latter was a Dreamer, and the former a Sage.

Very few People in *England* read *Descartes,* whose Works indeed are now useless. On the other Side, but a small Number peruse those of Sir *Isaac,* because to do this the Student must be deeply skill'd in the Mathematicks, otherwise those Works will be unintelligible to him. But notwithstanding this, these great Men are the Subject of every One's Discourse. Sir *Isaac Newton* is allow'd every Advantage, whilst *Des Cartes* is not indulg'd a single one. According to some, 'tis to the former that we owe the Discovery of a *Vacuum,* that the Air is a heavy Body, and the Invention of Telescopes. In a Word, Sir *Isaac Newton* is here as the *Hercules* of fabulous Story, to whom the Ignorant ascrib'd all the Feats of ancient Heroes.

In a Critique that was made in *London* on Mr. *de Fontenelle*'s Discourse, the Writer presum'd to assert that *Des Cartes* was not a great Geometrician. Those who make such a Declaration may justly be reproach'd with flying in their Master's Face. *Des Cartes* extended the Limits of Geometry as far beyond the Place where he found them, as Sir *Isaac* did after him. The former first taught the Method of expressing Curves by Equations. This Geometry which, Thanks to him for it, is now grown common, was so abstruse in his Time, that not so much as one Professor would undertake to explain it; and *Schotten* in *Holland*, and *Format* in *France*, were the only Men who understood it.

He applied this geometrical and inventive Genius to Dioptricks, which, when treated of by him, became a new Art. And if he was mistaken in some Things, the Reason of that is, a Man who discovers a new Tract of Land cannot at once know all the Properties of the Soil. Those who come after him, and make these Lands fruitful, are at least oblig'd to him for the Discovery. I will not deny but that there are innumerable Errors in the rest of *Des Cartes*'s Works.

Geometry was a Guide he himself had in some Measure fashion'd, which would have conducted him safely thro' the several Paths of natural Philosophy. Nevertheless he at last abandon'd this Guide, and gave entirely into the Humour of forming Hypotheses; and then Philosophy was no more than an ingenious Romance, fit only to amuse the Ignorant. He was mistaken in the Nature of the Soul, in the Proofs of the Existence of a God, in Matter, in the Laws of Motion, and in the Nature of Light. He admitted innate Ideas, he invented new Elements, he created a World; he made Man according to his own Fancy; and 'tis justly said, that the Man of *Des Cartes* is in Fact that of *Des Cartes* only, very different from the real one.

He push'd his metaphysical Errors so far, as to declare that two and two make four, for no other Reason but because God would have it so. However, 'twill not be making him too great a Compliment if we affirm that he was valuable even in his Mistakes. He deceiv'd himself, but then it was at least in a methodical Way. He destroy'd all the absurd Chimæra's with which Youth had been infatuated for two thousand Years. He taught his Cotemporaries how to reason, and enabled them to employ his own Weapons against himself. If *Des Cartes* did not pay in good Money, he however did great Service in crying down that of a base Alloy.

I indeed believe, that very few will presume to compare his Philosophy in any respect with that of Sir *Isaac Newton*. The former is an Essay, the latter a Master-Piece: But then the Man who first brought us to the Path of Truth, was perhaps as great a Genius as he who afterwards conducted us through it.

Des Cartes gave Sight to the Blind. These saw the Errors of Antiquity and of the Sciences. The Path he struck out is since become boundless. *Rohault*'s little Work was during some Years a complete System of Physicks; but now all the Transactions of the several Academies in *Europe* put together do not form so much as the Beginning of a System. In fathoming this Abyss no Bottom has been found. We are now to examine what Discoveries Sir *Isaac Newton* has made in it.

*   *   *

REVIEW QUESTIONS

1. How does Voltaire describe the scientific revolution?
2. What are its consequences?
3. What was the particular contribution of John Locke?
4. Why does Voltaire single out Descartes and Newton?
5. What differentiates their methods?
6. Why, according to Voltaire, was Descartes persecuted and Newton not?

BARON DE LA BRÈDE ET DE MONTESQUIEU

FROM *The Spirit of the Laws*

Charles-Louis de Secondat, baron de La Brède et de Montesquieu (1689–1755), was a French philosopher, historian, and satirist. He was born at the family chateau of La Brède near Bordeaux. His great-grandfather, a Calvinist, had been rewarded with a title of nobility for his service to Henry IV. In the next generation, however, the family had converted to Catholicism and had entered the judicial nobility by purchasing offices in the Parlement of Bordeaux. Charles-Louis de Secondat inherited one of these offices, that of presiding judge of the criminal division, in 1712 and held it for eleven years. Montesquieu studied law at the University of Bordeaux, and married Jeanne de Lartique, a practicing Calvinist who risked persecution for her faith. This and his own background may explain Montesquieu's lifelong championship of religious toleration. He entered the literary world with the publication of his Persian Letters (1721). Shortly thereafter Montesquieu moved to Paris and joined the intellectual world of the salon. His most influential work, at least among his contemporaries, was The Spirit of the Laws (1748). By 1750, twenty-two editions had appeared, and it had been translated into every major European language. Montesquieu explored the role of law in shaping political society and sought theoretical and practical responses to the problem of despotism. He envisioned political order as a human body, possessed of a dynamic balance among its various parts. A healthy political order contained inner mechanisms to maintain its balance. An ideal example of such separation and balance of power was the English system of monarch and parliament. These ideas made Montesquieu one of the most widely read and influential figures of the Enlightenment.

From *The Spirit of Laws*, vol. 1, Montesquieu, translated by Thomas Nugent (London: Bell, 1901).

Book XII
Of the Laws that Establish Political Liberty, in Relation to the Subject

I. It is not sufficient to have treated of political liberty in relation to the constitution; we must examine it likewise in the relation it bears to the subject.

We have observed that in the former case it arises from a certain distribution of the three powers; but in the latter we must consider it in another light. It consists in security, or in the opinion people have of their country.

The constitution may happen to be free, and the subject not. The subject may be free, and not the constitution. In those cases, the constitution will be free by right, and not in fact; the subject will be free in fact, and not by right.

It is the disposition only of the laws, and even of the fundamental laws, that constitutes liberty in relation to the constitution. But as it regards the subject: manners, customs, or received examples may give rise to it, and particular civil laws may encourage it, as we shall presently observe.

Further, as in most states liberty is more checked or depressed than their constitution requires, it is proper to treat of the particular laws that in each constitution are apt to assist or check the principle of liberty which each state is capable of receiving.

II. Philosophic liberty consists in the free exercise of the will; or at least, if we must speak agreeably to all systems, in an opinion that we have the free exercise of our will. Political liberty consists in securing, or, at least, in the opinion that we enjoy security.

This security is never more dangerously attacked than in public or private accusations. It is, therefore, on the goodness of criminal laws that the liberty of the subject principally depends.

Criminal laws did not receive their full perfection all at once. Even in places where liberty has been most sought after, it has not been always found. Aristotle informs us that at Cumae the parents of the accuser might be witnesses. So imperfect was the law under the kings of Rome, that Servius Tullius pronounced sentence against the children of Ancus Martius, who were charged with having assassinated the king, his father-in-law. Under the first kings of France, Clotarius made a law that nobody should be condemned without being heard, which shows that a contrary custom had prevailed in some particular case or among some barbarous people. It was Charondas that first established penalties against false witnesses. When the subject has no fence to secure his innocence, he has none for his liberty.

The knowledge already acquired in some countries, or that may be hereafter attained in others, concerning the surest rules to be observed in criminal judgments, is more interesting to mankind than any other thing in the world.

Liberty can be founded on the practice of this knowledge only; and supposing a state to have the best laws imaginable in this respect, a person tried under that state, and conto be hanged the next day, would have much more liberty than a pasha enjoys in Turkey.

Those laws which condemn a man to death on the deposition of a single witness are fatal to liberty. In reason there should be two, because a witness who affirms, and the accused who denies, make an equal balance, and a third must incline the scale.

The Greeks and Romans required one voice more to condemn; but our French laws insist upon two. The Greeks pretend that their custom was established by the gods; but this more justly may be said of ours.

III. Liberty is in perfection when criminal laws derive each punishment from the particular nature of the crime. There are then no arbitrary decisions; the punishment does not flow from the capriciousness of the legislator, but from the very nature of the thing; and man uses no violence to man.

There are four sorts of crimes. Those of the first species are prejudicial to religion, the second to morals, the third to the public tranquillity, and the fourth to the security of the subject. The punishments inflicted for these crimes ought to proceed from the nature of each of these species.

In the class of crimes that concern religion, I rank only those which attack it directly, such as all simple sacrileges. For as to crimes that disturb the exercise of it, they are of the nature of those which prejudice the tranquillity or security of the subject, and ought to be referred to those classes.

In order to derive the punishment of simple sacrileges from the nature of the thing, it should consist in depriving people of the advantages conferred by religion in expelling them out of the temples, in a temporary or perpetual exclusion from the society of the faithful, in shunning their presence, in execrations, comminations, and conjurations.

In things that prejudice the tranquillity or security of the state, secret actions are subject to human jurisdiction. But in those which offend the Deity, where there is no public act, there can be no criminal matter; the whole passes between man and God, who knows the measure and time of his vengeance. Now, if magistrates confounding things should inquire also into hidden sacrileges, this inquisition would be directed to a kind of action that does not at all require it; the liberty of the subject would be subverted by arming the zeal of timorous as well as of presumptuous consciences against him.

The mischief arises from a notion which some people have entertained of revenging the cause of the Deity. But we must honor the Deity and leave him to avenge his own cause. And, indeed, were we to be directed by such a notion, where would be the end of punishments? If human laws are to avenge the cause of an infinite Being, they will be directed by his infinity, and not by the weakness, ignorance, and caprice of man.

A historian of Provence relates a fact which furnishes us with an excellent description of the consequences that may arise in weak capacities from the notion of avenging the Deity's cause. A Jew was accused of having blasphemed against the Virgin Mary, and upon conviction was condemned to be flayed alive. A strange spectacle was then exhibited: gentlemen masked, with knives in their hands, mounted the scaffold, and drove away the executioner, in order to be the avengers themselves of the honor of the blessed Virgin. I do not here choose to anticipate the reflections of the reader.

The second class consists of those crimes which are prejudicial to morals. Such is the violation of public or private continence—that is, of the police directing the manner in which the pleasure annexed to the conjunction of the sexes is to be enjoyed. The punishment of those crimes ought to be also derived from the nature of the thing; the privation of such advantages as society has attached to the purity of morals, fines, shame, necessity of concealment, public infamy, expulsion from home and society, and, in fine, all such punishments as belong to a corrective jurisdiction, are sufficient to repress the temerity of the two sexes. In effect these things are less founded on malice than on carelessness and self-neglect.

We speak here of none but crimes which relate merely to morals, for as to those that are also prejudicial to the public security, such as rapes, they belong to the fourth species.

The crimes of the third class are those which disturb the public tranquillity. The punishments ought therefore to be derived from the nature of the thing, and to be in relation to this tranquillity: such as imprisonment, exile, and other like chastisements, proper for reclaiming turbulent spirits, and obliging them to conform to the established order.

I confine those crimes that injure the public tranquillity to things which imply a bare offense against the police; for as to those which by disturbing the public peace attack at the same time the security of the subject, they ought to be ranked in the fourth class.

The punishments inflicted upon the latter crimes are such as are properly distinguished by that name. They are a kind of retaliation, by which the society refuses security to a member who has actually or intentionally deprived another of his security. These punishments are derived from the nature of the thing, founded on reason, and drawn from the very source of good and evil. A man deserves death when he has violated the security of the subject so far as to deprive, or attempt to deprive, another man of his life. This punishment of death is the remedy, as it were, of a sick society. When there is a breach of security with regard to property, there may be some reasons for inflicting a capital punishment; but it would be much better, and perhaps more natural, that crimes committed against the security of property should be punished with the loss of property; and this ought, indeed, to be the case if men's fortunes were common or equal. But as those who have no property of their own are generally the readiest to attack that of others, it has been found necessary, instead of a pecuniary, to substitute a corporal, punishment.

All that I have here advanced is founded in Nature, and extremely favorable to the liberty of the subject.

IV. It is an important maxim that we ought to be very circumspect in the prosecution of witchcraft and heresy. The accusation of these two crimes may be vastly injurious to liberty, and productive of infinite oppression, if the legislator knows not how to set bounds to it. For as it does not directly point at a person's actions, but at his character, it grows dangerous in proportion to the ignorance of the people; and then a man is sure to be always in danger, because the most exceptional conduct, the purest morals, and the constant practice of every duty in life are not a sufficient security against the suspicion of his being guilty of the like crimes.

Under Manuel Comnenus, the Protestator was accused of having conspired against the emperor, and of having employed for that purpose some secrets that render men invisible. It is mentioned in the life of this emperor that Aaron was detected as he was poring over a book of Solomon's, the reading of which was sufficient to conjure up whole legions of devils. Now, by supposing a power in witchcraft to rouse the infernal spirits to arms, people look upon a man whom they call a sorcerer as the person in the world most likely to disturb and subvert society, and of course they are disposed to punish him with the utmost severity.

But their indignation increases when witchcraft is supposed to have the power of subverting religion. The history of Constantinople informs us that in consequence of a revelation made to a bishop of a miracle having ceased because of the magic practices of a certain person, both that person and his son were put to death. On how many surprising things did not this single crime depend!—that revelations should not be uncommon, that the bishop should be favored with one, that it was real, that there had been a miracle in the case, that this miracle had ceased, that there was an art magic, that magic could subvert religion, that this particular person was a magician, and, in fine, that he had committed that magic act.

The Emperor Theodorus Lascarus attributed his illness to witchcraft. Those who were accused of this crime had no other resource left than to handle a red-hot iron without being hurt. Thus among the Greeks a person ought to have been a sorcerer to be able to clear himself of the imputation of witchcraft. Such was the excess of their stupidity that to the most dubious crime in the world they joined the most dubious proofs of innocence.

Under the reign of Philip the Long, the Jews were expelled from France, being accused of having poisoned the springs with their lepers. So absurd an accusation ought to make us doubt all those that are founded on public hatred.

I have not here asserted that heresy ought not to be punished; I said only that we ought to be extremely circumspect in punishing it.

V. God forbid that I should have the least inclination to diminish the public horror against a crime which religion, morality, and civil government equally condemn. It ought to be proscribed, were it only for its communicating to one sex the weaknesses of the other, and for leading people by a scandalous prostitution of their youth to an ignominious old age. What I shall say concerning it will in no way diminish its infamy, being leveled only against the tyranny that may abuse the very horror we ought to have against the vice.

As a natural circumstance of this crime is secrecy, there are frequent instances of its having been punished by legislators upon the deposition of a child. This was opening a very wide door to calumny. "Justinian," says Procopius, "published a law against this crime; he ordered an inquiry to be made not only against those who were guilty of it, after the enacting of that law, but even before. The deposition of a single witness, sometimes of a child, sometimes of a slave, was sufficient, especially against such as were rich, and against those of the green faction."

It is very odd that these three crimes—witchcraft, heresy, and that against Nature, of which the first might easily be proved not to exist, the second to be susceptible of an infinite number of distinctions, interpretations, and limitations, the third to be often obscure and uncertain—it is very odd, I say, that these three crimes should among us be punished with fire.

I may venture to affirm that the crime against Nature will never make any great progress in society, unless people are prompted to it by some particular custom, as among the Greeks, where the youths of that country performed all their exercises naked; as among us, where domestic education is disused; as among the Asiatics, where particular persons have a great number of women whom they despise, while others can have none at all. Let there be no customs preparatory to this crime; let it, like every other violation of morals, be severely proscribed by the civil magistrate; and Nature will soon defend or resume her rights. Nature, that fond, that indulgent parent, has strewed her pleasures with a bounteous hand, and while she fills us with delights she prepares us, by means of our issue, in whom we see ourselves, as it were, reproduced—she prepares us, I say, for future satisfactions of a more exquisite kind than those very delights.

VI. It is determined by the laws of China that whosoever shows any disrespect to the emperor is to be punished with death. As they do not mention in what this disrespect consists, everything may furnish a pretext to take away a man's life, and to exterminate any family whatsoever.

Two persons of that country who were employed to write the court gazette, having inserted some circumstances relating to a certain fact that was not true, it was pretended that to tell a lie in the court gazette was a disrespect shown to the court, in consequence of which they were put to death. A prince of the blood having inadvertently made some mark on a memorial signed with the red pencil by the emperor, it was determined that he had behaved disrespectfully to the sovereign, which occasioned one of the most terrible persecutions against that family that ever was recorded in history.

If the crime of high treason be indeterminate, this alone is sufficient to make the government degenerate into arbitrary power. I shall descant more largely on this subject when I come to treat of the composition of laws.

VII. It is likewise a shocking abuse to give the appellation of high treason to an action that does not deserve it. By an imperial law it was decreed that those who called in question the prince's judgment, or doubted the merit of such as he had chosen for a public office, should be prosecuted as guilty of sacrilege. Surely it was the cabinet council and the prince's favorites who invented that crime. By another law it was determined that whosoever made any attempt to injure the ministers and officers belonging to the sovereign should be deemed guilty of high treason, as if he had attempted to injure the sovereign himself. This law is owing to two princes remarkable for their weaknesses—princes who were led by their ministers as flocks by shepherds; princes who were slaves in the palace, children in the council, strangers to the army; princes, in fine, who preserved their authority only by giving it away every day. Some of those favorites conspired against their sovereigns. Nay, they did more, they conspired against the empire—they called in barbarous nations; and when the emperors wanted to stop their progress the state was so enfeebled as to be under a necessity of infringing the law, and of exposing itself to the crime of high treason in order to punish those favorites.

And yet this is the very law which the judge of Monsieur de Cinq-Mars built upon when endeavoring to prove that the latter was guilty of the crime of high treason for attempting to remove Cardinal Richelieu from the ministry. He says: "Crimes that aim at the persons of ministers are deemed by the imperial constitutions of equal consequence with those which are leveled against the emperor's own person. A minister discharges his duty to his prince and to his country; to attempt, therefore, to remove him is endeavoring to deprive the former one of his arms, and the latter of part of its power." It is impossible for the meanest tools of power to express themselves in more servile language.

By another law of Valentinian, Theodosius, and Arcadius, false coiners are declared guilty of high treason. But is not this confounding the ideas of things? Is not the very horror of high treason diminished by giving that name to another crime?

Paulinus having written to the Emperor Alexander that "he was preparing to prosecute for high treason a judge who had decided contrary to his edict," the emperor answered that "under his reign there was no such thing as indirect high treason."

Faustinian wrote to the same emperor, that as he had sworn by the prince's life never to pardon his slave, he found himself thereby obliged to perpetuate his wrath, lest he should incur the guilt of *laesa majestas*. Upon which the emperor made answer, "Your fears are groundless, and you are a stranger to my principles."

It was determined by a senatus-consultum that whosoever melted down any of the emperor's statues which happened to be rejected should not be deemed guilty of high treason. The Emperors Severus and Antoninus wrote to Pontius that those who sold unconsecrated statues of the emperor should not be charged with high treason. The same princes wrote to Julius Cassianus that if a person in flinging a stone should by chance strike one of the emperor's statues he should not be liable to a prosecution for high treason. The Julian law requires this sort of limitations; for in virtue of this law the crime of high treason was charged not only upon those who melted down the emperor's statues, but likewise on those who committed any suchlike action, which made it an arbitrary crime. When a number of crimes of *laesa majestas* had been established, they were obliged to distinguish the several sorts. Hence Ulpian, the civilian, after saying that the accusation of *laesa majestas* did not die with the criminal, adds that this does not relate to all the treasonable acts established by the Julian law, but only to that which implies an attempt against the empire, or against the emperor's life.

There was a law passed in England under Henry VIII, by which whoever predicted the king's death was declared guilty of high treason. This law was extremely vague; the terror of despotic power is so great that it recoils upon those who exercise it. In this king's last illness, the physicians would not venture to say he was in danger; and surely they acted very right.

VIII. Marsyas dreamed that he had cut Dionysius' throat. Dionysius put him to death, pretending that he would never have dreamed of such a thing by night if he had not thought of it by day. This was a most tyrannical action, for though it had been the subject of his thoughts, yet he had made no attempt toward it. The laws do not take upon them to punish any other than overt acts.

IX. Nothing renders the crime of high treason more arbitrary than declaring people guilty of it for indiscreet speeches. Speech is so subject to interpretation; there is so great a difference between indiscretion and malice; and frequently so little is there of the latter in the freedom of expression, that the law can hardly subject people to a capital punishment for words unless it expressly declares what words they are.

Words do not constitute an overt act; they remain only in idea. When considered by themselves, they have generally no determinate signification, for this depends on the tone in which they are uttered. It often happens that in repeating the same words they have not the same meaning; this depends on their connection with other things, and sometimes more is signified by silence than by any expression whatever. Since there can be nothing so equivocal and ambiguous as all this, how is it possible to convert it into a crime of high treason? Wherever this law is established, there is an end not only of liberty, but even of its very shadow.

In the manifesto of the late Czarina against the family of the Dolgorukis, one of these princes is condemned to death for having uttered some indecent words concerning her person; another, for having maliciously interpreted her imperial laws, and for having offended her sacred person by disrespectful expressions.

Not that I pretend to diminish the just indignation of the public against those who presume to stain the glory of their sovereign; what I mean is, that if despotic princes are willing to moderate their power, a milder chastisement would be more proper on those occasions than the charge of high treason—a thing always terrible even to innocence itself.

Overt acts do not happen every day; they are exposed to the eye of the public, and a false charge with regard to matters of fact may be easily detected. Words carried into action assume the nature of that action. Thus a man who goes into a public marketplace to incite the subject to revolt incurs the guilt of high treason, because the words are joined to the action, and partake of its nature. It is not the words that are punished, but an action in which words are employed. They do not become criminal but when they are annexed to a criminal action; everything is confounded if words are construed into a capital crime, instead of considering them only as a mark of that crime.

The Emperors Theodosius, Arcadius, and Honorius wrote thus to Rufinus, who was *praefectus praetorio*: "Though a man should happen to speak amiss of our person or government, we do not intend to punish him. If he has spoken through levity, we must despise him; if through folly, we must pity him; and if he wrongs us, we must forgive him. Therefore, leaving things as they are, you are to inform us accordingly, that we may be able to judge of words by persons, and that we may duly consider whether we ought to punish or overlook them."

X. In writings there is something more permanent than in words, but when they are in no way preparative to high treason they cannot amount to that charge. . . .

* * *

REVIEW QUESTIONS

1. What kinds of liberty does Montesquieu distinguish?
2. On what basis does he make his distinctions?
3. What is the relation between liberty and reason?
4. What is the relation between crime and nature?
5. What role does a concept of nature play in Montesquieu's differentiation of crimes?

IMMANUEL KANT

"What Is Enlightenment?"

Immanuel Kant (1724–1804) was born, lived, and died in Königsberg, eastern Prussia, but wandered much more widely in his mind. A rationalist and disciple of Christian von Wolff, he set himself the task of working out the philosophical implications of Newtonian physics. Appointed to the chair of logic and metaphysics at the University of Königsberg in 1770, he began work on his great system of critical thought. His trilogy, Critique of Pure Reason *(1781),* Critique of Practical Reason *(1788), and* Critique of Judgment *(1790), provided the foundations for reliable human knowledge. In addition, he penned popular shorter essays that explained aspects of his thought. One of the most famous of these appears here. Publication of his last great work,* Religion in the Bounds of Reason *(1793), earned the censure of the Prussian government. Alone and silent, he died a decade later.*

From "What Is Enlightenment," translated by Peter Gay, in *Introduction to Contemporary Civilization*, vol. 1 (New York: Columbia University Press, 1954), pp. 1071–76.

Enlightenment is man's emergence from his self-imposed nonage. Nonage is the inability to use one's own understanding without another's guidance. This nonage is self-imposed if its cause lies not in lack of understanding but in indecision and lack of courage to use one's own mind without another's guidance. *Dare to know!* "Have the courage to use your own understanding," is therefore the motto of the enlightenment.

Laziness and cowardice are the reasons why such a large part of mankind gladly remain minors all their lives, long after nature has freed them from external guidance. They are the reasons why it is so easy for others to set themselves up as guardians. It is so comfortable to be a minor. If I have a book that thinks for me, a pastor who acts as my conscience, a physician who prescribes my diet, and so on—then I have no need to exert myself. I have no need to think, if only I can pay; others will take care of that disagreeable business for me. Those guardians who have kindly taken supervision upon themselves see to it that the overwhelming majority of mankind—among them the entire fair sex—should consider the step to maturity not only as hard, but as extremely dangerous. First, these guardians make their domestic cattle stupid and carefully prevent the docile creatures from taking a single step without the leading-strings to which they have fastened them. Then they show them the danger that would threaten them if they should try to walk by themselves. Now, this danger is really not very great; after stumbling a few times they would, at last, learn to walk. However, examples of such failures intimidate and generally discourage all further attempts.

Thus it is very difficult for the individual to work himself out of the nonage which has become almost second nature to him. He has even grown to like it and is at first really incapable of using his own understanding, because he has never been permitted to try it. Dogmas and formulas, these mechanical tools designed for reasonable use—or rather abuse—of his natural gifts, are the fetters of an everlasting nonage. The man who casts them off would make an uncertain leap over the narrowest ditch, because he is not used to such free movement. That is why there are only a few men who walk firmly, and who have emerged from nonage by cultivating their own minds.

It is more nearly possible, however, for the public to enlighten itself; indeed, if it is only given freedom, enlightenment is almost inevitable. There will always be a few independent thinkers, even among the self-appointed guardians of the multitude. Once such men have thrown off the yoke of nonage, they will spread about them the spirit of a reasonable appreciation of man's value and of his duty to think for himself. It is especially to be noted that the public which was earlier brought under the yoke by these men afterward forces these very guardians to remain in submission, if it is so incited by some of its guardians who are themselves incapable of any enlightenment. That shows how pernicious it is to implant prejudices: they will eventually revenge themselves upon their authors or their authors' descendants. Therefore, a public can achieve enlightenment only slowly. A revolution may bring about the end of a personal despotism or of avaricious and tyrannical oppression, but never a true reform of modes of thought. New prejudices will serve, in place of the old, as guidelines for the unthinking multitude.

This enlightenment requires nothing but *freedom*—and the most innocent of all that may be called "freedom": freedom to make public use of one's reason in all matters. Now I hear the cry from all sides: "Do not argue!" The officer says: "Do not argue—drill!" The tax collector: "Do not argue—pay!" The pastor: "Do not argue—believe!" Only one ruler in the world says: "Argue as much as you please, and about what you please, but obey!" We find restrictions on freedom everywhere. But which restriction is harmful to enlightenment? Which restriction is innocent, and which advances enlightenment? I reply: the public use of one's reason must be free at all times, and this alone can bring enlightenment to mankind.

On the other hand, the private use of reason may frequently be narrowly restricted without especially hindering the progress of enlightenment.

By "public use of one's reason" I mean that use which a man, as *scholar*, makes of it before the reading public. I call "private use" that use which a man makes of his reason in a civic post that has been entrusted to him. In some affairs affecting the interest of the community a certain governmental mechanism is necessary in which some members of the community remain passive. This creates an artificial unanimity which will serve the fulfillment of public objectives, or at least keep these objectives from being destroyed. Here arguing is not permitted: one must obey. Insofar as a part of this machine considers himself at the same time a member of a universal community— a world society of citizens—(let us say that he thinks of himself as a scholar rationally addressing his public through his writings) he may indeed argue, and the affairs with which he is associated in part as a passive member will not suffer. Thus, it would be very unfortunate if an officer on duty and under orders from his superiors should want to criticize the appropriateness or utility of his orders. He must obey. But as a scholar he could not rightfully be prevented from taking notice of the mistakes in the military service and from submitting his views to his public for its judgment. The citizen cannot refuse to pay the taxes levied upon him; indeed, impertinent censure of such taxes could be punished as a scandal that might cause general disobedience. Nevertheless, this man does not violate the duties of a citizen if, as a scholar, he publicly expresses his objections to the impropriety or possible injustice of such levies. A pastor too is bound to preach to his congregation in accord with the doctrines of the church which he serves, for he was ordained on that condition. But as a scholar he has full freedom, indeed the obligation, to communicate to his public all his carefully examined and constructive thoughts concerning errors in that doctrine and his proposals concerning improvement of religious dogma and church institutions. This is nothing that could burden his conscience. For what he teaches in pursuance of his office as representative of the church, he represents as something which he is not free to teach as he sees it. He speaks as one who is em-

ployed to speak in the name and under the orders of another. He will say: "Our church teaches this or that; these are the proofs which it employs." Thus he will benefit his congregation as much as possible by presenting doctrines to which he may not subscribe with full conviction. He can commit himself to teach them because it is not completely impossible that they may contain hidden truth. In any event, he has found nothing in the doctrines that contradicts the heart of religion. For if he believed that such contradictions existed he would not be able to administer his office with a clear conscience. He would have to resign it. Therefore the use which a scholar makes of his reason before the congregation that employs him is only a private use, for, no matter how sizable, this is only a domestic audience. In view of this he, as preacher, is not free and ought not to be free, since he is carrying out the orders of others. On the other hand, as the scholar who speaks to his own public (the world) through his writings, the minister in the public use of his reason enjoys unlimited freedom to use his own reason and to speak for himself. That the spiritual guardians of the people should themselves be treated as minors is an absurdity which would result in perpetuating absurdities.

But should a society of ministers, say a Church Council, . . . have the right to commit itself by oath to a certain unalterable doctrine, in order to secure perpetual guardianship over all its members and through them over the people? I say that this is quite impossible. Such a contract, concluded to keep all further enlightenment from humanity, is simply null and void even if it should be confirmed by the sovereign power, by parliaments, and by the most solemn treaties. An epoch cannot conclude a pact that will commit succeeding ages, prevent them from increasing their significant insights, purging themselves of errors, and generally progressing in enlightenment. That would be a crime against human nature, whose proper destiny lies precisely in such progress. Therefore, succeeding ages are fully entitled to repudiate such decisions as unauthorized and outrageous. The touchstone of all those decisions that may be made into law for a people lies in this question: Could a people impose such a law upon itself? Now, it might be possible to introduce a certain order for a definite short period of time in expectation of a better order. But while this provisional order continues, each citizen (above all, each pastor acting as a scholar) should be left free to publish his criticisms of the faults of existing institutions. This should continue until public understanding of these matters has gone so far that, by uniting the voices of many (although not necessarily all) scholars, reform proposals could be brought before the sovereign to protect those congregations which had decided according to their best lights upon an altered religious order, without, however, hindering those who want to remain true to the old institutions. But to agree to a perpetual religious constitution which is not to be publicly questioned by anyone would be, as it were, to annihilate a period of time in the progress of man's improvement. This must be absolutely forbidden.

A man may postpone his own enlightenment, but only for a limited period of time. And to give up enlightenment altogether, either for oneself or one's descendants, is to violate and to trample upon the sacred rights of man. What a people may not decide for itself may even less be decided for it by a monarch, for his reputation as a ruler consists precisely in the way in which he unites the will of the whole people within his own. If he only sees to it that all true or supposed improvement remains in step with the civic order, he can for the rest leave his subjects alone to do what they find necessary for the salvation of their souls. Salvation is none of his business; it *is* his business to prevent one man from forcibly keeping another from determining and promoting his salvation to the best of his ability. Indeed, it would be prejudicial to his majesty if he meddled in these matters and supervised the writings in which his subjects seek to bring their views into the open, even when he does this from his own highest insight, because then he exposes himself to the reproach: *Caesar non est supra grammaticos.*[1] It is worse when he

debases his sovereign power so far as to support the spiritual despotism of a few tyrants in his state over the rest of his subjects.

When we ask, Are we now living in an enlightened age? the answer is, No, but we live in an age of enlightenment. As matters now stand it is still far from true that men are already capable of using their own reason in religious matters confidently and correctly without external guidance. Still, we have some obvious indications that the field of working toward the goal of religious truth is now being opened. What is more, the hindrances against general enlightenment or the emergence from self-imposed nonage are gradually diminishing. In this respect this is the age of the enlightenment and the century of Frederick.

A prince ought not to deem it beneath his dignity to state that he considers it his duty not to dictate anything to his subjects in religious matters, but to leave them complete freedom. If he repudiates the arrogant word *tolerant,* he is himself enlightened; he deserves to be praised by a grateful world and posterity as that man who was the first to liberate mankind from dependence, at least on the government, and let everybody use his own reason in matters of conscience. Under his reign, honorable pastors, acting as scholars and regardless of the duties of their office, can freely and openly publish their ideas to the world for inspection, although they deviate here and there from accepted doctrine. This is even more true of every other person not restrained by any oath of office. This spirit of freedom is spreading beyond the boundaries of Prussia, even where it has to struggle against the external hindrances established by a government that fails to grasp its true interest. Frederick's Prussia is a shining example that freedom need not cause the least worry concerning public order or the unity of the community. When one does not deliberately attempt to keep men in barbarism, they will gradually work out of that condition by themselves.

I have emphasized the main point of the enlightenment—man's emergence from his self-imposed nonage—primarily in religious matters, because our rulers have no interest in playing the

---

[1] "Caesar is not above grammarians."

guardian to their subjects in the arts and sciences. Above all, nonage in religion is not only the most harmful but the most dishonorable. But the disposition of a sovereign ruler who favors freedom in the arts and sciences goes even further: he knows that there is no danger in permitting his subjects to make public use of their reason and to publish their ideas concerning a better constitution, as well as candid criticism of existing basic laws. We already have a striking example [of such freedom], and no monarch can match the one whom we venerate.

But only the man who is himself enlightened, who is not afraid of shadows, and who commands at the same time a well-disciplined and numerous army as guarantor of public peace—only he can say what a free state cannot dare to say: "Argue as much as you like, and about what you like, but obey!" Thus we observe here as elsewhere in human affairs, in which almost everything is paradoxical, a surprising and unexpected course of events: a large degree of civic freedom appears to be of advantage to the intellectual freedom of the people, yet at the same time it establishes insurmountable barriers. A lesser degree of civic freedom, however, creates room to let that free spirit expand to the limits of its capacity. Nature, then, has carefully cultivated the seed within the hard core—namely, the urge for and the vocation of free thought. And this free thought gradually reacts back on the modes of thought of the people, and men become more and more capable of acting in freedom. At last free thought acts even on the fundamentals of government, and the state finds it agreeable to treat man, who is now more than a machine, in accord with his dignity.

REVIEW QUESTIONS

1. What is enlightenment?
2. What is its relation to habit? To freedom? To revolution?
3. What is the relation of enlightenment to argument? Why?
4. Why should reasoning be public?
5. How does Kant define "public"?
6. Is the church public or private?

DAVID HUME

FROM *A Treatise of Human Nature*

David Hume (1711–1776) was born the younger son of a gentry family from Scotland. Though he attended the University of Edinburgh, he found formal education distasteful and applied himself instead to an intense program of reading. After a nervous breakdown in 1729 and an unsuccessful foray into business, Hume moved to France in 1734. During his stay there, which lasted until 1737, he devoted himself to studying and to writing the A Treatise of Human Nature (1739–1740). Though he later dismissed it as immature, it became his most influential work. In it, he introduced his notion of skepticism that restricted human knowledge to the experience of ideas and impression and denied the ability to verify their ultimate truth. Nonetheless, given the cautious, persistent exercise of reason, humankind could gather knowledge that was reliable and useful. As historian, economist, and essayist, Hume was one of the most influential figures of the middle years of the Enlightenment.

From *A Treatise of Human Nature*, by David Hume, edited by L. A. Selby-Biggs (Oxford, England: Clarendon Press, 1888), pp. xvii–xxiii.

Introduction

Nothing is more usual and more natural for those, who pretend to discover any thing new to the world in philosophy and the sciences, than to insinuate the praises of their own systems, by decrying all those, which have been advanced before them. And indeed were they content with lamenting that ignorance, which we still lie under in the most important questions, that can come before the tribunal of human reason, there are few, who have an acquaintance with the sciences, that would not readily agree with them. 'Tis easy for one of judgment and learning, to perceive the weak foundation even of those systems, which have obtained the greatest credit, and have carried their pretensions highest to accurate and profound reasoning. Principles taken upon trust, consequences lamely deduced from them, want of coherence in the parts, and of evidence in the whole, these are every where to be met with in the systems of the most eminent philosophers, and seem to have drawn disgrace upon philosophy itself.

Nor is there requir'd such profound knowledge to discover the present imperfect condition of the sciences, but even the rabble without doors may judge from the noise and clamour, which they hear, that all goes not well within. There is nothing which is not the subject of debate, and in which men of learning are not of contrary opinions. The most trivial question escapes not our controversy, and in the most momentous we are not able to give any certain decision. Disputes are multiplied, as if every thing was uncertain; and these disputes are managed with the greatest warmth, as if every thing was certain. Amidst all this bustle 'tis not reason, which carries the prize, but eloquence; and no man needs ever despair of gaining proselytes to the most extravagant hypothesis, who has art enough to represent it in any favourable colours. The victory is not gained by the men at arms, who manage the pike and the sword; but by the trumpeters, drummers, and musicians of the army.

From hence in my opinion arises that common prejudice against metaphysical reasonings of all kinds, even amongst those, who profess themselves scholars, and have a just value for every other part of literature. By metaphysical reasonings, they do not understand those on any particular branch of science, but every kind of argument, which is any way abstruse, and requires some attention to be comprehended. We have so often lost our labour in such researches, that we commonly reject them without hesitation, and resolve, if we must for ever be a prey to errors and delusions, that they shall at least be natural and entertaining. And indeed nothing but the most determined scepticism, along with a great degree of indolence, can justify this aversion to metaphysics. For if truth be at all within the reach of human capacity, 'tis certain it must lie very deep and abstruse; and to hope we shall arrive at it without pains, while the greatest geniuses have failed with the utmost pains, must certainly be esteemed sufficiently vain and presumptuous. I pretend to no such advantage in the philosophy I am going to unfold, and would esteem it a strong presumption against it, were it so very easy and obvious.

'Tis evident, that all the sciences have a relation, greater or less, to human nature; and that however wide any of them may seem to run from it, they still return back by one passage or another. Even *Mathematics, Natural Philosophy, and Natural Religion,* are in some measure dependent on the science of Man; since they lie under the cognizance of men, and are judged of by their powers and faculties. 'Tis impossible to tell what changes and improvements we might make in these sciences were we thoroughly acquainted with the extent and force of human understanding, and cou'd explain the nature of the ideas we employ, and of the operations we perform in our reasonings. And these improvements are the more to be hoped for in natural religion, as it is not content with instructing us in the nature of superior powers, but carries its views farther, to their disposition towards us, and our duties towards them; and consequently we ourselves are not only the beings, that reason, but also one of the objects, concerning which we reason.

If therefore the sciences of Mathematics, Natural Philosophy, and Natural Religion, have such a dependence on the knowledge of man, what may be expected in the other sciences, whose connexion with human nature is more close and intimate? The sole end of logic is to explain the principles and operations of our reasoning faculty, and the nature of our ideas: morals and criticism regard our tastes and sentiments: and politics consider men as united in society, and dependent on each other. In these four sciences of *Logic, Morals, Criticism, and Politics,* is comprehended almost every thing, which it can any way import us to be acquainted with, or which can tend either to the improvement or ornament of the human mind.

Here then is the only expedient, from which we can hope for success in our philosophical researches, to leave the tedious ling'ring method, which we have hitherto followed, and instead of taking now and then a castle or village on the frontier, to march up directly to the capital or center of these sciences, to human nature itself; which being once masters of, we may every where else hope for an easy victory. From this station we may extend our conquests over all those sciences, which more intimately concern human life, and may afterwards proceed at leisure to discover more fully those, which are the objects of pure curiosity. There is no question of importance, whose decision is not compriz'd in the science of man; and there is none, which can be decided with any certainty, before we become acquainted with that science. In pretending therefore to explain the principles of human nature, we in effect propose a compleat system of the sciences, built on a foundation almost entirely new, and the only one upon which they can stand with any security.

And as the science of man is the only solid foundation for the other sciences, so the only solid foundation we can give to this science itself must be laid on experience and observation. 'Tis no astonishing reflection to consider, that the application of experimental philosophy to moral subjects should come after that to natural at the distance of above a whole century; since we find in fact, that there was about the same interval betwixt the origins of these sciences; and that reckoning from Thales to Socrates, the space of time is nearly equal to that betwixt my Lord Bacon and some late philosophers in *England,* who have begun to put the science of man on a new footing, and have engaged the attention, and excited the curiosity of the public. So true it is, that however other nations may rival us in poetry, and excel us in some other agreeable arts, the improvements in reason and philosophy can only be owing to a land of toleration and of liberty.

Nor ought we to think, that this latter improvement in the science of man will do less honour to our native country than the former in natural philosophy, but ought rather to esteem it a greater glory, upon account of the greater importance of that science, as well as the necessity it lay under of such a reformation. For to me it seems evident, that the essence of the mind being equally unknown to us with that of external bodies, it must be equally impossible to form any notion of its powers and qualities otherwise than from careful and exact experiments, and the observation of those particular effects, which result from its different circumstances and situations. And tho' we must endeavour to render all our principles as universal as possible, by tracing up our experiments to the utmost, and explaining all effects from the simplest and fewest causes, 'tis still certain we cannot go beyond experience; and any hypothesis, that pretends to discover the ultimate original qualities of human nature, ought at first to be rejected as presumptuous and chimerical.

I do not think a philosopher, who would apply himself so earnestly to the explaining the ultimate principles of the soul, would show himself a great master in that very science of human nature, which he pretends to explain, or very knowing in what is naturally satisfactory to the mind of man. For nothing is more certain, than that despair has almost the same effect upon us with enjoyment, and that we are no sooner acquainted with the impossibility of satisfying any desire, than the desire itself vanishes. When we see, that we have arrived at the utmost extent of human reason, we sit down contented; tho' we be perfectly satisfied in the main of our ignorance, and perceive that we can give no reason for our most general and most refined principles, beside our experience of their reality; which is the reason of the mere vulgar, and what it required no study at first to have discovered for the most particular and most extraordinary phaenomenon. And as this impossibility of making any farther progress is enough to satisfy the reader, so the writer may derive a more delicate satisfaction from the free confession of his ignorance, and from his prudence in avoiding that error, into which so many have fallen, of imposing their conjectures and hypotheses on the world for the most certain principles. When this mutual contentment and satisfaction can be obtained betwixt the master and scholar, I know not what more we can require of our philosophy.

But if this impossibility of explaining ultimate principles should be esteemed a defect in the science of man, I will venture to affirm, that 'tis a defect common to it with all the sciences, and all the arts, in which we can employ ourselves, whether they be such as are cultivated in the schools of the philosophers, or practised in the shops of the meanest artizans. None of them can go beyond experience, or establish any principles which are not founded on that authority. Moral philosophy has, indeed, this peculiar disadvantage, which is not found in natural, that in collecting its experiments, it cannot make them purposely, with premeditation, and after such a manner as to satisfy itself concerning every particular difficulty which may arise. When I am at a loss to know the effects of one body upon another in any situation, I need only put them in that situation, and observe what results from it. But should I endeavour to clear up after the same manner any doubt in moral philosophy, by placing myself in the same case with that which I consider, 'tis evident this reflection and premeditation would so disturb the operation of my natural principles, as must render it impossible to form any just conclusion from the phaenomenon. We must therefore glean up our experiments in this science from a cautious observation of human life, and take them as they appear in the common course of the world, by men's behaviour in company, in affairs, and in their pleasures. Where experiments of this kind are judiciously collected and compared, we may hope to establish on them a science, which will not be inferior in certainty, and will be much superior in utility to any other of human comprehension.

*   *   *

REVIEW QUESTIONS

1. To what does Hume attribute all the disputes in the sciences?
2. What is the science of man, and what are its methods and goals?
3. Why must one understand human reason first?

Women's Role in the Enlightenment

Jeanne Manon Philipon Roland de la Platière (1754–1793), better known simply as Madame Roland, was a revolutionary and social figure of the late Enlightenment. Born in Paris, she married a government official, Jean Roland de la Platière. As the wife of a public figure, her intelligence, charm, and energy had a broader influence than might otherwise have been the case. With her husband, she became a member of the Girondist faction during the French Revolution, and her home became its headquarters. There she presided over a salon where the issues of the day were discussed. When the Girondists lost power to the more radical Jacobins, Madame Roland was arrested and condemned to death by a revolutionary tribunal for royalist sympathies. She wrote her Private Memoirs *(1795) while in prison awaiting execution. With the correspondence of other noteworthy salonnières, such as Julie de Lespinasse,* Private Memoirs *offers a perspective on the social and intellectual role of well-educated women during the Enlightenment. As hostesses in literary salons, where philosophes met to discuss philosophical issues, they facilitated discourse between schools and across classes.*

From *Private Memoirs of Madame Roland,* edited by E. Gilpin Johnson (Chicago: McGlurg, 1901).

Jeanne Manon Philipon Roland de la Platière

FROM *Private Memoirs*

*   *   *

The little library of my relations afforded me some resources. I found there the works of Puffendorf, tedious perhaps in his universal history, but interesting to me in his "Duties of the Man and the Citizen;" the "Maison Rustique," and other works of agriculture and economy, that I studied for want of better, because it was necessary that I should be always learning something; the pleasant and delicate rhymes that Berni wrote when he was not restrained by the Romish purple; a Life of Cromwell, and a medley of other productions.

I must here remind the reader of the fact that in mentioning casually the long list of books that chance or circumstances had caused to pass through my hands, I have as yet said nothing of Rousseau. The fact is I read him very late—and it was as well for me that I did so, since I might have been so completely engrossed with him as to have read no other author. Even as it is, he has but too much strengthened what I may venture to term my cardinal failing.

I have reason to believe that my mother had been solicitous to keep him out of my way; for, as his name was not unknown to me, I had sought after his works, but, previously to her death, had read only his "Letters from the Mountain," and his "Letter to Christopher de Beaumont;" whereas I had then read the whole of Voltaire and Boulanger and the Marquis d'Argens and Helvetius, besides many other philosophers and critics. Probably my worthy mother, who perceived the necessity of permitting me to exercise my head, was not averse to my studying philosophy even at the risk of a little incredulity; but she doubtless felt that my tender heart, already too impressible, needed no master in the school of sensibility. What a multitude of useless cares to avoid one's destiny! The same idea influenced her, when she interfered to prevent me from devoting myself to painting; and had made her also oppose my studying the harpsichord, though I had a most excellent opportunity for doing so. We had become acquainted in the neighborhood with an Abbé Jeauket, a musical amateur, good-natured, but frightfully ugly, and fond of the pleasures of the table. He was born in the environs of Prague, had passed many years at Vienna, and had given some lessons there to Marie Antoinette. Led by circumstances to Lisbon, he had at last settled at Paris, where he lived in independence on the pensions that composed his little fortune. He was extremely desirous that my mother would permit him to teach me the harpsichord. He contended that with such fingers and such a head I must have made a great performer, and that I ought not to fail to apply myself to composition. "What a shame," he cried, "to be jingling a guitar, when one might be composing and executing the finest pieces on the greatest of instruments!" But with all his enthusiasm and his repeated entreaties he could not overcome my mother's opposition. For myself, always ready to profit by an opportunity of instruction, but accustomed nevertheless to bow to her decisions, I did not press the matter. Besides, study, in general, afforded me so vast a field of occupation, that I never knew the lassitude of idleness. I often said to myself: When I shall be a mother in my turn it will then be my business to make use of what I shall have acquired; I shall then have no leisure for further studies; and I was the more earnest to employ my time, fearful of losing a single moment. The Abbé Jeauket was now and then visited by persons of some note, and whenever he invited them to his house, he was anxious to include us in his party. Thus, among others not worth remembering, I became acquainted with the learned Roussier, and the polite d'Odiment; but I have not forgotten the impertinent Paradelle and Madame de Puisieux. This Paradelle was a great scamp in the gown of an abbé, and the greatest coxcomb and braggart I have ever met with. He

pretended to have ridden in his carriage at Lyons for twenty years; and yet, that he might not starve at Paris, he was obliged to give lectures on the Italian language, of which he was wholly ignorant. Madame de Puisieux, posing as the author of the work entitled "Caractères," to which her name is prefixed, retained at the age of sixty, with a hunch back and a toothless mouth, the air and pretensions of which the affectation is scarcely pardonable even in youth. I had conceived that a literary woman must be a very respectable character, especially when morality was the subject of her writings. The absurdities of Madame de Puisieux furnished me with a topic for reflection. Her conversation was as little indicative of talent as her caprices were of sense. I began to perceive it was possible to store up reason for a public occasion, without making much use of it in one's own affairs; and I thought that perhaps the men who made a jest of female authors were not otherwise to blame than in applying exclusively to them what is equally true of themselves. Thus in a round of life very circumscribed did I find means to accumulate a fund of observations. I was placed in solitude, it is true, but yet on the confines of a world where I saw a variety of objects without being encumbered by any. The concerts of Madame Lépine offered me a fresh point of view. I have already said that Lépine was a pupil of Pigale: he was, indeed, his right hand. At Rome he had married a woman who, as I presume, had been a cantatrice, and whom his family had at first beheld with disfavor, but who proved by the propriety of her conduct that their disdain was ill-founded.

She had formed at her house a company of amateurs, skilled performers, to which none were admitted but those whom she called good company. It met every Thursday, and my mother often conducted me thither. It was here I heard Jarnowich, St. George, Duport, Guérin, and many others. Here too I saw the wits of both sexes: Mademoiselle Morville, Madame Benoît, Sylvain Maréchal, etc., together with haughty baronesses, smart abbés, old chevaliers, and young fops. What a pleasant magic lantern! The apartments of Madame Lépine, rue Neuve Saint Eustache, were not remarkably fine, nor was the concert room spacious; but it opened into another apartment, of which the folding-doors were kept open: there, placed in the circle, you had the combined advantage of hearing the music, seeing the authors, and conversing in the intervals. Seated close to my mother, and maintaining the silence that custom prescribes to young women, I was all eyes and ears—unless we chanced for a moment to be in private with Madame Lépine, when I put a few questions to her, in order to illustrate to myself by her answers such observations as I had made.

One day this lady proposed to my mother to accompany her to a "charming" assembly, held at the house of a man of wit, whom we had sometimes seen at Madame Lépine's. There was to be a feast of reason, a flow of soul, a reunion of the wits; there were to be readings "most delightful" —in short something "delicious" was promised. The proposal, however, was several times repeated before it was accepted. "Let us go," said I at last to my mother, "I begin to know enough of the world to presume that it must be either extremely agreeable or very absurd; and should the latter be the case, we shall be sure to find for once sufficient amusement in its novelty." The business is settled; and on the following Wednesday, which was the day of M. Vâse's literary assemblies, we set off with Madame Lépine for the *barrière* of the Temple, where he resided. We mount to the third story, and arrive at a spacious room indifferently furnished, where were placed rows of rush-bottomed chairs, already partly occupied; dirty brass chandeliers, with tallow candles, illumined this resort of the Muses, the grotesque simplicity of which did not belie what I had heard of the philosophical rigor and poverty of an author. Some agreeable women, young girls, old dowagers, with a number of minor poets, virtuosos, and men of intrigue, composed this brilliant circle.

The master of ceremonies, seated before a table which formed a desk, opened the *séance* by reading a poetic effusion of his own, the subject of which was a pretty little lap-dog that the old Marchioness de Préville always carried in her muff, and which she now exhibited to the company; for she was present, and thought herself obliged to gratify the auditors with a sight of the hero of the piece. The *bravos* and plaudits of the whole room paid homage to the fancy of M. Vâse, who, highly satisfied with himself, was to have yielded his seat to M. Delpêches, a poet who wrote little comic dramas for the theatre of Audinot, upon which he was accustomed to take the judgment of the society, or, in other words, the encouragement of its applause; but, either because of a sore throat, or the want of some verses in several of his scenes, or some other cause, he was prevented from attending. Imbert, author of the "Judgment of Paris," accordingly took the chair, and read an agreeable trifle, which was also extolled to the skies. A further distinction was in store for him. Mademoiselle de la Cossonnière succeeded him with a "Farewell to Colin," which, if not very ingenious, was at least meltingly tender. It was known that the lines were addressed to Imbert, who was about to undertake a journey; and compliments fell upon him in showers. Imbert acquitted his muse and himself by saluting all the females in the assembly. This brisk and gay ceremony, conducted however with decorum, was not at all pleasing to my mother, and appeared in so strange a light to me as to give me an air of embarrassment. After an epigram or couplet in which there was nothing remarkable, a pompous declaimer recited some verses in praise of Madame Benoît, who was present. Let me here say a word as to this lady, for the sake of those who have not read her romances, which were dead long before the Revolution, and upon which thick dust will have gathered long before these memoirs see the light.

*   *   *

Julie de Lespinasse

FROM *Letters of Julie de Lespinasse*

FROM MEMOIR OF BARON DE GRIMM

*   *   *

Her circle met daily from five o'clock until nine in the evening. There we were sure to find choice men of all orders in the State, the Church, the Court,—military men, foreigners, and the most distinguished men of letters. Every one agrees that though the name of M. d'Alembert may have drawn them thither, it was she alone who kept them there. Devoted wholly to the care of preserving that society, of which she was the soul and the charm, she subordinated to this purpose all her tastes and all her personal intimacies. She seldom went to the theatre or into the country, and when she did make an exception to this rule it was an event of which all Paris was notified in advance. . . . Politics, religion, philosophy, anecdotes, news, nothing was excluded from the conversation, and, thanks to her care, the most trivial little narrative gained, as naturally as possible, the place and notice it deserved. News of all kinds was gathered there in its first freshness.

*   *   *

FROM MEMOIR OF MARMONTEL

*   *   *

The circle was formed of persons who were not bound together. She had taken them here and there in society, but so well assorted were they that once there they fell into harmony like the strings of an instrument touched by an able hand. Following out that comparison, I may say that she played the instrument with an art that came of

genius; she seemed to know what tone each string would yield before she touched it; I mean to say that our minds and our natures were so well known to her that in order to bring them into play she had but to say a word. Nowhere was conversation more lively, more brilliant, or better regulated than at her house. It was a rare phenomenon indeed, the degree of tempered, equable heat which she knew so well how to maintain, sometimes by moderating it, sometimes by quickening it. The continual activity of her soul was communicated to our souls, but measurably; her imagination was the mainspring, her reason the regulator. Remark that the brains she stirred at will were neither feeble nor frivolous: the Coudillacs and Turgots were among them; d'Alembert was like a simple, docile child beside her. Her talent for casting out a thought and giving it for discussion to men of that class, her own talent in discussing it with precision, sometimes with eloquence, her talent for bringing forward new ideas and varying the topic—always with the facility and ease of a fairy, who, with one touch of her wand, can change the scene of her enchantment—these talents, I say, were not those of an ordinary woman. It was not with the follies of fashion and vanity that daily, during four hours of conversation, without languor and without vacuum, she knew how to make herself interesting to a wide circle of strong minds.

*   *   *

REVIEW QUESTIONS

1. Why did Madame Roland turn to the writings of Rousseau so late in her education?
2. What does this tell you about her attitude toward his opinions specifically and toward the education of women generally?
3. Were the salonnières more than simply hostesses at social gatherings?
4. What was their function in the salons?
5. Why do you suppose women rather than men fulfilled this role?

From *Letters of Julie de Lespinasse,* translated by Katherine Wormley (Boston: Hardy, Pratt, 1903).

6. What larger purpose did the salons serve?
7. What does the fact that the salons were among the foremost institutions of the Enlightenment tell you about the nature of the Enlightenment as a historical phenomenon?

MARQUIS DE CONDORCET

FROM *Sketch for a Historical Picture on the Progress of the Human Mind*

Marie-Jean-Antoine-Nicolas Caritat, marquis de Condorcet (1734–1794) came from an old noble family of the principality of Orange. His ancestors had converted to Calvinism and settled in the Dauphiné. During the repression of French Protestantism under Louis XIV, they reconverted to Roman Catholicism. He lost his father while still an infant and was raised by his mother in an atmosphere of intense Catholic piety. He was educated by Jesuits in Reims and the Collège de Navare. As an adult, Condorcet's thought showed strains of anticlericalism, and he opposed the Jesuit tradition of education. In 1758, he defied his family's wishes by traveling to Paris to pursue studies in mathematics. His work on integral calculus won him a seat in the French Academy of Sciences, where he advanced to assistant to the perpetual secretary in 1774 and to perpetual secretary in 1775. He retained this post until 1793, when his political enemies forced him into hiding. Condorcet espoused revolutionary ideas and was an early supporter of the goals of the French Revolution. Yet, he attacked the constitution proposed in the National Convention of 1793. This earned him the enmity of radicals, including a fellow academician, Chabot, who denounced him as an enemy of the revolution. He went into hiding and eventually fled Paris only to be caught and imprisoned. He committed suicide while in prison. Condorcet was a champion of the improvement of humankind through the proper use of reason. Rational laws governed human affairs just as they did nature. These laws could be discovered by reason and applied to improve the human condition. His Outline of a Historical View of the Progress of the Human Mind *(1795) was published posthumously, one year after Condorcet's death.*

From *Sketch for a Historical Picture on the Progress of the Human Mind,* by Jean Antoine Nicolas Caritat Marquis de Condorcet, translated by June Barraclough (London: Weidenfeld and Nicolson, 1955).

The Tenth Stage
The Future Progress of the Human Mind

If man can, with almost complete assurance, predict phenomena when he knows their laws, and if, even when he does not, he can still, with great expectation of success, forecast the future on the basis of his experience of the past, why, then, should it be regarded as a fantastic undertaking to sketch, with some pretence to truth, the future destiny of man on the basis of his history? The sole foundation for belief in the natural sciences is this idea, that the general laws directing the phenomena of the universe, known or unknown, are necessary and constant. Why should this principle be any less true for the development of the intellectual and moral faculties of man than for the other operations of nature? Since beliefs founded on past experience of like conditions provide the only rule of conduct for the wisest of men, why should the philosopher be forbidden to base his conjectures on these same foundations, so long as he does not attribute to them a certainty superior to that warranted by the number, the constancy, and the accuracy of his observations?

Our hopes for the future condition of the human race can be subsumed under three important heads: the abolition of inequality between nations, the progress of equality within each nation, and the true perfection of mankind. Will all nations one day attain that state of civilization which the most enlightened, the freest and the least burdened by prejudices, such as the French and the Anglo-Americans, have attained already? Will the vast gulf that separates these peoples from the slavery of nations under the rule of monarchs, from the barbarism of African tribes, from the ignorance of savages, little by little disappear?

Is there on the face of the earth a nation whose inhabitants have been debarred by nature herself from the enjoyment of freedom and the exercise of reason?

Are those differences which have hitherto been seen in every civilized country in respect of the enlightenment, the resources, and the wealth enjoyed by the different classes into which it is divided, is that inequality between men which was aggravated or perhaps produced by the earliest progress of society, are these part of civilization itself, or are they due to the present imperfections of the social art? Will they necessarily decrease and ultimately make way for a real equality, the final end of the social art, in which even the effects of the natural differences between men will be mitigated and the only kind of inequality to persist will be that which is in the interests of all and which favours the progress of civilization, of education, and of industry, without entailing either poverty, humiliation, or dependence? In other words, will men approach a condition in which everyone will have the knowledge necessary to conduct himself in the ordinary affairs of life, according to the light of his own reason, to preserve his mind free from prejudice, to understand his rights and to exercise them in accordance with his conscience and his creed; in which everyone will become able, through the development of his faculties, to find the means of providing for his needs; and in which at last misery and folly will be the exception, and no longer the habitual lot of a section of society?

Is the human race to better itself, either by discoveries in the sciences and the arts, and so in the means to individual welfare and general prosperity; or by progress in the principles of conduct or practical morality; or by a true perfection of the intellectual, moral, or physical faculties of man, an improvement which may result from a perfection either of the instruments used to heighten the intensity of these faculties and to direct their use or of the natural constitution of man?

In answering these three questions we shall find in the experience of the past, in the observation of the progress that the sciences and civilization have already made, in the analysis of the progress of the human mind and of the development of its faculties, the strongest reasons for believing that nature has set no limit to the realization of our hopes.

If we glance at the state of the world today we

see first of all that in Europe the principles of the French constitution are already those of all enlightened men. We see them too widely propagated, too seriously professed, for priests and despots to prevent their gradual penetration even into the hovels of their slaves; there they will soon awaken in these slaves the remnants of their common sense and inspire them with that smouldering indignation which not even constant humiliation and fear can smother in the soul of the oppressed.

As we move from nation to nation, we can see in each what special obstacles impede this revolution and what attitudes of mind favour it. We can distinguish the nations where we may expect it to be introduced gently by the perhaps belated wisdom of their governments, and those nations where its violence intensified by their resistance must involve all alike in a swift and terrible convulsion.

Can we doubt that either common sense or the senseless discords of European nations will add to the effects of the slow but inexorable progress of their colonies, and will soon bring about the independence of the New World? And then will not the European population in these colonies, spreading rapidly over that enormous land, either civilize or peacefully remove the savage nations who still inhabit vast tracts of its land?

Survey the history of our settlements and commercial undertakings in Africa or in Asia, and you will see how our trade monopolies, our treachery, our murderous contempt for men of another colour or creed, the insolence of our usurpations, the intrigues or the exaggerated proselytic zeal of our priests, have destroyed the respect and goodwill that the superiority of our knowledge and the benefits of our commerce at first won for us in the eyes of the inhabitants. But doubtless the moment approaches when, no longer presenting ourselves as always either tyrants or corrupters, we shall become for them the beneficent instruments of their freedom.

*   *   *

The time will therefore come when the sun will shine only on free men who know no other master but their reason; when tyrants and slaves,

priests and their stupid or hypocritical instruments will exist only in works of history and on the stage; and when we shall think of them only to pity their victims and their dupes; to maintain ourselves in a state of vigilance by thinking on their excesses; and to learn how to recognize and so to destroy, by force of reason, the first seeds of tyranny and superstition, should they ever dare to reappear amongst us.

In looking at the history of societies we shall have had occasion to observe that there is often a great difference between the rights that the law allows its citizens and the rights that they actually enjoy, and, again, between the equality established by political codes and that which in fact exists amongst individuals: and we shall have noticed that these differences were one of the principal causes of the destruction of freedom in the Ancient republics, of the storms that troubled them, and of the weakness that delivered them over to foreign tyrants.

These differences have three main causes: inequality in wealth; inequality in status between the man whose means of subsistence are hereditary and the man whose means are dependent on the length of his life, or, rather, on that part of his life in which he is capable of work; and, finally, inequality in education.

We therefore need to show that these three sorts of real inequality must constantly diminish without however disappearing altogether: for they are the result of natural and necessary causes which it would be foolish and dangerous to wish to eradicate; and one could not even attempt to bring about the entire disappearance of their effects without introducing even more fecund sources of inequality, without striking more direct and more fatal blows at the rights of man.

It is easy to prove that wealth has a natural tendency to equality, and that any excessive disproportion could not exist or at least would rapidly disappear if civil laws did not provide artificial ways of perpetuating and uniting fortunes; if free trade and industry were allowed to remove the advantages that accrued wealth derives from any restrictive law or fiscal privilege; if taxes on covenants, the restrictions placed on their free employment, their subjection to tiresome formalities and the uncertainty and inevitable expense involved in implementing them did not hamper the activity of the poor man and swallow up his meagre capital; if the administration of the country did not afford some men ways of making their fortune that were closed to other citizens; if prejudice and avarice, so common in old age, did not preside over the making of marriages; and if, in a society enjoying simpler manners and more sensible institutions, wealth ceased to be a means of satisfying vanity and ambition, and if the equally misguided notions of austerity, which condemn spending money in the cultivation of the more delicate pleasures, no longer insisted on the hoarding of all one's earnings.

Let us turn to the enlightened nations of Europe, and observe the size of their present populations in relation to the size of their territories. Let us consider, in agriculture and industry the proportion that holds between labour and the means of subsistence, and we shall see that it would be impossible for those means to be kept at their present level and consequently for the population to be kept at its present size if a great number of individuals were not almost entirely dependent for the maintenance of themselves and their family either on their own labour or on the interest from capital invested so as to make their labour more productive. Now both these sources of income depend on the life and even on the health of the head of the family. They provide what is rather like a life annuity, save that it is more dependent on chance; and in consequence there is a very real difference between people living like this and those whose resources are not at all subject to the same risks, who live either on revenue from land, or on the interest on capital which is almost independent of their own labour.

Here then is a necessary cause of inequality, of dependence and even of misery, which ceaselessly threatens the most numerous and most active class in our society.

We shall point out how it can be in great part eradicated by guaranteeing people in old age a means of livelihood produced partly by their own savings and partly by the savings of others who make the same outlay, but who die before they need to reap the reward; or, again, on the same principle of compensation, by securing for widows and orphans an income which is the same and costs the same for those families which suffer an early loss and for those which suffer it later; or again by providing all children with the capital necessary for the full use of their labour, available at the age when they start work and found a family, a capital which increases at the expense of those whom premature death prevents from reaching this age. It is to the application of the calculus to the probabilities of life and the investment of money that we owe the idea of these methods which have already been successful, although they have not been applied in a sufficiently comprehensive and exhaustive fashion to render them really useful, not merely to a few individuals, but to society as a whole, by making it possible to prevent those periodic disasters which strike at so many families and which are such a recurrent source of misery and suffering.

We shall point out that schemes of this nature, which can be organized in the name of the social authority and become one of its greatest benefits, can also be the work of private associations, which will be formed without any real risk, once the principles for the proper working of these schemes have been widely diffused and the mistakes which have been the undoing of a large number of these associations no longer hold terrors for us.

[We shall reveal other methods of ensuring this equality, either by seeing that credit is no longer the exclusive privilege of great wealth, but that it has another and no less sound foundation; or by making industrial progress and commercial activity more independent of the existence of the great capitalists. And once again, it is to the application of the calculus that we shall be indebted for such methods.]

The degree of equality in education that we can reasonably hope to attain, but that should be adequate, is that which excludes all dependence, either forced or voluntary. We shall show how this condition can be easily attained in the present state of human knowledge even by those who can study only for a small number of years in childhood, and then during the rest of their life in their few hours of leisure. We shall prove that, by a suitable choice of syllabus and of methods of education, we can teach the citizen everything that he needs to know in order to be able to manage his household, administer his affairs and employ his labour and his faculties in freedom; to know his rights and to be able to exercise them; to be acquainted with his duties and fulfil them satisfactorily; to judge his own and other men's actions according to his own lights and to be a stranger to none of the high and delicate feelings which honour human nature; not to be in a state of blind dependence upon those to whom he must entrust his affairs or the exercise of his rights; to be in a proper condition to choose and supervise them; to be no longer the dupe of those popular errors which torment man with superstitious fears and chimerical hopes; to defend himself against prejudice by the strength of his reason alone; and, finally, to escape the deceits of charlatans who would lay snares for his fortune, his health, his freedom of thought and his conscience under the pretext of granting him health, wealth and salvation.

From such time onwards the inhabitants of a single country will no longer be distinguished by their use of a crude or refined language; they will be able to govern themselves according to their own knowledge; they will no longer be limited to a mechanical knowledge of the procedures of the arts or of professional routine; they will no longer depend for every trivial piece of business, every insignificant matter of instruction on clever men who rule over them in virtue of their necessary superiority; and so they will attain a real equality, since differences in enlightenment or talent can no longer raise a barrier between men who understand each other's feelings, ideas and language, some of whom may wish to be taught by others but, to do so, will have no need to be controlled by them, or who may wish to confide the care of government to the ablest of their number but will

not be compelled to yield them absolute power in a spirit of blind confidence.

This kind of supervision has advantages even for those who do not exercise it, since it is employed for them and not against them. Natural differences of ability between men whose understanding has not been cultivated give rise, even in savage tribes, to charlatans and dupes, to clever men and men readily deceived. These same differences are truly universal, but now they are differences only between men of learning and upright men who know the value of learning without being dazzled by it; or between talent or genius and the common sense which can appreciate and benefit from them; so that even if these natural differences were greater, and more extensive than they are, they would be only the more influential in improving the relations between men and promoting what is advantageous for their independence and happiness.

These various causes of equality do not act in isolation; they unite, combine and support each other and so their cumulative effects are stronger, surer and more constant. With greater equality of education there will be greater equality in industry and so in wealth; equality in wealth necessarily leads to equality in education: and equality between the nations and equality within a single nation are mutually dependent.

So we might say that a well directed system of education rectifies natural inequality in ability instead of strengthening it, just as good laws remedy natural inequality in the means of subsistence, and just as in societies where laws have brought about this same equality, liberty, though subject to a regular constitution, will be more widespread, more complete than in the total independence of savage life. Then the social art will have fulfilled its aim, that of assuring and extending to all men enjoyment of the common rights to which they are called by nature.

The real advantages that should result from this progress, of which we can entertain a hope that is almost a certainty, can have no other term than that of the absolute perfection of the human race; since, as the various kinds of equality come to work in its favour by producing ampler sources of supply, more extensive education, more complete liberty, so equality will be more real and will embrace everything which is really of importance for the happiness of human beings.

It is therefore only by examining the progress and the laws of this perfection that we shall be able to understand the extent or the limits of our hopes.

*   *   *

The progress of the sciences ensures the progress of the art of education which in turn advances that of the sciences. This reciprocal influence, whose activity is ceaselessly renewed, deserves to be seen as one of the most powerful and active causes working for the perfection of mankind. At the present time a young man on leaving school may know more of the principles of mathematics than Newton ever learnt in years of study or discovered by dint of genius, and he may use the calculus with a facility then unknown. The same observation, with certain reservations, applies to all the sciences. As each advances, the methods of expressing a large number of proofs in a more economical fashion and so of making their comprehension an easier matter, advance with it. So, in spite of the progress of science, not only do men of the same ability find themselves at the same age on a level with the existing state of science, but with every generation, that which can be acquired in a certain time with a certain degree of intelligence and a certain amount of concentration will be permanently on the increase, and, as the elementary part of each science to which all men may attain grows and grows, it will more and more include all the knowledge necessary for each man to know for the conduct of the ordinary events of his life, and will support him in the free and independent exercise of his reason.

In the political sciences there are some truths that, with free people (that is to say, with certain generations in all countries) can be of use only if they are widely known and acknowledged. So the influence of these sciences upon the freedom and prosperity of nations must in some degree be measured by the number of truths that, as a result of elementary instruction, are common knowledge; the swelling progress of elementary instruction, connected with the necessary progress of these sciences promises us an improvement in the destiny of the human race, which may be regarded as indefinite, since it can have no other limits than that of this same progress.

We have still to consider two other general methods which will influence both the perfection of education and that of the sciences. One is the more extensive and less imperfect use of what we might call technical methods; the other is the setting up of a universal language.

I mean by technical methods the art of arranging a large number of subjects in a system so that we may straightway grasp their relations, quickly perceive their combinations, and readily form new combinations out of them.

We shall develop the principles and examine the utility of this art, which is still in its infancy, and which, as it improves, will enable us, within the compass of a small chart, to set out what could possibly not be expressed so well in a whole book, or, what is still more valuable, to present isolated facts in such a way as to allow us to deduce their general consequences. We shall see how by means of a small number of these charts, whose use can easily be learned, men who have not been sufficiently educated to be able to absorb details useful to them in ordinary life, may now be able to master them when the need arises; and how these methods may likewise be of benefit to elementary education itself in all those branches where it is concerned either with a regular system of truths or with a series of observations and facts.

A universal language is that which expresses by signs either real objects themselves, or well-defined collections composed of simple and general ideas, which are found to be the same or may arise in a similar form in the minds of all men, or the general relations holding between these ideas, the operations of the human mind, or the operations peculiar to the individual sciences, or the procedures of the arts. So people who become acquainted with these signs, the ways to combine them and the rules for forming them will understand what is written in this language and will be able to read it as easily as their own language.

It is obvious that this language might be used to set out the theory of a science or the rules of an art, to describe a new observation or experiment, the invention of a procedure, the discovery of a truth or a method; and that, as in algebra, when one has to make use of a new sign, those already known provide the means of explaining its import.

Such a language has not the disadvantages of a scientific idiom different from the vernacular. We have already observed that the use of such an idiom would necessarily divide society into two unequal classes, the one composed of men who, understanding this language, would possess the key to all the sciences, the other of men who, unable to acquire it, would therefore find themselves almost completely unable to acquire enlightenment. In contrast to this, a universal language would be learnt, like that of algebra, along with the science itself; the sign would be learnt at the same time as the object, idea or operation that it designates. He who, having mastered the elements of a science, would like to know more of it, would find in books not only truths he could understand by means of the signs whose import he has learnt, but also the explanation of such further signs as he needs in order to go on to other truths.

We shall show that the formation of such a language, if confined to the expression of those simple, precise propositions which form the system of a science or the practice of an art, is no chimerical scheme; that even at the present time it could be readily introduced to deal with a large number of objects; and that, indeed, the chief obstacle that would prevent its extension to others would be the humiliation of having to admit how very few precise ideas and accurate, unambiguous notions we actually possess.

We shall show that this language, ever improving and broadening its scope all the while, would be the means of giving to every subject embraced by the human intelligence, a precision and a rigour that would make knowledge of the truth easy and error almost impossible. Then the progress of every science would be as sure as that of mathematics, and the propositions that compose it would acquire a geometrical certainty, as far, that is, as is possible granted the nature of its aim and method.

All the causes that contribute to the perfection of the human race, all the means that ensure it must by their very nature exercise a perpetual influence and always increase their sphere of action. The proofs of this we have given and in the great work they will derive additional force from elaboration. We may conclude then that the perfectibility of man is indefinite. Meanwhile we have considered him as possessing the natural faculties and organization that he has at present. How much greater would be the certainty, how must vaster the scheme of our hopes if we could believe that these natural faculties themselves and this organization could also be improved? This is the last question that remains for us to ask ourselves.

Organic perfectibility or deterioration amongst the various strains in the vegetable and animal kingdom can be regarded as one of the general laws of nature. This law also applies to the human race. No-one can doubt that, as preventitive medicine improves and food and housing become healthier, as a way of life is established that develops our physical powers by exercise without ruining them by excess, as the two most virulent causes of deterioration, misery and excessive wealth, are eliminated, the average length of human life will be increased and a better health and a stronger physical constitution will be ensured. The improvement of medical practice, which will become more efficacious with the progress of reason and of the social order, will mean the end of infectious and hereditary diseases and illnesses brought on by climate, food, or working conditions. It is reasonable to hope that all other diseases may likewise disappear as their distant causes are discovered. Would it be absurd then to suppose that this perfection of the human species might be capable of indefinite progress; that the day will come when death will be due only to extraordinary accidents or to the decay of the vital forces, and that ultimately the average span between birth and decay will have no assignable value? Certainly man will not become immortal, but will not the interval between the first breath that he draws and the time when in the natural course of events, without disease or accident, he expires, increase indefinitely? Since we are now speaking of a progress that can be represented with some accuracy in figures or on a graph, we shall take this opportunity of explaining the two meanings that can be attached to the word *indefinite*.

In truth, this average span of life which we suppose will increase indefinitely as time passes, may grow in conformity either with a law such that it continually approaches a limitless length but without ever reaching it, or with a law such that through the centuries it reaches a length greater than any determinate quantity that we may assign to it as its limit. In the latter case such an increase is truly indefinite in the strictest sense of the word, since there is no term on this side of which it must of necessity stop. In the former case it is equally indefinite in relation to us, if we cannot fix the limit it always approaches without ever reaching, and particularly if, knowing only that it will never stop, we are ignorant in which of the two senses the term 'indefinite' can be applied to it. Such is the present condition of our knowledge as far as the perfectibility of the human race is concerned; such is the sense in which we may call it indefinite.

So, in the example under consideration, we are bound to believe that the average length of human life will for ever increase unless this is prevented by physical revolutions; we do not know what the limit is which it can never exceed. We cannot tell even whether the general laws of nature have determined such a limit or not.

But are not our physical faculties and the strength, dexterity and acuteness of our senses, to be numbered among the qualities whose perfection in the individual may be transmitted? Observation of the various breeds of domestic animals inclines us to believe that they are, and we can confirm this by direct observation of the human race.

Finally may we not extend such hopes to the intellectual and moral faculties? May not our parents, who transmit to us the benefits or disadvantages of their constitution, and from whom we receive our shape and features, as well as our tendencies to certain physical affections, hand on to us also that part of the physical organization which determines the intellect, the power of the brain, the ardour of the soul or the moral sensibility? Is it not probable that education, in perfecting these qualities, will at the same time influence, modify and perfect the organization itself? Analogy, investigation of the human faculties and the study of certain facts, all seem to give substance to such conjectures which would further push back the boundaries of our hopes.

These are the questions with which we shall conclude this final stage. How consoling for the philosopher who laments the errors, the crimes, the injustices which still pollute the earth and of which he is often the victim is this view of the human race, emancipated from its shackles, released from the empire of fate and from that of the enemies of its progress, advancing with a firm and sure step along the path of truth, virtue and happiness! It is the contemplation of this prospect that rewards him for all his efforts to assist the progress of reason and the defence of liberty. He dares to regard these strivings as part of the eternal chain of human destiny; and in this persuasion he is filled with the true delight of virtue and the pleasure of having done some lasting good which fate can never destroy by a sinister stroke of revenge, by calling back the reign of slavery and prejudice. Such contemplation is for him an asylum, in which the memory of his persecutors cannot pursue him; there he lives in thought with man restored to his natural rights and dignity, forgets man tormented and corrupted by greed, fear or envy; there he lives with his peers in an Elysium created by reason and graced by the purest pleasures known to the love of mankind.

*   *   *

REVIEW QUESTIONS

1. On what does Condorcet found his ability to predict the future?
2. Would Newton agree "that nature has set no limit to the realization of one's hopes"?
3. In what areas of human endeavor does Condorcet measure progress?
4. What are the standards by which he measures it?
5. What does Condorcet see as the end point of Enlightenment?
6. What is the nature of freedom? Equality?
7. How does Condorcet measure equality?
8. What is its relation to a universal language?

JEAN-JACQUES ROUSSEAU

FROM *The Social Contract*

Jean-Jacques Rousseau (1712–1778) was one of the most original writers of the Enlightenment. A native of Geneva, he was raised by his father, a watchmaker. At sixteen years of age, he left home and eventually settled in Paris. His first attempts to penetrate the world of philosophes and encyclopedists were not very successful. In 1750, however, he won a literary award from the Academy of Dijon for an essay that contrasted the corruption of modern civilization with the natural goodness of simple, uncivilized human beings. Rousseau eventually settled in the town of Montmorency. His years there proved to be the most fruitful of his life. In a two-year span he wrote his most significant works: La nouvelle Héloise *(1761),* Emile *(1761),* Le contrat social *(1762).*

In The Social Contract, *as well as his other works, Rousseau struggled with the freedom of the individual and how to balance it against the needs of the collectivity. He believed the preservation of liberty depended on the creation of a new society by means of a social contract. The idea was not new, having been adopted by other enlightened thinkers from the political theory of John Locke. Rousseau's interpretation was highly original, however. Locke believed that the social contract preserved freedom; Rousseau argued that the social contract preserved equality. Under his social contract, people voluntarily relinquished certain rights and submitted to the general will, a vague entity that found expression in a set of positive laws under a virtuous legislator. These laws had absolute authority and would preserve absolute equality between people.*

From *The Social Contract,* by Jean-Jacques Rousseau, translated by Henry J. Tozer (New York: Scribner's, 1898).

Book I

I mean to inquire if, in the civil order, there can be any sure and legitimate rule of administration, men being taken as they are and laws as they might be. In this inquiry I shall endeavour always to unite what right sanctions with what is prescribed by interest, in order that justice and utility may in no case be divided.

I enter upon my task without proving the importance of the subject. I shall be asked if I am a prince or a legislator, to write on politics. I answer that I am neither, and that is why I do so. If I were a prince or a legislator, I should not waste time in saying what wants doing; I should do it, or hold my peace.

As I was born a citizen of a free State, and a member of the Sovereign, I feel that, however feeble the influence my voice can have on public affairs, the right of voting on them makes it my duty to study them: and I am happy, when I reflect upon governments, to find my inquiries always furnish me with new reasons for loving that of my own country.

CHAPTER I
SUBJECT OF THE FIRST BOOK

Man is born free; and everywhere he is in chains. One thinks himself the master of others, and still remains a greater slave than they. How did this change come about? I do not know. What can make it legitimate? That question I think I can answer.

If I took into account only force, and the effects derived from it, I should say: "As long as a people is compelled to obey, and obeys, it does well; as soon as it can shake off the yoke, and shakes it off, it does still better; for, regaining its liberty by the same right as took it away, either it is justified in resuming it, or there was no justification for those who took it away." But the social order is a sacred right which is the basis of all rights. Nevertheless, this right does not come from nature, and must therefore be founded on con-

ventions. Before coming to that, I have to prove what I have just asserted.

CHAPTER II
THE FIRST SOCIETIES

The most ancient of all societies, and the only one that is natural, is the family: and even so the children remain attached to the father only so long as they need him for their preservation. As soon as this need ceases, the natural bond is dissolved. The children, released from the obedience they owed to the father, and the father, released from the care he owed his children, return equally to independence. If they remain united, they continue so no longer naturally, but voluntarily; and the family itself is then maintained only by convention.

This common liberty results from the nature of man. His first law is to provide for his own preservation, his first cares are those which he owes to himself; and, as soon as he reaches years of discretion, he is the sole judge of the proper means of preserving himself, and consequently becomes his own master.

The family then may be called the first model of political societies: the ruler corresponds to the father, and the people to the children; and all, being born free and equal, alienate their liberty only for their own advantage. The whole difference is that, in the family, the love of the father for his children repays him for the care he takes of them, while, in the State, the pleasure of commanding takes the place of the love which the chief cannot have for the peoples under him.

Grotius denies that all human power is established in favour of the governed, and quotes slavery as an example. His usual method of reasoning is constantly to establish right by fact. It would be possible to employ a more logical method, but none could be more favourable to tyrants.

It is then, according to Grotius, doubtful whether the human race belongs to a hundred men, or that hundred men to the human race: and, throughout his book, he seems to incline to the former alternative, which is also the view of

Hobbes. On this showing, the human species is divided into so many herds of cattle, each with its ruler, who keeps guard over them for the purpose of devouring them.

As a shepherd is of a nature superior to that of his flock, the shepherds of men, i.e. their rulers, are of a nature superior to that of the peoples under them. Thus, Philo tells us, the Emperor Caligula reasoned, concluding equally well either that kings were gods, or that men were beasts.

The reasoning of Caligula agrees with that of Hobbes and Grotius. Aristotle, before any of them, had said that men are by no means equal naturally, but that some are born for slavery, and others for dominion.

Aristotle was right; but he took the effect for the cause. Nothing can be more certain than that every man born in slavery is born for slavery. Slaves lose everything in their chains, even the desire of escaping from them: they love their servitude, as the comrades of Ulysses loved their brutish condition. If then there are slaves by nature, it is because there have been slaves against nature. Force made the first slaves, and their cowardice perpetuated the condition.

I have said nothing of King Adam, or Emperor Noah, father of the three great monarchs who shared out the universe, like the children of Saturn, whom some scholars have recognized in them. I trust to getting due thanks for my moderation; for, being a direct descendant of one of these princes, perhaps of the eldest branch, how do I know that a verification of titles might not leave me the legitimate king of the human race? In any case, there can be no doubt that Adam was sovereign of the world, as Robinson Crusoe was of his island, as long as he was its only inhabitant; and this empire had the advantage that the monarch, safe on his throne, had no rebellions, wars, or conspirators to fear.

CHAPTER III
THE RIGHT OF THE STRONGEST

The strongest is never strong enough to be always the master, unless he transforms strength into right, and obedience into duty. Hence the right of the strongest, which, though to all seeming meant ironically, is really laid down as a fundamental principle. But are we never to have an explanation of this phrase? Force is a physical power, and I fail to see what moral effect it can have. To yield to force is an act of necessity, not of will—at the most, an act of prudence. In what sense can it be a duty?

Suppose for a moment that this so-called "right" exists. I maintain that the sole result is a mass of inexplicable nonsense. For, if force creates right, the effect changes with the cause: every force that is greater than the first succeeds to its right. As soon as it is possible to disobey with impunity, disobedience is legitimate; and, the strongest being always in the right, the only thing that matters is to act so as to become the strongest. But what kind of right is that which perishes when force fails? If we must obey perforce, there is no need to obey because we ought; and if we are not forced to obey, we are under no obligation to do so. Clearly, the word "right" adds nothing to force: in this connection, it means absolutely nothing.

Obey the powers that be. If this means yield to force, it is a good precept, but superfluous: I can answer for its never being violated. All power comes from God, I admit; but so does all sickness: does that mean that we are forbidden to call in the doctor? A brigand surprises me at the edge of a wood: must I not merely surrender my purse on compulsion; but, even if I could withhold it, am I in conscience bound to give it up? For certainly the pistol he holds is also a power.

Let us then admit that force does not create right, and that we are obliged to obey only legitimate powers. In that case, my original question recurs.

CHAPTER IV
SLAVERY

Since no man has a natural authority over his fellow, and force creates no right, we must conclude that conventions form the basis of all legitimate authority among men.

If an individual, says Grotius, can alienate his liberty and make himself the slave of a master, why could not a whole people do the same and make itself subject to a king? There are in this passage plenty of ambiguous words which would need explaining; but let us confine ourselves to the word *alienate*. To alienate is to give or to sell. Now, a man who becomes the slave of another does not give himself; he sells himself, at the least for his subsistence: but for what does a people sell itself? A king is so far from furnishing his subjects with their subsistence that he gets his own only from them; and, according to Rabelais, kings do not live on nothing. Do subjects then give their persons on condition that the king takes their goods also? I fail to see what they have left to preserve.

It will be said that the despot assures his subjects civil tranquillity. Granted; but what do they gain, if the wars his ambition brings down upon them, his insatiable avidity, and the vexatious conduct of his ministers press harder on them than their own dissensions would have done? What do they gain, if the very tranquillity they enjoy is one of their miseries? Tranquillity is found also in dungeons; but is that enough to make them desirable places to live in? The Greeks imprisoned in the cave of the Cyclops lived there very tranquilly, while they were awaiting their turn to be devoured.

To say that a man gives himself gratuitously, is to say what is absurd and inconceivable; such an act is null and illegitimate, from the mere fact that he who does it is out of his mind. To say the same of a whole people is to suppose a people of madmen; and madness creates no right.

Even if each man could alienate himself, he could not alienate his children: they are born men and free; their liberty belongs to them, and no one but they has the right to dispose of it. Before they come to years of discretion, the father can, in their name, lay down conditions for their preservation and well-being, but he cannot give them irrevocably and without conditions: such a gift is contrary to the ends of nature, and exceeds the rights of paternity. It would therefore be necessary, in order to legitimize an arbitrary government, that in every generation the people should be in a position to accept or reject it; but, were this so, the government would be no longer arbitrary.

To renounce liberty is to renounce being a man, to surrender the rights of humanity and even its duties. For him who renounces everything no indemnity is possible. Such a renunciation is incompatible with man's nature; to remove all liberty from his will is to remove all morality from his acts. Finally, it is an empty and contradictory convention that sets up, on the one side, absolute authority, and, on the other, unlimited obedience. Is it not clear that we can be under no obligation to a person from whom we have the right to exact everything? Does not this condition alone, in the absence of equivalence or exchange, in itself involve the nullity of the act? For what right can my slave have against me, when all that he has belongs to me, and, his right being mine, this right of mine against myself is a phrase devoid of meaning?

Grotius and the rest find in war another origin for the so-called right of slavery. The victor having, as they hold, the right of killing the vanquished, the latter can buy back his life at the price of his liberty; and this convention is the more legitimate because it is to the advantage of both parties.

But it is clear that this supposed right to kill the conquered is by no means deducible from the state of war. Men, from the mere fact that, while they are living in their primitive independence, they have no mutual relations stable enough to constitute either the state of peace or the state of war, cannot be naturally enemies. War is constituted by a relation between things, and not between persons; and, as the state of war cannot arise out of simple personal relations, but only out of real relations, private war, or war of man with man, can exist neither in the state of nature, where there is no constant property, nor in the social state, where everything is under the authority of the laws.

Individual combats, duels, and encounters, are acts which cannot constitute a state; while the private wars, authorized by the Establishments of

Louis IX, King of France, and suspended by the Peace of God, are abuses of feudalism, in itself an absurd system if ever there was one, and contrary to the principles of natural right and to all good polity.

War then is a relation, not between man and man, but between State and State, and individuals are enemies only accidently, not as men, nor even as citizens, but as soldiers; not as members of their country, but as its defenders. Finally, each State can have for enemies only other States, and not men; for between things disparate in nature there can be no real relation.

Furthermore, this principle is in conformity with the established rules of all times and the constant practice of all civilized peoples. Declarations of war are intimations less to powers than to their subjects. The foreigner, whether king, individual, or people, who robs, kills, or detains the subjects, without declaring war on the prince, is not an enemy, but a brigand. Even in real war, a just prince, while laying hands, in the enemy's country, on all that belongs to the public, respects the lives and goods of individuals: he respects rights on which his own are founded. The object of the war being the destruction of the hostile State, the other side has a right to kill its defenders, while they are bearing arms; but as soon as they lay them down and surrender, they cease to be enemies or instruments of the enemy, and become once more merely men, whose life no one has any right to take. Sometimes it is possible to kill the State without killing a single one of its members; and war gives no right which is not necessary to the gaining of its object. These principles are not those of Grotius: they are not based on the authority of poets, but derived from the nature of reality and based on reason.

The right of conquest has no foundation other than the right of the strongest. If war does not give the conqueror the right to massacre the conquered peoples, the right to enslave them cannot be based upon a right which does not exist. No one has a right to kill an enemy except when he cannot make him a slave, and the right to enslave him cannot therefore be derived from the right to kill him. It is accordingly an unfair exchange to make him buy at the price of his liberty his life, over which the victor holds no right. Is it not clear that there is a vicious circle in founding the right of life and death on the right of slavery, and the right of slavery on the right of life and death?

Even if we assume this terrible right to kill everybody, I maintain that a slave made in war, or a conquered people, is under no obligation to a master, except to obey him as far as he is compelled to do so. By taking an equivalent for his life, the victor has not done him a favour; instead of killing him without profit, he has killed him usefully. So far then is he from acquiring over him any authority in addition to that of force, that the state of war continues to subsist between them: their mutual relation is the effect of it, and the usage of the right of war does not imply a treaty of peace. A convention has indeed been made; but this convention, so far from destroying the state of war, presupposes its continuance.

So, from whatever aspect we regard the question, the right of slavery is null and void, not only as being illegitimate, but also because it is absurd and meaningless. The words *slave* and *right* contradict each other, and are mutually exclusive. It will always be equally foolish for a man to say to a man or to a people: "I make with you a convention wholly at your expense and wholly to my advantage; I shall keep it as long as I like, and you will keep it as long as I like."

*   *   *

CHAPTER VI
THE SOCIAL COMPACT

I suppose men to have reached the point at which the obstacles in the way of their preservation in the state of nature show their power of resistance to be greater than the resources at the disposal of each individual for his maintenance in that state. That primitive condition can then subsist no longer; and the human race would perish unless it changed its manner of existence.

But, as men cannot engender new forces, but

only unite and direct existing ones, they have no other means of preserving themselves than the formation, by aggregation, of a sum of forces great enough to overcome the resistance. These they have to bring into play by means of a single motive power, and cause to act in concert.

This sum of forces can arise only where several persons come together: but, as the force and liberty of each man are the chief instruments of his self-preservation, how can he pledge them without harming his own interests, and neglecting the care he owes to himself? This difficulty, in its bearing on my present subject, may be stated in the following terms:

"The problem is to find a form of association which will defend and protect with the whole common force the person and goods of each associate, and in which each, while uniting himself with all, may still obey himself alone, and remain as free as before." This is the fundamental problem of which the *Social Contract* provides the solution.

The clauses of this contract are so determined by the nature of the act that the slightest modification would make them vain and ineffective; so that, although they have perhaps never been formally set forth, they are everywhere the same and everywhere tacitly admitted and recognized, until, on the violation of the social compact, each regains his original rights and resumes his natural liberty, while losing the conventional liberty in favour of which he renounced it.

These clauses, properly understood, may be reduced to one—the total alienation of each associate, together with all his rights, to the whole community; for, in the first place, as each gives himself absolutely, the conditions are the same for all; and, this being so, no one has any interest in making them burdensome to others.

Moreover, the alienation being without reserve, the union is as perfect as it can be, and no associate has anything more to demand: for, if the individuals retained certain rights, as there would be no common superior to decide between them and the public, each, being on one point his own judge, would ask to be so on all; the state of nature

would thus continue, and the association would necessarily become inoperative or tyrannical.

Finally, each man, in giving himself to all, gives himself to nobody; and as there is no associate over which he does not acquire the same right as he yields others over himself, he gains an equivalent for everything he loses, and an increase of force for the preservation of what he has.

If then we discard from the social compact what is not of its essence, we shall find that it reduces itself to the following terms:

"Each of us puts his person and all his power in common under the supreme direction of the general will, and, in our corporate capacity, we receive each member as an indivisible part of the whole."

At once, in place of the individual personality of each contracting party, this act of association creates a moral and collective body, composed of as many members as the assembly contains voters, and receiving from this act its unity, its common identity, its life, and its will. This public person, so formed by the union of all other persons, formerly took the name of *city,* and now takes that of *Republic* or *body politic;* it is called by its members *State* when passive, *Sovereign* when active, and *Power* when compared with others like itself. Those who are associated in it take collectively the name of *people,* and severally are called *citizens,* as sharing in the sovereign power, and *subjects,* as being under the laws of the State. But these terms are often confused and taken one for another: it is enough to know how to distinguish them when they are being used with precision.

CHAPTER VII
THE SOVEREIGN

This formula shows us that the act of association comprises a mutual undertaking between the public and the individuals, and that each individual, in making a contract, as we may say, with himself, is bound in a double capacity; as a member of the Sovereign he is bound to the individuals, and as a member of the State to the Sovereign. But the maxim of civil right, that no one is bound by undertakings made to himself, does not apply in this case; for there is a great difference between incurring an obligation to yourself and incurring one to a whole of which you form a part.

Attention must further be called to the fact that public deliberation, while competent to bind all the subjects to the Sovereign, because of the two different capacities in which each of them may be regarded, cannot, for the opposite reason, bind the Sovereign to itself; and that it is consequently against the nature of the body politic for the Sovereign to impose on itself a law which it cannot infringe. Being able to regard itself in only one capacity, it is in the position of an individual who makes a contract with himself; and this makes it clear that there neither is nor can be any kind of fundamental law binding on the body of the people—not even the social contract itself. This does not mean that the body politic cannot enter into undertakings with others, provided the contract is not infringed by them; for in relation to what is external to it, it becomes a simple being, an individual.

But the body politic or the Sovereign, drawing its being wholly from the sanctity of the contract, can never bind itself, even to an outsider, to do anything derogatory to the original act, for instance, to alienate any part of itself, or to submit to another Sovereign. Violation of the act by which it exists would be self-annihilation; and that which is itself nothing can create nothing.

As soon as this multitude is so united in one body, it is impossible to offend against one of the members without attacking the body, and still more to offend against the body without the members resenting it. Duty and interest therefore equally oblige the two contracting parties to give each other help; and the same men should seek to combine, in their double capacity, all the advantages dependent upon that capacity.

Again, the Sovereign, being formed wholly of the individuals who compose it, neither has nor can have any interest contrary to theirs; and consequently the sovereign power need give no guarantee to its subjects, because it is impossible for the body to wish to hurt all its members. We shall also see later on that it cannot hurt any in particular. The Sovereign, merely by virtue of what it is, is always what it should be.

This, however, is not the case with the relation of the subjects to the Sovereign, which, despite the common interest, would have no security that they would fulfil their undertakings, unless it found means to assure itself of their fidelity.

In fact, each individual, as a man, may have a particular will contrary or dissimilar to the general will which he has as a citizen. His particular interest may speak to him quite differently from the common interest: his absolute and naturally independent existence may make him look upon what he owes to the common cause as a gratuitous contribution, the loss of which will do less harm to others than the payment of it is burdensome to himself; and, regarding the moral person which constitutes the State as a *persona ficta,* because not a man, he may wish to enjoy the rights of citizenship without being ready to fulfil the duties of a subject. The continuance of such an injustice could not but prove the undoing of the body politic.

In order then that the social compact may not be an empty formula, it tacitly includes the undertaking, which alone can give force to the rest, that whoever refuses to obey the general will shall be compelled to do so by the whole body. This means nothing less than that he will be forced to be free; for this is the condition which, by giving each citizen to his country, secures him against all personal dependence. In this lies the key to the working of the political machine; this alone legitimizes civil undertakings, which, without it, would be absurd, tyrannical, and liable to the most frightful abuses.

CHAPTER VIII
THE CIVIL STATE

The passage from the state of nature to the civil state produces a very remarkable change in man, by substituting justice for instinct in his conduct, and giving his actions the morality they had formerly lacked. Then only, when the voice of duty takes the place of physical impulses and right of appetite, does man, who so far had considered only himself, find that he is forced to act on different principles, and to consult his reason before listening to his inclinations. Although, in this state, he deprives himself of some advantages which he got from nature, he gains in return others so great, his faculties are so stimulated and developed, his ideas so extended, his feelings so ennobled, and his whole soul so uplifted, that, did not the abuses of this new condition often degrade him below that which he left, he would be bound to bless continually the happy moment which took him from it for ever, and, instead of a stupid and unimaginative animal, made him an intelligent being and a man.

Let us draw up the whole account in terms easily commensurable. What man loses by the social contract is his natural liberty and an unlimited right to everything he tries to get and succeeds in getting; what he gains is civil liberty and the proprietorship of all he possesses. If we are to avoid mistake in weighing one against the other, we must clearly distinguish natural liberty, which is bounded only by the strength of the individual, from civil liberty, which is limited by the general will; and possession, which is merely the effect of force or the right of the first occupier, from property, which can be founded only on a positive title.

We might, over and above all this, add, to what man acquires in the civil state, moral liberty, which alone makes him truly master of himself; for the mere impulse of appetite is slavery, while obedience to a law which we prescribe to ourselves is liberty. But I have already said too much on this head, and the philosophical meaning of the word liberty does not now concern us.

*   *   *

Book II

*   *   *

CHAPTER III
WHETHER THE GENERAL WILL IS FALLIBLE

It follows from what has gone before that the general will is always right and tends to the public advantage; but it does not follow that the deliberations of the people are always equally correct. Our will is always for our own good, but we do not always see what that is; the people is never corrupted, but it is often deceived, and on such occasions only does it seem to will what is bad.

There is often a great deal of difference between the will of all and the general will; the latter considers only the common interest, while the former takes private interest into account, and is no more than a sum of particular wills: but take away from these same wills the pluses and minuses that cancel one another, and the general will remains as the sum of the differences.

If, when the people, being furnished with adequate information, held its deliberations, the citizens had no communication one with another, the grand total of the small differences would always give the general will, and the decision would always be good. But when factions arise, and partial associations are formed at the expense of the great association, the will of each of these associations becomes general in relation to its members, while it remains particular in relation to the State: it may then be said that there are no longer as many votes as there are men, but only as many as there are associations. The differences become less numerous and give a less general result. Lastly, when one of these associations is so great as to prevail over all the rest, the result is no longer a sum of small differences, but a single difference; in this case there is no longer a general will, and the opinion which prevails is purely particular.

It is therefore essential, if the general will is to be able to express itself, that there should be no partial society within the State, and that each citizen should think only his own thoughts: which was indeed the sublime and unique system established by the great Lycurgus. But if there are partial societies, it is best to have as many as possible and to prevent them from being unequal, as was done by Solon, Numa, and Servius. These precautions are the only ones that can guarantee that the general will shall be always enlightened, and that the people shall in no way deceive itself.

*   *   *

CHAPTER IV
THE LIMITS OF THE SOVEREIGN POWER

If the State is a moral person whose life is in the union of its members, and if the most important of its cares is the care for its own preservation, it must have a universal and compelling force, in order to move and dispose each part as may be most advantageous to the whole. As nature gives each man absolute power over all his members, the social compact gives the body politic absolute power over all its members also; and it is this power which, under the direction of the general will, bears, as I have said, the name of Sovereignty.

But, besides the public person, we have to consider the private persons composing it, whose life and liberty are naturally independent of it. We are bound then to distinguish clearly between the respective rights of the citizens and the Sovereign, and between the duties the former have to fulfil as subjects, and the natural rights they should enjoy as men.

Each man alienates, I admit, by the social compact, only such part of his powers, goods, and liberty as it is important for the community to control; but it must also be granted that the Sovereign is sole judge of what is important.

Every service a citizen can render the State he ought to render as soon as the Sovereign demands it; but the Sovereign, for its part, cannot impose upon its subjects any fetters that are useless to the community, nor can it even wish to do so; for no more by the law of reason than by the law of nature can anything occur without a cause.

The undertakings which bind us to the social body are obligatory only because they are mutual; and their nature is such that in fulfilling them we cannot work for others without working for ourselves. Why is it that the general will is always in the right, and that all continually will the happiness of each one, unless it is because there is not a man who does not think of "each" as meaning him, and consider himself in voting for all? This proves that equality of rights and the idea of justice which such equality creates originate in the preference each man gives to himself, and accordingly in the very nature of man. It proves that the general will, to be really such, must be general in its object as well as its essence; that it must both come from all and apply to all; and that it loses its natural rectitude when it is directed to some particular and determinate object, because in such a case we are judging of something foreign to us, and have no true principle of equity to guide us.

Indeed, as soon as a question of particular fact or right arises on a point not previously regulated by a general convention, the matter becomes contentious. It is a case in which the individuals concerned are one party, and the public the other, but in which I can see neither the law that ought to be followed nor the judge who ought to give the decision. In such a case, it would be absurd to propose to refer the question to an express decision of the general will, which can be only the conclusion reached by one of the parties and in consequence will be, for the other party, merely an external and particular will, inclined on this occasion to injustice and subject to error. Thus, just as a particular will cannot stand for the general will, the general will, in turn, changes its nature, when its object is particular, and, as general, cannot pronounce on a man or a fact. When, for instance, the people of Athens nominated or displaced its rulers, decreed honours to one, and imposed penalties on another, and, by a multitude of particular decrees, exercised all the functions of government indiscriminately, it had in such cases no longer a general will in the strict sense; it was acting no longer as Sovereign, but as magistrate. This will seem contrary to current views; but I must be given time to expound my own.

It should be seen from the foregoing that what makes the will general is less the number of voters than the common interest uniting them; for, under this system, each necessarily submits to the conditions he imposes on others: and this admirable agreement between interest and justice gives to the common deliberations an equitable character which at once vanishes when any particular question is discussed, in the absence of a common interest to unite and identify the ruling of the judge with that of the party.

From whatever side we approach our principle, we reach the same conclusion, that the social compact sets up among the citizens an equality of such a kind, that they all bind themselves to observe the same conditions and should therefore all enjoy the same rights. Thus, from the very nature of the compact, every act of Sovereignty, i.e. every authentic act of the general will, binds or favours all the citizens equally; so that the Sovereign recognizes only the body of the nation, and draws no distinctions between those of whom it is made up. What, then, strictly speaking, is an act of Sovereignty? It is not a convention between a superior and an inferior, but a convention between the body and each of its members. It is legitimate, because based on the social contract, and equitable, because common to all; useful, because it can have no other object than the general good, and stable, because guaranteed by the public force and the supreme power. So long as the subjects have to submit only to conventions of this sort, they obey no one but their own will; and to ask how far the respective rights of the Sovereign and the citizens extend, is to ask up to what point the latter can enter into undertakings with themselves, each with all, and all with each.

We can see from this that the sovereign power, absolute, sacred, and inviolable as it is, does not and cannot exceed the limits of general conventions, and that every man may dispose at will of such goods and liberty as these conventions leave him; so that the Sovereign never has a right to lay more charges on one subject than on another, because, in that case, the question becomes par-

ticular, and ceases to be within its competency.

When these distinctions have once been admitted, it is seen to be so untrue that there is, in the social contract, any real renunciation on the part of the individuals, that the position in which they find themselves as a result of the contract is really preferable to that in which they were before. Instead of a renunciation, they have made an advantageous exchange: instead of an uncertain and precarious way of living they have got one that is better and more secure; instead of natural independence they have got liberty, instead of the power to harm others security for themselves, and instead of their strength, which others might overcome, a right which social union makes invincible. Their very life, which they have devoted to the State, is by it constantly protected; and when they risk it in the State's defence, what more are they doing than giving back what they have received from it? What are they doing that they would not do more often and with greater danger in the state of nature, in which they would inevitably have to fight battles at the peril of their lives in defence of that which is the means of their preservation? All have indeed to fight when their country needs them; but then no one has ever to fight for himself. Do we not gain something by running, on behalf of what gives us our security, only some of the risks we should have to run for ourselves, as soon as we lost it?

*   *   *

REVIEW QUESTIONS

1. How does Rousseau's conception of the origin of political society compare with those of Filmer and Locke?
2. What is the relation between human slavery and human nature?
3. How do relations of subject and ruler come into being?
4. What is the social contract?
5. What is its relation to nature? To reason? To will?

JEAN-JACQUES ROUSSEAU

FROM *Emile*

Emile, written a year earlier than The Social Contract, *was in some ways more controversial. A study of education, it renounced the empiricism and rationalism of the Enlightenment to emphasize the value of emotions and impulses. Rousseau's goal was to educate a natural child, one preserved from the corrupting influences of formal education and contemporary society. Allowed to pursue his curiosity and inclination, according to his capacities and talents, such a child would grow into a social, moral, and rational being, one capable of doing whatever is needed in a given situation. His ideas so scandalized French authorities that they ordered his arrest. Fleeing at the last moment, Rousseau spent the rest of his life in exile. He died before the French Revolution, which adopted his thought and transferred his remains to the* Panthéon *in Paris.*

From *Emile,* by Jean-Jacques Rousseau, translated by Allan Bloom (New York: Basic Books, 1979), pp. 358–69.

*　*　*

Book V

Now we have come to the last act in the drama of youth, but we are not yet at the dénouement. It is not good for man to be alone.[1] Emile is a man. We have promised him a companion. She has to be given to him. That companion is Sophie. In what place is her abode? Where shall we find her? To find her, it is necessary to know her. Let us first learn what she is; then we shall better judge what places she inhabits. And even when we have found her, everything will still not have been done. "Since our young gentleman," says Locke, "is ready to marry, it is time to leave him to his beloved."[2] And with that he finishes his work. But as I do not have the honor of raising a gentleman, I shall take care not to imitate Locke on this point.

SOPHIE OR THE WOMAN

Sophie ought to be a woman as Emile is a man— that is to say, she ought to have everything which suits the constitution of her species and her sex in order to fill her place in the physical and moral order. Let us begin, then, by examining the similarities and the differences of her sex and ours.

In everything not connected with sex, woman is man. She has the same organs, the same needs, the same faculties. The machine is constructed in the same way; its parts are the same; the one functions as does the other; the form is similar; and in whatever respect one considers them, the difference between them is only one of more or less.

In everything connected with sex, woman and man are in every respect related and in every respect different. The difficulty of comparing them comes from the difficulty of determining what in their constitutions is due to sex and what is not. On the basis of comparative anatomy and even just by inspection, one finds general differences between them that do not appear connected with sex. They are, nevertheless, connected with sex, but by relations which we are not in a position to perceive. We do not know the extent of these relations. The only thing we know with certainty is that everything man and woman have in common belongs to the species, and that everything which distinguishes them belongs to the sex. From this double perspective, we find them related in so many ways and opposed in so many other ways that it is perhaps one of the marvels of nature to have been able to construct two such similar beings who are constituted so differently.

These relations and these differences must have a moral influence. This conclusion is evident to the senses; it is in agreement with our experience; and it shows how vain are the disputes as to whether one of the two sexes is superior or whether they are equal—as though each, in fulfilling nature's ends according to its own particular purpose, were thereby less perfect than if it resembled the other more! In what they have in common, they are equal. Where they differ, they are not comparable. A perfect woman and a perfect man ought not to resemble each other in mind any more than in looks, and perfection is not susceptible of more or less.

*   *   *

Here, then, is a third conclusion drawn from the constitution of the sexes—that the stronger appears to be master but actually depends on the weaker. This is due not to a frivolous practice of gallantry or to the proud generosity of a protector, but to an invariable law of nature which gives woman more facility to excite the desires than man to satisfy them. This causes the latter, whether he likes it or not, to depend on the former's wish and constrains him to seek to please her in turn, so that she will consent to let him be the stronger. Then what is sweetest for man in his victory is the doubt whether it is weakness which yields to strength or the will which surrenders. And the woman's usual ruse is always to leave this doubt between her and him. In this the spirit of women corresponds perfectly to their constitution. Far from blushing at their weakness, they make it their glory. Their tender muscles are without

resistance. They pretend to be unable to lift the lightest burdens. They would be ashamed to be strong. Why is that? It is not only to appear delicate; it is due to a shrewder precaution. They prepare in advance excuses and the right to be weak in case of need.

*   *   *

Observe how the physical leads us unawares to the moral, and how the sweetest laws of love are born little by little from the coarse union of the sexes. Women possess their empire not because men wanted it that way, but because nature wants it that way. It belonged to women before they appeared to have it. The same Hercules who believed he raped the fifty daughters of Thespitius was nevertheless constrained to weave while he was with Omphale; and the strong Samson was not so strong as Delilah.[5] This empire belongs to women and cannot be taken from them, even when they abuse it. If they could ever lose it, they would have done so long ago.

*   *   *

The strictness of the relative duties of the two sexes is not and cannot be the same. When woman complains on this score about unjust man-made inequality, she is wrong. This inequality is not a human institution—or, at least, it is the work not of prejudice but of reason. It is up to the sex that nature has charged with the bearing of children to be responsible for them to the other sex. Doubtless it is not permitted to anyone to violate his faith, and every unfaithful husband who deprives his wife of the only reward of the austere duties of her sex is an unjust and barbarous man. But the unfaithful woman does more; she dissolves the family and breaks all the bonds of nature. In giving the man children which are not his, she betrays both. She joins perfidy to infidelity. I have difficulty seeing what disorders and what crimes do not flow from this one. If there is a frightful condition in the world, it is that of an unhappy father who, lacking confidence in his wife, does not dare to yield to the sweetest sentiments of his heart, who wonders, in embracing his child, whether he is embracing another's, the token of his dishonor, the plunderer of his own children's property. What does the family become in such a situation if not a society of secret enemies whom a guilty woman arms against one another in forcing them to feign mutual love?

It is important, then, not only that a woman be faithful, but that she be judged to be faithful by her husband, by those near her, by everyone. It is important that she be modest, attentive, reserved, and that she give evidence of her virtue to the eyes of others as well as to her own conscience. If it is important that a father love his children, it is important that he esteem their mother. These are the reasons which put even appearances among the duties of women, and make honor and reputation no less indispensable to them than chastity. There follows from these principles, along with the moral difference of the sexes, a new motive of duty and propriety which prescribes especially to women the most scrupulous attention to their conduct, their manners, and their bearing. To maintain vaguely that the two sexes are equal and that their duties are the same, is to lose oneself in vain declaiming; it is to say nothing so long as one does not respond to these considerations.

*   *   *

Once it is demonstrated that man and woman are not and ought not to be constituted in the same way in either character or temperament, it follows that they ought not to have the same education. In following nature's directions, man and woman ought to act in concert, but they ought not to do the same things. The goal of their labors is common, but their labors themselves are different, and consequently so are the tastes directing them. After having tried to form the natural man, let us also see how the woman who suits this man ought to be formed so that our work will not be left imperfect.

Do you wish always to be well guided? Then always follow nature's indications. Everything that characterizes the fair sex ought to be respected as established by nature. You constantly say, "Women have this or that failing which we do not

have." Your pride deceives you. They would be failings for you; they are their good qualities. Everything would go less well if they did not have these qualities. Prevent these alleged failings from degenerating, but take care not to destroy them.

For their part, women do not cease to proclaim that we raise them to be vain and coquettish, that we constantly entertain them with puerilities in order to remain more easily their masters. They blame on us the failings for which we reproach them. What folly! And since when is it that men get involved in the education of girls? Who prevents their mothers from raising them as they please? They have no colleges. What a great misfortune! Would God that there were none for boys; they would be more sensibly and decently raised! Are your daughters forced to waste their time in silliness? Are they made in spite of themselves to spend half their lives getting dressed up, following the example you set them? Are you prevented from instructing them and having them instructed as you please? Is it our fault that they please us when they are pretty, that their mincing ways seduce us, that the art which they learn from you attracts us and pleases us, that we like to see them tastefully dressed, that we let them sharpen at their leisure the weapons with which they subjugate us? So, decide to raise them like men. The men will gladly consent to it! The more women want to resemble them, the less women will govern them, and then men will truly be the masters.

All the faculties common to the two sexes are not equally distributed between them; but taken together, they balance out. Woman is worth more as woman and less as man. Wherever she makes use of her rights, she has the advantage. Wherever she wants to usurp ours, she remains beneath us. One can respond to this general truth only with exceptions, the constant mode of argument of the gallant partisans of the fair sex.

To cultivate man's qualities in women and to neglect those which are proper to them is obviously to work to their detriment. Crafty women see this too well to be duped by it. In trying to usurp our advantages, they do not abandon theirs. But it turns out that they are unable to manage both well—because the two are incompatible—and they remain beneath their own level without getting up to ours, thus losing half their value. Believe me, judicious mother, do not make a decent man of your daughter, as though you would give nature the lie.[7] Make a decent woman of her, and be sure that as a result she will be worth more for herself and for us.

Does it follow that she ought to be raised in ignorance of everything and limited to the housekeeping functions alone? Will man turn his companion into his servant? Will he deprive himself of the greatest charm of society with her? In order to make her more subject, will he prevent her from feeling anything, from knowing anything? Will he make her into a veritable automaton? Surely not. It is not thus that nature has spoken in giving women such agreeable and nimble minds. On the contrary, nature wants them to think, to judge, to love, to know, to cultivate their minds as well as their looks. These are the weapons nature gives them to take the place of the strength they lack and to direct ours. They ought to learn many things but only those that are suitable for them to know.

Whether I consider the particular purpose of the fair sex, whether I observe its inclinations, whether I consider its duties, all join equally in indicating to me the form of education that suits it. Woman and man are made for one another, but their mutual dependence is not equal. Men depend on women because of their desires; women depend on men because of both their desires and their needs. We would survive more easily without them than they would without us. For them to have what is necessary to their station, they depend on us to give it to them, to want to give it to them, to esteem them worthy of it. They depend on our sentiments, on the value we set on their merit, on the importance we attach to their charms and their virtues. By the very law of nature women are at the mercy of men's judgments, as much for their own sake as for that of their children. It is not enough that they be estimable; they must be esteemed. It is not enough for them to be pretty; they must please. It is not enough for

them to be temperate; they must be recognized as such. Their honor is not only in their conduct but in their reputation; and it is not possible that a woman who consents to be regarded as disreputable can ever be decent. When a man acts well, he depends only on himself and can brave public judgment; but when a woman acts well, she has accomplished only half of her task, and what is thought of her is no less important to her than what she actually is. From this it follows that the system of woman's education ought to be contrary in this respect to the system of our education. Opinion is the grave of virtue among men and its throne among women.

The good constitution of children initially depends on that of their mothers. The first education of men depends on the care of women. Men's morals, their passions, their tastes, their pleasures, their very happiness also depend on women. Thus the whole education of women ought to relate to men. To please men, to be useful to them, to make herself loved and honored by them, to raise them when young, to care for them when grown, to counsel them, to console them, to make their lives agreeable and sweet—these are the duties of women at all times, and they ought to be taught from childhood. So long as one does not return to this principle, one will deviate from the goal, and all the precepts taught to women will be of no use for their happiness or for ours.

*   *   *

It is known that comfortable clothing which did not hinder the body contributed a great deal to leaving both sexes among the Greeks with those beautiful proportions seen in their statues—statues which still serve as models for art today, when disfigured nature has ceased furnishing art with models among us. They had not a single one of all these gothic shackles, these multitudes of ligatures which squeeze our bodies on all sides. Their women were ignorant of the use of these whalebone corsets with which our women counterfeit their waists rather than display them. I cannot believe that this abuse, pushed to an inconceivable extent in England, will not finally cause the species to degenerate, and I even maintain that the attraction that it offers is in bad taste. It is not attractive to see a woman cut in half like a wasp. That is shocking to the sight, and it makes the imagination suffer. The narrowness of the waist has, like everything else, its proportions, its limit, beyond which it is certainly a defect. This defect would even be an assault on the eye when seen naked. Why should it be a beautiful thing under clothing?

* * *

Everything that hinders and constrains nature is in bad taste. This is as true of the adornments of the body as it is of the ornaments of the mind. Life, health, reason, and well-being ought to go ahead of everything. Grace does not exist without comfort. Delicacy is not sickliness, and it is not requisite to be unhealthy in order to please. One arouses pity when one suffers, but pleasure and desire seek the freshness of health.

The children of both sexes have many common entertainments, and that ought to be so. Is this not also the case when they are grown up? They also have particular tastes which distinguish them. Boys seek movement and noise: drums, boots, little carriages. Girls prefer what presents itself to sight and is useful for ornamentation: mirrors, jewels, dresses, particularly dolls. The doll is the special entertainment of this sex. This is evidently its taste, determined by its purpose. The physical part of the art of pleasing lies in adornment. This is the only part of that art that children can cultivate.

* * *

This is a very definite primary taste. You have only to follow and regulate it. It is certain that the little girl would want with all her heart to know how to adorn her doll, to make its bracelets, its scarf, its flounce, its lace. For all of this she is put in such a harsh dependence on the good will of others that it would be far more convenient for weakening this attachment, only increase it; for dependence is a condition natural to women, and thus girls feel themselves made to obey.

For the same reason that they have—or ought to have—little freedom, they tend to excess in the freedom that is left to them. Extreme in everything, they indulge themselves in their games with even more intensity than boys do. This is the second difficulty of which I was just speaking. This intensity ought to be moderated, for it is the cause of several vices peculiar to women, such as, among others, the capriciousness and infatuation which cause a woman to be in transports today for some object she will not look at tomorrow. Inconstancy of tastes is as deadly for them as is excess, and both come from the same source. Do not deprive them of gaiety, laughter, noise, and frolicsome games, but prevent them from getting their fill of one in order to run to another; do not allow for a single instant in their lives that they no longer know any restraint. Accustom them to being interrupted in the midst of their games and brought back to other cares without grumbling. Habit alone suffices in this as well, because it does nothing other than to reinforce nature.

From this habitual constraint comes a docility which women need all their lives, since they never cease to be subjected either to a man or to the judgments of men and they are never permitted to put themselves above these judgments. The first and most important quality of a woman is gentleness. As she is made to obey a being who is so imperfect, often so full of vices, and always so full of defects as man, she ought to learn early to endure even injustice and to bear a husband's wrongs without complaining. It is not for his sake, it is for her own, that she ought to be gentle. The bitterness and the stubbornness of women never do anything but increase their ills and the bad behavior of their husbands. Men feel that it is not with these weapons that women ought to conquer them. Heaven did not make women ingratiating and persuasive in order that they become shrewish. It did not make them weak in order that they be imperious. It did not give them so gentle a voice in order that they utter insults. It did not give them such delicate features to be disfigured by anger. When they get upset, they forget themselves. They are often right to complain, but they are always wrong to scold. Each sex ought to keep to its own tone. A husband who is too gentle can make a woman impertinent; but unless a man is a monster, the gentleness of a woman brings him around and triumphs over him sooner or later.

*   *   *

REVIEW QUESTIONS

1. What, according to Rousseau, is the nature of woman, and how does her nature differ from that of man?

2. How and to what end ought women to be educated?
3. What is the purpose of education generally and for women specifically?
4. To what extent does Rousseau's notion of the basis of education set him apart from enlightened thinkers in general?
5. Why might Rousseau's discussion of education have struck French authorities as dangerously subversive?

MARY WOLLSTONECRAFT

FROM *A Vindication of the Rights of Women*

Mary Wollstonecraft (1759–1797) was a writer and advocate of social and educational equality for women. Born a farmer's daughter, she served as a teacher and governess, positions that shaped her thinking about education for young women. Her most mature and best-remembered work, A Vindication of the Rights of Women, *appeared in 1792. In it she argued for the equal education of men and women. An educational system that deliberately trained women to be inferior and subject to men should be replaced by a national system that allowed girls the same advantages and opportunities as boys. The result would be not only more able wives and mothers but also women capable of taking part in public life. Her interests in social equality and political change turned her attention to events in France. Inspired by the ideals of the revolution there, she traveled to Paris that same year to observe events and, returning to London in 1795, joined a circle of political radicals that included Thomas Paine. She died shortly after giving birth to her second daughter, the future Mary Wollstonecraft Shelley.*

From *A Vindication of the Rights of Women,* by Mary Wollstonecraft, edited by Ashley Tauchert (London: Everyman, 1997), pp. 22–26, 29–30, 41–42.

*　　*　　*

Chapter 2
The Prevailing Opinion of a Sexual Character Discussed

To account for, and excuse the tyranny of man, many ingenious arguments have been brought forward to prove, that the two sexes, in the acquirement of virtue, ought to aim at attaining a very different character: or, to speak explicitly, women are not allowed to have sufficient strength of mind to acquire what really deserves the name of virtue. Yet it should seem, allowing them to have souls, that there is but one way appointed by Providence to lead *mankind* to either virtue or happiness.

If then women are not a swarm of ephemeron triflers, why should they be kept in ignorance under the specious name of innocence? Men complain, and with reason, of the follies and caprices of our sex, when they do not keenly satirize our headstrong passions and groveling vices. Behold, I should answer, the natural effect of ignorance! The mind will ever be unstable that has only prejudices to rest on, and the current will run with destructive fury when there are no barriers to break its force. Women are told from their infancy, and taught by the example of their mothers, that a little knowledge of human weakness, justly termed cunning, softness of temper, *outward* obedience, and a scrupulous attention to a puerile kind of propriety, will obtain for them the protection of man; and should they be beautiful, every thing else is needless, for, at least, twenty years of their lives.

*　　*　　*

How grossly do they insult us who thus advise us only to render ourselves gentle, domestic brutes! For instance, the winning softness so warmly, and frequently, recommended, that governs by obeying. What childish expressions, and how insignificant is the being—can it be an immortal one? who will condescend to govern by such sinister methods! "Certainly," says Lord Bacon, "man is of kin to the beasts by his body; and

if he be not of kin to God by his spirit, he is a base and ignoble creature!" Men, indeed, appear to me to act in a very unphilosophical manner when they try to secure the good conduct of women by attempting to keep them always in a state of childhood. Rousseau was more consistent when he wished to stop the progress of reason in both sexes, for if men eat of the tree of knowledge, women will come in for a taste; but, from the imperfect cultivation which their understandings now receive, they only attain a knowledge of evil.

*　　*　　*

In treating, therefore, of the manners of women, let us, disregarding sensual arguments, trace what we should endeavour to make them in order to co-operate, if the expression be not too bold, with the supreme Being.

By individual education, I mean, for the sense of the word is not precisely defined, such an attention to a child as will slowly sharpen the senses, form the temper, regulate the passions as they begin to ferment, and set the understanding to work before the body arrives at maturity; so that the man may only have to proceed, not to begin, the important task of learning to think and reason.

To prevent any misconstruction, I must add, that I do not believe that a private education can work the wonders which some sanguine writers have attributed to it. Men and women must be educated, in a great degree, by the opinions and manners of the society they live in. In every age there has been a stream of popular opinion that has carried all before it, and given a family character, as it were, to the century. It may then fairly be inferred, that, till society be differently constituted, much cannot be expected from education. It is, however, sufficient for my present purpose to assert, that, whatever effect circumstances have on the abilities, every being may become virtuous by the exercise of its own reason; for if but one being was created with vicious inclinations, that is positively bad, what can save us from atheism? or if we worship a God, is not that God a devil?

Consequently, the most perfect education, in my opinion, is such an exercise of the understanding as is best calculated to strengthen the body and form the heart. Or, in other words, to enable the individual to attain such habits of virtue as will render it independent. In fact, it is a farce to call any being virtuous whose virtues do not result from the exercise of its own reason. This was Rousseau's opinion respecting men: I extend it to women, and confidently assert that they have been drawn out of their sphere by false refinement, and not by an endeavour to acquire masculine qualities. Still the regal homage which they receive is so intoxicating, that till the manners of the times are changed, and formed on more reasonable principles, it may be impossible to convince them that the illegitimate power, which they obtain, by degrading themselves, is a curse, and that they must return to nature and equality, if they wish to secure the placid satisfaction that unsophisticated affections impart. But for this epoch we must wait—wait, perhaps, till kings and nobles, enlightened by reason, and, preferring the real dignity of man to childish state, throw off their gaudy hereditary trappings: and if then women do not resign the arbitrary power of—they will prove that they have *less* mind than man.

I may be accused of arrogance; still I must declare what I firmly believe, that all the writers who have written on the subject of female education and manners from Rousseau to Dr Gregory, have contributed to render women more artificial, weak characters, than they would otherwise have been; and, consequently, more useless members of society. ✴ ✴ ✴

✴   ✴   ✴

Many are the causes that, in the present corrupt state of society, contribute to enslave women by cramping their understandings and sharpening their senses. One, perhaps, that silently does more mischief than all the rest, is their disregard of order.

To do every thing in an orderly manner, is a most important precept, which women, who, generally speaking, receive only a disorderly kind of education, seldom attend to with that degree of exactness that men, who from their infancy are

broken into method, observe. This negligent kind of guess-work, for what other epithet can be used to point out the random exertions of a sort of instinctive common sense, never brought to the test of reason? prevents their generalizing matters of fact—so they do today, what they did yesterday, merely because they did it yesterday.

✴   ✴   ✴

Women are, therefore, to be considered either as moral beings, or so weak that they must be entirely subjected to the superior faculties of men.

Let us examine this question. Rousseau declares that a woman should never, for a moment, feel herself independent, that she should be governed by fear to exercise her natural cunning, and made a coquettish slave in order to render her a more alluring object of desire, a *sweeter* companion to man, whenever he chooses to relax himself. He carries the arguments, which he pretends to draw from the indications of nature, still further, and insinuates that truth and fortitude, the corner stones of all human virtue, should be cultivated with certain restrictions, because, with respect to the female character, obedience is the grand lesson which ought to be impressed with unrelenting rigour.

What nonsense! when will a great man arise with sufficient strength of mind to puff away the fumes which pride and sensuality have thus spread over the subject! If women are by nature inferior to men, their virtues must be the same in quality, if not in degree, or virtue is a relative idea; consequently, their conduct should be founded on the same principles, and have the same aim.

Connected with man as daughters, wives, and mothers, their moral character may be estimated by their manner of fulfilling those simple duties; but the end, the grand end of their exertions should be to unfold their own faculties and acquire the dignity of conscious virtue. They may try to render their road pleasant; but ought never to forget, in common with man, that life yields not the felicity which can satisfy an immortal soul. I do not mean to insinuate, that either sex should be so lost in abstract reflections or distant views, as to forget the affections and duties that lie before them, and are, in truth, the means appointed to produce the fruit of life; on the contrary, I would warmly recommend them, even while I assert, that they afford most satisfaction when they are considered in their true, sober light.

*   *   *

Women ought to endeavour to purify their heart; but can they do so when their uncultivated understandings make them entirely dependent on their senses for employment and amusement, when no noble pursuit sets them above the little vanities of the day, or enables them to curb the wild emotions that agitate a reed over which every passing breeze has power? To gain the affections of a virtuous man is affectation necessary? Nature has given woman a weaker frame than man; but, to ensure her husband's affections, must a wife, who by the exercise of her mind and body whilst she was discharging the duties of a daughter, wife, and mother, has allowed her constitution to retain its natural strength, and her nerves a healthy tone, is she, I say, to condescend to use art and feign a sickly delicacy in order to secure her husband's affection? Weakness may excite tenderness, and gratify the arrogant pride of man; but the lordly caresses of a protector will not gratify a noble mind that pants for, and deserves to be respected. Fondness is a poor substitute for friendship!

*   *   *

If, I say, for I would not impress by declamation when Reason offers her sober light, if they be really capable of acting like rational creatures, let them not be treated like slaves; or, like the brutes who are dependent on the reason of man, when they associate with him; but cultivate their minds, give them the salutary, sublime curb of principle, and let them attain conscious dignity by feeling themselves only dependent on God. Teach them, in common with man, to submit to necessity, instead of giving, to render them more pleasing, a sex to morals.

Further, should experience prove that they cannot attain the same degree of strength of mind, perseverance, and fortitude, let their virtues be the same in kind, though they may vainly struggle for the same degree; and the superiority of man will be equally clear, if not clearer; and truth, as it is a simple principle, which admits of no modification, would be common to both. Nay, the order of society as it is at present regulated would not be inverted, for woman would then only have the rank that reason assigned her, and arts could not be practised to bring the balance even, much less to turn it.

These may be termed Utopian dreams. Thanks to that Being who impressed them on my soul, and gave me sufficient strength of mind to dare to exert my own reason, till, becoming dependent only on him for the support of my virtue, I view, with indignation, the mistaken notions that enslave my sex.

I love man as my fellow; but his sceptre, real, or usurped, extends not to me, unless the reason of an individual demands my homage; and even then the submission is to reason, and not to man. In fact, the conduct of an accountable being must be regulated by the operations of its own reason; or on what foundation rests the throne of God?

It appears to me necessary to dwell on these obvious truths, because females have been insulated, as it were; and, while they have been stripped of the virtues that should clothe humanity, they have been decked with artificial graces that enable them to exercise a short-lived tyranny. Love, in their bosoms, taking place of every nobler passion, their sole ambition is to be fair, to raise emotion instead of inspiring respect; and this ignoble desire, like the servility in absolute monarchies, destroys all strength of character. Liberty is the mother of virtue, and if women be, by their very constitution, slaves, and not allowed to breathe the sharp invigorating air of freedom, they must ever languish like exotics, and be reckoned beautiful flaws in nature.

As to the argument respecting the subjection in which the sex has ever been held, it retorts on man. The many have always been enthralled by the few; and monsters, who scarcely have shewn any discernment of human excellence, have tyr-

THE MALL (1783)　　　　　　　　　　　　　　　　　　THOMAS GAINSBOROUGH

Gainsborough is best remembered for his portraits of British aristocracy and gentry in the late eighteenth century, but The Mall *captures the sociability rather than the domesticity of the mercantile and landed elite. What aspects of enlightened thought might be rendered visible in* The Mall*? In particular, how do public spaces, nature, and reason correspond in* The Mall *and in the Enlightenment? Why do women predominate in the scene? What does this suggest about their role in enlightened society? Why might Gainsborough have taken up bourgeois sociability as a subject for painting?*

annized over thousands of their fellow-creatures. Why have men of superior endowments submitted to such degradation? For, is it not universally acknowledged that kings, viewed collectively, have ever been inferior, in abilities and virtue, to the same number of men taken from the common mass of mankind—yet, have they not, and are they not still treated with a degree of reverence that is an insult to reason? China is not the only country where a living man has been made a God. *Men* have submitted to superior strength to enjoy with impunity the pleasure of the moment— *women* have only done the same, and therefore till it is proved that the courtier, who servilely resigns the birthright of a man, is not a moral agent, it cannot be demonstrated that woman is essentially inferior to man because she has always been subjugated.

Brutal force has hitherto governed the world, and that the science of politics is in its infancy, is evident from philosophers scrupling to give the knowledge most useful to man that determinate distinction.

I shall not pursue this argument any further than to establish an obvious inference, that as sound politics diffuse liberty, mankind, including woman, will become more wise and virtuous.

*   *   *

REVIEW QUESTIONS

1. What does Wollstonecraft consider to be the then-present state of women?
2. Why should women, according to Wollstonecraft, be offered the same education as men?
3. What would the purpose of such an education be?
4. What does Wollstonecraft take to be the social role of women, and how does her conclusion differ from that of Rousseau?
5. What is virtue, according to Wollstonecraft, and how does it compare with Rousseau's conception?
6. How radical is Wollstonecraft's thought?

CESARE, MARCHESE DI BECCARIA BONESANA

FROM *An Essay on Crimes and Punishments*

Cesare, marchese di Beccaria Bonesana (1738–1794) was an economist and criminologist and one of the best-known Italian thinkers of the Enlightenment. Born the son of a Milanese aristocrat, he was educated by Jesuits and received a degree in law from the University of Pavia in 1755. He gravitated into the enlightened circle around Count Pietro Verri who encouraged him in 1763 to take up the study of criminal law. Beccaria's great work, An Essay on Crimes and Punishments, *appeared a year later. Arguing on the basis of utilitarian principles—the greatest good for the greatest number—he excoriated the barbaric and ineffective legal practices of his day, such as judicial torture, extreme punishment, and magisterial corruption. The effectiveness of the law, he reasoned, depended ultimately on its certainty rather than its severity. Thus, torture should be abolished, and punishments made proportional to the crimes. For the same reason Beccaria became the first modern writer to advocate the abolition of capital punishment. The work proved tremendously influ-*

ential, guiding legal reforms across Europe and winning champions like Jeremy Bentham.

From *An Essay on Crimes and Punishments,* by Cesare Beccaria-Bonesasa (Stanford, Calif.: Academic Reprints, 1953), pp. 15–19, 47, 59–67, 95–96.

Chapter 1
Of the Origin of Punishments

Laws are the conditions under which men, naturally independent, united themselves in society. Weary of living in a continual state of war, and of enjoying a liberty, which became of little value, from the uncertainty of its duration, they sacrificed one part of it, to enjoy the rest in peace and security. The sum of all these portions of the liberty of each individual constituted the sovereignty of a nation and was deposited in the hands of the sovereign, as the lawful administrator. But it was not sufficient only to establish this deposit; it was also necessary to defend it from the usurpation of each individual, who will always endeavour to take away from the mass, not only his own portion, but to encroach on that of others. Some motives therefore, that strike the senses were necessary to prevent the despotism of each individual from plunging society into its former chaos. Such motives are the punishments established against the infractors of the laws. I say that motives of this kind are necessary; because experience shows, that the multitude adopt no established principle of conduct; and because society is prevented from approaching to that dissolution, (to which, as well as all other parts of the physical and moral world, it naturally tends,) only by motives that are the immediate objects of sense, and which being continually presented to the mind, are sufficient to counterbalance the effects of the passions of the individual which oppose the general good. Neither the power of eloquence nor the sublimest truths are sufficient to restrain, for any length of time, those passions which are excited by the lively impressions of present objects.

Chapter 2
Of the Right to Punish

Every punishment which does not arise from absolute necessity, says the great Montesquieu, is tyrannical. A proposition which may be made more general thus: every act of authority of one man over another, for which there is not an absolute necessity, is tyrannical. It is upon this then that the sovereign's right to punish crimes is founded; that is, upon the necessity of defending the public liberty, entrusted to his care, from the usurpation of individuals; and punishments are just in proportion, as the liberty, preserved by the sovereign, is sacred and valuable.

Let us consult the human heart, and there we shall find the foundation of the sovereign's right to punish, for no advantage in moral policy can be lasting which is not founded on the indelible sentiments of the heart of man. Whatever law deviates from this principle will always meet with a resistance which will destroy it in the end; for the smallest force continually applied will overcome the most violent motion communicated to bodies.

No man ever gave up his liberty merely for the good of the public. Such a chimera exists only in romances. Every individual wishes, if possible, to be exempt from the compacts that bind the rest of mankind.

The multiplication of mankind, though slow, being too great, for the means which the earth, in its natural state, offered to satisfy necessities which every day became more numerous, obliged men to separate again, and form new societies. These naturally opposed the first, and a state of war was transferred from individuals to nations.

Thus it was necessity that forced men to give up a part of their liberty. It is certain, then, that every individual would choose to put into the public stock the smallest portion possible, as much only as was sufficient to engage others to defend it. The aggregate of these, the smallest portions possible, forms the right of punishing; all that extends beyond this, is abuse, not justice.

Observe that by *justice* I understand nothing more than that bond which is necessary to keep the interest of individuals united, without which men would return to their original state of barbarity. All punishments which exceed the necessity of preserving this bond are in their nature unjust. We should be cautious how we associate with the word *justice* an idea of any thing real, such as a physical power, or a being that actually exists. I do not, by any means, speak of the justice of God, which is of another kind, and refers immediately to rewards and punishments in a life to come.

*   *   *

Chapter 12
Of the Intent of Punishments

From the foregoing considerations it is evident that the intent of punishments is not to torment a sensible being, nor to undo a crime already committed. Is it possible that torments and useless cruelty, the instrument of furious fanaticism or the impotency of tyrants, can be authorised by a political body, which, so far from being influenced by passion, should be the cool moderator of the passions of individuals? Can the groans of a tortured wretch recall the time past, or reverse the crime he has committed?

The end of punishment, therefore, is no other than to prevent the criminal from doing further injury to society, and to prevent others from committing the like offence. Such punishments, therefore, and such a mode of inflicting them, ought to be chosen, as will make the strongest and most lasting impressions on the minds of others, with the least torment to the body of the criminal.

*   *   *

Chapter 16
Of Torture

The torture of a criminal during the course of his trial is a cruelty consecrated by custom in most nations. It is used with an intent either to make him confess his crime, or to explain some contradictions into which he had been led during his examination, or discover his accomplices, or for some kind of metaphysical and incomprehensible purgation of infamy, or, finally, in order to discover other crimes of which he is not accused, but of which he may be guilty.

No man can be judged a criminal until he be found guilty nor can society take from him the public protection until it have been proved that he has violated the conditions on which it was granted. What right, then, but that of power, can authorise the punishment of a citizen so long as there remains any doubt of his guilt? This dilemma is frequent. Either he is guilty, or not guilty. If guilty, he should only suffer the punishment ordained by the laws, and torture becomes useless, as his confession is unnecessary. If he be not guilty, you torture the innocent; for, in the eye of the law, every man is innocent whose crime has not been proved. Besides, it is confounding all relations to expect that a man should be both the accuser and accused; and that pain should be the test of truth, as if truth resided in the muscles and fibres of a wretch in torture. By this method the robust will escape, and the feeble be condemned. These are the inconveniencies of this pretended test of truth, worthy only of a cannibal, and which the Romans, in many respects barbarous, and whose savage virtue has been too much admired, reserved for the slaves alone.

What is the political intention of punishments? To terrify and be an example to others. Is this intention answered by thus privately torturing the guilty and the innocent? It is doubtless of importance that no crime should remain unpunished; but it is useless to make a public example of the author of a crime hid in darkness. A crime already committed, and for which there can be no remedy, can only be punished by a political society with an intention that no hopes of impunity should induce others to commit the same. If it be true, that the number of those who from fear or virtue respect the laws is greater than of those by whom they are violated, the risk of torturing an innocent person is greater, as there is a greater probability that, *cæteris paribus,* an individual hath observed, than that he hath infringed the laws.

There is another ridiculous motive for torture, namely, *to purge a man from infamy.* Ought such an abuse to be tolerated in the eighteenth century? Can pain, which is a sensation, have any connection with a moral sentiment, a matter of opinion? Perhaps the rack may be considered as the refiner's furnace.

It is not difficult to trace this senseless law to its origin; for an absurdity, adopted by a whole nation, must have some affinity with other ideas established and respected by the same nation. This custom seems to be the offspring of religion, by which mankind, in all nations and in all ages, are so generally influenced. We are taught by our infallible church, that those stains of sin contracted through human frailty, and which have not deserved the eternal anger of the Almighty, are to be purged away in another life by an incomprehensible fire. Now infamy is a stain, and if the punishments and fire of purgatory can take away all spiritual stains, why should not the pain of torture take away those of a civil nature? I imagine, that the confession of a criminal, which in some tribunals is required as being essential to his condemnation, has a similar origin, and has been taken from the mysterious tribunal of penitence, were the confession of sins is a necessary part of the sacrament. Thus have men abused the unerring light of revelation; and, in the times of tractable ignorance, having no other, they naturally had recourse to it on every occasion, making the most remote and absurd applications. Moreover, infamy is a sentiment regulated neither by the laws nor by reason, but entirely by opinion; but torture renders the victim infamous, and therefore cannot take infamy away.

Another intention of torture is to oblige the supposed criminal to reconcile the contradictions into which he may have fallen during his examination; as if the dread of punishment, the uncertainty of his fate, the solemnity of the court, the majesty of the judge, and the ignorance of the accused, were not abundantly sufficient to account for contradictions, which are so common to men even in a state of tranquility, and which must necessarily be multiplied by the perturbation of the mind of a man entirely engaged in the thoughts of saving himself from imminent danger.

This infamous test of truth is a remaining monument of that ancient and savage legislation, in which trials by fire, by boiling water, or the uncertainty of combats, were called *judgments of God;* as if the links of that eternal chain, whose beginning is in the breast of the first cause of all things, could ever be disunited by the institutions of men. The only difference between torture and trials by fire and boiling water is, that the event of the first depends on the will of the accused, and of the second on a fact entirely physical and external: but this difference is apparent only, not real. A man on the rack, in the convulsions of torture, has it as little in his power to declare the truth, as, in former times, to prevent without fraud the effects of fire or boiling water.

Every act of the will is invariably in proportion to the force of the impression on our senses. The impression of pain, then, may increase to such a degree, that, occupying the mind entirely, it will compel the sufferer to use the shortest method of freeing himself from torment. His answer, therefore, will be an effect as necessary as that of fire or boiling water, and he will accuse himself of crimes of which he is innocent: so that the very means employed to distinguish the innocent from the guilty will most effectually destroy all difference between them.

It would be superfluous to confirm these reflections by examples of innocent persons who, from the agony of torture, have confessed themselves guilty: innumerable instances may be found in all nations, and in every age. How amazing that mankind have always neglected to draw the natural conclusion! Lives there a man who, if he has carried his thoughts ever so little beyond the necessities of life, *when he reflects on such cruelty, is not tempted to fly from society, and return to his natural state of independence?*

The result of torture, then, is a matter of calculation, and depends on the constitution, which differs in every individual, and it is in proportion to his strength and sensibility; so that to discover truth by this method, is a problem which may be better solved by a mathematician than by a judge, and may be thus stated: *The force of the muscles and the sensibility of the nerves of an innocent person being given, it is required to find the degree of pain necessary to make him confess himself guilty of a given crime.*

The examination of the accused is intended to find out the truth: but if this be discovered with so much difficulty in the air, gesture, and countenance of a man at ease, how can it appear in a countenance distorted by the convulsions of torture? Every violent action destroys those small alterations in the features which sometimes disclose the sentiments of the heart.

These truths were known to the Roman legislators, amongst whom, as I have already observed, slaves only, who were not considered as citizens, were tortured. They are known to the English a nation in which the progress of science, superiority in commerce, riches, and power, its natural consequences, together with the numerous examples of virtue and courage, leave no doubt of the excellence of its laws. They have been acknowledged in Sweden, where torture has been abolished. They are known to one of the wisest monarchs in Europe, who, having seated philosophy on the throne by his beneficent legislation, has made his subjects free, though dependent on the laws; the only freedom that reasonable men can desire in the present state of things. In short, torture has not been thought necessary in the laws of armies, composed chiefly of the dregs of mankind, where its use should seem most necessary. Strange phenomenon! that a set of men, hardened by slaughter, and familiar with blood, should teach humanity to the sons of peace.

It appears also that these truths were known, though imperfectly, even to those by whom tor-

ture has been most frequently practised; for a confession made during torture, is null, if it be not afterwards confirmed by an oath, which if the criminal refuses, he is tortured again. Some civilians and some nations permit this infamous *petitio principii* to be only three times repeated, and others leave it to the discretion of the judge; therefore, of two men equally innocent, or equally guilty, the most robust and resolute will be acquitted, and the weakest and most pusillanimous will be condemned, in consequence of the following excellent mode of reasoning. *I, the judge, must find some one guilty. Thou, who art a strong fellow, hast been able to resist the force of torment; therefore I acquit thee. Thou, being weaker, hast yielded to it; I therefore condemn thee. I am sensible, that the confession which was extorted from thee has no weight; but if thou dost not confirm by oath what thou hast already confessed, I will have thee tormented again.*

A very strange but necessary consequence of the use of torture is, that the case of the innocent is worse than that of the guilty. With regard to the first, either he confesses the crime which he has not committed, and is condemned, or he is acquitted, and has suffered a punishment he did not deserve. On the contrary, the person who is really guilty has the most favourable side of the question; for, if he supports the torture with firmness and resolution, he is acquitted, and has gained, having exchanged a greater punishment for a less.

The law by which torture is authorised, says, *Men, be insensible to pain. Nature has indeed given you an irresistible self-love, and an unalienable right of self-preservation; but I create in you a contrary sentiment, an heroical hatred of yourselves. I command you to accuse yourselves, and to declare the truth, amidst the tearing of your flesh and the dislocation of your bones.*

*   *   *

Chapter 27
Of the Mildness of Punishments

The course of my ideas has carried me away from my subject, to the elucidation of which I now return. Crimes are more effectually prevented by the *certainty* than the *severity* of punishment. Hence in a magistrate the necessity of vigilance, and in a judge of implacability, which, that it may become an useful virtue, should be joined to a mild legislation. The certainty of a small punishment will make a stronger impression than the fear of one more severe, if attended with the hopes of escaping; for it is the nature of mankind to be terrified at the approach of the smallest inevitable evil, whilst hope, the best gift of Heaven, hath the power of dispelling the apprehension of a greater, especially if supported by examples of impunity, which weakness or avarice too frequently afford.

If punishments be very severe, men are naturally led to the perpetration of other crimes, to avoid the punishment due to the first. The countries and times most notorious for severity of punishments were always those in which the most bloody and inhuman actions and the most atrocious crimes were committed for the hand of the legislator and the assassin were directed by the same spirit of ferocity, which on the throne dictated laws of iron to slaves and savages, and in private instigated the subject to sacrifice one tyrant to make room for another.

In proportion as punishments become more cruel, the minds of men, as a fluid rises to the same height with that which surrounds it, grow hardened and insensible; and the force of the passions still continuing, in the space of an hundred years the *wheel* terrifies no more than formerly the *prison.* That a punishment may produce the effect required, it is sufficient that the *evil* it occasions should exceed the *good* expected from the crime, including in the calculation the certainty of the punishment, and the privation of the expected advantage. All severity beyond this is superfluous, and therefore tyrannical.

Men regulate their conduct by the repeated impression of evils they know, and not by those with which they are unacquainted. Let us, for example, suppose two nations, in one of which the greatest punishment is *perpetual slavery,* and in the other *the wheel:* I say, that both will inspire the same degree of terror, and that their can be no reasons for increasing the punishments of the first, which are not equally valid for augmenting those of the second to more lasting and more ingenious modes of tormenting, and so on to the most exquisite refinements of a science too well known to tyrants.

There are yet two other consequences of cruel punishments, which counteract the purpose of their institution, which was, to prevent crimes. The *first* arises from the impossibility of establishing an exact proportion between the crime and punishment; for though ingenious cruelty hath greatly multiplyed the variety of torments, yet the human frame can suffer only to a certain degree, beyond which it is impossible to proceed, be the enormity of the crime ever so great. The *second* consequence is impunity. Human nature is limited no less in evil than in good. Excessive barbarity can never be more than temporary, it being impossible that it should be supported by a permanent system of legislation; for if the laws be too cruel, they must be altered, or anarchy and impunity will succeed.

Is it possible without shuddering with horror, to read in history of the barbarous and useless torments that were cooly invented and executed by men who were called sages? Who does not tremble at the thoughts of thousands of wretches, whom their misery, either caused or tolerated by the laws, which favoured the few and outraged the many, had forced in despair to return to a state of nature, or accused of impossible crimes, the fabric of ignorance and superstition, or guilty only of having been faithful to their own principles; who, I say, can, without horror, think of their being torn to pieces, with slow and studied barbarity, by men endowed with the same passions and the same feelings? A delightful spectacle to a fanatic multitude!

REVIEW QUESTIONS

1. According to Beccaria, what is the proper basis of law in human society?
2. What is the legal purpose and function of punishment?
3. Why is torture irrational?
4. What does Beccaria's criminal theory reveal about his assumptions concerning human nature and human society?
5. What aspects of Beccaria's thought qualify as *enlightened* in the strict, historical sense of the term?

20 ❧ THE FRENCH REVOLUTION

The French revolutionary and Napoleonic eras, 1789–1815, launched the modern period in European history. Europe had so irrevocably changed after 1815 that contemporaries distinguished the period before 1789 as the old regime. To be sure, many features of the old regime continued into the new era, but the sentiment of sudden rupture was largely valid. In various dimensions of public life, the radical transformations of the French Revolution rendered many pre-revolutionary attitudes toward society and politics obsolete. Following the abolition of feudalism, the declaration of civic equality, and the subordination of monarchy to national political sovereignty, traditional authority became irretrievable.

The areas of French society (aristocrats, civil servants, professionals, merchants, artisans, urban workers, peasants) willing to reform, if not dismantle, absolutist monarchy established the revolution's legitimacy. The wide range of grievances that had accumulated in the French provinces and cities provided the broad social base for the upheaval of 1789, just as the prevailing emphasis of eighteenth-century letters on applying reason, natural law, and social utility to public affairs offered a general intellectual framework. To understand the revolution's development, however, one must recognize that, while the revolution inaugurated a new era of political rights and citizenship ideals, the specific content of "liberty, equality, brotherhood" remained contested. Consequently, the freshly constituted polity of France embarked on an uncharted course of political experimentation, the prominent milestones of which (dissolution of monarchy, regicide, radical republicanism, political terror, republican imperialism) subsequently defined the parameters of the modern political landscape.

The revolutionary impulses in Paris resonated throughout Europe. As the largest and most powerful continental state in Europe (one out of five Europeans lived in France), French politics affected all Europeans. The precedent of French constitutionalism and the Declaration of the Rights of Man and Citizen reconfigured the domestic political cultures of all European states. The level of political disputation intensified; contemporaries alternately celebrated or denounced the potential of widened political participation. Even Great Britain's stable political establishment of limited monarchy and parliamentary rule perceived French republicanism as a threat. The decision of Austria and Prussia to invade France in 1792 not only radicalized French politics but also expanded the revolutionary political sphere. Napoleon's military prowess further embedded French revolutionary influence abroad with the creation of new kingdoms, the appointment of new rulers, the institution of new laws, and the transmission of a new political outlook. Although the European great powers attempted to eradicate most of Napoleon's political reordering after 1815, the revolutionary challenge to traditional elites remained a permanent feature of European political life.

ARTHUR YOUNG

FROM *Travels in France During the Years 1787, 1788, 1789*

Arthur Young, an established author and one of the "improving landlords" of English agriculture, traveled through France prior to and during the French Revolution. His acute observations of the conditions of French society offer an invaluable contemporary testimony to the many problems that hindered both agricultural prosperity and political stability.

From *Travels in France During the Years 1787, 1788, 1789,* by Arthur Young, edited by Constantia Maxwell (Cambridge, Eng.: Cambridge University Press, 1950).

*   *   *

Of all the subjects of political economy, I know not one that has given rise to such a cloud of errors as this of population. It seems, for some centuries, to have been considered as the only sure test of national prosperity. I am clearly of opinion from the observations I made in every province of the Kingdom, that her population is so much beyond the proportion of her industry and labour, that she would be much more powerful, and infinitely more flourishing, if she had five or six millions less of inhabitants. From her too great population, she presents in every quarter such spectacles of wretchedness as are absolutely inconsistent with that degree of national felicity which she was capable of attaining even under her old government. A traveller much less attentive than I was to objects of this kind must see at every turn most unequivocal signs of distress. That these should exist, no one can wonder who considers the price of labour, and of provisions, and the misery into which a small rise in the price of wheat throws the lower classes. The causes of this great population were certainly not to be found in the benignity of the old government yielding a due protection to the lower classes, for, on the contrary, it abandoned them to the mercy of the privileged orders. This great populousness of France I attribute very much to the division of the lands into small properties, which takes place in that country to a degree of which we have in England but little conception. Whatever promises the appearance even of subsistence induces men to marry. The inheritance of 10 or 12 acres to be divided amongst the children of the proprietor will be looked to with the views of a permanent settlement, and either occasions a marriage, the infants of which die young for want of sufficient nourishment, or keeps children at home, distressing their relations, long after the time that they should have emigrated to towns.

*   *   *

V. MÉTAYERS is the tenure under which perhaps seven-eighths of the lands of France are held.

*   *   *

At the first blush, the great disadvantage of the *métayage* system is to landlords; but on a nearer examination, the tenants are found in the lowest state of poverty, and some of them in misery. At Vatan, in Berry, I was assured that the *métayers* almost every year borrowed their bread of the landlord before the harvest came round, yet hardly worth borrowing, for it was made of rye and barley mixed. I tasted enough of it to pity sincerely the poor people. In Limousin the *métayers* are considered as little better than menial servants, removable at pleasure, and obliged to conform in all things to the will of the landlords. It is commonly computed that half the tenantry are deeply in debt to the proprietor, so that he is often obliged to turn them off with the loss of these debts, in order to save his land from running waste.

In all the modes of occupying land, the great evil is the smallness of farms. There are large ones in Picardy, the Isle of France, the Pays de Beauce, Artois and Normandy; but in the rest of the kingdom such are not general. The division of the farms and population is so great, that the misery flowing from it is in many places extreme; the idleness of the people is seen the moment you enter a town on market day; the swarms of people are incredible. At Landivisiau in Bretagne, I saw a man who walked 7 miles to bring 2 chickens, which would not sell for 24 *sous* the couple, as he told me himself. At Avranches, men attending each a horse, with a pannier load of sea ooze, not more than 4 bushels. Near Isenheim in Alsace, a rich country, women, in the midst of harvest, where their labour is nearly as valuable as that of men, reaping grass by the road side to carry home to their cows.

*   *   *

In this most miserable of all the modes of letting land, after running the hazard of such losses, fatal in many instances, the defrauded landlord receives a contemptible rent; the farmer is in the lowest state of poverty; the land is miserably cultivated; and the nation suffers as severely as the parties themselves.

*   *   *

The abuses attending the levy of taxes were heavy and universal. The kingdom was parcelled into *généralités*, with an Intendant at the head of each, into whose hands the whole power of the Crown was delegated for everything except the military authority; but particularly for all affairs of finance. The *généralités* were sub-divided into *élections*, at the head of which was a *subdélégué*, appointed by the Intendant. The rolls of the *taille*, *capitation*, *vingtièmes*, and other taxes, were distributed among districts, parishes, and individuals, at the pleasure of the Intendant, who could exempt, change, add, or diminish, at pleasure. Such an enormous power, constantly acting, and from which no man was free, must, in the nature of things, degenerate in many cases into absolute tyranny. It must be obvious, that the friends, acquaintances, and dependents of the Intendant, and of all his *subdélégués*, and the friends of these friends, to a long chain of dependence, might be favoured in taxation at the expense of their miserable neighbours; and that noblemen, in favour at court, to whose protection the Intendant himself would naturally look up, could find little difficulty in throwing much of the weight of their taxes on others, without a similar support. Instances, and even gross ones, have been reported to me in many parts of the kingdom, that made me shudder at the oppression to which numbers must have been condemned, by the undue favours granted to such crooked influence.

*   *   *

The *corvées*, or police of the roads, were annually the ruin of many hundreds of farmers; more than 300 were reduced to beggary in filling up one vale in Lorraine. All these oppressions fell on the *tiers état* only; the nobility and clergy having been equally exempted from *tailles*, militia, and *corvées*.

The penal code of finance makes one shudder at the horrors of punishment inadequate to the crime. A few features will sufficiently characterize the old government of France.

1. Smugglers of salt, armed and assembled to the number of five, in Provence, *a fine of 500 livres and nine years galleys*; in all the rest of the kingdom, *death*.
2. Smugglers armed, assembled, but in number under five, *a fine of 300 livres and three years galleys*. Second offence, *death*.
3. Smugglers, without arms, but with horses, carts, or boats, *a fine of 300 livres; if not paid, three years galleys*. Second offence, *400 livres and nine years galleys*. In Dauphiné, second offence, *galleys for life*. In Provence, *five years galleys*.
4. Smugglers, who carry the salt on their backs, and without arms, *a fine of 200 livres, and, if not paid, are flogged and branded*. Second offence, *a fine of 300 livres and six years galleys*.
5. Women, married and single, smugglers, first offence, *a fine of 100 livres*. Second, *300 livres*. Third, *flogged, and banished the kingdom for life. Husbands responsible both in fine and body*.
6. Children smugglers, the same as women. *Fathers and mothers responsible; and for defect of payment flogged*.

*   *   *

But these were not all the evils with which the people struggled. The administration of justice was partial, venal, infamous. I have, in conversation with many very sensible men, in different parts of the kingdom, met with something of content with their government, in all other respects than this; but upon the question of expecting justice to be really and fairly administered, everyone confessed there was no such thing to be looked for. The conduct of the parliaments was profligate and atrocious. Upon almost every cause that came before them, interest was openly made with the judges; and woe betided the man who, with a cause to support, had no means of conciliating favour, either by the beauty of a handsome wife, or by other methods. It has been said, by many writers, that property was as secure under the old government of France as it is in England; and the assertion might possibly be true, as far as any violence from the King, his ministers, or the great was concerned; but for all that mass of property, which comes in every country to be litigated in courts of justice, there was not even the shadow of security, unless the parties were totally and equally unknown, and totally and equally honest; in every other case, he who had the best interest with the judges was sure to be the winner. To reflecting minds, the cruelty and abominable practice attending such courts are sufficiently apparent.

*   *   *

The true judgment to be formed of the French revolution must surely be gained from an attentive consideration of the evils of the old government. When these are well understood, and when the extent and universality of the oppression under which the people groaned, oppression which bore upon them from every quarter, it will scarcely be attempted to be urged that a revolution was not absolutely necessary to the welfare of the kingdom. Not one opposing voice can, with reason, be raised against this assertion; abuses ought certainly to be corrected, and corrected effectually. This could not be done without the establishment of a new form of government; whether the form that has been adopted were the best, is another question absolutely distinct.

*　　*　　*

REVIEW QUESTIONS

1. For Arthur Young, what are the chief problems in the French countryside?
2. What are the specific problems imposed on the small farmer by the nobility, the legal system, and the government?
3. How are public affairs conducted?
4. How did these problems in the countryside contribute to the success of the revolution?

THOMAS JEFFERSON

The Declaration of Independence

The successful attempt of the original thirteen states of the union to break their colonial allegiance to Great Britain was an important antecedent to the French Revolution. Not only did France's financial support of the insurgent colonies precipitate the financial crisis that would compel Louis XVI to convene the Estates General, but the American War of Independence also produced a political culture that celebrated principles of popular sovereignty and "unalienable" individual liberties. The Declaration of Independence, among the noblest of United States documents, arose out of the need to attach a preamble to a resolution by Congress moved June 1776 "that these United Colonies are, and of right ought to be, free and independent States." Congress appointed a committee of five representatives to write the preamble, but one member, Thomas Jefferson, actually drafted the document, which was adopted by Congress on 4 July 1776.

When in the course of human events, it becomes necessary for one people to dissolve the political bands which have connected them with another, and to assume the Powers of the earth, the separate and equal station to which the Laws of Nature and of Nature's God entitle them, a decent respect to the opinions of mankind requires that they should declare the causes which impel them to the separation.

We hold these truths to be self-evident, that all men are created equal, that they are endowed by their Creator with certain unalienable rights, that among these are Life, Liberty, and the pursuit of Happiness. That to secure these rights, Governments are instituted among Men, deriving their just powers from the consent of the governed. That whenever any Form of Government becomes destructive of these ends, it is the Right of the

People to alter or to abolish it, and to institute new Government, laying its foundation on such principles and organizing its powers in such form, as to them shall seem most likely to effect their Safety and Happiness. Prudence, indeed, will dictate that Governments long established should not be changed for light and transient causes; and accordingly all experience hath shown, that mankind are more disposed to suffer, while evils are sufferable, than to right themselves by abolishing the forms to which they are accustomed. But when a long train of abuses and usurpations, pursuing invariably the same Object evinces a design to reduce them under absolute Despotism, it is their right, it is their duty, to throw off such Government, and to provide new Guards for their future security—Such has been the patient sufferance of these Colonies; and such is now the necessity which constrains them to alter their former Systems of Government. The history of the present King of Great Britain is a history of repeated injuries and usurpations, all having in direct object the establishment of an absolute Tyranny over these States. To prove this, let Facts be submitted to a candid world.

He has refused his Assent to Laws, the most wholesome and necessary for the public good.

He has forbidden his Governors to pass Laws of immediate and pressing importance, unless suspended in their operation till his Assent should be obtained; and when so suspended, he has utterly neglected to attend to them.

He has refused to pass other Laws for the accommodation of large districts of people, unless those people would relinquish the right of Representation in the Legislature, a right inestimable to them and formidable to tyrants only.

He has called together legislative bodies at places unusual, uncomfortable, and distant from the depository of their public Records, for the sole purpose of fatiguing them into compliance with his measures.

He has dissolved Representative Houses repeatedly, for opposing with manly firmness his invasions on the rights of the people.

He has refused for a long time, after such dissolutions, to cause others to be elected; whereby the Legislative powers, incapable of Annihilation, have returned to the People at large for their exercise; the State remaining in the mean time exposed to all dangers of invasion from without, and convulsions within.

He has endeavoured to prevent the population of these States; for that purpose obstructing the Laws of Naturalization of Foreigners; refusing to pass others to encourage their migrations hither, and raising the conditions of new Appropriations of Lands.

He has obstructed the Administration of Justice, by refusing his Assent to Laws for establishing Judiciary powers.

He has made Judges dependent on his Will alone, for the tenure of their offices, and the amount and payment of their salaries.

He has erected a multitude of New Offices, and sent hither swarms of Officers to harass our People, and eat out their substance.

He has kept among us, in times of peace, Standing Armies without the Consent of our legislature.

He has affected to render the Military independent of and superior to the Civil Power.

He has combined with others to subject us to a jurisdiction foreign to our constitution, and unacknowledged by our laws; giving his Assent to their Acts of pretended Legislation:

For quartering large bodies of armed troops among us:

For protecting them, by a mock Trial, from Punishment for any Murders which they should commit on the Inhabitants of these States:

For cutting off our Trade with all parts of the world:

For imposing taxes on us without our Consent:

For depriving us of many cases, of the benefits of Trial by jury:

For transporting us beyond Seas to be tried for pretended offences:

For abolishing the free System of English Laws in a neighbouring Province, establishing therein an Arbitrary government, and enlarging its Boundaries so as to render it at once an example and fit instrument for introducing the same absolute rule into these Colonies:

For taking away our Charters, abolishing our most valuable Laws, and altering fundamentally the Forms of our Governments:

For suspending our own Legislatures, and declaring themselves in vested with Power to legislate for us in all cases whatsoever.

He has abdicated Government here, by declaring us out of his Protection and waging War against us.

He has plundered our seas, ravaged our Coasts, burnt our towns, and destroyed the lives of our people.

He is at this time transporting large armies of foreign mercenaries to compleat the works of death, desolation, and tyranny, already begun with circumstances of Cruelty & perfidy scarcely paralleled in the most barbarous ages, and totally unworthy the Head of a civilized nation.

He has constrained our fellow Citizens taken Captive on the high Seas to bear Arms against their Country, to become the executioners of their friends and Brethren, or to fall themselves by their Hands.

He has excited domestic insurrections amongst us, and has endeavoured to bring on the inhabitants of our frontiers, the merciless Indian Savages, whose known rule of warfare, is an undistinguished destruction of all ages, sexes, and conditions.

In every stage of these Oppressions We have Petitioned for Redress in the most humble terms: Our repeated Petitions have been answered only by repeated injury. A Prince, whose character is thus marked by every act which may define a Tyrant, is unfit to be the ruler of a free people.

Nor have We been wanting in attention to our British brethren. We have warned them from time to time of attempts by their legislature to extend an unwarrantable jurisdiction over us. We have reminded them of the circumstances of our emigration and settlement here. We have appealed to

their native justice and magnanimity, and we have conjured them by the ties of our common kindred to disavow these usurpations, which, would inevitably interrupt our connections and correspondence. They too must have been deaf to the voice of justice and of consanguinity. We must, therefore, acquiesce in the necessity, which denounces our Separation, and hold them, as we hold the rest of mankind, Enemies in War, in Peace Friends.

WE, THEREFORE, the Representatives of the UNITED STATES OF AMERICA, in General Congress, Assembled, appealing to the Supreme Judge of the world for the rectitude of our intentions, do, in the Name, and by Authority of the good People of these Colonies, solemnly publish and declare, That these United Colonies are, and of Right ought to be FREE AND INDEPENDENT STATES; that they are Absolved from all Allegiance to the British Crown, and that all political connection between them and the State of Great Britain, is and ought to be totally dissolved; and that as Free and Independent States, they have full Power to levy War, conclude Peace, contract Alliances, establish Commerce, and to do all other Acts and Things which Independent States may of right do. And for the support of this Declaration, with a firm reliance on the Protection of Divine Providence, we mutually pledge to each other our Lives, our Fortunes, and our sacred Honor.

The foregoing Declaration was, by order of Congress, engrossed, and signed by the following members: ＊ ＊ ＊

REVIEW QUESTIONS

1. On what grounds does the Declaration of Independence justify a break from Great Britain?
2. Why is this document often viewed as a prominent example of the Enlightenment's political outlook?
3. Compare Locke's *Two Treatises on Government* with the American Declaration of Independence. What Lockian influences can be detected in the declaration?

Abbé Emmanuel Sieyes

FROM *What Is the Third Estate?*

King Louis XVI's announcement in the summer of 1788 convening the Estates General, compounded by bread riots and widespread economic hardship, heated up political debate about reform and the future of France. Because the Estates General had not met since 1614, members of the Third Estate protested against the custom that the estates meet separately and vote by order. They insisted that the estates should instead deliberate in united sessions and vote as individuals, not as corporate bodies. Equally important, the Third Estate demanded that its votes be doubled, so that it could counter the votes of the First and Second Estates. In January 1789 Abbé Emmanuel Sieyes, a radical clergyman, sought to mobilize public support for these causes with the pamphlet What Is the Third Estate? *Its influence was pervasive and contributed to the plan to transform the Estates General into the National Constituent Assembly.*

From *A Documentary Survey of the French Revolution*, edited by John Hall Stewart (Upper Saddle River, N.J.: Prentice-Hall, 1951).

*   *   *

The plan of this pamphlet is very simple. We have three questions to ask:

1st. What is the third estate? Everything.

2nd. What has it been heretofore in the political order? Nothing.

3rd. What does it demand? To become something therein.

We shall see if the answers are correct. Then we shall examine the measures that have been tried and those which must be taken in order that the third estate may in fact become *something*. Thus we shall state:

4th. What the ministers have *attempted*, and what the privileged classes themselves *propose* in its favor.

5th. What *ought* to have been done.

6th. Finally, what *remains* to be done in order that the third estate may take its rightful place.

Chapter I
The Third Estate Is a Complete Nation

What are the essentials of national existence and prosperity? *Private* enterprise and *public* functions.

Private enterprise may be divided into four classes: 1st. Since earth and water furnish the raw material for man's needs, the first class will comprise all families engaged in agricultural pursuits. 2nd. Between the original sale of materials and their consumption or use, further workmanship, more or less manifold, adds to these materials a second value, more or less compounded. Human industry thus succeeds in perfecting the benefits of nature and in increasing the gross produce twofold, tenfold, one hundredfold in value. Such is the work of the second class. 3rd. Between production and consumption, as well as among the different degrees of production, a group of intermediate agents, useful to producers as well as to consumers, comes into being; these are the dealers and merchants. . . . 4th. In addition to these three classes of industrious and useful citizens concerned with goods for consumption and use, a society needs many private undertakings and endeavors which are *directly* useful or agreeable to the *individual*. This fourth class includes from the most distinguished scientific and liberal professions to the least esteemed domestic services. Such are the labors which sustain society. Who performs them? The third estate.

Public functions likewise under present circumstances may be classified under four well known headings: the Sword, the Robe, the Church, and the Administration. It is unnecessary to discuss them in detail in order to demonstrate that the third estate everywhere constitutes nineteen-twentieths of them, except that it is burdened with all that is really arduous, with all the tasks that the privileged order refuses to perform. Only the lucrative and honorary positions are held by members of the privileged order. . . . nevertheless they have dared lay the order of the third estate under an interdict. They have said to it: "Whatever be your services, whatever your talents, you shall go thus far and no farther. It is not fitting that you be honored." . . .

. . .

It suffices here to have revealed that the alleged utility of a privileged order to public service is only a chimera; that without it, all that is arduous in such service is performed by the third estate; that without it, the higher positions would be infinitely better filled; that they naturally ought to be the lot of and reward for talents and recognized services; and that if the privileged classes have succeeded in usurping all the lucrative and honorary positions, it is both an odious injustice to the majority of citizens and a treason to the commonwealth.

Who, then, would dare to say that the third estate has not within itself all that is necessary to constitute a complete nation? It is the strong and robust man whose one arm remains enchained. If the privileged order were abolished, the nation would be not something less but something more. Thus, what is the third estate? Everything; but an everything shackled and oppressed. What would it

be without the privileged order? Everything; but an everything free and flourishing. Nothing can progress without it; everything would proceed infinitely better without the others. It is not sufficient to have demonstrated that the privileged classes, far from being useful to the nation, can only enfeeble and injure it; it is necessary, moreover, to prove that the nobility does not belong to the social organization at all; that, indeed, it may be a *burden* upon the nation, but that it would not know how to constitute a part thereof.

. . .

What is a nation? a body of associates living under a *common* law and represented by the same *legislature.*

Is it not exceedingly clear that the noble order has privileges, exemptions, even rights separate from the rights of the majority of citizens? Thus it deviates from the common order, from the common law. Thus its civil rights already render it a people apart in a great nation. It is indeed *imperium in imperio.*

Also, it enjoys its political rights separately. It has its own representatives, who are by no means charged with representing the people. Its deputation sits apart; and when it is assembled in the same room with the deputies of ordinary citizens, it is equally true that its representation is essentially distinct and separate; it is foreign to the nation in principle, since its mandate does not emanate from the people, and in aim, since its purpose is to defend not the general but a special interest.

The third estate, then, comprises everything appertaining to the nation; and whatever is not the third estate may not be regarded as being of the nation. What is the third estate? Everything!

Chapter III
What Does the Third Estate Demand? To Become Something

* * * The true petitions of this order may be appreciated only through the authentic claims directed to the government by the large municipalities of the kingdom. What is indicated therein? That the people wishes to be *something*, and, in truth, the very least that is possible. It wishes to have real representatives in the Estates General, that is to say, deputies *drawn from its order,* who are competent to be interpreters of its will and defenders of its interests. But what will it avail it to be present at the Estates General if the predominating interest there is contrary to its own! Its presence would only consecrate the oppression of which it would be the eternal victim. Thus, it is indeed certain that it cannot come to vote at the Estates General unless it is to have in that body *an influence at least equal to that of the privileged classes*; and it demands a number of representatives equal to that of the first two orders together. Finally, this equality of representation would become completely illusory if every chamber voted separately. The third estate demands, then, that votes be taken *by head and not by order*. This is the essence of those claims so alarming to the privileged classes, because they believed that thereby the reform of abuses would become inevitable. The real intention of the third estate is to have an influence in the Estates General equal to that of the privileged classes. I repeat, can it ask less? And is it not clear that if its influence therein is less than equality, it cannot be expected to emerge from its political nullity and become *something*?

But what is indeed unfortunate is that the three articles constituting the demand of the third estate are insufficient to give it this equality of influence which it cannot, in reality, do without. In vain will it obtain an equal number of representatives drawn from its order; the influence of the privileged classes will establish itself and dominate even in the sanctuary of the third estate. . . .

. . .

Besides the influence of the aristocracy . . . there is the influence of property. This is natural. I do not proscribe it at all; but one must agree that it is still all to the advantage of the privileged classes . . .

. . .

The more one considers this matter, the more obvious the insufficiency of the three demands of the third estate becomes. But finally, such as they are, they have been vigorously attacked. Let us examine the pretexts for this hostility.

*   *   *

I have only one observation to make. Obviously there are abuses in France; these abuses are profitable to someone; they are scarcely advantageous to the third estate—indeed, they are injurious to it in particular. Now I ask if, in this state of affairs, it is possible to destroy any abuse so long as those who profit therefrom control the *veto*? All justice would be powerless; it would be necessary to rely entirely on the sheer generosity of the privileged classes. Would that be your idea of what constitutes the social order?

*   *   *

REVIEW QUESTIONS

1. What is Sieyes's tone of voice and how does it affect the argument?
2. What reasons does Sieyes provide for his claim that the Third Estate constitutes the nation?
3. What kind of political and social order does he advocate?

THIRD ESTATE OF DOURDAN

FROM Grievance Petitions

After summoning the Estates General, the king charged each estate with the task of drawing up grievance petitions, which in turn acted as suggestions for reform. Local assemblies throughout France, which appointed the Third Estate's deputies for the Estates General, wrote the grievance petitions, which are among the most valuable documents for assessing the moods of France's many regions and social groups just prior to the revolution. This particular petition is from the Third Estate of Dourdan, a town north of Paris in the Pan's basin.

From *A Documentary Survey of the French Revolution,* edited by John Hall Stewart (Upper Saddle River, NJ: Prentice-Hall, 1951).

*   *   *

The order of the third estate of the City, *Bailliage,* and County of Dourdan, imbued with gratitude prompted by the paternal kindness of the King, who deigns to restore its former rights and its former constitution, forgets at this moment its misfortunes and impotence, to harken only to its foremost sentiment and its foremost duty, that of sacrificing everything to the glory of the *Patrie* and the service of His Majesty. It supplicates him to accept the grievances, complaints, and remonstrances which it is permitted to bring to the foot of the throne, and to see therein only the expression of its zeal and the homage of its obedience.

It wishes:

1. That his subjects of the third estate, equal by such status to all other citizens, present themselves before the common father without other distinction which might degrade them.

2. That all the orders, already united by duty and a common desire to contribute equally to the needs of the State, also deliberate in common concerning its needs.

3. That no citizen lose his liberty except according to law; that, consequently, no one be arrested by virtue of special orders, or, if imperative circumstances necessitate such orders, that the prisoner be handed over to the regular courts of justice within forty-eight hours at the latest.

4. That no letters or writings intercepted in the post be the cause of the detention of any citizen, or be produced in court against him, except in case of conspiracy or undertaking against the State.

5. That the property of all citizens be inviolable, and that no one be required to make sacrifice thereof for the public welfare, except upon assurance of indemnification based upon the statement of freely selected appraisers.

*   *   *

9. That the national debt be verified; that the payment of arrears of said debt be assured by such indirect taxes as may not be injurious to the husbandry, industry, commerce, liberty, or tranquillity of the citizens.

10. That an annual reimbursement fund be established to liquidate the capital of the debt.

11. That as one part of the debt is liquidated, a corresponding part of the indirect tax also be liquidated.

12. That every tax, direct or indirect, be granted only for a limited time, and that every collection

beyond such term be regarded as peculation, and punished as such.

13. That no loan be contracted, under any pretext or any security whatsoever, without the consent of the Estates General.* * *

15. That every personal tax be abolished; that thus the *capitation* and the *taille* and its accessories be merged with the *vingtièmes* in a tax on land and real or nominal property.

16. That such tax be borne equally, without distinction, by all classes of citizens and by all kinds of property, even feudal and contingent rights.

17. That the tax substituted for the *corvée* be borne by all classes of citizens equally and without distinction. That said tax, at present beyond the capacity of those who pay it and the needs to which it is destined, be reduced by at least one-half.

18. That provincial Estates, subordinate to the Estates General, be established and charged with the assessment and levying of subsidies, with their deposit in the national treasury, with the administration of all public works, and with the examination of all projects conducive to the prosperity of lands situated within the limits of their jurisdiction.

19. That such Estates be composed of freely elected deputies of the three orders from the cities, boroughs, and parishes subject to their administration, and in the proportion established for the next session of the Estates General.

*   *   *

Justice

1. That the administration of justice be reformed, either by restoring strict execution of ordinances, or by reforming the sections thereof that are contrary to the dispatch and welfare of justice.

2. That every royal *bailliage* have such jurisdiction that persons be not more than three or four leagues distant from their judges, and that these pass judgment in the last resort up to the value of 300 *livres.*

3. That seigneurial courts of justice created by purely gratuitous right be suppressed.

4. That seigneurial courts of justice separated from the jurisdiction of royal *bailliages* . . . be returned thereto.

5. That seigneurial courts of justice, the creation of which has not been gratuitous, or usurpation of which is not proved, be suppressed with reimbursement.

*   *   *

8. That the excessive number of offices in the necessary courts be reduced in just measure, and that no one be given an office of magistracy if he is not at least twenty-five years of age, and until after a substantial public examination has verified his morality, integrity, and ability.

*   *   *

10. That the study of law be reformed; that it be directed in a manner analogous to our legislation, and that candidates for degrees be subjected to rigorous tests which may not be evaded; that no dispensation of age or time be granted.

*   *   *

12. That deliberations of courts and companies of magistracy which tend to prevent entry of the third estate thereto be rescinded and annulled as injurious to the citizens of that order, in contempt of the authority of the King, whose choice they limit, and contrary to the welfare of justice, the administration of which would become the patrimony of those of noble birth instead of being entrusted to merit, enlightenment, and virtue.

13. That military ordinances which restrict entrance to the service to those possessing nobility be reformed.

*   *   *

Finances

1. That if the Estates General considers it necessary to preserve the fees of *aides,* such fees be made uniform throughout the entire kingdom and reduced to a single denomination; that, accordingly, all ordinances and declarations in force be re-

voked . . . ; that the odious tax of *trop-bu* especially, a source of constant annoyance in rural districts, be abolished forever.

2. That the tax of the *gabelle* be eliminated if possible, or that it be regulated among the several provinces of the kingdom . . .

*   *   *

Agriculture

1. That exchange fees, disastrous to husbandry, . . . be suppressed.

*   *   *

3. That the privilege of hunting be restricted within its just limits; that the decrees of the *parlement* of the years 1778 and 1779, which tend rather to obstruct the claims of the cultivator than to effect his indemnification, be rescinded and annulled; that after having declared the excessive amount of game and summoned the seigneur to provide therefor, the landowner and the cultivator be authorized to destroy said game on their own lands and in their own woods—without permission, however, to use firearms, the carrying of which is forbidden by ordinances; that, moreover, a simple and easy method be established whereby every cultivator may have the damage verified and obtain compensation therefor.

4. That the right to hunt may never affect the property of the citizen; that, accordingly, he may at all times travel over his lands, have injurious herbs uprooted, and cut *luzernes, sainfoins,* and other produce whenever it suits him; and that stubble may be freely raked immediately after the harvest.

5. That, in conformity with former ordinances, gamekeepers be forbidden to carry arms, even in the retinue of their masters.

6. That hunting offences be punished only by pecuniary fines.

7. That His Majesty be supplicated to have enclosed the parks and forests which are reserved for his enjoyment; also to authorize elsewhere the destruction of wild beasts which ruin the rural dis-

tricts, and particularly that bordering on this forest of Dourdan.

8. That every individual who, without title or valid occupancy, has dovecotes or aviaries, be required to destroy them; that those who have title or valid occupancy be required to confine their pigeons at seedtime and harvest.

*   *   *

10. That no cultivator be permitted . . . several farms or farmings, if the total thereof necessitates the use of more than two ploughs.

*   *   *

15. That the militia, which devastates the country, takes workers away from husbandry, produces premature and ill-matched marriages, and imposes secret and arbitrary taxes upon those who are subject thereto, be suppressed and replaced by voluntary enlistment at the expense of the provinces.

*   *   *

17. That the ordinance and regulation concerning woods and forests be reformed so as to preserve property rights, encourage plantings, and prevent deforestation.

*   *   *

Commerce

1. That every regulation which tends to impede the business of citizens be revoked.

2. That the exportation and circulation of grain be directed by the provincial Estates, which shall correspond among themselves in order to prevent sudden and artificial increases in the price of provisions.

3. That when wheat reaches the price of twenty-five *livres* per *septier* in the markets, all day laborers be forbidden to buy any, unless it be for their sustenance.

4. That if circumstances necessitate the revenue from certificates and letters of mastership in the arts and crafts, no member be admitted into cor-

porations except upon condition of residing in the place of his establishment; that widows may carry on the profession of their husbands without new letters; that their children be admitted thereto at a moderate price; that all persons without an established and recognized domicile be forbidden to peddle.

5. That fraudulent bankruptcy be considered a public crime; that the public prosecutor be enjoined to prosecute it as such, and that privileged positions no longer serve as a refuge for bankrupts.

6. That all toll rights and other similar ones be suppressed throughout the interior of the kingdom, that customhouses be moved back to the frontiers, and that rights of *traite* be entirely abolished.

7. That, within a given time, weights and measures be rendered uniform throughout the entire kingdom.

REVIEW QUESTIONS

1. In the petitions, what are the principal targets of criticism?
2. What groups and institutions are cited as the recurring causes of hardship?
3. How extensive are the proposals for reform?
4. On the basis of this petition, how would you characterize the relationship between the French state and its people?

NATIONAL ASSEMBLY

The Tennis Court Oath

On 20 June 1789 the Third Estate, after refusing to meet separately and vote by order, was barred from its hall. Seeking a chamber, deputies reconvened on a nearby tennis court, where they deliberated and vowed to remain in session as the National Assembly until a French constitution was drafted. Toward this end, they swore an oath, which remains among the most important documents of the French Revolution.

The National Assembly, considering that it has been summoned to establish the constitution of the kingdom, to effect the regeneration of public order, and to maintain the true principles of monarchy; that nothing can prevent it from continuing its deliberations in whatever place it may be forced to establish itself; and, finally, that wheresoever its members are assembled, *there* is the National Assembly;

Decrees that all members of this Assembly shall immediately take a solemn oath not to separate, and to reassemble wherever circumstances require, until the constitution of the kingdom is established and consolidated upon firm foundations; and that, the said oath taken, all members and each one of them individually shall ratify this steadfast resolution by signature.

REVIEW QUESTIONS

1. What is the significance of the Third Estate calling itself the National Assembly?

2. What role does this document assign to the National Assembly?

3. How did this oath radically alter the nature of political sovereignty in eighteenth-century France?

NATIONAL ASSEMBLY

FROM Declaration of the Rights of Man and Citizen

This declaration, adopted on 27 August 1789, was a revolutionary clarion call to the people of France. Its subsequent impact on European political culture cannot be underestimated.

From *A Documentary Survey of the French Revolution* by John Hall Stewart (Upper Saddle River, N.J.: Prentice-Hall, 1951).

*   *   *

The representatives of the French people, organized in National Assembly, considering that ignorance, forgetfulness, or contempt of the rights of man are the sole causes of public misfortunes and of the corruption of governments, have resolved to set forth in a solemn declaration the natural, inalienable, and sacred rights of man, in order that such declaration, continually before all members of the social body, may be a perpetual reminder of their rights and duties; in order that the acts of the legislative power and those of the executive power may constantly be compared with the aim of every political institution and may accordingly be more respected; in order that the demands of the citizens, founded henceforth upon simple and incontestable principles, may always be directed towards the maintenance of the Constitution and the welfare of all.

Accordingly, the National Assembly recognizes and proclaims, in the presence and under the auspices of the Supreme Being, the following rights of man and citizen.

1. Men are born and remain free and equal in rights; social distinctions may be based only upon general usefulness.

2. The aim of every political association is the preservation of the natural and inalienable rights of man; these rights are liberty, property, security, and resistance to oppression.

3. The source of all sovereignty resides essentially in the nation; no group, no individual may exercise authority not emanating expressly therefrom.

4. Liberty consists of the power to do whatever is not injurious to others; thus the enjoyment of the natural rights of every man has for its limits only those that assure other members of society the enjoyment of those same rights; such limits may be determined only by law.

5. The law has the right to forbid only actions which are injurious to society. Whatever is not forbidden by law may not be prevented, and no

TENNIS COURT OATH (1792)   JACQUES-LOUIS DAVID

David's painting of the birth of the French nation strove not for authentic representation but, rather, for mythic grandeur. In depicting this disparate group of bourgeois men committed to take an oath to transform France into a constitutional monarchy, what was David implying about the political foundation of the new nation?

one may be constrained to do what it does not prescribe.

6. Law is the expression of the general will; all citizens have the right to concur personally, or through their representatives, in its formation; it must be the same for all, whether it protects or punishes. All citizens, being equal before it, are equally admissible to all public offices, positions, and employments, according to their capacity, and without other distinction than that of virtues and talents.

7. No man may be accused, arrested, or detained except in the cases determined by law, and according to the forms prescribed thereby. Whoever solicit, expedite, or execute arbitrary orders, or have them executed, must be punished; but every citizen summoned or apprehended in pursuance of the law must obey immediately; he renders himself culpable by resistance.

8. The law is to establish only penalties that are absolutely and obviously necessary; and no one may be punished except by virtue of a law established and promulgated prior to the offence and legally applied.

9. Since every man is presumed innocent until declared guilty, if arrest be deemed indispensable, all unnecessary severity for securing the person of the accused must be severely repressed by law.

10. No one is to be disquieted because of his opinions, even religious, provided their manifestation does not disturb the public order established by law.

11. Free communication of ideas and opinions is one of the most precious of the rights of man. Consequently, every citizen may speak, write, and print freely, subject to responsibility for the abuse of such liberty in the cases determined by law.

12. The guarantee of the rights of man and citizen necessitates a public force; such a force, therefore, is instituted for the advantage of all and not for the particular benefit of those to whom it is entrusted.

13. For the maintenance of the public force and for the expenses of administration a common tax is indispensable; it must be assessed equally on all citizens in proportion to their means.

14. Citizens have the right to ascertain, by themselves or through their representatives, the necessity of the public tax, to consent to it freely, to supervise its use, and to determine its quota, assessment, payment, and duration.

15. Society has the right to require of every public agent an accounting of his administration.

16. Every society in which the guarantee of rights is not assured or the separation of powers not determined has no constitution at all.

17. Since property is a sacred and inviolable right, no one may be deprived thereof unless a legally established public necessity obviously requires it, and upon condition of a just and previous indemnity.

*   *   *

REVIEW QUESTIONS

1. What similarities in issues do you see in the grievance petitions and in this declaration?
2. What are the principal differences between this declaration and the American Declaration of Independence?
3. How does this document reconcile the rights of the individual with the rights of government?
4. What civil liberties are missing here?
5. Assess the influence of the American Declaration of Independence on the Declaration of the Rights of Man and Citizen.

NATIONAL CONVENTION

FROM Levée en Masse Edict

This decree of 23 August 1793 mobilized the French nation for war, marking a new era in the modern history of warfare. Numerous setbacks of the French revolutionary army after its initial victories in 1792 compelled the government to pass a universal levy to repulse the enemy. The government's ability to conscript soldiers, requisition supplies, and organize the economy for war reveals the nationalist spirit that gripped France and provides one critical reason for success in the government's subsequent military campaigns.

From *A Documentary Survey of the French Revolution,* edited by John Hall Stewart (Upper Saddle River, N.J.: Prentice-Hall, 1951).

*   *   *

1. Henceforth, until the enemies have been driven from the territory of the Republic, the French people are in permanent requisition for army service.

The young men shall go to battle; the married men shall forge arms and transport provisions; the women shall make tents and clothes, and shall serve in the hospitals; the children shall turn old linen into lint; the old men shall repair to the public places, to stimulate the courage of the warriors and preach the unity of the Republic and hatred of kings.

2. National buildings shall be converted into barracks; public places into armament workshops; the soil of cellars shall be washed in lye to extract saltpeter therefrom.

3. Arms of caliber shall be turned over exclusively to those who march against the enemy; the service of the interior shall be carried on with fowling pieces and sabers.

4. Saddle horses are called for to complete the cavalry corps; draught horses, other than those employed in agriculture, shall haul artillery and provisions.

5. The Committee of Public Safety is charged with taking all measures necessary for establishing, without delay, a special manufacture of arms of all kinds, in harmony with the *élan* and the energy of the French people. Accordingly, it is authorized to constitute all establishments, manufactories, workshops, and factories deemed necessary for the execution of such works, as well as to requisition for such purpose, throughout the entire extent of the Republic, the artists and workmen who may contribute to their success. For such purpose a sum of 30,000,000, taken from the 498,200,000 livres in *assignats* in reserve in the "Fund of the Three Keys," shall be placed at the disposal of the Minister of War. The central establishment of said special manufacture shall be established at Paris.

6. The representatives of the people dispatched for the execution of the present law shall have similar authority in their respective *arrondissements,* acting in concert with the Committee of Public Safety; they are invested with the unlimited powers attributed to the representatives of the people with the armies.

7. No one may obtain a substitute in the service to which he is summoned. The public functionaries shall remain at their posts.

8. The levy shall be general. Unmarried citizens or childless widowers, from eighteen to twenty-

five years, shall go first; they shall meet, without delay, at the chief town of their districts, where they shall practice manual exercise daily, while awaiting the hour of departure.

9. The representatives of the people shall regulate the musters and marches so as to have armed citizens arrive at the points of assembling only in so far as supplies, munitions, and all that constitutes the material part of the army exist in sufficient proportion.

10. The points of assembling shall be determined by circumstances, and designated by the representatives of the people dispatched for the execution of the present decree, upon the advice of the generals, in co-operation with the Committee of Public Safety and the provisional Executive Council.

11. The battalion organized in each district shall be united under a banner bearing the inscription: *The French people risen against tyrants.*

12. Such battalions shall be organized according to established decrees, and their pay shall be the same as that of the battalions at the frontiers.

13. In order to collect supplies in sufficient quantity, the farmers and managers of national property shall deposit the produce of such property, in the form of grain, in the chief town of their respective districts.

14. Owners, farmers, and others possessing grain shall be required to pay, in kind, arrears of taxes, even the two-thirds of those of 1793, on the rolls which have served to effect the last payment.

*   *   *

17. The Minister of War is responsible for taking all measures necessary for the prompt execution of the present decree; a sum of 50,000,000, from the 498,200,000 *livres* in *assignats* in the "Fund of the Three Keys," shall be placed at his disposal by the National Treasury.

18. The present decree shall be conveyed to the departments by special messengers.

REVIEW QUESTIONS

1. Which social groups and areas of the economy did this edict affect, and what roles were they assigned?
2. How is this organization for war different from warfare under the old regime?
3. How does this document evoke the sense of emergency and crisis that characterized the years of the republic?

NATIONAL CONVENTION

FROM The Law of Suspects

Amid the chaos wreaked by foreign invasion, internal rebellion, inflation, and intense political factionalism, the republican government, dominated by the Jacobin club, erected political machinery in the form of emergency committees to monitor and suppress antirepublican activity. In 1793–1794 the fear of enemies of the revolution reached a fever pitch, endowing the revolutionary tribunals with an almost religious fervor as they sent their victims to the guillotine. The following law of 17 December 1793 gave the government the necessary legal authorization to suspend certain civil liberties in order to proceed with the extraordinary "revolutionary" measures of rescuing the republic from its actual and perceived enemies.

From *A Documentary Survey of the French Revolution,* edited by John Hall Stewart (Upper Saddle River, N.J.: Prentice-Hall, 1951).

* * *

1. Immediately after the publication of the present decree, all suspected persons within the territory of the Republic and still at liberty shall be placed in custody.

2. The following are deemed suspected persons: 1st, those who, by their conduct, associations, talk, or writings have shown themselves partisans of tyranny or federalism and enemies of liberty; 2nd, those who are unable to justify, in the manner prescribed by the decree of 21 March last, their means of existence and the performance of their civic duties; 3rd, those to whom certificates of patriotism have been refused; 4th, public functionaries suspended or dismissed from their positions by the National Convention or by its commissioners, and not reinstated, especially those who have been or are to be dismissed by virtue of the decree of 14 August last; 5th, those former nobles, husbands, wives, fathers, mothers, sons or daughters, brothers or sisters, and agents of the *émigrés,* who have not steadily manfested their devotion to the Revolution; 6th, those who have emigrated during the interval between 1 July, 1789, and the publication of the decree of 30 March–8 April, 1792, even though they may have returned to France within the period established by said decree or prior thereto.

3. The Watch Committees established according to the decree of 21 March last, or those substituted therefor, either by orders of the representatives of the people dispatched to the armies and the departments, or by virtue of particular decrees of the National Convention, are charged with drafting, each in its own *arrondissement,* a list of suspected persons, with issuing warrants of arrest against them, and with having seals placed on their papers. Commanders of the public force to whom such warrants are remitted shall be required to put them into effect immediately, under penalty of dismissal.

4. The members of the committee may order the arrest of any individual only if seven are present, and only by absolute majority of votes.

5. Individuals arrested as suspects shall be taken first to the jails of the place of their detention; in default of jails, they shall be kept under surveillance in their respective dwellings.

6. Within the following week, they shall be transferred to national buildings, which the departmental administrations shall be required to designate and to have prepared for such purpose immediately after the receipt of the present decree.

7. The prisoners may have their absolutely essential belongings brought into said buildings; they shall remain there under guard until the peace.

8. The expenses of custody shall be charged to the prisoners, and shall be divided among them equally: such custody shall be confided preferably to fathers of families and to the relatives of citizens who are at or may go to the frontiers. The salary therefor is established, for each man of the guard, at the value of one and one-half days of labor.

9. The Watch Committees shall dispatch to the Committee of General Security of the National Convention, without delay, the list of persons whom they have arrested, with the reasons for their arrest and with the papers they have seized in such connection.

10. If there is occasion, the civil and criminal courts may have detained, in custody, and dispatched to the jails above stated, those who are accused of offences with regard to which it has been declared that there was no occasion for indictment or who have been acquitted of charges brought against them.

*   *   *

REVIEW QUESTIONS

1. For which social groups was this law intended?
2. What was the correct procedure for arresting suspects?
3. Did the suspect have rights?
4. Are there checks against potential abuses in this law?
5. On the basis of this document, what kind of social and political atmosphere pervaded France during the Jacobin republic?

OLYMPE DE GOUGES

FROM Declaration of the Rights of Woman

The revolution politicized millions of French men by transforming their status from subjects to citizens, but revolutionaries of all political stripes displayed extreme reluctance to incorporate women into the national political body. Heeding the new political discourse of equality, inalienable rights, and universal liberties, Olympe de Gouges, the self-educated daughter of a butcher, pointed up the revolutionaries' patent contradiction of applying tenets of natural law philosophy to one half of the human race but not to the other. This pamphlet, published in September 1791, documents an important discussion during the revolution over the public roles and duties of women in civil society. Olympe de Gouges engaged her critical pen over a number of issues, which led to her arrest as a counterrevolutionary and her execution in 1793.

From *The French Revolution and Human Rights: A Brief Documentary History*, edited by Lynn Avery Hunt (New York: St. Martin's Press, 1996), pp. 124–29.

To be decreed by the National Assembly in its last sessions or by the next legislature.

Preamble

Mothers, daughters, sisters, female representatives of the nation ask to be constituted as a national assembly. Considering that ignorance, neglect, or contempt for the rights of woman are the sole causes of public misfortunes and governmental corruption, they have resolved to set forth in a solemn declaration the natural, inalienable, and sacred rights of woman: so that by being constantly present to all the members of the social body this declaration may always remind them of their rights and duties; so that by being liable at every moment to comparison with the aim of any and all political institutions the acts of women's and men's powers may be the more fully respected; and so that by being founded henceforward on simple and incontestable principles the demands of the citizenesses may always tend toward maintaining the constitution, good morals, and the general welfare.

In consequence, the sex that is superior in beauty as in courage, needed in maternal sufferings, recognizes and declares, in the presence and under the auspices of the Supreme Being, the following rights of woman and the citizeness.

1. Woman is born free and remains equal to man in rights. Social distinctions may be based only on common utility.

2. The purpose of all political association is the preservation of the natural and imprescriptible rights of woman and man. These rights are liberty, property, security, and especially resistance to oppression.

3. The principle of all sovereignty rests essentially in the nation, which is but the reuniting of woman and man. No body and no individual may exercise authority which does not emanate expressly from the nation.

4. Liberty and justice consist in restoring all that belongs to another; hence the exercise of the natural rights of woman has no other limits than those that the perpetual tyranny of man opposes to them; these limits must be reformed according to the laws of nature and reason.

5. The laws of nature and reason prohibit all actions which are injurious to society. No hindrance should be put in the way of anything not prohibited by these wise and divine laws, nor may anyone be forced to do what they do not require.

6. The law should be the expression of the general will. All citizenesses and citizens should take part, in person or by their representatives, in its formation. It must be the same for everyone. All citizenesses and citizens, being equal in its eyes, should be equally admissible to all public dignities, offices, and employments, according to their ability, and with no other distinction than that of their virtues and talents.

7. No woman is exempted; she is indicted, arrested, and detained in the cases determined by the law. Women like men obey this rigorous law.

8. Only strictly and obviously necessary punishments should be established by the law, and no one may be punished except by virtue of a law established and promulgated before the time of the offense, and legally applied to women.

9. Any woman being declared guilty, all rigor is exercised by the law.

10. No one should be disturbed for his fundamental opinions; woman has the right to mount the scaffold, so she should have the right equally to mount the tribune, provided that these manifestations do not trouble public order as established by law.

11. The free communication of thoughts and opinions is one of the most precious of the rights of woman, since this liberty assures the recognition of children by their fathers. Every citizeness may therefore say freely, I am the mother of your child; a barbarous prejudice should not force her to hide the truth, so long as responsibility is accepted for any abuse of this liberty in cases determined by the law.

12. The safeguard of the rights of woman and citizeness requires public powers. These powers are instituted for the advantage of all and not for the private benefit of those to whom they are entrusted.

13. For maintenance of public authority and for expenses of administration, taxation of women and men is equal; she takes part in all forced labor service, in all painful tasks; she must therefore have the same proportion in the distribution of places, employments, offices, dignities, and in industry.

14. The citizenesses and citizens have the right, by themselves or through their representatives, to have demonstrated to them the necessity of public taxes. The citizenesses can only agree to them upon admission of an equal division, not only in wealth, but also in the public administration, and to determine the means of apportionment, assessment, and collection, and the duration of the taxes.

15. The mass of women, joining with men in paying taxes, have the right to hold accountable every public agent of the administration.

16. Any society in which the guarantee of rights is not assured or the separation of powers not settled has no constitution. The constitution is null and

void if the majority of individuals composing the nation has not cooperated in its drafting.

17. Property belongs to both sexes whether united or separated; it is for each of them an inviolable and sacred right, and no one may be deprived of it as a true patrimony of nature, except when public necessity, certified by law, obviously requires it, and then on condition of a just compensation in advance.

Postscript

Women, wake up; the tocsin of reason sounds throughout the universe; recognize your rights. The powerful empire of nature is no longer surrounded by prejudice, fanaticism, superstition, and lies. The torch of truth has dispersed all the clouds of folly and usurpation. Enslaved man has multiplied his force and needs yours to break his chains. Having become free, he has become unjust toward his companion. Oh women! Women, when will you cease to be blind? What advantages have you gathered in the revolution? A scorn more marked, a disdain more conspicuous. During the centuries of corruption you only reigned over the weakness of men. Your empire is destroyed; what is left to you then? Firm belief in the injustices of men. The reclaiming of your patrimony founded on the wise decrees of nature; why should you fear such a beautiful enterprise? . . . Whatever the barriers set up against you, it is in your power to overcome them; you only have to want it. Let us pass now to the appalling account of what you have been in society; and since national education is an issue at this moment, let us see if our wise legislators will think sanely about the education of women.

*   *   *

If giving my sex an honorable and just consistency is considered to be at this time paradoxical on my part and an attempt at the impossible, I leave to future men the glory of dealing with this matter; but while waiting, we can prepare the way with national education, with the restoration of morals and with conjugal agreements.

Form for a Social Contract between Man and Woman

We, _____ and _____, moved by our own will, unite for the length of our lives and for the duration of our mutual inclinations under the following conditions: We intend and wish to make our wealth communal property, while reserving the right to divide it in favor of our children and of those for whom we might have a special inclination, mutually recognizing that our goods belong directly to our children, from whatever bed they come, and that all of them without distinction have the right to bear the name of the fathers and mothers who have acknowledged them, and we impose on ourselves the obligation of subscribing to the law that punishes any rejection of one's own blood. We likewise obligate ourselves, in the case of a separation, to divide our fortune equally and to set aside the portion the law designates for our children. In the case of a perfect union, the one the one who dies first will give up half his property in favor of the children; and if there are no children, the survivor will inherit by right, unless the dying person has disposed of his half of the common property in favor of someone he judges appropriate.

*   *   *

REVIEW QUESTIONS

1. Compare de Gouges's declaration with the Declaration of the Rights of Man and Citizen and determine the parallel and divergent aspects of the two documents.
2. How does de Gouges envision women in civil society, and how does this projected role differ from the social realities of eighteenth-century France?
3. What traditional institutions and mores does de Gouges criticize, and what does she exhort women to do?

NATIONAL CONVENTION

FROM Dissolution of Clubs and Popular Societies of Women

The political clubs and associations that mushroomed in France after 1789 played a significant role in revolutionary political culture. Because women had participated in critical events in the early phases of the revolution (e.g., the October Days), it is not surprising that women formed associations and participated in the public life of the republic. When the Society of Revolutionary Republican Women, an association that was initially supportive of Jacobin republicanism, grew critical of Jacobin government in 1793, it fell out of favor with the Jacobin-dominated National Convention, the nation's legislature. When a delegation of market women issued a formal complaint to the convention regarding the society's brusque insistence that they wear revolutionary garb (pantaloons and red bonnets), the convention used the incident to dissolve all women's societies.

From *Women in Revolutionary Paris, 1789–1795,* edited by John Robertson, Steven Epstein, Thomas Max Safley, James Brophy, and Cat Nilan (Champaign: University of Illinois Press, 1979), pp. 213–17.

National Convention Moise Bayle, Presiding Session of 9 Brumaire

. . . *Amar, for the Committee of General Security:* Citizens, your Committee has been working without respite on means of warding off the consequences of disorders which broke out the day before yesterday in Paris at the Marché des Innocents, near Saint-Eustache. It spent the night receiving deputations, listening to various reports which were made to it, and taking measures to maintain public order. Several women, calling themselves Jacobines, from an allegedly revolutionary society, were going about in the morning, in the market and under the ossuaries of les Innocents, in pantaloons and red bonnets. They intended to force other *citoyennes* to wear the same costume; several testified that they had been insulted by them. A mob of nearly six thousand women gathered. All the women were in agreement that violence and threats would not make them dress in a costume they respected but which

they believed was intended for men; they would obey laws passed by the legislators and acts of the people's magistrates, but they would not give in to the wishes and caprices of a hundred lazy and suspect women. They all cried out, "*Vive la Republique, une et indivisible!*"

Municipal officers and members of the Revolutionary Committee of the Section du Contrat Social quieted people down and dispersed the mobs. In the evening the same disturbance broke out with greater violence. A brawl started. Several self-proclaimed Revolutionary Women were roughed up. Some members of the crowd indulged themselves in acts of violence towards them which decency ought to have proscribed. Several remarks reported to your Committee show that this disturbance can be attributed only to a plot by enemies of the state. Several of these self-proclaimed Revolutionary Women may have been led astray by an excess of patriotism, but others, doubtless, were motivated only by malevolence.

Right now, when Brissot and his accomplices are being judged, they want to work up some disorders in Paris, as was the case whenever you were about to consider some important matter and when it was a question of taking measures useful for the Fatherland.

The Section des Marchés, informed of these events, drew up a resolution in which it informs your Committee that it believes several malevolent persons have put on the mask of an exaggerated patriotism to foment disturbances in the Section and a kind of counterrevolution in Paris. This Section requests that it be illegal to hinder anyone's freedom of dress and that popular societies of women be strictly prohibited, at least during the revolution.

The Committee thought it should carry its investigation further. It raised the following questions: (1) Is it permissible for citizens or for an individual society to force other citizens to do what the law does not prescribe? (2) Should meetings of women gathered together in popular societies in Paris be allowed? Don't the disorders already occasioned by these societies argue against tolerating their existence any longer?

Naturally, these questions are complicated, and their resolution must be preceded by two more general questions, which are: (1) Can women exercise political rights and take an active part in affairs of government? (2) Can they deliberate together in political associations or popular societies?

With respect to these two questions, the Committee decided in the negative. Time does not allow for the full development to which these major questions—and the first, above all—lend themselves. We are going to put forward a few ideas which may shed light on them. In your wisdom you will know how to submit them to thorough examination.

1. Should women exercise political rights and meddle in affairs of government? To govern is to rule the commonwealth by laws, the preparation of which demands extensive knowledge, unlimited attention and devotion, a strict immovability, and self-abnegation; again, to govern is to direct and ceaselessly to correct the action of constituted authorities. Are women capable of these cares and of the qualities they call for? In general, we can answer, no. Very few examples would contradict this evaluation.

The citizen's political rights are to debate and to have resolutions drawn up, by means of comparative deliberations, that relate to the interest of the state, and to resist oppression. Do women have the moral and physical strength which the exercise of one and the other of these rights calls for? Universal opinion rejects this idea.

2. Should women meet in political associations? The goal of popular associations is this: to unveil the maneuvers of the enemies of the commonwealth; to exercise surveillance both over citizens as individuals and over public functionaries—even over the legislative body; to excite the zeal of one and the other by the example of republican virtues; to shed light by public and in-depth discussion concerning the lack or reform of political laws. Can women devote themselves to these useful and difficult functions? No, because they would be obliged to sacrifice the more important cares to which nature calls them. The private functions for which women are destined by their very nature are related to the general order of society; this social order results from the differences between man and woman. Each sex is called to the kind of occupation which is fitting for it; its action is circumscribed within this circle which it cannot break through, because nature, which has imposed these limits on man, commands imperiously and receives no law.

Man is strong, robust, born with great energy, audacity, and courage; he braves perils and the intemperance of seasons because of his constitution; he resists all the elements; he is fit for the arts, difficult labors; and as he is almost exclusively destined for agriculture, commerce, navigation, voyages, war—everything that calls for force, intelligence, capability, so in the same way, he alone seems to be equipped for profound and serious thinking which calls for great intellectual effort and long studies which it is not granted to women to pursue.

What character is suitable for woman? Morals

and even nature have assigned her functions to her. To begin educating men, to prepare children's minds and hearts for public virtues, to direct them early in life towards the good, to elevate their souls, to educate them in the political cult of liberty: such are their functions, after household cares. Woman is naturally destined to make virtue loved. When they have fulfilled all these obligations, they will have deserved well of the Fatherland. Doubtless they must educate themselves in the principles of liberty in order to make their children cherish it; they can attend the deliberations of the Sections and discussions of the popular societies, but as they are made for softening the morals of man, should they take an active part in discussions the passion of which is incompatible with the softness and moderation which are the charm of their sex?

We must say that this question is related essentially to morals, and without morals, no republic. Does the honesty of woman allow her to display herself in public and to struggle against men? to argue in full view of a public about questions on which the salvation of the republic depends? In general, women are ill suited for elevated thoughts and serious meditations, and if, among ancient peoples, their natural timidity and modesty did not allow them to appear outside their families, then in the French Republic do you want them to be seen coming into the gallery to political assemblies as men do? abandoning both reserve—source of all the virtues of their sex—and the care of their family?

They have more than one alternative way of rendering service to the Fatherland; they can enlighten their husbands, communicating precious reflections, the fruit of the quiet of a sedentary life, and work to fortify their love of country by means of everything which intimate love gives them in the way of empire. And the man, enlightened by peaceful family discussions in the midst of his household, will bring back into society the useful ideas imparted to him by an honest woman.

We believe, therefore, that a woman should not leave her family to meddle in affairs of government.

There is another sense in which women's associations seem dangerous. If we consider that the political education of men is at its beginning, that all its principles are not developed, and that we are still stammering the word liberty, then how much more reasonable is it for women, whose moral education is almost nil, to be less enlightened concerning principles? Their presence in popular societies, therefore, would give an active role in government to people more exposed to error and seduction. Let us add that women are disposed by their organization to an over-excitation which would be deadly in public affairs and that interests of state would soon be sacrificed to everything which ardor in passions can generate in the way of error and disorder. Delivered over to the heat of public debate, they would teach their children not love of country but hatreds and suspicions.

We believe, therefore, and without any doubt you will think as we do, that it is not possible for women to exercise political rights. You will destroy these alleged popular societies of women which the aristocracy would want to set up to put them at odds with men, to divide the latter by forcing them to take sides in these quarrels, and to stir up disorder.

Charlier. Notwithstanding the objections just cited, I do not know on what principle one could lean in taking away women's right to assemble peaceably. (Murmurs.) Unless you are going to question whether women are part of the human species, can you take away from them this right which is common to every thinking being? When a popular society is negligent with respect to general order, to laws, then the members, accused of the offense, or the entire association, if it has made itself guilty, will be pursued by the police. And you have examples of the dissolution of several societies which had been taken over by the aristocracy. But may fear of a few abuses to which an institution is susceptible not force you to destroy the institution itself? For what institution is exempt from inconveniences?

Bazire. There is not anyone who does not sense the danger of abandoning to the police the surveillance and the overseeing of the popular societies. Thus, this remedy, which is itself an abuse, should not be cited against the all too real drawbacks of women's societies. Here is how the suspension of these societies can be justified. You declared yourselves a revolutionary government; in this capacity you can take all measures dictated by the public safety. For a brief period you have thrown a veil over principles out of fear that they might be abused to lead us into counterrevolution. Therefore, it is only a question of knowing whether women's societies are dangerous. Experience has shown these past days how deadly they are to the public peace. That granted, let no one say anything more to me about principles. I ask that in a revolutionary spirit and by way of a measure of public security these associations be prohibited, at least during the revolution.

The decree proposed by Amar is adopted in these terms:

The National Convention, after having heard the report of its Committee of General Security, decrees:

Article 1: Clubs and popular societies of women, whatever name they are known under, are prohibited. 2: All sessions of popular societies must be public.

*   *   *

REVIEW QUESTIONS

1. How did the national convention justify the abolition of women's clubs, and why was it threatened by women's political activities?
2. How does this document portray the behavior of women in public life?
3. What distinctions are made between the private functions of women and the social order of male public life?
4. Why are the two incompatible?
5. In this document, what is the role of nature in constructing the boundaries of civil society?

Opposing Views of the Revolution: Edmund Burke AND Thomas Paine

Although Edmund Burke, an Irish Whig member of parliament, had supported the American cause against Great Britain in the 1770s, he denounced the French Revolution with a sustained rhetorical elegance that has few, if any, rivals. The circumstance that provoked Burke's essay was a speech in 1789 by Dr. Richard Price, who posited a close affinity between England's Glorious Revolution of 1688 and the recent French Revolution. Burke's scathing attack on the premises and principles of the French Revolution in his Reflections on the Revolution in France *(1790) incited an equally engaging rejoinder by Thomas Paine, a committed English democrat, whose earlier* Common Sense *had become a central political tract supporting the American Revolution. His* Rights of Man *(1791), in response to Burke, assumed the status in Britain of a primer for democratic republicanism. The British government prohibited its publication and sale in vain.*

Edmund Burke

FROM **Reflections on the Revolution in France**

*   *   *

No experience has taught us that in any other course or method than that of an *hereditary crown* our liberties can be regularly perpetuated and preserved sacred as our *hereditary right*. An irregular, convulsive movement may be necessary to throw off an irregular, convulsive disease. But the course of succession is the healthy habit of the British constitution. Was it that the legislature wanted, at the act for the limitation of the crown in the Hanoverian line, drawn through the female descendants of James the First, a due sense of the inconveniences of having two or three, or possibly more, foreigners in succession to the British throne? No!—they had a due sense of the evils which might happen from such foreign rule, and more than a due sense of them. But a more decisive proof cannot be given of the full conviction of the British nation that the principles of the Revolution did not authorize them to elect kings at their pleasure, and without any attention to the ancient fundamental principles of our government, than their continuing to adopt a plan of hereditary Protestant succession in the old line, with all the dangers and all the inconveniences of its being a foreign line full before their eyes and operating with the utmost force upon their minds.

A few years ago I should be ashamed to overload a matter so capable of supporting itself by the then unnecessary support of any argument; but this seditious, unconstitutional doctrine is now publicly taught, avowed, and printed. The

From *Reflections on the Revolution in France,* edited by J. G. A. Pocock (Cambridge, Eng.: Hackett, 1987).

dislike I feel to revolutions, the signals for which have so often been given from pulpits; the spirit of change that is gone abroad; the total contempt which prevails with you, and may come to prevail with us, of all ancient institutions when set in opposition to a present sense of convenience or to the bent of a present inclination: all these considerations make it not unadvisable, in my opinion, to call back our attention to the true principles of our own domestic laws; that you, my French friend, should begin to know, and that we should continue to cherish them. We ought not, on either side of the water, to suffer ourselves to be imposed upon by the counterfeit wares which some persons, by a double fraud, export to you in illicit bottoms as raw commodities of British growth, though wholly alien to our soil, in order afterwards to smuggle them back again into this country, manufactured after the newest Paris fashion of an improved liberty.

The people of England will not ape the fashions they have never tried, nor go back to those which they have found mischievous on trial. They look upon the legal hereditary succession of their crown as among their rights, not as among their wrongs; as a benefit, not as a grievance; as a security for their liberty, not as a badge of servitude. They look on the frame of their commonwealth, *such as it stands,* to be of inestimable value, and they conceive the undisturbed succession of the crown to be a pledge of the stability and perpetuity of all the other members of our constitution.

I shall beg leave, before I go any further, to take notice of some paltry artifices which the abettors of election, as the only lawful title to the crown, are ready to employ in order to render the support of the just principles of our constitution a task somewhat invidious. These sophisters substitute a fictitious cause and feigned personages, in whose favor they suppose you engaged whenever you defend the inheritable nature of the crown. It is common with them to dispute as if they were in a conflict with some of those exploded fanatics of slavery, who formerly maintained what I believe no creature now maintains, "that the crown is held by divine hereditary and indefeasible right." These old fanatics of single arbitrary power dogmatized as if hereditary royalty was the only lawful government in the world, just as our new fanatics of popular arbitrary power maintain that a popular election is the sole lawful source of authority. The old prerogative enthusiasts, it is true, did speculate foolishly, and perhaps impiously too, as if monarchy had more of a divine sanction than any other mode of government; and as if a right to govern by inheritance were in strictness *indefeasible* in every person who should be found in the succession to a throne, and under every circumstance, which no civil or political right can be. But an absurd opinion concerning the king's hereditary right to the crown does not prejudice one that is rational and bottomed upon solid principles of law and policy. If all the absurd theories of lawyers and divines were to vitiate the objects in which they are conversant, we should have no law and no religion left in the world. But an absurd theory on one side of a question forms no justification for alleging a false fact or promulgating mischievous maxims on the other.

*   *   *

I almost venture to affirm that not one in a hundred amongst us participates in the "triumph" of the Revolution Society. If the king and queen of France, and their children, were to fall into our hands by the chance of war, in the most acrimonious of all hostilities (I deprecate such an event, I deprecate such hostility), they would be treated with another sort of triumphal entry into London. We formerly have had a king of France in that situation; you have read how he was treated by the victor in the field, and in what manner he was afterwards received in England. Four hundred years have gone over us, but I believe we are not materially changed since that period. Thanks to our sullen resistance to innovation, thanks to the cold sluggishness of our national character, we still bear the stamp of our forefathers. We have not (as

I conceive) lost the generosity and dignity of thinking of the fourteenth century, nor as yet have we subtilized ourselves into savages. We are not the converts of Rousseau; we are not the disciples of Voltaire; Helvetius has made no progress amongst us. Atheists are not our preachers; madmen are not our lawgivers. We know that *we* have made no discoveries, and we think that no discoveries are to be made in morality, nor many in the great principles of government, nor in the ideas of liberty, which were understood long before we were born, altogether as well as they will be after the grace has heaped its mold upon our presumption and the silent tomb shall have imposed its law on our pert loquacity. In England we have not yet been completely embowelled of our natural entrails; we still feel within us, and we cherish and cultivate, those inbred sentiments which are the faithful guardians, the active monitors of our duty, the true supporters of all liberal and manly morals. We have not been drawn and trussed, in order that we may be filled, like stuffed birds in a museum, with chaff and rags and paltry blurred shreds of paper about the rights of men. We preserve the whole of our feelings still native and entire, unsophisticated by pedantry and infidelity. We have real hearts of flesh and blood beating in our bosoms. We fear God; we look up with awe to kings, with affection to parliaments, with duty to magistrates, with reverence to priests, and with respect to nobility. Why? Because when such ideas are brought before our minds, it is *natural* to be so affected; because all other feelings are false and spurious and tend to corrupt our minds, to vitiate our primary morals, to render us unfit for rational liberty, and, by teaching us a servile, licentious, and abandoned insolence, to be our low sport for a few holidays, to make us perfectly fit for, and justly deserving of, slavery through the whole course of our lives.

You see, Sir, that in this enlightened age I am bold enough to confess that we are generally men of untaught feelings, that, instead of casting away all our old prejudices, we cherish them to a very considerable degree, and, to take more shame to ourselves, we cherish them because they are prejudices; and the longer they have lasted and the more generally they have prevailed, the more we cherish them. We are afraid to put men to live and trade each on his own private stock of reason, because we suspect that this stock in each man is small, and that the individuals would do better to avail themselves of the general bank and capital of nations and of ages. Many of our men of speculation, instead of exploding general prejudices, employ their sagacity to discover the latent wisdom which prevails in them. If they find what they seek, and they seldom fail, they think it more wise to continue the prejudice, with the reason involved, than to cast away the coat of prejudice and to leave nothing but the naked reason; because prejudice, with its reason, has a motive to give action to that reason, and an affection which will give it permanence. Prejudice is of ready application in the emergency; it previously engages the mind in a steady course of wisdom and virtue and does not leave the man hesitating in the moment of decision skeptical, puzzled, and unresolved. Prejudice renders a man's virtue his habit, and not a series of unconnected acts. Through just prejudice, his duty becomes a part of his nature.

Your literary men and your politicians, and so do the whole clan of the enlightened among us, essentially differ in these points. They have no respect for the wisdom of others, but they pay it off by a very full measure of confidence in their own. With them it is a sufficient motive to destroy an old scheme of things because it is an old one. As to the new, they are in no sort of fear with regard to the duration of a building run up in haste, because duration is no object to those who think little or nothing has been done before their time, and who place all their hopes in discovery. They conceive, very systematically, that all things which give perpetuity are mischievous, and therefore they are at inexpiable war with all establishments. They think that government may vary like modes of dress, and with as little ill effect; that there needs no principle of attachment, except a sense of present convenience, to any constitution of the

state. They always speak as if they were of opinion that there is a singular species of compact between them and their magistrates which binds the magistrate, but which has nothing reciprocal in it, but that the majesty of the people has a right to dissolve it without any reason but its will. Their attachment to their country itself is only so far as it agrees with some of their fleeting projects; it begins and ends with that scheme of polity which falls in with their momentary opinion.

These doctrines, or rather sentiments, seem prevalent with your new statesmen. But they are wholly different from those on which we have always acted in this country.

*   *   *

Thomas Paine

FROM *Rights of Man*

*   *   *

Mr. Burke talks about what he calls an hereditary crown, as if it were some production of Nature; or as if, like Time, it had a power to operate, not only independently, but in spite of man; or as if it were a thing or a subject universally consented to. Alas! it has none of those properties, but is the reverse of them all. It is a thing in imagination, the propriety of which is more than doubted, and the legality of which in a few years will be denied.

But, to arrange this matter in a clearer view than what general expressions can convey, it will be necessary to state the distinct heads under which (what is called) an hereditary crown, or, more properly speaking, an hereditary succession to the Government of a Nation, can be considered; which are,

First, The right of a particular Family to establish itself.

From *Rights of Man, Common Sense, and Other Political Writings,* by Thomas Paine (New York: Oxford University Press, 1995).

Secondly, The right of a Nation to establish a particular Family.

With respect to the *first* of these heads, that of a Family establishing itself with hereditary powers on its own authority, and independent of the consent of a Nation, all men will concur in calling it despotism; and it would be trespassing on their understanding to attempt to prove it.

But the *second* head, that of a Nation establishing a particular Family with *hereditary powers,* does not present itself as despotism on the first reflection; but if men will permit a second reflection to take place, and carry that reflection forward but one remove out of their own persons to that of their offspring, they will then see that hereditary succession becomes in its consequences the same despotism to others, which they reprobated for themselves. It operates to preclude the consent of the succeeding generation; and the preclusion of consent is despotism. When the person who at any time shall be in possession of a Government, or those who stand in succession to him, shall say to a Nation, I hold this power in 'contempt' of you, it signifies not on what authority he pretends to say it. It is no relief, but an aggravation to a person in slavery, to reflect that he was sold by his parent; and as that which heightens the criminality of an act cannot be produced to prove the legality of it, hereditary succession cannot be established as a legal thing.

In order to arrive at a more perfect decision on this head, it will be proper to consider the generation which undertakes to establish a Family with *hereditary powers,* a-part and separate from the generations which are to follow; and also to consider the character in which the *first* generation acts with respect to succeeding generations.

The generation which first selects a person, and puts him at the head of its Government, either with the title of King, or any other distinction, acts its *own choice,* be it wise or foolish, as a free agent for itself. The person so set up is not hereditary, but selected and appointed; and the generation who sets him up, does not live under an hereditary government, but under a government of its own choice and establishment. Were the generation

who sets him up, and the person so let up, to live for ever, it never could become hereditary succession; and of consequence, hereditary succession can only follow on the death of the first parties.

As therefore hereditary succession is out of the question with respect to the *first* generation, we have now to consider the character in which *that* generation acts with respect to the commencing generation, and to all succeeding ones.

It assumes a character, to which it has neither right nor title. It changes itself from a *Legislator* to a *Testator,* and affects to make its Will, which is to have operation after the demise of the makers, to bequeath the Government; and it not only attempts to bequeath, but to establish on the succeeding generation, a new and different form of government under which itself lived. Itself, as is already observed, lived not under an hereditary Government, but under a Government of its own choice and establishment; and it now attempts, by virtue of a will and testament, (and which it has not authority to make), to take from the commencing generation, and all future ones, the rights and free agency by which itself acted.

But, exclusive of the right which any generation has to act collectively as a testator, the objects to which it applies itself in this case, are not within the compass of any law, or of any will or testament.

The rights of men in society, are neither deviseable, nor transferable, nor annihilable, but are descendable only; and it is not in the power of any generation to intercept finally, and cut off the descent. If the present generation, or any other, are disposed to be slaves, it does not lessen the right of the succeeding generation to be free: wrongs cannot have a legal descent. When Mr. Burke attempts to maintain, that the *English Nation did at the Revolution of 1688, most solemnly renounce and abdicate their rights for themselves, and for all their posterity for ever;* he speaks a language that merits not reply, and which can only excite contempt for his prostitute principles, or pity for his ignorance.

In whatever light hereditary succession, as growing out of the will and testament of some former generation, presents itself, it is an absurdity. A cannot make a will to take from B the property of B, and give it to C; yet this is the manner in which (what is called) hereditary succession by law operates. A certain former generation made a will, to take away the rights of the commencing generation, and all future ones, and convey those rights to a third person, who afterwards comes forward, and tells them, in Mr. Burke's language, that they have *no rights,* that their rights are already bequeathed to him, and that he will govern in *contempt* of them. From such principles, and such ignorance, Good Lord deliver the world!

But, after all, what is this metaphor called a crown, or rather what is monarchy? Is it a thing, or is it a name, or is it a fraud? Is it "a contrivance of human wisdom," or of human craft to obtain money from a nation under specious pretences? Is it a thing necessary to a nation? If it is, in what does that necessity consist, what services does it perform, what is its business, and what are its merits? * * * It appears to be a something going much out of fashion, falling into ridicule, and rejected in some countries both as unnecessary and expensive. In America it is considered as an absurdity; and in France it has so far declined, that the goodness of the man, and the respect for his personal character, are the only things that preserve the appearance of its existence.

* * *

If there is any thing in monarchy which we people of America do not understand, I wish Mr. Burke

would be so kind as to inform us. I see in America, a government extending over a country ten times as large as England, and conducted with regularity, for a fortieth part of the expence which government costs in England. If I ask a man in America, if he wants a King? he retorts, and asks me if I take him for an ideot? How is it that this difference happens? are we more or less wise than others? I see in America, the generality of people living in a stile of plenty unknown in monarchical countries; and I see that the principle of its government, which is that of the *equal Rights of Man,* is making a rapid progress in the world.

* * *

REVIEW QUESTIONS

1. What is Burke's position on tradition and monarchy, and what is Paine's response to it?
2. What is Burke's response to the Enlightenment and its primacy of reason?
3. How does Paine characterize the use of reason in politics?
4. How did the issue of the French Revolution have a direct bearing on British domestic politics in the 1790s?

WILLIAM WORDSWORTH

FROM *The Prelude*

William Wordsworth, one of the outstanding voices of English Romantic poetry, exemplified the unbounded optimism with which he and many other European artists embraced the French Revolution. Although Wordsworth's enthusiasm for the revolution faded, this excerpt from The Prelude *(1805), an epic poem of his youth and development as a poet, recaptures the initial sublime hope that he projected on the revolution. Because Wordsworth was not alone among poets, writers, and artists in finding inspiration in the promise of justice and freedom, one must recognize the revolution as an all-embracing cultural event.*

From *The Prelude* (Norton Critical Edition), by William Wordsworth, edited by Jonathan Wordsworth, M. H. Abrams, and Stephen Gill (New York: Norton, 1979).

*   *   *

But from these bitter truths I must return
To my own History. It hath been told
That I was led to take an eager part
In arguments of civil polity
Abruptly, and indeed before my time:
I had approach'd, like other Youth, the Shield
Of human nature from the golden side
And would have fought, even to the death, to
   attest
The quality of the metal which I saw.
What there is best in individual Man,
Of wise in passion, and sublime in power,
What there is strong and pure in household
   love,
Benevolent in small societies,
And great in large ones also, when call'd forth
By great occasions, these were things of which
I something knew, yet even these themselves,
Felt deeply, were not thoroughly understood
By Reason; nay, far from it, they were yet,
As cause was given me afterwards to learn,
Not proof against the injuries of the day,
Lodged only at the Sanctuary's door,
Not safe within its bosom. Thus prepared,
And with such general insight into evil,
And of the bounds which sever it from good,
As books and common intercourse with life
Must needs have given; to the noviciate mind,
When the world travels in a beaten road,
Guide faithful as is needed, I began
To think with fervour upon management
Of Nations, what it is and ought to be,
And how their worth depended on their
   Laws
And on the Constitution of the State.

O pleasant exercise of hope and joy!
For great were the auxiliars which then stood
Upon our side, we who were strong in love;
Bliss was it in that dawn to be alive,
But to be young was very heaven; O times,
In which the meagre, stale, forbidding ways
Of custom, law, and statute took at once
The attraction of a Country in Romance;
When Reason seem'd the most to assert her
   rights
When most intent on making of herself
A prime Enchanter to assist the work,
Which then was going forwards in her name,
Not favour'd spots alone, but the whole earth
The beauty wore of promise, that which sets,
To take an image which was felt, no doubt,
Among the bowers of paradise itself,
The budding rose above the rose full blown.
What temper at the prospect did not wake
To happiness unthought of? The inert
Were rouz'd, and lively natures rapt away:
They who had fed their childhood upon dreams,
The Play-fellows of Fancy, who had made
All powers of swiftness, subtlety, and strength
Their ministers, used to stir in lordly wise
Among the grandest objects of the sense,
And deal with whatsoever they found there
As if they had within some lurking right
To wield it; they too, who, of gentle mood
Had watch'd all gentle motions, and to these
Had fitted their own thoughts, schemers more
   mild,
And in the region of their peaceful selves,
Did now find helpers to their hearts' desire,
And stuff at hand, plastic as they could wish,
Were call'd upon to exercise their skill,
Not in Utopia, subterraneous Fields,

Or some secreted Island, Heaven knows where,
But in the very world which is the world
Of all of us, the place in which, in the end,
We find our happiness, or not at all.

    Why should I not confess that earth was then
To me what an inheritance new-fallen
Seems, when the first time visited, to one
Who thither comes to find in it his home?
He walks about and looks upon the place
With cordial transport, moulds it, and remoulds,
And is half pleased with things that are amiss,
'Twill be such joy to see them disappear.

    An active partisan, I thus convoked
From every object pleasant circumstance
To suit my ends; I moved among mankind
With genial feelings still predominant;
When erring, erring on the better part,
And in the kinder spirit; placable,
Indulgent oft-times to the worst desires
As on one side not uninform'd that men
See as it hath been taught them, and that time
Gives rights to error; on the other hand

That throwing off oppression must be work
As well of license as of liberty;
And above all, for this was more than all,
Not caring if the wind did now and then
Blow keen upon an eminence that gave
Prospect so large into futurity;
In brief, a child of nature, as at first,
Diffusing only those affections wider
That from the cradle had grown up with me,
And losing, in no other way than light
Is lost in light, the weak in the more strong.

*   *   *

REVIEW QUESTIONS

1. What were young Wordsworth's sentiments on civil polity?
2. Why did Wordsworth remember 1789 as bliss?
3. What positive characteristics did he ascribe to the revolution?
4. What are the implicit criticisms of the revolution and his own attitudes?

AL-JABARTI

FROM *Chronicle of the French Occupation, 1798*

In May 1798, 400 French ships, carrying Napoleon and 36,000 men, set sail for Egypt. In an attempt to extend France's colonial empire and undermine Britain's economic dominance in the eastern Mediterranean, the French revolutionary army established control in Egypt in June 1798 after defeating the Mamluks, the military caste governing Egypt for the Ottoman Empire. In 1799 a superior British navy destroyed the French fleet in Alexandria, spurring Napoleon to return to France in the same year and leave behind a trapped, defeated French army, which finally returned in 1801. Although brief, the French occupation of Egypt significantly changed Arab life, alerting the Arab world to the West's formidable military might and its advances in learning. Al-Jabarti, a learned Egyptian born into a family of religious scholars, captured the upheaval and suffering of the Egyptian population. In the fol-

lowing section Al-Jabarti cites and critiques Napoleon's announcement of French occupation.

From *Al-Jabarti's Chronicle of the French Occupation,* translated by S. Moreh (1798), pp. 24, 26–33.

*   *   *

On Monday news arrived that the French had reached Damanhūr and Rosetta, bringing about the flight of their inhabitants to Fuwwa and its surroundings. Contained in this news was mention of the French sending notices throughout the country demanding impost for the upkeep of the military. Furthermore they printed a large proclamation in Arabic, calling on the people to obey them and to raise their "Bandiera." In this proclamation were inducements, warnings, all manner of wiliness and stipulations. Some copies were sent from the provinces to Cairo and its text is:

In the name of God, the Merciful, the Compassionate. There is no god but God. He has no son, nor has He an associate in His Dominion.

On behalf of the French Republic which is based upon the foundation of liberty and equality, General Bonaparté, Commander-in-Chief of the French armies makes known to all the Egyptian people that for a long time the Ṣanjaqs who lorded it over Egypt have treated the French community basely and contemptuously and have persecuted its merchants with all manner of extortion and violence. Therefore the hour of punishment has now come.

Unfortunately this group of Mamlūks, imported from the mountains of Circassia and Georgia have acted corruptly for ages in the fairest land that is to be found upon the face of the globe. However, the Lord of the Universe, the Almighty, has decreed the end of their power.

O ye Egyptians, they may say to you that I have not made an expedition hither for any other object than that of abolishing your religion; but this is a pure falsehood and you must not give credit to it, but tell the slanderers that I have not come to you except for the purpose of restoring your rights from the hands of the oppressors and that I more than the Mamlūks, serve God—may He be praised and exalted—and revere His Prophet Muhammad and the glorious Qur'ān.

And tell them also that all people are equal in the eyes of God and the only circumstances which distinguish one from the other are reason, virtue, and knowledge. But amongst the Mamlūks, what is there of reason, virtue, and knowledge, which would distinguish them from others and qualify them alone to possess everything which sweetens life in this world? Wherever fertile land is found it is appropriated to the Mamlūks; and the handsomest female slaves, and the best horses, and the most desirable dwelling-places, all these belong to them exclusively. If the land of Egypt is a fief of the Mamlūks, let them then produce the title-deed, which God conferred upon them. But the Lord of the Universe is compassionate and equitable toward mankind, and with the help of the Exalted, from this day forward no Egyptian shall be excluded from admission to eminent positions nor from acquiring high ranks, therefore the intelligent and virtuous and learned ("*ulamā*") amongst them, will regulate / their affairs, and thus the state of the whole population will be rightly adjusted.

Formerly, in the lands of Egypt there were great cities, and wide canals and extensive commerce and nothing ruined all this but the avarice and the tyranny of the Mamlūks.

O ye Qādis, Shaykhs and Imāms; O ye Shurbājiyya and men of circumstance tell your nation that the French are also faithful Muslims, and in confirmation of this they invaded Rome and destroyed there the Papal See, which was always exhorting the Christians to make war with Islam. And then they went to the island of Malta, from where they expelled the Knights, who claimed that God the Exalted required them to fight the Muslims. Furthermore, the French at all times have declared themselves to be the most sincere friends of the Ottoman Sultan and the enemy of his enemies, may God ever perpetuate his empire! And on the contrary the Mamlūks have withheld their obeisance from the Sultan, and have not followed his orders. Indeed they never obeyed anything but their own greed!

Blessing on blessing to the Egyptians who will act in concert with us, without any delay, for their condition shall be rightly adjusted, and their rank raised. Blessing also, upon those who will abide in their habitations, not siding with either of the two hostile parties, yet when they know us better, they will hasten to us with all their hearts. But woe upon woe to those who will unite with the Mamlūks and assist them in the war against us, for they will not find the way of escape, and no trace of them shall remain.

First Article

All the villages, situated within three hours' distance from the places through which the French army passes, are required to send to the Commander-in-Chief some persons, deputed by them, to announce to the aforesaid, that they submit and that they have hoisted the French flag, which is white, blue, and red.

Second Article

Every village that shall rise against the French army, shall be burnt down.

Third Article

Every village that submits to the French army must hoist the French flag and also the flag of our friend the Ottoman Sultan, may he continue for ever.

Fourth Article

The Shaykh of each village must immediately seal all property, houses, and possessions, belonging to the Mamlūks, making the most strenuous effort that not the least thing be lost.

Fifth Article

The Shaykhs, Qāḍīs, and Imāms must remain / at their posts, and every countryman shall remain peaceably in his dwelling, and also prayers shall be performed in the mosques as customary and the Egyptians, all of them shall render thanks for God's graciousness, praise be to Him and may He be exalted, in extirpating the power of the Mamlūks, saying with a loud voice, May God perpetuate the glory of the Ottoman Sultan! May God preserve the glory of the French army! May God curse the Mamlūks and rightly adjust the condition of the Egyptian people.

Written in the Camp at Alexandria on the 13th of the month Messidor [the 6th year] of the founding of the French Republic, that is to say toward the end of the month Muharram in the year [1213] of the Hijra [2 July 1798].

It ends here word for word. Here is an explanation of the incoherent words and vulgar constructions which he put into this miserable letter.

His statement "In the name of God, the Merciful, the Compassionate. There is no god but God. He has no son, nor has He an associate in His Dominion." In mentioning these three sentences there is an indication that the French agree with the three religions, but at the same time they do not agree with them, nor with any religion. They are consistent with the Muslims in stating the formula "In the name of God," in denying that He has a son or an associate. They disagree with the Muslims in not mentioning the two Articles of Faith, in rejecting the mission of Muhammad, and the legal words and deeds which are necessarily recognized by religion. They agree with the Christians in most of their words and deeds, but disagree with them by not mentioning the Trinity, and denying the mission and furthermore in rejecting their beliefs, killing the priests, and destroying the churches. Then, their statement "On behalf of the French Republic, etc.," that is, this proclamation is sent from their Republic, that means their body politic, because they have no chief or sultan with whom they all agree, like others, whose function is to speak on their behalf. For when they rebelled against their sultan six years ago and killed him, the people agreed unanimously that there was not to be a single ruler but that their state, territories, laws, and administration of their affairs, should be in the hands of the intelligent and wise men among them. They appointed persons chosen by them and made them heads of the army, and below them generals and commanders of thousands, two hundreds, and tens, administrators and advisers, on condition that they were all to be equal and none superior to any other in view of the equality of creation and nature. They made this the foundation and basis of their system. This is the meaning of their statement "based upon the foundation of liberty and equality." Their term "liberty" means that they are not slaves like the Mamlūks; "equality" has the aforesaid meaning. Their officials are distinguished by the cleanliness of their garments. They wear emblems on their uniforms and upon their heads. For example an Amir of ten has a large rosette of silk upon his head / like a big rose. If he is a commander of twenty-five his rosette is of two colours, and if he is a commander of a hundred his rosette is of three colours. His hat which is known as *burnayṭa* (It. *borreta*) is embroidered with gold brocade, or he may bear upon his shoulders an emblem of the same. If he has a reputation for daring and is well-known for his heroism and has been wounded several times he receives two badges on his shoulder. They follow this rule: great and small, high and low, male and female are all equal. Sometimes they break this rule according to their whims and inclinations or reasoning. Their women do not veil themselves and have no modesty; they do not care whether they uncover their private parts. Whenever a Frenchman has to perform an act of nature he does so wherever he happens to be, even in full view of people, and he goes away as he is, without washing his private parts after defecation. If he is a man of taste and refinement he wipes himself with whatever he finds, even with a paper with writing on it, otherwise he remains as he is. They have intercourse with any woman who pleases

them and vice versa. Sometimes one of their women goes into a barber's shop, and invites him to shave her pubic hair. If he wishes he can take his fee in kind. It is their custom to shave both their moustaches and beard. Some of them leave the hair of their cheeks only.

They do not shave their heads nor their pubic hair. They mix their foods. Some might even put together in one dish coffee, sugar, arrack, raw eggs, limes, and so on. As for the name "Bonaparté" this is the title of their general, it is not a name. Its meaning is "the pleasant gathering," because *Bona* (*Būnā*) means "pleasant" and *parté* means "gathering." * * *

*   *   *

His saying *fī hādhā 'l-taraf* (hither), means "this part of the earth." His statement *wa-qūlū li 'l-muftariyīn* (but tell the slanderers) is the plural of *muftarī* (slanderer) which means liar, and how worthy of this description they are. The proof of that is his saying "I have not come to you except for the purpose of restoring your rights from the hands of the oppressors," which is the first lie he uttered and a falsehood which he invented. Then he proceeds to something even worse than that, may God cast him into perdition, with his words: "I more than the Mamlūks serve God. . . ." There is no doubt that this is a derangement of his mind, and an excess of foolishness. What a worship he is speaking about, however great its intensity, *kufr* (disbelief) had dulled his heart, and prevented him from reaching the way of his salvation. There is inversion in the words which should read *innanī a'budu Allāh akthar min al-Mamālīk* (I serve God more than the Mamlūks do). However, it is possible that there is no inversion, and that the meaning is "I have more troops or more money than the Mamlūks" and that the accusative of specification has been omitted. So his words "I serve God" are a new sentence and a new lie.

His statement "[I] revere His Prophet" is conjoined to what goes before, as one lie joined to another, because if he respected him he would believe in him, accept his truth, and respect his nation. His statement *al-Qur'ān al-'aẓim* (the glorious Qur'ān) is joined to "His Prophet," that is, "I respect the glorious Qur'ān," and this too is a lie, because to respect the Qur'ān means to glorify it, and one glorifies it by believing / in what it contains. The Qur'ān is one of the miracles of the Prophet which proves his truth, and that he is the Prophet to the end of time, and that his nation is the most noble of all nations. These people deny all that and lie in every thing they enumerate, "And many as are the signs in the Heavens and on the Earth, yet they will pass them by, and turn aside from them."

His saying "[all people] are equal in the eyes of God" the Almighty, this is a lie and stupidity. How can this be when God has made some superior to others as is testified by the dwellers in the Heavens and on the Earth?

*　　*　　*

His statement *al-manāṣib al-sāmiya* (eminent positions), that means *al-murtafi'a* (elevated). This is in order to avert blame from themselves by giving high posts of authority to the low and vulgar people among them, as for example their appointment of Barṭulmān (Barthélemy) the artilleryman to the post of Katkhudā Mustaḥfiẓān. He says "and thus the state of the whole population will be rightly adjusted." Yes, that is to say, under the administration of wise and intelligent men. But they did not appoint them. The word *Muslimīn* should be *Muslimūn* in the nominative. The point of putting the word in the *naṣb* (accusative) has already been mentioned. There is another point namely: that their Islam is *naṣb* (fraud).

As for his statement "and destroyed there the Papal See," by this deed they have gone against the Christians as has already been pointed out. So those people are opposed to both Christians and Muslims, and do not hold fast to any religion. You see that they are materialists, who deny all God's attributes, the Hereafter and Resurrection, and who reject Prophethood and Messengership. They believe that the world was not created, and that the heavenly bodies and the occurrences of the Universe are influenced by the movement of the stars, and that nations appear and states decline, according to the nature of the conjunctions and the aspects of the moon. Some believe in transmigration of souls, or other fantasies. For this reason they do not slaughter ritually any animal they eat / or behead any man, before having killed them, so that the parts of his soul may not be separated and scattered, so as not to be whole in another body, and similar nonsense and erroneous beliefs. * * *

*　　*　　*

REVIEW QUESTIONS

1. In what ways does the French announcement accommodate Islamic culture? Is it successful?
2. What are Al-Jabarti's political, religious, and social views of the French, and how are these views interconnected?
3. What makes the French invasion and colonization of an Islamic culture more difficult than conquests in Europe?
4. What is the manner and method of Al-Jabarti's critique of Napoleon's announcement?

GLOIRE NATIONALE NAPOLEON

Lithographic prints and woodcuts popularized the French Revolution and Napoleon's empire. Inexpensive and easily vended, visual images of the revolution enabled both illiterate and rural social groups to participate in the new political culture of the revolution. What attributes of Napoleon and the French nation did the artist emphasize in this print, and what does it suggest about early-nineteenth-century popular nationalism?

The *Code Napoleon*

The Civil Code, promulgated in 1804 and renamed the Code Napoleon *in 1807, marked a domestic triumph of the French Revolution, uniting France with one code of law that above all guaranteed civic equality and property rights. In doing so, it swept away centuries of legal privileges for the aristocracy, clergy, and government. Accompanied by commercial, criminal, penal, and civil procedure codes (1806–1810), the Civil Code quickly became a legal model for modern civil society, which was widely borrowed and adapted throughout continental Europe and other regions of the world. Dubbed the "bourgeois bible," the code embodied the beliefs and values of the nineteenth-century middle classes, including their biases toward women, children, and the unpropertied. The following section centers on the code's definition of women's legal status.*

From *The Code Napoleon,* translated by Bryant Barrett (London: Reed, 1811), pp. 47–50, 57–58.

Title V
Of Marriage

Chapter VI
Of the Rights and Respective Duties of Husband and Wife

212. Husband and wife mutually owe to each other fidelity, succour, and assistance.

213. The husband owes protection to his wife, the wife obedience to her husband.

214. The wife is obliged to live with her husband, and to follow him wherever he may think proper to dwell: the husband is bound to receive her, and to furnish her with every thing necessary for the purposes of life, according to his means and condition.

215. The wife can do no act in law without the authority of her husband, even where she shall be a public trader, or not in community, or separate in property.

216. The authority of the husband is not necessary where a woman is prosecuted for criminal matters, or matters of police.

217. The wife, even not in community or separate in property, cannot give, alien, mortgage, or acquire, either gratuitously or subject to condition, without the concurrence of her husband in the acts, or his consent in writing.

218. If the husband refuses to authorize his wife to proceed at law, a judge may give authority.

219. If the husband refuse to authorize his wife to pass an act, the wife may cause her husband to be cited directly before the tribunal of first instance of the district of their common domicile, which may give or refuse the authority, after the husband shall have been heard or duly summoned to the council chamber.

220. The wife, if she is a public trader, may without the authority of her husband, bind herself in what concerns her business; and, in such case, she also binds her husband, if there is community between them. She is not reputed a public trader, if she merely retails the merchandize of her husband in his business, but only where she carries on a separate trade.

221. Where the husband has incurred a condemnation carrying afflictive or infamous punishment, although it shall only have been pronounced for

contempt, the wife, even of full age, cannot, during the continuance of the punishment, do any act in law, nor contract, until after being authorized by the judge, who may, in such case, give authority, without the husband being heard or summoned.

222. If the husband is interdicted or absent, the judge may, on cognizance of the matter, authorize the wife, either to do acts in law, or to contract.

223. No general authority, even though stipulated by a marriage contract, is valid but as to administration of the property of the wife.

224. If the husband is a minor, the authority of a judge is necessary to the wife, either to do acts in law, or to contract.

225. Nullity founded on want of authority can only be set up by the wife, by the husband, or by their heirs.

226. The wife may make a will without the authority of her husband.

Chapter VII
Of Dissolution of Marriage

227. Marriage is dissolved,

> By the death of one of the parties;
> By divorce legally pronounced;
> By the condemnation, become definitive, of one of the parties, to a punishment carrying civil death.

Chapter VIII
Of Second Marriages

228. The wife cannot contract a new marriage until ten months have elapsed since the dissolution of the preceding marriage.

Title VI
Of Divorce

Chapter the First
Of Causes of Divorce

229. The husband may demand divorce for cause of adultery on the part of his wife.

230. The wife may demand divorce for cause of adultery on the part of her husband, where he shall have kept his concubine in their common house.

231. The married parties may reciprocally demand divorce for cause of excess, cruelty, or grievous injuries, by the one of them towards the other.

232. Condemnation of one of the married parties to an infamous punishment, shall be to the other party a cause of divorce.

233. The mutual and persevering consent of the parties, expressed in the manner prescribed by the law, under the conditions and after the trials the law prescribes, shall sufficiently prove that living in common is insupportable to them, and that there exists, in respect to them, a peremptory cause of divorce.

Chapter II
Of Divorce for Cause Defined

*   *   *

SECTION II

OF THE PROVISIONAL MEASURES TO WHICH THE DEMAND OF DIVORCE FOR CAUSE DEFINED MAY GIVE RISE

267. The provisional administration of the children shall remain with the husband plaintiff or defendant in divorce, unless it shall be otherwise ordered by the tribunal, at the request either of the mother, or of the family, or of the imperial proctor, for the greater benefit of the children.

268. The wife plaintiff or defendant in divorce, may quit the domicile of her husband during the suit, and demand as alimentary pension propor-

tioned to the means of the husband. The tribunal shall point out the house in which the wife shall be obliged to reside, and shall fix, if that is ground for it, the alimentary pension which the husband shall be obliged to pay her.

269. The wife shall be bound to prove her residence in the house pointed out for her, as often as she shall be required so to do: in default of such proof, the husband may refuse the alimentary provision, and, if the wife is demandant in divorce, may cause her to be declared incapable to continue her suit.

270. The wife, plaintiff or defendant in divorce, being in community of property, may, in every state of the cause, commencing from the date of the order of which mention is made in article 238, require, for the preservation of her rights, the affixing of seals upon the moveable effects in community. These seals shall not be taken of without an inventory being made with a valuation, and at the charge on the part of the husband of produc-ing the things inventoried, or making good their value as judiciary guardian.

271. Every obligation upon the community contracted by the husband, and every alienation made by him of the immoveables belonging to the community subsequently to the date of the order of which mention is made in article 238, shall be declared null, if proved to have been made or contracted in fraud of the rights of the wife.

*   *   *

Review Questions

1. What civic rights did the code accord women?
2. How did the code fix the relationship of married women to property?
3. What were the distinctions between the rights of men and women in divorce proceedings?
4. What does this law code tell us about nineteenth-century social relations between men and women?

21 ⅋ THE INDUSTRIAL REVOLUTION

The economic transition from mercantile to industrial capitalism in Britain and Europe constitutes one of the momentous structural revolutions in modern civilization. Industrialization not only expanded the material culture of the West but also penetrated and transformed most spheres of economic activity. The industrial revolution unleashed an unprecedented dynamism of sustained economic growth. It introduced a new scale and scope of economic activity, and the resulting need for new markets, better infrastructure, greater capitalization, and technological innovation came to characterize the modern world.

Early industrialization is largely associated with laissez faire political economy, a doctrine of economic liberalism that championed free trade, private enterprise, meritocratic individualism, and the sanctity of private property. Grounded in the writings of the political economist Adam Smith, this doctrine roundly attacked any interference with the "natural laws" of the marketplace and advocated separation of government and economy. Although Adam Smith was not the first to criticize mercantilism and advocate unrestricted trade, his treatise, by associating free trade with the "natural rights" of other individual liberties, provided the philosophical underpinnings for the political demands of Great Britain's capitalist classes, whose enfranchisement after 1832 exerted influence on state policy. By dint of the vast wealth accumulated through private enterprise, the middle classes espoused the notion that commerce and industry were the twin pillars of civil society. Liberals confidently embraced the belief that these two spheres of public life provided the material basis for progress and prosperity. Yet the new industrial economy benefited from Britain's empire, whose institution of slavery did not conform to the progressive ideals of economic liberalism.

In spite of England's self-proclaimed status as the "workshop of the world," industrialism clearly moved in both positive and negative directions. Contemporaries dubbed the new discipline of political economy the "dismal science," for its studies on population growth and wage levels suggested the impossibility of general happiness and welfare. Little consensus existed on the extent to which laissez faire principles should be applied and how industrial society should be organized. Consequently, the industrialization of Europe did not follow any single model. European governments, accustomed to directing economic activity, proved reluctant to surrender to the "invisible hand," Smith's tenet that individual self-interest promoted general welfare. In contrast to England, these European governments nurtured domestic industry with subventions and protective tariffs, mobilized state capital to assist in railroad construction, promoted economic development through technical education, and oversaw the management of large-scale industrial enterprises. Moreover, the majority of European society remained predominantly rural throughout most of the nineteenth century. Hence, while one speaks of an industrial revolution, one must envision small handicraft workshops alongside mechanized factories and vital rural economies serving dynamic urban centers.

The onset of early industrialization also generated an extraordinary range of criticism against the premise that captitalism would benefit the majority of society. Saint-Simon, Robert Owen, and Karl Marx are but three observers who acknowledged capitalism's material benefits but nonetheless emphasized its elemental flaws in its treatment of wage workers. Their concerns for the material, moral, and creative dimensions of workers' lives compelled them to offer alternative visions to the dominant principles of competition and individual self-interest. Such critical voices sharpened the debate on ethics and social justice, thus exerting force over the next century—through rational argument and political struggle—on Europe's elite to incorporate the interests of unpropertied workers into their statecraft.

ADAM SMITH

FROM *The Wealth of Nations*

Adam Smith (1723–1790), a professor of logic and moral philosophy as well as rector of Glasgow University, wrote on moral philosophy, rhetoric, astronomy, and the formation of languages, but his reputation rests on his work of political economy, An Inquiry into the Nature and Causes of the Wealth of Nations (1776). The treatise's wide-ranging discussions on wages, profit, capital, and industry influenced political economists for the next century, but the book's attack on mercantilism and its corresponding advocacy of free trade heralded a new economic age. The following selections center on the division of labor, the productive "orders" of society, the "invisible hand" of individual interest, and the role of the state in political economy.

From *An Inquiry into the Nature and Causes of the Wealth of Nations,* by Adam Smith (Oxford, Eng.: Oxford University Press, 1993).

Book I
Of the Causes of Improvement in the Productive Powers of Labour, and of the Order According to Which Its Produce Is Naturally Distributed among the Different Ranks of the People

CHAPTER I
OF THE DIVISION OF LABOUR

The greatest improvement in the productive powers of labour, and the greater part of the skill, dexterity, and judgment with which it is any where directed, or applied, seem to have been the effects of the division of labour.

*   *   *

To take an example, therefore, from a very trifling manufacture; but one in which the division of labour has been very often taken notice of, the trade of the pin-maker; a workman not educated to this business (which the division of labour has rendered a distinct trade), nor acquainted with the use of the machinery employed in it (to the invention of which the same division of labour has probably given occasion), could scarce, perhaps, with his utmost industry, make one pin in a day, and certainly could not make twenty. But in the way in which this business is now carried on, not only the whole work is a peculiar trade, but it is divided into a number of branches, of which the greater part are likewise peculiar trades. One man draws out the wire, another straights it, a third cuts it, a fourth points it, a fifth grinds it at the top for receiving the head; to make the head requires two or three distinct operations; to put it on, is a peculiar business, to whiten the pins is another; it is even a trade by itself to put them into the paper; and the important business of making a pin is, in this manner, divided into about eighteen distinct operations, which, in some manufactories, are all performed by distinct hands, though in others the same man will sometimes perform two or three of them. I have seen a small manufactory of this kind where ten men only were employed, and where some of them consequently performed two or three distinct operations. But though they were very poor, and therefore but indifferently accommodated with the necessary machinery, they could, when they exerted themselves, make among them about twelve pounds of pins in a day. There are in a pound upwards of four thousand pins of a middling size. Those ten persons, therefore, could make among them upwards of forty-eight thousand pins in a day. Each person, therefore, making a tenth part of forty-eight thousand pins, might be considered as making four thousand eight hundred pins in a day. But if they had all wrought separately and independently, and without any of them having been educated to this peculiar business, they certainly could not each of them have made twenty, perhaps not one pin in a day; that is, certainly, not the two hundred and fortieth, perhaps not the four thousand eight hundredth part of what they are at present capable of performing, in consequence of a proper division and combination of their different operations.

*   *   *

It is the great multiplication of the productions of all the different arts, in consequence of the division of labour, which occasions, in a well-governed society, that universal opulence which extends itself to the lowest ranks of the people.

Every workman has a great quantity of his own work to dispose of beyond what he himself has occasion for; and every other workman being exactly in the same situation, he is enabled to exchange a great quantity of his own goods for a great quantity, or, what comes to the same thing, for the price of a great quantity of theirs. He supplies them abundantly with what they have occasion for, and they accommodate him as amply with what he has occasion for, and a general plenty diffuses itself through all the different ranks of the society.

*   *   *

* * * The whole annual produce of the land and labour of every country, or what comes to the same thing, the whole price of that annual produce, naturally divides itself, it has already been observed, into three parts; the rent of land, the wages of labour, and the profits of stock; and constitutes a revenue to three different orders of people; to those who live by rent, to those who live by wages, and to those who live by profit. These are the three great, original and constituent orders of every civilized society, from whose revenue that of every other order is ultimately derived.

The interest of the first of those three great orders, it appears from what has been just now said, is strictly and inseparably connected with the general interest of the society. Whatever either promotes or obstructs the one, necessarily promotes or obstructs the other. When the publick deliberates concerning any regulation of commerce or police, the proprietors of land never can mislead it, with a view to promote the interest of their own particular order; at least, if they have any tolerable knowledge of that interest. They are, indeed, too often defective in this tolerable knowledge. They are the only one of the three orders whose revenue costs them neither labour nor care, but comes to them, as it were, of its own accord, and independent of any plan or project of their own. That indolence, which is the natural effect of the ease and security of their situation, renders them too often, not only ignorant, but incapable of that application of mind which is necessary in order to foresee and understand the consequences of any publick regulation.

The interest of the second order, that of those who live by wages, is as strictly connected with the interest of the society as that of the first. The wages of the labourer, it has already been shewn, are never so high as when the demand for labour is continually rising, or when the quantity employed is every year increasing considerably. When this real wealth of the society becomes stationary, his wages are soon reduced to what is barely enough to enable him to bring up a family, or to continue the race of labourers. When the society declines, they fall even below this. The order of proprietors may, perhaps, gain more by the prosperity of the society, than that of labourers: but there is no order that suffers so cruelly from its decline. But though the interest of the labourer is strictly connected with that of the society, he is incapable either of comprehending that interest, or of understanding its connection with his own. His condition leaves him no time to receive the necessary information, and his education and habits are commonly such as to render him unfit to judge even though he was fully informed. In the publick deliberations, therefore, his voice is little heard and less regarded, except upon some particular occasions, when his clamour is animated, set on, and supported by his employers, not for his, but their own particular purposes.

His employers constitute the third order, that of those who live by profit. It is the stock that is employed for the sake of profit, which puts into motion the greater part of the useful labour of every society. The plans and projects of the employers of stock regulate and direct all the most important operations of labour, and profit is the end proposed by all those plans and projects. But the rate of profit does not, like rent and wages, rise with the prosperity, and fall with the declension of the society. On the contrary, it is naturally low in rich, and high in poor countries, and it is always highest in the countries which are going fastest to ruin. The interest of this third order therefore, has not the same connection with the general interest of the society as that of the other two. Merchants and master manufacturers are, in this order, the two classes of people who commonly employ the largest capitals, and who by their weakness draw to themselves the greatest share of the publick consideration. As during their whole lives they are engaged in plans and projects, they have frequently more acuteness of understanding than the greater part of country gentlemen. As their thoughts, however, are commonly exercised rather about the interest of their own particular branch of business, than about that of the society, their judgment, even when given with the greatest candour (which it has not been upon every occasion) is much more to be depended upon with regard to the former of those two objects, than with regard to the latter. Their superiority over the country gentleman is, not so much in their knowledge of the publick interest, as in their having a better knowledge of their own interest than he has of his. It is by this superior knowledge of their own interest that they have frequently imposed upon his generosity, and persuaded him to give up both his own interest and that of the publick, from a very simple but honest conviction, that their interest, and not his, was the interest of the publick. The interest of the dealers, however, in any particular branch of trade or manufactures, is always in some respects different from, and even opposite to, that of the publick. To widen the market and to narrow the competition, is always the interest of the dealers. To widen the market may frequently be agreeable enough to the interest of the publick; but to narrow the competition must always be against it, and can serve only to enable the dealers, by raising their profits above what they naturally would be, to levy, for their own benefit, an absurd tax upon the rest of their fellow-citizens. The proposal of any new law or regulation of commerce which comes from this order, ought always to be listened to with great precaution, and ought never to be adopted till after having been long and carefully examined, not only with the most scrupulous, but with the most suspicious attention. It comes from an order of men, whose interest is never exactly the same with that of the publick, who have generally an interest to deceive and even to oppress the publick, and who accordingly have, upon many occasions, both deceived and oppressed it. * * *

*   *   *

But the annual revenue of every society is always precisely equal to the exchangeable value of the whole annual produce of its industry, or rather is precisely the same thing with that exchangeable value. As every individual, therefore, endeavours as much as he can both to employ his capital in the support of domestick industry, and so to direct that industry that its produce may be of the greatest value; every individual necessarily labours to render the annual revenue of the society as great as he can. He generally, indeed, neither intends to promote the publick interest, nor knows how much he is promoting it. By preferring the support of domestick to that of foreign industry, he intends only his own security; and by directing that industry in such a manner as its produce may be of the greatest value, he intends only his own gain, and he is in this, as in many other cases, led by an invisible hand to promote an end which was no part of his intention. Nor is it always the worse for the society that it was no part of it. By pursuing his own interest he frequently promotes that of the society more effectually than when he really intends to promote it. I have never known much good done by those who affected to trade for the publick good. It is an affectation, indeed, not very common among merchants, and very few words need be employed in dissuading them from it.

What is the species of domestick industry which his capital can employ, and of which the produce is likely to be of the greatest value, every individual, it is evident, can, in his local situation, judge much better than any statesman or lawgiver can do for him. The stateman, who should attempt to direct private people in what manner they ought to employ their capitals, would not only load himself with a most unnecessary attention, but assume an authority which could safely be trusted, not only to no single person, but to no council or senate whatever, and which would nowhere be so dangerous as in the hands of a man who had folly and presumption enough to fancy himself fit to exercise it.

To give the monopoly of the home-market to the produce of domestick industry, in any particular art or manufacture, is in some measure to direct private people in what manner they ought to employ their capitals, and must, in almost all cases, be either a useless or a hurtful regulation. If the produce of domestick can be brought there as cheap as that of foreign industry, the regulation is evidently useless. If it cannot, it must generally be hurtful. It is the maxim of every prudent master of a family, never to attempt to make at home what it will cost him more to make than to buy. The taylor does not attempt to make his own shoes, but buys them of the shoemaker. The shoemaker does not attempt to make his own cloaths, but employs a taylor. The farmer attempts to make neither the one nor the other, but employs those different artificers. All of them find it for their interest to employ their whole industry in a way in which they have some advantage over their neighbours, and to purchase with a part of its produce, or what is the same thing, with the price of a part of it, whatever else they have occasion for.

What is prudence in the conduct of every private family, can scarce be folly in that of a great kingdom.

*   *   *

The expence of defending the society, and that of supporting the dignity of the chief magistrate, are both laid out for the general benefit of the whole society. It is reasonable, therefore, that they should be defrayed by the general contribution of the whole society, all the different members contributing, as nearly as possible, in proportion to their respective abilities.

The expence of the administration of justice too, may, no doubt, be considered as laid out for the benefit of the whole society. There is no impropriety, therefore, in its being defrayed by the general contribution of the whole society. The persons, however, who give occasion to this expence are those who, by their injustice in one way or another, make it necessary to seek redress or protection from the courts of justice. The persons again most immediately benefited by this expence, are those whom the courts of justice either restore to their rights, or maintain in their rights. The expence of the administration of justice, therefore, may very properly be defrayed by the particular contribution of one or other, or both of those two different sets of persons, according as different occasions may require, that is, by the fees of court. It cannot be necessary to have recourse to the general contribution of the whole society, except for the conviction of those criminals who have not themselves any estate or fund sufficient for paying those fees.

Those local or provincial expences of which the benefit is local or provincial (what is laid out, for example, upon the police of a particular town or district) ought to be defrayed by a local or provincial revenue, and ought to be no burden upon the general revenue of the society. It is unjust that the whole society should contribute towards an expence of which the benefit is confined to a part of the society.

The expence of maintaining good roads and communications is, no doubt, beneficial to the whole society, and may, therefore, without any injustice, be defrayed by the general contribution of the whole society. This expence, however, is most immediately and directly beneficial to those who travel or carry goods from one place to another, and to those who consume such goods. The turnpike tolls in England, and the duties called peages in other countries, lay it altogether upon those two different sets of people, and thereby discharge the general revenue of the society from a very considerable burden.

The expence of the institutions for education and religious instruction, is likewise, no doubt, beneficial to the whole society, and may, therefore, without injustice, be defrayed by the general contribution of the whole society. This expence, however, might perhaps with equal propriety, and even with some advantage, be defrayed altogether by those who receive the immediate benefit of such education and instruction, or by the voluntary contribution of those who think they have occasion for either the one or the other.

When the institutions or publick works which are beneficial to the whole society, either cannot be maintained altogether, or are not maintained altogether by the contribution of such particular members of the society as are most immediately benefited by them, the deficiency must in most cases be made up by the general contribution of the whole society. The general revenue of the society, over and above defraying the expence of defending the society, and of supporting the dignity of the chief magistrate, must make up for the deficiency of many particular branches of revenue. The sources of this general or publick revenue, I shall endeavour to explain in the following chapter.

* * *

REVIEW QUESTIONS

1. What is the organizational innovation of the pin factory and what, according to Smith, is its significance for society?
2. What are Smith's three productive orders and what political roles does he assign these orders?
3. How is Smith both praiseworthy and suspicious of businessmen's ability to serve the public good?
4. Why did Smith's metaphor of the "invisible hand" grip the minds of nineteenth-century capitalists?
5. Why does it continue to exert force today?
6. What is, for Smith, the importance of government in civil society?
7. Who should maintain state costs?

ANDREW URE

FROM *The Philosophy of Manufactures*

A doctor by training, Andrew Ure gained fame by his speeches and writings that advocated the great benefits of industrial capitalism. His Philosophy of Manufactures *(1835) played an important role in molding a positive public opinion on the factory system amid critical debates on factory reform and new poor laws.*

From *The Philosophy of Manufactures*, by Andrew Ure (London: Knight, 1835).

* * *

This island is pre-eminent among civilized nations for the prodigious development of its factory wealth, and has been therefore long viewed with a jealous admiration by foreign powers. This very pre-eminence, however, has been contemplated in a very different light by many influential members of our own community, and has been even denounced by them as the certain origin of innumerable evils to the people, and of revolutionary convulsions to the state. If the affairs of the kingdom be wisely administered, I believe such allegations and fears will prove to be groundless, and to proceed more from the envy of one ancient and powerful order of the commonwealth, towards another suddenly grown into political importance than from the nature of things.

In the recent discussions concerning our factories, no circumstance is so deserving of remark,

POWER LOOMS IN A BRITISH COTTON FACTORY (1830)

The number of power looms in England rose from 2,400 in 1813 to 224,000 in 1850, bringing about the full mechanization of textile production. The work of spinning and weaving was now concentrated in factories, a shift that had profound consequences for urbanization and the future of industrial labor. While Andrew Ure and other publicists praised the new system with words, artists illustrated the new manufacturing processes. This drawing of a cotton mill, for example, underscores the prominence of women workers, denoting a signal change in the weaving industry that excluded skilled male weavers. Yet the illustration also conveys work conditions that the viewer should question. What elements of factory life might the artist have chosen not to represent?

as the gross ignorance evinced by our leading legislators and economists, gentlemen well informed in other respects, relative to the nature of those stupendous manufactures which have so long provided the rulers of the kingdom with the resources of war, and a great body of the people with comfortable subsistence; which have, in fact, made this island the arbiter of many nations, and the benefactor of the globe itself. Till this ignorance be dispelled, no sound legislation need be expected on manufacturing subjects. To effect this purpose is a principal, but not the sole aim of the present volume, for it is intended also to convey specific information to the classes directly concerned in the manufactures, as well as general knowledge to the community at large, and particularly to young persons about to make the choice of a profession.

The blessings which physico-mechanical science has bestowed on society, and the means it has still in store for ameliorating the lot of mankind, have been too little dwelt upon; while, on the other hand, it has been accused of lending itself to the rich capitalists as an instrument for harassing the poor, and of exacting from the operative an accelerated rate of work. It has been said, for example, that the steam-engine now drives the power-looms with such velocity as to urge on their attendant weavers at the same rapid pace; but that the handweaver, not being subjected to this restless agent, can throw his shuttle and move his treddles at his convenience. There is, however, this difference in the two cases, that in the factory, every member of the loom is so adjusted, that the driving force leaves the attendant nearly nothing at all to do, certainly no muscular fatigue to sustain, while it procures for him good, unfailing wages, besides a healthy workshop *gratis:* whereas the nonfactory weaver, having everything to execute by muscular exertion, finds the labour irksome, makes in consequence innumerable short pauses, separately of little account, but great when added together; earns therefore proportionally low wages, while he loses his health by poor diet and the dampness of his hovel.

*   *   *

In its precise acceptation, the Factory system is of recent origin, and may claim England for its birthplace.

*   *   *

When the first water-frames for spinning cotton were erected at Cromford, in the romantic valley of the Derwent, about sixty years ago, mankind were little aware of the mighty revolution which the new system of labour was destined by Providence to achieve, not only in the structure of British society, but in the fortunes of the world at large. Arkwright alone had the sagacity to discern, and the boldness to predict in glowing language, how vastly productive human industry would become, when no longer proportioned in its results to muscular effort, which is by its nature fitful and capricious, but when made to consist in the task of guiding the work of mechanical fingers and arms, regularly impelled with great velocity by some indefatigable physical power. What his judgment so clearly led him to perceive, his energy of will enabled him to realize with such rapidity and success, as would have done honour to the most influential individuals, but were truly wonderful in that obscure and indigent artisan. The main difficulty did not, to my apprehension, lie so much in the invention of a proper self-acting mechanism for drawing out and twisting cotton into a continuous thread, as in the distribution of the different members of the apparatus into one co-operative body, in impelling each organ with its appropriate delicacy and speed, and above all, in training human beings to renounce their desultory habits of work, and to identify themselves with the unvarying regularity of the complex automaton. To devise and administer a successful code of factory discipline, suited to the necessities of factory diligence, was the Herculean enterprise, the noble achievement of Arkwright. Even at the present day, when the system is perfectly organized, and its labour lightened to the utmost, it is found nearly impossible to convert persons past the age of puberty, whether drawn from rural or from handicraft occupations, into useful factory hands.

*　　*　　*

In my recent tour, continued during several months, through the manufacturing districts, I have seen tens of thousands of old, young, and middle-aged of both sexes, many of them too feeble to get their daily bread by any of the former modes of industry, earning abundant food, raiment, and domestic accommodation, without perspiring at a single pore, screened meanwhile from the summer's sun and the winter's frost, in apartments more airy and salubrious than those of the metropolis, in which our legislative and fashionable aristocracies assemble. In those spacious halls the benignant power of steam summons around him his myriads of willing menials, and assigns to each the regulated task, substituting for painful muscular effort on their part, the energies of his own gigantic arm, and demanding in return only attention and dexterity to correct such little aberrations as casually occur in his workmanship. The gentle docility of this moving force qualifies it for impelling the tiny bobbins of the lace-machine with a precision and speed inimitable by the most dexterous hands, directed by the sharpest eyes. Hence, under its auspices, and in obedience to Arkwright's polity, magnificent edifices, surpassing far in number, value, usefulness, and ingenuity of construction, the boasted monuments of Asiatic, Egyptian, and Roman despotism, have, within the short period of fifty years, risen up in this kingdom, to show to what extent, capital, industry, and science may augment the resources of a state, while they meliorate the condition of its citizens. Such is the factory system, replete with prodigies in mechanics and political economy.

*　　*　　*

The principle of the factory system then is, to substitute mechanical science for hand skill, and the partition of a process into its essential constituents, for the division or graduation of labour among artisans. On the handicraft plan, labour more or less skilled, was usually the most expensive element of production—*Materiam superabat opus;* but on the automatic plan, skilled labour gets progressively superseded, and will, eventually, be replaced by mere overlookers of machines.

By the infirmity of human nature it happens, that the more skilful the workman, the more self-willed and intractable he is apt to become, and, of course, the less fit a component of a mechanical system, in which, by occasional irregularities, he may do great damage to the whole. The grand object therefore of the modern manufacturer is, through the union of capital and science, to reduce the task of his work-people to the exercise of vigilance and dexterity—faculties, when concentred to one process, speedily brought to perfection in the young. In the infancy of mechanical engineering, a machine-factory displayed the division of labour in manifold gradations—the file, the drill, the lathe, having each its different workmen in the order of skill: but the dexterous hands of the filer and driller are now superseded by the planing, the key-groove cutting, and the drilling-machines; and those of the iron and brass turners, by the self-acting slide-lathe. Mr. Anthony Strutt, who conducts the mechanical department of the great cotton factories of Belper and Milford, has so thoroughly departed from the old routine of the schools, that he will employ no man who has learned his craft by regular apprenticeship; but in contempt, as it were, of the division of labour principle, he sets a ploughboy to turn a shaft of perhaps several tons weight, and never has reason to repent his preference, because he infuses into the turning apparatus a precision of action, equal, if not superior, to the skill of the most experienced journeyman.

*　　*　　*

REVIEW QUESTIONS

1. How does Ure compare the tempo and rewards of factory work with those of traditional labor?
2. How are factory work conditions characterized and how is factory work different from traditional labor?
3. What kind of persons are better suited for factory discipline?
4. What were the implications of the factory system for English laborers?

THOMAS MALTHUS

FROM *An Essay on the Principle of Population*

In 1798 Thomas Malthus (1766–1834), a minister and an economist, published this essay, which challenged the Enlightenment's indomitable belief in the perfectibility of humankind. The essay raised much controversy in the early nineteenth century. It not only resigned some social groups to the inevitability of poverty but also encouraged them to abandon traditional charity. The custom of indiscriminately aiding all indigent people with satisfactory relief, argued Malthusians, only exacerbated the problem. The following passage on food supply and population increase laid the foundation for his bleak argument.

From *An Essay on the Principle of Population,* by Thomas Malthus (London: Murray, 1826).

In an inquiry concerning the improvement of society, the mode of conducting the subject which naturally presents itself, is,

1. To investigate the causes that have hitherto impeded the progress of mankind towards happiness; and,

2. To examine the probability of the total or partial removal of these causes in future.

To enter fully into this question, and to enumerate all the causes that have hitherto influenced human improvement, would be much beyond the power of an individual. The principal object of the present essay is to examine the effects of one great cause intimately united with the very nature of man; which, though it has been constantly and powerfully operating since the commencement of society, has been little noticed by the writers who have treated this subject. The facts which establish the existence of this cause have, indeed, been repeatedly stated and acknowledged; but its natural and necessary effects have been almost totally overlooked; though probably among these effects may be reckoned a very considerable portion of that vice and misery, and of that unequal distribution of the bounties of nature, which it has been the unceasing object of the enlightened philanthropist in all ages to correct.

The cause to which I allude, is the constant tendency in all animated life to increase beyond the nourishment prepared for it.

It is observed by Dr. Franklin, that there is no bound to the prolific nature of plants or animals, but what is made by their crowding and interfering with each other's means of subsistence. Were the face of the earth, he says, vacant of other plants, it might be gradually sowed and overspread with one kind only, as for instance with fennel: and were it empty of other inhabitants, it might in a few ages be replenished from one nation only, as for instance with Englishmen.

This is incontrovertibly true. Through the animal and vegetable kingdoms Nature has scattered the seeds of life abroad with the most profuse and liberal hand; but has been comparatively sparing in the room and the nourishment necessary to rear them. The germs of existence contained in this earth, if they could freely develop themselves, would fill millions of worlds in the course of a few thousand years. Necessity, that imperious, all-pervading law of nature, restrains them within the prescribed bounds. The race of plants and the race of animals shrink under this great restrictive law; and man cannot by any efforts of reason escape from it.

In plants and irrational animals, the view of the subject is simple. They are all impelled by a powerful instinct to the increase of their species; and this instinct is interrupted by no doubts about providing for their offspring. Wherever therefore there is liberty, the power of increase is exerted; and the superabundant effects are repressed afterwards by want of room and nourishment.

The effects of this check on man are more complicated. Impelled to the increase of his species by an equally powerful instinct, reason interrupts his career, and asks him whether he may not bring beings into the world, for whom he cannot provide the means of support. If he attend to this natural suggestion, the restriction too frequently produces vice. If he hear it not, the human race will be constantly endeavouring to increase beyond the means of subsistence. But as, by that law of our nature which makes food necessary to the life of man, population can never actually increase beyond the lowest nourishment capable of supporting it, a strong check on population, from the difficulty of acquiring food, must be constantly in operation. This difficulty must fall somewhere, and must necessarily be severely felt in some or other of the various forms of misery, or the fear of misery, by a large portion of mankind.

That population has this constant tendency to increase beyond the means of subsistence, and that it is kept to its necessary level by these causes, will sufficiently appear from a review of the different states of society in which man has existed. But, before we proceed to this review, the subject will, perhaps, be seen in a clearer light, if we endeavour to ascertain what would be the natural increase of population, if left to exert itself with perfect freedom; and what might be expected to be the rate of increase in the productions of the earth, under the most favourable circumstances of human industry.

*   *   *

According to a table of Euler, calculated on a mortality of 1 in 36, if the births be to the deaths in the proportion of 3 to 1, the period of doubling will be only 12 years and 4-5ths. And this proportion is not only a possible supposition, but has actually occurred for short periods in more countries than one.

*   *   *

It may safely be pronounced, therefore, that population, when unchecked, goes on doubling itself every twenty-five years, or increases in a geometrical ratio.

The rate according to which the productions of the earth may be supposed to increase, it will not be so easy to determine. Of this, however, we may be perfectly certain, that the ratio of their increase in a limited territory must be of a totally different nature from the ratio of the increase of population. A thousand millions are just as easily doubled every twenty-five years by the power of population as a thousand. But the food to support the increase from the greater number will by no means be obtained with the same facility. Man is necessarily confined in room. When acre has been added to acre till all the fertile land is occupied, the yearly increase of food must depend upon the melioration of the land already in possession. This is a fund, which, from the nature of all soils, instead of increasing, must be gradually diminishing. But population, could it be supplied with food, would go on with unexhausted vigour; and the increase of one period would furnish the power of a greater increase the next, and this without any limit.

*   *   *

It may be fairly pronounced, therefore, that, considering the present average state of the earth, the means of subsistence, under circumstances the most favourable to human industry, could not possibly be made to increase faster than in an arithmetical ratio.

The necessary effects of these two different rates of increase, when brought together, will be very striking. Let us call the population of this island eleven millions; and suppose the present produce equal to the easy support of such a number. In the first twenty-five years the population would be twenty-two millions, and the food being also doubled, the means of subsistence would be equal to this increase. In the next twenty-five years, the population would be forty-four millions, and the means of subsistence only equal to the support of thirty-three millions. In the next period the population would be eighty-eight millions, and the means of subsistence just equal to the support of half that number. And, at the conclusion of the first century, the population would be a hundred and seventy-six millions, and the means of subsistence only equal to the support of fifty-five millions, leaving a population of a hundred and twenty-one millions totally unprovided for.

Taking the whole earth, instead of this island, emigration would of course be excluded; and,

supposing the present population equal to a thousand millions, the human species would increase as the numbers, 1, 2, 4, 8, 16, 32, 64, 128, 256, and subsistence as 1, 2, 3, 4, 5, 6, 7, 8, 9. In two centuries the population would be to the means of subsistence as 256 to 9; in three centuries as 4096 to 13, and in two thousand years the difference would be almost incalculable.

In this supposition no limits whatever are placed to the produce of the earth. It may increase for ever and be greater than any assignable quantity; yet still the power of population being in every period so much superior, the increase of the human species can only be kept down to the level of the means of subsistence by the constant operation of the strong law of necessity, acting as a check upon the greater power.

*   *   *

REVIEW QUESTIONS

1. For Malthus, how does nature check the happiness of human society?
2. What are his assumptions regarding food supply and demography, and are they valid?
3. How might this argument affect discussions on public relief of the poor?
4. How does this essay contribute to the emerging laissez-faire philosophy of the early nineteenth century?

A JAMAICA PROPRIETOR

Letter to the Duke of Wellington on the Subject of West India Slavery

Britain's empire and industrial ascendancy were closely connected. Although indus-trialization is associated with free trade, private property, and the contractual wage system, England also launched its industrial supremacy through the economic ad-vantages of colonies. Such colonial possessions as India and the West Indies supplied the British metropole with raw materials, monopolies of trade, and a general accu-mulation of wealth for industrial investment. Yet Britain's imperial slave economy did not always sit well with the moral claims of a reforming society. Having deliber-ated over the blemish of slavery since 1788, Parliament banned the trade of slaves in 1807 but left intact existing slave labor serving West Indian sugar plantations. In the 1820s, however, abolition became a prominent public issue, leading to the 1833 law that banned slavery with compensation for planters. Written in 1829 as an open letter to the duke of Wellington (the current prime minister), the following excerpt presents the planters' arguments in favor of slavery, pointing out the contra-dictions of aligning civic freedoms with both the hallowed rights of property and the older structures of the Atlantic economy.

From *Letter to the Duke of Wellington on the Subject of West India Slavery,* by a Jamaica Proprietor (London: Ridgway, 1829), pp. 2–10, 12–21.

*   *   *

I cannot hope to add any thing but an echo to the voices of those who have preceded me. But there is a general view of a subject which every man is capable of forming, and of putting, per-haps, in a somewhat different light from his pred-ecessors. Moreover, I may add, it is the duty, not less than the interest of every one who is con-nected with the Colonies, and who is daily de-nounced by a vilifying press, and viler periodical publications, to stand forth fearlessly, and call upon his Brother Colonists, "older and abler," to awaken from their apathy, and to meet their ac-cusers front to front, whether they come forward in the guise of religion, or under the brand of infidelity. My Lord, there is a point beyond which patience is pusillanimity; and we have reached it.

I profess no impartiality on the subject of Negro Emancipation—I own myself the direct unshrink-ing advocate for the present continuance of Slav-ery. I hold that this country has no right to interfere in the question, otherwise than by advice or remonstrance; and I claim your Grace's atten-tion as one of the many who have succeeded to the inheritance of West India property, and of the few who are not ashamed to avow it.

Are we then advocates of Slavery *per se.* I an-swer, No. We are told that we speak of Slavery as Slave Owners, and that if it was otherwise we should hold a different language. I deny it. Do *we* pray for the destruction of the British Empire in India? Do *we* send Missionaries to urge the native Princes to rebel? Do *we* desire that the *rights,* the unquestioned rights of the Nabobs to their own territories, rights just as clear as the rights of the Negro to his freedom, should be restored?

My Lord, we preach no such crusade against common sense—we proclaim no such indiscriminate Emancipation; whether it be of native Princes who are vassals in their own country, or of African Negroes who are slaves in another, All we say is—"There it exists, you encouraged us to plant it there; you have nursed it into existence. Get rid of it if you can, but with justice to the master as well as mercy to the slave; or let it remain, till Time has effected those changes which have heretofore taken place in other countries."

It is not my intention, my Lord Duke, to enter upon an elaborate discussion of the origin of Slavery, or the rights of property, albeit the former is traceable through all antiquity; and the latter have no foundation save in *Law*. It matters not in these times whether Slavery was allowed by Jew or Gentile; whether it was fostered by Radical Sparta and Republican Rome; or whether it is still cherished by Revolutionary America. It is sufficient to know that it exists; a bad practice needs no precedents. That Slavery is an evil, a very great evil, and in the abstract utterly indefensible, no one can gainsay; but what of this! Does it prove, that being an evil, (an evil, be it observed, which we the nation, in the aggregate, have encouraged and benefited by for nearly two centuries), does it show that, being an evil, the nation ought to do another evil; in other words, to ruin a portion of ourselves, of men, women, and children, with whom we are connected by the ties of blood and the bonds of marriage, in order to get rid of the first evil? Does it not rather become any *honest* man, however borne along he may be by the torrent of philanthropy and philosophy, previously to guarantee and ultimately to pay the full price for his experiment; and does it not become any *rational* man, *at least,* to approach the subject with the wisdom of a Statesman, and not with the wildness of an Enthusiast?

My Lord, as to the right of property, whether in men or matter, I shall say little. Paley has given us, long since, the true definition, viz. the *Law of the Land;* and even Mr. Hume (I mean of Aberdeen) has admitted the Slave to be, to all intents and purposes, the property of his master. On Acts of Parliament all title to all property is founded, whether it be derived from the enfeebled fingers of the cotton spinner, or the stronger sinews of the African. If all contracts could be annulled at the caprice or convenience of the country, of what avail is public faith? it is little better than an *ignis fatuus* held up to defrand us or a narcotic drug administered for the purpose of pillaging us. The origin of the right of property is unquestionable; and how far the nation has the right of cancelling its own bonds at pleasure, to the prejudice of a portion of the community, is another question.

* * *

* * * The slaves in the West Indies *were* declared *property* by the nation, and now the nation is urged to declare them not so. The emancipation of the Negro now, or twenty years hence, is the destruction of the property. If the back sinews of my horse are cut, he is rendered useless—if the means of cultivating my land are not given to me, the land itself is taken. "You take my life when you do take the means by which I live." It is little less than folly to say, "We leave you your estate, but you must till it as you can, for you shall have neither horses nor ploughs." It may be said, that I proceed on the hypothesis that free labour is unavailable. I do. It is useless for me to remind your Grace that all persons at all conversant with the subject, even unto the democrat of the United States, maintain, 1st, That Europeans are incapable of manual labour under a tropical sun: 2ndly, That with a free Negro population, and a comparatively uncultivated country, no hope could be entertained of continuing the cultivation of sugar, because the facilities for procuring food, the grand stimulus to labour, are too great: 4thly, That the example of St. Domingo is decisive. The question then is, Are we to keep the West Indian Islands as sugar islands, or abandon the cultivation altogether? If the former, slavery *must* continue; if the latter—if the emancipationists should carry their philanthropic scheme—let the whole Negro population be removed to Sierra Leone; and if we cannot command their labour, let us at least be freed from their presence. Better were it at once, when the "one cheer more" of the philanthropists has been heard, to re-export the Negro to his native shores, to the full enjoyment of the freedom of the Foulahs and the Felatahs, and leave the owners of the soil in our islands to contemplate the desertion of their fields, and the dilapidation of their towns—the sublime consequences of British benevolence! My Lord, we are told that the West India colonies are a burthen to this country, or, to use the words of the wild enthusiast who has dispersed his slanders through the medium of the Westminster Review, "If the West India Islands, with all their abominations, were to sink into the sea to-morrow, the British people, instead of being losers, would be immense gainers."[1] That this is false, your Grace must be perfectly aware. Let any man look at the quantity of shipping employed in the trade, the vast supplies of cotton goods alone annually sent out for the black population; and last, not least, at the seven-and-twenty shillings duty wrung from the scanty profits of the proprietor, and then let him ask himself whether we, the people of England, are losers by the West Indian possessions? But, my Lord, is it only by a miserable calculation of pounds, shillings, and pence, that we are to estimate the value of a colony? Is a country to balance its accounts like a banker? Are there no advantages to be derived from the possession of an island, unless it enables us to put down a *per contra* to our credit? Is Malta a burthen, and is Gibraltar an incubus? "Ships, colonies, and commerce," was the cry of the all-seeing Emperor of France; and shall we degrade his mighty mind, by acknowledging the superior sagacity of a writer in one of the least read of our Quarterly Journals? The feeling on the continent against this country is universal and notorious;

envy, hatred, malice, and all uncharitableness, and why? Solely on account of our commercial greatness and naval superiority. There is not a single nation that would not give "one cheer more," if our foolish philanthropy should induce us to amputate that arm which enables us to hold the other hemisphere in our grasp. * * * My Lord, speaking as a West Indian, I heartily wish we were under the dominion of America. Then, at least, we should be freed from the trans-atlantic labours of the Anti-Slavery Society—the annual *exposé* of Mr. Buxton—and the periodical ravings of a third-rate reviewer. Old women might subscribe their six-pences, and young women might sell their pin-cushions with innocent and even praiseworthy impunity.

*   *   *

* * * Is there any *impartial* man, who *has been* in the West Indies, who will say that the acts of barbarity which the mercenary malice of our enemies imputes to us, are of constant occurrence and notoriety? If there is, let us hear him. I protest, my Lord Duke, against the production of *partial* acts as proofs for *general* accusation. Are we to denounce the whole fraternity of chimney-sweepers because some few are tyrants? Let any man look at the *gangs* of wretched victims who labour in the cotton factories—pallid, consumptive, haggard; in religion, untaught; and, in habits, immoral. Are we to call them the slaves of mercantile rapacity, and to denounce their employers as "the Hibners" of commerce? Let him look at the gangs of Negroes working in a sugar plantation. It is true, that the latter "labour under the lash," if the occasional infliction of punishment on the idle, can be called so. What is the stimulus of the former? Starvation. It is true, they *may* go elsewhere. Yes, my Lord they *may* go elsewhere, certainly. They may labour on the roads, or emigrate to Canada, or bind themselves in bondage at Swan River. The mental throbbings of a starving mechanic *may* be more acute than those of a Negro. Are his bodily privations less so? My Lord, in mere bodily comfort, there is no comparison. All the Englishman's superiority consists in the men-

---

[1] *If* they were to sink, we might not, as a nation, be so materially affected; but, as we cannot calculate upon the contingency of their submersion, we have only to consider what they are *now*, what they *might be* with a free black population; and what they *would be* if they fell into the hands of any other Power.

tal feeling that he *can* go elsewhere, *if* his legs can carry him. Servitude and a full stomach at Swan River, *may* be better than liberty and an empty one at Manchester. My Lord, the punishment of the whip is deemed an outrage on human nature,[2] and the administration of thirty-nine lashes to the shoulders of the black is thought less philanthropic than the infliction of three hundred on the back of the British soldier. The Negro is a slave—the British soldier, who is ordered, at the peril of the cat-o'-nine-tails, or the musket-ball, to execute his orders, right or wrong, is a free agent! The Negro is a slave—The British sailor, who has been dragged from the bosom of his family by a press-gang, and who, after he has been so kidnapped, is doomed to the self-same stimulating process for promoting obedience as the free British soldier, is likewise a free agent! My Lord, they are neither free agents, neither soldier, sailor, nor Negro, and the punishment of the two former is only rather less obnoxious, inasmuch as it proceeds, not indeed from a trial by his peers, but from the loftier judgment of his superiors. I have only, my Lord, to add, on the subject of Negro treatment, that if the country is not satisfied by the representations of the Bishop and Governors, and other persons calculated to give *impartial* information, let a Commission be sent out to make inquiries. In the mean time I could wish your Grace to look over some of the lists of supplies which are annually sent out to the different estates, as evidence, at least, of the *intentions* of the Masters, unless, indeed, and it is not improbable, some ingenious slanderer should insinuate, in any subsequent Review, that we must physic where we wound, and that we waste our resources in alternate exportations of whip-cord and diaculum.

My Lord I claim your attention on the subject of our situation as Proprietors; and let the false and foul-mouthed libeller who asserts that "we," the nation, "pay a tax to enable the Hibners of the West Indies to ride, not in a cart, but in their coaches"; that we pay "one penny in every shilling that Slavery may be carried on"; that "it is a robbery on a great scale"; let him recollect, that we, the West India Proprietors, have paid to the Government of this Country 27s. for every cwt. of sugar for six-and-twenty years; that the duty of 7s. was a war tax; and that for the last eleven years, *we* have been absolutely robbed of that sum per cwt. annually; but, my Lord, this was the plundering of a West India Proprietor, and not the robbery of a Rajah. After the payment of duties, freight, insurance, supplies, &c. even in the highest times, our receipts, as your Grace may easily ascertain, were only one-half of the actual value of the produce. At the present time, we may think ourselves fortunate if we secure a fourth. My Lord, I maintain that we are entitled to some protection—we have been pillaged for some years by high duties, and we have been forced to get all our supplies from this country. Let us have a restoration of our rights, viz. a duty of 20s. instead of 27s.; and if the sugar of "the slaves of the peasants" in the East Indies, as Sir Henry Colebrooke calls them, is to be admitted on an equal duty, extend to us, my Lord, the blessings of free trade for our supplies.

My Lord, in conclusion, all we ask is *Justice* and *Enquiry;* but enquiry, unaccompanied by excitement. We ask it at the hands of the Country, and of the Government, and not at the hands of the Anti-Slavery Society, and the Westminster Review. We ask it of the Minister who acknowledges our rights, and not of the Missionary who denies them. Property in the West Indies is held by the same, and just as sacred a title as the property of any other individual subject in His Majesty's dominions, whether he be the Lord of confiscated monasteries in England, or the owner of forfeited acres in Ireland, whether his wealth is dated from the first efforts of a Factory, or is still engendered by the protecting embraces of a Company. If the country, in the fulness of its philanthropy, is determined on Emancipation, let the slaves be valued according to the price they bore for some years preceding, and let a tax be imposed for the pay-

---

[2]He is a brute who would practise unnecessary cruelty; but it is evident that there *must* be some compulsory mode of exacting obedience: you must either starve, whip, or confine. *Utrum horum mavis.*

ment. The idea of emancipating them after a certain date, or of emancipating all children born after a certain date, is a visionary scheme.[3] "The truth is," says even Paley, "the emancipation of slaves should be gradual, and be carried on by provisions of law, and under the protection of civil government." "In this way, the Greek and Roman slavery, and since then, the feudal tyranny has declined before it." We ask no better termination; let it perish like the feudal system; let it die away gradually; as the Whites, the People of Colour, and the Blacks, progressively intermix; but when we are insultingly told that it is a system "which every one knows it would be an honour and glory to demolish with the bayonet"; that the people of this country consider the rebellious slave "as a soldier fallen in the advance guard of that combat, which is only kept from themselves because somebody else is exposed to it further off." There is something so flagitiously sanguinary in the first passage, and something so exquisitely ludicrous in the second, that Hogarth's Portrait of Garrick is the only thing emblematical of the reader's situation; and while I am upon the subject of the ludicrous, it would be unfair towards the writer to rob him of his *few* pleasing features; and equally unfair towards your Grace, not to put you on your guard against the consequences of not following that writer's advice. "It may be *necessary*," he says, "to obey a Government that supports slaves by law; but it can never be *desirable* longer than it is *necessary*." "Resistance becomes a question of discretion," as Mr. Fox said. This highly constitutional alarmist then goes on to observe, that nothing but our "physical force" stands between us "and the infliction." Moreover, that the "hired press"

would write in favour "of reducing the working classes to the same slavery, if any body saw chance enough of effecting the object to make it worth while to pay." This is all infinitely amusing, and would savour of having been concocted at Saint Luke's, if the general phraseology of the essay did not bear such strong testimony to the vocabulary of Billingsgate. Every vilifying epithet has been exhausted. "All creatures of ill omen, every odious and foul bird," he says "nestles and roosts in the question of West Indian Slavery." He then goes on, in a strain of frantic fanaticism, blasphemously proclaiming "The Truce of God!!! Cry havoc, and let slip the dogs of war;" and ends with the utmost tranquillity in proposing to pull us down "by old women's six-pences!" And is it by such as these that we are to be calumniated?—"There is no terror, Cassius in your threats."—The undisguised humbug (I can use no more appropriate expression) of the petitioning practice is notorious. Every little village now has its petition; and good honest creatures, who know as much of the West Indies as they do of the Satellites of Jupiter, are told, after the assiduous attentions of the emissary have been duly administered, that their names are enrolled as part and parcel of those who are capable of admonishing the British Parliament as to the course of its colonial policy; and then, good easy souls, having signed their petition in the morning, they stir up their sugar in the evening, hardly knowing for what place the former is destined, and little caring from which hemisphere the latter is derived.

My Lord, but a few words more, and I have done. I have no wish to shrink from the question, whether it be the rights of ownership, or the evils of servitude. The national faith is pledged for the payment of the National Debt. The national faith is pledged for the continuance of Slavery. The nation may compromise with its creditors in either case, if the creditor chuses to consent to an equitable adjustment; but, until that adjustment is recognized, I deny that the country has the right of interference. The very voices that were the loudest *against* the invasion of the rights of America, are now the loudest in *favour* of the invasion

---

[3]The objection to the first proposition, (putting rights out of the question,) is, that you do that by one blow, which ought to proceed by an imperceptible process; you give the owner *a term of years* in his property, and induce him, viewing it in that light, to work it to its utmost. The objection to the second is, that you condemn a Negro to Slavery who is born on the 30th of December, and proclaim him free who is born on the 1st of January; thus producing division in families, and every sort of confusion.

of the rights of her neighbours. The West Indians are oppressed and insulted; but, my Lord, a second American war may show that they are not helpless; and it may then be seen, too late, that the opinion of Nelson is entitled to as much respect as that of an East Indian Essay writer, a writer who is infamous enough to think, and insolent enough to declare, that our "claim for compensation is a fraud."

"Malignity is the mint of slander"; and I must be excused for resorting to the vocabulary of that writer for words to express my indignant contempt for his opinions. When we see ourselves maligned; trampled upon, spurned at, pointed at as the refuse of society—"The Hibners of the West Indies!!"—Are we, for ever and a day, to practise the same miserable mediocrity of conduct, and, in all "modest stillness and humility," to smile and not strike at the insolent calumniators who assail us? Are they to go unscathed in the undisturbed presumption that *their* scorpion lash is a monopoly?

If the scrapings of a Monthly Reporter—if the wild effusions of an itinerant orator—if the periodical outpourings of a rancorous and malignant partisan—if the frantic and friendlike propositions of a Quarterly Journalist, are circulated against us; are we to sit in more than Turkish apathy to await our destiny? If we are pelted with ordure, are we to return it with ottar of roses? "Good Sirs, kind Sirs, you spat upon us yesterday." No, my Lord, we have shewn too much of the "milk of human kindness." If we *are* the blood-thirsty monsters they speak of, let them prove it. If we *are* the Hibners of another hemisphere, let it be shewn. We stand at the bar of public opinion. In many of our accusers we blame, not the intention, but the ignorance. We call upon the country to do us simple *justice.* The evil of Slavery is one of its *own creation;* and we call upon it not to sacrifice its honour and our fortunes on speculative projects, founded on insulated cases of oppression, which may and must exist under any system, and in any country; and we conjure it, lastly, not to

heal the canker of one angry wound
By making many and worse.

With the highest sense of your Grace's services, the greatest respect for your judgment, and in the fullest confidence of your justice, I have the honour to subscribe myself,

&c. &c.

REVIEW QUESTIONS

1. How does this planter justify the continued practice of slavery? Why does he see the defense of slavery as rational?
2. What argument does he make about political rights in colonies? Why does he refer to India and what point does it serve?
3. What role does the issue of property rights play in the planter's argument?
4. Are the tensions between modern economic and political rights of the West and the colonial economies of sugar, cotton, and coffee still existent? If so, how have they changed since the early nineteenth century?

FRIEDRICH LIST

FROM *National System of Political Economy*

Whereas British political economy largely stressed individual enterprise and free trade, Friedrich List (1789–1846), a German political economist, recognized disadvantages for German states in aligning themselves completely with British trade policies. Instead he centered on the nation as an economic unit, emphasizing the need for protectionist measures to create domestic free trade within the German Confederation (a union of thirty-nine political states) before Germany could become a mature, internationally competitive economy. List's National System of Political Economy *(1840) thus manifests the concerns of German politics of the 1840s, linking liberal nationalism with questions of economic unity and power. Friedrich List's liberalism forced him to emigrate to the United States between 1825 and 1832. On returning to Germany, his promotion of railroad and commercial reform was tireless but not always heeded.*

From *Metternich's Europe*, edited by Mack Walker (New York: Harper and Row, 1968).

No BRANCH of political economy presents a greater diversity of views between men of theory and men of practice, than that which treats of international commerce and commercial policy. There is, however, in the domain of this science no topic, which, in regard to the well-being and civilization of nations, as well as to their independence, power and duration, presents the same degree of importance. Poor, weak, and uncivilized countries have not unfrequently attained power and wealth by a judicious commercial system, whilst others have sunk from a high rank for want of such a system; nations have even lost their independence, and their political existence, because their commercial policy had not aided the development and the consolidation of their nationality.

In our day, more than at any former period, among all the questions which belong to political economy, that of international commerce has acquired a preponderant interest; for the more rapidly the genius of discovery and of industrial improvement, as well as that of social and political progress advances, the more rapidly is the distance between stationary nations and those which are progressive increased, and the greater is the peril of remaining behind. If in time past it required centuries to monopolize that important branch of industry, the manufacture of wool, some ten years have sufficed in our time to obtain ascendency in the much more considerable manufacture of cotton; and now the start of a few years may enable England to absorb all the flax industry of the continent of Europe.

At no other epoch has the world seen a manufacturing and commercial power possessing resources so immense as those in the control of the power which now holds sway, pursuing designedly a system so consistently selfish, absorbing with such untiring energy the manufacturing and commercial industry of the world, the important colonies, the domination of the seas, and subjecting so many people, as in the case of the Hindoos, to a manufacturing and commercial yoke.

Alarmed by the consequences of that policy, nay, constrained by the convulsions it has occasioned, we have seen in our century, Prussia, a continental nation, as yet imperfectly prepared for manufacturing industry, seeking her welfare in the prohibitory system so condemned by theorists. And what has been her reward? National prosperity.

On the other hand, encouraged by promises of theory, the United States of America, which had made a rapid growth under the protective system, have been induced to open their ports to the manufacturers of England; and what fruits has this competition borne? A periodical visitation of commercial disaster.

*   *   *

The author will begin, as theory does not begin, by interrogating History, and deducing from it his fundamental principles; this being done, an examination of former systems will follow, and his tendency being especially practical, he will, in conclusion, furnish a sketch of the later phases of commercial policy.

For greater clearness, we give here a cursory view of the principal results of his researches and meditations:

The association of individuals for the prosecution of a common end is the most efficacious mode towards ensuring the happiness of individuals. Alone, and separated from his fellow-creatures, man is feeble and destitute. The greater the number of those who are united, the more perfect is the association, and the greater and the more perfect is the result, which is the moral and material welfare of individuals.

The highest association of individuals now realized, is that of the state, the nation; and the highest imaginable, is that of the whole human race. Just as the individual is happier in the bosom of the state than in solitude, all nations would be more prosperous if they were united together by law, by perpetual peace, and by free interchange.

Nature leads nations gradually to the highest degree of association; inviting them to commerce by variety of climate, soil, and productions; and by overflowing population, by superabundance of capital and talents, it leads them to emigration and the founding of distant colonies. International trade, by rousing activity and energy, by the new wants it creates, by the propagation among nations of new ideas and discoveries, and by the diffusion of power, is one of the mightiest instruments of civilization and one of the most powerful agencies in promoting national prosperity.

The association of nations by means of trade is even yet very imperfect, for it is interrupted, or at least weakened, by war or selfish measures on the part sometimes of one and sometimes of another nation.

*   *   *

The elevation of an agricultural people to the condition of countries at once agricultural, manufacturing, and commercial, can only be accomplished under the law of free trade when the various nations engaged at the time in manufacturing industry shall be in the same degree of progress and civilization; when they shall place no obstacle in the way of the economical development of each other, and not impede their respective progress by war or adverse commercial legislation.

But some of them, favored by circumstances, having distanced others in manufactures, commerce, and navigation, and having early perceived that this advanced state was the surest mode of acquiring and keeping political supremacy, have adopted and still persevere in a policy so well adapted to give them the monopoly of manufactures, of industry and of commerce, and to impede the progress of less advanced nations or those in a lower degree of culture. The measures enforced by such nations, taken as a whole, the prohibitions, the duties on imports, the maritime restrictions, premiums upon exports, &c., are called the protective system.

The anterior progress of certain nations, foreign commercial legislation and war have compelled inferior countries to look for special means of effecting their transition from the agricultural to the manufacturing stage of industry, and as far as practicable, by a system of duties, to restrain their trade with more advanced nations aiming at manufacturing monopoly.

The system of import duties is consequently not, as has been said, an invention of speculative minds; it is a natural consequence of the tendency of nations to seek for guarantees of their existence and prosperity, and to establish and increase their weight in the scale of national influence.

Such a tendency is legitimate and reasonable only so far as it renders easy, instead of retarding, the economical development of a nation; and it is not in opposition to the higher objects of society, the universal confederation of the future.

*　　*　　*

No commercial policy is more dangerous and reprehensible than a sudden resort to absolute prohibition of foreign products. It may, however, be justified when a country, separated from others by a long war, finds itself almost in a compulsory state of prohibitions in regard to foreign products, and under the absolute necessity of offering a high premium to the industry which will enable it to supply its own wants.

The return from such a condition must be by gradual transition from the prohibitive to the protective system, and should be effected by means of duties fixed by anticipation and decreasing gradually. On the other hand, a nation which is to pass from free trade to the protective system should commence with low duties to be afterwards raised by degrees according to a suitable scale.

Duties thus fixed by anticipation must be strictly maintained by the government; it must be careful not to diminish them before the appointed time, and equally careful to raise them if they should prove insufficient.

Duties upon imports so high as absolutely to exclude foreign competition are prejudicial to the country which adopts them; for they suppress all rivalry between domestic and foreign manufactures, and encourage indolence among the former.

When, under the rule of suitable and progressive duties, the manufactures of a country do not thrive, it is an evidence that the country does not yet possess the conditions requisite to a manufacturing people.

Duties designed to favor an industry should never be put so low as to endanger the existence of the latter from foreign competition. It should be a rule to preserve what exists—to protect national industry in its trunk and in its roots.

Foreign competition should not have more than its share in the annual increase of consumption. Duties should be raised when foreign commodities supply the greatest part or the whole of the increased annual consumption.

A country like England, which is far in advance of all its competitors, cannot better maintain and extend its manufacturing and commercial industry than by a trade as free as possible from all restraints. For such a country, the cosmopolitan and the national principle are one and the same thing.

This explains the favor with which the most enlightened economists of England regard free trade, and the reluctance of the wise and prudent of other countries to adopt this principle in the actual state of the world.

A quarter of a century since, the prohibitive and protective system of England operated to her detriment and to the advantage of her rivals.

Nothing could be more prejudicial to England than her restrictions upon the importation of raw material and food.

Union of customs and commercial treaties are the most efficient means of facilitating national exchanges.

But treaties of commerce are legitimate and durable only when the advantages are reciprocal. They are fatal and illegitimate when they sacrifice one country to another. * * *

If protective duties enhance for a time the price of domestic manufactures, they secure afterwards lower prices by means of internal competition; for an industry that has reached its full development can safely reduce its prices far below those which were necessary to ensure its growth, and thus save to its consumers the whole expense of transportation and the whole profits of trade which are consequent upon imports of the same articles from other countries.

The loss occasioned by protective duties consists, after all, only in values; whilst the country thus acquires a power by which it is enabled to produce a great mass of values. This loss in values must be considered as the price of the industrial training of the country.

Protective duties upon manufactured products do not press heavily upon the agriculture of a country. By the development of manufacturing industry the wealth, population, consumption of agricultural products, rent, and exchangeable value of real estate are vastly increased, whilst the manufactured products consumed by farmers gradually fall in price. The gain thus realized exceeds, in the proportion of ten to one, the loss which agriculturalists incur by the transient rise of manufactured products.

Internal and external trade flourish alike under the protective system; these have no importance but among nations supplying their own wants by their own manufacturing industry, consuming their own agricultural products, and purchasing foreign raw materials and commodities with the surplus of their manufactured articles. Home and foreign trade are both insignificant in the merely agricultural countries of temperate climes, and their external commerce is usually in the hands of the manufacturing and trading nations in communication with them.

A good system of protection does not imply any monopoly in the manufacturers of a country; it only furnishes a guarantee against losses to those who devote their capital, their talents, and their exertions to new branches of industry.

There is no monopoly, because internal competition comes in the place of foreign competition, and every individual has the privilege of taking his share in the advantages offered by the country to its citizens; it is only an advantage to citizens as against foreigners, who enjoy in their own country a similar advantage.

But this protection is useful not only because it awakens the sleeping energies of a country and puts in motion its productive power, but because it attracts the productive power of foreign countries, including capital, both material and moral, and skilful masters as well as skilful men.

*   *   *

History is not without examples of entire nations having perished, because they knew not and seized not the critical moment for the solution of the great problem of securing their moral, economical, and political independence by the establishment of manufacturing industry and the formation of a powerful class of manufacturers and tradesmen.

REVIEW QUESTIONS

1. How does List characterize Britain's economic relationship to Europe, and what is his advice to German states?
2. What are the roles of nations in economic life for List?
3. What are List's views of trade barriers and how do they compare with those of Adam Smith?
4. How applicable are List's views to the economic conditions in western society today?

Rules of a Factory in Berlin

The transition for Europeans from agricultural and artisanal labor to factory work was by no means an easy change. The task-oriented world of traditional labor clashed radically with the time-oriented, strictly routinized world of industrial capitalism. The following set of rules from a Berlin foundry and engineering works in the 1840s denotes the new demands of industrial discipline.

From *Documents of Economic European History,* Vol. 1, *The Process of Industrialization, 1750–1870,* edited by Sidney Pollard and C. Holmes (New York: Arnold, 1968), pp. 534–36.

In every large works, and in the co-ordination of any large number of workmen, good order and harmony must be looked upon as the fundamentals of success, and therefore the following rules shall be strictly observed.

Every man employed in the concern named below shall receive a copy of these rules, so that no one can plead ignorance. Its acceptance shall be deemed to mean consent to submit to its regulations.

1. The normal working day begins at all seasons at 6 a.m. precisely and ends, after the usual break of half an hour for breakfast, an hour for dinner and half an hour for tea, at 7 p.m., and it shall be strictly observed.

Five minutes before the beginning of the stated hours of work until their actual commencement, a bell shall ring and indicate that every worker employed in the concern has to proceed to his place of work, in order to start as soon as the bell stops.

The doorkeeper shall lock the door punctually at 6 a.m., 8.30 a.m., 1 p.m. and 4.30 p.m.

Workers arriving 2 minutes late shall lose half an hour's wages; whoever is more than 2 minutes late may not start work until after the next break, or at least shall lose his wages until then. Any disputes about the correct time shall be settled by the clock mounted above the gatekeeper's lodge.

These rules are valid both for time- and for piece-workers, and in cases of breaches of these rules, workmen shall be fined in proportion to their earnings. The deductions from the wage shall be entered in the wage-book of the gatekeeper whose duty they are; they shall be unconditionally accepted as it will not be possible to enter into any discussions about them.

2. When the bell is rung to denote the end of the working day, every workman, both on piece- and on day-wage, shall leave his workshop and the yard, but is not allowed to make preparations for his departure before the bell rings. Every breach of this rule shall lead to a fine of five silver groschen to the sick fund. Only those who have obtained special permission by the overseer may stay on in the workshop in order to work.—If a workman has worked beyond the closing bell, he must give his name to the gatekeeper on leaving, on pain of losing his payment for the overtime.

3. No workman, whether employed by time or piece, may leave before the end of the working day, without having first received permission from the overseer and having given his name to the gatekeeper. Omission of these two actions shall lead to a fine of ten silver groschen payable to the sick fund.

4. Repeated irregular arrival at work shall lead to dismissal. This shall also apply to those who are found idling by an official or overseer, and refuse to obey their order to resume work.

5. Entry to the firm's property by any but the

designated gateway, and exit by any prohibited route, e.g. by climbing fences or walls, or by crossing the Spree, shall be punished by a fine of fifteen silver groschen to the sick fund for the first offences, and dismissal for the second.

6. No worker may leave his place of work otherwise than for reasons connected with his work.

7. All conversation with fellow-workers is prohibited; if any worker requires information about his work, he must turn to the overseer, or to the particular fellow-worker designated for the purpose.

8. Smoking in the workshops or in the yard is prohibited during working hours; anyone caught smoking shall be fined five silver groschen for the sick fund for every such offence.

9. Every worker is responsible for cleaning up his space in the workshop, and if in doubt, he is to turn to his overseer.—All tools must always be kept in good condition, and must be cleaned after use. This applies particularly to the turner, regarding his lathe.

10. Natural functions must be performed at the appropriate places, and whoever is found soiling walls, fences, squares, etc., and similarly, whoever is found washing his face and hands in the workshop and not in the places assigned for the purpose, shall be fined five silver groschen for the sick fund.

11. On completion of his piece of work, every workman must hand it over at once to his foreman or superior, in order to receive a fresh piece of work. Pattern makers must on no account hand over their patterns to the foundry without express order of their supervisors. No workman may take over work from his fellow-workman without instruction to that effect by the foreman.

12. It goes without saying that all overseers and officials of the firm shall be obeyed without question, and shall be treated with due deference. Disobedience will be punished by dismissal.

13. Immediate dismissal shall also be the fate of anyone found drunk in any of the workshops.

14. Untrue allegations against superiors or officials of the concern shall lead to stern reprimand, and may lead to dismissal. The same punishment shall be meted out to those who knowingly allow errors to slip through when supervising or stock-taking.

15. Every workman is obliged to report to his superiors any acts of dishonesty or embezzlement on the part of his fellow workmen. If he omits to do so, and it is shown after subsequent discovery of a misdemeanour that he knew about it at the time, he shall be liable to be taken to court as an accessory after the fact and the wage due to him shall be retained as punishment. Conversely, anyone denouncing a theft in such a way as to allow conviction of the thief shall receive a reward of two Thaler, and, if necessary, his name shall be kept confidential.—Further, the gatekeeper and the watchman, as well as every official, are entitled to search the baskets, parcels, aprons etc. of the women and children who are taking the dinners into the works, on their departure, as well as search any worker suspected of stealing any article whatever. * * *

*   *   *

18. Advances shall be granted only to the older workers, and even to them only in exceptional circumstances. As long as he is working by the piece, the workman is entitled merely to his fixed weekly wage as subsistence pay; the extra earnings shall be paid out only on completion of the whole piece contract. If a workman leaves before his piece contract is completed, either of his own free will, or on being dismissed as punishment, or because of illness, the partly completed work shall be valued by the general manager with the help of two overseers, and he will be paid accordingly. There is no appeal against the decision of these experts.

19. A free copy of these rules is handed to every workman, but whoever loses it and requires a new one, or cannot produce it on leaving, shall be fined 2½ silver groschen, payable to the sick fund.

Moabit, August, 1844.

REVIEW QUESTIONS

1. What does the specificity of these regulations suggest about the social realities of early factory work?

2. Judging from the rules' injunctions and monetary fines, what areas of factory work are for newcomers the most difficult to learn?

3. What kind of relationship is established between factory hands and their superiors?

4. How do these regulations distinguish the work experience of factories from those of agriculture, domestic service, or the traditional crafts?

5. How does this document compare with Ure's discussion of factory work?

COMTE DE SAINT-SIMON

FROM "The Incoherence and Disorder of Industry"

European observers of early industrialization were not always enamored with the spirit of rugged individualism and minimalist governmental control. Claude Henri de Rouvroy (1760–1825), comte de Saint-Simon, roundly criticized laissez-faire political economy, advocating instead an industrialized state directed by science, and an enlightened class of industrialists to address the needs of the poor. Saint-Simon, who fought in the American Revolution, used a self-made fortune to promote numerous large-scale industrial enterprises which left him an impoverished man. His writings, especially The New Christianity, *had little impact during his lifetime but influenced subsequent generations of French social theorists. His most enduring legacy was perhaps his influence on Auguste Comte, who founded the doctrine of Positivism.*

From *Documents of Economic European History*, Vol. 1, *The Process of Industrialization, 1750–1870*, edited by Sidney Pollard and C. Holmes (New York: Arnold, 1968), pp. 545–46.

In industry, as in science, emphasis is centred entirely on individualism; the sole sentiment which dominates all thinking is egotism. The industrialist is very little concerned about society's interests. His family, his capital and the personal fortune he strives to attain, constitute his humanity, his universe, his god. All those pursuing the same career are inevitably enemies . . . and it is by ruining them that he attains personal happiness and glory.

Problems which are no less serious exist regarding the organisation of work. Industry possesses a theory, which it might be believed holds the key to the harmonisation of production and consumption. Now this theory itself is the principal cause of disorder; the economists seem to pose the following problem:

"If it is accepted that leaders of society are more ignorant than those they govern; if it is supposed, moreover, that far from favouring the development of industry, these leaders wished to hinder its development, and their representatives

THE CRYSTAL PALACE (1851)

England's Great Exhibition of 1851, the first world fair, displayed over 100,000 objects from all over the world. For Prince Albert, the royal sponsor, the fair stood for the hope and welfare that industrial power would bring to the world. The prominent display of British locomotives, steam engines, luxury manufactures, and imperial splendor further called attention to England's preeminence as the "workshop of the world" and its arrival as an urbanized, industrial power. Joseph Paxton's vast exhibition hall of steel and glass, which occupied a total floor area of 990,000 square feet, was hailed as a symbol of the new era. Dubbed the Crystal Palace, the building became a prototype for industrial design in the second half of the nineteenth century. What kind of economic and political ideals might Paxton have hoped to endorse with his Crystal Palace?

were the born enemies of the producers, what kind of industrial organisation is suited to society?"

Laissez-faire, laissez-passer! Such has been the inevitable solution; such has been the single, general principle which they have proclaimed. The economists have thought by this to resolve with a stroke of the pen all questions relating to the production and distribution of wealth; they have entrusted the realisation of their schemes to *personal interest,* without realising that the individual, irrespective of his insight, is incapable of assessing total situations. . . . Well then! what is the picture we see before us? Each industry, deprived of direction, without any guidance other than personal observation, which is always imperfect . . . strives to become informed about consumer needs. Rumour has it that a branch of production offers wonderful prospects; all endeavour and capital are directed towards it, everyone dashes blindly into it. . . . The economists immediately applaud the stampede because in it they recognise the principle of competition. . . . Alas! What results from this struggle to the death? Several fortunate individuals triumph . . . the price is the complete ruin of innumerable victims. A necessary consequence of this over-production in certain sectors, this uncoordinated activity, is that the equilibrium between production and consumption is always affected. Innumerable crises result, those commercial crises which terrify speculators and frustrate worthwhile projects. Honest and hard-working men are ruined and morale is injured by such events; such people come to believe that to succeed something

more than honesty and hard work are needed. They become cunning, shrewd and sly; they even boast about these characteristics; once they have assumed this position, they are lost to humanity.

Let us add now that the fundamental principle, *laissez-faire, laissez-passer,* assumes that personal and social interests always coincide, a supposition which is disproved by innumerable facts. To select only one example, is it not clear that if society sees its interest in the establishment of a steam engine, the worker who lives by his hands cannot share this sentiment? The reply to the workers' objection is well-known; for example, printing is cited, and it is true that today it occupies more men than there were transcribers before its invention, therefore it is concluded and stated that in the long run a new equilibrium is obtained. An admirable conclusion! And until then what will happen to the thousands of hungry men? Will our reasoning console them? Will they bear their misery patiently because statistical calculations prove that in future years they will have food to appease their hunger?

REVIEW QUESTIONS

1. How does Saint-Simon's view of individual interest differ from Adam Smith's notion of the "invisible hand"?
2. Why does Saint-Simon reject competitive capitalism?
3. What social interests should capitalists aspire to embrace?

ROBERT OWEN

FROM *A New View of Society*

Robert Owen (1771–1858), a highly successful manager and partner of a cotton mill in Manchester, grew disenchanted early in his life with the deplorable material and moral standards of factory workers. Resolved to direct a capitalist enterprise that could ameliorate the lives of factory workers, Owen convinced his partners to buy cotton mills in New Lanaark and set up a model community. Workers received salubrious housing, quality goods from low-cost cooperative stores, and education for their children; in turn, Owen inculcated the moral virtues of cleanliness, order, thrift, and sobriety. Because New Lanaark combined moral improvement with commercial success, Owen's communitarian project achieved international fame, and it still ranks among the most important examples of utopian socialism. In 1813, Owen delineated his views on the importance of human capital in his A New View of Society. *The following speech is included in this work.*

From *A New View of Society*, by Robert Owen (Friends of the New System, 1826).

An Address
To the Superintendants of Manufactories, and to Those Individuals Generally, Who, by Giving Employment to an Aggregated Population, May Easily Adopt the Means to Form the Sentiments and Manners of Such a Population

Like you, I am a manufacturer for pecuniary profit. But having for many years acted on principles the reverse in many respects of those in which you have been instructed, and having found my procedure beneficial to others and to myself, even in a pecuniary point of view, I am anxious to explain such valuable principles, that you and those under your influence may equally partake of their advantages.

In two Essays, already published, I have developed some of these principles, and in the following pages you will find still more of them explained, with some detail of their application to practice, under the particular local circumstances in which I undertook the direction of the New Lanark Mills and Establishment.

By those details you will find that from the commencement of my management I viewed the population, with the mechanism and every other part of the establishment, as a system composed of many parts, and which it was my duty and interest so to combine, as that every hand, as well as every spring, lever, and wheel, should effectually co-operate to produce the greatest pecuniary gain to the proprietors.

Many of you have long experienced in your manufacturing operations the advantages of substantial, well-contrived, and well-executed machinery.

Experience has also shewn you the difference of the results between mechanism which is neat, clean, well arranged, and always in a high state of repair; and that which is allowed to be dirty, in disorder, without the means of preventing unnecessary friction, and which therefore becomes, and works, much out of repair.

In the first case, the whole economy and management are good; every operation proceeds with ease, order, and success. In the last, the reverse must follow, and a scene be presented of counteraction, confusion, and dissatisfaction among all the agents and instruments interested or occupied in the general process, which cannot fail to create great loss.

If then due care as to the state of your inanimate machines can produce such beneficial results, what may not be expected if you devote equal attention to your vital machines, which are far more wonderfully constructed?

When you shall acquire a right knowledge of these, of their curious mechanism, of their self-adjusting powers; when the proper main spring shall be applied to their varied movements, you will become conscious of their real value, and you will be readily induced to turn your thoughts more frequently from your inanimate to your living machines; you will discover that the latter may be easily trained and directed to procure a large increase of pecuniary gain, while you may also derive from them high and substantial gratification.

Will you then continue to expend large sums of money to procure the best devised mechanism of wood, brass, or iron; to retain it in perfect repair; to provide the best substance for the prevention of unnecessary friction, and to save it from falling into premature decay? Will you also devote years of intense application to understand the connection of the various parts of these lifeless machines, to improve their effective powers, and to calculate with mathematical precision all their minute and combined movements? And when in these transactions you estimate time by minutes, and the money expended for the chance of increased gain by fractions, will you not afford some of your attention to consider whether a portion of your time and capital would not be more advantageously applied to improve your living machines?

From experience which cannot deceive me, I venture to assure you that your time and money,

so applied, if directed by a true knowledge of the subject, would return you, not five, ten, or fifteen per cent. for your capital so expended, but often fifty, and in many cases a hundred per cent.

I have expended much time and capital upon improvements of the living machinery; and it will soon appear that the time and money so expended in the manufactory at New Lanark, even while such improvements are in progress only, and but half their beneficial effects attained, are now producing a return exceeding fifty per cent., and will shortly create profits equal to cent. per cent. on the original capital expended in them.

Indeed, after experience of the beneficial effects, from due care and attention to the mechanical implements, it became easy to a reflecting mind to conclude at once, that at least equal advantages would arise from the application of similar care and attention to the living instruments. And when it was perceived that inanimate mechanism was greatly improved by being made firm and substantial; that it was the essence of economy to keep it neat, clean, regularly supplied with the best substance to prevent unnecessary friction, and, by proper provision for the purpose, to preserve it in good repair; it was natural to conclude that the more delicate, complex, living mechanism, would be equally improved by being trained to strength and activity; and that it would also prove true economy to keep it neat and clean; to treat it with kindness, that its mental movements might not experience too much irritating friction; to endeavour by every means to make it more perfect; to supply it regularly with a sufficient quantity of wholesome food and other necessaries of life, that the body might be preserved in good working condition, and prevented from being out of repair, or falling prematurely to decay.

These anticipations are proved by experience to be just.

Since the general introduction of inanimate mechanism into British manufactories, man, with few exceptions, has been treated as a secondary and inferior machine; and far more attention has been given to perfect the raw materials of wood and metals than those of body and mind. Give but due reflection to the subject, and you will find that man, even as an instrument for the creation of wealth, may be still greatly improved.

But, my friends, a far more interesting and gratifying consideration remains. Adopt the means which ere long shall be rendered obvious to every understanding, and you may not only partially improve those living instruments, but learn how to impart to them such excellence as shall make them infinitely surpass those of the present and all former times.

Here then is an object which truly deserves your attention; and instead of devoting all your faculties to invent improved inanimate mechanism, let your thoughts be, at least in part, directed to discover how to combine the more excellent materials of body and mind, which, by a well devised experiment, will be found capable of progressive improvement.

Thus seeing with the clearness of noon-day light, thus convinced with the certainty of conviction itself, let us not perpetuate the really unnecessary evils which our present practices inflict on this large proportion of our fellow subjects.⋆ ⋆ ⋆ But when you may have ocular demonstration, that, instead of any pecuniary loss, a well-directed

attention to form the character and increase the comforts of those who are so entirely at your mercy, will essentially add to your gains, prosperity, and happiness, no reasons, except those founded on ignorance of your self-interest, can in future prevent you from bestowing your chief care on the living machines which you employ; and by so doing you will prevent an accumulation of human misery, of which it is now difficult to form an adequate conception.

That you may be convinced of this most valuable truth, which due reflection will shew you is founded on the evidence of unerring facts, is the sincere wish of

The Author.

REVIEW QUESTIONS

1. Who is the intended audience, and why is Owen's analogy of workers as machines especially effective for this social group?
2. How does Owen reconcile social improvement with capitalist principles?
3. Why was Owen's argument largely dismissed by his peers as radical and unacceptable?

KARL MARX

FROM "Estranged Labour"

As an intellectual and a political activist, Karl Marx (1818–1883) represents a remarkable synthesis of European thought. Combining a rigorous philosophical training in German idealism and Hegelian dialectics with the revolutionary spirit of French politics and the materialist concerns of British political economy, Karl Marx not only wrote the most formidable critique of capitalism in the nineteenth century (Das Kapital) but also established a socialist ideology that profoundly altered the course of modern world history. The following passage captures the concerns of the early Marx, exiled in Paris in 1844, seeking to understand why wage labor and commodity production devalued and ultimately alienated workers. These writings, sometimes referred to as the Paris Manuscripts, evoke Marx's concerns with the philosophical essence of work and how it constructs identity. Implicitly comparing nineteenth-century wage work with the craft traditions of the early modern era, Marx saw a dehumanizing process inherent in capitalist commodity production, thus provoking him to envision capitalism as merely a stage in human development which would be superseded by an economic system that would restore human integrity to labor.

From *The Marx-Engels Reader,* edited by Robert C. Tucker (2d ed.; New York: Norton, 1978), pp. 56–62.

We have proceeded from the premises of political economy. We have accepted its language and its laws. We presupposed private property, the separation of labour, capital and land, and of wages, profit of capital and rent of land—likewise division of labour, competition, the concept of exchange-value, etc. On the basis of political economy itself, in its own words, we have shown that the worker sinks to the level of a commodity and becomes indeed the most wretched of commodities; that the wretchedness of the worker is in inverse proportion to the power and magnitude of his production; that the necessary result of competition is the accumulation of capital in a few hands, and thus the restoration of monopoly in a more terrible form; that finally the distinction between capitalist and land-rentier, like that between the tiller of the soil and the factory-worker, disappears and that the whole of society must fall apart into the two classes—the property-*owners* and the propertyless *workers.*

Political economy proceeds from the fact of private property, but it does not explain it to us. It expresses in general, abstract formulae the *material* process through which private property actually passes, and these formulae it then takes for *laws.* It does not *comprehend* these laws—i.e., it does not demonstrate how they arise from the very nature of private property. Political economy does not disclose the source of the division between labour and capital, and between capital and land. When, for example, it defines the relationship of wages to profit, it takes the interest of the capi-

talists to be the ultimate cause; i.e., it takes for granted what it is supposed to evolve. Similarly, competition comes in everywhere. It is explained from external circumstances. As to how far these external and apparently fortuitous circumstances are but the expression of a necessary course of development, political economy teaches us nothing. We have seen how, to it, exchange itself appears to be a fortuitous fact. The only wheels which political economy sets in motion are *avarice* and the *war amongst the avaricious—competition.*

*   *   *

Do not let us go back to a fictitious primordial condition as the political economist does, when he tries to explain. Such a primordial condition explains nothing. He merely pushes the question away into a grey nebulous distance. He assumes in the form of fact, of an event, what he is supposed to deduce—namely, the necessary relationship between two things—between, for example, division of labour and exchange. Theology in the same way explains the origin of evil by the fall of man: that is, it assumes as a fact, in historical form, what has to be explained.

We proceed from an *actual* economic fact.

The worker becomes all the poorer the more wealth he produces, the more his production increases in power and range. The worker becomes an ever cheaper commodity the more commodities he creates. With the *increasing value* of the world of things proceeds in direct proportion the *devaluation* of the world of men. Labour produces not only commodities; it produces itself and the worker as a *commodity*—and does so in the proportion in which it produces commodities generally.

This fact expresses merely that the object which labour produces—labour's product—confronts it as *something alien,* as a *power independent* of the producer. The product of labour is labour which has been congealed in an object, which has become material: it is the *objectification* of labour. Labour's realization is its objectification. In the conditions dealt with by political economy this realization of labour appears as *loss of reality* for the workers; objectification as *loss of the object* and *object-bondage;* appropriation as *estrangement,* as *alienation.*

So much does labour's realization appear as loss of reality that the worker loses reality to the point of starving to death. So much does objectification appear as loss of the object that the worker is robbed of the objects most necessary not only for his life but for his work. Indeed, labour itself becomes an object which he can get hold of only with the greatest effort and with the most irregular interruptions. So much does the appropriation of the object appear as estrangement that the more objects the worker produces the fewer can he possess and the more he falls under the dominion of his product, capital.

All these consequences are contained in the definition that the worker is related to the *product of his labour* as to an *alien* object. For on this premise it is clear that the more the worker spends himself, the more powerful the alien objective world becomes which he creates over-against himself, the poorer he himself—his inner world—becomes, the less belongs to him as his own. It is the same in religion. The more man puts into God, the less he retains in himself. The worker puts his life into the object; but now his life no longer belongs to him but to the object. Hence, the greater this activity, the greater is the worker's lack of objects. Whatever the product of his labour is, he is not. Therefore the greater this product, the less is he himself. The *alienation* of the worker in his product means not only that his labour becomes an object, an *external* existence, but that it exists *outside him,* independently, as something alien to him, and that it becomes a power of its own confronting him; it means that the life which he has conferred on the object confronts him as something hostile and alien.

*   *   *

Political economy conceals the estrangement inherent in the nature of labour by not considering the direct relationship between the worker (labour) *and production.* It is true that labour produces for the rich wonderful things—but for the worker it produces privation. It produces palaces—but for the worker, hovels. It produces beauty—but for the worker, deformity. It replaces labour by machines—but some of the workers it throws back to a barbarous type of labour, and the other workers it turns into machines. It produces intelligence—but for the worker idiocy, cretinism.

The direct relationship of labour to its produce is the relationship of the worker to the objects of his production. The relationship of the man of means to the objects of production and to production itself is only a *consequence* of this first relationship—and confirms it. We shall consider this other aspect later.

When we ask, then, what is the essential relationship of labour we are asking about the relationship of the *worker* to production.

Till now we have been considering the estrangement, the alienation of the worker only in one of its aspects, i.e., the worker's *relationship to the products of his labour.* But the estrangement is manifested not only in the result but in the *act of production*—within the *producing activity* itself. How would the worker come to face the product of his activity as a stranger, were it not that in the very act of production he was estranging himself from himself? The product is after all but the summary of the activity of production. If then the product of labour is alienation, production itself must be active alienation, the alienation of activity, the activity of alienation. In the estrangement of the object of labour is merely summarized the estrangement, the alienation, in the activity of labour itself.

What, then, constitutes the alienation of labour?

First, the fact that labour is *external* to the worker, i.e., it does not belong to his essential being; that in his work, therefore, he does not affirm himself but denies himself, does not feel content but unhappy, does not develop freely his physical and mental energy but mortifies his body and ruins his mind. The worker therefore only feels himself outside his work, and in his work feels outside himself. He is at home when he is not working, and when he is working he is not at home. His labour is therefore not voluntary, but coerced; it is *forced labour*. It is therefore not the satisfaction of a need; it is merely a *means* to satisfy needs external to it. Its alien character emerges clearly in the fact that as soon as no physical or other compulsion exists, labour is shunned like the plague. External labour, labour in which man alienates himself, is a labour of self-sacrifice, of mortification. Lastly, the external character of labour for the worker appears in the fact that it is not his own, but someone else's, that it does not belong to him, that in it he belongs, not to himself, but to another. Just as in religion the spontaneous activity of the human imagination, of the human brain and the human heart, operates independently of the individual—that is, operates on him as an alien, divine or diabolical activity—in the same way the worker's activity is not his spontaneous activity. It belongs to another; it is the loss of his self.

As a result, therefore, man (the worker) no longer feels himself to be freely active in any but his animal functions—eating, drinking, procreating, or at most in his dwelling and in dressing-up, etc.; and in his human functions he no longer feels himself to be anything but an animal. What is animal becomes human and what is human becomes animal.

Certainly eating, drinking, procreating, etc., are also genuinely human functions. But in the abstraction which separates them from the sphere of all other human activity and turns them into sole and ultimate ends, they are animal.

We have considered the act of estranging practical human activity, labour, in two of its aspects. (1) The relation of the worker to the *product of labour* as an alien object exercising power over him. This relation is at the same time the relation to the sensuous external world, to the objects of nature as an alien world antagonistically opposed to him. (2) The relation of labour to the *act of production* within the *labour* process. This relation is the relation of the worker to his own activity as an alien activity not belonging to him; it is activity as suffering, strength as weakness, begetting as emasculating, the worker's *own* physical and mental energy, his personal life or what is life other than activity—as an activity which is turned against him, neither depends on nor belongs to him. Here we have *self-estrangement*, as we had previously the estrangement of the *thing*.

We have yet a third aspect of *estranged labour* to deduce from the two already considered.

Man is a species being, not only because in practice and in theory he adopts the species as his object (his own as well as those of other things), but—and this is only another way of expressing it—but also because he treats himself as the actual, living species; because he treats himself as a *universal* and therefore a free being.

The life of the species, both in man and in animals, consists physically in the fact that man (like the animal) lives on inorganic nature; and the more universal man is compared with an animal, the more universal is the sphere of inorganic nature on which he lives. Just as plants, animals, stones, the air, light, etc., constitute a part of human consciousness in the realm of theory, partly as objects of natural science, partly as objects of art—his spiritual inorganic nature, spiritual nourishment which he must first prepare to make it palatable and digestible—so too in the realm of practice they constitute a part of human life and human activity. Physically man lives only on these products of nature, whether they appear in the form of food, heating, clothes, a dwelling, or whatever it may be. The universality of man is in practice manifested precisely in the universality which makes all nature his *inorganic* body—both inasmuch as nature is (1) his direct means of life, and (2) the material, the object, and the instrument of his life-activity. Nature is man's *inorganic body*—nature, that is, in so far as it is not itself the human body. Man *lives* on nature—means that nature is his *body,* with which he must remain in continuous intercourse if he is not to die. That man's physical and spiritual life is linked to nature means simply that nature is linked to itself, for man is a part of nature.

̄In estranging from man (1) nature, and (2) himself, his own active functions, his life-activity, estranged labour estranges the *species* from man. It turns for him the *life of the species* into a means of individual life. First it estranges the life of the species and individual life, and secondly it makes individual life in its abstract form the purpose of the life of the species, likewise in its abstract and estranged form.

For in the first place labour, *life-activity, productive life* itself, appears to man merely as a *means* of satisfying a need—the need to maintain the physical existence. Yet the productive life is the life of the species. It is life-engendering life. The whole character of a species—its species character—is contained in the character of its life-activity; and free, conscious activity is man's species character. Life itself appears only as *a means to life.*

The animal is immediately identical with its life-activity. It does not distinguish itself from it. It is *its life-activity*. Man makes his life-activity itself the object of his will and of his consciousness. He has conscious life-activity. It is not a determination with which he directly merges. Conscious life-activity directly distinguishes man from animal life-activity. It is just because of this that he is a species being. Or it is only because he is a species being that he is a Conscious Being, i.e., that his own life is an object for him. Only because of that is his activity free activity. Estranged labour reverses this relationship, so that it is just because man is a conscious being that he makes his life-activity, his *essential* being, a mere means to his *existence.*

*   *   *

REVIEW QUESTIONS

1. What are, for Marx, the actual economic facts of labor, and why are they so deleterious to the happiness of the worker?
2. When can labor free the "physical and mental energy" of a worker, and why does this not occur under wage labor?
3. According to Marx, why is work an indispensable component of human freedom?
4. What are the social and political ramifications of estranged labor?

22 ❧ CONSEQUENCES OF INDUSTRIALIZATION: URBANIZATION AND CLASS CONSCIOUSNESS, 1800–1850

The legacy of revolutionary republicanism combined with the harsh economic conditions of early industrial capitalism produced a new era in social relations and political struggle. For many contemporary observers, industrial society had established an unbridgeable chasm between propertied classes and wage-earning workers—two nations deeply divided in their political, cultural, and social outlooks.

The transition from agricultural and handicraft economies to the new urban industrial society produced pervasive dislocation and suffering. In the countryside, the erosion of traditional authority and social stability preceded large-scale industrialization. The enclosure of common lands and the increasing demand for profitable harvests replaced the paternalistic ties that bound together lords and tenant farmers with the more callous contractual relationship of wages and rents. Reduced to the penury of day laborers, many farmers migrated to the young industrial towns offering work. Similarly, cottage weavers throughout Europe, a proud class of skilled artisans, faced ruin when mechanized spinning and weaving drove down rates to starvation levels.

Squalor and grueling factory work offered little solace in the city. Unencumbered by any legal restraints, employers imposed insufferable working conditions on men, women, and children. In the 1830s, reformers likened the circumstances in English mill towns to colonial slavery and ridiculed the blind spots of bourgeois society, which fervently proselytized for the abolition of slavery but could not see similar misery and exploitation in their own cities. Because of the pervasive wretchedness of English urban life, with its heightened problems of malnutrition, disease, alcohol abuse, prostitution, and theft, engaged commentators questioned whether laissez-faire capitalism possessed a moral center.

The social question of early industrialization inexorably took on political dimensions. Privation and bitterness produced machine breaking, hayrick burning, and violent confrontations with masters, all early manifestations of political action. Bloody interventions of governments against workers articulated the differences of class interests between political elites and workers, who gradually developed their own political organizations. Chartism emerged as one of the earliest independent working-class movements, a national network of committees in Britain that agitated for workers' enfranchisement through colossal petition drives. Although unsuccessful in its immediate goals (Parliament rejected all demands), the movement alerted the nation to a mature, responsible working class, thus laying the groundwork for a subsequent liberal-labor alliance and eventual integration into Britain's political body. On the continent, however, unremitting state hostility toward workers' rights produced more resolute positions against bourgeois capitalism, most vividly expressed in the classic pamphlet, The Communist Manifesto (1848). Influenced by the widespread poverty of the 1840s and the growing concentration of capital, Karl Marx and Friedrich Engels asserted the axiomatic existence of class struggle and the eventual triumph of workers' socialism. The manifesto launched the political movement of Marxist socialism, which anchored class antagonism as a central issue in European political life.

In spite of the growing specter of socialism, this period is still labeled the bourgeois century. The growth of industrial capitalism brought with it a confident, well-defined middle-class culture, whose values of thrift, meritocracy, and hard work looked askance on indolent aristocrats and improvident laborers. The credo of self-reliance loomed large in the crowded Victorian marketplace of ideas. In the hands of popular writers, the appealing tales of rags-to-riches success through personal discipline and moral improvement enshrined a fundamental bourgeois tenet: social mobility for the deserving. Equally central to bourgeois life was the sharpened division between home and work as gender roles grew more pronounced. Bourgeois society expected women to preside over the private sphere's social and material complexities, while raising children and providing husbands with domestic sanctuary from the rigors of public life.

The divisions between employers and wage earners and the separation of private and public spheres constitute two fundamental shifts caused by the industrial revolution. While industrialization reconfigured the roles of bourgeois women and domesticity, class determined the new framework of social relations. Political affinities became class specific, and expectations in life depended on one's relationship to the market.

ANONYMOUS

An Address by a Journeyman Cotton Spinner

The factory system in northern England brought with it new social relations and political tensions. This anonymous address of 1818, published in the radical demo-cratic newspaper the Black Dwarf, *highlights the growing political divide between the two principal classes of Manchester: employers, who owned factories and con-trolled the market for commissioned work from weavers working from their homes, and workers, either factory hands or independent, reduced to accepting ever-lower rates for their skills. The article's sharp invective against the new moneyed class of Manchester points up the power of the public sphere to mobilize public opinion against wealth and political power. The* Black Dwarf, *one among a handful of prominent radical democratic newspapers, boasted a circulation of more than 12,000 in 1820, which, compared with the 7,000 of the* Times, *the newspaper of record, suggests a literate, informed working class capable of political organization.*

From *The Making of the English Working Class,* by E. P. Thompson (London: Penguin, 1968), quoting *Black Dwarf,* 30 September 1818.

First, then, as to the employers: with very few exceptions, they are a set of men who have sprung from the cotton-shop without edu-cation or address, except so much as they have acquired by their intercourse with the little world of merchants on the exchange at Manchester; but to counterbalance that deficiency, they give you enough of appearances by an ostentatious display of elegant mansions, equipages, liveries, parks, hunters, hounds, &c. which they take care to shew off to the merchant stranger in the most pompous manner. Indeed their houses are gorgeous palaces, far surpassing in bulk and extent the neat charm-ing retreats you see round London . . . but the chaste observer of the beauties of nature and art combined will observe a woeful deficiency of taste. They bring up their families at the most costly schools, determined to give their offspring a dou-ble portion of what they were so deficient in them-selves. Thus with scarcely a second idea in their heads, they are literally petty monarchs, absolute and despotic, in their own particular districts; and

to support all this, their whole time is occupied in contriving how to get the greatest quantity of work turned off with the least expence. . . . In short, I will venture to say, without fear of contradiction, that there is a greater distance observed between the master there and the spinner, than there is between the first merchant in London and his lowest servant or the lowest artisan. Indeed there is no comparison. I know it to be a fact, that the greater part of the master spinners are anxious to keep wages low for the purpose of keeping the spinners indigent and spiritless . . . as for the pur-pose of taking the surplus to their own pockets.

The master spinners are a class of men unlike all other master tradesmen in the kingdom. They are ignorant, proud, and tyrannical. What then must be the men or rather beings who are the instruments of such masters? Why, they have been for a series of years, with their wives and their families, patience itself—bondmen and bond-women to their cruel taskmasters. It is in vain to insult our common understandings with the observation that such men are free; that the law protects the rich and poor alike, and that a spinner can leave his master if he does not like the wages. True; so he can: but where must he go? why to another, to be sure. Well: he goes; he is asked where did you work last: 'did he discharge you?' No; we could not agree about wages. Well I shall not employ you nor anyone who leaves his master in that manner. Why is this? Because there is an abominable *combination existing amongst the masters,* first established at Stockport in 1802, and it has since become so general, as to embrace all the great masters for a circuit of many miles round Manchester, though not the little masters: they are excluded. They are the most obnoxious beings to the great ones that can be imagined. . . . When the combination first took place, one of their first articles was, that no master should take on a man until he had first ascertained whether his last master had discharged him. What then is the man to do? If he goes to the parish, that grave of all independence, he is there told—We shall not relieve you; if you dispute with your master, and don't support your family, we will send you to prison; so that the man is bound, by a combination of circumstances, to submit to his master. He cannot travel and get work in any town like a shoe-maker, joiner, or taylor; he is confined to the district.

The workmen in general are an inoffensive, unassuming, set of well-informed men, though how they acquire their information is almost a mystery to me. They are docile and tractable, if not goaded too much; but this is not to be wondered at, when we consider that they are trained to work from six years old, from five in a morning to eight and nine at night. Let one of the advocates for obedience to his master take his stand in an avenue leading to a factory a little before five o'clock in the morning, and observe the squalid appearance of the little infants and their parents taken from their beds at so early an hour in all kinds of weather; let him examine the miserable pittance of food, chiefly composed of water gruel and oatcake broken into it, a little salt, and sometimes coloured with a little milk, together with a few potatoes, and a bit of bacon or fat for dinner;

would a London mechanic eat this? There they are, (and if late a few minutes, a quarter of a day is stopped in wages) locked up until night in rooms heated above the hottest days we have had this summer, and allowed no time, except three-quarters of an hour at dinner in the whole day: whatever they eat at any other time must be as they are at work. The negro slave in the West Indies, if he works under a scorching sun, has probably a little breeze of air sometimes to fan him: he has a space of ground, and time allowed to cultivate it. The English spinner slave has no enjoyment of the open atmosphere and breezes of heaven. Locked up in factories eight stories high, he has no relaxation till the ponderous engine stops, and then he goes home to get refreshed for the next day; no time for sweet association with his family; they are all alike fatigued and exhausted. This is no over-drawn picture: it is literally true. I ask again, would the mechanics in the South of England submit to this?

When the spinning of cotton was in its infancy, and before those terrible machines for superseding the necessity of human labour, called steam engines, came into use, there were a great number of what were then called *little masters;* men who with a small capital, could procure a few machines, and employ a few hands, men and boys (say to twenty or thirty), the produce of whose labour was all taken to Manchester central mart, and put into the hands of brokers. . . . The brokers sold it to the merchants, by which means the master spinner was enabled to stay at home and work and attend to his workmen. The cotton was then always given out in its raw state from the bale to the wives of the spinners at home, when they heat and cleansed it ready for the spinners in the factory. By this they could earn eight, ten, or twelve shillings a week, and cook and attend to their families. But none are thus employed now; for all the cotton is broke up by a machine, turned by the steam engine, called a devil: so that the spinners wives have no employment, except they go to work in the factory all day at what can be done by children for a few shillings, four or five per week. If a man then could not agree with his master, he left him, and could get employed elsewhere. A few years, however, changed the face of things. Steam engines came into use, to purchase which, and to erect buildings sufficient to contain them and six or seven hundred hands, required a great capital. The engine power produced a more marketable (though not a better) article than the little master could at the same price. The consequence was their ruin in a short time; and the overgrown capitalists triumphed in their fall; for they were the only obstacle that stood between them and the complete control of the workmen.

Various disputes then originated between the workmen and masters as to the fineness of the work, the workmen being paid according to the number of hanks or yards of thread he produced from a given quantity of cotton, which was always to be proved by the overlooker, whose interest made it imperative on him to lean to his master, and call the material coarser than it was. If the workman would not submit *he must summon his employer before a magistrate;* the whole of the acting magistrates in that district, with the exception of two worthy clergymen, being gentlemen who have sprung from the *same* source with the master

cotton spinners. The employer generally contented himself with sending his overlooker to answer any such summons, thinking it beneath him to meet his servant. The magistrate's decision was generally in favour of the master, though on the statement of the overlooker only. The workman dared not appeal to the sessions on account of the expense. . . .

These evils to the men have arisen from that dreadful monopoly which exists in those districts where wealth and power are got into the hands of the few, who, in the pride of their hearts, think themselves the lords of the universe.

REVIEW QUESTIONS

1. Why are employers characterized as "petty monarchs, absolute and despotic"?
2. Why is this a new attitude among employers?
3. How does this address compare the lives of Manchester workers with prior times and with workers elsewhere in Britain?
4. What is the perceived attitude of the state in this conflict between employers and workers?

ANONYMOUS

FROM *The Life & History of Captain Swing, the Kent Rick Burner, Written by Himself*

The mechanization of spinning and weaving and the introduction of threshing machines in the English countryside brought waves of machine breakings and barn burnings in the 1820s and 1830s. Although this violence is often characterized as the futile resistance to inevitable change, these uprisings are more accurately seen as highly organized, disciplined political events. Under such fictional leaders as Ned Ludd or Captain Swing, weavers, artisans, and sharecroppers organized themselves into bands and destroyed private property that they believed had stripped them of

their livelihoods and dignity. The following story, which circulated as a popular po-
litical tract in the early 1830s, compresses the major political grievances of England's
agricultural workers into the life of Swing, a fictional hard-working tenant farmer
driven to destitution and despair by social and political change in the early nine-
teenth century.

From *The Life & History of Captain Swing, the Kent Rick Burner, Written by Himself,* by Anonymous (Chubb, 1830).

I WAS born on the day William Pitt became Prime Minister of England. My father was one of the class of small farmers, then so numerous in England, but whom the system of large farms has now altogether extinguished in the country. My father had two sons, of whom I was the younger; and as the savings of his predecessors had rendered him wealthy in his way, he determined educating me for a profession, and sent me to a grammar school in the neighbourhood; from whence I was removed in due time to a public school, preparatory to my entering college. When I was about to enter college, my elder brother died,—in consequence of which my father changed his intention of bringing me up to a profession, and took me home to attend to the farm. As I considered my future path in life was now definitively marked out for me, I gave up my entire time and attention to acquire a thorough knowledge of agriculture, and soon became one of the best farmers in that part of the kingdom. Soon after my father died, and bequeathed to me the farm and greater part of his effects. Some time after this I became acquainted with the daughter of a neighbouring curate, * * * and after a short period I proposed marriage to her, and she became my wife. I, of course, got no fortune with her, but she had that which surpasseth riches,—a most kind and amiable disposition; and if industry and integrity on the one side, and virtue and humility on the other, were sufficient to render our union a happy one, never was there a couple bid fairer for it than we did.

A few years passed as happily as I could wish, and three little ones added to my felicity. Although working hard all day, I at night forgot my toil and trouble when I returned to my fireside and family; and as soon as my children began to lisp, the first words I taught them to utter were the same I had myself learned when I was their age, namely, "To fear God and honour the King—to give every man his due, and behave uprightly to all." A short time after the birth of my fourth child, our old landlord died, and was succeeded by his son.

About two years after our young landlord returned home, (he had been on the Continent since the death of his father) I received a notice to quit,—the receipt of which astonished me beyond measure, as I owed no rent, and had always supported the character of being the best and most improving tenant on the estate. * * * As I found it impossible to see the lord, I called on the steward, and asked him what fault I had committed, or what crime I had been guilty of, that I should be turned out of the farm where my forefathers had lived for centuries, and which they and I had done so much to improve? "There is no fault to be found with you," replied the steward, "you have always paid your rent regularly, and conducted yourself correctly; but my lord wants your to make a fox-cover, and you must leave it next settling day."

"Good God!" exclaimed I, "are my wife and children to be turned out to make room for wild beasts?"—"There is no use in talking," said the steward, "your land is the best site on the estate for a fox-cover, and you must give it up."

The lord himself happened to pass by, and with tears in my eyes, I beseeched him not to turn out my family, in order to replace them with foxes. "Every man," said the lord, "*can do what he pleases with his own,*" and he walked away and left me.

*   *   *

Time, which flies equally fast whether we are miserable or happy, soon brought about the settling day, and as I found all appeals to the landlord utterly useless, I was prepared to give him possession, I had not sufficient capital to take a large farm, and small ones were not to be had, so I was obliged to dispose of my horses, black cattle, and farming machinery; and as the period I sold them was one of unusual depression, I did not receive one half their value.

As soon as my first burst of grief for the loss of my farm was over, I again applied myself to labour in my garden, (which I had taken with a cottage in the neighbourhood) and by dint of industry and exertion supported my family, by supplying a neighbouring village with vegetables. Up to this period I had never attended a political meeting in my life, nor took any part whatever in politics; I thought our laws and legislators too good to require alteration or change; and if I hated one thing more than another, it was Radicalism, the abettors of which I considered no better than rebels and revolutionists, who wanted to destroy our glorious constitution, and cause anarchy in the country. I begun, however, now to think otherwise. I had seen all around me, my neighbours reduced from comfort to poverty, and from poverty to the poor-rates; and as, in the greater number of cases, it had arisen from no fault of their own, it occurred to me that some change was necessary; as had England been governed as it ought, those things could never have taken place. Reflections of this sort determined me to attend the great meeting at Manchester, then about to be held, and I accordingly went there. Every thing passed quietly off until noon, when, to my horror and surprise, a charge was made by the military and yeomanry on the peaceable and unarmed multitude that were assembled, and I, amongst others, was wounded by a sabre-cut in the arm. Bleeding profusely, and with my arm hanging uselessly by my side, I went into Manchester and got it dressed; I was kept awake the entire night by the pain of my wound, but consoled myself with

the reflection that immediate and condign punishment would be inflicted on the lawless soldiery who had dared to massacre a peaceable multitude assembled to petition Parliament. "The King," said I, "will certainly send down a commission to have the monsters tried for their blood-thirsty outrage." What was my astonishment and indignation, in ten days after, when I saw a letter from the Secretary of State, thanking in the King's name, the military and magistrates, for massacring the people at Manchester.

I no longer wanted a proof that our country was sadly misgoverned—that a great change was necessary—and that the Reformers were the only real friends of the people.

*   *   *

[Swing is wrongfully accused of poaching and serves eighteen months in prison] When I was permitted to leave prison, I again commenced working in my garden, hoping my troubles were now over, and that, for the rest of my life, though poor, I should be allowed to rear my children peaceably and without persecution. A new and unexpected misfortune, however, arose; the parson of the parish considered his tithes not sufficiently productive, and made a claim for small tithes, which none of his predecessors had done, and demanded of me not only tithes for the current year, but also for that of the preceding one. I was unable to pay it, and was served with a law process, and, in a few weeks after, my cow sold by auction for the parson's tithes. I was now no longer able to keep my cottage and garden, and gave it up to the landlord, and rented a smaller one, having half an acre of ground attached to it. My present holding, though situated in the same parish, was two miles farther in the country than the former one, and adjoining it was a slip of uncultivated land, containing about an acre. My present landlord proposed that I should take this piece of land, in addition to what I had already; and, as an encouragement to me to do so, told me that he would not ask rent for the two first years, as during that time, he was perfectly well aware, the land would produce nothing. As I considered his proposal a fair one, I accepted it, and became his tenant for the piece of land, which I immediately set about enclosing with a ditch: having no person to assist me in making it, it was a considerable time before I had it finished: and I then commenced digging it with a spade, as I had no money to pay for getting it ploughed. In this way I fallowed it for two successive seasons; and in the beginning of the third spring I contrived, by parting with a good deal of my furniture to purchase some manure, which I carried in a basket on my head to the land: thus prepared, I sowed a crop in it, and nothing could succeed better than it did. When the time nearly came for gathering it, I was one day standing admiring it, with a gratification proportionate to the immense labour and time I had expended in bringing it about. "Although it had cost me three years labour," said I, "to grow this crop, it will nevertheless amply remunerate me." I had scarcely uttered the words, when two men rode up to me, one of whom I found to be the parson, whom I had never before seen in the parish, and the other his tithe valuator. After the latter had examined the crop, the parson asked me whether I would pay in kind or money?

"How much is it parson?" asked I.—"Only the tenth of the crop," replied he; "you must be very ignorant to ask such a question."

"But," said I, "if your reverence takes the tenth of the crop, it will be three-tenths of the produce of my laud; for I have been three years bringing the land into cultivation before it could grow any thing."—"I don't understand you," said the parson; "I must have my tithe."

"Why surely," said I, "your reverence will not rob my poor little children, by taking two-tenths more than you have a right to?"—"Rob them!" roared out the parson; "I see, my good fellow, you are a Radical, but I'll make you pay me my right; you shall not defraud the church of its lawful dues."

The parson went away, and the overseers came and demanded the poor-rates; the churchwardens called for an applotment, made to repair and beautify the church, and the landlord took his rent, and I was a ruined man. My whole three years' labour went amongst them, without leaving me one shilling for myself. I was now broken in purse and spirit, and could no longer bear up against the misfortunes that had fallen upon me. I gave up my land, and as I could procure no employment, I was obliged to apply to the parish. In order to lessen the poor-rates as much as possible, the overseers and farmers met each Sunday, and every able-bodied labourer was set up to auction, and the farmer who bid most for him had him to work for him during the ensuing week. One farmer bid three shillings a week for me, and I was ordered to work for him for that sum, and four shillings that the overseer gave me, making together seven shillings a week, to support my wife, five children, and myself. At the end of a week the farmer had no further occasion for my services, and I was on the following Monday, in company with some others, yoked to a cart, and made to draw gravel to the road. "Good God!" exclaimed I, when I found the harness upon me, "what is England reduced to, when, without any fault of my own, in the same parish that so many generations of my forefathers lived comfortable and happy, I am obliged to submit so be treated as a beast of burthen!" The work of drawing stones was so dreadfully severe, and so unlike what I had been accustomed to, that a few weeks' trial soon convinced me it would soon kill me; and I determined leaving my native parish, and seeking employment elsewhere; and with this intention I came into Kent. * * *

In Kent I found myself still worse off than at home, for I could procure no employment whatever, and as I had no claim on the poor-rates, I was in danger of starving, and felt myself compelled to return home; before, however, I could do so, my poor wife fell ill of fever, and in order to prevent her perishing from want, I was obliged to go and beg—downright hunger having conquered my reluctance to ask charity. I proceeded along the road in order to do so, and saw a fat man, dressed in black, approaching me, to whom I applied for something to prevent my wife and children dying of starvation.—"I cannot *afford* to give you any thing," replied he; "go to your parish." His manner was so repulsive, that I considered it useless to make a second application, and passed on: when I had walked a few yards, I began to think I had somewhere before seen the gentleman in black, and, after a few minutes recollection, remembered he was the Rev. Mr. Saint Paul, who had taken my cow in payment of his small tithes, and who afterwards took three-tenths of my crop for his tithe of my plot of ground: he was a pluralist; and, having five livings, seldom or never came to the parish I had lived in, except to receive his tithes, so that I did not at first recognise him. I walked on for some time longer, and not meeting any person, was obliged to return to the cottage that my wife was in, without any thing to give her; as I could not bring myself to enter the cottage and behold my wife dying for want, I sat down on the road, a little distance from the door, and soon beheld the parson returning from his walk. He had a cake in his hand, which, as he had no inclination to eat, he threw to a large pampered dog that walked beside him. The dog, having no better appetite than his master, took the cake in his mouth, played with it for a moment, then tossed it in the dirt and left it there, A little child of mine beheld the scene from the cottage door, and ran and picked the cake out of the gutter, when the parson demanded how dare she take it from his dog? "Oh, Sir!" said the little girl, "the dog will not eat it, and I wish to bring it to my poor mother, who is starving."—"Your mother and yourself ought to be in the workhouse," said the parson; "it is a shame for the parish officers to allow little naked vagabonds like you to be running about the roads."

"Can this man," thought I, "be a descendant of the Apostles, who carried nothing with them but scrip and staff, and who preached that we should consider every man as our brother, and relieve the necessities of our fellow-creatures?" Such an impression did his conduct make on me, that I got a piece of paper, and wrote a few lines, cautioning him against the consequences of his cruelty, and having signed it with my real name, "SWING," I left it at his hall-door during the night, and the following day the village rung with the report of the parson's having received a threatening notice, and that if the author could be detected, he would certainly be transported.

When writing the notice, I had not the most distant intention of making myself the instrument of punishment to the parson; it was an ebullition of the moment, called forth by my suffering, and I though no more about it. In a few days after the serving of the notice my wife died, and I was obliged to procure a coffin from the parish to bury her; no person attended her remains to the grave but a man who helped me to carry the coffin, and my five motherless children; it was late in the afternoon when we reached the churchyard, and as the man was obliged to leave me before the grave was entirely covered in, it became quite dark ere I could finish it, and I was obliged to procure a lantern to enable me to do so. When I completed it, I beheld my five children starving and shivering with cold beside the grave of their poor mother, without the smallest prospect of obtaining any food for them before morning; and in this condition I returned towards the cottage from whence I had that day carried my wife to be buried; the idea of passing the night on the straw on which she had expired was so repugnant to me, that I determined not to do so, and as the parson's haggard was only a short distance from me, I brought my children to pass the night on some loose straw that was lying on the ground. I was too much overwhelmed with grief and misery to attend to any thing, and I forgot to extinguish the light in the lantern which was carried by one of my children; the child incautiously placed the candle close to a rick, which caught fire, and was in a few minutes in a blaze; frightened and confounded at the accident, I immediately left the place, and the next morning journeyed homewards, begging for subsistence along the road: every where I went I heard of fires and notices signed "SWING." "How happens this," thought I. "I am not the author of these burnings!—What can have caused them?" A few minutes' reflection on the history of my own life, which without any alteration may stand for that of thousands of others, enabled me to give myself a satisfactory answer. "Those fires," said I, "are caused by farmers having been turned out of their lands to make room for foxes—peaceable people assembled to petition Parliament, massacred by the military—peasants confined two years in prison for picking up a dead partridge, English labourers set up to auction like slaves, and treated as beasts of burthen,—and pluralist parsons taking a poor man's only cow for the tythe of his cabbage garden. These are the things that have caused the burnings, and not unfortunate 'SWING!'" I continued my route, reached home, and am again harnessed like a horse to a gravel cart. But I bear it with patience, under the conviction that, in a very short time, Reform or Revolution must release me from it.

REVIEW QUESTIONS

1. What change initially uprooted Swing from his prosperity, and what factors continue to cause him misfortune?
2. How had traditional authority changed in the countryside?
3. What are Swing's political sympathies at the story's beginning, and how do they evolve?
4. How does this story blur the boundaries of criminality and social justice?

RICHARD OASTLER

"Yorkshire Slavery"

Richard Oastler (1789–1861), a conservative church-and-king Tory, became a prominent social reformer in the 1830s after a factory owner exposed him to the ills of child employment. His letter to the liberal Leeds Mercury *in October 1830, "Yorkshire Slavery," launched a long campaign agitating for factory reform, which resulted in the Ten Hours Bill. His stirring oratory and his efforts to fuse a Radical-Tory alliance for factory legislation earned him the title the Factory King. Imprisoned in 1840 for debt, Oastler published from prison the weekly* Fleet Papers, *which renewed the effort for factory reform and criticized the government's treatment of the poor. In the following letter, Oastler compares his cause to the antislavery movement of the 1820s, a cause embraced by religious associations and many elements of bourgeois society.*

From *The Factory System*, Vol. 2, *The Factory System and Society*, edited by J. T. Ward (New York: Barnes and Noble, 1970).

To the Editors of the Leeds Mercury

"It is the pride of Britain that a slave cannot exist on her soil; and if I read the genius of her constitution aright, I find that slavery is most abhorrent to it—that the air which Britons breathe is free—the ground on which they tread is sacred to liberty." *Rev. R. W. Hamilton's Speech at the Meeting held in the Cloth-hall Yard, September 22d, 1830.*

Gentlemen—No heart responded with truer accents to the sounds of liberty which were heard in the Leeds Cloth-hall Yard, on the 22d instant, than did mine, and from none could more sincere and earnest prayers arise to the throne of Heaven, that hereafter slavery might only be known to Britain in the pages of her history. One shade alone obscured my pleasure, arising not from any difference in principle, but from the want of application of the general principle *to the whole empire.* The pious and able champions of *negro* liberty and *colonial* rights should, if I mistake not, have gone farther than they did; or perhaps, to speak more correctly, before they had travelled so far as the West Indies, should, at least for a few moments, have sojourned in our own immediate neighbourhood, and have directed the attention of the meeting to scenes of misery, acts of oppression, and victims of slavery, even on the threshold of our homes.

Let truth speak out, appalling as the statement may appear. The fact is true. Thousands of our fellow-creatures and fellow-subjects, both male and female, the miserable inhabitants of a *Yorkshire town,* (Yorkshire now represented in Parliament by the giant of anti-slavery principles) are this very moment existing in a state of slavery, *more horrid* than are the victims of that hellish system "*colonial slavery.*" These innocent creatures drawl out, unpitied, their short but miserable existence, in a place famed for its profession of religious zeal, whose inhabitants are ever foremost in *professing* "temperance" and "reformation," and are striving to outrun their neighbours in missionary exertions, and would fain send the Bible to the farthest corner of the globe—aye, in the very place where the anti-slavery fever rages most furiously, her *apparent charity* is not more admired on earth, than her *real cruelty* is abhorred in Heaven. The very streets which receive the droppings of an "Anti-Slavery Society" are every morning wet by the tears of innocent victims at the accursed shrine of avarice, who are *compelled* (not by the cart-whip of the negro slave-driver) but by the dread of the equally appalling thong or strap of the over-looker, to hasten, half-dressed,

but not half-fed, to those magazines of British infantile slavery—*the worsted mills in the town and neighbourhood of Bradford! ! !*

Would that I had Brougham's eloquence, that I might rouse the hearts of the nation, and make every Briton swear, "These innocents shall be free!"

Thousands of little children, both male and female, *but principally female,* from seven to fourteen years of age, are daily *compelled* to *labour* from six o'clock in the morning to seven in the evening, with only—Britons, blush while you read it!—*with only thirty minutes allowed for eating and recreation.* Poor infants! ye are indeed sacrificed at the shrine of avarice, *without even the solace of the negro slave;* ye are no more than he is, *free agents;* ye are compelled to work as long as the *necessity* of your needy parents may require, or the cold-blooded avarice of your worse than barbarian masters *may demand!* Ye live in the boasted land of freedom, and *feel* and mourn that *ye are slaves,* and slaves without the only comfort which the negro has. He knows it is his sordid, mercenary master's interest that he should *live,* be *strong* and *healthy.* Not so with you. Ye are doomed to labour from morning to night for one who cares not how soon your weak and tender frames are stretched to breaking! You are not mercifully valued at so much per head; this would assure you at least (even with the worst and most cruel masters) of the mercy shown to their own labouring beasts. No, no! your soft and delicate limbs are tired and fagged, and jaded, at only *so much per week,* and when your joints can act no longer, your emaciated frames are cast aside, the boards on which you lately toiled and wasted life away, are instantly supplied with other victims, who in this boasted land of liberty are HIRED—not sold—as slaves and daily forced to hear that they are free. Oh! Duncombe! Thou hatest slavery—I know thou dost resolve that "Yorkshire children shall no more be slaves!" And Morpeth! who justly glorieth in the Christian faith—Oh, Morpeth! listen to the cries and count the tears of these poor babes, and let St. Stephen's hear thee swear "they shall no longer groan in slavery!" And Bethell, too! who swears eternal hatred to the name of slave, whene'er thy manly voice is heard in Britain's senate, assert the rights and liberty of Yorkshire youths. And Brougham! thou who are the chosen champion of liberty in every clime! oh bend thy giant's mind, and listen to the sorrowing accents of these poor Yorkshire little ones, and note their tears; then let thy voice rehearse their woes, and touch the chord thou only holdest—the chord that sounds above the silvery notes in praise of heavenly liberty, and down descending at thy will, groans in the horrid caverns of the deep in muttering sounds of misery accursed to hellish bondage; and as thou sound'st these notes, let Yorkshire hear thee swear, "Her children shall be free!" Yes, all ye four protectors of our rights, chosen by freemen to destroy oppression's rod,

"Vow one by one, vow altogether, vow
With heart and voice, eternal enmity
Against oppression by your brethren's hands;
Till man nor woman under Britain's laws,
Nor son nor daughter born within her empire,
Shall buy, or sell, or HIRE, or BE A SLAVE!"

The nation is now most resolutely determined that negroes shall be free. Let them, however, not forget that Britons have common rights with Afric's sons.

The blacks may be fairly compared to beasts of burden, *kept for their master's use;* the whites, to those *which others keep and let for hire.* If I have succeeded in calling the attention of your readers to the horrid and abominable system on which the worsted mills in and near Bradford is conducted, I have done some good. Why should not children working in them be protected by legislative enactments, as well as those who work in cotton mills? Christians should feel and act for those whom Christ so eminently loved, and declared that "of such is the Kingdom of Heaven."—I remain, yours, etc.,

A Briton.

REVIEW QUESTIONS

1. In what ways does Oastler expose the hypocrisy of English politics?
2. How does he compare colonial and domestic politics?
3. What are the author's rhetorical devices and tone of voice that make the letter such a powerful text?

MICHAEL RYAN

FROM *Prostitution in London, with a Comparative View of That of Paris and New York*

The rapid urbanization of Europe in the nineteenth century brought new concerns and fears over the rise of prostitution. Although prostitution long antedated the nineteenth century, many contemporaries believed that modern urban poverty increased it. Not surprisingly, the issue of prostitution consequently became a leading cause for middle-class reformers throughout the nineteenth century. In 1839 Michael Ryan, a doctor and member of the Royal College of Physicians, published a work which compared prostitution in three major Western cities to underscore the need for legislative and moral reform. The following excerpt on Paris throws light on the approach and analytical categories of Victorian reformers.

From *Prostitution in London with a Comparative View of That of Paris and New York,* by Michael Ryan (London: Bailliere, 1839), pp. 42–51.

*   *   *

* * * M. Duchatelet's work is entitled to all the praise it has received, because it is highly calculated to effect great improvement in public morals; and being strongly impressed with this conviction, I quote it freely, and imitate the author in giving an account of prostitution in London and America, with the most sanguine hope of doing good to mankind.

The laudable object of the author of Prostitution in Paris, was to obtain information from the medical profession, the magistracy, and the police, so that the subject of his inquiry has been examined in all its bearings; and the legislator, the magistrate, the physician, the surgeon, and the philanthropist, now possess a store of knowledge to guide them in their amelioration of the social intellectual, and pathological conditions of a deeply degraded but important class—important from the influence it may exert upon the rest of society. It is important to state that the author expended no less than eight years in collecting his materials, and not only describes the causes of prostitution, but what is the best policy to be adopted towards the wretched victims, for the preservation of their health, and for the diminution of the amount of evil, which they inflict on the whole community, without, at the same time giving encouragement to a vice, which prevails to so great an extent at present.

It appears that the happy results of the sanitary surveillance exercised by the police in Paris since 1800, have led the authorities of Rome, Naples, Milan, the chief towns in Germany, Holland, Belgium, the Brazils, and the United States, to request information respecting the management and treatment of prostitutes in the French capital; but there was no source from the records of which satisfactory and conclusive replies could be given.

M. Duchatelet found, on a careful examination of all the records on the subject, that these were for the most part, replete with errors, and the falsest notions, with the exception of some few historical notices. He, therefore, examined for himself, and refuted or confirmed the received opinions.

I cannot however follow him through his minute details, but shall only notice his leading conclusions, strongly recommending every legislator, judge, magistrate, and medical practitioner to carefully peruse the original production.

NUMBER OF PROSTITUTES IN PARIS

According to this author, the number of prostitutes in Paris in 1836, was about 18,000, one half of whom were kept women. The number was about 30,000 during the republic after 1793. The number in London, according to the reports of the police superintendents is from 8,000 to 10,000.

The variations of those in Paris from 1812 to 1832 are remarkable; in 1812 there were only 1,293; in 1832, 3,558; and the increase is to be attributed to the invasion of foreign armies, and various other causes.

Four hundred and fifty-one were Europeans not natives of France—of these, Belgium supplied 161, Switzerland 59; Prussia; 58; Holland; 23; England, 23; Savoy, 22; Austria, 15; Spain, 14; Piedmont, 11; Rome, 7; Poland, 6; Ireland, 4; Naples, 3; Scotland, 1.

The regularity with which foreigners of this class arrive every year in Paris is very remarkable. The number of prostitutes, natives of France, were, from 10th April, 1816, to April 30, 1831, a period of fifteen years, 12,201, including 506 foreigners, in all 12,707.

NATIONS WHICH FURNISH THESE WOMEN

The prostitutes born in Paris are almost exclusively of the class of artisans, and only four belonging to respectable families. The families of the labourers and others, who cannot attend to the education of their daughters, nor watch, nor provide for their wants when they attain a certain age, are those which supply servants, and women of the workshops.

A third of the fathers were men who could not write their names; and those of the departments were still more illiterate. The prostitutes of Paris and the departments belong to the poorest and most miserable families. A great majority of the former were legitimate, and not illegitimate or foundling infants, as many imagine.

"The influence of the sedentary employments of the manufactory and workshop is very remarkable upon certain classes. The smallness of the remuneration of their labouring inmates is well known; and as the workpeople have frequently no resource but their labour, it may well be asked, how is it possible for them, with such means, to obtain even the merest necessaries of life? It should be observed, too, that a number of causes continually occur to suspend the works of these establishments, and throw out of employment, for two or three months at a time, work-women, who find it impossible to put by any part of their receipts, and who frequently, from the division of labour introduced into our manufactures, only know how to produce one particular thing. Destitute girls, under such circumstances—isolated, and without friends, without having received even the commonest education, a prey to many passions, surrounded with temptations and bad examples, frequently a prey to every privation, and having in perspective the cruellest of deaths, that of hunger—fly to resources the most repugnant to the wealthy and virtuous, in whose minds their condition is well calculated to arouse philanthropic reflection."

The reader will admit, that the author from whom I quote, has accurately described the actual condition of those numerous girls and women in this country, who are compelled to work or earn the means of their support.

EDUCATION

The education of prostitutes is very defective. Of 4,470 born and brought up in Paris, 1,780 signed very badly, 110 signed well, 248 doubtful, 2,232 could not sign their names; and of 7,600 born in the departments, 4,352 were unable to sign.

AGES

Of 3,245, 2 were registered above 10 years; 3 at 11; 3 at 12; 6 at 13; 20 at 14; 51 at 15; 111 at 16; 149 at 17; 279 at 18; 322 at 19; 389 at 20; 303 at 21; 300 at 22; 215 at 23; 179 at 24; 136 at 25; 140 at 26; 122 at 27; 101 at 28; 57 at 29; 56 at 30; 52 at 31; 27 at 32; 32 at 33; 31 at 34; 26 at 35; 24 at 36; 15 at 37; 12 at 38; 11 at 39; 9 at 40; 5 at 41; so on, diminishing to 52; when there was at this age, not more than 1 in each year from 52 to 63 years.

CAUSES OF PROSTITUTION

The chief causes of prostitution deserve attentive reflection. In the space of ten years, not more than three or four presented themselves at the dispensary in Paris for registration, who had not been previously SEDUCED. Seduction is the most common cause of prostitution in all nations.

M. Duchatelet gives the following detail of the causes, and as it applies to all countries, I shall condense it.

Laziness may be placed in the first rank; it is the desire of procuring enjoyments without working, that causes many young women to leave their places, or to refrain from seeking others when out of service. The laziness, carelessness, and cowardice of prostitutes, have become almost proverbial. Misery, proceeding to a frightful extreme, is also one of the most active causes of this evil. How many young women, abandoned by their families, without relations or friends, are obliged to have recourse to prostitution? One unhappy girl, alive to all the feelings of honour, struggled to the last extremity against this wretched alternative, and, when she came to be registered, it was proved that she had not eaten for nearly three days! Vanity, and the desire of being finely dressed, is another active cause of prostitution, particularly in Paris, where simplicity in dress is actually a subject of reproach, and shabbiness is still more despised. It is hardly, then, surprising, that so many girls allow themselves to be seduced by the desire to possess a dress, which, while its display would gratify their vanity, would help to remove them from the station in which they were born, and allow them to mingle with a class by whom they consider themselves regarded with hauteur. Those who know the extent to which love of dress and finery exists in some women, will easily judge of the activity of such a cause of prostitution in Paris.

There are, also, a great number of young women, who, being seduced in the departments by military officers, students, commercial travellers, and others, are induced to come to Paris by various deceptive promises, and being there afterwards abandoned, follow, in the destitute condition which afflicts them, the suggestions of the first person whom they encounter; and it is proved, that it is upon this description of girls, that those abominable women whose trade it is to corrupt youth, particularly fix their attention. These wretches seek them every where, exhibiting, in the pursuit of their infernal art, the most remarkable address. Other young women, being seduced in the country, voluntarily seek refuge in Paris, where they can conceal their disgrace from their friends. Domestic trouble, also, and ill-treatment received from their family and friends, determine some to adopt this course of life.

A long sojourn in a hospital, or in the low lodging-houses, where servants out of place are assembled, is likewise one of the causes of prostitution; and, finally, the misconduct of parents and relations, and bad examples of every kind, must be considered to exercise a very great influence in the promotion of this vice.

But of all the causes of prostitution there is none more active, particularly in Paris, and, prob-

ably, in all the other great towns, than an insufficiency of wages. Let the profits of the cleverest of our sempstresses, our laundresses, and, in general, of all those who live by the use of the needle, be compared with the profits of individuals who possess inferior skill, and it will be seen, that it is scarcely possible for the latter to obtain the barest necessaries of life. More especially, let the reward of their labour be compared with the price of their dishonour, and surprise will no longer be felt that so great a number abandon themselves to this wretched state of life.

It is difficult and painful to believe, that this career is occasionally embraced by certain women, as the only means of performing the duties imposed upon them by the title of "mother" or "daughter." Nothing, however, is more true. It is not uncommon for married women, abandoned by, or deprived of their husbands, and, consequently, of all support, to become prostitutes, with the sole intention of preserving a numerous family from starvation; and it is still more common to see girls, who are unable by their labour to support aged or infirm parents, add, by prostitution at night, to their limited means. I have too often obtained exact particulars of these two classes of prostitutes, not to be convinced that they are very numerous in Paris.

There are, lastly, some women who become prostitutes from a spirit of licentiousness, which can only be explained by ascribing it to the operation of a violent mental disease, but, in general, these Messalinas are rare.

"Is prostitution," inquires M. Duchatelet, "to be attributed to the extreme degree of civilization which we have reached? Were we only to regard the preceding details, this opinion might be maintained; but if we look back to the times of the ancients, and to the barbarous middle ages, we shall find that prostitution was then very common. If we consult modern travellers, who have penetrated to the most remote parts of America and Africa, where civilization is scarcely dawning, we find the same custom prevailing. In all those regions prostitutes have been observed to abound. No doubt our social state is the cause of the ruin of many young women; but, on the other hand, it provides resources for a great number, which they would not possess under other circumstances, and which allows them to lead a life of regularity.

"The following details, which partly belong to this question, will serve to throw some light upon it. Of the 5,183 individuals already alluded to, there have been found inscribed on the registers—

Two sisters,   164 times.
Three ditto,   4 ditto.
Four ditto,   3 ditto.

"Besides which, there have been found—

Mother and daughter,   16 times.
Aunt and Niece,   4 ditto.
Two cousins,   22 ditto.

"It must not be supposed, that these 436 persons were all prostitutes at the same time; this number is to be distributed through a period of eight years. By this, the complete immorality of the families, from which these women issue, is exposed. Their degradation is most frequently owing to the pernicious examples which are placed before their eyes during infancy."

It may be asked, on seeing these sad results, whether society has sufficiently inquired into the fate of these unhappy women, who so much need its care, and who exercise so great an influence upon the mechanism (if the term may be allowed) of a state? In this respect, many reforms and improvements remain to be accomplished; and these important matters, though difficult to discuss, are as worthy of attention, on the part of the friends of humanity, as of the meditations of the statesman."

OPINIONS ENTERTAINED OF THEMSELVES

According to our author, prostitutes entertain the most abject opinion of themselves. The sight of a mother of a family, or of any woman of good character, is insupportable to them; and they often feel pleasure in insulting these, to revenge, in some degree, the contempt and disgust with which virtuous women regard them. They often become suddenly ill on seeing any of their former acquaintances; and one girl lost her senses, by the sight of one of her countrymen. They most acutely feel their abject state, and are a subject of horror to themselves; their contempt for themselves often surpasses that in which they are held by persons of moral character; they bitterly regret their fall, and form plans and make exertions to quit their mode of life; but all efforts are useless; they are driven to despair by the tyranny of their keepers and of the world, which renders them the very dregs of society; while their heartless seducers, who are much more depraved and guilty, are approved by society. It is obvious that I have justly censured male seducers, and the inhuman law in their favour, in my work on the Philosophy of Marriage, even against a popular Government, but all right-minded individuals are now of my opinion. No one can suffer, without dread and the greatest dejection, to be entirely forgotten by the world; and to be hated, despised, and universally disdained. "The thought alone of this state, often causes many prostitutes to become lunatics."

RELIGIOUS FEELINGS OF PROSTITUTES

Most of this unhappy class, are in a profound state of ignorance with respect to religion. A great number have scarcely an idea of the commonest sentiment of the Divinity; and they are not sparing of jests and sarcasms upon matters of religion. Many of them refrain from all religious duties, on account of their unworthiness; though most of them are anxious for religious consolation when dangerous or fatal illness assails them. I have known many examples.

FEELING OF SHAME

M. Duchatelet attests, by many facts, that there is a feeling of shame in prostitutes, notwithstanding their habits and their vices. He states, that at the examinations and demonstrations of their diseases, before a numerous audience, at the dispensary in Paris—a most indecent and reprehensible proceeding—"all, without exception, even the most shameless, became of the colour of crimson;

they hid their faces, and considered this inspection a real punishment." This equally applies to public examinations in our hospitals. A remarkable change for the better has taken place of late years. Before and during the Revolution, mention is frequently made of women dancing, and walking in the daylight, in a state of nature. "But by degrees," says our author, "as we approach the present time, I found fewer details of scenes of disgusting indecency." This improvement is to be attributed to the enforcement of the police regulations, and to the laudable perseverance with which it carries into effect its wise measures of correction and reform.

TURN AND CHARACTER OF MIND

There are other traits in the conduct of the unfortunate class of beings now under consideration, which deserve to be noticed. Their volatile and changeable turn of mind is so great, that nothing can fix their attention, which is distracted by the most trifling occurrence. This will, in some degree, account for their many errors and misconduct, and extenuate, in a great degree, their culpability in the eyes of all men of understanding.

Loquacity, noise, tumult, and agitation, appear to be indispensable to their existence, in the prisons, the hospitals, and penitentiaries; but even in this respect, many improvements have taken place of late years.

MANNER OF PASSING THEIR LEISURE HOURS

The manner of passing their leisure hours is very remarkable. Nine-tenths of them do nothing at all, and pass their time in idleness. Those of the better class rise late, go to baths, live very well, or, rather too freely, and amuse themselves with skipping, recline on a bed or couch, or walk in the open air. Those of the lower class frequent wine shops (*Anglicè*, "gin-palaces") and converse with all the bad characters that visit such places. Those of this class often sell articles in the streets.

M. Duchatelet has ascertained, that the first class read romances and tales of a tragical nature, which excite lively emotions; but they never chose those obscene and licentious works, which most young and depraved persons seek for with such ardour. Satiety renders that insipid and monotonous, which, under other circumstances, would be a powerful, and, too often, a ruinous stimulant. Many informants, upon whose veracity I can rely, assure me to the contrary; and it is proved beyond all doubt, and I have seen the works which were seized in brothels, that this is not true as regards London, nor do I believe as regards Paris. The better class are fond of balls, theatres, and other amusements; as many of them only exercise their vocation from ten to four o'clock in the afternoon.

*　　*　　*

REVIEW QUESTIONS

1. According to Ryan, to what extent had prostitution increased in Paris and what were the reasons for this numerical rise?
2. For Ryan, what is the relationship between civilization and prostitution?
3. What economic, cultural, and social influences does Ryan attribute to women's susceptibility to prostitution?
4. How does he characterize prostitutes and what attention does he give to men?
5. What moral assumptions frame this social analysis?

SATANIC MILLS, MANCHESTER, ENGLAND (1851)

Among the most prominent social consequences of industrialization were urbanization and mechanization. Between 1750 and 1850, the English city of Manchester swelled from 20,000 to 400,000, becoming a notorious example of overcrowding and squalor. What two ways of life are contrasted in this painting?

FRIEDRICH ENGELS

FROM *The Condition of the Working Class in England*

Friedrich Engels (1820–1895), the son of a pietistic textile manufacturer from the Rhenish town of Elberfeld, completed his apprenticeship as a textile entrepreneur in Manchester in 1842–1844. Prior to this apprenticeship, Engels read critical philosophy as a student in Berlin and published articles in the opposition Cologne paper, Rheinische Zeitung. In 1842 in Cologne Engels met Karl Marx for the first time. Manchester nurtured Engel's radical political spirit: he joined the Chartists, the movement agitating for universal suffrage and workingmen's rights; published articles in the Owenite newspaper The New Moral World; *and wrote "Outlines of a Critique of Political Economy," which Marx published in his new Paris-based journal,* Deutsch-Französische Jahrbücher. *In 1844 he gathered material for a social history of England's working class, which became* The Condition of the Working Class in England *(first published in German in 1845), a descriptive work of English industrial life that amounted to an empirical indictment of capitalism's immorality. The following passage examines Manchester, a city whose population increase of seventy thousand between 1831 and 1841 produced deplorable living conditions for the city's poor.*

From *The Condition of the Working Class in England,* by Friedrich Engels, edited by David McLellan (Oxford, Eng.: Oxford University Press, 1993), pp. 60–65.

*   *   *

The south bank of the Irk is here very steep and between 15 and 30, feet high. On this declivitous hillside there are planted three rows of houses, of which the lowest rise directly out of the river, while the front walls of the highest stand on the crest of the hill in Long Millgate. Among them are mills on the river, in short, the method of construction is as crowded and disorderly here as in the lower part of Long Millgate. Right and left a multitude of covered passages lead from the main street into numerous courts, and he who turns in thither gets into a filth and disgusting grime, the equal of which is not to be found—especially in the courts which lead down to the Irk, and which contain unqualifiedly the most horrible dwellings which I have yet beheld. In one of these courts there stands directly at the entrance, at the end of the covered passage, a privy without a door, so dirty that the inhabitants can pass into and out of the court only by passing through foul pools of stagnant urine and excrement. This is the first court on the Irk above Ducie Bridge—in case anyone should care to look into it. Below it on the river there are several tanneries which fill the whole neighbourhood with the stench of animal putrefaction. Below Ducie Bridge the only entrance to most of the houses is by means of narrow, dirty stairs and over heaps of refuse and filth. The first court below Ducie Bridge, known as Allen's Court, was in such a state at the time of the cholera that the sanitary police ordered it evacuated, swept, and disinfected with chloride of lime. Dr Kay gives a terrible description of the state of this court at that time. Since then, it seems to have been partially torn away and rebuilt; at least looking down from Ducie Bridge, the passer-by sees several ruined walls and heaps of debris with some newer houses. The view from this bridge, mercifully concealed from mortals of small stature by a parapet as high as a man, is characteristic for the whole district. At the bottom flows, or rather stagnates, the Irk, a narrow, coal-black, foul-smelling stream, full of debris and refuse, which it deposits on the shallower right bank. In dry weather, a long string of the most disgusting, blackish-green, slime pools are left standing on this bank, from the depths of which bubbles of miasmatic gas constantly arise and give forth a stench unendurable even on the bridge 40 or 50 feet above the surface of the stream. But besides this, the stream itself is checked every few paces by high weirs, behind which slime and refuse accumulate and rot in thick masses. Above the bridge are tanneries, bonemills, and gasworks, from which all drains and refuse find their way into the Irk, which receives further the contents of all the neighbouring sewers and privies. It may be easily imagined, therefore, what sort of residue the stream deposits. Below the bridge you look upon the piles of debris, the refuse, filth, and offal from the courts on the steep left bank; here each house is packed close behind its neighbour and a piece of each is visible, all black, smoky, crumbling, ancient, with broken panes and window-frames. The background is furnished by old barrack-like factory buildings. On the lower right bank stands a long row of houses and mills; the second house being a ruin without a roof, piled with debris; the third stands so low that the lowest floor is uninhabitable, and therefore without windows or doors. Here the background embraces the pauper burial-ground, the station of the Liverpool and Leeds railway, and, in the rear of this, the Workhouse, the "Poor-Law Bastille" of Manchester, which, like a citadel, looks threateningly down from behind its high walls and parapets on the hilltop, upon the working-people's quarter below.

Above Ducie Bridge, the left bank grows more flat and the right bank steeper, but the condition of the dwellings on both banks grows worse rather than better. He who turns to the left here from the main street, Long Millgate, is lost; he wanders from one court to another, turns countless corners, passes nothing but narrow, filthy nooks and alleys, until after a few minutes he has lost all clue, and knows not whither to turn. Everywhere half or wholly ruined buildings, some of them actually uninhabited, which means a great deal here; rarely a wooden or stone floor to be seen in the houses, almost uniformly broken, ill-fitting windows and doors, and a state of filth! Everywhere heaps of debris, refuse, and offal; standing pools for gutters, and a stench which alone would make it impossible for a human being in any degree civilized to live in such a district.

*   *   *

Enough! The whole side of the Irk is built in this way, a planless, knotted chaos of houses, more or less on the verge of uninhabitableness, whose unclean interiors fully correspond with their filthy external surroundings. And how could the people be clean with no proper opportunity for satisfying the most natural and ordinary wants? Privies are so rare here that they are either filled up every day, or are too remote for most of the inhabitants to use. How can people wash when they have only the dirty Irk water at hand, while pumps and water-pipes can be found in decent parts of the city alone? In truth, it cannot be charged to the account of these helots of modern society if their dwellings are not more clean than the pigsties which are here and there to be seen among them. The landlords are not ashamed to let dwellings like the six or seven cellars on the quay directly below Scotland Bridge, the floors of which stand at least 2 feet below the low-water level of the Irk that flows not 6 feet away from them; or like the upper floor of the corner-house on the opposite shore directly above the bridge, where the ground floor, utterly uninhabitable, stands deprived of all fittings for doors and windows, a case by no means rare in this region, when this open ground floor is used as a privy by the whole neighbourhood for want of other facilities!

If we leave the Irk and penetrate once more

on the
midst
come
stretche
Grove
better
find at
courts,
square.
built a
court is
of the
directio
the war
a corne
certainl
time in
If I
district
is, in c
perfect
may, n
over th
the stre
house
which i
of the
of the l
offal he
mon to
der dis
the clea
of pigs
the off
Here, a
Manch
build p
or eve

whelming burden on the *compagnons*. From 4 or 6 francs, the wages of the intelligent and hard-working man fell gradually to 40, 36 and 25 sous; in November 1831 the worker employed in the manufacture of plain material earned only 18 sous for an 18 hour day . . . complaint became general; *chefs d'atelier* and *compagnons* shared their troubles; and from the depths of the Croix Rousse sector, which bore the misery, at first a confused clamour was heard, but this soon became solemn, formidable and immense.

For some time the Prefect in Lyons had been a man who was skilled in soothing and handling popular passions. M. Douvier Dumolard understood immediately that no solution was possible in such a state of affairs, other than that of exterminating the working population, or satisfying its legitimate grievances. He took the latter course. . . .

M. Douvier began work . . . and on 11 October 1831 the Conseil des Prud'hommes had issued the following declaration:

"Considering that it is public knowledge that many manufacturers pay too low wages, it is expedient to establish a minimum wage."

M. Douvier Dumolard resolved to deal with this resolution, which fell perfectly within his province; and on the 15th, under his Chairmanship, the Chamber of Commerce, the Mayor of Lyons and mayors of the three town suburbs met to discuss the situation. It became clear at this meeting that the bases of the wage structure would be discussed in a contradictory fashion by the twenty-two workers, twelve of whom had already been delegated by their comrades, and the twenty-two manufacturers whom the Chamber of Commerce designated as representatives.

M. Douvier Dumolard could have, and ought to have, fixed the tariff himself; he did not have the courage; he contented himself with putting the two parties together.

On 21 October a new meeting was convoked at the Prefecture. The 25th of October had been fixed as a date for the definitive discussion of the rates of pay.

Among the delegates of both parties discussion centred upon the crying abuses which had crept into the factories, but particularly on the reduction of wage rates; and such was the moderation of the workers that those whom twelve years before the manufacturers were pleased to pay 8 sous had their wages reduced by one eighth. . . . The agreement was signed . . . and the Conseil des Prud'hommes was charged with supervising its execution, and one day per week was fixed to listen to the complaints which might arise through bad faith.

Among the manufacturers there were men who were honest and enlightened; they regarded the tariff as a necessary brake on the cupidity of several large speculators, and as a sure method of moderating disastrous market fluctuations resulting from competition. But this was the sentiment of a minority, and the news of the establishment of a tariff was no sooner known than the anger of most of the manufacturers spilled over into recriminations and menaces.

Infractions of the tariff were increasingly numerous; the Conseil des Prud'hommes, retracting its former decisions, refused to take action against those who violated the agreement; in this extreme situation the unfortunate weavers resolved to cease all work for a week; during this period they were to walk around the town calmly and without creating any disturbance, and they agreed that they would greet all those manufacturers who had kept the agreement. But this very moderation inflated the pride of their enemies. . . .

On Sunday, 20 November, a review of the National Guard was to take place on the Place Bellecour. This review brought out all the elements of the discord which existed deep within the Lyons population. . . .

Everything seemed then to announce a battle on the morrow. At the meeting held at the Prefecture . . . it was decided that the five gate-ways which led from Lyons to Croix-Rousse would be occupied from day-break; that a battalion of the National Guard of Croix-Rousse and 300 men of the line would meet at 7.00 in the morning to prevent the formation of any mobs; that four battalions of the National Guard of Lyons and one from La Guillotière would assemble at the same time in their respective positions.

On Monday, 21 November, at 7.00 or 8.00 in the morning, the workers in a body of about three or four thousand, gathered together at the Croix-Rousse.

At their head they had one of their leaders, and they were armed with sticks. Their aim was not in any sense to engage the manufacturers in battle. All they wanted was a cessation of work until the tariff was recognized, and some workers went through the workshops to bring out those of their mates who were still at work. In the meantime, fifty or sixty guards appeared, and the Commanding Officer having cried "My friends, we must sweep away that *canaille*," they advanced with bayonets. The indignant workers dashed forward, surrounded the platoon, disarmed some of the guards, and caused some of the others to flee. Soon the groups became more numerous, but they were not hostile. They spoke only of recommencing the peaceful demonstration of 25 October. With this in mind, the weavers, joining arms and walking four abreast, descended the Grand'Côte. The Infantry of the First Legion, specially formed by the manufacturers, resolutely advanced to meet the columns. Their anger had reached its highest point and several drew their cartridges from their pouches. Towards the middle of the Grand'Côte the two groups met face to face; the Infantry fired and eight workers fell seriously wounded; immediately, the column of which they were members retreated in disorder, up the Grand'Côte and back into the Croix-Rousse. In an instant the cry went up, combatants emerged from every house, armed with picks, shovels, stones, forks; some had rifles. Some individuals ran from side to side crying "To arms! Our brothers are being killed!" Barricades were erected by women and children in every street; the insurgents, in possession of two cannons belonging to the National Guard of the Croix-Rousse, began to march on Lyons, preceded by drums, and waving in the air a black banner, bearing the inscription. "Live by working or die by fighting!" It was eleven o'clock. . . .

REVIEW QUESTIONS

1. How does Blanc characterize the economic structure of Lyons's industry and the factors that produced the insurrection of 1831?
2. What were the procedures to mediate disputes between manufacturers and workers, and why did they break down?
3. What is the relationship of the state with the two disputing sides?
4. What does this account suggest about the place of workers in France's political structure?

FRANCIS PLACE

The People's Charter and National Petition

As the first movement that explicitly advocated the political rights of unpropertied laborers, Chartism is a watershed moment in European political history. Following the Reform Act of 1832, which enfranchised the upper echelons of the bourgeoisie, radical democrats broke allegiance with liberals and sought ways to renew the call for political reform. With unions outlawed in 1834, reformers turned to the strategy of petitioning parliament for reform. In 1838, Francis Place, a venerable figure in English radical politics, drew up a statement entitled the People's Charter, a set of demands presented in the National Petition submitted to parliament in 1839. Committees throughout England and Wales circulated the charter as a petition, and collected millions of signatures. The charter was presented to parliament in 1839 and 1842, and rejected. In 1848, with revolution rampant on the continent, Chartists organized six million signatures for a final petition; its submission to Parliament was demonstratively attended by 500,000 workers. England's political establishment did not bow to Chartism, but the dignity and discipline of most Chartist demonstrations commanded respect and paved the way for trade associations in 1855 and a second reform act in 1867.

From *The People's Charter and National Petition,* by Francis Place (Quigley, 1839).

Unto the Honourable the Commons of the United Kingdom of Great Britain and Ireland, in Parliament assembled, the Petition of the undersigned, their suffering Countrymen,

Humbly Sheweth,

That we, your Petitioners, dwell in a land whose merchants are noted for enterprise, whose manufacturers are very skilful, and whose workmen are proverbial for their industry.

The land itself is goodly, the soil rich, and the temperature wholesome; it is abundantly furnished with the materials of commerce and trade; it has numerous and convenient harbours; in facility of internal communication it exceeds all others.

For three-and-twenty years we have enjoyed a profound peace.

Yet, with all these elements of national prosperity, and with every disposition and capacity to take advantage of them, we find ourselves overwhelmed with public and private suffering.

We are bowed down under a load of taxes; which, notwithstanding, fall greatly short of the wants of our rulers; our traders are trembling on the verge of bankruptcy; our workmen are starving; capital brings no profit, and labour no remuneration; the home of the artificer is desolate, and the warehouse of the pawnbroker is full; the workhouse is crowded, and the manufactory is deserted.

We have looked on every side, we have searched diligently, in order to find out the causes of a distress so sore and so long continued.

We can discover none in nature, or in providence.

Heaven has dealt graciously by the people; but the foolishness of our rulers has made the goodness of God of none effect.

The energies of a mighty kingdom have been wasted in building up the power of selfish and ignorant men, and its resources squandered for their aggrandisement.

The good of a party has been advanced to the sacrifice of the good of the nation; the few have governed for the interest of the few, while the interest of the many has been neglected, or insolently and tyrannously trampled upon.

It was the fond expectation of the people that a remedy for the greater part, if not for the whole, of their grievances, would be found in the Reform Act of 1832.

They were taught to regard that Act as a wise means to a worthy end; as the machinery of an improved legislation, where the will of the masses would be at length potential.

They have been bitterly and basely deceived.

The fruit, which looked so fair to the eye, has turned to dust and ashes when gathered.

The Reform Act has effected a transfer of

power from one domineering faction to another, and left the people as helpless as before.

Our slavery has been exchanged for an apprenticeship to liberty, which has aggravated the painful feeling of our social degradation, by adding to it the sickening of still deferred hope.

We come before your Honourable House to tell you, with all humility, that this state of things must not be permitted to continue, that it cannot long continue without very seriously endangering the stability of the throne, and the peace of the kingdom; that if, by God's help, and all lawful and constitutional appliances, an end can be put to it, we are fully resolved that it shall speedily come to an end.

We tell your Honourable House, that the capital of the master must no longer be deprived of its due profit; that the labour of the workman must no longer be deprived of its due reward; that the laws which make food dear, and those which, by making money scarce, make labour cheap, must be abolished; that taxation must be made to fall on property, not on industry; that the good of the many, as it is the only legitimate end, so must it be the sole study of the government.

As a preliminary essential to these and other requisite changes; as the means by which alone the interests of the people can be effectually vindicated and secured, we demand that those interests be confided to the keeping of the people.

When the State calls for defenders, when it calls for money, no consideration of poverty or ignorance can be pleaded in refusal or delay of the call.

Required as we are, universally, to support and to obey the laws, nature and reason entitle us to demand that, in the making of the laws, the universal voice shall be implicitly listened to.

We perform the duties of freemen: we must have the privileges.

We Demand Universal Suffrage.

The Suffrage, to be exempt from the corruption of the wealthy and the violence of the powerful, must be secret.

The assertion of our right necessarily involves the power of its uncontrolled exercise.

We ask for the reality of a good, not for its semblance.

We Demand the Ballot.

The connection between the representatives and the people, to be beneficial, must be intimate.

The legislative and constituent powers, for correction and for instruction, ought to be brought into frequent contact.

Errors, which are comparatively light when susceptible of a speedy popular remedy, may produce the most disastrous effect when permitted to grow inveterate through years of compulsory endurance.

To public safety, as well as public confidence, frequent elections are essential.

We Demand Annual Parliaments.

With power to choose, and freedom in choosing, the range of our choice must be unrestricted.

We are compelled by the existing law, to take for our representatives, men who are incapable of appreciating our difficulties, or who have little sympathy with them; merchants who have retired from trade, and no longer feel its harassings; proprietors of land, who are alike ignorant of its evils and their cures; lawyers, by whom the honours of the Senate are sought after only as a means of obtaining notice in the Courts.

The labours of a representative, who is sedulous in the discharge of his duty, are numerous and burdensome.

It is neither just, nor reasonable, nor safe, that they should continue to be gratuitously rendered.

We demand that, in the future election of Members of your Honourable House, the approbation of the constituency shall be the sole qualification; and that, to every representative so chosen, shall be assigned, out of the public taxes, a fair and adequate remuneration for the time which he is called upon to devote to the public service.

Finally, we would most earnestly impress on your Honourable House, that this petition has not been dictated by any idle love of change; that it springs out of no inconsiderate attachment to fanciful theories—but that it is the result of much and long deliberation, and of convictions, which the events of each succeeding year tend more and more to strengthen.

The management of this mighty kingdom has hitherto been a subject for contending factions, to try their selfish experiments upon.

We have felt the consequences, in our sorrowful experience—short glimmerings of uncertain enjoyment, swallowed up by long and dark seasons of suffering.

If the self-government of the people should not remove their distresses, it will at least remove their repinings.

Universal Suffrage will, and it alone can, bring true and lasting peace to the nation; we firmly believe that it will bring prosperity.

May it, therefore, please your Honourable House to take this our Petition into your most serious consideration; and to use your utmost endeavours, by all constitutional means, to have a law passed granting to every male of lawful age, sane mind, and unconvicted of crime, the right of voting for Members of Parliament; and directing all future elections of Members of Parliament to be in the way of secret ballot; and ordaining that the duration of Parliament so chosen shall in no case exceed one year; and abolishing all property qualifications in the Members: and providing for their due remuneration while in attendance on their Parliamentary duties.

And your Petitioners, &c.

REVIEW QUESTIONS

1. What were, according to the petition, the economic and political circumstances that occasioned this plea?
2. What are the specific points of the petition, and what do these demands implicitly reveal about British political culture in the 1830s?
3. How radical were these demands, and why were they unacceptable to Parliament?

HEINRICH HEINE

"The Silesian Weavers"

In the following poem of 1844, Heinrich Heine, an exiled German writer and poet, aimed his satiric scorn at the Prussian state, which showed little aptitude in handling the widespread economic desperation of its provinces in the "hungry forties." The poem immortalized the plight of a once-proud class of Silesian linen weavers reduced to starvation wages because of mechanized cotton weaving and a declining demand in linen. In June 1844 Silesian weavers assembled before prominent merchants' houses to protest starvation wages; government intervention left eleven protesters dead. The poem, which follows the rhythm of a loom, exemplifies a body of politically engaged literature of the 1840s that adumbrated the social necessity of revolution.

From *The Norton Anthology of World Masterpieces*, edited by Mack, et al., translated by Aaron Kramer (New York: Norton, 1992).

In gloomy eyes there wells no tear.
Grinding their teeth, they are sitting here:
"Germany, your shroud's on our loom;
And in it we weave the threefold doom.
  We weave; we weave.

"Doomed be the God who was deaf to our prayer
In Winter's cold and hunger's despair.
All in vain we hoped and bided;
He only mocked us, hoaxed, derided—
  We weave; we weave.

"Doomed be the king, the rich man's king,
Who would not be moved by our suffering,
Who tore the last coin out of our hands,
And let us be shot by his blood-thirsty bands—
  We weave; we weave.

"Doomed be the fatherland, false name,
Where nothing thrives but disgrace and shame,

Where flowers are crushed before they unfold,
Where the worm is quickened by rot and mold—
  We weave; we weave.

"The loom is creaking, the shuttle flies;
Nor night nor day do we close our eyes.
Old Germany, your shroud's on our loom,
And in it we weave the threefold doom;
  We weave; we weave!"

REVIEW QUESTIONS

1. What is the "threefold doom," and how is the poem politically charged?
2. How does Heine evoke desperation and despair?
3. What does Heine mean by "Old Germany" in the last stanza?

KARL MARX AND FRIEDRICH ENGELS

FROM *Manifesto of the Communist Party*

Written in 1847 to proclaim the existence of a newly constituted—and miniscule—revolutionary party, the manifesto subsequently became the most widely read political pamphlet in modern European history. Written by Karl Marx and Friedrich Engels, the manifesto's success is grounded in its dramatic, confident presentation of the socialist blueprint for social development and political emancipation. Divided into three sections, the pamphlet outlines the class struggle between the bourgeoisie and the proletariat, the final stage of history under communism, and, finally, the false promises of competing socialist doctrines. The passage below is an excerpt of the first section, which boldly lays out the economic process by which the bourgeoisie and the capitalist mode of production would falter and surrender to the next stage of history.

From *The Marx-Engels Reader,* edited by Robert C. Tucker (2d ed.; New York: Norton, 1978), pp. 56–62.

A spectre is haunting Europe—the spectre of Communism. All the Powers of old Europe have entered into a holy alliance to exorcise this spectre: Pope and Czar, Metternich and Guizot, French Radicals and German police-spies.

To this end, Communists of various nationalities have assembled in London, and sketched the following Manifesto, to be published in the English, French, German, Italian, Flemish and Danish languages.

*   *   *

I. Bourgeois and Proletarians

The history of all hitherto existing society is the history of class struggles.

Freeman and slave, patrician and plebeian, lord and serf, guild-master and journeyman, in a word, oppressor and oppressed, stood in constant opposition to one another, carried on an uninterrupted, now hidden, now open fight, a fight that each time ended, either in a revolutionary reconstitution of society at large, or in the common ruin of the contending classes.

In the earlier epochs of history, we find almost everywhere a complicated arrangement of society into various orders, a manifold gradation of social rank. In ancient Rome we have patricians, knights, plebeians, slaves; in the Middle Ages, feudal lords, vassals, guild-masters, journeymen, apprentices, serfs; in almost all of these classes, again, subordinate gradations.

The modern bourgeois society that has sprouted from the ruins of feudal society has not done away with clash antagonisms. It has but established new classes, new conditions of oppression, new forms of struggle in place of the old ones.

Our epoch, the epoch of the bourgeoisie, possesses, however, this distinctive feature: it has simplified the class antagonisms: Society as a whole is more and more splitting up into two great hostile camps, into two great classes directly facing each other: Bourgeoisie and Proletariat.

*   *   *

The feudal system of industry, under which industrial production was monopolised by closed guilds, now no longer sufficed for the growing wants of the new markets. The manufacturing system took its place. The guild-masters were pushed on one side by the manufacturing middle class; division of labour between the different corporate guilds vanished in the face of division of labour in each single workshop.

*   *   *

Modern industry has established the world-market, for which the discovery of America paved the way. This market has given an immense development to commerce, to navigation, to communication by land. This development has, in its turn, reacted on the extension of industry; and in proportion as industry, commerce, navigation, railways extended, in the same proportion the bourgeoisie developed, increased its capital, and pushed into the background every class handed down from the Middle Ages.

*   *   *

The bourgeoisie, historically, has played a most revolutionary part.

The bourgeoisie, wherever it has got the upper hand, has put an end to all feudal, patriarchal, idyllic relations. It has pitilessly torn asunder the motley feudal ties that bound man to his "natural superiors," and has left remaining no other nexus between man and man than naked self-interest, than callous "cash payment." It has drowned the most heavenly ecstasies of religious fervour, of chivalrous enthusiasm, of philistine sentimentalism, in the icy water of egotistical calculation. It has resolved personal worth into exchange value, and in place of the numberless indefeasible chartered freedoms, has set up that single, unconscionable freedom—Free Trade. In one word, for exploitation, veiled by religious and political illusions, it has substituted naked, shameless, direct, brutal exploitation.

* * *

The bourgeoisie cannot exist without constantly revolutionising the instruments of production, and thereby the relations of production, and with them the whole relations of society. Conservation of the old modes of production in unaltered form, was, on the contrary, the first condition of existence for all earlier industrial classes. Constant revolutionising of production, uninterrupted disturbance of all social conditions, everlasting uncertainty and agitation distinguish the bourgeois epoch from all earlier ones. All fixed, fast-frozen relations, with their train of ancient and venerable prejudices and opinions, are swept away, all new-formed ones become antiquated before they can ossify. All that is solid melts into air, all that is holy is profaned, and man is at last compelled to face with sober senses, his real conditions of life, and his relations with his kind.

The need of a constantly expanding market for its products chases the bourgeoisie over the whole surface of the globe. It must nestle everywhere, settle everywhere, establish connexions everywhere.

* * *

The bourgeoisie, during its rule of scarce one hundred years, has created more massive and more colossal productive forces than have all preceding generations together. Subjection of Na-

ture's forces to man, machinery, application of chemistry to industry and agriculture, steam-navigation, railways, electric telegraphs, clearing of whole continents for cultivation, canalisation of rivers, whole populations conjured out of the ground—what earlier century had even a presentiment that such productive forces slumbered in the lap of social labour?

We see then: the means of production and of exchange, on whose foundation the bourgeoisie built itself up, were generated in feudal society. At a certain stage in the development of these means of production and of exchange, the conditions under which feudal society produced and exchanged, the feudal organisation of agriculture and manufacturing industry, in one word, the feudal relations of property became no longer compatible with the already developed productive forces; they became so many fetters. They had to be burst asunder; they were burst asunder.

Into their place stepped free competition, accompanied by a social and political constitution adapted to it, and by the economical and political sway of the bourgeois class.

* * *

Modern bourgeois society with its relations of production, of exchange and of property, a society that has conjured up such gigantic means of production and of exchange, is like the sorcerer, who is no longer able to control the powers of the nether world whom he has called up by his spells. For many a decade past the history of industry and commerce is but the history of the revolt of modern productive forces against modern conditions of production, against the property relations that are the conditions for the existence of the bourgeoisie and of its rule. It is enough to mention the commercial crises that by their periodical return put on its trial, each time more threateningly, the existence of the entire bourgeois society. In these crises a great part not only of the existing products, but also of the previously created productive forces, are periodically destroyed. In these crises there breaks out an epidemic that, in all earlier epochs, would have seemed an absurdity—the epidemic of over-production. Society suddenly finds itself put back into a state of momentary barbarism; it appears as if a famine, a universal war of devastation had cut off the supply of every means of subsistence; industry and commerce seem to be destroyed; and why? Because there is too much civilisation, too much means of subsistence, too much industry, too much commerce. The productive forces at the disposal of society no longer tend to further the development of the conditions of bourgeois property; on the contrary, they have become too powerful for these conditions, by which they are fettered, and so soon as they overcome these fetters, they bring disorder into the whole of bourgeois society, endanger the existence of bourgeois property. The conditions of bourgeois society are too narrow to comprise the wealth created by them. And how does the bourgeoisie get over these crises? On the one hand by enforced destruction of a mass of productive forces; on the other, by the conquest of new markets, and by the more thorough exploitation of the old ones. That is to say, by paving the way for more extensive and more destructive crises, and by diminishing the means whereby crises are prevented.

The weapons with which the bourgeoisie felled feudalism to the ground are now turned against the bourgeoisie itself.

But not only has the bourgeoisie forged the weapons that bring death to itself; it has also called into existence the men who are to wield those weapons—the modern working class—the proletarians.

In proportion as the bourgeoisie, i.e., capital, is developed, in the same proportion is the proletariat, the modern working class, developed—a class of labourers, who live only so long as they find work, and who find work only so long as their labour increases capital. These labourers, who must sell themselves piece-meal, are a commodity, like every other article of commerce, and are consequently exposed to all the vicissitudes of competition, to all the fluctuations of the market.

*   *   *

The proletariat goes through various stages of development. With its birth begins its struggle with the bourgeoisie. At first the contest is carried on by individual labourers, then by the workpeople of a factory, then by the operatives of one trade, in one locality, against the individual bourgeois who directly exploits them. They direct their attacks not against the bourgeois conditions of production, but against the instruments of production themselves; they destroy imported wares that compete with their labour, they smash to pieces machinery, they set factories ablaze, they seek to restore by force the vanished status of the workman of the Middle Ages.

*   *   *

But with the development of industry the proletariat not only increases in number; it becomes concentrated in greater masses, its strength grows, and it feels that strength more. The various interests and conditions of life within the ranks of the proletariat are more and more equalised, in proportion as machinery obliterates all distinctions of labour, and nearly everywhere reduces wages to the same low level. The growing competition among the bourgeois, and the resulting commercial crises, make the wages of the workers ever more fluctuating. The unceasing improvement of machinery, ever more rapidly developing, makes their livelihood more and more precarious; the collisions between individual workmen and individual bourgeois take more and more the character of collisions between two classes. Thereupon the workers begin to form combinations (Trades Unions) against the bourgeois; they club together in order to keep up the rate of wages; they found permanent associations in order to make provision beforehand for these occasional revolts. Here and there the contest breaks out into riots.

*   *   *

This organisation of the proletarians into a class, and consequently into a political party, is continually being upset again by the competition between the workers themselves. But it ever rises up again, stronger, firmer, mightier. It compels legislative recognition of particular interests of the workers, by taking advantage of the divisions among the bourgeoisie itself. Thus the ten-hours' bill in England was carried.

*   *   *

Of all the classes that stand face to face with the bourgeoisie today, the proletariat alone is a really revolutionary class. The other classes decay and finally disappear in the face of Modern Industry; the proletariat is its special and essential product.

*   *   *

All previous historical movements were movements of minorities, or in the interests of minorities. The proletarian movement is the self-conscious, independent movement of the immense majority, in the interests of the immense majority. The proletariat, the lowest stratum of our present society, cannot stir, cannot raise itself up, without the whole superincumbent strata of official society being sprung into the air.

Though not in substance, yet in form, the struggle of the proletariat with the bourgeoisie is at first a national struggle. The proletariat of each country must, of course, first of all settle matters with its own bourgeoisie.

In depicting the most general phases of the development of the proletariat, we traced the more or less veiled civil war, raging within existing society, up to the point where that war breaks out into open revolution, and where the violent overthrow of the bourgeoisie lays the foundation for the sway of the proletariat.

Hitherto, every form of society has been based, as we have already seen, on the antagonism of oppressing and oppressed classes. But in order to oppress a class, certain conditions must be assured to it under which it can, at least, continue its slavish existence. The serf, in the period of serfdom, raised himself to membership in the commune, just as the petty bourgeois, under the yoke of feudal absolutism, managed to develop into a bour-

geois. The modern labourer, on the contrary, instead of rising with the progress of industry, sinks deeper and deeper below the conditions of existence of his own class. He becomes a pauper, and pauperism develops more rapidly than population and wealth. And here it becomes evident, that the bourgeoisie is unfit any longer to be the ruling class in society, and to impose its conditions of existence upon society as an over-riding law. It is unfit to rule because it is incompetent to assure an existence to its slave within his slavery, because it cannot help letting him sink into such a state, that it has to feed him, instead of being fed by him. Society can no longer live under this bourgeoisie, in other words, its existence is no longer compatible with society.

The essential condition for the existence, and for the sway of the bourgeois class, is the formation and augmentation of capital; the condition for capital is wage-labour. Wage-labour rests exclusively on competition between the labourers. The advance of industry, whose involuntary promoter is the bourgeoisie, replaces the isolation of the labourers, due to competition, by their revolutionary combination, due to association. The development of Modern Industry, therefore, cuts from under its feet the very foundation on which the bourgeoisie produces and appropriates products. What the bourgeoisie, therefore, produces, above all, is its own grave-diggers. Its fall and the victory of the proletariat are equally inevitable.

*   *   *

REVIEW QUESTIONS

1. According to Marx, what is the role of the bourgeoisie in world history?
2. How does Marx characterize the evolution of working-class political consciousness?
3. What does Marx mean by saying the bourgeoisie are their "own gravediggers"?

LONDON NOMADES (1877)   John Thomson

*Since the early nineteenth century descriptions about the "dangerous classes" of urban slums
had developed a consciousness of class difference in modern cities. With the advent of photography, however, a new medium emerged that claimed to document truth. In spite of the
camera's "objective" lens, early photography of the London poor manifested the same subjectivity of urban lower classes as did earlier drawings and narrative accounts. John Thomson's photograph,* London Nomades, *printed in his popular* Street Life in London *(1877)
is a case in point. What assumptions about the urban poor might images such as this have
fostered or reinforced?*

SAM SMILES

FROM *Thrift*

One of the most powerful ideological buttresses of the bourgeois social order was the doctrine of self-help. The Scottish author Sam Smiles (1812–1904) achieved enormous success in a number of books that presented the virtues of self-reliance and self-education in an appealing and accessible manner. His biography of George Stephenson, the self-made railroad engineer, was followed by Self-Help *(1859), a primer on individualism that was translated into seventeen languages. The book's success spawned similar works:* Character *(1871),* Thrift *(1875), and* Duty *(1880). The following section from* Thrift *is particularly characeristic of his avuncular style and his themes of sobriety and frugality.*

From *Thrift,* by Sam Smiles (London: Murray, 1875).

Improvidence

*   *   *

England is one of the richest countries in the world. Our merchants are enterprizing, our manufacturers are industrious, our labourers are hardworking. There is an accumulation of wealth in the country to which past times can offer no parallel. The Bank is gorged with gold. There never was more food in the empire; there never was more money. There is no end to our manufacturing productions, for the steam-engine never tires. And yet, notwithstanding all this wealth, there is an enormous mass of poverty. Close alongside the Wealth of Nations, there gloomily stalks the Misery of Nations,—luxurious ease resting upon a dark background of wretchedness.

Parliamentary reports have again and again revealed to us the miseries endured by certain portions of our working population. They have described the people employed in factories, workshops, mines, and brick-fields, as well as in the pursuits of country life. We have tried to grapple with the evils of their condition by legislation, but it seems to mock us. Those who sink into poverty are fed, but they remain paupers. Those who feed them, feel no compassion; and those who are fed, return no gratitude. There is no bond of sympathy between the givers and the receivers. Thus the Haves and the Have-nots, the opulent and the indigent, stand at the two extremes of the social scale, and a wide gulf is fixed between them.

*   *   *

With respect to the poorer classes, * * *

They work, eat, drink, and sleep: that constitutes their life. They think nothing of providing for to-morrow, or for next week, or for next year. They abandon themselves to their sensual appetites; and make no provision whatever for the future. The thought of adversity, or of coming sorrow, or of the helplessness that comes with years and sickness, never crosses their minds. In these respects, they resemble the savage tribes, who know no better, and do no worse. Like the North American Indians, they debase themselves by the vices which accompany civilization, but make no use whatever of its benefits and advantages.

*   *   *

No one can reproach the English workman with want of industry. He works harder and more skilfully than the workman of any other country; and he might be more comfortable and independent in his circumstances, were he as prudent as he is laborious. But improvidence is unhappily the defect of the class. Even the best-paid English workmen, though earning more money than the average of professional men, still for the most part belong to the poorer classes because of their thoughtlessness. In prosperous times they are not accustomed to make provision for adverse times; and when a period of social pressure occurs, they are rarely found more than a few weeks ahead of positive want.

*   *   *

Though trade has invariably its cycles of good and bad years, like the lean and fat kine in Pharaoh's dream—its bursts of prosperity, followed by glut, panic, and distress—the thoughtless and spendthrift take no heed of experience, and make no better provision for the future. Improvidence seems to be one of the most incorrigible of faults. "There are whole neighbourhoods in the manufacturing districts," says Mr. Baker in a recent Report, "where not only are there no savings worth mentioning, but where, within a fortnight of being out of work, the workers themselves are starving for want of the merest necessaries." Not a strike takes place, but immediately the workmen are plunged in destitution; their furniture and watches are sent to the pawnshop, whilst deplorable appeals are made to the charitable, and numerous families are cast upon the poor-rates.

This habitual improvidence—though of course there are many admirable exceptions—is the real cause of the social degradation of the artizan. This too is the prolific source of social misery. But the misery is entirely the result of human ignorance and self-indulgence. For though the Creator has ordained poverty, the poor are not necessarily, nor as a matter of fact, the miserable. Misery is the result of moral causes, most commonly of individual vice and improvidence.

*   *   *

We have certainly had numerous "Reforms." We have had household suffrage, and vote by ballot. We have relieved the working classes of the taxes on corn, cattle, coffee, sugar, and provisions generally; and imposed a considerable proportion of the taxes from which they have been relieved on the middle and upper ranks. Yet these measures have produced but little improvement in the condition of the working people. They have not applied the principle of Reform to themselves. They have not begun at home. Yet the end of all Reform is the improvement of the individual. Everything that is wrong in Society results from that which is wrong in the Individual. When men are bad, society is bad.

*   *   *

Complaining that the laws are bad, and that the taxes are heavy, will not mend matters. Aristocratic government, and the tyranny of masters, are nothing like so injurious as the tyranny of vicious appetites. Men are easily led away by the parade of their miseries, which are for the most part voluntary and self-imposed, the results of idleness, thriftlessness, intemperance, and misconduct. To blame others for what we suffer, is always more agreeable to our self-pride, than to blame ourselves. But it is perfectly clear that people who live from day to day without plan, without rule, without forethought—who spend all their earnings, without saving anything for the future—are preparing beforehand for inevitable distress. To provide only for the present, is the sure means of sacrificing the future. What hope can there be for a people whose only maxim seems to be, "Let us eat and drink, for to-morrow we die"?

All this may seem very hopeless; yet it is not entirely so. The large earnings of the working classes is an important point to start with. The gradual diffusion of education will help them to use, and not abuse, their means of comfortable living. The more extended knowledge of the uses of economy, frugality, and thrift, will help them to spend their lives more soberly, virtuously, and religiously.

*   *   *

REVIEW QUESTIONS

1. What does Smiles attribute to most workers' impoverished condition?
2. What worth does Smile ascribe to reform laws for the worker, and what is for him the genuine source of improvement?
3. How does Smiles's argument compare with Engels's or Tristan's account of workers' improvidence?

ISABELLA BEETON

FROM *The Book of Household Management*

First published in serial form in 1859–1861, The Book of Household Management *remained in print for the remainder of the century, establishing itself as a self-evident necessity for bourgeois Victorian households. Today the book serves as an excellent example of prescriptive literature: a source documenting how proper bourgeois families ought to have led their social and domestic lives. The book provided a broad window on Victorian tastes in food, bourgeois attitudes toward other classes, and proper comportment in and outside the home. The following section is taken from the book's first chapter, which sets rules of conduct for the mistress of the household.*

From *Mrs. Beeton's Book of Household Management,* by Isabella Beeton (London: Chancellor Press, 1982).

The Mistress

*   *   *

1. As with the Commander of an Army, or the leader of any enterprise, so is it with the mistress of a house. Her spirit will be seen through the whole establishment; and just in proportion as she performs her duties intelligently and thoroughly, so will her domestics follow in her path. Of all those acquirements, which more particularly belong to the feminine character, there are none which take a higher rank, in our estimation, than such as enter into a knowledge of household duties; for on these are perpetually dependent the happiness, comfort, and well-being of a family. In this opinion we are borne out by the author of "The Vicar of Wakefield," who says: "The modest virgin, the prudent wife, and the careful matron, are much more serviceable in life than petticoated philosophers, blustering heroines, or virago queens. She who makes her husband and her children happy, who reclaims the one from vice and trains up the other to virtue, is a much greater character than ladies described in romances, whose whole occupation is to murder mankind with shafts from their quiver, or their eyes."

2. Pursuing this Picture, we may add, that to be a good housewife does not necessarily imply an abandonment of proper pleasures or amusing recreation; and we think it the more necessary to express this, as the performance of the duties of a mistress may, to some minds, perhaps seem to be incompatible with the enjoyment of life. Let us,

however, now proceed to describe some of those home qualities and virtues which are necessary to the proper management of a Household, and then point out the plan which may be the most profitably pursued for the daily regulation of its affairs.

3. Early Rising is one of the most Essential Qualities which enter into good Household Management, as it is not only the parent of health, but of innumerable other advantages. Indeed, when a mistress is an early riser, it is almost certain that her house will be orderly and well-managed. On the contrary, if she remain in bed till a late hour, then the domestics, who, as we have before observed, invariably partake somewhat of their mistress's character, will surely become sluggards. To self-indulgence all are more or less disposed, and it is not to be expected that servants are freer from this fault than the heads of houses. The great Lord Chatham thus gave his advice in reference to this subject:—"I would have inscribed on the curtains of your bed, and the walls of your chamber, 'If you do not rise early, you can make progress in nothing.'"

4. Cleanliness is also indispensable to Health, and must be studied both in regard to the person and the house, and all that it contains. Cold or tepid baths should be employed every morning, unless, on account of illness or other circumstances, they should be deemed objectionable. The bathing of *children* will be treated of under the head of "MANAGEMENT OF CHILDREN."

5. Frugality and Economy are Home Virtues, without which no household can prosper. Dr. Johnson says: "Frugality may be termed the daughter of Prudence, the sister of Temperance, and the parent of Liberty. He that is extravagant will quickly become poor, and poverty will enforce dependence and invite corruption." The necessity of practising economy should be evident to every one, whether in the possession of an income no more than sufficient for a family's requirements, or of a large fortune, which puts financial adversity out of the question. We must always remember that it is a great merit in housekeeping to manage a little well. "He is a good waggoner," says Bishop Hall, "that can turn in a little room. To

live well in abundance is the praise of the estate, not of the person. I will study more how to give a good account of my little, than how to make it more." In this there is true wisdom, and it may be added, that those who can manage a little well, are most likely to succeed in their management of larger matters. Economy and frugality must never, however, be allowed to degenerate into parsimony and meanness.

* * *

13. The Dress of the Mistress should always be adapted to her circumstances, and be varied with different occasions. Thus, at breakfast she should be attired in a very neat and simple manner, wearing no ornaments. If this dress should decidedly pertain only to the breakfast-hour, and be specially suited for such domestic occupations as usually follow that meal, then it would be well to exchange it before the time for receiving visitors, if the mistress be in the habit of doing so. It is still to be remembered, however, that, in changing the dress, jewellery and ornaments are not to be worn until the full dress for dinner is assumed. Further information and hints on the subject of the toilet will appear under the department of the "LADY'S-MAID."

* * *

16. A Housekeeping Account-book should invariably be kept, and kept punctually and precisely. The plan for keeping household accounts, which we should recommend, would be to make an entry, that is, write down into a daily diary every amount paid on that particular day, be it ever so small; then, at the end of the month, let these various payments be ranged under their specific heads of Butcher, Baker, &c.; and thus will be seen the proportions paid to each tradesman, and any one month's expenses may be contrasted with another. The housekeeping accounts should be balanced not less than once a month; so that you may see that the money you have in hand tallies with your account of it in your diary. Judge Haliburton never wrote truer words than when he said,

No man is rich whose expenditure exceeds his means, and no one is poor whose incomings exceed his outgoings.

When, in a large establishment, a housekeeper is kept, it will be advisable for the mistress to examine her accounts regularly. Then any increase of expenditure which may be apparent, can easily be explained, and the housekeeper will have the satisfaction of knowing whether her efforts to manage her department well and economically, have been successful.

17. Engaging Domestics is one of those duties in which the judgment of the mistress must be keenly exercised. There are some respectable registry-offices, where good servants may sometimes be hired; but the plan rather to be recommended is, for the mistress to make inquiry amongst her circle of friends and acquaintances, and her tradespeople. The latter generally know those in their neighbourhood, who are wanting situations, and will communicate with them, when a personal interview with some of them will enable the mistress to form some idea of the characters of the applicants, and to suit herself accordingly.

We would here point out an error—and a grave one it is—into which some mistresses fall. They do not, when engaging a servant, expressly tell her all the duties which she will be expected to perform. This is an act of omission severely to be reprehended. Every portion of work which the maid will have to do, should be plainly stated by the mistress, and understood by the servant. If this plan is not carefully adhered to, domestic contention is almost certain to ensue, and this may not be easily settled; so that a change of servants, which is so much to be deprecated, is continually occurring.

18. In obtaining a Servant's Character, it is not well to be guided by a written one from some unknown quarter; but it is better to have an interview, if at all possible, with the former mistress. By this means you will be assisted in your decision of the suitableness of the servant for your place, from the appearance of the lady and the state of her house. Negligence and want of cleanliness in her and her household generally, will naturally lead you to the conclusion, that her servant has suffered from the influence of the bad example.

The proper course to pursue in order to obtain a personal interview with the lady is this:—The servant in search of the situation must be desired to see her former mistress, and ask her to be kind enough to appoint a time, convenient to herself, when you may call on her; this proper observance of courtesy being necessary to prevent any unseasonable intrusion on the part of a stranger. Your first questions should be relative to the honesty and general morality of her former servant; and if no objection is stated in that respect, her other qualifications are then to be ascertained. Inquiries should be very minute, so that you may avoid disappointment and trouble, by knowing the weak points of your domestic.

19. The Treatment of Servants is of the highest possible moment, as well to the mistress as to the domestics themselves. On the head of the house the latter will naturally fix their attention; and if they perceive that the mistress's conduct is regulated by high and correct principles, they will not fail to respect her. If, also, a benevolent desire is shown to promote their comfort, at the same time that a steady performance of their duty is exacted, then their respect will not be unmingled with affection, and they will be still more solicitous to continue to deserve her favour.

*   *   *

REVIEW QUESTIONS

1. According to Beeton, what are the duties and expectations of bourgeois women?
2. What virtues and attitudes are extolled?
3. What does she reveal about the way bourgeois families lived?
4. What are the shortcomings of such prescriptive literature?

ELIZABETH POOLE SANFORD

FROM *Woman in Her Social and Domestic Character*

The widened separation of domestic and public spheres in the nineteenth century brought with it fundamental changes in the economic and social roles of bourgeois women. No longer expected to work in the productive sphere, middle-class married women took on domestic, motherly, and religious duties. Not surprisingly, character-ological assumptions accompanied this role of the "angel in the house." Alongside purity, delicacy, and virtue, subservience to husbands was foremost among the traits considered desirable for women. The following excerpt from Elizabeth Poole San-ford's book (1833) is an early example of the prescriptive literature aimed at middle-class women of the Victorian era.

From *Woman in Her Social and Domestic Character,* by Elizabeth Poole Sanford (Boston: Bowles, 1833).

*   *   *

Domestic comfort is the chief source of her influence, and the greatest debt society owes her; for happiness is almost an element of virtue, and nothing conduces more to improve the character of men than domestic peace. A woman may make a man's home delightful, and may thus increase his motives for virtuous exertion. She may refine and tranquillise his mind,—may turn away his anger or allay his grief. Her smile may be the happy influence to gladden his heart, and to disperse the cloud that gathers on his brow. And she will be loved in proportion as she makes those around her happy,—as she studies their tastes, and sympathises in their feelings. In social relations adaptation is therefore the true secret of her influence.

*   *   *

Domestic life is a woman's sphere, and it is there that she is most usefully as well as most appropriately employed. But society, too, feels her influence, and owes to her, in great measure, its balance and its tone. She may be here a corrective of what is wrong, a moderator of what is unruly, a restraint on what is indecorous. Her presence may be a pledge against impropriety and excess, a check on vice, and a protection to virtue.

And it is her delicacy which will secure to her such an influence, and enable her to maintain it. It is the policy of licentiousness to undermine where it cannot openly attack, and to weaken by stratagem what it may not rudely assail. But a delicate woman will be as much upon her guard against the insidious as against the direct assault, and will no more tolerate the innuendo than the avowal. She will shrink from the licentiousness which is couched in ambiguous phrase or veiled in covert allusion, and from the immorality which, though it may not offend the ear, is meant to corrupt the heart. And though a depraved taste may relish the condiments of vice, or an unscrupulous palate receive them without detection, her virtue will be too sensitive not to reject the poison, and to recoil spontaneously from the touch.

Delicacy is, indeed, the point of honor in woman. And her purity of manner will ensure to her deference, and repress, more effectually than any other influence, impropriety of every kind. A delicate woman, too, will be more loved, as well as more respected, than any other; for affection can scarcely be excited, and certainly cannot long subsist, unless it is founded on esteem.

Yet such delicacy is neither prudish nor insipid. Conversation, for instance, is one great source of a woman's influence; and it is her province, and her peculiar talent, to give zest to it. She is, and ought to be, the enlivener of society: if she restrains impropriety, she may promote cheerfulness; and it is not because her conversation is innocent that it need therefore be dull. The sentiment of woman contributes much to social interest: her feeling imparts life, and her gentleness a polish.

*   *   *

Again, to be agreeable, a woman must avoid egotism. It is no matter how superior she is, she will never be liked, if she talks chiefly of herself. The impression of her own importance can convey no pleasure to others: on the contrary, as a desire for distinction is always mutual, a sense of inferiority must be depressing.

If we would converse pleasingly, we must endeavor to set others at ease: and it is not by flattery that we can succeed in doing so, but by a courteous and kind address, which delicately avoids all needless irritation, and endeavors to infuse that good humor of which it is itself the result.

In woman this is a Christian duty. How often should they suppress their own claims rather than interfere with those of others! How often should they employ their talent in developing that of their associates, and not for its own display! How invariably should they discard pretension, and shun even the appearance of conceit; and seek to imbibe the spirit of that lovely religion, of which sympathy is the characteristic feature, and humility the pre-eminent grace!

*   *   *

It is seldom, indeed, that women are great proficients. The *chefs-d'œuvre* of the sculptress need the polish of the master chisel; and the female pencil has never yet limned the immortal forms of beauty. The mind of woman is, perhaps, incapable of the originality and strength requisite for the sublime. Even Saint Cecilia exists only in an elegant legend, and the poetry of music, if often felt and expressed, has seldom been conceived by a female adept. But the practical talents of women are far from contemptible; and they may be both the encouragers and the imitators of genius. They should not grasp at too much, nor be content with superficial attainment; they should not merely daub a few flowers, or hammer out a few tunes, or trifle away their time in inept efforts, which at best claim only indulgence; but they should do well what they do attempt, and do it without affectation or display.

*   *   *

Review Questions

1. According to Sanford, what were the character traits assigned to women, and for what goals should women strive?
2. What attributes constituted the domestic sphere of women?
3. What is the ideal relationship between husband and wife, and how is this justified?

23 ⚬⌁ REVOLUTION AND LIBERAL REFORM, 1815–1870

At the core of most discussions explaining change from the traditional to the modern world lies an evolving form of liberalism. After the Glorious Revolution in England, elements of a liberal social contract emerged, many of which have been accented in earlier chapters: individual liberties guaranteed by constitutional law; the sanctity of private property; unrestricted movement of individuals, ideas, and goods; and, finally, social advancement based on merit. Such beliefs irreparably undermined the social foundations of the old regime.

The principles of the Enlightenment and liberalism largely overlap. Liberalism, for example, inherited the Enlightenment's emphasis on reason, social utility, pragmatic reform, and aversion to arbitrary rule. Above all, both embraced the indomitable belief in progress. The French Revolution, however, significantly affected liberalism's development. Shaped by the experiences of the Terror and Napoleonic demagoguery, liberals reasserted the Lockian emphasis on the limits of power that public authority held over the individual. Governments based on popular will, they argued, could be as despotic as absolutist monarchy, for they sacrificed individual liberties in the name of general welfare and collective happiness. For liberals, the whole could never be greater than the sum of its parts; the irreducible unit of a free civil society remained the individual, not the general will. Following classical economic theory, liberals averred that the "invisible hand" of individual self-interest best secured the greater good of society. Liberalism further distinguished itself from democracy by rejecting universal human suffrage, assigning those classes lacking property and education merely passive rights of citizenship. Consequently, liberalism evolved into a solidly bourgeois ideology.

For the traditional elite, liberalism remained a subversive threat. Its advocacy of constitutions, civil liberties, and centralized government challenged the post-Napoleonic restoration of dynastic legitimacy and aristocratic privilege. Be-

cause liberals in the Italian, German, and eastern European states coupled their ideals of constitutionalism with a unified nation-state, the doctrine was doubly alarming. In the first half of the nineteenth century, conservative statesmen and rulers vigorously strove to contain the spread of liberal national ideals.

The economic and cultural dimensions of liberalism are particularly important in understanding the doctrine's impact on European society. Economically, Europeans largely associated liberalism as the promoter of laissez faire capitalism. Liberals believed that society and government were compelled to acquiesce in the natural laws of the market. Between 1840 and 1870 the doctrine of free trade assumed the status of a moral imperative for British and European liberals, who associated material wealth with the advance of civilization. If governments minimized their presence in the marketplace, liberals argued, industry and commerce could expand markets, lower the costs of food and goods, and thus lift the diligent out of privation. Culturally, liberalism advocated a secular civil society in which religion played little or no role in public affairs. Liberals viewed the Catholic Church as obscurantist, an outmoded institution that hindered the diffusion of rational, materialist knowledge. Education, the battle for childrens' minds, was a particularly devisive issue. Denying the church its traditional role as educator by instituting state-supervised school systems with national curricula and state-trained teachers became a central plank in the platform of many liberal parties.

In all its facets, liberalism was a critical agent of change in the first century of the modern era after 1789. By locating its role in such overarching themes as individualism, constitutional rights, capitalism, free trade, nationalism, and secular statebuilding, one sees liberalism as a preponderant force in nineteenth-century civil society.

MARY WOLLSTONECRAFT

FROM *A Vindication of the Rights of Woman*

Mary Wollstonecraft (1759–1797), a teacher and writer, wrote this essay as a critical response to the French Revolution. An enthusiastic supporter of the revolution, she was nonetheless angered that the national assembly did not extend the same liberties to women as to men. Her essay, appealing to reason, utility, and natural law, exhorted both men and women to reform education for women and enable them to *participate in civil society as useful members. Scorned as a radical francophile by contemporaries, her essay convincingly applies liberal reasoning to the cause of women at a critical juncture in European history.*

From *A Vindication of the Rights of Woman,* by Mary Wollstonecraft (New York: Norton, 1970).

After considering the historic page, and viewing the living world with anxious solicitude, the most melancholy emotions of sorrowful indignation have depressed my spirits, and I have sighed when obliged to confess that either Nature has made a great difference between man and man, or that the civilization which has hitherto taken place in the world has been very partial. I have turned over various books written on the subject of education, and patiently observed the conduct of parents and the management of schools; but what has been the result?— a profound conviction that the neglected education of my fellow-creatures is the grand source of the misery I deplore, and that women, in particular, are rendered weak and wretched by a variety of concurring causes, originating from one hasty conclusion. The conduct and manners of women, in fact, evidently prove that their minds are not in a healthy state; for, like the flowers which are planted in too rich a soil, strength and usefulness are sacrificed to beauty; and the flaunting leaves, after having pleased a fastidious eye, fade, disregarded on the stalk, long before the season when they ought to have arrived at maturity. One cause of this barren blooming I attribute to a false system of education, gathered from the books written on this subject by men who, considering females rather as women than human creatures, have been more anxious to make them alluring mistresses than affectionate wives and rational mothers; and the understanding of the sex has been so bubbled by this specious homage, that the civilized women of the present century, with a few exceptions, are only anxious to inspire love, when they ought to cherish a nobler ambition, and by their abilities and virtues exact respect.

In a treatise, therefore, on female rights and manners, the works which have been particularly written for their improvement must not be overlooked, especially when it is asserted, in direct terms, that the minds of women are enfeebled by false refinement; that the books of instruction, written by men of genius, have had the same tendency as more frivolous productions; and that, in the true style of Mahometanism, they are treated as a kind of subordinate beings, and not as a part of the human species, when improvable reason is allowed to be the dignified distinction which raises men above the brute creation, and puts a natural sceptre in a feeble hand.

Yet, because I am a woman, I would not lead my readers to suppose that I mean violently to agitate the contested question respecting the quality or inferiority of the sex; but as the subject lies in my way, and I cannot pass it over without subjecting the main tendency of my reasoning to misconstruction, I shall stop a moment to deliver, in a few words, my opinion. In the government of the physical world it is observable that the female in point of strength is, in general, inferior to the male. This is the law of Nature; and it does not appear to be suspended or abrogated in favour of woman. A degree of physical superiority cannot, therefore, be denied, and it is a noble prerogative! But not content with this natural pre-eminence, men endeavour to sink us still lower, merely to render us alluring objects for a moment; and women, intoxicated by the adoration which men, under the influence of their senses, pay them, do not seek to obtain a durable interest in their hearts, or to become the friends of the fellow-creatures who find amusement in their society.

I am aware of an obvious inference. From every quarter have I heard exclamations against masculine women, but where are they to be found? If by this appellation men mean to inveigh against their ardour in hunting, shooting, and gaming, I shall most cordially join in the cry; but if it be against the imitation of manly virtues, or, more properly speaking, the attainment of those talents and virtues, the exercise of which ennobles the human character, and which raises females in the scale of animal being, when they are comprehensively termed mankind, all those who view them with a philosophic eye must, I should think, wish with me, that they may every day grow more and more masculine.

This discussion naturally divides the subject. I shall first consider women in the grand light of human creatures, who, in common with men, are placed on this earth to unfold their faculties; and afterwards I shall more particularly point out their peculiar designation.

I wish also to steer clear of an error which many respectable writers have fallen into; for the instruction which has hitherto been addressed to women, has rather been applicable to *ladies,* if the little indirect advice that is scattered through "Sandford and Merton" be excepted; but, addressing my sex in a firmer tone, I pay particular attention to those in the middle class, because they appear to be in the most natural state. Perhaps the seeds of false refinement, immorality, and vanity, have ever been shed by the great. Weak, artificial beings, raised above the common wants and affections of their race, in a premature unnatural manner, undermine the very foundation of virtue, and spread corruption through the whole mass of society! As a class of mankind they have the strongest claim to pity; the education of the rich tends to render them vain and helpless, and the unfolding mind is not strengthened by the practice of those duties which dignify the human character. They only live to amuse themselves, and by the same law which in Nature invariably produces certain effects, they soon only afford barren amusement.

But as I purpose taking a separate view of the different ranks of society, and of the moral character of women in each, this hint is for the present sufficient; and I have only alluded to the subject because it appears to me to be the very essence of an introduction to give a cursory account of the contents of the work it introduces.

My own sex, I hope, will excuse me, if I treat them like rational creatures, instead of flattering their *fascinating* graces, and viewing them as if they were in a state of perpetual childhood, unable to stand alone. I earnestly wish to point out in what true dignity and human happiness consists. I wish to persuade women to endeavour to acquire strength, both of mind and body, and to convince them that the soft phrases, susceptibility of heart, delicacy of sentiment, and refinement of taste, are almost synonymous with epithets of weakness, and that those beings who are only the objects of pity, and that kind of love which has been termed its sister, will soon become objects of contempt.

Dismissing, then, those pretty feminine phrases, which the men condescendingly use to soften our slavish dependence, and despising that weak elegancy of mind, exquisite sensibility, and sweet docility of manners, supposed to be the sexual characteristics of the weaker vessel, I wish to show that elegance is inferior to virtue, that the first object of laudable ambition is to obtain a character as a human being, regardless of the distinction of sex, and that secondary views should be brought to this simple touchstone.

This is a rough sketch of my plan; and should I express my conviction with the energetic emotions that I feel whenever I think of the subject, the dictates of experience and reflection will be felt by some of my readers. Animated by this important object, I shall disdain to cull my phrases or polish my style. I aim at being useful, and sincerity will render me unaffected; for wishing rather to persuade by the force of my arguments than dazzle by the elegance of my language, I shall not waste my time in rounding periods, or in fabricating the turgid bombast of artificial feelings, which, coming from the head, never reach the heart. I shall be employed about things, not words! and, anxious to render my sex more respectable members of society, I shall try to avoid that flowery diction which has slided from essays into novels, and from novels into familiar letters and conversations.

These pretty superlatives, dropping glibly from the tongue, vitiate the taste, and create a kind of sickly delicacy that turns away from simple unadorned truth; and a deluge of false sentiments and overstretched feelings, stifling the natural emotions of the heart, render the domestic pleasures insipid, that ought to sweeten the exercise of those severe duties, which educate a rational and immortal being for a nobler field of action.

The education of women has of late been more attended to than formerly; yet they are still reckoned a frivolous sex, and ridiculed or pitied by the writers who endeavour by satire or instruction to improve them. It is acknowledged that they spend many of the first years of their lives in acquiring a smattering of accomplishments; meanwhile strength of body and mind are sacrificed to libertine notions of beauty, to the desire of establishing themselves—the only way women can rise in the world—by marriage. And this desire making mere animals of them, when they marry they act as such children may be expected to act—they dress, they paint, and nickname God's creatures. Surely these weak beings are only fit for a seraglio! Can they be expected to govern a family with judgement, or take care of the poor babes, whom they bring into the world?

If, then, it can be fairly deduced from the present conduct of the sex, from the prevalent fondness for pleasure which takes place of ambition and those nobler passions that open and enlarge the soul, that the instruction which women have hitherto received has only tended, with the constitution of civil society, to render them insignificant objects of desire—mere propagators of fools!—if it can be proved that in aiming to accomplish them, without cultivating their understandings, they are taken out of their sphere of duties, and made ridiculous and useless when the short-lived bloom of beauty is over, I presume that *rational* men will excuse me for endeavouring to persuade them to become more masculine and respectable.

Indeed the word masculine is only a bugbear; there is little reason to fear that women will acquire too much courage or fortitude, for their apparent inferiority with respect to bodily strength must render them in some degree dependent on men in the various relations of life; but why should it be increased by prejudices that give a sex to virtue, and confound simple truths with sensual reveries?

Women are, in fact, so much degraded by mistaken notions of female excellence, that I do not mean to add a paradox when I assert that this artificial weakness produces a propensity to tyrannize, and gives birth to cunning, the natural opponent of strength, which leads them to play off those contemptible infantine airs that undermine esteem even whilst they excite desire. Let men become more chaste and modest, and if women do not grow wiser in the same ratio it will be clear that they have weaker understandings. It seems scarcely necessary to say that I now speak of the sex in general. Many individuals have more sense than their male relatives; and, as nothing preponderates where there is a constant struggle for an equilibrium without it has naturally more gravity, some women govern their husbands without degrading themselves, because intellect will always govern.

REVIEW QUESTIONS

1. Why is Wollstonecraft's emphasis on education critical for her argument?
2. What are the similarities and differences between this essay and Olympe de Gouges's declaration?
3. At which social classes was this essay aimed, and what are Wollstonecraft's criticisms of the women from these classes?
4. What distinctions does Wollstonecraft make between men and women, and what is her point in drawing such distinctions?

BENJAMIN CONSTANT

FROM *The Principles of Politics*

The political writings of Benjamin Constant de Rebecque (1767–1830) addressed critical issues of popular sovereignty and individual liberty in the immediate post-revolutionary period. An advocate of parliamentary monarchy, Constant sought in his many essays to check the abuses of the general will against individual rights. The following passage, written weeks before Napoleon's final defeat at Waterloo, constitutes a classic liberal argument, distinguishing between sovereignty, authority, and individual freedom.

From *The Liberal Tradition in European Thought*, edited by David Sidorsky (New York: Putnam, 1970).

Of the Sovereignty of the People

The error of those who, sincere in their love of freedom, have attributed unlimited power to the sovereign people, comes of the manner in which their ideas about politics have been formed. They have seen in history a few men, or even one man alone, possessed of immense and very harmful power; and their anger has turned against the possessors of power and not against power itself. Instead of destroying it, they dreamt only of displacing it. It was a scourge, but they looked upon it as something to be conquered. They endowed society as a whole with it. And it passed perforce from the whole to the majority, and from the majority into the hands of a few men, and often of one man alone; and it has done as much harm as before. Manifold examples, objections, arguments and facts have been used to condemn all political institutions.

Certainly, in a society where the people's sovereignty is accepted as a basic principle, no man and no class may subject the others to his or their particular will; but it is not true that society as a whole possesses over its members an unlimited sovereignty.

The generality of citizens constitute the sov-ereign in the sense that no individual, no fraction, no partial association can assume the sovereignty unless it has been delegated to him or them. But it does not follow that the citizens generally, or those in whom they have vested the sovereignty, may dispose absolutely of the lives of individuals. On the contrary, there is a part of life which necessarily remains personal and independent, which of right is beyond the competence of society. Sovereignty can be only limited and relative. At the point where personal independence and life begin, the jurisdiction of the sovereign ceases. If society goes beyond this point, it is as guilty as the despot whose only title is the sword of the destroyer; society cannot pass beyond the sphere of its competence without usurpation, nor the majority without factiousness. The assent of the majority is not always enough to make its acts legitimate: there are some which nothing can justify. When authority commits such actions, it matters little from what source the authority is alleged to come, or whether it belongs to an individual or a nation; even when it is exercised by the whole nation, except for the citizen oppressed, it is not the more legitimate for that.

Rousseau failed to recognize this truth, and his error has made of his *Social Contract,* so often invoked in favour of liberty, the most terrible support of all kinds of despotism. He defines the contract made by society with its members as the complete and unreserved alienation of each individual with all his rights to the community. To reassure us about the consequences of so absolute a surrender of all aspects of our life to an abstract being, he tells us that the sovereign, that is to say the social body, cannot injure either its members in general or any one of them in particular; that, since each gives himself entire, the condition is the same for all, and none has an interest in making it burdensome to others; that each in giving himself to all gives himself to nobody, that each acquires over all his associates the rights which he grants to them, and gains the equivalent of all that he loses together with greater power to preserve what he has. But he forgets that all these preservative attributes which he confers on the abstract being he calls the sovereign derive from its including within it all individuals without exception. But, as soon as the sovereign has to make use of the power belonging to him—that is to say, as soon as authority has to be organized for practical purposes—the sovereign, since he cannot himself exercise it, must delegate it; and all these attributes disappear. Since the action taken in the name of all is willy nilly done by one person or by a few, it is not true that in giving oneself to all one gives oneself to no one; on the contrary, one gives oneself to those who act in the name of all. Whence it follows that, in giving oneself entire, one does not enter a condition which is equal for all, because there are some who alone benefit from the sacrifice of the others. It is not true that no one has an interest in making the condition a burden to others, since there are associates to whom the condition does not apply. It is not true that all the associates acquire over others the rights which they grant to them over themselves; they do not all gain the equivalent of what they lose, and what results from their sacrifice is, or may be, the establishment of a power which takes from them what they have.

Rousseau himself took fright at these consequences. Appalled by the immensity of the social power he had created, he did not know in what hands to place that monstrous power, and could find as a safeguard against the danger inseparable from sovereignty thus conceived only an expedient which made its exercise impossible. He declared that sovereignty could not be alienated or delegated or represented; which amounted to saying that it could not be exercised. This was to annihilate the principle he had just proclaimed. . . .

Where sovereignty is unlimited, there is no way of protecting the individual against the government. It is in vain that you claim to subject governments to the general will. It is they who give utterance to that will, and all precautions become illusory.

The people, says Rousseau, are sovereign in one respect, and subjects in another: but in practice these two respects merge into one another. Authority can easily oppress the people taken as subjects in order to compel them in their sovereign capacity to express a will prescribed to them by authority.

No political organization can remove this danger. It is in vain that you separate the powers: if the sum total of power is unlimited, the separate powers have only to make an alliance, and there is despotism without a remedy. What matters is not that our rights should be inviolable by one power without the approval of another, but that the violation be forbidden to all the powers. It is not enough that executive agents should have to invoke a grant of authority by the legislator; the legislator must be able to grant them authority to act only within a legitimate sphere. It is of little moment that the executive power should not have the right to act without the backing of the law, if limits are not set to that backing; if it is not laid down that there are matters about which the lawmaker may not make law—or, in other words, that sovereignty is limited, and there are decisions which neither the people nor their delegates have the right to make.

It is this that must be proclaimed; this, the important truth, the essential principle, to be established.

No authority on earth is unlimited; whether it

resides in the people, or in the men who claim to be their representatives, or in kings, whatever their title to rule, or in the law, which, being only the expression of the people's or the prince's will (depending on the form of government), must be confined within the same limits as that will.

Citizens possess rights independently of all social or political authority, and every authority which violates these rights becomes illegitimate. These rights are freedom of person, of religious worship, and of opinion (including its publication), the enjoyment of property, and security against arbitrary power. No one in authority can infringe these rights without destroying his own title to authority. . . .

We owe to public tranquillity many sacrifices; and we should be morally to blame if, by holding inflexibly to our rights, we resisted all laws which appeared to us to impair them; but no duty binds us to those pretended laws whose corrupting influence threatens the noblest aspects of life, to the laws which not only restrict our legitimate rights but require of us actions contrary to the eternal principles of justice and compassion which man cannot cease to observe without degrading and belying his nature.

So long as a law, though a bad one, does not tend to deprave us, so long as the encroachments of authority require only sacrifices which do not make us vile or cruel, we can submit. We then make compromises which affect only ourselves. But if the law should require us to tread underfoot our affections or our duties; if, on the pretext of an extraordinary and factitious sacrifice, in favour either of the monarchy or the republic (as the case may be), it should forbid loyalty to friends in misfortune; if it should require us to betray our allies, or even to persecute vanquished enemies, anathema upon the promotion of injustices and crimes thus covered with the name of law!

Whenever a law appears unjust, it is a positive, general unrestricted duty not to become an executor of it. This force of inertia entails neither upheavals, nor revolutions, nor disorders.

Nothing justifies the man who gives his support to a law which he believes is iniquitous. . . .

*　　*　　*

REVIEW QUESTIONS

1. What are Constant's reservations about sovereignty of the people, and what are his criticisms of Rousseau?
2. According to Constant, on what individual liberties may no authority trespass?
3. What justifications does Constant cite for obeying and breaking laws?

ALEXIS DE TOCQUEVILLE

FROM *Democracy in America*

Alexis Charles Henri Clerel de Tocqueville (1805–1859) ranks as one of the brilliant political minds of the liberal era, a politician and writer who was among the first to compare and systematize the liberal political systems of the postrevolutionary era. De Tocqueville balanced an active career as a magistrate and legislative deputy during the July Monarchy (1830–1848) with extensive trips to the United States and England. These trips allowed him to observe the customs and manners of two politi-

THE NEWSPAPER READER IN THE TAVERN (1835)   Johann Peter Hasenclever

In this canvas, the artist Johann Peter Hasenclever strove to depict the growing participation of popular classes—artisans, farmers, factory hands—in the political questions of the day. Set in a tavern in the Rhineland, the newspaper reader holds a copy of the Düsseldorfer Zeitung, *one of Germany's leading liberal newspapers, and reads aloud to a rapt audience, whose gestures convey varying degrees of disagreement with the article. In an era of restricted voting rights, what revolutionary tensions did Hasenclever evoke with his depiction of politically informed common people?*

cal systems that differed significantly from France's inherited tradition of centralized authority. His Democracy in America *(1835) and* The Old Regime and the French Revolution *(1856) are enduring works on the relationship of individual liberty and equality to central and federal political power. Both combine pragmatic political experience with a detached analytical grasp of differing political systems and their respective benefits. His observations on the civic culture of democratic politics are evinced in the following sections on political associations and freedom of the press from* Democracy in America.

From *Democracy in America,* by Alexis de Tocqueville (Chicago: University of Chicago Press, 1951), pp. 81–84, 88–90.

*   *   *

Political Associations in the United States

In no country in the world has the principle of association been more successfully used, or more unsparingly applied to a multitude of different objects, than in America. Besides the permanent associations which are established by law under the names of townships, cities, and counties, a vast number of others are formed and maintained by the agency of private individuals. . . .

The most natural privilege of man, next to the right of acting for himself, is that of combining his exertions with those of his fellow-creatures, and of acting in common with them. I am therefore led to conclude that the right of association is almost as inalienable as the right of personal liberty. No legislator can attack it without impairing the very foundations of society. Nevertheless, if freedom of association is a fruitful source of advantages and prosperity to some nations, it may be perverted or carried to excess by others, and a source of vigor may be changed into one of destruction. A comparison of the different methods which associations pursue, in those countries in which they are managed with discretion, as well as in those where liberty degenerates into license, may perhaps be thought useful both to governments and to parties.

The greater part of Europeans look upon an association as a weapon which is to be hastily fashioned, and immediately tried in conflict. A society is formed for discussion, but the idea of impending action prevails in the minds of those who constitute it: it is, in fact, an army; and the time given to parley serves to reckon up the strength and to inspire the troops, after which they march against the enemy. Resources which lie within the bounds of the law may suggest themselves to the persons who compose it as means, but never as the only means, of success.

Such, however, is not the manner in which the right of association is understood in the United States. In America the citizens who form the minority associate, in order, in the first place, to show their numerical strength, and so to diminish the moral authority of the majority; and, in the second place, to stimulate competition, and to discover those arguments which are most fitted to act upon the majority: for they always entertain hopes of drawing over their opponents to their own side, and of afterwards disposing of the supreme power in their name. Political associations in the United States are therefore peaceable in their intentions, and strictly legal in the means which they employ; and they assert with perfect truth, that they only aim at success by lawful expedients.

The difference which exists between the Americans and ourselves depends on several causes. In Europe there are numerous parties so diametrically opposed to the majority, that they can never hope to acquire its support, and at the same time they think that they are sufficiently strong in themselves to struggle and to defend their cause. When a party of this kind forms an association, its object is, not to conquer, but to fight. In America, the individuals who hold opinions very much opposed to those of the majority are no sort of impediment to its power; and all other parties hope to win it over to their own principles in the end. The exercise of the right of association becomes dangerous in proportion to the impossibility which excludes great parties from acquiring the majority. In a country like the United States, in which the differences of opinion are mere differences of hue, the right of association may remain unrestrained without evil consequences. The inexperience of many of the European nations in the enjoyment of liberty, leads them only to look upon freedom of association as a right of attacking the Government. The first notion which presents itself to a party, as well as to an individual, when it has acquired a consciousness of its own strength, is that of violence: the notion of persuasion arises at a later period, and is only derived from experience. The English, who are divided into parties which differ most essentially from each other, rarely abuse the right of association, because they have long been accustomed to exercise it. In France, the passion for war is so intense that there is no undertaking so mad, or so injurious to the welfare of the State, that a man does not consider himself honoured in defending it, at the risk of his life.

But perhaps the most powerful of the causes which tend to mitigate the excesses of political association in the United States is universal suffrage. In countries in which universal suffrage exists, the majority is never doubtful, because neither party can pretend to represent that portion of the community which has not voted. The associations which are formed are aware, as well as the nation at large, that they do not represent the majority. This is, indeed, a condition inseparable from their existence, for if they did represent the preponderating power, they would change the law instead of soliciting its reform. The consequence of this is that the moral influence of the Government which

they attack is very much increased, and their own power is very much enfeebled.

In Europe there are few associations which do not affect to represent the majority, or which do not believe that they represent it. This belief or pretence tends greatly to increase their power, and serves admirably to legitimate their actions. For what is more excusable than violence in a righteous cause against oppression? Thus it is, in the vast labyrinth of human laws, that extreme liberty sometimes corrects the abuses of license, and that extreme democracy obviates the dangers of democratic government. In Europe, associations consider themselves in some degree the legislative and executive councils of the people, which is unable to speak for itself. In America, where they only represent a minority of the nation, they argue and they petition.

The means which the associations of Europe employ are in accordance with the end which they propose to obtain. As the principle aim of these bodies is to act, and not to debate, to fight rather than to persuade, they are naturally led to adopt a form of organization which differs from the ordinary customs of civil bodies, and which assumes the habits and the maxims of military life. They centralize the direction of their resources as much as possible, and they entrust the power of the whole party to a very small number of leaders.

The members of these associations reply to a watchword, like soldiers on duty; they profess the doctrine of passive obedience, or rather in uniting together they at once abjure the exercise of their own judgment and free will. And the tyrannical control which these societies exercise, is often far more insupportable than the authority possessed over society by the Government which they attack. Their moral force is much diminished by these excesses. They lose the sacred quality which always characterises a struggle between oppressors and the oppressed. The man who in given cases consents to obey his fellows with servility, and who submits his actions and even his opinions to their control, can have no claim to rank as a free citizen.

The Americans have also established certain

forms of government for their associations, but these are invariably borrowed from the forms of the civil administration. The independence of each individual is formally recognized. As in society at large, all the members work towards the same end, but they are not obliged to follow exactly the same track. No-one abjures the exercise of his reason and his free will; rather everyone exercises that reason and that will for the benefit of a common undertaking.

*   *   *

Freedom of the Press

There are certain nations which have peculiar reasons for cherishing the freedom of the press. For in certain countries which profess to enjoy the privileges of freedom, every individual agent of the Government may violate the laws with impunity, since those whom he oppresses cannot prosecute him before the courts of justice. In this case the freedom of the press is not merely a guarantee, but the *only* guarantee of their liberty and their security which the citizens possess. If the rulers of these nations proposed to abolish the independence of the press, the people would be justified in saying: Give us the right of prosecuting your offences before ordinary tribunals, and perhaps we may then waive our right of appeal to the tribunal of public opinion.

But in the countries in which the doctrine of the sovereignty of the people ostensibly prevails, the censorship of the press is not only dangerous, it is absurd. When the right of every citizen to cooperate in the government of society is acknowledged, every citizen must be presumed to possess the power of discriminating between the different opinions of his contemporaries, and of appreciating the different facts from which inferences may be drawn. The sovereignty of the people and the freedom of the press may therefore be looked upon as inseparable institutions; the censorship of the press and universal suffrage are two things which are irreconcileably opposed, and which cannot long be retained among the insti-

tutions of the same people. Not a single individual of the twelve millions who inhabit the territory of the United States has as yet dared to propose any restrictions to the liberty of the press. . . .

In France it is not uncommonly imagined that the virulence of the press originates in the uncertain social condition, in the political excitement, and the consequent sense of general malaise which prevail in that country; and it is therefore supposed that as soon as society has resumed a certain degree of composure, the press will abandon its present vehemence. I am inclined to think that these causes explain the extraordinary ascendency it has acquired over the nation, but that they do not exercise much influence upon the tone of its language. The periodical press appears to me to be actuated by passions and propensities independent of the circumstances in which it is placed; and the present position of America corroborates this opinion.

America is perhaps, at this moment, the country of the whole world which contains the fewest germs of revolution, but the press is no less destructive in its principles than in France, and it displays the same violence without the same reasons for indignation. In America, as in France, it constitutes a singular power, so strangely composed of mingled good and evil, that it is at the same time indispensable to the existence of freedom, and nearly incompatible with the maintenance of public order. Its power is certainly much greater in France than in the United States; though nothing is more rare in the latter country than to hear of a prosecution having been instituted against it. The reason for this is perfectly simple: the Americans having once accepted the doctrine of the sovereignty of the people, apply it with perfect consistency. They never intended to establish laws for all eternity on foundations which change from day to day. There is consequently nothing criminal in an attack upon the existing laws, provided it be not attended with a violent infraction of them. They are moreover of the opinion that Courts of Justice are unable to check the abuses of the press; and that as the subtlety of human language perpetually eludes the severity of judicial analysis, offences of this nature are apt to escape the hand which attempts to apprehend them. They hold that to act with efficacy upon the press, it would be necessary to find a tribunal not only devoted to the existing order of things, but capable of surmounting the influence of public opinion, a tribunal which should conduct its proceedings without publicity, which should pronounce its decrees without assigning its motives, and punish the intentions even more than the language of the author. Whoever had the power of creating and maintaining a tribunal of this kind would be wasting his time in prosecuting the liberty of the press, for he would be the supreme master of the whole community, and he would be as free to rid himself of the authors as of their writings. In this question, therefore, there is no middle way between servitude and extreme licence. In order to enjoy the inestimable benefits which the freedom of the press ensures, it is necessary to submit to the inevitable evils which it engenders. To expect to acquire the former, and to escape the latter, is to cherish one of those illusions which commonly mislead nations in their times of sickness, when, tired with faction and exhausted by effort, they attempt to combine hostile opinions and contrary opinions upon the same soil. . . .

The influence of the press upon America is immense. It is the power which impels the circulation of political life through all the districts of that vast territory. Its eye is constantly open to detect the secret springs of political designs, and to summon the leaders of all parties to the bar of public opinion. It rallies the interests of the community round certain principles, and it draws up the creed which factions adopt. It affords a means of intercourse between parties which hear, and which address each other, without ever having been in immediate contact. When a great number of the organs of the press adopt the same line of conduct, their influence becomes irresistible; and public opinion, when it is perpetually assailed from the same side, eventually yields to the attack. In the United States each separate journal exercises but little authority: but the power of the periodical press is only second to that of the people.

*   *   *

REVIEW QUESTIONS

1. Why does de Tocqueville find the right of association as important as rights of personal liberty?
2. According to de Tocqueville, what role do associations play for minority views?
3. How did French and American political associations differ?
4. Why is the press, for de Tocqueville, "indispensable to the existence of freedom"?
5. Why did de Tocqueville consider the power of the press greater in France than in the United States?

KLEMENS VON METTERNICH

Letter to Neuman in London, Vienna, 24 June 1832

Prince Klemens Lothar von Metternich (1773–1859), who served the Austrian Empire from 1809 to 1848, ranked as one of the most influential statesmen of his time. Following the defeat of Napoleon, Metternich, a staunch conservative, sought to restore aristocratic privilege and legitimate royal authority in Europe. His efforts to use laws, police surveillance, and military intervention to uncover and suppress movements advocating constitutional liberties and national unity were unsurpassed. In 1819, Metternich authorized the Carlsbad Decrees, laws in the German Confederation that clamped down on the liberal politics of students and secret political associations. In July 1832 these were reenforced with the Six Articles, which strengthened censorship and prohibited all associations, assemblies, and festivals with political character. Metternich wrote the following letter on the eve of the Six Article's promulgation. In this missive Metternich instructs his ambassador how to justify these laws to the British government, whose regard for civil liberties offered potential problems to Metternich's German policies.

From *Memoirs of Prince Metternich, 1830–35,* Vol. 3, translated by Gerard Smith (New York: Harper, 1882).

The position of the German Governments has at all times deservedly engaged our anxious care and attention.

Germany has long suffered from the evil which is now spread over the whole of Europe. In some sense, the evil may be said to have been in existence there previous to the outbreak in France of 1789. The sect of the *Illuminati*, the first *Radical* association, owed its existence, long before that time, to the weakness of the Bavarian Government and the complicity of several men who were among its members from the first. This sect, in spite of all endeavors on the part of the same Government to put it down by the severest measures of repression, has never ceased to exist from that time forward, and has assumed in turn, according to circumstances and the requirements of the moment, the names of *Tugendbund, Burschenschaft,* etc.

Several Princes have committed the unpardonable error of giving their States institutions copied from those of France. This error they followed up by a second, in preserving, side by side with the new institutions, the *Dienst-Pragmatik* (Pragmatic of Service), an institution of great efficacy under the laws of the old German Empire, but absolutely incompatible with institutions of a different character. The modern representative system, which makes Ministers responsible *to the nation* for the acts of the Government, necessarily demands that the *employés* should be removable at will; in the German Constitutional States, the Ministers are *responsible* and the *employés* of all classes are *not removable.* Thence the Governments have no longer the means of enforcing obedience among their own agents, and experience shows that in these countries obedience still exists among the people, but that it has long since disappeared among those who form the intermediate class between the throne and the people. If to all this we add the extraordinary influence exercised by the Universities at all times in Germany, the respect which was paid to those learned bodies, and the extraordinary privileges which they never ceased to enjoy, it is evident that nothing more was needed than the liberty of the Press and the right of public discussion, to reduce the German States to the condition in which we now find them.

I have entered into these details with a view to presenting, in as brief a space as possible, a sketch which it may be well to bring before the English Cabinet. That Cabinet, engrossed by very different cares, has no means of forming an accurate judgment on the condition of things in Germany, and yet the fate which awaits this part of the Continent will decide that of the whole of Europe.

Our action upon the Confederation, as, in fact, any influence which the Emperor permits himself to exert on foreign political bodies, has consistently been confined within strictly lawful limits. Austria is a member of the Confederation. As such she holds the foremost place in it, and her representative acts as President of the Diet. Like Prussia, Bavaria, etc., she has only a single vote.

Our constant endeavor has been to maintain order in the proceedings of this central body, and to preach *Justice* and *Strength* to the German Courts. The evil which has been done and which has reached such a pitch of intensity, is none of our doing. It is the result of the grave errors into which the German Governments have fallen, and is partly owing to their want of judgment. When this defeat is aggravated by a vicious system of legislation, it becomes difficult to uphold and ensure public order. If this be the case at all times, what far greater proportions does the danger threaten to assume, in face of the examples which France continues to set before Germany, and an influence so potent as that of the Directing Committee has become since the Revolution of 1830! The affiliation between the German sectaries and those of Paris is no longer a mystery; it was celebrated by a public banquet, under the presidency of General Lafayette, on the same day that the Hambach scandal came upon the Governments like a final trump of warning. The question which the latter have to decide is, whether they shall continue to exist or yield to inevitable ruin. The German Princes who have been most blind hitherto have now opened their eyes to their true position, and are firmly resolved not to let themselves be beguiled into taking the course which foolish or perfidious advisers have marked out for them.

They applied to us. The Emperor, convinced as he had been for a long time of the existence of the danger, had foreseen this contingency. A full understanding had been come to with the King of Prussia, and the two monarchs have shown no hesitation as to the means to be employed. The complementary Act of 1820 contained all that was requisite. The German Governments have had their attention called to laws which already existed, and it is these which are about to be set in motion at Frankfort.

You will find, Baron, in the documents enclosed ample information as to the course affairs are about to take at the Diet. That course is clear and decided; in adopting it there will be no need to have recourse to exceptional laws or measures; there is nothing in it against which an objection could be raised, and its effects should be proportionably great.

Be pleased to put these facts before Lord Palmerston in a friendly way. I should be loath to take up his time, occupied as he is by other pressing cares, by inviting his attention to legislative details, to which, moreover, the fullest publicity will shortly be given. It is from a political point of view that the British Cabinet should be interested in the success of the undertaking. The question to be settled reduces itself to this: whether Germany is to remain an independent country, or whether she is to be absorbed into the French Revolution and so become dependent on France. If the members of the Confederation only know how to do their duty, their triumph is assured, for it will be at the same time the triumph of patriotism and true liberty.

REVIEW QUESTIONS

1. What was the "evil . . . spread over the whole of Europe," and why was Germany particularly beset with this "evil"?
2. What was Metternich's opinion of the press, public discussion, and the universities?
3. What political activities did Metternich find so threatening, and why?

SATIRE OF LIBERAL REFORMS (1833)

This anonymous cartoon satirically underscores one of the glaring contradictions of English life during the early years of the liberal era. Following the Reform Act of 1832, which enfranchised the propertied middle classes, Parliament abolished slavery in the British Empire in 1833, the year of this cartoon. The illustration juxtaposes the conditions of a common English worker and a Jamaican slave (who's condition is cruelly misrepresented), reversing the labels of slavery and freedom. The man in the middle, presumably a bourgeois politician, states: "Think of the poor suffering African called a Slave unpossess'd of any of the rights & privileges that you enjoy, while you sit under the vine of your Reform Bill and the fig-tree of your Magna Chart. He knows nothing of such blessings." How is this cartoon a parody of Britain's liberal reforms?

509

WILLIAM WILBERFORCE

FROM *An Appeal to the Religion, Justice, Humanity of the Inhabitants of the British Empire, in Behalf of the Negro Slaves in the West Indies*

William Wilberforce (1759–1833) was the principal herald of a sustained political campaign to abolish both the slave trade and slavery in the British Empire. An evangelical Christian whose advocacy of social reform was based on Christian ethics, Wilberforce embodied the progressive religious reform movement of the early-nineteenth-century bourgeoisie. As a member of Parliament between 1780 and 1825, Wilberforce unrelentingly exposed the horror and tyranny of slavery. In 1823, the year of the tract printed below, he founded and became co-president of the Anti-Slavery Society, an association that agitated for public support of the Emancipation Bill, thus bringing together conservatives and liberals alike to espouse the universal right to personal liberty. A month after Wilberforce died, his bill became law.

From *An Appeal to the Religion, Justice, Humanity of the Inhabitants of the British Empire, in Behalf of the Negro Slaves in the West Indies*, by William Wilberforce (London: Printed for J. Hatchard, 1823), pp. 9–14.

*   *   *

But though the evils which have been already enumerated are of no small amount, in estimating the physical sufferings of human beings, especially of the lower rank, yet, to a Christian eye, they shrink almost into insignificance when compared with the moral evils that remain behind—with that, above all, which runs through the whole of the various cruel circumstances of the Negro Slave's condition, and is at once the effect of his wrongs and sufferings, their bitter aggravation, and the pretext for their continuance—his extreme degradation in the intellectual and moral scale of being, and in the estimation of his White oppressors.

The proofs of the extreme degradation of the slaves, in the latter sense, are innumerable; and indeed it must be confessed, that in the minds of Europeans in general, more especially in vulgar minds, whether vulgar from the want of education, or morally vulgar (a more inwrought and less curable vulgarity), the personal peculiarities of the Negro race could scarcely fail, by diminishing sympathy, to produce impressions, not merely of contempt, but even of disgust and aversion. But how strongly are these impressions sure to be confirmed and augmented, when to all the effects of bodily distinctions are superadded all those arising from the want of civilization and knowledge, and still more, all the hateful vices that slavery never fails to engender or to aggravate. Such, in truth, must naturally be the effect of these powerful causes, that even the most ingeniously constructed system which humanity and policy combined could have devised, would in vain have endeavoured to counteract them: how much more powerfully then must they operate, especially in low and uneducated minds, when the whole system abounds with institutious and practices which tend to confirm and strengthen their efficiency, and to give to a contemptuous aversion for the Negro race the sanction of manners and of law.

It were well if the consequences of these impressions were only to be discovered among the inferior ranks of the privileged class, or only to be found in the opinions and conduct of individuals. But in the earlier laws of our colonies they are expressed in the language of insult, and in characters of blood. And too many of these laws still remain unrepealed, to permit the belief that the same odious spirit of legislation no longer exists, or to relieve the injured objects of them from their degrading influence. The slaves were systematically depressed below the level of human beings. And though I confess, that it is of less concern to a slave, under what laws he lives, than what is the character of his master, yet if the laws had extended to them favour and protection instead of degradation, this would have tended to raise them in the social scale, and, operating insensibly on the public mind, might, by degrees, have softened the extreme rigour of their bondage. Such, however, had been the contrary effects of an opposite process, on the estimation of the Negro race, before the ever-to-be-honoured Granville Sharpe, and his followers, had begun to vindicate their claim to the character and privileges of human nature, that a writer of the highest authority on all West-India subjects, Mr. Long, in his celebrated History of Jamaica, though pointing out some of the particulars of their ill treatment, scrupled not to state it as his opinion, that in the gradations of being, Negroes were little elevated above the oran ou-tang, "that type of man." Nor was this an unguarded or a hastily thrown-out assertion. He institutes a laborious comparison of the Negro race with that species of baboon; and declares, that, "ludicrous as the opinion may seem, he does not think that an oran outang husband would be any dishonour to a Hottentot female." When we find such sentiments as these to have been unblushingly avowed by an author of the highest estimation among the West India colonists, we are prepared for what we find to have been, and, I grieve to say, still continues to be, the practical effects of these opinions.

The first particular of subsisting legal oppression that I shall notice, and which is at once a decisive proof of the degradation of the Negro race, in the eyes of the Whites, and a powerful cause of its continnance, is of a deeply rooted character, and often productive of the most cruel effects. In the contemplation of law they are not persons, but mere chattels; and as such are liable to be seized and sold by creditors and by executors, in payment of their owner's debts; and this separately from the estates on which they are settled. By the operation of this system, the most meritorious slave who may have accumulated a little peculium, and may be living with his family in some tolerable comfort, who by long and faithful services may have endeared himself to his proprietor or manager—who, in short, is in circumstances that mitigate greatly the evils of his condition—is liable at once to be torn for ever from his home, his family, and his friends, and to be sent to serve a new master, perhaps in another island, for the rest of his life.

Another particular of their degradation by law, which, in its effects, most perniciously affects their whole civil condition, and of which their inadequate legal protection is a sure and necessary consequence, is their evidence being inadmissible against any free person. The effect of this cannot be stated more clearly or compendiously than in the memorable evidence of a gentleman eminently distinguished for the candour with which he gave to the Slave-Trade Committee the result of his long personal experience in the West Indies, the late Mr. Otley, Chief-justice of St. Vincent's, himself a planter: "As the evidence of Slaves is never admitted against White men, the difficulty of legally establishing the facts is so great, that White men are in a manner put beyond the reach of the law." It is due also to the late Sir William Young, long one of the most active opponents of the abolition, to state, that he likewise, when Governor of Tobago, acknowledged, as a radical defect in the administration of justice, that the law of evidence "covered the most guilty European with impunity."

The same concession was made by both houses of the legislature of Grenada, in the earliest inquiries of the Privy Council. The only difficulty, as they stated, that had been found in putting an effectual stop to gross and wanton cruelty towards slaves, was that of bringing home the proof of the fact against the delinquent by satisfactory evidence, those who were capable of the guilt, being in general artful enough to prevent any but slaves being witnesses of the fact. "As the matter stands," they add, "though we hope the instances in this island are at this day not frequent, yet it must be admitted with regret, that the persons prosecuted, and who certainly were guilty, have escaped for want of legal proof."

It is obvious that the same cause must produce the same effect in all our other slave colonies, although there has not been found the same candour in confessing it.

The next evil which I shall specify, for which the extreme degradation of these poor beings, in the eyes of their masters, can alone account, is the driving system. Not being supposed capable of being governed like other human beings, by the hope of reward, or the fear of punishment, they are subjected to the immediate impulse or present terror of the whip, and are driven at their work like brute animals. Lower than this it is scarcely possible for man to be depressed by man. If such treatment does not find him vile and despised, it must infallibly make him so. Let it not however be supposed, that the only evil of this truly odious system is its outraging the moral character of the human species, or its farther degrading the slaves in the eyes of all who are in authority over them, and thereby extinguishing that sympathy which would be their best protection. The whip is itself a dreadful instrument of punishment; and the mode of inflicting that punishment shockingly indecent and degrading. The drivers themselves, commonly, or rather always slaves, are usually the strongest and stoutest of the Negroes; and though they are forbidden to give more than a few lashes at a time, as the immediate chastisement of faults

committed at their work, yet the power over the slaves which they thus possess unavoidably invests them with a truly formidable tyranny, the consequences of which, to the unfortunate subjects of it, are often in the highest degree oppressive and pernicious. No one who reflects on the subject can be at a loss to anticipate one odious use which is too commonly made of this despotism, in extorting, from the fears of the young females who are subject to it, compliances with the licentious desires of the drivers, which they might otherwise have refused from attachment to another, if not from moral feelings and restraints. It is idle and insulting to talk of improving the condition of these poor beings, as rational and moral agents, while they are treated in a manner which precludes self-government, and annihilates all human motives but such as we impose on a maniac, or on a hardened and incorrigible convict.

Another abuse, which shows, like the rest, the extreme degradation of the Negro race, and the apathy which it creates in their masters, is the cruel, and, at least in the case of the female sex, highly indecent punishments inflicted in public, and in the face of day, often in the presence of the gang, or of the whole assembled population of an estate. From their low and ignominious condition it doubtless proceeds, that they are in some degree regarded as below the necessity of observing towards others the proper decencies of life, or of having those decencies observed by others towards them.

It is no doubt also chiefly owing to their not being yet raised out of that extreme depth in which they are sunk, so much below the level of the human species, that no attempts have been made to introduce among them the Christian institution of marriage, that blessed union which the Almighty himself established as a fundamental law at the creation of man, to be as it were the wellspring of all the charities of life—the source of all domestic comfort and social improvement—the moral cement of civilized society.

*   *   *

REVIEW QUESTIONS

1. What are the "moral evils" of slavery that Wilberforce refers to?

2. How were slaves degraded, and why did Wilberforce find this so offensive?

3. Why is slavery incompatible with the political doctrine of liberalism?

W. J. FOX

FROM *Speech on Corn Laws*

Following the enfranchisement of the British middle class in 1832, the greatest indicator of bourgeois political influence was the repeal of the Corn Laws in 1846. In 1815, parliamentary landed interests levied tariffs on cheap imported wheat to ensure that domestic grain would not be undersold, thus promoting the continued prosperity of England's landed elite. Businessmen, however, sharply criticized the tariff. They argued that it kept bread prices artificially high and, in turn, raised the cost level of a worker's sustenance, by which employers set wages. Claiming that the Corn Laws blunted the competitive edge of British manufactured exports, business interests formed the Anti–Corn Law League in 1839. This pressure group tirelessly promoted free trade as a policy benefiting the entire nation. Bad harvests and the specter of famine in the 1840s magnified the league's charge that cheap, plentiful bread was a moral necessity. The following anti–Corn Law speech from 1844 typifies the arguments of free traders.

From *Speech on Corn Laws*, by W. J. Fox (New York: Kelley, 1903).

*   *   *

Who that lives by eating bread has not an interest in the repeal of the bread tax? Who that is endeavouring to support himself and his family by commerce has not an interest in Free Trade? Who has not an interest in what advances the general prosperity of the country, even though his pursuits are artistical or intellectual, ministering to the spiritual rather than the material portions of our nature? For as one thrives will all thrive—they react the one upon the other—the starving do not encourage literature and art—they are bound together by the ties which Providence formed to uphold society; and it is because they and we have an interest in this matter that we are determined the question shall not drop until it is satisfactorily settled.

I say all classes have an interest in this matter; even they who are represented as the great opposing class—the landlord class. For what has made England the paradise of landowners but its being the workshop of the world? In the progress of manufacture, if machinery has enabled one man to do the work of two hundred, it has also employed two hundred, and two thousand, where one was employed; all bread eaters, coming to the landowner for his produce. And while the manufacturers of this country have been thus advancing in the last century, its growth of wheat has been tripled, and the rents of the farmers have been in many cases quadrupled. The landlords gain by railways enhancing the worth of their property; they gain by the rich and flourishing community arising around them; and if for a while they should have to make some slight sacrifice—if at first their rents should fall in the change—why, they will still be gaining that which gold could never buy. By the graceful concession they would be gaining the goodwill and gratitude of their fellow-countrymen; they would gain for themselves an exemption from the execration that pursues their class—from the infamy of their names in history—from the reprobation of their consciences, and the pollution of their souls.

*   *   *

Some affect to sneer at abstract principles; but abstract good is the real, practical good, after all; the exceptions made to it are some little, dirty contrivances of those who would have trade free for others, but would reserve the monopoly for themselves—would have free trade as to what they buy, but restrictions as to what they sell; and who tell us that those principles are sound and excellent things in reference to all other commodities whatever, but that there is some one exception left—the exception of that in which the exceptor deals; and each in turn will tell you that Free Trade is the noblest thing in the world, except for corn, except for sugar, except for coffee, and except for this, that, and the other, till once, even in the House of Commons, it came to an exception of second-hand glass bottles. I say this is a principle recognized by all—recognized even by the Government in its measures of last year, however paltry their nature and limited their operation; recognized in their Canada Corn Bill; recognized in the repeal of the laws against the exportation of machinery, the last rag of that form of monopoly; and the repeal of the duties on imports must follow that of restriction on exports. A principle thus practically recognized by foes, as well as by friends, is certain of success. Thus was it that the

great principle of Negro liberty was recognized, and thus eventually carried. And did not the recognition of a principle emancipate the Roman Catholics of Ireland? Ask Sir Robert Peel and the Duke of Wellington whether this was not the secret of the success of that measure.

*   *   *

Why, the corn laws and the policy of our agricultural legislators hunt poverty and wretchedness from their own districts into ours. The landlord class call themselves feeders of the people. They speak of their ability, if properly encouraged and protected, to feed the nation. What feeds the people? Not the growing of corn, but the people being able to buy it. The people are no more fed, for all the wheat that is grown, than as if there were so many stones covering the rich valleys of the country. It is in the price required of the people who eat it; and if that is beyond the power of the multitude to give, the landlords become starvers instead of feeders of the people. Agriculture cannot support its own population; it is not in the course of nature that it should, for one man is vested with the ability to raise food for the many. Twenty-eight per cent of the population are amply sufficient to cultivate the ground so as to yield food for the remainder of the hundred. How are the rest to be fed? By opening markets for the products of their industry, that they may obtain the means.

*   *   *

Wisely has the Council appealed to the great towns, for there is the power. What can the poor farmer do? His money is in his landlord's ground, and the man who has money in another man's ground must needs be a slave. His freedom is buried there with it, not, like the grain, to germinate, but only to rot and dissolve in corruption. It is where great bodies are congregated that they can stand by one another; where not the importance of the individual, but the importance of the many, is the great thing for all. And how independent are such places, if they but knew their position, of all that aristocracy is, or can do! Landlords! They built not this magnificent metropolis; they covered not these forty square miles with the great mass of human dwellings that spread over them; they crowd not our ports with shipping; they filled not your city with its monuments of science and art, with its institutions of literature and its temples of religion; they poured not that stream of commercial prosperity into the country which during the last century has made the grandeur of London, quadrupling its population, and showing that it has one heart with the entire community.

* * *

The time is opportune for the appeal which has been made to the inhabitants of this metropolis, and for the appeal to those among you who enjoy the franchise of the city of London. There will, in a very short period, be an opportunity for you to show decidedly that the principle of Free Trade is consecrated in your hearts and guides your votes. I trust the contest will be by no means a personal one, but one wholly of principle, and that no ambiguous pretensions, no praise of Free Trade, with certain qualifications and accommodations necessary to the hustings, will be tolerated for an instant; but that the plain and simple test will be the complete, total, and immediate abolition of the monopoly of food.* * * Here, then, I hope, will one of the first great electoral experiments be tried, that not merely every member of the League, but every inhabitant of London, who can honourably influence the result of that election, should feel himself bound to do so, as amongst his earliest pledges of adherence to this great cause—the commencement of his answer to the appeal which has now been made to him for support. Other ways will soon open themselves; and I trust that its past backwardness will be amply redeemed by the metropolis in the readiness with which it will respond to the great call now made for its pecuniary liberality, and in the ardour

which many will manifest in other modes of co-operating in this great work, showing that we look to yet higher principles and considerations than any that belong either to rural districts or to particular classes, and that we regard this as the common cause of humanity. And so it is; for Free-Trade principles are the dictates of Nature plainly written on the surface of land and ocean, so that the simplest may read them and imbibe their spirit. For that Power which stretched abroad the land, poured forth the ocean, and piled up the mountains; that Power which gave Western America its broad prairies, and reared the gigantic and boundless forests of the north; that Power which covered with rich vineyards the smiling hills of France, which wafts sweet odours from the 'spicy shores of Araby the blest,' which has endowed this country with its minerals and its insular advantages, and its people with their indomitable Saxon energy, with their skill, their hardihood, their perseverance, their enterprise;—that Power which doth all this, evidently designed it for the common good, for the reciprocal advantage of all; it intended that all should enrich all by the freest interchange, thus making the world no longer the patrimony of a class, but the heritage and the paradise of humanity.

REVIEW QUESTIONS

1. In Fox's speech, what are the principal criticisms raised against the landlord class?
2. What are the chief differences between the commercial and agriculture interests?
3. Why is free trade more than just an economic doctrine?
4. What attributes are projected onto this trade policy?
5. Why is London considered so important for the repeal?

JOHN STUART MILL

FROM *On Liberty*

In 1859 J. S. Mill (1806–1873) presented to Victorian society the now-classic statement on individual freedom, On Liberty. *Mill, however, should not be mistaken for a typical liberal. He not only abandoned classical economic theory early in his career, advocating certain forms of government regulation, but also foresaw the moral necessity of extending the vote to workers and women. Yet he continued to harbor distrust in state authority and in governments' inability to guarantee the rights of minorities. His passages on individual liberty, freedom of opinion, and limits of authority over the individual are critical to the canon of liberal political philosophy.*

From *On Liberty*, by John Stuart Mill, edited by David Spitz (New York: Norton, 1975).

Chapter I
Introductory

The subject of this Essay is not the so-called Liberty of the Will so unfortunately opposed to the misnamed doctrine of Philosophical Necessity; but Civil, or Social Liberty: the nature and limits of the power which can be legitimately exercised by society over the individual. A question seldom stated, and hardly ever discussed, in general terms, but which profoundly influences the practical controversies of the age by its latent presence, and is likely soon to make itself recognised as the vital question of the future. It is so far from being new, that, in a certain sense, it has divided mankind, almost from the remotest ages; but in the stage of progress into which the more civilised portions of the species have now entered, it presents itself under new conditions, and requires a different and more fundamental treatment.

The struggle between Liberty and Authority is the most conspicuous feature in the portions of history with which we are earliest familiar, particularly in that of Greece, Rome, and England. But in old times this contest was between subjects, or some classes of subjects, and the Government. By liberty, was meant protection against the tyranny of the political rulers. The rulers were conceived (except in some of the popular governments of Greece) as in a necessarily antagonistic position to the people whom they ruled. They consisted of a governing One, or a governing tribe or caste, who derived their authority from inheritance or conquest, who, at all events, did not hold it at the pleasure of the governed, and whose supremacy men did not venture, perhaps did not desire, to contest, whatever precautions might be taken against its oppressive exercise. Their power was regarded as necessary, but also as highly dangerous; as a weapon which they would attempt to use against their subjects, no less than against external enemies. To prevent the weaker members of the community from being preyed upon by innumerable vultures, it was needful that there should be an animal of prey stronger than the rest, commissioned to keep them down. But as the king of the vultures would be no less bent upon preying on the flock than any of the minor harpies, it was indispensable to be in a perpetual attitude of defence against his beak and claws. The aim, therefore, of patriots was to set limits to the power which the ruler should be suffered to exercise over the community; and this limitation was what they meant by liberty. It was attempted in two ways.

First, by obtaining a recognition of certain immunities, called political liberties or rights, which it was to be regarded as a breach of duty in the ruler to infringe, and which if he did infringe, specific resistance, or general rebellion, was held to be justifiable. A second, and generally a later expedient, was the establishment of constitutional checks, by which the consent of the community, or of a body of some sort, supposed to represent its interests, was made a necessary condition to some of the more important acts of the governing power. To the first of these modes of limitation, the ruling power, in most European countries, was compelled, more or less, to submit. It was not so with the second; and, to attain this, or when already in some degree possessed, to attain it more completely, became everywhere the principal object of the lovers of liberty. And so long as mankind were content to combat one enemy by another, and to be ruled by a master, on condition of being guaranteed more or less efficaciously against his tyranny, they did not carry their aspirations beyond this point.

A time, however, came, in the progress of human affairs, when men ceased to think it a necessity of nature that their governors should be an independent power, opposed in interest to themselves. It appeared to them much better that the various magistrates of the State should be their tenants or delegates, revocable at their pleasure. In that way alone, it seemed, could they have complete security that the powers of government would never be abused to their disadvantage. By degrees this new demand for elective and temporary rulers became the prominent object of the exertions of the popular party, wherever any such party existed; and superseded, to a considerable extent, the previous efforts to limit the power of rulers. As the struggle proceeded for making the ruling power emanate from the periodical choice of the ruled, some persons began to think that too much importance had been attached to the limitation of the power itself. *That* (it might seem) was a resource against rulers whose interests were habitually opposed to those of the people. What was now wanted was, that the rulers should be iden-

tified with the people; that their interest and will should be the interest and will of the nation. The nation did not need to be protected against its own will. There was no fear of its tyrannising over itself. Let the rulers be effectually responsible to it, promptly removable by it, and it could afford to trust them with power of which it could itself dictate the use to be made. Their power was but the nation's own power, concentrated, and in a form convenient for exercise. This mode of thought, or rather perhaps of feeling, was common among the last generation of European liberalism, in the Continental section of which it still apparently predominates. Those who admit any limit to what a government may do, except in the case of such governments as they think ought not to exist, stand out as brilliant exceptions among the political thinkers of the Continent. A similar tone of sentiment might by this time have been prevalent in our own country, if the circumstances which for a time encouraged it, had continued unaltered.

But, in political and philosophical theories, as well as in persons, success discloses faults and infirmities which failure might have concealed from observation. The notion, that the people have no need to limit their power over themselves, might seem axiomatic, when popular government was a thing only dreamed about, or read of as having existed at some distant period of the past. Neither was that notion necessarily disturbed by such temporary aberrations as those of the French Revolution, the worst of which were the work of a usurping few, and which, in any case, belonged, not to the permanent working of popular institutions, but to a sudden and convulsive outbreak against monarchical and aristocratic depotism. In time, however, a democratic republic came to occupy a large portion of the earth's surface, and made itself felt as one of the most powerful members of the community of nations; and elective and responsible government became subject to the observations and criticisms which wait upon a great existing fact. It was now perceived that such phrases as "self-government," and "the power of the people over themselves," do not express the true state of the case. The "people" who exercise the power are not always the same people with those over whom it is exercised; and the "self-government" spoken of is not the government of each by himself, but of each by all the rest. The will of the people, moreover, practically means the will of the most numerous or the most active *part* of the people; the majority, or those who succeed in making themselves accepted as the majority; the people, consequently, *may* desire to oppress a part of their number; and precautions are as much needed against this as against any other abuse of power. The limitation, therefore, of the power of government over individuals loses none of its importance when the holders of power are regularly accountable to the community, that is, to the strongest party therein. This view of things, recommending itself equally to the intelligence of thinkers and to the inclination of those important classes in European society to whose real or supposed interests democracy is adverse, has had no difficulty in establishing itself; and in political speculations "the tyranny of the majority" is now generally included among the evils against which society requires to be on its guard.

*   *   *

The object of this Essay is to assert one very simple principle, as entitled to govern absolutely the dealings of society with the individual in the way of compulsion and control, whether the means used be physical force in the form of legal penalties, or the moral coercion of public opinion. That principle is, that the sole end for which mankind are warranted, individually or collectively, in interfering with the liberty of action of any of their number, is self-protection. That the only purpose for which power can be rightfully exercised over any member of a civilised community, against his will, is to prevent harm to others. His own good, either physical or moral, is not a sufficient warrant. He cannot rightfully be compelled to do or forbear because it will be better for him to do so, because it will make him happier, because, in the opinions of others, to do so would be wise, or even right. These are good reasons for remonstrat-

ing with him, or reasoning with him, or persuading him, or entreating him, but not for compelling him, or visiting him with any evil in case he do otherwise. To justify that, the conduct from which it is desired to deter him must be calculated to produce evil to some one else. The only part of the conduct of any one, for which he is amenable to society, is that which concerns others. In the part which merely concerns himself, his independence is, of right, absolute. Over himself, over his own body and mind, the individual is sovereign.

*   *   *

We have now recognised the necessity to the mental well-being of mankind (on which all their other well-being depends) of freedom of opinion, and freedom of the expression of opinion, on four distinct grounds; which we will now briefly recapitulate.

First, if any opinion is compelled to silence, that opinion may, for aught we can certainly know, be true. To deny this is to assume our own infallibility.

Secondly, though the silenced opinion be an error, it may, and very commonly does, contain a portion of truth; and since the general or prevailing opinion on any subject is rarely or never the whole truth, it is only by the collision of adverse opinions that the remainder of the truth has any chance of being supplied.

Thirdly, even if the received opinion be not only true, but the whole truth; unless it is suffered to be, and actually is, vigorously and earnestly contested, it will, by most of those who receive it, be held in the manner of a prejudice, with little comprehension or feeling of its rational grounds. And not only this, but, fourthly, the meaning of the doctrine itself will be in danger of being lost, or enfeebled, and deprived of its vital effect on the character and conduct; the dogma becoming a mere formal profession, inefficacious for good, but cumbering the ground, and preventing the growth of any real and heartfelt conviction, from reason or personal experience.

* * *

Chapter IV
Of the Limits to the Authority
of Society over the Individual

What, then, is the rightful limit to the sovereignty of the individual over himself? Where does the authority of society begin? How much of human life should be assigned to individuality, and how much to society?

Each will receive its proper share, if each has that which more particularly concerns it. To individuality should belong the part of life in which it is chiefly the individual that is interested; to society, the part which chiefly interests society.

Though society is not founded on a contract, and though no good purpose is answered by inventing a contract in order to deduce social obligations from it, every one who receives the protection of society owes a return for the benefit, and the fact of living in society renders it indispensable that each should be bound to observe a certain line of conduct towards the rest. This conduct consists, first, in not injuring the interests of one another; or rather certain interests, which, either by express legal provision, or by tacit understanding, ought to be considered as rights; and secondly, in each person's bearing his share (to be fixed on some equitable principle) of the labours and sacrifices incurred for defending the society or its members from injury and molestation. These conditions society is justified in enforcing, at all costs to those who endeavour to withhold fulfilment. Nor is this all that society may do. The acts of an individual may be hurtful to others, or wanting in due consideration for their welfare, without going to the length of violating any of their constituted rights. The offender may then be justly punished by opinion, though not by law. As soon as any part of a person's conduct affects prejudicially the interests of others, society has jurisdiction over it, and the question whether the general welfare will or will not be promoted by interfering with it, becomes open to discussion. But there is no room for entertaining any such question when a person's conduct affects the interests of no persons besides himself, or needs not affect them unless they like (all the persons concerned being of full age, and the ordinary amount of understanding). In all such cases, there should be perfect freedom, legal and social, to do the action and stand the consequences.

It would be a great misunderstanding of this doctrine to suppose that it is one of selfish indifference, which pretends that human beings have no business with each other's conduct in life, and that they should not concern themselves about the well-doing or well-being of one another, unless their own interest is involved. Instead of any diminution, there is need of a great increase of disinterested exertion to promote the good of others. But disinterested benevolence can find other instruments to persuade people to their good than whips and scourges, either of the literal or the metaphorical sort. I am the last person to undervalue the self-regarding virtues; they are only second in importance, if even second, to the social. It is equally the business of education to cultivate both. But even education works by conviction and persuasion as well as by compulsion, and it is by the former only that, when the period of education is passed, the self-regarding virtues should be inculcated. Human beings owe to each other help to distinguish the better from the worse, and encouragement to choose the former and avoid the latter. They should be forever stimulating each other to increased exercise of their higher faculties, and increased direction of their feelings and aims towards wise instead of foolish, elevating instead of degrading, objects and contemplations. But neither one person, nor any number of persons, is warranted in saying to another human creature of ripe years, that he shall not do with his life for his own benefit what he chooses to do with it. He is the person most interested in his own well-being: the interest which any other person, except in cases of strong personal attachment, can have in it, is trifling, compared with that which he himself has; the interest which society has in him individually (except as to his conduct to others) is fractional, and altogether indirect; while with respect to his own feelings and circumstances, the most ordinary man or woman has means of knowledge immeasurably surpassing those that can be possessed by any one else. The interference of society to overrule his judgment and purposes in what only regards himself must be grounded on general presumptions; which may be altogether wrong, and even if right, are as likely as not to be misapplied to individual cases, by persons no better acquainted with the circumstances of such cases than those are who look at them merely from without. In this department, therefore, of human affairs, Individuality has its proper field of action. In the conduct of human beings towards one another it is necessary that general rules should for the most part be observed, in order that people may know what they have to expect: but in each person's own concerns his individual spontaneity is entitled to free exercise.

* * *

REVIEW QUESTIONS

1. According to Mill, what are the liberties of the individual, and what is the relationship of these liberties to society?
2. What is the importance of freedom of opinion for society?
3. Why would Mill consider the "tyranny of the majority" one of the prominent ills of nineteenth-century society?

ALEXANDER II

FROM Manifesto Emancipating the Serfs

The emancipation of 22 million serfs in 1861 constitutes the most ambitious social reform of nineteenth-century Russia. Although Russia's socioeconomic structure did not undergo radical change after 1861, the abolition of serfdom inaugurated a series of judicial, military, and governmental reforms that liberalized Russian society. Extending basic civil liberties to Russians was the necessary first step in the effort to westernize Russia within the Tsarist autocratic tradition.

From *Major Problems in the History of Imperialist Russia*, edited by James Cracraft (Boston: Houghton Mifflin, 1994), pp. 340–44.

Called by Divine Providence and the sacred law of succession to Our ancestral All-Russian Throne, in response to which call We vowed in Our heart to embrace in Our Royal love and Solicitude all Our faithful of every rank and estate . . . ; investigating the condition of [those] who comprise the State, We saw that State law, while actively promoting the welfare of the higher and middle estates defining their obligations, rights, and privileges, has not equally favored the bonded people, so called because as a matter partly of old laws and partly of current custom they have been hereditarily bound to the authority of landlords, who are obliged accordingly to see to their welfare. Hitherto the rights of the lords were broad and not precisely defined in law, wherefore tradition, custom, and the lord's good will prevailed. At best this [system] produced good patriarchal relations of sincere solicitude and benevolence on the part of the lords and good-natured submission from the peasants. But owing to the decline of morals, an increase in the variety of relationships, and a lessening of the lords' direct paternal relations with their peasants, whereupon landlord rights sometimes fell into the hands of persons seeking only their own advantage; good relations weakened, and the way was opened to an arbitrariness that has been burdensome for the peasants and not conducive to their welfare, whence they have shown indifference to any improvement in their lives.

Such was perceived by Our Predecessors of worthy memory, and they took steps to improve the condition of the peasantry. But these steps were only partly successful, depending as they did on the good will and voluntary action of landlords and applicable as they were only to certain localities, as required by special circumstances or by way of experiment. . . .

We were therefore convinced that the task of improving the condition of the bonded people is a legacy to Us from Our Predecessors, and a destiny conferred upon Us in the course of events by the hand of Providence.

We began this task by an act of trust in the Russian Nobility, knowing of its great proofs of loyalty to the Throne and of its readiness to make sacrifices for the good of the Fatherland. We left it to the Nobility Itself to assemble and consider a new arrangement of peasant affairs, whereupon it was proposed to the Nobles to limit their rights over peasants and to bear the difficulties of a transformation that would entail losses to themselves. And Our trust was justified. Through its representatives in the Provincial Committees chosen by the whole Nobility of every province, the Nobility voluntarily renounced any rights to the person of the bonded ones. These Committees, af-

ter collecting the needed information, drew up proposals regarding a new order for people living in bondage and relations with lords.

*   *   *

Having called on God for assistance, We are resolved to complete this task.

Pursuant to these new Statutes, the bonded people are to receive in due course the full rights of free rural inhabitants.

The landlords, preserving their right of ownership of all lands belonging to them, are to grant to the peasants, in return for a certain obligation, perpetual use of their homestead as well as such quantity of plowland and other goods as is provided in the Statutes, so that they may be secure in their livelihood and fulfill their duties to the Government.

In taking advantage of this land allotment, the peasants are thereby required to fulfill the obligations to lords specified in the Statutes. In this condition, which is transitional, the peasants are temporarily obligated.

They are also to be given the right to buy their homestead; and with their lord's agreement they may acquire ownership of the plowland and other goods assigned to their perpetual use. On acquiring ownership of said land, the peasants are freed of any duties owed on it to the lord, and thus enter the well-defined estate of free peasant proprietors.

A Special Statute defines the transitional status of domestic folk, as appropriate to their duties and needs. Two years after publication of this Statute, they will receive complete freedom and certain temporary privileges.

*   *   *

Although these Statutes, the General, Local, and Supplementary Rules for certain special localities, for small landowners, and for peasants working in their lords' factories or industries, have been adapted as far as possible to local economic needs and practices; nevertheless, to preserve the customary order where it is mutually advantageous We leave it to the lords to reach voluntary understandings with peasants and to conclude agreements regarding the extent of the peasants' land allotments and corresponding obligations, observing therein the rules laid down for preserving the inviolability of such agreements.

As this new arrangement, given the inescapable complexity of the changes required by it, cannot be introduced at once, but rather needs time for that, meaning not less than two years: so in the course of this time, to avoid confusion, and to maintain the public and private good, the order hitherto existing on seigneurial estates should be preserved until, on completion of the necessary preparations, the new order will begin.

*   *   *

Considering the inescapable difficulties involved in this transformation, We place Our hope first of all in the surpassing goodness of Divine Providence, which protects Russia.

Then do We rely on the valiant zeal for the common good of the Well-born Noble estate, to whom We cannot fail to express, on behalf of Ourselves and the whole Fatherland, well-deserved recognition of unselfish execution of Our designs. Russia will not forget that, prompted only by respect for human dignity and Christian love of neighbor, they voluntarily renounced the law of bondage and laid the basis of a new economic future for peasants. We assuredly expect that with like nobility they will exhibit the utmost care in seeing that the new Statutes are carried out in good order, and in a spirit of peace and benevolence; that every landowner will complete, on his own land, the great civic act of his entire estate; and that, having arranged the affairs of the peasants settled on his land and of his domestic folk on terms advantageous to both sides, he will thus give a good example to the rural people and an incentive to exact and conscientious fulfillment of State regulations.

Mindful of examples of the landowners' generous solicitude for the good of peasants, and of the peasants' recognition of same, We are confirmed in Our hope that mutual voluntary agreements will resolve most of the difficulties

that are unavoidable when general rules are applied to the varying circumstances of individual estate lands. In this way the transition from the old order to the new will be alleviated, and mutual trust, good accord, and a unanimous aspiration for the common good will be strengthened in the future.

*   *   *

And We place Our hope in the good sense of Our people.

When word of the Government's plan to abolish the law of bondage reached peasants unprepared for it, there arose a partial misunderstanding. Some thought about freedom and forgot about obligations. But the general good sense was not disturbed in the conviction that anyone freely enjoying the goods of society correspondingly owes it to the common good to fulfill certain obligations, both by natural reason and by Christian law, according to which "every soul must be subject to the governing authorities" and "pay all of them their dues," in particular "labor, tribute, fear, and honor" * * * rights legally acquired by the landlords cannot be taken from them without a decent return or voluntary concession; and that it would be contrary to all justice to make use of the lords' land without bearing the corresponding obligations.

And now We hopefully expect that the bonded people, as a new future opens before them, will understand and accept with gratitude the important sacrifice made by the Well-born Nobility for the improvement of their lives.

They will understand that, receiving the advantages of ownership and the freedom to conduct their own affairs, they owe it to society and to themselves to realize the beneficence of the new law by a loyal, judicious, and diligent exercise of the rights granted to them. The most beneficent law cannot make people happy if they do not themselves labor to build their happiness under the protection of the law. Prosperity is acquired and increased only by hard work, the judicious use of strength and resources, strict economy, and, overall, by an honest, God-fearing life.

* * *

Make the sign of the cross, Orthodox people, and invoke with Us God's blessing on thy free labor, the pledge of thine own prosperity and of the public good.

Given at St. Petersburg in the year of Our Lord one thousand eight hundred sixty-one, and of Our Reign the seventh.

Alexander

REVIEW QUESTIONS

1. According to the manifesto, what social changes provoked emancipation?
2. What role does the aristocracy play in the execution of emancipation, and how realistic is this prescribed role?
3. How is religion invoked to unify Russian society in this period of change?

JULES FERRY

FROM The State Must Be Secular AND Letter to Teachers

The clash of views between clerics and liberals over the proper role of religion in civil society endured throughout the nineteenth century. Liberals associated progress with a secular state's promoting rational, materialist knowledge and criticized the meddling of the Catholic Church in such temporal public affairs as government and education. In France liberals attacked the Catholic Church as a royalist institution that undermined the values of the republic. Clerics and others, however, averred that a society bereft of spirituality and Christian mores in public life tokened a cold, increasingly insensitive world. In 1882 Jules Ferry (1832–1893), a statesman of the French Third Republic, secured a law that made primary education obligatory, free, and nonclerical. In the following speech and letter, Ferry outlined the classic liberal position on secular society and education.

From *Nineteenth Century Europe: Liberalism and its Critics,* edited by Jan Goldstein and John W. Boyer (Chicago: University of Chicago Press, 1988).

The State Must Be Secular
Given before the Chamber
of Deputies, 3 June 1876

I pronounce the words *secular state* without any trepidation, even though, for some of our honorable colleagues they would seem to have a certain radical, anarchist, or revolutionary flavor. Yet I am not saying anything new, revolutionary, or

anarchist when I maintain that the state must be secular, that the totality of society is necessarily represented by secular organizations.

What, exactly, is this principle? It is a doctrine that [the Catholic church] prides itself on having introduced into the world: the doctrine of the separation of temporal and spiritual power. Yes, Christianity introduced the doctrine of the separation of these two domains, the realm of the state and that of conscience, the temporal and the spiritual. It was successful, after centuries of struggle, in the midst of full-blown paganism. However, there is one reproach we could make against the church in this matter. After taking four or five centuries to introduce this doctrine, the church has then spent seven or eight centuries vehemently attacking it.

Gentlemen, what was the key accomplishment, the major concern, the great passion and service of the French Revolution? To have built this secular state, to have succeeded in making the social organisms of society exclusively secular, to have taken away from the clergy its political organization and role as a cadre within the state—that, precisely, is the French Revolution in its full reality. Well now, we do not presume to convert the honorable members seated on this side of the Chamber [i.e., on the right] to the doctrines of the revolution. We only wish it to be well understood that we do not deviate from these doctrines. Convinced that the first concern, the first duty of a democratic government is to maintain incessant, powerful, vigilant and efficient control over public education, we insist that this control belong to no authority other than the state. We cannot admit, we will never admit, and this country of France will never admit that the State can be anything but a secular one.

*   *   *

Letter to Teachers, 17 November 1883

The law of 28 March[1] is marked by two tendencies that complement without contradicting each other: on the one hand, the law excludes the teaching of any particular dogma from the required program; on the other, it accords moral and civic education the highest rank. Religious instruction belongs to the home and the church; moral instruction belongs to the school. The legislator thus did not intend to undertake a purely negative project. Undoubtedly, his first goal was to separate school and church, to assure the freedom of conscience for both masters and pupils, to distinguish at last between two domains that have been for too long confused: that of beliefs, which are personal, free, and variable; and that of knowledge, which is common and indispensable to all, consensual. But there is something else in the law of 28 March. It is a declaration of our will to found our own national education and base it on those notions of duty and right that the lawmaker does not hesitate to place among the first truths no one can fail to know. For this keystone of education, it is upon you, gentlemen, that the public powers have counted.

By dispensing you from religious instruction, we have no thoughts of freeing you from the teaching of morals. That would be removing the dignity of your profession. On the contrary, it seemed completely natural that the teacher, while teaching children to read and write, teach them as well the elementary rules of the moral life, which are no less universally accepted than those of grammar and mathematics.

. . . You do not, strictly speaking, have to teach anything new, anything that is not already as familiar to you as it is to all good people. And when we speak to you of your mission and apostolate, you should not misunderstand us. You are not the apostles of a new gospel. The legislator did not wish to transform you into philosophers or makeshift theologians. He asks of you what one may ask of any man of heart and sense. It is impossible for you to see all these children who gather around you every day to listen to your lessons, who observe your conduct and are inspired by your example, at the age when the mind awakens, the heart opens, the memory becomes enriched, without your having the idea of taking advantage of this docility and this confidence for purposes of moral instruction. You cannot help but give, along with what is strictly speaking, scholarly knowledge, the very principles of morality—by which I mean that good, simple, and ancient morality that we received from our parents and that in our rela-

---

[1] The law of 28 March 1882, often called the Ferry Law, made primary education in France free, nonclerical, and obligatory. [Editor.]

tionships in life we all pride ourselves on following without troubling to examine its philosophical basis.

You are the auxiliary and, in some respects, the substitute for the father of the family. Speak then to his son as you would wish one to speak to your own: with force and authority every time it is a question of an incontestable truth, of a matter of common morality: with the greatest reserve the moment you risk touching upon a religious feeling of which you are not the judge.

If at times you are at a loss to know exactly how far you may go in your moral teaching, here is a practical rule for you to follow. The moment you are planning to propose any precept or maxim to your students, ask yourself if you know of any good man who could be offended by what you are going to say. Ask yourself if any family man present in your class and hearing you could with good faith refuse to assent to what you say. If the answer is yes, refrain from saying it. If not, speak boldly, for what you are going to communicate to the child is not your own wisdom, but that of the human race. It is one of the ideas of a universal order that centuries of human civilization have bequeathed us. However narrow this cir-

cle of action may seem, make it a point of honor never to leave it. Remain within its boundaries rather than overstepping them. You can never be too scrupulous about touching that delicate and sacred thing that is a child's conscience. But, once you are thus loyally confined to the humble and secure role of everyday morality, what do we ask of you? Speeches? Wise explanations? Brilliant exposés, scholarly teaching? No! Family and society ask you to help raise their children, to make honest people of them. That is to say that they expect not words but acts, not another course added to the program but a completely practical service that you can render to the country more as a man than as a teacher.

REVIEW QUESTIONS

1. According to Ferry, what was the history of the secular state in Europe, and why did the secular state represent progress?
2. Why was a secular education so critical for Ferry?
3. What is Ferry's advice to teachers regarding morality and knowledge?

POPE LEO XIII

FROM *Rerum Novarum*

Throughout the modern era, the Catholic Church's position on modern science, secular civil society, and republican politics remained critical and oppositional. In 1864 Pope Pius IX issued the Syllabus of Errors, *an enyclical that reinforced the Church's irresolvable differences on progress, liberalism, and modern civilization. A subsequent declaration of papal infallibility in 1870 inflamed anew the tension between church and state. Pope Leo XIII (1878–1903), however, took a different tack. He accepted the principal features of the modern age but strove to offer moral leadership with constructive criticism of civil society's disregard for social justice and economic morals. His encyclical of 1896,* Rerum Novarum *(About New Things), critiqued both capitalism and socialism, and its influence unintentionally spawned a wave of Christian socialist movments throughout Europe.*

From *Rerum Novarum, Encyclical Letter of Pope Leo XIII on the Condition of Labor,* by Pope Leo XIII (Mahwah, N.J.: Paulist Press, 1939), pp. 3–6, 9–10, 12–13, 14–15, 29–31.

It is not surprising that the spirit of revolutionary change, which has long been predominant in the nations of the world, should have passed beyond politics and made its influence felt in the cognate field of practical economy. The elements of a conflict are unmistakable: the growth of industry, and the surprising discoveries of science; the changed relations of masters and workmen; the enormous fortunes of individuals and the poverty of the masses; the increased self-reliance and the closer mutual combination of the working population; and, finally, a general moral deterioration. The momentous seriousness of the present state of things just now fills every mind with painful apprehension; wise men discuss it; practical men propose schemes; popular meetings, legislatures, and sovereign princes, all are occupied with it—and there is nothing which has a deeper hold on public attention.

Therefore, Venerable Brethren, as on former occasions, when it seemed opportune to refute false teaching, We have addressed you in the interests of the Church and of the commonwealth, and have issued Letters on Political Power, on Human Liberty, on the Christian Constitution of the State, and on similar subjects, so now We have thought it useful to speak on

The Condition of Labor

It is a matter on which we have touched once or twice already. But in this Letter the responsibility of the Apostolic office urges Us to treat the question expressly and at length, in order that there may be no mistake as to the principles which truth and justice dictate for its settlement. The discussion is not easy, nor is it free from danger. It is not easy to define the relative rights and the mutual duties of the wealthy and of the poor, of capital and of labor. And the danger lies in this, that crafty agitators constantly make use of these disputes to pervert men's judgments and to stir up the people to sedition.

But all agree, and there can be no question whatever, that some remedy must be found, and quickly found, for the misery and wretchedness which press so heavily at this moment on the large majority of the very poor. The ancient workmen's Guilds were destroyed in the last century, and no other organization took their place. Public institutions and the laws have repudiated the ancient religion. Hence by degrees it has come to pass that Working Men have been given over, isolated and defenceless, to the callousness of employers and the greed of unrestrained competition. The evil has been increased by rapacious Usury, which, although more than once condemned by the Church, is nevertheless, under a different form but with the same guilt, still practiced by avaricious and grasping men. And to this must be added the custom of working by contract, and the concentration of so many branches of trade in the hands of a few individuals, so that a small number of very rich men have been able to lay upon the masses of the poor a yoke little better than slavery itself.

To remedy these evils the *Socialists,* working on the poor man's envy of the rich, endeavor to destroy private property, and maintain that individual possessions should become the common property of all, to be administered by the State or by municipal bodies. They hold that, by thus transferring property from private persons to the community, the present evil state of things will be set to rights, because each citizen will then have his equal share of whatever there is to enjoy. But their proposals are so clearly futile for all practical purposes, that if they were carried out the working man himself would be among the first to suffer. Moreover they are emphatically unjust, because they would rob the lawful possessor, bring the State into a sphere that is not its own, and cause complete confusion in the community.

Private Ownership

It is surely undeniable that, when a man engages in remunerative labor, the very reason and motive of his work is to obtain property, and to hold it as his own private possession. If one man hires out to another his strength or his industry, he does this for the purpose of receiving in return what is necessary for food and living; he thereby expressly proposes to acquire a full and real right, not only to the remuneration, but also to the disposal of that remuneration as he pleases. Thus, if he lives sparingly, saves money, and invests his savings, for greater security, in land, the land in such a case is only his wages in another form; and, consequently, a working man's little estate thus purchased should be as completely at his own disposal as the wages he receives for his labor. But it is precisely in this power of disposal that ownership consists, whether the property be land or movable goods. The *Socialists,* therefore, in endeavoring to transfer the possessions of individuals to the community, strike at the interests of every wage earner, for they deprive him of the liberty of disposing of his wages, and thus of all hope and possibility of increasing his stock and of bettering his condition in life.

What is of still greater importance, however, is that the remedy they propose is manifestly against justice. For every man has by nature the right to possess property as his own. This is one of the *chief points of distinction* between man and the animal creation. For the brute has no power of self-direction, but is governed by two chief instincts, which keep his powers alert, move him to use his strength, and determine him to action without the power of choice. These instincts are self-preservation and the propagation of the species. Both can attain their purpose by means of things which are close at hand; beyond their sur-

roundings the brute creation cannot go, for they are moved to action by sensibility alone, and by the things which sense perceives. But with man it is different indeed. He possesses, on the one hand, the full perfection of animal nature, and therefore he enjoys, at least, as much as the rest of the animal race, the fruition of the things of the body. But animality, however perfect, is far from being the whole of humanity, and is indeed humanity's humble handmaid, made to serve and obey. It is the mind, or the reason, which is the chief thing in us who are human beings; it is this which makes a human being human, and distinguishes him essentially and completely from the brute. And on this account—viz., that man alone among animals possesses reason—it must be within his right to have things not merely for temporary and momentary use, as other living beings have them, but in stable and permanent possession; he must have not only things which perish in the using, but also those which, though used, remain for use in the future.

*   *   *

Socialism Rejected

The idea, then, that the civil government should, at its own discretion, penetrate and pervade the family and the household, is a great and pernicious mistake. True, if a family finds itself in great difficulty, utterly friendless, and without prospect of help, it is right that extreme necessity be met by public aid; for each family is a part of the commonwealth. In like manner, if within the walls of the household there occur grave disturbance of mutual rights, the public power must interfere to force each party to give the other what is due; for this is not to rob citizens of their rights, but justly and properly to safeguard and strengthen them. But the rulers of the State must go no further: nature bids them stop here. Paternal authority can neither be abolished by the State nor absorbed; for it has the same source as human life itself; "the child belongs to the father," and is, as it were, the continuation of the father's personality; and, to speak with strictness, the child takes its place in civil society not in its own right, but in its quality as a member of the family in which it is begotten. And it is for the very reason that "the child belongs to the father," that, as St. Thomas of Aquin says, "before it attains the use of free-will, it is in the power and care of its parents." The Socialists, therefore, in setting aside the parent and introducing the providence of the State, act *against natural justice,* and threaten the very existence of family life.

And such interference is not only unjust, but is quite certain to harass and disturb all classes of citizens, and to subject them to odious and intolerable slavery. It would open the door to envy, to evil speaking, and to quarrelling; the sources of wealth would themselves run dry, for no one would have any interest in exerting his talents or his industry; and that ideal equality of which so much is said would, in reality, be the leveling down of all to the same condition of misery and dishonor.

Thus it is clear *that the main tenet of Socialism, the community of goods, must be utterly rejected;* for it would injure those whom it is intended to benefit, it would be contrary to the natural rights of mankind, and it would introduce confusion, and disorder into the commonwealth. Our first and most fundamental principle, therefore, when we undertake to alleviate the condition of the masses, must be the inviolability of private property This laid down, We go on to show where we must find the remedy that we seek.

*　　*　　*

Employer and Employee

The great mistake that is made in the matter now under consideration, is to possess oneself of the idea that class is naturally hostile to class; that rich and poor are intended by nature to live at war with one another. So irrational and so false is this view, that the exact contrary is the truth. Just as the symmetry of the human body is the result of the disposition of the members of the body, so in

a State it is ordained by nature that these two classes should exist in harmony and agreement, and should, as it were, fit into one another, so as to maintain the equilibrium of the body politic. Each requires the other; capital cannot do without labor, nor labor without capital. Mutual agreement results in pleasantness and good order; perpetual conflict necessarily produces confusion and outrage. Now, in preventing such strife as this, and in making it impossible, the efficacy of Christianity is marvelous and manifold. First of all, there is nothing more powerful than Religion (of which the Church is the interpreter and guardian) in drawing rich and poor together, by reminding each class of its duties to the other, and especially of the duties of justice. Thus Religion teaches the laboring man and the workman to carry out honestly and well all equitable agreements freely made, never to injure capital, nor to outrage the person of an employer; never to employ violence in representing his own cause, nor to engage in riot and disorder; and to have nothing to do with men of evil principles, who work upon the people with artful promises, and raise foolish hopes which usually end in disaster and in repentance when too late. Religion teaches the rich man and the employer that their work people are not their slaves; that they must respect in every man his dignity as a man and as a Christian; that labor is nothing to be ashamed of, if we listen to right reason and to Christian philosophy, but is an honorable employment, enabling a man to sustain his life in an upright and creditable way, and that it is shameful and inhuman to treat men like chattels to make money by, or to look upon them merely as so much muscle or physical power.

*　　*　　*

The Right Use of Money

Therefore, those whom fortune favors are warned that freedom from sorrow and abundance of earthly riches, are no guarantee of that beatitude that shall never end, but rather the contrary; that the rich should tremble at the threatenings of Jesus Christ—threatenings so strange in the mouth of our Lord; and that a most strict account must be given to the Supreme Judge for all that we possess. The chiefest and most excellent rule for the right use of money is one which the heathen philosophers indicated, but which the Church has traced out clearly, and has not only made known to men's minds, but has impressed upon their lives. It rests on the principle that it is one thing to have a right to the possession of money, and another to have a right to use money as one pleases. Private ownership, as we have seen, is the natural right of man; and to exercise that right, especially as members of society, is not only lawful but absolutely necessary. "It is lawful," says St. Thomas of Aquin, "for a man to hold private property; and it is also necessary for the carrying on of human life." But if the question be asked, How must one's possessions be used? the Church replies without hesitation in the words of the same holy Doctor: "Man should not consider his outward possessions as his own, but as common to all, so as to share them without difficulty when others are in need. Whence the Apostle saith, Command the rich of this world . . . to give with ease, to communicate." True, no one is commanded to distribute to others that which is required for his own necessities and those of his household; nor even to give away what is reasonably required to keep up becomingly his condition in life; "for no one ought to live unbecomingly." But when necessity has been supplied, and one's position fairly considered, it is a duty to give to the indigent out of that which is over. "That which remaineth give alms." It is a duty, not of justice (except in extreme cases), but of Christian Charity—a duty which is not enforced by human law.

*   *   *

Workmen's Associations

In the first place—employers and workmen may themselves effect much in the matter of which We treat, by means of those institutions and or-ganizations which afford opportune assistance to those in need, and which draw the two orders more closely together. Among these may be enumerated: societies for mutual help; various foundations established by private persons for providing for the workman, and for his widow or his orphans, in sudden calamity, in sickness, and in the event of death; and what are called "patronages," or institutions for the care of boys and girls, for young people, and also for those of more mature age.

The most important of all are Workmen's Associations; for these virtually include all the rest. History attests what excellent results were affected by the Artificer's Guilds of a former day. They were the means not only of many advantages to the workmen, but in no small degree of the advancement of art, as numerous monuments remain to prove. Such associations should be adapted to the requirements of the age in which we live—an age of greater instruction, of different customs, and of more numerous requirements in daily life. It is gratifying to know that there are actually in existence not a few societies of this nature, consisting either of workmen alone, or of workmen and employers together; but it were greatly to be desired that they should multiply and become more effective. We have spoken of them more than once; but it will be well to explain here how much they are needed, to show that they exist by their own right, and to enter into their organization and their work.

*   *   *

These lesser societies and the society which constitutes the State differ in many things, because their immediate purpose and end is different. Civil society exists for the common good, and, therefore, is concerned with the interests of all in general, and with the individual interests in their due place and proportion. Hence, it is called *public* society, because by its means, as St. Thomas of Aquin says, "Men communicate with one another in the setting up of a commonwealth." But the societies which are formed in the bosom of the State are called *private,* and justly so, because their immediate purpose is the private advantage of the associates. "Now, a private society," says St. Thomas again, "is one which is formed for the purpose of carrying out private business; as when two or three enter into partnership with the view of trading in conjunction." Particular societies, then, although they exist within the State, and are each a part of the State, nevertheless cannot be prohibited by the State absolutely and as such. For to enter into a "society" of this kind is the natural right of man; and the State must protect natural rights, not destroy them; and if it forbids its citizens to form associations, it contradicts the very principle of its own existence; for both they and it exist in virtue of the same principle, viz., the natural propensity of man to live in society.

*   *   *

Conclusion

We have now laid before you, Venerable Brethren, who are the persons, and what are the means, by which this most difficult question must be solved. Every one must put his hand to work which falls to his share, and that at once and immediately, lest the evil which is already so great may by delay become absolutely beyond remedy. Those who rule the State must use the law and the institutions of the country; masters and rich men must remember their duty; the poor, whose interests are at stake, must make every lawful and proper effort; since Religion alone, as We said at the beginning, can destroy the evil at its root, all men must be persuaded that the primary thing needful is to return to real Christianity, in the absence of which all the plans and devices of the wisest will be of little avail.

*   *   *

REVIEW QUESTIONS

1. What was the position of the Catholic Church on the condition of labor?
2. What were Leo XIII's criticisms of capitalism and socialism?
3. How did the Catholic Church's view of civil society differ from those two doctrines?
4. What reforms of market economy did the encyclical propose, and how were these critical of liberalism?

24 ❧ REVOLUTION, NATIONALISM, AND NATION BUILDING, 1815–1870

Nationalism is strictly a modern phenomenon. Arising as a cultural doctrine in the late eighteenth century, the sentiment of nationalism quickly became a widespread political force, constantly evolving over time and adapting to particular needs. Its impact was registered at all levels of public life. As one of the chief solvents of the old regime, the principle of national unity not only realigned the European state system but also radically recast political culture with a new consciousness of citizenship. Political and economic change eroded older forms of local and regional loyalties, enabling the ideal of national citizenship to embed itself as a self-evident assumption for millions of Europeans.

The cultural dominance of the French Enlightenment, and its insistence on uniform standards, produced a wave of cultural resistance among European writers. In contrast to the Enlightenment's search for social and artistic norms applicable to all societies, select intellectuals celebrated instead the teeming heterogeneity of European language, customs, and culture. Each culture or people, they argued, embodied a national spirit: unique manifestations of geography, climate, and language that defied qualitative comparison. Humanitas, argued cultural nationalists, was not reducible to core characteristics, but rather was the aggregate of humankind's cultural diversity. By honoring all cultures and nations and conferring on them the self-evident right to develop of their own accord, early forms of cultural nationalism perceived the nation within a tolerant, cosmopolitan worldview.

The French Revolution converted this cultural sentiment into political strength. By endowing the nation with political sovereignty and transforming subjects into citizens, the French Revolution evinced the enormous potential of nationalism to wield political and military power. Reaffirmed in flags, anthems, emblems, festivals, and dress, the words nation *and* Fatherland *("la patrie") stirred the blood of patriots, enabling the revolutionary government to mobilize its citizenry to serve the nation-state with unprecedented engagement. Under the leadership of Napoleon, the massive revolutionary armies of citizen soldiers stood out as a superior fighting force, compelling the great powers of Europe to adapt or perish.*

Napoleonic occupation, in turn, awakened national consciousness in other European cultures. The traditional elite initially tapped patriotism to counter Napoleon's armies, but unwittingly set in motion popular movements whose ideals of national sovereignty, unified nation-states, and constitutional liberties challenged kingdoms, multinational empires, and conservative principles of social hierarchy. Emancipating peoples from the injustice of imposed foreign rule gripped the imagination of artists, writers, and poets, who depicted nationalist movements as romantic quests for liberty and freedom. In the first half of the nineteenth century, liberals, democrats, and nationalists formed strong bonds, for they saw a constitutional nation-state as the vehicle of progress for all social groups. The struggle to unify a people under modern principles of citizenship assumed an ethical, humanitarian character. Advocates of nationalism adopted rhetoric, imagery, and ceremonies once reserved exclusively for religions. The ideal of self-sacrifice further sanctified nationalist movements; bloodshed consecrated the nation as a higher purpose for which to die.

The principle of nationalism shaped the course of nineteenth-century state building, but not in the manner envisioned by liberals. Statesmen reworked nationalism into a conservative mold, using patriotism and nationalist sentiment to support conservative monarchism and authoritarian government. Calculating that rural voters were inherently resistant to innovative change, conservative rulers shrewdly introduced constitutions and universal manhood suffrage to lend popular legitimacy to their conservative policies, thereby checking the reformist impulses of urban liberals. Yet nationalism did not remain the manipulative tool of conservative statesmen. Urbanization, improved communications, and the vote produced grassroots political movements that used nationalism to protect domestic industry, agitate for imperial expansion, and brand socialists, Jews, and foreigners as pernicious influences on the nation's political body. The numerous hybrid forms of nationalisms circulating in Europe by the end of the nineteenth century contributed to the increasingly chauvinistic political culture that condoned aggressive militarism, xenophobia, and racial exclusion.

In the wake of the Industrial and French Revolutions, political consciousness underwent radical change. Traditional authority was either modified or replaced by political communities whose legitimacy and power hinged on their representation of the nation. Yet the meaning of nationalism never became fixed; it remained a protean ideology serving a wide array of political interests and social classes over the long period from 1789 to 1914.

JOHANN GOTTFRIED HERDER

FROM *Reflections on the Philosophy of the History of Mankind*

Johann Gottfried Herder (1744–1803), a theologian by training and profession, greatly influenced German letters with his literary criticism and his philosophy of history. In his later years, Herder resided in the Duchy of Weimar and his presence, along with those of J. W. Goethe and F. Schiller, made Weimar the seat of German neohumanism. His analogy of national cultures as organic beings had an enormous impact on modern historical consciousness. Nations, he argued, possessed not only the phases of youth, maturity, and decline but also singular, incomparable worth. His mixture of anthropology and history, as witnessed in the passage below, is characteristic of the age.

From *Reflections on the Philosophy of the History of Mankind,* by Johann Gottfried Herder, edited by Frank E. Manuel (Chicago: University of Chicago Press, 1970).

Chapter 1
Notwithstanding the Varieties of the Human Form, There Is But One and the Same Species of Man throughout the Whole of Our Earth

No two leaves of any one tree in nature are to be found perfectly alike; and still less do two human faces, or human frames, resemble each other. Of what endless variety is our artful structure susceptible! Our solids are decomposable into such minute and multifariously interwoven fibres, as no eye can trace; and these are connected by a gluten of such a delicate composition, as the utmost skill is insufficient to analyse. Yet these constitute the least part of us: they are nothing more than the containing vessels and conduits of the variously compounded, highly animated fluid, existing in much greater quantity, by means of which we live and enjoy life. "No man," says Haller, "is exactly similar to another in his internal structure: the courses of the nerves and blood vessels differ in millions and millions of cases, so that amid the variations of these delicate parts, we are scarcely able to discover in what they agree." But if the eye of the anatomist can perceive this infinite variety, how much greater must that be, which dwells in the invisible powers of such an artful organization! So that every man is ultimately a world, in external appearance indeed similar to others, but internally an individual being, with whom no other coincides.

And since man is no independent substance, but is connected with all the elements of nature; living by inspiration of the air, and deriving nutriment from the most opposite productions of the Earth, in his meats and drinks; consuming fire, while he absorbs light, and contaminates the air he breathes; awake or asleep, in motion or at rest, contributing to the change of the universe; shall not he also be changed by it? It is far too little, to compare him to the absorbing sponge, the sparkling tinder: he is a multitudinous harmony, a living self, on whom the harmony of all the powers that surround him operates.

The whole course of a man's life is change: the different periods of his life are tales of transformation, and the whole species is one continued metamorphosis. Flowers drop and wither; others sprout out and bud: the vast tree bears at once all the seasons on its head. If, from a calculation of the insensible perspiration alone, a man of eighty have renovated his whole body at least four and twenty times; who can trace the variations of matter and its forms through all the race of mankind upon the Earth, amid all the causes of change; when not one point on our complicated Globe, not one wave in the current of time, resembles another? A few centuries only have elapsed since the inhabitants of Germany were Patagonians: but they are so no longer, and the inhabitants of its future climates will not equal us. If now we go back to those times, when every thing upon Earth was apparently so different; the times for instance, when elephants lived in Siberia and North America, and those large animals existed, the bones of which are to be found on the Ohio; if men then lived in those regions, how different must they have been from those, who now inhabit them! Thus the history of man is ultimately a theatre of transformations, which He alone can review, who animates all these figures, and feels and enjoys in them all. He builds up and destroys, improves and alters forms, while he changes the World around them. The wanderer upon Earth, the transient ephemeron, can only admire the wonders of this great spirit in a narrow circle, enjoy the form that belongs to him in the general choir, adore, and disappear with this form. "I too was in Arcadia": is the monumental inscription of all living beings in the ever-changing, ever-renewing creation.

As the human intellect, however, seeks unity in every kind of variety, and the divine mind, its prototype, has stamped the most innumerable multiplicity upon the Earth with unity, we may venture from the vast realm of change to revert to the simplest position: *all mankind are only one and the same species.*

*   *   *

For each genus Nature has done enough, and to each has given its proper progeny. The ape she has divided into as many species and varieties as possible, and extended these as far as she could: but thou, O man, honour thyself: neither the pongo nor the gibbon is thy brother: the American and the Negro are: these therefore thou shouldst not oppress, or murder, or steal; for they are men, like thee: with the ape thou canst not enter into fraternity.

Lastly, I could wish the distinctions between the human species, that have been made from a laudable zeal for discriminating science, not carried beyond due bounds. Some for instance have thought fit, to employ the term of *races* for four or five divisions, originally made in consequence of country or complexion: but I see no reason for this appellation. Race refers to a difference of origin, which in this case either does not exist, or in each of these countries, and under each of these complexions, comprises the most different races. For every nation is one people, having its own national form, as well as its own language: the climate, it is true, stamps on each its mark, or spreads over it a slight veil, but not sufficient to destroy the original national character. This originality of character extends even to families, and its transitions are as variable as imperceptible. In short, there are neither four or five races, nor exclusive varieties, on this Earth. Complexions run into each other: forms follow the genetic character: and upon the whole, all are at last but shades of the same great picture, extending through all ages, and over all parts of the Earth. They belong not, therefore, so properly to systematic natural history, as to the physico-geographical history of man.

*   *   *

Now as mankind, both taken as a whole, and in its particular individuals, societies, and nations, is a permanent natural system of the most multifarious living powers; let us examine, wherein its stability consists; in what point its highest beauty, truth, and goodness, unite; and what course it takes, in order to reapproach its permanent condition, on every aberration from it, of which many are exhibited to us by history and experience.

1. The human species is such a copious scheme of energies and capacities, that, as every thing in nature rests on the most determinate individuality, its great and numerous capacities could not appear on our planet otherwise than *divided among millions.* Every thing has been born, that could be born upon it; and every thing has maintained itself, that could acquire a state of permanence according to the laws of Nature. Thus every individual bears within himself that symmetry, for which he is made, and to which he must mould himself, both in his bodily figure, and mental capacities. Human existence appears in every shape and kind, from the most sickly deformity, that can scarcely support life, to the superhuman form of a Grecian demigod; from the passionate ardour of the Negro brain, to the capacity for consummate wisdom. Through faults and errours, through education, necessity, and exercise, every mortal seeks the symmetry of his powers; as in this alone the most complete enjoyment of his existence lies: yet few are sufficiently fortunate, to attain it in the purest, happiest manner.

2. As an individual man can subsist of himself but very imperfectly, *a superiour maximum of cooperating powers* is formed with every society. These powers contend together in wild confusion, till, agreeably to the unfailing laws of nature, opposing regulations limit each other, and a kind of equilibrium and harmony of movement takes place. Thus nations modify themselves, according to time, place, and their internal character: each bears in itself the standard of its perfection, totally independent of all comparison with that of others. Now the more pure and fine the maximum on which a people hit, the more useful the objects to which it applied the exertions of its nobler powers, and, lastly, the more firm and exact the bond of union, which most intimately connected all the members of the state, and guided them to this good end; the more stable was the nation itself, and the more brilliant the figure it made in history. The course that we have hitherto taken through certain nations shows how different, ac-

cording to place, time, and circumstances, was the object for which they strove. With the Chinese it was refined political morality; with the Hindoos, a kind of retired purity, quiet assiduity in labour, and endurance; with the Phoenicians, the spirit of navigation, and commercial industry. The culture of the Greeks, particularly at Athens, proceeded on the maximum of sensible beauty, both in arts and manners, in science and in political institutions. In Sparta, and in Rome, men emulated the virtues of the patriot and hero; in each, however, in a very different mode. Now as in all these most depended on time and place, the ancients will scarcely admit of being compared with each other in the most distinguished features of national fame.

3. In all, however, we see the operation of *one principle*, namely *human reason*, which endeavours to produce unity out of multiplicity, order out of disorder, and out of variety of powers and designs one symmetrical and durably beautiful whole. From the shapeless artificial rocks, with which the Chinese ornaments his garden, to the Egyptian pyramid, or the ideal beauty of Greece, the plan and design of a reflecting understanding is every where observable, though in very different degrees. The more refined the reflections of this understanding were, and the nearer it came to the point, which is the highest in its kind, and admits no deviation to the right or to the left; the more were its performances to be considered as models, for they contain eternal rules for the human understanding in all ages. Thus nothing of the kind can be conceived superiour to an Egyptian pyramid, or to several Greek and Roman works of art. They are simple solutions of certain problems of the understanding, which admit no arbitrary supposition, that the problems are perhaps not yet solved, or might be solved in a better way, for in them the simple idea of what they ought to be is displayed in the easiest, fullest, and most beautiful manner. Every deviation from them would be a fault; and were they to be repeated and diversified in a thousand modes, we must still return to that single point, which is the highest of its kind.

4. Thus through all the polished nations, that we have hitherto considered, or shall hereafter con-

sider, *a chain of cultivation* may be drawn, flying off in extremely divergent curves. In each it designates increasing and decreasing greatness, and has maximums of every kind. Many of these exclude or limit one another, till at length a certain symmetry takes place in the whole; so that were we to reason from one perfection of any nation concerning another, we should form very treacherous conclusions. Thus, because Athens had exquisite orators, it does not follow, that its form of government must likewise have been the best possible; or that, because the Chinese moralize so excellently, their state must be a pattern for all others. Forms of government refer to a very different maximum, from that of beautiful morals, or a pathetic oration; notwithstanding, at bottom, all things in any nation have a certain connexion, if it be only that of exclusion and limitation. No other maximum, but that of the most perfect bond of union, produces the most happy states; even supposing the people are in consequence obliged to dispense with many shining qualities.

5. But in one and the same nation every maximum of its commendable endeavours ought not and cannot endure for ever; since it is but one point in the progress of time. This incessantly moves on; and the more numerous the circumstances, on which the beautiful effect depends, the sooner is it liable to pass away. Happy if its master pieces remain as rules for future ages.

*   *   *

REVIEW QUESTIONS

1. What is Herder's argument regarding difference and similarity in the human race?
2. What is the role of time, place, and climate in Herder's view of civilizations?
3. How is Herder's presentation of cultural development different from that of the Enlightenment?

JOHANN GOTTLIEB FICHTE

FROM *Addresses to the German Nation*

One of the most important ramifications of the revolutionary era was the awakening of nationalist sentiment in Europe. The origin of German national consciousness provides a good example. Following the stunning victories of France over Germany between 1802 and 1807, Napoleon redrew the map of Germany, reducing the great power status of Prussia, erecting a federation of satellite states, and creating new kingdoms. Faced with this humiliation, German rulers, statesmen, and intellectuals realized that reform from above was necessary so that the untapped energies of German citizenry could be summoned to defeat the French foe. In the occupied Prussian capital of Berlin in the winter of 1807–1808, the philosopher Johann Gottlieb Fichte held a series of lectures that called for the spiritual renewal of Germany through a program of reformed education that stressed the German nation's character and strength. It typified the idealism and romanticism of German patriotism in this era.

From *Addresses to the German Nation,* translated by R. F. Jones and G. H. Turnbull (Ashland, Ohio: Open Court, 1922).

*   *   *

Fourteenth Address

*   *   *

CONCLUSION

In the addresses which I conclude today, I have spoken aloud to you first of all, but I have had in view the whole German nation, and my intention has been to gather round me, in the room in which you are bodily present, everyone in the domain of the German language who is able to understand me. If I have succeeded in throwing into any heart which has beaten here in front of me a spark which will continue to glow there and to influence its life, it is not my intention that these hearts should remain apart and lonely; I want to gather to them from over the whole of our common soil men of similar sentiments and resolutions, and to link them together, so that at this central point a single, continuous, and unceasing flame of patriotic disposition may be kindled, which will spread over the whole soil of the fatherland to its utmost boundaries. These addresses have not been meant for the entertainment of indolent ears and eyes in the present age; on the contrary, I want to know once for all, and everyone of like disposition shall know it with me, whether there is anyone besides ourselves whose way of thinking is akin to ours. Every German who still believes himself to be a member of a nation, who thinks highly and nobly of that nation, hopes for it, ventures, endures, and suffers for it, shall at last have the uncertainty of his belief removed; he shall see clearly whether he is right or is only a fool and a dreamer; from now on he shall either pursue his way with the glad consciousness of certainty, or else firmly and vigorously renounce a fatherland here below, and find in the heavenly one his only consolation. To them, not as individuals in our everyday limited life, but as representatives of the nation, and so through their ears to the whole nation, these addresses make this appeal:

Centuries have come and gone since you were last convoked as you are to-day; in such numbers; in a cause so great, so urgent, and of such concern to all and everyone; so entirely as a nation and as Germans. Never again will the offer come to you in this way. If you now take no heed and withdraw into yourselves, if you again let these addresses go by you as if they were meant merely to tickle your ears, or if you regard them as something strange and fabulous, then no human being will ever take you into account again. Hearken now at last; reflect now at last. Go not from your place this time at least without first making a firm resolution; and let everyone who hears my voice make this resolution by himself and for himself, just as if he were alone and had to do everything alone. If very many individuals think in this way, there will soon be formed a large community which will be fused into a single close-connected force. But if, on the contrary, each one, leaving himself out, puts his hope in the rest and leaves the matter to others, then there will be no others, and all together will remain as they were before. Make it on the spot, this resolution.

*   *   *

To all you Germans, whatever position you may occupy in society, these addresses solemnly appeal; let every one of you, who can think, think first of all about the subject here suggested, and let each do for it what lies nearest to him individually in the position he occupies.

Your forefathers unite themselves with these addresses, and make a solemn appeal to you. Think that in my voice there are mingled the voices of your ancestors of the hoary past, who with their own bodies stemmed the onrush of Roman world-dominion, who with their blood won the independence of those mountains, plains, and rivers which under you have fallen a prey to the foreigner. They call to you: "Act for us; let the memory of us which you hand on to posterity be just as honourable and without reproach as it was when it came to you, when you took pride in it and in your descent from us. Until now, the resistance we made has been regarded as great and wise and noble; we seemed the consecrated and the inspired in the divine world-purpose. If our race dies out with you, our honour will be turned to shame and our wisdom to foolishness. For if, indeed, the German stock is to be swallowed up in Roman civilization, it were better that it had fallen before the Rome of old than before a Rome of to-day. The former we resisted and conquered; by the latter you have been ground to dust. Seeing that this is so, you shall now not conquer them with temporal weapons; your spirit alone shall rise up against them and stand erect. To you has fallen the greater destiny, to found the empire of the spirit and of reason, and completely to annihilate the rule of brute physical force in the world. If you do this, then you are worthy of your descent from us."

Then, too, there mingle with these voices the spirits of your more recent forefathers, those who fell in the holy war for the freedom of belief and of religion. "Save our honour too," they cry to you. "To us it was not entirely clear what we fought for; besides the lawful resolve not to let ourselves be dictated to by external force in matters of conscience, there was another and a higher spirit driving us, which never fully revealed itself to us. To you it is revealed, this spirit, if you have the power of vision in the spiritual world; it beholds you with eyes clear and sublime. The varied and confused mixture of sensuous and spiritual motives that has hitherto ruled the world shall be displaced, and spirit alone, pure and freed from all sensuous motives, shall take the helm of human affairs. It was in order that this spirit might have freedom to develop and grow to independent existence—it was for this that we poured forth our blood. It is for you to justify and give meaning to our sacrifice, by setting this spirit to fulfil its purpose and to rule the world. If this does not come about as the final goal to which the whole previous development of our nation has been tending, then the battles we fought will turn out to be a vain and fleeting farce, and the freedom of conscience and of spirit that we won is a vain word, it from now onwards spirit and conscience are to be no more."

*   *   *

All ages, all wise and good men who have ever breathed upon this earth, all their thoughts and intuitions of something loftier, mingle with these voices and surround you and lift up imploring hands to you; even, if one may say so, providence and the divine plan in creating a race of men, a plan which exists only to be thought out by men and to be brought by men into the actual world —the divine plan, I say, solemnly appeals to you to save its honour and its existence. Whether those were right who believed that mankind must always grow better, and that thoughts of a true order and worth of man were no idle dreams, but the prophecy and pledge of the real world that is to be— whether they are to be proved right, or those who continue to slumber in an animal and vegetable existence and mock at every flight into higher worlds—to give a final and decisive judgment on this point is a work for you. The old world with its glory and its greatness, as well as its defects, has fallen by its own unworthiness and by the violence of your fathers. If there is truth in what has been expounded in these addresses, then are you of all modern peoples the one in whom the seed of human perfection most unmistakably lies, and to whom the lead in its development is committed. If you perish in this your essential nature, then there perishes together with you every hope of the whole human race for salvation from the depths of its miseries. Do not console yourselves with an opinion based on thin air and depending on the mere recurrence of cases that have already happened; do not hope that when the old civilization has fallen a new one will arise once more out of a semi-barbarous nation on the ruins of the first. In ancient times there was such a people in existence, equipped with every requirement for such a destiny and quite well known to the civilized people, who have left us their description of it; and they themselves, if they had been able to imagine their own downfall, would have been able to discover in this people the means of reconstruction. To us also the whole surface of the globe is quite well known and all the peoples that dwell thereon. But do we know a people akin to the ancestral stock of the modern world, of whom we may have the same expectation? I think that everyone who does not merely base his hopes and beliefs on idle dreaming, but investigates thoroughly and thinks, will be bound to answer this question with a NO. There is, therefore, no way out; if you go under, all humanity goes under with you, without hope of any future restoration.

This it was, gentlemen, which at the end of these addresses I wanted and was bound to impress upon you, who to me are the representatives of the nation, and through you upon the whole nation.

REVIEW QUESTIONS

1. How does Fichte define the nation? What is the significance of Fichte's stress on continuity between contemporary Germans and their forefathers?
2. What is the relationship of Fichte's nationalism to humanity?

LORD BYRON

"On This Day I Complete My Thirty-sixth Year"

George Gordon, Lord Byron (1788–1824), one of the prominent English Romantic poets, took up the cause of liberating Greece from the Ottoman empire, lending his money, time, and pen to the cause of independence. In 1823 he sailed to Greece, where he partook in preparation for the Greek uprising. Before he had the chance to fight and find "a soldier's grave," Byron fell ill and died. Just prior to his death, however, he composed the following poem, which immortalized the Greek nationalist movement. The engagement of such intellectuals as Byron for national freedom generated widespread support among western European bourgeois circles for nationalist movements.

From *The Best of Byron*, edited by Richard Ashley Rice (New York: Ronald Press, 1942).

Tis time this heart should be unmoved,
　　Since others it hath ceased to move:
Yet, though I cannot be beloved,
　　Still let me love!

My days are in the yellow leaf;
　　The flowers and fruits of love are gone;
The worm, the canker, and the grief
　　Are mine alone!

The fire that on my bosom preys
　　Is lone as some volcanic isle;
No torch is kindled at its blaze—
　　A funeral pile.

The hope, the fear, the jealous care,
　　The exalted portion of the pain
And power of love, I cannot share,
　　But wear the chain.

But 'tis not *thus*—and 'tis not *here*—
　　Such thoughts should shake my soul nor
　　now,
Where glory decks the hero's bier,
　　Or binds his brow.

The sword, the banner, and the field,
　　Glory and Greece, around me see!
The Spartan, borne upon his shield,
　　Was not more free.

Awake! (not Greece—she *is* awake!)
　　Awake, my spirit! Think through *whom*
Thy life-blood tracks its parent lake,
　　And then strike home!

Tread those reviving passions down,
　　Unworthy manhood!—unto thee
Indifferent should the smile or frown
　　Of beauty be.

If thou regrett'st thy youth, *why live?*
　　The land of honourable death
Is here:—up to the field, and give
　　Away thy breath!

Seek out—less often sought than found—
　　A soldier's grave, for thee the best;
Then look around, and choose thy ground,
　　And take thy rest.

REVIEW QUESTIONS

1. What does the poem exhort the reader to do?
2. How does Byron romanticize the Greek cause?
3. How are immortality, manhood, and honor achieved in this poem, and how are these attributes related to nationalism?

GREECE ON THE RUINS OF MISSOLONGHI (1826)   Eugène Delacroix

Many nationalist movements in Europe fashioned the Greek struggle for emancipation against the Ottoman Empire in the 1820s as a romantic, epic struggle for national freedom and statehood. And in a period of reaction and censorship in Europe, artists, authors, and poets used the Greek emancipation and pan-Hellenic movement as larger metaphors for the political aspirations of liberal nationalism throughout Europe. Eugène Delacroix painted a number of allegories of Greek enslavement in the 1820s; this painting was inspired after the Greek fortress of Missolonghi fell to Turkish forces. In personifying Greece through the female figure in the foreground, what does Delacroix imply about the nature of nation-statehood?

ADAM MICKIEWICZ

FROM *The Books of the Polish Nation*

The Polish uprising of 1830–1831 against Russian imperial control produced an outpouring of sympathy in western Europe. Adam Mickiewicz (1798–1855), a Polish patriot living in Paris, wrote the following poem in 1832. The heroic epic typifies the histrionic nature of patriotic Romantic verse, but the poem is further significant in its attempt to breathe religious spirituality into the cause of Polish nationalism.

From *Metternich's Europe,* edited by Mack Walker (New York: Harper and Row, 1968).

In the beginning there was belief in one God, and there was freedom in the world. And there were no laws, only the will of God, and there were no lords and slaves, only patriarchs and their children.

But later the people denied the one God, and made for themselves idols, and bowed themselves down to them, and slew in their honor bloody offerings, and waged war for the honor of their idols.

Therefore God sent upon the idolaters the greatest punishment, which is slavery.

*   *   *

Finally in idolatrous Europe there rose three rulers; the name of the first was *Frederick the Second* of Prussia, the name of the second was *Catherine the Second* of Russia, the name of the third was *Maria Theresa* of Austria.

And this was a Satanic trinity, contrary to the Divine Trinity, and was in the manner of a mock and a derision of all that is holy.

Frederick, whose name signifieth *friend of peace,* contrived wars and pillage throughout his whole life, and was like Satan eternally panting for war, who in derision should be called Christ, the God of peace.

*   *   *

Now *Catherine* signifieth in Greek pure, but she was the lewdest of women, and it was as though the shameless Venus had called herself a pure virgin.

And this Catherine assembled a council for the establishing of laws, that she might turn lawmaking into a mockery, for the rights of her neighbors she overthrew and destroyed.

And this Catherine proclaimed that she protected freedom of conscience or tolerance, that she might make a mock of freedom of conscience, for she forced millions of her neighbors to change their faith. And *Maria Theresa* bore the name of the most meek and immaculate Mother of the Savior, that she might make a mock of humility and holiness.

For she was a proud she-devil, and carried on war to make subject the lands of others.

*   *   *

Then this trinity, seeing that not yet were the people sufficiently foolish and corrupt, fashioned a new idol, the most abominable of all, and they called this idol *Interest,* and this idol was not known among the pagans of old.

*   *   *

But the Polish nation alone did not bow down to the new idol, and did not have in its language the expression for christening it in Polish, neither for christening its worshipers, whom it calls by the French word *egoists*.

The Polish nation worshiped God, knowing that he who honoreth God giveth honor to everything that is good.

The Polish nation then from the beginning to the end was true to the God of its ancestors.

Its kings and men of knightly rank never assaulted any believing nation, but defended Christendom from the pagans and barbarians who brought slavery.

And the Polish kings went to the defense of Christians in distant lands, King Wladislaw to Varna, and King Jan to Vienna, to the defense of the east and the west.

And never did their kings and men of knightly rank seize neighboring lands by force, but they received the nations into brotherhood, uniting them with themselves by the gracious gift of faith and freedom.

And God rewarded them, for a great nation, Lithuania, united itself with Poland, as husband with wife, two souls in one body. And there was never before this such a union of nations. But hereafter there shall be.

For that union and marriage of Lithuania and Poland is the symbol of the future union of all Christian peoples in the name of faith and freedom.

And God gave unto the Polish kings and knights freedom, that all might be called brothers, both the richest and the poorest. And such freedom never was before. But hereafter there shall be.

The king and the men of knightly rank received into their brotherhood still more people; they received whole armies and whole tribes. And the number of brothers became as great as a nation, and in no nation were there so many people free and calling each other brothers as in Poland.

And finally, on the Third of May, the king and the knightly body determined to make all Poles brothers, at first the burghers and later the peasants.

And they called the brothers the nobility, because they had become noble, that is had become brothers with the Lachs, who were men free and equal.

And they wished to bring it about that every Christian in Poland should be ennobled and called a Nobleman, for a token that he should have a noble soul and always be ready to die for freedom.

Just as of old they called each man accepting the gospel a Christian, for a token that he was ready to shed his blood for Christ.

Nobility then was to be the baptism of freedom, and every one who was ready to die for freedom was to be baptized of the law and of the sword.

And finally Poland said: "Whosoever will come to me shall be free and equal, for I am FREEDOM."

But the kings when they heard of this were terrified in their hearts and said: "We banished freedom from the earth; but lo, it returneth in the person of a just nation, that doth not bow down to our idols! Come, let us slay this nation." And they plotted treachery among themselves.

And the King of Prussia came and kissed the Polish Nation and greeted it, saying: "My ally," but already he had sold it for thirty cities of Great Poland, even as Judas for thirty pieces of silver.

And the two other rulers fell upon and bound the Polish Nation. And Gaul was judge and said: "Verily I find no fault in this nation, and France my wife, a timid woman, is tormented with evil dreams; nevertheless, take for yourselves and martyr this nation." And he washed his hands.

And the ruler of France said: "We cannot ransom this innocent nation by our blood or by our money, for my blood and my money belong to me, but the blood and money of my nation belong to my nation."

And this ruler uttered the last blasphemy against Christ, for Christ taught that the blood of the Son of Man belongeth to all our brother men.

And when the ruler had uttered these words, then the crosses fell from the towers of the godless capital, for the sign of Christ could no longer shine upon a people worshiping the idol *Interest.*

And this ruler was called Casimir-Périer, a Slavic first name and a Roman last name. His first name signifieth corrupter or annihilator of peace, and his last name signifieth, from the word *perire* or *périr,* destroyer or son of destruction. And these two names are anti-Christian. And they shall be alike accursed among the Slavic race and among the Roman race.

And this man rent the league of peoples as that Jewish priest rent his clothes upon hearing the voice of Christ.

And they martyred the Polish Nation and laid it in the grave, and the kings cried out: "We have slain and we have buried Freedom."

But they cried out foolishly, for in committing the last sin they filled up the measure of their iniquities, and their power was coming to an end at the time when they exulted most.

For the Polish Nation did not die: its body lieth in the grave, but its spirit hath descended from the earth, that is from public life, to the abyss, that is to the private life of people who suf-fer slavery in their country and outside of their country, that it may see their sufferings.

But on the third day the soul shall return to the body, and the Nation shall arise and free all the peoples of Europe from slavery.

And already two days have gone by. One day passed with the first capture of Warsaw, and the second day passed with the second capture of Warsaw, and the third day shall begin, but shall not pass.

And as after the resurrection of Christ bloody offerings ceased in all the world, so after the resurrection of the Polish Nation wars shall cease in all Christendom.

REVIEW QUESTIONS

1. Why is the poem's biblical cadence significant?
2. How does Christianity serve the cause of Polish nationalism?
3. How does the poem recount Poland's plight in the history of eastern Europe?

FREDERICK DOUGLASS

FROM *The Life*

The transformation from bonded subject to political participant—a critical feature of modern citizenship and nation building—took many forms over the course of the nineteenth century. In the United States the most dramatic step toward a republic of free citizens was the emancipation of slaves by President Lincoln in 1863. Yet political activity for African Americans began long before Lincoln's proclamation, as demonstrated by the thousands who chose to escape southern slavery. Frederick Douglass's narrative of his life as a slave and his escape to the North illustrates well how the search for basic liberty politicized a generation of African Americans who underwent the transformation from slave to fugitive slave to citizen. A former Maryland slave who taught himself to read and write, Frederick Douglas became a powerful orator for the abolitionist movement in the 1840s and, eventually, the first African American citizen to hold high office in the U.S. government, including U.S.

FREDERICK DOUGLASS: FROM *The Life*   **545**

*minister to Haiti (1889–1891). His narrative, which centers principally on the phys-
ical horrors and moral degradation of slaves' lives, concludes with his first days in
the North and his decision to embark on a political career as an orator for the abolitionist movement.*

From *Narrative of the Life of Frederick Douglass, an American Slave,* by Frederick Douglass
(Boston: Anti-Slavery Office, 1845).

*   *   *

I have been frequently asked how I felt when I found myself in a free State. I have never been able to answer the question with any satisfaction to myself. It was a moment of the highest excitement I ever experienced. I suppose I felt as one may imagine the unarmed mariner to feel when he is rescued by a friendly man-of-war from the pursuit of a pirate. In writing to a dear friend, immediately after my arrival at New York, I said I felt like one who had escaped a den of hungry lions. This state of mind, however, very soon subsided; and I was again seized with a feeling of great insecurity and loneliness. I was yet liable to be taken back, and subjected to all the tortures of slavery. This in itself was enough to damp the ardor of my enthusiasm. But the loneliness overcame me. There I was in the midst of thousands, and yet a perfect stranger; without home and without friends, in the midst of thousands of my own brethren—children of a common Father, and yet I dared not to unfold to any of them my sad condition. I was afraid to speak to any one for fear of speaking to the wrong one, and thereby falling into the hands of money-loving kidnappers, whose business it was to lie in wait for the panting fugitive, as the ferocious beasts of the forest lie in wait for their prey. The motto which I adopted when I started from slavery was this—"Trust no man!" I saw in every white man an enemy, and in almost every colored man cause for distrust. It was a most painful situation; and, to understand it, one must needs experience it, or imagine himself in similar circumstances. Let him be a fugitive slave in a strange land—a land given up to be the hunting-ground for slaveholders—whose inhabitants are legalized kidnappers—where he is every

moment subjected to the terrible liability of being seized upon by his fellowmen, as the hideous crocodile seizes upon his prey! I say, let him place himself in my situation—without home or friends—without money or credit—wanting shelter, and no one to give it—wanting bread, and no money to buy it—and at the same time let him feel that he is pursued by merciless men-hunters, and in total darkness as to what to do, where to go, or where to stay—perfectly helpless both as to the means of defence and means of escape—in the midst of plenty, yet suffering the terrible gnawings of hunger—in the midst of houses, yet having no home—among fellowmen, yet feeling as if in the midst of wild beasts, whose greediness to swallow up the trembling and half-famished fugitive is only equalled by that with which the monsters of the deep swallow up the helpless fish upon which they subsist—I say, let him be placed in this most trying situation—the situation in which I was placed—then, and not till then, will he fully appreciate the hardships of, and know how to sympathize with, the toil-worn and whip-scarred fugitive slave.

*   *   *

* * * Upon reaching New Bedford, we were directed to the house of Mr. Nathan Johnson, by whom we were kindly received, and hospitably provided for. Both Mr. and Mrs. Johnson took a deep and lively interest in our welfare. They proved themselves quite worthy of the name of abolitionists. When the stage driver found us unable to pay our fare, he held on upon our baggage as security for the debt. I had but to mention the fact to Mr. Johnson, and he forthwith advanced the money.

We now began to feel a degree of safety, and

to prepare ourselves for the duties and responsibilities of a life of freedom. On the morning after our arrival at New Bedford, while at the breakfast-table, the question arose as to what name I should be called by. The name given me by my mother was, "Frederick Augustus Washington Bailey." I, however, had dispensed with the two middle names long before I left Maryland so that I was generally known by the name of "Frederick Bailey." I started from Baltimore bearing the name of "Stanley." When I got to New York, I again changed my name to "Frederick Johnson," and thought that would be the last change. But when I got to New Bedford, I found it necessary again to change my name. The reason of this necessity was, that there were so many Johnsons in New Bedford, it was already quite difficult to distinguish between them. I gave Mr. Johnson the privilege of choosing me a name, but told him he must not take from me the name of "Frederick." I must hold on to that, to preserve a sense of my identity. Mr. Johnson had just been reading the "Lady of the Lake," and at once suggested that my name be "Douglass." From that time until now I have been called "Frederick Douglass;" and as I am more widely known by that name than by either of the others, I shall continue to use it as my own.

I was quite disappointed at the general appearance of things in New Bedford. The impression which I had received respecting the character and condition of the people of the north, I found to be singularly erroneous. I had very strangely supposed, while in slavery, that few of the comforts, and scarcely any of the luxuries, of life were enjoyed at the north, compared with what were enjoyed by the slaveholders of the south. I probably came to this conclusion from the fact that northern people owned no slaves. I supposed that they were about upon a level with the non-slaveholding population of the south. I knew *they* were exceedingly poor, and I had been accustomed to regard their poverty as the necessary consequence of their being non-slaveholders. I had somehow imbibed the opinion that, in the absence of slaves, there could be no wealth, and very little refinement. And upon coming to the north, I

expected to meet with a rough, hard-handed and uncultivated population, living in the most Spartan-like simplicity, knowing nothing of the ease, luxury, pomp, and grandeur of southern slaveholders. Such being my conjectures, any one acquainted with the appearance of New Bedford may very readily infer how palpably I must have seen my mistake.

In the afternoon of the day when I reached New Bedford, I visited the wharves, to take a view of the shipping. Here I found myself surrounded with the strongest proofs of wealth. Lying at the wharves, and riding in the stream, I saw many ships of the finest model, in the best order, and of the largest size. Upon the right and left, I was walled in by granite warehouses of the widest dimensions, stowed to their utmost capacity with the necessaries and comforts of life. Added to this, almost every body seemed to be at work, but noiselessly so, compared with what I had been accustomed to in Baltimore. There were no loud songs heard from those engaged in loading and unloading ships. I heard no deep oaths or horrid curses on the laborer. I saw no whipping of men; but all seemed to go smoothly on. Every man appeared to understand his work, and went at it with a sober, yet cheerful earnestness, which betokened the deep interest which he felt in what he was doing, as well as a sense of his own dignity as a man. To me this looked exceedingly strange. From the wharves I strolled around and over the town, gazing with wonder and admiration at the splendid churches, beautiful dwellings, and finely-cultivated gardens; evincing an amount of wealth, comfort, taste and refinement, such as I had never seen in any part of slaveholding Maryland.

Every thing looked clean, new, and beautiful. I saw few or no dilapidated houses, with poverty-stricken inmates; no half-naked children and bare-footed women, such as I had been accustomed to see in Hillsborough, Easton, St. Michael's, and Baltimore. The people looked more able, stronger, healthier, and happier, than those of Maryland. I was for once made glad by a view of extreme wealth, without being saddened by seeing extreme poverty. But the most astonishing as well as the most interesting thing to me was the condition of the colored people, a great many of whom, like myself, had escaped thither as a refuge from the hunters of men. I found many, who had not been seven years out of their chains, living in finer houses, and evidently enjoying more of the comforts of life, than the average slaveholders in Maryland. I will venture to assert, that my friend Mr. Nathan Johnson (of whom I can say with a grateful heart, "I was hungry, and he gave me meat; I was thirsty, and he gave me drink; I was a stranger, and he took me in.") lived in a neater house; dined at a better table; took, paid for, and read, more newspapers; better understood the moral, religious, and political character of the nation—than nine tenths of the slaveholders in Talbot county Maryland. Yet Mr. Johnson was a working man. His hands were hardened by toil, and not his alone, but those also of Mrs. Johnson. I found the colored people much more spirited than I had supposed they would be. I found among them a determination to protect each other from the blood-thirsty kidnapper, at all hazards. Soon after my arrival, I was told of a circumstance which illustrated their spirit. A colored man and a fugitive slave were on unfriendly terms. The former was heard to threaten the latter with informing his master of his whereabouts. Straightway a meeting was called among the colored people, under the stereotyped notice, "Business of importance!" The betrayer was invited to attend. The people came at the appointed hour, and organized the meeting by appointing a very religious old gentleman as president, who, I believe, made a prayer, after which he addressed the meeting as follows: *"Friends, we have got him here, and I would recommend that you young men just take him outside the door, and kill him!"* With this, a number of them bolted at him; but they were intercepted by some more timid than themselves, and the betrayer escaped their vengeance, and has not been seen in New Bedford since. I believe there have been no more such threats, and should there be hereafter, I doubt not that death would be the consequence.

I found employment, the third day after my arrival, in stowing a sloop with a load of oil. It was new, dirty, and hard work for me; but I went at it with a glad heart and a willing hand. I was now my own master. It was a happy moment, the rapture of which can be understood only by those who have been slaves. It was the first work, the reward of which was to be entirely my own. There was no Master Hugh standing ready, the moment I earned the money, to rob me of it. I worked that day with a pleasure I had never before experienced. I was at work for myself and newly-married wife. It was to me the starting-point of a new existence. When I got through with that job, I went in pursuit of a job of calking; but such was the strength of prejudice against color, among the white calkers, that they refused to work with me, and of course I could get no employment.[1] Finding my trade of no immediate benefit, I threw off my calking habiliments, and prepared myself to do any kind of work I could get to do. Mr. Johnson kindly let me have his woodhorse and saw, and I very soon found myself a plenty of work. There was no work too hard—none too dirty. I was ready to saw wood, shovel coal, carry wood, sweep the chimney, or roll oil casks—all of which I did for nearly three years in New Bedford, before I became known to the anti-slavery world.

In about four months after I went to New Bedford, there came a young man to me, and inquired if I did not wish to take the "Liberator." I told him I did; but, just having made my escape from slavery, I remarked that I was unable to pay for it then. I, however, finally became a subscriber to it. The paper came, and I read it from week to week with such feelings as it would be quite idle for me to attempt to describe. The paper became my meat and my drink. My soul was set all on fire. Its sympathy for my brethen in bonds—its scathing denunciations of slaveholders—its faithful exposures of slavery—and its powerful attacks upon the upholders of the institution—sent a thrill of joy through my soul, such as I had never felt before!

---

[1] I am told that colored persons can now get employment at calking in New Bedford—a result of anti-slavery effort.

I had not long been a reader of the "Liberator," before I got a pretty correct idea of the principles, measures and spirit of the anti-slavery reform. I took right hold of the cause. I could do but little; but what I could, I did with a joyful heart, and never felt happier than when in an anti-slavery meeting. I seldom had much to say at the meetings, because what I wanted to say was said so much better by others. But, while attending an anti-slavery convention at Nantucket, on the 11th of August, 1841, I felt strongly moved to speak, and was at the same time much urged to do so by Mr. William C. Coffin, a gentleman who had heard me speak in the colored people's meeting at New Bedford. It was a severe cross, and I took it up reluctantly. The truth was, I felt myself a slave, and the idea of speaking to white people weighed me down. I spoke but a few moments, when I felt a degree of freedom, and said what I desired with considerable ease. From that time until now, I have been engaged in pleading the cause of my brethren—with what success, and with what devotion, I leave those acquainted with my labors to decide.

REVIEW QUESTIONS

1. According to Douglass, what hardships did fugitive slaves encounter in the free North?
2. Why was Douglass surprised at the economic prosperity of the North?
3. How did Douglass come to participate in abolitionist meetings?
4. What does the participation of a fugitive slave in public meetings in the 1840s tell us about American citizenship at that time?

ALEXEI STEPANOVICH KHOMYAKOV

FROM To the Serbs: An Epistle from Moscow

Alongside national consciousness arose two allied movements in eastern Europe: Panslavism and Slavophilism. The former explored the means for political and cultural unity of Europe's Slavic cultures; the Pan-Slav Congress in June 1848, for example, sought ways to unite Slav interests in the Austrian Empire. Slavophilism, however, was largely a Russian intellectual movement in the second half of the nineteenth century that sought to bring southern and western Slav cultures back into the orbit of Eastern Orthodox Church thinking. Alexei Khomyakov, one of the chief exponents of this doctrine, argued forcefully that the overarching religious influence of orthodoxy was more critical than national roots for the proper development of Slavic identity, whose cultural and political communities transcended national borders. The epistle below, written in 1860, captures the mood and substance of the Slavophilism movement.

From *A Documentary History of Russian Thought: From the Enlightenment to Marxism*, edited by W. J. Leatherbarrow and C. C. Offord (Dana Point, Calif.: Ardis Books, 1987).

* * *

* * * In truth, O Serbs, God has bestowed great favors upon you, greater, we think, than you yourselves know. A healthy body is one of man's greatest blessings, but he realizes this only when he loses it, or when he observes the illnesses of others and compares them with his own healthy state. In the same way you can come to know your advantages only through comparison with the shortcomings of other societies (and you have not yet attended to such a comparison), or through the frank confession of such other societies, who know from experience their sicknesses and their causes. Let this knowledge serve as a warning to you, so that you might avoid the errors which other nations have not been able to avoid, and so that, in adopting what is good and useful, you will not be infected by those malignant principles which often accompany good things, unnoticed by the inexperienced eye.

The first, most important and priceless blessing which you, the Serbs, possess is your unity in Orthodoxy, that highest wisdom and highest truth, the root of all spiritual and moral growth. Such is your unity in the faith that for the Turk the words "Serb" and "Orthodox" are synonymous. You must value this finest of all blessings above all others, and guard it as you would the pupil of your eye; after all, what is Orthodoxy if not the pupil of one's inner, spiritual eye?

Christianity was not sown by force in the world; nor did it develop through violence, but by overcoming all violence. Thus it must not be preserved by violence, and woe to him who seeks to protect the might of Christ with the feebleness of human weapons! Faith is a matter of spiritual freedom, and it tolerates no compulsion. True faith is conquering the world, but it does not seek the temporal sword for its triumph. Therefore, respect all freedom of conscience and faith, in order that no one should offend against the truth by saying that it fears falsehood and does not dare compete with falsehood armed only with thought and words. Defend God's honor, not with timidity and

doubt as to its might, but boldly and with a calm confidence in its victory.

But, on the other hand, always bear in mind the significance and dignity of the faith. Those who think that it is simply a matter of creed, rituals, or even the direct communion of man with God, are quite wrong. No, faith penetrates man's whole being and all his relations with his neighbor. As if with invisible threads or roots it binds together all his feelings, all his convictions and all his aspirations. It is a sort of rarefied air, recreating and transforming within him every mundane principle, or a luminous light, illuminating all his moral conceptions and all his views on other people and the inner laws which bind him to them. Therefore, faith is also the highest social principle; for society itself is precisely the visible manifestation of our inner relations with other people and our union with them.

A healthy civil society is based on its citizens' understanding of brotherhood, truth, justice and mercy; but this understanding cannot be the same among men if their faiths are different. The Jew and the Mohammedan profess one God, just like the Christian, but is their understanding of truth and mercy the same as ours? Of course, it will be said that they know neither the Sacrament of the Holy and Ever-Worshipful Trinity, nor the love of God, which is our salvation through Christ, and that consequently the difference between them and us is too great. But we know that even Christians, apart from the true Orthodox Church, possess neither a totally clear understanding nor a totally sincere sense of brotherhood. Such an understanding and such a sense develop and strengthen only in Orthodoxy. It is no accident that the commune, the sanctity of the communal verdict and the unquestioning submission of each individual to the unanimous decision of his brethren are preserved only in Orthodox countries. The teachings of the faith cultivate the soul even in social life. The Papist seeks extraneous and personal authority, just as he is used to submitting to such authority in matters of faith; the Protestant takes personal freedom to the extreme of blind arrogance, just as in his sham worship. Such is the spirit of their teaching. Only the Orthodox Christian, preserving his freedom, yet humbly acknowledging his weakness, subordinates his freedom to the unanimous resolution of the collective conscience. It is for this reason that the local commune has not been able to preserve its laws outside Orthodox countries. And it is for this reason that the Slav cannot be fully a Slav without Orthodoxy. Even our brethren who have been led astray by the Western falsehood, be they Papists or Protestants, acknowledge this with grief. This principle applies to all matters of justice and truth, and to all conceptions about society; for at the root of it lies brotherhood.

*   *   *

REVIEW QUESTIONS

1. In this letter, how is the Eastern Orthodox Church portrayed as the superior religion?
2. What are the cultural advantages for Serbs to embrace the Eastern Orthodox religion and way of life?
3. What is promised?
4. How does this Eastern doctrine undermine Western notions of nationalism?
5. What are the implications of this doctrine for relations between the Austrian and Russian empires?

GIUSEPPE MAZZINI

FROM *Duties of Man*

Giuseppe Mazzini (1805–1872) was one of the most well known liberal national revolutionaries of the nineteenth century. Mazzini achieved international renown for his founding of Young Italy in 1831, an organization that strove for an Italian republic, which spawned the parallel associations Young Poland, Young Germany, and Young Ireland. In 1849 he assisted Garibaldi in defending the Roman republic, and after its defeat was compelled to flee Italy. In exile he continued his efforts as a writer for a unified Italian republic. The eventual unification of Italy during the period 1859–1871 brought him little satisfaction, because it was realized under the conservative political settlement of a constitutional monarchy. His Duties of Man, *first begun in weekly installments in 1840, best characterized Mazzini's liberal-democratic humanitarian spirit, which endowed the nationalism of this period with an ethical core.*

From *The Liberal Tradition in European Thought*, edited by David Sidorsky (New York: Putnam, 1970).

To the Italian Working Class

To you, sons and daughters of the people, I dedicate this little book, wherein I have pointed out the principles in the name and strength of which you may, if you so will, accomplish your mission in Italy; a mission of republican progress for all and of emancipation for yourselves. Let those who are specially favoured by circumstances or in understanding, and able to comprehend these principles more easily, explain and comment on them to the others, and may that spirit of love inspire them with which, as I wrote, I thought on your griefs and on your virgin aspirations towards the new life which—once the unjust inequality now stifling your faculties is overcome—you will kindle in the Italian country.

I loved you from my first years. The republican instincts of my mother taught me to seek out among my fellows the Man, not the merely rich and powerful individual; and the simple unconscious virtue of my father accustomed me to admire, rather than conceited and pretentious semi-knowledge, the silent and unnoticed virtue of self-sacrifice so often found in you. Later on I gathered from the history of our country that the true life of Italy is the life of the people, and that the slow work of the centuries has constantly tended, amid the shock of different races and the superficial transitory changes wrought by usurpations and conquests, to prepare the great democratic National Unity. . . .

DUTIES TO COUNTRY

Your first Duties—first, at least, in importance—are, as I have told you, to Humanity. You are *men* before you are *citizens* or *fathers*. If you do not embrace the whole human family in your love, if you do not confess your faith in its unity —consequent on the unity of God—and in the brotherhood of the Peoples who are appointed to reduce that unity for fact—if wherever one of your fellowmen groans, wherever the dignity of human nature is violated by falsehood or tyranny, you are not prompt, being able, to succour that wretched one, or do not feel yourself called, being able, to fight for the purpose of relieving the deceived or oppressed—you disobey your law of life, or do not comprehend the religion which will bless the future.

But what can *each* of you, with his isolated powers, *do* for the moral improvement, for the progress of Humanity? . . . God gave you this means when he gave you a Country, when, like a wise overseer of labour, who distributes the different parts of the work according to the capacity of the workmen, he divided Humanity into distinct groups upon the face of our globe, and thus planted the seeds of nations. Bad governments have disfigured the design of God, which you may see clearly marked out, as far, at least, as regards Europe, by the courses of the great rivers, by the lines of the lofty mountains, and by other geographical conditions; they have disfigured it by conquest, by greed, by jealousy of the just sovereignty of others; disfigured it so much that today there is perhaps no nation except England and France whose confines correspond to this design. They did not, and they do not, recognise any country except their own families and dynasties, the egoism of caste. But the divine design will infallibly be fulfilled. Natural divisions, the innate spontaneous tendencies of the people will replace the arbitrary divisions sanctioned by bad governments. The map of Europe will be remade. The Countries of the People will rise, defined by the voice of the free, upon the ruins of the Countries of Kings and privileged castes. Between these Countries there will be harmony and brotherhood. And then the work of Humanity for the general amelioration, for the discovery and application of the real law of life, carried on in association and distributed according to local capacities, will be accomplished by peaceful and progressive development; then each of you, strong in the affections and in the aid of many millions of men speaking the same language, endowed with the same tendencies, and educated by the same historic tradition, may hope by your personal effort to benefit the whole of Humanity.

To you, who have been born in Italy, God has

allotted, as if favouring you specially, the best-defined country in Europe. In other lands, marked by more uncertain or more interrupted limits, questions may arise which the pacific vote of all will one day solve, but which have cost, and will yet perhaps cost, tears and blood; in yours, no. God has stretched round you sublime and indisputable boundaries; on one side the highest mountains of Europe, the Alps; on the other the sea, the immeasurable sea. Take a map of Europe and place one point of a pair of compasses in the north of Italy on Parma; point the other to the mouth of the Var, and describe a semicircle with it in the direction of the Alps; this point, which will fall, when the semicircle is completed, upon the mouth of the Isonzo, will have marked the frontier which God has given you. As far as this frontier your language is spoken and understood; beyond this you have no rights. Sicily, Sardinia, Corsica, and the smaller islands between them and the mainland of Italy belong undeniably to you. Brute force may for a little while contest these frontiers with you, but they have been recognised from of old by the tacit general consent of the peoples; and the day when, rising with one accord for the final trial, you plant your tricoloured flag upon that frontier, the whole of Europe will acclaim re-risen Italy, and receive her into the community of the nations. To this final trial all your efforts must be directed.

Without Country you have neither name, token, voice, nor rights, no admission as brothers into the fellowship of the Peoples. You are the bastards of Humanity. Soldiers without a banner, Israelites among the nations, you will find neither faith nor protection; none will be sureties for you. Do not beguile yourselves with the hope of emancipation from unjust social conditions if you do not first conquer a Country for yourselves; where there is no Country there is no common agreement to which you can appeal; the egoism of self-interest rules alone, and he who has the upper hand keeps it, since there is no common safeguard for the interests of all. Do not be led away by the idea of improving your material conditions without first solving the national question. You cannot

do it. Your industrial associations and mutual help societies are useful as a means of educating and disciplining yourselves; as an economic fact they will remain barren until you have an Italy. The economic problem demands, first and foremost, an increase of capital and production; and while your Country is dismembered into separate fragments—while shut off by the barrier of customs and artificial difficulties of every sort, you have only restricted markets open to you—you cannot hope for this increase. Today—do not delude yourselves—you are not the working-class of Italy; you are only fractions of that class; powerless, unequal to the great task which you propose to yourselves. Your emancipation can have no practical beginning until a National Government, understanding the signs of the times, shall, seated in Rome, formulate a Declaration of Principles to be the guide for Italian progress, and shall insert into it these words, *Labour is sacred, and is the source of the wealth of Italy.*

Do not be led astray, then, by hopes of material progress which in your present conditions can only be illusions. Your Country alone, the vast and rich Italian Country, which stretches from the Alps to the farthest limit of Sicily, can fulfil these hopes. You cannot obtain your *rights* except by obeying the commands of *Duty.* Be worthy of them, and you will have them. O my Brothers! love your Country. Our Country is our home, the home which God has given us, placing therein a numerous family which we love and are loved by, and with which we have a more intimate and quicker communion of feeling and thought than with others; a family which by its concentration upon a given spot, and by the homogeneous nature of its elements, is destined for a special kind of activity. Our Country is our field of labour; the products of our activity must go forth from it for the benefit of the whole earth; but the instruments of labour which we can use best and most effectively exist in it, and we may not reject them without being unfaithful to God's purpose and diminishing our own strength. In labouring according to true principles for our Country we are labouring for Humanity; our Country is the fulcrum of the lever which we have to wield for the common good. If we give up this fulcrum we run the risk of becoming useless to our Country and to Humanity. Before *associating* ourselves with the Nations which compose Humanity we must exist as a Nation. There can be no association except among equals; and you have no recognised collective existence.

Humanity is a great army moving to the conquest of unknown lands, against powerful and wary enemies. The Peoples are the different corps and divisions of that army. Each has a post entrusted to it; each a special operation to perform; and the common victory depends on the exactness with which the different operations are carried out. Do not disturb the order of the battle. Do not abandon the banner which God has given you. Wherever you may be, into the midst of whatever people circumstances may have driven you, fight for the liberty of that people if the moment calls for it; but fight as Italians, so that the blood which you shed may win honour and love, not for you only, but for your Country. And may the constant thought of your soul be for Italy, may all the acts of your life be worthy of her, and may the standard beneath which you range yourselves to work for Humanity be Italy's. Do not say *I*; say *we*. Be every one of you an incarnation of your Country, and feel himself and make himself responsible for his fellow-countrymen; let each one of you learn to act in such a way that in him men shall respect and love his Country.

Your Country is one and indivisible. As the members of a family cannot rejoice at the common table if one of their number is far away, snatched from the affection of his brothers, so you should have no joy or repose as long as a portion of the territory upon which your language is spoken is separated from the Nation.

*   *   *

A Country is a fellowship of free and equal men bound together in a brotherly concord of labour towards a single end. You must make it and maintain it such. A Country is not an aggregation, it is an *association*. There is no true Country without a uniform right. There is no true Country where the uniformity of that right is violated by the existence of caste, privilege, and inequality—where the powers and faculties of a large number of individuals are suppressed or dormant—where there is no common principle accepted, recognised, and developed by all. In such a state of things there can be no Nation, no People, but only a multitude, a fortuitous agglomeration of men whom circumstances have brought together and different circumstances will separate. In the name of your love of your Country you must combat without truce the existence of every privilege, every inequality, upon the soil which has given you birth.

*   *   *

The laws made by one fraction of the citizens only can never by the nature of things and men do otherwise than reflect the thoughts and aspirations and desires of that fraction; they represent, not the whole country, but a third, a fourth part, a class, a zone of the country. The law must express the general aspiration, promote the good of all, respond to a beat of the nation's heart. The whole nation therefore should be, directly or indirectly, the legislator. By yielding this mission to a few men, you put the egoism of one class in the place of the Country, which is the union of *all* the classes.

A Country is not a mere territory; the particular territory is only its foundation. The Country is the idea which rises upon that foundation; it is the sentiment of love, the sense of fellowship which binds together all the sons of that territory. So long as a single one of your brothers is not represented by his own vote in the development of the national life—so long as a single one vegetates uneducated among the educated—so long as a single one able and willing to work languishes in poverty for want of work—you have not got a Country such as it ought to be, the Country of all and for all. *Votes, education, work* are the three main pillars of the nation; do not rest until your hands have solidly erected them.

*   *   *

REVIEW QUESTIONS

1. How is Mazzini's nationalism related to the larger issue of humanity?

2. For Mazzini what is necessary to achieve progress in humanity?

3. How does Mazzini define a country?

4. Why might Mazzini's nationalism be termed utopian?

OTTO VON BISMARCK

FROM *The Memoirs*

Otto von Bismarck (1815–1898), a Prussian noble, served the Prussian crown as its premier statesmen from 1862 to 1890. Under his aegis, Prussia united Germany, creating the German Empire in 1871, a nation-state whose power and size significantly altered the European state system. Prussia's bid to unite Germany brought armed conflict with Austria in 1866. Yet Prussia's military victory was only partly successful, for Prussia's role as unifier could only become legitimate with popular support. On the eve of war with Austria, Bismarck promulgated a constitution that included a bicameral legislation and universal manhood suffrage, a political move that sought to shift public opinion in favor of Prussia. The move achieved the intended effect, enabling Bismarck to sever the once-indivisible bond between nationalism and liberalism. The following passage, written at the end of his life, throws light on a conservative's views of popular politics and nationalism.

From *The Memoirs*, by Otto von Bismarck, translated by A. J. Butler (New York: Fertig, 1890).

* * *

Looking to the necessity, in a fight against an overwhelming foreign Power, of being able, in extreme need, to use even revolutionary means, I had had no hesitation whatever in throwing into the frying-pan, by means of the circular dispatch of June 10, 1866, the most powerful ingredient known at that time to liberty-mongers, namely, universal suffrage, so as to frighten off foreign monarchies from trying to stick a finger into our national omelette. I never doubted that the German people would be strong and clever enough to free themselves from the existing suffrage as soon as they realised that it was a harmful institution.

If it cannot, then my saying that Germany can ride when once it has got into the saddle was erroneous. The acceptance of universal suffrage was a weapon in the war against Austria and other foreign countries, in the war for German Unity, as well as a threat to use the last weapons in a struggle against coalitions. In a war of this sort, when it becomes a matter of life and death, one does not look at the weapons that one seizes, nor the value of what one destroys in using them: one is guided at the moment by no other thought than the issue of the war, and the preservation of one's external independence; the settling of affairs and reparation of the damage has to take place after the peace. Moreover, I still hold that the principle of universal suffrage is a just one, not only in theory but also in practice, provided always that voting be not secret, for secrecy is a quality that is indeed incompatible with the best characteristics of German blood.

The influence and the dependence on others that the practical life of man brings in its train are God-given realities which we cannot and must not ignore. If we refuse to transfer them to political life, and base that life on a faith in the secret insight of everybody, we fall into a contradiction between public law and the realities of human life which practically leads to constant frictions, and finally to an explosion, and to which there is no theoretical solution except by way of the insanities of social-democracy, the support given to which rests on the fact that the judgment of the masses is sufficiently stultified and undeveloped to allow them, with the assistance of their own greed, to be continually caught by the rhetoric of clever and ambitious leaders.

The counterpoise to this lies in the influence of the educated classes, which would be greatly strengthened if voting were public, as for the Prussian Diet. It may be that the greater discretion of the more intelligent classes rests on the material basis of the preservation of their possessions. The other motive, the struggle for gain, is equally justifiable; but a preponderance of those who represent property is more serviceable for the security and development of the state. A state, the control of which lies in the hands of the greedy, of the *novarum rerum cupidi,* and of orators who have in a higher degree than others the capacity for deceiving the unreasoning masses, will constantly be doomed to a restlessness of development, which so ponderous a mass as the commonwealth of the state cannot follow without injury to its organism. Ponderous masses, and among these the life and development of great nations must be reckoned, can only move with caution, since the road on which they travel to an unknown future has no smooth iron rails. Every great state-commonwealth that loses the prudent and restraining influence of the propertied class, whether that influence rests on material or moral grounds,

will always end by being rushed along at a speed which must shatter the coach of state, as happened in the development of the French Revolution. The element of greed has the preponderance arising from large masses which in the long run must make its way. It is in the interests of the great mass itself to wish decision to take place without dangerous acceleration of the speed of the coach of state, and without its destruction. If this should happen, however, the wheel of history will revolve again, and always in a proportionately shorter time, to dictatorship, to despotism, to absolutism, because in the end the masses yield to the need of order; if they do not recognise this need *a priori,* they always realise it eventually after manifold arguments *ad hominem;* and in order to purchase order from a dictatorship and Caesarism they cheerfully sacrifice that justifiable amount of freedom which ought to be maintained, and which the political society of Europe can endure without ill-health.

I should regard it as a serious misfortune, and as an essential weakening of our security in the future, if we in Germany are driven into the vortex of this French cycle. Absolutism would be the ideal form of government for an European political structure were not the King and his officials ever as other men are to whom it is not given to reign with superhuman wisdom, insight and justice. The most experienced and well-meaning absolute rulers are subject to human imperfections, such as overestimation of their own wisdom, the influence and eloquence of favourites, not to mention petticoat influence, legitimate and illegitimate. Monarchy and the most ideal monarch, if in his idealism he is not to be a common danger, stand in need of criticism; the thorns of criticism set him right when he runs the risk of losing his way. Joseph II is a warning example of this.

Criticism can only be exercised through the medium of a free press and parliaments in the modern sense of the term. Both correctives may easily weaken, and finally lose their efficacy if they abuse their powers. To avert this is one of the tasks of a conservative policy, which cannot be accomplished without a struggle with parliament and press. The measuring of the limits within which such a struggle must be confined, if the control of the government, which is indispensable to the country, is neither to be checked nor allowed to gain a complete power, is a question of political tact and judgment.

It is a piece of good fortune for his country if a monarch possess the judgment requisite for this—a good fortune that is temporary, it is true, like all human fortune. The possibility of establishing ministers in power who possess adequate qualifications must always be granted in the constitutional organism; but also the possibility of maintaining in office ministers who satisfy these requirements in face of occasional votes of an adverse majority and of the influence of courts and camarillas. This aim, so far as human imperfections in general allow its attainment, was approximately reached under the government of William I.

* * *

REVIEW QUESTIONS

1. What was Bismarck's opinion of universal suffrage?
2. What political system and balance of social forces did Bismarck advocate?
3. Why is Bismarck often viewed as a conservative revolutionary?

ERNEST RENAN

What Is a Nation?

First delivered as a lecture in 1882 at the University of Paris, this essay by Ernest Renan, a prolific French author on philosophical and historical subjects, provided a remarkably detached critique of theories that defined and legitimized European nationalisms. By dismantling the dominant explanations of nationalism in his time, Renan pointed toward viewing nations as cultural entities willed into existence by the "daily plebiscite" of believing communities. For Renan, nations had less to do with authentic historical development than with the contemporary cultural needs of social groups seeking an idealistic collective identity. For this reason Renan's argument has greatly influenced contemporary theories on nationalism.

From *What Is a Nation?* by Ernest Renan, edited by Homi K. Bhabba, translated by Martin Thom (London: Routledge, 1990), pp. 42, 46–54.

What I propose to do today is to analyse with you an idea which, though seemingly clear, lends itself to the most dangerous misunderstandings. * * *

* * *

If one were to believe some political theorists, a nation is above all a dynasty, representing an earlier conquest, one which was first of all accepted, and then forgotten by the mass of the people. According to the above-mentioned theorists, the grouping of provinces effected by a dynasty,

BATTLE OF NATIONS MONUMENT IN LEIPZIG (1913)

Modern nation-states require mass civic participation to acclaim the legitimacy of nations and the states that rule in their name. In this regard, national monuments became important components of nineteenth-century national movements, acting as physical markers and sacred spaces of collective national memory. The Battle of Nations Monument in Leipzig, Germany, illustrates well the function of national monuments in late-nineteenth-century Europe. Designed by Bruno Schmitz and constructed between 1894 and 1913, this structure not only commemorates the important milestone for German nationhood—the defeat of Napoleon in 1813—but also acts as a pantheon of German heroes and nation builders. What characteristics do this monument and its surrounding space project about the German nation?

by its wars, its marriages, and its treaties, ends with the dynasty which had established it. It is quite true that the majority of modern nations were made by a family of feudal origin, which had contracted a marriage with the soil and which was in some sense a nucleus of centralization. France's frontiers in 1789 had nothing either natural or necessary about them. The wide zone that the House of Capet had added to the narrow strip of land granted by the partition of Verdun was indeed the personal acquisition of this House. During the epoch when these acquisitions were made, there was no idea of natural frontiers, nor of the rights of nations, nor of the will of provinces. The union of England, Ireland, and Scotland was likewise a dynastic fact. Italy only tarried so long before becoming a nation because, among its numerous reigning houses, none, prior to the present century, constituted itself as the centre of [its] unity, Strangely enough, it was through the obscure island of Sardinia, a land that was scarcely Italian, that [the house of Savoy] assumed a royal title. Holland, which—through an act of heroic resolution—created itself, has nevertheless contracted an intimate marriage with the House of Orange, and it will run real dangers the day this union is compromised.

Is such a law, however, absolute? It undoubtedly is not. Switzerland and the United States, which have formed themselves, like conglomerates, by successive additions, have no dynastic basis. I shall not discuss this question in relation to France, for I would need to be able to read the secrets of the future in order to do so. Let me simply say that so loftily national had this great French royal principle been that, on the morrow of its fall, the nation was able to stand without her. Furthermore, the eighteenth century had changed everything. Man had returned, after centuries of abasement, to the spirit of antiquity, to [a sense of] respect for himself, to the idea of his own rights. The words *patrie* and citizen had recovered their former meanings. Thus it was that the boldest operation ever yet put into effect in history was brought to completion, an operation

which one might compare with the attempt, in physiology, to restore to its original identity a body from which one had removed the brain and the heart.

It must therefore be admitted that a nation can exist without a dynastic principle, and even that nations which have been formed by dynasties can be separated from them without therefore ceasing to exist. The old principle, which only takes account of the right of princes, could no longer be maintained; apart from dynastic right, there is also national right. Upon what criterion, however, should one base this national right? By what sign should one know it? From what tangible fact can one derive it?

Several confidently assert that it is derived from race. The artificial divisions, resulting from feudalism, from princely marriages, from diplomatic congresses are, [these authors assert], in a state of decay. It is a population's race which remains firm and fixed. This is what constitutes a right, a legitimacy. The Germanic family, according to the theory I am expounding here, has the right to reassemble the scattered limbs of the Germanic order, even when these limbs are not asking to be joined together again. The right of the Germanic order over such-and-such a province is stronger than the right of the inhabitants of that province over themselves. There is thus created a kind of primordial right analogous to the divine right of kings: an ethnographic principle is substituted for a national one. This is a very great error, which, if it were to become dominant, would destroy European civilization. The primordial right of races is as narrow and as perilous for genuine progress as the national principle is just and legitimate.

*   *   *

The truth is that there is no pure race and that to make politics depend upon ethnographic analysis is to surrender it to a chimera. The noblest countries, England, France, and Italy, are those where the blood is the most mixed. Is Germany an exception in this respect? Is it a purely Germanic country? This is a complete illusion. The whole of the south was once Gallic; the whole of the east, from the river Elbe on, is Slav. Even those parts which are claimed to be really pure, are they in fact so? We touch here on one of those problems in regard to which it is of the utmost importance that we equip ourselves with clear ideas and ward off misconceptions.

*   *   *

The fact of race, which was originally crucial, thus becomes increasingly less important. Human history is essentially different from zoology, and race is not everything, as it is among the rodents or the felines, and one does not have the right to go through the world fingering people's skulls, and taking them by the throat saying: "You are of our blood; you belong to us!" Aside from anthropological characteristics, there are such things as reason, justice, the true, and the beautiful, which are the same for all. Be on your guard, for this ethnographic politics is in no way a stable thing and, if today you use it against others, tomorrow you may see it turned against yourselves. Can you be sure that the Germans, who have raised the banner of ethnography so high, will not see the Slavs in their turn analyse the names of villages in Saxony and Lusatia, search for any traces of the Wiltzes or of the Obotrites, and demand recompense for the massacres and the wholesale enslavements that the Ottoss inflicted upon their ancestors? It is good for everyone to know how to forget.

*   *   *

What we have just said of race applies to language too. Language invites people to unite, but it does not force them to do so. The United States and England, Latin America and Spain, speak the same languages yet do not form single nations. Conversely, Switzerland, so well made, since she was made with the consent of her different parts, numbers three or four languages. There is something in man which is superior to language, namely, the will. The will of Switzerland to be united, in spite of the diversity of her dialects, is a fact of far greater importance than a similitude often obtained by various vexatious measures.

*   *   *

Religion cannot supply an adequate basis for the constitution of a modern nationality either. Originally, religion had to do with the very existence of the social group, which was itself an extension of the family. Religion and the rites were family rites. * * *

* * * In our own time, the situation is perfectly clear. There are no longer masses that believe in a perfectly uniform manner. Each person believes and practises in his own fashion what he is able to and as he wishes. There is no longer a state religion; one can be French, English, or German, and be either Catholic, Protestant, or orthodox Jewish, or else practise no cult at all. Religion has become an individual matter; it concerns the conscience of each person. The division of nations into Catholics and Protestants no longer exists. Religion, which, fifty-two years ago, played so substantial a part in the formation of Belgium, preserves all of its [former] importance in the inner tribunal of each; but it has ceased almost entirely to be one of the elements which serve to define the frontiers of peoples.

A community of interest is assuredly a powerful bond between men. Do interests, however, suffice to make a nation? I do not think so. Community of interest brings about trade agreements, but nationality has a sentimental side to it; it is both soul and body at once; a *Zollverein* is not a *patrie.*

*   *   *

A nation is a soul, a spiritual principle. Two things, which in truth are but one, constitute this soul or spiritual principle. One lies in the past, one in the present. One is the possession in common of a rich legacy of memories; the other is present-day consent, the desire to live together, the will to perpetuate the value of the heritage that one has received in an undivided form. Man, Gentlemen, does not improvise. The nation, like the individual, is the culmination of a long past of endeavours, sacrifice, and devotion. Of all cults, that of the ancestors is the most legitimate, for the ancestors have made us what we are. A heroic past, great men, glory (by which I understand genuine glory), this is the social capital upon which one bases a national idea. To have common glories in the past and to have a common will in the present; to have performed great deeds together, to wish to perform still more—these are the essential conditions for being a people. One loves in proportion to the sacrifices to which one has consented, and in proportion to the ills that one has suffered. One loves the house that one has built 'and that one has handed down. The Spartan song—"We are what you were; we will be what you are"— is, in its simplicity, the abridged hymn of every *patrie.*

More valuable by far than common customs posts and frontiers conforming to strategic ideas is the fact of sharing, in the past, a glorious heritage and regrets, and of having, in the future, [a shared] programme to put into effect, or the fact of having suffered, enjoyed, and hoped together. These are the kinds of things that can be understood in spite of differences of race and language. I spoke just now of "having suffered together" and, indeed, suffering in common unifies more than joy does. Where national memories are concerned, griefs are of more value than triumphs, for they impose duties, and require a common effort.

A nation is therefore a large-scale solidarity, constituted by the feeling of the sacrifices that one has made in the past and of those that one is prepared to make in the future. It presupposes a past; it is summarized, however, in the present by a tangible fact, namely, consent, the clearly expressed desire to continue a common life. A nation's existence is, if you will pardon the metaphor, a daily plebiscite, just as an individual's existence is a perpetual affirmation of life. That, I know full well, is less metaphysical than divine right and less brutal than so-called historical rights. According to the ideas that I am outlining

to you, a nation has no more right than a king does to say to a province: "You belong to me. I am seizing you." A province, as far as I am concerned, is its inhabitants; if anyone has the right to be consulted in such an affair, it is the inhabitant. A nation never has any real interest in annexing or holding on to a country against its will. The wish of nations is, all in all, the sole legitimate criterion, the one to which one must always return.

*   *   *

Let me sum up, Gentlemen. Man is a slave neither of his race nor his language, nor of his religion, nor of the course of rivers nor of the direction taken by mountain chains. A large aggregate of men, healthy in mind and warm of heart, creates the kind of moral conscience which we call a nation. So long as this moral consciousness gives proof of its strength by the sacrifices which demand the abdication of the individual to the advantage of the community, it is legitimate and has the right to exist. If doubts arise regarding its frontiers, consult the populations in the areas under dispute. They undoubtedly have the right to a say in the matter. This recommendation will bring a smile to the lips of the transcendants of politics, these infallible beings who spend their lives deceiving themselves and who, from the height of their superior principles, take pity upon our mundane concerns. "Consult the populations, for heaven's sake! How naive! A fine example of those wretched French ideas which claim to replace diplomacy and war by childishly simple methods." Wait a while, Gentlemen; let the reign of the transcendants pass; bear the scorn of the powerful with patience. It may be that, after many fruitless gropings, people will revert to our more modest empirical solutions. The best way of being right in the future is, in certain periods, to know how to resign oneself to being out of fashion.

REVIEW QUESTIONS

1. Which explanations for nationalism does Renan reject and why?

2. How does Renan finally view nationalism, and does he reject the doctrine?

3. What implications does Renan's argument have for the making and unmaking of nation-states?

ÉDOUARD DRUMONT

FROM *Jewish France*

During the first half of the nineteenth century, European Jews won many new guarantees of legal and political equality, largely as a result of political liberalism and the growing secularization of European society. In western Europe especially, it almost seemed that centuries of anti-Semitism would be brought to an end through the quiet assimilation of Jews into mainstream national cultures. However, in the final quarter of the century, a new and very virulent form of anti-Semitism emerged, threatening Jewish communities' fragile political and social gains.

In France as elsewhere, Jews served as scapegoats for deep-seated cultural anxieties stimulated by the political instability of the Third Republic, as well as the massive social and economic changes generated by French industrialization. During the Dreyfus affair, French anti-Semites were rallied to the cause by Édouard Drumont (1844–1917), the editor of La Libre parole *("The Free Word"), a conservative anti-Semitic journal, and the founder of the French Anti-Semitic League. Drumont's* Jewish France, *published in 1885, enjoyed immense popularity: at least 150,000 copies were sold within two years of its first appearance and it remained in print long into the twentieth century. As the following excerpt from his work demonstrates, Drumont's anti-Semitism took the form of an argument that "old France" was being "conquered" by an alien and parasitic Jewish culture.*

From *La France juive: Essai d'histoire contemporaine*, by Édouard Drumont, translated by Cat Nilan (Paris: Marpon and Flammarion, 1997).

The only one who has benefitted from the Revolution [of 1789] is the Jew. Everything comes from the Jew; everything returns to the Jew.

We have here a veritable conquest, an entire nation returned to serfdom by a minute but cohesive minority, just as the Saxons were forced into serfdom by William the Conqueror's 60,000 Normans.

The methods are different, the result is the same. One can recognize all the characteristics of a conquest: an entire population working for another population, which appropriates, through a vast system of financial exploitation, all of the profits of the other. Immense Jewish fortunes, castles, Jewish townhouses, are not the fruit of any actual labor, of any production: they are the booty taken from an enslaved race by a dominant race.

It is certain, for example, that the Rothschild family, whose French branch alone possesses a declared fortune of three billion [francs], did not have that money when it arrived in France; it has invented nothing, it has discovered no mine, it has tilled no ground. It has therefore appropriated these three billion francs from the French without giving them anything in exchange.

*   *   *

All Jewish fortunes have been built up in the same manner, through an appropriation of the work of others.

*   *   *

Today, thanks to the Jew, money—to which the Christian world attached only a secondary importance and assigned only a subordinate role—has become all powerful. Capitalist power concentrated in a tiny number of hands governs at will the entire economic life of the people, enslaves their labor, and feasts on iniquitous profits acquired without labor.

These problems, familiar to all thinking Europeans, are all but unknown in France. The reason is simple. The Jew Lassalle himself has noted how slender are the intellectual foundations of the bourgeoisie, whose opinions are fabricated by the newspapers. * * *

Now, since almost all newspapers and all organs of publicity in France are in the hands of Jews or belong to them indirectly, it is not surprising that the significance and the scope of the immense anti-Semitic movement that has begun to organize itself everywhere is being carefully hidden from us.

*   *   *

In any case, it seems to me interesting and useful to describe the successive phases of this *Jewish Conquest,* to indicate how, little by little, as a result of Jewish activities, old France has been dissolved, broken up, how its unselfish, happy, loving people has been replaced by a hateful people, hungry for gold and soon to be dying of hunger.

*   *   *

Thanks to the Jews' cunning exploitation of the principles of '89, France was collapsing into dissolution. Jews had monopolized all of the public wealth, had invaded everything, except the army. The representatives of the old [French] families, whether noble or bourgeois, had divided themselves into two camps. Some gave themselves up to pleasure, and were corrupted by the Jewish prostitutes they had taken as mistresses or were ruined by the horse-sellers and money-lenders, also Jews, who aided the prostitutes. The others obeyed the attraction exercised over the Aryan race by the infinite, the Hindu Nirvana, Odin's paradise. They became almost uninterested in contemporary life, they lost themselves in ecstasy, they barely had one foot still planted in the real world.

If the Semites could have been patient for a few years they would have achieved their goal. Jules Simon, one of the few truly wise men they count among their ranks * * * , told them exactly what they needed to do: quietly take over the earth and let the Aryans migrate up to heaven.

The Jews never wanted to listen to this message: they preferred the Semite Gambetta to the Semite Simon. * * * they believed that [Gambetta] was going to help them get rid of Christ, whom they still hated just as much as they had on the day they crucified him. Freemasonry made its contribution, Jewish journals stirred up public opinion, gold was freely distributed, police superintendents were richly paid off, although they refused to make themselves guilty of a crime up to the last minute.

What happened? * * * The Aryan—provoked, troubled, wounded in his innate feelings of nobility and generosity—felt his blood rise to his face when he saw unfortunate old [monks] dragged from their cells by the dregs of the police. He took a while to deliberate, to gather his thoughts, to reflect.

"In the name of what principle are you acting?" he asked.

"In the name of the principal of liberty," replied in unison the newspapers of Porgès, Reinach, Dreyfus, Eugène Mayer, Camille Sée, Naquet.

"And what does this principle consist of?"

"Of this: some Jew or another leaves Hamburg, Frankfurt, Vilna, or anyplace else, and he amasses a certain number of millions at the expense of the *goyim* [gentiles]. He can take his carriage out for a ride, his domicile is inviolable, unless a warrant is issued, and naturally it never is. On the other hand, a native Frenchman, a *natural Frenchman,* to use the words of Saint-Simon, gives away everything he owns to help the poor; he goes barefoot, he lives in a narrow, whitewashed cell that the servant of Rothschild's servant wouldn't want. He is the outlaw. He can be thrown out in the street like a dog.

The Aryan, roused from his slumbers, decides, not without reason, that once this so precious tolerance—talked about so much for the last hundred years—is interpreted in this way, it is better to strike back than be struck. He decides that it is more than time to wrest the country from such impatient masters. "Since the monk's rough robe is so annoying to your frock-coat, we'll give you back the yellow rag, my old Shem." Such was the upshot of [the Aryan's] meditations. It is from that moment that one can date the establishment of the first anti-Semitic—or, to be more precise, anti-Jewish—committee.

*   *   *

∗ ∗ ∗ The fatherland, in the sense that we attach to that word, has no meaning for the Semite. The Jew, to use the energetic expression of the *Israelite Alliance,* is characterized by an *inexorable universalism.*

I can see no reason for reproaching the Jews for thinking this way. What does the word "Fatherland" mean? Land of the fathers. One's feelings for the Fatherland are engraved in one's heart in the same way that a name carved in a tree is driven deeper into the bark with each passing year, so that the tree and the name eventually become one. You can't become a patriot through improvization; you are a patriot in your blood, in your marrow.

Can the Semite, a perpetual nomad, ever experience such enduring impressions?

∗ ∗ ∗ The first requirement for adopting a new fatherland, is to renounce the old one. Now, the Jew has a fatherland he never renounces: Jerusalem, the holy and mysterious city Jerusalem. In triumph or persecution, joyous or sad, it serves as a link uniting all of those children who say every year at Rosh Hashanah: "next year in Jerusalem!"

Aside from Jerusalem, every other country, whether France, or Germany, or England, is only a residence for the Jew, any old place, a social agglomeration, in the midst of which he may find himself at home, whose interests he may even find it profitable to serve for the moment, but which he joins only as a free agent, as a temporary member.

*   *   *

To succeed in their attack against Christian civilization, the Jews of France had to use deceit, to lie, to disguise themselves as freethinkers. If they had said frankly: "We want to destroy that France of old, so glorious, so beautiful, and replace it with domination by a fistful of Hebrews from many lands," our fathers, less soft than ourselves, would not have let this happen. For a long time [the Jews] kept things vague, working with Freemasonry, hiding behind sonorous words: emancipation, enfranchisement, the struggle against superstition and the prejudices of another age.

*   *   *

∗ ∗ ∗ Among the Jews, religious persecution takes on a particularly bitter character. For them, nothing has changed: they hate Christ as much in 1885 as they hated him at the time of Tiberius Augustus, and they heap the same outrages upon him. Whipping the crucifix on Good Friday, profaning the host, besmirching sacred images: such was the great joy of the medieval Jew, and such is his great joy today. Then, he attacked the bodies of children; today, he tries to get at their souls through atheist education. Then, he bled them; today, he poisons their minds: which is worse?

*   *   *

Despite everything, it is difficult to escape the influence of what one hears from morning to night, from the impression of the artificial intellectual climate created by the Jewish press, and even the best sometimes are subject, despite themselves, to what we have already named the *prejudices of modernism*.

*   *   *

As for myself, I repeat that I claim to have done nothing more than to attempt a work of good will, to demonstrate by what an underhanded and crafty enemy France has been invaded, corrupted, and brutalized, to such a point that she has broken with her proper hands everything that once made her powerful, respected, and happy. Have I written our last will and testament? Have I laid the foundations for our re-

birth? I do not know. I have done my duty, in any case, by responding with insults to the numberless insults that the Jewish press directs at Christians. In proclaiming the Truth, I have obeyed the imperious command of my conscience: *liberavi animam meam* [free my soul]. * * *

*   *   *

REVIEW QUESTIONS

1. Of what "crimes" were the Jews of France guilty, according to Drumont?
2. How did they get away with these crimes?
3. What does Drumont mean by "tolerance"? Why does he reject it?
4. What are the "prejudices of modernism"?
5. Why does Drumont associate Jews with modernism?
6. On the basis of this reading, why do you think Drumont hated Jews?
7. Why do you think his arguments might have appealed to many late-nineteenth-century Europeans?

25 ♊ IMPERIALISM AND COLONIALISM, 1870–1914

The striking escalation of Europe's formal political control over other lands and peoples during the last half of the nineteenth century is often called the new imperialism. The term refers to the West's renewed enthusiasm and drive for colonial empires—a calculus of political power, economic exploitation, and cultural superiority—that first began in the early modern era. The shift from informal economic advantages to direct political control began slowly after 1850 but gathered a frenetic momentum in the 1870s with widespread European competition for new colonies. Following the Indian Mutiny in 1857, Britain first changed its informal economic relationship with the subcontinent by introducing direct colonial rule. Between the years 1880 and 1914 European powers radically increased their dominion in Africa, expanding their formal control of the continent from 10 to 90 percent. Similarly, by 1900 nearly all of Asia had been divided among the British, French, Dutch, Germans, and Americans. The feverish pace of colonization in this period erected unstable structures within which twentieth-century global economies, politics, and cultural exchanges would operate. Modern world history is simply inexplicable without an understanding of nineteenth-century imperialism.

Colonies assumed a new status in European culture: economically, colonies promised cheap raw materials, high yields on investments, and markets for finished goods; culturally, they provided the points of entry for the spread of Christianity and European civilization; and politically, they signified great-power status and offered a glorious, nation-uniting mission to European publics seeking solace from contentious domestic politics. Contemporaries, however, usually perceived the various justifications for imperialism as a totality: the civilizing effects of commerce and religion followed the glory of the flag. Thus proceeded the "friendly competition" among European nations to carve up Africa and penetrate the Far East.

Prior to the First World War, Europe almost exclusively viewed imperialism in terms of its own interests and needs, presuming that non-Western peoples benefited from the "civilizing mission" of the "white man's burden." Some contemporaries, however, criticized such arrogance, pointing out the crushing "black man's burden" that had accumulated from the imperialist legacy. Similarly, Near Eastern writers took note of the large discrepancy between the West's notions of the "exotic" Orient and the lived realities of the Near East, a dichotomy explained in part by Europe's desire to articulate cultural difference between Western "civilization" and Eastern "barbarism." Indeed, the Western imperial gaze saw the world as a vast space in need of transformation. In meeting that challenge to remake the world in its own image, the West redefined itself and its role in the world.

The legacies of colonial ruling classes, imperial plantation economies, and European mass consumer markets on non-Western manufactures forever changed indigenous societies. In creating a new set of economic, political, and social relationships between the West and the world, imperialism interpenetrated and irrevocably transformed European and non-Western cultures. Metropole and colony, once separate entities, became fused over time into an imperial alloy, rendering desires to return to precolonial conditions impossible. For this reason the multifaceted phenomenon of imperialism is a central element of modernity. It not only defined the national and cultural identities of European states but also shaped colonials' aspirations for independence and their visions of postcolonial society.

ISAAC BUTT

FROM "A Voice for Ireland"

Out of a nation of eight million, approximately one million Irish starved to death in the Great Famine between 1845 and 1851. Following the famine, close to another two million emigrated to England or the United States, thus constituting a social catastrophe of immeasurable magnitude for Ireland. The immediate cause of the famine was a potato blight, a fungus that rotted the potato and rendered it unfit for consumption. But the larger explanatory framework of the Great Famine must also include Britain's long-term imperial policy in Ireland, which encouraged the export of wheat for the profits of absentee landlords, discouraged investment in Irish farms, and turned a blind eye to a century of abject poverty for Irish tenant farmers. Critics also charged that Britain's responses to the famine were aloof, addressing famine within English political frameworks of ending grain tariffs (the so-called Corn Laws) and poor laws, measures which proved to be woefully inadequate for Irish conditions. The passage below offers a reasoned, contemporary Irish perspective on British policy.

From *A Voice for Ireland,* by Isaac Butt (Dublin: McGlashan, 1847), pp. 2–11.

*   *   *

We will not take up our space by repeating the testimonies, which prove incontestably that this is no exaggeration. It is not, perhaps, the least appalling feature of this calamity, that it is difficult, if not impossible, to obtain accurate information upon the extent of devastation that has already taken place. Nearly a month ago, the deaths that had resulted in one shape or other from starvation were estimated at 240,000. Long before the sam period, the deaths that were occurring each day in Ireland, beyond those of the same period in the preceding year, were estimated at 1,000—1,000 each day—a number, we apprehend, below the truth. In many of the workhouses deaths occurred in numbers that would lead to a much greater estimate of the loss of life in the entire country. In one electoral poor-law division of the county Cork—one not within the fatal district of Schull or Skibbereen—out of a population of 16,000, the deaths in the early part of March were averaging seventy a-day, a rate of mortality that would sweep away the entire population in about eight months. There are parts of Mayo, Galway, and Sligo, in which the deaths were nearly in the same proportion. It is impossible, however, to form more than an approximation to the real extent of the calamity. It is an incident of the neglect with which the people, when living, have been treated, that we have no note of them when dead. The occupation of Death has not been interfered with, even by registering the number he has carried off.

It is, however, enough, to say that multitudes in Ireland are starving—that each day is striking down new victims of want of food, and that there is not in Ireland sufficient food to supply her whole population with subsistence for many weeks to come.

So many topics press upon us in relation to the fearful subject we have undertaken, that we scarcely know how to commence its treatment. Let us recall the attention of our readers to the commencement of the potato blight.

In the autumn of 1845, it was discovered that a disease had attacked the potato in Ireland, and in several other parts of the world. Of the actual existence of such a disease there was no doubt. Its extent was, like most questions in Ireland, made a party one—and, we grieve to say, the Tory party were in the wrong. Some of the journals in Ireland, supposed most to represent the aristocracy, persisted in vigorously denying the existence of any failure to more than a very partial extent. The question of the corn laws, then pending, gave this question an imperial interest. The potato famine in Ireland was represented as the invention of the agitators on either side of the water. So far was party feeling carried, that the Conservative mayor of Liverpool, honestly we are sure, refused to convene a meeting for the relief of Irish distress—a committee which sat at the Mansion House, in Dublin, and first declared their belief in the approach of an overwhelming calamity, were stigmatized as deluding the public with a false alarm. Men's politics determined their belief. To profess belief in the fact of the existence of a formidable potato blight, was as sure a method of being branded as a radical, as to propose to destroy the Church.

Thus in the very outset of this sore trial did Ireland encounter that which has ever been her bitterest curse—that questions of fact are made party questions, and the belief or disbelief of matters of fact is regulated in each man's mind, not by the real state of the case, but by his own political prejudices or opinions.

Sir Robert Peel was then at the head of affairs, and the ministry certainly foresaw the coming calamity. Inquiries were made as to the substance that would be the best and cheapest substitute for the potato. Indian corn was adopted, and without any public excitement on the subject, orders were given by the government for the importation of Indian corn to the amount of £100,000. This timely precaution, and the subsequent judicious distribution of this store, had the effect of bringing the people through the winter that closed the year 1845, without exposing them to any very severe privations. Arrangements were made by the government for the supply of provisions in biscuit and rice, to a much greater extent, if needed. However men may differ as to the merits of Sir Robert Peel as a politician, whatever estimate may be formed of his measures, it is impossible to deny that for the limited distress that existed consequent upon the partial failure of the potato crop of 1845, provision was made with the most consummate skill—at least with the most complete success. Uninfluenced by party representations, the minister had evidently accurately informed himself of the nature of the calamity, and clearly foresaw its extent. That he erred in fixing too early a period for its full realization, subsequent events have proved; but this was an error on the right side: and all that Sir Robert Peel predicted of the fearful extent of calamity which he anticipated in the summer of 1846, has been more than realized in the spring of 1847. There is no man of any party in Ireland who does not now feel the debt which Ireland owes to the minister for the precautions that enabled us to meet the difficulties of 1846, or who is not thoroughly convinced that an imitation, and, with the extended occasion, an extension of that policy last autumn, would have obviated most, if not all, of the suffering in which Ireland is now paying the penalty of the adherence of the present ministry, not to the doctrines of political economy, but to an utterly mistaken application of them.

It was, however, the misfortune of famine-stricken Ireland, and a deep misfortune almost all men in Ireland now feel it to be, that party combinations (we say not now, how justifiable or honorable) removed from office the man who had

shown himself alone, perhaps, of living statesmen, alive to the exigencies of the crisis, and capable of boldly and efficiently meeting them. It was an occasion upon which no statesman could efficiently serve the country out of office—a lamentable proof of this we have later in this sad history, in the rejection of Lord George Bentinck's bill; and with the removal of Peel from office he lost the power of even assisting to obviate the danger, which, we do believe, had he remained in office, he would successfully have met.

Our sketch of this part of our history would be incomplete without alluding to the repeal of the corn laws, by which the session of 1846 was ushered in. On that question, this periodical has already strongly and distinctly expressed its opinion, and that opinion it forms no part of the object of this article to qualify or retract. Sir Robert Peel stated, however, in parliament, that the determination of ministers to settle the question was forced on by their anticipation of an Irish famine—that he and his colleagues felt it would be impossible to maintain the protection during that famine—and that the ports once opened to avert starvation, never could be closed—that the agitation of the question of corn laws in a famine, when arguments in favour of cheap bread could carry with them such a deep appeal to the passions and sympathies of the human heart, would go far to break up society altogether. The coming of the Irish famine was that which he stated forced the ministry to perhaps a premature decision upon this question—and we well remember the deep and solemn warning in which, with all the authority of premier, he predicted the coming of a calamity in Ireland; of which no one could know or measure the extent.

*　　*　　*

The summer of 1846 saw the place of Sir Robert Peel filled by Lord John Russell, and upon the present premier and his colleagues devolved the responsibility of meeting the heaviest calamities of the famine. Scarcely had the present cabinet been formed, when men began to be convinced that all hope of the preservation of the potato crop of that year must be given up. As in the former year, the question was made, indeed, a party one. Those who wished to see Peel disparaged, persisted in representing his alarm as groundless. Confident reports were still published of the probability of an average supply. The journals, who had from the very beginning appeared to make it a point of political conscience to disbelieve in the existence of the scarcity, persevered in their delusive hopes of abundance. It was elaborately calculated that the abundance of the produce of the potato and the great excess of the wheat and hay crops, for which last harvest was remarkable, would at least make up for the potatoes that were lost, and thus Ireland still have her ordinary supply of food, while in the increased prices obtained for their oats, the farmers would find the year one of profit. Alas! the representations of party cannot stay the progress of nature's blight.

While these calculations were amusing and deluding the public mind, the potatoes were rotting in the ground, and before the end of September the conviction had been fixed upon the mind of the most sceptical that the potato crop, as a means of support for the people, was destroyed, and that of the ordinary food of the people there was not a supply to support them for many weeks to come.

*   *   *

Before the prorogation of parliament, ministers announced the mode in which they proposed to deal with Irish distress. The means of purchasing provisions were to be secured to the poor by an enactment which enabled, or, perhaps, we ought to say, obliged the cess-payers, in districts which the Lord Lieutenant proclaimed as distressed, to tax themselves for what were termed public works—the money for the expenditure to be advanced by the Treasury, but to be repaid by a rate upon the taxed districts in a period not exceeding twenty years. A sum of £50,000 was voted by way of grant, and in this measure was summed up the whole of the ministerial plan for meeting the exigencies of Irish distress!!

The introduction of the Labour Rate Act was coupled by a declaration on the part of the pre-

mier, which appeared almost to amount to a pledge that with the supply of food to the country government did not intend to interfere; that this should be left entirely to the ordinary resources of commercial enterprise; and that government was resolved in no manner to interfere with the ordinary operations of the speculators or traffickers in human food.

This fatal declaration of the minister was the grand mistake of his policy—it was the doom of myriads of the Irish people to death. Combined with measures of a character very different from any that ministers have ventured to propose, this determination would still have perilled, upon an experiment of social economy, the lives of thousands of Irishmen. Coupled only with such a remedial measure as the Labour Rate Act, it was consigning this ill-fated country to the horrors of starvation.

The expectation that the enterprise of merchants would bring to Ireland, under the circumstances in which the country was then placed, the additional supply of food that was needed for her people, appears to us, we confess, to have been one of the most unnatural expectations which an ignorance of the principles of social economy could permit any man to entertain, supposing the extent of the calamity to have been fully understood.

There can be no doubt that if any change in the circumstances of Ireland were to cause Ireland permanently to need an importation of Indian corn, and if the same change of circumstances were to endow her people with the means of paying for it, in a few years trade would accommodate itself to this new market, so as to afford the required supply. Shipping, probably, would be built to carry on the new transit—capital would be gradually withdrawn from other occupations, to be embarked in the trade—merchants would build stores, and carriers establish conveyances, to distribute the imported produce through the country; retail dealers in the towns and villages would gradually spring up, and in the course of a few years the new social machinery which the altered habits of the people demanded would be called into existence.

But all this must be, in any event, the work of time, and it could only be the work of time where there was a market existing, and people with the means of purchase known to exist in their hands; but to expect all this to be done as if by magic, to meet a sudden emergency, and this to supply the wants of a people known not to have the means of purchase in their hands, whose ability to pay must depend upon the successful application of the provisions of a questionable statute—to expect this economic miracle to be wrought, would indicate the most miserable misapprehension of every principle and law that regulates the system by which the wants of mankind are supplied.

The process by which extraordinary demand produces within certain limits additional supply, is one not very difficult to understand. The retail dealer of an article finds the calls of his customers for that article increasing; he correspondingly increases his orders to the merchant, who again, if the article be one of importation, gives larger orders to his correspondents abroad. By what delusion could any man persuade himself, that by the natural operation of this process, Indian corn could find its way to the wilds of Mayo, or the village of Carberry? There were neither retail dealers nor merchants in the article required. The people whose food was gone were, in fact, beyond the pale of all mercantile system—they had lived upon the produce of their potato gardens, and had been customers of no shop. To trust to mercantile enterprise to supply a country so circumstanced, was to expect men suddenly to embark in the trade of supplying Ireland with food, not by any of the ordinary processes by which merchants are led into the affording of additional supplies, by orders coming in the usual way of trade, but upon some vague and uncertain speculation that a country of which they knew nothing would have a demand for corn, and the still more uncertain speculation that the pauper inhabitants of that country would have the means of paying for that demand.

We say nothing of the difficulty, upon such a sudden emergency, of finding in the ordinary way of trade the shipping necessary for the additional transit; from what other branch of commercial marine were they to be withdrawn? what trade was to have all its contracts disturbed—its promised freights retarded—its orders for importation disregarded? and all this to meet an emergency for which no calculation had prepared men. While this difficulty was aggravated by the obstinate refusal of ministers, up to the very meeting of parliament, to suspend the navigation laws, and permit foreign vessels to assist in the task of transit, to which the British marine was inadequate.

The refusal or neglect to suspend the navigation laws, was the climax of infatuation. While food was deficient in the country, and the freight of corn from America had risen to three times its ordinary rate, not a vessel of any foreign nation would have been permitted to unload a cargo of grain in any one of our ports.

If ministers resolved to trust the lives of the Irish people to private enterprize, was it not common sense and common justice to them that private enterprize should be unencumbered by any restrictions in the execution of the task of supplying, at the notice of a few months, provisions to five millions of people; yet, during the months in which food might have been imported into the country, the ministry left the importation of corn impeded by the restrictions of the navigation laws, and subject to a duty on importation which an order in council might have removed.

It is difficult to trace this history without indignation. We can understand the verdict of the coroner's jury, who, in days when inquests were held in Ireland upon the bodies of men found dead upon the highway, returned upon the body of a man who died of starvation while toiling at the public works, and fell dead of exhaustion with the implements of labour in his hand, a verdict of murder against the ministers who had neglected the first responsibility of government. Can we wonder if the Irish people believe—*and believe it they do*—that the lives of those who have perished, and who will perish, have been sacrificed by a deliberate compact to the gains of English merchants, and if this belief has created among all classes a feeling of deep dissatisfaction, not only with the ministry but with English rule.

Let us not be misunderstood. Of any such compact we acquit the ministers. In the resolution they originally formed, they were actuated by a sincere, but most mistaken belief, that they could best secure a supply of food to Ireland by declaring their determination to leave all to be done by the ordinary operations of trade. But these must be excused, who, while they witness the scenes of horror that too many in Ireland are daily seeing, believe that the subsequent deliberations of the cabinet were too much influenced by the fear of offending powerful British interests—that the omission to remove the duty from the importation on corn—to suspend the navigation laws—and to import provisions into Ireland at government expense, when it became manifest that by no other means could the emergency be met, indicated a tender regard for the interests that might have been affected by a change in their policy, which gave too much weight to those interests, and too little to the safety of the Irish people, and which, in all probability, would not long have delayed remedial measures, had the interests to be sacrificed been Irish ones.

The folly of relying on private enterprize to supply the deficiency, is proved incontestably by the result. Private enterprize has not saved us from the horrors of the famine. With Indian corn at the price of 15s. 4d. a quarter on the other side of the Atlantic, and 60s. in London! with wheat 32s. and 73s.! private enterprize has failed to import it. The applications of the best established principles of political economy would have enabled any man of ordinary sagacity to have foreseen this result. All the ordinary demands of civilized life are, doubtless, best met by those spontaneous processes in which the self-interest of man directs his activity and energy in the channels best adapted to supply these demands; but sudden and extraordinary emergencies must be met by other means. These are the occasions upon which it is of value to all that great resources should be wielded by the governing power to effect rapidly great ends.

If ever there was an occasion upon which practical proof could be given of the value to every member of the state of that association of men into states, that permits the government to wield mighty powers for the common good—if ever there were a time when men in the remotest corners of Ireland might have been taught the lesson that they have a deep interest in the strength and greatness of the United Empire, this famine presented that occasion. Tell us not that it was beyond the power of the combinations which the strength of the British empire could have wielded, to have brought to the ports of Ireland subsistence for all her people. Who is there that will say, that in such an empire all that strength should not have been put forth? What nobler triumph of British greatness could be imagined, than to have collected in the ports of famine-stricken Ireland, vessels of all nations laden with food? This would have been an exhibition of British power and British greatness, compared with which the most glorious of her fleets, or the vastest of her arsenals, would bring to the mind but a poor idea of majesty and strength. Six months ago it was possible to have done all this. The opportunity was lost; and Britain is now branded as the only civilized nation which would permit her subjects to perish of famine, without making a national effort to supply them with food.

In what parallel case do we find statesmen willing to trust to the ordinary operations of commerce, to supply in any country a sudden and unexpected demand for human subsistence? If England had occasion to send an army into some country destitute of food, would her statesmen content themselves with seeing that the soldiers were provided regularly with their pay, and trust to the speculations of private enterprize to follow them with the necessary articles of food? Multiply that army to four millions, and you have exactly the case of the starving Irish in this year.

REVIEW QUESTIONS

1. Why does Butt call "party questions" the "bitterest curse" for Ireland?
2. What was the relationship of the famine to the parliamentary repeal of the Corn Laws in 1846?
3. How did Parliament propose to end the famine?
4. How did Butt suggest that Ireland had suffered because of its colonial status?

DAVID LIVINGSTONE

FROM Cambridge Speech of 1857

David Livingstone (1813–1873), the Scottish missionary and explorer of Africa, personified for Britain the higher cause of imperialism. Between 1840 and 1873, Livingstone traversed nearly a third of Africa, missionizing Christianity, opposing the persistent slave trade, and recording the geography and ethnographic customs of its peoples. His achievement and his self-effacing devotion to opening up Africa to commerce and Christianity provided inspiration to a nineteenth-century British public in search of a moral center to its imperialist policies in Africa.

From *Dr. Livingstone's Cambridge Lectures,* edited by William Monk (Cambridge, Eng.: Bell, 1858).

*   *   *

My object in going into the country south of the desert was to instruct the natives in a knowledge of Christianity, but many circumstances prevented my living amongst them more than seven years, amongst which were considerations arising out of the slave system carried on by the Dutch Boers. I resolved to go into the country beyond, and soon found that, for the purposes of commerce, it was necessary to have a path to the sea. I might have gone on instructing the natives in religion, but as civilization and Christianity must go on together, I was obliged to find a path to the sea, in order that I should not sink to the level of the natives. The chief was overjoyed at the suggestion, and furnished me with twenty-seven men, and canoes, and provisions, and presents for the tribes through whose country we had to pass.

*   *   *

In a commercial point of view communication with this country is desirable. Angola is wonderfully fertile, producing every kind of tropical plant in rank luxuriance. Passing on to the valley of Quango, the stalk of the grass was as thick as a quill, and towered above my head, although I was mounted on my ox; cotton is produced in great abundance, though merely woven into common cloth; bananas and pine-apples grow in great luxuriance; but the people having no maritime communication, these advantages are almost lost. The country on the other side is not quite so fertile, but in addition to indigo, cotton, and sugar-cane, produces a fibrous substance, which I am assured is stronger than flax.

The Zambesi has not been thought much of as a river by Europeans, not appearing very large at its mouth; but on going up it for about seventy miles, it is enormous. The first three hundred miles might be navigated without obstacle: then there is a rapid, and near it a coal-field of large extent. The elevated sides of the basin, which form the most important feature of the country, are far different in climate to the country nearer the sea, or even the centre. Here the grass is short, and the Angola goat, which could not live in the centre, had been seen on the east highland by Mr Moffat.

My desire is to open a path to this district, that civilization, commerce, and Christianity might find their way there. I consider that we made a great mistake, when we carried commerce into India, in being ashamed of our Christianity; as a matter of common sense and good policy, it is always best to appear in one's true character. In travelling through Africa, I might have imitated certain Portuguese, and have passed for a chief; but I never attempted anything of the sort, although endeavouring always to keep to the lessons of cleanliness rigidly instilled by my mother long ago; the consequence was that the natives respected me for that quality, though remaining dirty themselves.

I had a pass from the Portuguese consul, and on arriving at their settlement, I was asked what I was. I said, "A missionary, and a doctor too." They asked, "Are you a doctor of medicine?"—"Yes."—"Are you not a doctor of mathematics too?"—"No."—"And yet you can take longitudes and latitudes."—Then they asked me about my moustache; and I simply said I wore it, because men had moustaches to wear, and ladies had not. They could not understand either, why a sacerdote should have a wife and four children; and many a joke took place upon that subject. I used to say, "Is it not better to have children with than without a wife?" Englishmen of education always command respect, without any adventitious aid. A Portuguese governor left for Angola, giving out that he was going to keep a large establishment, and taking with him quantities of crockery, and about five hundred waistcoats; but when he arrived in Africa, he made a 'deal' of them. Educated Englishmen seldom descend to that sort of thing.

A prospect is now before us of opening Africa for commerce and the Gospel. Providence has been preparing the way, for even before I proceeded to the Central basin it had been conquered and rendered safe by a chief named Sebituane, and the language of the Bechuanas made the fashionable tongue, and that was one of the languages into which Mr Moffat had translated the Scriptures. Sebituane also discovered Lake Ngami some time previous to my explorations in that part. In going back to that country my object is to open up traffic along the banks of the Zambesi, and also to preach the Gospel. The natives of Central Africa are very desirous of trading, but their only traffic is at present in slaves, of which the poorer people have an unmitigated horror: it is therefore most desirable to encourage the former principle, and thus open a way for the consumption of free productions, and the introduction of Christianity and commerce. By encouraging the native propensity for trade, the advantages that might be derived in a commercial point of view are incalculable; nor should we lose sight of the inestimable blessings it is in our power to bestow upon the unenlightened African, by giving him the light of Christianity. Those two pioneers of civilization—Christianity and commerce—should ever be inseparable; and Englishmen should be warned by the fruits of neglecting that principle as exemplified in the result of the management of Indian affairs. By trading with Africa, also, we should at length be independent of slave-labour, and thus discountenance practices so obnoxious to every Englishman.

Though the natives are not absolutely anxious to receive the Gospel, they are open to Christian influences. Among the Bechuanas the Gospel was well received. These people think it a crime to shed a tear, but I have seen some of them weep at the recollection of their sins when God had opened their hearts to Christianity and repentance. It is true that missionaries have difficulties to encounter; but what great enterprise was ever accomplished without difficulty? It is deplorable to think that one of the noblest of our missionary societies, the Church Missionary Society, is compelled to send to Germany for missionaries, whilst other societies are amply supplied. Let this stain be wiped off. The sort of men who are wanted for missionaries are such as I see before me; men of education, standing, enterprise, zeal, and piety. It is a mistake to suppose that *any one*, as long as he is pious, will do for this office. Pioneers in every thing should be the ablest and best qualified men, not those of small ability and education. This remark especially applies to the first teachers of Christian truth in regions which may never have before been blest with the name and Gospel of Jesus Christ. In the early ages the monasteries were the schools of Europe, and the monks were not ashamed to hold the plough. The missionaries now take the place of those noble men, and we should not hesitate to give up the small luxuries of life in order to carry knowledge and truth to them that are in darkness. I hope that many of those whom I now address will embrace that honourable career. Education has been given us from above for the purpose of bringing to the benighted the knowledge of a Saviour. If you knew the satisfaction of performing such a duty, as well as the gratitude to God which the missionary must always feel, in being chosen for so noble, so sacred a calling, you would have no hesitation in embracing it.

For my own part, I have never ceased to rejoice that God has appointed me to such an office.

People talk of the sacrifice I have made in spending so much of my life in Africa. Can that be called a sacrifice which is simply paid back as a small part of a great debt owing to our God, which we can never repay?—Is that a sacrifice which brings its own blest reward in healthful activity, the consciousness of doing good, peace of mind, and a bright hope of a glorious destiny hereafter?—Away with the word in such a view, and with such a thought! It is emphatically no sacrifice. Say rather it is a privilege. Anxiety, sickness, suffering, or danger, now and then, with a foregoing of the common conveniences and charities of this life, may make us pause, and cause the spirit to waver, and the soul to sink, but let this only be for a moment. All these are nothing when compared with the glory which shall hereafter be revealed in, and for, us. I never made a sacrifice. Of this we ought not to talk, when we remember the great sacrifice which HE made who left His Father's throne on high to give Himself for us.

* * *

REVIEW QUESTIONS

1. What was for Livingstone the relationship between commerce and missionary work?
2. What were Livingstone's perceptions of African culture?
3. Judging from this speech, how did Livingstone inspire a generation to enter into missionary work?

MUHAMMED AS-SAFFAR

FROM *Travels of a Moroccan Scholar in France in 1845–46*

Between 1841 and 1844, the French army, in its attempt to consolidate political control in Algeria, engaged in a border war with Morocco so that France could win wider Arab recognition of its sovereignty over Algeria. Following a naval bombardment of Tangiers in August 1844, the Moroccans confronted the decision of choosing either a holy war or a diplomatic conciliation with the French. The Moroccan sultan chose the latter and sent a mission to Paris to effect a diplomatic compromise. As the secretary to the sultan's ambassador to France, Muhammed As-Saffar traveled to Paris. A learned scholar in law, Hadith, and Arabic grammar, As-Saffar kept a precise diary of his journey to Paris in 1845–1846. Through this invaluable source, one sees an Arabian scholar's perception of Europe as an alien civilization. Passages on Christianity and the press provide a glimpse into this foreigner's impressions, at once critical and admiring.

From *Disorienting Encounters: Travels of a Moroccan Scholar in France in 1845–46,* by Muhammed As-Saffar, translated by Susan Gilson Miller (Berkeley: University of California Press, 1992), pp. 108–10, 150–53.

*   *   *   *

In Aix we saw a huge cross made of wood standing on one side of the town square. At its top was a smaller bit of wood made into the likeness of a crucified man, naked except for a cloth covering his maleness. What a sight it was! We were terrified to see it and thought that he was a criminal they had hung there, for without a doubt, whoever saw it [would think it] was a crucified man. I asked about this and they told me that it was the deity and the crucifix which they worshipped. They claim he is Jesus, that is to say, a likeness of him crucified. And there is no doubt that they believe in his divinity just as the Koran tells us, and there is no doubt about the untruth of their claim and the falsity of their belief. *"For they have no knowledge of it, and only follow conjecture."*[1] Those are the words of their mouths, which is [false] like the speech of those who become infi-

dels just before they die. My God how they lie! This is the cross set up in their churches to worship and glorify, and which Jesus, may peace be unto him, will break upon his return, refuting the falsehood of their belief and the wrongheadedness of the Christian religion.

Al-Qasṭallānī in his commentary on the *Ṣaḥīḥ* mentions the tradition about breaking the cross as follows: It is said that its origin is that a group of Jews insulted Jesus and his mother, peace be unto them, and God called upon the [Jews] and changed them into pigs and monkeys. Then the Jews decided to kill [Jesus]. God warned him and said he would raise him to heaven. Then [Jesus] said to his companions, "Which of you wishes to take on my likeness, be killed and crucified, and so enter the Garden of Eden?" One of them got up and God cast upon him the likeness [of Jesus], so that it would be he who was killed and crucified. And then people said, perhaps this man is a dissembler, and tried to prove it by entering the

[1] Koran 4:157.

house of Jesus, but Jesus had already left and his likeness was cast on the other. So that when the Jews entered, they killed [the dissembler], claiming he was Jesus. Then they disagreed and some said that he was God and could not be killed; and others said that a dissembler had been killed and crucified; and others said that if it was Jesus, then where was his companion; and if it was his companion, then where was Jesus? And some said he was raised to heaven, and others said his face is the face of Jesus, and his body the body of the companion. Then the Jews oppressed the companions of Jesus, peace be unto him, by killing and crucifying and jailing [them], until the matter came before the Master of Rome. He was told that the Jews were oppressing the companions of Jesus, because he said he was the Messenger of God, he was giving life to the dead, he was healing the dumb and the leprous, and working miracles, and that the Jews had killed him and crucified him. And [the Master of Rome] sent for the crucified body, which was taken down from the wooden pieces. The pieces of wood on which he was crucified were brought to the Master of Rome, who began to worship them. From them they made many crosses and from that day on Christians have worshiped the cross. The end.

The cross of the crucifixion appears there in different guises, but always in the same form. Sometimes it is large, at other times it is small. It may be of wood, stone, metal, brass, or gold, or in a picture. Sometimes the form of the crucified Jesus is on it, sometimes it is the cross alone, as was mentioned by al-Qastallānî. Many are sold in the shops. The figure of Jesus is portrayed in various ways: as a grown man, or a small boy in the lap or arms of Mary. In the church they pray to them both. If you ask one of them about this likeness, he will explain to you that it is God, or His son, or His mother if Mary is there. May [God] preserve them from that, and may He be raised high above what the sinners say. The proof of our eyes only increased our insight into their unbelief, the falsity of their creed, and the stupidity of their reasoning. Thanks be to God who guided us to the true religion. We ask God, praise be unto Him,

to keep us in the true faith until death. Amen. With the help of our faithful prophet, may prayers and the purest peace be upon him until the Day of Judgment.

*　　*　　*

The Gazettes

The people of Paris, like all the French—indeed, like all of Rūm—are eager to know the latest news and events that are taking place in other parts. For this purpose they have the gazette. These are papers in which they write all the news that has reached them that day about events in their own country and in other lands both near and far.

This is the way it is done. The owner of a newspaper dispatches his people to collect everything they see or hear in the way of important events or unusual happenings. Among the places where they collect the news are the two Chambers, the Great and the Small, where they come together to make their laws. When the members of the Chamber meet to deliberate, the men of the gazette sit nearby and write down everything that is said, for all debating and ratifying of laws is matter for the gazette and is known to everyone. No one can prevent them from doing this. However, if their words are about a disgraceful subject, they must conceal them from the public, and are not allowed [to write them].

They also have correspondents and reporters in other lands, who know what is happening there. You will find that the newspaper people are advised about unusual events before anyone else. [They] spend their day collecting news, handing in at night what they have gathered during the day. The owner of the newspaper then prints it, making numerous sheets by means of the printing press, which will be explained later. Then it is distributed to everyone who takes it, each receiving a set. All the leaders of France, and especially in Paris, make a contract with the owner of the newspaper to receive a new gazette each day, in return for a fixed sum paid annually. Likewise, all the cafés receive numerous gazettes each day from many places. When someone enters a café, first the waiter brings him a newspaper so he may learn what is new, and then he serves him his coffee. The newspapers are handed back and kept there. Whoever wishes to know what has happened in the past can hunt around in the café for a gazette from that time, and read about it.

On the front of the gazette is written its price each year. Every day during our stay in Paris, a new gazette with the most correct news arrived at our house. Written at the top was its price—sixteen *riyals* per year. One makes a contract with the owner [of the newspaper] and receives it for a short or long period, but never less than a month. They say that about fifteen thousand copies are printed daily. Each [sheet] is a piece of paper about two cubits long, written on both sides. In it you will find the news from Paris and the rest of the land of the French; from all the lands of the Christians; from the lands of the East and the West; in fact, from everywhere. Some copies even travel to other countries. Whenever you enter another part of France you will find the gazette of Paris, just as in Paris you find gazettes from the provinces.

For this reason they are well acquainted with all the news, whether it is local or foreign. Nor is it all necessarily true; it may be that the lies in it are more numerous than the truths, because it includes news that human nature loves to hear. But there are benefits in it too, such as learning what is new. Moreover, if someone has an idea about a subject but he is not a member of the press, he may write about it in the gazette and make it known to others, so that the leaders of opinion learn about it. If the idea is worthy they may follow it, and if its author was out of favor it may bring him recognition. As the poet says:

Don't reject an idea if it is suitable,
Or Truth even if it comes from error.
Pearls are precious to acquire,
But it is not the diver who decides their worth.

Among the many laws which their Sultan Louis XVIII has made for them and they are obliged to follow is that no person in France is prohibited from expressing his opinion or from writing it and printing it, on condition that he does not violate

the law. If he does, it is erased. One of the reasons they were so hostile to their King Charles X, who preceded the present king, and a cause for their overthrow of his rule, is that he proclaimed a ban on anyone expressing ideas, or writing them, or printing them in the newspapers, unless one of the men of state had read it [first]. Therefore nothing appeared except what he wanted to appear.

In the newspapers they write rejoinders to the men of the two Chambers about the laws they are making. If their Sultan demands gifts from the notables or goes against the law in any way, they write about that too, saying that he is a tyrant and in the wrong. He cannot confront them or cause them harm. Also, if someone behaves out of the ordinary, they write about that too, making it common knowledge among people of every rank. If his deeds were admirable, they praise and delight in him, lauding his example; but if he behaved badly, they revile him to discourage the like.

Moreover, if someone is being oppressed by another, they write about that too, so that everyone will know the story from both sides just as it happened, until it is decided in court. One can also read in it what their courts have decided. Whoever wishes to advertise his wares can write about them in the newspaper, praising them and mentioning their location and price in the hope of selling them; and whoever wishes to sell a house or property can publish it in the gazette to inform people. All in all, the gazette is of such importance that one of them would do without food or drink sooner than do without reading the newspaper.

*   *   *

REVIEW QUESTIONS

1. Why was As-Saffar so disturbed by the crucifix as a religious symbol?
2. What were his perceptions of Christianity?
3. How is the French press described, and was the author disturbed that the lies may be "more numerous than the truths"?
4. Why is an outsider's perspective on Western religion, manners, and customs instructive?

F. A. STEEL AND G. GARDINER

FROM *The Complete Indian Housekeeper & Cook*

Following the institution of formal political rule in India in 1857, British colonial life expanded and grew as generations of administrators, merchants, and missionaries pursued their careers in the colonies. British women, too, increasingly followed their husbands on their colonial tours, bringing with them British notions of cuisine and domestic order. The following primer on keeping a proper household in imperial India throws light on how Victorian perceptions of class intersected with imperial notions of foreign cultures.

From *The Complete Indian Housekeeper & Cook,* by F. A. Steel and G. Gardiner (London: Heinemann, 1898), pp. 1–4, 9.

This book, it is hoped, will meet the very generally felt want for a practical guide to young housekeepers in India. A large proportion of English ladies in this country come to it newly married, to begin a new life, and take up new responsibilities under absolutely new conditions.

Few, indeed, have had any practical experience of housekeeping of any sort or kind; whilst those who have find themselves almost as much at sea as their more ignorant sisters. How can it be otherwise, when the familiar landmarks are no longer visible, and, amid the crowd of idle, unintelligible servants, there seems not one to carry on the usual routine of household work, which in England follows as a matter of course?

The kitchen is a black hole, the pantry a sink. The only servant who will condescend to tidy up is a skulking savage with a reed broom; whilst pervading all things broods the stifling, enervating atmosphere of custom, against which energy beats itself unavailingly, as against a feather bed.

The authors themselves know what it is to look round on a large Indian household, seeing that all things are wrong, all things slovenly, yet feeling paralysed by sheer inexperience in the attempt to find a remedy.

* * *

Housekeeping in India, when once the first strangeness has worn off, is a far easier task in many ways than it is in England, though it none the less requires time, and, in this present transitional period, an almost phenomenal patience; for, while one mistress enforces cleanliness according to European methods, the next may belong to the opposite faction, who, so long as the dinner is nicely served, thinks nothing of it being cooked in a kitchen which is also used as a latrine; the result being that the servants who serve one and then the other stamp of mistress, look on the desire for decency as a mere personal and distinctly disagreeable attribute of their employer, which, like a bad temper or stinginess, may be resented or evaded.

And, first, it must be distinctly understood that it is not necessary, or in the least degree desirable, that an educated woman should waste the best years of her life in scolding and petty supervision. Life holds higher duties, and it is indubitable that friction and over-zeal is a sure sign of a bad housekeeper. But there is an appreciable difference between the careworn Martha vexed with many things, and the absolute indifference displayed by many Indian mistresses, who put up with a degree of slovenliness and dirt which would disgrace a den in St. Giles, on the principle that it is no use attempting to teach the natives.

They never go into their kitchens, for the simple reason that their appetite for breakfast might be marred by seeing the *khitmutgâr*[1] using his toes as an efficient toast-rack (*fact*); or their desire for dinner weakened by seeing the soup strained through a greasy *pugri*.

*   *   *

Easy, however, as the actual housekeeping is in India, the personal attention of the mistress is quite as much needed here as at home. The Indian servant, it is true, learns more readily, and is guiltless of the sniffiness with which Mary Jane receives suggestions, but a few days of absence or neglect on the part of the mistress, results in the servants falling into their old habits with the inherited conservatism of dirt. This is, of course, disheartening, but it has to be faced as a necessary condition of life, until a few generations of training shall have started the Indian servant on a new inheritance of habit. It must never be forgotten that at present those mistresses who aim at anything beyond keeping a good table are in the minority, and that pioneering is always arduous work.

The first duty of a mistress is, of course, to be able to give intelligible orders to her servants; therefore it is necessary she should learn to speak Hindustani. No sane Englishwoman would dream of living, say, for twenty years, in Germany, Italy, or France, without making the *attempt*, at any rate, to learn the language. She would, in fact, feel that by neglecting to do so she would write herself down an ass. It would be well, therefore, if ladies in India were to ask themselves if a difference in longitude increases the latitude allowed in judging of a woman's intellect.

The next duty is obviously to insist on her orders being carried out. And here we come to the burning question, "How is this to be done?" Certainly, there is at present very little to which we can appeal in the average Indian servant, but then, until it is implanted by training, there is very little sense of duty in a child; yet in some well-regulated nurseries obedience is a foregone conclusion. The secret lies in making rules, and *keeping to them*. The Indian servant is a child in everything save age, and should be treated as a child; that is to say, kindly, but with the greatest firmness. The laws of the household should be those of the Medes and Persians, and first faults should never go unpunished. By overlooking a first offence, we lose the only opportunity we have of preventing it becoming a habit.

But it will be asked, How are we to punish our servants when we have no hold either on their minds or bodies?—when cutting their pay is illegal, and few, if any, have any real sense of shame.

The answer is obvious. Make a hold.

In their own experience the authors have found a system of rewards and punishments perfectly easy of attainment. One of them has for years adopted the plan of engaging her servants at so much a month—the lowest rate at which such servant is obtainable—and so much extra as *buksheesh*, conditional on good service. For instance, a *khitmutgâr* is engaged permanently on Rs. 9 a month, but the additional rupee which makes the wage up to that usually demanded by good servants is a fluctuating assessment! From it small fines are levied, beginning with one pice for forgetfulness, and running up, through degrees of culpability, to one rupee for lying. The money thus returned to imperial coffers may very well be spent on giving small rewards; so that each servant knows that by good service he can get back his own fines. That plan has never been objected to, and such a thing as a servant giving up his place has never been known in the author's experience. On the contrary, the household quite enters into the spirit of the idea, infinitely preferring it to volcanic eruptions of fault-finding.

To show what absolute children Indian ser-

---

[1] The object of this book being to enable a person who is absolutely unacquainted with India, its language and people, to begin housekeeping at once, the authors have decided on adhering throughout to purely phonetic spelling. The only accent used will be the circumflex.

vants are, the same author has for years adopted castor oil as an ultimatum in all obstinate cases, on the ground that there must be some physical cause for inability to learn or to remember. This is considered a great joke, and exposes the offender to much ridicule from his fellow-servants; so much so, that the words, "*Mem Sahib tum ko zuroor kâster ile pila dena hoga*" (*The Mem Sahib will have to give you castor oil*), is often heard in the mouths of the upper servants when newcomers give trouble. In short, without kindly and reasonable devices of this kind, the usual complaint of a want of hold over servants *must* remain true until they are educated into some sense of duty. Of course, common-sense is required to adjust the balance of rewards and punishments, for here again Indian servants are like children, in that they have an acute sense of justice. A very good plan for securing a certain amount of truthfulness in a servant is to insist that any one who has been caught out in a distinct falsehood should invariably bring witnesses to prove the truth of the smallest detail. It is a great disgrace and worry, generally producing a request to be given another chance after a few days. These remarks, written ten years ago, are still applicable, though the Indian mistress has now to guard against the possibility of impertinence. It should never be overlooked for an instant.

*   *   *

We do not wish to advocate an unholy haughtiness; but an Indian household can no more be governed peacefully, without dignity and prestige, than an Indian Empire. * * *

*   *   *

REVIEW QUESTIONS

1. What differences do Steel and Gardiner see between Indian and British servants and why?
2. What must an English lady have done with her servants to have kept a well-run household?
3. How would you characterize the authors' attitude toward Indian workers?
4. What differences and similarities do you see between this colonial household manual and Mrs. Beeton's manual for Britain (see Chapter 22)?

LORD GEORGE NATHANIEL CURZON

Indian Art Exhibition at Delhi Speech

European imperialism affected the colonial world in manifold ways. In the sphere of culture and the arts, European economic and political dominance often led to the decline in non-Western arts and handicrafts. Equally significant, colonized cultures in India, Africa, China, and Latin America adapted their goods and artistic tastes to suit metropoles and European mass markets. This led sometimes to innovative fusions but more usually to products of inferior quality and beauty. In this speech in 1902, Lord Curzon, viceroy of India from 1898 to 1905, who once pronounced the British Empire to be "under Providence, the greatest instrument for good that the world has seen," acknowledged that the empire produced a deleterious effect on Indian material culture. In sponsoring a government-funded exhibition to reverse the adverse transformation of Indian domestic arts, Curzon sought to cultivate a taste for what was perhaps irretrievable—authentic and uncorrupted Indian art.

From *Lord Curzon in India,* by Sir Thomas Raleigh (London: Macmillan and Co., 1906), pp. 204–8.

One of the principal features of the Delhi Durbar was the Art Exhibition in the Kudsia Gardens, where a special building had been erected for the accommodation of a large collection of the finest art products of modern India. The Exhibition was opened by the Viceroy on December 30, 1902, with the following speech:

*   *   *

Perhaps you will expect me to say a few words about the circumstances in which this Exhibition started into being. Ever since I have been in India I have made a careful study of the art industries and handicrafts of this country, once so famous and beautiful, and I have lamented, as many others have done, their progressive deterioration and decline. When it was settled that we were to hold this great gathering at Delhi, at which there would be assembled representatives of every Province and State in India, Indian Princes and Chiefs and nobles, high officials, native gentlemen, and visitors from all parts of the globe, it struck me that here at last was the long-sought opportunity of doing something to resuscitate these threatened handicrafts, to show to the world of what India is still capable, and, if possible, to arrest the process of decay. I accordingly sent for Dr. Watt, and I appointed him my right hand for the purpose. Far and wide throughout India have he and his assistant, Mr. Percy Brown, proceeded, travelling thousands of miles, everywhere interviewing the artisans, selecting specimens, giving orders, where necessary supplying models, and advancing money to those who needed it. Three conditions I laid down to be observed like the laws of the Medes and Persians.

First, I stipulated that this must be an Art Exhibition, and nothing else. We could easily have given you a wonderful show illustrating the industrial and economic development of India. Dr. Watt has such an exhibition, and a very good one too, at Calcutta. We could have shown you timbers, and minerals, and raw stuffs, and hides, and manufactured articles to any extent that you pleased. It would all have been very satisfying, but also very ugly. But I did not want that. I did not mean this to be an industrial or economic Exhibition. I meant it to be an Art Exhibition, and that only.

My second condition was that I would not have anything European or quasi-European in it. I declined to admit any of those horrible objects, such as lamps on gorgeous pedestals, coloured-glass lustres, or fantastic statuettes, that find such a surprising vogue among certain classes in this country, but that are bad anywhere in the world, and worst of all in India, which has an art of its own. I laid down that I wanted only the work that represented the ideas, the traditions, the instincts, and the beliefs of the people. It is possible that a few articles that do not answer to my definition may have crept in, because the process of Europeanisation is going on apace in this country, and the number of teapots, cream jugs, napkin rings, salt cellars, and cigarette cases that the Indian artisan is called upon to turn out is appalling. But, generally speaking, my condition has been observed.

Then my third condition was that I would only have the best. I did not want cheap cottons and waxcloths, vulgar lacquer, trinkets and tinsel, brass gods and bowls made to order in Birmingham, or perhaps made in Birmingham itself. What I desired was an exhibition of all that is rare, characteristic, or beautiful in Indian art, our gold and silver ware, our metal work and enamels and jewellery, our carving in wood and ivory and stone, our best pottery and tiles, our carpets of old Oriental patterns, our muslins and silks and embroideries, and the incomparable Indian brocades. All of these you will see inside this building. But please remember it is not a bazaar, but an Exhibition. Our object has been to encourage and revive good work, not to satisfy the requirements of the thinly lined purse.

Such is the general character of the Exhibition. But we have added to it something much more important. Conscious that taste is declining, and that many of our modern models are debased and bad, we have endeavoured to set up alongside the products of the present the standards and samples of the past. This is the meaning of the Loan Collection, which has a hall to itself, in which you will see many beautiful specimens of old Indian art ware, lent to us by the generosity of Indian Chiefs and connoisseurs, some of it coming from our own Indian Museums, and some from the unrivalled collection in the South Kensington Museum in London. Many of these objects are beautiful in themselves; but we hope that the Indian workmen who are here, and also the patrons who employ them, will study them not merely as objects of antiquarian or even artistic interest, but as supplying them with fresh or rather resuscitated ideas which may be useful to them in inspiring their own work in the future. For this may be laid down as a truism, that Indian art will never be revived by borrowing foreign ideals, but only by fidelity to its own.

And now I may be asked, What is the object of this Exhibition, and what good do I expect to result from it? I will answer in a very few words. In so far as the decline of the Indian arts represents the ascendancy of commercialism, the superiority of steam power to hand power, the triumph of the test of utility over that of taste, then I have not much hope. We are witnessing in India only one aspect of a process that is going on throughout the world, that has long ago extinguished the old manual industries of England, and that is rapidly extinguishing those of China and Japan. Nothing can stop it. The power loom will

drive out the hand loom, and the factory will get the better of the workshop, just as surely as the steam car is superseding the horse carriage, and as the hand-pulled punkah is being replaced by the electric fan. All that is inevitable, and in an age which wants things cheap and does not mind their being ugly, which cares a good deal for comfort and not much for beauty, and which is never happy unless it is deserting its own models and traditions, and running about in quest of something foreign and strange, we may be certain that a great many of the old arts and handicrafts are doomed.

There is another symptom that to my mind is even more ominous. I am one of those, as I have said, who believe that no national art is capable of continued existence unless it satisfies the ideals, and expresses the wants, of the nation that has produced it. No art can be kept alive by globe-trotters or curio-hunters alone. If it has got to that point, it becomes a mere mechanical reproduction of certain fashionable patterns; and when fashion changes, and they cease to be popular, it dies. If Indian art, therefore, is to continue to flourish, or is to be revived, it can only be if the Indian Chiefs and aristocracy, and people of culture and high degree, undertake to patronise it. So long as they prefer to fill their palaces with flaming Brussels carpets, with Tottenham Court Road furniture, with cheap Italian mosaics, with French oleographs, with Austrian lustres, and with German tissues and cheap brocades, I fear there is not much hope. I speak in no terms of reproach, because I think that in England we are just as bad in our pursuit of anything that takes our fancy in foreign lands. But I do say that if Indian arts and handicrafts are to be kept alive, it can never be by outside patronage alone. It can only be because they find a market within the country and express the ideas and culture of its people. I should like to see a movement spring up among the Indian Chiefs and nobility for the expurgation, or at any rate the purification, of modern tastes, and for a reversion to the old-fashioned but exquisite styles and patterns of their own country. Some day I have not a doubt that it will come. But it may then be too late.

If these are the omens, what then is the aim of this Exhibition, and what purpose do I think that it will serve? I can answer in a word. The Exhibition is intended as an object lesson. It is meant to show what India can still imagine, and create, and do. It is meant to show that the artistic sense is not dead among its workmen, but that all they want is a little stimulus and encouragement. It is meant to show that for the beautification of an Indian house or the furniture of an Indian home there is no need to rush to the European shops at Calcutta or Bombay, but that in almost every Indian State and Province, in most Indian towns, and in many Indian villages, there still survives the art and there still exist the artificers who can satisfy the artistic as well as the utilitarian tastes of their countrymen, and who are competent to keep alive this precious inheritance that we have received from the past. It is with this object that Dr. Watt and I have laboured in creating this Exhibition; and in now declaring it open, it only remains for me to express the earnest hope that it may in some measure fulfil the strictly patriotic purpose for which it has been designed.

REVIEW QUESTIONS

1. Why had Indian arts and handicrafts declined?
2. Why had European or quasi-European objects had a surprising vogue among Indian people? Why did Curzon object to this?
3. What socioeconomic forces worked against Curzon's government revival of traditional Indian handicrafts?
4. What does this speech suggest about the impact of imperial life on the arts of a colonized culture?

HALIL HALID

FROM *The Diary of a Turk*

The harem, an area of a Muslim household set apart for women, remains a wholly misunderstood Eastern social practice. The misconception stems largely from the cultural legacy of imperialism, the composite product of writers, painters, missionaries, and state officials who characterized the large harems of royalty and wealthy families as a signal example of Oriental moral decadence. In the Victorian era, the harem especially gripped the prurient imagination of Western commentators, who characterized women and their social spaces as sites of sensuality and concubinary pleasure. In emphasizing harems as exotic mysteries of the Orient, Western culture forged a motif with which to distinguish Eastern and Western civilization. Written in 1903 by a Turkish man conversant with both English and Turkish customs, the excerpt below redresses the misconceptions of the Muslim harem.

From *The Diary of a Turk,* by Halil Halid (London: Black, 1903).

ODALISQUE WITH SLAVE (1839)   Jean August Dominique Ingres

Over the course of the eighteenth and nineteenth centuries, literary and visual representations of the Orient became bound up in a larger colonial project of defining cultural difference between East and West. French artists particularly developed the odalisque as a genre of the imperial exotic. Odalik is the Turkish word for the slave attendant to women of the harem, but it entered into the French language as a word signifying a harem temptress. Odalisque paintings typify the West's eroticized fantasies of the Orient, which mix the sensually delightful with the tyrannical. Jean August Dominique Ingres' Odalisque with Slave, presented in 1839, is a classic example of the genre. How did this fantasy of Middle Eastern culture help define the West?

* * *

The Harem and Women in the East

* * *

There are many people in England whose ideas on the subject of the harem are but a confused misconception, based on what they may have heard about Eastern polygamy. In this chapter, that I may correct these mistaken conceptions, I will give some more exact information on the subject of the harem and its inmates, as well as on the position of women in Turkey in general.

Although the word harem is known and used by the people of Western Europe, the true meaning of the term is understood by but few persons in this country. As a matter of fact, many subjects concerning the East are much misunderstood in the West, just as there are certain manners and customs of Western Europe that cause prejudice in the Eastern mind. When an Englishman uses the word harem, he means thereby the numerous wives whom a man in our part of the East is supposed to shut up in his house. He, moreover, believes that every man in the Mohammedan East may marry as many women as he pleases. This idea is not only mistaken, but grotesque. There are thousands of men who would consider themselves fortunate if they could marry even a single woman; while, on the other hand, there are thousands who would be happy to get rid of the single wife they have. Any man who can manage to keep two, not to say more, wives in peace, and can cope with the requirements of each, must be an exceptionally brave person. Wives are not all religiously obedient in the East, just as all men are not tyrants. Religion, law, and custom impose upon men many duties to be discharged towards their wives. An honest man must discharge these duties, and indeed it is very difficult to find many men who are able to fulfil their obligations as husbands towards more than one wife. It has been proved that in many parts of the Ottoman empire the number of women does not exceed that of men, a fact which alone is enough to show the absurdity of the notion prevailing in England about the plurality of wives in that country. As a matter of fact, there is no law against the practice of polygamy, but the feeling of decent people condemns it. A man who is once married to a gentleman's daughter would find it no light matter to add another wife to his home circle. There are nowadays many men of Western education who marry in order to find a life-companion, and they quite understand that were they so injudicious as to take another wife, they would very likely render their lives the reverse of peaceful.

After pointing out the absurdity of the notion that a man's harem is his collection of wives, I will now explain what it really is.

In Mohammedan countries, where the seclusion of women is a deeply rooted and religiously observed custom, every house is divided into two separate parts. In Turkey the section of a house where the ladies reside is called the *harem,* and the men's portion is named the *selamlik*—that is to say, the reception-place. Though the female inmates of a house are also collectively called the harem, this does not mean that they are all the wives of the master of the house. A man's wife, his mother, his sister, his daughter, and such other women as may lawfully appear unveiled in his presence, all belong to his harem.

The male members of a family who are permitted to enter the harem are the master of the house, his sons, his father, his father-in-law, and his wife's brother. In large cities such as Constantinople, Smyrna, and Adrianople, the advanced class of people may even permit their more distant relatives to enter. Those who adopt European customs may even admit their intimate friends. But in the old-fashioned families, such as form the great bulk of the population, no male relation of the master is allowed to enter the harem portion of his house after he has reached his thirteenth or fourteenth year if marriage between such male relation and the master's daughter, or other young marriageable inmates of his house, be possible.

The restrictions are greater in the house of the well-to-do. In these houses, all communication, and sending and receiving parcels and dishes between the inmates of the harem and male members of the household, are effected through a kind of turning cupboard. This contrivance is fixed in a hole in the wall which separates the harem apartments from the men's quarter. As another measure to ensure the seclusion of women, to the windows of all harems is fastened a lattice; so while the inmates can see everything outside from behind this barrier, no man in the neighbouring streets, gardens, and houses can see them. As boys above the age of thirteen or fourteen are not allowed to see any women except those very near relatives I have enumerated, so girls, after the same age, must not appear unveiled in the presence of men, excepting their very near relatives; and if they have been attending mixed schools, they will then be taken away; if they go to girls' schools, they must go there, as anywhere else, carefully veiled. It must not be supposed that the veils used are similar to the light veils used by the ladies in this country. A woman must go out wrapped from head to foot in a long cloak, somewhat resembling a sheet.

The seclusion of women cannot be wholly attributed to the precepts of the religion of Islam. In the time of Prophet Mohammed, and for generations after, women used to accompany the armies to the battlefield, singing stirring melodies to encourage the fighting men, and tending those who were wounded. Even nowadays among the tribal people, such as nomadic Arabs, and among the Circassians, there is no such absurdly strict seclusion of women as is fostered by the harem system; yet those primitive people are much more earnestly devoted to that religion than the advanced Ottomans. According to some of my countrymen who are better judges than I am of these matters, the custom of veiling women's faces so thickly was adopted by the Ottomans from the Byzantine Greeks, and I think it was man's despotic jealousy in olden days which brought about the existing practice of covering up and veiling women out of doors, and also their strict seclusion in the houses.

The life in most Turkish harems is very simple, and, if we leave out the case of the few polygamists who still remain, very peaceful and happy. The absolute authority of the husband does not interfere with the recognized privileges of the wife; while the obedience of the wife, which is regarded by more advanced women in Western Europe with such contempt, in most cases strengthens the affection and respect of the husband for her. Wives are not slaves of their husbands, as some people in this country fancy them to be.[1] The inmates of harems live mostly indoors, but they are not entirely shut up. They go out in groups of two, three, and more to pay visits to other harems, and they receive visitors from the harems of friends and relations. Of course their gatherings are almost always unmixed, but, like the women of other countries, some of them sing and play to entertain others. Dancing has been introduced recently, but it is confined only to very advanced private families. Among the people of the old school the dancing of young ladies in the presence of others is considered shocking. At weddings and other similar festivities only hired professional women amuse the guests by dancing, and these professional dancers are not regarded as respectable. In my time, reading aloud was a favourite pastime in many harems. The number of educated women was much less than it is now. The most learned among them used to read sacred legends, or religious traits, or recite hymns to the other ladies, who would listen attentively for hours. I believe this social pastime is still in favour in the provinces.

Turkish women, according to their social po-

---

[1]If the detractors of Islam would take the trouble to find out what is the exact position of women under Mohammedan law, they might feel ashamed of their contention that she is treated like a slave. Laws protecting the rights of women were promulgated under Islam when no such laws existed in Europe. As far back as five hundred years ago women in Turkey had begun to dispute men's superiority openly. As proof of this I will quote a few lines of the poetess Mihri, who lived in the last half of the fifteenth century:

Since they cry that woman lacketh wit alway,
Need must they excuse whatever word she say.
Better far one female, if she worthy be,
Than a thousand males, if all unworthy they.

sition, have various duties to discharge. No qualities are so much sought after in an average marriageable woman as the domestic ones. In the provinces the peasant women, besides managing their humble domestic affairs, have to work in the fields, more especially when their brothers and husbands are away discharging their compulsory military service. The daughters of well-to-do people, besides attending to the business of their households, are indefatigable with their needles, and are always busy with needlework or embroidery; while the daughters of high dignitaries must, among other duties, learn what their instructors or governesses teach them.

It will be understood from the details I have given that the popular notion prevailing in this country of the harem and the life in the harem is much mistaken. Women in Turkish harems do not really pass their time lying on sofas or couches, eating sweetmeats and smoking waterpipes all day long. Of course they are as fond of sweetstuffs as most ladies of this country. But to lie down on a couch in presence of others is considered by Turkish women vulgarity of the most disgraceful kind.

The representation of harem life given in books and on the stage, or shown in exhibitions, is either the work of Turkey's detractors, or simply the work of imaginative persons who know nothing about it, and whose object is to attract the curiosity of English people by exhibiting grotesque sights, and thus to make money.

*   *   *

REVIEW QUESTIONS

1. How does Halid characterize English perceptions of Turkish marriages and Turkish households?
2. What were the functions and practices of the harem?
3. Did women in harems have rights?
4. How does Hadid characterize Muslim marriages?

FRIEDRICH FABRI

FROM *Does Germany Need Colonies?*

The small pamphlet Does Germany Need Colonies? *by F. Fabri, a former inspector of the Rhenish Missionary Association, was published in 1879 and was one among many publications that generated a widespread public debate in Germany regarding its need for colonies. Fabri cited overpopulation as a motivating factor, and his emphasis on Germany's "cultural mission" infused imperialism with an idealism that enthused the general public. The domestic agitation for colonial expansion by pressure groups and grassroots associations radically affected domestic politics. Germany's decision in the 1880s to enter the race for colonial territories in Africa and Asia had, moreover, a profound impact on the European balance of power.*

From *The Imperialism Reader*, edited by Louis L. Snyder (New York: Van Nostrand, 1962).

* * *

Should not the German nation, so seaworthy, so industrially and commercially minded, more than other peoples geared to agricultural colonization, and possessing a rich and available supply of labor, all these to a greater extent than other modern culture-peoples, should not this nation successfully hew a new path on the road of imperialism? We are convinced beyond doubt that the colonial question has become a matter of life or death for the development of Germany. Colonies will have a salutary effect on our economic situation as well as on our entire national progress.

Here is a solution for many of the problems that face us. In this new Reich of ours there is so much bitterness, so much unfruitful, sour, and poisoned political wrangling, that the opening of a new, promising road of national effort will act as a kind of liberating influence. Our national spirit will be renewed, a gratifying thing, a great asset. A people that have been led to a high level of power can maintain its historical position only as long as it understands and proves itself to be *the bearer of a culture mission*. At the same time, this is the only way to stability and to the growth of national welfare, the necessary foundation for a lasting expansion of power.

At one time Germany contributed only intellectual and literary activity to the tasks of our century. That era is now over. As a people we have become politically minded and powerful. But if political power becomes the primal goal of a nation, it will lead to harshness, even to barbarism. We must be ready to serve for the ideal, moral, and economic culture-tasks of our time. The French national-economist, Leroy Beaulieu, closed his words on colonization with these words: "That nation is the greatest in the world which colonizes most; if she does not achieve that rank today, she will make it tomorrow."

No one can deny that in this direction England has by far surpassed all other countries. Much has been said, even in Germany, during the last few decades about the "disintegrating power of England." Indeed, there seems to be something to it

when we consider the Palmerston era and Gladstonian politics. It has been customary in our age of military power to evaluate the strength of a state in terms of its combat-ready troops. But anyone who looks at the globe and notes the steadily increasing colonial possessions of Great Britain, how she extracts strength from them, the skill with which she governs them, how the Anglo-Saxon strain occupies a dominant position in the overseas territories, he will begin to see the military argument as the reasoning of a philistine.

The fact is that England tenaciously holds on to its world-wide possessions with scarcely one-fourth the manpower of our continental military state. That is not only a great economic advantage but also a striking proof of the solid power and cultural fiber of England. Great Britain, of course, isolates herself far from the mass warfare of the continent, or only goes into action with dependable allies; hence, the insular state has suffered and will suffer no real damage. In any case, it would be wise for us Germans to learn about colonial skills from our Anglo-Saxon cousins and to begin a friendly competition with them. When the German Reich centuries ago stood at the pinnacle of the states of Europe, it was the Number One trade and sea power. If the New Germany wants to protect its newly won position of power for a long time, it must heed its *Kultur*-mission and, above all, delay no longer in the task of renewing the call for colonies.

* * *

REVIEW QUESTIONS

1. Why does Fabri consider the acquisition of colonies "a matter of life or death for the development of Germany"?
2. How does Fabri compare Germany's political status with England?
3. What political, economic, and cultural uses will, according to Fabri, be derived from colonies?

HOUSTON STEWART CHAMBERLAIN

FROM *Foundations of the Nineteenth Century*

In 1890, Houston Stewart Chamberlain (1855–1926), an Englishman who lived and wrote in Germany, published Foundations of the Nineteenth Century, *which went through numerous German editions and earned him widespread notoriety in Germany. Although English contemporaries resented the anti-British tone of the book, more disturbing were the rambling arguments that ridiculed Western humanitarianism and posited the superiority of the Teutonic race, which possessed the self-evident right to assert itself against lesser cultures. The book marks a watershed moment in the early discourse of pseudoscientific racial theory.*

From *Foundations of the Nineteenth Century*, edited by H. S. Chamberlain, translated by John Lees (London: Head, 1913).

*   *   *

Historical Criterion

If we then free ourselves from the delusion of a progressive or retrogressive humanity, and content ourselves with the realisation of the fact that our culture is specifically North-European, *i.e.*, Teutonic, we shall at once gain a sure standard by which to judge our own past and our present, and at the same time a very useful standard to apply to a future which has yet to come. For nothing Individual is limitless. So long as we regard ourselves as the responsible representatives of all humanity, the more clear-seeing minds must be driven to despair by our poverty and obvious incapacity to pave the way for a golden age; at the same time, however, all shallow-brained phrase-makers turn us from those earnest aims which we might attain, and undermine what I should like to call historical morality, in that, shutting their eyes, blind to our universal limitation, and totally failing to realise the value of our specific talents, they dangle before our eyes the Impossible, the Absolute: natural rights, eternal peace, universal broth-

erhood, mutual fusion, &c. But if we know that we Northern Europeans are a definite individuality, responsible, not for humanity, but certainly for our own personality, we shall love and value our work as something individual, we shall recognise the fact that it is by no means complete, but still very defective, and, above all, far from being sufficiently independent; no vision of an "absolute" perfection will mislead us, but we shall, as Shakespeare wished, remain true to ourselves, and be satisfied with doing our very best within the limits of the Teuton's power of achievement; we shall deliberately defend ourselves against the un-Teutonic, and seek not only to extend our empire farther and farther over the surface of the globe and over the powers of nature, but above all unconditionally to subject the inner world to ourselves by mercilessly overthrowing and excluding those who are alien to us, and who, nevertheless, would fain gain the mastery over our thought. It is often said that politics can know no scruples; nothing at all can know scruples; scruples are a crime against self. Scruple is the soldier who in the battle takes to his heels, presenting his back as a target to the enemy. The most sacred duty of the Teuton is to serve the Teutonic cause. This fact supplies us with an historical standard of measurement. In all spheres that man and that deed will be glorified as greatest and most important which most successfully advance specific Teutonism or have most vigorously supported its supremacy. Thus and thus only do we acquire a limiting, organising, absolutely positive principle of judgment. To refer to a well-known instance; why is it that, in spite of the admiration which his genius inspires, the personality of the great Byron has something repulsive in it for every thorough Teuton? Treitschke has answered this question in his brilliant essay on Byron: it is "because nowhere in this rich life do we encounter the idea of duty." That is an unsympathetic, un-Teutonic feature.

*   *   *

Inner Contrasts

There is yet a word to be said, and one of great importance, if we would clearly recognise and distinguish what is thoroughly Teutonic. In the matters which I have just mentioned, as in a thousand others, we discover everywhere that specific characteristic of the Teuton, the close association—as though they were twin brothers, walking hand in hand—of the Practical and the Ideal* * * At all points we shall encounter similar contradictions in the Teuton, and shall learn to value them equally highly. For when we realise that we have to deal with something individual, we shall, in forming our judgment, refrain above all from taking into consideration the logical notions of abstract theories about Good and Evil, Higher and Lower, and direct our attention simply to the individuality; but an individuality is always best recognised from its inner contrasts; where it is uniform, it is also without shape, without individuality. Thus, for example, the Teutons are characterised by a power of expansion possessed by no race before them, and at the same time by an inclination to concentration which is equally new. We see the expansive power at work—in the practical sphere, in the gradual colonisation of the whole surface of the globe;—in the scientific sphere, in the revelation

of the infinite Cosmos, in the search for ever remoter causes;—in the ideal sphere, in the conception of the Transcendent, in the boldness of hypotheses, and in sublime artistic flights which lead to more and more comprehensive means of expression. At the same time, however, we are inclined to return within more and more narrowly circumscribed limits, carefully cut off from everything external by ramparts and trenches; we return to the idea of blood-relationships of the Fatherland, of the native district, of the village of our birth, of the inviolable home (*my home is my castle*, as in Rome), of the closest family circle; finally we return to the innermost central point of the individual, who now, purified and elevated to consciousness of absolute isolation, faces the outer world as an invisible, independent being, a supreme lord of freedom, as was the case with the Indians; this is that concentration which in other spheres reveals itself as division of countries into small Principalities, as limitation to a special "field," whether in science or industry, as inclination to form sects and schools as in Greece, as poetical effects of the innermost nature, *e.g.*, the woodcut, engraving, chamber music. In character these contrasted qualities which are held in coherence by the higher individuality of the race, signify a spirit of enterprise allied to conscientiousness, or they lead—if misguided—to speculation (on the Stock Exchange or in philosophy, it is all the same), to narrow-minded pedantry and pusillanimity.

I cannot on this occasion be expected to attempt an exhaustive description of Teutonic individuality; everything individual—however manifest and recognisable beyond all doubt it may be—is inexhaustible. As Goethe says, "Words cannot clearly reveal the Best," and if personality is the highest gift which we children of earth receive, then truly the individuality of our definite race is one of those "best" things. It alone carries along all separate personalities, as the ship is borne by the flood, and without it (or when this flood is too shallow easily to float anything great) even the strongest character must lie helpless and impotent, like a barque stranded and capsized.

*   *   *

REVIEW QUESTIONS

1. What does Chamberlain mean by *retrogressive humanity*?

2. What attributes are ascribed to the Teutonic race?
3. What is the Teutonic race explicitly exhorted to do with its talents?
4. How do Chamberlain's views of races and peoples differ from those of Herder or Mazzini?

RUDYARD KIPLING

"The White Man's Burden"

Rudyard Kipling (1865–1936), a prolific poet, novelist, and short-story author who won the Nobel Prize for literature in 1907, was born in Bombay to parents of high Anglo-Indian society. Schooled in England, Kipling returned to India and used its imperial atmosphere in his fiction and verse to great success. Alongside his literary feats, Kipling also championed the "civilizing mission" of empire throughout his life, devoutly believing in Britain's and the West's duty to educate and govern the "Sloth and heathen Folly" of the non-Western world. "The White Man's Burden" originally appeared in McClure's Magazine *in February 1899 during the Spanish-American War. Composed as an exhortation to the United States to fulfill its imperial role in the Pacific, the phrase was immediately coined as a slogan by imperialists.*

From *Rudyard Kipling's Verse*, by Rudyard Kipling (New York: Doubleday, Doran, 1934), pp. 373–74.

Take up the White Man's burden—
    Send forth the best ye breed—
    Go bind your sons to exile
To serve your captives' need;
To wait in heavy harness,
    On fluttered folk and wild—
Your new-caught, sullen peoples,
    Half-devil and half-child.

Take up the White Man's burden—
    In patience to abide,
To veil the threat of terror
    And check the show of pride;

By open speech and simple,
    An hundred times made plain,
To seek another's profit,
    And work another's gain.

Take up the White Man's burden—
    The savage wars of peace—
Fill full the mouth of Famine
    And bid the sickness cease;
And when your goal is nearest
    The end for others sought,
Watch Sloth and heathen Folly
    Bring all your hope to nought.

The first step towards lightening

The White Man's Burden

is through teaching the virtues of cleanliness.

Pears' Soap

is a potent factor in brightening the dark corners of the earth as civilization advances, while amongst the cultured of all nations it holds the highest place—it is the ideal toilet soap.

"LIGHTENING THE WHITE MAN'S BURDEN" (1899)

Popular culture in the late nineteenth century articulated Western imperial themes in numerous ways. This soap advertisement in 1899, which plays on Kipling's "White Man's Burden," offers a clear illustration of the negative characterization of non-Western peoples in the high imperial era. Admiral Dewey, a hero of the Spanish-American War, is featured washing with Pears' Soap; the corner illustrations and the text express the advertisement's sentiment. Alongside steamboats and commerce, soap and hygiene are characterized as new items, which the West can introduce to the non-Western world. The word lighten *works, then, as a racist pun. How does this advertisement help us understand how the beliefs of imperial politics became a self-evident, everyday practice?*

Take up the White Man's burden—
    No tawdry rule of kings,
But toil of serf and sweeper—
    The tale of common things.
The ports ye shall not enter,
    The roads ye shall not tread,
Go make them with your living,
    And mark them with your dead.

Take up the White Man's burden—
    And reap his old reward:
The blame of those ye better,
    The hate of those ye guard—
The cry of hosts ye humour
    (Ah, slowly!) toward the light:—
"Why brought ye us from bondage,
    "Our loved Egyptian night?"

Take up the White Man's burden—
    Ye dare not stoop to less—
Nor call too loud on Freedom
    To cloak your weariness;
By all ye cry or whisper,
    By all ye leave or do,
The silent, sullen peoples
    Shall weigh your Gods and you.

Take up the White Man's burden—
    Have done with childish days—
The lightly proffered laurel,
    The easy, ungrudged praise.
Comes now, to search your manhood
    Through all the thankless years,
Cold, edged with dear-bought wisdom,
    The judgment of your peers!

REVIEW QUESTIONS

1. What was the burden of the white man?
2. How does Kipling glorify the white man's role?
3. How are Kipling's imperial subjects characterized?
4. What were the civil and military aspects of the "white man's burden"?

EDMUND D. MOREL

FROM *The Black Man's Burden*

Alongside the dominant ideological assertion that moral responsibility obliged the West to build empires, critics of imperialism voiced their dissent. Although the most consistent denunciation came from socialists, liberals also criticized imperialism on a number of economical and political principles. E. D. Morel, a British journalist writing in the immediate aftermath of the First World War, offers here a stinging indictment of imperialism's fatal impact on Africa. Written in 1920, Morel's scathing criticism of Britain must be situated in the postwar debate concerning the future of the colonies and the question of African self-determination.

From *The Black Man's Burden*, Edmund D. Morel (Northbrook, Ill.: Metro Books, 1972).

* * *

It is with the peoples of Africa, then, that our inquiry is concerned. It is they who carry the "Black man's" burden. They have not withered away before the white man's *occupation*. Indeed, if the scope of this volume permitted, there would be no difficulty in showing that Africa has ultimately absorbed within itself every Caucasian and, for that matter, every Semitic invader too. In hewing out for himself a fixed abode in Africa, the white man has massacred the African in heaps. The African has survived, and it is well for the white settlers that he has.

In the process of imposing his political dominion over the African, the white man has carved broad and bloody avenues from one end of Africa to the other. The African has resisted, and persisted.

For three centuries the white man seized and enslaved millions of Africans and transported them, with every circumstance of ferocious cruelty, across the seas. Still the African survived and, in his land of exile, multiplied exceedingly.

But what the partial occupation of his soil by the white man has failed to do; what the mapping out of European political "spheres of influence" has failed to do; what the maxim and the rifle, the slave gang, labour in the bowels of the earth and the lash, have failed to do; what imported measles, smallpox and syphilis have failed to do; what even the oversea slave trade failed to do, the power of modern capitalistic exploitation, assisted by modern engines of destruction, may yet succeed in accomplishing.

For from the evils of the latter, scientifically applied and enforced, there is no escape for the African. Its destructive effects are not spasmodic: they are permanent. In its permanence resides its fatal consequences. It kills not the body merely, but the soul. It breaks the spirit. It attacks the African at every turn, from every point of vantage. It wrecks his polity, uproots him from the land, invades his family life, destroys his natural pursuits and occupations, claims his whole time, enslaves him in his own home.

Economic bondage and wage slavery, the grinding pressure of a life of toil, the incessant demands of industrial capitalism—these things a landless European proletariat physically endures, though hardly.* * * The recuperative forces of a temperate climate are there to arrest the ravages, which alleviating influences in the shape of prophylactic and curative remedies will still further circumscribe. But in Africa, especially in tropical Africa, which a capitalistic imperialism threatens and has, in part, already devastated, man is incapable of reacting against unnatural conditions. In those regions man is engaged in a perpetual struggle against disease and an exhausting climate, which tells heavily upon child-bearing; and there is no scientific machinery for salving the weaker members of the community. The African of the tropics is capable of tremendous physical labours. But he cannot accommodate himself to the European system of monotonous, uninterrupted labour, with its long and regular hours, involving, moreover, as it frequently does, severance from natural surroundings and nostalgia, the condition of melancholy resulting from separation from home, a malady to which the African is specially prone. Climatic conditions forbid it. When the system is forced upon him, the tropical African droops and dies.

Nor is violent physical opposition to abuse and injustice henceforth possible for the African in any part of Africa. His chances of effective resistance have been steadily dwindling with the increasing perfectibility in the killing power of modern armament. Gunpowder broke the effectiveness of his resistance to the slave trade, although he continued to struggle. He has forced and, on rare occasions and in exceptional circumstances beaten, in turn the old-fashioned musket, the elephant gun, the seven-pounder, and even the repeating rifle and the gatling gun. He has been known to charge right down repeatedly, foot and horse, upon the square, swept on all sides with the pitiless and continuous hail of maxims. But against the latest inventions, physical bravery, though associated with a perfect knowledge of the country, can do nothing. The African cannot face the high-explosive shell and the bomb-dropping aeroplane. He has inflicted sanguinary reverses upon picked

European troops, hampered by the climate and by commissariat difficulties. He cannot successfully oppose members of his own race free from these impediments, employed by his white adversaries, and trained in all the diabolical devices of scientific massacre. And although the conscripting of African armies for use in Europe or in Africa as agencies for the liquidation of the white man's quarrels must bring in its train evils from which the white man will be the first to suffer, both in Africa and in Europe; the African himself must eventually disappear in the process. Winter in Europe, or even in Northern Africa, is fatal to the tropical or sub-tropical African, while in the very nature of the case anything approaching real European control in Africa, of hordes of African soldiery armed with weapons of precision is not a feasible proposition. The Black man converted by the European into a scientifically-equipped machine for the slaughter of his kind, is certainly not more merciful than the white man similarly equipped for like purposes in dealing with unarmed communities. And the experiences of the civilian population of Belgium, East Prussia, Galicia and Poland is indicative of the sort of visitation involved for peaceable and powerless African communities if the white man determines to add to his appalling catalogue of past misdeeds towards the African, the crowning wickedness of once again, as in the day of the slave trade, supplying him with the means of encompassing his own destruction.

Thus the African is really helpless against the material gods of the white man, as embodied in the trinity of imperialism, capitalistic-exploitation, and militarism. If the white man retains these gods and if he insists upon making the African worship them as assiduously as he has done himself, the African will go the way of the Red Indian, the Amerindian, the Carib, the Guanche, the aboriginal Australian, and many more. And this would be at once a crime of enormous magnitude, and a world disaster.

*　　*　　*

An endeavour will now be made to describe the nature, and the changing form, which the bur-

den inflicted by the white man in modern times upon the black has assumed. It can only be sketched here in the broadest outline, but in such a way as will, it is hoped, explain the differing causes and motives which have inspired white activities in Africa and illustrate, by specific and notable examples, their resultant effects upon African peoples. It is important that these differing causes and motives should be understood, and that we should distinguish between them in order that we may hew our way later on through the jungle of error which impedes the pathway to reform. Diffused generalities and sweeping judgments generate confusion of thought and hamper the evolution of a constructive policy based upon clear apprehension of the problem to be solved.

The history of contact between the white and black peoples in modern times is divisible into two distinct and separate periods: the period of the slave trade and the period of invasion, political control, capitalistic exploitation, and, the latest development, militarism. Following the slave trade period and preceding the period of invasion, occurs the trade interlude which, indeed, had priority of both periods, as when the Carthagenians bartered salt and iron implements for gold dust on the West Coast. But this interlude concerns our investigations only when we pass from destructive exposure to constructive demonstration.

The first period needs recalling, in order to impress once more upon our memories the full extent of the African's claim upon us, the white imperial peoples, for tardy justice, for considerate and honest conduct.

Our examination of the second period will call for sectional treatment. The history of contact and its consequences during this period may be roughly sub-divided thus:

a. The struggle for supremacy between European invading *Settlers* and resident African peoples in those portions of Africa where the climate and other circumstances permit of Europeans rearing families of white children.

b. *Political action* by European Governments aiming at the assertion of sovereign rights over particular areas of African territory.

c. *Administrative policy,* sanctioned by European Governments, and applied by their local representatives in particular areas, subsequent to the successful assertion of sovereign rights.

These sub-divisions are, perhaps, somewhat arbitrary. The distinctiveness here given to them cannot be absolutely preserved. There is, for instance, a natural tendency for both *a* and *b* to merge into *c* as, through efflux of time, the originating cause and motive of contact is obscured by developments to which contact has given rise. Thus racial contention for actual possession of the soil, and political action often resulting in so-called treaties of Protectorate thoroughly unintelligible to the African signees, are both landmarks upon the road leading to eventual administrative policy: *i.e.,* to direct government of the black man by the white.

*   *   *

It is often argued that the agricultural and arboricultural methods of the African are capable of improvement. The statement is undoubtedly true. It applies with equal force to the land of Britain. There is no difference of opinion among British agricultural experts as to the capacities for improvement in the methods of British agriculture. As for British arboriculture it is still an almost entirely neglected field of British home enterprise. We can afford to be patient with the African if he has not yet attained perfection. Why, it is only since the beginning of the 18th century that the rotation of crops has been practised in England! But the Kano farmers in Northern Nigeria have understood rotation of crops and grass manuring for at least five hundred years.

To advance such truisms as an excuse for robbing the native communities of their land, degrading farmers in their own right to the level of hired labourers urged on by the lash, and conferring monopolistic rights over the land and its fruits to private corporations, is to make truth the stalking horse of oppression and injustice. The statement of fact may be accurate. The claim put forward on the strength of it is purely predatory.

Those who urge this and kindred arguments only do so to assist the realisation of their purpose. That purpose is clear. It is to make of Africans all over Africa a servile race; to exploit African labour, and through African labour, the soil of Africa for their own exclusive benefit. They are blind to the cost in human suffering. They are indifferent to the fact that in the long run their policy must defeat its own ends. They care only for the moment, and for the objects of the moment they are prepared to sacrifice the future. But since their purpose is selfish, short-sighted and immoral it must be striven against without pause or relaxation. There can be no honest or safe compromise with these people and their policy. A great moral issue is involved. But although that issue comes first, and must come first, it is not the only issue.

For a time it may be possible for the white man to maintain a white civilisation in the colonisable, or partly colonisable, areas of the African Continent based on servile or semi-servile labour: to build up a servile State. But even there the attempt can be no more than fleeting. The days of Roman imperialism are done with for ever. Education sooner or later breaks all chains, and knowledge cannot be kept from the African. The attempt will be defeated in the north by Islam, which confers power of combination in the political sphere, and a spiritual unity which Europe has long lost in the mounting tides of her materialism. It will fail in the south through the prolificness of the African, through the practical impossibility of arresting his intellectual advance and through race admixture, which is proceeding at a much more rapid rate than most people realise. In the great tropical regions the attempt must fail in the very nature of things, if for no other reason, because it can only be enforced by employing the black man, trained in the art of modern warfare as the medium through which to coerce his unarmed brother. The former will be well content to play that part for a period more or less prolonged, but when he becomes alive to his power the whole fabric of European domination will fall to pieces in shame and ruin. From these failures the people of Europe will suffer moral and material damage of a far-reaching kind.

And the criminal folly of it! The white imperial peoples have it in their power, if their rulers will cultivate vision and statesmanship enough to thrust aside the prompting of narrow, ephemeral interests—anti-national in the truest sense—to make of Africa the home of highly-trained and prosperous peoples enriching the universe as their prosperity waxes, dwelling in plains and valleys, in forests and on plateaux made fruitful by their labours, assisted by science; a country whose inhabitants will be enterprising and intelligent, loving their land, looking to it for inspiration, co-operating faithfully in the work of the world, developing their own culture, independent, free, self-respecting, attaining to higher mental growth as the outcome of internal evolutionary processes. Why cannot the white imperial peoples, acknowledging in some measure the injuries they have inflicted upon the African, turn a new leaf in their treatment of him? For nearly two thousand years they have professed to be governed by the teachings of Christ. Can they not begin in the closing century of that era, to practise what they profess —and what their missionaries of religion teach the African? Can they not cease to regard the African

as a producer of dividends for a selected few among their number, and begin to regard him as a human being with human rights? Have they made such a success of their own civilisation that they can contemplate with equanimity the forcing of all its social failures upon Africa—its hideous and devastating inequalities, its pauperisms, its senseless and destructive egoisms, its vulgar and soulless materialism? It is in their power to work such good to Africa—and such incalculable harm! Can they not make up their minds that their strength shall be used for noble ends? Africa demands at their hands, justice, and understanding sympathy—not ill-informed sentiment. And when these are dealt out to her she repays a thousandfold.

*   *   *

REVIEW QUESTIONS

1. How does Morel outline the history of gradual European domination over indigenous Africans?
2. What is the extent of blame that Morel lays at Europe's door?
3. List the range of abuse and exploitation that Morel ascribes to the Western imperial powers.
4. What does Morel's criticism of Europe's use of industrial work habits in Africa suggest about European attitudes toward colonies?
5. Why does Morel call the preservation of colonies in Africa a criminal folly?

VLADIMIR LENIN

FROM *Imperialism, The Highest Stage of Capitalism*

Imperialists' justification for formal control of colonies in the last half of the nine-teenth century often carried the economic rationale of securing monopoly outlets for domestic-made goods and capital investment. Hence, although Marx never inte-grated imperialism into his critique of capitalism, second-generation socialists per-ceived capitalism in the imperial era as having entered a new phase, which witnessed the anxious attempts of banking consortiums and large-scale industrial enterprises to stake out high-yielding investments, new markets, and cheaper raw materials. In the highly influential pamphlet, Imperialism, the Highest Stage of Capitalism, *first written in 1917 (and posthumously revised in the 1920s and 1930s), Lenin argued that imperialism must be viewed as "parasitic or decaying capitalism." The apparent success of combining empire and capitalism, he argued, hid profound structural contradictions that brought on not only the First World War but also the imminent revolt of the colonial world from capitalist exploitation. The following passage, drawn from the pamphlet's final chapter, summarizes his principal arguments for viewing imperialism as the highest—that is, the final— stage of capitalism.*

From *Imperialism, The Highest Stage of Capitalism*, by V. I. Lenin (New York: International, 1939), pp. 123–27.

*   *   *

We have seen that the economic quintessence of imperialism is monopoly capitalism. This very fact determines its place in history, for monopoly that grew up on the basis of free competition, and precisely out of free competition, is the transition from the capitalist system to a higher social-economic order. We must take special note of the four principal forms of monopoly, or the four principal manifestations of monopoly capitalism, which are characteristic of the epoch under review.

Firstly, monopoly arose out of the concentra-tion of production at a very advanced stage of de-velopment. This refers to the monopolist capitalist combines, cartels, syndicates and trusts. We have seen the important part that these play in modern economic life. At the beginning of the twentieth century, monopolies acquired complete suprem-acy in the advanced countries. And although the first steps towards the formation of the cartels were first taken by countries enjoying the protec-tion of high tariffs (Germany, America), Great Britain, with her system of free trade, was not far behind in revealing the same basic phenomenon, namely, the birth of monopoly out of the concen-tration of production.

Secondly, monopolies have accelerated the cap-ture of the most important sources of raw mate-rials, especially for the coal and iron industries, which are the basic and most highly cartelised in-dustries in capitalist society. The monopoly of the most important sources of raw materials has enor-mously increased the power of big capital, and has sharpened the antagonism between cartelised and non-cartelised industry.

Thirdly, monopoly has sprung from the banks.

The banks have developed from modest intermediary enterprises into the monopolists of finance capital. Some three or five of the biggest banks in each of the foremost capitalist countries have achieved the "personal union" of industrial and bank capital, and have concentrated in their hands the disposal of thousands upon thousands of millions which form the greater part of the capital and income of entire countries. A financial oligarchy, which throws a close net of relations of dependence over all the economic and political institutions of contemporary bourgeois society without exception—such is the most striking manifestation of this monopoly.

Fourthly, monopoly has grown out of colonial policy. To the numerous "old" motives of colonial policy, finance capital has added the struggle for the sources of raw materials, for the export of capital, for "spheres of influence," *i.e.*, for spheres for profitable deals, concessions, monopolist profits and so on; in fine, for economic territory in general. When the colonies of the European powers in Africa, for instance, comprised only one-tenth of that territory (as was the case in 1876) colonial policy was able to develop by methods other than those of monopoly—by the "free grabbing" of territories, so to speak. But when nine-tenths of Africa had been seized (approximately by 1900), when the whole world had been divided up, there was inevitably ushered in a period of colonial monopoly and, consequently, a period of particularly intense struggle for the division and the redivision of the world.

The extent to which monopolist capital has intensified all the contradictions of capitalism is generally known. It is sufficient to mention the high cost of living and the oppression of the cartels. This intensification of contradictions constitutes the most powerful driving force of the transitional period of history, which began from the time of the definite victory of world finance capital.

Monopolies, oligarchy, the striving for domination instead of the striving for liberty, the exploitation of an increasing number of small or weak nations by an extremely small group of the richest or most powerful nations—all these have given birth to those distinctive characteristics of imperialism which compel us to define it as parasitic or decaying capitalism. More and more prominently there emerges, as one of the tendencies of imperialism, the creation of the "bond-holding" (rentier) state, the usurer state, in which the bourgeoisie lives on the proceeds of capital exports and by "clipping coupons." It would be a mistake to believe that this tendency to decay precludes the possibility of the rapid growth of capitalism. It does not. In the epoch of imperialism, certain branches of industry, certain strata of the bourgeoisie and certain countries betray, to a more or less degree, one or other of these tendencies. On the whole, capitalism is growing far more rapidly than before. But this growth is not only becoming more and more uneven in general; its unevenness also manifests itself, in particular, in the decay of the countries which are richest in capital (such as England).

In regard to the rapidity of Germany's economic development, Riesser, the author of the book on the big German banks, states:

> The progress of the preceding period (1848–70), which had not been exactly slow, stood in about the same ratio to the rapidity with which the whole of Germany's national economy, and with it German banking, progressed during this period (1870–1905) as the mail coach of the Holy Roman Empire of the German nation stood to the speed of the present-day automobile . . . which in whizzing past, it must be said, often endangers not only innocent pedestrians in its path, but also the occupants of the car.

In its turn, this finance capital which has grown so rapidly is not unwilling (precisely because it has grown so quickly) to pass on to a more "tranquil" possession of colonies which have to be seized—and not only by peaceful methods—from richer nations. In the United States, economic development in the last decades has been even more rapid than in Germany, and *for this very reason* the parasitic character of modern American capitalism has stood out with particular prominence. On the other hand, a comparison of, say, the republican

American bourgeoisie with the monarchist Japanese or German bourgeoisie shows that the most pronounced political distinctions diminish to an extreme degree in the epoch of imperialism—not because they are unimportant in general, but because in all these cases we are discussing a bourgeoisie which has definite features of parasitism.

The receipt of high monopoly profits by the capitalists in one of the numerous branches of industry, in one of numerous countries, etc., makes it economically possible for them to corrupt certain sections of the working class, and for a time a fairly considerable minority, and win them to the side of the bourgeoisie of a given industry or nation against all the others. The intensification of antagonisms between imperialist nations for the division of the world increases this striving. And so there is created that bond between imperialism and opportunism, which revealed itself first and most clearly in England, owing to the fact that certain features of imperialist development were observable there much earlier than in other countries.

Some writers, L. Martov, for example, try to evade the fact that there is a connection between imperialism and opportunism in the labour movement—which is particularly striking at the present time—by resorting to "official optimistic" arguments (*à la* Kautsky and Huysmans) like the following: the cause of the opponents of capitalism would be hopeless if it were precisely progressive capitalism that led to the increase of opportunism, or, if it were precisely the best paid workers who were inclined towards opportunism, etc. We must have no illusion regarding "optimism" of this kind. It is optimism in regard to opportunism; it is optimism which serves to conceal opportunism. As a matter of fact the extraordinary rapidity and the particularly revolting character of the development of opportunism is by no means a guarantee that its victory will be durable: the rapid growth of a malignant abscess on a healthy body only causes it to burst more quickly and thus to relieve the body of it. The most dangerous people of all in this respect are those who do not wish to understand that the fight against imperialism is a sham and humbug unless it is inseparably bound up with the fight against opportunism.

From all that has been said in this book on the economic nature of imperialism, it follows that we must define it as capitalism in transition, or, more precisely, as moribund capitalism. It is very instructive in this respect to note that the bourgeois economists, in describing modern capitalism, frequently employ terms like "interlocking," "absence of isolation," etc.; "in conformity with their functions and course of development," banks are "not purely private business enterprises; they are more and more outgrowing the sphere of purely private business regulation." And this very Riesser, who uttered the words just quoted, declares with all seriousness that the "prophecy" of the Marxists concerning "socialisation" has "not come true"!

What then does this word "interlocking" express? It merely expresses the most striking feature of the process going on before our eyes. It shows that the observer counts the separate trees, but cannot see the wood. It slavishly copies the superficial, the fortuitous, the chaotic. It reveals the observer as one who is overwhelmed by the mass of raw material and is utterly incapable of appreciating its meaning and importance. Ownership of shares and relations between owners of private property "interlock in a haphazard way." But the underlying factor of this interlocking, its very base, is the changing social relations of production. When a big enterprise assumes gigantic proportions, and, on the basis of exact computation of mass data, organises according to plan the supply of primary raw materials to the extent of two-thirds, or three-fourths of all that is necessary for tens of millions of people; when the raw materials are transported to the most suitable place of production, sometimes hundreds or thousands of miles away, in a systematic and organised manner; when a single centre directs all the successive stages of work right up to the manufacture of numerous varieties of finished articles; when these products are distributed according to a single plan among tens and hundreds of millions of consumers (as in the case of the distribution of oil in

America and Germany by the American "oil trust")—then it becomes evident that we have so-cialisation of production, and not mere "inter-locking"; that private economic relations and private property relations constitute a shell which is no longer suitable for its contents, a shell which must inevitably begin to decay if its destruction be delayed by artificial means; a shell which may continue in a state of decay for a fairly long period (particularly if the cure of the opportunist abscess is protracted), but which will inevitably be removed.

REVIEW QUESTIONS

1. According to Lenin, why are monopolies a contradiction and a problem for capitalism?
2. Why does Lenin emphasize finance (as opposed to industrial) capital in his interpretation of imperialism?
3. How would imperial monopolies spur the collapse of capitalism?

26 ò THE CHALLENGE OF THE MODERN WEST

In the period 1870–1914, the West's prosperity as an industrial powerhouse and its maturity as a modern civil society produced an array of economic, political, and cultural challenges. Although Europe stood at the zenith of its power, its political turmoil and intellectual developments nonetheless questioned and mitigated the bourgeoisie's triumphant belief in progress and civilization.

Industrialization entered into a second, more mature stage, which produced innovative technologies and greater scales of economy. Department stores marked the arrival of mass consumer culture, with its breadth of goods and its new sales techniques. Newly invented machinery, which sewed, cut, pressed, and molded with labor-saving efficiency, allowed entrepreneurs to meet increased demands at lower prices. Employers furthermore maximized profit margins with "scientific" time-work studies, producing more efficient, rationalized regimens of work. Although hardly proportional to employers' gains, the living standards of workers rose, demonstrating capitalism's innovative abilities to adapt and prosper. But the new economic growth also brought keener competition for markets and national wealth, which sharpened political rivalries. While Britain remained the undisputed leader of the first Industrial Revolution, the emergence of such new leading sectors as steel, chemicals, and electrical engineering enabled German companies to achieve explosive economic expansion and thus vie with England and France for a greater share of world markets. After 1890 Britain felt the sting of its free-trade policy when other countries, especially Germany, competed in her own colonies and in Britain itself. The ubiquitous label "made in Germany" vexed British industrialists, reminding them of their relative decline. Economic nationalism became an increasingly important component of political discussions.

The widespread introduction of universal male suffrage after 1870 launched the era of mass politics. The enfranchisement of unpropertied laborers significantly broadened the political landscape, producing a range of political views that shook the delicate equilibrium of bourgeois and aristocratic governance. Syndicalists, anarchists, socialists, communists, and democratic labor parties now competed for workers' political loyalty. In this period Marxism also ceased to be a monolithic tenet. While such socialists as Eduard Bernstein argued that socialism should revise its belief in the imminent collapse of capitalism and start to participate in parliamentary politics for incremental reform, Lenin and other radical socialists continued to embrace Marx's tenet of class struggle for new revolutionary programs.

Women also emerged as a new political constituency. No longer content with the "natural" roles of reproduction and domesticity, women contested the right arrogated by men to deny them political citizenship and control over their property and legal affairs. Awakening to new identities, women demanded the vote, the right to a higher education, and overall respect for their intelligence and ability to serve society. The failure of the political establishment to initiate change for women abetted the rise of women's associations to agitate for the vote. And when peaceful petitioning failed to produce parliamentary debates, English women resorted to civil disobedience and militancy. Hunger strikes, destruction of property, and contentious demonstrations by women scandalized Europeans and disturbed ideals of peaceful, evolutionary change. Rejecting bourgeois movements, socialist feminists advocated the economic and political mobilization of women as an important weapon for the working-class movement.

In the last third of the nineteenth century, Europe's leading intellectuals, artists, and scientists also shook the foundations of the bourgeois world, questioning the fundamental premises by which bourgeois values and norms organized society and politics. Scientific discussion of Charles Darwin's theory of natural selection threw doubt on the ordered harmony of a divine, moral universe and furthermore became susceptible to false analogies to social behavior. Philosophers attacked Judeo-Christian values of social justice as spiritually enervating and culturally debilitating. The fledgling science of psychoanalysis further challenged the bourgeoisie's belief in rational, purposive action by demonstrating that behavior was largely determined by the inner mechanisms of the unconscious. Although the richness of European letters defies simple generalization, many of the enduring voices from this period felt increasingly detached from normative bourgeois assumptions, especially those grounded in rationality and progress.

ÉMILE ZOLA

FROM *The Ladies' Paradise*

Throughout his literary career Émile Zola (1840–1902) strove to address the social issues of his day. In a twenty-novel cycle, centered on the fictitious Rougon-Macquart family, he attempted to sketch a cross-section of French society, offering his readers grim portrayals of coal miners, peasants, urban workers, and Parisian prostitutes. Ever alert to shifts in the economic and cultural trends of Paris, Zola also perceived the innovation of Parisian department stores to be more than just a marketing breakthrough. By 1880 the Bon Marché, the Paris department store on which the novel is modeled, was turning over an unprecedented sum of 80 million francs annually, thus embodying the new rhythm and tempo of mass culture. Department stores' vast range of goods represented a revolution in personal consumption. The Ladies' Paradise (1883) develops a multilayered theme about the inexorable drive of modern capitalism, personified in Mouret, owner of the Ladies' Paradise department store, to purvey more goods at lower prices in faster business cycles. In addition the novel examines small shop owners driven to bankruptcy, as well as the shopping habits of women from all social classes. The section below illustrates Zola's knowledge of modern retail strategies as well as the manner in which he characterized female consumers.

From *The Ladies' Paradise*, by Émile Zola, translated by Brian Nelson (New York: Oxford University Press, 1995), pp. 232–40.

*   *   *

⋆ ⋆ ⋆ It was the cathedral of modern business, strong and yet light, built for vast crowds of customers. In the central gallery on the ground floor, after the bargains near the door, came the tie, glove, and silk departments; the Monsigny Gallery was occupied by the household linen and the printed cotton goods, the Michodière Gallery by the haberdashery, hosiery, cloth, and woollen departments. Then, on the first floor, there were the ready-made clothes, lingerie, shawls, lace, and other new departments, while the bedding, carpets, and furnishing materials, all the bulky goods and those which were difficult to handle, had been relegated to the second floor. By this time there were thirty-nine departments and eighteen hundred employees, of whom two hundred were

women. A whole world was springing up amidst the life echoing beneath the high metal naves.

Mouret's sole passion was the conquest of Woman. He wanted her to be queen in his shop; he had built this temple for her in order to hold her at his mercy. His tactics were to intoxicate her with amorous attentions, to trade on her desires, and to exploit her excitement. He racked his brains night and day for new ideas. Already, to spare delicate ladies the trouble of climbing the stairs, he had installed two lifts lined with velvet. In addition, he had just opened a buffet, where fruit cordials and biscuits were served free of charge, and a reading-room, a colossal gallery decorated with excessive luxury, in which he even ventured to hold picture exhibitions. But his most inspired idea, which he deployed with women devoid of coquetry, was that of conquering the mother through the child; he exploited every kind of force, speculated on every kind of feeling, created departments for little boys and girls, stopped the mothers as they were walking past by offering pictures and balloons to their babies. Presenting a balloon as a free gift to each customer who bought something was a stroke of genius; they were red balloons, made of fine indiarubber and with the name of the shop written on them in big letters; when held on the end of a string they travelled through the air, parading a living advertisement through the streets!

Mouret's greatest source of power was publicity. He spent as much as three hundred thousand francs a year on catalogues, advertisements, and posters. For his sale of summer fashions he had sent out two hundred thousand catalogues, of which fifty thousand, translated into every language, were sent abroad. He now had them illustrated with drawings, and even enclosed samples with them, glued on to the pages. His displays appeared everywhere. The Ladies' Paradise was staring the whole world in the face, invading walls, newspapers, and even the curtains of theatres. He declared that Woman was helpless against advertisements; in the end she inevitably went to see what all the noise was about. And he set even more cunning snares for her, analysing her like a great moralist. For example, he had discovered that she could not resist a bargain, that she bought things without needing them if she thought she was getting them cheaply; and on this observation he based his system of price reductions, progressively lowering the prices of unsold items, preferring to sell them at a loss, faithful to the principle of the rapid turnover of stocks. Then, penetrating even further into women's hearts, he had recently conceived of 'returns', a masterpiece of Jesuitical seduction. 'Take it all the same, madam: you can return the article to us if you find you don't like it.' And a woman who was resisting was thus given a final excuse, the possibility of going back on an act of folly; her conscience satisfied, she would buy it. Returns and price reductions were now part of the standard methods of the new business.

But it was in the interior arrangement of the shops that Mouret revealed himself to be an unrivalled master. He laid it down as a law that not a corner of the Ladies' Paradise was to remain deserted; everywhere he insisted upon noise, crowds, life; for life, he would say, attracts life, gives birth and multiplies. He put this law into practice in a whole variety of ways. First of all, there should be a crush at the entrance; it should seem to people in the street that there was a riot in the shop; and he obtained this crush by placing bargains at the entrance, shelves and baskets overflowing with articles at very low prices, so that working-class people began to congregate there, barring the threshold, and giving the impression that the shop was bursting with customers, when often it was only half full. Then, all through the galleries, he had the art of hiding the departments in which business was slack—the shawl department in summer and the cotton materials in winter, for example; he would surround them with active departments, drowning them with blaring noise. It was he alone who had thought of putting the carpet and furniture departments on the second floor, for in those departments customers were rarer, and their presence on the ground floor would have created cold, empty gaps. If he could have found a way of making the street run right through his shop, he would have done so.

Just now Mouret was undergoing one of his fits of inspiration. On Saturday evening, as he was casting a last glance over the preparations for Monday's big sale, which they had been working on for a month, he had suddenly realized that the way he had arranged the departments was stupid. It was, however, an absolutely logical arrangement—materials on one side, manufactured goods on the other, an intelligent system which should enable the customers to find their own way about. He had dreamed of this system while he was still working in the muddle of Madame Hedouin's little shop; and now, on the day when he was putting it into effect, he felt his faith in it shaken. Suddenly he had shouted that he wanted it all changed. This meant moving half the shop, and they had forty-eight hours to do it in. The staff, bewildered and working at full stretch, had had to spend two nights and the whole of Sunday in the midst of an appalling mess. Even on Monday morning, an hour before the opening, the goods were not yet in place. The governor was surely losing his mind; no one could understand it, and there was general consternation.

"Come on! Let's hurry!" Mouret shouted, with the calm assurance born of his genius. "Here are some more suits I want taken upstairs . . . And are the Japanese things installed on the central landing? . . . One last effort, lads, and you'll see what a sale we're going to have!"

Bourdoncle, too, had been there since dawn. He understood no better than the others, and was watching the governor most anxiously. He hadn't dated to question him, knowing how he responded in such moments of crisis. All the same, he decided to risk it, and asked gently:

"Was it really necessary to turn everything upside-down like that, on the eve of our exhibition?"

At first Mouret shrugged his shoulders without replying. Then, since Bourdoncle insisted, he burst out:

"So that the customers should all huddle together in the same corner, perhaps? An excellent geometrical idea I had when I thought of that! I'd never have forgiven myself . . . Can't you see that I'd have localized the crowd? A woman would have come in, gone straight to where she wanted, passed from the petticoat department to the dress department, from the dresses to the coats, and then left, without even having got a bit lost! Not one of them would really have seen our shop!"

"But," Bourdoncle pointed out, "now that you've mixed everything up and thrown everything all over the place, the staff will wear their legs out taking customers from department to department."

Mouret made a gesture of supreme contempt.

"I don't care a damn! They're young; it'll make them grow. So much the better if they walk about! They'll look more numerous, they'll swell the crowd. As long as there's a crush, all will be well!"

He was laughing, and deigned to explain his idea, lowering his voice:

"Listen, Bourdoncle, this is what will happen . . . First, this continual circulation of customers scatters them all over the place, multiplies them, and makes them lose their heads; secondly, as they have to be conducted from one end of the shop to the other—for example, if they want a lining after having bought a dress—these journeys in every direction triple, as they see it, the size of the shop; thirdly, they're forced to go through departments where they'd never have set foot, temptations present themselves as they pass, and they succumb; fourthly . . ."

*   *   *

Finally the doors were opened again, and the crowd streamed in. From the beginning, even before the shop was full, there was such a crush in the entrance hall that the police had to be called in to keep people moving along on the pavement. Mouret's calculations had been right: all the housewives, a serried band of shopkeepers' and workmen's wives, were assaulting the bargains and remnants, which were displayed right into the street. Outstretched hands were continually feeling the materials hanging at the entrance, a calico at thirty-five centimes, a wool and cotton grey material at forty-five centimes, and above all an Orleans cloth at thirty-eight centimes which was playing havoc with the poorer purses. There was much elbowing, a feverish scrimmage round the racks and baskets in which piles of goods at reduced prices—lace at ten centimes, ribbons at twenty-five centimes, garters at fifteen, gloves, petticoats, ties, cotton socks and stockings—were collapsing and disappearing, as if devoured by the voracious crowd. In spite of the cold weather, the assistants who were selling to the crowd on the pavement could not serve fast enough. A fat woman screamed. Two little girls nearly suffocated.

*   *   *

REVIEW QUESTIONS

1. In *The Ladies' Paradise*, what marketing innovations did the new department store create, and which made it different from the traditional shop?

2. What character traits does Zola assign women shoppers?

3. How did the innovation of the department fit into the larger economic transformation known as the second industrial revolution?

FREDERICK W. TAYLOR

FROM *The Principles of Scientific Management*

In its later phase the second industrial revolution introduced innovative management methods for increasing worker productivity, which would eventually culminate in Henry Ford's assembly lines. But the new philosophy of "scientific management" was often labeled Taylorism, named after F. W. Taylor, who presented his precepts for greater discipline and worker efficiency in his Principles of Scientific Management *(1912), which became an international model for large-scale businesses. The following excerpt centers on the now-classic example of Schmidt the pig-iron worker.*

From *The Principles of Scientific Management*, by Frederick W. Taylor (New York: Norton, 1967).

*   *   *

Perhaps the most prominent single element in modern scientific management is the task idea. The work of every workman is fully planned out by the management at least one day in advance, and each man receives in most cases complete written instructions, describing in detail the task which he is to accomplish, as well as the means to be used in doing the work. And the work planned in advance in this way constitutes a task which is to be solved, as explained above, not by the workman alone, but in almost all cases by the joint effort of the workman and the management. This task specifies not only what is to be done but how it is to be done and the exact time allowed for doing it. And whenever the workman succeeds in doing his task right, and within the time limit specified, he receives an addition of from 30 per cent. to 100 per cent. to his ordinary wages. These tasks are carefully planned, so that both good and careful work are called for in their performance, but it should be distinctly understood that in no case is the workman called upon to work at a pace which would be injurious to his health. The task is always so regulated that the man who is well suited to his job will thrive while working at this rate during a long term of years and grow happier and more prosperous, instead of being overworked. Scientific management consists very largely in preparing for and carrying out these tasks.

*   *   *

The first illustration is that of handling pig iron, and this work is chosen because it is typical of perhaps the crudest and most elementary form of labor which is performed by man. This work is done by men with no other implements than their hands. The pig-iron handler stoops down, picks up a pig weighing about 92 pounds, walks for a few feet or yards and then drops it on to the ground or upon a pile. This work is so crude and elementary in its nature that the writer firmly believes that it would be possible to train an intelligent gorilla so as to become a more efficient pig-iron handler than any man can be. Yet it will be shown that the science of handling pig iron is so great and amounts to so much that it is impossible for the man who is best suited to this type of work to understand the principles of this science, or even to work in accordance with these principles without the aid of a man better educated than he is. And the further illustrations to be given will make it clear that in almost all of the mechanic arts the science which underlies each workman's act is so great and amounts to so much that the workman who is best suited actually to do the work is incapable (either through lack of education or through insufficient mental capacity) of understanding this science. This is announced as a general principle, the truth of which will become apparent as one illustration after another is given. After showing these four elements in the handling of pig iron, several illustrations will be given of their application to different kinds of work in the field of the mechanic arts, at intervals in a rising scale, beginning with the simplest and ending with the more intricate forms of labor.

One of the first pieces of work undertaken by us, when the writer started to introduce scientific management into the Bethlehem Steel Company, was to handle pig iron on task work. The opening of the Spanish War found some 80,000 tons of pig iron placed in small piles in an open field adjoining the works. Prices for pig iron had been so low that it could not be sold at a profit, and it therefore had been stored. With the opening of the Spanish War the price of pig iron rose, and this large accumulation of iron was sold. This gave us

a good opportunity to show the workmen, as well as the owners and managers of the works, on a fairly large scale the advantages of task work over the old-fashioned day work and piece work, in doing a very elementary class of work.

The Bethlehem Steel Company had five blast furnaces, the product of which had been handled by a pig-iron gang for many years. This gang, at this time, consisted of about 75 men. They were good, average pig-iron handlers, were under an excellent foreman who himself had been a pig-iron handler, and the work was done, on the whole, about as fast and as cheaply as it was anywhere else at that time.

A railroad switch was run out into the field, right along the edge of the piles of pig iron. An inclined plank was placed against the side of a car, and each man picked up from his pile a pig of iron weighing about 92 pounds, walked up the inclined plank and dropped it on the end of the car.

We found that this gang were loading on the average about 12½ long tons per man per day. We were surprised to find, after studying the matter, that a first-class pig-iron handler ought to handle between 47 and 48 long tons per day, instead of 12½ tons. This task seemed to us so very large that we were obliged to go over our work several times before we were absolutely sure that we were right. Once we were sure, however, that 47 tons was a proper day's work for a first-class pig-iron handler, the task which faced us as managers under the modern scientific plan was clearly before us. It was our duty to see that the 80,000 tons of pig iron was loaded on to the cars at the rate of 47 tons per man per day, in place of 12½ tons, at which rate the work was then being done. And it was further our duty to see that this work was done without bringing on a strike among the men, without any quarrel with the men, and to see that the men were happier and better contented when loading at the new rate of 47 tons than they were when loading at the old rate of 12½ tons.

Our first step was the scientific selection of the workman. In dealing with workmen under this type of management, it is an inflexible rule to talk to and deal with only one man at a time, since each workman has his own special abilities and limitations, and since we are not dealing with men in masses, but are trying to develop each individual man to his highest state of efficiency and prosperity. Our first step was to find the proper workman to begin with. We therefore carefully watched and studied these 75 men for three or four days, at the end of which time we had picked out four men who appeared to be physically able to handle pig iron at the rate of 47 tons per day. A careful study was then made of each of these men. We looked up their history as far back as practicable and thorough inquiries were made as to the character, habits, and the ambition of each of them. Finally we selected one from among the four as the most likely man to start with. He was a little Pennsylvania Dutchman who had been observed to trot back home for a mile or so after his work in the evening about as fresh as he was when he came trotting down to work in the morning. We found that upon wages of $1.15 a day he had succeeded in buying a small plot of ground, and that he was engaged in putting up the walls of a little house for himself in the morning before starting to work and at night after leaving. He also had the reputation of being exceedingly "close," that is, of placing a very high value on a dollar. As one man whom we talked to about him said, "A penny looks about the size of a cart-wheel to him." This man we will call Schmidt.

The task before us, then, narrowed itself down to getting Schmidt to handle 47 tons of pig iron per day and making him glad to do it. This was done as follows. Schmidt was called out from among the gang of pig-iron handlers and talked to somewhat in this way:

"Schmidt, are you a high-priced man?"

"Vell, I don't know vat you mean."

"Oh yes, you do. What I want to know is whether you are a high-priced man or not."

"Vell, I don't know vat you mean."

"Oh, come now, you answer my questions. What I want to find out is whether you are a high-priced man or one of these cheap fellows here. What I want to find out is whether you want to

earn $1.85 a day or whether you are satisfied with $1.15, just the same as all those cheap fellows are getting."

"Did I vant $1.85 a day? Vas dot a high-priced man? Vell, yes, I vas a high-priced man."

"Oh, you're aggravating me. Of course you want $1.85 a day—every one wants it! You know perfectly well that that has very little to do with your being a high-priced man. For goodness' sake answer my questions, and don't waste any more of my time. Now come over here. You see that pile of pig iron?"

"Yes."

"You see that car?"

"Yes."

"Well, if you are a high-priced man, you will load that pig iron on that car to-morrow for $1.85. Now do wake up and answer my question. Tell me whether you are a high-priced man or not."

"Vell—did I got $1.85 for loading dot pig iron on dot car to-morrow?"

"Yes, of course you do, and you get $1.85 for loading a pile like that every day right through the year. That is what a high-priced man does, and you know it just as well as I do."

"Vell, dot's all right. I could load dot pig iron on the car to-morrow for $1.85, and I get it every day, don't I?"

"Certainly you do—certainly you do."

"Vell, den, I vas a high-priced man."

"Now, hold on, hold on. You know just as well as I do that a high-priced man has to do exactly as he's told from morning till night. You have seen this man here before, haven't you?"

"No, I never saw him."

"Well, if you are a high-priced man, you will do exactly as this man tells you to-morrow, from morning till night. When he tells you to pick up a pig and walk, you pick it up and you walk, and when he tells you to sit down and rest, you sit down. You do that right straight through the day. And what's more, no back talk. Now a high-priced man does just what he's told to do, and no back talk. Do you understand that? When this man tells you to walk, you walk; when he tells you to sit down, you sit down, and you don't talk back at him. Now you come on to work here to-morrow morning and I'll know before night whether you are really a high-priced man or not."

This seems to be rather rough talk. And indeed it would be if applied to an educated mechanic, or even an intelligent laborer. With a man of the mentally sluggish type of Schmidt it is appropriate and not unkind, since it is effective in fixing his attention on the high wages which he wants and away from what, if it were called to his attention, he probably would consider impossibly hard work.

What would Schmidt's answer be if he were talked to in a manner which is usual under the management of "initiative and incentive"? say, as follows:

"Now, Schmidt, you are a first-class pig-iron handler and know your business well. You have been handling at the rate of 12½ tons per day. I have given considerable study to handling pig iron, and feel sure that you could do a much larger day's work than you have been doing. Now don't you think that if you really tried you could handle 47 tons of pig iron per day, instead of 12½ tons?"

What do you think Schmidt's answer would be to this?

Schmidt started to work, and all day long, and at regular intervals, was told by the man who stood over him with a watch, "Now pick up a pig and walk. Now sit down and rest. Now walk— now rest," etc. He worked when he was told to work, and rested when he was told to rest, and at half-past five in the afternoon had his 47½ tons loaded on the car. And he practically never failed to work at this pace and do the task that was set him during the three years that the writer was at Bethlehem. And throughout this time he averaged a little more than $1.85 per day, whereas before he had never received over $1.15 per day, which was the ruling rate of wages at that time in Bethlehem. That is, he received 60 per cent. higher wages than were paid to other men who were not working on task work. One man after another was picked out and trained to handle pig iron at the rate of 47½ tons per day until all of the pig iron was handled at this rate, and the men were receiving 60 per cent. more wages than other workmen around them.

* * *

REVIEW QUESTIONS

1. According to Taylor, what are the management's objectives and how are they achieved?
2. Why is this management "scientific"?
3. How is Schmidt the worker handled, and what are the advantages for both him and the management?
4. What are Taylor's assumptions about workers?
5. How does Taylor's prescription for a new industrial discipline compare with the Rules of a Factory in Berlin (Chapter 21)?
6. What are the ramifications of this method for industrial production and industrial relations?

ERNEST EDWIN WILLIAMS

FROM *Made in Germany*

The dynamism of German economic growth after 1870 caused concern in England. Comparing the output of pig iron—a reliable index of industrial production—in Germany and England reveals the relative decline of England as an industrial power. Whereas German pig iron production increased from 1.56 million metric tons in 1871 to 14.8 million metric tons in 1910, English pig iron rose in the same time period from 6.5 million metric tons in 1871 to 10.1 million metric tons in 1910. Germany also surpassed the United Kingdom in metallurgical and steel production, while developing a world reputation for its machines, tools, cutlery, optics, and precision instruments. Consequently, economic competition sharpened the edge of the political rivalry that developed between England and Germany after 1890. Ernest Edwin William's enormously popular book, which went through numerous editions in the 1890s, exemplifies the popular literature that fueled the economic nationalism of this period.

From *Made in Germany*, by Ernest Edwin Williams (London: Heinemann, 1896).

THE Industrial Supremacy of Great Britain has been long an axiomatic commonplace; and it is fast turning into a myth, as inappropriate to fact as the Chinese Emperor's computation of his own status. This is a strong statement. But it is neither wide nor short of the truth. The industrial glory of England is departing, and England does not know it. There are spasmodic outcries against foreign competition, but the impression they leave is fleeting and vague. The phrase, "Made in Germany," is raw material for a jape at the pantomime, or is made the text for a homily by the official guardians of some particular trade, in so far as the matter concerns themselves. British Consuls, too, send words of warning home, and the number of these is increasing with significant frequency. But the nation at large is yet as little alive to the impending danger as to the evil already wrought. The man in the shop or the factory has plenty to say about the Armenian Question and the House of Lords, but about commercial and industrial matters which concern him vitally he is generally much less eloquent. The amount of interest evinced by the amateur politician seems invariably to advance with the remoteness of the matter from his daily bread. It is time to disturb the fatal torpor: even though the moment be, in one sense, unhappily chosen. The pendulum between depression and prosperity has swung to the latter, and manufacturers and merchants are flushed with the joyful contemplation of their order-books. Slackness has given way to briskness; the lean years have been succeeded by a term of fat ones. The prophet of evil commands his most attentive audiences when the times are with him. When they are good—though the good be fleeting—his words are apt to fall unheeded.

*   *   *

As It Was

There was a time when our industrial Empire was unchallenged. It was England which first emerged from the Small-Industry stage. She produced the Industrial Revolution about the middle of the last century, and well-nigh until the middle of this she developed her multitude of mills, and factories, and mines, and warehouses, undisturbed by war at home, and profiting by wars abroad. The great struggles which drained the energies of the Continental nations, sealed her industrial supremacy, and made her absolute mistress of the world-market. Thanks to them, she became the Universal Provider. English machinery, English pottery, English hardware, guns, and cutlery, English rails and bridge-work, English manufactures of well-nigh every kind formed the material of civilisation all over the globe. She covered the dry land with a network of railways, and the seas were alive with her own ships freighted with her own merchandise. Between 1793 and 1815 the value of her exports had risen from £17,000,000 to £58,000,000. Her industrial dominion was immense, unquestioned, unprecedented in the history of the human race; and not unnaturally we have come to regard her rule as eternal. But careless self-confidence makes not for Empire. While she was throwing wide her gates to the world at large, her sisters were building barriers of protection against her; and, behind those barriers, and aided often by State subventions, during the middle and later years of the century, they have developed industries of their own. Of course, this was to a certain extent inevitable. England could not hope for an eternal monopoly of the world's manufactures; and industrial growths abroad do not of necessity sound the knell of her greatness. But she must discriminate in her equanimity. And most certainly she must discriminate against Germany. For Germany has entered into a deliberate and deadly rivalry with her, and is battling with might and main for the extinction of her supremacy.

In estimating England's industrial position, regard must also be had to her function as the world's middleman. Not only is she a manufacturer for other peoples: she is likewise their agent for distribution. There is scarce a nation—certainly not one of any importance—which does not come to England to buy goods sent in for sale from elsewhere. She sells those nations hams from her Colonies, coffee from Arabia, gloves from France, currants from Greece, cotton from America—in fact it would be hard to name an article produced abroad which is not on sale in those universal market-places, the Mersey and the Thames. In this retail business, also, the Germans are setting themselves to beat us; and South Americans are already buying their Irish linen through Hamburg houses. If there be an advance in this form of competition on the part of Germany, we shall lose the little benefit accruing from the German export trade, for in all other respects it is wholly baneful to us.

The German Revolution

Up to a couple of decades ago, Germany was an agricultural State. Her manufactures were new and unimportant; her industrial capital was small; her export trade was too insignificant to merit the attention of the official statistician; she imported largely for her own consumption. Now she has changed all that. Her youth has crowded into English houses, has wormed its way into English manufacturing secrets, and has enriched her establishments with the knowledge thus purloined. She has educated her people in a fashion which has made it in some branches of industry the superior, and in most the equal of the English. Her capitalists have been content with a simple style, which has enabled them to dispense with big immediate profits, and to feed their capital. They have toiled at their desks, and made their sons do likewise; they have kept a strict controlling hand on all the strings of their businesses; they have obtained State aid in several ways—as special rates to shipping ports; they have insinuated themselves into every part of the world—civilised, barbarian, savage—learning the languages, and patiently studying the wants and tastes of the several peoples. Not content with reaping the advantages of

British colonisation—this was accomplished with alarming facility—Germany has "protected" the simple savage on her own account, and the Imperial Eagle now floats on the breezes of the South Sea Islands, and droops in the thick air of the African littoral. Her diplomatists have negotiated innumerable commercial treaties. The population of her cities has been increasing in a manner not unworthy of England in the Thirties and Forties. Like England, too, she is draining her rural districts for the massing of her children in huge factory towns. Her yards (as well as those of England) too, are ringing with the sound of hammers upon ships being built for the transport of German merchandise. Her agents and travellers swarm through Russia, and wherever else there is a chance of trade on any terms—are even supplying the foreigner with German goods *at a loss*, that they may achieve their purpose in the end. In a word, an industrial development, unparalleled, save in England a century ago, is now her portion. A gigantic commercial State is arising to menace our prosperity, and contend with us for the trade of the world. It is true that this mad rush towards industrialism does not meet with universal approval; and the Agrarian Party is energetic in its denunciation of the ruin wrought thereby to Germany as an agricultural State. But its protests have nothing availed it yet, nor are ever likely to avail it anything.

Made in Germany

The phrase is fluent in the mouth: how universally appropriate it is, probably no one who has not made a special study of the matter is aware. Take observations, Gentle Reader, in your own surroundings: the mental exercise is recommended as an antidote to that form of self-sufficiency which our candid friends regard as indigenous to the British climate. Your investigations will work out somewhat in this fashion. You will find that the material of some of your own clothes was probably woven in Germany. Still more probable is it that some of your wife's garments are German importations; while it is practically beyond a doubt that the magnificent mantles and jackets wherein her maids array themselves on their Sundays out are German-made and German-sold, for only so could they be done at the figure. Your governess's *fiancé* is a clerk in the City; but he also was made in Germany. The toys, and the dolls, and the fairy books which your children maltreat in the nursery are made in Germany: nay, the material of your favourite (patriotic) newspaper had the same birthplace as like as not. Roam the house over, and the fateful mark will greet you at every turn, from the piano in your drawing-room to the mug on your kitchen dresser, blazoned though it be with the legend, *A Present from Margate*. Descend to your domestic depths, and you shall find your very drain-pipes German made. You pick out of the grate the paper wrappings from a book consignment, and they also are "Made in Germany." You stuff them into the fire, and reflect that the poker in your hand was forged in Germany. As you rise from your hearthrug you knock over an ornament on your mantlepiece; picking up the pieces you read, on the bit that formed the base, "Manufactured in Germany." And you jot your dismal reflections down with a pencil that was made in Germany. At midnight your wife comes home from an opera which was made in Germany, has been here enacted by singers and conductor and players made in Germany, with the aid of instruments and sheets of music made in Germany. You go to bed, and glare wrathfully at a text on the wall; it is illuminated with an English village church, and it was "Printed in Germany." If you are imaginative and dyspeptic, you drop off to sleep only to dream that St. Peter (with a duly stamped halo round his head and a bunch of keys from the Rhineland) has refused you admission into Paradise, because you bear not the Mark of the Beast upon your forehead, and are not of German make. But you console yourself with the thought that it was only a Bierhaus Paradise any way; and you are awakened in the morning by the sonorous brass of a German band.

Is the picture exaggerated? Bear with me, while I tabulate a few figures from the Official Returns of Her Majesty's Custom House, where, at any rate, fancy and exaggeration have no play. In '95 Germany sent us linen manufactures to the value of £91,257; cotton manufactures to the value of £536,471; embroidery and needlework to the value of £11,309; leather gloves to the value of £27,934 (six times the amount imported six years earlier); and woollen manufactures to the value of £1,016,694. Despite the exceeding cheapness of toys, the value of German-made playthings for English nurseries amounted, in '95, to £459,944. In the same year she sent us books to the value of £37,218, and paper to the value of £586,835. For musical instruments we paid her as much as £563,018; for china and earthenware £216,876; for prints, engravings, and photographs, £111,825. This recital of the moneys which *in one year* have come out of John Bull's pocket for the purchase of his German-made household goods is, I submit disproof enough of any charge of alarmism. For these articles, it must be remembered, are not like oranges and guano. They are not products which we must either import or lack:—*they all belong to the category of English manufactures,* the most important of them, indeed, being articles in the preparation of which Great Britain is held pre-eminent. The total value of manufactured goods imported into the United Kingdom by Germany rose from £16,629,987 in '83 to £21,632,614 in '93: an increase of 30.08 per cent.

A few figures more. I said that a little while since Germany was a large importer of manufactures needed for her own consumption. Take as a first example, the iron and steel industries. In '78 the make of pig-iron in Germany was 2,147,000 tons; in '95 it was 5,788,000 tons. Germany made in '78 492,512 tons of steel; in '94 3,617,000 tons. Her import and export statistics tell the same tale. In '80 her iron exports only totalled 1,301,000 tons; in '94 they stood at 2,008,000 tons. (In the same period England's exports of iron had decreased.) In the matter of cottons Germany exported 14,666,100 kilogs. in '83; in '93, 33,350,800 kilogs., an increase of more than 127 per cent. (England's increase in the same period was only

about 2½ per cent.) Shipping returns are a pretty sure test of commercial prosperity: it is therefore significant that in '93 the total tonnage of the seagoing ships which touched at Hamburg for the first time left Liverpool behind, and in '94 Hamburg cut her record of the year before.

*　　*　　*

The Significance of These Facts

These are the sober—to believers in our eternal rule, the sobering—facts. They are picked almost at random from a mass of others of like import, and I think they are sufficient to prove that my general statements are neither untrue nor unduly emphatic. And yet the data needed for the purpose of showing the parlous condition into which our trade is drifting are still largely to seek. Germany is yet in her industrial infancy; and the healthiest infant can do but poor battle against a grown man. England, with her enormous capital, and the sway she has wielded for a century over the world-market, is as that strong man. Now, to tell a strong man, conscious of his strength to an over-weening degree, that he is in peril from a half-grown youngster, is to invite his derision; and yet if a strong man, as the years advance on him, neglect himself and abuse his strength, he may fall before an energetic stripling. Germany has already put our trade in a bad way; but the worst lies in the future, and it is hard to convince the average Englishman of this.

*　　*　　*

REVIEW QUESTIONS

1. In what stages of growth did Williams perceive both England and Germany?
2. Why had German products flooded Britain's domestic market?
3. Does Williams's economic argument have political ramifications?

EDUARD BERNSTEIN

FROM *Evolutionary Socialism*

At the turn of the century, Eduard Bernstein (1850–1932) was a leading member of the Social Democratic Party of Germany (SPD), Europe's largest, best-organized Marxist party. In 1899 Bernstein published The Premises of Socialism and the Tasks of Social Democracy, *which called attention to the evolutionary changes in capitalism that rendered orthodox Marxist doctrine obsolete. In the book Bernstein argued for the need to revise tactics and goals for working-class constituencies. Bernstein's treatise, which sparked an important debate among socialists, is a useful document, for it throws light not only on the revisionist political strategies of socialists but also on the changing nature of late nineteenth-century capitalist political economy.*

From *Evolutionary Socialism: A Criticism and Affirmation,* by Edward Bernstein, translated by Edith C. Harvey (New York: Schocken Books, 1963).

*   *   *

It has been maintained in a certain quarter that the practical deductions from my treatises would be the abandonment of the conquest of political power by the proletariat organised politically and economically. That is quite an arbitrary deduction, the accuracy of which I altogether deny.

I set myself against the notion that we have to expect shortly a collapse of the bourgeois economy, and that social democracy should be induced by the prospect of such an imminent, great, social catastrophe to adapt its tactics to that assumption. That I maintain most emphatically.

The adherents of this theory of a catastrophe, base it especially on the conclusions of the *Communist Manifesto.* This is a mistake in every respect.

The theory which the *Communist Manifesto* sets forth of the evolution of modern society was correct as far as it characterised the general tendencies of that evolution. But it was mistaken in several special deductions, above all in the estimate of the *time* the evolution would take. The

last has been unreservedly acknowledged by Friedrich Engels, the joint author with Marx of the *Manifesto,* in his preface to the *Class War in France.* But it is evident that if social evolution takes a much greater period of time than was assumed, it must also take upon itself *forms* and lead to forms that were not foreseen and could not be foreseen then.

Social conditions have not developed to such an acute opposition of things and classes as is depicted in the *Manifesto.* It is not only useless, it is the greatest folly to attempt to conceal this from ourselves. The number of members of the possessing classes is to-day not smaller but larger. The enormous increase of social wealth is not accompanied by a decreasing number of large capitalists but by an increasing number of capitalists of all degrees. The middle classes change their character but they do not disappear from the social scale.

The concentration in productive industry is not being accomplished even to day in all its departments with equal thoroughness and at an equal rate. In a great many branches of production it certainly justifies the forecasts of the socialist critic of society; but in other branches it lags even to-day behind them. The process of concentration in agriculture proceeds still more slowly. Trade statistics show an extraordinarily elaborated graduation of enterprises in regard to size. No rung of the ladder is disappearing from it. The significant changes in the inner structure of these enterprises and their interrelationship cannot do away with this fact.

In all advanced countries we see the privileges of the capitalist bourgeoisie yielding step by step to democratic organisations. Under the influence of this, and driven by the movement of the working classes which is daily becoming stronger, a social reaction has set in against the exploiting tendencies of capital, a counteraction which, although it still proceeds timidly and feebly, yet does exist, and is always drawing more departments of economic life under its influence. Factory legislation, the democratising of local government, and the extension of its area of work, the freeing of trade unions and systems of co-operative trading from legal restrictions, the consideration of standard conditions of labour in the work undertaken by public authorities—all these characterise this phase of the evolution.

But the more the political organisations of modern nations are democratised the more the needs and opportunities of great political catastrophes are diminished. He who holds firmly to the catastrophic theory of evolution must, with all his power, withstand and hinder the evolution described above, which, indeed, the logical defenders of that theory formerly did. But is the conquest of political power by the proletariat simply to be by a political catastrophe? Is it to be the appropriation and utilisation of the power of the State by the proletariat exclusively against the whole non-proletarian world?

He who replies in the affirmative must be reminded of two things. In 1872 Marx and Engels announced in the preface to the new edition of the *Communist Manifesto* that the Paris Commune had exhibited a proof that "the working classes cannot simply take possession of the ready-made State machine and set it in motion for their own aims." And in 1895 Friedrich Engels stated in detail in the preface to *War of the Classes* that the time of political surprises, of the "revolutions of small conscious minorities at the head of unconscious masses" was to-day at an end, that a collision on a large scale with the military would be the means of checking the steady growth of social democracy and of even throwing it back for a time—in short, that social democracy would flourish far better by lawful than by unlawful means and by violent revolution. And he points out in conformity with this opinion that the next task of the party should be "to work for an uninterrupted increase of its votes" or to carry on a slow *propaganda of parliamentary activity*.

Thus Engels, who, nevertheless, as his numerical examples show, still somewhat overestimated the rate of process of the evolution! Shall we be told that he abandoned the conquest of political power by the working classes, because he wished to avoid the steady growth of social democracy secured by lawful means being interrupted by a political revolution?

If not, and if one subscribes to his conclusions, one cannot reasonably take any offence if it is declared that for a long time yet the task of social democracy is, instead of speculating on a great economic crash, "to organise the working classes politically and develop them as a democracy and to fight for all reforms in the State which are adapted to raise the working classes and transform the State in the direction of democracy."

That is what I have said in my impugned article and what I still maintain in its full import. As far as concerns the question propounded above it is equivalent to Engel's dictum, for democracy is, at any given time, as much government by the working classes as these are capable of practising according to their intellectual ripeness and the degree of social development they have attained. Engels, indeed, refers at the place just mentioned to the fact that the *Communist Manifesto* has "proclaimed the conquest of the democracy as one of the first and important tasks of the fighting proletariat."

In short, Engels is so thoroughly convinced that the tactics based on the presumption of a catastrophe have had their day, that he even considers a revision of them necessary in the Latin countries where tradition is much more favourable to them than in Germany. "If the conditions of war between nations have altered," he writes, "no less have those for the war between classes." Has this already been forgotten?

No one has questioned the necessity for the working classes to gain the control of government. The point at issue is between the theory of a social cataclysm and the question whether with the given social development in Germany and the present advanced state of its working classes in the towns and the country, a sudden catastrophe would be desirable in the interest of the social democracy. I have denied it and deny it again, because in my judgment a greater security for lasting success lies in a steady advance than in the possibilities offered by a catastrophic crash.

And as I am firmly convinced that important periods in the development of nations cannot be leapt over I lay the greatest value on the next tasks of social democracy, on the struggle for the political rights of the working man, on the political activity of working men in town and country for the interests of their class, as well as on the work of the industrial organisation of the workers.

In this sense I wrote the sentence that the movement means everything for me and that what is *usually* called "the final aim of socialism" is nothing; and in this sense I write it down again to-day. Even if the word "usually" had not shown that the proposition was only to be understood conditionally, it was obvious that it *could* not express indifference concerning the final carrying out of socialist principles, but only indifference— or, as it would be better expressed, carelessness— as to the form of the final arrangement of things. I have at no time had an excessive interest in the future, beyond general principles; I have not been able to read to the end any picture of the future. My thoughts and efforts are concerned with the duties of the present and the nearest future, and I only busy myself with the perspectives beyond so far as they give me a line of conduct for suitable action now.

The conquest of political power by the working classes, the expropriation of capitalists, are no ends in themselves but only means for the accomplishment of certain aims and endeavours. As such they are demands in the programme of social democracy and are not attacked by me. Nothing can be said beforehand as to the circumstances of their accomplishment; we can only fight for their realisation. But the conquest of political power necessitates the possession of political *rights*; and the most important problem of tactics which German social democracy has at the present time to solve, appears to me to be to devise the best ways for the extension of the political and economic rights of the German working classes.

* * *

That which concerns me, that which forms the chief aim of this work, is, by opposing what is left of the utopian mode of thought in the socialist theory, to strengthen equally the realistic and the idealistic element in the socialist movement.

REVIEW QUESTIONS

1. According to Bernstein, in what ways was the *Communist Manifesto* incorrect?
2. What aspects of political and economic life had alleviated class conflict?
3. What is Bernstein's solution, and how does it differ from orthodox Marxism?

VLADIMIR LENIN

FROM *Our Programme*

The extreme conservatism of government officials such as Pobedonostsev found its answer in the revolutionary aspirations of late-nineteenth-century Russian political activists. While populists—the narodniki—*sought to mobilize the Russian peasantry as a revolutionary force, the emergence of an industrial working class convinced Marxist socialists that the urban proletariat would spearhead a revolution against the capitalist development being fostered by the tsarist state itself.*

Vladimir Ilich Ulyanov, better known as Lenin (1870–1924), was drawn into the Russian opposition movement after his brother was executed in 1887 for conspiring to assassinate Tsar Alexander III. In subsequent years, Lenin became one of the leading theorists of the Russian Social Democratic Workers' Party. In 1899, at the end of a period of exile in Siberia, he wrote the following statement of revolutionary principles, affirming his adherence to revolutionary Marxism and rejecting "reformist" tendencies within the international socialist movement. Four years prior to the historic schism between the Social Democratic Party's revolutionary Bolsheviks and reformist Mensheviks, it is clear that Lenin had already begun to reject worker cooperation with the liberal bourgeoisie and that he was becoming committed to the idea that a "vanguard" of professional revolutionaries must lead the workers' revolution.

From *Our Programme*, by Vladimir Lenin (1899), Internet Modern History Sourcebook, www.fordham.edu/halsall/mod/modsbook.html [accessed 11/21/01].

International social democracy is at present going through a period of theoretical vacillations. Up to the present the doctrines of Marx and Engels were regarded as a firm foundation of revolutionary theory—nowadays voices are raised everywhere declaring these doctrines to be inadequate and antiquated. Anyone calling himself a social-democrat and having the intention to publish a social-democratic organ, must take up a definite attitude as regards this question, which by no means concerns German social-democrats alone.

We base our faith entirely on Marx's theory; it was the first to transform socialism from a Utopia into a science, to give this science a firm foundation and to indicate the path which must be trodden in order further to develop this science and to elaborate it in all its details. It discovered the nature of present-day capitalist economy and explained the way in which the employment of workers—the purchase of labour power—the enslavement of millions of those possessing no property by a handful of capitalists, by the owners of the land, the factories, the mines, etc., is concealed. It has shown how the whole development of modern capitalism is advancing towards the large producer ousting the small one, and is creating the prerequisites which make a socialist order of society possible and necessary. It has taught us to see, under the disguise of ossified habits, political intrigues, intricate laws, cunning theories, the class struggle, the struggle between, on the one hand, the various species of the possessing classes, and, on the other hand, the mass possessing no property, the proletariat, which leads all those who possess nothing. It has made clear what is the real task of a revolutionary socialist party—not to set up projects for the transformation of society, not to preach sermons to the capitalists and their admirers about improving the position of the workers, not the instigation of conspiracies, but the organisation of the class struggle of the proletariat and the carrying on of this struggle, the final aim of which is the seizure of political power by the proletariat and the organisation of a socialist society.

We now ask: What new elements have the touting "renovators" introduced into this theory, they who have attracted so much notice in our day and have grouped themselves round the German socialist Bernstein? Nothing, nothing at all; they have not advanced by a single step the science which Marx and Engels adjured us to develop; they have not taught the proletariat any new methods of fighting; they are only marching backwards in that they adopt the fragments of antiquated theories and are preaching to the proletariat not the theory of struggle but the theory of submissiveness—submissiveness to the bitterest enemies of the proletariat, to the governments and bourgeois parties who never tire of finding new methods of persecuting socialists. Plekhanov, one of the founders and leaders of Russian social-democracy, was perfectly right when he subjected to merciless criticism the latest "Criticism" of Bernstein, whose views have now been rejected even by the representatives of the German workers at the Party Congress in Hanover [1899].

We know that on account of these words we shall be drenched with a flood of accusations; they will cry out that we want to turn the Socialist Party into a holy order of the "orthodox," who persecute the "heretics" for their aberrations from the "true dogma," for any independent opinion, etc. We know all these nonsensical phrases which have become the fashion nowadays. Yet there is no shadow of truth in them, no iota of sense. There can be no strong socialist party without a revolutionary theory which unites all socialists, from which the socialists draw their whole conviction, which they apply in their methods of fighting and working. To defend a theory of this kind, of the

truth of which one is completely convinced, against unfounded attacks and against attempts to debase it, does not mean being an enemy of criticism in general. We by no means regard the theory of Marx as perfect and inviolable; on the contrary, we are convinced that this theory has only laid the foundation stones of that science on which the socialists must continue to build in every direction, unless they wish to be left behind by life. We believe that it is particularly necessary for Russian socialists to work out the Marxist theory independently, for this theory only gives general precepts, the details of which must be applied in England otherwise than in France, in France otherwise than in Germany, and in Germany otherwise than in Russia. * * *

What are the main questions which arise in applying the common programme of all social-democrats to Russia?

We have already said that the essence of this programme consists in the organisation of the class struggle of the proletariat and in carrying on this struggle, the final aim of which is the seizure of political power by the proletariat and the construction of a socialist society. The class struggle of the proletariat is divided into: the economic fight (the fight against [the] individual capitalist, or against the individual groups of capitalists by the improvement of the position of the workers) and the political fight (the fight against the Government for the extension of the rights of the people, i.e., for democracy, and for the expansion of the political power of the proletariat). Some Russian social-democrats * * * regard the economic fight as incomparably more important and almost go so far as to postpone the political fight to a more or less distant future. This standpoint is quite wrong. All social-democrats are unanimous in believing that it is necessary to carry on an agitation among the workers on this basis, i.e., to help the workers in their daily fight against the employers, to direct their attention to all kinds and all cases of chicanery, and in this way to make clear to them the necessity of unity. To forget the political for the economic fight would, however, mean a digression from the most important principle of international social-democracy; it would mean forgetting what the whole history of the Labour movement has taught us. Fanatical adherents of the bourgeoisie and of the government which serves it, have indeed repeatedly tried to organise purely economic unions of workers and thus to deflect them from the "politics" of socialism. It is quite possible that the Russian Government will also be clever enough to do something of the kind, as it has always endeavored to throw some largesse or other sham presents to the people in order to prevent them becoming conscious that they are oppressed and are without rights.

No economic fight can give the workers a permanent improvement of their situation, it cannot, indeed, be carried on on a large scale unless the workers have the free right to call meetings, to join in unions, to have their own newspapers and to send their representatives to the National Assembly as do the workers in Germany and all European countries (with the exception of Turkey and Russia). In order, however, to obtain these rights, a political fight must be carried on. In Russia, not only the workers but all the citizens are deprived of political rights. Russia is an absolute monarchy. The Tsar alone promulgates laws, nominates officials and controls them. For this reason it seems as though in Russia the Tsar and the Tsarist Government were dependent on no class and cared for all equally. In reality, however, all the officials are chosen exclusively from the possessing class, and all are subject to the influence of the large capitalists who obtain whatever they want—the Ministers dance to the tune the large capitalists play. The Russian worker is bowed under a double yoke; he is robbed and plundered by the capitalists and the landowners, and, lest he should fight against them, he is bound hand and foot by the police, his mouth is gagged and any attempt to defend the rights of the people is followed by persecution. Any strike against a capitalist results in the military and police being let loose on the workers. Every economic fight of necessity turns into a political fight, and social-democracy must indissolubly combine the economic with the political fight into a united class struggle of the proletariat.

The first and chief aim of such a fight must be the conquest of political rights, the conquest of political freedom. Since the workers of St. Petersburg alone have succeeded, in spite of the inadequate support given them by the socialists, in obtaining concessions from the Government within a short time—the passing of a law for shortening the hours of work—the whole working class, led by a united "Russian Social-Democratic Labour Party," will be able, through obstinate fighting, to obtain incomparably more important concessions.

The Russian working class will see its way to carrying on an economic and political fight alone, even if no other class comes to its help. The workers are not alone, however, in the political fight. The fact that the people is absolutely without rights and the unbridled arbitrary rule of the officials rouses the indignation of all who have any pretensions to honesty and educations, who cannot reconcile themselves with the persecution of all free speech and all free thought; it rouses the indignation of the persecuted Poles, Finns, Jews, Russian sects, it rouses the indignation of small traders, of the industrialists, the peasants, of all who can nowhere find protection against the chicanery of the officials and the police. All these groups of the population are incapable of carrying on an obstinate political fight alone; if, however, the working class raises the banner of a fight of this kind it will be supported on all sides. Russian social-democracy will place itself at the head of all fights for the rights of the people, of all fights for democracy, and then it will be invincible.

*   *   *

REVIEW QUESTIONS

1. What tendencies within the socialist movement does Lenin reject here? Why?
2. Why, according to Lenin, must workers combine the fight for economic rights with the fight for political rights?

CLARA ZETKIN

FROM "Women's Work and the Organization of Trade Unions"

The German socialist Clara Zetkin (1857–1933) was well known throughout Europe for her ardent support of working women. Unlike the many left wing activists who rejected feminism in the belief that the workers' revolution would inevitably bring gender equality in its wake, Zetkin argued that an active commitment to women's rights must go hand in hand with the socialist struggle against capitalism. Although Zetkin was a strong supporter of women's right to vote, as a socialist she rejected the liberal feminism of middle-class suffragettes such as the Pankhursts (after the next selection) and instead focused her efforts on seeking solutions to the specific forms of economic oppression suffered by women as workers.

The following article appeared in Gleichheit *("Equality"), the highly successful German Socialist women's newspaper that Zetkin edited between 1892 and 1917. Responding to male labor organizers who saw low-paid women workers as competitors and who wished to exclude women from the industrial work force, Zetkin argues here that the socialist movement would benefit more if male workers sought to bring working women into trade union organizations.*

From *Clara Zetkin: Selected Writings,* edited by Phillip S. Foner, translated by Kai Schoenhals (New York: International, 1984).

*   *   *

In all capitalist countries, women's work in industry plays an ever larger role. The number of industrial branches in which women nowadays toil and drudge from morning till night increases with every year. Factories which have traditionally employed women, employ more and more women workers. It is not only that the number of all industrially employed women is constantly growing, but their number in relation to the men who are working in industry and trade is also on the increase.

Some branches of industry (one has only to think of clothing) are virtually dominated by women's labor which constantly reduces and replaces men's labor.

For understandable reasons, particularly during periods of recession (like the one we are experiencing right now), the number of women workers has increased in both relative and absolute terms whereas the number of employed male laborers has decreased.

*   *   *

The reasons for the constantly growing use of female laborers have been repeatedly pointed out: their cheapness and the improvement of the mechanical means and methods of production. The automatic machine, which in many cases does not even stand in need of having to be regulated, works with the powers of a giant, possesses unbelievable skill, speed and exactness and renders muscle power and acquired skills superfluous. The capitalist entrepreneur can employ only female labor at those places where he previously had to use male employees. And he just loves to hire women because female labor is cheap, much cheaper than male labor.

Even though the productive capacity of female workers does not lag behind that of male workers, the difference between men's and women's wages is very significant. The latter is often only half of the former and often only a third.

*　　*　　*

* * * [T]he living conditions of these female workers correspond to their miserable earnings. It is easily understandable that these customary starvation wages for female laborers push thousands of them from the proletariat into the lumpenproletariat.[1] Their dire straits force some of them to take up part-time or temporary prostitution so that by selling their bodies, they may earn the piece of bread that they cannot secure by the sale of their labor.

But it is not just the women workers who suffer because of the miserable payment of their labor. The male workers, too, suffer because of it. As a consequence of their low wages, the women are transformed from mere competitors into unfair competitors who push down the wages of men. Cheap women's labor eliminates the work of men and if the men want to continue to earn their daily bread, they must put up with low wages. Thus women's work is not only a cheap form of labor, it also cheapens the work of men and for that reason it is doubly appreciated by the capitalist, who craves profits.

*　　*　　*

The transfer of hundreds of thousands of female laborers to the modernized means of production that increase productivity ten or even a hundredfold should have resulted (and did result

in some cases) in a higher standard of living for the proletariat, given a rationally organized society. But as far as the proletariat is concerned, capitalism has changed blessing into curse and wealth into bitter poverty. The economic advantages of the industrial activity of proletarian women only aid the tiny minority of the sacrosanct guild of coupon clippers and extortionists of profit.

Frightened by the economic consequences of women's work and the abuses connected with it, organized labor demanded for a while the prohibition of female labor. It was viewing this question merely from the narrow viewpoint of the wage question. Thanks to Socialist propaganda, the class-conscious proletariat has learned to view this question from another angle, from the angle of its historical importance for the liberation of women and the liberation of the proletariat. It understands now how impossible it is to abolish the industrial labor of women. Thus it has dropped its former demand and it attempts to lessen the bad economic consequences of women's work within capitalist society (and only within it!) by two other means; by the legal protection of female workers and by their inclusion in trade union organizations. We have already mentioned above the necessity and the advantageous effects of the legal protection of women workers. * * *

Given the fact that many thousands of female workers are active in industry, it is vital for the trade unions to incorporate them into their movement. In individual industries where female labor plays an important role, any movement advocating better wages, shorter working hours, etc., would be doomed from the start because of the attitude of those women workers who are not organized. Battles which began propitiously enough, ended up in failure because the employers were able to play off non-union female workers against those that are organized in unions. These non-union workers continued to work (or took up work) under any conditions, which transformed them from competitors in dirty work to scabs.

It is not only because of the successful economic battles of trade unions that women should be included in them. The improvement of the

---

[1] In Marxist terminology, the *lumpenproletariat* consists of the lowest ranks of the working class. It verges on being a criminal underclass and is disinclined to join with honest workers in the struggle against capitalism.

starvation wages of female workers and the limitation of competition among them requires their organization into unions.

The fact that the pay for female labor is so much lower than that of male labor has a variety of causes. Certainly one of the reasons for these poor wages for women is the circumstance that female workers are practically unorganized. They lack the strength which comes with unity. They lack the courage, the feeling of power, the spirit of resistance and the ability to resist which is produced by the strength of an organization in which the individual fights for everybody and everybody fights for the individual. Furthermore, they lack the enlightenment and the training which an organization provides. Without an understanding of modern economic life in whose machinery they are inextricably caught up, they will neither be able to take advantage of periods of boom through conscious, calculating and unified conduct nor will they be able to protect themselves against the disadvantages occurring during periods of economic recession. If, under the pressure of unbearable conditions they finally fight back, they usually do so at an inopportune moment and in a disorganized fashion.

This situation exercises a great influence upon the miserable state of women's work and is further reflected by the bitterness that male workers feel about women's competition. Thus in the interest of both men and women workers, it is urgently recommended that the latter be included in the trade unions. The larger the number of organized female workers who fight shoulder to shoulder with their comrades from the factory or workshop for better working conditions, the sooner and the greater will women's wages rise so that soon there may be the realization of the principle: Equal pay for equal work regardless of the difference in sex. The organized female worker who has become the equal of the male worker ceases to be his scab competitor.

The unionized male workers realize more and more just how important it is that the female workers are accepted into the ranks of their organization. During these past few years, there was no lack of effort on the part of the unions in regard to this endeavor. And yet how little has been accomplished and how incredibly much remains to be done in this respect.

*   *   *

Even in those industrial branches in which the trade union organization of women began, these organizations are still in their infancy.

*   *   *

As far as the percentage of female membership is concerned, the Tobacco Workers rank first, and yet these women workers do not even constitute a fourth of its entire membership. In 1882, 43.1% of all tobacco industry workers were women. In the other four trade unions which come next, as far as the percentage of women that work in the industries they represent are concerned, women workers do not even constitute 10% of the membership. The Organization of Gold and Silver Workers does not have a female membership of even 5% even though there are large numbers of women workers who are employed by the gold and silver industry. In 1882, 60% of all laborers in spinning mills and 30% of all laborers in weaving mills happened to be women, yet the percentage of them who were unionized amounted to only 9½%. These numbers, in conjunction with the slave wages which generally prevail in the textile industry, speak whole volumes about the necessity of unionizing women.

In recognition of this necessity, the trade unions should use all of their energies to work for the inclusion of women in their organizations.

We certainly do not fail to recognize the difficulties raised by women workers which are detrimental to the solution of this problem. Stupid resignation, lack of a feeling of solidarity, shyness, prejudices of all kinds and fear of the factory tyrant keep many women from joining unions. Even more than the just mentioned factors, the lack of time on the part of female workers represents a major obstacle against their mass organization because women are house as well as factory slaves and are forced to bear a double workload. The economic developments, however, as well as the increasing acuteness of the class struggle, educate both male and female laborers and force them to overcome the above-mentioned difficulties. * * *

Theoretically, most male union members admit that the common unionization of both male and female workers of the same trade has become an unavoidable necessity. In practice, however, many of them do not make the effort that they could be making. Rather there are only a few unions and within them only certain individuals who pursue with energy and perseverance the organization of female workers. The majority of trade union members give them precious little support. They treat such endeavors as a hobby which should be tolerated but not supported "as long as there are still so many indifferent non-union male workers." This point of view is totally wrong.

The unionization of women workers will make significant progress only when it is no longer merely aided by the few, but by every single union member making every effort to enlist their female colleagues from factory and workshop. In order to fulfill this task, two things are necessary. The male workers must stop viewing the female worker primarily as a woman to be courted if she is young, beautiful, pleasant and cheerful (or not). They must stop (depending on their degree of culture or lack of it) molesting them with crude and fresh sexual advances. The workers must rather get accustomed to treat female laborers primarily as

female proletarians, as working-class comrades fighting class slavery and as equal and indispensable co-fighters in the class struggle. The unions make such a big thing out of having all of the members and followers of the political party become members of the unions. It seems to us that it would be much more important to put the emphasis on enrolling the broad, amorphous masses in the labor movement. In our opinion, the main task of the unions is the enlightenment, disciplining and education of all workers for the class struggle. In view of the increasing use of female labor and the subsequent results, the labor movement will surely commit suicide if, in its effort to enroll the broad masses of the proletariat, it does not pay the same amount of attention to female workers as it does to male ones.

REVIEW QUESTIONS

1. To what extent does Zetkin's discussion of women's work reflect the changes in industrial work conditions brought about by the second industrial revolution?
2. According to Zetkin, what factors cause divisions between male and female workers?
3. How does Zetkin suggest that socialist workers build solidarity within their ranks?
4. What sort of socialist is Zetkin? What sort of feminist is she?

GEORGES SOREL

FROM *Reflections on Violence*

Although Marxist socialism was the dominant political ideology of workers, syndicalism was widely preferred in areas of France, Spain, and Italy. Syndicalism grew out of trade union associations that espoused the utopian vision of one day controlling their industries and, eventually, the political state. The strike became the central weapon of syndicalism, but it was the general strike that made syndicalism revolu-

tionary. The thousands of strikes in Europe at the end of the century offered the potential of one mighty, total work stoppage that would ruin capitalism and dismantle the state. Georges Sorel (1847–1922) wrote his treatise on syndicalism in 1908. The following excerpt includes Sorel's important notion of the general strike as a mythic belief, the widespread acceptance of which would prompt collective action by workers as well as soften employers' resolve against concessions.

From *Reflections on Violence,* by Georges Sorel, edited by T. E. Hulme (New York: Huebsch, 1914).

*　　*　　*

Against this noisy, garrulous, and lying Socialism, which is exploited by ambitious people of every description, which amuses a few buffoons, and which is admired by decadents—revolutionary Syndicalism takes its stand, and endeavours, on the contrary, to leave nothing in a state of indecision; its ideas are honestly expressed, without trickery and without mental reservations; no attempt is made to dilute doctrines by a stream of confused commentaries. Syndicalism endeavours to employ methods of expression which throw a full light on things, which put them exactly in the place assigned to them by their nature, and which bring out the whole value of the forces in play. Oppositions, instead of being glozed over, must be thrown into sharp relief if we desire to obtain a clear idea of the Syndicalist movement; the groups which are struggling one against the other must be shown as separate and as compact as possible; in short, the movements of the revolted masses must be represented in such a way that the soul of the revolutionaries may receive a deep and lasting impression.

These results could not be produced in any very certain manner by the use of ordinary language; use must be made of a body of images which, *by intuition alone,* and before any considered analyses are made, is capable of evoking as an undivided whole the mass of sentiments which corresponds to the different manifestations of the war undertaken by Socialism against modern society. The Syndicalists solve this problem perfectly, by concentrating the whole of Socialism in the drama of the general strike; there is thus no longer any place for the reconciliation of contraries in the equivocations of the professors; everything is clearly mapped out, so that only one interpretation of Socialism is possible. This method has all the advantages which "integral" knowledge has over analysis, according to the doctrine of Bergson; and perhaps it would not be possible to cite another example which would so perfectly demonstrate the value of the famous professor's doctrines.

The possibility of the actual realisation of the general strike has been much discussed; it has been stated that the Socialist war could not be decided in one single battle. To the people who think themselves cautious, practical, and scientific the difficulty of setting great masses of the proletariat in motion at the same moment seems prodigious; they have analysed the difficulties of detail which such an enormous struggle would present. It is the opinion of the Socialist-sociologists, as also of the politicians, that the general strike is a popular dream, characteristic of the beginnings of a working-class movement; we have had quoted against us the authority of Sidney Webb, who has decreed that the general strike is an illusion of youth, of which the English workers—whom the monopolists of sociology have so often presented to us as the depositaries of the true conception of the working-class movement—soon rid themselves.

*　　*　　*

And yet without leaving the present, without reasoning about this future, which seems for ever condemned to escape our reason, we should be unable to act at all. Experience shows that the *framing of a future, in some indeterminate time,* may, when it is done in a certain way, be very effective, and have very few inconveniences; this happens when the anticipations of the future take the form of those myths, which enclose with them all the strongest inclinations of a people, of a party or of a class, inclinations which recur to the mind with the insistence of instincts in all the circumstances of life; and which give an aspect of complete reality to the hopes of immediate action by which, more easily than by any other method, men can reform their desires, passions, and mental activity. We know, moreover, that these social myths in no way prevent a man profiting by the observations which he makes in the course of his life, and form no obstacle to the pursuit of his normal occupations.

The truth of this may be shown by numerous examples.

The first Christians expected the return of Christ and the total ruin of the pagan world, with the inauguration of the kingdom of the saints, at the end of the first generation. The catastrophe did not come to pass, but Christian thought profited so greatly from the apocalyptic myth that certain contemporary scholars maintain that the whole preaching of Christ referred solely to this one point. The hopes which Luther and Calvin had formed of the religious exaltation of Europe were by no means realised; these fathers of the Reformation very soon seemed men of a past era; for present-day Protestants they belong rather to the Middle Ages than to modern times, and the problems which troubled them most occupy very little place in contemporary Protestantism. Must we for that reason deny the immense result which came from their dreams of Christian renovation?

*   *   *

In our own times Mazzini pursued what the wiseacres of his time called a mad chimera; but it can no longer be denied that, without Mazzini, Italy would never have become a great power, and

that he did more for Italian unity than Cavour and all the politicians of his school.

*   *   *

The myth must be judged as a means of acting on the present; any attempt to discuss how far it can be taken literally as future history is devoid of sense. *It is the myth in its entirety which is alone important:* its parts are only of interest in so far as they bring out the main idea. No useful purpose is served, therefore, in arguing about the incidents which may occur in the course of a social war, and about the decisive conflicts which may give victory to the proletariat; even supposing the revolutionaries to have been wholly and entirely deluded in setting up this imaginary picture of the general strike, this picture may yet have been, in the course of the preparation for the Revolution, a great element of strength, if it has embraced all the aspirations of Socialism, and if it has given to the whole body of Revolutionary thought a precision and a rigidity which no other method of thought could have given.

To estimate, then, the significance of the idea of the general strike, all the methods of discussion which are current among politicians, sociologists, or people with pretensions to political science, must be abandoned. Everything which its opponents endeavour to establish may be conceded to them, without reducing in any way the value of the theory which they think they have refuted. The question whether the general strike is a partial reality, or only a product of popular imagination, is of little importance. All that it is necessary to know is, whether the general strike contains everything that the Socialist doctrine expects of the revolutionary proletariat.

To solve this question we are no longer compelled to argue learnedly about the future; we are not obliged to indulge in lofty reflections about philosophy, history, or economics; we are not on the plane of theories, and we can remain on the level of observable facts. We have to question men who take a very active part in the real revolutionary movement amidst the proletariat, men who do not aspire to climb into the middle class and whose mind is not dominated by corporative prejudices. These men may be deceived about an infinite number of political, economical, or moral questions; but their testimony is decisive, sovereign, and irrefutable when it is a question of knowing what are the ideas which most powerfully move them and their comrades, which most appeal to them as being identical with their socialistic conceptions, and thanks to which their reason, their hopes, and their way of looking at particular facts seem to make but one indivisible unity.

Thanks to these men, we know that the general strike is indeed what I have said: the *myth* in which Socialism is wholly comprised, *i.e.* a body of images capable of evoking instinctively all the sentiments which correspond to the different manifestations of the war undertaken by Socialism against modern society. Strikes have engendered in the proletariat the noblest, deepest, and most moving sentiments that they possess; the general strike groups them all in a co-ordinated picture, and, by bringing them together, gives to each one of them its maximum of intensity; appealing to their painful memories of particular conflicts, it colours with an intense life all the details of the composition presented to consciousness. We thus obtain that intuition of Socialism which language cannot give us with perfect clearness—and we obtain it as a whole, perceived instantaneously.

We may urge yet another piece of evidence to prove the power of the idea of the general strike. If that idea were a pure chimera, as is so frequently said, Parliamentary Socialists would not attack it with such heat; I do not remember that they ever attacked the senseless hopes which the Utopists have always held up before the dazzled eyes of the people.

*   *   *

They struggle against the conception of the general strike, because they recognise, in the course of their propagandist rounds, that this conception is so admirably adapted to the working-class mind that there is a possibility of its dominating the latter in the most absolute manner, thus leaving no place for the desires which the Parliamentarians are able to satisfy. They perceive that this idea is so effective as a motive force that once it has entered the minds of the people they can no longer be controlled by leaders, and that thus the power of the deputies would be reduced to nothing. In short, they feel in a vague way that the whole Socialist movement might easily be absorbed by the general strike, which would render useless all those compromises between political groups in view of which the Parliamentary régime has been built up.

The opposition it meets with from official Socialists, therefore, furnishes a confirmation of our first inquiry into the scope of the general strike.

*   *   *

REVIEW QUESTIONS

1. How does Sorel differentiate between socialism and syndicalism?
2. For Sorel, what is the real significance of the general strike?
3. How is syndicalism compared with Christianity and nationalism?
4. What is the importance of myth in political struggle?

"THE PREVENTION OF HUNGER STRIKES"

In the decade prior to the First World War, the political campaign for women's suffrage reached a feverish pitch in Great Britain. Emmeline Pankhurst and followers of the Women's Social and Political Union (WSPU) embarked on a course of militant action that included damaging private property, disrupting meetings, and attempting entry into Parliament. When imprisoned and denied the status of political prisoners, WSPU women organized hunger strikes to press their case. In response, the government ordered force feedings of the prisoners, a role that cast the Liberal government of England as a cruel political hypocrite. The cartoon captures the horrific dimensions of English political life on the eve of the war. How did this cartoon criticize both the British government and the suffragette movement?

EMMELINE PANKHURST

FROM The Why We Are Militant Speech

In 1903, Emmeline Pankhurst (1858–1928) founded the Women's Social and Political Union, an organization that advocated militancy and direct action to promote the cause of female suffrage, which had become an international movement since the 1890s. Angered by the insouciance of the British political establishment, which remained unphased by the massive petitions and peaceful demonstrations of suffragettes, Pankhurst's association organized hunger strikes and assaults on private property to signify the gravity of the matter. In the following speech of 21 October 1913, delivered in New York, Pankhurst justified the tactics of the Women's Social and Political Union.

From *Suffrage and the Pankhursts,* edited by Jane Marcus (London: Routledge and Paul, 1987).

I know that in your minds there are questions like these; you are saying, "Woman Suffrage is sure to come; the emancipation of humanity is an evolutionary process, and how is it that some women, instead of trusting to that evolution, instead of educating the masses of people of their country, instead of educating their own sex to prepare them for citizenship, how is it that these militant women are using violence and upsetting the business arrangements of the country in their undue impatience to attain their end?"

Let me try to explain to you the situation.

Although we have a so-called democracy, and so called representative government there, England is the most conservative country on earth. Why, your forefathers found that out a great many years ago! If you had passed your life in England as I have, you would know that there are certain words which certainly, during the last two generations, certainly till about ten years ago, aroused a feeling of horror and fear in the minds of the mass of the people. The word revolution, for instance, was identified in England with all kind of horrible ideas. The idea of change, the idea of unsettling the established order of things was repugnant.

*   *   *

The extensions of the franchise to the men of my country have been preceded by very great violence, by something like a revolution, by something like civil war. In 1832, you know we were on the edge of a civil war and on the edge of revolution, and it was at the point of the sword —no, not at the point of the sword—it was after the practice of arson on so large a scale that half the city of Bristol was burned down in a single night, it was because more and greater violence and arson were feared that the Reform Bill of 1832 was allowed to pass into law. In 1867, John Bright urged the people of London to crowd the approaches to the Houses of Parliament in order to show their determination, and he said that if they did that no Parliament, however obdurate, could resist their just demands. Rioting went on all over the country, and as the result of that rioting, as the result of that unrest, which resulted in the pulling down of the Hyde Park railings, as a result of the fear of more rioting and violence the Reform Act of 1867 was put upon the statute books.

In 1884 came the turn of the agricultural labourer. Joseph Chamberlain, who afterwards became a very conservative person, threatened that, unless the vote was given to the agricultural labourer, he would march 100,000 men from Birmingham to know the reason why. Rioting was threatened and feared, and so the agricultural labourers got the vote.

Meanwhile, during the '80's, women, like men, were asking for the franchise. Appeals, larger and more numerous than for any other reform, were presented in support of Woman's Suffrage. Meetings of the great corporations, great town councils, and city councils, passed resolutions asking that women should have the vote. More meetings were held, and larger, for Woman Suffrage than were held for votes for men, and yet the women did not get it. Men got the vote because they were and would be violent. The women did not get it because they were constitutional and law-abiding. Why, is it not evident to everyone that people who are patient where mis-government is concerned may go on being patient! Why should anyone trouble to help them? I take to myself some shame that through all those years, at any rate from the early '80's, when I first came into the Suffrage movement, I did not learn my political lessons.

I believed, as many women still in England believe, that women could get their way in some mysterious manner, by purely peaceful methods. We have been so accustomed, we women, to accept one standard for men and another standard for women, that we have even applied that variation of standard to the injury of our political welfare.

Having had better opportunities of education, and having had some training in politics, having in political life come so near to the "superior" being as to see that he was not altogether such a fount of wisdom as they had supposed, that he had his human weaknesses as we had, the twentieth century women began to say to themselves. "Is it not time, since our methods have failed and the men's have succeeded, that we should take a leaf out of their political book?"

We were led to that conclusion, we older women, by the advice of the young—you know there is a French proverb which says, "If youth knew; if age could," but I think that when you can bring together youth and age, as we have done, and get them to adopt the same methods and take the same point of view, then you are on the high road to success.

Well, we in Great Britain, on the eve of the General Election of 1905, a mere handful of us— why, you could almost count us on the fingers of both hands—set out on the wonderful adventure of forcing the strongest Government of modern times to give the women the vote. Only a few in number; we were not strong in influence, and we had hardly any money, and yet we quite gaily made our little banners with the words "Votes for Women" upon them, and we set out to win the enfranchisement of the women of our country.

The Suffrage movement was almost dead. The women had lost heart. You could not get a Suffrage meeting that was attended by members of the general public. We used to have about 24 adherents in the front row. We carried our resolutions and heard no more about them.

Two women changed that in a twinkling of an eye at a great Liberal demonstration in Manchester, where a Liberal leader, Sir Edward Grey, was explaining the programme to be carried out during the Liberals' next turn of office. The two women put the fateful question, "When are you going to give votes to women?" and refused to sit down until they had been answered. These two women were sent to gaol, and from that day to this the women's movement, both militant and constitutional, has never looked back. We had little more than one moribund society for Woman Suffrage in those days. Now we have nearly 50 societies for Woman Suffrage, and they are large in membership, they are rich in money, and their ranks are swelling every day that passes. That is how militancy has put back the clock of Woman Suffrage in Great Britain.

Now, some of you have said how wicked it is (the immigration commissioners told me that on Saturday afternoon), how wicked it is to attack the property of private individuals who have done us no harm. Well, you know there is a proverb which says that you cannot make omelettes without breaking eggs. I wish we could.

I want to say here and now that the only justification for violence, the only justification for damage to property, the only justification for risk to the comfort of other human beings is the fact that you have tried all other available means and have failed to secure justice, and as a law-abiding person—and I am by nature a law-abiding person, as one hating violence, hating disorder—I want to say that from the moment we began our militant agitation to this day I have felt absolutely guiltless in this matter.

I tell you that in Great Britain there is no other way. We can show intolerable grievances. The Chancellor of the Exchequer, Mr Lloyd George, who is no friend of the woman's movement, although a professed one, said a very true thing when speaking of the grievances of his own country, of Wales. He said that there comes a time in the life of human beings suffering from intolerable grievances when the only way to maintain their self respect is to revolt against that injustice.

Well, I say the time is long past when it became necessary for women to revolt in order to maintain their self respect in Great Britain. The women who are waging this war are women who would fight, if it were only for the idea of liberty—if it were only that they might be free citizens of a free country—I myself would fight for that idea alone. But we have, in addition to this love of freedom, intolerable grievances to redress.

*   *   *

All my life I have tried to understand why it is that men who value their citizenship as their dearest possession seem to think citizenship ridiculous when it is to be applied to the women of their race. And I find an explanation, and it is the only one I can think of. It came to me when I was in a prison cell, remembering how I had seen men laugh at the idea of women going to prison. Why they would confess they could not bear a cell door to be shut upon themselves for a single hour without asking to be let out. A thought came to me in my prison cell, and it was this: that to men women

are not human beings like themselves. Some men think we are superhuman; they put us on pedestals; they revere us; they think we are too fine and too delicate to come down into the hurly-burly of life. Other men think us sub-human; they think we are a strange species unfortunately having to exist for the perpetuation of the race. They think that we are fit for drudgery, but that in some strange way our minds are not like theirs, our love for great things is not like theirs, and so we are a sort of sub-human species.

We are neither superhuman nor are we sub-human. We are just human beings like yourselves.

*   *   *

When we were patient, when we believed in argument and persuasion, they said, "You don't really want it because, if you did, you would do something unmistakable to show you were determined to have it." And then when we did something unmistakable they said, "You are behaving so badly that you show you are not fit for it."

Now, gentlemen, in your heart of hearts you do not believe that. You know perfectly well that there never was a thing worth having that was not worth fighting for. You know perfectly well that if the situation were reversed, if you had no constitutional rights and we had all of them, if you had the duty of paying and obeying and trying to look as pleasant, and we were the proud citizens who could decide our fate and yours, because we knew what was good for you better than you knew yourselves, you know perfectly well that you wouldn't stand it for a single day, and you would be perfectly justified in rebelling against such intolerable conditions.

Well, in Great Britain, we have tried persuasion, we have tried the plan of showing (by going upon public bodies, where they allowed us to do work they hadn't much time to do themselves) that we are capable people. We did it in the hope that we should convince them and persuade them to do the right and proper thing. But we had all our labour for our pains, and now we are fighting for our rights, and we are growing stronger and better women in the process. We are getting more fit to use our rights because we have such difficulty in getting them.

* * *

People have said that women could never vote, never share in the government, because government rests upon force. We have proved that is not true. Government rests not upon force; government rests upon the consent of the governed; and the weakest woman, the very poorest woman, if she withholds her consent cannot be governed.

They sent me to prison, to penal servitude for three years. I came out of prison at the end of nine days. I broke my prison bars. Four times they took me back again; four times I burst the prison door open again. And I left England openly to come and visit America, with only three or four weeks of the three years' sentence of penal servitude served. Have we not proved, then, that they cannot govern human beings who withhold their consent?

And so we are glad we have had the fighting experience, and we are glad to do all the fighting for all the women all over the world. All that we ask of you is to back us up. We ask you to show that although, perhaps, you may not mean to fight as we do, yet you understand the meaning of our fight; that you realise we are women fighting for a great idea; that we wish the betterment of the human race, and that we believe this betterment is coming through the emancipation and uplifting of women.

REVIEW QUESTIONS

1. What precedents in history does Pankurst cite to justify her cause and tactics?
2. According to Pankhurst, what is the catalyst of political reform?
3. Why were contemporaries outraged by the idea of women's undertaking militant civil disobedience and going to prison for political beliefs?
4. Compare the positions and pleas of Wollstonecraft (Chapter 19) and Pankhurst.
5. What had changed over the course of the century?

HENRIK IBSEN

FROM *A Doll's House*

Henrik Ibsen (1828–1906) had a keen eye for the plight of individuals trapped in the conventions and institutions of bourgeois life. His drama A Doll's House *(1879) confronts the legal and financial restrictions that subordinated women to their husbands and how such limitations affected individual lives. The play was controversial in its time for its depiction of the bourgeois marriage as hypocritical and hollow. The scene below follows an epiphany of Nora, the wife of a respectable bourgeois banker, who slowly grasps that she does not genuinely know her husband. This realization grows out the complex set of events that produces the play's climax. Her husband, Torvald Helmer, learns that his wife is faced with the prospect of arrest for forging her father's signature for a loan. Nora took on this debt to save her hus-*

band's finances during his long illness and kept it a secret from him to preserve his sense of honor. Expecting gratitude and a chivalrous defense of her actions and motives, Nora received instead a severe rebuke for her moral turpitude. Yet when the threat of exposure, arrest, and public shame vanish, he forgives her and considers the matter forgotten. The incident, however, produces a profound change of heart for Nora.

From *Plays: Two*, by Henrik Ibsen, translated by Michael Meyer (London: Methuen, 1990).

*   *   *

HELMER. No, don't go—(*Looks in.*) What are you doing there?

NORA (*offstage*). Taking off my fancy dress.

HELMER (*by the open door*). Yes, do that. Try to calm yourself and get your balance again, my frightened little songbird. Don't be afraid. I have broad wings to shield you. (*Begins to walk around near the door.*) How lovely and peaceful this little home of ours is, Nora. You are safe here; I shall watch over you like a hunted dove which I have snatched unharmed from the claws of the falcon. Your wildly beating little heart shall find peace with me. It will happen, Nora; it will take time, but it will happen, believe me. Tomorrow all this will seem quite different. Soon everything will be as it was before. I shall no longer need to remind you that I have forgiven you; your own heart will tell you that it is true. Do you really think I could ever bring myself to disown you, or even to reproach you? Ah, Nora, you don't understand what goes on in a husband's heart. There is something indescribably wonderful and satisfying for a husband in knowing that he has forgiven his wife—forgiven her unreservedly, from the bottom of his heart. It means that she has become his property in a double sense; he has, as it were, brought her into the world anew; she is now not only his wife but also his child. From now on that is what you shall be to me, my poor, helpless, bewildered little creature. Never be frightened of anything again, Nora. Just open your heart to me. I shall be both your will and your conscience. What's this? Not in bed? Have you changed?

NORA (*in her everyday dress*). Yes, Torvald. I've changed.

HELMER. But why now—so late—?

NORA. I shall not sleep tonight.

HELMER. But, my dear Nora—

NORA (*looks at her watch*). It isn't that late. Sit down there, Torvald. You and I have a lot to talk about.

She sits down on one side of the table.

HELMER. Nora, what does this mean? You look quite drawn—

NORA. Sit down. It's going to take a long time. I've a lot to say to you.

HELMER (*sits down on the other side of the table*). You alarm me, Nora. I don't understand you.

NORA. No, that's just it. You don't understand me. And I've never understood you—until this evening. No, don't interrupt me. Just listen to what I have to say. You and I have got to face facts, Torvald.

HELMER. What do you mean by that?

NORA (*after a short silence*). Doesn't anything strike you about the way we're sitting here?

HELMER. What?

NORA. We've been married for eight years. Does it occur to you that this is the first time we two, you and I, man and wife, have ever had a serious talk together?

HELMER. Serious? What do you mean, serious?

NORA. In eight whole years—no, longer—ever since we first met—we have never exchanged a serious word on a serious subject.

HELMER. Did you expect me to drag you into all my worries—worries you couldn't possibly have helped me with?

NORA. I'm not talking about worries. I'm simply

saying that we have never sat down seriously to try to get to the bottom of anything.

HELMER. But, my dear Nora, what on earth has that got to do with you?

NORA. That's just the point. You have never understood me. A great wrong has been done to me, Torvald. First by papa, and then by you.

HELMER. What? But we two have loved you more than anyone in the world!

NORA (*shakes her head*). You have never loved me. You just thought it was fun to be in love with me.

HELMER. Nora, what kind of a way is this to talk?

NORA. It's the truth, Torvald. When I lived with papa, he used to tell me what he thought about everything, so that I never had any opinions but his. And if I did have any of my own, I kept them quiet, because he wouldn't have liked them. He called me his little doll, and he played with me just the way I played with my dolls. Then I came here to live in your house—

HELMER. What kind of a way is that to describe our marriage?

NORA (*undisturbed*). I mean, then I passed from papa's hands into yours. You arranged everything the way you wanted it, so that I simply took over your taste in everything—or pretended I did—I don't really know—I think it was a little of both—first one and then the other. Now I look back on it, it's as if I've been living here like a pauper, from hand to mouth. I performed tricks for you, and you gave me food and drink. But that was how you wanted it. You and papa have done me a great wrong. It's your fault that I have done nothing with my life.

HELMER. Nora, how can you be so unreasonable and ungrateful? Haven't you been happy here?

NORA. No; never. I used to think I was. But I haven't ever been happy.

HELMER. Not—not happy?

NORA. No. I've just had fun. You've always been very kind to me. But our home has never been anything but a playroom. I've been your doll-wife, just as I used to be papa's doll-child. And the children have been my dolls. I used to think

it was fun when you came in and played with me, just as they think it's fun when I go in and play games with them. That's all our marriage has been, Torvald.

HELMER. There may be a little truth in what you say, though you exaggerate and romanticize. But from now on it'll be different. Playtime is over. Now the time has come for education.

NORA. Whose education? Mine or the children's?

HELMER. Both yours and the children's, my dearest Nora.

NORA. Oh, Torvald, you're not the man to educate me into being the right wife for you.

HELMER. How can you say that?

NORA. And what about me? Am I fit to educate the children?

HELMER. Nora!

NORA. Didn't you say yourself a few minutes ago that you dare not leave them in my charge?

HELMER. In a moment of excitement. Surely you don't think I meant it seriously?

NORA. Yes. You were perfectly right. I'm not fitted to educate them. There's something else I must do first. I must educate myself. And you can't help me with that. It's something I must do by myself. That's why I'm leaving you.

HELMER (*jumps up*). What did you say?

NORA. I must stand on my own feet if I am to find out the truth about myself and about life. So I can't go on living here with you any longer.

HELMER. Nora, Nora!

NORA. I'm leaving you now, at once. Christine will put me up for tonight—

HELMER. You're out of your mind! You can't do this! I forbid you!

NORA. It's no use your trying to forbid me any more. I shall take with me nothing but what is mine. I don't want anything from you, now or ever.

HELMER. What kind of madness is this?

NORA. Tomorrow I shall go home—I mean, to where I was born. It'll be easiest for me to find some kind of a job there.

HELMER. But you're blind! You've no experience of the world—

NORA. I must try to get some, Torvald.

HELMER. But to leave your home, your husband, your children! Have you thought what people will say?

NORA. I can't help that. I only know that I must do this.

HELMER. But this is monstrous! Can you neglect your most sacred duties?

NORA. What do you call my most sacred duties?

HELMER. Do I have to tell you? Your duties towards your husband, and your children.

NORA. I have another duty which is equally sacred.

HELMER. You have not. What on earth could that be?

NORA. My duty towards myself.

HELMER. First and foremost you are a wife and mother.

NORA. I don't believe that any longer. I believe that I am first and foremost a human being, like you—or anyway, that I must try to become one. I know most people think as you do, Torvald, and I know there's something of the sort to be found in books. But I'm no longer prepared to accept what people say and what's written in books. I must think things out for myself, and try to find my own answer.

HELMER. Do you need to ask where your duty lies in your own home? Haven't you an infallible guide in such matters—your religion?

NORA. Oh, Torvald, I don't really know what religion means.

HELMER. What are you saying?

NORA. I only know what Pastor Hansen told me when I went to confirmation. He explained that religion meant this and that. When I get away from all this and can think things out on my own, that's one of the questions I want to look into. I want to find out whether what Pastor Hansen said was right—or anyway, whether it is right for me.

HELMER. But it's unheard of for so young a woman to behave like this! If religion cannot guide you, let me at least appeal to your conscience. I presume you have some moral feelings left? Or—perhaps you haven't? Well, answer me.

NORA. Oh, Torvald, that isn't an easy question to answer. I simply don't know. I don't know where I am in these matters. I only know that these things mean something quite different to me from what they do to you. I've learned now that certain laws are different from what I'd imagined them to be; but I can't accept that such laws can be right. Has a woman really not the right to spare her dying father pain, or save her husband's life? I can't believe that.

HELMER. You're talking like a child. You don't understand how society works.

NORA. No, I don't. But now I intend to learn. I must try to satisfy myself which is right, society or I.

HELMER. Nora, you're ill. You're feverish. I almost believe you're out of your mind.

NORA. I've never felt so sane and sure in my life.

*   *   *

REVIEW QUESTIONS

1. What are Helmer's assumptions about the relationship between husband and wife?
2. What disturbs Nora most about her relationship with Helmer?
3. What does Nora realize about herself and her life?
4. What social criticisms are embedded in this dialogue?

MAN · IS · BVT · A · WORM·

"MAN IS BUT A WORM" (1881)

Charles Darwin's path-breaking Origin of the Species *(1859) was followed up with his* Descent of Man *in 1871, which applied his theory of natural selection to the evolution of the human species. The implication that man descended from apes was by far the most controversial aspect of his larger argument on natural selection. Illustrating the cultural disquiet about the reconfigured relationship of humankind to the animal world, this cartoon from* Punch, *an English satirical magazine, parodied Darwin with its version of evolution, from worm to gentleman. What beliefs and social structures might Darwin's theories have threatened to undermine?*

CHARLES DARWIN

FROM *The Origin of Species*

The impact of the work of Charles Darwin (1809–1882) cannot be underestimated. The theory of natural selection not only framed the modern view of evolution but also diminished the authority of the Bible in modern thinking. Darwin's theory of how species adapted and evolved over time grew out of his five-year journey on the HMS Beagle *(1831–1836) as the ship's naturalist. Published in 1859,* The Origin of Species *was followed by* The Descent of Man *in 1871, which applied the theory of evolution to humans. Darwin's argument that humans descended from apes shocked a Victorian society teethed on Genesis, the biblical creation myth. The following selection comes from the conclusion of* The Origin of Species.

From *The Origin of Species,* by Charles Darwin (New York: Penguin Books, 1859).

*　　*　　*

Chapter XIV
Recapitulation and Conclusion

*　　*　　*

As this whole volume is one long argument, it may be convenient to the reader to have the leading facts and inferences briefly recapitulated.

That many and grave objections may be advanced against the theory of descent with modification through natural selection, I do not deny. I have endeavoured to give to them their full force. Nothing at first can appear more difficult to believe than that the more complex organs and instincts should have been perfected, not by means superior to, though analogous with, human reason, but by the accumulation of innumerable slight variations, each good for the individual possessor. Nevertheless, this difficulty, though appearing to our imagination insuperably great, cannot be considered real if we admit the following propositions, namely, that gradations in the perfection of any organ or instinct, which we may consider, either do now exist or could have existed, each good of its kind, that all organs and instincts are, in ever so slight a degree, variable, and, lastly, that there is a struggle for existence leading to the preservation of each profitable deviation of structure or instinct. The truth of these propositions cannot, I think, be disputed.

It is, no doubt, extremely difficult even to conjecture by what gradations many structures have been perfected, more especially amongst broken and failing groups of organic beings; but we see so many strange gradations in nature, as is proclaimed by the canon, 'Natura non facit saltum,' that we ought to be extremely cautious in saying that any organ or instinct, or any whole being, could not have arrived at its present state by many graduated steps. There are, it must be admitted, cases of special difficulty on the theory of natural selection; and one of the most curious of these is the existence of two or three defined castes of workers or sterile females in the same community of ants; but I have attempted to show how this difficulty can be mastered.

*　　*　　*

As on the theory of natural selection an interminable number of intermediate forms must have existed, linking together all the species in each group by gradations as fine as our present varieties, it may be asked, Why do we not see these linking forms all around us? Why are not all organic beings blended together in an inextricable chaos? With respect to existing forms, we should remember that we have no right to expect (excepting in rare cases) to discover *directly* connecting links between them, but only between each and some extinct and supplanted form. Even on a wide area, which has during a long period remained continuous, and of which the climate and other conditions of life change insensibly in going from a district occupied by one species into another district occupied by a closely allied species, we have no just right to expect often to find intermediate varieties in the intermediate zone. For we have reason to believe that only a few species are undergoing change at any one period; and all changes are slowly effected. I have also shown that the intermediate varieties which will at first probably exist in the intermediate zones, will be liable to be supplanted by the allied forms on either hand; and the latter, from existing in greater numbers, will generally be modified and improved at a quicker rate than the intermediate varieties, which exist in lesser numbers; so that the intermediate varieties will, in the long run, be supplanted and exterminated.

*　　*　　*

As each species tends by its geometrical ratio of reproduction to increase inordinately in number; and as the modified descendants of each species will be enabled to increase by so much the more as they become more diversified in habits and structure, so as to be enabled to seize on many and widely different places in the economy of nature, there will be a constant tendency in natural selection to preserve the most divergent offspring of any one species. Hence during a long-continued course of modification, the slight differences, characteristic of varieties of the same species, tend to be augmented into the greater differences characteristic of species of the same genus. New and improved varieties will inevitably supplant and exterminate the older, less improved and intermediate varieties; and thus species are rendered to a large extent defined and distinct objects. Dominant species belonging to the larger groups tend to give birth to new and dominant forms; so that each large group tends to become still larger, and at the same time more divergent in character. But as all groups cannot thus succeed in increasing in size, for the world would not hold them, the more dominant groups beat the less dominant. This tendency in the large groups to go on increasing in size and diverging in character, together with the almost inevitable contingency of much extinction, explains the arrangement of all the forms of life, in groups subordinate to groups, all within a few great classes, which we now see everywhere around us, and which has prevailed throughout all time. This grand fact of the grouping of all organic beings seems to me utterly inexplicable on the theory of creation.

As natural selection acts solely by accumulating slight, successive, favourable variations, it can produce no great or sudden modification; it can act only by very short and slow steps. Hence the canon of 'Natura non facit saltum,' which every fresh addition to our knowledge tends to make more strictly correct, is on this theory simply intelligible. We can plainly see why nature is prodigal in variety, though niggard in innovation. But why this should be a law of nature if each species has been independently created, no man can explain.

Many other facts are, as it seems to me, explicable on this theory. How strange it is that a bird, under the form of woodpecker, should have been created to prey on insects on the ground; that upland geese, which never or rarely swim, should have been created with webbed feet; that a thrush should have been created to dive and feed on sub-aquatic insects; and that a petrel should have been created with habits and structure fitting it for the life of an auk or grebe! and so on in endless other cases. But on the view of each species constantly trying to increase in number, with natural selection always ready to adapt the slowly varying descendants of each to any unoccupied or ill-occupied place in nature, these facts cease to be strange, or perhaps might even have been anticipated.

As natural selection acts by competition, it adapts the inhabitants of each country only in relation to the degree of perfection of their associates; so that we need feel no surprise at the inhabitants of any one country, although on the ordinary view supposed to have been specially created and adapted for that country, being beaten and supplanted by the naturalised productions from another land. Nor ought we to marvel if all the contrivances in nature be not, as far as we can judge, absolutely perfect; and if some of them be abhorrent to our ideas of fitness. We need not marvel at the sting of the bee causing the bee's own death; at drones being produced in such vast numbers for one single act, and being then slaughtered by their sterile sisters; at the astonishing waste of pollen by our fir-trees; at the instinctive hatred of the queen bee for her own fertile daughters; at ichneumonidae feeding within the live bodies of caterpillars; and at other such cases. The wonder indeed is, on the theory of natural selection, that more cases of the want of absolute perfection have not been observed.

* * *

The fact, as we have seen, that all past and present organic beings constitute one grand natural system, with group subordinate to group, and with extinct groups often falling in between recent groups, is intelligible on the theory of natural selection with its contingencies of extinction and divergence of character. On these same principles we see how it is, that the mutual affinities of the species and genera within each class are so complex and circuitous. We see why certain characters are far more serviceable than others for classification; why adaptive characters, though of paramount importance to the being, are of hardly any importance in classification; why characters derived from rudimentary parts, though of no service to the being, are often of high classificatory value; and why embryological characters are the most valuable of all. The real affinities of all organic

beings are due to inheritance or community of descent. The natural system is a genealogical arrangement, in which we have to discover the lines of descent by the most permanent characters, however slight their vital importance may be.

The framework of bones being the same in the hand of a man, wing of a bat, fin of the porpoise, and leg of the horse—the same number of vertebrae forming the neck of the giraffe and of the elephant—and innumerable other such facts, at once explain themselves on the theory of descent with slow and slight successive modifications. The similarity of pattern in the wing and leg of a bat, though used for such different purposes, in the jaws and legs of a crab, in the petals, stamens, and pistils of a flower, is likewise intelligible on the view of the gradual modification of parts or organs, which were alike in the early progenitor of each class. On the principle of successive variations not always supervening at an early age, and being inherited at a corresponding not early period of life, we can clearly see why the embryos of mammals, birds, reptiles, and fishes should be so closely alike, and should be so unlike the adult forms. We may cease marvelling at the embryo of an air-breathing mammal or bird having branchial slits and arteries running in loops, like those in a fish which has to breathe the air dissolved in water, by the aid of well-developed branchiae.

* * *

In the distant future I see open fields for far more important researches. Psychology will be based on a new foundation, that of the necessary acquirement of each mental power and capacity by gradation. Light will be thrown on the origin of man and his history.

Authors of the highest eminence seem to be fully satisfied with the view that each species has been independently created. To my mind it accords better with what we know of the laws impressed on matter by the Creator, that the production and extinction of the past and present inhabitants of the world should have been due to secondary causes, like those determining the birth and death of the individual. When I view all beings not as special creations, but as the lineal descendants of some few beings which lived long before the first bed of the Silurian system was deposited, they seem to me to become ennobled. Judging from the past, we may safely infer that not one living species will transmit its unaltered likeness to a distant futurity. And of the species now living very few will transmit progeny of any kind to a far distant futurity; for the manner in which all organic beings are grouped, shows that the greater number of species of each genus, and all the species of many genera, have left no descendants, but have become utterly extinct. We can so far take a prophetic glance into futurity as to fortell that it will be the common and widely-spread species, belonging to the larger and dominant groups, which will ultimately prevail and procreate new and dominant species. As all the living forms of life are the lineal descendants of those which lived long before the Silurian epoch, we may feel certain that the ordinary succession by generation has never once been broken, and that no cataclysm has desolated the whole world. Hence we may look with some confidence to a secure future of equally inappreciable length. And as natural selection works solely by and for the good of each being, all corporeal and mental endowments will tend to progress towards perfection.

It is interesting to contemplate an entangled bank, clothed with many plants of many kinds, with birds singing on the bushes, with various insects flitting about, and with worms crawling through the damp earth, and to reflect that these elaborately constructed forms, so different from each other, and dependent on each other in so complex a manner, have all been produced by laws acting around us. These laws, taken in the largest sense, being Growth with Reproduction; Inheritance which is almost implied by reproduction; Variability from the indirect and direct action of the external conditions of life, and from use and disuse; a Ratio of Increase so high as to lead to a Struggle for Life, and as a consequence to Natural Selection, entailing Divergence of Character and the Extinction of less-improved forms. Thus, from the war of nature, from famine and death, the most exalted object which we are capable of conceiving, namely, the production of the higher animals, directly follows. There is grandeur in this view of life, with its several powers, having been originally breathed into a few forms or into one; and that, whilst this planet has gone cycling on according to the fixed law of gravity, from so simple a beginning endless forms most beautiful and most wonderful have been, and are being, evolved.

REVIEW QUESTIONS

1. According to Darwin, what are the driving forces of natural selection?
2. What is the relationship between heredity and environment?
3. Why is the last paragraph so successful in conveying the gist of his argument?
4. Why was the theory of natural selection so threatening to Christianity?

FRIEDRICH NIETZSCHE

FROM *The Genealogy of Morals*

Over the course of his numerous writings, the German philosopher Friedrich Nietzsche (1844–1900) leveled an impressively sustained attack on Western values. Although his philosophical inquiries ranged over a wide area, his devastating criticisms of Judeo-Christian values of individual worth and social justice are probably the most disturbing of his literary corpus. Nietzsche countered his scorn for the "slave mentality" of Judeo-Christian ethics with a wholly different set of ethics that dismissed guilt and a moral conscience as corrosive to life-affirming creativity, what he called the will to power. Written in a vivid aphoristic prose and organized loosely in detached paragraphs, Nietzsche's writings were frequently misunderstood and often abused in the twentieth century. He remains one of the influential writers of the modern era.

From *The Genealogy of Morals,* by Friedrich Nietzsche (New York: Bantam Doubleday Dell, 1956), pp. 166–73, 177–78.

* * *

IX

"But what is all this talk about nobler values? Let us face facts: the people have triumphed—or the slaves, the mob, the herd, whatever you wish to call them—and if the Jews brought it about, then no nation ever had a more universal mission on this earth. The lords are a thing of the past, and the ethics of the common man is completely triumphant. I don't deny that this triumph might be looked upon as a kind of blood poisoning, since it has resulted in a mingling of the races, but there can be no doubt that the intoxication has succeeded. The "redemption" of the human race (from the lords, that is) is well under way; everything is rapidly becoming Judaized, or Christianized, or mob-ized—the word makes no difference. The progress of this poison throughout the body of mankind cannot be stayed. * * *

* * *

X

The slave revolt in morals begins by rancor turning creative and giving birth to values—the rancor of beings who, deprived of the direct outlet of action, compensate by an imaginary vengeance. All truly noble morality grows out of triumphant self-affirmation. Slave ethics, on the other hand, begins by saying *no* to an "outside," an "other," a non-self, and that *no* is its creative act. This reversal of direction of the evaluating look, this invariable looking outward instead of inward, is a fundamental feature of rancor. Slave ethics requires for its inception a sphere different from and hostile to its own. Physiologically speaking, it requires an outside stimulus in order to act at all; all its action is reaction. The opposite is true of aristocratic valuations: such values grow and act spontaneously, seeking out their contraries only in order to affirm themselves even more gratefully and delightedly. Here the negative concepts, *humble, base, bad,* are late, pallid counterparts of the positive, intense and passionate credo, "We noble, good, beautiful, happy ones." Aristocratic valuations may go amiss and do violence to reality, but this happens only with regard to spheres which they do not know well, or from the knowledge of which they austerely guard themselves: the aristocrat will, on occasion, misjudge a sphere which he holds in contempt, the sphere of the common man, the people. On the other hand we should remember that the emotion of contempt, of looking down, provided that it falsifies at all, is as nothing compared with the falsification which suppressed hatred, impotent vindictiveness, effects upon its opponent, though only in effigy. There is in all contempt too much casualness and nonchalance, too much blinking of facts and impatience, and too much inborn gaiety for it ever to make of its object a downright caricature and monster. Hear the almost benevolent nuances the Greek aristocracy, for example, puts into all its terms for the commoner; how emotions of compassion, consideration, indulgence, sugar-coat these words until, in the end, almost all terms referring to the common man survive as expressions for "unhappy," "pitiable" * * * ; how, on the other hand, the words *bad, base, unhappy* have continued to strike a similar note for the Greek ear, with the timbre "unhappy" preponderating. The "well-born" really felt that they were also the "happy." They did not have to construct their happiness factitiously by looking at their enemies, as all rancorous men are wont to do, and being fully active, energetic people they were incapable of divorcing happiness from action. They accounted activity a necessary part of happiness. * * *

All this stands in utter contrast to what is called happiness among the impotent and oppressed, who are full of bottled-up aggressions. Their happiness is purely passive and takes the form of drugged tranquillity, stretching and yawning, peace, "sabbath," emotional slackness. Whereas the noble lives before his own conscience with confidence and frankness * * * , the rancorous person is neither truthful nor ingenuous nor honest and forthright with himself. His soul squints; his mind loves hide-outs, secret paths, and back doors; everything that is hidden seems

to him his own world, his security, his comfort; he is expert in silence, in long memory, in waiting, in provisional self-depreciation, and in self-humiliation. A race of such men will, in the end, inevitably be cleverer than a race of aristocrats, and it will honor sharp-wittedness to a much greater degree, i.e., as an absolutely vital condition for its existence. Among the noble, mental acuteness always tends slightly to suggest luxury and overrefinement. The fact is that with them it is much less important than is the perfect functioning of the ruling, unconscious instincts or even a certain temerity to follow sudden impulses, court danger, or indulge spurts of violent rage, love, worship, gratitude, or vengeance. When a noble man feels resentment, it is absorbed in his instantaneous reaction and therefore does not poison him. Moreover, in countless cases where we might expect it, it never arises, while with weak and impotent people it occurs without fail. It is a sign of strong, rich temperaments that they cannot for long take seriously their enemies, their misfortunes, their *misdeeds;* for such characters have in them an excess of plastic curative power, and also a power of oblivion. * * * Such a man simply shakes off vermin which would get beneath another's skin—and only here, if anywhere on earth, is it possible to speak of "loving one's enemy." The noble person will respect his enemy, and respect is already a bridge to love. . . . Indeed he requires his enemy for himself, as his mark of distinction, nor could he tolerate any other enemy than one in whom he finds nothing to despise and much to esteem. Imagine, on the other hand, the "enemy" as conceived by the rancorous man! For this is his true creative achievement: he has conceived the "evil enemy," the Evil One, as a fundamental idea, and then as a pendant he has conceived a Good One—himself.

*   *   *

XII

Here I want to give vent to a sigh and a last hope. Exactly what is it that I, especially, find intolerable; that I am unable to cope with; that asphyxiates me? A bad smell. The smell of failure, of a soul that has gone stale. God knows it is possible to endure all kinds of misery—vile weather, sickness, trouble, isolation. All this can be coped with, if one is born to a life of anonymity and battle. There will always be moments of re-emergence into the light, when one tastes the golden hour of victory and once again stands foursquare, unshakable, ready to face even harder things, like a bowstring drawn taut against new perils. But, you divine patronesses—if there are any such in the realm beyond good and evil—grant me now and again the sight of something perfect, wholly achieved, happy, magnificently triumphant, something still capable of inspiring fear! Of a man who will justify the existence of mankind, for whose sake one may continue to believe in mankind! . . . The leveling and diminution of European man is our greatest danger; because the sight of him makes us despond. . . . We no longer see anything these days that aspires to grow greater; instead, we have a suspicion that things will continue to go downhill, becoming ever thinner, more placid, smarter, cosier, more ordinary, more indifferent, more Chinese, more Christian—without doubt man is getting "better" all the time. . . . This is Europe's true predicament: together with the fear of man we have also lost the love of man, reverence for man, confidence in man, indeed the *will to man*. Now the sight of man makes us despond. What is nihilism today if not that?

*   *   *

XVI

Let us conclude. The two sets of valuations, good/bad and good/evil, have waged a terrible battle on this earth, lasting many millennia; and just as surely as the second set has for a long time now

been in the ascendant, so surely are there still places where the battle goes on and the issue remains in suspension. It might even be claimed that by being raised to a higher plane the battle has become much more profound. Perhaps there is today not a single intellectual worth his salt who is not divided on that issue, a battleground for those opposites. The watchwords of the battle, written in characters which have remained legible throughout human history, read: "Rome vs. Israel, Israel vs. Rome." No battle has ever been more momentous than this one. Rome viewed Israel as a monstrosity; the Romans regarded the Jews as *convicted* of hatred against the whole of mankind—and rightly so if one is justified in associating the welfare of the human species with absolute supremacy of aristocratic values. But how did the Jews, on their part, feel about Rome? A thousand indications point to the answer. It is enough to read once more the Revelations of St. John, the most rabid outburst of vindictiveness in all recorded history. (We ought to acknowledge the profound consistency of the Christian instinct in assigning this book of hatred and the most extravagantly doting of the Gospels to the same disciple. There is a piece of truth hidden here, no matter how much literary skulduggery may have gone on.) The Romans were the strongest and most noble people who ever lived. Every vestige of them, every least inscription, is a sheer delight, provided we are able to read the spirit behind the writing. The Jews, on the contrary, were the priestly, rancorous nation *par excellence*, though possessed of an unequaled ethical genius; we need only compare with them nations of comparable endowments, such as the Chinese or the Germans, to sense which occupies the first rank. Has the victory so far been gained by the Romans or by the Jews? But this is really an idle question. Remember who it is before whom one bows down, in Rome itself, as before the essence of all supreme values—and not only in Rome but over half the globe, wherever man has grown tame or desires to grow tame: before three Jews and one Jewess (Jesus of Nazareth, the fisherman Peter, the rug weaver Paul, and Maria, the mother of that Jesus).

This is very curious: Rome, without a doubt, has capitulated. It is true that during the Renaissance men witnessed a strange and splendid awakening of the classical ideal; like one buried alive, Rome stirred under the weight of a new Judaic Rome that looked like an ecumenical synagogue and was called the Church. But presently Israel triumphed once again, thanks to the plebeian rancor of the German and English Reformation, together with its natural corollary, the restoration of the Church—which also meant the restoration of ancient Rome to the quiet of the tomb. In an even more decisive sense did Israel triumph over the classical ideal through the French Revolution. For then the last political nobleness Europe had known, that of seventeenth- and eighteenth-century France, collapsed under the weight of vindictive popular instincts. A wilder enthusiasm was never seen. And yet, in the midst of it all, something tremendous, something wholly unexpected happened: the ancient classical ideal appeared incarnate and in unprecedented splendor before the eyes and conscience of mankind. Once again, stronger, simpler, more insistent than ever, over against the lying shibboleth of the rights of the majority, against the furious tendency toward lev-

eling out and debasement, sounded the terrible yet exhilarating shibboleth of the "prerogative of the few." Like a last signpost to an *alternative* route Napoleon appeared, most isolated and anachronistic of men, the embodiment of the noble ideal. It might be well to ponder what exactly Napoleon, that synthesis of the brutish with the more than human, did represent. ⋆ ⋆ ⋆

⋆   ⋆   ⋆

REVIEW QUESTIONS

1. What are slave morals, and why is Nietzsche so critical of them?
2. In contrast, what are construed as "noble" values?
3. Is Nietzsche criticizing or endorsing the spirit of the Enlightenment?
4. What is Nietzsche's relationship with European society?
5. What does he not like about modern times?
6. Where is there room for abuse in such an argument?

SIGMUND FREUD

FROM *Five Lectures on Psychoanalysis*

Sigmund Freud (1856–1939), an Austrian doctor, is largely credited as the first scientist of psychoanalysis, a discipline that seeks to understand the mechanisms of the unconscious and to explain the role of suppressed desire in determining people's actions and dysfunctions. In doing so, Freud fundamentally changed the way humankind perceived itself, thus affecting numerous disciplines of knowledge and a wide range of literary and art movements. Perhaps it is impossible to interpret twentieth-century culture without first weighing Freud's impact. Psychoanalysis arose in 1895 when Freud and Josef Breuer, a physician friend, published a case study that posited the link between hysteria and sexual malfunctions, and the need to uncover re-

pressed memory for recovery. Freud outlined the early development of his under-standing of resistance and repression in five lectures, excerpted below, presented at Clark University, Worcester, Massachussets, in 1912.

From *Five Lectures on Psychoanalysis*, by Sigmund Freud, translated by James Strachey (London: Hogarth Press, 1976).

*　　*　　*

When, later on, I set about continuing on my own account the investigations that had been begun by Breuer, I soon arrived at another view of the origin of hysterical dissociation (the splitting of consciousness). A divergence of this kind, which was to be decisive for everything that followed, was inevitable, since I did not start out, like Janet, from laboratory experiments, but with therapeutic aims in mind.

I was driven forward above all by practical necessity. The cathartic procedure, as carried out by Breuer, presupposed putting the patient into a state of deep hypnosis; for it was only in a state of hypnosis that he attained a knowledge of the pathogenic connections which escaped him in his normal state. But I soon came to dislike hypnosis, for it was a temperamental and, one might almost say, a mystical ally. When I found that, in spite of all my efforts, I could not succeed in bringing more than a fraction of my patients into a hypnotic state, I determined to give up hypnosis and to make the cathartic procedure independent of it. Since I was not able at will to alter the mental state of the majority of my patients, I set about working with them in their *normal* state. At first, I must confess, this seemed a senseless and hopeless undertaking. I was set the task of learning from the patient something that I did not know and that he did not know himself. How could one hope to elicit it? But there came to my help a recollection of a most remarkable and instructive experiment which I had witnessed when I was with Bernheim at Nancy. Bernheim showed us that people whom he had put into a state of hypnotic somnambulism, and who had had all kinds of experiences while they were in that state, only *appeared* to have lost the memory of what they had experienced during somnambulism; it was possible to revive these memories in their normal state. It is true that, when he questioned them about their somnambulistic experiences, they began by maintaining that they knew nothing about them; but if he refused to give way, and insisted, and assured them that they *did* know about them, the forgotten experiences always reappeared.

So I did the same thing with my patients. When I reached a point with them at which they maintained that they knew nothing more, I assured them that they *did* know it all the same, and that they had only to say it; and I ventured to declare that the right memory would occur to them at the moment at which I laid my hand on their forehead. In that way I succeeded, without using hypnosis, in obtaining from the patients whatever was required for establishing the connection between the pathogenic scenes they had forgotten and the symptoms left over from those scenes. But it was a laborious procedure, and in the long run an exhausting one; and it was unsuited to serve as a permanent technique.

I did not abandon it, however, before the observations I made during my use of it afforded me decisive evidence. I found confirmation of the fact that the forgotten memories were not lost. They were in the patient's possession and were ready to emerge in association to what was still known by him; but there was some force that prevented them from becoming conscious and compelled them to remain unconscious. The existence of this force could be assumed with certainty, since one became aware of an effort corresponding to it if, in opposition to it, one tried to introduce the unconscious memories into the patient's consciousness. The force which was maintaining the pathological condition became apparent in the form of *resistance* on the part of the patient.

It was on this idea of resistance, then, that I based my view of the course of psychical events in hysteria. In order to effect a recovery, it had proved necessary to remove these resistances. Starting out from the mechanism of cure, it now became possible to construct quite definite ideas of the origin of the illness. The same forces which, in the form of resistance, were now offering opposition to the forgotten material's being made conscious, must formerly have brought about the forgetting and must have pushed the pathogenic experiences in question out of consciousness. I gave the name of "*repression*" to this hypothetical process, and I considered that it was proved by the undeniable existence of resistance.

The further question could then be raised as to what these forces were and what the determinants were of the repression in which we now recognized the pathogenic mechanism of hysteria. A comparative study of the pathogenic situations which we had come to know through the cathartic procedure made it possible to answer this question. All these experiences had involved the emergence of a wishful impulse which was in sharp contrast to the subject's other wishes and which proved incompatible with the ethical and aesthetic standards of his personality. There had been a short conflict, and the end of this internal struggle was that the idea which had appeared before consciousness as the vehicle of this irreconcilable wish fell a victim to repression, was pushed out of consciousness with all its attached memories, and was forgotten. Thus the incompatibility of the wish in question with the patient's ego was the motive for the repression; the subject's ethical and other standards were the repressing forces. An acceptance of the incompatible wishful impulse or a prolongation of the conflict would have produced a high degree of unpleasure; this unpleasure was avoided by means of repression, which was thus revealed as one of the devices serving to protect the mental personality.

To take the place of a number of instances, I will relate a single one of my cases, in which the determinants and advantages of repression are sufficiently evident. For my present purpose I shall have once again to abridge the case history and omit some important underlying material. The patient was a girl, who had lost her beloved father after she had taken a share in nursing him—a situation analogous to that of Breuer's patient. Soon afterwards her elder sister married, and her new brother-in-law aroused in her a peculiar feeling of sympathy which was easily masked under a disguise of family affection. Not long afterwards her sister fell ill and died, in the absence of the patient and her mother. They were summoned in all haste without being given any definite information of the tragic event. When the girl reached the bedside of her dead sister, there came to her for a brief moment an idea that might be expressed in these words: 'Now he is free and can marry me.' We may assume with certainty that this idea, which betrayed to her consciousness the intense love for her brother-in-law of which she had not herself been conscious, was surrendered to repression a moment later, owing to the revolt of her feelings. The girl fell ill with severe hysterical symptoms; and while she was under my treatment it turned out that she had completely forgotten the scene by her sister's bedside and the odious egoistic impulse that had emerged in her. She remembered it during the treatment and reproduced the pathogenic moment with signs of the most violent emotion, and, as a result of the treatment, she became healthy once more.

Perhaps I may give you a more vivid picture of repression and of its necessary relation to resistance, by a rough analogy derived from our actual situation at the present moment. Let us suppose that in this lecture-room and among this audience, whose exemplary quiet and attentiveness I cannot sufficiently commend, there is nevertheless someone who is causing a disturbance and whose ill-mannered laughter, chattering and shuffling with his feet are distracting my attention from my task. I have to announce that I cannot proceed with my lecture; and thereupon three or four of you who are strong men stand up and, after a short struggle, put the interrupter outside the door. So now he is "repressed," and I can continue my lecture. But in order that the interruption shall not be repeated, in case the individual who has been expelled should try to enter the room once more, the gentlemen who have put my will into effect place their chairs up against the door and thus establish a "resistance" after the repression has been accomplished. If you will now translate the two localities concerned into psychical terms as the "conscious" and the "unconscious," you will have before you a fairly good picture of the process of repression.

You will now see in what it is that the difference lies between our view and Janet's. We do not derive the psychical splitting from an innate incapacity for synthesis on the part of the mental apparatus; we explain it dynamically, from the conflict of opposing mental forces and recognize it as the outcome of an active struggling on the part of the two psychical groupings against each other. But our view gives rise to a large number of fresh problems. Situations of mental conflict are, of course, exceedingly common; efforts by the ego to ward off painful memories are quite regularly to be observed without their producing the result of a mental split. The reflection cannot be escaped that further determinants must be present if the conflict is to lead to dissociation. I will also readily grant you that the hypothesis of repression leaves us not at the end but at the beginning of a psychological theory. We can only go forward step by step however, and complete knowledge must await the results of further and deeper researches.

*   *   *

To put the matter more directly. The investigation of hysterical patients and of other neurotics

leads us to the conclusion that their repression of the idea to which the intolerable wish is attached has been a *failure*. It is true that they have driven it out of consciousness and out of memory and have apparently saved themselves a large amount of unpleasure. *But the repressed wishful impulse continues to exist in the unconscious.* It is on the look-out for an opportunity of being activated, and when that happens it succeeds in sending into consciousness a disguised and unrecognizable *substitute* for what had been repressed, and to this there soon become attached the same feelings of unpleasure which it was hoped had been saved by the repression. This substitute for the repressed idea—the *symptom*—is proof against further attacks from the defensive ego; and in place of the short conflict an ailment now appears which is not brought to an end by the passage of time. Alongside the indication of distortion in the symptom, we can trace in it the remains of some kind of indirect resemblance to the idea that was originally repressed. The paths along which the substitution was effected can be traced in the course of the patient's psychoanalytic treatment; and in order to bring about recovery, the symptom must be led back along the same paths and once more turned into the repressed idea. If what was repressed is brought back again into conscious mental activity—a process which presupposes the overcoming of considerable resistances—the resulting psychical conflict, which the patient had tried to avoid, can, under the physician's guidance, reach a better outcome than was offered by repression. There are a number of such opportune solutions, which may bring the conflict and the neurosis to a happy end, and which may in certain instances be combined. The patient's personality may be convinced that it has been wrong in rejecting the pathogenic wish and may be led into accepting it wholly or in part; or the wish itself may be directed to a higher and consequently unobjectionable aim (this is what we call its "sublimation"); or the rejection of the wish may be recognized as a justifiable one, but the automatic and therefore inefficient mechanism of repression may be replaced by a condemning judgement with the help of the highest human mental functions—conscious control of the wish is attained.

*   *   *

REVIEW QUESTIONS

1. How does Freud view the pathology of hysteria and its solution?
2. What does the theory of repression imply for individuals' identities and actions?
3. What were the implications of Freud's theory of the unconscious for bourgeois culture?

27 ❧ THE FIRST WORLD WAR

The assassination of Archduke Franz Ferdinand in Sarajevo in 1914 unleashed a cataclysm of unparalleled magnitude. For four years the European combatants and their allies confronted one another in a war of global dimensions. By 1918 millions of soldiers had been killed on the battlefront, and the lives of civilians living behind the lines on the home front had been unalterably disrupted.

Europeans initially responded to the outbreak of war with jubilation and enthusiasm. Young men rushed to enlist, worried that the war—which everyone expected to be over by Christmas—would end before they could reach the front lines. But soldiers who had yearned for high drama and the chance to prove what one poet-soldier called their "untested manhood" soon discovered the sullen face of modern warfare. The ideal of personal heroism wilted as soldiers alternated between long drab days spent huddling in the trenches and brief but murderous bouts of combat. The new technologies of war, especially the machine gun and heavy artillery, reduced the individual soldier to insignificance, making a mockery of his bravery and leading him to fear not only the clean death brought by bullets but the utter annihilation of being blown to bits or the long, drawn out agony of gas poisoning. For those who survived this ordeal, the Great War was a fundamental experience, forever separating them from the prewar world—and from noncombatants—and leaving deep physical and psychological scars.

Although civilians were protected from the worst horrors of the trenches, they too were deeply affected by the war. The lines between the home front and the battlefront blurred as production of armaments and munitions made civilian workers crucial to the military effort and as government-sponsored propaganda campaigns encouraged noncombatants to do their part for the war effort. While the war brought hardships to civilians, it also brought new opportunities and even adventure, especially to young women who were suddenly freed from the restraints of prewar society.

When the war ended, Europeans were eager to believe that they had, in fact, fought "the war to end all wars." But the end of hostilities did not bring an end to the trauma and dislocation occasioned by the war. The peace settlement itself, promoted by its framers as a new, more hopeful beginning, was widely condemned as an inadequate guarantee of international security and stability.

The Trench Poets of the First World War

The outbreak of the First World War inspired a spate of poetry; one historian estimates that more than one million poems were written in 1914 alone. Like Rupert Brooke (1887–1915), many poets initially greeted the war as a release from the dreariness of civilian life. Educated at Cambridge, Brooke finely crafted idealistic wartime poems, especially the sonnet series "1914," which earned him lasting fame. However, as the war dragged on, soldier-poets' initial enthusiasm gave way to resignation. The stately verse of Alan Seeger (1888–1916), an American educated at Harvard, reflects the new acceptance of the tragic inevitability of death.

Some poets eventually expressed their outrage at the cost of the war. British poet Wilfred Owen (1893–1918), a graduate of the University of London, condemned the older generation that had allowed the war to happen and that was now refusing to end the slaughter of "half the seed of Europe, one by one." Owen's "Dulce et Decorum est," perhaps the most famous of all the First World War poems, is noteworthy not only for its antiwar sentiments but also for its stylistic innovation. The same disenchantment and modernist tone is found in "Trench Poets," written by a lesser known British author, John Edgell Rickword (1898–1982). Of the four poets whose verse is reproduced here, only Rickword survived the war.

From *The Collected Poems*, by Rupert Brooke, edited by George E. Woodbury (New York: Lane, 1916).

Rupert Brooke

FROM "1914"

I. PEACE

Now, God be thanked Who has matched us with
    His hour,
  And caught our youth, and wakened us from
    sleeping,

With hand made sure, clear eye, and sharpened
    power,
  To turn, as swimmers into cleanness leaping,
Glad from a world grown old and cold and weary,
  Leave the sick hearts that honour could not
    move,
And half-men, and their dirty songs and dreary,
  And all the little emptiness of love!

Oh! we, who have known shame, we have found
    release there,

Where there's no ill, no grief, but sleep has
   mending,
    Naught broken save this body, lost but
     breath;
Nothing to shake the laughing heart's long peace
   there
But only agony, and that has ending;
    And the worst friend and enemy is but
     Death.

*   *   *

V. THE SOLDIER

If I should die, think only this of me:
   That there's some corner of a foreign field
That is for ever England. There shall be
   In that rich earth a richer dust concealed;
A dust whom England bore, shaped, made
   aware,
    Gave, once, her flowers to love, her ways to
    roam,
A body of England's, breathing English air,
   Washed by the rivers, blest by suns of home.

And think, this heart, all evil shed away,
   A pulse in the eternal mind, no less
    Gives somewhere back the thoughts by
    England given;
Her sights and sounds; dreams happy as her day;
   And laughter, learnt of friends; and gentleness,
    In hearts at peace, under an English heaven.

*   *   *

Alan Seeger

"Rendezvous"

I have a rendezvous with Death
At some disputed barricade,
I have a rendezvous with Death
At some disputed barricade,

When Spring comes back with rustling shade
And apple-blossoms fill the air—
I have a rendezvous with Death
When Spring brings back blue days and fair.

It may be he shall take my hand
And lead me into his dark land
And close my eyes and quench my breath—
It may be I shall pass him still.
I have a rendezvous with Death
On some scarred slope of battered hill,
When Spring comes round again this year
And the first meadow-flowers appear.

God knows 'twere better to be deep
Pillowed in silk and scented down,
Where love throbs out in blissful sleep,
Pulse nigh to pulse, and breath to breath,
Where hushed awakenings are dear . . .
But I've a rendezvous with Death
At midnight in some flaming town,
When Spring trips north again this year,
And I to my pledged word am true,
I shall not fail that rendezvous.

Wilfred Owen

"Dulce et decorum est"

Bent double, like old beggars under sacks,
Knock-kneed, coughing like hags, we cursed
    through sludge,
Till on the haunting flares we turned our backs
And towards our distant rest began to trudge.
Men marched asleep. Many had lost their boots
But limped on, blood-shod. All went lame; all
   blind;
Drunk with fatigue; deaf even to the hoots
Of tired, outstripped Five-Nines that dropped
   behind.

Gas! GAS! Quick, boys!

From *Poems,* by Alan Seeger (Scribner's, 1916).

From *Poems,* by Wilfred Owen (Huebsch, 1921).

An ecstasy of fumbling,
Fitting the clumsy helmets just in time;
But someone still was yelling out and stumbling,
And flound'ring like a man in fire or lime . . .
Dim, through the misty panes and thick green
    light,
As under a green sea, I saw him drowning.
In all my dreams, before my helpless sight,
He plunges at me, guttering, choking, drowning.
If in some smothering dreams you too could
    pace
Behind the wagon that we flung him in,
And watch the white eyes writhing in his face,
His hanging face, like a devil's sick of sin;
If you could hear, at every jolt, the blood
Come gargling from the froth-corrupted lungs,
Obscene as cancer, bitter as the cud
Of vile, incurable sores on innocent tongues,
My friend, you would not tell with such high
    zest
To children ardent for some desperate glory,
The old Lie: *Dulce et decorum est*
Pro patria mori.[1]

like "Get with child a mandrake-root."
But you can tell he was far gone,
for he lay gaping, mackerel-eyed,
and stiff, and senseless as a post
even when that old poet cried
"I long to talk with some old lover's ghost."

I tried the Elegies one day,
but he, because he heard me say:
"What needst thou have more covering than a
    man?"
grinned nastily, and so I knew
the worms had got his brains at last.
There was one thing that I might do
to starve the worms; I racked my head
for healthy things and quoted Maud.
His grin got worse and I could see
he sneered at passion's purity.
He stank so badly, though we were great chums
I had to leave him; then rats ate his thumbs.

Edgell Rickword

"Trench Poets"

I knew a man, he was my chum,
but he grew blacker every day,
and would not brush the flies away,
nor blanch however fierce the hum
of passing shells; I used to read,
to rouse him, random things from Donne—[2]

---

[1] "It is sweet and fitting to die for one's country." A line taken from the *Odes* of Horace (65–8 B.C.E.).

From *Behind the Eyes*, by Edgell Rickword (Sidgwick and Jackson, 1921).

[2] John Donne (1572–1631), an English poet of the late Renaissance. The citations in this poem are taken from Donne's works.

REVIEW QUESTIONS

1. Why does Rupert Brooke welcome war?
2. What virtues does he find in death on the battlefield?
3. How does this compare with Seeger's attitude toward his own impending "rendezvous with Death"?
4. How does Wilfred Owen's perception of warfare differ from Brooke's?
5. How do Owen's and Brooke's attitudes about patriotism differ?
6. What point about Western culture is Edgell Rickword trying to make in "Trench Poets"?

BATTLE OF VERDUN (1916)

On 21 February 1916, the German army laid siege to the fortress town of Verdun, France. The attack, although initially successful, subsided into a long-term battle, claiming over 400,000 French casualties and approximately as many German. The town was never taken, and the German high command ended the campaign in July. For contemporaries and subsequent generations, the massive expense of life at the Battle of Verdun, which witnessed the use of gas and flamethrowers, epitomized the cruelty and futility of modern war. This still photograph is taken from front-line film footage of a French officer leading his men in a charge across "no-man's land" and confronting the deadly efficiency of machine guns. How did this image of the western front undermine Western idealism for war and military valor?

HENRI BARBUSSE

FROM *Under Fire: The Story of a Squad*

French author Henri Barbusse (1873–1935) enlisted voluntarily in 1914 but was discharged as a result of battlefield injuries in 1917. Already a successful poet when the war began, Barbusse published Under Fire: The Story of a Squad, *a fictionalized account of his wartime experiences, in 1916. The novel won the Prix Goncourt, the highest French literary honor. Barbusse's antiwar sentiments, evident in the bitter sarcasm of* Under Fire, *inspired him to become a pacifist and to join the Communist Party after the war. He was living in the Soviet Union at the time of his death.*

Under Fire documents the life of the poilu, *the "hairy" French World War I soldier, through a group portrait of a squadron of men drawn from all walks of life. In the following excerpt from the opening of the novel, Barbusse introduces the soldiers and reveals their single, overwhelming preoccupation—the quality of their grub.*

From *Under Fire: The Story of a Squad*, by Henri Barbusse, translated by Fitzwater Wray (New York: Dutton, 1917).

* * *

Mesnil Joseph drowses; Blaire yawns; Marthereau smokes, "eyes front." Lamuse scratches himself like a gorilla, and Eudore like a marmoset. Volpatte coughs, and says, "I'm kicking the bucket." Mesnil André has got out his mirror and comb and is tending his fine chestnut beard as though it were a rare plant. The monotonous calm is disturbed here and there by the outbreaks of ferocious resentment provoked by the presence of parasites—endemic, chronic, and contagious.

Barque, who is an observant man, sends an itinerant glance around, takes his pipe from his mouth, spits, winks, and says—

"I say, we don't resemble each other much."

"Why should we?" says Lamuse. "It would be a miracle if we did."

* * *

Our ages? We are of all ages. Ours is a regiment in reserve which successive reinforcements have renewed partly with fighting units and partly with Territorials. In our half-section there are reservists of the Territorial Army, new recruits, and *demi-poils*. Fouillade is forty; Blaire might be the father of Biquet, who is a gosling of Class 1913. The corporal calls Marthereau "Grandpa" or "Old Rubbish-heap," according as in jest or in earnest. Mesnil Joseph would be at the barracks if there were no war. It is a comical effect when we are in charge of Sergeant Vigile, a nice little boy, with a dab on his lip by way of mustache. When we were in quarters the other day, he played at skipping-rope with the kiddies. In our ill-assorted flock, in this family without kindred, this home without a hearth at which we gather, there are three generations side by side, living, waiting, standing still, like unfinished statues, like posts.

Our races? We are of all races; we come from everywhere. I look at the two men beside me. Poterloo, the miner from the Calonne pit, is pink; his eyebrows are the color of straw, his eyes flax-blue. His great golden head involved a long search in the stores to find the vast steel-blue tureen that bonnets him. Fouillade, the boatman from Cette, rolls his wicked eyes in the long, lean face of a musketeer, with sunken cheeks and his skin the color of a violin. In good sooth, my two neighbors are as unlike as day and night.

Cocon, no less, a slight and desiccated person in spectacles, whose tint tells of corrosion in the chemical vapors of great towns, contrasts with Biquet, a Breton in the rough, whose skin is gray and his jaw like a paving-stone; and Mesnil André, the comfortable chemist from a country town in Normandy, who has such a handsome and silky beard and who talks so much and so well—he has little in common with Lamuse, the fat peasant of Poitou, whose cheeks and neck are like underdone beef. The suburban accent of Barque, whose long legs have scoured the streets of Paris in all directions, alternates with the semi-Belgian cadence of those Northerners who came from the 8th Territorial; with the sonorous speech, rolling on the syllables as if over cobblestone, that the 144th pours out upon us; with the dialect blown from those ant-like clusters that the Auvergnats so obstinately form among the rest. I remember the first words of that wag, Tirette, when he arrived—"I, *mes enfants,* I am from Clichy-la-Garenne! Can any one beat that?"—and the first grievance that Paradis brought to me, "They don't give a damn for me, because I'm from Morvan!"

*   *   *

Our callings? A little of all—in the lump. In those departed days when we had a social status, before we came to immure our destiny in the molehills that we must always build up again as fast as rain and scrap-iron beat them down, what were we? Sons of the soil and artisans mostly. Lamuse was a farm-servant, Paradis a carter. Cadilhac, whose helmet rides loosely on his pointed head, though it is a juvenile size—like a dome on a steeple, says Tirette—owns land. Papa Blaire was a small farmer in La Brie. Barque, porter and mes-

senger, performed acrobatic tricks with his carrier-tricycle among the trams and taxis of Paris, with solemn abuse (so they say) for the pedestrians, fleeing like bewildered hens across the big streets and squares. Corporal Bertrand, who keeps himself always a little aloof, correct, erect, and silent, with a strong and handsome face and forthright gaze, was foreman in a case-factory. Tirloir daubed carts with paint—and without grumbling, they say. Tulacque was barman at the Throne Tavern in the suburbs; and Eudore of the pale and pleasant face kept a roadside café not very far from the front lines. It has been ill-used by the shells—naturally, for we all know that Eudore has no luck. Mesnil André, who still retains a trace of well-kept distinction, sold bicarbonate and infallible remedies at his pharmacy in a *Grande Place.* His brother Joseph was selling papers and illustrated story-books in a station on the State Railways at the same time that, in far-off Lyons, Cocon, the man of spectacles and statistics, dressed in a black smock, busied himself behind the counters of an ironmongery, his hands glittering with plumbago; while the lamps of Bécuwe Adolphe and Poterloo, risen with the dawn, trailed about the coalpits of the North like weakling Will-o'-th'-wisps.

And there are others amongst us whose occupations one can never recall, whom one confuses with one another; and the rural nondescripts who peddled ten trades at once in their packs, without counting the dubious Pépin, who can have had none at all. (While at the depot after sick leave, three months ago, they say, he got married—to secure the separation allowance.)

The liberal professions are not represented among those around me. Some teachers are subalterns in the company or Red Cross men. In the regiment a Marist Brother is sergeant in the *Service de Santé;* a professional tenor is cyclist dispatch-rider to the Major; a "gentleman of independent means" is mess corporal to the C.H.R. But here there is nothing of all that. We are fighting men, we others, and we include hardly any intellectuals, or men of the arts or of wealth, who during this war will have risked their faces only at the loop-holes, unless in passing by, or under gold-laced caps.

Yes, we are truly and deeply different from each other. But we are alike all the same. In spite of this diversity of age, of country, of education, of position, of everything possible, in spite of the former gulfs that kept us apart, we are in the main alike. Under the same uncouth outlines we conceal and reveal the same ways and habits, the same simple nature of men who have reverted to the state primeval.

The same language, compounded of dialect and the slang of workshop and barracks, seasoned with the latest inventions, blends us in the sauce of speech with the massed multitudes of men who (for seasons now) have emptied France and crowded together in the North-East.

Here, too, linked by a fate from which there is no escape, swept willy-nilly by the vast adventure into one rank, we have no choice but to go as the weeks and months go—alike. The terrible narrowness of the common life binds us close, adapts us, merges us one in the other. It is a sort of fatal contagion. Nor need you, to see how alike we soldiers are, be afar off—at that distance, say, when we are only specks of the dust-clouds that roll across the plain.

We are waiting. Weary of sitting, we get up, our joints creaking like warping wood or old hinges. Damp rusts men as it rusts rifles; more slowly, but deeper. And we begin again, but not in the same way, to wait. In a state of war, one is always waiting. We have become waiting-machines. For the moment it is food we are waiting for. Then it will be the post. But each in its turn. When we have done with dinner we will think about the letters. After that, we shall set ourselves to wait for something else.

Hunger and thirst are urgent instincts which formidably excite the temper of my companions. As the meal gets later they become grumblesome and angry. Their need of food and drink snarls from their lips—

"That's eight o'clock. Now, why the hell doesn't it come?"

*   *   *

"There's the grub!" announces a poilu who was on the look-out at the corner.

"Time, too!"

And the storm of revilings ceases as if by magic. Wrath is changed into sudden contentment.

Three breathless fatigue men, their faces streaming with tears of sweat, put down on the ground some large tins, a paraffin can, two canvas buckets, and a file of loaves, skewered on a stick. Leaning against the wall of the trench, they mop their faces with their handkerchiefs or sleeves. And I see Cocon go up to Pépère with a smile, and forgetful of the abuse he had been heaping on the other's reputation, he stretches out a cordial hand towards one of the cans in the collection that swells the circumference of Pépère after the manner of a life-belt.

"What is there to eat?"

"It's there," is the evasive reply of the second fatigue man, whom experience has taught that a proclamation of the menu always evokes the bitterness of disillusion. So they set themselves to panting abuse of the length and the difficulties of the trip they have just accomplished: "Some crowds about, everywhere! It's a tough job to get along—got to disguise yourself as a cigarette paper, sometimes."—"And there are people who say they're shirkers in the kitchens!" As for *him,* he would a hundred thousand times rather be with the company in the trenches, to mount guard and dig, than earn his keep by *such* a job, twice a day during the night!

Paradis, having lifted the lids of the jars, surveys the recipients and announces, "Kidney beans in oil, bully, pudding, and coffee—that's all."

"*Nom de Dieu!*" bawls Tulacque. "And wine?" He summons the crowd: "Come and look here, all of you! That—that's the limit! We're done out of our wine!"

Athirst and grimacing, they hurry up; and from the profoundest depths of their being wells up the chorus of despair and disappointment, "Oh, Hell!"

"Then what's that in there?" says the fatigue man, still ruddily sweating, and using his foot to point at a bucket.

"Yes," says Paradis, "my mistake, there *is* some."

The fatigue man shrugs his shoulders, and hurls at Paradis a look of unspeakable scorn—"Now you're beginning! Get your gig-lamps on, if your sight's bad." He adds, "One cup each—rather less perhaps—some chucklehead bumped against me, coming through the Boyau du Bois, and a drop got spilled. "Ah!" he hastens to add, raising his voice, "if I hadn't been loaded up, talk about the boot-toe he'd have got in the rump! But he hopped it on his top gear, the brute!"

In spite of this confident assurance, the fatigue man makes off himself, curses overtaking him as he goes, maledictions charged with offensive reflections on his honesty and temperance, imprecations inspired by this revelation of a ration reduced.

All the same, they throw themselves on the food, and eat it standing, squatting, kneeling, sitting on tins, or on haversacks pulled out of the holes where they sleep—or even prone, their backs on the ground, disturbed by passers-by, cursed at and cursing. Apart from these fleeting insults and jests, they say nothing, the primary and universal interest being but to swallow, with their mouths and the circumference thereof as greasy as a rifle-breech. Contentment is theirs.

*   *   *

Review Questions

1. How different from one another are the soldiers in this squad?
2. What social characteristics do they share?
3. How democratic was the First World War according to Barbusse?
4. Why is food so important to these men?
5. What point is Barbusse trying to make about the military experience in this passage?

Ernst Jünger

FROM *The Storm of Steel: From the Diary of a German Storm-Troop Officer on the Western Front*

German author Ernst Jünger (born 1895) was so eager for adventure that he ran away from home and joined the French Foreign Legion at the age of eighteen. Still only nineteen when the First World War was declared, Jünger volunteered immediately and served with considerable distinction as an officer. The Storm of Steel, Jünger's autobiographical account of his life in the trenches, was published in 1920 and is still recognized as one of the great wartime memoirs.

The following excerpt from The Storm of Steel *provides a description of the German soldier's experience during the futile but extremely deadly First Battle of the Somme in 1916. In an attempt to relieve the French line during the German assault on Verdun, British and French troops first bombarded the German line north of the*

Somme River with heavy artillery and then launched an all-out assault. In the course of this battle 650,000 Germans were killed or wounded; French and British casualties totaled 195,000 and 420,000, respectively.

From *The Storm of Steel: From the Diary of a German Storm-Troop Officer on the Western Front,* by Ernst Jünger, translated by Basil Creighton (London: Chatto and Windus, 1929).

*   *   *

In the evening we sat up a long while drinking coffee that two Frenchwomen made for us in a neighboring house. It was the strongest drink we could procure. We knew that we were on the verge this time of a battle such as the world had never seen. Soon our excited talk rose to a pitch that would have rejoiced the hearts of any freebooters, or of Frederick's Grenadiers. A few days later there were very few of that party still alive.

Guillemont

On the 23d of August we were transported in lorries to Le Mesnil. Our spirits were excellent, though we knew we were going to be put in where the battle of the Somme was at its worst. Chaff and laughter went from lorry to lorry. We marched from Le Mesnil at dusk to Sailly-Saillisel, and here the battalion dumped packs in a large meadow and paraded in battle order.

Artillery fire of a hitherto unimagined intensity rolled and thundered on our front. Thousands of twitching flashes turned the western horizon into a sea of flowers. All the while the wounded came trailing back with white, dejected faces, huddled into the ditches by the gun and ammunition columns that rattled past.

A man in a steel helmet reported to me as guide to conduct my platoon to the renowned Combles, where for the time we were to be in reserve. Sitting with him at the side of the road, I asked him, naturally enough, what it was like in the line. In reply I heard a monotonous tale of crouching all day in shell holes with no one on either flank and no trenches communicating with the rear, of unceasing attacks, of dead bodies lit-

tering the ground, of maddening thirst, of wounded and dying, and of a lot besides. The face half-framed by the steel rim of the helmet was unmoved; the voice accompanied by the sound of battle droned on, and the impression they made on me was one of unearthly solemnity. One could see that the man had been through horror to the limit of despair and there had learned to despise it. Nothing was left but supreme and superhuman indifference.

"Where you fall, there you lie. No one can help you. No one knows whether he will come back alive. They attack every day, but they can't get through. Everybody knows it is life and death."

One can fight such with fellows. We marched on along a broad paved road that showed up in the moonlight as a white band on the dark fields. In front of us the artillery fire rose to a higher and higher pitch. *Lasciate ogni speranza!*[1]

Soon we had the first shells on one side of the road and the other. Talk died down and at last ceased. Everyone listened—with that peculiar intentness that concentrates all thought and sensation in the ear—for the long-drawn howl of the approaching shell. Our nerves had a particularly severe test passing Frégicourt, a little hamlet near Combles cemetery, under continuous fire.

As far as we could see in the darkness, Combles was utterly shot to bits. The damage seemed to be recent, judging from the amount of timber among the ruins and the contents of the houses slung over the road. We climbed over numerous heaps of débris—rather hurriedly, owing to a few shrapnel shells—and reached our quarters. They were in a large, shot-riddled house. Here I estab-

---

[1] "Abandon all hope!" These words are written on the gate of Hell in Dante Alighieri's *Inferno*. [Editor.]

lished myself with three sections. The other two occupied the cellar of a ruin opposite.

At 4 A.M. we were aroused from our rest on the fragments of bed we had collected, in order to receive steel helmets. It was also the occasion of discovering a sack of coffee beans in a corner of the cellar; whereupon there followed a great brewing of coffee.

After breakfast I went out to have a look round. Heavy artillery had turned a peaceful little billeting town into a scene of desolation in the course of a day or two. Whole houses had been flattened by single direct hits or blown up so that the interiors of the rooms hung over the chaos like the scenes on a stage. A sickly scent of dead bodies rose from many of the ruins, for many civilians had been caught in the bombardment and buried beneath the wreckage of their homes. A little girl lay dead in a pool of blood on the threshold of one of the doorways.

* * *

In the course of the afternoon the firing increased to such a degree that single explosions were no longer audible. There was nothing but one terrific tornado of noise. From seven onward the square and the houses round were shelled at intervals of half a minute with fifteen-centimeter shells. There were many duds among them, which all the same made the houses rock. We sat all this while in our cellar, round a table, on armchairs covered in silk, with our heads propped on our hands, and counted the seconds between the explosions. Our jests became less frequent, till at last the foolhardiest of us fell silent, and at eight o'clock two direct hits brought down the next house.

From nine to ten the shelling was frantic. The earth rocked and the sky boiled like a gigantic cauldron.

Hundreds of heavy batteries were concentrated on and round Combles. Innumerable shells came howling and hurtling over us. Thick smoke, ominously lit up by Very lights, veiled everything. Head and ears ached violently, and we could only make ourselves understood by shouting a word at a time. The power of logical thought and the force of gravity seemed alike to be suspended. One had the sense of something as unescapable and as unconditionally fated as a catastrophe of nature. An N. C. O. of No. 3 platoon went mad.

At ten this carnival of hell gradually calmed down and passed into a steady drum fire. It was still certainly impossible to distinguish one shell from another.

* * *

At last we reached the front line. It was held by men cowering close in the shell holes, and their dead voices trembled with joy when they heard that we were the relief. A Bavarian sergeant major briefly handed over the sector and the Very-light pistol.

My platoon front formed the right wing of the position held by the regiment. It consisted of a shallow sunken road which had been pounded by shells. It was a few hundred meters left of Guillemont and a rather shorter distance right of Bois-de-Trônes. We were parted from the troops on our right, the Seventy-sixth Regiment of Infantry, by a space about five hundred meters wide. This space was shelled so violently that no troops could maintain themselves there.

The Bavarian sergeant major had vanished of a sudden, and I stood alone, the Very-light pistol in my hand, in the midst of an uncanny sea of shell holes over which lay a white mist whose swaths gave it an even more oppressive and mysterious appearance. A persistent, unpleasant smell came from behind. I was left in no doubt that it came from a gigantic corpse far gone in decay. * * *

When day dawned we were astonished to see, by degrees, what a sight surrounded us.

The sunken road now appeared as nothing but a series of enormous shell holes filled with pieces of uniform, weapons, and dead bodies. The ground all round, as far as the eye could see, was plowed by shells. You could search in vain for one wretched blade of grass. This churned-up battlefield was ghastly. Among the living lay the dead. As we dug ourselves in we found them in layers stacked one upon the top of another. One company after another had been shoved into the drum fire and steadily annihilated. The corpses were covered with the masses of soil turned up by the shells, and the next company advanced in the place of the fallen.

The sunken road and the ground behind were full of German dead; the ground in front, of English. Arms, legs, and heads stuck out stark above the lips of the craters. In front of our miserable defenses there were torn-off limbs and corpses over many of which cloaks and ground sheets had been thrown to hide the fixed stare of their distorted features. In spite of the heat no one thought for a moment of covering them with soil.

The village of Guillemont was distinguished from the landscape around it only because the shell holes there were of a whiter color by reason of the houses which had been ground to powder. Guillemont railway station lay in front of us. It was smashed to bits like a child's plaything. Delville Wood, reduced to matchwood, was farther behind.

*   *   *

It was the days at Guillemont that first made me aware of the overwhelming effects on the war of material. We had to adapt ourselves to an entirely new phase of war. The communications between the troops and the staff, between the artillery and the liaison officers, were utterly crippled by the terrific fire. Dispatch carriers failed to get through the hail of metal, and telephone wires were no sooner laid than they were shot into pieces. Even light-signaling was put out of action by the clouds of smoke and dust that hung over the field of battle. There was a zone of a kilometer behind the front line where explosives held absolute sway.

Even the regimental staff only knew exactly where we had been and how the line ran when we came back after three days and told them. Under such circumstances accuracy of artillery fire was out of the question. We were also entirely in the dark about the English line, though often, without our knowing it, it was only a few meters from us. Sometimes a Tommy, feeling his way from one shell hole to another like an ant along a track in the sand, landed in one that we occupied, and *vice versa*, for our front line consisted merely of isolated and unconnected bits that were easily mistaken.

Once seen, the landscape is an unforgettable one. In this neighborhood of villages, meadows, woods, and fields there was literally not a bush or a tiniest blade of grass to be seen. Every hand's-breadth of ground had been churned up again and again; trees had been uprooted, smashed, and ground to touchwood, the houses blown to bits and turned to dust; hills had been leveled and the arable land made a desert.

And yet the strangest thing of all was not the horror of the landscape in itself, but the fact that these scenes, such as the world had never known before, were fashioned by men who intended them to be a decisive end to the war. Thus all the frightfulness that the mind of man could devise was brought into the field; and there, where lately had been the idyllic picture of rural peace, there was as faithful a picture of the soul of scientific war. In earlier wars, certainly, towns and villages had been burned, but what was that compared with this sea of craters dug out by machines? For even in this fantastic desert there was the sameness of the machine-made article. A shell hole strewn with bully tins, broken weapons, fragments of uniform, and dud shells, with one or two dead bodies on its edge—this was the never-changing scene that surrounded each one of all these hundreds of thousands of men. And it seemed that man, on this landscape he had himself created, became different, more mysterious and hardy and callous than in any previous battle. The spirit and the tempo of the fighting altered, and after the battle of the Somme the war had its own peculiar impress that distinguished it from all other wars. After this battle the German soldier wore the steel helmet, and in his features there were chiseled the lines of an energy stretched to the utmost pitch, lines that future generations will perhaps find as fascinating and imposing as those of many heads of classical or Renaissance times.

For I cannot too often repeat, a battle was no longer an episode that spent itself in blood and fire; it was a condition of things that dug itself in remorselessly week after week and even month after month. What was a man's life in this wilderness whose vapor was laden with the stench of thousands upon thousands of decaying bodies? Death lay in ambush for each one in every shell hole, merciless, and making one merciless in turn. Chivalry here took a final farewell. It had to yield to the heightened intensity of war, just as all fine and personal feeling has to yield when machinery gets the upper hand. The Europe of today ap-

peared here for the first time on the field of battle. . . .

*   *   *

REVIEW QUESTIONS

1. What impact did the British bombardment have on the battle zone described by Jünger?
2. What affect does the bombardment seem to have had on the psyche of individual soldiers?
3. How does the kind of warfare described here differ from that of the past?
4. In what sense is this warfare a product of "the Europe of today"?

R. SCOTLAND LIDDELL

FROM *On the Russian Front*

British journalist R. Scotland Liddell (dates unknown) served on the eastern front as a medic for the Seventh Group of Polish Red Cross Volunteers. Liddell witnessed firsthand both the bravery of the Russian troops and the woeful inadequacy of their arms and provisions. On the Russian Front, *his report on the military campaign in the East, was published in 1916 with the intention of bolstering the western Allies' sympathy for their Russian partners and convincing the British public that the tsar's army remained firmly committed to the Allied effort.*

In May of 1915, Liddell was stationed at a Red Cross camp in Russian Poland, near the ongoing German offensive in western Galicia. His account provides a rare glimpse at the distinctive difficulties of warfare on the eastern front and the hardships being suffered by Russian soldiers less than two years prior to the collapse of the tsarist regime.

From *On the Russian Front*, by R. Scotland Liddell (London: Simpkin, Marshall, 1916).

Staro-Radziwillow Broken Rifles

Somewhere in Poland there was a smiling plain fringed by dark woods from which the roar of guns was heard by day and night.

*   *   *

At the edge of the wood there was a Red Cross camp where wounded men were brought from hour to hour. Two hundred yards across the field, behind a little grove, stood a cottage where broken rifles were repaired. The broken men came to be patched that they might go to fight again. The broken rifles were mended that once more they might be levelled against the invading foe. Some men—some rifles—were beyond repair. . . .

To the little cottage arsenal amongst the trees were brought six thousand rifles in a dozen weeks. Perhaps three thousand rifles were made good. Sometimes three broken guns were needed for the production of one serviceable weapon. One rifle, for instance, would have all its parts complete except the cartridge magazine and the firing bolt. Two other rifles would be wholly smashed except those needed parts. From three—one.

In the cottage itself, the kitchen had become a grimy foundry. The fire was now a tiny furnace. The pans of Polish *zur* and *kluski* had given way to pots of molten metal and bars of red-hot iron. Outside the kitchen window, the workmen sat on rough benches in the open air. The cottage folk stood idly by. Half of their house was still unoccupied by soldiers. An old man, undressed on head and neck and feet, apathetically watched the work. His poor old brain could scarcely understand it all. A wagon stood in the dusty yard, its clumsy wheels rusty from disuse. By the straw-strewn door of the cottage stable an old dog growled fiercely at each stranger's arrival. The working men hummed simple tunes and sang to the accompaniment of hammer and rasp. The boom of cannon seemed to shake the air.

There was a shed at one end of the yard—a wooden shed with many ragged gaps. The mended guns stood in it piled in neat stacks. Heaps of the various parts were all around. Here, a box of tiny screws; there, a pile of bayonets; and again, a heaped-up mass of firing bolts and other units of the gun. Each mended rifle was tested before it left the arsenal. When I was there I aimed one rifle at a small, fleecy cloud and fired a bullet up into the sky.

Across the field—the broken men. Across the woods—the broken land. And here—the broken rifles with their histories of varying tragedy.

*   *   *

This turning of the cottage into a workshop was significant of one of the greatest difficulties that Russia had to contend with—distance. The nearest town in which the rifles could have been repaired was too far away from the firing line to be convenient. The means of communication, moreover, were not sufficiently good. And yet again, there was a shortage of rifles. The broken ones had to be repaired with all speed. Hence the cottage arsenal, within sound of the rifle fire itself, within range of the German guns.

In England, it's a long, long way to Tipperary. On the Eastern front, it's a longer way to anywhere at all. New roads had to be cut through virgin forest—great straight roads that ran for miles without a turn. Little tramways were laid across the fields for the easier transport of guns and ammunition and wounded men. Later on, when we had retreated out of Poland into Lithuania, there were great stretches of country with no roads except mere rough tracks. For many versts there were no villages. It was possible to ride for hours across bleak country without encountering a single house.

Russia's lack of good routes was almost as bad as another enemy. I was told, when we were still west of Warsaw, that there were seventeen railway routes from Berlin to the Eastern front. This means of communication was almost as good as an ally for Germany.

*   *   *

One night, May 30, the firing was very heavy. Big guns boomed all the time, making the rifle volleys almost unheard. I stood on the top of the reserve trench embankment and thought of all the scenes beyond the wood. Then I went to my tent to sleep. Tired as I was, I could not. The noise of the battle was too great. It was the heaviest bombardment I had heard. ✳ ✳ ✳

Grey morning came and with the coming of the light we saw a wagon rumbling on the little tram-way over the fields towards us. There were six soldiers hanging over the sides, coughing and gasping for breath. The enemy had attacked with gas shells and the men were poisoned. Their lungs were terribly burned. We put the men on stretchers in the open sandy space between our sleeping tent and that in which the wounded men were placed. A doctor hurried to attend to them. To see these men choking was an awful sight. Three died in agony. It was very terrible to watch them, but it was nothing to what we were to witness that day.

More wagons came, and then an almost constant stream. Many of the poisoned men were dead before they arrived at our camp. In one wagon three dead lay on three dying. Before an hour had passed we had five hundred men, but hundreds more arrived. In all, that day, we had two thousand one hundred poisoned men, and many others who were wounded. One hundred and forty-three men died in our camp. Nearly five hundred died after we had sent them off to Zyrardow and Warsaw.

✳   ✳   ✳

It was really almost impossible to do anything for the worst cases. We tried artificial respiration, but without much success. As the men choked for life they grew purple in the face—their tongues grew almost black. They died most painfully. I myself saw sixty-seven men die. I helped to carry their bodies to the large tent that we used as a mortuary. We found that not only had the brass parts of the men's equipment been turned green with the gas, but their clips of bullets were also all coated with a green film. Later on it was discovered that the gas used was a mixture of chloride and sulphur. The effect on the lungs was terrible. Doctor Sklodowski, a brother of Madame Curie of Radium fame, told me that he feared that even should the men live, most of them would have tuberculosis. Very few poisoned men would escape the disease.

✳   ✳   ✳

We dug graves for the men next day. One very large one and another. In the former were buried one hundred and eight men, and in the latter, thirty-five. Such graves are called "fraternal." The men were buried in their clothes—just as they had died. But first we took their belongings from their pockets, in order, if possible, to send them to their relatives. They were pathetically interesting. Almost every man had a purse, but very little money. The whole number had not a hundred roubles amongst them. There were watches of all sizes and metals. Silver rings—the favourite ones were fashioned in the form of a skull with green and red stones in the place of eyes. One man had only a brass button and a soiled piece of loaf sugar in his pocket. Another had a faded photograph of a woman, wrapped in a piece of coloured cloth. Some had pocket-books with letters in them and photographs of their folks and of themselves. These latter were of fine, brave, clean-looking men, moustaches well waxed and faces looking very proudly from out of the glossy card. The difference was striking—the men as they had been and as they now were. There were little trinkets, too, and nails and pieces of string and all manner of odds and ends. The heap of articles might have been treasure trove from schoolboys' pockets.

✳   ✳   ✳

REVIEW QUESTIONS

1. What does Liddell's account suggest about Russian military preparedness?
2. How did conditions on the eastern front differ from those on the western front?
3. What special problems confronted the Russian military?
4. How do Liddell and Wilfred Owen describe the effects of poison gas on soldiers?

BONNIE SMITH

FROM *Confessions of a Concierge*

The First World War produced a dramatic break in the continuity of soldiers' lives, but its effects on civilian populations were often less immediate, especially in the early stages of the war. Those living in close proximity to the battlefront suffered substantial loss of life and property, but those living safely behind the lines experienced the hardships of war in a less direct manner, in the form of food rationing, long hours of work in armaments factories, or the dreaded telegram announcing the death of a loved one. Madame Lucie (1896–1981), an elderly Parisian interviewed by American historian Bonnie Smith in the 1970s, remembered the war less as a major "historical" event than as an important element in her developing personal life. When the war broke out in 1914, Madame Lucie and her mother were running a small hat shop in the garrison city of Lisieux in northwestern France. Madame Lucie was eighteen years old and, despite her mother's scolding, eager to flirt with the young soldiers who had been stationed in the town prior to their departure for the front.

From *Confessions of a Concierge: Madame Lucie's History of Twentieth Century France,* by Bonnie Smith (New Haven, Conn.: Yale University Press, 1985), pp. 32–34, 38–41.

*   *   *

Madame Lucie Gets Married

*   *   *

* * * right under Maman's eyes, I met soldiers. They talked to me while I brought our waste to the doorstop. In those days, it was natural to say a little *bonjour* to one's neighbor while holding a chamber pot, whose contents would soon be fertilizing Norman fields. As I opened the shutters or watered the flowers in the windowboxes, a passing soldier might stop for a second, and I was polite. Often the young men quartered on the second floor of the house facing ours waved to me. How could one avoid soldiers in a city like this?

On my excursions to fetch water, I tried to see as much as I could, especially the pilgrims, and also the goods in shop windows. One day, rather preoccupied with the sights and with the water jar, I saw two soldiers approaching. Not alert enough to the situation, we met at a point where the sidewalk was narrow, bounded by a building on one side and a horsehitch on the other. The first soldier leaned politely toward the building while I navigated past the horsehitch, my water jar not making things easier. Suddenly we were bottlenecked, for my skirt had caught in the hitch. I remained its prisoner, spilling water in my effort to move, until the soldier released me. The soldier was Philippe, friend of the young men across the street. Later, he said he had vowed to marry me at that very moment he saw me blushing and discomfited by our unexpected brush together.

From that time on Philippe passed by our boutique whenever possible, and I arranged to be at the counter, or even better, out watering the plants when I thought he might be passing. I looked for him and thought of him almost continually. Maman did not help matters any by singing her romantic songs, like the "Polka à Moustache," while we worked. I knew it was wrong to be thinking of soldiers, to meet a beau in this way, but there was no help for me. After weeks of this, one day I came into the store, having talked to Philippe while I (slowly, very slowly) closed the shutters.

"Who was that young man with you out there?" Maman asked sternly.

"Just a passing soldier, Maman," I replied.

"Enough of these stories. You are not to leave this building, and above all you are not to talk to that soldier again."

There was nothing to say. One didn't argue with parents in those days. But that evening I wrote a note to Philippe explaining our problem. Next morning, the apprentice, sent to do my usual errands, took the note to a café where Philippe had told me he could be found in emergencies. She returned and, when Maman left the workroom, reported that he had indeed been in the café but had said nothing after reading the note.

My heart began to break. A dream of Philippe had taken over my life, and I couldn't accept that this, too, would have to end. I was sitting, desperate at the possibility, when a letter arrived for my parents. Maman took a long time reading it, then tucked it away. When Papa came home she handed it to him. Somehow I knew it was from Philippe, so much had Maman looked at me that day. Finally, they told me that he might visit me at home. Philippe had explained himself so finely that Maman called him "honorable."

In those visits, while we all sat and talked together, Philippe won my parents over, and before I knew it we were engaged to be married. What a time! How improbable! Philippe was an orphan, a soldier, a stranger to all of us. Yet we were going to get married. Maman and I started sewing, and the first thing we made was a new dress and hat for me to wear on an engagement trip to my grandmother's in Caen. Philippe wore his best uniform and met us at the train station with a white bouquet and a tiny ring for me. I have never been so happy and will always remember the day —July 14, the *fête nationale*, 1914. Three weeks later Philippe went off to war.

I did something unusual for our family by writing letters every day for three months until, in October, Philippe was killed. Some time later we held a family reunion and had our picture taken: Papa and his brother with their joking smiles; Maman in mourning out of respect and love for my fiancé; I, in mourning also, having vowed never to marry.

The death of Philippe made this war the most important and least significant event of my life. That moment—his death—lasted forever; and then nothing else about wartime touched me. Besides, compared to the regions north and east of us we hardly suffered. Battles weren't fought on our fields; we weren't occupied; neither combatants nor wounded, nor ambulances nor munitions crossed our paths. Maman and I continued making hats, but our ingenuity was tested as luxury fabrics became scarce. We sewed with felt instead of silk, and especially we made mourning hats until, after a couple of years, every woman in Lisieux and the countryside had one. So you can see that while many people would thereafter be obsessed by the story of the war, for me it would always and only mean the death of Philippe.

*   *   *

But I was young, and one day in 1916 I met another soldier, with whom, as the expression goes, I fell in love at first sight. Entering our boutique to find corporal's stripes, Pierre was handsome in his uniform and his curled moustache.

*   *   *

We had only one problem: Pierre was married.

At any other time, I wouldn't have thought of looking at a married man, but war was different. Besides, being spoiled and headstrong, I felt that I should have the person I loved no matter what. From the first Pierre had explained his situation. Before the war he had worked for the Pathé brothers, our great film makers. He had set up their theaters around France, and while doing this work in Nancy had met a woman with whom he eloped. But war came, and when he went home on his first leave, his wife had left without a trace. Pierre was now in the process of getting a divorce, and even though it was not his fault, as one would say, still the whole business was scandalous.

My parents were astonished when we finally told them. Maman looked grim, even though Pierre was so obviously upset at having to talk of his own humiliation over the divorce procedure. Seeing my determination, Papa did nothing more than give his assent, but after Pierre left, he fumed.

"Oh, it's unfortunate to have an only daughter, and her about to marry a divorced man."

In spite of everything I was happy.

*　　*　　*

Then, right in the middle of it all, the war took Pierre to Salonika on the Balkan front—even though he was unfit, so the army decreed, for active service.

*　　*　　*

Suddenly the war ended, and my fiancé was on his way home.

*　　*　　*

Pierre returned, and together we waited for his divorce to be settled. Meanwhile, news of my impending marriage traveled the neighborhood, though we tried to keep it secret because of the circumstances. Our priest stopped me one day to offer his congratulations.

"This will be a fine marriage for the parish, Mlle Brun."

"I'm afraid not, Father. My fiancé is divorced." I explained the desertion by Pierre's wife, but that didn't soften his stern look.

"Well, Mademoiselle, I'm going to have to excommunicate you. Come back after the wedding and we'll see what it takes to straighten things out. I'll be waiting for you."

With that he turned back to the church, probably to start filling the forms and counting the costs for my reinstatement. I can assure you, he's still waiting for me.

We were married July 22, 1919, in a small and quiet ceremony because of this new scandal.

*　　*　　*

For three days the family celebrated. Pierre, now my excellent husband, and I spent our wedding night at my parents'. It was a shock, I can tell you, because except for my few months as an apprentice, I had never heard much about sex.

But we had good customs in Normandy. People sang all the time in those days. * * *

that night after my husband and I had gone to our room, after things began to seem strange to me, suddenly clanging and singing broke out, my father's voice louder than all the rest:

Said the mattress to the sheets
I have never seen such feats.
Said the pillow to the case
We've been shaken to the base.

Pierre and I giggled, holding one another until we went to sleep.

*　　*　　*

REVIEW QUESTIONS

1. How was Madame Lucie affected by the war?
2. What do her experiences tell you about the relationship between the homefront and the battlefront?
3. To what extent were traditions regulating marriage and the family transformed by the war?
4. What benefits might young women like Madame Lucie have derived from the social changes brought by the war?

VERA BRITTAIN

FROM *Testament of Youth*

Despite an eminently respectable "provincial young ladyhood," British author Vera Brittain (1893–1970) rebelled early against the constraints imposed by age, class, and sex. Brittain insisted on pursuing her education, despite her parents' protests, and attended Sommerville, a college for women affiliated with Oxford. She experienced the outbreak of the First World War as "an infuriating personal interruption rather than a world-wide catastrophe," but this attitude changed dramatically after her fiancé, brother, and best male friends enlisted and then died, one by one. Frustrated by her inability to become a soldier and share the hardships of her male peers, she chose the nearest thing: service as a Voluntary Aid Detachment nurse. After a period of training in England, she attended wounded soldiers on the island of Malta and the western front. The following excerpts from Brittain's widely read memoir, Testament of Youth, *demonstrate the various ways in which the lives of ordinary individuals were disrupted and transformed during the course of the war.*

From *Testament of Youth: An Autobiographical Study of the Years 1900–1925,* by Vera Brittain (London: V. Gollancz, 1933).

*   *   *

Nurse's Training

On Sunday morning, June 27th, 1915, I began my nursing at the Devonshire Hospital. * * *

From our house above the town I ran eagerly downhill to my first morning's work, not knowing, fortunately for myself, that my servitude would last for nearly four years. The hospital had originally been used as a riding-school, but a certain Duke of Devonshire, with exemplary concern for the welfare of the sick but none whatever for the feet of the nursing staff, had caused it to be converted to its present charitable purpose. The main part of the building consisted of a huge dome, with two stone corridors running one above the other round its quarter-mile circumference. The nurses were not allowed to cross its diameter, which contained an inner circle reserved for convalescent patients, so that everything forgotten or newly required meant a run round the circumference. * * *

My hours there ran from 7.45 a.m. until 1 p.m., and again from 5.0 p.m. until 9.15 p.m.—a longer day, as I afterwards discovered, than that normally required in many Army hospitals. No doubt the staff was not unwilling to make the utmost use of so enthusiastic and unsophisticated a probationer. Meals, for all of which I was expected to go home, were not included in these hours. As our house was nearly half a mile from the hospital on the slope of a steep hill, I never completely overcame the aching of my back and the soreness of my feet throughout the time that I worked there, and felt perpetually as if I had just returned from a series of long route marches.

I never minded these aches and pains, which appeared to me solely as satisfactory tributes to my love for Roland. What did profoundly trouble and humiliate me was my colossal ignorance of the simplest domestic operations. Among other "facts of life," my expensive education had omitted to teach me the prosaic but important essentials of egg-boiling, and the Oxford cookery classes had triumphantly failed to repair the omission. I imagined that I had to bring the saucepan to the boil, then turn off the gas and allow the egg to lie for three minutes in the cooling water. The remarks of a lance-corporal to whom I presented an egg "boiled" in this fashion led me to make shamefaced inquiries of my superiors, from whom I learnt, in those first few days, how numerous and devastating were the errors that it was possible to commit in carrying out the most ordinary functions of everyday life. To me, for whom meals had hitherto appeared as though by clockwork and the routine of a house had seemed to be worked by some invisible mechanism, the complications of sheer existence were nothing short of a revelation.

Despite my culinary shortcomings, the men appeared to like me; none of them were very ill, and no doubt my youth, my naïve eagerness and the clean freshness of my new uniform meant more to them than any amount of common sense and efficiency. Perhaps, too, the warm and profoundly surprising comfort that I derived from their presence produced a tenderness which was able to communicate back to them, in turn, something of their own rich consolation.

Throughout my two decades of life, I had never looked upon the nude body of an adult male; I had never even seen a naked boy-child since the nursery days when, at the age of four or five, I used to share my evening baths with Edward. I had therefore expected, when I first started nursing, to be overcome with nervousness and embarrassment, but, to my infinite relief, I was conscious of neither. Towards the men I came to feel an almost adoring gratitude for their simple and natural acceptance of my ministrations. Short of actually going to bed with them, there was hardly an intimate service that I did not perform for one or another in the course of four years, and I still have reason to be thankful for the knowledge of masculine functioning which the care of them gave me, and for my early release from the sex-

inhibitions that even to-day—thanks to the Victorian tradition which up to 1914 dictated that a young woman should know nothing of men but their faces and their clothes until marriage pitchforked her into an incompletely visualised and highly disconcerting intimacy—beset many of my female contemporaries, both married and single.

In the early days of the War the majority of soldier patients belonged to a first-rate physical type which neither wounds nor sickness, unless mortal, could permanently impair, and from the constant handling of their lean, muscular bodies, I came to understand the essential cleanliness, the innate nobility, of sexual love on its physical side. Although there was much to shock in Army hospital service, much to terrify, much, even, to disgust, this day-by-day contact with male anatomy was never part of the shame. Since it was always Roland whom I was nursing by proxy, my attitude towards him imperceptibly changed; it became less romantic and more realistic, and thus a new depth was added to my love.

In addition to the patients, I managed to extract approval from most of the nurses—no doubt because, my one desire being to emulate Roland's endurance, I seized with avidity upon all the unpleasant tasks of which they were only too glad to be relieved, and took a masochistic delight in emptying bed-pans, washing greasy cups and spoons, and disposing of odoriferous dressings in the sink-room. The Matron described as "a slave-driver" by one of the elegant lady V.A.D.s who intermittently trotted in to "help" in the evenings after the bulk of the work was done—treated me with especial kindness, and often let me out through her private gate in order to save me a few yards of the inter-minable miles upon my feet.

My particular brand of enthusiasm, the nurses told me later, was rare among the local V.A.D.s, most of whom came to the hospital expecting to hold the patients' hands and smooth their pillows while the regular nurses fetched and carried everything that looked or smelt disagreeable. Probably this was true, for my diary records of one Buxton girl a month later: "Nancy thinks she would like to take up Red Cross work but does not want to go where she would have to dust wards and clean up as she does not think she would like that."

*   *   *

At the Western Front

Only a day or two afterwards I was leaving quarters to go back to my ward, when I had to wait to let a large contingent of troops march past me along the main road that ran through our camp. They were swinging rapidly towards Camiers, and though the sight of soldiers marching was now too familiar to arouse curiosity, an unusual quality of bold vigour in their swift stride caused me to stare at them with puzzled interest.

They looked larger than ordinary men; their tall, straight figures were in vivid contrast to the under-sized armies of pale recruits to which we had grown accustomed. At first I thought their spruce, clean uniforms were those of officers, yet obviously they could not be officers, for there were too many of them; they seemed, as it were, Tommies in heaven. Had yet another regiment been conjured out of our depleted Dominions? I wondered, watching them move with such rhythm, such dignity, such serene consciousness of self-respect. But I knew the colonial troops so well, and these were different; they were assured where the Australians were aggressive, self-possessed where the New Zealanders were turbulent.

Then I heard an excited exclamation from a group of Sisters behind me.

"Look! Look! Here are the Americans!"

I pressed forward with the others to watch the United States physically entering the War, so god-like, so magnificent, so splendidly unimpaired in comparison with the tired, nerve-racked men of the British Army. So these were our deliverers at last, marching up the road to Camiers in the spring sunshine! There seemed to be hundreds of them, and in the fearless swagger of their proud strength they looked a formidable bulwark against the peril looming from Amiens.

Somehow the necessity of packing up in a hurry, the ignominious flight to the coast so long imagined, seemed to move further away. An uncontrollable emotion seized me—as such emotions often seized us in those days of insufficient sleep; my eyeballs pricked, my throat ached, and a mist swam over the confident Americans going to the front. The coming of relief made me realise all at once how long and how intolerable had been the tension, and with the knowledge that we were not, after all, defeated, I found myself beginning to cry.

*   *   *

War's End

When the sound of victorious guns burst over London at 11 a.m. on November 11th, 1918, the men and women who looked incredulously into each other's faces did not cry jubilantly: "We've won the War!" They only said "The War is over."

From Millbank I heard the maroons crash with terrifying clearness, and, like a sleeper who is determined to go on dreaming after being told to wake up, I went on auto-matically washing the dressing bowls in the annex outside my hut. Deeply buried beneath my consciousness there stirred the vague memory of a letter that I had written Roland in those legendary days when I was still at Oxford and could spend my Sundays in thinking of him while the organ echoed grandly through New College Chapel. It had been a warm May evening, when all the city was sweet with the scent of wallflowers and lilac, and I had walked back to Micklem Hall after hearing an Occasional Oratorio by Handel, which described the mustering of troops for battle, the lament for the fallen and the triumphant return of the victors.

"As I listened," I told him, "to the organ swelling forth into a final triumphant burst in the song of victory, after the solemn and mournful dirge over the dead, I thought with what mockery and irony the jubilant celebrations which we hail the coming of peace will fall upon the ears of those to whom their best will never return, upon whose sorrow victory is built, who have paid with their mourning for the others' joy. I wonder if I shall be one of those who take happy part in the triumph—or if I shall listen to the merriment with a heart that breaks and ears that try to keep out the mirthful sounds."

And as I dried the bowls, I thought: "It's come too late for me. Somehow I knew, even at Oxford, that it would. Why couldn't it have ended rationally, as it might have ended, in 1916, instead of all that trumpet-blowing against a negotiated peace, and the ferocious talk of secure civilians about marching to Berlin? It's come five months too late—or is it three years? It might have ended last June, and let Edward, at least, be saved! Only five months—it's such a little time, when Roland died nearly three years ago."

But on Armistice Day not even a lonely survivor drowning in black waves of memory could be left alone with her thoughts. A moment after the guns had subsided into sudden, palpitating silence, the other V.A.D. from my ward dashed excitedly into the annex.

"Brittain! Brittain! Did you hear the maroons? It's over—it's all over! Do let's come out and see what's happening!" Mechanically, I followed her into the road, as I stood there, stupidly rigid, long after the triumphant explosions from Westminster had turned into a distant crescendo of shouting, I saw a taxicab turn swiftly in from the Embankment toward the hospital. The next moment there was a cry for doctors and nurses from passers-by, for in rounding the corner the taxi had knocked down a small elderly woman who in listening, like myself, to the wild noise of a world released from nightmare, had failed to observe its approach.

As I hurried to her side I realised that she was all but dead and already past speech. Like Victor in the mortuary chapel, she seemed to have shrunk to the dimensions of a child with the sharp features of age, but on the tiny chalk-white face an expression of shocked surprise still lingered, and she stared hard at me as Geoffrey had stared at his orderly in those last moments of conscious silence beside the Scarpe. Had she been thinking, I wondered, when the taxi struck her, of her sons at the front, now safe? The next moment a medical officer and some orderlies came up, and I went back to my ward.

But I remembered her at intervals throughout that afternoon, during which, with a half-masochistic notion of "seeing the sights," I made a circular tour to Kensington by way of the intoxicated West End. With aching persistence my thoughts went back to the dead and the strange irony of their fates—to Roland, gifted, ardent, ambitious, who had died without glory in the conscientious performance of a routine job; to Victor and Geoffrey, gentle and diffident, who, conquering nature by resolution, had each gone down bravely in a big "show"; and finally to Edward, musical, serene, a lover of peace, who had fought courageously through so many battles and at last had been killed while leading a vital counter-attack in one of the few decisive actions of the War. As I struggled through the waving, shrieking crowds in Piccadilly and Regent Street on the overloaded top of a 'bus, some witty enthusiast for contemporary history symbolically turned upside down the sign-board "Seven Kings."

Late that evening, when supper was over, a group of elated V.A.D.s who were anxious to walk through Westminster and Whitehall to Buckingham Palace prevailed upon me to join them. Outside the Admiralty a crazy group of convalescent Tommies were collecting specimens of different uniforms and bundling their wearers into flag-strewn taxis; with a shout they seized two of my companions and disappeared into the clamorous crowd, waving flags and shaking rattles. Wherever we went a burst of enthusiastic cheering greeted our Red Cross uniform, and complete strangers adorned with wound stripes rushed up and shook me warmly by the hand. After the long, long blackness, it seemed like a fairy-tale to see the street lamps shining through the chill November gloom.

I detached myself from the others and walked slowly up Whitehall, with my heart sinking in a sudden cold dismay. Already this was a different world from the one that I had known during four life-long years, a world in which people would be light-hearted and forgetful, in which themselves and their careers and their amusements would blot out political ideals and great national issues. And in that brightly lit, alien world I should have no part. All those with whom I had really been intimate were gone; not one remained to share with me the heights and the depths of my memories. As the years went by and youth departed and remembrance grew dim, a deeper and ever deeper darkness would cover the young men who were once my contemporaries.

For the first time I realised, with all that full realisation meant, how completely everything that had hitherto made up my life had vanished with Edward and Roland, with Victor and Geoffrey. The War was over; a new age was beginning; but the dead were dead and would never return.

REVIEW QUESTIONS

1. How did Brittain's experiences as a nurse change her attitude toward human sexuality?
2. Why did she so willingly accept the hard and sometimes unpleasant work nursing entailed?
3. How does Brittain describe the newly arrived American troops?
4. In a letter to her fiancé, Brittain expressed the fear that the war would put "a barrier of indescribable experience between men and the women whom they loved." Do you think this concern was valid?

FROM The Versailles Treaty

Toward the end of the war, the American president Woodrow Wilson began to lobby for a "peace without victory" and proposed a set of Fourteen Points as the basis for eventual peace negotiations. Wilson envisioned a just settlement that would permanently eradicate recourse to armed conflict by striking at the root causes of all wars and not simply at the incidental factors that had precipitated this particular war. He called for an end to the arms races and secret diplomacy of the prewar era, and he proposed that the new international order be based on the principles of democracy, international free trade, and the right of ethnic minorities to self-determination, all of which would be guaranteed by a league of nations. When the new German government sued for peace in late 1918, it did so in the hopes that the peace settlement would be negotiated on the basis of Wilson's proposals. However, Germany was not allowed to send representatives to the Versailles Conference, and the representatives of the European Allies—Clemenceau for France, Lloyd George for Britain, and Orlando for Italy—produced a rather different treaty than that suggested by the Fourteen Points. Despite Wilson's very active role in the framing of the settlement, the Versailles Treaty, 1919, was not ratified by the U.S. Congress, and the United States never joined Wilson's cherished League of Nations.

From The Versailles Treaty, World War I Document Archive web page, www.lib.byu.edu/~rdh/wwi/ [accessed 11/21/01].

WAR PROPAGANDA (1917)

Poster art was a leading form of propaganda used by all belligerents in the First World War to enlist men, sell war bonds, and sustain morale on the home front. In addition, many posters demonized the enemy to rationalize the unprecedented loss of life and national wealth. This U.S. poster from 1917 exemplifies the hate mongering that war posters promoted. How is the enemy characterized in this poster and how might such characterizations have affected the postwar political climate?

*   *   *

The Covenant of the League of Nations

The HIGH CONTRACTING PARTIES, In order to promote international cooperation and to achieve international peace and security

by the acceptance of obligations not to resort to war by the prescription of open, just and honourable relations between nations

by the firm establishment of the understandings of international law as the actual rule of conduct among Governments, and

by the maintenance of justice and a scrupulous respect for all treaty obligations in the dealings of organised peoples with one another

Agree to this Covenant of the League of Nations.

*   *   *

ARTICLE 8

The Members of the League recognise that the maintenance of peace requires the reduction of national armaments to the lowest point consistent with national safety and the enforcement by common action of international obligations. The Council, taking account of the geographical situation and circumstances of each State, shall formulate plans for such reduction for the consideration and action of the several Governments. Such plans shall be subject to reconsideration and revision at least every ten years.

*   *   *

ARTICLE 10

The Members of the League undertake to respect and preserve as against external aggression the ter-ritorial integrity and existing political independence of all Members of the League. *   *   *

ARTICLE 11

Any war or threat of war, whether immediately affecting any of the Members of the League or not, is hereby declared a matter of concern to the whole League, and the League shall take any action that may be deemed wise and effectual to safeguard the peace of nations. *   *   *

ARTICLE 12

The Members of the League agree that if there should arise between them any dispute likely to lead to a rupture, they will submit the matter either to arbitration or to inquiry by the Council, and they agree in no case to resort to war until three months after the award by the arbitrators or the report by the Council.

*   *   *

ARTICLE 16

Should any Member of the League resort to war in disregard of its covenants *   *   *, it shall ipso facto be deemed to have committed an act of war against all other Members of the League, which hereby undertake immediately to subject it to the severance of all trade or financial relations, the prohibition of all intercourse between their nations and the nationals of the covenant-breaking State, and the prevention of all financial, commercial, or personal intercourse between the nationals of the covenant-breaking State and the nationals of any other State, whether a Member of the League or not. *   *   * Any Member of the League which has violated any covenant of the League may be declared to be no longer a Member of the League by a vote of the Council concurred in by the Representatives of all the other Members of the League represented thereon.

* * *

ARTICLE 18

Every treaty or international engagement entered into hereafter by any Member of the League shall be forthwith registered with the Secretariat and shall as soon as possible be published by it. No such treaty or international engagement shall be binding until so registered.

* * *

ARTICLE 22

To those colonies and territories which as a consequence of the late war have ceased to be under the sovereignty of the States which formerly governed them and which are inhabited by peoples not yet able to stand by themselves under the strenuous conditions of the modern world, there should be applied the principle that the well-being and development of such peoples form a sacred trust of civilisation and that securities for the performance of this trust should be embodied in this Covenant. The best method of giving practical effect to this principle is that the tutelage of such peoples should be entrusted to advanced nations who by reason of their resources, their experience or their geographical position can best undertake this responsibility, and who are willing to accept it, and that this tutelage should be exercised by them as Mandatories on behalf of the League. The character of the mandate must differ according to the stage of the development of the people, the geographical situation of the territory, its economic conditions, and other similar circumstances. Certain communities formerly belonging to the Turkish Empire have reached a stage of development where their existence as independent nations can be provisionally recognised subject to the rendering of administrative advice and assistance by a Mandatory until such time as they are able to stand alone. The wishes of these communities must be a principal consideration in the selection of the Mandatory. Other peoples, especially those of Central Africa, are at such a stage that the Mandatory must be responsible for the administration of the territory under conditions which will guarantee freedom of conscience and religion, subject only to the maintenance of public order and morals, the prohibition of abuses such as the slave trade, the arms traffic, and the liquor traffic, and the prevention of the establishment of fortifications or military and naval bases and of military training of the natives for other than police purposes and the defence of territory, and will also secure equal opportunities for the trade and commerce of other Members of the League. There are territories, such as South-West Africa and certain of the South Pacific Islands, which, owing to the sparseness of their population, or their small size, or their remoteness from the centres of civilisation, or their geographical contiguity to the territory of the Mandatory, and other circumstances, can be best administered under the laws of the Mandatory as integral portions of its territory, subject to the safeguards above mentioned in the interests of the indigenous population. In every case of mandate, the Mandatory shall render to the Council an annual report in reference to the territory committed to its charge. * * *

ARTICLE 23

* * * The Members of the League: (a) will endeavour to secure and maintain fair and humane conditions of labour for men, women, and children, both in their own countries and in all countries to which their commercial and industrial relations extend, and for that purpose will establish and maintain the necessary international organisations; (b) undertake to secure just treatment of the native inhabitants of territories under their control; (c) will entrust the League with the general supervision over the execution of agreements with regard to the traffic in women and children, and the traffic in opium and other dangerous drugs; (d) will entrust the League with the general supervision of the trade in arms and ammunition with the countries in which the control of this traffic is necessary in the common interest; (e) will make provision to secure and maintain freedom of communications and of transit and equitable treatment for the commerce of all Members of the League. In this connection, the special necessities of the regions devastated during the war of 1914–1918 shall be borne in mind; (f) will endeavour to take steps in matters of international concern for the prevention and control of disease.

*　　*　　*

ARTICLE 25

The Members of the League agree to encourage and promote the establishment and co-operation of duly authorised voluntary national Red Cross organisations having as purposes the improvement of health, the prevention of disease, and the mitigation of suffering throughout the world.

*　　*　　*

ARTICLE 42

Germany is forbidden to maintain or construct any fortifications either on the left bank of the Rhine or on the right bank to the west of a line drawn 50 kilometres to the East of the Rhine.

ARTICLE 43

In the area defined above the maintenance and the assembly of armed forces, either permanently or temporarily, and military maneuvers of any kind, as well as the upkeep of all permanent works for mobilization, are in the same way forbidden.

ARTICLE 44

In case Germany violates in any manner whatever the provisions of Articles 42 and 43, she shall be regarded as committing a hostile act against the Powers signatory of the present Treaty and as calculated to disturb the peace of the world.

ARTICLE 45

As compensation for the destruction of the coal-mines in the north of France and as part payment towards the total reparation due from Germany for the damage resulting from the war, Germany cedes to France in full and absolute possession, with exclusive rights of exploitation, unencumbered and free from all debts and charges of any kind, the coal-mines situated in the Saar Basin. * * *

*　　*　　*

ARTICLE 49

* * * At the end of fifteen years from the coming into force of the present Treaty the inhabitants of the [Saar Basin] shall be called upon to indicate the sovereignty under which they desire to be placed.

*　　*　　*

ARTICLE 51

The territories [of Alsace and Lorraine] which were ceded to Germany in accordance with the Preliminaries of Peace signed at Versailles on February 26, 1871, and the Treaty of Frankfort of May 10, 1871, are restored to French sovereignty as from the date of the Armistice of November 11, 1918. * * *

*　　*　　*

ARTICLE 80

Germany acknowledges and will respect strictly the independence of Austria * * * ; she agrees that this independence shall be inalienable, except with the consent of the Council of the League of Nations.

ARTICLE 81

Germany * * * recognises the complete independence of the Czecho-Slovak State. * * *

*   *   *

ARTICLE 84

German nationals habitually resident in any of the territories recognised as forming part of the Czecho-Slovak State will obtain Czecho-Slovak nationality ipso facto and lose their German nationality.

*   *   *

ARTICLE 87

Germany, in conformity with the action already taken by the Allied and Associated Powers, recognises the complete independence of Poland. * * *

*   *   *

ARTICLE 102

The Principal Allied and Associated Powers undertake to establish the town of Danzig, together with the rest of the territory described in Article 100, as a Free City. It will be placed under the protection of the League of Nations.

*   *   *

ARTICLE 116

Germany acknowledges and agrees to respect as permanent and inalienable the independence of all the territories which were part of the former Russian Empire on August 1, 1914.

* * * Germany accepts definitely the abrogation of the Brest-Litovsk Treaties and of all other treaties, conventions, and agreements entered into by her with the Maximalist Government in Russia.

The Allied and Associated Powers formally reserve the rights of Russia to obtain from Germany restitution and reparation based on the principles of the present Treaty.

*   *   *

ARTICLE 119

Germany renounces in favour of the Principal Allied and Associated Powers all her rights and titles over her oversea possessions.

*   *   *

ARTICLE 160

* * * The total number of effectives in the Army of the States constituting Germany must not exceed one hundred thousand men, including officers and establishments of depots. The Army shall be devoted exclusively to the maintenance of order within the territory and to the control of the frontiers.

The total effective strength of officers, including the personnel of staffs, whatever their composition, must not exceed four thousand. * * *

*   *   *

ARTICLE 168

The manufacture of arms, munitions, or any war material, shall only be carried out in factories or works the location of which shall be communicated to and approved by the Governments of the Principal Allied and Associated Powers, and the number of which they retain the right to restrict. * * *

*   *   *

ARTICLE 173

Universal compulsory military service shall be abolished in Germany.

The German Army may only be constituted and recruited by means of voluntary enlistment.

*   *   *

ARTICLE 176

On the expiration of two months from the coming into force of the present Treaty there must only exist in Germany the number of military schools which is absolutely indispensable for the recruitment of the officers of the units allowed. * * *

*   *   *

ARTICLE 181

* * * The German naval forces in commission must not exceed:

6 battleships of the Deutschland or Lothringen type, 6 light cruisers, 12 destroyers, 12 torpedo boats. * * *

No submarines are to be included.

All other warships, except where there is provision to the contrary in the present Treaty, must be placed in reserve or devoted to commercial purposes.

*   *   *

ARTICLE 198

The armed forces of Germany must not include any military or naval air forces. * * *

*   *   *

ARTICLE 227

The Allied and Associated Powers publicly arraign William II of Hohenzollern, formerly German Emperor, for a supreme offence against international morality and the sanctity of treaties. * * *

*   *   *

ARTICLE 231

The Allied and Associated Governments affirm and Germany accepts the responsibility of Germany and her allies for causing all the loss and damage to which the Allied and Associated Governments and their nationals have been subjected as a consequence of the war imposed upon them by the aggression of Germany and her allies. * * *

ARTICLE 232

The Allied and Associated Governments recognise that the resources of Germany are not adequate, after taking into account permanent diminutions of such resources which will result from other provisions of the present Treaty, to make complete reparation for all such loss and damage.

The Allied and Associated Governments, however, require, and Germany undertakes, that she will make compensation for all damage done to the civilian population of the Allied and Associated Powers and to their property during the period of the belligerency of each as an Allied or Associated Power against Germany. * * *

ARTICLE 233

The amount of the above damage for which compensation is to be made by Germany shall be determined by an Inter-Allied Commission. * * *

*   *   *

Organisation of Labour

Whereas the League of Nations has for its object the establishment of universal peace, and such a peace can be established only if it is based upon social justice;

And whereas conditions of labour exist involving such injustice, hardship, and privation to large numbers of people as to produce unrest so great that the peace and harmony of the world are imperilled; and an improvement of those conditions is urgently required; * * *

Whereas also the failure of any nation to adopt humane conditions of labour is an obstacle in the way of other nations which desire to improve the conditions in their own countries;

The HIGH CONTRACTING PARTIES, moved by sentiments of justice and humanity as well as by the desire to secure the permanent peace of the world, agree to the following:

ARTICLE 387

A permanent organisation is hereby established for the promotion of the objects set forth in the Preamble. * * *

*   *   *

ARTICLE 427

[The HIGH CONTRACTING PARTIES] recognise that differences of climate, habits, and customs, of economic opportunity and industrial tradition, make strict uniformity in the conditions of labour difficult of immediate attainment. But, holding as they do, that labour should not be regarded merely as an article of commerce, they think that there are methods and principles for regulating labour conditions which all industrial communities should endeavour to apply, so far as their special circumstances will permit.

Among these methods and principles, the following seem to the High Contracting Parties to be of special and urgent importance:

First. The guiding principle above enunciated that labour should not be regarded merely as a commodity or article of commerce.

Second. The right of association for all lawful

purposes by the employed as well as by the employers.

Third. The payment to the employed of a wage adequate to maintain a reasonable standard of life as this is understood in their time and country.

Fourth. The adoption of an eight hours day or a forty-eight hours week as the standard to be aimed at where it has not already been attained.

Fifth. The adoption of a weekly rest of at least twenty-four hours, which should include Sunday wherever practicable.

Sixth. The abolition of child labour and the imposition of such limitations on the labour of young persons as shall permit the continuation of their education and assure their proper physical development.

Seventh. The principle that men and women should receive equal remuneration for work of equal value.

Eighth. The standard set by law in each country with respect to the conditions of labour should have due regard to the equitable economic treatment of all workers lawfully resident therein.

Ninth. Each State should make provision for a system of inspection in which women should take part, in order to ensure the enforcement of the laws and regulations for the protection of the employed. * * *

ARTICLE 428

As a guarantee for the execution of the present Treaty by Germany, the German territory situated to the west of the Rhine, together with the bridgeheads, will be occupied by Allied and Associated troops for a period of fifteen years from the coming into force of the present Treaty.

*   *   *

ARTICLE 430

In case either during the occupation or after the expiration of the fifteen years referred to above the Reparation Commission finds that Germany refuses to observe the whole or part of her obliga-

tions under the present Treaty with regard to reparation, the whole or part of the areas specified in Article 429 will be reoccupied immediately by the Allied and Associated forces.

ARTICLE 431

If before the expiration of the period of fifteen years Germany complies with all the undertakings resulting from the present Treaty, the occupying forces will be withdrawn immediately.

✳   ✳   ✳

ARTICLE 434

Germany undertakes to recognise the full force of the Treaties of Peace and Additional Conventions which may be concluded by the Allied and Associated Powers with the Powers who fought on the side of Germany and to recognise whatever dispositions nay be made concerning the territories of the former Austro-Hungarian Monarchy, of the Kingdom of Bulgaria and of the Ottoman Empire, and to recognise the new States within their frontiers as there laid down.

REVIEW QUESTIONS

1. What guarantees of permanent international peace are incorporated into this treaty?
2. Assuming that all of the clauses in this treaty were to be enforced, does it provide the basis for a lasting peace?
3. Is this a "peace without victors"?
4. How do you think Germans responded to this treaty?
5. To what extent are the rights and liberties of disenfranchised minorities—whether ethnic minorities in eastern Europe, colonial subjects, or the world's laborers—guaranteed by this treaty?

JOHN MAYNARD KEYNES

FROM *The Economic Consequences of the Peace*

Criticism of the Versailles Treaty began almost immediately after it was signed. German outrage at this "dictated" peace was predictable, but objections were also voiced on the Allied side. One of the most stinging indictments came from British economist John Maynard Keynes (1883–1946), who believed that the economic clauses of the treaty had laid shaky foundations for a lasting peace. Keynes served as an economic adviser to Lloyd George at the Versailles Conference, but he abandoned this post in despair over the terms being imposed on Germany, and then quickly made public his concerns in the highly influential book, The Economic Consequences of the Peace *(1919). Keynes was especially critical of the reparations settlement, arguing that punishing Germany by seriously weakening its economy would only serve to destabilize the European economy as a whole. After dissecting the characters and motives of the chief negotiators, he offered his own solutions to the economic crisis produced by the war, arguing that these remedies would benefit not*

only Europe but also the United States, which would enjoy increased international trade with healthy trading partners.

From *The Economic Consequences of the Peace,* by John Maynard Keynes (New York: Harcourt, Brace and Howe, 1920).

The Conference

* * * The lead was taken by the French, in the sense that it was generally they who made in the first instance the most definite and the most extreme proposals. This was partly a matter of tactics. When the final result is expected to be a compromise, it is often prudent to start from an extreme position; and the French anticipated at the outset—like most other persons—a double process of compromise, first of all to suit the ideas of their allies and associates, and secondly in the course of the Peace Conference proper with the Germans themselves. These tactics were justified by the event.

* * *

Clemenceau was by far the most eminent member of the Council of Four, and he had taken the measure of his colleagues. He alone both had an idea and had considered it in all its consequences. His age, his character, his wit, and his appearance joined to give him objectivity and a defined outline in an environment of confusion. One could not despise Clemenceau or dislike him, but only take a different view as to the nature of civilized man, or indulge, at least, a different hope.

* * *

His principles for the peace can be expressed simply. In the first place, he was a foremost believer in the view of German psychology that the German understands and can understand nothing but intimidation, that he is without generosity or remorse in negotiation, that there is no advantage he will not take of you, and no extent to which he will not demean himself for profit, that he is without honor, pride, or mercy. Therefore you must never negotiate with a German or conciliate him; you must dictate to him. On no other terms will he respect you, or will you prevent him from cheating you. But it is doubtful how far he thought these characteristics peculiar to Germany, or whether his candid view of some other nations was fundamentally different. His philosophy had, therefore, no place for "sentimentality" in international relations. Nations are real things, of whom you love one and feel for the rest indifference—or hatred. The glory of the nation you love is a desirable end,—but generally to be obtained at your neighbor's expense. The politics of power are inevitable, and there is nothing very new to learn about this war or the end it was fought for; England had destroyed, as in each preceding century, a trade rival; a mighty chapter had been closed in the secular struggle between the glories of Germany and of France. Prudence required some measure of lip service to the "ideals" of foolish Americans and hypocritical Englishmen; but it would be stupid to believe that there is much room in the world, as it really is, for such affairs as the League of Nations, or any sense in the principle of self-determination except as an ingenious formula for rearranging the balance of power in one's own interests.

* * *

* * * [President Wilson] was like a Nonconformist minister, perhaps a Presbyterian. His thought and his temperament were essentially theological not intellectual, with all the strength and the weakness of that manner of thought, feeling, and expression.

* * *

The President's program for the World, as set forth in his speeches and his Notes, had displayed a spirit and a purpose so admirable that the last

desire of his sympathizers was to criticize details, —the details, they felt, were quite rightly not filled in at present, but would be in due course. It was commonly believed at the commencement of the Paris Conference that the President had thought out, with the aid of a large body of advisers, a comprehensive scheme not only for the League of Nations, but for the embodiment of the Fourteen Points in an actual Treaty of Peace. But in fact the President had thought out nothing; when it came to practice his ideas were nebulous and incomplete. He had no plan, no scheme, no constructive ideas whatever for clothing with the flesh of life the commandments which he had thundered from the White House. He could have preached a sermon on any of them or have addressed a stately prayer to the Almighty for their fulfilment; but he could not frame their concrete application to the actual state of Europe.

He not only had no proposals in detail, but he was in many respects, perhaps inevitably, ill-informed as to European conditions. And not only was he ill-informed—that was true of Mr. Lloyd George also—but his mind was slow and unadaptable.

* * *

After a display of much principle and dignity in the early days of the Council of Ten, he discovered that there were certain very important points in the program of his French, British, or Italian colleague, as the case might be, of which he was incapable of securing the surrender by the methods of secret diplomacy. What then was he to do in the last resort?

* * *

Having decided that some concessions were unavoidable, he might have sought by firmness and address and the use of the financial power of the United States to secure as much as he could of the substance, even at some sacrifice of the letter. But the President was not capable of so clear an understanding with himself as this implied. He was too conscientious. Although compromises were now necessary, he remained a man of prin-

ciple and the Fourteen Points a contract absolutely binding upon him. He would do nothing that was not honorable; he would do nothing that was not just and right; he would do nothing that was contrary to his great profession of faith. Thus, without any abatement of the verbal inspiration of the Fourteen Points, they became a document for gloss and interpretation and for all the intellectual apparatus of self-deception,

* * *

The subtlest sophisters and most hypocritical draftsmen were set to work, and produced many ingenious exercises which might have deceived for more than an hour a cleverer man than the President.

Thus instead of saying that German-Austria is prohibited from uniting with Germany except by leave of France (which would be inconsistent with the principle of self-determination), the Treaty, with delicate draftsmanship, states that "Germany acknowledges and will respect strictly the independence of Austria, within the frontiers which may be fixed in a Treaty between that State and the Principal Allied and Associated Powers; she agrees that this independence shall be inalienable, except with the consent of the Council of the League of Nations," which sounds, but is not, quite different. And who knows but that the President forgot that another part of the Treaty provides that for this purpose the Council of the League must be *unanimous*.

* * *

Such instances could be multiplied. The honest and intelligible purpose of French policy, to limit the population of Germany and weaken her economic system, is clothed, for the President's sake, in the august language of freedom and international equality.

* * *

Remedies

*   *   *

By fixing the Reparation payments well within Germany's capacity to pay, we make possible the renewal of hope and enterprise within her territory, we avoid the perpetual friction and opportunity of improper pressure arising out of Treaty clauses which are impossible of fulfilment, and we render unnecessary the intolerable powers of the Reparation Commission.

*   *   *

It would be objected, I suppose, by some critics that such an arrangement might go some way in effect towards realizing the former German dream of Mittel-Europa.

*   *   *

If we take the view that for at least a generation to come Germany cannot be trusted with even a modicum of prosperity, that while all our recent Allies are angels of light, all our recent enemies, Germans, Austrians, Hungarians, and the rest, are children of the devil, that year by year Germany must be kept impoverished and her children starved and crippled, and that she must be ringed round by enemies; then we shall reject all the proposals of this chapter, and particularly those which may assist Germany to regain a part of her former material prosperity and find a means of livelihood for the industrial population of her towns. But if this view of nations and of their relation to one another is adopted by the democracies of Western Europe, and is financed by the United States, heaven help us all.

*   *   *

The Settlement of Inter-Ally Indebtedness

In proposing a modification of the Reparation terms, I have considered them so far only in relation to Germany. But fairness requires that so great a reduction in the amount should be accompanied by a readjustment of its apportionment between the Allies themselves.

*   *   *

I suggest, therefore, that we should by our acts prove ourselves sincere and trustworthy, and that accordingly Great Britain should waive altogether her claims for cash payment in favor of Belgium, Serbia, and France. The whole of the payments made by Germany would then be subject to the prior charge of repairing the material injury done to those countries and provinces which suffered actual invasion by the enemy. * * *

*   *   *

With the Reparation problem thus cleared up it would be possible to bring forward with a better grace and more hope of success two other financial proposals, each of which involves an appeal to the generosity of the United States.

The first is for the entire cancellation of Inter-Ally indebtedness (that is to say, indebtedness between the Governments of the Allied and Associated countries) incurred for the purposes of the war.

*   *   *

On the one hand, Europe must depend in the long run on her own daily labor and not on the largesse of America; but, on the other hand, she will not pinch herself in order that the fruit of her daily labor may go elsewhere. In short, I do not believe that any of these tributes will continue to be paid, at the best, for more than a very few years. They do not square with human nature or agree with the spirit of the age.

*   *   *

An International Loan

I pass to a second financial proposal. The requirements of Europe are *immediate*. The prospect of being relieved of oppressive interest payments to England and America over the whole life of the next two generations (and of receiving from Germany some assistance year by year to the costs of restoration) would free the future from excessive anxiety. But it would not meet the ills of the immediate present,—the excess of Europe's imports over her exports, the adverse exchange, and the disorder of the currency. It will be very difficult for European production to get started again without a temporary measure of external assistance. I am therefore a supporter of an international loan in some shape or form, such as has been advocated in many quarters in France, Germany, and England, and also in the United States. In whatever way the ultimate responsibility for repayment is distributed, the burden of finding the immediate resources must inevitably fall in major part upon the United States.

*   *   *

But if America recalls for a moment what Europe has meant to her and still means to her, what

Europe, the mother of art and of knowledge, in spite of everything, still is and still will be, will she not reject these counsels of indifference and isolation, and interest herself in what may prove decisive issues for the progress and civilization of all mankind?

*   *   *

REVIEW QUESTIONS

1. How did the characters and motives of Clemenceau and Wilson differ?
2. What problems were produced by the incompatability of their attitudes toward the peace settlement according to Keynes?
3. How would Keynes have revised the economic clauses of the treaty?
4. What benefit did he believe Britain would derive from sacrificing its demand for reparations payments?
5. What benefit would the United States have derived from sacrificing its demand for repayment of wartime loans?

28 ❧ TURMOIL BETWEEN THE WARS

The Great War was not only physically devastating, but it also did considerable psychological and spiritual damage. During the war, the trauma of trench warfare sometimes pushed soldiers over the edge of sanity into madness, a condition euphemistically known as shell shock. In the aftermath of the war, it almost seemed as if European society as a whole was suffering from a nervous breakdown of monumental proportions. Peace, so long desired, did not bring the security and prosperity for which so many yearned. Instead, the European nations lurched from one crisis to the next during the 1920s and 1930s, and another episode of international warfare erupted at the end of these two short decades of uneasy peace.

The crisis of "total" war produced conditions conducive to the rise of totalitarianism, a distinctively modern form of authoritarian government. In Russia, the initial stages of the Soviet Revolution generated hopes for the creation of a modern communist utopia, hopes shared both by Russian revolutionaries and by many progressives outside of Russia. However, Stalin's rise to power and his imposition of a Communist Party dictatorship put an end to this dream. Stalin's authoritarianism of the left was paralleled by fascist movements in eastern and central Europe. Mussolini's fascism and Hitler's Nazism shared many elements of traditional right-wing ideology, but they also sought to incorporate elements of left-wing theory and practice, producing a revolutionism of the right. Many Europeans, disillusioned with liberalism and democracy, greeted charismatic dictatorship as a new and attractive political option.

The tendency to look to extremist political movements for solutions to social problems was greatly reinforced by the economic crisis brought on by the Great Depression of the 1930s. Throughout Europe, the Depression caused a dramatic polarization of the political spectrum and a realignment of political allegiances. The greatest losers were the centrist parties still committed to liberalism and parliamentary democracy.

In response to the dislocations of the era, many intellectuals subjected traditional orthodoxies to ruthless scrutiny. Philosophers, scientists, and artists all puzzled over the purpose of human existence in a cosmos that seemed bereft of transcendent meaning, and many wondered whether God was dead, or at least unwilling to intervene in human affairs. The pointless carnage of the war had crushed the optimism of Belle Époque culture. That Europeans had allowed such a cataclysm to occur at all suggested that irrational impulses played an important role in human behavior and that progress was not as inevitable as nineteenth-century positivists had thought. Technological and scientific advances, while impressive, brought new dangers—including devastating increases in the destructiveness of military weapons—and they did not provide answers to human beings' deepest yearnings for spiritual knowledge and sustenance.

JOHN REED

FROM *Ten Days That Shook the World*

Despite his upper-class origins, the American John Reed (1887–1920) was drawn to the socialist and labor movements of the prewar era. After graduating from Harvard in 1910, he traveled extensively as a reporter, covering the Mexican Revolution, worker protests in the United States, and the battlefronts of World War I. After the February Revolution in Russia, Reed set off for Petrograd, arriving in time to personally witness the Bolshevik takeover in late 1917. On the basis of his experiences, and using documents collected during his stay in Russia, Reed wrote Ten Days That Shook the World, *one of the best-known accounts of the Soviet Revolution, which was first published in 1919. For all its historical value,* Ten Days That Shook the World *is an intensely personal account of the revolutionary events of 1917, what Reed himself called a "slice of intensified history—history as I saw it." Recreating the swirling drama of unfolding events, Reed's book provides a blow-by-blow account of the key events of the revolution.*

On 8 November 1917, the day after the successful Bolshevik overthrow of the liberal provisional government, Lenin—who had only returned to Russia from exile two weeks before—gave a critically important speech to the All-Russia Congress of Soviets. In an attempt to rally support for the fledgling Communist regime, Lenin offered Russian soldiers, peasants, and workers what they most wanted: an end to the war and a redistribution of land.

From *Ten Days That Shook the World,* by John Reed (New York: Boni and Liveright, 1919).

＊　＊　＊

It was just 8.40 when a thundering wave of cheers announced the entrance of the presidium, with Lenin—great Lenin—among them. A short, stocky figure, with a big head set down in his shoulders, bald and bulging. Little eyes, a snubbish nose, wide, generous mouth, and heavy chin; clean-shaven now, but already beginning to bristle with the well-known beard of his past and future. Dressed in shabby clothes, his trousers much too long for him. Unimpressive, to be the idol of a mob, loved and revered as perhaps few leaders in history have been. A strange popular leader—a leader purely by virtue of intellect; colourless, humourless, uncompromising and detached, without picturesque idiosyncrasies—but with the power of explaining profound ideas in simple terms, of analysing a concrete situation. And combined with shrewdness, the greatest intellectual audacity.

＊　＊　＊

Now Lenin, gripping the edge of the reading stand, letting his little winking eyes travel over the crowd as he stood there waiting, apparently oblivious to the long-rolling ovation, which lasted several minutes. When it finished, he said simply, "We shall now proceed to construct the Socialist order!" Again that overwhelming human roar.

"The first thing is the adoption of practical measures to realise peace. . . . We shall offer peace to the peoples of all the belligerent countries upon the basis of the Soviet terms—no annexations, no indemnities, and the right of self-determination of peoples. At the same time, according to our promise, we shall publish and repudiate the secret treaties. . . . The question of War and Peace is so clear that I think that I may, without preamble, read the project of a Proclamation to the Peoples of All the Belligerent Countries. . . ."

His great mouth, seeming to smile, opened wide as he spoke; his voice was hoarse—not unpleasantly so, but as if it had hardened that way after years and years of speaking—and went on monotonously, with the effect of being able to go

on forever. . . . For emphasis he bent forward slightly. No gestures. And before him, a thousand simple faces looking up in intent adoration.

PROCLAMATION TO THE PEOPLES AND GOVERNMENTS OF ALL THE BELLIGERENT NATIONS

The Workers' and Peasants' Government, created by the revolution of November 6th and 7th and based on the Soviets of Workers', Soldiers' and Peasants' Deputies, proposes to all the belligerent peoples and to their Governments to begin immediately negotiations for a just and democratic peace.

The Government means by a just and democratic peace, which is desired by the immense majority of the workers and the labouring classes, exhausted and depleted by the war—that peace which the Russian workers and peasants, after having struck down the Tsarist monarchy, have not ceased to demand categorically—immediate peace without annexations (that is to say, without conquest of foreign territory, without forcible annexation of other nationalities), and without indemnities.

＊　＊　＊

To continue this war in order to permit the strong and rich nations to divide among themselves the weak and conquered nationalities is considered by the Government the greatest possible crime against humanity; and the Government solemnly proclaims its decision to sign a treaty of peace which will put an end to this war upon the above conditions, equally fair for all nationalities without exception.

＊　＊　＊

In addressing this offer of peace to the Governments and to the peoples of all the belligerent countries, the Provisional Workers' and Peasants' Government of Russia addresses equally and in particular the conscious workers of the three nations most devoted to humanity and the three most important nations among those taking part in the present war—England,

France, and Germany. The workers of these countries have rendered the greatest services to the cause of progress and of Socialism. The splendid examples of the Chartist movement in England, the series of revolutions, of world-wide historical significance, accomplished by the French proletariat—and finally, in Germany, the historic struggle against the Laws of Exception, an example for the workers of the whole world of prolonged and stubborn action, and the creation of the formidable organisations of German proletarians—all these models of proletarian heroism, these monuments of history, are for us a sure guarantee that the workers of these countries will understand the duty imposed upon them to liberate humanity from the horrors and consequences of war; and that these workers, by decisive, energetic and continued action, will help us to bring to a successful conclusion the cause of peace—and at the same time, the cause of the liberation of the exploited working masses from all slavery and all exploitation.

When the grave thunder of applause had died away, Lenin spoke again:

"We propose to the Congress to ratify this declaration. We address ourselves to the Governments as well as to the peoples, for a declaration which would be addressed only to the peoples of the belligerent countries might delay the conclusion of peace. The conditions of peace, drawn up during the armistice, will be ratified by the Constituent Assembly. In fixing the duration of the armistice at three months, we desire to give to the peoples as long a rest as possible after this bloody extermination, and ample time for them to elect their representatives. This proposal of peace will meet with resistance on the part of the imperialist governments—we don't fool ourselves on that score. But we hope that revolution will soon break out in all the belligerent countries; that is why we address ourselves especially to the workers of France, England and Germany. . . .

"The revolution of November 6th and 7th,"

he ended, "has opened the era of the Social Revolution. . . . The labour movement, in the name of peace and Socialism, shall win, and fulfil its destiny. . . ."

There was something quiet and powerful in all this, which stirred the souls of men. It was understandable why people believed when Lenin spoke. . . .

*   *   *

"We want a just peace, but we are not afraid of a revolutionary war. . . . Probably the imperialist Governments will not answer our appeal—but we shall not issue an ultimatum to which it will be easy to say no. . . . If the German proletariat realises that we are ready to consider all offers of peace, that will perhaps be the last drop which overflows the bowl—revolution will break out in Germany. . . .

"We consent to examine all conditions of peace, but that doesn't mean that we shall accept them. . . . For some of our terms we shall fight to the end—but possibly for others will find it impossible to continue the war. . . . Above all, we want to finish the war. . . ."

It was exactly 10:35 when Kameniev asked all in favour of the proclamation to hold up their cards. One delegate dared to raise his hand against, but the sudden sharp outburst around him brought it swiftly down. . . . Unanimous.

Suddenly, by common impulse, we found ourselves on our feet, mumbling together into the smooth lifting unison of the *Internationale*. A grizzled old soldier was sobbing like a child. Alexandra Kollontai rapidly winked the tears back. The immense sound rolled through the hall, burst windows and doors and seared into the quiet sky. "The war is ended! The war is ended!" said a young workman near me, his face shining. And when it was over, as we stood there in a kind of awkward hush, some one in the back of the room shouted, "Comrades! Let us remember those who have died for liberty!" So we began to sing the Funeral March, that slow, melancholy and yet-triumphant chant, so Russian and so moving. The

Internationale is an alien air, after all. The Funeral March seemed the very soul of those dark masses whose delegates sat in this hall, building from their obscure visions a new Russia—and perhaps more.

> You fell in the fatal fight
> For the liberty of the people, for the honour of
>   the people. . . .
> You gave up your lives and everything dear to
>   you,
> You suffered in horrible prisons,
> You went to exile in chains. . . .
>
>   Without a word you carried your chains be-
>   cause you could not ignore your suffering
>   brothers,
>   Because you believed that justice is stronger
>   than the sword. . . .
>   The time will come when your surrendered
>   life will count.
>   That time is near; when tyranny falls the
>   people will rise, great and free!
>   Farewell, brothers, you chose a noble path,
>   You are followed by the new and fresh army
>   ready to die and to suffer. . . .
>
>   Farewell, brothers, you chose a noble path,
>   At your grave we swear to fight, to work for
>   freedom and the people's happiness. . . .

For this did they lie there, the martyrs of March, in their cold Brotherhood Grave on Mars Field; for this thousands and tens of thousands had died in the prisons, in exile, in Siberian mines. It had not come as they expected it would come, nor as the *intelligentzia* desired it; but it had come—rough, strong, impatient of formulas, contemptuous of sentimentalism; *real*. . . .

Lenin was reading the Decree on Land:

1. All private ownership of land is abolished immediately without compensation.
2. All land-owners' estates, and all lands belonging to the Crown, to monasteries, church lands with all their live stock and inventoried property, buildings and all appurtenances, are transferred to the disposition of the township Land Committees and the district Soviets of Peasants' Deputies until the Constituent Assembly meets.
3. Any damage whatever done to the confiscated property which from now on belongs to the whole People, is regarded as a serious crime, punishable by the revolutionary tribunals. The district Soviets of Peasants' Deputies shall take all necessary measures for the observance of the strictest order during the taking over of the land-owners' estates, for the determination of the dimensions of the plots of land and which of them are subject to confiscation, for the drawing up of an inventory of the entire confiscated property, and for the strictest revolutionary protection of all the farming property on the land, with all buildings, implements, cattle, supplies of products, etc., passing into the hands of the People.
4. * * * The lands of peasants and of Cossacks serving in the Army shall not be confiscated.

"This is not," explained Lenin, "the project of former Minister Tchernov, who spoke of 'erecting a frame-work' and tried to realise reforms from above. From below, on the spot, will be decided the questions of division of the land. The amount of land received by each peasant will vary according to the locality. . . ."

*   *   *

REVIEW QUESTIONS

1. What kind of peace does Lenin propose?
2. How do you think the other governments of the belligerent nations would have responded to this proposal?
3. What policies were instituted by the Decree on Land? Why?
4. What does this document tell you about the aspirations of the Bolshevik revolutionaries?

OCTOBER (1927)   Sergei Eisenstein

The reconstruction of history through film often treads the fine line between art and political persuasion. Created in 1927 for the tenth anniversary of the Bolshevik Revolution, Sergei Eisenstein's October *depicted the Bolshevik storming of the Winter Palace on 25 October 1917 as a spectacular expression of popular will and revolutionary valor. Yet, in reality, the event had little dramatic flair; the Winter Palace, the seat of Aleksandr Kerensky's provisional government, was guarded by only a handful of cadets who offered little or no resistance. How might this film have influenced Soviet citizens' perception and memory of the October Revolution?*

ALEXANDRA KOLLONTAI

FROM *The Autobiography of a Sexually Emancipated Communist Woman*

Alexandra Kollontai (1872–1952) grew up in an educated, affluent, and fairly liberal Russian family. She married young, but left her husband and son to study political economy in Switzerland, where she became actively involved in socialist organizing. Originally a Menshevik, Kollontai became a Bolshevik in 1915, largely because of the Bolshevik opposition to the war, and entered into a friendly correspondence with Lenin.

After the October Revolution, Kollontai was named people's commissar of social welfare, becoming the only woman to hold a cabinet post in the new Bolshevik government. As director of the Women's Bureau (Zhenotdel), she agitated in favor of economic liberty for working women and state welfare benefits for mothers. Her advocacy of women's rights and free love was not universally popular, and in the years following the revolution she found herself increasingly at odds with the Communist Party leadership. In 1922, Kollontai was assigned a diplomatic post in Norway—a gentle form of exile—and she spent much of the rest of her life outside of Russia. In memoirs written in 1926, she recounted the heady early days of the revolution, when a total transformation of Russian society still seemed possible.

From *The Autobiography of a Sexually Emancipated Communist Woman*, Alexandra Kollontai, translated by Salvator Attanasio (New York: Herder and Herder, 1971).

*   *   *

When one recalls the first months of the Workers' Government, months which were so rich in *magnificent illusions*,[1] plans, ardent initiatives to improve life, to organize the world anew, months of the real romanticism of the Revolution, one would in fact like to write about all else save about one's self. I occupied the post of Minister of Social Welfare from October of 1917 *to March of 1918.* It was not without opposition that I was received by the former officials of the Ministry. Most of them sabotaged us openly and simply did not show up for work. But precisely this office could not interrupt its work, come what may, since in itself it was an extraordinarily complicated operation. It included the whole welfare program for the war-disabled, hence for hundreds of thousands of crippled soldiers and officers, the pension system in general, foundling homes, homes for the aged, orphanages, hospitals for the needy, the work-shops making artificial limbs, the administration of playing-card factories (the manufacture of playing cards was a State monopoly), *the educational system,* clinical hospitals for women. In addition a whole series of educational institutes for young

---

[1] By 1926, it was already necessary to be cautious about how one described one's involvement in the revolution, and Kollontai censored her own writing. Italics indicate passages in the original manuscript that were not included in the published version of her memoirs.

girls were also under the direction of this Ministry. One can easily imagine the enormous demands these tasks made upon a small group of people who, at the same time, were novices in State administration. In a clear awareness of these difficulties *I formed,* immediately, an auxiliary council in which experts such as physicians, jurists, pedagogues were represented alongside the workers and the minor officials of the Ministry. The sacrifice, the energy with which the minor employees bore the burden of this difficult task was truly exemplary. It was not only a matter of keeping the work of the Ministry going, but also of initiating reforms and improvements. New, fresh forces replaced the sabotaging officers of the old regime. A new life stirred in the offices of the formerly highly conservative Ministry. Days of grueling work! And at night the sessions of the councils of the People's Commissar (of the cabinet) under Lenin's chairmanship. A small, modest room and only one secretary who recorded the resolutions which changed Russia's life to its bottommost foundations.

*   *   *

My main work as People's Commissar consisted in the following: by decree to improve the situation of the war-disabled, to abolish religious instruction in the schools for young girls which were under the Ministry (this was still before the general separation of Church and State), and to transfer priests to the civil service, to introduce the right of self-administration for pupils in the schools for girls, to reorganize the former orphanages into government Children's Homes (*no distinction was to be made between orphaned children and those who still had fathers and mothers*), to set up the first hostels for the needy and street-urchins, to convene a committee, composed *only* of doctors, which was to be commissioned *to elaborate* the free public health system for the whole country. In my opinion the most important accomplishment of the People's Commissariat, however, was the legal foundation of a Central Office for Maternity and Infant Welfare. The draft of the bill relating to this Central Office was signed by me in January of 1918. A second decree followed in which *I* changed all maternity hospitals into free Homes for Maternity and Infant Care, in order thereby to set the groundwork for a comprehensive government system of pre-natal care. I was greatly assisted in coping with these tasks by Dr. Korolef. We also planned a "Pre-Natal Care Palace," a model home with an exhibition room in which courses for mothers would be held *and, among many other things,* model day nurseries were also to be established. We were just about completing preparations for such a facility in the building of a girls' boarding school at which formerly young girls of the nobility had been educated and which was still under the direction of a countess, when a fire destroyed our work, which had barely begun! Had the fire been set deliberately? . . . I was dragged out of bed in the middle of the night. I rushed to the scene of the fire; the beautiful exhibition room was totally ruined, as were all the other rooms. Only the huge nameplate "Pre-Natal Care Palace" still hung over the entrance door.

My efforts to nationalize maternity and infant care set off a new wave of insane attacks against me. All kinds of lies were related about the "nationalization of women," *about my legislative proposals which assertedly ordained that little girls of 12 were to become mothers.* A special fury gripped the religious followers of the old regime when, *on my own authority (the cabinet later criticized me for this action),* I transformed the famous Alexander Nevsky monastery into a home for war-invalids. The monks resisted and a shooting fray ensued. The press again raised a loud hue and cry against me. The Church organized street demonstrations *against my action* and also pronounced "anathema" against me. . . .

I received countless threatening letters, but I never requested military protection. I always went out alone, unarmed and without any kind of a bodyguard. In fact I never gave a thought to any kind of danger, being all too engrossed in matters of an utterly different character. In February of 1918 a first State delegation of the Soviets was sent to Sweden in order to clarify different economic and political questions. As Peoples' Commissar I headed this delegation. But our vessel was shipwrecked; we were saved by landing on the Aland Islands which belonged to Finland. At this very time the struggle between the Whites and the Reds in the country had reached its most crucial moment and the German Army was also making ready to wage war against Finland.

*   *   *

Now began a *dark time* of my life which I cannot treat of here since the events are still too fresh in my mind. *But the day will also come when I will give an account of them.*

There were differences of opinion in the Party. I resigned from my post as People's Commissar *on the ground of total disagreement with the current policy. Little by little I was also relieved of all my other tasks. I again gave lectures and espoused my ideas on "the new woman" and "the new morality."* The Revolution was in full swing. The struggle was becoming increasingly irreconcilable and bloodier, *much of what was happening did not fit in with my outlook.* But after all there was still the unfinished task, women's liberation. Women, of course, had received all rights but in practice, of course, they still lived under the old yoke: without authority in family life, enslaved by a thousand menial household chores, bearing the whole burden of maternity, even the material cares, because many women now found life alone as a result of the war and other circumstances.

*   *   *

A flood of new work was waiting for me. The question now was one of drawing women into the people's kitchens and of educating them to devote their energies to children's homes and day-care centers, the school system, household reforms, and still many other pressing matters. The main thrust of all this activity was to implement, in fact, equal rights for women as a labor unit in the national economy and as a citizen in the political sphere and, of course, with the special proviso: maternity was to be appraised as a social function and therefore protected and provided for by the State.

*   *   *

A serious illness tore me away from the exciting work for months. Hardly having recovered—at that time I was in Moscow—I took over the direction of the Coordinating Office for Work among Women and again a new period of intensive, grueling work began. A communist women's *newspaper* was founded, conferences and congresses of women workers were convoked. The foundation was laid for work with the women of the East (Mohammedans). Two world conferences of communist women took place in Moscow. The law liberalizing abortion was put through and a number of regulations of benefit to women were introduced by our Coordinating Office and legally confirmed. *At this time I had to do more writing and speaking than ever before. . . .* Our work received wholehearted support from Lenin. And Trotsky, although he was overburdened with military tasks, unfailingly and gladly appeared at our conferences. Energetic, gifted women, two of whom are no longer alive, sacrificially devoted all their energies to the work of the Coordinating Office.

At the eighth Soviet Congress, as a member of the Soviet executive (*now there were already several women on this body*), I proposed a motion that the Soviets in all areas contribute to the creation of a consciousness of the struggle for equal rights for women and, accordingly, to involve them in State and communal work. I managed to push the motion through and to get it accepted but not without resistance. It was a great, an enduring victory.

A heated debate flared up when I published my thesis on the new morality. *For our Soviet marriage law, separated from the Church to be sure, is not essentially more progressive than the same laws that after all exist in other progressive democratic countries.* * * * [A]lthough the illegitimate child *was* placed on a legal par with the legitimate child, in practice a great deal of hypocrisy and injustice still exists in this area. When one speaks of the "immorality" which the Bolsheviks purportedly propagated, it suffices to submit our marriage laws to a close scrutiny to note that in the divorce question we are on a par with North America whereas in the question of the illegitimate child we have *not yet even* progressed as far as the Norwegians.

The most radical wing of the Party was formed around this question. My theses, my *sexual and moral* views, were bitterly fought *by many Party comrades of both sexes: as were still other differences of opinion in the Party regarding political guiding principles.* Personal and family cares were added thereto and thus months in 1922 went by without fruitful work. Then in the autumn of 1922 came my official appointment to the legation of the Russian Soviet representation in Norway. I really believed that this appointment would be purely formal and that therefore in Norway I would find time to devote to myself, to my literary activity. Things turned out quite differently. With the day of my entry into office in Norway I also entered upon a wholly new course of work in my life which drew upon all my energies to the highest degree.

*   *   *

REVIEW QUESTIONS

1. What kind of work did Kollontai do as people's commissar of social welfare?
2. What does her work tell you about the social welfare policies of the revolutionary government?
3. Who opposed Kollontai's efforts in favor of women's liberation? Why?

NADEZHDA MANDELSTAM

FROM *Hope Against Hope*

The Soviet revolution also generated considerable excitement about revitalizing the arts in Russia. In the early 1920s a vibrant and sometimes contentious artistic culture emerged, a culture typified by experimentation and considerable optimism about the future of the new workers' state. However, as Stalin consolidated his grip on power, artists and writers were forced either to produce works that supported Stalinist orthodoxy or to retreat into silence. By the 1930s, any expression of resistance to the regime was firmly suppressed and the avant-gardism of the early revolution gave way to state-imposed socialist realism. During the great purges, many artists and intellectuals were imprisoned or executed.

Osip Mandelstam (1891–1938?), widely recognized as one of the greatest Russian poets of the twentieth century, was already an established author in 1917. As a poet, Mandelstam tended to be apolitical, but in 1934 he read a poem about Stalin to a private gathering, describing the Soviet dictator as having "cockroach whiskers" and "fingers . . . as fat as grubs." In retaliation, Stalin had Mandelstam and his wife, Nadezhda, exiled to the provinces. In 1938 Mandelstam was arrested and sent east to a prison camp, where he soon died. In the 1970s, Nadezhda Mandelstam (1899–1980) wrote two volumes of memoirs about her life with and without Osip. In Hope Against Hope, *she documented the circumstances surrounding her hus-*

reduced to these highlights, which were intended to show that although it was almost impossible to survive, man's will to live was such that he came through nevertheless. Listening to these accounts, I was horrified at the thought that there might be nobody who could ever properly bear witness to the past. Whether inside or outside the camps, we had all lost our memories. But it later turned out that there were people who had made it their aim from the beginning not only to save themselves, but to survive as witnesses. These relentless keepers of the truth, merging with all the other prisoners, had bided their time—there were probably more such people in the camps than outside, where it was all too common to succumb to the temptation to make terms with reality and live out one's life in peace. Of course those witnesses who have kept a clear memory of the past are few in number, but their very survival is the best proof that good, not evil, will prevail in the end.

* * *

One Final Account

* * *

There is nowhere I can make inquiries and nobody who will tell me anything. Who is likely to search through those grisly archives just for the sake of Mandelstam, when they won't even publish a volume of his work? * * *

All I can do, therefore, is to gather what meager evidence there is and speculate about the date of his death. As I constantly tell myself: the sooner he died, the better. There is nothing worse than a slow death. I hate to think that at the moment when my mind was set at rest on being told in the post office that he was dead, he may actually have been still alive and on his way to Kolyma. The date of death has not been established. And it is beyond my power to do anything more to establish it.

* * *

REVIEW QUESTIONS

1. Why do you think it was so important to Nadezhda Mandelstam that she reconstruct the exact details of her husband's death?
2. Why do you think Nadezhda Mandelstam wrote her memoirs?
3. Why is she so concerned with remembering and documenting the past?
4. What does this document tell you about conditions in Stalin's prison camps?

BENITO MUSSOLINI

FROM "Born of a Need for Action"

Fascism emerged during the 1920s as a response to the unsettled political, economic, and social climate of the postwar period. While it was a global phenomenon, it enjoyed its greatest successes in Germany and Italy.

As the first fascist head of state, Benito Mussolini (1883–1945) was an inspiration to other would-be dictators throughout the 1920s. Mussolini began his political career as a socialist journalist, but his ardent support for Italian participation in the First World War caused him to be expelled from the Socialist Party. In the chaos of the immediate postwar years in Italy, Mussolini created his own Fascist Party, encouraging his followers to silence political opponents through the use of violence. The Italian ruling elite, confronted with widespread strike activity and the threat of a communist takeover, handed over the reins of government to Mussolini in 1922, after he demonstrated the strength of the fascist movement through a march on Rome. Many Italians welcomed this development, seeing Mussolini as a great leader— Duce—whose forceful rule would bring order, prosperity, and a renewal of national strength and pride. In 1932, ten years after his seizure of power, Mussolini wrote an article on fascism for an Italian encyclopedia, setting down in writing for the first time the ideological premises of the movement.

From *The Estate of Benito Mussolini,* translated by Jane Soames (London: Hogarth Press, 1933).

*   *   *

Fascism was not the nursling of a doctrine worked out beforehand with detailed elaboration; it was born of the need for action and it was itself from the beginning practical rather than theoretical; it was not merely another political party but, even in the first two years, in opposition to all political parties as such, and itself a living movement.

*   *   *

The years which preceded the march to Rome were years of great difficulty, during which the necessity for action did not permit of research or any complete elaboration of doctrine. The battle had to be fought in the towns and villages. There was much discussion, but—what was more important and more sacred—men died. They knew how to die. Doctrine, beautifully defined and carefully elucidated, with headlines and paragraphs, might be lacking; but there was to take its place something more decisive—Faith.

*   *   *

Fascism is now a completely individual thing, not only as a regime but as a doctrine. And this means that to-day Fascism, exercising its critical sense upon itself and upon others, has formed its own distinct and peculiar point of view, to which it can refer and upon which, therefore, it can act in the face of all problems, practical or intellectual, which confront the world.

And above all, Fascism, the more it considers and observes the future and the development of humanity quite apart from political considerations of the moment, believes neither in the possibility nor the utility of perpetual peace. It thus repudiates the doctrine of Pacifism—born of a renunciation of the struggle and an act of cowardice in the face of sacrifice. War alone brings up to its highest tension all human energy and puts the stamp of nobility upon the peoples who have the courage to meet it. All other trials are substitutes, which never really put men into the position where they have to make the great decision—the alternative of life or death. Thus a doctrine which is founded upon this harmful postulate of peace is hostile to Fascism.

*   *   *

* * * Fascism [is] the complete opposite of * * * so-called scientific and Marxian Socialism, the materialist conception of history; according to which the history of human civilization can be explained simply through the conflict of interests among the various social groups and by the change and development in the means and instruments of production. That the changes in the economic field—new discoveries of raw materials, new methods of working them, and the inventions of science—have their importance no one can deny; but that these factors are sufficient to explain the history of humanity excluding all others is an absurd delusion. Fascism, now and always, believes in holiness and in heroism; that is to say, in actions influenced by no economic motive, direct or indirect.

*   *   *

* * * Fascism repudiates the conception of "economic" happiness, to be realized by Socialism and, as it were, at a given moment in economic evolution to assure to everyone the maximum of well-being. Fascism denies the materialist conception of happiness as a possibility,* * *: that is to say, Fascism denies the validity of the equation, well-being-happiness, which would reduce men to the level of animals, caring for one thing only—to be fat and well-fed—and would thus degrade humanity to a purely physical existence.

After Socialism, Fascism combats the whole complex system of democratic ideology, and repudiates it, whether in its theoretical premises or in its practical application. Fascism denies that the majority, by the simple fact that it is a majority, can direct human society; it denies that numbers alone can govern by means of a periodical consultation, and it affirms the immutable, beneficial and fruitful inequality of mankind, which can never be permanently levelled through the mere operation of a mechanical process such as universal suffrage.

*   *   *

* * * Fascism denies, in democracy, the absurd conventional untruth of political equality dressed out in the garb of collective irresponsibility, and the myth of "happiness" and indefinite progress. But, if democracy may be conceived in diverse forms—that is to say, taking democracy to mean a state of society in which the populace are not reduced to impotence in the State—Fascism may

write itself down as "an organized, centralized and authoritative democracy."

*   *   *

A party which entirely governs a nation is a fact entirely new to history, there are no possible references or parallels. Fascism uses in its construction whatever elements in the Liberal, Social or Democratic doctrines still have a living value* * *

*   *   *

* * * If the nineteenth century was a century of individualism (Liberalism always signifying individualism) it may be expected that this will be the century of collectivism, and hence the century of the State.

*   *   *

The foundation of Fascism is the conception of the State, its character, its duty, and its aim. Fascism conceives of the State as an absolute, in comparison with which all individuals or groups are relative, only to be conceived of in their relation to the State. * * * In 1929, at the first five-yearly assembly of the Fascist regime, I said:

"For us Fascists, the State is not merely a guardian, preoccupied solely with the duty of assuring the personal safety of the citizens; nor is it an organization with purely material aims, such as to guarantee a certain level of well-being and peaceful conditions of life; for a mere council of administration would be sufficient to realize such objects. Nor is it a purely political creation, divorced from all contact with the complex material reality which makes up the life of the individual and the life of the people as a whole. The State, as conceived of and as created by Fascism, is a spiritual and moral fact in itself, since its political, juridical and economic organization of the nation is a concrete thing: and such an organization must be in its origins and development a manifestation of the spirit. The State is the guarantor of security both internal and external, but it is also the custodian and transmitter of the spirit of the people, as it has grown up through the centuries in language, in customs and in faith. And the State is not only a living reality of the present, it is also linked with the past and above all with the future, and thus transcending the brief limits of individual life, it represents the immanent spirit of the nation. The forms in which States express themselves may change, but the necessity for such forms is eternal. It is the State which educates its citizens in civic virtue, gives them a consciousness of their mission and welds them into unity; harmonizing their various interests through justice, and transmitting to future generations the mental conquests of science, of art, of law and the solidarity of humanity. It leads men from primitive tribal life to that highest expression of human power which is Empire: it links up through the centuries the names of those of its members who have died for its existence and in obedience to its laws, it holds up the memory of the leaders who have increased its territory and the geniuses who have illumined it with glory as an example to be followed by future generations. When the conception of the State declines, and disunifying and centrifugal tendencies prevail, whether of individuals or of particular groups, the nations where such phenomena appear are in their decline."

*   *   *

* * * The Fascist State is unique, and an original creation. It is not reactionary, but revolutionary, in that it anticipates the solution of the universal political problems which elsewhere have to be settled in the political field by the rivalry of parties, the excessive power of the Parliamentary regime and the irresponsibility of political assemblies; while it meets the problems of the economic field by a system of syndicalism which is continually increasing in importance, as much in the sphere of labour as of industry: and in the moral field enforces order, discipline, and obedience to that which is the determined moral code of the country. Fascism desires the State to be a strong and organic body, at the same time reposing upon broad and popular support. The Fascist State has drawn into itself even the economic activities of the nation, and, through the corporative social and educational institutions created by it, its influence reaches every aspect of the national life and includes, framed in their respective organizations, all the political, economic and spiritual forces of the nation. A State which reposes upon the support of millions of individuals who recognize its authority, are continually conscious of its power and are ready at once to serve it, is not the old tyrannical State of the medieval lord nor has it anything in common with the absolute governments either before or after 1789. The individual in the Fascist State is not annulled but rather multiplied, just in the same way that a soldier in a regiment is not diminished but rather increased by the number of his comrades. The Fascist State organizes the nation, but leaves a sufficient margin of liberty to the individual; the latter is deprived of all useless and possibly harmful freedom, but retains what is essential; the deciding power in this question cannot be the individual, but the State alone.

*   *   *

REVIEW QUESTIONS

1. Why did Mussolini reject pacifism?
2. What implications do his comments about war have for the policies of the fascist state?
3. Which aspects of socialism and democracy does Mussolini reject? Which does he retain?
4. What exactly does Mussolini mean when he defines the fascist state as "an organized, centralized and authoritative democracy"?
5. What role does the individual play in this state?

ADOLF HITLER

FROM *Mein Kampf*

German Nazism shared many of the tenets of Italian fascism. Like Mussolini, Adolf Hitler (1889–1945) rejected democracy as bankrupt and promoted an authoritarian politics based on the "leadership principle." Hitler was also an ardent militarist who believed that war was a crucial test of a nation's vigor. Germany's defeat in 1918 was not the result of military failure, he insisted, but rather the product of the diseased condition of German society in general. This corruption and weakness was caused by the diabolical machinations of the Jewish people, whom Hitler portrayed as a degenerate "race" engaged in an international conspiracy designed to destroy the "national principle" binding the German people together as a "master race." In response to this threat, Hitler offered himself as the leader—Führer—of a revitalized, militantly nationalist Germany purged of all those who would weaken or diminish the racial purity of the German people.

Hitler was jailed for nine months after a failed coup d'état, the Beer Hall Putsch of 1923. During his imprisonment, he wrote Mein Kampf *("My Struggle"), a massive, rambling political memoir detailing the political agenda of the Nazi Party. Many of the political arguments presented in* Mein Kampf *parallel those underpinning Italian fascism. What distinguishes Hitler's thought is his obsessive preoccupation with racial "hygiene" as the basis of national strength.*

From *Mein Kampf,* by Adolf Hitler, translated by Alvin Johnson (New York: Reynal and Hitchcock, 1940).

*   *   *

What we have to fight for is the security of the existence and the increase of our race and our people, the nourishment of its children and the preservation of the purity of the blood, the freedom and independence of the fatherland in order to enable our people to mature for the fulfillment of the mission which the Creator of the universe has allotted also to them.

*   *   *

A further example for the half-heartedness and the weakness of the leading authority in pre-War Germany in the most important vital questions of the nation can be the following: Parallel with the political and moral infection of the people went a no less terrible poisoning of the health of the national body. Syphilis began to spread more and more, especially in the great cities. * * *

*   *   *

The cause * * * lies primarily in our prostitution of love. Even if the result of this were not this terrible disease, yet it would still be of deepest danger for the people, for the moral devastation which this depravity brings with it are sufficient to destroy a people slowly but surely. The Judaization of our spiritual life and the mammonization of our mating impulse sooner or later befouls our entire new generation, for instead of vigorous children of natural feeling, only the miserable specimens of financial expedience come forth. For this becomes more and more the basis and the only prerequisite for our marriages. Love, however, finds an outlet somewhere else.

Naturally, one can also here mock Nature for a certain time, but the revenge will not fail to appear, it only will appear later, or rather, it is often recognized too late by the people.

*   *   *

The sin against the blood and the degradation of the race are the hereditary sin of this world and the end of a mankind surrendering to them.

*   *   *

Prostitution is a disgrace to mankind, but one cannot abolish it by moral lectures, pious intentions, etc., but its limitation and its final elimination warrant the abolition of quite a number of preliminary conditions. But the first is and remains the creation of the possibility of early marriage, according to human nature, above all for the man; because the woman is here only the passive part, anyhow.

*   *   *

Marriage also cannot be an end in itself, but has to serve the one greater aim, the propagation and preservation of the species and the race. Only this is its meaning and its task.

*   *   *

*** Education and training have to eliminate quite a series of evils about which one hardly cares at all today. Above all, in our present-day education a balance between intellectual instruction and physical training has to take place. What today calls itself a *gymnasium* is an insult to the Greek example. With our education one has entirely forgotten that in the long run a healthy mind is able to dwell only in a healthy body. Especially when, with a few exceptions, one looks at the great masses of the people, this principle receives absolute validity.

In pre-War Germany there was a time when one no longer cared for this truth. One simply went on sinning against the body, and one thought that in the one-sided training of the 'mind' one possessed a safe guaranty for the greatness of the nation. A mistake which began to avenge itself much sooner than one thought. It is no accident that the bolshevistic wave found nowhere a better ground than in those places where a population, degenerated by hunger and constant undernourishment, lives: in Central Germany, Saxony, and the Ruhr district. In all these districts, however, a serious resistance on the part of the so-called "intelligentsia" to this Jewish disease hardly takes place any longer for the simple reason that the intelligentsia itself is physically completely degenerated, though less by reasons of distress than by reasons of education. The exclusively intellectual attitude of our education of the higher classes makes them unable—in a time where not the mind but the fist decides—even to preserve themselves, let alone to hold their ground. In physical deficiencies there lies not infrequently the first cause of personal cowardice.

The exceeding stress on a purely intellectual training and the neglect of physical training favor also in much too early youth the formation of sexual conceptions. The boy who, by sports and gymnastics, is brought to an ironlike inurement succumbs less to the need of sensual gratification than the stay-at-home who is fed exclusively on intellectual food. A reasonable education, however, must take this into consideration. Further, it must not forget that on the part of the healthy young man the expectations of the woman will be different than on the part of a prematurely corrupted weakling.

Thus the entire education has to be directed towards employing the free time of the boy for the useful training of his body. He has no right to loaf about idly in these years, to make streets and movie theaters insecure, but after his daily work he has to steel and harden his young body so that life will not find him too soft some day. To get this under way and also to carry it out, to guide and to lead is the task of the education of youth, and not the exclusive infiltration of so-called wisdom. It has also to do away with the conception that the treatment of the body were the concern of each individual. There is no liberty to sin at the expense of posterity and, with it, of the race.

*   *   *

It is a half measure to allow incurably ill people the permanent possibility of contaminating the other healthy ones. But this corresponds entirely to a humaneness which, in order not to hurt one individual, lets hundreds of others perish. The demand that for defective people the propagation of an equally defective offspring be made impossible is a demand of clearest reason and in its planful execution it means the most humane act of mankind. It will spare undeserved suffering to millions of unfortunates, but in the future it will lead to an increasing improvement of health on the whole. The determination to proceed in this direction will also put up a dam against the further spreading of venereal diseases. For here, if necessary, one will have to proceed to the pitiless isolation of incurably diseased people; a barbaric measure for one who was unfortunate enough to be stricken with it, but a blessing for the contemporaries and for posterity. The temporary pain of a century may and will redeem millenniums from suffering.

*   *   *

Any crossing between two beings of not quite the same high standard produces a medium between the standards of the parents. That means: the young one will probably be on a higher level than the racially lower parent, but not as high as the higher one. Consequently, it will succumb later on in the fight against the higher level. But such a mating contradicts Nature's will to breed life as a whole towards a higher level.

*   *   *

Just as little as Nature desires a mating between weaker individuals and stronger ones, far less she desires the mixing of a higher race with a lower one, as in this case her entire work of higher breeding, which has perhaps taken hundreds of thousands of years, would tumble at one blow.

Historical experience offers countless proofs of this. It shows with terrible clarity that with any mixing of the blood of the Aryan with lower races the result was the end of the culture-bearer. North America, the population of which consists for the greatest part of Germanic elements—which mix only very little with the lower, colored races—displays a humanity and a culture different from those of Central and South America, where chiefly the Romanic immigrants have sometimes mixed with the aborigines on a large scale. By this example alone one may clearly and distinctly recognize the influence of the race mixture. The Germanic of the North American continent, who has remained pure and less intermixed, has become the master of that continent, he will remain so until he, too, falls victim to the shame of blood-mixing.

*   *   *

Everything that today we admire on this earth—science and art, technique and inventions—is only the creative product of a few peoples and perhaps originally of *one* race. On them now depends also the existence of this entire culture. If they perish, then the beauty of this earth sinks into the grave with them.

*   *   *

All great cultures of the past perished only because the originally creative race died off through blood-poisoning.

*   *   *

He who wants to live should fight, therefore, and he who does not want to battle in this world of eternal struggle does not deserve to be alive.

*   *   *

What we see before us of human culture today, the results of art, science, and techniques, is almost exclusively the creative product of the Aryan.

* * *

If one were to divide mankind into three groups: culture-founders, culture-bearers, and culture-destroyers, then, as representative of the first kind, only the Aryan would come in question. It is from him that the foundation and the walls of all human creations originate, and only the external form and color depend on the characteristics of the various peoples involved. He furnishes the gigantic building-stones and also the plans for all human progress, and only the execution corresponds to the character of the people and races in the various instances.

* * *

But if it is ascertained that a people receives, takes in, and works over the essential basic elements of its culture from other races, and if then, when a further external influence is lacking, it stiffens again and again, then one can perhaps call such a race a *"culture-bearing"* one but never a *"culture-creating"* one.

* * *

The Jew forms the strongest contrast to the Aryan. Hardly in any people of the world is the instinct of self-preservation more strongly developed than in the so-called "chosen people." The fact of the existence of this race alone may be looked upon as the best proof of this. Where is the people that in the past two thousand years has been exposed to so small changes of the inner disposition, of character, etc., as the Jewish people? Which people finally has experienced greater changes than this one—and yet has always come forth the same from the most colossal catastrophes of mankind? What an infinitely persistent will for life, for preserving the race do these facts disclose!

Also the intellectual abilities were schooled in the course of centuries. Today the Jew is looked upon as "clever," and in a certain sense he has been so at all times. But his reason is not the result of his own development, but that of object lessons from without.

* * *

As now the Jew (for reasons which will immediately become evident from the following) was never in the possession of a culture of his own, the bases for his spiritual activity have always been furnished by others. At all times his intellect has developed through the culture that surrounds him.

* * *

In the Jewish people, the will to sacrifice oneself does not go beyond the bare instinct of self-preservation of the individual. The seemingly great feeling of belonging together is rooted in a very primitive herd instinct, as it shows itself in a similar way in many other living beings in this world. Thereby the fact is remarkable that in all these cases a common herd instinct leads to mutual support only as long as a common danger makes this seem useful or unavoidable. The same pack of wolves that jointly falls upon its booty dissolves when its hunger abates.

* * *

The Jew remains united only if forced by a common danger or is attracted by a common booty; if both reasons are no longer evident, then the qualities of the crassest egoism come into their own, and, in a moment, the united people becomes a horde of rats, fighting bloodily among themselves.

If the Jews were alone in this world, they would suffocate as much in dirt and filth, as they would carry on a detestable struggle to cheat and to ruin each other, although the complete lack of the will to sacrifice, expressed in their cowardice, would also in this instance make the fight a comedy.

Thus it is fundamentally wrong to conclude, merely from the fact of their standing together in a fight, or, more rightly expressed, in their exploiting their fellow human beings, that the Jews have a certain idealistic will to sacrifice themselves.

* * *

* * * The Jewish people, with all its apparent intellectual qualities, is nevertheless without any true culture, especially without a culture of its own. For the sham culture which the Jew possesses today is the property of other peoples, and is mostly spoiled in his hands.

* * *

No, the Jew possesses no culture-creating energy whatsoever, as the idealism, without which there can never exist a genuine development of man towards a higher level, does not and never did exist in him. His intellect, therefore, will never have a constructive effect, but only a destructive one. * * *

* * *

The Jews were always a people with definite racial qualities and never a religion, only their progress made them probably look very early for a means which could divert disagreeable attention from their person. But what would have been more useful and at the same time more harmless than the "purloining" of the appearance of being a religious community? For here, too, everything is purloined, or rather, stolen. But resulting from his own original nature the Jew cannot possess a religious institution for the very reason that he lacks all idealism in any form and that he also does not recognize any belief in the hereafter.

* * *

The State is a means to an end. Its end is the preservation and the promotion of a community of physically and psychically equal living beings. This very preservation comprises first the racial stock and thereby it permits the free development of all the forces slumbering in this race. Again and again a part of them will primarily serve the preservation of the physical life and only another part will serve the promotion of a further mental development. But actually the one always creates the presumption for the other.

States that do not serve this purpose are faulty specimens, even miscarriages.

* * *

Thus the highest purpose of the folkish State is the care for the preservation of those racial primal elements which, supplying culture, create the beauty and dignity of a higher humanity. We, as Aryans, are therefore able to imagine a State only to be the living organism of a nationality which not only safeguards the preservation of that nationality, but which, by a further training of its spiritual and ideal abilities, leads it to the highest freedom.

* * *

REVIEW QUESTIONS

1. What were the greatest threats to the racial purity of Germans according to Hitler?
2. What solutions did he propose?
3. What were the fundamental goals of education in the Nazi state?
4. In what sense did Jews pose a threat to Aryans?
5. On what evidence did Hitler base his arguments?

GEORGE ORWELL

FROM *The Road to Wigan Pier*

Europeans had hoped that the end of the war would signal a renewed prosperity: instead they experienced one economic crisis after another in the 1920s and 1930s. A feverish period of economic revival began in 1925, but it was brought to a precipitous halt by the crash of the U.S. stock market in 1929. While the global economy was gradually stabilized during the middle to late 1930s, the Depression did not truly come to an end until a new world war—and a tremendous increase in the production of armaments—kicked the economies of the industrialized nations back into high gear.

The United States and Germany endured the greatest hardships during the Depression, but all of the industrialized nations of western Europe suffered from high rates of unemployment and the demoralization caused by economic collapse. In the mid-1930s, George Orwell (pseudonym of Eric Arthur Blair, 1903–1950), was asked by the Left Book Club to travel through northern England and write a report on workers' conditions for the book club's members. Already known to progressive readers as the author of Down and Out in Paris and London *(1933), a sympathetic account of life among the transient poor, Orwell was an unorthodox socialist whose perceptions of workers were strongly shaped by his rejection of the prejudices of the "shabby-genteel" lower middle class into which he had been born. In* The Road to Wigan Pier *(1937), Orwell describes the lives of unemployed workers living "on the dole," the welfare benefits provided by the British government.*

From *The Road to Wigan Pier*, by George Orwell (New York: Harcourt, Brace, 1958), pp. 76–77, 79–82, 85–90.

*   *   *

When you see the unemployment figures quoted at two millions, it is fatally easy to take this as meaning that two million people are out of work and the rest of the population is comparatively comfortable. I admit that till recently I was in the habit of doing so myself. I used to calculate that if you put the registered unemployed at round about two millions and threw in the destitute and those who for one reason and another were not registered, you might take the number of underfed people in England (for *everyone* on the dole or thereabouts is underfed) as being, at the very most, five millions.

This is an enormous under-estimate, because, in the first place, the only people shown on unemployment figures are those actually drawing the dole—that is, in general, heads of families. An unemployed man's dependants do not figure on the list unless they too are drawing a separate allowance. A Labour Exchange officer told me that to get at the real number of people *living on* (not drawing) the dole, you have got to multiply the official figures by something over three. This alone brings the number of unemployed to round about six millions. But in addition there are great numbers of people who are in work but who, from a financial point of view, might equally well be unemployed, because they are not drawing anything that can be described as a living wage. Allow for these and their dependants, throw in as before the old-age pensioners, the destitute and other nondescripts, and you get an *underfed* population of well over ten millions. ✳ ✳ ✳

Take the figures for Wigan, which is typical enough of the industrial and mining districts. The number of insured workers is round about 36,000 (26,000 men and 10,000 women). Of these, the number unemployed at the beginning of 1936 was about 10,000. But this was in winter when the mines are working full time; in summer it would probably be 12,000. Multiply by three, as above, and you get 30,000 or 36,000. The total population of Wigan is a little under 87,000; so that at any moment more than one person in three out of the whole population—not merely the registered workers—is either drawing or living on the dole. Those ten or twelve thousand unemployed contain a steady core of from four to five thousand miners who have been continuously unemployed for the past seven years. And Wigan is not especially badly off as industrial towns go. Even in Sheffield, which has been doing well for the last year or so because of wars and rumours of war, the proportion of unemployment is about the same—one in three of registered workers unemployed.

✳   ✳   ✳

Nevertheless, in spite of the frightful extent of unemployment, it is a fact that poverty—extreme poverty—is less in evidence in the industrial North than it is in London. Everything is poorer and shabbier, there are fewer motor-cars and fewer well-dressed people; but also there are fewer people who are obviously destitute. Even in a town the size of Liverpool or Manchester you are struck by the fewness of the beggars. London is a sort of whirlpool which draws derelict people towards it, and it is so vast that life there is solitary and anonymous. Until you break the law nobody will take any notice of you, and you can go to pieces as you could not possibly do in a place where you had neighbours who knew you. But in the industrial towns the old communal way of life has not yet broken up, tradition is still strong and almost everyone has a family—potentially, therefore, a home. In a town of 50,000 or 100,000 inhabitants there is no casual and as it were unaccounted-for population; nobody sleeping in the streets, for instance. Moreover, there is just this to be said for the unemployment regulations, that they do not discourage people from marrying. A man and wife on twenty-three shillings a week are not far from the starvation line, but they can make a home of sorts; they are vastly better off than a single man on fifteen shillings.

✳   ✳   ✳

But there is no doubt about the deadening, debilitating effect of unemployment upon everybody, married or single, and upon men more than upon women.

✳   ✳   ✳

Take a miner, for instance, who has worked in the pit since childhood and has been trained to be a miner and nothing else. How the devil is he to fill up the empty days? It is absurd to say that he ought to be looking for work. There is no work to look for, and everybody knows it. You can't go on looking for work every day for seven years.

✳   ✳   ✳

I first became aware of the unemployment problem in 1928. ✳ ✳ ✳ At that time nobody cared to admit that unemployment was inevitable, because this meant admitting that it would probably continue. The middle classes were still talking about "lazy idle loafers on the dole" and saying that "these men could all find work if they wanted to," and naturally these opinions percolated to the working class themselves. I remember the shock of astonishment it gave me, when I first mingled with tramps and beggars, to find that a fair proportion, perhaps a quarter, of these beings whom I had been taught to regard as cynical parasites, were decent young miners and cotton-workers gazing at their destiny with the same sort of dumb amazement as an animal in a trap. They simply could not understand what was happening to them. They had been brought up to work, and behold! it seemed as if they were never going to have the chance of working again. In their circumstances it was inevitable, at first, that they should be haunted by a feeling of personal degradation. That was the attitude towards unemployment in those days: it was a disaster which happened to *you* as an individual and for which *you* were to blame.

When a quarter of a million miners are unemployed, it is part of the order of things that Alf Smith, a miner living in the back streets of Newcastle, should be out of work. Alf Smith is merely one of the quarter million, a statistical unit.

* * *

When people live on the dole for years at a time they grow used to it, and drawing the dole, though it remains unpleasant, ceases to be shameful. * * * The people have at any rate grasped that unemployment is a thing they cannot help. It is not only Alf Smith who is out of work now; Bert Jones is out of work as well, and both of them have been "out" for years. It makes a great deal of difference when things are the same for everybody.

* * *

But they don't necessarily lower their standards by cutting out luxuries and concentrating on necessities; more often it is the other way about—the more natural way, if you come to think of it. Hence the fact that in a decade of unparalleled depression, the consumption of all cheap luxuries has increased. The two things that have probably made the greatest difference of all are the movies and the mass-production of cheap smart clothes since the war. The youth who leaves school at fourteen and gets a blind-alley job is out of work at twenty, probably for life; but for two pounds ten on the hire-purchase system he can buy himself a suit which, for a little while and at a little distance, looks as though it had been tailored in Savile Row. The girl can look like a fashion plate at an even lower price. You may have three halfpence in your pocket and not a prospect in the world, and only the corner of a leaky bedroom to go home to; but in your new clothes you can stand on the street corner, indulging in a private daydream of yourself as Clark Gable or Greta Garbo, which compensates you for a great deal. And even at home there is generally a cup of tea going—a "nice cup of tea"—and Father, who has been out of work since 1929, is temporarily happy because he has a sure tip for the Cesarewitch.

Trade since the war has had to adjust itself to meet the demands of underpaid, underfed people, with the result that a luxury is nowadays almost always cheaper than a necessity. One pair of plain solid shoes costs as much as two ultra-smart pairs. For the price of one square meal you can get two pounds of cheap sweets. You can't get much meat for threepence, but you can get a lot of fish-and-chips. Milk costs threepence a pint and even "mild" beer costs fourpence, but aspirins are seven a penny and you can wring forty cups of tea out of a quarter-pound packet. And above all there is gambling, the cheapest of all luxuries. Even people on the verge of starvation can buy a few days' hope ("Something to live for," as they call it) by having a penny on a sweepstake.

* * *

Of course the post-war development of cheap luxuries has been a very fortunate thing for our rulers. It is quite likely that fish and chips, art-silk stockings, tinned salmon, cut-price chocolate (five two-ounce bars for sixpence), the movies, the radio, strong tea and the Football Pools have between them averted revolution. Therefore we are sometimes told that the whole thing is an astute manœuvre by the governing class—a sort of "bread and circuses" business—to hold the unemployed down. What I have seen of our governing class does not convince me that they have that much intelligence. The thing has happened, but by an unconscious process—the quite natural interaction between the manufacturer's need for a market and the need of half-starved people for cheap palliatives.

*   *   *

REVIEW QUESTIONS

1. Why, according to Orwell, was extreme poverty less common in the north of England than in the south?
2. What impact did long-term unemployment have on workers in northern England?
3. Why were the poor addicted to cheap luxuries?

SIGMUND FREUD

FROM *Civilization and Its Discontents*

The interwar years witnessed a generalized collapse of confidence in the values and practices promoted by nineteenth-century liberalism. Many Europeans rejected the principles of parliamentary democracy, individualism, and reason in favor of authoritarianism, collectivism, and the reign of instinct. Writing in the late 1920s, Sigmund Freud asked himself, "How has it happened that so many people have come to take up this strange attitude of hostility to civilization?" Freud was puzzled and disturbed by the rise of irrationalist political movements, and he sought psychological explanations for the seething discontent with civilized society expressed by so many Europeans during this period. While Freud's earlier writings had focused on the expression—and repression—of the sexual instinct, Civilization and its Discontents *(1930), dealt with what Freud identified as a countervailing aggressive instinct.*

Freud's own perspective on civilization revealed a deep pessimism about human nature. While he conceived of modern European society as marking a high point in human cultural development, he argued that Western "Civilization" could only be realized and maintained through the painful repression of the individual's instinctual sexual and aggressive drives. When instinct was successfully sublimated—redirected into socially beneficial ends—it produced art, literature, science, industry, and stable government. On the other hand, no amount of human progress could ever compensate the individual for the loss of the spontaneous expression of these primordial impulses.

From *Civilization and Its Discontents,* by Sigmund Freud, translated by James Strachey (New York: Norton, 1961), pp. 55–59.

* * *

* * * Sexual love is a relationship between two individuals in which a third can only be superfluous or disturbing, whereas civilization depends on relationships between a considerable number of individuals. When a love-relationship is at its height there is no room left for any interest in the environment; a pair of lovers are sufficient to themselves, and do not even need the child they have in common to make them happy. * * *

So far, we can quite well imagine a cultural community consisting of double individuals like this, who, libidinally satisfied in themselves, are connected with one another through the bonds of common work and common interests. If this were so, civilization would not have to withdraw any energy from sexuality. But this desirable state of things does not, and never did, exist. Reality shows us that civilization is not content with the ties we have so far allowed it. It aims at binding the members of the community together in a libidinal way as well and employs every means to that end. It favours every path by which strong identifications can be established between the members of the community, and it summons up aim-inhibited libido on the largest scale so as to strengthen the communal bond by relations of friendship. In order for these aims to be fulfilled, a restriction upon sexual life is unavoidable. But we are unable to understand what the necessity is which forces civilization along this path and which causes its antagonism to sexuality. There must be some disturbing factor which we have not yet discovered.

The clue may be supplied by one of the ideal demands, as we have called them, of civilized society. It runs: "Thou shalt love thy neighbour as thyself." It is known throughout the world and is undoubtedly older than Christianity, which puts it forward as its proudest claim. Yet it is certainly not very old; even in historical times it was still strange to mankind. Let us adopt a naïve attitude towards it, as though we were hearing it for the first time; we shall be unable then to suppress a feeling of surprise and bewilderment. Why should we do it? What good will it do us? But, above all, how shall we achieve it? How can it be possible? My love is something valuable to me which I ought not to throw away without reflection. It imposes duties on me for whose fulfilment I must be ready to make sacrifices. If I love someone, he must deserve it in some way. (I leave out of account the use he may be to me, and also his possible significance for me as a sexual object, for neither of these two kinds of relationship comes into question where the precept to love my neighbour is concerned.) He deserves it if he is so like me in important ways that I can love myself in him; and he deserves it if he is so much more perfect than myself that I can love my ideal of my own self in him. Again, I have to love him if he is my friend's son, since the pain my friend would feel if any harm came to him would be my pain too—I should have to share it. But if he is a stranger to me and if he cannot attract me by any worth of his own or any significance that he may already have acquired for my emotional life, it will be hard for me to love him. Indeed, I should be wrong to do so, for my love is valued by all my own people as a sign of my preferring them, and it is an injustice to them if I put a stranger on a par with them. But if I am to love him (with this universal love) merely because he, too, is an inhabitant of this earth, like an insect, an earthworm or a grass-snake, then I fear that only a small modicum of my love will fall to his share—not by any possibility as much as, by the judgement of my reason, I am entitled to retain for myself. What is the point of a precept enunciated with so much solemnity if its fulfilment cannot be recommended as reasonable?

On closer inspection, I find still further difficulties. Not merely is this stranger in general unworthy of my love; I must honestly confess that he has more claim to my hostility and even my hatred. He seems not to have the least trace of love for me and shows me not the slightest consideration. If it will do him any good he has no hesitation in injuring me, nor does he ask himself whether the amount of advantage he gains bears any proportion to the extent of the harm he does to me. Indeed, he need not even obtain an advantage; if he can satisfy any sort of desire by it, he thinks nothing of jeering at me, insulting me, slandering me and showing his superior power; and the more secure he feels and the more helpless I am, the more certainly I can expect him to behave like this to me. If he behaves differently, if he shows me consideration and forbearance as a stranger, I am ready to treat him in the same way, in any case and quite apart from any precept. Indeed, if this grandiose commandment had run "Love thy neighbour as thy neighbour loves thee," I should not take exception to it. And there is a second commandment, which seems to me even more incomprehensible and arouses still stronger opposition in me. It is "Love thine enemies." If I think it over, however, I see that I am wrong in treating it as a greater imposition. At bottom it is the same thing.

I think I can now hear a dignified voice admonishing me: "It is precisely because your neighbour is not worthy of love, and is on the contrary your enemy, that you should love him as yourself." ⁎ ⁎ ⁎

Now it is very probable that my neighbour, when he is enjoined to love me as himself, will answer exactly as I have done and will repel me for the same reasons. I hope he will not have the same objective grounds for doing so, but he will have the same idea as I have.

⁎   ⁎   ⁎

The element of truth behind all this, which people are so ready to disavow, is that men are not gentle creatures who want to be loved, and who at the most can defend themselves if they are attacked; they are, on the contrary, creatures among whose instinctual endowments is to be reckoned a powerful share of aggressiveness. As a result, their neighbour is for them not only a potential helper or sexual object, but also someone who tempts them to satisfy their aggressiveness on him, to exploit his capacity for work without compensation, to use him sexually without his consent, to seize his possessions, to humiliate him, to cause him pain, to torture and to kill him. *Homo*

homini lupus.[1] Who, in the face of all his experience of life and of history, will have the courage to dispute this assertion? As a rule this cruel aggressiveness waits for some provocation or puts itself at the service of some other purpose, whose goal might also have been reached by milder measures. In circumstances that are favourable to it, when the mental counter-forces which ordinarily inhibit it are out of action, it also manifests itself spontaneously and reveals man as a savage beast to whom consideration towards his own kind is something alien. Anyone who calls to mind the atrocities committed during the racial migrations or the invasions of the Huns, or by the people known as Mongols under Jenghiz Khan and Tamerlane, or at the capture of Jerusalem by the pious Crusaders, or even, indeed, the horrors of the recent World War—anyone who calls these things to mind will have to bow humbly before the truth of this view.

The existence of this inclination to aggression, which we can detect in ourselves and justly assume to be present in others, is the factor which disturbs our relations with our neighbour and which forces civilization into such a high expenditure [of energy]. In consequence of this primary mutual hostility of human beings, civilized society is perpetually threatened with disintegration. The interest of work in common would not hold it together; instinctual passions are stronger than reasonable interests. Civilization has to use its utmost efforts in order to set limits to man's aggressive instincts and to hold the manifestations of them in check by psychical reaction-formations. Hence, therefore, the use of methods intended to incite people into identifications and aim-inhibited relationships of love, hence the restriction upon sexual life, and hence too the ideal's commandment to love one's neighbour as oneself—a commandment which is really justified by the fact that nothing else runs so strongly counter to the original nature of man. In spite of every effort, these endeavours of civilization have not so

---

[1] "Man is a wolf to man."

far achieved very much. It hopes to prevent the crudest excesses of brutal violence by itself assuming the right to use violence against criminals, but the law is not able to lay hold of the more cautious and refined manifestations of human aggressiveness. The time comes when each one of us has to give up as illusions the expectations which, in his youth, he pinned upon his fellow-men, and when he may learn how much difficulty and pain has been added to his life by their ill-will.

*   *   *

REVIEW QUESTIONS

1. Why is it so difficult to love one's neighbor as oneself?
2. Why is this commandment a necessary requirement of civilized society?
3. What is human nature like according to Freud?
4. What specific historical events and developments might be explained by Freud's theory of aggression?

ALBERT EINSTEIN

FROM *Science and Religion*

Soon after the publication of Civilization and Its Discontents, *Freud and German physicist Albert Einstein (1879–1955) exchanged letters commenting on the origins of war (published as* Why War? *in 1932). Both Freud and Einstein agreed that war was perhaps an inevitable, if undesirable, expression of instinctual aggression. When Hitler became chancellor of Germany in 1933, Einstein relocated to the United States and began teaching at Princeton. When Hitler sent troops into Austria in 1938, Freud, aging and very ill, was forced to flee Vienna and settle in London. As Jews and as purveyors of disturbingly modern scientific and psychological theories, neither of these great thinkers were welcome in Nazi-controlled territories.*

Perhaps the most famous scientist of the twentieth century, Einstein revolutionized physics in 1905 when he published a series of papers that forced a fundamental rethinking of the basic laws governing the properties of space, time, light, and motion. The best known of his discoveries was the special theory of relativity, according to which both time and motion are not absolutes but relative to the observer. Einstein's passionate commitment to science was matched by an equally passionate commitment to the international peace movement and to spiritual growth. While Freud was an atheist who studied the psychology of religion from a strictly secular perspective, Einstein saw no incompatibility between religious faith and a scientific understanding of the cosmos. He rejected traditional revealed religion but continued to believe in a "clockmaker" God "who reveals himself in the harmony of what exists."

From *Science and Religion*, by Albert Einstein (New York: Bonanza Books, 1954).

* * *

It would not be difficult to come to an agreement as to what we understand by science. Science is the century-old endeavor to bring together by means of systematic thought the perceptible phenomena of this world into as thorough-going an association as possible. To put it boldly, it is the attempt at the posterior reconstruction of existence by the process of conceptualization. But when asking myself what religion is I cannot think of the answer so easily. And even after finding an answer which may satisfy me at this particular moment, I still remain convinced that I can never under any circumstances bring together, even to a slight extent, the thoughts of all those who have given this question serious consideration.

At first, then, instead of asking what religion is I should prefer to ask what characterizes the aspirations of a person who gives me the impression of being religious: a person who is religiously enlightened appears to me to be one who has, to the best of his ability, liberated himself from the fetters of his selfish desires and is preoccupied with thoughts, feelings, and aspirations to which he clings because of their superpersonal value. It seems to me that what is important is the force of this superpersonal content and the depth of the conviction concerning its overpowering meaningfulness, regardless of whether any attempt is made to unite this content with a divine Being, for otherwise it would not be possible to count Buddha and Spinoza as religious personalities. Accordingly, a religious person is devout in the sense that he has no doubt of the significance and loftiness of those superpersonal objects and goals which neither require nor are capable of rational foundation. They exist with the same necessity and matter-of-factness as he himself. In this sense religion is the age-old endeavor of mankind to become clearly and completely conscious of these values and goals and constantly to strengthen and extend their effect. If one conceives of religion and science according to these definitions then a conflict between them appears impossible. For science can only ascertain what *is,* but not what *should be,* and outside of its domain value judgments of all kinds remain necessary. Religion, on the other hand, deals only with evaluations of human thought and action: it cannot justifiably speak of facts and relationships between facts. According to this interpretation the well-known conflicts between religion and science in the past must all be ascribed to a misapprehension of the situation which has been described.

For example, a conflict arises when a religious community insists on the absolute truthfulness of all statements recorded in the Bible. This means an intervention on the part of religion into the sphere of science; this is where the struggle of the Church against the doctrines of Galileo and Darwin belongs. On the other hand, representatives of science have often made an attempt to arrive at fundamental judgments with respect to values and ends on the basis of scientific method, and in this way have set themselves in opposition to religion. These conflicts have all sprung from fatal errors.

Now, even though the realms of religion and science in themselves are clearly marked off from each other, nevertheless there exist between the two strong reciprocal relationships and dependencies. Though religion may be that which determines the goal, it has, nevertheless, learned from science, in the broadest sense, what means will contribute to the attainment of the goals it has set up. But science can only be created by those who are thoroughly imbued with the aspiration toward truth and understanding. This source of feeling, however, springs from the sphere of religion. To this there also belongs the faith in the possibility that the regulations valid for the world of existence are rational, that is, comprehensible to reason. I cannot conceive of a genuine scientist without that profound faith. The situation may be expressed by an image: science without religion is lame, religion without science is blind.

Though I have asserted above that in truth a legitimate conflict between religion and science cannot exist, I must nevertheless qualify this assertion once again on an essential point, with reference to the actual content of historical religions.

This qualification has to do with the concept of God. During the youthful period of mankind's spiritual evolution human fantasy created gods in man's own image, who, by the operations of their will were supposed to determine, or at any rate to influence, the phenomenal world. Man sought to alter the disposition of these gods in his own favor by means of magic and prayer. The idea of God in the religions taught at present is a sublimation of that old concept of the gods. Its anthropomorphic character is shown, for instance, by the fact that men appeal to the Divine Being in prayers and plead for the fulfillment of their wishes.

Nobody, certainly, will deny that the idea of the existence of an omnipotent, just, and omnibeneficent personal God is able to accord man solace, help, and guidance; also, by virtue of its simplicity it is accessible to the most undeveloped mind. But, on the other hand, there are decisive weaknesses attached to this idea in itself, which have been painfully felt since the beginning of history. That is, if this being is omnipotent, then every occurrence, including every human action, every human thought, and every human feeling and aspiration is also His work; how is it possible to think of holding men responsible for their deeds and thoughts before such an almighty Being? In giving out punishment and rewards He would to a certain extent be passing judgment on Himself. How can this be combined with the goodness and righteousness ascribed to Him?

The main source of the present-day conflicts between the spheres of religion and of science lies in this concept of a personal God. It is the aim of science to establish general rules which determine the reciprocal connection of objects and events in time and space. For these rules, or laws of nature, absolutely general validity is required—not proven. It is mainly a program, and faith in the possibility of its accomplishment in principle is only founded on partial successes. But hardly anyone could be found who would deny these partial successes and ascribe them to human self-deception. The fact that on the basis of such laws we are able to predict the temporal behavior of phenomena in certain domains with great precision and certainty is deeply embedded in the consciousness of the modern man, even though he may have grasped very little of the contents of those laws. He need only consider that planetary courses within the solar system may be calculated in advance with great exactitude on the basis of a limited number of simple laws. In a similar way, though not with the same precision, it is possible to calculate in advance the mode of operation of an electric motor, a transmission system, or of a wireless apparatus, even when dealing with a novel development.

To be sure, when the number of factors coming into play in a phenomenological complex is too large, scientific method in most cases fails us. One need only think of the weather, in which case prediction even for a few days ahead is impossible. Nevertheless no one doubts that we are confronted with a causal connection whose causal components are in the main known to us. Occurrences in this domain are beyond the reach of exact prediction because of the variety of factors in operation, not because of any lack of order in nature.

We have penetrated far less deeply into the regularities obtaining within the realm of living things, but deeply enough nevertheless to sense at least the rule of fixed necessity. One need only think of the systematic order in heredity, and in the effect of poisons, as for instance alcohol, on the behavior of organic beings. What is still lacking here is a grasp of connections of profound generality, but not a knowledge of order in itself.

The more a man is imbued with the ordered regularity of all events the firmer becomes his conviction that there is no room left by the side of this ordered regularity for causes of a different nature. For him neither the rule of human nor the rule of divine will exists as an independent cause of natural events. To be sure, the doctrine of a personal God interfering with natural events could never be *refuted*, in the real sense, by science, for this doctrine can always take refuge in those domains in which scientific knowledge has not yet been able to set foot.

But I am persuaded that such behavior on the part of the representatives of religion would not only be unworthy but also fatal. For a doctrine which is able to maintain itself not in clear light but only in the dark, will of necessity lose its effect on mankind, with incalculable harm to human progress. In their struggle for the ethical good, teachers of religion must have the stature to give up the doctrine of a personal God, that is, give up that source of fear and hope which in the past placed such vast power in the hands of priests. In their labors they will have to avail themselves of those forces which are capable of cultivating the Good, the True, and the Beautiful in humanity itself. This is, to be sure, a more difficult but an incomparably more worthy task. After religious teachers accomplish the refining process indicated they will surely recognize with joy that true religion has been ennobled and made more profound by scientific knowledge.

If it is one of the goals of religion to liberate mankind as far as possible from the bondage of egocentric cravings, desires, and fears, scientific reasoning can aid religion in yet another sense. Although it is true that it is the goal of science to discover rules which permit the association and foretelling of facts, this is not its only aim. It also seeks to reduce the connections discovered to the smallest possible number of mutually independent conceptual elements. It is in this striving after the rational unification of the manifold that it encounters its greatest successes, even though it is precisely this attempt which causes it to run the greatest risk of falling a prey to illusions. But whoever has undergone the intense experience of successful advances made in this domain is moved by profound reverence for the rationality made manifest in existence. By way of the understanding he achieves a far-reaching emancipation from the shackles of personal hopes and desires, and thereby attains that humble attitude of mind toward the grandeur of reason incarnate in existence, and which, in its profoundest depths, is inaccessible to man. This attitude, however, appears to me to be religious, in the highest sense of the word. And so it seems to me that science not only purifies the religious impulse of the dross of its anthropomorphism but also contributes to a religious spiritualization of our understanding of life.

The further the spiritual evolution of mankind advances, the more certain it seems to me that the path to genuine religiosity does not lie through the fear of life, and the fear of death, and blind faith, but through striving after rational knowledge. In this sense I believe that the priest must become a teacher if he wishes to do justice to his lofty educational mission.

*   *   *

REVIEW QUESTIONS

1. Why, according to Einstein, are religion and science not mutually incompatible?
2. What sort of God did Einstein believe in?
3. How acceptable would this conception of God be to traditional Jews, Christians, or Muslims?
4. To what extent do you think Einstein's arguments were a product of his specific historical experience?

THE JOURNALIST SYLVIA VON HARDEN (1927)   Otto Dix

Interwar artists, writers, poets, and dramatists redefined the individual subject in radically critical ways, making the interwar decades a watershed era for modern cultural expression. Among the many art movements that arose in the 1920s was the New Objectivity movement, a brand of realism that stripped away ideals and illusions to render people and things in unadorned objectivity. What does this painting suggest about interwar artistic aesthetics and about the function of art for interwar society?

T. S. ELIOT

The Love Song of J. Alfred Prufrock

Freud and Einstein expressed their concerns about interwar culture in the form of tightly reasoned essays, but many artists and writers were drawn to new forms of expression that attempted to convey the nonlinearity and irrationality of lived experience. T. S. Eliot (1888–1965), one of the most prominent exponents of the modernist style, produced several collections of poetry, including The Waste Land *(1922) and* Four Quartets *(1943), that had a profound impact on both the form and content of interwar literature. Eliot, like John Reed (see first reading, this chapter), had been born into an affluent American family and attended Harvard, graduating one year before Reed in 1909. Eliot moved to Europe just prior to the First World War and spent most of the rest of his life in Britain.*

Eliot's first major work, The Love Song of J. Alfred Prufrock, *published in 1915, is one of the great masterpieces of modernist poetry. Eliot's verse is steeped in the traditions of European high art culture—"Prufrock" contains numerous references to the works of other poets, including Hesiod, Dante, Andrew Marvell, and Shakespeare—but it also seeks to apply this literary tradition to the description of everyday life, uniting the heroic and the prosaic, the transcendent and the mundane, solemn drama and tawdry melodrama. In this poem, Eliot's skillful use of language lends a certain tragic grandeur to the thoughts and turns of phrase of a very ordinary and unromantic protagonist. It is the tortured complexity of J. Alfred Prufrock's mental processes, his agonized self-consciousness and even self-deprecation, that make him such an apt representative of the complex and tortured interwar years.*

From *Prufrock and Other Observations*, by T. S. Eliot (London: Egoist, 1917).

S'io credesse che mia risposta fossè
A persona che mai tornasse al mondo,
Questa fiamma staria senza piu scosse.
Ma perciocche giammai di questo fondo
Non torno vivo alcun, s'i'odo il vero,
Senza tema d'infamia ti rispondo[1]

---

[1] "If I thought that my reply would be to one who would ever return to the world, this flame would stay without further movement; but since none has ever returned alive from this depth, if what I hear is true, I answer you without fear of infamy" (Dante, *Inferno* 27. 61–66).

Let us go then, you and I,
When the evening is spread out against the sky
Like a patient etherized upon a table;
Let us go, through certain half-deserted streets,
The muttering retreats
Of restless nights in one-night cheap hotels
And sawdust restaurants with oyster shells:
Streets that follow like a tedious argument
Of insidious intent
To lead you to an overwhelming question . . .
Oh, do not ask, "What is it?"
Let us go and make our visit.

In the room the women come and go
Talking of Michelangelo.

The yellow fog that rubs its back upon the
　windowpanes,
The yellow smoke that rubs its muzzle on the
　windowpanes
Licked its tongue into the corners of the
　evening,
Lingered upon the pools that stand in drains,
Let fall upon its back the soot that falls from
　chimneys,
Slipped by the terrace, made a sudden leap,
And seeing that it was a soft October night,
Curled once about the house, and fell asleep.

And indeed there will be time
For the yellow smoke that slides along the street,
Rubbing its back upon the windowpanes;
There will be time, there will be time
To prepare a face to meet the faces that you
　meet;
There will be time to murder and create,
And time for all the works and days of hands
That lift and drop a question on your plate;
Time for you and time for me,
And time yet for a hundred indecisions,
And for a hundred visions and revisions,
Before the taking of a toast and tea.

In the room the women come and go
Talking of Michelangelo.

And indeed there will be time
To wonder, "Do I dare?" and, "Do I dare?"
Time to turn back and descend the stair,
With a bald spot in the middle of my hair—
(They will say: "How his hair is growing thin!")
My morning coat, my collar mounting firmly to
　the chin,
My necktie rich and modest, but asserted by a
　simple pin—
(They will say: "But how his arms and legs are
　thin!")
Do I dare
Disturb the universe?

In a minute there is time
For decisions and revisions which a minute will
　reverse.

For I have known them all already, known
　them all—
Have known the evenings, mornings, afternoons,
I have measured out my life with coffee spoons;
I know the voices dying with a dying fall
Beneath the music from a farther room.
　So how should I presume?

And I have known the eyes already, known
　them all—
The eyes that fix you in a formulated phrase,
And when I am formulated, sprawling on a pin,
When I am pinned and wriggling on the wall,
Then how should I begin
To spit out all the butt-ends of my days and
　ways?
　And how should I presume?

And I have known the arms already, known
　them all—
Arms that are braceleted and white and bare
(But in the lamplight, downed with light brown
　hair!)
Is it perfume from a dress
That makes me so digress?
Arms that lie along a table, or wrap about a
　shawl.
　And should I then presume?
　And how should I begin?

• • •

Shall I say, I have gone at dusk through
　narrow streets
And watched the smoke that rises from the pipes
Of lonely men in shirt-sleeves, leaning out of
　windows? . . .

I should have been a pair of ragged claws
Scuttling across the floors of silent seas

• • •

And the afternoon, the evening, sleeps so
　peacefully!
Smoothed by long fingers,

Asleep . . . tired . . . or it malingers,
Stretched on the floor, here beside you and me.
Should I, after tea and cakes and ices,
Have the strength to force the moment to its
    crisis?
But though I have wept and fasted, wept and
    prayed,
Though I have seen my head (grown slightly
    bald) brought in upon a platter,
I am no prophet—and here's no great matter;
I have seen the moment of my greatness flicker,
And I have seen the eternal Footman hold my
    coat, and snicker,
And in short, I was afraid.

    And would it have been worth it, after all,
After the cups, the marmalade, the tea,
Among the porcelain, among some talk of you
    and me,
Would it have been worth while,
To have bitten off the matter with a smile,
To have squeezed the universe into a ball
To roll it toward some overwhelming question,
To say: "I am Lazarus, come from the dead,
Come back to tell you all, I shall tell you all"—
If one, settling a pillow by her head,
    Should say: "That is not what I meant at all.
    That is not it, at all."

    And would it have been worth it, after all,
Would it have been worth while,
After the sunsets and the dooryards and the
    sprinkled streets,
After the novels, after the teacups, after the skirts
    that trail along the floor—
And this, and so much more?—
It is impossible to say just what I mean!
But as if a magic lantern threw the nerves in
    patterns on a screen:
Would it have been worth while
If one, settling a pillow or throwing off a shawl,
And turning toward the window, should say:
"That is not it at all,
That is not what I meant, at all."

    . . .

    No! I am not Prince Hamlet, nor was meant
    to be;
Am an attendant lord, one that will do
To swell a progress, start a scene or two,
Advise the prince; no doubt, an easy tool,
Deferential, glad to be of use,
Politic, cautious, and meticulous;
Full of high sentence, but a bit obtuse;
At times, indeed, almost ridiculous—
Almost, at times, the Fool.

    I grow old . . . I grow old . . .
I shall wear the bottoms of my trousers rolled.

    Shall I part my hair behind? Do I dare to eat
    a peach?
I shall wear white flannel trousers, and walk
    upon the beach.
I have heard the mermaids singing, each to each.

I do not think that they will sing to me.

I have seen them riding seaward on the waves
Combing the white hair of the waves blown back
When the wind blows the water white and black.

We have lingered in the chambers of the sea
By sea-girls wreathed with seaweed red and
    brown
Till human voices wake us, and we drown.

REVIEW QUESTIONS

1. Who are the "you and I" introduced in the first line of the poem?
2. Where are they going and why?
3. What exactly is it that Prufrock is afraid to presume to do?
4. What might Freud have to say about Prufrock's neurotic anxieties?

29 ❧ THE SECOND WORLD WAR

The Great War had been disastrous, but its outbreak could be blamed on the errors of political leaders and military planners who had allowed diplomatic arrangements and mobilization timetables to take on a life of their own. That a second world war could occur so soon after the first suggested that periodic outbreaks of global warfare were perhaps essential elements in the functioning of modern industrial societies. Similarly, that the nations of the world had again failed to avoid armed conflict suggested that human beings were incapable of controlling their innate aggressivity and learning from their past mistakes. The Second World War was a total war, and its worst horrors—the Holocaust and the bombing of major urban areas—resulted in the slaughter of civilians on a scale hitherto unimagined. Once again, the war made painfully clear the astounding degree of devastation that might occur when humans directed the technologies of industry toward destructive ends.

Yet, if the Second World War was dishearteningly destructive it was not as absurd as the First World War had been. In 1914, the outbreak of war seemed almost arbitrary, and even the War Guilt Clause of the Versailles Treaty could not dispel the postwar conviction that the war had been the fault of no one and everyone. In 1939, on the other hand, the outbreak of war took the form of an overt act of aggression on the part of Germany. Many attempts had been made to appease Hitler, but all diplomatic negotiations had failed in the face of his determination to go to war. During the Great War, the military leadership's adoption of a strategy of attrition had served to strip the individual soldier's death of meaning, depriving military service of all heroism. During the Second World War, the German army's lightning war strategy returned the elements of speed and mobility to warfare. Military engagements once again reached decisive conclusions, producing clear winners and losers.

However, from the start, the Second World War was most clearly distinguished from the First World War by its ideological component. To both soldiers and civilians, this new conflict presented itself as a struggle not merely between competing nations but between two fundamentally opposed political and social philosophies, between fascism and antifascism. On the level of the individual, this meant that the war presented clear choices, even if these choices often took the form of extremely difficult ethical decisions. On both sides, government propaganda fanned the flames of political passions, producing a strong sense of conviction among fascists and antifascists alike. At the same time, the increasingly manifest viciousness and brutality of the fascist regime generated intense opposition both within Germany and Italy and in the territories the two states occupied. Participants in resistance movements experienced an acute sense of human agency: having committed themselves to the antifascist cause, they engaged in actions that exposed them to the risk of imprisonment, torture, and execution.

The defeat of the Axis powers seemed like a triumph for the principles of democracy, tolerance, and individual liberty. After the war, the world's nations renewed their commitment to international governance through the creation of the United Nations, but many people continued to fear that the twentieth century was doomed to experience yet another global cataclysm, especially as growing tensions between the Soviet Union and the United States developed into an ominously tense cold war. Any optimism generated by the return of peace was quickly overshadowed by the emergence of a bipolar system of international relations: the world's two superpowers, armed to the teeth with devastating weapons of destruction, insisted that the rest of the world choose sides.

Constancia de la Mora

FROM *In Place of Splendor: The Autobiography of a Spanish Woman*

Spain suddenly became the subject of considerable international attention in 1936, after civil war broke out between the Republican Popular Front government and conservative nationalists under the leadership of General Francisco Franco. France and Britain failed to intervene in support of the Spanish republic, abiding by the terms of an international nonintervention agreement, but Germany and Italy eagerly supplied the nationalist uprising with troops, tanks, and airplanes. The Soviet Union sent some armaments to the loyalists, but this aid was inadequate and often served only to reinforce divisions between communists and other political factions within the ranks of the republicans. European and American leftists viewed the Spanish Civil War as a first opportunity to take a strong stand against the rise of fascism, and many of them fought on the loyalist side as volunteers in international brigades.

Constancia de la Mora (1906–1950) was born into an aristocratic family with a long history of service to the Spanish crown. As a young woman she broke with her family, both by divorcing her first husband and by becoming an ardent supporter of the republican government. In 1933, she married an air force officer, Ignacio Hidalgo de Cisneros, an aristocrat who had also gone over to the republican side. During the Spanish Civil War, Constancia served the loyalist cause by running an orphanage, while her husband desperately tried to scrape together an air force to protect the republic from attack by Italian and German bombers.

From *In Place of Splendor: The Autobiography of a Spanish Woman,* by Constancia de la Mora (New York: Harcourt, Brace, 1939), pp. 254–55, 256, 272–75.

*　　*　　*

It never occurred to us that the legal, democratically elected, recognized Government of Spain would have any difficulty buying the arms and supplies it needed to crush the remaining Rebel forces. We felt that the revolt was nearly over—the Spanish generals had no popular support whatsoever. The people were solidly behind the Government. It was a matter of buying rifles, artillery, supplies, and the like—then the Rebels would probably surrender and the whole thing would be over, with the minimum amount of loss of life.

On July 27, the news broke like a bomb in Madrid. The French Government has refused to sell us arms!

Why? We couldn't understand. We knew the British and the French reactionaries had put pressure on the Popular Front Government of France, but that a Socialist premier should deny a legal, recognized Government the right to buy arms to crush a fascist rebellion! It was monstrous! Worse, it was mad. What were the French thinking of?

On July 31, Ignacio brought me more terrible news: the Italians are invading Spain! Italian airplanes had been sighted flying to Rebel territory, some had been forced down in French Morocco, having lost the way. The orders found on them were dated July 16—the day before the rebellion broke out. Mussolini promptly denied this news,

just as Hitler denied he was sending arms, men, and guns. After the war was over, both dictators boasted that they helped prepare the plot and sent supplies and all kinds of aid, from troops to bandages, airplanes to trucks, the moment the traitor generals moved.

But in the early August days, Spaniards tried to convince the world—and especially France, England, and the United States—that our country was being invaded by fascists. The democracies turned a deaf ear to our pleas while the fascists strangled democracy in Spain.

When André Malraux arrived with a group of Frenchmen and some planes too old to be used by the French Air Force, we imagined that France was ready to sell us the planes that we so badly needed. It was common knowledge that Italy had sent and was sending Savoias, Capronis, and Fiats—four Savoias crashed in French Moroccan territory on their way to the Rebels—and that Germany's pocket battleships prevented bombardments of Rebel towns in Spanish Morocco by our Navy. On August 3, for instance, the *Deutschland* together with another German destroyer steamed slowly up and down the harbor of Ceuta, making it impossible for the *Jaime I* and other units of the Spanish Fleet to fire on their objectives.

German bombers and pursuit planes—Junkers 52 and Heinkels manned by German pilots—had already landed in Seville and Cadiz. They were helping to carry officers and troops of the Foreign

Legion to the Peninsula, speeding the human cargo of Moors and white mercenaries coming across in great numbers every day.

But we were very innocent in those days. We thought France had realized her own danger and was willing to sell us the things we needed to defend ourselves. We did not know then that certain powerful people in France and England had made up their minds, even before the war had started.

* * *

Only one country in the world printed the truth about Spain, from the beginning and until the end—the Soviet Union. Spaniards who had never heard of the Soviet Union before suddenly awoke in those days in August, when we were being betrayed everywhere else in the world, to realize that at least one nation had not abandoned us in our struggle for democracy. Every Spanish newspaper carried the news in great headlines that the Soviet workers had levied a one per cent tax on their salaries and collected 14,000,000 rubles for the Spanish people within the first month of the rebellion.

The news helped us to bear the loss of Badajoz, a little town on the Portugal frontier. For Badajoz fell on August 13, with the "honor" of being the first Spanish town to be bombarded by Italian and German planes. The people of Badajoz will bear the distinction in history of being the first Spaniards to have been blown to eternity by the conquering bombs of foreign fascists. We grew more accustomed to stories of horror later on in the war—but at that time we could hardly bear to read the eyewitness accounts and see the few photographs of the terrible massacre the Moors and foreign legionnaires had committed in this peaceful town when they entered after the bombardment. The slaughter in the bull ring at Badajoz horrified the whole world.

* * *

I turned on the radio for the Government news reports.

And then I first heard the voice of Dolores Ibarruri, "La Pasionaria." This woman of the people, this living symbol of Spanish courage, spoke to the people of Spain at the grave moment when Madrid faced the enemy at its very gates.

The children at my home gathered around the radio. The cook came in from the kitchen. Paco came from the garage. We clustered around the little wireless set.

"They shall not pass! No pasarán!" Her beautiful voice, vibrant, strong, filled the room. We straightened up. After the long day of panic and fear, after the weeks of tense waiting which had weighed on even the children, this stirring voice called us all back to our faith in Spain, to our faith in ourselves.

"The fascists will not pass! They will not pass because we are not alone!"

I glanced at our cook. She had clasped her hands together in that beautiful, unconscious gesture which is native to all women of Spain. She was leaning toward the radio, her lips moving a little, repeating without sound, the words of "La Pasionaria."

"We must not conceal the fact that Madrid is in danger! The removal of this danger depends on the people of Madrid, and on them alone. . . . All the people of Madrid, men and women, must learn the use of arms."

Paco was nearly in tears. His hand covered his mouth. I saw him gulping hard.

The strong voice, powerful and sure, went on, growing more vibrant, more electric. *"The lives and future of our children are at stake! This is not the time for hesitation; this is not the time for timidity. We women must demand that our men be courageous. We must inspire them with the thought that a man must know how to die worthily. Preferimos ser viudas de héroes antes que esposas de cobardes!"*

"We prefer to be the widows of heroes rather than wives of cowards!"

November 5, 1936.

In Alicante we did not know that this day Madrid fought for its life. I had the use of a car and a holiday at long last. I had not seen Ignacio for almost two months. He was stationed at Albacete, the new air base the Government had built slightly away from Madrid. I started early in the afternoon, before the radio began to broadcast the news of the attack on Madrid. The drive took four hours and when we reached Albacete, the parched ugly little town was almost dark. Ignacio was not in when I went to the Central Hotel but the porter led me to his room. I was just inspecting the dreary, dusty metal furniture, the taps marked hot and cold from which only cold water and very little of that ever came, when the door opened and Ignacio came in.

I turned to face him with a lump in my throat. Two months. We had never even been separated for two weeks until the war came.

His hair had turned from premature gray to white. That was the first thing I noticed. His face had grown thinner. His eyes mirrored a heavy worry.

For a moment, while he stood still, I was afraid he was ill. Then when he spoke, his voice was full of energy. He had just been promoted from major to lieutenant-colonel, but he still wore his old overalls with a sweater sticking out under his collar and his old major's insignias.

I think we were so happy to see each other that for a minute or so, we actually forgot the war.

At last, Ignacio said, "I must work tonight, but now we can have dinner, alone, and we will talk."

We had our coffee in the lobby. The place had the air of a family encampment. The wives of the Air Force officers sat in rocking chairs, knitting. The children played on the floor. Foreign correspondents sat at little tables, drinking and talking. French, German, Italian, English rose from corner tables all around the room—conversation of the international volunteers, exiles from fascist countries, young doctors, lawyers, workers, from the democratic countries, men who had come hundreds and thousands of miles to fight for democracy in Spain.

Next day, Ignacio, who could spare no time from his work, sent me to visit the hospitals newly moved to Albacete. I found conditions very bad. The town had a very poor water supply and almost no plumbing. The doctors and nurses were struggling with inadequate buildings and supplies. Ignacio had asked me to visit the wounded of the Air Force, and that night I said thoughtfully to him, "We need some sort of a convalescent home for the pilots. Some place where they could grow strong after the first weeks at a regular hospital."

Ignacio grinned. "I wouldn't want to ask you, darling. . . ." I had the plans made in my mind for a convalescent home that first day in Albacete.

And then, for forty-eight hours, everyone in Albacete forgot everything else but Madrid.

Madrid!

The Moors and the "blond Moors," as Franco called his German troops, and the Italians were at the very gates of the city. Fascists fought at the barricades the people of Madrid had built. The whole city rose. Every man, every woman, leaped to the defense of their native Madrid.

And then, in this critical hour, on November 6, 1936, as the fascist planes rose over the city, defenseless from the air, a miracle (or so it seemed to all of Spain) happened.

For flying with impossible speed, swift, deadly, fierce, came a squadron of new planes, planes of the Spanish Government. While all Madrid looked on choking with excitement, the Government planes fought off the fascists.

Ignacio told me about it first. His face shone like a child's. "Connie! One country at least understands our fight. They sold us planes!"

I could hardly believe his story. The planes Spain had bought from Russia arrived at Cartagena on November 2—in parts of course. The mechanics, working almost without stop for four solid days, had assembled a whole squadron of pursuit planes, enough to save the capital from the merciless bombing Franco planned to synchronize with his attack on the gates of the city.

"The people call them *Chatos*, the pug noses," Ignacio said, grinning.

And that night, November 7, I had dinner with the young Russian pilots who had just arrived. The Spanish aviators were almost delirious with joy. Planes! At last! Ignacio had been trying to build an Air Force out of thin air, trying to train men with no planes to fly with. Now there were planes to save Madrid from bombing, pilots to teach ours how to operate the new planes, mechanics to school our mechanics and help us in our factories.

The dinner started off with a joke. One of the Spanish aviators turned to me with great pride and said, "I have already learned a Russian word. Listen!" Then, carefully setting his lips, he said, "Propeller!"

He was most crestfallen when I explained that the word was English. Probably some early American engineer had taught it to the Russians.

But although we laughed, our dinner was not hilarious but very solemn. Ignacio made a little speech, only saying that the people of Madrid were dying tonight, dying with the words, *"No pasarán"* on their lips. He did not need, he said, to ask his men to make the same great sacrifice. He knew that they were always willing to give their lives for freedom. But now, more than ever, the Republic faced danger. The Russian pilots who had come as volunteers to help the people of Madrid were an heroic example.

"Viva la República!" Ignacio said quietly. *"No pasarán."*

"No pasarán," the men at the table answered solemnly.

Then everyone went back to the air field.

*   *   *

REVIEW QUESTIONS

1. What problems confronted the loyalist military effort?
2. To what extent was the Spanish Civil War shaped by international factors?
3. What role did the Soviet Union play in the civil war?
4. How did de la Mora respond to the military aid provided by the Soviet government?
5. How did Dolores Ibarruri attempt to rally Spaniards to the republican cause in her radio speech?

FROM Treaty of Non-Aggression between Germany and the Soviet Union

In early 1939, Germany absorbed the western half of Czechoslovakia and Hitler then prepared to proceed with the conquest of additional lebensraum ("living space") in eastern Europe. Bismarck and his generals had been plagued by the dilemma of Germany's encirclement and its vulnerability to a two-front war with France and Russia. In an attempt to solve this problem of military strategy, Hitler began negotiations with Stalin.

Hitler and Stalin were ideological enemies, but they were also opportunists willing to cooperate, if only temporarily, in the interest of their own nation's power. Stalin's great purges of 1936 and 1937 had seriously weakened the Red Army, depriving it of much of its officer corps, and Stalin was eager to buy time to rebuild the strength of the Soviet military. At the same time, Stalin's expressions of interest

in an alliance with France and Britain had gone largely unheeded, and he contin-
ued to distrust the Western democracies almost as much as Nazi Germany.

Late in August of 1939 the international community was shocked to learn that
Joachim von Ribbentropp and Vyacheslav Molotov, respectively the German and So-
viet foreign ministers, had signed a nonaggression pact on 23 August between their
two governments. One week later, Hitler invaded Poland.

From *Nazi-Soviet Relations 1939–1941, Documents from the Archives of the German Foreign Office* (Washington, D.C.: U.S. Department of State, 1948).

The Government of the German Reich and the Government of the Union of Soviet Socialist Republics desirous of strengthening the cause of peace between Germany and the U.S.S.R., and proceeding from the fundamental provisions of the Neutrality Agreement concluded in April 1926 between Germany and the U.S.S.R., have reached the following agreement:

ARTICLE I

Both High Contracting Parties obligate themselves to desist from any act of violence, any aggressive action, and any attack on each other, either individually or jointly with other powers.

ARTICLE II

Should one of the High Contracting Parties become the object of belligerent action by a third power, the other High Contracting Party shall in no manner lend its support to this third power.

ARTICLE III

The Governments of the two High Contracting Parties shall in the future maintain continual contact with one another for the purpose of consultation in order to exchange information on problems affecting their common interests.

ARTICLE IV

Neither of the two High Contracting Parties shall participate in any grouping of powers whatsoever that is directly or indirectly aimed at the other party.

ARTICLE V

Should disputes or conflicts arise between the High Contracting Parties over problems of one kind or another, both parties shall settle these disputes or conflicts exclusively through friendly exchange of opinion or, if necessary, through the establishment of arbitration commissions.

ARTICLE VI

The present treaty is concluded for a period of ten years, with the proviso that, in so far as one of the High Contracting Parties does not denounce it one year prior to the expiration of this period, the validity of this treaty shall automatically be extended for another five years.

ARTICLE VII

The present treaty shall be ratified within the shortest possible time. The ratifications shall be exchanged in Berlin. The agreement shall enter into force as soon as it is signed.

*　　*　　*

Secret Additional Protocol

On the occasion of the signature of the Non-aggression Pact between the German Reich and the Union of Socialist Soviet Republics the undersigned plenipotentiaries of each of the two parties discussed in strictly confidential conversations the question of the boundary of their respective spheres of influence in Eastern Europe. These conversations led to the following conclusions:

1. In the event of a territorial and political rearrangement in the areas belonging to the Baltic States (Finland, Estonia, Latvia, Lithuania), the northern boundary of Lithuania shall represent the boundary of the spheres of influence of Germany and the U.S.S.R. In this connection the interest of Lithuania in the Vilna area is recognized by each party.

2. In the event of a territorial and political rearrangement of the areas belonging to the Polish state the spheres of influence of Germany and the U.S.S.R. shall be bounded approximately by the line of the rivers Narew, Vistula, and San.

The question of whether the interests of both parties make desirable the maintenance of an independent Polish state and how such a state should be bounded can only be definitely determined in the course of further political developments.

In any event both Governments will resolve this question by means of a friendly agreement.

3. With regard to Southeastern Europe attention is called by the Soviet side to its interest in Bessarabia. The German side declares its complete political disinterestedness in these areas.

4. This protocol shall be treated by both parties as strictly secret.

*   *   *

REVIEW QUESTIONS

1. To what terms did this treaty bind Germany and the Soviet Union?
2. Who do you think derived the most advantage from the treaty? Why?
3. Using a map of Eastern Europe, locate the various spheres of influence designated by the secret protocol.
4. What territories in Eastern Europe did Hitler and Stalin expect to gain as a result of this agreement?

MARC BLOCH

FROM *Strange Defeat*

After an extended period of inactivity on the west front—known to the French as the drôle de guerre *("funny war")—Hitler's armies attacked France on 10 May 1940. The defeat of the combined French and British forces was astoundingly rapid, and France signed its surrender on June 22. French generals had expected a long war of attrition along the lines of the First World War. Instead, they discovered that Hitler and his strategists had formulated a new offensive strategy: Blitzkrieg ("lightning war"). Quickly moving massed tank formations, supported by aerial bombardment, were used to overwhelm enemy troops and smash through their lines. While this approach relied on an intensive deployment of troops and weapons, it was not intended to annihilate opponents but rather to immobilize them in the face of a swift and crushing assault.*

In the immediate aftermath of the French military collapse, historian Marc Bloch (1886–1944), wrote an extended essay on this "strange defeat," combining an account of his personal experience as a captain in charge of fuel supplies with a more general analysis of French military preparedness. Bloch had served with distinction in the First World War and then worked as a university professor during the interwar years, publishing several extremely influential studies of medieval society. In 1939, at the age of 53, he enlisted once again, serving until the French surrender in 1940. As a Jew and as an ardent patriot, he soon became active in the French resistance movement. In 1944 he was captured by the Germans and executed before a firing squad.

From *Strange Defeat: A Statement of Evidence Written in 1940,* by Marc Bloch, translated by Gerard Hopkins (Oxford, Eng.: Oxford University Press, 1968), pp. 25, 36–37, 44–45, 54–56, 125.

*   *   *

We have just suffered such a defeat as no one would have believed possible. On whom or on what should the blame be laid?

*   *   *

What drove our armies to disaster was the cumulative effect of a great number of different mistakes. One glaring characteristic is, however, common to all of them. Our leaders, or those who acted for them, were incapable of thinking in terms of a *new* war. In other words, the German triumph was, essentially, a triumph of intellect—and it is that which makes it so peculiarly serious.

*   *   *

The ruling idea of the Germans in the conduct of this war was speed. We, on the other hand, did our thinking in terms of yesterday or the day before. Worse still: faced by the undisputed evidence of Germany's new tactics, we ignored, or wholly failed to understand, the quickened rhythm of the times. So true is this, that it was as though the two opposed forces belonged, each of them, to an entirely different period of human history. We interpreted war in terms of assagai *versus* rifle made familiar to us by long years of colonial expansion.

But this time it was we who were cast for the rôle of the savage!

*   *   *

Did we ever, really, in the whole course of the campaign know the precise location of the enemy at any given time? That our commanders should have had a very imperfect idea of his intentions, and, worse still, of his material resources, can easily be explained by the faulty organization of our Intelligence Service. But the fact that we were never quite certain of his movements was due mainly to a persistent failure ever to judge distances correctly. Our own rate of progress was too slow and our minds were too inelastic for us ever to admit the possibility that the enemy might move with the speed which he actually achieved. When we left Lens on 22 June, H.Q. was split into two sections—an "advanced" group at Estaires, with a less mobile organization at Merville, where it was thought that it would be at a safe distance from the theatre of operations. What was our surprise when it was borne in upon us that, in fact, the so-called "rear" H.Q. was a great deal closer to the line than its advanced brother! When the Germans crashed through the Meuse defences, we were compelled to improvise at short notice alternative rail-heads for the division which we were preparing to rush into the lion's mouth in the hope of blocking egress from the pocket.

*   *   *

It can be seen from what I have said that the war was a constant succession of surprises. The effect of this on morale seems to have been very serious. And here I must touch on a delicate subject. I have no right to do more than record impressions which are those only of a looker-on. But there are some things that must be said, even at the risk of hurting a good many feelings. Men are so made that they will face expected dangers in expected places a great deal more easily than the sudden appearance of deadly peril from behind a turn in the road which they have been led to suppose is perfectly safe. Years ago, shortly after the Battle of the Marne, I saw men who the day before had gone into the line under murderous fire without turning a hair, run like rabbits just because three shells fell quite harmlessly on a road where they had piled arms in order to furnish a water-fatigue. "We cleared out because the Germans came." Again and again I heard that said in the course of last May and June. Analysed, the words mean no more than this: "Because the Germans turned up where we didn't expect them and where we had never been told we ought to expect them." Consequently, certain breakdowns, which cannot, I fear, be denied, occurred mainly because men had been trained to use their brains too slowly. Our soldiers were defeated and, to some extent, let themselves be too easily defeated, principally because their minds functioned far too sluggishly.

Not only did we meet the enemy too often in unexpected places, but for the most part, especially, and with increasing frequency, *in a way* which neither the High Command nor, as a result, the rank and file had anticipated. We should have been perfectly prepared to spend whole days potting at one another from entrenched positions, even if the lines had been only a few yards apart as they were in the Argonne during the last war. It would have seemed to us the most natural thing in the world to carry out raids on occupied saps.

It would have been well within our capacity to stand firm in face of an assault through a curtain of wire more or less cut by "Minenwerfer," or to have gone over the top courageously in an attempt to rush a position that had already been flattened—though, as a rule, not very completely—by artillery fire. In short, we could have played our part without difficulty in operations beautifully planned by our own staff and the enemy's, if only they had been in accordance with the well-digested lessons learned at peace-time manœuvres. It was much more terrifying to find ourselves suddenly at grips with a section of tanks in open country. The Germans took no account of roads. They were everywhere. They felt their way forward, stopping whenever they ran up against serious resistance. Where, however, the resistance was not serious and they could find a "soft spot," they drove ahead, exploiting their gains, and using them as a basis from which to develop the appropriate tactical movement or, rather, as it seemed, to take their choice of a number of alternative possibilities already envisaged in accordance with that methodical opportunism which was so characteristic of Hitler's methods. They relied on action and on improvisation. We, on the other hand, believed in doing nothing and in behaving as we always had behaved.

*   *   *

Is it true to say that by then—the precise moment at which Pétain announced that he had asked for an armistice—all hope of resistance had become impossible? Several officers thought not, especially the younger officers, for, with the quickened pace of events, a wider gulf began to show between the generations. Unfortunately, our leaders were not drawn from among those who suffered least from a hardening of the arteries. I am still strongly of the opinion to-day that what we called, in 1918, our "last-ditchers" were right. They dreamed of a modern type of warfare waged by guerrillas against tanks and motorized detachments. Some of them, if I am not wrong, had drawn up plans for such a war, plans which will never now see the light of day. The motorcyclists, of whom the enemy made such extensive and such excellent use, could move rapidly, and without too many accidents, only on metalled roads. Even vehicles equipped with caterpillar treads proceed less slowly on macadamized highways than across open country, and mobile guns and tractors of the normal type must have a good hard surface on which to manœuvre. That is why the Germans, true to their doctrine of speed, tended more and more to move their shock elements along the main arteries. It was, therefore, absolutely unnecessary to cover our front with a line extending for hundreds of kilometres, almost impossible to man, and terribly easy to pierce. On the other hand, the invader might have been badly mauled by a few islands of resistance well sited along the main roads, adequately camouflaged, sufficiently mobile, and armed with a few machine-guns and anti-tank artillery, or even with the humble 75!

*   *   *

The story goes that Hitler, before drawing up his final plans for the campaign, summoned a number of psychologists to his headquarters and asked their advice. I cannot vouch for the truth of this, but it does not seem to be altogether beyond the bounds of probability. However that may be, the air offensive, conducted with such dash by the Germans, does seem to prove that they had gone very deeply into the whole question of nerves and the best way of breaking them. Nobody who has ever heard the whistling scream made by dive-bombers before releasing their load is ever likely to forget the experience. It is not only that the strident din made by the machines terrifies the victim by awakening in his mind associated images of death and destruction. In itself, and by reason of what I may call its strictly acoustic qualities, it can so work upon the nerves that they become wrought to a pitch of intolerable tension whence it is a very short step to panic.

*   *   *

I am going to relate one small experience of my own, and without mincing words. I underwent my baptism of fire in 1940 (my earlier baptism of 1914 took place at the Marne) on 22 May on a road in Flanders—for I do not count the bombing of Douai and of the environs of Lens, in neither of which was I closely concerned. On the morning of the day in question, the convoy of which my car formed part was first machine-gunned from the air and then bombed. The machine-gunning, though it killed a man quite close to me, left me more or less unmoved. Of course, it is never very pleasant to be within touching-distance of death, and I do not mind admitting that I was a good deal relieved when the storm of bullets passed. But all through that particular episode my uneasiness had been much more a matter of intellect than of instinct. It was a sort of *cold* fear, with nothing in it of the quality of genuine *terror*. The bombing attack, so far as I am aware, killed no one, or no one who was anywhere near me. Nevertheless, it left me profoundly shaken, and when I crept out of the ditch where I had been crouching I was trembling pretty badly. During the latter part of the campaign I came under a number of artillery bombardments. I have known worse, and should be the last to exaggerate their violence. Still, they were quite nasty enough. But I stood up to them without much difficulty, and I think I can say that they never made me lose my presence of mind. But under air bombing I was never able to retain anything like the same calmness except by making a very considerable effort of will.

*   *   *

* * * Our war, up to the very end, was a war of old men, or of theorists who were bogged down in errors engendered by the faulty teaching of history. It was saturated by the smell of decay rising from the Staff College, the offices of a peace-time General Staff, and the barrack-square. The world belongs to those who are in love with the new. That is why our High Command, finding itself face to face with novelty, and being quite incapable of seizing its opportunities, not only experienced defeat, but, like boxers who have run to fat and are thrown off their balance by the first unexpected blow, accepted it.

*　　*　　*

REVIEW QUESTIONS

1. According to Bloch, what specific failings of French military leaders contributed to the French defeat?

2. What made Hitler's Blitzkrieg strategy so successful?

3. How might the French military have fended off the German assault according to Bloch?

4. What did Bloch's personal experience of aerial bombardment teach him about Hitler's military strategy?

WINSTON CHURCHILL

FROM *Wars Are Not Won by Evacuation*

Having defeated France, Hitler turned his attention to Britain. Before the amphibious landing of German troops, known as Operation Sea-Lion, could proceed, it was necessary for the German air force to establish control of the airways above the English Channel. Beginning in June 1940, the German Luftwaffe began a series of bombing raids on air fields and other strategic military targets. However, following a retaliatory British bombing raid on Berlin, Hitler called for the bombing of civilian targets, against the advice of many of his military advisors. Beginning in September, the city of London was bombed for almost two months, and tens of thousands of Londoners were killed. Hitler expected this blitz to break civilian morale, but it only served to rally support to the wartime effort. Unable to dominate the British skies, Hitler turned his attention to the invasion of the Soviet Union, planned for mid-1941.

The British victory was at least in part the result of the forceful leadership provided by Winston Churchill (1874–1965). Churchill, long an opponent of Neville Chamberlain's policy of appeasement, had become prime minister in May 1940, and then led Britain in its struggle against the German assault. In June, after the collapse of the combined British and French counteroffensive on the western front, Churchill readied the British people for the coming battle, calling on them to prepare to stand alone against the German onslaught. Just after every available seaworthy vessel had been drafted into service to ferry the more than 300,000 British and French troops trapped at Dunkirk back to Britain, Churchill gave a rousing speech to Parliament, announcing his firm resolve to resist German occupation of his island nation.

From *Wars Are Not Won by Evacuation*, vol. 6, by Winston Churchill, edited by R. R. James (New York: Chelsea House, 1940).

*   *   *

When, a week ago today, I asked the House to fix this afternoon as the occasion for a statement, I feared it would be my hard lot to announce the greatest military disaster in our long history. I thought—and some good judges agreed with me —that perhaps 20,000 or 30,000 men might be re-embarked. But it certainly seemed that the whole of the French First Army and the whole of the British Expeditionary Force north of the Amiens-Abbeville gap would be broken up in the open field or else would have to capitulate for lack of food and ammunition. These were the hard and heavy tidings for which I called upon the House and the nation to prepare themselves a week ago.

*   *   *

* * * The Royal Navy, with the willing help of countless merchant seamen, strained every nerve to embark the British and Allied troops; 220 light warships and 650 other vessels were engaged. They had to operate upon the difficult coast, often in adverse weather, under an almost ceaseless hail of bombs and an increasing concentration of artillery fire. Nor were the seas, as I have said, themselves free from mines and torpedoes. It was in conditions such as these that our men carried on, with little or no rest, for days and nights on end, making trip after trip across the dangerous waters, bringing with them always men whom they had rescued. The numbers they have brought back are the measure of their devotion and their courage. The hospital ships, which brought off many thousands of British and French wounded, being so plainly marked were a special target for Nazi bombs; but the men and women on board them never faltered in their duty.

*   *   *

* * * The Navy, using nearly 1,000 ships of all kinds, carried over 335,000 men, French and British, out of the jaws of death and shame, to their native land and to the tasks which lie immediately ahead. We must be very careful not to assign to this deliverance the attributes of a victory. Wars are not won by evacuations. * * * Can you conceive a greater objective for the Germans in the air than to make evacuation from these beaches impossible, and to sink all these ships which were displayed, almost to the extent of thousands? Could there have been an objective of greater military importance and significance for the whole purpose of the war than this? They tried hard, and they were beaten back; they were frustrated in their task. We got the Army away; and they have paid fourfold for any losses which they have inflicted. Very large formations of German aeroplanes—and we know that they are a very brave race—have turned on several occasions from the attack of one-quarter of their number of the Royal Air Force, and have dispersed in different directions. Twelve aeroplanes have been hunted by two. One aeroplane was driven into the water and cast away by the mere charge of a British aeroplane, which had no more ammunition. All of our types—the Hurricane, the Spitfire and the new Defiant—and all our pilots have been vindicated as superior to what they have at present to face.

When we consider how much greater would be our advantage in defending the air above this Island against an overseas attack, I must say that I find in these facts a sure basis upon which practical and reassuring thoughts may rest. I will pay my tribute to these young airmen. The great French Army was very largely, for the time being, cast back and disturbed by the onrush of a few thousands of armored vehicles. May it not also be that the cause of civilization itself will be defended by the skill and devotion of a few thousand airmen? There never has been, I suppose, in all the world, in all the history of war, such an opportunity for youth. * * *

I return to the Army. In the long series of very fierce battles, now on this front, now on that, fighting on three fronts at once, battles fought by two or three divisions against an equal or somewhat larger number of the enemy, and fought fiercely on some of the old grounds that so many of us knew so well—in these battles our losses in men have exceeded 30,000 killed, wounded and missing. I take occasion to express the sympathy of the House to all who have suffered bereavement or who are still anxious.

*   *   *

* * * Our losses in material are enormous. We have perhaps lost one-third of the men we lost in the opening days of the battle of 21st March, 1918, but we have lost nearly as many guns—nearly one thousand—and all our transport, all the armored vehicles that were with the Army in the north. * * * An effort the like of which has never been seen in our records is now being made. Work is proceeding everywhere, night and day, Sundays and week days. Capital and Labor have cast aside their interests, rights, and customs and put them into the common stock. Already the flow of munitions has leaped forward. There is no reason why we should not in a few months overtake the sudden and serious loss that has come upon us, without retarding the development of our general program.

Nevertheless, our thankfulness at the escape of our Army and so many men, whose loved ones have passed through an agonizing week, must not blind us to the fact that what has happened in France and Belgium is a colossal military disaster. * * * The whole of the Channel ports are in his hands, with all the tragic consequences that follow from that, and we must expect another blow to be struck almost immediately at us or at France. We are told that Herr Hitler has a plan for invading the British Isles. This has often been thought of before. When Napoleon lay at Boulogne for a year with his flat-bottomed boats and his Grand Army, he was told by someone. "There are bitter weeds in England." There are certainly a great many more of them since the British Expeditionary Force returned.

The whole question of home defense against invasion is, of course, powerfully affected by the fact that we have for the time being in this Island incomparably more powerful military forces than we have ever had at any moment in this war or the last. But this will not continue. We shall not be content with a defensive war. We have our duty to our Ally. We have to reconstitute and build up the British Expeditionary Force once again, under its gallant Commander-in-Chief, Lord Gort. All this is in train; but in the interval we must put our defenses in this Island into such a high state of organization that the fewest possible numbers will be required to give effective security and that the largest possible potential of offensive effort may be realized. On this we are now engaged. * * *

We have found it necessary to take measures of increasing stringency, not only against enemy aliens and suspicious characters of other nationalities, but also against British subjects who may become a danger or a nuisance should the war be transported to the United Kingdom. I know there are a great many people affected by the orders which we have made who are the passionate enemies of Nazi Germany. I am very sorry for them, but we cannot, at the present time and under the present stress, draw all the distinctions which we should like to do. * * *

Turning once again, and this time more generally, to the question of invasion, I would observe that there has never been a period in all these long centuries of which we boast when an absolute guarantee against invasion, still less against serious raids, could have been given to our people. In the days of Napoleon the same wind which would have carried his transports across the Channel might have driven away the blockading fleet. There was always the chance, and it is that chance which has excited and befooled the imaginations of many Continental tyrants. Many are the tales that are told. We are assured that novel methods will be adopted, and when we see the originality of malice, the ingenuity of aggression, which our enemy displays, we may certainly prepare ourselves for every kind of novel stratagem and every kind of brutal and treacherous maneuver. I think that no idea is so outlandish that it should not be considered and viewed with a searching, but at the same time, I hope, with a steady eye. We must never forget the solid assurances of sea power and those which belong to air power if it can be locally exercised.

I have, myself, full confidence that if all do their duty, if nothing is neglected, and if the best arrangements are made, as they are being made, we shall prove ourselves once again able to defend our Island home, to ride out the storm of war, and to outlive the menace of tyranny, if necessary for years, if necessary alone. At any rate, that is what we are going to try to do. That is the resolve of His Majesty's Government—every man of them. That is the will of Parliament and the nation. The British Empire and the French Republic, linked together in their cause and in their need, will defend to the death their native soil, aiding each other like good comrades to the utmost of their strength. Even though large tracts of Europe and many old and famous States have fallen or may fall into the grip of the Gestapo and all the odious apparatus of Nazi rule, we shall not flag or fail. We shall go on to the end, we shall fight in France, we shall fight on the seas and oceans, we shall fight with growing confidence and growing strength in the air, we shall defend our Island, whatever the cost may be, we shall fight on the beaches, we shall fight on the landing grounds, we shall fight in the fields and in the streets, we shall fight in the hills; we shall never surrender, and even if, which I do not for a moment believe, this Island or a large part of it were subjugated and starving, then our Empire beyond the seas, armed and guarded by the British Fleet, would carry on the struggle, until, in God's good time, the New World, with all its power and might, steps forth to the rescue and the liberation of the old.

REVIEW QUESTIONS

1. According to Churchill, what problems confronted Britain in its approaching battle with Germany?
2. What advantages did Britain enjoy?
3. What was the purpose of Churchill's speech?
4. What message was he attempting to convey to both Parliament and the British people?

HILDE MARCHANT

FROM *Women and Children Last: A Woman Reporter's Account of the Battle of Britain*

Initial bombing raids on London targeted armament factories and other strategically sensitive sites, most of which were concentrated in the poorer East End. London's working class resented the fact that even in war the rich seemed to escape from hardship. However, the bombing of Buckingham Palace, the royal residence, brought an end to any hard feelings. Princess Elizabeth commented, "I'm glad we've been bombed. It makes me feel I can look the East End in the face."

Having grown up in northern England, young journalist Hilde Marchant (dates unknown) admitted that she did not feel at home in London prior to the war. However, her experience covering the blitz gradually changed her opinion of the city and its people. With an eye toward encouraging Americans to come to the aid of

THE BOMBING OF DRESDEN

The term total war *acquired new meaning in the Second World War with the aerial bombardment of civilian populations. Tens of thousands of civilian deaths resulted from direct aerial bombardment, and millions of other civilians were evacuated and uprooted from their homes. The firebombing of Dresden during the night of February 13–14, 1945, killed over 25,000 people, destroyed the baroque splendor of the inner city, and displaced hundreds of thousands of residents, including recently arrived East European evacuees. This conventional bombing mission was the most severe in the European theater of war, even though the city played no outstanding military or industrial roles. This photo, taken from city hall by Walther Hahn, poignantly contrasts a graceful statue—personifying here the* humanitas *of another era—against the charred, empty shell of a once-great city. What political messages are implied by the composition and subject matter of this photograph?*

the British war effort, Marchant published Women and Children Last: A Woman Reporter's Account of the Battle of Britain *in 1941. It contains a lively account of Londoners' stoicism in the face of devastating bombing raids and of the quiet heroism of ordinary people in extraordinary circumstances.*

From *Women and Children Last: A Woman Reporter's Account of the Battle of Britain,* by Hilde Marchant (London: V. Gollancz, 1941).

*   *   *

Mr. Smith is not a big man, not a handsome man, not a strong man. Mr. Smith is a little man. He is rather narrow across the chest, his face is deflated of its youth, his hair is as thin as the grass in a London park. First of all, Mr. Smith would describe himself as a Cockney, and secondly he would describe himself as a Londoner. For his affection and civic patriotism is for those tightly packed miles of wavering roof tops that make a shabby border for the South side of the river Thames. He has lived there all his life and when he goes West for a Saturday night treat with his wife he is like a provincial on the loose. And Mr. Smith would tell you that he loved every one of those narrow, suppurating streets that miraculously bulge with life. Though looking at the blackened mortar, and ruptured walls you might wonder why.

So just before the war Mr. Smith decided to express his fervent love for these homes and people who dwell there and became one of the war's new soldiers—a warden of Stepney. His uniform is a pair of blue overalls, a tin hat and a gasmask and he is a veteran member of the civilian defence force that has defended and saved the citizens of London. Mr. Smith would not regard himself as a particularly brave man, because in his peace time life there was never any occasion to be brave. It was just a routine, unnoticed fight, to survive such things as unemployment, rent and a fourth child.

At first Smith was very uncomfortable about his chosen job as nursemaid to the streets. Khaki broke the everyday street scene and he had to take a lot of unpleasant remarks about dodging the army and taking £3 5s. 0d. for sitting by a telephone that never rang and polishing a whistle that never played a tune. He was either a comedian or a coward. Until one day in September when he fell flat on his face in a road. He was covered with bricks and dust.

From that day it was Smith's war. From that day Mr. Smith was the hero of the streets to everybody but Mr. Smith. He regards himself as a "trained officer of incidents"—that delightful piece of under-statement that so fits his character. For an "incident" can mean climbing into fires, burrowing under crushed homes, or comforting a broken spirit.

But perhaps the greatest battle of all in those early days was a personal one. Smith had to adjust his warm, sentimental, domestic nature to the grim agonising sights of the night. He loves humanity, in all its virtue and vice, and it was a shock for him to see the pain and distortion of life around him. Yet he corseted his sentimentality with the months of training he had had and became the handyman of the blitz.

Smith's post is in a basement on the corner of a street in Stepney. He was resting—not sleeping—when I met him. He can only sleep in the daytime now.

There were half a dozen other men at the post who, apart from their names, were no more distinctive than Smith. There was a tailor, a food porter, a driver, a fishmonger, men who until the September days had not been able to express their desire for action.

Smith began to tell me about that first night, the night he fell in the road and broke his glasses. A bomb just a few yards from him had hit a block of buildings, and there were eleven people trapped on the ground floor.

"It was a noisy night, but every time we bent low we could hear the groans of the people underneath. I thought I'd be sick. I held a man's hand that was clear. It took us nine hours to get him out. An hour later we got a woman out. They were in a bad way. There was dirt and blood caked on the woman's face. We wiped it off. She must have been about thirty. They both died. We were all a bit quiet. It was the first we'd seen. We couldn't have got them out quicker—we'd torn our hands up dragging the stones away. But it was awful seeing them take the last gasps as they lifted them into the ambulance."

Smith was quiet, even retelling the story, and one of the men said:

"It was the first, you see."

Then Smith told me about the next night—the night when he was really "blooded". Incendiaries had started a fire in one of the smaller streets and high explosives began to fall into the fire. Smith approached the houses from the back and got through to the kitchen of one of the houses.

"I fell over something. I picked it up and it was a leg. I stood there with it in my hand wondering what I should do with it. I knew it was a woman's leg. I put it down and went to look for the ambulance. They had got the fire out at the front. The ambulance men brought a stretcher and I showed them the leg. Then we looked farther in and there were pieces all over. All they said was they didn't need a stretcher."

As Smith sat thinking, his whole body seemed to pause . . .

"Funny, I don't seem to remember what I thought that night. Surprising how you forget things."

It would be slighting Smith's imagination to say that the sight in the kitchen did not affect him. It did.

"You see, how we look at things now is like this. If they're alive you work like the devil to keep 'em alive and get 'em out. We listen to their groans and know they have breath in them. If they're dead there's nothing we can do. Getting upset hampers your work."

So Smith learned not to over-indulge his sensitivity on seeing death, or torn limb and flesh. His job was with the spark of life that survived.

* * *

The next day he took me round his streets in a baby car, showing me the damage. Damage has been described over and over again, but I still like Smith's own description of a house:

"Cut in two like a slice of cheese, showing all the little holes where the maggots crawled in and out."

It has a touch of that high-flown philosophising that the Cockney is so fond of twisting into his own flamboyant phrases.

The house was neatly cut. It was the usual scene—the waxed flowers still on the mantelpiece, the portrait of Grandma still hanging from the bedroom wall, the clock still ticking on the wall. Yet in every house strange things remain intact. In this one there was a mirror hanging in a shattered hall and the glass had not broken, china cups hanging over the kitchen sink were still whole, the beer glasses on the sideboard were covered with plaster, but unbroken. I pointed this out to Smith.

"Same as the 'umans. Some of the skinniest get through all right and some of the big ones come off worst."

* * *

As we wandered through these broken streets people called out to Smith.

"Any more bombs?" or "When do we get the roof mended?" They all knew Mr. Smith the Warden. He walked through the streets like the squire of a village, smiling and chatting to the people standing at their doors.

* * *

A woman came out of the huddle round the canteen.

"We looked for you on Wednesday and couldn't find you. My husband wants to say thank you and buy you a pint," she said.

Smith told me that story as we went back to

his post. They had discovered a D.A. bomb in a garden. They knew there were people in the house, so they went round knocking at the door, telling them to get out. At the end of the street a small high explosive had broken one house. They thought the house was empty until they were moving the others. Then one of the men said he had heard a sound from the back of the garden. With the delayed action bomb only a few yards away, the wardens began to investigate. They found that a huge piece of the wall had locked a man and wife in the Anderson. For two hours they worked, wondering all the time if the delayed action was going up. They got the man and wife out and then ran down the street. And an hour later the bomb exploded.

"Lucky to be alive," said Smith casually. Smith is a little man but only in his size.

We had a cup of tea at the post and Smith went over to a box marked "Biscuits." He shook it. There was no sound, so he cursed.

"If there's one thing I like it's a chocolate biscuit with my tea."

*   *   *

REVIEW QUESTIONS

1. What were the duties of a warden? What impact did the blitz have on Mr. Smith's ward?
2. How did it affect Mr. Smith himself?
3. What point was Marchant trying to make through her pencil portrait of this "little man"?
4. To what extent did her reporting support the sentiments expressed in Churchill's speech?

VASSILY GROSSMAN

FROM "In the Line of the Main Attack"

By mid-1942, the Germans had advanced deep into the Soviet Union. To the north, the Red Army fought desperately to hold Moscow; to the southeast, Soviet troops took their stand at Stalingrad, an industrial city and a significant source of armaments for the Russian war effort, standing between the German army and the rich oil fields of the Caucasus. In some of the fiercest fighting of the war, Red Army troops successfully defended Stalingrad, despite intense bombardment by the Germans. During the battle, which marked a decisive turning point in the war on the eastern front, as many as 800,000 combined Axis troops and as many as one million Soviet troops died.

Vassily Grossman (1905–1964) was a wartime correspondent for the Soviet periodical Krasnaya Zvezda. In late 1942 he wrote a report on the battle of Stalingrad, documenting the valiant efforts of a division of Siberian troops under the command of Coloniel Gurtiev. Like all wartime reporting, including Hilde Marchant's stories of the blitz, Grossman's account was shaped by its propagandistic aims. In this particular case, the Siberian troops are described in much the same manner as the "heroes of labor" whose astounding acts of industrial production were celebrated during the 1930s. However, Grossman's eyewitness testimony also provides a lively and sympathetic portrait of the Red Army, conveying the dogged determination and loy-alty of the many soldiers who died defending Russia—if not necessarily Stalinism—from the ferocious Nazi onslaught.

From "In the Line of the Main Attack," by Vassily Grossman, in *Moscow-Stalingrad, 1941–1942: Recollections, Stories, Reports*, compiled by Vladimir Sevruk (Moscow: Progress, 1970).

* * *

Colonel Gurtiev is a lean man of fifty. When the First World War broke out in 1914 he left the St. Petersburg Polytechnic where he was studying in his second year to volunteer for the army, and fought as a gunner at Warsaw, Baranovichi and Chartoriisk.

Gurtiev has been in the army for twenty-eight years, seeing active service and training officers. His two sons went off to the front as lieutenants. He has left his wife and daughter behind in far-away Omsk. On this terrible and solemn day he thought of his lieutenant sons, his daughter and his wife, and the many young officers he had trained, and his whole long, hard, Spartan life. The time has come when all the principles of military science, morale and duty which he taught his sons, his pupils and fellow soldiers will be put to the test, and he looked anxiously at the faces of the Siberians—the men from Omsk, Novosibirsk, Krasnoyarsk and Barnaul—the men with whom it was his destiny to repel the enemy onslaught.

The Siberians came to the Volga well-prepared. The Division had been well-trained before being sent to the front. Colonel Guttiev had trained his men thoroughly and wisely, had never stood for any nonsense and if anything had been over-exacting. He knew that however hard military training might be—the night practice raids, the lying in trenches and slits being "ironed" by tanks, the long forced marches—the real thing was far grimmer. He had faith in the fortitude and stamina of his Siberians. He had tested it on the way to the front, when throughout the whole long journey there had been only one incident: one of the soldiers had dropped his rifle from the moving train, and had leapt down, picked it up and run

three kilometres to the next station to rejoin his regiment. He had tested their stamina in the Stalingrad steppes, where his men had had their baptism of fire and calmly repelled a surprise attack of thirty German tanks. He had tested their endurance during the last leg of the march to Stalingrad, when they had covered two hundred kilometres in forty-eight hours. Yet he still looked anxiously at the faces of the men, now that they were there on the front line, where they would be bearing the brunt of the main attack.

* * *

Hardly had the division had time to entrench itself in the stony ground of Stalingrad, hardly had the command post moved into a deep gallery cut in the sandy escarpment above the Volga, the communications lines been laid and the transmitters begun to tap out their messages to the artillery positions on the other side of the river, hardly had the first pale light of dawn pierced the darkness, than the Germans opened fire. For eight hours solid the German Junkers dive-bombed the Division's positions, for eight hours, without a moment's pause, wave after wave of German planes passed over, for eight hours the sirens wailed, the bombs whistled through the air, the earth trembled and what was left of the brick buildings crashed to the ground. For eight hours the air was dark with smoke and dust and deadly splinters zipped everywhere. Anyone who has heard the whine of the air rent by falling bomb, anyone who has experienced an intense ten-minute bombing raid by the Luftwaffe will understand what eight hours of solid aerial bombardment by dive-bombers means. For eight hours the Siberians kept up a constant barrage of fire at the enemy aircraft, and the Germans doubtless felt something like despair as the whole area of the plant, burning and shrouded in a black cloud of dust and smoke, crackled with rifle shots, rattled with machine-gun fire, the short thuds of anti-tank rifles and the regular, angry fire of ack-ack guns. It would seem that everything living must be broken, annihilated; yet there were the Siberian Division, dug into the ground, uncowed and unbroken, keeping up a continuous deadly barrage of fire. The Germans had thrown in their heavy mortars and artillery. The monotonous hiss of mines and the crash of shells merged with the whine of sirens and the roar of exploding bombs. So it continued until nightfall. Then in solemn silence the Red Army men buried their dead comrades. That was the first day, the "house-warming." The German mortar-batteries kept up their racket all night, and few of the men got any sleep.

*   *   *

In the course of a month the enemy launched one hundred and seventeen attacks against the Siberian Division.

There was one terrible day when the German tanks and infantry attacked twenty-three times. And all twenty-three attacks were repulsed. Every day except three for a month, the Luftwaffe was in the air over the Division's positions for ten to twelve hours—three hundred and twenty hours in the whole month. The operations department counted up the astronomical number of bombs dropped on the Division. It ran into tens of thousands; so did the number of Luftwaffe sorties. All this on a front little over a mile long! The roar of explosions was enough to deafen the whole of mankind, the fire and metal was enough to wipe a whole country off the map. The Germans thought they were breaking the morale of the Siberians. They thought they had exceeded the limits of human endurance, the power of human hearts and nerves to stand up to such punishment. But, amazingly, the men had not crumpled, had not gone insane, had not lost control of their hearts and nerves, but had instead become stronger and calmer. The sturdy, tight-lipped Siberians had become even sterner, even more tight-lipped; their

cheeks had become hollow, and their eyes more determined. Here where the brunt of the German attack was borne there was no singing, no accordions, no light conversation in the short lulls in the fighting. Here men were undergoing a superhuman strain. There were times when no one slept for three or four days and nights, and talking with his men Gurtiev was pained to hear a soldier say quietly:

"We've got everything, Comrade Colonel; nine hundred grammes of bread, and hot meals in thermoses twice a day without fail—but we're just not hungry."

Gurtiev loved and respected his men, and he knew that when a soldier is "not hungry," he's really finding the going hard. But now Gurtiev's mind was at ease. He realised that there was no power on earth that could shake his Siberians.

*   *   *

After almost twenty days the Germans launched a "decisive" attack on the plant. Never in history had an assault been preceded by such massive preparation. The Luftwaffe and the heavy mortars and artillery showered the Division with bombs and shells for eighty hours solid: three days and nights that were a chaos of smoke, fire and thunder. The whistle of falling bombs, the scream of mortar shells from the six-barrel "goofies," the thunder of heavy shells and the protracted wail of the sirens was alone enough to deafen people— but they were only the prelude to the thunder of explosions. Jagged tongues of flame spurted up and the air was rent by the howl of tormented metal. For eighty hours it went on, then the preparation finished suddenly at five in the morning and immediately German tanks and infantry advanced to the attack. The Germans managed to penetrate into the plant workshops, their tanks roared at its very walls, they broke through our defences and cut off the command posts from the forward lines. It would have seemed that deprived of their commanders, further resistance by the troops would have been impossible, and that the command posts, under direct enemy attack, would be wiped out. But an extraordinary thing happened: every trench, every dugout, every firing-point and every fortified ruin became a separate, isolated fortress with its own command, its own communications. Sergeants and rank-and-file soldiers assumed command, and skilfully repulsed all attacks. And in this bitter, critical hour, the commanders and HQ staff turned the command posts into fortified strong-points, and fought like rank-and-file soldiers to repulse the enemy attacks. Chamov beat off ten attacks. A giant, red-haired tank commander defending Chamov's command post used up all his grenades and ammunition and then took to hurling stones at the advancing Germans. Chamov himself manned a mortar. The golden boy of the Division, Mikhalyev, was killed by a direct bomb hit on the command post. "They've killed our father," said the men. Major Kushnaryov, who replaced Mikhalyev, transferred his command post to a concrete pipe that passed beneath the workshops. Along with his Chief-of-Staff, Dyatlenko, and six other staff officers he successfully defended the entrance to the pipe for several hours with a few boxes of grenades, repulsing numerous German attacks.

This battle, unequalled in its cruelty and ferocity, lasted for several days and nights uninterrupted. It was fought for every step of a staircase, for every corner in a dark passage, for every machine and the space between them, for every gas pipe. No one took a step back in this battle. And if the Germans gained some ground it meant that there was nobody left alive to defend it. Everyone fought like the giant red-haired tankman, whose name Chamov was never to learn; like the sapper Kosichenko, who, his left arm broken, took to removing the pin of his grenades with his teeth. It was as if the fallen were giving added strength to the living, and there were moments when ten men held a line that had been defended by a whole battalion. The workshops changed hands many times in the course of the battle. The Germans succeeded in occupying several buildings and workshops. It was in this battle that the German offensive reached its climax. This was the high-water mark of their main attack. As if they had

lifted a weight that was too heavy for them, they overstrained some inner spring that had set their battering-ram in motion.

The German onslaught began to falter. They had three divisions, the 94th, the 305th and the 389th, fighting the Siberians. Their hundred and seventeen infantry attacks cost 5,000 German lives. The Siberians withstood this superhuman pressure. Two thousand tons of scrap metal from enemy tanks littered the ground in front of the plant. Thousands of tons of bombs, mines and shells had fallen on the factory yard and on the workshops, but still the Division held out. The troops faced death, without ever once looking back, for they knew that behind them lay the Volga and the fate of Russia.

One cannot help wondering how this tremendous strength was forged. It was partly the national character, the tremendous sense of responsibility, and that stolid Siberian stubbornness, excellent military and political training and strict discipline. But there was something else I should like to mention as having played no mean role in this great, tragic epic—and that was the amazingly fine morale and the strong bond of love that united all the men of the Siberian Division. A spirit of Spartan simplicity was characteristic of the whole staff. It was reflected in ordinary, everyday details, in the refusal to accept the rationed hundred grammes of vodka that was theirs by right throughout the whole long Stalingrad battle, and in their sensible, calm, business-like manner. I saw the love that united the men of the Division, in the deep distress with which they mourned the loss of their fallen comrades.

I saw it in the moving meeting between the grey-haired Colonel Gurtiev and the battalion nurse, Zoya Kalganova, when she returned to duty after her second wound. "Hello, my dear child," Gurtiev said quietly, and quickly went forward with outstretched hands to greet the thin girl with close-cropped hair—just like a father greeting his own daughter.

This love and faith in one another was what helped the soldiers in the heat of battle to take the place of their commander and the commanders and staff to take up machine-guns, hand-grenades, and incendiary bottles to repulse the German tanks approaching the command post.

The wives and children of these men will never forget their husbands and fathers who fell in the great battle on the Volga. They cannot be forgotten, these fine, true men. There is only one worthy way in which our Red Army can honour the sacred memory of the men who bore the brunt of the enemy's main attack—and that is by an unlimited, liberating offensive. We believe that the hour of this offensive is at hand.

*   *   *

REVIEW QUESTIONS

1. How did the warfare described by Grossman differ from that described by First World War soldiers Henri Barbusse and Ernst Jünger?
2. How did it differ from Marc Bloch's description of the western front engagements of 1940?
3. On the basis of this account, why do you think that the Soviet troops were able to hold Stalingrad?

ANNY LATOUR

FROM *The Jewish Resistance in France, 1940–1944*

Despite the brutal treatment that the Nazi government meted out to its opponents, organized resistance to Hitler's regime began almost immediately after he seized power in 1933, and it developed into an important component of the military effort during the Second World War. Resistance took many forms, including espionage, sabotage, the smuggling of refugees, and armed assaults on occupying forces. Resisters were drawn from all walks of life, but active resistance to Nazism tended to flourish among those with strong preexisting political, ideological, or religious allegiances. Armed resistance was most successful in regions whose terrain was conducive to guerrilla warfare, from the rugged maquis *of southern France to the mountains of Yugoslavia.*

European Jews had strong incentives for joining resistance movements, for they were the first to be targeted for imprisonment and deportation when German troops occupied a country or region. On the other hand, Jews were also subject to heavy surveillance and were often deported or imprisoned immediately after German occupation, making overt acts of resistance difficult and very dangerous. Despite these obstacles, many Jews joined the resistance, often at great personal cost. In 1970, Anny Latour, a historian and a former resister, published a study of the Jewish resistance in France, based on the testimony of survivors and on her own experiences as a resister. In the following excerpt from this study, Latour describes some of the tactics of the Groupes Francs, *the assault units of the armed Jewish resistance.*

From *The Jewish Resistance in France, 1940–1944,* by Anny Latour, translated by Irene R. Ilton (New York: Schocken Books, 1981).

* * *

The more the networks of the Jewish Resistance developed, the harder the Gestapo tried to destroy them. Arrests became more and more frequent.

But didn't the Jews have excellent false papers?

The Gestapo relied on another weapon: treacherous informers. They are paid 5,000 francs for each Jew they denounce—a handsome sum for that time.

These who are something of "physiognomists" are particularly valuable to the Germans, and are placed on their payroll; these individuals are talented at distinguishing Jews from non-Jews, and are sent to roam the streets and mingle in crowds—until they pounce upon their prey!

Another method—though it only works on men—is conducting "undressing sessions," as we referred to them; men would be stopped in the middle of the street, and told to pull down their pants, so as to be examined for circumcision.

Means of self-defense were needed. The Jewish Army forms its own Groupes Francs in all the great urban centers.

Unmask the traitors—strike them down without pity!

The "specialty" of the commandos is surprise attack. Targets range from the traitors themselves, to German military installations.

Today, conversing with men and women who seem incapable of hurting a fly, I am dumbfounded as I listen to their exploits: former killers they certainly were; and yet, striking down men whose actions were a threat to so many, clearly seems an act of legitimate self-defense. Blowing up German munition dumps, removing bolts from the rail tracks so as to delay German trains bound for the front after D-Day—all these were acts of patriotism.

But executing traitors, sabotaging ammunition

dumps and fighting in the maquis—these all required bombs and weapons.

The Groupes Francs had their own suppliers, particularly in Marseille. The real problem was of transport: baggage was subject to inspection; officials were often on the lookout for black marketeers—what if, instead of a nice cut of ham, or chunk of butter, they found a few guns . . .

Moreover, police informers are posted at all the outskirts of the stations keeping an alert eye out for suspects. Just the way in which a traveler holds his suitcase, can give him away—and a heavy-looking bag he's having trouble with, could be stuffed with arms.

Women were less often the target than men, so it was they who were assigned the job of arms transport. There are "specialists" in the field: Reine Roman; Betty Knout (daughter of Ariane Knout), who is just sixteen, Evelyne Gottlieb, and Nina Jefroykin, to name but a few.

Tommy-guns and rifles for the maquis groups; revolvers and incendiary bombs for executing the traitors—they were conveyed in suitcases, bicycle "saddlebags" and even the huge housings of radios.

Reine, in particular, is extremely daring. Radiantly beautiful, she sails shamelessly through all obstacles. It seems miraculous that she survived— I recall one particularly dramatic plan we devised. At the time, she was carrying a revolver of her own: "I don't surrender without a fight," she liked to say.

Brazen it out—it was the only way to emerge unscathed. Tony Gryn tells a story about Betty Knout:

It was shortly before the Liberation. The railroad bridge crossing the Loire had been

EINSATZGRUPPEN (MOBILE KILLING UNITS) MASSACRES IN EASTERN EUROPE JUNE 1941— NOVEMBER 1942

MILES
0   400

Legend:
- Einsatzgruppen area of operation
- Greater Germany and occupied territories
- German allies or dependent states
- Neutral
- Allies

N

Atlantic Ocean

GREAT BRITAIN

NORWAY
SWEDEN
FINLAND

DENMARK
NETHERLANDS
BELGIUM
GREATER GERMANY
SWITZERLAND
FRANCE
SPAIN
PORTUGAL

ITALY
Corsica
Sardinia
Sicily

MOROCCO
ALGERIA
TUNISIA

Mediterranean Sea

1941 INTERNATIONAL BOUNDARIES

SOVIET UNION

Farthest German Army Advance

German-Soviet Demarcation Line

GENERAL-GOVERNMENT

SLOVAKIA
HUNGARY
CROATIA
SERBIA
ROMANIA
BULGARIA
GREECE
TURKEY

Baltic Sea
Black Sea

Tallinn
Riga
Dvinsk
Kovno
Vilna
Bialystok
Minsk
Vitebsk
Smolensk
Gomel
Rovno
Kiev
Kharkov
Lvov
Kamenets-Podolski
Mogilev-Podolski
Chernovtsy
Kishinev
Odessa
Kherson
Rostov
Krasnodar

MAP OF EINSATZGRUPPEN MASSACRES (1941–42)

Barbed wire, diseased barracks, malnourished prisoners, gas chambers, and crematoria are the principal images of the Holocaust inflicted on Jews and other Europeans by the racial genocide of Nazi Germany. Yet before such death camps as Auschwitz and Treblinka were put into full operation, approximately 1.2 millions Jews were killed with rifles by mobile killing units in 1941–42. Four select groups, composed of approximately 1,000 SS and auxiliary police units, swept behind the advancing German army in its invasion of the Soviet Union in August 1941 to carry out the first massive wave of racial and political murder, primarily Russian Jews and Soviet partisans. Typically, victims were rounded up, forced to dig a mass grave, and then executed with rifles at the gravesite. This map of eastern Central Europe, which constituted the cultural center of European Jewry, locates the principal massacre sites by the mobile killing units. What does this map convey about the geographic breadth of Nazi genocide before the death camps were put into operation?

blown up. To get to Paris, then, we had to get off the train, cross the river on foot via another bridge, and get back on a different train north of the river.—No easy matter when you're loaded down with a suitcase of arms!

A German officer spies this cute young thing with a roguish look to her, and sees her laboring with the large suitcases.

"Need some help, mademoiselle?" Then: "These weigh a ton! What have you got here—butter? cheese? some ham?"

Betty adopts a knowing look: "Shh! I've got weapons in there!—tommy guns, and revolvers!"

The officer breaks out into a hearty laugh. "Allow me!" He lifts both suitcases and carries them all the way to the new train, even going so far as to help Betty get comfortably settled. . . .

*   *   *

REVIEW QUESTIONS

1. How did the German occupying forces identify Jewish resisters?
2. How did Jews respond to the threat of discovery?
3. How did Jewish resisters procure guns?
4. What special advantages did women have as gunrunners?

TADEUSZ BOROWSKI

FROM "This Way for the Gas, Ladies and Gentlemen"

In the years following the Second World War, the resistance movement inspired a certain optimism about the fundamental goodness of human nature. On the other hand, the unparalleled brutality of the Nazi's "final solution"—the systematic extermination of European Jews—provided crushing evidence of the depths of depravity to which civilized societies might sink. While some explained away the mechanized genocide of the concentration camps as the result of German barbarism, others rejected this approach, analyzing the Holocaust as the product of social pathologies to which all human beings might succumb, given the proper circumstances.

Polish author Tadeusz Borowski (1922–1951) was born in the Soviet Ukraine and both of his parents were imprisoned in Siberia during the Stalinist terror of the 1930s. The family was reunited in Poland before the Second World War, and Borowski began his literary career in Warsaw. He was arrested as a political dissident in 1943 and was interned in the concentration camps of Dachau and Auschwitz until 1945. Because he was young, healthy, and not a Jew, Borowski managed to survive in the camps, performing services that facilitated the extermination of Jewish prisoners. After the war he was haunted by this coerced collaboration and published several collections of fictionalized stories about his camp experiences. Not long after he returned to Warsaw, now under the control of a pro-Soviet communist regime, Borowski committed suicide, at least in part out of a deep despair over what he perceived as the survival of the concentration camp mentality in Cold War Poland.

In the short story, "This Way for the Gas, Ladies and Gentleman," Borowski describes unloading the cattle cars that brought Jews to Auschwitz.

From *This Way for the Gas, Ladies and Gentlemen,* by Tadeusz Borowski, translated by Barbara Vedder (New York: Viking Penguin, 1967), pp. 33–39.

*   *   *

"Want to come with us on the ramp?"

"Sure, why not?"

"Come along then, grab your coat! We're short of a few men. I've already told the Kapo," and he shoves me out of the barracks door.

We line up. Someone has marked down our numbers, someone up ahead yells, "March, march," and now we are running towards the gate, accompanied by the shouts of a multilingual throng that is already being pushed back to the barracks. Not everybody is lucky enough to be going on the ramp. We have almost reached the gate. *Links, zwei, drei, vier! Mützen ab!* Erect, arms stretched stiffly along our hips, we march past the gate briskly, smartly, almost gracefully. A sleepy S.S. man with a large pad in his hand checks us off, waving us ahead in groups of five.

"*Hundert!*" he calls after we have all passed.

"*Stimmt!*" comes a hoarse answer from out front.

We march fast, almost at a run. There are guards all around, young men with automatics. We pass camp II B, then some deserted barracks and a clump of unfamiliar green—apple and pear trees. We cross the circle of watchtowers and, running, burst on to the highway. We have arrived. Just a few more yards. There, surrounded by trees, is the ramp.

A cheerful little station, very much like any other provincial railway stop: a small square framed by tall chestnuts and paved with yellow gravel. Not far off, beside the road, squats a tiny wooden shed, uglier and more flimsy then the ugliest and flimsiest railway shack; farther along lie stacks of old rails, heaps of wooden beams, barracks parts, bricks, paving stones. This is where they load freight for Birkenau: supplies for the construction of the camp, and people for the gas chambers. Trucks drive around, load up lumber, cement, people—a regular daily routine.

And now the guards are being posted along the rails, across the beams, in the green shade of the Silesian chestnuts, to form a tight circle around the ramp. They wipe the sweat from their faces and sip out of their canteens. It is unbearably hot; the sun stands motionless at its zenith.

"Fall out."

We sit down in the narrow streaks of shade along the stacked rails. The hungry Greeks (several of them managed to come along, God only knows how) rummage underneath the rails. One of them finds some pieces of mildewed bread, another a few half-rotten sardines. They eat.

"*Schweinedreck,*" spits a young, tall guard with corn-coloured hair and dreamy blue eyes. "For God's sake, any minute you'll have so much food to stuff down your guts, you'll bust!" He adjusts his gun, wipes his face with a handkerchief.

"Hey you fatso!" His boot lightly touches Henri's shoulder. "*Pass mal auf,* want a drink?"

"Sure, but I haven't got any marks," replies the Frenchman with a professional air.

"*Schade,* too bad."

"Come, come, Herr Posten, isn't my word good enough any more? Haven't we done business before? How much?"

"One hundred. *Gemacht?*"

"*Gemacht.*"

We drink the water, lukewarm and tasteless. It will be paid for by the people who have not yet arrived.

"Now you be careful," says Henri, turning to me. He tosses away the empty bottle. It strikes the rails and bursts into tiny fragments. "Don't take any money, they might be checking. Anyway, who the hell needs money? You've got enough to eat. Don't take suits, either, or they'll think you're planning to escape. Just get a shirt, silk only, with a collar. And a vest. And if you find something to drink, don't bother calling me. I know how to shift for myself, but you watch your step or they'll let you have it."

"Do they beat you up here?"

"Naturally. You've got to have eyes in your ass. *Arschaugen.*"

Around us sit the Greeks, their jaws working greedily, like huge human insects. They munch on stale lumps of bread. They are restless, wondering what will happen next. The sight of the large beams and the stacks of rails has them worried. They dislike carrying heavy loads.

"*Was wir arbeiten?*" they ask.

"*Niks. Transport kommen, alles Krematorium, compris?*"

"*Alles verstehen,*" they answer in crematorium Esperanto. All is well—they will not have to move the heavy rails or carry the beams.

In the meantime, the ramp has become increasingly alive with activity, increasingly noisy. The crews are being divided into those who will open and unload the arriving cattle cars and those who will be posted by the wooden steps. They receive instructions on how to proceed most efficiently. Motor cycles drive up, delivering S.S. officers, bemedalled, glittering with brass, beefy men with highly polished boots and shiny, brutal faces. Some have brought their briefcases, others hold thin, flexible whips. This gives them an air of military readiness and agility. They walk in and out of the commissary—for the miserable little shack by the road serves as their commissary, where in the summertime they drink mineral water, *Studentenquelle,* and where in winter they can warm up with a glass of hot wine. They greet each other in the state-approved way, raising an arm Roman fashion, then shake hands cordially, exchange warm smiles, discuss mail from home, their children, their families. Some stroll majestically on the ramp. The silver squares on their collars glitter, the gravel crunches under their boots, their bamboo whips snap impatiently.

We lie against the rails in the narrow streaks of shade, breathe unevenly, occasionally exchange a few words in our various tongues, and gaze listlessly at the majestic men in green uniforms, at the green trees, and at the church steeple of a distant village.

"The transport is coming," somebody says. We spring to our feet, all eyes turn in one direction. Around the bend, one after another, the cattle cars begin rolling in. The train backs into the station, a conductor leans out, waves his hand, blows a whistle. The locomotive whistles back with a shrieking noise, puffs, the train rolls slowly alongside the ramp. In the tiny barred windows appear pale, wilted, exhausted human faces, terror-stricken women with tangled hair, unshaven men. They gaze at the station in silence. And then, suddenly, there is a stir inside the cars and a pounding against the wooden boards.

"Water! Air!"—weary, desperate cries.

Heads push through the windows, mouths gasp frantically for air. They draw a few breaths, then disappear; others come in their place, then also disappear. The cries and moans grow louder.

A man in a green uniform covered with more glitter than any of the others jerks his head impatiently, his lips twist in annoyance. He inhales deeply, then with a rapid gesture throws his cigarette away and signals to the guard. The guard removes the automatic from his shoulder, aims, sends a series of shots along the train. All is quiet now. Meanwhile, the trucks have arrived, steps are being drawn up, and the Canada men[1] stand ready at their posts by the train doors. The S.S. officer with the briefcase raises his hand.

"Whoever takes gold, or anything at all besides food, will be shot for stealing Reich property. Understand? *Verstanden?*"

"*Jawohl!*" we answer eagerly.

---

[1] Canada men were those prisoners fortunate enough to be assigned to transport duty. Canada, to which many Europeans had immigrated prior to the war, was imagined by camp inmates as an ideal land of peace and plenty.

"*Also los!* Begin!"

The bolts crack, the doors fall open. A wave of fresh air rushes inside the train. People . . . inhumanly crammed, buried under incredible heaps of luggage, suitcases, trunks, packages, crates, bundles of every description (everything that had been their past and was to start their future). Monstrously squeezed together, they have fainted from heat, suffocated, crushed one another. Now they push towards the opened doors, breathing like fish cast out on the sand.

"Attention! Out, and take your luggage with you! Take out everything. Pile all your stuff near the exits. Yes, your coats too. It is summer. March to the left. Understand?"

"Sir, what's going to happen to us?" They jump from the train on to the gravel, anxious, worn-out.

"Where are you people from?"

"Sosnowiec-Będzin. Sir, what's going to happen to us?" They repeat the question stubbornly, gazing into our tired eyes.

"I don't know, I don't understand Polish."

It is the camp law: people going to their death must be deceived to the very end. This is the only permissible form of charity. The heat is tremendous. The sun hangs directly over our heads, the white, hot sky quivers, the air vibrates, an occasional breeze feels like a sizzling blast from a furnace. Our lips are parched, the mouth fills with the salty taste of blood, the body is weak and heavy from lying in the sun. Water!

A huge, multicoloured wave of people loaded down with luggage pours from the train like a blind, mad river trying to find a new bed. But before they have a chance to recover, before they can draw a breath of fresh air and look at the sky, bundles are snatched from their hands, coats ripped off their backs, their purses and umbrellas taken away.

"But please, sir, it's for the sun, I cannot . . ."

"*Verboten!*" one of us barks through clenched teeth. There is an S.S. man standing behind your back, calm, efficient, watchful.

"*Meine Herrschaften,* this way, ladies and gentlemen, try not to throw your things around,

please. Show some goodwill," he says courteously, his restless hands playing with the slender whip.

"Of course, of course," they answer as they pass, and now they walk alongside the train somewhat more cheerfully. A woman reaches down quickly to pick up her handbag. The whip flies, the woman screams, stumbles, and falls under the feet of the surging crowd. Behind her, a child cries in a thin little voice "Mamele!"—a very small girl with tangled black curls.

The heaps grow. Suitcases, bundles, blankets, coats, handbags that open as they fall, spilling coins, gold, watches; mountains of bread pile up at the exits, heaps of marmalade, jams, masses of meat, sausages; sugar spills on the gravel. Trucks, loaded with people, start up with a deafening roar and drive off amidst the wailing and screaming of the women separated from their children, and the stupefied silence of the men left behind. They are the ones who had been ordered to step to the right—the healthy and the young who will go to the camp. In the end, they too will not escape death, but first they must work.

Trucks leave and return, without interruption, as on a monstrous conveyor belt. A Red Cross van drives back and forth, back and forth, incessantly: it transports the gas that will kill these people. The enormous cross on the hood, red as blood, seems to dissolve in the sun.

The Canada men at the trucks cannot stop for a single moment, even to catch their breath. They shove the people up the steps, pack them in tightly, sixty per truck, more or less. Near by stands a young, cleanshaven "gentleman," an S.S. officer with a notebook in his hand. For each departing truck he enters a mark; sixteen gone means one thousand people, more or less. The gentleman is calm, precise. No truck can leave without a signal from him, or a mark in his notebook: *Ordnung muss sein.* The marks swell into thousands, the thousands into whole transports, which afterwards we shall simply call "from Salonica," "from Strasbourg," "from Rotterdam." This one will be called "Sosnowiec-Będzin." The new prisoners from Sosnowiec-Będzin will receive serial numbers 131–2—thousand, of course, though afterwards we shall simply say 131–2, for short.

The transports swell into weeks, months, years. When the war is over, they will count up the marks in their notebooks—all four and a half million of them. The bloodiest battle of the war, the greatest victory of the strong, united Germany. *Ein Reich, ein Volk, ein Führer*—and four crematoria.

* * *

REVIEW QUESTIONS

1. Why does the narrator consider himself lucky to be doing this work?
2. What were the benefits of unloading the cattle cars?
3. In the story, what will happen to the people in the Sosnowiec-Będzin transport?
4. Why won't the camp inmates unloading the trains explain what is going to happen to these new arrivals?
5. Compare Borowski's depictions of the unloading crew ("Canada men"), the camp administrators, and the Jews arriving in Auschwitz.
6. What message is conveyed by Borowski's portrayal of these distinct concentration camp subpopulations?

FROM *Trials of War Criminals before the Nuremberg Military Tribunals*

Borowski's detached, even clinical, descriptions of life in the concentration camps offered little solace to a world desperate for a renewed sense of decency and justice. While many postwar philosophers emphasized the moral ambiguities of human action and the relativism of all moral and ethical systems, these postmodern approaches were counterbalanced by a desire to reaffirm the existence of clear lines between good and evil, right and wrong. Survivors sought to ensure that all of humanity would know about the murder of millions of concentration camp inmates, and they called for a judgment on those who had committed crimes against humanity.

Beginning in 1945, many surviving members of the Nazi leadership were put on trial in the city of Nuremberg. The "doctors' trial," which began in December 1946, involved the prosecution of twenty-three German doctors and administrators who had used concentration camp inmates as unwilling volunteers in a variety of gruesome and often pointless experiments, including intentional infection with contagious diseases like malaria and spotted fever, experimental surgery, and exposure to extreme cold, mustard gas, and various poisons. On 6 December 1946, Brigadier General Telford Taylor presented the opening statement for the prosecution, detailing both the specific crimes committed by the defendants and the broader significance of their trial.

From *Trials of War Criminals before the Nuremberg Military Tribunals under Control Council Law No. 10. Nuremberg, October 1946–April 1949* (Washington, D.C.: U.S. Government Printing Office, 1949–1953).

Opening Statement of the Prosecution by Brigadier General Telford Taylor, 9 December 1946

The defendants in this case are charged with murders, tortures, and other atrocities committed in the name of medical science. The victims of these crimes are numbered in the hundreds of thousands. A handful only are still alive; a few of the survivors will appear in this courtroom. But most of these miserable victims were slaughtered outright or died in the course of the tortures to which they were subjected.

For the most part they are nameless dead. To their murderers, these wretched people were not individuals at all. They came in wholesale lots and were treated worse than animals. They were 200 Jews in good physical condition, 50 gypsies, 500 tubercular Poles, or 1,000 Russians. The victims of these crimes are numbered among the anonymous millions who met death at the hands of the Nazis and whose fate is a hideous blot on the page of modern history.

*   *   *

The mere punishment of the defendants, or even of thousands of others equally guilty, can never redress the terrible injuries which the Nazis visited on these unfortunate peoples. For them it is far more important that these incredible events be established by clear and public proof, so that no one can ever doubt that they were fact and not fable; and that this Court, as the agent of the United States and as the voice of humanity, stamp these acts, and the ideas which engendered them, as barbarous and criminal.

We have still other responsibilities here. The defendants in the dock are charged with murder, but this is no mere murder trial. We cannot rest content when we have shown that crimes were committed and that certain persons committed them. To kill, to maim, and to torture is criminal under all modern systems of law. These defendants did not kill in hot blood, nor for personal enrichment. Some of them may be sadists who killed and tortured for sport, but they are not all perverts. They are not ignorant men. Most of them are trained physicians and some of them are distinguished scientists. Yet these defendants, all of whom were fully able to comprehend the nature of their acts, and most of whom were exceptionally qualified to form a moral and professional judgment in this respect, are responsible for wholesale murder and unspeakably cruel tortures. It is our deep obligation to all peoples of the world to show why and how these things happened. It is incumbent upon us to set forth with conspicuous clarity the ideas and motives which moved these defendants to treat their fellow men as less than beasts.

*   *   *

To the German people we owe a special responsibility in these proceedings. Under the leadership of the Nazis and their war lords, the German nation spread death and devastation throughout Europe. This the Germans now know. So, too, do they know the consequences to Germany: defeat, ruin, prostration, and utter demoralization. Most German children will never, as long as they live, see an undamaged German city.

*   *   *

This case, and others which will be tried in this building, offer a signal opportunity to lay before the German people the true cause of their present misery. The walls and towers and churches of Nuremberg were, indeed, reduced to rubble by Allied bombs, but in a deeper sense Nuremberg had been destroyed a decade earlier, when it became the seat of the annual Nazi Party rallies, a focal point for the moral disintegration in Germany. * * *

*   *   *

That murder should be punished goes without the saying, but the full performance of our task requires more than the just sentencing of these defendants. Their crimes were the inevitable result of the sinister doctrines which they espoused, and these same doctrines sealed the fate of Germany, shattered Europe, and left the world in ferment. Wherever those doctrines may emerge and prevail, the same terrible consequences will follow. That is why a bold and lucid consummation of these proceedings is of vital importance to all nations. That is why the United States has constituted this Tribunal.

*   *   *

Before taking up these experiments one by one, let us look at them as a whole. Are they a heterogeneous list of horrors, or is there a common denominator for the whole group?

A sort of rough pattern is apparent on the face of the indictment. Experiments concerning high altitude, the effect of cold, and the potability of processed sea water have an obvious relation to aeronautical and naval combat and rescue problems. The mustard gas and phosphorous burn experiments, as well as those relating to the healing value of sulfanilamide for wounds, can be related to air raid and battlefield medical problems. It is well known that malaria, epidemic jaundice, and typhus were among the principal diseases which had to be combated by the German Armed Forces and by German authorities in occupied territories.

To some degree, the therapeutic pattern outlined above is undoubtedly a valid one, and explains why the Wehrmacht, and especially the German Air Force, participated in these experiments. Fanatically bent upon conquest, utterly ruthless as to the means or instruments to be used in achieving victory, and callous to the sufferings of people whom they regarded as inferior, the German militarists were willing to gather whatever scientific fruit these experiments might yield.

But our proof will show that a quite different and even more sinister objective runs like a red thread through these hideous researches. We will show that in some instances the true object of these experiments was not how to rescue or to cure, but how to destroy and kill. The sterilization experiments were, it is clear, purely destructive in purpose. The prisoners at Buchenwald who were shot with poisoned bullets were not guinea pigs to test an antidote for the poison; their murderers really wanted to know how quickly the poison would kill.

*   *   *

The 20 physicians in the dock range from leaders of German scientific medicine, with excellent international reputations, down to the dregs of the German medical profession. All of them have in common a callous lack of consideration and human regard for, and an unprincipled willingness to abuse their power over the poor, unfortunate, defenseless creatures who had been deprived of their rights by a ruthless and criminal government. All of them violated the Hippocratic commandments which they had solemnly sworn to uphold and abide by, including the fundamental principles never to do harm. * * *

*   *   *

I intend to pass very briefly over matters of medical ethics, such as the conditions under which a physician may lawfully perform a medical experiment upon a person who has voluntarily subjected himself to it, or whether experiments may lawfully be performed upon criminals who have been condemned to death. This case does not present such problems. No refined questions confront us here.

None of the victims of the atrocities perpetrated by these defendants were volunteers, and this is true regardless of what these unfortunate people may have said or signed before their tortures began. Most of the victims had not been condemned to death, and those who had been were not criminals, unless it be a crime to be a Jew, or a Pole, or a gypsy, or a Russian prisoner of war.

Whatever book or treatise on medical ethics we may examine, and whatever expert on forensic medicine we may question, will say that it is a fundamental and inescapable obligation of every physician under any known system of law not to perform a dangerous experiment without the subject's consent. In the tyranny that was Nazi Germany, no one could give such a consent to the medical agents of the State; everyone lived in fear and acted under duress. I fervently hope that none of us here in the courtroom will have to suffer in silence while it is said on the part of these defendants that the wretched and helpless people whom they froze and drowned and burned and poisoned were volunteers.

*　　*　　*

This case is one of the simplest and clearest of those that will be tried in this building. It is also one of the most important. It is true that the defendants in the box were not among the highest leaders of the Third Reich. They are not the war lords who assembled and drove the German military machine, nor the industrial barons who made the parts, nor the Nazi politicians who debased and brutalized the minds of the German people. But this case, perhaps more than any other we will try, epitomizes Nazi thought and the Nazi way of life, because these defendants pursue the savage promises of Nazi thought so far. The things that these defendants did, like so many other things that happened under the Third Reich, were the result of the noxious merger of German militarism and Nazi racial objectives.

*　　*　　*

Germany surrendered herself to this foul conjunction of evil forces. The nation fell victim to the Nazi scourge because its leaders lacked the wisdom to foresee the consequences and the courage to stand firm in the face of threats. Their failure was the inevitable outcome of that sinister undercurrent of German philosophy which preaches the supreme importance of the state and the complete subordination of the individual. A nation in which the individual means nothing will find few leaders courageous and able enough to serve its best interests.

*　　*　　*

The Nazis have, to a certain extent, succeeded in convincing the peoples of the world that the Nazi system, although ruthless, was absolutely efficient; that although savage, it was completely scientific; that although entirely devoid of humanity, it was highly systematic—that "it got things done." The evidence which this Tribunal will hear will explode this myth. The Nazi methods of investigation were inefficient and unscientific, and their techniques of research were unsystematic.

These experiments revealed nothing which civilized medicine can use. It was, indeed, ascertained that phenol or gasoline injected intravenously will kill a man inexpensively and within 60 seconds. *　*　* There is no doubt that a number of these new methods may be useful to criminals everywhere and there is no doubt that they may be useful to a criminal state.

*　　*　　*

Apart from these deadly fruits, the experiments were not only criminal but a scientific failure. *　*　* The moral shortcomings of the defendants and the precipitous ease with which they decided to commit murder in quest of "scientific results," dulled also that scientific hesitancy, that thorough thinking-through, that responsible weighing of every single step which alone can insure scientifically valid results. Even if they had merely been forced to pay as little as two dollars for human experimental subjects, such as American investigators may have to pay for a cat, they might have thought twice before wasting unnecessary numbers, and thought of simpler and better ways to solve their problems. The fact that these investigators had free and unrestricted access to human beings to be experimented upon misled them to the dangerous and fallacious conclusion that the results would thus be better and more quickly obtainable than if they had gone through the labor of preparation, thinking, and meticulous preinvestigation.

*   *   *

In short, this conspiracy was a ghastly failure as well as a hideous crime. The creeping paralysis of Nazi superstition spread through the German medical profession and, just as it destroyed character and morals, it dulled the mind.

Guilt for the oppressions and crimes of the Third Reich is widespread, but it is the guilt of the leaders that is deepest and most culpable. Who could German medicine look to to keep the profession true to its traditions and protect it from the ravaging inroads of Nazi pseudo-science? This was the supreme responsibility of the leaders of German medicine. * * * That is why their guilt is greater than that of any of the other defendants

in the dock. They are the men who utterly failed their country and their profession, who showed neither courage nor wisdom nor the vestiges of moral character. It is their failure, together with the failure of the leaders of Germany in other walks of life, that debauched Germany and led to her defeat. It is because of them and others like them that we all live in a stricken world.

REVIEW QUESTIONS

1. Why, according to General Taylor, was it so important that the defendants be tried for their crimes?
2. Other then punishing specific guilty individuals, what purpose was being served by these trials?
3. To what extent is Taylor's statement an indictment of Nazi science in general?
4. How does Taylor's perspective on Nazi atrocities differ from Borowski's?
5. What can account for this difference?

TADATAKA KURIBAYASHI

FROM *A Child's Experience: My Experience of the Atomic Bomb*

On 6 August 1945, an atomic bomb was dropped on the Japanese city of Hiroshima, killing 66,000 people outright. On 9 August another bomb was dropped on Nagasaki, killing 39,000. In the following weeks and months, many more died as a result of radiation exposure and of injuries sustained at the time of the explosions.

The decision to drop the newly developed atomic bomb on Japan continues to generate heated debate among philosophers, historians, and the general public. Those who defend this particular deployment of nuclear weapons argue that it brought a more rapid end to the war, thereby saving the lives of countless American soldiers and Japanese civilians. Others counter that the Japanese government was al-

ready on the verge of surrender and that the targeting of civilian populations for military ends is, in any case, indefensible. Evaluation of this event is further complicated by the fact that the decision to use the atomic bomb was made in the context of emerging Cold War hostilities. Truman was eager to end the war with Japan and keep the Soviet Union out of the Asian theater, and he may also have wished to provide Stalin with a graphic demonstration of the enhanced military might of the United States.

During the war years, Allied propaganda supplied Americans and Europeans with highly stereotyped and racist caricatures of the Japanese. In the postwar period, this dehumanized image was challenged by movies and books documenting the tragic consequences of the use of nuclear weapons. In the 1960s, Tadataka Kuribayashi recounted his own experience of the bombing of Hiroshima. In early 1945, Kuribayashi had been attending school in Hiroshima. In April of that year he was evacuated to the nearby peasant village of Tsutsuga, along with eighteen other children.

From *A Child's Experience: My Experience of the Atomic Bomb,* by Tadataka Kuribayashi, A-Bomb web page, www.csi.ad.jp/ABOMB/ [accessed 11/21/01].

The Fatal Day (6 August)

The weather was fine in the village on the morning of the 6 August, which was more than one month after the parents-visiting day. In the precincts of a shrine adjacent to the school, we boys in the 6th grade were undergoing training in the Morse signals. Cool breeze blew under ginkgo trees, and the cicadas seemed to be singing the joys of summer. Suddenly I felt something warm on my left cheek and turned back. It seemed like a strong reflection from a mirror. Then a roaring sound shook the whole village. While I was wondering what had happened, a column of clouds appeared above the mountains in the south. That was not an ordinary cloud but of a superb pink color. Gradually it assumed the shape of a mushroom and rose to the sky.

When I returned to the temple, the matron said she had felt a strong tremor even in the temple. As time passed, the fine sky gradually became dark, and in the late afternoon, a lot of cinders of paper and other things fell down from the sky. First a rumor said that an arsenal had exploded, but I later heard that a fire engine from an adjacent village had gone to Hiroshima City for rescue, but because of the strong fire, could not go beyond Yokogawa and returned. Thus, though I was small, I felt something unusual had happened. However, I didn't even imagine that the big city of Hiroshima had instantaneously become a sheet of fire.

Soon I heard that many people with severe burns had returned to the village. All of these people were from the village and were working in Hiroshima. Since then, there was no communication from the parents. After more than a week, a teacher told us that there had been an important announcement and that Japan had lost the war, but now I cannot remember sorrow or anxiety at that time. We might have been too young to have any direct emotion about the big change for the nation. Even though the war ended, we couldn't do anything. No one came to fetch us, and everyone lived anxiously from day to day.

At the beginning of September, I received a wrinkled-up postcard. Though my mother's name was mentioned, the handwriting with a pencil, some parts of which were blurred, was not my mother's. The card simply said, "I am in the reception center in Miyajima. Come here immediately." and a simple map of the place was shown.

I wondered why my mother had not written it herself, but was glad to know where she was. However, the date on the card showed that many days had passed since it had been written. Next day, I, accompanied by Mr. Yamakawa, left for Miyajima. That was the 2 September.

I looked at the town of Hiroshima while I proceeded from Yokogawa to Koi. It was a field of charred ruins. The city streetcar which just began to run between Koami-cho and Koi had numerous flies on the ceiling. It was a strange sight. We took a boat from Miyajima-guchi. I saw the old big torii (Shinto shrine archway) and the beautiful Itsukushima Shrine, but they just looked a faded landscape painting to me. I wanted to go to the reception center and see the face of my mother as soon as possible. I was so eager to see her that I felt the boat was extremely slow. Soon we arrived at the center, which was a big building to the north of the shrine. When I stood at the entrance, I felt some kind of anxiety, which was an emotion difficult to express.

Attending on Mother

I looked for Mother with my teacher. It was a big room with tens of tatami mats, and the spaces between A-bomb survivors lying on futon (bedclothes) produced a forlorn atmosphere. We took one round, but couldn't find her. While I took the second round, looking into the face of each person, I was astonished to find Mother, lying on her face and exhausted. She was a small person, but she looked even smaller. Suppressing the tremor of my voice, I called her quietly. There was no answer. I called her again. Then she noticed and slightly raised her head. She saw the teacher behind me, and took out some bills to give to him. He refused to receive them, and left there after a short while saying that he had business at the school.

When Mother told me about the death of Father, I was not so surprised. I might have been somewhat ready to hear the news. Deprived of a flush of hope, I imagined my father being burnt to death in agony. My heart was wrung. We didn't know if my elder brother, who had gone abroad to war was dead or alive. I naturally had a dark prospect about our future, but resolved firmly to continue to live with my mother no matter how poor we would be. Mother told me to take the cloth off her back. I found brown burns all over her back. Because of the burns, she couldn't lie on her back. Why does my mother, as innocent as a person could be, have to be tortured like this? I could not suppress the anger I felt. From that day, I took care of her for 2 nights and 3 days. However, the only medicine provided was mercurochrome. We were even short of cresol. When Mother arrived at the center, she was fine and even washed other people's clothes, but when I got there she couldn't even move her body.

She was engaged in building-demolition work near the Tsurumi Bridge when she was exposed to the flash. She couldn't do anything for Mrs. Takai, who was immediately burned to death in front of her, and climbed the Hijiyama Hill in a hurry with her back burned. From the hill, she looked at the city, which was a hell on earth. With other people, she was first accommodated in the reception center in Ninoshima, and moved to Miyajima. The terrible gas which entered to the depth of her body gradually damaged her bones and organs. She had completely lost her appetite.

Remorse

No one had disposed of my mother's urine, so her lower body gave out a stench. Her stool was not like that of a human being. Its color and smell were like those of internal organs that had been melted and had become a sticky liquid. I felt that the only way to give humaneness back to her was to clean the chamber pot often. Though I was eager to care for her, I became negligent once. On the second night at the center, I heard Mother's small voice calling me, but I was so sleepy that I pretended as though I didn't hear her. She called me twice, but didn't say anything more. Whenever I remember this, there is a sharp pain in my heart.

At the camp, simple food such as salty soup with one dumpling was served three times. No boiled rice was served. We were allowed to drink as many cups of soup as we liked, and I had three or four more cups of soup. My mother smiled wryly. At that time, she was too weak to speak. I saw the front of a big torii, gateway to a Shinto shrine, from the window of the lavatory. Looking at the B-29 bomber which sometimes came flying, I shouted to myself "Idiot!" It was all the resistance I, as a boy, could offer. And I sometimes cried secretly in the lavatory.

Death of Mother

At lunch-time on 4 September, the third day, Mother started to writhe in pain. Her unusual action completely upset me. All I could do was to absentmindedly look at my suffering Mother. After suffering for 30 minutes, she regained her calmness. However, it was the last calmness, the sign of the end of life. I continued calling her name, clinging to her body. Tears welled up in the eyes of my speechless mother and tears rolled down her cheek. I wondered if the tears were from the sorrow of eternal parting between mother and child or from an anxiety about my future. I shall never forget the tears of my Mother I saw on that day.

I continued crying even after a white cloth was placed over Mother's face. Some irritated people reproached me, saying "Be quiet!" Shouldn't I feel sorry for the death of my most precious mother? My tears seemed to have forgotten to stop until evening.

Return to Tsutsuga Village

There was a middle-aged man who happened to come to the camp as an attendant. He was kind enough to offer to take charge of me, probably in pity of me who had been left an orphan. I answered I would decide after consulting with my teacher at the Saihoji Temple where I had been evacuated. He decided to take me there. Wrapping my mother's personal belongings, I had rice ball made for lunch. The man and I left Miyajima Island, leaving what had to be done including the burial of my dead mother to the officials at the camp.

Arriving at the Miyajima-guchi streetcar station, I found a streetcar already there. The streetcar was about to leave the station. I had a return ticket but the man did not have one and bought his own ticket. He hurried to the platform after he had his ticket punched. I tried to follow him, but a man at the gate told me that the ticket I had was for a train, not for a streetcar and showed me the way to the railway station. I started walking toward the station at once, never thinking of anything. There is no way of knowing if the man left for Hiroshima by streetcar or returned to Miyajima. The fact that the one ticket I had served as the turning point of my fate still makes me think of the mysteriousness of fate.

The train I got on took me close to Tsutsuga Village; from Miyajima-guchi to Yokogawa and from Yokogawa to Kabe to Aki-imuro. I felt relieved when I was picked up by a truck driver at Aki-imuro who took me to Kake. An old man who shared the ride had a water bottle and gave me some water. The water tasted so good and I felt the water coursing down through my bowels. The old man was returning to Tsutsuga Village and I asked him to take me there.

It was very far from Kake to Tsutsuga. The road along a river seemed to be endless. I tottered after several persons while half sleeping late at night. When I reached Tsutsuga Village, I noticed there were no other people except the old man who had given me water. We walked for another 40 minutes and finally reached the front of the Saihoji Temple at dawn. At that time I felt undescribably happy. I expressed my thanks and said farewell to the old man. I entered the main hall of the temple. I thought I had to report to my teacher that I had returned, but I decided to do so later in the morning because I did not want to wake him up. I stole into a mosquito net, under which some children were sleeping, carrying my bedclothes and lay down. In the morning, my teacher was very surprised to learn that I had returned. I had never experienced such a long trip.

Left Alone

I resumed my life at the temple. An increasing number of children were leaving the temple together with their parent or sibling or relative who came there to take them home. However, traffic was completely paralyzed due to a heavy flood caused by an unprecedented typhoon which hit the prefecture. So, there was no choice but to walk all the way to Hiroshima.

Children who had homes to return to were happy. Most of the children had lost either a parent or other family members. It was only I that had lost both parents and had no relatives. I had nowhere to go except an orphanage where I was taken care of. In spite of sheer unhappiness, I, as a child, did not think so seriously of it.

In the end, only three children including myself stayed behind at the temple. The temple was too big for the three of us. I heard that the relatives of Yoshihiro Inoue and Yoko Minematsu would come to the temple later for some reason. Then, it was decided that children including those living in neighboring villages who had no home to return would be accommodated in a temple at Togouchi adjacent to Tsutsuga. I was hurriedly

crossing a mountain pass when it began to get dark on 3 October. There was no one to be seen and everything was ominously still and silent.

I, an 11-year-old boy, only thought of running out of the weird trees, not being afraid of my future life which would bring me loneliness and starvation. Frequently frightened at the sound of my footsteps, I kept running, only wishing I could reach the village as soon as possible.

* * *

REVIEW QUESTIONS

1. What does this account tell you about the Japanese experience in the Second World War?
2. How does Kuribayashi's ordeal compare with Mr. Smith's experience during the London blitz, for example?
3. To what extent might the testimony of survivors like Kuribayashi influence historical interpretations of the use of atomic weapons?
4. How should historians approach the analysis of events heavily charged with moral significance, such as the Holocaust and the deployment of nuclear weapons?
5. How do the bombings of Hiroshima and Nagasaki differ from the Holocaust?

FROM Charter of the United Nations

Before the atomic bomb brought the war in the Pacific to a dramatic close, a new international peacekeeping organization was already being organized to replace the League of Nations. On 26 June 1945, the United Nations was established by a formal charter drawn up at an international congress held in San Francisco. Vested with the authority to maintain and deploy peacekeeping forces, the United Nations was intended to be a more effective agency for world peace than its predecessor had been. And, while the United Nations was not able to solve the many problems generated by the Cold War, it nevertheless served as an important arena for the negoti-

ation of conflicts between member nations. The preamble and first chapter of the United Nations Charter sets out the primary goals of the organization.

From Charter of the United Nations, United Nations web page, www.un.org/[accessed 11/21/01].

Preamble

WE THE PEOPLES OF THE UNITED NATIONS DETERMINED

to save succeeding generations from the scourge of war, which twice in our lifetime has brought untold sorrow to mankind, and

to reaffirm faith in fundamental human rights, in the dignity and worth of the human person, in the equal rights of men and women and of nations large and small, and

to establish conditions under which justice and respect for the obligations arising from treaties and other sources of international law can be maintained, and

to promote social progress and better standards of life in larger freedom,

AND FOR THESE ENDS

to practice tolerance and live together in peace with one another as good neighbours, and

to unite our strength to maintain international peace and security, and

to ensure, by the acceptance of principles and the institution of methods, that armed force shall not be used, save in the common interest, and

to employ international machinery for the promotion of the economic and social advancement of all peoples,

HAVE RESOLVED TO COMBINE OUR EFFORTS TO ACCOMPLISH THESE AIMS

Accordingly, our respective Governments, through representatives assembled in the city of San Francisco, who have exhibited their full powers found to be in good and due form, have agreed to the present Charter of the United Nations and do hereby establish an international organization to be known as the United Nations.

ARTICLE 1

The Purposes of the United Nations are:
1. To maintain international peace and security, and to that end: to take effective collective measures for the prevention and removal of threats to the peace, and for the suppression of acts of aggression or other breaches of the peace, and to bring about by peaceful means, and in conformity with the principles of justice and international law, adjustment or settlement of international disputes or situations which might lead to a breach of the peace;
2. To develop friendly relations among nations based on respect for the principle of equal rights and self-determination of peoples, and to take other appropriate measures to strengthen universal peace;
3. To achieve international co-operation in solving international problems of an economic, social, cultural, or humanitarian character, and in promoting and encouraging respect for human rights and for fundamental freedoms for all without distinction as to race, sex, language, or religion; and
4. To be a centre for harmonizing the actions of nations in the attainment of these common ends.

ARTICLE 2

The Organization and its Members, in pursuit of the Purposes stated in Article 1, shall act in accordance with the following Principles.
1. The Organization is based on the principle of the sovereign equality of all its Members.
2. All Members, in order to ensure to all of them the rights and benefits resulting from membership, shall fulfill in good faith the obligations as-

sumed by them in accordance with the present Charter.

3. All Members shall settle their international disputes by peaceful means in such a manner that international peace and security, and justice, are not endangered.

4. All Members shall refrain in their international relations from the threat or use of force against the territorial integrity or political independence of any state, or in any other manner inconsistent with the Purposes of the United Nations.

* * *

REVIEW QUESTIONS

1. How does this preamble compare with the Covenant of the League of Nations (see Chapter 27)?

2. To what extent was this statement of goals formulated as a response to the Second World War experience?

30 ✦ COLD WAR POLITICS, ECONOMIC BOOM, AND CULTURAL CHANGE

At the beginning of the twentieth century, the European great powers dominated the world, both materially and—at least in the opinion of Europeans—culturally. Even after the First World War, European power seemed only slightly diminished, especially when the newest contender for world power status, the United States, chose to retreat again into isolationism after the war.

After the Second World War, the world was a dramatically different place. A second great cataclysm had left much of Europe in ruins, and the former great powers found themselves confronted with the enormous task of reconstructing what they themselves had destroyed. The new bipolar balance of world power, pitting the United States against the Soviet Union, decreased the global power and prestige of individual European nations, drawing them into the orbits of the two competing superpowers. Europe was divided in two by an "iron curtain," and the cultures, economies, and political systems of the two Europes were deeply marked by the new realities of the cold war.

European dominance had ended, but the Western European nations soon rallied, achieving general levels of prosperity, technological sophistication, and democratic participation never before experienced in their histories. American economic aid reinvigorated western European economies, greatly increasing the material well-being of ordinary people. Cradle-to-grave social welfare programs provided education, medical care, and guarantees that no citizen would be deprived of the minimum necessities of life. The appurtenances of consumer culture—radios, cars, televisions, dishwashers, seaside vacations—became available to the majority of Western Europeans.

The economic "miracle" did not come to Eastern Europe. Always underdeveloped by Western standards, Eastern Europe's poverty and technological backwardness were only reinforced by the domination of the powerful Soviet Union. Communist regimes throughout Eastern Europe retained their hold on *power not through popular support but through the threat of Soviet invasion. Communist heads of state were forced to follow the dictates of economic and military planners in Moscow, often to the detriment of their own citizens. The death of Stalin in 1953 brought some easing of repression, and standards of living did improve, if more gradually and less opulently than in the West. But Stalin's successors continued to rule Eastern Europe with a firm hand, stifling dissent and emphasizing heavy industrial and military production at the expense of consumer goods. When the Soviet bloc collapsed in the late 1980s, bringing a surprisingly sudden end to the cold war, Eastern Europe remained burdened with the bitter legacy of economic underdevelopment and political immaturity.*

In both the East and the West, postwar culture was unsettled and complex. The war had demonstrated the moral bankruptcy of fascism (even if nostalgia for militarism, nationalism, and racial cleansing lingered in the hearts of many), but no other alternative ideologies won unqualified support. For many, the simple joys of life were enough. After the hardships of the war, consumerism and leisure culture offered a welcome respite from ideology. On the other hand, intellectuals struggled to come to terms with the implications of wartime genocide, economic and political globalization, and the Americanization of European culture. While the cold war left many feeling powerless in the face of impersonal forces such as superpower politics and the threat of nuclear annihilation, others drew renewed hope from the anticolonial struggles of third world peoples and the protests of civil rights activists around the world.

WINSTON CHURCHILL

FROM "The Sinews of Peace"

During the Second World War, long-standing tensions between the Soviet Union and the other Allied states were set aside in favor of a unified war effort. However, even before the war had ended, mutual suspicions were revived, especially as Allied leaders began to negotiate postwar territorial settlements. The United States and Great Britain promoted the creation of capitalist democracies throughout Europe, while Stalin sought to establish communist satellite states in the East.

One of the defining moments of the emerging Cold War came on 5 March 1946, when Winston Churchill (1874–1965), who had been voted out of office as prime minister by war-weary Britons that year, gave a speech at Westminster College in Fulton, Missouri, attended by the U.S. president Harry S Truman. In this speech, entitled "The Sinews of Peace," Churchill called on Americans and western Europeans to maintain a unified front against the Soviet threat.

From *The Sinews of Peace,* vol. 7, edited by R. R. James (New York: Chelsea House, 1946).

*   *   *

A shadow has fallen upon the scenes so lately lighted by the Allied victory. Nobody knows what Soviet Russia and its Communist international organisation intends to do in the immediate future, or what are the limits, if any, to their expansive and proselytising tendencies. I have a strong admiration and regard for the valiant Russian people and for my wartime comrade, Marshal Stalin. There is deep sympathy and goodwill in Britain— and I doubt not here also—towards the peoples of all the Russias and a resolve to persevere through many differences and rebuffs in establishing lasting friendships. We understand the Russian need to be secure on her western frontiers by the removal of all possibility of German aggression. We welcome Russia to her rightful place among the leading nations of the world. We welcome her flag upon the seas. Above all, we welcome constant, frequent and growing contacts between the Russian people and our own people on both sides of the Atlantic. It is my duty however, for I am sure you would wish me to state the facts as I see them to you, to place before you certain facts about the present position in Europe.

From Stettin in the Baltic to Trieste in the Adriatic, an iron curtain has descended across the Continent. Behind that line lie all the capitals of the ancient states of Central and Eastern Europe. Warsaw, Berlin, Prague, Vienna, Budapest, Belgrade, Bucharest and Sofia, all these famous cities and the populations around them lie in what I must call the Soviet sphere, and all are subject in one form or another, not only to Soviet influence but to a very high and, in many cases, increasing measure of control from Moscow. Athens alone— Greece with its immortal glories—is free to decide its future at an election under British, American

and French observation. The Russian-dominated Polish Government has been encouraged to make enormous and wrongful inroads upon Germany, and mass expulsions of millions of Germans on a scale grievous and undreamed-of are now taking place. The Communist parties, which were very small in all these Eastern States of Europe, have been raised to pre-eminence and power far beyond their numbers and are seeking everywhere to obtain totalitarian control. Police governments are prevailing in nearly every case, and so far, except in Czechoslovakia, there is no true democracy.

*   *   *

The safety of the world requires a new unity in Europe, from which no nation should be permanently outcast. It is from the quarrels of the strong parent races in Europe that the world wars we have witnessed, or which occurred in former times, have sprung. Twice in our own lifetime we have seen the United States, against their wishes and their traditions, against arguments, the force of which it is impossible not to comprehend, drawn by irresistible forces, into these wars in time to secure the victory of the good cause, but only after frightful slaughter and devastation had occurred. Twice the United States has had to send several millions of its young men across the Atlantic to find the war; but now war can find any nation, wherever it may dwell between dusk and dawn. Surely we should work with conscious purpose for a grand pacification of Europe, within the structure of the United Nations and in accordance with its Charter. That I feel is an open cause of policy of very great importance.

*   *   *

From what I have seen of our Russian friends and Allies during the war, I am convinced that there is nothing they admire so much as strength, and there is nothing for which they have less respect than for weakness, especially military weakness. For that reason the old doctrine of a balance of power is unsound. We cannot afford, if we can help it, to work on narrow margins, offering temptations to a trial of strength. If the Western Democracies stand together in strict adherence to the principles of the United Nations Charter, their influence for furthering those principles will be immense and no one is likely to molest them. If however they become divided or falter in their duty and if these all-important years are allowed to slip away then indeed catastrophe may overwhelm us all.

* * *

REVIEW QUESTIONS

1. What was the "iron curtain"? Where was it?
2. What policies was Churchill promoting in this speech?
3. What specific response do you think he hoped to elicit from his U.S. audience?
4. To what extent were his remarks shaped by the existence of nuclear weapons? By the U.S. tradition of isolationism?

GEORGE C. MARSHALL

FROM The Marshall Plan Speech

Following the Second World War, the United States broke decisively with its pre-1945 foreign policy, rejecting the isolationism that had typified U.S. international relations throughout the first half of the twentieth century. In the military arena, this was demonstrated through U.S. participation in the North Atlantic Treaty Organization (NATO). But the United States did not limit its active engagement in international affairs to a purely military role. Amid anxiety about the appeal of communist parties to the population of devastated postwar Europe, many U.S. policymakers called for the U.S. government to provide economic aid to the European states. Healthy democracies with viable economies, they argued, would serve as bulwarks against further Soviet expansion and would also be rewarding trading partners for U.S. businesses.

In a speech given at Harvard University in 1947, the U.S. secretary of state George C. Marshall (1880–1959) signaled the Truman administration's readiness to engage in a massive European Recovery Program, which came to be known as the Marshall Plan. Between 1948 and 1951, the United States proceeded to distribute almost $13,000,000,000 to seventeen European nations, greatly stimulating the economies of western and southern Europe.

From The Marshall Plan Speech, by George C. Marshall, For European Recovery: The Fiftieth Anniversary of the Marshall Plan web page, www.loc.gov/exhibits/marshall/ [accessed 11/21/01].

*   *   *

I need not tell you that the world situation is very serious. That must be apparent to all intelligent people. I think one difficulty is that the problem is one of such enormous complexity that the very mass of facts presented to the public by press and radio make it exceedingly difficult for the man in the street to reach a clear appraisement of the situation. Furthermore, the people of this country are distant from the troubled areas of the earth and it is hard for them to comprehend the plight and consequent reactions of the long-suffering peoples, and the effect of those reactions on their governments in connection with our efforts to promote peace in the world.

In considering the requirements for the rehabilitation of Europe, the physical loss of life, the visible destruction of cities, factories, mines, and railroads was correctly estimated, but it has become obvious during recent months that this visible destruction was probably less serious than the dislocation of the entire fabric of European economy. For the past ten years conditions have been abnormal. The feverish preparation for war and the more feverish maintenance of the war effort engulfed all aspects of national economies. Machinery has fallen into disrepair or is entirely obsolete. Under the arbitrary and destructive Nazi rule, virtually every possible enterprise was geared into the German war machine. Long-standing commercial ties, private institutions, banks, insurance companies, and shipping companies disappeared through loss of capital, absorption through nationalization, or by simple destruction. In many countries, confidence in the local currency has been severely shaken. The breakdown of the business structure of Europe during the war was complete. Recovery has been seriously retarded by the fact that two years after the close of hostilities a peace settlement with Germany and Austria has not been agreed upon. But even given a more prompt solution of these difficult problems, the rehabilitation of the economic structure of Europe quite evidently will require a much longer time and greater effort than has been foreseen.

There is a phase of this matter which is both interesting and serious. The farmer has always produced the foodstuffs to exchange with the city dweller for the other necessities of life. This division of labor is the basis of modern civilization. At the present time it is threatened with breakdown. The town and city industries are not producing adequate goods to exchange with the food-producing farmer. Raw materials and fuel are in short supply. Machinery is lacking or worn out. The farmer or the peasant cannot find the goods for sale which he desires to purchase. So the sale of his farm produce for money which he cannot use seems to him an unprofitable transaction. He, therefore, has withdrawn many fields from crop cultivation and is using them for grazing. He feeds more grain to stock and finds for himself and his family an ample supply of food, however short he may be on clothing and the other ordinary gadgets of civilization. Meanwhile, people in the cities are short of food and fuel, and in some places approaching the starvation levels. So the governments are forced to use their foreign money and credits to procure these necessities abroad. This process exhausts funds which are urgently needed for reconstruction. Thus a very serious situation is rapidly developing which bodes no good for the world. The modern system of the division of labor upon which the exchange of products is based is in danger of breaking down.

The truth of the matter is that Europe's requirements for the next three or four years of foreign food and other essential products—principally from America—are so much greater than her present ability to pay that she must have substantial additional help or face economic, social, and political deterioration of a very grave character.

The remedy lies in breaking the vicious circle and restoring the confidence of the European people in the economic future of their own countries and of Europe as a whole. The manufacturer and the farmer throughout wide areas must be able and willing to exchange their product for currencies, the continuing value of which is not open to question.

Aside from the demoralizing effect on the world at large and the possibilities of disturbances arising as a result of the desperation of the people concerned, the consequences to the economy of the United States should be apparent to all. It is logical that the United States should do whatever it is able to do to assist in the return of normal economic health in the world, without which there can be no political stability and no assured peace. Our policy is directed not against any country or doctrine but against hunger, poverty, desperation, and chaos. Its purpose should be the revival of a working economy in the world so as to permit the emergence of political and social conditions in which free institutions can exist. Such assistance, I am convinced, must not be on a piecemeal basis as various crises develop. Any assistance that this Government may render in the future should provide a cure rather than a mere palliative. Any government that is willing to assist in the task of recovery will find full cooperation, I am sure, on the part of the United States Government. Any government which maneuvers to block the recovery of other countries cannot expect help from us. Furthermore, governments, political parties, or groups which seek to perpetuate human misery in order to profit therefrom politically or otherwise will encounter the opposition of the United States.

It is already evident that, before the United States Government can proceed much further in its efforts to alleviate the situation and help start the European world on its way to recovery, there must be some agreement among the countries of Europe as to the requirements of the situation and the part those countries themselves will take in order to give proper effect to whatever action might be undertaken by this Government. It would be neither fitting nor efficacious for this Government to undertake to draw up unilaterally a program designed to place Europe on its feet economically. This is the business of the Europeans. The initiative, I think, must come from Europe. The role of this country should consist of friendly aid in the drafting of a European program and of later support of such a program so far as it may be practical for us to do so. The program

should be a joint one, agreed to by a number, if not all, European nations.

An essential part of any successful action on the part of the United States is an understanding on the part of the people of America of the character of the problem and the remedies to be applied. Political passion and prejudice should have no part. With foresight, and a willingness on the part of our people to face up to the vast responsibility which history has clearly placed upon our country the difficulties I have outlined can and will be overcome.

I am sorry that on each occasion I have said something publicly in regard to our international situation, I've been forced by the necessities of the case to enter into rather technical discussions. But to my mind, it is of vast importance that our people reach some general understanding of what the complications really are, rather than react from a passion or a prejudice or an emotion of the moment. As I said more formally a moment ago, we are remote from the scene of these troubles. It is virtually impossible at this distance merely by reading, or listening, or even seeing photographs or motion pictures, to grasp at all the real significance of the situation. And yet the whole world of the future hangs on a proper judgment. It hangs, I think, to a large extent on the realization of the American people, of just what are the various dominant factors. What are the reactions of the people? What are the justifications of those reactions? What are the sufferings? What is needed? What can best be done? What must be done?

REVIEW QUESTIONS

1. Why, according to Marshall, should the United States have offered economic aid to Europe?
2. What advantages would the United States derive from this aid?
3. What were the risks of not providing aid? To what extent is this speech marked by cold war concerns?
4. How does Marshall's speech compare with Churchill's?

HUNGARIAN UPRISING, BUDAPEST (23 OCTOBER 1956)

Emboldened by Nikita Khrushchev's speech, February 1956, denouncing Stalin's cult of personality as well as by Polish demands for reform in the spring and summer of that year, Hungarian students presented a petition to Soviet officials demanding political freedoms, economic reforms, rule of law, and greater parity between the Soviet Union and Hungary. The petition also requested the removal of Soviet troops, the reappointment of Imre Nagy as premier, and the removal of Stalin's statue, a reviled symbol of the Soviet yoke. Captured in this photo is the momentous beginning to the uprising: During an official parade, a group of marchers broke off in a second formation to pull down the statue of Stalin. On 4 November, after a revolutionary government attempted to withdraw from the Warsaw Pact, Soviet tanks entered the city. In spite of a general strike and armed resistance, the Soviets crushed the rebellion. How does this photo convey the aims of the Hungarian uprising?

NIKITA KHRUSHCHEV

FROM "On the Cult of Personality and Its Consequences"

Stalin's death in 1953 was followed by an intense struggle for power within the Soviet leadership. At midnight on the night of 25 February 1956, the victor of this contest, first secretary Nikita Khrushchev (1894–1971), gave a "secret speech" to the twentieth congress of the Communist Party. In blunt language, Khrushchev denounced Stalin's authoritarianism as a deviation from the Marxist-Leninist principles of the Bolshevik revolution. Later that year, Khrushchev reestablished friendly relations with Yugoslavia's independent communist leader, Tito, demonstrating a new willingness on the part of the Soviet state to tolerate "different roads to Socialism." When he became premier in 1958, Khrushchev rejected the inevitability of war with non-Communist states, cultivating a foreign policy based on "peaceful coexistence."

As a loyal communist, Khrushchev remained committed to single-party rule, the planned economy, and state censorship, but his de-Stalinization campaign produced a notable thaw within the Soviet Union. Many political prisoners were released, and many of those who had died or been imprisoned during Stalin's reign of terror were exonerated of any crimes. Greater intellectual freedom was granted to artists, while ordinary Soviet citizens, who had long suffered as a result of Stalin's single-minded focus on the development of heavy industry, benefited from a redirection of the economy toward greater production of consumer goods.

From *The Stalin Dictatorship: Khrushchev's "Secret Speech" and Other Documents*, edited by T. H. Rigby (Sydney: Sydney University Press, 1968), pp. 23–25, 29–32, 36–37, 52–53, 58–62, 65, 84.

Comrades! In the report of the Central Committee of the party at the 20th Congress, in a number of speeches by delegates to the Congress, as well as before this during plenary sessions of the CPSU Central Committee, quite a lot has been said about the cult of the individual and about its harmful consequences.

After Stalin's death the Central Committee of the party began to implement a policy of explaining concisely and consistently that it is impermissible and foreign to the spirit of Marxism-Leninism to elevate one person, to transform him into a superman possessing supernatural characteristics akin to those of a god. Such a man supposedly knows everything, sees everything, thinks for everyone, can do anything, and is infallible in his behaviour.

This kind of belief about a man, namely about Stalin, was cultivated among us for many years.

*　　*　　*

The great modesty of the genius of the revolution, Vladimir Ilyich Lenin, is known. Lenin always stressed the role of the people as the creator of history, the directing and organizational role of the party as a living and creative organism, and also the role of the Central Committee.

Marxism does not negate the role of the leaders of the workers' class in directing the revolutionary liberation movement.

While ascribing great importance to the role of the leaders and organizers of the masses, Lenin at the same time mercilessly stigmatized every manifestation of the cult of the individual, inexorably combated views which are foreign to Marxism, about the "hero" and the "crowd," and countered all efforts to oppose the 'hero' to the masses and to the people.

*   *   *

In addition to the great accomplishments of V. I. Lenin for the victory of the working class and of the working peasants, for the victory of our party and for the application of the ideas of scientific communism to life, his acute mind expressed itself also, in the fact that he detected in Stalin in time those negative characteristics which resulted later in grave consequences.

*   *   *

Stalin acted not through persuasion, explanation, and patient co-operation with people, but by imposing his concepts and demanding absolute submission to his opinion. Whoever opposed this concept or tried to prove his viewpoint, and the correctness of his position, was doomed to removal from the leading collective and to subsequent moral and physical annihilation. This was especially true during the period following the 17th Party Congress [in 1934], when many prominent party leaders and rank-and-file party workers, honest and dedicated to the cause of communism, fell victim to Stalin's despotism.

*   *   *

It was precisely during this period (1935–1937–1938) that the practice of mass repression through the government apparatus was born, first against the enemies of Leninism—Trotskyites, Zinovievites, Bukharinites, long since politically defeated by the party, and subsequently also against many honest communists, against those party cadres who had borne the heavy load of the Civil War and the first and most difficult years of industrialization and collectivization, who actively fought against the Trotskyites and the rightists for the Leninist party line.

Stalin originated the concept "enemy of the people." This term automatically rendered it unnecessary that the ideological errors of a man or men engaged in a controversy be proven; this term made possible the employment of the most cruel repression, violating all norms of revolutionary legality, against anyone who in any way disagreed with Stalin, against those who were only suspected of hostile intent, against those who had bad reputations. This concept, "enemy of the people," actually eliminated the possibility of any kind of ideological struggle or the making of one's views known on this or that issue, even those of a practical character. In the main, and in actuality, the only proof of guilt used, against all norms of current legal science, was the "confession" of the accused himself; and, as subsequent probing proved, "confessions" were acquired through physical pressures against the accused.

*   *   *

[Stalin] discarded the Leninist method of convincing and educating; he abandoned the method of ideological struggle for that of administrative violence, mass repressions, and terror. He acted on an increasingly larger scale and more stubbornly through punitive organs, at the same time often violating all existing norms of morality and of Soviet laws.

Arbitrary behavior by one person encouraged and permitted arbitrariness in others. Mass arrests and deportations of many thousands of people, execution without trial and without normal investigation created conditions of insecurity, fear and even desperation.

This, of course, did not contribute toward unity of the party ranks and of all strata of working people, but on the contrary brought about the annihilation and expulsion from the party of workers who were loyal but inconvenient to Stalin.

*   *   *

Were our party's sacred Leninist principles observed after the death of Vladimir Ilyich?

Whereas during the first few years after Lenin's death party congresses and Central Committee plenums took place more or less regularly, later, when Stalin began increasingly to abuse his power, these principles were crudely violated. This was especially evident during the last 15 years of his life. Was it a normal situation when over 13 years elapsed between the 18th and 19th Party Congresses, years during which our party and our country experienced so many important events? These events demanded categorically that the party pass resolutions pertaining to the country's defense during the Patriotic War and to peacetime construction after the war. Even after the end of the war a congress was not convened for over 7 years.

*   *   *

In practice Stalin ignored the norms of party life and trampled on the Leninist principle of collective party leadership.

Stalin's arbitrariness *vis-à-vis* the party and its Central Committee became fully evident after the 17th Party Congress which took place in 1934.

*   *   *

It has been established that of the 139 members and candidates of the Party's Central Committee who were elected at the 17th Congress, 98 persons, i.e. 70 percent, were arrested and shot (mostly in 1937–1938). *(Indignation in the hall.)*

*   *   *

The power accumulated in the hands of one person, Stalin, led to serious consequences during the Great Patriotic War.

When we look at many of our novels, films and historical "scientific studies," the role of Stalin in the Patriotic War appears to be entirely improbable. Stalin had foreseen everything. The So-

viet Army, on the basis of a strategic plan prepared by Stalin long before, used the tactics of so-called "active defense," i.e., tactics which, as we know, allowed the Germans to come up to Moscow and Stalingrad. Using such tactics the Soviet Army, supposedly thanks only to Stalin's genius, turned to the offensive and subdued the enemy. The epic victory gained through the armed might of the Land of the Soviets, through our heroic people is ascribed in this type of novel, film and "scientific study" as being completely due to the strategic genius of Stalin.

*   *   *

During the war and after the war Stalin put forward the thesis that the tragedy which our nation experienced in the first part of the war was the result of the "unexpected" attack of the Germans against the Soviet Union. But, Comrades, this is completely untrue. As soon as Hitler came to power in Germany he assigned himself the task of liquidating communism. The fascists were saying this openly; they did not hide their plans. In order to attain this aggressive end all sorts of pacts and blocs were created, such as the famous Berlin-Rome-Tokyo axis. Many facts from the pre-war period clearly showed that Hitler was going all out to begin a war against the Soviet state and that he had concentrated large armed units, together with armored units, near the Soviet borders.

Documents which have now been published show that by April 3, 1941, Churchill, through his ambassador to the U.S.S.R., Cripps, personally warned Stalin that the Germans had begun regrouping their armed units with the intent of attacking the Soviet Union. It is self-evident that Churchill did not do this at all because of his friendly feeling toward the Soviet nation. He had in this his own imperialistic goals—to bring Germany and the U.S.S.R. into a bloody war and thereby to strengthen the position of the British Empire. Just the same, Churchill affirmed in his writings that he sought to "warn Stalin and call his attention to the danger which threatened him." Churchill stressed this repeatedly in his dispatches of April 18 and in the following days. However,

Stalin took no heed of these warnings. What is more, Stalin ordered that no credence be given to information of this sort, in order not to provoke the initiation of military operations.

* * *

When there developed an exceptionally serious situation for our army in 1942 in the Kharkov region, we correctly decided to drop an operation whose objective had been to encircle Kharkov, because the real situation at that time would have threatened our army with fatal consequences if this operation had been proceeded with.

We communicated this to Stalin, stating that the situation demanded changes in operational plans in order to prevent the enemy from liquidating a sizable concentration of our army.

Contrary to common sense, Stalin rejected our suggestion and issued the order to continue the operation aimed at the encirclement of Kharkov, despite the fact that at this time many army concentrations were themselves actually threatened with encirclement and liquidation.

* * *

And what was the result of this? The worst that we had expected. The Germans surrounded our army concentrations and consequently we lost hundreds of thousands of our soldiers. This is Stalin's military "genius"; this what it cost us. (*Movement in the hall.*)

* * *

In the same vein, let us take, for instance, our historical and military films and some works of literature; they make us feel sick. Their true objective is the propagation of the theme of praising Stalin as a military genius. Let us recall the film, "The Fall of Berlin." Here only Stalin acts; he issues orders in the hall in which there are many empty chairs and only one man approaches him and reports something to him—that is Poskrebyshev, his loyal shieldbearer. (*Laughter in the hall.*)

And where is the military command? Where is the Political Bureau? Where is the Government? What are they doing and with what are they engaged? There is nothing about them in the film. Stalin acts for everybody; he does not reckon with anyone, he asks no one for advice. Everything is shown to the nation in this false light. Why? In order to surround Stalin with glory, contrary to the facts and contrary to historical truth.

* * *

Not Stalin, but the party as a whole, the Soviet Government, our heroic army, its talented leaders and brave soldiers, the whole Soviet nation— these are the ones who assured the victory in the Great Patriotic War. (*Tempestuous and prolonged applause.*)

* * *

Comrades, let us reach for some other facts. The Soviet Union is justly considered as a model of a multi-national state because we have in practice assured the equality and friendship of all nations which live in our great fatherland.

All the more monstrous are the acts whose initiator was Stalin and which represent crude violations of the basic Leninist principles of the nationality policy of the Soviet state. We refer to the mass deportations from their native places of whole nations, together with all communists and komsomol members without any exception; this deportation action was not dictated by any military considerations.

Thus, as early as the end of 1943, when there occurred a permanent breakthrough at the fronts of the Great Patriotic War benefiting the Soviet Union, a decision was taken and carried out concerning the deportation of all the Karachai from the lands on which they lived. In the same period, at the end of December 1943, the same lot befell the whole population of the Kalmyk Autonomous Republic. In March 1944 all the Chechen and Ingush peoples were deported and the Chechen-Ingush Autonomous Republic was liquidated. In April 1944, all Balkars were deported to faraway places from the territory of the Kabardino-Balkar Autonomous Republic and the Republic itself was renamed the Karbardin Autonomous Republic.

The Ukrainians avoided meeting this fate only because there were too many of them and there was no place to which to deport them. Otherwise, he would have deported them also. *(Laughter and animation in the hall.)*

*   *   *

The willfulness of Stalin showed itself not only in decisions concerning the internal life of the country but also in the international relations of the Soviet Union.

The July plenary session of the Central Committee studied in detail the reasons for the development of conflict with Yugoslavia. It was a shameful role which Stalin played here. The "Yugoslav affair" contained no problems which could not have been solved through party discussions among comrades. There was no significant basis for the development of this "affair"; it was completely possible to have prevented the rupture of relations with that country. This does not mean, however, that the Yugoslav leaders did not make mistakes or did not have shortcomings. But these mistakes and shortcomings were magnified in a monstrous manner by Stalin, which resulted in a break of relations with a friendly country.

*   *   *

Comrades! The 20th Congress of the Communist Party of the Soviet Union has manifested with a new strength the unshakable unity of our party, its cohesiveness around the Central Committee, its resolute will to accomplish the great task of building communism. *(Tumultuous applause.)* And the fact that we present in all their ramifications the basic problems of overcoming the cult of the individual which is alien to Marxism-Leninism, as well as the problem of liquidating its burdensome consequences, is evidence of the great moral and political strength of our party. *(Prolonged applause.)*

We are absolutely certain that our party, armed with the historical resolutions of the 20th Congress, will lead the Soviet people along the Leninist path to new successes, to new victories. *(Tumultuous, prolonged applause.)*

Long live the victorious banner of our party —Leninism! *(Tumultuous, prolonged applause ending in ovation. All rise.)*

REVIEW QUESTIONS

1. What was the cult of personality?
2. In what sense did Stalin's style of rule represent a violation of Marxist-Leninist theory according to Khrushchev?
3. What specific errors is Stalin accused of in this speech?
4. What do these accusations tell you about Khrushchev's intentions as the new leader of the Soviet Union?

French Students and Workers Unite in Protest

In the Soviet bloc, the brief easing in state repression initiated by Khrushchev came to an end with his abrupt fall from power in 1964. Under Leonid Brezhnev the Soviet political leadership returned to more traditional policies, although Stalinism was not revived. When the Czechoslovakian leadership sought to loosen its ties to the Soviet Union in 1968, tanks and Soviet troops soon put an end to the Prague Spring.

During this same period, the centrist governments and white-collar bureaucrats of Western Europe cooperated to produce unprecedentedly prosperous economies. Yet

STUDENT UPRISING IN PARIS (MAY 1968)

In May 1968, sparked by the government's announcement to close a French university in Nanterre, students of the Sorbonne University in Paris protested with street demonstrations, which quickly broadened into political protests against the French state. The protests escalated into a national crisis after thousands of workers went on strike to support the students' grievances. Although government officials sought to deny the magnitude and significance of the May protests, such photos as the one here were instrumental in eliciting popular support by communicating the revolutionary mood of Paris to a national audience. Following revolts in communist Europe and colonial Africa in the 1950s and 1960s, why did this image of Paris shock the French nation in 1968?

affluence and political stability generated their own frustrations: young people, especially, rejected the stodgy conformity of their elders, calling for a radical recasting of social, political, and economic relations. De-Stalinization in the East had stimulated the revival of Socialist and Communist Parties in the West, and this inspired a new generation of radical activists operating outside of the established left-wing parties. In 1968, French students in Paris followed the lead of their Czechoslovakian counterparts, engaging in violent protests against the stifling traditionalism of the universities and against the conservatism of Charles de Gaulle's government. They were eventually joined by as many as ten million striking workers, bringing France to a virtual standstill in mid-1968.

From *Writing on the Wall, France 1968: A Documentary Anthology,* by Vladimir Fisera (New York: St. Martin's Press, 1978), pp. 133–34, 138–39.

Your Struggle Is Our Struggle!

We are occupying the faculties, you are occupying the factories. Aren't we fighting for the same thing? Higher education only contains 10 per cent workers' children. Are we fighting so that there will be more of them, for a democratic university reform? That would be a good thing, but it's not the most important. These workers' children would just become like other students. We are not aiming for a worker's son to be a manager. We want to wipe out segregation between workers and management.

There are students who are unable to find jobs on leaving university. Are we fighting so that they'll find jobs, for a decent graduate employment policy? It would be a good thing, but it is not vital. Psychology or sociology graduates will become the selectors, the planners and psycho-technicians who will try to organise your working conditions; mathematics graduates will become engineers, perfecting maximum-productivity machines to make your life even more unbearable. Why are we, students who are products of a middle-class life, criticising capitalist society? The son of a worker who becomes a student leaves his own class. For the son of a middle-class family, it could be his opportunity to see his class in its true light, to question the role he is destined for in society and the organisation of our society. We refuse to become scholars who are out of touch

with real life. We refuse to be used for the benefit of the ruling class. We want to destroy the separation that exists between those who organise and think and those who execute their decisions. We want to form a classless society; your cause is the same as ours.

You are asking for a minimum wage of 1,000 francs in the Paris area, retirement at sixty, a 40-hour week for 48 hours' pay.

These are long-standing and just demands: nevertheless, they seem to be out of context with our aims. Yet you have gone on to occupy factories, take your managers as hostages, strike without warning. These forms of struggle have been made possible by perseverence and lengthy action in various enterprises, and because of the recent student battles.

These struggles are even more radical than our official aims, because they go further than simply seeking improvements for the worker within the capitalist system, they imply the destruction of the system. They are political in the true sense of the word: you are fighting not to change the Prime Minister, but so that your boss no longer retains his power in business or society. The form that your struggle has taken offers us students the model for true socialist activity: the appropriation of the means of production and of the decision-making power by the workers.

Our struggles converge. We must destroy everything that seeks to alienate us (everyday habits, the press, etc.). We must combine our occupations in the faculties and factories.

Long live the unification of our struggles!

The Workers' Red Flag Is Flying over Renault: Down with the Anti-Popular Gaullist Régime

For ten years the working class has gradually fought to gain unity in each factory; to defend in each company its working conditions, which are systematically attacked by the big capitalists. Workers' fights have succeeded in containing the bosses' offensive, but the division of the workers' forces and the policy of class collaboration which has become the rule *even at the level of the confederate leadership of the CGT*[1] have prevented the mass struggles from bringing about the downfall of the anti-popular régime of unemployment and poverty.

For a month now the progressive students who reject the bourgeois university, who want to be on the side of the people struggling against the bosses' régime, have put their full strength into the battle. *By their tenacity, their resolution, their desire to link their struggle with that of the working class, which is the main force in the struggle against the big capitalist bosses and the government,* the mass of progressive students has been able to strike a resounding blow against Gaullism. The workers have understood this: the progressive current in the student movement reflects the desire of the people to fight, its desire to get rid of Gaullism. The progressive students' determination has reminded the workers that only forceful action pays off. The class-collaborating unions which have encouraged the workers to demonstrate peacefully and with dignity only in order to receive alms, the unions which have sabotaged the mass strug-

gles at Caen, at La Rhodia in Lyon, at Schwarz-Haumont, at Alluvac, at Alès in the ceramics industry, at Dassault, at Renault, *can today no longer resist the drive of the working masses.*

The battle flag has passed into the hands of the proletariat. The leaders of the CGT have first of all attacked the students' progressive movement in a disgusting way, using the same phrases as the government is using. Then, when the workers demonstrated their desire to intervene in force to take the lead in the battle against capitalism and its régime, the CGT and PCF[2] leaderships called for a strike with petty-bourgeois, academic slogans. But the workers understood, and put all their strength into the battle.

The government wishes to quell the revolt; Pompidou has just said so. The government is panic-stricken. The repression of the workers and the progressive students, the repression of the real communists who are fighting for popular victory, will change nothing. People's hatred of the class enemy will increase tenfold. A tremendous force is rising today. *The people will win!*

Against unemployment, starvation wages, fiendish work rates. Against police and bosses' repression. Freedom for the people!

REVIEW QUESTIONS

1. In what sense was the workers' struggle also the students' struggle?
2. What specific reforms were students and workers seeking?
3. What were their broader goals?
4. Why did radical workers at Renault reject the leadership of the General Confederation of Labor and the French Communist Party?
5. Why did they seek to ally their movement with that of the student protesters?

---

[1] *Confédération Générale du Travail* ("General Confederation of Labor"), a communist labor union.

[2] *Parti Communiste Français* ("French Communist Party").

MARGARET THATCHER

FROM Speech to the Conservative Party Conference

*The international financial crisis precipitated by the Arab oil embargo of 1973
served to revitalize conservative movements in the mid- to late 1970s. In the face of
tightened economic circumstances, the right wing in the United States and much of
Western Europe sought to dismantle the social welfare systems created by postwar
governments. In the United States, this trend resulted in the election of Ronald Reagan (born 1911), who served as president from 1980 to 1988. In Britain, it brought
the conservative Tories to power from 1979 to 1997.*

*In 1975, Margaret Thatcher (born 1925) was chosen as the new leader of the
British Conservative Party. The first woman ever to be elected prime minister in a
European nation, she served in this position for three consecutive terms, from 1979
to 1990. Thatcher was a new conservative, committed to breaking with the tax-and-
spend policies of previous governments, whether right or left. A fierce opponent of
trade unions, she drew her support largely from the upper and upper-middle classes,
although a critical minority of Tory workers gave Conservatives an edge in elections.
During her tenure in office, Thatcher limited state intervention in the British economy, privatized many state-owned industries, and reduced taxes by substantially decreasing government spending, especially for social services and welfare.
Unemployment increased substantially during her years in power, but many members of her upper-class constituency benefited from lower taxes and the government's
probusiness policies. The following speech, her first as head of the Conservative
Party, given 10 October 1975, provides a blueprint for the Thatcher Revolution, and
demonstrates the often biting wit of the Iron Lady.*

From *The Revival of Britain: Speeches on Home and European Affairs, 1975–1988*, by Margaret
Thatcher, edited by Alastair Cooke (London: Aurum Press, 1989), pp. 19–28.

*   *   *

Our Leaders have been different men with different qualities and different styles, but they all
had one thing in common: each met the challenge
of his time.

Now, what is the challenge of our time? I believe there are two: to overcome the country's
economic and financial problems, and to regain
our confidence in Britain and ourselves.

*   *   *

Whatever could I say about Britain that is half
as damaging as what this Labour Government has
done to our country? Let us look at the record. It
is the Labour Government that has caused prices
to rise at a record rate of 26 per cent a year. They
told us the Social Contract would solve everything,
but now everyone can see that the so-called Contract was a fraud—a fraud for which the people
of this country have had to pay a very high price.
It is the Labour Government whose past policies
are forcing unemployment higher than it need
ever have been. Thousands more men and women

are losing their jobs every day, and there are going to be men and women, many of them youngsters straight out of school, who will be without a job this winter because Socialist Ministers spent last year attacking us instead of attacking inflation.

It is the Labour Government that brought the level of production below that of the three-day week in 1974. We have really got a three-day week now, only it takes five days to do it. It is the Labour Government that has brought us record peace-time taxation. They have the usual Socialist disease: they have run out of other people's money. It is the Labour Government that has pushed public spending to record levels. How have they done it? By borrowing and borrowing. Never in the field of human credit has so much been owed.

Serious as the economic challenge is, the political and moral challenge is just as grave and perhaps even more so, because economic problems never start with economics. They have much deeper roots in human nature and roots in politics, and they do not finish at economics either. Labour's failure to cope, to look at the nation's problems from the viewpoint of the whole nation, and not just one section of it, has led to a loss of confidence, and to a sense of helplessness; and with it goes a feeling that Parliament, which ought to be in charge, is not in charge, and that the actions and decisions are taken elsewhere.

It goes even deeper than that, to the voices that seem anxious not to overcome our economic difficulties, but to exploit them, to destroy the free enterprise society and put a Marxist system in its place. Today those voices form a sizeable chorus in the parliamentary Labour Party, a chorus which, aided and abetted by the many constituency Labour Parties, seems to be growing in numbers.

*　　*　　*

I sometimes think the Labour Party is like a pub where the mild is running out. If someone does not do something soon all that is left will be bitter, and all that is bitter will be Left.

Whenever I visit Communist countries their politicians never hesitate to boast about their achievements. They know them all by heart; they reel off the facts and figures, claiming this is the rich harvest of the Communist system. Yet they are not prosperous as we in the West are prosperous, and they are not free as we in the West are free.

Our capitalist system produces a far higher standard of prosperity and happiness because it believes in incentive and opportunity, and because it is founded on human dignity and freedom. Even the Russians have to go to a capitalist country—America—to buy enough wheat to feed their people—and that after more than fifty years of a State-controlled economy. Yet they boast incessantly, while we, who have so much more to boast about, for ever criticize and decry. Is it not time we spoke up for our way of life? After all, no Western nation has to build a wall round itself to keep its people in.

So let us have no truck with those who say the free enterprise system has failed. What we face today is not a crisis of capitalism but of Socialism. No country can flourish if its economic and social life is dominated by nationalization and State control.

The cause of our shortcomings does not, therefore, lie in private enterprise. Our problem is not that we have too little Socialism. It is that we have too much. If only the Labour Party in this country would act like Social Democrats in West Germany. If only they would stop trying to prove their Socialist virility by relentlessly nationalizing one industry after another.

Of course, a halt to further State control will not on its own restore our belief in ourselves, because something else is happening to this country. We are witnessing a deliberate attack on our values, a deliberate attack on those who wish to promote merit and excellence, a deliberate attack on our heritage and our great past, and there are those who gnaw away at our national self-respect, rewriting British history as centuries of unrelieved gloom, oppression and failure—as days of hopelessness, not days of hope. And others, under the shelter of our education system, are ruthlessly attacking the minds of the young. Everyone who believes in freedom must be appalled at the tactics employed by the far Left in the systematic destruction of the North London Polytechnic—blatant tactics of intimidation designed to undermine the fundamental beliefs and values of every student, tactics pursued by people who are the first to insist on their own civil rights while seeking to deny them to the rest of us.

We must not be bullied or brainwashed out of our beliefs. No wonder so many of our people, some of the best and the brightest, are depressed and talking of emigrating. Even so, I think they are wrong. They are giving up too soon. Many of the things we hold dear are threatened as never before, but none has yet been lost, so stay here, stay and help us defeat Socialism so that the Britain you have known may be the Britain your children will know.

These are the two great challenges of our time—the moral and political challenge, and the economic challenge. They have to be faced together and we have to master them both.

What are our chances of success? It depends on what kind of people we are. What kind of people are we? We are the people that in the past made Great Britain the workshop of the world, the people who persuaded others to buy British, not by begging them to do so but because it was best.

*   *   *

We export more of what we produce than either West Germany, France, Japan or the United States, and well over 90 per cent of these exports come from private enterprise. It is a triumph for the private sector and all who work in it, and let us say so loud and clear.

With achievements like that who can doubt that Britain can have a great future, and what our friends abroad want to know is whether that future is going to happen.

Well, how can we Conservatives make it happen? Many of the details have already been dealt with in the Conference debates. But policies and programmes should not just be a list of unrelated items. They are part of a total vision of the kind of life we want for our country and our children. Let me give you my vision: a man's right to work as he will, to spend what he earns, to own property, to have the State as servant and not as master—these are the British inheritance. They are the essence of a free country and on that freedom all our other freedoms depend.

But we want a free economy, not only because it guarantees our liberties, but also because it is the best way of creating wealth and prosperity for the whole country, and it is this prosperity alone which can give us the resources for better services for the community, better services for those in need.

By their attack on private enterprise, this Labour Government has made certain that there will be next to nothing available for improvements in our social services over the next few years. We must get private enterprise back on the road to recovery, not merely to give people more of their own money to spend as they choose, but to have more money to help the old and the sick and the handicapped. And the way to recovery is through profits, good profits today leading to high investment, leading to well-paid jobs, leading to a better standard of living tomorrow. No profits mean no investment and that means a dying industry geared to yesterday's world, and that means fewer jobs tomorrow. Other nations have recognized that for years now, and because they have recognized it they are going ahead faster than we are; and the gap between us will continue to increase unless we change our ways. The trouble here is that for years the Labour Party has made people feel that profits are guilty unless proved innocent.

When I visit factories and companies I do not find that those who actually work in them are against profits; on the contrary, they want to work for a prosperous concern, a concern with a future—their future.

Governments must learn to leave these companies with enough of their own profits to produce the goods and jobs for tomorrow. If the Socialists will not, or cannot, there will be no profit-making industry left to support the losses caused by fresh bouts of nationalization. If anyone should murmur that I am preaching *laissez-faire,* let me say I am not arguing, and have never argued, that all we have to do is to let the economy run by itself. I believe that, just as each of us has an obligation to make the best of his talents, so Governments have an obligation to create the framework within which we can do so—not only individual people, but individual firms and particularly small firms. If they concentrated on doing that, they would do a lot better than they are doing now. Some of the small firms will stay small, but others will expand and become the great companies of the future. The Labour Government has pursued a disastrous vendetta against small businesses and the self-employed. We will reverse its damaging policies.

*   *   *

So today what is the picture? Depressed profits, low investment, no incentive, and, overshadowing everything, Government spending, spending, spending far beyond the taxpayers' means.

To recover, to get from where we are to where we want to be—and I admit we would rather not be here—will take time. "Economic policy," wrote Maynard Keynes, "should not be a matter of tearing up by the roots but of slowly training a plant to grow in a different direction."

It will take time to reduce public spending, to rebuild profits and incentives, and to benefit from the investments which must be made. But the sooner that time starts, the better it will be for Britain's unemployed and for Britain as a whole.

One of the reasons why this Labour Government has incurred more unemployment than any Conservative Government since the war is because they have concentrated too much on distributing what we have and too little on seeing that we have more.

We Conservatives hate unemployment. We hate the idea of men and women not being able to use their abilities. We deplore the waste of natural resources and the deep affront to people's dignity from being out of work through no fault

of their own. It is ironic that we should be accused of wanting unemployment to solve our economic problems by the very Government which has produced a record post-war unemployment and is expecting more.

*   *   *

Now let me turn to something I spoke about in America. Some Socialists seem to believe that people should be numbers in a State computer. We believe they should be individuals. We are all unequal. No one, thank heavens, is quite like anyone else, however much the Socialists may pretend otherwise. We believe that everyone has the right to be unequal. But to us, every human being is equally important. Engineers, miners, manual workers, shop assistants, farmworkers, postmen, housewives—these are the essential foundations of our society, and without them there would be no nation. But there are others with special gifts who should also have their chance, because if the adventurers who strike out in new directions in science, technology, medicine, commerce and industry are hobbled, there can be no advance. The spirit of envy can destroy; it can never build. Everyone must be allowed to develop the abilities he knows he has within him, and she knows she has within her, in the way they choose.

Freedom to choose is something we take for granted until it is in danger of being taken away. Socialist Governments set out perpetually to restrict the area of choice, and Conservative Governments to increase it. We believe that you become a responsible citizen by making decisions for yourself, not by having them made for you. But they are made for you by Labour all right!

*   *   *

When the next Conservative Government comes to power many trade unionists will have put it there. Millions of them vote for us at every election. I want to say this to them and to all of our supporters in industry: go out and join in the work of your unions; go to their meetings and stay to the end, and learn the union rules as well as the far Left knows them. Remember that if parliamentary democracy dies, free trade unions die with it.

* * *

There is one part of this country where, tragically, defiance of the law is costing life day after day. In Northern Ireland our troops have the dangerous and thankless task of trying to keep the peace and hold a balance. We are proud of the way they have discharged their duty. This party is pledged to support the unity of the United Kingdom, to preserve that unity and to protect the people, Catholic and Protestant alike. We believe our Armed Forces must remain until a genuine peace is made. Our thoughts are with them and our pride is with them, too.

I have spoken of the challenges which face us here in Britain—the challenge to recover economically and the challenge to recover our belief in ourselves—and I have shown our potential for recovery. I have dealt with some aspects of our strength and approach and I have tried to tell you something of my personal vision and my belief in the standards on which this nation was greatly built, on which it greatly thrived and from which in recent years it has greatly fallen away. I believe

we are coming to yet another turning point in our long history. We can go on as we have been going and continue down, or we can stop and with a decisive act of will say "Enough."

Let all of us here today, and others far beyond this hall who believe in our cause, make that act of will. Let us proclaim our faith in a new and better future for our party and our people; let us resolve to heal the wounds of a divided nation, and let that act of healing be the prelude to a lasting victory.

REVIEW QUESTIONS

1. In what ways, according to Thatcher, had Labour Party rule undermined the British economy?
2. In what ways had it undermined British confidence?
3. On the basis of this speech, what specific policies would Thatcher be likely to pursue once elected as prime minister?
4. To what extent might Thatcher's conservatism be considered a product of the general economic malaise of the 1970s?

JEAN-YVES POTEL

FROM *The Promise of Solidarity: Inside the Polish Workers' Struggle, 1980–82*

While conservatives in the West lashed out at organized labor, in Poland a revitalized and independent workers' movement pitted itself against the entrenched communist authorities. Poland's weak and backward economy produced simmering unrest among workers. When the government announced food price increases in 1970, a wave of strikes broke out; force was used to end these protests, resulting in the deaths of one hundred workers. A second wave of strikes in 1976, again sparked by food costs, was also firmly repressed, but this time without bloodshed.

In August 1980, scattered strikes broke out across industrialized Poland, again in response to increased food prices. In mid-August, 17,000 workers at the Lenin Ship-yards in Gdansk went out on strike, at first demanding increased wages but eventually expanding their demands to include greater political liberties and the right to organize independent trade unions. Under the leadership of Lech Walesa, a shipyard electrician who had been fired for his participation in the worker protests of 1976, the strikers won concessions from management on bread-and-butter issues but then decided to continue their protest in solidarity with other Polish workers. French journalist Jean-Yves Potel, who witnessed these events, provided the following report on the early stages of the Gdansk strike.

From *The Promise of Solidarity: Inside the Polish Workers' Struggle, 1980–82*, by Jean-Yves Potel, translated by Phil Markham (New York: Praeger, 1982).

*   *   *

The strike that had broken out on the shores of the Baltic Sea one day in August 1980 was an event capable of reviving abandoned hopes. Like an unexpected breeze, it breathed life into them. It set them buzzing. It confounded the sceptics, and worried the strategists. Because this was a most unusual strike. It was innovative, capable of astounding and transforming. It was strong and unified. It shook up a system many had thought immovable. It revived prospects and desires that people had almost forgotten. The march of history was set in motion again.

Such was Poland in the summer of 1980. A Poland where the strike arrived, quietly, and spread, gathering strength, and consuming all around it. Calmly and peacefully.

For the third time, the trigger seemed clear enough. As in the two preceding times food prices were to go up.

*   *   *

Andrzej stood there with seven posters rolled under his arm. It was 5.00 am at the *Lenin* ship-yard, Thursday 14 August. He was waiting for Bogdan. Kazik arrived—whom he had also arranged to meet the previous evening. Kazik worked in the W3 section. They went over to the section. A few minutes later, workers changing in that section's locker room saw a poster stuck up

under the clock which read: "We demand a 1,000 zloty wage rise, a cost-of-living bonus, and news on the sacking of Anna Walentynowicz!" Groups of workers gathered and asked for more detailed information.

*   *   *

In the central square there were by now several thousand men and women, cheerfully waiting there. Neither Andrzej and Kazik, nor Jurek and Bogdan, who eventually arrived with the workers from their department, imagined that this spot would give birth to the most important strike in the history of "people's" Poland.

*   *   *

The procession set off again, with the banner at its head. It was a fine morning. They strolled along, whistling, singing, and calling out those who were still in their sections. At the far end of the shipyard, Wojcik, the yard's director, or at least, the man who thought he was still director of the yard, waited. His first words were:

"What's all this about?"

"It's a strike," they all choroused.

"Why?"

"Because you've sacked Anna Walentynowicz."

"Anna Walentynowicz?" replied the director, with feigned surprise.

Somebody refreshed his memory: "She's been

sacked without warning. It's disgraceful, somebody like her . . . A woman who's been decorated with three Orders of Merit—bronze, silver and gold. She's got 30 years of work behind her, and only five months to go before she retires." The director made as if to protest. "We don't want to talk with you now!" shouted Bogdan in his direction. And the crowd set off again, leaving the director to his own thoughts.

The workers began to organise. Some people remained on the canal bridge, to make sure this route was not cut off. Then they all went to Gate No. 2, where, in 1970, four workers had fallen to police gunfire, and a minute's silence was observed to honour their memory. Before long, thousands of workers of all ages were gathered in the square, around the mechanical excavator. Somebody climbed up and made the first speech: "We must elect a strike committee. We need trusted people from each squad . . ." At that moment the director appeared, with his entourage. They set him up on the excavator, and for a few moments he was able to speak: "What more do you want? You get 9,000 zloty per month—isn't that enough?" He was unable to say much more. From the crowd came a great roar of protest, whistling and people speaking all at the same time. Was the director really so unaware of the huge disparities in rates of pay?!

It was at this point that Lech Walesa came out of the ranks. He had got into the shipyard by shinning over one of the gates. "Do you recognise me? I worked here for ten years. You sacked me in 1976 for being involved in a strike. But I still consider myself a dockworker. I have everyone's trust!" The crowd roared its approval. A number of workers hoisted him on their shoulders, and he said: "We are going on strike and occupying the plant!" The director could not get another word in—he was drowned out by the "Hurrah! Hurrah!" which rose from the crowd. They demanded that the loudspeakers of the yard's internal broadcast system be connected up, so that everybody could hear what was said.

Somebody shouted: "We must go and find Anna Walentynowicz." Another chimed in: "With

the manager's car . . ." The manager protested, but the strikers were determined, and the driver had to do what they said.

They still had to negotiate the rest of their demands, so they needed to elect delegates and draw up a list of priority demands. They decided to go back into their sections. There were more than a hundred sections in that enormous shipyard. Each section elected one or two delegates, mandated on a set of precise demands, and at the start of the afternoon they got up one after another, perched on the excavator, to present their section's case to the crowd. People cheered and sang, in a kind of relaxed party atmosphere. Then the 200 delegates assembled in the conference hall next to the canteen. This general assembly laid out 11 basic demands, which were far more radical than those of the July strikes. They were both political and economic demands with the former taking priority. They took as their starting point the advanced demand of the Lublin workers for the dissolution of the (official) trade union factory council. Other demands already pointed to the Gdansk strikers' role as leading the whole of the Polish working class. They demanded the release of political prisoners; the reinstatement of all those sacked; family allowance parity with the militia; and the erection of a monument in front of the shipyard gates to the memory of the martyrs of 1970.

The delegates also set up a 'negotiating committee' of about 20 workers, headed by Lech Walesa. Anna Walentynowicz was also on it. She had just arrived, and visibly moved by this first victory, she spoke to the strikers: "We are firmly resolved to carry forward our movement until our demands are satisfied," she concluded. A workers' militia was set up to make sure that everything went smoothly in each section, and to prevent provocations. Stewards were stationed at the entrances to the shipyard. The 1970 massacres were still fresh in everyone's minds: the shipyard was to be occupied, but they were not venturing out into the streets.

At the start of the afternoon, negotiations began in the conference hall, under the dull gaze of a statue of Lenin erected by the authorities. Facing the workers' delegates sat the yard's manager, accompanied by Tadeusz Fiszbach, First Secretary of the Party in Gdansk. The discussions were stormy, and continued till daybreak. Management gave way very fast on the question of reinstating those sacked, and on the construction of a monument in memory of the victims of 1970. They also undertook that there would be no reprisals against the strike committee, and that family allowances would be brought in line with those of the militia. On the other demands they suggested a fresh meeting two or three weeks later.

This was unacceptable: "If we are going to negotiate, we do it here and now!" said one delegate. The manager would have none of it. He would only agree to a 1,200 zloty wage rise (the workers were demanding 2,000), and said that he was not authorised to negotiate on the other points. Talks were broken off. Management agreed to return at five in the morning. They never came back. The workers were already settling in for their first night in the shipyard.

In Gdansk itself the news of a strike at the *Lenin* shipyard—already the symbol of so many important struggles—spread like wildfire. By four in the morning tram drivers were stopping work in sympathy. Only the electric train serving the Three Towns continued to run. As usual, it unloaded thousands of workers in front of their factory gates. That Friday morning, everybody knew that they would be discussing strike action. For example, the morning shift at the *Paris Commune* yard in Gdynia: from the moment they arrived there was an air of expectancy, and nobody really started working. They talked among themselves. At around 7.30 am, groups of workers gathered in the two largest departments, the K2 and K3 hull-construction sections. A group of them came out and marched towards the management office. Almost immediately the other departments emptied, with workers downing tools and following the demonstration.

Andrzej Kolodziej, a young 20-year old worker, was at the head of the march. He didn't work at the Gdynia yard, but had just spent the night at the *Lenin* shipyard, from which he had been sacked in January 1980. Everyone knew him from his earlier activities. They listened to him and they trusted him. The demonstration marched towards the management building. "This is too soon," Kolodziej explained. "We are not ready. They may organise a provocation to divide us." He led the crowd towards the central square, next to the main gate. This spot was to become the venue for all meetings in the weeks to come. The workers needed to get organised, to decide on their objectives. They elected a 20-person strike committee, of which Andrzej Kolodziej was naturally elected President, and before negotiating they decided to get in touch with the Gdansk workers. *Act together*—that was their main principle.

*   *   *

At the *Lenin* shipyard, negotiations resumed at seven o'clock on Saturday morning, but proved fruitless. Once again, talks were broken off. They began again at 11 o'clock. This time management offered a 1,500 zloty wage rise plus a cost of living bonus. Outside, the workers, who were following every word of the negotiations, began to shout: "Two thousand! Two thousand!" The negotiator asked for a delegate vote. The majority of delegates accepted the compromise offered by the management, but first it had to be put into writing. After a brief withdrawal, the management returned with a document. It was signed. At 3.00 pm, in line with the majority vote, Lech Walesa announced that the occupation of the shipyard had ended.

At this point the movement entered a critical phase. The decision to end the occupation was not accepted. People wanted to continue.

*   *   *

Delegations from other factories arrived at the yard. They were alarmed: "If you return to work," explained a representative from a bus depot, "nobody else will win anything." He was applauded. Walesa stood up to speak, and in a quiet voice this 40-year old man turned the situation on its head: "We must respect democracy," he said, "and therefore accept the compromise, even if it is not brilliant; but we do not have the right to abandon others. We must continue the strike, out of solidarity, until everyone has won."

*   *   *

It was at this moment that the name "Solidarity" was born. Leszek said: "We will continue, in solidarity with all workers in Poland." The gates were closed again, and the strike began anew.

This was a historic moment. Effectively the strike was no longer a simple collective protest, a defence against rising prices. That phase, which had begun at the start of July had now come to an end. In its place came a political offensive by the whole of the Polish working class, an offensive that was better organised and more resolute than ever before.

*   *   *

REVIEW QUESTIONS

1. Why did the workers at Gdansk go out on strike?
2. What were their initial demands? What new demands did they make after winning concessions from the shipyard's managers?
3. What is the significance of the name Solidarity?

MIKHAIL GORBACHEV

FROM "On Restructuring the Party's Personnel Policy"

The Polish reform movement's eventual triumph in the late 1980s would have been unimaginable if it had not been for the dramatic changes taking place in the Soviet Union. After the ouster of Khrushchev in 1964, the aging Soviet political bureaucracy had returned to business as usual, under the leadership of Leonid Brezhnev. This ended when Mikhail Gorbachev (born 1931), the youngest member of the Politburo, was elected general secretary of the Communist Party in 1985, a position he held until the collapse of the Soviet Union in 1991. Beginning in 1987, Gorbachev initiated an extensive reform campaign, intended to revitalize the Soviet economy through increased democracy, greater "openness" (glasnost) and a substantial "restructuring" (perestroika) of the political and economic institutions of the Soviet state. At the same time, he encouraged reform movements within other Eastern European states, allowing organizations such as Solidarity and Civic Forum in Czechoslovakia to emerge as powerful and influential forces for change.

Although Gorbachev embraced democratization and economic modernization, he was not ready to relinquish state control over the Soviet economy. Restructuring introduced limited free-market mechanisms, but it also upheld the fundamental premise of the state-planned economy. In an important speech given to the Communist

Party Central Committee in January 1987, Gorbachev laid out his critiques of the existing Soviet system and his plans for reforming that system.

From *Speeches and Writings,* by Mikhail Gorbachev (New York: Pergamon Press, 1986).

Restructuring Is an Objective Necessity

Our Plenary Meeting is taking place in the year of the 70th anniversary of the Great October Socialist Revolution. Almost seven decades ago the Leninist Party raised over the country the victorious banner of Socialist revolution, of struggle for Socialism, freedom, equality, social justice and progress and against oppression and exploitation, poverty and the subjugation of minority nationalities.

For the first time in world history, the working man and his interests and needs were made the focal point of state policy. The Soviet Union achieved truly epoch-making successes in political, economic, social, cultural and intellectual development as it built Socialist society. Under the leadership of the Party, the Soviet people built Socialism, won the victory over Nazism in the Great Patriotic War, rehabilitated and strengthened the national economy and made their homeland a mighty power.

Our achievements are immense and indubitable and the Soviet people rightfully take pride in their successes. They constitute a firm base for the fulfilment of our current programmes and our plans for the future. But the Party must see life in its entirety and complexity. No accomplishments, not even the most impressive, should obscure either contradictions in societal development or our mistakes and failings.

* * *

A need for change was coming to a head in the economy and other fields—but it was not realized through the political and practical work of the Party and the State.

What was the reason for that complex and controversial situation?

The main cause—and the Politburo considers it necessary to say so with utmost frankness at the Plenary Meeting—was that the CPSU Central Committee and the leadership of the country failed, primarily for subjective reasons, to see in time and in full the need for change and the danger of the intensification of crisis phenomena in society, and to formulate a clear policy for overcoming them and making better use of the opportunities intrinsic to the Socialist system.

* * *

In fact, a whole system of weakening the economic tools of government emerged and a mechanism of retarding socio-economic development and hindering progressive change developed, which made it possible to tap and use the advantages of Socialism. That retarding process was rooted in serious shortcomings in the functioning of the institutions of Socialist democracy, outdated political and theoretical concepts, that often did not correspond to reality, and conservative managerial machinery.

All this adversely affected development in many spheres in the life of society. Take material production: the growth rates of the national income in the past three five-year plan periods dropped by more than half. Most plan targets have not been met since the early 1970s. The economy as a whole became cumbersome and relatively unreceptive to innovation. The quality of a considerable part of the output no longer met current requirements, and imbalances in production became aggravated.

* * *

Having successfully resolved the question of employment and provided basic social guarantees, at the same time we failed to realize in full the potential of Socialism to improve housing conditions, food supply, transport, health care and education, and to solve a number of other vital problems.

There were violations of the most important principle of Socialism—distribution according to work. Efforts to control unearned income were indecisive. The policy of material and moral incentive to work efficiently was inconsistent. Large, unjustified bonuses and various additional incentives were paid and figure-padding for profit was allowed to take place. Parasitic sentiments grew stronger and the mentality of "wage levelling" began to take hold, and that hit workers who could work better and wanted to work better, while making life easier for the idle.

The violation of the organic relationship between the measure of work and measure of consumption not only perverts the attitude to work, holding back the growth of productivity, but leads to distortion of the principle of social justice— and that is a question of great political importance.

Elements of social corrosion that emerged in the past few years had a negative effect on society's morale and inconspicuously eroded the lofty moral values which have always been characteristic of our people and of which we are proud—ideological dedication, labour enthusiasm and Soviet patriotism.

As an inevitable consequence of all this, interest in the affairs of society slackened, manifestations of callousness and scepticism appeared and the role of moral incentive to work declined. The stratum of people, some of them young people, whose ultimate goal in life was material wellbeing and gain by any means, grew wider. Their cynical stand acquired more and more aggressive forms, poisoning the mentality of those around them and triggering a wave of consumerism. The spread of alcohol and drug abuse and a rise in crime became indicators of the decline of social mores.

Disregard for laws, report-padding, bribe-taking and the encouragement of toadyism and sycophancy had a deleterious influence on the moral atmosphere in society.

Real care for people, for the conditions of their life and work and for social wellbeing were often replaced with political flirtation—the mass distribution of awards, titles and prizes. An atmosphere of permissiveness was taking shape, and exactingness, discipline and responsibility were declining.

Serious shortcomings in ideological and political education were in many cases disguised with ostentatious activities and campaigns and celebrations of numerous jubilees at the centre and in the provinces. The world of day-to-day realities and that of make-believe wellbeing were increasingly parting ways.

The ideology and mentality of stagnation had their effect on culture, literature and the arts. Criteria in appraising artistic creative work were debased. As a consequence, quite a few mediocre, faceless works appeared, which did not give anything to the mind or the heart, along with works which raised serious social and moral problems and reflected true to life conflicts. Stereotypes from capitalist mass culture, with its propagation of vulgarity, primitive tastes and spiritual callousness, began to infiltrate Soviet society to a larger extent.

*　　*　　*

The situation in the Party was also influenced by the fact that in a number of cases the Party bodies did not attach proper attention to strict compliance with the Leninist principles and norms of Party life. This made itself especially manifest, perhaps, in breaches of the principle of collective leadership. What I mean is the weakening of the role of Party meetings and elective bodies, which denied Communists the opportunity to contribute energetically to the discussion of vital issues and, in the analysis, actually to influence the atmosphere in work collectives and in society as a whole.

The principle of equality between Communists was often violated. Many Party members in senior executive positions were beyond control or criticism, which resulted in failures in work and serious breaches of Party ethics.

We cannot overlook the just indignation of

working people at the conduct of senior officials in whom trust and authority had been vested and who were called upon to stand guard over the interests of the state and its citizens, and who themselves abused their authority, suppressed criticism and sought personal gain, some even becoming accomplices in—if not organizers of—criminal activities.

*   *   *

It was in this situation that the question of accelerating the socio-economic development of the country—the question of restructuring—was raised. The case in point is actually a radical turn, comprising measures of a revolutionary character. When we talk about restructuring and associated processes of profound democratization, we mean truly revolutionary and comprehensive transformations in society.

We need to make this decisive turn because we simply do not have the choice of any other way. We must not retreat and do not have anywhere to retreat to.

*   *   *

The main purport of our strategy is to combine the achievements of the scientific and technological revolution with a plan-based economy and set the entire potential of Socialism going again.

Restructuring is reliance on the creative endeavour of the masses, all-round extension of democracy and Socialist self-government, encouragement of initiative and self-organized activities, better discipline and order, greater openness, criticism and self-criticism in all fields of public life, and high respect for the value and dignity of the individual.

Restructuring means the ever greater role of intensive growth factors in Soviet economic development, reinstatement and enhancement of Leninist principles of democratic centralism in the management of the national economy, employment of cost benefit methods of management everywhere, renunciation of the domineering style of management and administration by decree, con-

version of all units of the economy to the principles of full-scale economic accountability and new forms of organizing labour and production, and every kind of incentive for innovation and Socialist enterprise.

Restructuring means a decisive turn to science, the businesslike partnership of science and practice for the sake of the highest possible end-results, the ability to ground any undertaking on sound scientific basis, readiness and keen desire on the part of scientists to assist the Party's policy of revitalizing society, and concern for the development of science and research personnel and for their active engagement in the process of change.

Restructuring means the priority development of the social sphere, increasingly satisfying the Soviet people's requirements for adequate working and living conditions, recreational facilities, education and medical services. It means unfailing concern for raising the intellectual and cultural standards of every person and of society as a whole: it is the ability to combine decision making on the major, cardinal problems of public life with that on the current issues of immediate interest to the people.

Restructuring means vigorously ridding society of any deviations from Socialist morals, consistently enforcing the principles of social justice, harmony between words and deeds, indivisibility of rights and duties, promotion of conscientious, high quality work, and overcoming pay-levelling and consumerism.

The final aim of the restructuring effort is, I believe, clear: it is to effect a thorough going change in all aspects of public life, to give Socialism the most advanced forms of social organization, and to bring out the humane nature of our system in all decisive aspects—economic, social, political and moral—to the fullest possible degree.

This is, comrades, the task we have in motion. The restructuring effort is unfolding along the entire front. It is acquiring a new quality, not only gaining in scope but also penetrating the deepest fibres of life.

*   *   *

To Deepen Socialist Democratism and Develop Self-government by the People

We now understand better than ever before the profundity of Lenin's thought about the vital, inner link between Socialism and democracy.

The entire historical experience of our country has convincingly demonstrated that the Socialist System has in practice ensured citizens' political and socio-economic rights and personal freedoms, demonstrated the advantages of Soviet democracy and given each person confidence in the morrow.

But in conditions of restructuring, when the task of intensifying the human factor has become so urgent, we must return once again to Lenin's approach to the question of the maximum democratism of the Socialist system under which people feel that they are their own masters and creators.

"We must be guided by experience, we must allow complete freedom to the creative faculties of the masses," Vladimir Lenin said.

Indeed, democracy, the essence of which is the power of the man of labour, is the form of realizing his extensive political and civil rights, his interest in transformations and practical participation in their implementation.

A simple and lucid thought is becoming increasingly entrenched in social consciousness: a house can be put in order only by a person who feels that he owns this house. This truth is correct not only in the wordly sense but also in the sociopolitical one.

This truth must be undeviatingly applied in practice. I repeat, in practice. Otherwise the human factor will be ineffectual.

It is only through the consistent development of the democratic forms inherent in Socialism, through a broadening of self-government, that our advancement in production, science and technol-ogy, literature, culture and the arts, in all areas of social life, is possible. It is only this way that ensures conscientious discipline. The restructuring itself is possible only through democracy and due to democracy. It is only this way that is is possible to give scope to Socialism's most powerful creative force—free labour and free thought in a free country.

Therefore the further democratization of Soviet society is becoming the Party's urgent task. Herein, properly speaking, lies the essence of the course of the April Plenum, of the 27th Congress of the CPSU for deepening Socialist self-government by the people. The point at issue is, certainly, not any break up of our political system. We should make use of all its potentialities with maximum effectiveness, fill the work of the Party, the Soviets and the government bodies, public organizations and work collectives with deep democratic contents, breathe new life into all cells of the social organism.

This process is already under way in the country. The life of the Party organizations is becoming more full-blooded. Criticism and self-criticism are broadening. The mass media have begun working more actively. The Soviet people can sense the salutary effect of openness, which is becoming a norm of society's life.

The congresses of the creative unions proceeded in an atmosphere of principledness and criticism. New public organizations are being set up. The All-Union Organization of War and Labour Veterans has come into being. The Soviet Cultural Fund has been set up. Work is under way to set up women's councils. All these facts indicate the growing participation of the working people in social affairs and in the administration of the country.

*   *   *

We wish to turn our country into a model of a highly developed state, into a society with the most advanced economy, the broadest democracy, the most humane and lofty ethics, where the working man will feel that he is master, will enjoy all the benefits of material and spiritual culture, where the future of his children will be secure, where he will have everything that is necessary for a full and interesting life. And even sceptics would be forced to say: yes, the Bolsheviks can accomplish anything. Yes, truth is on their side. Yes, Socialism is a system serving man, working for his benefit, in his social and economic interests, for his spiritual elevation.

REVIEW QUESTIONS

1. Why, according to Gorbachev, was restructuring an objective necessity?

2. What social, political, and economic forms would this restructuring take?
3. Why was it crucial that social, political, and economic reform go hand in hand?
4. What elements of free-market capitalism were included in Gorbachev's economic restructuring?
5. In what ways did Gorbachev remain a traditional communist in his economic thinking?

FROM **Treaty on European Union**

In the late nineteenth century, French author Victor Hugo expressed the hoped that the twentieth century would witness the birth of a "United States of Europe," followed by a "United States of the World." In fact, the history of twentieth-century Europe has been shaped more by the hostilities generated by aggressive nationalism than by Hugo's internationalist utopianism. Yet, despite the battles that have raged and continue to rage in Europe, the desire for peaceful cooperation has lingered. After 1945, Europe was divided between East and West, but regional cooperation flourished. Cooperative agreements created competing regional economic associations (the European Community and the European Free Trade Association in the West; the Council for Mutual Economic Assistance in the East) and defense alliances (the North Atlantic Treaty Organization; the Warsaw Pact).

Interest in integrating the European economy has been greatly stimulated in recent years by both economic globalization and the end of the Cold War. In an effort to make Europe more competitive in the world economy, the twelve members of the European Community—Belgium, Denmark, France, Germany, Greece, Ireland, Italy, Luxembourg, the Netherlands, Portugal, Spain, and the United Kingdom—signed a treaty establishing the European Union in the Dutch city of Maastricht in December 1991, which was amended on 7 February 1992. The European Union is designed to create a single free trade zone, sharing a common currency (the "euro"), to grant shared citizenship to residents of participating nations, and to coordinate the member states' common trade, defense, justice, and financial needs.

From Treaty on European Union, Europa web site.

The signatory heads of state:
Resolved to mark a new stage in the process of European integration undertaken with the establishment of the European Communities,

Recalling the historic importance of the ending of the division of the European continent and the need to create firm bases for the construction of the future Europe,

Confirming their attachment to the principles of liberty, democracy and respect for human rights and fundamental freedoms and of the rule of law,

Desiring to deepen the solidarity between their peoples while respecting their history, their culture and their traditions,

Desiring to enhance further the democratic and efficient functioning of the institutions so as to enable them better to carry out, within a single institutional framework, the tasks entrusted to them,

Resolved to achieve the strengthening and the convergence of their economies and to establish an economic and monetary union including, in accordance with the provisions of this Treaty, a single and stable currency,

Determined to promote economic and social progress for their peoples, within the context of the accomplishment of the internal market and of reinforced cohesion and environmental protection, and to implement policies ensuring that advances in economic integration are accompanied by parallel progress in other fields,

Resolved to establish a citizenship common to the nationals of their countries,

Resolved to implement a common foreign and security policy including the eventual framing of a common defense policy, which might in time lead to a common defense, thereby reinforcing the European identity and its independence in order to promote peace, security and progress in Europe and in the world,

Reaffirming their objective to facilitate the free movement of persons while ensuring the safety and security of their peoples, by including provisions on justice and home affairs in this Treaty,

Resolved to continue the process of creating an ever closer union among the peoples of Europe, in which decisions are taken as closely as possible to the citizen in accordance with the principle of subsidiarity,

In view of further steps to be taken in order to advance European integration,

Have decided to establish a European Union. * * *

*   *   *

Title V
Provisions on a Common Foreign and Security Policy

ARTICLE J

A common foreign and security policy is hereby established which shall be governed by the following provisions.

ARTICLE J.1

1. The union and its Member States shall define and implement a common foreign and security policy, governed by the provisions of the Title and covering all areas of foreign and security policy.
2. The objectives of the common foreign and security policy shall be:
   to safeguard the common values, fundamental interests and independence of the Union;
   to strengthen the security of the Union and its Member States in all ways;
   to preserve peace and strengthen international security, in accordance with the principles of the United Nations Charter as well as the principles of the Helsinki Final Act and the objectives of the Paris Charter;
   to promote international cooperation;
   to develop and consolidate democracy and the rule of law, and respect for human rights and fundamental freedoms.
3. The Union shall pursue these objectives;
   by establishing systematic cooperation between Member States in the conduct of policy; * * *

by gradually implementing * * * joint action in the areas in which the Member States have important interests in common.

4. The Member States shall support the Union's external and security policy actively and unreservedly in a spirit of loyalty and mutual solidarity. They shall refrain from any action which is contrary to the interests of the Union or likely to impair its effectiveness as a cohesive force in international relations. The Council shall ensure that these principles are complied with.

*   *   *

Provisions on Cooperation in the Fields of Justice and Home Affairs

ARTICLE K

Cooperation in the fields of justice and home affairs shall be governed by the following provisions.

ARTICLE K.1

For the purposes of achieving the objectives of the Union, in particular the free movement of persons, and without prejudice to the powers of the European Community, Member States shall regard the following areas as matters of common interest:

1. asylum policy;
2. rules governing the crossing by persons of the external borders of the Member States and the exercise of controls thereon;
3. immigration policy and policy regarding nationals of third countries;
a. conditions of entry and movement by nationals of third countries on the territory of Member States;
b. conditions of residence by nationals of third countries on the territory of Member States, including family reunion and access to employment;
c. combating unauthorized immigration, residence and work by nationals of third countries on the territory of Member States;
4. combating drug addiction in so far as this is not covered by 7 to 9;
5. combating fraud on an international scale in so far as this is not covered by 7 to 9;
6. judicial cooperation in civil matters;
7. judicial cooperation in criminal matters;
8. customs cooperation;
9. police cooperation for the purposes of preventing and combating terrorism, unlawful drug trafficking and other serious forms of international crime, including if necessary certain aspects of customs cooperation, in connection with the organization of a Union-wide system for exchanging information within a European Police Office (Europol).

REVIEW QUESTIONS

1. On the basis of your reading of this treaty, why do you think the European Union was created?
2. What advantages will it provide to member states?
3. What disadvantages might there be to participation?
4. Does the treaty create a *fully* integrated Europe?
5. To what extent does it maintain the individual sovereignty of participating nations?
6. Why might the inclusion of former Soviet bloc states in the European Union be problematic?

SIMONE DE BEAUVOIR

FROM *The Second Sex*

During the twentieth century, the traditional divisions between the experiences of men and women started to blur. New technologies decreased the premium once placed on men's greater physical strength, making it possible for women to do jobs once reserved only for men. At the same time, female fertility decreased substantially: as improved health conditions allowed more children to survive to adulthood, couples increasingly sought to have fewer children and new birth-control technologies made this increasingly easy. Whereas reproductive and child-rearing duties had once played a predominant role in most women's adult lives, motherhood now became only one aspect of a more-varied lifetime experience.

However, if the material conditions of women's lives had changed significantly, attitudes toward women had not. If anything, the immediate postwar period saw a resurrection of traditional models of femininity and masculinity. On the other hand, the popularization of existentialist philosophy, which argued that every individual has responsibility to be an active agent, to create the self through "engagement" with other human beings, helped to fuel a growing resistance to "objectification"— entrapment in the limiting conceptual categories of outside society—whether on the basis of race, gender, or class. In 1949 the French novelist and existential philosopher Simone de Beauvoir (1908–1986) published The Second Sex, *an extended philosophical essay that called on women to reject socially imposed models of appropriate feminine identity and to become authentic individuals in their own right.* The Second Sex *was initially greeted with outrage and howls of derision, but the revival of feminism in the 1960s brought de Beauvoir a new, more sympathetic audience, and her arguments exercised a strong influence over the U.S. and European women's movements.*

From *The Second Sex*, by Simone de Beauvoir, translated by Cat Nilan (Paris: Gallimard, 1997).

I f being female is not a sufficient definition of woman, if we also refuse to explain her through "the eternal feminine," and if we nevertheless admit (if only provisionally), that there are women on this planet, then we are forced to ask ourselves the question: what is a woman?

Simply stating the problem suggests one immediate response. It is significant that I ask this question. A man would never think of writing a book about the peculiar position that males oc- cupy in the ranks of humanity. If I want to define myself, I am first obligated to declare: "I am a woman." That truth constitutes the foundation upon which all other affirmations will be based. A man never begins by declaring himself an individual of a certain sex: that he is a man goes without saying. It is only as a formality that "male" and "female" appear as symmetrical terms in town hall records and identification papers. The relationship between the sexes is not that of two electrical poles: the man represents both the positive and the neutral to such an extent that in French one says "*les hommes*" ("men") to designate all human beings. * * * Woman is so strongly associated with the negative that her every trait is imputed to her as a limitation, without reciprocity. It annoys me when, during the course of an abstract discussion, a man says: "You think such and such a thing because you are a woman." I know that my only defense is to reply: "I believe it because it is true," eliminating in that manner my own subjectivity. It's out of the question to answer: "And you think the contrary because you are a man," because it is understood that the fact of being a man is not a peculiarity. A man is in the right in being a man; it is the woman who is in the wrong. In practice, just as the ancients identified an absolute vertical against which the oblique was defined, there is an absolute human type that is masculine. Woman has ovaries, a uterus; these are the peculiarities that enclose her in her subjectivity. It is often said that she thinks with her glands. Man arrogantly forgets that his own anatomy also includes hormones, testicles. He experiences his body as being in a direct and normal relationship with the world, which he believes he apprehends objectively, whereas he considers the body of a woman to be weighted down by all of its specificities: an obstacle, a prison. * * * Humanity is male and man defines woman not in and of herself but relative to him; she is not considered an autonomous being. * * * And she is nothing other than what man decides; thus she is called "the sex," meaning that she appears to the male, in essence, as a sexuated being. For him, she is sex, and therefore she is so absolutely. She is defined and differentiated in relation to man and not he in relation to her; she is the inessential as compared with the essential. He is the Subject, he is the Absolute: she is the Other.

The category of the *Other* is as old as consciousness itself. * * * No collectivity ever defines itself as the One without immediately positing an Other in opposition to it. If three travelers happen to be gathered together by chance in the same cabin, that is enough to make all other travelers vaguely hostile "others." For the villager, all of the

people who do not belong to his village are suspect "others"; for the native of one country, the inhabitants of other countries are "foreigners." Jews are "others" to the antisemite; Blacks are "others" to American racists; indigenous peoples are "others" to the colonizers; proletarians are "others" to the propertied classes. * * *

But the other consciousness opposes to this claim a reciprocal claim: when he travels, the native is shocked to discover that the natives of neighboring countries regard him in his turn as a foreigner. Between villages, clans, nations, and classes there are wars, potlatches, markets, treaties, and conflicts that deprive the idea of the Other of its absolute sense and reveal its relativity. Willingly or not, individuals and groups are forced to recognize the reciprocity of their relations. How then has it happened that between the sexes that reciprocity has not been admitted, that one of the terms has affirmed itself as the only essential one, denying all relativity in relation to its corollary, defining it as pure otherness? Why don't women contest male sovereignty? No subject spontaneously admits, from the first, that it is the inessential. It is not the Other who by defining himself as Other defines the One: he is posited as Other by the One posing himself as One. But in order for the return from Other to One not to happen, it is necessary that he submit to this foreign point of view. Where does woman's submission come from?

*   *   *

* * * The parallel established by Bebel between women and the proletariat is the most apt: like women, proletarians are not a minority and they have never constituted a separate collectivity. Nevertheless, in the absence of a *single* event, it is a historical development that explains their existence as a class and which accounts for the distribution of *these* individuals in that class. There have not always been proletarians; there have always been women. Women are women through their physiology. However far one goes back into history, women have always been subordinated to man. Their dependency is not the consequence of

an event or a development; it did not *happen*. It is in part because otherness escapes the accidental character of a historical fact in this case that it appears here as an absolute. Something that happened over time can be undone at another time. The Blacks of Haiti, among others, have proved this. On the other hand, it would appear that a natural condition defies change. In truth, nature is no more an immutable given than historical reality. If woman reveals herself as the inessential that never returns to the essential, it is because she herself does not set that reversal into motion. Proletarians say "We." Blacks too. Positing themselves as subjects they change the bourgeoisie and Whites into "others." * * * Women do not say "we." Men say "women" and women use this word to designate themselves, but they do not posit themselves authentically as Subject. Proletarians made a revolution in Russia, the Blacks in Haiti, the Indochinese are fighting in Indochina. Women's action has never been anything more than a symbolic disturbance. They have won only what men were willing to concede to them. They have taken nothing: they have merely received.

*   *   *

There are deep analogies between the situation of women and that of Blacks. Today both are emancipating themselves from the same paternalism and the former master class wishes to keep them in "their place," that is to say, the place it has chosen for them. In both cases, that master class lavishes more or less sincere praise on the virtues of the "good Black," childish, happy-go-lucky, his soul slumbering, and on "the real woman," who is frivolous, puerile, irresponsible, submissive to man. In both cases, it derives its argument from the situation it has in fact created. George Bernard Shaw's witticism is well known: "The white American," he said, in essence, "relegates the Black to the rank of shoeshine boy and he concludes from this that the Black is good for nothing but shining shoes." This vicious circle is found in all analogous circumstances; when an in-

dividual, or a group of individuals, is held in a situation of inferiority, the fact is that he *is* inferior. But we must be clear about what we mean by *to be*. It is in bad faith to give it a substantial meaning, when it should be read in the dynamic, Hegelian sense: *to be* is to have become, it is to have been made that which one appears to be. Yes, as a whole women today *are* inferior to men, which is to say that their situation is offered them fewer opportunities. The problem is determining whether or not this state of affairs should continue.

Many men hope that it will; not all of them have disarmed themselves yet. The conservative bourgeoisie continues to see women's emancipation as a menace to its morality and its interests. Certain males fear feminine competition. Just the other day, a male student declared in the *Hebdo-Latin:* "Every female student who takes a position as a doctor or a lawyer *steals* a place from us." He certainly doesn't have any questions about his rights over this world. But it is not only economic concerns that are at play here. One of the benefits that oppression guarantees to the oppressors is that the humblest among them feels himself *superior:* a "poor White" in the Southern United States consoles himself by saying that he is not a "dirty Negro," and more affluent Whites skillfully exploit this pride. In the same way, the most mediocre of males believes himself a demigod compared with women.

REVIEW QUESTIONS

1. What *is* a woman according to de Beauvoir?
2. How has woman become an "Other"?
3. How can she become a "Self"?
4. In what ways are the conditions of blacks, Jews, workers, and women similar? In what ways are they different?
5. Why do you think de Beauvoir chose to make these particular comparisons?

REINHOLD WAGNLEITNER

FROM *The Coca-Colonization and the Cold War*

Western Europeans greatly appreciated the influx of Marshall Plan money after the Second World War, but they were far more ambivalent about the cultural Americanization that seemed to accompany this aid. As European domination of the globe receded in the face of superpower conflict and as the great European empires crumbled in the face of third world independence movements, many Europeans, in both the East and the West, continued to cling to a belief in the enduring supremacy of European cultural traditions. Yet even in this area, the European cultural elite soon found itself powerless to influence a general public more interested in dancing to the rock and roll of Elvis Presley than the waltzes of Strauss.

On one level, ordinary Europeans welcomed the brash vibrancy of U.S. pop culture as a relief from the horrors of the Second World War. In the immediate postwar period, U.S. movies and radio programs filled the void left by the collapse of the European entertainment industry, offering a diversion from the hardships of the reconstruction era. On a deeper level, the appeal of U.S. culture lay also in its mythic qualities. Especially for young people, "America" represented an idealized embodiment of democracy in stark contrast to the authoritarian fascism that had been accepted, or at least tolerated, by their parents' generation. In his recent historical study of U.S. cultural policies in occupied Austria, Reinhold Wagnleitner begins with an account of the ways in which his own childhood was affected by the "coca-colonization" of European culture.

From *The Coca-Colonization and the Cold War: The Cultural Mission of the United States in Austria after the Second World War,* by Reinhold Wagnleitner, translated by Diana M. Wolf (Chapel Hill: University of North Carolina Press, 1994), pp. 9–11.

*   *   *

When I was born in Upper Austria in 1949, Mauerkirchen was a small, sleepy market town—but it was also situated in the American occupation zone of Austria. Although during the period of occupation, 1945–55, the U.S. Army was barely visible in our part of the woods, we children religiously waited for the best action of the year: the annual U.S. Army maneuvers and our rations of chewing gum.

For us, the horrors of the Second World War were in the distant past, but still they were everywhere. Our everyday experience included quite a few mutilated men, and for the nicer ones we picked up cigarette butts from the streets. It seemed absolutely normal that most men and many women looked old and tired—and not only because we were children and they wore dark clothes. But what a contrast when we saw pictures of GIs or, even better, met "the real thing." Somehow, they clashed with our images of soldiers. They looked young and healthy. Contrasted to our poverty, they seemed incredibly rich, and many were generous to us kids. Of course, their casualness and loudness were proverbial—but we admired them precisely for that.

Although most families with a Nazi past repressed and hid this past from the children, the war remained everywhere—and we did not need a war memorial to be reminded of the many ghosts roaming our streets. Unspoken Nazi-past or not, it was clear that most adults objected to those crass boys from across the Atlantic. "We" had indeed lost the war, but look at those uncultured American guys who chewed gum and put their feet on the table. (This, it seemed, was the utmost crime!) How could an army manned by such unmilitaristic, childish, and undisciplined boys (even blacks!) win a war, especially one against Germany! A few of us children, however, secretly suspected that an army advancing to the rhythm of swing music *deserved* to win the war. It did not help our elders to warn us that if we chewed gum we would look like Americans: that was exactly what we wanted to look like!

In my family, I was spared this routine of Austrian cultural superiority versus American cultural inferiority mostly for two reasons. First, my parents and grandparents had not been Nazis, and my mother loved American music, while my father enjoyed American action movies, which had returned to Mauerkirchen's little cinema in the wake of the U.S. Army. Second, a traumatic incident in my father's childhood—he had lost one foot in a car accident at age thirteen—spared him the fate of having to fight in the Second World War. It was rather rare, indeed, to grow up in Austria during the 1950s with parents like that. (Of course, for most of my teenage friends, American pop culture became *the* major vehicle of protest against their parents.)

While our household was uncharacteristically open to what parents of my friends despised as "American trash," I was far from being the vanguard of American popular culture in our family. It is my only brother, Günter, born in 1940, who has to take the main responsibility for my un-Austrian behavior. Günter is extremely musical. He started to take piano lessons at age four and passed the entrance exam to the Vienna Boys Choir at age six—we still possess a 78 shellac recording of Günter's voice, which my father had ordered for this occasion. But in the end, my par-

ents decided against sending him to Vienna. They did not want to hand over their six-year-old boy to a boarding school, especially to a boarding school in Vienna, which was surrounded by the Soviet occupation zone. (After all, we lived in the *Goldenen Westen* of Austria.)

Yet, my parents had no idea that they built the perfect stage for American music for their still-unborn second child. Günter, who had a voracious appetite for any kind of good music, did more than simply improve his playing of Mozart and Beethoven, Bach and Brahms, Schubert and Strauss; he also discovered Frank Sinatra and Ray Charles, Dizzy Gillespie and Miles Davis. And when he discovered rock 'n' roll in the middle of the 1950s, nothing remained the same. While he worked the piano and made our living room rock like a jailhouse, I would work the matchboxes and pretend I was something like a rock 'n' roll drum machine. Many were the sighs of my poor parents—not because we played American music, but because we didn't do *anything else*. And then one day Günter really became the King. A friend of my mother gave him the absolutely most yearned for article of clothing imaginable: the first and only pair of Levi's in Mauerkirchen, which she had received as a present from an American officer.

While my brother was lost for good to any "respectable profession" and became a musician in dance bands, I finished *Gymnasium* (high school), although I had been playing in amateur dance bands since the age of fourteen. After copying my major role model's rock 'n' roll, however, I had my second awakening in 1963 when the British beat bands confronted us—just as they simultaneously confronted white American teenagers, to the annoyance of *their* parents—with the Liverpool, Birmingham, and London version of American blues and rhythm and blues.

So it happened that shortly before entering university, I already had a sort of final graduation: my brother picked me as the bass player for his band. Hardly a weekend passed during my teenage years when our living room was not transformed into a rehearsal room for a band of screaming and strumming kids. Still, I will always be grateful for the proud look on my parents' faces when they saw their sons on stage together for the first time.

Of course, I had no money to buy records, and the Austrian radio stations still pretended that we lived in an age before "Roll Over Beethoven." My major source of musical information about British and American groups consisted of the daily fix of three hours of rock programs that were aired by Radio Free Europe every weekday afternoon. The political messages of Radio Svobodna Evropa (ten minutes of news to fifty minutes of music for three hours) were directed at Czechoslovakian listeners and, as bait, had far and away the best music program of any European station. It really worked like a commercially sponsored program, only here the commercials were the news and the political commentaries. As their reactions showed, the Czechoslovak and other Eastern European governments had not the least inkling of what was really going on. Otherwise they would have jammed the music, not the news.

Contemporary parallels must not be overlooked; the present transformations in Eastern Europe should remind us of the developments in Western Europe after the Second World War. It is of the utmost political significance that practically the whole East German population chose to emigrate to the West every night via television. The effects of such a temporary electronic emigration, the impact of thus becoming quasi-Americans by tuning in to modern mass media, should not be underrated. The Iron Curtain—is not its name already symbolic for an outdated industrial sector, largely connoting the nineteenth century?—in the end was no match for the messages produced by the electronic-consciousness industry in the West, the real heavy industry of the twentieth century (in the apt words of Hans Mag-

nus Enzensberger). Or what does it really mean that during the weekend of February 19–21, 1993, only 6 Russian movies were shown in the cinemas of Moscow compared with 111 American films?

During my student days, I soon learned that there was another side to the United States. Just like many of my peer group on American campuses, I objected to American involvement in Indochina and other foreign policy adventures as well as the repression of minorities in the United States. Yet, we demonstrated in blue jeans and T-shirts and attended sit-ins and teach-ins. What's more, quite a few of us understood what it meant to be able to demonstrate against a war in wartime without being court-martialed. Some of us were also aware that we had learned our peaceful tactics of democratic protest and opposition from the American civil rights movement and the anti-nuclear-armament movement. After all, we did not intone the "Internationale" but instead sang "We Shall Overcome."

*   *   *

REVIEW QUESTIONS

1. Why did so many Austrian adults dislike U.S. culture?
2. Why did this same U.S. culture appeal so strongly to Austrian children and teenagers?
3. What specific aspects of U.S. culture appealed to young Europeans?
4. What sorts of values did these cultural expressions seem to embody?
5. Why do you think youth culture became such an important phenomenon after the Second World War?

31 ❧ PROBLEMS OF WORLD CIVILIZATION

At the beginning of recorded human history, the entire population of the world probably consisted of fewer than ten million people. Ten thousand years later, the world population is rapidly approaching six billion. Human ingenuity has made possible the production of enough food and material goods to sustain this enormous population, but this achievement puts serious strains on the environment and creates intense competition for limited resources.

Innovations in transportation and communication have made it possible for people around the world to have far more intimate and informed relations with one another than ever before. Earth's surface remains subdivided by national boundaries, but the problems confronting humanity are, increasingly, international problems that can only be solved through global cooperation. From a historical perspective, it is already clear that human history has become world history and that even the most isolated regions are no longer insulated from the general trend toward global integration.

One of the most important factors in the emerging history of the contemporary world is the deep divide separating developed and developing nations. Most of the inhabitants of affluent and technologically advanced regions such as Japan, the United States, and western Europe enjoy extremely high standards of living and can expect to live long and healthy lives. The four-fifths of Earth's people who live in developing regions regularly suffer from a lack of basic necessities, including adequate food, clean drinking water, and a bare minimum of health care.

The reasons for this dramatic disparity in the distribution of wealth are complex, but they are closely linked to the historical processes of colonization and decolonization. During the late nineteenth century, imperialist powers acquired colonies in the hopes of procuring raw materials, cheap labor, and national grandeur. The builders of empire were largely uninterested in modernizing the economies or political systems of their colonies, and they often destroyed indigenous industries and governments at the same time that they crushed expressions of cultural resistance. After the Second World War, most of these colonies regained their independence, as a result of either more or less voluntary withdrawal on the part of the colonizers or violent conflict.

The newly independent states of Africa and Asia faced substantial challenges, not the least of which were the international tensions generated by the cold war. When the Soviet Union and the United States sought allies in the third world, both superpowers tended to support dictators friendly to their strategic aims, thereby discouraging the emergence of independent democracies. In addition, most former colonies were strongly disadvantaged in the economic arena by technological backwardness, a legacy of colonial rule. The developed nations have been slow to come to the aid of struggling third world nations, and the political instability produced by desperate poverty and often-violent competition for land and resources continues to threaten global peace and prosperity.

As developing regions struggle to come to terms with the legacies of colonialism and superpower conflict, they are also called on to share in the project of forging global solutions to global problems. Uncontrolled population growth, the exploitation and mismanagement of natural resources, and unregulated industrial and commercial development pose serious dangers to the survival of all humanity. Similarly, the international transfer of people, capital, consumer goods, and land, air, and water pollution can no longer be contained within national boundaries. While individual identity remains deeply rooted in local cultural traditions, the future history of humanity may hinge on our ability to develop a model of global citizenship that balances the rights of the individual with the responsibilities of all human beings to both the local and the global community.

MAHATMA GANDHI

FROM *The Essential Writings*

The Indian struggle for independence from Great Britain can be traced back to the early nineteenth century, but it first became a mass movement after the First World War. Indian nationalists supported India's participation in the war on the Allied side, but they were angered by Britain's failure to reward this service with a greater degree of self-government. Under the charismatic leadership of Mahatma ("Great

Soul") Gandhi (1869–1948), the Indian independence movement became a model for other colonial independence struggles.

Having trained as a lawyer in Britain, the young Mohandas Gandhi worked for many years among the East Indian community of South Africa, where he experienced the effects of racial discrimination in the acute form of apartheid. As he struggled to maintain his human dignity in a system that looked on him as nothing more than a coolie, he drew sustenance from the Hindu religious traditions of India, building his "soul force" through a commitment to truth, love, and ascetic practices (such as vegetarianism, sexual abstinence, and manual labor). When he returned to India in 1913, Gandhi became active in the Indian National Congress and directed the fledgling independence movement toward adopting a strategy of peaceful noncooperation. At the same time, he also lobbied for economic self-sufficiency. Taking as his symbol the spinning wheel, he argued that the spiritual and material poverty of the Indian masses could be alleviated through the revival of indigenous traditions of small-scale, low-tech textile production.

From *The Essential Writings of Mahatma Gandhi*, edited by Raghavan Iyer (Oxford, Eng.: Oxford University Press, 1991).

FROM The Doctrine of the Sword

In this age of the rule of brute force, it is almost impossible for anyone to believe that anyone else could possibly reject the law of the final supremacy of brute force. And so I receive anonymous letters advising me that I must not interfere with the progress of non-co-operation even though popular violence may break out. Others come to me and assuming that secretly I must be plotting violence, inquire when the happy moment for declaring open violence will arrive. They assure me that the English will never yield to anything but violence secret or open. Yet others, I am informed, believe that I am the most rascally person living in India because I never give out my real intention and that they have not a shadow of a doubt that I believe in violence just as much as most people do.

Such being the hold that the doctrine of the sword has on the majority of mankind, and as success of non-co-operation depends principally on absence of violence during its pendency and as my views in this matter affect the conduct of a large number of people, I am anxious to state them as clearly as possible.

I do believe that where there is only a choice between cowardice and violence I would advise violence. Thus when my eldest son asked me what he should have done, had he been present when I was almost fatally assaulted in 1908, whether he should have run away and seen me killed or whether he should have used his physical force which he could and wanted to use, and defended me, I told him that it was his duty to defend me even by using violence. Hence it was that I took part in the Boer War, the so-called Zulu rebellion and the late War. Hence also do I advocate training in arms for those who believe in the method of violence. I would rather have India resort to arms in order to defend her honour than that she should in a cowardly manner become or remain a helpless witness to her own dishonour.

But I believe that non-violence is infinitely superior to violence, forgiveness is more manly than punishment. *Kshama virasya bhushanam.* "Forgiveness adorns a soldier." But abstinence is forgiveness only when there is the power to punish; it is meaningless when it pretends to proceed from a helpless creature. A mouse hardly forgives a cat when it allows itself to be torn to pieces by her. I, therefore, appreciate the sentiment of those who cry out for the condign punishment of General Dyer and his ilk. They would tear him to pieces if they could. But I do not believe India to be helpless. I do not believe myself to be a helpless creature. Only I want to use India's and my strength for a better purpose.

Let me not be misunderstood. Strength does not come from physical capacity. It comes from an indomitable will. An average Zulu is any way more than a match for an average Englishman in bodily capacity. But he flees from an English boy, because he fears the boy's revolver or those who will use it for him. He fears death and is nerveless in spite of his burly figure. We in India may in a moment realize that one hundred thousand Englishmen need not frighten three hundred million human beings. A definite forgiveness would therefore mean a definite recognition of our strength. With enlightened forgiveness must come a mighty wave of strength in us, which would make it impossible for a Dyer and a Frank Johnson to heap affront upon India's devoted head. It matters little to me that for the moment I do not drive my point home. We feel too downtrodden not to be angry and revengeful. But I must not refrain from saying that India can gain more by waiving the right of punishment. We have better work to do, a better mission to deliver to the world.

I am not a visionary. I claim to be a practical idealist. The religion of non-violence is not meant merely for the * * * saints. It is meant for the common people as well. Non-violence is the law of our species as violence is the law of the brute. The spirit lies dormant in the brute and he knows no law but that of physical might. The dignity of man requires obedience to a higher law—to the strength of the spirit.

I have therefore ventured to place before India the ancient law of self-sacrifice. * * *

Non-violence in its dynamic condition means conscious suffering. It does not mean meek submission to the will of the evil-doer, but it means the putting of one's whole soul against the will of the tyrant. Working under this law of our being, it is possible for a single individual to defy the whole might of an unjust empire to save his honour, his religion, his soul and lay the foundation for that empire's fall or its regeneration.

And so I am not pleading for India to practise non-violence because it is weak. I want her to practise non-violence being conscious of her strength and power. No training in arms is required for realization of her strength. We seem to need it because we seem to think that we are but a lump of flesh. I want India to recognize that she has a soul that cannot perish and that can rise triumphant above every physical weakness and defy the physical combination of a whole world. What is the meaning of Rama, a mere human being, with his host of monkeys, pitting himself against the insolent strength of ten-headed Ravana surrounded in supposed safety by the raging waters on all sides of Lanka? Does it not mean the conquest of physical might by spiritual strength? However, being a practical man, I do not wait till India recognizes the practicability of the spiritual life in the political world. India considers herself to be powerless and paralysed before the machine-guns, the tanks and the aeroplanes of the English. And she takes up non-co-operation out of her weakness. It must still serve the same purpose, namely, bring her delivery from the crushing weight of British injustice if a sufficient number of people practise it.

* * * I invite even the school of violence to give this peaceful non-co-operation a trial. It will not fail through its inherent weakness. It may fail because of poverty of response. Then will be the time for real danger. The high-souled men, who are unable to suffer national humiliation any longer, will want to vent their wrath. They will take to violence. So far as I know, they must perish without delivering themselves or their country from the wrong. If India takes up the doctrine of the sword, she may gain momentary victory. Then India will cease to be the pride of my heart. I am wedded to India because I owe my all to her. I believe absolutely that she has a mission for the world. She is not to copy Europe blindly. India's acceptance of the doctrine of the sword will be the hour of my trial. I hope I shall not be found wanting. My religion has no geographical limits. If I

have a living faith in it, it will transcend my love for India herself. My life is dedicated to service of India through the religion of non-violence which I believe to be the root of Hinduism.

Meanwhile I urge those who distrust me, not to disturb the even working of the struggle that has just commenced, by inciting to violence in the belief that I want violence. I detest secrecy as a sin. Let them give non-violent non-co-operation a trial and they will find that I had no mental reservation whatsoever.

FROM Non-Violence — The Greatest Force

*   *   *

The cry for peace will be a cry in the wilderness, so long as the spirit of non-violence does not dominate millions of men and women.

An armed conflict between nations horrifies us. But the economic war is no better than an armed conflict. This is like a surgical operation. An economic war is prolonged torture. And its ravages are no less terrible than those depicted in the literature on war properly so called. We think nothing of the other because we are used to its deadly effects.

Many of us in India shudder to see blood spilled. Many of us resent cow-slaughter, but we think nothing of the slow torture through which by our greed we put our people and cattle. But because we are used to this lingering death, we think no more about it.

The movement against war is sound. I pray for its success. But I cannot help the gnawing fear that the movement will fail, if it does not touch the root of all evil—man's greed.

Will America, England and the other great nations of the West continue to exploit the so-called weaker or uncivilized races and hope to attain peace that the whole world is pining for? Or will Americans continue to prey upon one an-

other, have commercial rivalries and yet expect to dictate peace to the world?

Not till the spirit is changed can the form be altered. The form is merely an expression of the spirit within. We may succeed in seemingly altering the form but the alteration will be a mere make-believe if the spirit within remains unalterable. A whited sepulchre still conceals beneath it the rotting flesh and bone.

Far be it from me to discount or under-rate the great effort that is being made in the West to kill the war-spirit. Mine is merely a word of caution as from a fellow-seeker who has been striving in his own humble manner after the same thing, maybe in a different way, no doubt on a much smaller scale. But if the experiment demonstrably succeeds on the smaller field and, if those who are working on the larger field have not overtaken me, it will at least pave the way for a similar experiment on a large field.

I observe in the limited field in which I find myself, that unless I can reach the hearts of men and women, I am able to do nothing. I observe further that so long as the spirit of hate persists in some shape or other, it is impossible to establish peace or to gain our freedom by peaceful effort. We cannot love one another, if we hate Englishmen. We cannot love the Japanese and hate Englishmen. We must either let the Law of Love rule us through and through or not at all. Love among ourselves based on hatred of others breaks down under the slightest pressure. The fact is such love is never real love. It is an armed peace. And so it will be in this great movement in the West against war. War will only be stopped when the conscience of mankind has become sufficiently elevated to recognize the undisputed supremacy of the Law of Love in all the walks of life. Some say this will never come to pass. I shall retain the faith till the end of my earthly existence that it shall come to pass.

REVIEW QUESTIONS

1. Why must the strategy of nonviolence proceed from a position of strength according to Gandhi?
2. In what ways were Indians strong?
3. What does Gandhi mean by *economic war*?
4. How can human beings bring an end to *all* wars?
5. Why do you think the strategy of passive resistance to oppression was so popular among many participants in the independence and civil rights movements of the mid–twentieth century?

FRANTZ FANON

FROM *The Wretched of the Earth*

Gandhi's strategy of peaceful resistance had a profound impact on other twentieth-century movements for social change. Yet many independence activists rejected this approach, arguing that the imperial powers would never relinquish their control over colonial holdings without violence. Instead, these activists looked for inspiration to the armed struggles led by Ho Chi Minh in Vietnam and Fidel Castro in Cuba. Militant anti-imperialists recognized that resistance movements could never outgun the colonizers, but they were convinced that sustained guerilla warfare would eventually convince the imperial powers that the costs of maintaining control over a colony were simply too high.

For Frantz Fanon (1925–1961), violence was not simply a tactic in anti-imperial conflicts: it also served an important role in the psychological decolonization of subject peoples. Born in the French colony of Martinique, Fanon trained as a psychiatrist in Martinique and France before becoming an active participant in the Algerian independence movement of the 1950s. Fanon argued that the physical and psychological violence of the colonial system had traumatized colonized peoples, generating individual and communal mental illness. Violent resistance to imperialism would permit subject peoples to purge this trauma and to build a new and independent community based on this shared experience of retaliation. In The Wretched of the Earth, *published in 1961 shortly before his untimely death from cancer, Fanon analyzed anti-imperial violence as a pathological response to a pathological system and as a necessary therapy for the social maladies generated by colonialism.*

From *The Wretched of the Earth,* by Frantz Fanon, translated by Constance Farrington (New York: Grove/Atlantic, 1963), pp. 83–84, 88–90, 96–98, 102.

GANDHI AT SPINNING WHEEL

Margaret Bourke-White

Mahatma Gandhi's strategy of achieving independence for India through boycotts and non-participation in civil institutions marks a high point in nonviolent political struggles in the twentieth century. A cornerstone of Gandhi's political program was the assertion that when Indians could break their economic dependence on British manufacturers (of textiles, for example), Indian political independence could be achieved. How does this photograph of Gandhi capture the philosophy and program of his politics?

*   *   *

The existence of an armed struggle shows that the people are decided to trust to violent methods only. He of whom *they* have never stopped saying that the only language he understands is that of force, decides to give utterance by force. In fact, as always, the settler has shown him the way he should take if he is to become free. The argument the native chooses has been furnished by the settler, and by an ironic turning of the tables it is the native who now affirms that the colonialist understands nothing but force. The colonial regime owes its legitimacy to force and at no time tries to hide this aspect of things. Every statue, whether of Faidherbe or of Lyautey, of Bugeaud or of Sergeant Blandan—all these conquistadors perched on colonial soil do not cease from proclaiming one and the same thing: "We are here by the force of bayonets. . . ."

*   *   *

The violence of the colonial regime and the counter-violence of the native balance each other and respond to each other in an extraordinary reciprocal homogeneity. This reign of violence will be the more terrible in proportion to the size of the implantation from the mother country. The development of violence among the colonized people will be proportionate to the violence exercised by the threatened colonial regime. In the first phase of this insurrectional period, the home governments are the slaves of the settlers, and these settlers seek to intimidate the natives and their home governments at one and the same time. They use the same methods against both of them. The assassination of the Mayor of Evian, in its method and motivation, is identifiable with the assassination of Ali Boumendjel. For the settlers, the alternative is not between *Algérie algérienne* and *Algérie française* but between an independent Algeria and a colonial Algeria, and anything else is mere talk or attempts at treason. The settler's logic is implacable and one is only staggered by the counter-logic visible in the behavior of the native insofar as one has not clearly understood beforehand the mechanisms of the settler's ideas. From the moment that the native has chosen the methods of counter-violence, police reprisals automatically call forth reprisals on the side of the nationalists. However, the results are not equivalent, for machine-gunning from airplanes and bombardments from the fleet go far beyond in horror and magnitude any answer the natives can make. This recurring terror de-mystifies once and for all the most estranged members of the colonized race. They find out on the spot that all the piles of speeches on the equality of human beings do not hide the commonplace fact that the seven Frenchmen killed or wounded at the Col de Sakamody kindles the indignation of all civilized consciences, whereas the sack of the douars of Guergour and of the dechras of Djerah and the massacre of whole populations—which had merely called forth the Sakamody ambush as a reprisal—all this is of not the slightest importance. Terror, counter-terror, violence, counter-violence: that is what observers bitterly record when they describe the circle of hate, which is so tenacious and so evident in Algeria.

In all armed struggles, there exists what we might call the point of no return. Almost always it is marked off by a huge and all-inclusive repression which engulfs all sectors of the colonized people. This point was reached in Algeria in 1955 with the 12,000 victims of Phillippeville. * * *

*   *   *

Then it became clear to everybody, including even the settlers, that "things couldn't go on as before." Yet the colonized people do not chalk up the reckoning. They record the huge gaps made in their ranks as a sort of necessary evil. Since they have decided to reply by violence, they therefore are ready to take all its consequences. They only insist in return that no reckoning should be kept, either, for the others. To the saying "All natives are the same" the colonized person replies, "All settlers are the same."

*   *   *

The appearance of the settler has meant in the terms of syncretism the death of the aboriginal society, cultural lethargy, and the petrification of individuals. For the native, life can only spring up again out of the rotting corpse of the settler. This then is the correspondence, term by term, between the two trains of reasoning.

But it so happens that for the colonized people this violence, because it constitutes their only work, invests their characters with positive and creative qualities. The practice of violence binds them together as a whole, since each individual forms a violent link in the great chain, a part of the great organism of violence which has surged upward in reaction to the settler's violence in the beginning. The groups recognize each other and the future nation is already indivisible. The armed struggle mobilizes the people; that is to say, it throws them in one way and in one direction.

The mobilization of the masses, when it arises out of the war of liberation, introduces into each man's consciousness the ideas of a common cause, of a national destiny, and of a collective history. In the same way the second phase, that of the building-up of the nation, is helped on by the existence of this cement which has been mixed with blood and anger. Thus we come to a fuller appreciation of the originality of the words used in these underdeveloped countries. During the colonial period the people are called upon to fight against oppression; after national liberation, they are called upon to fight against poverty, illiteracy, and underdevelopment. The struggle, they say, goes on. The people realize that life is an unending contest.

We have said that the native's violence unifies the people. By its very structure, colonialism is separatist and regionalist. Colonialism does not simply state the existence of tribes; it also reinforces it and separates them. The colonial system encourages chieftaincies and keeps alive the old Marabout confraternities. Violence is in action all-inclusive and national. It follows that it is closely involved in the liquidation of regionalism and of tribalism. Thus the national parties show no pity at all toward the caids and the customary chiefs.

Their destruction is the preliminary to the unification of the people.

At the level of individuals, violence is a cleansing force. It frees the native from his inferiority complex and from his despair and inaction; it makes him fearless and restores his self-respect. Even if the armed struggle has been symbolic and the nation is demobilized through a rapid movement of decolonization, the people have the time to see that the liberation has been the business of each and all and that the leader has no special merit.

*   *   *

Today, national independence and the growth of national feeling in underdeveloped regions take on totally new aspects. In these regions, with the exception of certain spectacular advances, the different countries show the same absence of infrastructure. The mass of the people struggle against the same poverty, flounder about making the same gestures and with their shrunken bellies outline what has been called the geography of hunger. It is an underdeveloped world, a world inhuman in its poverty; but also it is a world without doctors, without engineers, and without administrators. Confronting this world, the European nations sprawl, ostentatiously opulent. This European opulence is literally scandalous, for it has been founded on slavery, it has been nourished with the blood of slaves and it comes directly from the soil and from the subsoil of that underdeveloped world. The well-being and the progress of Europe have been built up with the sweat and the dead bodies of Negroes, Arabs, Indians, and the yellow races. We have decided not to overlook this any longer. When a colonialist country, embarrassed by the claims for independence made by a colony, proclaims to the nationalist leaders: "If you wish for independence, take it, and go back to the Middle Ages," the newly independent people tend to acquiesce and to accept the challenge; in fact you may see colonialism withdrawing its capital and its technicians and setting up around the young State the apparatus of economic pressure. The apotheosis of independence is transformed into the curse of independence, and the colonial power through its immense resources of coercion condemns the young nation to regression. In plain words, the colonial power says: "Since you want independence, take it and starve." The nationalist leaders have no other choice but to turn to their people and ask from them a gigantic effort. A regime of austerity is imposed on these starving men; a disproportionate amount of work is required from their atrophied muscles. An autarkic regime is set up and each state, with the miserable resources it has in hand, tries to find an answer to the nation's great hunger and poverty. We see the mobilization of a people which toils to exhaustion in front of a suspicious and bloated Europe.

*   *   *

* * * The imperialist states would make a great mistake and commit an unspeakable injustice if they contented themselves with withdrawing from our soil the military cohorts, and the administrative and managerial services whose function it was to discover the wealth of the country, to extract it and to send it off to the mother countries. We are not blinded by the moral reparation of national independence; nor are we fed by it. The wealth of the imperial countries is our wealth too. On the universal plane this affirmation, you may be sure, should on no account be taken to signify that we feel ourselves affected by the creations of Western arts or techniques. For in a very concrete way Europe has stuffed herself inordinately with the gold and raw materials of the colonial countries: Latin America, China, and Africa. From all these continents, under whose eyes Europe today raises up her tower of opulence, there has flowed out for centuries toward that same Europe diamonds and oil, silk and cotton, wood and exotic products. Europe is literally the creation of the Third World. The wealth which smothers her is that which was stolen from the underdeveloped peoples. The ports of Holland, the docks of Bordeaux and Liverpool were specialized in the Negro slave trade, and owe their renown to millions of deported slaves. So when we hear the head of a European state declare with his hand on his heart that he must come to the aid of the poor underdeveloped peoples, we do not tremble with gratitude. Quite the contrary; we say to ourselves: "It's a just reparation which will be paid to us."

*   *   *

REVIEW QUESTIONS

1. In what ways did colonial regimes breed violence?
2. What were the positive benefits of anti-imperial violence for the community? For the individual?
3. According to Fanon, how did Europe compare with its former colonies?
4. In what sense is the wealth of Europe the "creation of the Third World"?

RUHOLLAH KHOMEINI

FROM *Islamic Government*

Throughout his lifetime, Mahatma Gandhi sought to universalize traditional Hindu religious concepts in the interest of uniting Indians of diverse religious backgrounds in a nonviolent independence movement. Iranian nationalist leader Ruhollah Khomeini (1900?–1989) took a radically different approach, formulating a narrow and highly conservative Islamic fundamentalism intended to unite Iranian Moslems in violent opposition to the Western-supported government of the shah of Iran and against Western culture in general. While Khomeini's version of Islam is not representative of more liberal mainstream traditions in the Moslem world, it has had a powerful influence on those Moslems seeking an alternative to Western cultural, political, and economic hegemony.

Born into a family of Shi'ite Moslem religious leaders, Khomeini was recognized as the leading Iranian religious authority—the Grand Ayatollah—in the 1950s. Forced out of Iran in the early 1960s, Khomeini continued to voice his opposition to the Iranian government from exile. After the shah was expelled from Iran in early 1979, Khomeini returned to his homeland and served as both religious and political head of state until his death in 1989. In Islamic Government, *written in the early 1970s, Khomeini had already outlined his own model of theocratic government based in a rigid, antimodern reading of Islamic political and legal doctrines.*

From *Islamic Government,* by Ruhollah Khomeini, translated by Joint Publications Research Service (New York: Manor Books, 1979).

The Islamic government is not similar to the well-known systems of government. It is not a despotic government in which the head of state dictates his opinion and tampers with the lives and property of the people. The prophet, may God's prayers be upon him, and 'Ali, the amir of the faithful, and the other imams had no power to tamper with people's property or with their lives.[1] The Islamic government is not despotic but constitutional. However, it is not constitutional in the well-known sense of the word, which is represented in the parliamentary system or in the people's councils. It is constitutional in the sense that those in charge of affairs observe a number of conditions and rules underlined in the Koran and in the Sunna and represented in the necessity of observing the system and of applying the dictates and laws of Islam.[2] This is why the Islamic government is the government of the divine law. The difference between the Islamic government and the constitutional governments, both monarchic and republican, lies in the fact that the people's representatives or the king's representatives are the ones who codify and legislate, whereas the power of legislation is confined to God, may He be praised, and nobody else has the right to legislate and nobody may rule by that which has not been given power by God. This is why Islam replaces the legislative council by a planning council that works to run the affairs and work of the ministries so that they may offer their services in all spheres.

All that is mentioned in the book (Koran) and in the Sunna is acceptable and obeyed in the view of the Moslems. This obedience facilitates the state's responsibilities, however when the majorities in the constitutional monarchic or republican governments legislate something, the government has to later exert efforts to compel people to obey, even if such obedience requires the use of force.

The Islamic government is the government of the law and God alone is the ruler and the legislator. God's rule is effective among all the people and in the state itself. All individuals—the prophet, his successors and other people—follow what Islam, which descended through revelation

---

[1] "The prophet" refers to Muhammed; 'Ali was Muhammed's son-in-law and, according to the Shi'ite tradition, his legitimate heir; an amir is a high military official; and an imam, in the Shi'ite tradition, is an important spiritual leader with sole power to make decisions about doctrine.

[2] The Koran is the book of the holy scriptures of Islam; the Sunna is the body of customary Islamic law second only to the Koran in authority.

and which God has explained through the Koran and through the words of His prophet, has legislated for them.

*   *   *

Yes, government in Islam means obeying the law and making it the judge. The powers given to the prophet, may God's peace and prayers be upon him, and to the legitimate rulers after him are powers derived from God. God ordered that the prophet and the rulers after him be obeyed: "Obey the prophet and those in charge among you." There is no place for opinions and whims in the government of Islam. The prophet, the imams and the people obey God's will and Shari'a.[3]

The government of Islam is not monarchic, * * * and not an empire, because Islam is above squandering and unjustly undermining the lives and property of people. This is why the government of Islam does not have the many big palaces, the servants, the royal courts, the crown prince courts and other trivial requirements that consume half or most of the country's resources and that the sultans and the emperors have. The life of the great prophet was a life of utter simplicity, even though the prophet was the head of the state, who ran and ruled it by himself. * * * Had this course continued until the present, people would have known the taste of happiness and the country's treasury would not have been plundered to be spent on fornication, abomination and the court's costs and expenditures. You know that most of the corrupt aspects of our society are due to the corruption of the ruling dynasty and the royal family. What is the legitimacy of these rulers who build houses of entertainment, corruption, fornication and abomination and who destroy houses which God ordered be raised and in which His name is mentioned? Were it not for what the court wastes and what it embezzles, the country's budget would not experience any deficit that forces the state to borrow from America and En-

gland, with all the humiliation and insult that accompany such borrowing. Has our oil decreased or have our minerals that are stored under this good earth run out? We possess everything and we would not need the help of America or of others if it were not for the costs of the court and for its wasteful use of the people's money. This is on the one hand. On the other hand, there are state agencies that are not needed and that consume money, resources, paper and equipment. This is a waste banned by our religion because such waste escalates the people's problems, wastes their time and effort and consumes monies of which they are in the direct need. In Islam, when Islam was the ruler, justice was dispensed, restrictions established and disputes settled with utter simplicity. The qadi (judge) saw to it that all this was done by a handful of persons with some pencils and a little ink and paper. Behind all this, the qadi directed people to work for an honorable and virtuous life. But now, only God knows the number of the justice departments, bureaus and employees—all of which are futile and do the people no good, not to mention the hardship, difficulties, waste of time and monies, and, consequently, the loss of justice and rights that they cause the people.

Qualifications of Ruler

The qualifications that must be available to the ruler emanate from the nature of the Islamic government. Regardless of the general qualifications, such as intelligence, maturity and a good sense of management, there are two important qualifications:

1. Knowledge of Islamic Law

2. Justice

A. In view of the fact that the Islamic government is a government of law, it is a must that the ruler of the Moslems be knowledgeable in the law. * * * Knowledge of the law and of justice are among the most important mainstays of the imamate. If

---

[3] Shari'a is Islamic law as a whole, including the Koran and the Sunna.

a person knows a lot about nature and its secrets and masters many arts but is ignorant of the law, then his knowledge does not qualify him for the caliphate and does not put him ahead of those who know the law and deal with justice. It is an acknowledged fact among the Moslems since the first days and until our present day that the ruler or the caliph must know the law and possess the faculty of justice with a sound faith and good ethics. This is what sound reason requires, especially since we know that the Islamic government is an actual embodiment of the law and not a matter of whims.

*   *   *

B. The ruler must have the highest degree of faith in the creed, good ethics, the sense of justice and freedom from sins, because whoever undertakes to set the strictures, to achieve the rights, and to organize the revenues and expenditures of the treasury house must not be unjust. God says in his precious book: "The unjust shall not have my support." Thus, if the ruler is not just, he cannot be trusted not to betray the trust and not to favor himself, his family and his relatives over the people.

*   *   *

REVIEW QUESTIONS

1. What prevents Islamic government from becoming despotic according to Khomeini?
2. In what sense is Islamic government constitutional?
3. Why is there no legislative branch in Islamic government?
4. What is the role of the executive and the judiciary in this form of government?
5. What qualifications must a Moslem ruler have?
6. How will his method of governing differ from that of a traditional monarch?

TOMÁS BORGE

FROM "The New Education in the New Nicaragua"

The small nations of Central America gained their independence in the early nineteenth century but were subject to the informal economic and political imperialism of the United States well into the late twentieth century. Saddled with weak, single-commodity economies vulnerable to the fluctuations of the international market, these "banana republics" remained poor and undeveloped. For the most part, they were ruled by dictators whose expressions of anticommunism and subservience to U.S. foreign policy objectives won them the money and weapons they needed to suppress internal dissent.

In 1979, Nicaragua's Sandinista National Liberation Front (FSLN) overthrew the dictatorial regime of Anastasio Somoza, replacing it with a hybrid synthesis of political democracy, an economy combining elements of socialism and capitalism, and a Christian radicalism based in Catholic liberation theology. Despite fierce opposition on the part of the Reagan administration, the Sandinista's struggled throughout the 1980s to solidify their claim to power through improving the basic living conditions of ordinary Nicaraguans. But as Tomás Borge, one of the original founders of the FSLN, argued, the transformation of Nicaragua was to be not only material but also intellectual. In 1983, Borge addressed the National Association of Nicaraguan Educators and called on them to apply their skills in support of the revolution.

From "The New Education in the New Nicaragua," by Tomás Borge, in *Nicaragua: The Sandinista People's Revolution, Speeches by Sandinista Leaders,* edited by Bruce Marcus (New York: Pathfinder Press, 1985), pp. 70–72, 75, 77–81.

*   *   *

It is not at all unusual that teachers who yesterday fought the *somocista* dictatorship today defend the revolution they helped make, that they do not stand apart from the heroic struggle of the peoples of Central America. In February 1979 Nicaraguan teachers did not struggle, could not struggle, for a new system of education. They had to fight to create the conditions of struggle for a new education.

Right now that struggle is the order of the day. A new philosophy, a new structure, a new strategy of education constitute the most important task of this revolutionary process, a task that belongs to the entire society but whose fundamental responsibility lies with the teachers.

Of course, when we speak of the new education, we are not only referring to academic programs or to the social priorities of this great challenge. We are referring to the quest for the new man, to the transformation of man through education. We are referring to the unpostponable task of converting our people into a nation of students and teachers—that is, a country where the students learn to be teachers and the teachers learn to be students.

One of the most important challenges is to create in teachers the consciousness that they too must be students. To be capable of teaching others, the teacher must learn to be his own instructor as well.

*   *   *

But how can teachers raise the cultural level of their students if they haven't mastered new teaching techniques; if they lack culture adequate to the level that should be imparted in their teaching? How can teachers form patriotic and revolutionary consciousness in their students if they lack the basic elements for projecting this capacity as architects or sculptors of consciousness?

How can teachers explain the politics of the revolution to their students if they have no basis on which to form an opinion, if they themselves don't know what the revolution is? How can teachers explain to their students the essence of exploitation, exploitation that has stripped part of their own hides, if they don't know how to explain exploitation conceptually? How can they create profoundly anti-imperialist consciousness if they are ignorant of the essence of imperialism?

How can they speak to their students of the perspectives of the new society if they don't know what pillars the new society must be built on? How can they involve their students in conceiving a strategy of education if they don't have the remotest idea of what the new education is?

To answer all these problems we must understand their roots. Before speaking about what the new education means, it's essential that we understand what the role of education has been in the social process. It's necessary for us to define education in the full sense in order to later place it in the context of the revolutionary process.

Education is the process through which society reproduces the ideas, values, moral and ethical principles, and behavioral habits of the successive generations. All social organization is a function of the class interests that hold state power. Education is a process of forming individuals in ideology, in a complex system of values and ideas that justifies the interests of the class that wields state power.

*   *   *

In Nicaragua, at the time it was incorporated into the capitalist world market, at the end of the last century when massive coffee production began, the oligarchy's vehicle of ideological domination was fundamentally the church. The great masses of urban and rural workers, the so-called marginal sectors, and the great mass of the peasantry were denied access to education at any level.

This paved the way for an almost bloodcurdling illiteracy in our country. It was the rich coffee growers and landlords, the political sectors that controlled the government, and the rich merchants who sent their sons to the national and foreign universities.

*   *   *

After victory in the war of liberation against all the material means of domination, all our people and you teachers in particular opened up a second battle, just as important, in the field of ideological liberation. I am referring to the National Literacy Crusade.

However, other battles remain to be opened, perhaps some of the most difficult battles and confrontations, battles in the sphere of ideological formation. And you, teachers, you who can carry in your knapsacks the reproduction of ideology, science, and culture should be part of the vanguard in this battle for the new education and the formation of the new man.

This battle is going to complete the liberation of Nicaragua. It will open the way for the formation of a society where man can unleash all his physical, spiritual, scientific, and artistic faculties, that is, a society that develops man's freedom to create, construct, and fabricate beauty and culture, to master science.

*   *   *

* * * You should teach all those who enter your area of influence to be patriots, revolution-

aries, exemplars of solidarity, dedicated to the interests of the workers and peasants and of all the toiling masses. You should teach them to be anti-imperialist, to fight discrimination and oppression, and encourage love for justice, liberty, and defense of the homeland.

You should help create a new man who is responsible, disciplined, creative, cooperative, an efficient worker, with high moral, civic, and spiritual principles, endowed with a critical and self-critical capacity, and with a scientific view of the world and society.

Teachers should help to create a new man who will know how to appreciate beauty and who will recognize and value the dignity of sweat and daily labor, to create a new man who is profoundly humanitarian, reliable, and selfless, a man ready to fight in the quest for the great joining together of individual and collective interests.

*   *   *

At this point the importance of the links between education and work is perhaps all too obvious. One time we put it this way: We should create a society where all students work and all workers study.

*   *   *

To create a new education we must create a new teacher. What should this new teacher be like? The teacher should:

1. Be revolutionary—that is, master of the new morality, archetype of the new man.

2. Have a high degree of commitment.

3. Identify with the interests of the workers.

4. Be a bearer of critical and self-critical attitudes.

5. Be capable of teaching and capable of learning.

6. Give each student the same love as would be given to his or her own children.

7. Be responsible and disciplined.

8. Be a teacher in the classroom and in the community.

9. Participate in defense of the homeland.

10. Participate in and bring participation from the community into all decision making.

These are principles that cannot be negotiated. Sovereignty of the homeland cannot be negotiated. The arms that defend this sovereignty are not negotiable.

And what are these arms? The cannons, the tanks, the rifles. We don't ever want to use them, and it is to be hoped that we won't have to. The violent fire of these arms will be used only to defend ourselves. We are sure that one day, when the ferocious fangs of imperialism have been pulled, we are not going to need these arms any more.

But there are other arms, ideological arms, that also defend the sovereignty of our homeland. The main ideological arm our people possess is the new education. This is an arm that cannot be laid down. The imperialists can shout all they want.

Even if they shout their heads off we will hold tight to our ideological arms with the same tenacity that we hang on to our rifles.

*   *   *

REVIEW QUESTIONS

1. Why is education critical to the revolutionary project according to Borge?
2. On the basis of Borge's remarks, what kind of society were the Sandinistas hoping to build?
3. What would the "new man" of the post-revolutionary period be like?
4. How would the "new teacher" help to create this "new man"?
5. How does the "new education" differ from the old?

CHAI LING

FROM "I Am Still Alive"

The growing liberalization of Soviet policies in the late 1980s generated new hopes for political reform and increased civil liberties in Communist China. After the death of Mao Zedong in 1976, the new Chinese leadership under Deng Xiaoping (1904–1997) had begun to introduce limited economic reforms, including a greater willingness to condone small-scale private industry, and had ended the Cultural Revolution, permitting somewhat greater freedom of cultural expression. Many hoped that the aging Chinese leadership would follow the lead of the Soviet "gerontocracy" and move to institute a more democratic system of government.

In the spring of 1989, the seventieth anniversary of the 4 May 1919 student movement sparked prodemocracy protests in Beijing. At the height of the demonstrations, China's capital was occupied by as many as one million protesters. In Tiananmen Square, long a focal point for political protests, 100,000 demonstrators gathered, led by students who served as leaders of the protest movement. Despite strong international pressure to deal gently with the protesters, Deng Xiaoping declared martial law on 20 May. Trustworthy troops recruited from the countryside were called in and on 4 June they put an end to the demonstrations by firing on the protesters, killing hundreds and arresting thousands. A few days later, Chai

Ling, one of the student leaders, wrote a description of the massacre in the hopes of stirring international indignation over this incident.

From "I Am Still Alive," by Chai Ling, in *Voices from Tiananmen Square: Beijing Spring and the Democracy Movement*, edited by Mok Chiu Yu and J. Frank Harrison (Montreal: Black Rose Books, 1990), pp. 194–200.

Today is June 8th, 1989. It is now 4:00 p.m. I am Chai Ling, Commander-in-Chief in Tiananmen Square. I am still alive.

I believe I am the best qualified witness to the situation in the Square during the period from June 2nd to 4th June, and I also have the responsibility to tell that truth to everyone, every single countryman, every single citizen.

At about 10 p.m. on the night of June 2nd, the first warning of what was to come was given when a police car knocked down four innocent persons, three of whom died. The second signal immediately followed when soldiers abandoned whole truckloads of armaments, military uniforms and other equipment, leaving them behind for the people and my college mates who had blocked their way. We were very suspicious of this act; so we immediately collected together everything that had been abandoned and sent them to the Public Security Bureau, retaining a receipt as proof. The third signal occurred at 2:10 p.m. on June 3rd, when large numbers of military police beat up students and citizens at Xinhuamen. At that time, the students were standing on top of cars, using microphones to cry out to the police: "The people's police love the people," "The people's police won't beat people up." Instantly, a soldier rushed towards a student, kicked him in the stomach, and scoffed: "Who loves you?" He then gave him another bash in the head and the student collapsed.

*   *   *

At 9:00 p.m. sharp, all of the students in the Square stood up and with their right hands raised, declared: "I vow that, for the promotion of our nation's process of democratization, for the true prosperity of our nation, for our great nation, for defense against a handful of schemers, for the sal-vation of our 1.1 billion countrymen from White Terror, that I will give up my young life to protect Tiananmen Square, to protect the Republic. Heads can fall, blood can run, but the people's Square can never be abandoned. We are willing to sacrifice our young lives in a fight to the death of the very last person."

At 10:00 p.m. sharp, the Democratic University was formally established in the Square, with vice-commander Jiang Deli becoming the principal, and people from all sides celebrated the occasion enthusiastically. At that time, the commanding unit was receiving many urgent warnings, as the situation became very tense. On one hand, there was the thunderous applause for the establishment of our Democratic University in the northern part of the Square near the Statue of the Goddess of Liberty; whereas along the Boulevard of Eternal Peace at the eastern edge of the Square, there was a river of blood. Murderers, those soldiers of the 27th Battalion, used tanks, heavy machine guns, bayonets (tear gas being already outdated) on people who did no more than utter a slogan, or throw a stone. They chased after the people, shooting with their machine guns. All the corpses along the Boulevard of Eternal Peace bled heavily from their chests; and all the students who ran to us were bleeding in the arms, chests and legs. They did this to their own countrymen, taking their life's blood. The students were very angry and held their dead friends in their arms.

After 10:00 p.m. we, the commanding unit, made a request based upon the principle that our Patriotic-Democratic Movement, as both a Student Movement and People's Movement, had always been to demonstrate peacefully. In opposition, therefore, to the many students and citizens who angrily declared that it was time to use weapons, we proposed the supreme principle of peace and sacrifice.

In this way, hands joined together, shoulder to shoulder, singing "The International," we slowly came out from our tents. Hands joined, we came to the western, northern and the southern sides of the Monument of the People's Heroes, and sat there quietly, with serenity in our eyes, waiting for the attack by murderers. What we were involved in was a battle between love and hate, not one between violence and military force. We all knew that if we used things like clubs, gasoline bottles and the like (which are hardly weapons) against those soldiers, who were holding machine guns or riding in tanks, and who were out of their minds, then this would have been the greatest tragedy for our Democracy Movement.

So the students sat there silently, waiting to give up their lives. There were loudspeakers next to the commanding unit's tent playing "The Descendants of the Dragon." We sang along with it, with tears in our eyes. We embraced each other, shook hands, because we knew that the last moment of our lives, the moment to give up our lives for our nation, had arrived.

There was this student called Wang Li, who was fifteen. He had written his will. I have forgotten the exact wording, but I remember him saying: "Life is strange. The difference between life and death is just a split second. If you see an insect crawling toward you, all you have to do is to think about killing it and the insect will instantly stop crawling." He was only fifteen, and yet he was thinking about death. People of the Republic, you must not forget the children who fought for you.

*   *   *

I chatted with the students and told them the old story that goes: "There were these 1.1 billion ants living on a mountain top. One day, the mountain was ablaze. To survive, the ants had to get down the mountain. They gathered themselves into a giant ball and rolled down the mountain. The ants on the outside were burnt to death. But the lives of many more were saved. My fellow students, we at the Square are the outermost layer, because in our hearts we understand that only by dying can we ensure the survival of the Republic." * * * The hunger strikers went to negotiate with the soldiers, with the so-called Martial Law Command Post, to tell them we were leaving. It was hoped that they would ensure the students' safety and peaceful retreat. Our headquarters consulted students on whether to leave or to stay. We decided to leave.

But the executioners didn't keep their word. As students were leaving, armed troops charged up to the third level of the Monument. * * * We only found out later, that some students still had hope in the Government and they thought that, at worst, they would be removed.

Then the tanks made "mincemeat" of them. Some say more than 200 students died. Some say more than 4000 died in the Square alone. I don't know the total. But the members of the Independent Workers' Union were on the outside. They stood their ground and they're all dead. There were twenty to thirty of them. I heard that, after the students left, tanks and armoured personnel carriers flattened tents with bodies inside. They poured gasoline over them and burned them. Then they washed away the traces with water. Our movement's symbol, the Goddess of Democracy, was crushed to bits.

*   *   *

The radio kept saying that the troops had come to Beijing to deal with riotous elements and to maintain order in the capital. I think I'm most qualified to say that we students are not riotous elements. Anyone with a conscience should put his hand on his chest and think of children, arm in arm, shoulder to shoulder, sitting quietly under the Monument, their eyes awaiting the executioner's blade. Can they be riotous elements? If they were riotous elements, would they sit there quietly? How far have the fascists gone? They can turn their backs on their conscience and tell the biggest lie under the sky. If you say soldiers who kill innocent people with their rifles are animals, what do you call those who sit in front of the camera and lie?

As we left the Square, arm in arm, as we walked along Changan Avenue, a tank charged at us and fired tear gas at the students. Then the tank rolled toward us, rolled over the students' heads, and legs. We couldn't find any of our classmates' bodies intact. Who's the riotous element? In spite of this, we in the front continued on our way. Students put on masks because the tear gas hurt their throats. What can we do to bring back those students who were sacrificed? Their souls will always remain on Changan Avenue. We who walked away from Tiananmen Square, arrived at Beijing University, still alive. Many students from other universities, students from out of town, had prepared beds to welcome us. But we were very, very sad. We were alive. Many more were left in the Square, and on Changan Avenue. They'll never come back. Some of them were very young. They will never come back.

As we entered Beijing University, our hunger strike turned sit-in, our peaceful protest, came to an end. Later we heard that Li Peng, at 10 p.m. on June 3rd, had handed down three orders: First, troops can open fire. Second, military vehicles must go forward without stopping. They must take back the Square by June 4th. Third, the leaders and organizers of the Movement must be killed.

My compatriots, this is the frenzied, puppet government that initiated a slaughter and is still commanding troops and ruling China. But my compatriots, even at the darkest moment, dawn will still break. Even with the frenzied, fascist crackdown, a true people's democratic republic will be born. The critical moment has come. My compatriots, all Chinese nationals with a conscience, all Chinese people, wake up! The ultimate victory must be the people's! Yang Shangkun, Li Peng, Wang Zhen and Bo Yibo, the final hour of your puppet regime is near!

Down with Fascism!
Down with Military Rule!
Long Live the Republic!

REVIEW QUESTIONS

1. According to Chai Ling, what were the goals of the student protesters?
2. How does Chai Ling characterize the actions of the political leadership and the troops sent in to put down the protests?
3. Why were Chinese students willing to die for their cause?
4. To what extent did the Chinese student protesters accept Gandhi's principles of non-violent resistance?
5. Why do you think that strategy failed in this particular case?

THE UNITED NATIONS

FROM *Global Outlook 2000*

Whereas population growth rates were once largely controlled by local conditions such as the fertility of the soil, the availability of natural resources, and local weather conditions, the globalization of production and distribution have created a situation in which a region's population growth rate is directly affected by the operation of the international market. Better distribution of food surpluses now makes it possible for local famines to be averted, while the transfer of medical technologies can have a dramatic impact on decreasing the number of deaths caused by disease and accidents. On the other hand, political instability and weak infrastructures can interfere with the distribution of available resources to threatened populations. In this sense, the global outlook for the world's population is determined as much by politics as by the productive capacity of humankind.

As the following excerpts from a recent United Nations report demonstrate, the demographic history of late-twentieth-century human populations is strongly shaped by continuing economic disparities between the developed and developing regions of the world.

From *Global Outlook 2000: An Economic, Social and Environmental Perspective,* by United Nations (New York: United Nations, 1990), pp. 202–8.

*   *   *

Demographic trends are fairly predictable and provide a good basis for the analysis of structural economic change and the associated economic and social policy issues of the next decade. Against a background of generally slower population growth, which will result in a world population of 6 billion just before the turn of the century, there will be considerable regional diversity. The fastest growth (an annual rate of 3 per cent) will occur in Africa, where the task of economic recovery and restoration of self-sustained growth will be particularly difficult. There will be less dispersion, however, in labour force growth rates in the developing world. The rate will average 2.5 to 3 per cent. In contrast, labour force growth rates in developed countries will be less than 1 per cent. Employment is likely to grow more slowly than the labour force in most countries, and unemployment will be a concern for all groups of countries.

For the world as a whole, the dependency ratio is expected to fall, but this is the result of opposing trends in major world regions. In the developing countries, the total dependency ratio should fall as fertility declines. In the developed countries it is expected to rise, mainly as a result of the increase in the elderly population. This increase will raise the level of the real and financial resources needed for health care and other support of the elderly.

The pressure for international migration should accelerate in the 1990s as income differentials increase and the cost of transportation declines relative to incomes. Urban population will continue to grow faster than rural population in all regions of the world, due principally to rural-urban migration, and the number and size of "megacities" is expected to increase rapidly in developing countries.

*   *   *

The world's population surpassed 5 billion in the middle of 1987 and is projected to grow to 6 billion just before the turn of the century. In the previous 13 years, it grew from 4 to 5 billion. The quarter century from 1975 to 2000 will have witnessed the greatest absolute expansion of the global population in such a short time. From 1980 to 1985 the annual rate of population growth was 1.7 per cent, compared with the peak rate of 2.0 per cent in the period from 1965 to 1970. It is expected to continue to decline slowly in the future. Only in the next century, however, will there be a significant decline in the size of the net annual increments to the world total.

There was a clear dichotomy in the 1960s between slow growth of population in the developed countries (the average annual rate was 1.1 per cent) and rapid growth in the developing countries (the average annual rate was about 2.5 per cent). The major developing regions showed little diversity, ranging from 2.4 per cent in Asia (excluding Japan) to 2.7 per cent in Latin America.

Since the 1960s, however, the rates of population increase have become more diverse among the developing regions and their constituent countries, and the divergence is expected to increase in the 1990s. Population growth in Africa began to accelerate in the 1950s and continued to do so through the 1980s, while in most of the other developing regions it began to decelerate in the 1970s. The drop in the growth rate was particularly notable in China and the Asian planned economies; the drop is expected to continue in the 1990s, falling to little more than half the rate of the 1960s. Projected population growth rates for the 1990s are now about 3 per cent in Africa and Western Asia, 2 per cent in South and East Asia (excluding Japan and the Asian planned economies), 1.9 per cent in Latin America, and 1.3 per cent in China together with the Asian planned economies. The growth rate in the developed countries as a whole has fallen to 0.6 per cent in the 1980s and is projected to be only 0.5 per cent in the 1990s (0.8 per cent or less in North America and Eastern Europe and 0.3 to 0.5 per cent in the European market economies and Japan). These differential growth rates will result in quite different age structures that, in turn, will affect many aspects of development.

The shift in the regional shares of global population is dominated by the growth of developing Africa and West Asia. Their combined share was 10 per cent in 1960 and 12 per cent in 1980. It is projected to reach 16 per cent in 2000. In contrast, the proportion of world population accounted for by the developed countries declined from 31.4 per cent in 1960 to 25.8 per cent in 1980, and is projected to be only 20.6 per cent in 2000.

Population growth in the least developed countries has accelerated from an average rate of 2.4 per cent in the 1960s to 2.6 per cent in the 1980s. This is in contrast to a dramatic drop in China together with the Asian planned economies, from 2.4 per cent to 1.3 per cent, and a slight decline in the other developing countries as a whole. The difference is expected to be even greater in the 1990s—2.9 per cent in the least de-

veloped countries versus 1.3 per cent in China and the Asian planned economies and 2.3 per cent in the developing countries as a whole.

* * *

Population growth rates are affected by trends in mortality and fertility. Mortality has declined unevenly in most countries during recent decades. Although it remains high in most of the developing countries, the mortality rate has declined very rapidly in some and has reached levels as low, or nearly as low, as those in developed countries. In the past decade, there have been decreases in infant mortality rates in nearly all countries, but more than one quarter, representing 29 per cent of world population, still have rates above 100 per 1,000 live births. Between 1985 and 1990, the average in the least developed countries is estimated at 123 per 1,000. In Africa as a whole it is 106, while the average in the developed countries (excluding South Africa) is about 15.

Mortality levels and trends are influenced by many social, economic, and cultural factors, including policies and programmes outside the health sector. Economic development is usually associated with mortality decline, since improved economic conditions imply higher living standards and increased financial resources for health services. But low mortality levels have also been achieved in some low-income countries where Governments are committed to reducing mortality; China, Cuba, Sri Lanka, and the state of Kerala in India are well-known examples, as is Costa Rica among middle-income countries.

Deaths of young children in developing countries constitute a large share of all deaths, and children are considered the major target in efforts to reduce overall mortality. The factors having the greatest effect on the mortality of children are those related to parental education, especially of mothers. Analysis of data from the World Fertility Surveys show that infant and child mortality generally decreases as the average number of years of the mother's education increases. Survey results suggest that the effect of parental education may be greater than that of income-related factors and access to health facilities combined.

One of the most important findings from the World Fertility Surveys concerns the exceptionally high mortality among children born after a short birth interval. This suggests that family planning programmes aimed at spacing births and avoiding high-risk pregnancies could help to reduce infant, child, and also maternal mortality. Other interventions that can lower mortality in developing countries include efforts to improve the nutritional level of the population, immunization programmes, and other health measures.

*   *   *

In the developed countries, life expectancy at birth has increased from 66 years in the early 1950s to 73 years in the late 1980s, while in the developing countries as a whole (including China), it has increased from 41 to 60. There was a dramatic increase in China, from 41 years in the early 1950s to 69 in the late 1980s; in Africa, it increased from 35 years to 49. The average life expectancy in the least developed countries in the period from 1985 to 1990 is also about 49 years. The low life expectancy and high infant mortality in the least developed countries reflect their unfavourable living conditions and imply that their population may increase even more rapidly in the future if mortality conditions improve and fertility remains unchanged.

Life expectancy at birth is generally several years longer for women than for men, especially in the developed countries: 77 years for women versus 70 years for men in the late 1980s. In the developing countries (including China), it is about 61 years for women and 59 years for men. The region where average expectancy for women is the same as for men is South Asia, although improvements in female life expectancy in Sri Lanka in the past two decades have resulted in a more normal pattern in that country. By the year 2000, the difference is projected to increase to three years in the developing countries as a whole, and to remain constant in the developed countries.

*   *   *

The most rapid fertility declines have occurred in developing countries with a combination of profound improvements in child survival, increases in educational levels, and strong family planning programmes. Since the late 1950s, total fertility rates have declined by 2 to 3 children per woman in China, the Republic of Korea, Thailand, Malaysia, Sri Lanka, Brazil, Mexico, and Colombia. The proportion of married women of childbearing age currently using contraception in all these countries grew rapidly since at least the mid-1960s, gaining 2 to 3 percentage points a year. In the 1980s, it reached levels of 50 to 70 per cent. Simultaneously, under-five mortality (i.e., the combined mortality of infants and children under age 5) declined in China from 240 per thousand to 55, and from a range of 120 to 190 per thousand in the other seven countries to a range of 40 to 90. Gross enrolment ratios of females for the second level of education rose from less than 15 per cent in all these countries to between 30 and 35 per cent in Thailand, Brazil, and China. It rose to about 50 per cent in Sri Lanka, Malaysia, Mexico, and Colombia and to 90 per cent in the Republic of Korea.

Conversely, low rates of child survival, low levels of education, and insufficient access to birth control methods impede the transformation to lower fertility in most countries of sub-Saharan Africa, as well as in such Asian countries as Pakistan, Bangladesh, Nepal, and Afghanistan. Total fertility rates in many of these countries average 6 or 7 children per woman. They show few signs of decline despite significant government initiatives in immunization and family planning. Under-five mortality is still well above 150 per 1000 in most of them and often exceeds 250; the female gross enrolment ratio for the second level of education and the proportion of married women currently using contraception are typically below 10 per cent and rarely above 20 per cent.

*   *   *

REVIEW QUESTIONS

1. According to the United Nations, what general trends can the world population be expected to follow in coming years?
2. What are the most important differences between the demographic trends of the developed and developing regions of the globe?
3. Why are population growth rates higher in developing regions than in developed regions?
4. How do the population profiles of developing and developed regions differ?
5. What role does infant mortality play in the demographic patterns of developed and developing regions?
6. Why is a decrease in infant mortality usually associated with economic development?
7. What is the relationship between family planning and infant mortality?

NIGEL HARRIS

FROM *The New Untouchables: Immigration and the New World Worker*

The geographic distribution of the human population is increasingly determined by economic trends favoring the transfer of substantial numbers of people from one region to another. Immigration has always played an important role in human experience—the history of the United States is, in its very essence, a history of migration—but greatly enhanced opportunities for long-distance travel make migration an especially significant factor in the late twentieth century.

Labor migration has long been a highly contentious social and political issue. When shortages of workers threaten to limit the economic development of a nation or region, as they did in western Europe during the 1950s and 1960s, for example, skilled and unskilled workers are often recruited and encouraged to relocate to host countries. However, when an economic downturn occurs, as happened around the world in the 1970s, native workers often come to resent immigrants, even when those immigrants hold jobs that native workers do not want. At the same time, cultural differences between natives and immigrants may breed hostility, especially when the language, religion, or ethnicity of immigrants sets them apart from the native majority. Yet, as Nigel Harris argues in a recent study of labor migration, legislation intended to stem the influx of migrant workers runs counter to processes of global economic integration which tend to break down existing national boundaries and blur the lines separating citizens from noncitizens.

From *The New Untouchables: Immigration and the New World Worker,* by Nigel Harris (London: Tauris, 1995), pp. 104–9.

In the case of Britain, workers had been recruited from the West Indies, Asia and Africa during the Second World War (the restrictions on their entry to Britain were removed in 1942). In the immediate postwar years, while emigration continued to be encouraged, the government made significant efforts to recruit displaced—but white—persons in Europe (for example, 170,000 Poles and Italians were brought in). However, from 1948, the spontaneous arrival of West Indian workers began a process that expanded to include those from the Indian subcontinent, parts of Africa, Cyprus, and so on, and continued up to the ending of the automatic right of entry for Empire subjects in 1962. Up to that time, immigrants from the Empire were automatically citizens with the same rights as those born in Britain (including the right to vote and stand for public office).

The 1962 measure by no means settled the issue, since many groups in the former Empire retained the status of British nationality, and it was thus necessary to remove from this status any right to enter Britain. Through successive crises, leading to the flight of British passport holders—particularly those of Indian origin living in Kenya, Uganda, Malawi and, later, Chinese from Hong Kong—two types of British passport were created: one carrying the right to enter and live in Britain, one without it. The unfortunates who gained the second type were thus unilaterally deprived of their former rights. For the first time, a specific British nationality was invented, based upon a quasi-ethnic origin or "patriality," turning upon the nationality of a parent or grandparent.

*   *   *

If the British, at least in theory, accepted Empire or Commonwealth citizens resident in Britain as British, and then sought to identify newcomers as foreigners (other than those entering for family reunification), France identified those with French identity cards (including, for example, the inhabitants of the four main cities of Senegal) as having the right to settle in the country. Further-

more, the efforts to incorporate Algeria into France led in 1947 to the recognition of Muslim Algerians as French citizens. Yet severe conflicts of interest remained: the French Algerian authorities at various stages discouraged migration to protect the local labour supply; however, as the movement for an independent Algeria developed, they began to encourage movement to France as a safety valve, while Paris shifted from seeking labour to trying to discourage the spread of sedition to metropolitan France. Later, under the Evian Agreements (1962) which ended the war in Algeria, Paris agreed to the free movement of labour to France in return for Algerian protection of French interests and population in Algeria, and in particular, French oil and gas installations; in the event, the Algerian government nationalized these assets in 1971. Only two years after the Evian Agreements, Paris tried to restrict the movement in a new bilateral agreement with Algiers—an annual quota of 35,000 was laid down as from 1968 (under separate agreements with the relevant governments, France agreed to accept 150,000 workers from Morocco and 100,000 from Tunisia). In practice, the Algerian government saw the outflow of workers, particularly the skilled, as deleterious to Algeria's economic development, and eventually suspended the arrangement just ahead of a decision by Paris to do so.

For Germany, * * * under the federal constitution, workers drawn in by the extraordinary growth of the economy remained temporary or "guest workers" *(Gastarbeiter)*. Political and economic status, citizen and worker, remained distinct. While by 1960 possibly a quarter of West Germany's population had been born abroad, by 1990 there were some 5 million "immigrants" (including those born in Germany of non-German parents). The initial movement had been started and regulated by bilateral government agreements. The rush of agreements came after the main supply of labour, from East Germany, ended with the building of the Berlin Wall in 1961. However, once established, direct relationships between employers and source areas tended to take over—up to 35 per cent of the migration of Turkish workers to Germany took place outside the bilateral agreements, and two-fifths of these were requested by companies rather than being recruited by German government agents. ∗ ∗ ∗ The agreements, however, restricted the freedom of the government to act unilaterally on the flows.

What had been created by government action tended to be sustained by employers, even after the government had reversed its position. As we have seen, as controls tightened, so the exceptions increased, particularly for seasonal workers in construction and agriculture from Poland and the Czech and Slovak Republics. Companies also recruited workers from Albania, Bulgaria, Poland and Hungary. It was still insufficient and reputedly the numbers of illegal entrants continued to rise.

In Europe generally, from the early 1970s and shortly before the onset of the largest recession since the Second World War, increasing attempts were made to end immigration, deter the arrival of newcomers with a right of entry, and encourage immigrants to leave. Britain was among the first to seek to suspend the process with the 1962 Commonwealth Immigration Act; Denmark temporarily suspended new arrivals in 1970; Norway increased the restrictions on the issue of work permits in 1971; West Germany ended the right of foreign tourists to apply for work permits in 1972, with other disincentives to those with the right to enter Germany under family reunification privileges; the Netherlands restricted entries from 1973, France from 1974. Thus, within a very short space of time, the desperate search for workers was replaced by a no less desperate struggle to exclude them. In December 1978, the French government suspended the granting of extensions to ten-year residents' permits which were due to expire in 1979, affecting some half a million North Africans; in the spring of the following year, Paris eased the provisions to expel immigrants without judicial appeal (the same innovation took place in Britain), and tried to introduce summary detention (a measure subsequently defeated in the Assembly). Governments tried also—unsuccessfully—to pressurize governments in source countries to restrict emigration (without an increase in foreign aid to compensate for the loss in emigrant remittances). Some also penalized the carriers, forcing airline officials to implement immigration legislation, and thus avoided the legal complexities of expelling landed immigrants (the US Coastguards, for similar reasons, arrested suspected immigrants on the high seas and expelled them—acts that might be construed as acts of piracy). As we have seen, employers were also used to help implement immigration law by making them liable to charges for hiring illegal immigrants.

Governments also, as we have seen, tried to encourage existing immigrants to give up voluntarily their residential rights and leave. Britain made provision for this under the 1971 Act, but, as has been frequently noted, those who utilized the provisions usually intended to leave the country in any case. Similarly under the West German regulations of 1984–85, most of the 180,000 immigrants who left seemed to have decided to do so independently of any incentives offered. In 1977–78, the French government offered financial help to encourage unemployed immigrants and their families to leave; out of the targeted 100,000, some 45,000—mainly Portuguese and Spaniards —responded, but again, it was thought the beneficiaries had already decided to leave.

The context of increased control, in conditions of world recession from 1973, ensured that the question of immigration was interwoven with increased economic insecurity among the population at large. If this were not enough, in almost all European countries there were political leaders to urge on the process, to seek to stimulate sudden waves of panic at the "foreign invasion" (the words used by former President of France, Giscard d'Estaing). Former British cabinet minister Enoch Powell spoke in 1968 of British decline in terms of the fall of the Roman Empire, overwhelmed by barbarians. Edith Cresson, prime minister of France, promised the mass expulsion of illegal immigrants. Some British borough councils refused to implement their legal obligation to rehouse the homeless if they were foreign-born; French local authorities also refused the citizens of French overseas territories the right to public housing.

Having established the context of the public debate, governments feel obliged to proclaim, at one- or two-year intervals, a complete end to immigration, knowing full well that the promise cannot be fulfilled. In the jostling for a political edge, the lies are traded without a flicker of shame. French minister Charles Pasqua in mid-1993, preparing for the presidential elections of 1995, announced the government's target as "zero immigration" and promised legislation to legalize random identity checks and introduce an accelerated expulsion procedure; such measures were necessary because illegal immigrants were responsible for crime and drug dealing.

This verbal froth may have been effective in directing public attention to some of the more defenceless members of society, but it had little impact on the number of arrivals. According to one of the better estimates, the entries for residence of non-Europeans into the European Union increased from 1 million per year in 1985 to 3 million in 1992—with legal immigration increasing from 700,000 to 1 million; the number applying for asylum from 170,000 to 690,000; citizens of former Yugoslavia with temporary protected status from 100,000 to 300,000; the entry of "ethnic" Germans (nationals of countries other than Germany but claiming German descent) from 100,000 to 300,000; and illegals from 50,000 to 400,000. ＊ ＊ ＊ Of course, figures for arrivals say nothing about the stock of foreign residents, since the numbers leaving were also rising; by 1990, there were only about 8 million resident aliens, or just over 2 for every 100 of the population of the European Union.

The numbers of illegal entrants seemed to be rising and, as in the case of Canada and the United States, governments in Europe were periodically obliged to regularize their status in order that they could be brought into the area of public supervision. Regularization was a recognition of the failure of immigration regulation to control the labour market.

＊   ＊   ＊

REVIEW QUESTIONS

1. According to Harris, why did European governments allow immigration after the Second World War?
2. Why have they sought to discourage it since the 1970s?
3. Where did immigrants to Britain, France, and Germany come from?
4. What factors influenced non-European workers' decisions about where to relocate?
5. Why is it difficult for European governments to enforce "zero immigration" policies?

KATHRYN KOPINAK

FROM *Desert Capitalism*

In recent years, many manufacturers have also become migrants, having transferred production facilities from their home country to other regions. Seeking large pools of low-cost workers and freedom from government labor and environmental regulations, these corporations have broken their ties to a single nation or region, taking a transnational approach to doing business. European, Japanese, or U.S. consumers benefit from this system because manufactured goods made in China, the Philip-

pines, or Honduras tend to be cheaper; corporate shareholders benefit from increased profits. On the other hand, workers in developed regions suffer from a loss of jobs, while workers in the developing world suffer from low pay, long hours, and dangerous or abusive conditions.

In the mid-1960s, the Mexican government passed legislation allowing foreign-owned companies to establish duty-free production facilities—known as maquiladoras—*on the U.S.-Mexico border. Car parts manufactured in the United States, for example, might be transported across the border to be assembled by unskilled or semiskilled Mexican laborers, and then be returned for sale in the United States. Japanese and U.S. corporations would be able to take advantage of the low cost of hiring Mexican workers, and Mexican peasants would benefit from access to new, better-paid jobs in the industrial sector. In theory, a dual-technology transfer would occur:* maquiladoras *would provide not only unskilled jobs but also some highly paid and highly skilled managerial and technical positions. However, as Kathryn Kopinak demonstrates in her recent study of Nogales-area* maquiladoras, *the migration of production facilities does not necessarily result in the creation of an affluent consumer economy in Mexico, although it could create incentives for migrant laborers to remain within their country of origin.*

From *Desert Capitalism: Maquiladoras in North America's Western Industrial Corridor,* by Kathryn Kopinak (Tucson: University of Arizona Press, 1996), pp. 111–14.

*   *   *

Biological reproduction and migration are alternative ways of constituting a labor force, and the household is an important structure facilitating either option. While Mexico as a country has no difficulty in biologically reproducing itself, the economic restructuring of the eighties—which culminated in NAFTA—meant that for many Mexicans, employment was available at home less often than it used to be. Journalists * * * have observed that the media have been used by the state as vehicles "for convincing people to change their reproductive behavior, to control or encourage migration—like migration toward the northern border—and it has been those media . . . which propagate the idea that it would be a better life with a small family, without questioning what women or couples want."

* * * The individuals who get the Nogales and Imuris transport-equipment jobs advertised in the newspaper actively organize their lives outside of work to take the most advantage of whatever opportunity maquila employment offers. Many have left their families and traveled from Nayarit, Sinaloa, and from locations within Sonora to work at the border. Most of them come from within the western industrial corridor, rather than outside of it. Even though most were not employed before their first maquila job, or worked marginally in agriculture, they now comprise an industrial labor force that this corridor internally generates. (The central corridor also generates its own maquila labor force, but the Pacific corridor does not.)

Workers organize themselves into households which attempt to mediate some of the sharpest difficulties of the economy. The household is especially important in this attempted mediation due to the absence * * * of effective trade-union organizations that might help defend workers' rights and represent their interests. The others with whom workers undertake the active organization of their lives are in most cases members of their families.

Given Mexico's economic crisis in the eighties, and the concomitant drop in real wages, the average maquiladora worker's household must be seen as an organization promoting family survival, rather than one whose goal is to accumulate consumer goods. The goal of subsistence is accomplished better by some maquila households than others, and the optimum form seems to be a household with both men and women wage earners, as opposed to a household with only male wage earners or only female wage earners. Households with both male and female wage earners had the highest total household and per capita incomes, the least dependence on the income of any one worker, and the lowest proportion of economically active members working in maquilas. They were also larger than households that had only male or only female workers, indicating that the slogan used by family-planning promoters that "between fewer burros, there are more cobs of corn" is not necessarily a valid assumption. * * *

While Nogales has one of the lowest proportions of women in its maquila labor force of any maquiladora center, the wages of women transport-equipment workers were found to be about the same as anyone else's wages in their households. Women workers who identified themselves as wives or daughters of the head of the household in which they lived were definitely not supplementary wage earners, as is often assumed. Women workers also headed their own households, and sometimes could not count on any income brought home by men. Households without any economic support from men probably provide for the most precarious existence.

Perhaps if maquiladoras paid workers higher wages, there would be more reason for workers to separate their work life from their family life. * * * However, such a wage increase would have to be quite substantial to make up for the drop in real wages that occurred in the eighties. Even if wages did increase to a level that could provide the material possibility for living independently from family, Mexicans might very well not choose such a lifestyle, since there is strong cultural support for family economies. * * * At present, this question is not dependent on culture, as many managers indicated, but on the material basis that

would make it a possibility. Maquiladoras do not pay workers enough for them to put work before family even if they valued their work more highly than their families, which, in general, they do not.

While household organization enhances the well-being of the family group as a unit, it may also create and maintain inequalities structured internally on the basis of age and gender. Other authors have argued that women maquila workers are subordinated by their families. Although redistribution of income within the household was not specifically investigated in this study, I think there is no doubt that the household is one site of women's subordination. The fact that some men said they had migrated because of curiosity or for excitement, whereas women never gave such a reason for migrating, is an indication of the greater choices available to men for acting outside of family structures. The household, however, is not the only source of women's subordination. * * *

Even those households with both men and women wage earners, the best type of household for pooling income, often failed to meet basic standards set by Mexicans for decent living. Evidence for this is the finding that the average maquila household in Nogales, including all wage earners, only brought together enough income to be considered "absolutely poor" by prevailing standards. Moreover, many of the households evaluated as having achieved an effective structure for group survival share housing that is overcrowded, built of inadequate materials, and poorly serviced by utilities like water and electricity.

In general, employment in Nogales transport-equipment maquilas does not serve workers very well. If the dual-technology thesis were becoming a reality, more workers would be expected to live in households that were accumulating consumer goods rather than merely surviving. Also, more workers would be expected to have better housing due to an increase in skilled jobs, which should be better rewarded.

The existence of the border to stop migration means that maquila workers' main cross-border travel is for shopping to take advantage of lower prices, greater variety, and better quality in the

United States. Most Nogales workers buy their groceries and other basic supplies in the United States in dollar-denominated values. * * * With little to spend, they are limited to stores in the immediate Nogales area. They may, however, consider more permanent trips farther into the United States if maquila employment provides them with enough resources. On the other hand, higher wages might help Mexicans establish a better standard of living south of the border and root them there.

* * *

REVIEW QUESTIONS

1. According to Kopinak, where do *maquiladora* workers come from?
2. Why have they migrated to Nogales?
3. How do *maquiladora* workers organize their lives once they arrive in Nogales?
4. What sort of family structure allows these workers to maximize their standard of living?
5. Why do these workers remain absolutely poor?

THE UNITED NATIONS

FROM *Report of the Fourth World Conference on Women*

> *In September 1995, women representing 185 of the world's nations gathered in Beijing to attend the United Nations' Fourth World Conference on Women. Delegates to the conference adopted a platform for action that outlined the various problems confronting women around the world, established a set of strategic objectives, and listed the specific actions to be taken to achieve these objectives. Working from a general consensus in favor of women's empowerment, participants discussed the ways in which women are affected by poverty, violence, armed conflict, human rights violations, pollution, and differing access to medical treatment, education, economic advancement, and political power.*
>
> *Certain issues addressed by the conference were highly controversial and drew formal reservations from the governments of participating nations. Language intended to guarantee access to abortion and contraceptive technologies or to protect the rights of lesbians, for example, was rejected by many who attended the conference. Representatives of Islamic nations also refused to accept clauses that were seen as violating Muslim practice in the area of marriage, female sexuality, and inheritance. On the other hand, few reservations were expressed about one of the key issues addressed by the conference: the fact that women (and children) are disproportionately represented among the world's poor.*

From *Report of the Fourth World Conference on Women, Beijing, 4–15 September 1995,* United Nations web page, www.undp.org/fwcw/daw1.htm [accessed 11/21/01].

FROM **Platform for Action**

*   *   *

A. WOMEN AND POVERTY

47. More than 1 billion people in the world today, the great majority of whom are women, live in unacceptable conditions of poverty, mostly in the developing countries. * * *

48. In the past decade the number of women living in poverty has increased disproportionately to the number of men, particularly in the developing countries. The feminization of poverty has also recently become a significant problem in the countries with economies in transition as a short-term consequence of the process of political, economic and social transformation. In addition to economic factors, the rigidity of socially ascribed gender roles and women's limited access to power, education, training and productive resources as well as other emerging factors that may lead to insecurity for families are also responsible. The failure to adequately mainstream a gender perspective in all economic analysis and planning and to address the structural causes of poverty is also a contributing factor.

49. Women contribute to the economy and to combating poverty through both remunerated and unremunerated work at home, in the community and in the workplace. The empowerment of women is a critical factor in the eradication of poverty.

50. While poverty affects households as a whole, because of the gender division of labour and responsibilities for household welfare, women bear a disproportionate burden, attempting to manage household consumption and production under conditions of increasing scarcity. Poverty is particularly acute for women living in rural households.

51. Women's poverty is directly related to the absence of economic opportunities and autonomy, lack of access to economic resources, including credit, land ownership and inheritance, lack of access to education and support services and their minimal participation in the decision-making process. Poverty can also force women into situations in which they are vulnerable to sexual exploitation.

52. In too many countries, social welfare systems do not take sufficient account of the specific conditions of women living in poverty, and there is a tendency to scale back the services provided by such systems. The risk of falling into poverty is greater for women than for men, particularly in old age, where social security systems are based on the principle of continuous remunerated employment. In some cases, women do not fulfil this requirement because of interruptions in their work, due to the unbalanced distribution of remunerated and unremunerated work. Moreover, older women also face greater obstacles to labour-market re-entry.

53. In many developed countries, where the level of general education and professional training of women and men are similar and where systems of protection against discrimination are available, in some sectors the economic transformations of the past decade have strongly increased either the unemployment of women or the precarious nature of their employment. The proportion of women among the poor has consequently increased. In countries with a high level of school enrolment of girls, those who leave the educational system the earliest, without any qualification, are among the most vulnerable in the labour market.

*   *   *

55. Particularly in developing countries, the productive capacity of women should be increased through access to capital, resources, credit, land, technology, information, technical assistance and training so as to raise their income and improve nutrition, education, health care and status within the household. The release of women's productive potential is pivotal to breaking the cycle of poverty so that women can share fully in the benefits of development and in the products of their own labour.

56. Sustainable development and economic

growth that is both sustained and sustainable are possible only through improving the economic, social, political, legal and cultural status of women. Equitable social development that recognizes empowering the poor, particularly women, to utilize environmental resources sustainably is a necessary foundation for sustainable development.

*   *   *

F. WOMEN AND THE ECONOMY

150. There are considerable differences in women's and men's access to and opportunities to exert power over economic structures in their societies. In most parts of the world, women are virtually absent from or are poorly represented in economic decision-making, including the formulation of financial, monetary, commercial and other economic policies, as well as tax systems and rules governing pay. * * *

151. In many regions, women's participation in remunerated work in the formal and non-formal labour market has increased significantly and has changed during the past decade. While women continue to work in agriculture and fisheries, they have also become increasingly involved in micro, small and medium-sized enterprises and, in some cases, have become more dominant in the expanding informal sector. Due to, inter alia, difficult economic situations and a lack of bargaining power resulting from gender inequality, many women have been forced to accept low pay and poor working conditions and thus have often become preferred workers. On the other hand, women have entered the workforce increasingly by choice when they have become aware of and demanded their rights. Some have succeeded in entering and advancing in the workplace and improving their pay and working conditions. However, women have been particularly affected by the economic situation and restructuring processes, which have changed the nature of employment and, in some cases, have led to a loss of jobs, even for professional and skilled women. In ad-

dition, many women have entered the informal sector owing to the lack of other opportunities. Women's participation and gender concerns are still largely absent from and should be integrated in the policy formulation process of the multilateral institutions that define the terms and, in cooperation with Governments, set the goals of structural adjustment programmes, loans and grants.

152. Discrimination in education and training, hiring and remuneration, promotion and horizontal mobility practices, as well as inflexible working conditions, lack of access to productive resources and inadequate sharing of family responsibilities, combined with a lack of or insufficient services such as child care, continue to restrict employment, economic, professional and other opportunities and mobility for women and make their involvement stressful. Moreover, attitudinal obstacles inhibit women's participation in developing economic policy and in some regions restrict the access of women and girls to education and training for economic management.

153. Women's share in the labour force continues to rise and almost everywhere women are working more outside the household, although there has not been a parallel lightening of responsibility for unremunerated work in the household and community. Women's income is becoming increasingly necessary to households of all types. In some regions, there has been a growth in women's entrepreneurship and other self-reliant activities, particularly in the informal sector. In many countries, women are the majority of workers in non-standard work, such as temporary, casual, multiple part-time, contract and home-based employment.

154. Women migrant workers, including domestic workers, contribute to the economy of the sending country through their remittances and also to the economy of the receiving country through their participation in the labour force. However, in many receiving countries, migrant women experience higher levels of unemployment compared with both non-migrant workers and male migrant workers.

*   *   *

156. * * * Women contribute to development not only through remunerated work but also through a great deal of unremunerated work. On the one hand, women participate in the production of goods and services for the market and household consumption, in agriculture, food production or family enterprises. * * * This unremunerated work—particularly that related to agriculture—is often undervalued and underrecorded. On the other hand, women still also perform the great majority of unremunerated domestic work and community work, such as caring for children and older persons, preparing food for the family, protecting the environment and providing voluntary assistance to vulnerable and disadvantaged individuals and groups. This work is often not measured in quantitative terms and is not valued in national accounts. Women's contribution to development is seriously underestimated, and thus its social recognition is limited. The full visibility of the type, extent and distribution of this unremunerated work will also contribute to a better sharing of responsibilities.

157. Although some new employment opportunities have been created for women as a result of the globalization of the economy, there are also trends that have exacerbated inequalities between women and men. At the same time, globalization, including economic integration, can create pressures on the employment situation of women to adjust to new circumstances and to find new sources of employment as patterns of trade change. More analysis needs to be done of the impact of globalization on women's economic status.

158. These trends have been characterized by low wages, little or no labour standards protection, poor working conditions, particularly with regard to women's occupational health and safety, low skill levels, and a lack of job security and social security, in both the formal and informal sectors. Women's unemployment is a serious and increasing problem in many countries and sectors. Young workers in the informal and rural sectors and migrant female workers remain the least protected by labour and immigration laws. Women, particularly those who are heads of households with young children, are limited in their employment opportunities for reasons that include inflexible working conditions and inadequate sharing, by men and by society, of family responsibilities.

159. In countries that are undergoing fundamental political, economic and social transformation, the skills of women, if better utilized, could constitute a major contribution to the economic life of their respective countries. Their input should continue to be developed and supported and their potential further realized.

160. Lack of employment in the private sector and reductions in public services and public service jobs have affected women disproportionately. In some countries, women take on more unpaid work, such as the care of children and those who are ill or elderly, compensating for lost household income, particularly when public services are not available. In many cases, employment creation strategies have not paid sufficient attention to occupations and sectors where women predominate; nor have they adequately promoted the access of women to those occupations and sectors that are traditionally male.

161. For those women in paid work, many experience obstacles that prevent them from achieving their potential. While some are increasingly found in lower levels of management, attitudinal discrimination often prevents them from being promoted further. The experience of sexual harassment is an affront to a worker's dignity and prevents women from making a contribution commensurate with their abilities. The lack of a family-friendly work environment, including a lack of appropriate and affordable child care, and inflexible working hours further prevent women from achieving their full potential.

162. In the private sector, including transnational and national enterprises, women are largely absent from management and policy levels, denoting discriminatory hiring and promotion policies and

practices. The unfavourable work environment as well as the limited number of employment opportunities available have led many women to seek alternatives. Women have increasingly become self-employed and owners and managers of micro, small and medium-scale enterprises. The expansion of the informal sector, in many countries, and of self-organized and independent enterprises is in large part due to women, whose collaborative, self-help and traditional practices and initiatives in production and trade represent a vital economic resource. When they gain access to and control over capital, credit and other resources, technology and training, women can increase production, marketing and income for sustainable development.

163. ∗ ∗ ∗ To realize fully equality between women and men in their contribution to the economy, active efforts are required for equal recognition and appreciation of the influence that the work, experience, knowledge and values of both women and men have in society.

164. In addressing the economic potential and independence of women, Governments and other actors should promote an active and visible policy of mainstreaming a gender perspective in all policies and programmes so that before decisions are taken, an analysis is made of the effects on women and men, respectively.

REVIEW QUESTIONS

1. According to this report, why are women more likely to be poor than men?
2. What role does the increasing integration of the global economy play in female poverty?
3. What specific types of difficulties do women confront as workers?
4. Which of the problems addressed in this document are more likely to be confronted by women in developing regions?
5. Which are specific to developed regions?

LYUBOV SIROTA

FROM "Chernobyl Poems"

On the night of 25 April 1986, one of the reactors at the Chernobyl nuclear power station in the Soviet Ukraine exploded during a poorly implemented experiment, releasing a substantial amount of radiation and resulting in a partial meltdown of the reactor's core. The Soviet government initially attempted to keep news of this disaster from the public but was later forced to acknowledge the magnitude of the incident. While the long-term effects of this serious nuclear accident remain to be seen, those living in the immediate vicinity of Chernobyl were exposed to substantial levels of radiation. Thirty-two people died immediately from massive radiation exposure, but many others in the general vicinity suffered from a variety of radiation-related illnesses. Thyroid cancer rates among the children in the region, for example, are abnormally high.

The 30,000 residents of Pripyat, the town closest to the Chernobyl plant, were not evacuated immediately and suffered exposure to radiation and lingering illness. Lyubov Sirota, an employee of the Chernobyl Atomic Energy Station, was one of the

NUCLEAR DISASTER AT CHERNOBYL (1986)

On 26 April 1986, an uncontrolled fire in a Ukrainian nuclear reactor in Chernobyl un-leashed the worst accident in the history of nuclear power. Thirty-one workers died from fatalities stemming from the incident, thousands died from thyroid cancer in the following years, and the high incidence of cancer in the Ukraine persists. The accident galvanized Europe's antinuclear movement and prompted a new international awareness of environ-mental pollution as a critical issue facing the contemporary world. How does this photograph heighten the viewer's alarm about the magnitude of nuclear disasters?

few who actually saw the explosion on that April night. Both she and her son were eventually evacuated to Kiev, but they continue to suffer from the aftereffects of radiation exposure. The following poems by Sirota, from a collection of her poems on the Chernobyl accident, entitled Burden, *serve as a farewell to her home town.*

From "Chernobyl Poems," in *Burden,* by Lyubov Sirota, translated by Leonid Levin and Elisavietta Ritchie, Chernobyl Poems web site, www.wsu.edu/~brians/chernobyl_poems.html [accessed 11/21/01].

To Pripyat

1.

We can neither expiate nor rectify
the mistakes and misery of that April.
The bowed shoulders of a conscience awakened
must bear the burden of torment for life.
It's impossible, believe me,
to overpower
or overhaul
our pain for the lost home.
Pain will endure in the beating hearts
stamped by the memory of fear.
There,
surrounded by prickly bitterness,
our puzzled town asks:
since it loves us
and forgives everything,
why was it abandoned forever?

2.

At night, of course, our town
though emptied forever, comes to life.
There, our dreams wander like clouds,
illuminate windows with moonlight.
live by unwavering memories,
remember the touch of hands.
How bitter for them to know
there will be no one for their shade
to protect from the scorching heat!
At night their branches quietly rock
our inflamed dreams.
Stars thrust down
onto the pavement,

to stand guard until morning . . .
But the hour will pass . . .
Abandoned by dreams,
the orphaned houses
whose windows
have gone insane
will freeze and bid us farewell! . . .

3.

We've stood over our ashes;
now what do we take on our long journey?
The secret fear that wherever we go
we are superfluous?
The sense of loss
that revealed the essence
of a strange and sudden kinlessness,
showed that our calamity is not
shared by those who might, one day,
themselves face annihilation?
. . . We are doomed to be left behind by the
            flock
in the harshest of winters . . .
You, fly away!
But when you fly off
don't forget us, grounded in the field!
And no matter to what joyful faraway lands
your happy wings bear you,
may our charred wings
protect you from carelessness.

At the Crossing

A century of universal decay.
In cyclotrons nuclei are split;
souls are split,

sounds are split
insanely.

While behind a quiet fence
on a bench in someone's garden
Doom weighs
a century of separation
on the scales.

And her eyes are ancient,
and her palms are taut with nerves,
and her words clutch
in her throat . . .

Nearby and cynical, death
brandishes a hasty spade.
Here, whispers are worse than curses,
offer no consolation.

Yet out on the festive streets
the mixed chorus
of pedestrians and cars
never stops.
The stoplight
winks with greed,
gobbles the fates of those it meets
in the underground passageways
of eternity.

How long
the bureaucrats
babbled on
like crows
about universal good . . .
Yet somehow
that universal good
irreversibly
seeps away.
Have we slipped up?

In the suburbs, choke-cherries
came out with white flowers
like gamma fluorescence.
What is this—a plot by mysterious powers?
Are these intrigues?
We have slipped up!

Choke-cherries are minor.
They are not vegetables . . .
Here, tomatoes ripened too early:
someone just ate one—the ambulance
had to be called in a rush.
We have slipped up.

We came to the sea—
the eternal source of healing . . .
And—we were stunned.
The sea is an enormous waste dump.
What happened?
Have we slipped up?

How masterfully
the blind promoters
of gigantic plans
manipulated us so far!
Now the bitter payment
for what we so easily
overlooked yesterday.

Has day died?
Or is this the end of the world?
Morbid dew on pallid leaves.
By now it's unimportant
whose the fault,
what the reason,
the sky is boiling only with crows . . .
And now—no sounds, no smells.
And no more peace in this world.
Here, we loved . . .
Now, eternal separation
reigns on the burnt out Earth . . .

These dreams are dreamed
ever more often.
Ever more often I am sad for no reason,
when flocks of crows
circle over the city
in skies, smoky, alarmed . . .

REVIEW QUESTIONS

1. What do Lyubov Sirota's poems tell you about individual reactions to this sort of nuclear accident?
2. Why do you think Sirota chose to write about this experience in the form of poetry?
3. On the basis of your reading of these poems, how has the relationship between human beings and nature been transformed by Chernobyl and other ecological disasters?
4. What shared concerns appear in these poems and Mikhail Gorbachev's restructuring speech (Chapter 30)?
5. In what ways might Sirota's poems be read as a critique of the Soviet system?

HOWARD H. FREDERICK

FROM "Computer Networks and the Emergence of Global Civil Society"

As the Chernobyl disaster demonstrates, the benefits of new technologies are sometimes offset by substantial local and global risks. However, certain recent advances in communication technologies promise to greatly enhance the quality of human interaction, making it possible for the world's people to enter into far more intimate and informed relationships with one another than ever before. Dramatic increases in the ease and rapidity of information transfer—through the use of satellite transmission and the internet, an international computer network—now make it possible for people almost anywhere in the world to communicate freely with one another.

Certain autocratic regimes have sought to impose strict regulations on access to these new forms of communications, fearful that their citizens will be able to use fax machines and modems to circumvent the state's monopoly over the media. Even nations with a traditionally strong allegiance to the freedom of speech and the freedom of the press have sought to place some restrictions on the free flow of information. In the United States, for example, the Computer Decency Act—recently overturned by the U.S. Supreme Court—was passed into law with the intent of limiting children's exposure to pornography. However, the potential benefits of the "information superhighway" are readily apparent, even to those who believe that it must be subject to a certain degree of government control. In 1992, Howard H. Frederick, of the Institute for Global Communications, presented a paper to the Annual Conference of the Peace Studies Association, arguing that modern communications technologies may have an important role to play in maintaining world peace.

From "Computer Networks and the Emergence of Global Civil Society: The Case of the Association for Progressive Communications (APC)," by Howard H. Frederick, in *Globalizing Networks: Computers and International Communications*, edited by Linda Harasim and Jan Walls (Cambridge, Mass.: MIT Press, 1997).

*   *   *

What we call "community" used to be limited to face-to-face dialogue among people in the same physical space, a dialogue that reflected mutual concerns and a common culture. For thousands of years, people had little need for long-distance communication because they lived very close to one another. The medieval peasant's entire life was spent within a radius of no more than twenty-five miles from the place of birth. Even at the beginning of our century, the average person still lived in the countryside and knew of the world only through travelers' tales.

Today, of course, communications technologies have woven parts of the world together into an electronic web. No longer is community or dialogue restricted to a geographical place. With the advent of the fax machine, telephones, international publications, and computers, personal and professional relationships can be maintained irrespective of time and place. Communication relationships are no longer restricted to place, but are distributed through space. Today we are all members of many global "non-place" communities.

In the last decade there has emerged a new kind of global community, one that has increasingly become a force in international relations. We speak of the emergence of a global civil society, that part of our collective lives that is neither market nor government but is so often inundated by them. Still somewhat inarticulate and flexing its muscles, global civil society is best represented in the global "NGO Movement," nongovernmental organizations and citizens advocacy groups uniting to fight planetary problems whose scale confound local or even national solutions. Previously isolated from one another, nongovernmental organizations (NGOs) are flexing their muscles at the United Nations and other world forums as their power and capacity to communicate increase.

The concept of civil society arose with John Locke, the English philosopher and political theorist. It implied a defense of human society at the national level against the power of the state and the inequalities of the marketplace. For Locke, civil society was that part of civilization—from the family and the church to cultural life and education—that was outside of the control of government or market but was increasingly marginalized by them. Locke saw the importance of social movements to protect the public sphere from these commercial and governmental interests.

From the industrial age to the present, mercantilist and power-political interests pushed civil society to the edge. In most countries, civil society even lacked its own channels of media communication. It was speechless and powerless, isolated behind the artifice of national boundaries, rarely able to reach out and gain strength in contact with counterparts around the world. What we now call the "NGO Movement" began in the middle of the last century with a trickle of organizations and has now become a flood of activity. Nongovernmental organizations (NGOs) today encompass private citizens and national interest groups from all spheres of human endeavor. Their huge increase in number and power is due in no small measure to the development of globe-girdling communications technologies.

As Dutch social theorist Cees J. Hamelink has written, we are seeing a new phenomenon emerging on the world scene—global civil society, best articulated by the NGO movement. New communications technologies now facilitate communication among and between the world's national civil societies, especially within the fields of human rights, consumer protection, peace, gender equality, racial justice, and environmental protection.

*   *   *

The continued growth and influence of global civil society face two fundamental problems: increasing monopolization of global information and communication by transnational corporations; and the increasing disparities between the world's info-rich and info-poor populations. Global computer networking makes an electronic "end-run" around the first problem and provides an appropriate technological solution to overcome the second.

Hamelink observed that the very powers that obstructed civil society at the national level—markets and governments—also controlled most of the communication flows at the global level. Government monopolies still control a huge share of the world's air waves and telecommunications flows. Even worse, a handful of immense corporations now dominate the world's mass media. If present trends continue, [Ben] Bagdikian predicted, by the turn of the century "five to ten corporate giants will control most of the world's important newspapers, magazines, books, broadcast stations, movies, recordings and videocassettes." Telecommunications infrastructures and data networks must also be included in this gloomy account. Today's "lords of the global village" are huge corporations that "exert a homogenizing power over ideas, culture and commerce that affects populations larger than any in history. Neither Caesar nor Hitler, Franklin Roosevelt nor any Pope, has commanded as much power to shape the information on which so many people depend to make decisions about everything from whom to vote for to what to eat."

Why is this happening? The most fundamental reason is that fully integrated corporate control of media production and dissemination reaps vast profits and creates huge corporate empires. Already more than two-thirds of the U.S. work force is now engaged in information-related jobs. * * * While there are more than one hundred news agencies around the world, only five—Associated Press, United Press International, Reuters, Agence France Presse, and TASS—control about ninety-six percent of the world's news flows. * * *

In addition to transnational control of information, global civil society and the NGO movements confront the increasing gap between the world's info-rich and info-poor populations. In virtually every medium, the disparities are dramatic.

Ninety-five percent of all computers are in the developed countries.

While developing countries have three-quarters the world's population, they can manage only thirty percent of the world's newspaper output.

* * *

Only seventeen countries in the world had a Gross National Product larger than total U.S. advertising expenditures.

* * *

Ten developed countries, with 20 percent of the world's population, accounted for almost three-quarters of all telephone lines. * * *

Even within the United States we have the info-rich and the info-poor. From the streets of Manhattan to the barrios of Los Angeles, from the homeless to the immigrant populations, from Appalachia to the inner cities, there are millions upon millions of our fellow Americans who cannot read or type, do not have access to computers, do not consume newsprint, cannot afford a book.

* * *

To counter these twin trends that threaten to engulf civil society with a highly controlled form of commercialization, there has arisen a worldwide metanetwork of highly decentralized technologies—computers, fax machines, amateur radio, packet data satellites, VCRs, video cameras and the like. They are "decentralized" in the sense that they democratize information flow, break down hierarchies of power, and make communication from top and bottom just as easy as from horizon to horizon. For the first time in history, the forces of peace and environmental preservation have acquired the communication tools and intelligence gathering technologies previously the province of the military, government and transnational corporations.

* * *

[Association for Progressive Communication (APC)] members are fond of saying that they "dial locally and act globally." * * *

The APC Networks can now set up complete electronic mail and conferencing systems on small, inexpensive appropriate-technology microcomputers. * * * Individual users typically make a local phone call to connect to their host machine, which stores up mail and conference postings until contacted by a partner computer in the network, typically about every two hours. Aside from its low cost, this technological configuration is appropriate for countries whose telecommunications infrastructure is still poor.

*   *   *

One user, let's say a peace researcher in Finland, uses her computer to dial into a local data network (analogous to the telephone network but for data traffic instead of voice). She either types in a message or "uploads" a prepared text, into her host computer, in this case, NordNet in Stockholm. Within a short time that message is transferred via high-speed modems through the telephone lines to the host system of her correspondent, a university peace studies professor in Hawaii. His host system is the PeaceNet computer in California. At his convenience, he connects to his host and "downloads" the message. This miraculous feat, near instantaneous communication across half the globe, costs each user only the price of a local phone call plus a small transmission charge.

Unlike systems used by the large commercial services, the APC Networks are highly decentralized and preserve local autonomy. One microcomputer serves a geographical region and is in turn connected with other "nodes."

*   *   *

The first large-scale impact of these decentralizing technologies on international politics happened in 1989. When the Chinese government massacred its citizens near Tianamen Square, Chinese students transmitted the most detailed, vivid reports instantly by fax, telephone and computer networks to activists throughout the world. They organized protests[,] meetings, fundraising, speaking tours and political appeals. Their impact was so immense and immediate that the Chinese government tried to cut telephone links to the exterior and started to monitor the Usenet com-

puter conferences where much of this was taking place.

Another example is the 1991 Gulf War, where computer networks such as PeaceNet and its partner networks in the APC exploded with activity. While mainstream channels of communication were blocked by Pentagon censorship, the APC Networks were carrying accurate reports of the effects of the Gulf War on the Third World, Israel and the Arab countries and the worldwide anti-war movement.

*   *   *

During the attempted coup in the Soviet Union in August 1990, the APC partners used telephone circuits to circumvent official control. Normally, the outdated Russian telephone system requires hordes of operators to connect international calls by hand, and callers must compete fiercely for phone lines. But the APC partner networks found other routes for data flow.

*   *   *

Around the globe, other APC networks are working on issues of peace, social justice, and environmental protection. In Australia, the members of the Pegasus network are working to hook up the affluent 18 percent of the electorate that votes Green, which would make the party more powerful. Back in the United States, EcoNet is helping high school students monitor water quality in local rivers. One such experiment involved 50 students along the Rouge River in Michigan. When in 1991 neo-Nazi skinheads ransacked a Dresden neighborhood populated by foreigners, users of the German partner network ComLink posted news of the event. Soon Dresden newspapers were flooded with faxes from around the world deploring the action. All in all, tens of thousands of messages a day pass back and forth within the "APC village," and the number grows every day.

*   *   *

The partner networks of the Association for Progressive Communications have built a truly global network dedicated to the free and balanced flow of information. The APC Charter mandates its partners to serve people working toward "peace, the prevention of warfare, elimination of militarism, protection of the environment, furtherance of human rights and the rights of peoples, achievement of social and economic justice, elimination of poverty, promotion of sustainable and equitable development, advancement of participatory democracy, and nonviolent conflict resolution."

The APC Networks are trying to make an "end-run" around the information monopolies and to construct a truly alternative information infrastructure for the challenges that lie ahead. By providing a low-cost, appropriate solution for nongovernmental organizations and poor countries, they are attempting to civilize and democratize cyberspace.

We are moving into a "new world order." The age of democracy may have had its beginnings in the French and the American revolutions, but only today is it finally reaching the hearts and minds of sympathetic populations around the world. This "preferred" world order of democratic change depends heavily on the efficiency of communication systems.

* * *

REVIEW QUESTIONS

1. According to Frederick, what is a "global civil society"?
2. How is it being created?
3. What might threaten its continued expansion and development?
4. In what ways does access to computer technologies reflect existing disparities between rich and poor countries?
5. How might the existence of a global information infrastructure undercut this division?
6. In what ways do new information and communications technologies lessen the importance of existing national borders?
7. What might be the benefits of the emergence of a global culture?
8. What dangers are there to an ever-increasing integration of the cultures of the world?

Credits

Images

Page 34: Ministero per i Beni e le Attivita Culturali, Soprintendenza Speciale al Museo Nazionale Preistorico ed Etnografico "L. Pigorini," Roma; **40:** Courtesy of the University of Utah Press; **63:** Scala/Art Resource, NY; **68:** Scala/Art Resource, NY; **98:** Scala/Art Resource, NY; **120:** By permission of the British Library; **135:** Giraudon/Art Resource, NY; **175:** (*top*) Photo by Josie Piller and Debra Doty, University Art Gallery, University of Pittsburgh; (*middle*) Bettmann/Corbis; (*bottom*) Photo by Josie Piller and Debra Doty, University Art Gallery, University of Pittsburgh; **188:** Rijksmuseum, Amsterdam; **195:** Erich Lessing/Art Resource, NY; **239:** Giraudon/Art Resource, NY; **255:** Scala/Art Resource, NY; **278:** Art Resource, NY; **308:** Erich Lessing/Art Resource, NY; **316:** Bibliotheque Nationale de France; **369:** Copyright The Frick Collection, New York; **392:** Reunion des Musées Nationaux/Art Resource, NY; **415:** Copyright Imagerie d'Epinal 2001; **426:** Manchester City Council, Department of Libraries and Theatres; **448:** Art Resource, NY; **474:** The Royal Collection 2001, Copyright HM Queen Elizabeth II; **489:** National Library of Scotland; **505:** Courtesy of Stadtgeschich Hiches Museum, Dusseldorf; **512:** from *The Looking Glass*, 1832; **541:** Erich Lessing/Art Resource, NY; **557:** Foto Marburg/Art Resource, NY; **584:** Courtesy of the Fogg Art Museum, Harvard University Art Museums, Bequest of Grenville L. Winthrop; **592:** © 1997 North Winds Pictures; **628:** From the book *Spectacle of Women* by Lisa Tickner; **636:** Punch Limited; **653:** Hulton-Deutsch Collection/Corbis; **672:** Hoover Institution Archives; **689:** Ullstein Bild, Berlin; **715:** Giraudon/Art Resource, NY; **734:** Sächsische Landesbibliothek—Staats- und Universitätsbibliothek Dresden; **765:** Ullstein Bild, Berlin; **771:** Hulton-Deutsch Collection/Corbis; **802:** Keystone Pressedienst, Hamburg; **829:** Ullstein Bilderdienst, Berlin.

Text Selections

Page 3: From *Mission to Asia*, Medieval Academy of America, 1980. **10:** From *The Travels of Ibn Battuta*. Copyright © 1958 Cambridge University Press. Reprinted with the permission of Cambridge University Press. **15:** From *Decline and Fall of Byzantium to the Ottoman Turks*. Copyright © 1975 by permission of the Wayne State University Press. **21:** From *Islam: From the Prophet Muhammad to the Capture of Constantinople*, vol. 1, Oxford University Press, 1987. **23:** From *Medieval Russia's Epics, Chronicals and Tales*, edited by Serge A. Zenkovsky, translated by Serge A. Zenkovsky. Copyright © 1963, 1974 by Serge A. Zenkovsky; renewed © 1991 by Betty Jean Zenkovsky. Used by permission of Dutton, a division of Penguin Putnam, Inc. **28:** From *The Voyage of Cadamosto*. Copyright © the Hakluyt Society. Reprinted by the permission of the publisher. **33:** From *Selected Documents Illustrating the Four Voyages of Columbus*. Copyright © the Hakluyt Society. Reprinted by the permission of the publisher. **39:** From *The Voyage of Pedro Alvares Cabal to Brazil and India*. Copyright © the Hakluyt Society. Reprinted by the permission of the publisher. **47:** From *I Libri della Famiglia*, University of South Carolina Press, 1969. Reprinted by permission of the publisher. **52:** From *The Autobiography of Benvenuto Cellini*, Modern Library, 1995. Reprinted by permission of the publisher. **55:** From *The Lives of Artists*, Penguin Books, 1965. Reprinted by permission of the publisher. **59:** From *The Notebooks of Leonardo da Vinci*, Cape, 1958. Reprinted by permission of the publisher. **62:** From *The Book of the Courtier*, Bantam Doubleday Dell, 1959. Reprinted by permission of the publisher. **69:** From *Philosophy of Man*, University of Chicago Press, 1948. Reprinted by permission of the publisher. **71:** From *The Prince*, W. W. Norton, 1977. Reprinted by permission of the publisher. **75:** From *Ten Colloquies*, Prentice-Hall, 1986. Reprinted by permission of the publisher. **80:** From *Utopia*, W. W. Norton, 1975. Reprinted by permission of the publisher. **87:** From *The Pursuit of Power: Venetian Ambassadors' Reports* by James C. Davis, editor & translator. English translation copyright © 1970 by James C. Davis. Reprinted by permission of HarperCollins Publishers Inc. **89:** From *The Spiritual Exercises of St. Ignatius* by Anthony Mottola, copyright © 1964 by Doubleday, a division of Random House, Inc. Used by permission of Doubleday, a division of Random House, Inc. **92:** From *The Trial of Klaus Hottinger of Zurich*, translated by L. P. Wandel, Staatsarchiv, Zurich. **95:** From *The Life of Theresa of Jesus: The Autobiography of Teresa Avila*, Bantam Doubleday Dell, 1991. Reprinted by permission of the publisher. **97:** From *The Revolution of 1525: The German Peasants from a New Perspective*, Johns Hopkins University Press, 1981. **102:** From *Canons and Decrees of the Council of Trent*, translated by H. J. Schroeder, Herder, 1941. **109:** From